Naomi Elizabeth (Oma) Breshears Huckaby and her husband William Thomas (Buck) Huckaby, taken about 1925.

In front, Roy and Rosa Overcash holding Leroy. In back seat, Verna Overcash, daughter of Roy and Rosa and Wilma Overcash, sister of Roy.

Jacob Overcash, 1918

History & Families
Polk County, Missouri

Home of the Polk County Genealogical Society

TURNER PUBLISHING COMPANY

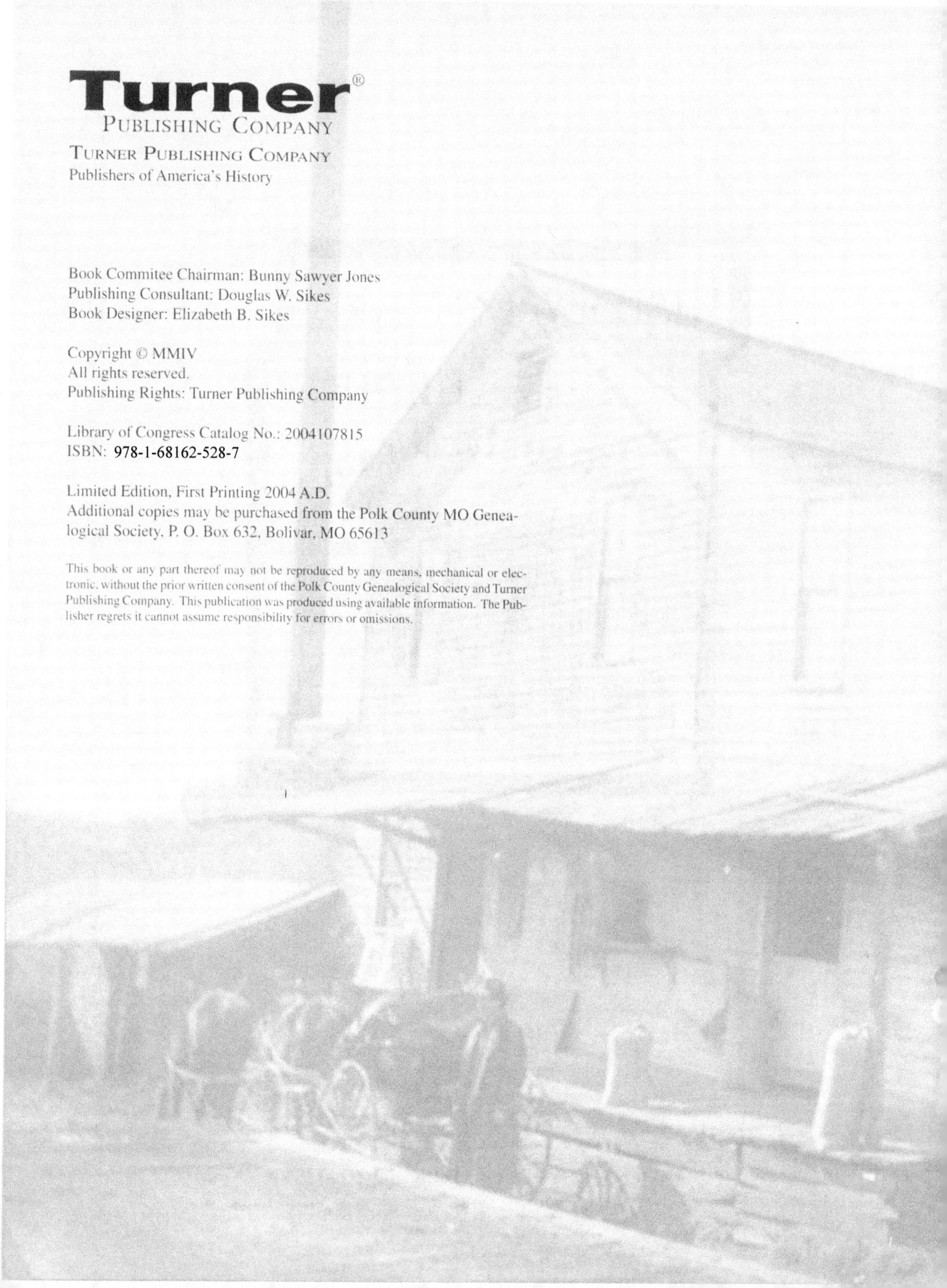

Turner Publishing Company
Publishers of America's History

Book Commitee Chairman: Bunny Sawyer Jones
Publishing Consultant: Douglas W. Sikes
Book Designer: Elizabeth B. Sikes

Copyright © MMIV
All rights reserved.
Publishing Rights: Turner Publishing Company

Library of Congress Catalog No.: 2004107815
ISBN: 978-1-68162-528-7

Limited Edition, First Printing 2004 A.D.
Additional copies may be purchased from the Polk County MO Genealogical Society, P. O. Box 632, Bolivar, MO 65613

This book or any part thereof may not be reproduced by any means, mechanical or electronic, without the prior written consent of the Polk County Genealogical Society and Turner Publishing Company. This publication was produced using available information. The Publisher regrets it cannot assume responsibility for errors or omissions.

Table of Contents

Preface 4
Polk County Genealogical Society 5
History of Polk County, Missouri 6
Towns, Communities, Mills and Post Offices 22
Polk County Churches–Past and Present 38
Cemeteries 50
Schools, Academies, Colleges And Institutes 52
Businesses, Churches and Organizations 76
Family Histories 114
Index 380

John W. Pursselley's flour mill at Brighton, MO circa 1907

Preface

Thanks to my late aunt Ruby Ross Booher for piquing my interest in genealogy at a young age, I was, in the Spring of 2002, ready to take on a project I had dreamed of doing for many years, that being to help create the first county and family history book of its kind for Polk County since 1889. I had purchased several county history books over the years that pertained to our families from other counties and had always wanted to be part of a team that would help to preserve Polk County history for the future generations to read. My thinking was that if someone does not do this while we have older family members living, a large amount of history could be lost forever.

I presented the idea to the Polk County Genealogical Society members, and as chairman of the committee I chose to have as committee members, Susan Sparks, as she had been the president of the society for the past four years and Linda Crawford, the secretary for the past four years. We interviewed companies and chose to have Turner Publishing as our partner. Thank you Turner for sending us Doug Sikes for this project. He has been an excellent mentor.

When you take on a project like this you know that it will be big, but none of us realized just how much impact it would have on our lives.

A special thank you goes first to my husband Mike and our son Charles Michael for all their support at home during this two and one half year time frame. They gave up our dining room for the duration, so that I could process the bushels of mail as it came in consisting of histories and book orders, e-mails and phone calls, and helped in many other ways. I love you both.

Linda Crawford volunteered for the position of gathering the county history for the book. She has done an excellent job compiling more history than space would allow. She had many people that helped her with facts and photos, which was much appreciated, the main contributors being her husband Jack and PCGS member Bob Phillips. Thank you Linda for all your hard work on the history.

Susan Sparks, your vision for this book and the PCGS has carried us far. You have been a true asset with both the book and the group.

A huge thanks goes to the following people, who in their own special ways, contributed greatly with this project. Those being, Joyce Burkhart, who gave me the needed encouragement when things would get overwhelming, critiquing of my press releases, confidence and friendship. You were a real cheerleader.

Julie Trout and Judy Kallenbach, what can I say? This book would never have made it to press without you and the staff of the *Bolivar Herald Free Press*. Polk Countians need to realize what an asset we have in the *Bolivar Herald Free Press*. To Rena Smith and Lou Kemp for all your help with the sponsored pages, thank you.

To all the faithful society members who helped countless hours with proofreading, you came through for me at the critical times.

There have been too many people to name separately that have contributed with information and photos. But you know who you are and will always be remembered fondly.

To Leota Ross Recknor, thank you for being the first person to purchase a book you would not see for at least two or three years. And thank you for being my mom, the world's best in my opinion.

And one last thanks to my cousin JoAnne Booher, you went above and beyond the call of duty, living in Greene County and persuading so many former Polk Countians to write their stories. Your heart was in this book as much as mine has been. You all are champions in your own ways. Thank you to everyone who had a part in this book, you helped make it what it is.

The Polk County Genealogical Society, Inc. is proud to have such a wonderful compilation of history for everyone to read and enable us to remember the various aspects of peoples' lives that have made Polk County what it is today.

I am happy to have served my native county by helping preserve its history. May its future be as rich as its past.

Very sincerely,
Bunny Sawyer Jones, PCGS Librarian and PC History Book Chairman

Left: Linda Crawford, PCGS Vice President and Compiler of county history. **Seated:** *Susan Sparks, PCGS President.* **Right:** *Bunny Sawyer Jones, PCGS Librarian and History Book Chairman.*

Polk County Genealogical Society

The Polk County Genealogical Society was established in 1994 in Bolivar, MO. Interested parties first met for an organizational meeting in February 1994. The first program and business meeting was held in April 1994. At that time the society was a special interest group of the Friends of the Polk County Library and was supported financially by the Friends. The society was first called the Bolivar Genealogy Group, but the name was soon changed to the Polk County Genealogical Society. PCGS is the name most commonly used by its members.

In 1996 the society became independent of the Friends of the Library. The first publication for sale by the society was published in 1998. The society was incorporated in August 1999. In January 2001 the society became a not-for-profit corporation.

As PCGS grew it became apparent there was a need for a permanent library. Materials and equipment had been housed in a number of locations, therefore making it hard for PCGS members to use any of the collection. A campaign was started to raise money to purchase the Carnegie Library building which had previously housed the Polk County Public Library. On October 31, 2001 the purchase was finalized. Renovation was started on the lower level of the building and the Polk County Genealogical Society Library was opened to the public in July 2002.

In January 2003 PCGS received a grant from the Delarue Trust. A lift was installed and other remodeling work was begun on the upper floor. On July 27, 2003 the National Park Service declared the library building as a historic site. It is now listed on the National Register of Historic Places and it has the distinction of being the first historic site in Polk County to be listed on the Register.

Monthly business meetings are held at the library and a program is presented at that time also. In the spring of the year an all day conference is held with speakers and workshops available.

PCGS now has over 50 publications for sale. A 10 page bi-monthly newsletter is mailed to members of the society. The library collection continues to grow with gifts of valuable resource materials. The collection contains census records, maps, pictures, church records, school records, family histories and court records. These can be found in books, microfilm or on CD. A microfilm reader and computers are an important part of this library and they are available for anyone doing research there. A vertical file is also kept with many miscellaneous records. There is always an ongoing project to promote Polk County genealogy and preserve records for the future. PCGS volunteers spend many hours donating time to the library and working on future projects for generations to come.

History of Polk County, Missouri

Halfway, MO MFA

History of Polk County Missouri

On March 9 and 10 of 1804 an agreement for the Louisiana Purchase was signed. The purchase was divided in two sections. The southern half was called the Territory of Orleans and the northern half was known as the District of Louisiana. In 1805 the District of Louisiana was changed to the Territory of Louisiana. In 1812 Missouri became a second class territory and in 1818 it became the Territory of Missouri. On March 6, 1820 Congress authorized the citizens to write a state constitution and establish a state government.

As a territory, Missouri had five districts and some of these districts reached almost across the state. In 1810 the area that was to become Polk County was located in two districts. The northern half was in the St. Louis District or possibly the St. Genevieve District. The southern half of the area was in the Cape Girardeau District. In 1812 the districts in Missouri became counties. More people settled in the territory so there was a need for closer local government representation. In 1818 Franklin County was formed out of St. Louis County. This would take in all of what would be Polk County. Gasconade County was formed out of Franklin County in 1820. Crawford County was formed out of Gasconade County in 1829. In 1833 Greene County was formed out of Crawford County. The southern part of what was to be Greene County had also been in Wayne County for a time.

James Smithson, John Mooney and their families were perhaps two of the earliest families who would try to settle the area of the future county of Polk. They settled near to each other and since water was a necessity, each man settled by a good sized spring that would supply their needs. Mr. Smithson camped by the spring just to the south of the present day Bolivar square which is now known as Keeling Spring. Mr. Mooney camped by the spring that is located near the Bolivar Middle School campus which was later called the Clark/Finley Spring.

This was still Kickapoo Indian territory at the time of their arrival. Had they remained for any period of time, they would have to have paid rent to the Kickapoo who were occupying the land. The two families were not happy in their new homes and wanted to be closer to a white settlement. They packed up and went south to a white settlement near the James River.

After the move they were in Delaware Indian territory, but among other white people. John Mooney was listed as residing on the James River in 1827. After sometime, both families became dissatisfied at that location and decided to go back north where they had first settled when arriving in the new country. This time neither family went as far north as Bolivar. They arrived in what would become the Brighton area about the same time as the Campbells first arrived in the territory in 1829. John Mooney settled east of the future Brighton. James Smithson settled this time near the Pomme de Terre river, northwest of the future Pleasant Hope.

The Jackson Wright family and Reuben Smith family also arrived in 1829. Both families settled in the area west of what would become Aldrich near the Davis Mill which was later called Strain's Mill on the Little Sac River. John Smith was born to the Smith family in 1832 and was said to have been the first white child born in the area. Mr. Wright and Mr. Smith were brothers-in-law, coming from Tennessee.

John and Mary Jane Russell Williams arrived in 1830 and settled west of the future Brighton. They are considered the first permanent white settlers of the future county because they did not settle in the area and leave to come back again as did many of the earlier arrivals. They were living in Indian territory and paid rent to the Kickapoo tribe until a government treaty moved the tribe westward.

Cyrus Patterson and Absalom Renfrow along with their families arrived shortly after the Williams family. They settled close by to the other families. This was near where John Mooney settled when he returned from the James River settlement. About 1831 the Akard family left Tennessee and settled on Bear Creek about two miles south of what is now Fair Play. John Polk Campbell and his brother, Ezekial Madison Campbell left their homes in Tennessee in 1829. After arriving in southwest Missouri, they marked their claims and went back to Tennessee to get their families for a return to Missouri. John Polk Campbell returned around 1830 with other family members.

The area was still at that time legally owned by the Kickapoo tribe. In 1832 the government bought the land from them so they could prepare the way for more white emigrants. In that year Ezekial and William Campbell arrived from Tennessee along with the Fox, Lemmon, Ruyle, Batten and Slagle families. It wasn't long before mills were erected and trading posts were opened to accommodate the new arrivals. The names of some of those places have been lost to time.

Parts of Jackson, Osage and Mooney Townships of Greene County would later become Polk County. The description of these boundaries was set forth in the Greene County Court in 1833.

Jackson Township: Beginning at the north boundary line of Greene County, as now established, running with the dividing ridge between the North Fork of Sack river and the Pomada Tarr river, *without limit,* or so as to include all the settlements on both sides of Sack river. Elections to be held at Ezekial Campbell's.

Mooney Township: Beginning at Pomada Tarr river where the Niangua Trace crosses; thence taking the waters of Pomada Tarr to the mouth of Little Pomada Tarr; thence up the Little Pomada Tarr to the dividing ridge between it and Sack river; thence along the line of Jackson Township, to Sack river; elections, James Smithson, Aaron Ruyle and John West.

Osage Township: Beginning at the mouth of Little Niangua river running so as to include the place where William Montgomery now lives thence to the mouth of Little Pomada Tarr river; thence west to Sack river and down Sack to the Osage river. Thence down the Osage river to the beginning. Elections to be held at William Brinegar's ferry, on Pomada Tarr.

Polk County was formed on January 5, 1835 from Greene County. This was done by an act of the State Legislature of Missouri. The county court officials were Judge Jeremiah N. Sloan and Judge Richard Saye, who had both served as justices for Greene County. They met on February 9, 1835 for the first time at the home of Daniel M. Stockton which was located five miles southwest of Bolivar on the West Bend Road. In a few places remnants of the old road can still be seen running mostly north and south to the west of Highway U.

The new county was named after Ezekial Polk, a Revolutionary War Colonel and grandfather of James Knox Polk who was the 11th president of the United States. He only served one term which ran from 1845 to 1849. John Polk, Ezekiel Madison and William C. Campbell were cousins of President Polk. Their mother was a sister of the president's father. John Polk attended the inauguration of his cousin to the office of president of the United States.

At the first meeting, county court officials appointed Joseph English as sheriff and William Henry as clerk. Other officials appointed that day were Ezekial Madison Campbell as surveyor, Rodham Payne as assessor and John C. Montgomery as commissioner to select a site for the new county seat. They were to select the seat for the county at a meeting the following day. They met at the home of William C. Campbell. It was decided that Ezekial Madison Campbell was to meet on the 25th of that month with the Greene County surveyor to mark the boundaries between the two counties. At that time, the county was divided into three townships which were Washington, Marion and Jackson Township.

William and Ezekial Campbell, along with other family and friends, asked the county court to name the new county seat Bolivar for the home of their grandfather Polk in Hardeman County, Tennessee. This was done on November 10, 1835, but a site had not been decided on for the location of the town.

William Campbell, family and friends had decided the site should be near where Aldrich was later located. Robert E. Acock and friends wanted the site to be where a town already had its beginnings at the present site of Bolivar. Another faction proposed the seat should be at West Bend where the first meeting was held in the Stockton home. William Campbell lost his bid for the site but he built a trading post there and called it New Market. West Bend did not come into existence as a town. Some residents of the Humansville area wanted the county seat to be located there. The county officials felt that was too far from the center of the county.

John C. Montgomery did not fill the seat he was appointed to as commissioner so that seat was filled by William Jamison, who chose Bolivar as the site for the county seat because it was the intersection of the Fort Scott to Lebanon and the Springfield to Sedalia trails.

William Marlin was the county's first representative in the state legislature. He resided in the far southeast corner of Polk County and that would later become Dallas County. He was followed by Robert E. Acock who lived near Brighton.

The first building erected by the county as a courthouse was built in 1837 at a cost of $125. This building was a log structure that measured 20 x 20 and was located four blocks west of the present courthouse. It sat on the south side of the present West Broadway. The county grew quickly and the first building was not adequate to take care of the needs of the county. A new building was begun in 1841. It was a two-story brick structure which was completed in 1842. It served the county for more than 60 years until the growth of the county called for yet another bigger and better structure.

On May 24, 1906 the cornerstone for the new Polk County courthouse was laid. On October 1, 1907 the courthouse was occupied with the dedication held on November 25, 1907. The cost for the new building, its furniture and fixtures was $53,250.00. It is still an impressive building and has served the county for almost 100 years. Records from the beginning of the county are housed at the courthouse.

When the county was organized, the population was about 200 residents and it was a much larger county area wise at the time it was formed than it is at the present time. All of Dallas County, the far northwest corner of Webster County, the south half of Hickory County, the far southeast corner of St. Clair County, the eastern half of Cedar County and the northeast quarter of Dade County all were part of Polk County. The county measured 54 miles from east to west and 33 miles from north to south containing 1700 square miles. After the other counties were formed, there were only 640 square miles remaining.

Polk County is almost a perfect rectangle in shape except for the northern part of the county. This was caused by early land surveyors in marking the boundaries. Johnson Township extends farther to the west than the other western townships. Part of the township also extends farther north than the other northern townships. On the northeast side of the county, North Green and part of South Green Townships do not extend as far east as the remaining townships on the eastern boundary.

Osage Indians had occupied the area for many years and were still in residence when the Federal Government entered into a treaty with

Early picture of the present Polk County Courthouse, north entrance.

Second Polk County Courthouse with the door on the east.

them in 1808. The Osage tribe was then pushed into the southwest corner of the state and into what is now Kansas and Oklahoma. This land was then given to tribes who had given up their homeland on the east side of the Mississippi River which included the Kickapoo Tribe. Their area was between the Pomme de Terre and Sac Rivers. Sac River was named for the Sac Indian Tribe which was one of the last tribes to move to new territory.

Alexander Isham Brown is buried at Brock Cemetery south of Brighton, not far from the Greene County line. He is buried by his wife Sarah Canoe. Alexander was the brother-in-law of Dragging Canoe, a highly respected Chickamauga Cherokee Warrior. Dragging Canoe had helped lead the fight to save their homeland. Their land had originally been in the Carolinas, Tennessee, Kentucky, Virginia and part of Mississippi and Alabama. They had fought for many years to protect their homeland but the many battles left them devastated. They asked for a peace agreement and were forced to give up large tracts of their tribal lands, hunting and fishing territory. Eventually they began moving westward. Among those who can show proof of belonging to the Chickamauga Cherokee are the Shawnee, Delaware, Osage and the Sac Osage or Quapaw. It has been stated that Chickamauga means "Where the Chief Sleeps". Others say the meaning of the name is lost.

The state of Missouri estimated that by the year 2003 there would be 35,000 American Indians living in the state. Polk County has many members who have proven their eligibility. It is believed within the boundaries of Polk, Cedar, Dade and Hickory Counties there are more than 2,000 people with Indian background. The Chickamauga Nation of today is made up of two separate and distinct bands of families. Polk County is part of the Sac River Band.

In 1850 the State of Arkansas and State of Missouri issued a statement announcing that all Indians had been removed from those two states. This became a "Period of Silence" when an Indian living in these two states would not admit being Indian. Missouri passed laws to keep the Indians from living in the state and it was in effect until the 1930s. After Missouri achieved statehood, a rush was on to inhabit the land by those coming from the east. Many Indians rented land to the new settlers. The Indian did not consider himself to be the owner of the land. He felt it was lent to him for his use. White settlers did not see it this way and wanted the land for themselves. Eventually the Indians had to give it all up and move onward. Indian mounds may still be seen in many areas of Polk County. Many have been plowed over and under through the years until they are no longer visible. A few of the visible sites that still remain in the county are believed to be Indian worship sites.

Some of the Osage Indians were not happy with their new homes that they had been moved to farther southwest and they were unhappy with the government. By 1837 they were beginning to cause trouble and threatened to return to their old home which included Polk County. Judge Jeremiah Sloan was appointed to contact the governor and ask for military protection for area citizens. Lilburn W. Boggs was the governor.

He sent out an order to mobilize the militia in this area and they were sent to Barry County where the trouble was settled. Brigadier General A.F. Neill was in command of the 18-day campaign. The militia was mustered out, discharged and paid in Bolivar. The following men served under Neill: Aide de Camp, Nicholas Munn; Brigade Inspector, William Jamison; Brigade Judge Advocate, William Henry; Brigade Quarter Master, L.H. Bunch; Brigade Paymaster, John Shannon; Brigade Commissary, E. M. Campbell; Brigade Surgeon, Louis Polk; Colonel, T.J. Shannon; Adjutant, I. W. Davis; Lieutenant-Colonel, J.L. Young; Major, Levi A. Williams; Judge Advocate, C. Luttrell; Quarter Master Sergeant, William Owens; Color Bearer, Mart Morgan; Trumpeter, William Jones; Quarter Master, Hugh Boyd; Sergeant Major, William R. Hill; Paymaster, Winfrey Owens.

The companies' officers were as follows: 1. Captain, A. Morgan; Lieutenant, J.W. Jamison; Ensign, J. H. Smallman. 2. Captain, Richard Saye; Lieutenant, James R. Alsup; Ensign, Davis Fields; Sergeant, James Appleby. 3. Captain, Gran C. Clark; Lieutenant, William Odell; Ensign, Samuel W. Davis; 2nd Lieutenant, Joseph McBroom; Sergeant, William K. Latham. 4. Captain, Michael Randleman; Lieutenant, Elijah Benton; Ensign, Zion S. Pritchett; Sergeant, Elias Parrot. 5. Captain, Levi A. Williams; Lieutenant, M.C. Campbell, Ensign, A. Looney; Sergeant, Alex Morgan.

As far as is known there is no listing for the noncommissioned officers and privates who took part in the campaign or whether or not they were from Polk County, but it is believed that many of them were from the area. The five companies included more than 400 men. The records relating to this incident were destroyed when Missouri's capitol building burned on February 5, 1911.

Many of the above names will be seen again and again in the history of Polk County. William Jamison was the commissioner of the permanent seat of government and he entered the land on which Bolivar stands. William Henry was the first county clerk. Louis Polk was a cousin of the Campbells and of President John Polk.

It wasn't long before the original three townships of Madison, Washington and Jackson were divided. The present-day Looney Township was the earliest settled part of the county. It was named for Benjamin Looney and is in the south-central part of the county. The names of those living in that area at the time of the county organization can be found in Greene County records as early as the forming of Greene County in 1833 and earlier in Crawford County records.

Mrs. Martha "Patsy" Smith, wife of J. H. M. Smith wove the first cloth in Looney Township on her loom. This was believed to have been about 1830. In 1832 Rev. William Slavens, a Methodist minister, preached the first sermon in the area at the home of Aaron Ruyle located two miles east of the present Morrisville.

The first schools were also opened in Looney Township in 1835. The southern-most school was taught by a Mr. Wilson and the one near Three Mound Prairie was taught by Mr. B.W. Goodrich.

Thomas Smith Woodard was a Methodist Circuit Rider preacher in southwest Missouri. He was from Polk County. In 1838 he wrote about the condition of the county. It is included in an old book in the Methodist Archives at Fayette, MO. The book is titled *Methodism in Missouri*.

"Bolivar is a little village of about twelve families, one store, and two doggeries. The current court is in session here, Judge Wright is on the throne, and a number of lawyers at the bar, in a little cabin about sixteen feet square. There is a crowd and many look sickly. A great fuss-playing the fiddle, dancing, drinking, swearing, etc. is kept up in one of the doggeries. The community seems in a very degraded and immoral state. The brethren have begun to build here a very pretty little log meeting house, well suited to the present condition of the country and the church. The land around this place is so very poor that I think it can never be a place of much importance." A doggery was a saloon and generally its patrons were not the most upstanding citizens.

In late 1857 the first telegraph office in the southwest part of the state was established. In 1858 the first stage coach went through the county in Looney Township. It was from the Atlantic and Pacific Railroad Company at Tipton, MO. Colonel Butterfield entered into a contract with the U.S. Government to carry the mail by this stage line. The telegraph and stage both followed the north and south route through the county in the same basic area as the old State Road and present day Highway 13. This township is now divided into east and west sections.

Mooney Township is located in the southeast corner of the county and was named for John Mooney. The eastern part of Mooney Township at one time was Van Buren Township and included part of present day Dallas County and a small section of Webster County. Early residents other than John Mooney were William and Cyrus Patterson, Dr. Hamilton Bradford, John McClure, James Smithson, Hartwell Weaver, Caleb Murray, Fullertons, Cowdens and Burns. After a few years Mr. Mooney moved to Kansas. James Smithson died in 1841. A sale bill to settle his estate is included in his probate file. It shows names of many of the early settlers of the area and the items they purchased.

Gustave Gunter is said to have built the first house about 1832 in what is now Marion Township and the city of Bolivar. Both William Jamison and Joseph Montgomery were early residents there. Marion Township is located in the center of the county. As the township grew, it was divided into four separate districts. The townships are Northwest Marion, Northeast Marion, Southeast Marion and Southwest Marion. One corner of each township is in the city of Bolivar.

Jackson Township is located to the west of Looney Township in the southwest corner of the county. It also was settled early because of the waterways. Orleans Mill was in the northeast corner of the township. Eudora and Graydon Springs are in Jackson Township.

Union Township is between Jackson and Madison Townships. That area was also the home to early settlers because of Sac River and a number of the early mills were located there. Aldrich is located there.

Madison Township has been divided into an east section and a west section. Fair Play was located near the center of the original township which extends to the Cedar County line. The earliest settlers there were the families of Akards, Crains, Hopkins, Foxs, Campbells and Dunnegans.

Johnson Township is located in the northwest corner of the county and continued east to the Pomme de Terre River. In 1834 James G. Human settled near a big spring which later would be in the town of Humansville which was named for Mr. Human. It is credited with being the first town formed in what would be Polk County. The first recorded murder happened in Johnson Township near the big spring in 1833. Joseph Ferguson shot and killed Jacob Sigler. Mr. Ferguson was also injured in the affray. He was arrested and tried before Squire Stinson. He escaped while the trial was in progress and was never heard from after the escape. Some early residents wanted Humansville to be the county seat, but other citizens felt it should be more centrally located.

To the east of Johnson Township was Green Township in the far northeast corner of the county. It continues on to the Dallas County line and adjoins Hickory County. Most of its earliest settlers arrived later than those who settled in the southern part of the county. Like other townships it was later divided and has a north and a south section.

As the northern area of the county grew, other townships were taken from Johnson and Green Townships. Flemington, Jefferson and McKinley Townships are on the far northern edge of the county between Johnson and Green Townships. Benton Township is between Green and Mooney Townships on the east side of the county and it was later divided into a north and south section.

Wishart Township is situated between Jackson, West Looney, Union and Southwest Marion Townships. The town of Wishart is located there.

Campbell Township is just to the south of Johnson Township and the town of Dunnegan is located there on Highway 123.

Cliquot Township is to the east of Campbell Township with the town of Cliquot being located in the center. Highway 13 goes through the southwest corner and Highway 83 goes through the east side of the township.

The 1837 Tax Receipt Book of Polk County lists 668 names as paying taxes in the county, but at this time the other counties had not been taken from Polk County and many of the names can be recognized as names still seen in other counties to this day. It lists the number of free males, slaves, horses, cattle, mules, etc. and their value. In the early years of the county, clocks and watches were considered a luxury and as such were included in the tax assessment.

In the late 1830s, residents of the far eastern part of the county felt the need for their own separate county. The area had been growing with many new settlers and it was a long trip to the county seat at Bolivar. Near the Martin Randleman Spring east of Buffalo there was a big political campaign going on to elect a state representative for all of Polk County. A Mr. Jones from the western part of Polk County and Mr. Robert Acock from near Brighton were in the political race for the office. Both men wished to divide the county near the center leaving the east half for the residents to have their own county seat. Each man promised that if he was elected he would work to form a new county. Robert Acock won the election and he followed through with his promise. Just after the election in 1840 Niangua County was formed out of the eastern half of Polk County. In 1844 the boundaries changed slightly and the name was changed to Dallas County.

Dade County was formed in 1841 and its northeast corner was taken out of Polk County. St. Clair County was also formed in 1841. A small southeast section was taken from Polk County. Cedar County was formed in 1845. Its east half was taken from Polk County. Hickory County was formed in 1845. Almost half of that county was taken from Polk County. Webster County was not formed until 1855. The northwest corner of that county was taken from Dallas County, but that land had originally been a part of Polk County also.

On the 1848 tax list there was a space for remarks. The following is what was found on that list. Overage–109, Over 45–80, Underage–85, Widow–47, Cripple–22, Preacher–11, Hard of hearing–4, Eye out–3, Breast compl.–5, Weakly–2, Sickly–5, Rheumatic Pains–5, Arm broken–3, Leg broken–1, ASPM–1, Weak in arms–1, Affected Nerves–1, White Swelling–3, Rupture–1, Kidney Compl.–1, Eyes affected–1, Lame–1, Cap.n–1, Lungs affected–1, Dumb-1, Dispapsia-1, Fits–1, Pains–2, Weak back–1, Wounded, War(Joseph Derick)–1, Stage Driver–2, Road Overseer–3, In the Army–1, Mail carrier–1. Persons of color–2.

Those "In the United States Service": John Hart, Robert Morrow, J. E. Mooney, Nathan Rains, R. F. Saye, John T. Self, Adam Zumwalt and John Zumwalt Jr.

In 1856 former Missourians living in Kansas Territory had been threatened by abolitionists who had invaded parts of the territory. A group of Polk County citizens met to show their support for those who had migrated. J.F. Snyder and "Jake" Clark were considered leaders in organizing a group of about 50 to 60 men who would go to Kansas to help the families move back to Missouri. They were successful in bringing the families back to Missouri with no conflict in the process.

By 1860 the rumblings of war and the slavery problem were heard in the county. There was a population of just less than 10,000 residents. Four hundred and nine slaves were listed on the 1860 census which was an increase from 1850 when 358 were listed. The 1861 County Assessment shows 341 slaves that were held by 158 owners. There were 637 county property owners.

A number of early settlers brought slaves with them to their new homes. The southeast area of the county had a strong leaning to the southern cause, but very few of the residents there had slaves. There did not seem to be much division over the issue prior to the firing on Fort Sumter. At this point President Lincoln called for volunteers to help in the fight against the rebellion. Governor Claiborne Jackson called for volunteers to help defend the state of Missouri against a federal invasion.

Many Polk County men began signing up on one side or the other. On the streets of Bolivar preparations were being made for war. Both sides of the conflict could be seen practicing at the same time. Rebels in the county were expected to sign a list denoting them as rebels. Six hundred and seventy five names are on that list.

There were four units organized for the Union forces in the county. The Polk County Regiment Home Guard Infantry was organized in June 1861, This unit served in duty in the county until December 1861. It was formed to protect county citizens. This unit was authorized by General Nathaniel Lyon. In the *History of Polk County* by Goodspeed it is stated as the Fifteenth Regiment, United States Reserve Corps. Part of the companies performed guard duty at Jefferson City and on the railroad. The regiment was commanded by Colonel James W. Johnson with Thomas W. Cunnyingham as lieutenant colonel.

The Eighth Regiment State Militia Cavalry was organized December 18, 1861 and was disbanded July 17, 1865. Some of the same men who served in the Fifteenth Regiment also served with the Eighth Regiment. The Eighth was under the command of Joseph J. Gravely of Polk County. They did guard and escort duty and helped to keep the communications open between Springfield and Rolla.

The following was taken from the 1841 tax list of Polk County. It is the total of taxable property for that year.

		Value	State Tax	County Tax	Total
Slaves	226	$ 85,175	$ 106.46 3/4	$ 212.93 1/4	$ 319.401 1/2
Horses	1388	$ 60,716	$ 75.89 1/2	$ 151.79	$ 227.68
Cattle	2659	$ 35,599	$ 44.49 1/4	$ 88.99 1/2	$ 134.49 1/4
Mules	54	$ 2,245	$ 2.80 1/2	$ 5.61	$ 8.41 1/2
Asses	9	$ 1,480	$ 1.85	$ 3.70	$ 5.55
Carriages	13	$ 830	$ 1.02 1/2	$ 2.07	$ 3.11 1/4
Clocks	132	$ 2040	$ 2.55	$ 5.10	$ 7.60
Watches	36	$ 725	$ 0.90 1/2	$ 1.81	$ 2.71 1/2
Money at interest		$23,640.$23,640	$ 29.55	$ 59.30	$ 88.75
Free white males	b716		$ 179.00	$ 358.00	$ 537.00

Totals State tax $ 444.15 1/4 County $ 889.31 1/4 Total $ 1333.82 1/2
Jesse Mitchell was the assessor. Israel N. Davis was Clerk of the County Court. A. McMinn was the collector.

J.J. Akard and family. He enlisted with Co A, Fifteenth Reserve Corps and then Co A, Eighth Missouri State Militia Cavalry and became captain of his company.

The Twenty-Sixth Regiment Enrolled Missouri Militia was authorized July 22, 1862 to help control guerrilla warfare in Missouri. The provisional governor was Hamilton Gamble. Those men were only paid and received food when they were called to active duty. Most of their time was spent in their home communities, but on call when and if they were needed. Most of these men had also served in the Polk County Home Guard Infantry. James W. Johnson served as the colonel.

The Fifteenth Missouri Calvary was organized November 1, 1863 and mustered out July 1, 1865. Many of its members had served in the Twenty-Sixth Enrolled Missouri Militia. Its main purpose was to control the activities of the bushwhackers.

Two Polk County companies organized which would later become part of the Confederate Army. Captain Asbury C. Bradford commanded a company that was attached to Major Gibbons' battalion. Captain Bradford's company was in the Battle of Wilson's Creek and the Battle of Lexington. The company also served as body guard for General Sterling Price.

Captain Alexander Campbell Lemmons commanded the other company. That company became part of the Fifth Regiment, C. S. A.

"Butternut Boys" was the name given to the Missouri State Guard as they did not have regular uniforms to wear in service. Their homespun clothing was dyed using butternut juice so they could be differentiated from the Union soldiers. Some State Guards began wearing large clay-colored head pieces made of felt.

Although Polk County did not have a large destructive battle in its boundaries, it had many conflicts all through the county. The courthouse was not burned such as happened in many of the surrounding counties.

On March 26, 1862, a battle took place in Humansville near the present George Dimmit Memorial Hospital. Several companies of the Eighth Missouri Cavalry were stationed nearby. Mrs. Hannah George was visiting her sister

Colonel Dewitt Hunter of Hunter's Regiment C.S.A. and Shelby's Iron Brigade. Colonel Hunter is in a lodge uniform after the war. He lived at Nevada, MO before and after the war. He led part of Shelby's troops through Humansville on the retreat to Arkansas in 1863.

Catherine Kennedy near Humansville when a Confederate soldier came to the home and demanded a meal. Mrs. George used an excuse to get firewood and ran into town to warn the Union army of the nearby Confederates. The following is the official report given by Lieutenant Colonel Joseph W. McClurg, Missouri Cavalry, Militia from the *War of the Rebellion* official records.

"Headquarters Missouri State Militia,
Linn Creek, Mo., March 31, 1862.
GENERAL: I have the honor to submit, for your perusal and consideration, the following report of the fight at Humansville, Polk county. I make it from the official report of Captain Stockton, made out on the 28 instant. His language is about as follows:

About 2 o'clock in the afternoon of the 26th instant a lady came into town and informed Captain Gravely that a large force of rebels were marching upon us. The alarm was given and the officers and men of Companies A (Captain Stockton), B (Captain Cosgrove), D (Captain Gravely), and E (Captain Smith) were soon in line ready for battle. In a few minutes the enemy were seen passing town from west to east on the south of us. On the east of town is a thicket of underbrush, coming up within 50 paces and extending east and south about a mile. Believing it was the intention of the rebels to attack us from the east merely to draw the attention of our forces and that the main body would attack us from the west and north, Company A marched to the east of town, taking position along the fence running east and south. Captain Cosgrove, of Company B, and 70 men of his own and Captain Melton's company (both of these companies being at Warsaw, and Captain Cosgrove having gone to the assistance of the Humansville companies by request, as they were anticipating an attack or intended to make one) were in the rear of Captain Stockton, Company A, on the east of town. Company D (Captain Gravely) was paraded near the center of town on their horses, and ordered to watch the enemy and prevent flanking. Company E (Captain Smith) was on the west of town.

By this time the guard fired on the right of Company A, and the enemy were seen in the front and were fired on by Company A. The fire was returned and a charge ordered by the enemy, who rushed up through the underbrush, firing and taking shelter under fencing and behind trees. Company A fired several rounds, which told with considerable effect. Captain Cosgrove marched his company to the assistance of Company A under a severe fire, and took position on the right of Company A and opened fire upon the enemy with his whole company. Twenty-five men of Company A, under Lieutenant Wakefield, kept up a brisk fire from the left, and the main body of Company A, with Captain Stockton and Lieutenant Akard, fought on from the center. The enemy was seen to begin to retreat and Captain Cosgrove gave them a galling fire from the right. Captain Stockton's leg was broken when the charge was ordered by the enemy, and Lieutenant Akard remained and continued the fire from the center and was severely wounded in the arm as he moved to the right of Company A, but continued to command his men and superintend the battle (Captain Stockton being disabled by a broken leg.) When the enemy retreated Captain Cosgrove ordered Captain Gravely to follow them and ascertain if they had men back, thinking still that they had a reserve in the brush and intended to decoy us from our position. He promptly obeyed, fired upon their rear guard several times in the brush, until all were known to be retreating with great rapidity, but in good order.

The enemy's force was said to be 250 men by themselves after the fight and before it 400. Captain Gravely, who saw them in the prairie 4 miles south of town, estimates the number at least 400. We lost none killed. Captain Stockton, of Company A was badly wounded in the leg; Corporal Smith dangerously wounded in the breast; Privates A. Gordon and Wyatt were slightly wounded. Of Company B, Captain Cosgrove severely but not dangerously wounded in the arm; Private Divine severely wounded, and Halbert, Evans, Parker, and Kidwell slightly. Of Company D, Captain Gravely, Private Roberson severely wounded.

So far as known of the enemy Colonel Frazier was killed, Captain McMinn killed, 4 others dead on the ground, 4 mortally wounded and left, 6 others reported by their surgeon, who came in next morning, as certain to die, and not less that 20 others wounded in various degrees. We took 3 prisoners and a number of their horses. The officers and men in the fight behaved bravely, did their duty and so well that the rebels themselves acknowledge they were badly whipped. Captain Smith kept his position, and was not needed to drive the enemy from the brush. There was no flinching in ranks anywhere.

The wagon of Captain Stockton's company was 5 miles south of town, and the rebels took it and made their escape. Captain Stockton has very little doubt about recovering it. He sent out 150 men for that purpose on the 28th instant.

A view of the 1892 Civil War Reunion at Fair Play from the water tower hill looking southeast. The campground was located in the corner of the present Highways 32 and 123.

Private William Jasper Flint is seventh from the right. He was age 20 and had enlisted for 20 months. He was mustered in August 11, 1864 at Humansville and was a private in Co. D, 15th Regiment, Missouri Cavalry. His horse was valued at $135 and horse equipment at $20.

At the fight we took 13 horses. The men are rejoicing, and the ladies of the town (except for a few rebel wives) are jubilant. Drs. Holbert, of Hickory County, and Frazier, of Stockton, Cedar County, are present and administering to the wants and comfort of the wounded, and are entitled to the thanks of the command.

General you will see that in the command there is some good material. I feel that these brave men and officers have given us a name of which we may be proud and be assured I will use every effort to add new luster. While I sympathize with the wounded, I congratulate them on the honor of having received scars in the holy cause in which we have enlisted.

I have honor to be, most respectfully, your obedient servant, J. W. McClurg, Lieutenant-Colonel Commanding Battalion MO. S. M. Brig. Gen. James Totten, Jefferson City, Mo."

There had been some action in the Humansville area previous to the above action. The Union Troops were being moved toward Springfield. General Fremont's headquarters were at Humansville. The Confederates were occupying Springfield. Major Zagony was successful in driving the rebels from the city and he went back to Polk County to meet with General Fremont and the next day they left the area for Springfield.

On August 28, 1864 another incident happened in Polk County. There is not much information available about it. The following came from the *War of the Rebellion* official records.

"From Brigadier-General John B. Sanborn to Major O.D. Greene. Captain Pace, of the tenth Missouri (Rebel) Calvary, formerly of Saint Joseph, was attacked on last Sunday, in Polk County while proceeding north with seven men, by Captain Headlee and fifteen men of the Sixth Provisional Regiment, and Captain Pace and one man were killed, one wounded in arm and hands, and one taken prisoner. All in regular Confederate uniforms. Said they were going north to take part in the election this fall."

No description was given as to their location in the county, but some believe it was just to the west of Pleasant Hope where tales had been told of a skirmish. There have been rumors of a cemetery where soldiers were buried near Pleasant Hope. At one time a family was supposed to have come and removed the remains of their soldier and taken it home for burial. No names or dates are available to verify the happening. The above skirmish in recent years has been called the Battle of Lick Skillet.

One incident was called "Affair at Bolivar". It was a raid to round up rebel soldiers of which very few were taken prisoners. This happened on February 8, 1862.

Many stories are told of men in Polk County who were killed or wounded during the war years by guerrillas or bushwhackers. Homes were burned. Food was confiscated and livestock stolen. It is most likely that some of these acts were not perpetrated by guerrillas or bushwhackers but by those who used the war as an excuse to do their own dirty deeds.

Men were shot standing in the door of their homes. Several incidents were reported in the Bolivar newspaper. A baby was held over a flaming fireplace in an attempt to get the mother to tell where her husband was at the time. A nine-year-old boy was killed by Union gunfire while his brother hid to protect himself. Their father had been killed earlier at Fair Grove. Families in the county were divided by the war, but many were able to return and go on with life after the war.

A number of lawsuits were filed in Polk County after the war. Many of those suits were against the "Rebels of Polk County" and "Colonel Coffee's Rebels". The causes of action were for horses and mules taken; tobacco, clothing, a mill belt and sundrys being stolen.

On September 20, 21 and 22 of 1893 there was a Grand Army of the Republic Reunion of the old soldiers held in Polk County near Bolivar. Soldiers from areas other than Polk County were also invited. Those from the north were requested to camp at the Pomme de Terre bridge on the Jefferson City and Bolivar road. Those from the central and

Colonel J.J. Gravely, Eighth Missouri State Militia

Old Soldiers Reunion, with Polk County residents, 2035 Ramsey Ave. Springfield, MO

Old Soldiers' G.A.R. Reunion held in Humansville.

southern areas were to camp at the bridge on the Buffalo and Bolivar road. On the morning of September 20 they met at the forks of the road one-half mile east of Bolivar and marched as one body to the reunion grounds. This was the sixth annual reunion of ex Federal soldiers and sailors from Hickory, Polk, Dallas, Camden, Cedar and St. Clair Counties. It was considered the largest and most successful reunion to date. The people of the Bolivar area contributed greatly to the event. This event not only drew thousands of old soldiers but many other visitors at the same time.

In August 1908 a reunion for the survivors of the Eighth Missouri State Militia was held at Bolivar. It was a three-day meeting. At that time it was decided to hold another reunion in the next year which would begin on Monday, August 30 and close on Saturday, September 4 of 1909.

"All veterans of whatever service are cordially invited to join with the eighth in this meeting and are assured of full consideration and comradeship. Camp will be made in the splendid grove adjoining Bolivar on the north. Appropriate programs for each day have been arranged and the entertainment and comfort of all veterans will be looked after. Free tents and free firewood will be furnished to all old soldiers. There is an abundance of good spring water on the grounds. Applications for tents and further information may be made to the secretary. Executive Committee: John P. Tracy; Wm Underwood; Thos. Greer; Wm. McCracken; T. B. Evans; J.J. Akard, President; T.H. B. Dunnegan, Secretary."

After the war was over there were still many bitter memories. Veterans from both sides returned home to settle down and go on with their lives. Although memories remained of past differences, they knew it was time to move on. In many cases a family had to start over as they had lost their homes, outbuildings, livestock and crops.

The provisional government of Missouri made things hard for former rebel soldiers. They were not allowed to run for public office, vote, attend college, become professional men, act as deacon or preach. Union soldiers were forgiven for their atrocities while the rebels were held accountable and would be for many years. Young men had ridden with William Quantrill, "Bloody Bill" Anderson and George Todd in their guerilla bands. Some were ex-Confederate soldiers and others were just boys. They could not or would not turn their lives around. It wasn't long after the war when they returned to crime again.

The infamous Jesse James was one of those who rode with the above. He and others blamed the Civil War for their troubles. By 1874 Jesse was in the headlines of many newspapers including the *Bolivar Free Press*. After the train robbery at Gad's Hill, Jesse and his men had ridden into the Ozarks. They were known to be in the areas of Reynolds and Shannon Counties and heading west, probably to St. Clair County where they would meet the Younger brothers who had friends in the area of Monegaw Springs, Roscoe and Osceola.

Jesse and his gang went through Laclede and Dallas Counties and into Polk County. Just after midnight on February 18, 1874 they were seen passing through Bolivar. They were headed west. A map of that time period shows a crossroad about eight miles west of Bolivar and fourteen miles south of the St. Clair County line. It is believed they headed north at that junction. It was also rumored that Jesse and his gang watered their horses at the Big Spring in Humansville at some time during his career of crime. He was also supposed to have purchased merchandise from a store nearby in Humansville.

W.R. Cowan was appointed as the first Polk County probate judge. Until that time the county court took care of probate cases. A probate court proceedings book beginning in 1859 has many cases listed that are not probate court cases. James M. Jones and I.W. Davis were two early court clerks. One case taken before the court was when Peter Plugugly paid the sum of five dollars and fifty cents to keep a dram shop in the town of Bolivar for six months from the 8th day of February 1860.

The following two wills were filed before the first probate judge had been appointed. They are printed here exactly as they were in the court files.

BUNCH, JOHN

will dated 6 Mar 1837. Wife, Margaret M. Bunch, formerly Margaret M. Clay, to have all property her lifetime; consideration amounts some of them have already received. (children not named). Authorizes exrx. To sell to E.M. Campbell a certain tract of land provided the patent is received from the Government. Exrs

Erwin Family in 1897. William Erwin, Molly Frost Erwin and daughter Alma are standing in front of the home. Henry Erwin is at the top of the house. The house was torn down in 1904. At the time the picture was taken the verandah had been removed from the house. This was located at Walnut Hill Farm to the west of Wilson School House and north of Highway KK.

Molasses Making, Ervin Buckner, Willard Steel, Kelcy Buckner and Vis Laney making molasses in southern Polk County.

Jim McConnell home near Lindley Creek, about 1910

to be his son, Samuel H. Bunch, and son-in-law, Benjamin Craighead. (AA 11-14). Samuel H. Bunch, surviving exr. Of John Bunch, posted bond 7 Sept 1840. (AA 41)

AILSTOCK, HENRY

Will dated 17, Oct. 1851. Exr. To be Ezekiel M. Campbell. The 160 acres he got of Stephen Mitchell in Hickory Co. to be divided between wife, Pamelopy and her mother Susan Mitchell. Balance of property to be divided between wife and "my son Thomas Ailstock" and that he live on my place until 21 and "then he is to be a free man agreeable to the bill of sale that I got of E.M. Campbell." "I will that if there is any law allowing my mother's brother and sisters any part of my estate, only will them enough of my estate to cut them out of my estate or debar them." He mentioned a "rone" mare that Stephen Mitchell gave to his mother and sister, Penelopy Ailstock. Wit: James Watson & Charles Crain, Jr. filed for probate 15 Nov. 1851(WA 57-58) Court confirmed Ezekiel M. Campbell as exr., 26 Dec 1851. (AA 178-179)

Judge Richard Saye kept a ledger of cases brought before him as a justice. This ledger was

During 1936 Polk County farmers were paid $125,000 in benefit payments to assist them in returning some of their land to conserving crops. Then in 1937 $165,630 of payments were offered to farmers. The United States Department of Agriculture was in charge of this program. In 1938 Polk County was to have an election in each township to elect a committee of three members and two alternates. The elections were all held in November 1937.

Township	Town	Chairman	Date	Hour
McKinley	Polk	Ray Vest	Nov. 15	9:00 A.M.
Madison	Fair Play	Oren McCrory	Nov. 15	2:00 P.M.
Cliquot	Cliquot	I.M.Garretson	Nov. 15	7:30 P.M.
Johnson	Humansville	Francis Roberts	Nov. 16	9:00 A.M.
Flemington	Flemington	Neil McShane	Nov. 16	2:00 P.M.
Campbell	Dunnegan	R.C.Wollard	Nov. 16	7:30 P.M.
Benton	Halfway	Walter Roweton	Nov. 18	9:00 A.M.
Marion	Bolivar	A.L.Hutcheson	Nov. 18	2:00 P.M.
Wishart	Wishart	George Morrison	Nov. 18	7:30 P.M.
Looney	Morrisville	O.C. Jackson	Nov. 19	9:00 A.M.
Mooney	Pleasant Hope	Finis Laney	Nov. 19	2:00 P.M.
Union	Aldrich	H.O. Taylor	Nov. 19	2:00 P.M.
Jefferson	Rondo	Joe S. Allison	Nov. 20	9:00 A.M.
Jackson	Eudora	J.E. Wheeler	Nov. 20	2:00 P.M.
Greene	Rimby	Otus Black	Nov. 20	2:00 P.M.

Jess Breshears and his horse in far Northeast Polk County, 1912

later used by William Patterson. The ledger has entries for as early as 1822 and some of those names are that of early county settlers. Judge Saye served as justice for Mooney Township of Greene County previous to becoming a justice for Mooney Township in the new Polk County. He was probably a merchant or a shipper previous to or at the same time as a justice of either county.

Entries from Judge Richard Saye's ledger.

The words are spelled the way they are written in the ledger.

Ann Saye account–To one dollars worth of thread–$1.00, to one trunk bought in Nashville $2.12 1/2.

June the 27th 1832 bought at the Osage for Ann Saye–To one dollars worth of sugar–$1.00, to one dollars worth of coffee–$1.00, to one sack of salt, 200 lbs–$5.00, to one ax–$3.00

March the 7th day 1835, E.M. Campbell debtor to Richard Saye for eleven days service in running the county line between Green and Polk County at seventy five cents per day making in the whole $8.45.

September the 17th day 1835, received of James Smithson fourteen pounds of bacon at eight cents, $1.22.

June the 15th day 1835, received of Aaron Rule one ten dollar bank bill of the following discreption letter E No 2340 on the Bank of the United States at office of Discount Deposit at New Orleans and also one five dollars bank bill of the following discription letter F No 5632 on the Bank of the United States at the office of Discount of Deposit in New Orleans.

State of Missouri, county of Green. I Richard Saye a Justice of Peace within and for said county joined in matrimony on the 1th day of August 1833 Nelson rule & Elsey Luney by concent of parrents August the 1th day 1833, Richard Saye JP.

November 1834, I Richard Saye a Justice of the Peace within and for the county of Green joined in matrimoney on the 2nd day of November 1834 John Smith and Martha Luny both of the county of Green and state of Missouri this the 3 day of November 1834.

Febuary the 20 day 1835, State of Missouri, County of Polk. I Richard Saye a Justice of the Peace within and for the county of Polk joined in matrimoney on the 20th day of Febuary 1835 Joel Starkey and Mary Wilkerson both of the county of Polk and the state of Missouri. Richard Saye JP.

January term 1835, January the 17 1835. John P. Campbell, plantiff vs Green Gay and Joshua Davison, defendents. Now this day the plantiff have judgement against the defendents for three dollars & 67 1/4 cent and all cost him about this suit laid out and expended and the said plaintiff have execution there for, Richard Say JP. Now this day execution ishued on the above judgement for debt–$3.67 1/4, for original cost–$1.36 1/4, justice fees for execution $ .25, constable fees for execution $ .50, for three percent $ .07, total $5.87 1/2, Richard Saye.

April term, 1835, April 18th day 1835. Epraim Jamison, plantiff vs B. W. Goodrich and Joseph H. Miller defendents in debt. This day the constable of Jackson Township made his return of the above case and the plantiff requested the justice to let the constable stop farther_____ on the above cause and by the plantiff paying all cost. Richard Saye, JP.

September the 12 day 1835. This day the constable of Marian Township brought R.K. Pane and Therin Crosslin before me Richard Saye a Justice of the peace within and for the county of Polk and returned them for breaking the peace. The said R. K. Pane and Therin Crosslin dispenced with a jury and submitted them selves to the judgement of the justice therefore it is considered here by the justice that the said R.K. Pane and Therin Crosslin be fined in the sum of one dollar each. Richard Saye JP

February term 17 day 1838, precept ishued this 30 day of January 1838. John Whelchel, plantiff vs William A. Allen, defendant, in debt on account. This day came the parties in ther own proper persons and went into the trial and there upon came a jury to wit: John Allsup, John T. Self, George H. Ervin, Cyrus Patterson, Thomas Brown & William Tindle. The jury returned with the following verdict. "We the jury find for the defendent four dollars & 47 1/2 cents after all just demand being made. Thomas Brown foreman therefore it is considered here by the justice that the defendent have judgement against the plantiff for the sum four dollars & 47 1/2 for his debt and all cost of suit by him laid out and he have execution therefore. The above case stayed this 17 day of February 1838, Richard Saye, execution ishued this 26 day of March 1838 on the above judgement. Debt–$4.47 1/2, justice fees–$1.98, for this writ– $ .25, constable fees–$2.50, for this writ witness fees–Wm Whelchel–$ .50, Davis Fields–$ .50, James _ather–$ .50, Robert_____ $ .20 1/2, three per $ .33. $11.53 1/2.

November the 26 day 1836. State of Missouri, County of Polk. We the undersigned appraisers appointed and duly sworn to appraise without partiality favour or affection a certin mare and colt taken up by William Montgomery as strayes and brought before Richard Saye a Justice of the peace for Marian Township County of Polk do certify that we have viewed the said strayes and find them to be a bay mare and sorrel mare colt the bay mare judege to be thirteen hands three inches high and some white heires under her four top and a few white hares over her left eye and supposed on her ner thigh to be a brand but not plaine enough to tell what letter supposed to be five years old and do appraise said strayes to the sum of forty five dollars. Certified under our hands this the 26 day of November 1836. John _ Williams, James H. M. Smith. Richard Saye, JP.

The state of Missouri County of Polk. Taken up by Thomas C. Reed of Mooney Township Polk County Missouri one mile south east of Keels Mill one light brindle steer with some white in his forehead with a little white on his back, some while on his belley also a little white on his hind legs the bush part of his tail off a yoke on mark with a crop and underbit in each ear supposed to be six or seven years old appraised to 25 dollars by William C. Rogers and George C. Reed before the undersigned Justice according to law this the 16th day of January 1857, William Patterson JP. (Keel's Mill was previously Hugh Boyd's Mill and later Goodnight Mill.)

A coure for the agure–One ounce of alloum one ounce of lyum Goar one half ounce of ascitify in one Gallon of sperrets.

A cure for horses with the slow fever or the yellow wather–take one gill of camphere and a small quantity of assifity and one pint of used piper(?)____ mix them together and give the dose three days in succession and then ____three days.

Miscellaneous Events and Pictures

M. Waldo Hatler is Polk County's only Congressional Medal of Honor winner. He was born in 1894 and died in 1967. He was born in Polk County, but his family moved to Neosho, MO when he was a small boy. During his military career he was given several other military awards. While living in Bolivar, the Hatler family ran a flour mill.

Polk County Revolutionary War Soldiers

There are three known soldiers buried in the county.

W.M. Murphy is buried at Enon Cemetery. March 31, 1760-August 15, 1850.

Morris Mitchell is buried at Mitchell Campground Cemetery.

James Hopkins is buried at Hopkins-Cave Springs Cemetery.

Southwest Regional Library

At the time these two pictures were taken, the library district consisted of Cedar, Polk

Waldo Hatler

Southwest Regional Library bookmobile in 1950

Southwest Regional Library bookmobile in 1948

Frank Ashcroft and his jack rabbit in the Barren Creek area.

and Dallas Counties. Hickory County joined the system later. Each county now has its own library system. The new Polk County Library is on West Broadway Street with a branch library in Humansville. The old Carnegie building which housed the county library previously is now the home of the Polk County Genealogical Society. The building was erected in 1914.

The old county farm was located where the county fairgrounds are now located near Rt. T and South 100th Rd.

On June 25, 1835, the first double wedding of the county took place. A brother and sister married another brother and sister. Alfred M. Frieze married Amanda Ann Campbell and William Campbell married Matilda Frieze. The marriage ceremony was performed by Rev. James Mitchell.

POLK COUNTY CENTURY FARMS

Included are the current farm owners and the date of the original acquisition of the family farm.

Earl E. and Kathleen Coffman Adams–1897; David L. and Debra R. Agee–1890; Jack W. and Peggy J. Barham–1891; John Herbert Brock–1840; Brock Brothers–1840; Mr. and Mrs. Willard Choate–1874; Daniel E. and Frances Cornelius–1887; George Crussell by Danielle Richter, Kathy, Casey and Nick Shuler–1840; Leo M. Dodd–1849; Clyde K. Doke and Mary E. Standley Doke–1852; Donald and Barbara Dunseth–1896; Mrs. Ben Edmondson–1848; Glen E. Gamble–1842; Louis Gorden–1839, 1845, 1868; Toney Allen and Janet L. Gott–1892 and 1884; Edgar Hamilton Jr.–1861; Danny Hawk farm, partly in Greene County; Fred V. and Lois Hogan–1881; John F. and Richard A. Hogan; Bruce N. and JoAnne Hopkins–1868; Joann Elwyn Landers–1870; Jay, Jr. and Annabel Lyman–1895; MBF Farm Properties, George L. Battmer, Barbara A. Atkins, Hobart P. McPheeters and Richards P. McPheeters–1852-1857; Mike McGuire–1865; Dale Mitchell–1850; Dale and Betty J. Mitchell–1866, 1870 and 1871; Donald D. and Wilma Mitchell–1901; Kate Mitchell King and Bill Mitchell–1896; Bill Joe and Letha Moore–1862; Harold Moore–1834; Joe W. and Betty Parrish–1894; Emma Lorene Redd and Marilyn K. Dunseth–1869; Bert Summers–1860; Ralph Tillery–1866; Idotha P. (Hope) Vest–1877; Dean Voris–1839; Wilby Dean Voris–1854; Bruce Wheeler, Ginger Wheeler, Dawn Wheeler Buck, Sandy Wheeler Lininger and Paula Wheeler Ledford–1871;

APPRAISAL OF SAMUEL BECKLEY ESTATE IN 1863

1 2 horse wagon	$40
3 cows	$15
1 steer and heifer	$8
1 calf	$1.50
1 yearlin colt	$17.50
1 sorrel mare	$50
18 head of sheep	$22.50
1 light bay horse mule	$35
1 horse plow	$20
1 log chain	$2
1 1 horse plow	$3
1 bull tongue plow	$ .50
1 1 horse diamond plow	$1.25
Part of a set of blacksmith tools	$10
1 grindstone	$1
1 set wagon harness	$10
2 mowing blades	$2
1 clock	$5
1 bureau	$6
1 bureau with looking glass	$15
3 beds and bedding	$45.

Towns, Communities, Mills and Post Offices

This is a listing of the known towns, communities, mills and post offices which came from many sources such as old maps, newspapers, family histories, official documents, gazetteers and local history. In some cases an exact location could not be pinpointed.

Lumber and grist mills were very important to any area and as the county grew so did the number of these mills. Most of these were located on Little Sac River or Pomme de Terre River, but they can be found on small streams as well. In many instances the names of mills changed with each owner. Sometimes a mill was washed out in a flood or burned. The owner might sell to someone else and the mill then changed names. It is hard to determine which mills were in the same location, but with different names. Some of the mills were very near to each other on the same stream and some men seemed to have owned different mills which make it hard to determine for sure which mill was the correct mill. Some families even had their own small family mill just for their own use or that of just a few close neighbors. They wanted only to provide for their own family needs.

When water was at a low point in some streams, those needing services of many of the mills would find they must go 50 miles to have their grain ground. They would go to mills on streams that were spring fed, such as the mills to the east on the Niangua River or mills on other spring fed streams. Until 1841 when Niangua County was formed most of the Niangua River flowed through Polk County.

Some Polk County towns had steam mills as there was not a stream that would support a traditional water mill. This was most generally a later type mill.

A post office did not always have the same name as the town where it was located. The offices were located in businesses or homes and were moved from place to place with different officials in charge. Some of those offices were only in service for as little as a month. The post office information included in this section came from a microfilm copy of a government listing of post offices for Polk County.

ADONIS

An early town located northwest of Bolivar on the Pomme de Terre River. Known businesses were the post office, a blacksmith shop, two general stores and a farm implement dealer. Ambrose Bradley was a gunsmith during the 1850s and owned an early mill on the river. Nearby on the river was also the Flower's Mill. The Oak Grove Missionary Baptist Church still has regular services there and the cemetery is nearby. Oak Grove School was nearby. The post office was in service from 1895-1935. William Belknap was the postmaster from November 7, 1895 to February 19, 1900. Then Joseph M. Roberts assumed the position as postmaster. He was succeeded by Alonzo J. Price. James R. Roberts and James W. Mead were two other early postmasters.

ALDRICH

Located seven miles south of Fair Play on Highway 123 and near the Sac River in the southwest part of the county. Aldrich was not one of the earlier towns in the county. The K.C. C. & S. railroad began building a track through the area in the 1880s that was to run from Springfield to Clinton. They needed a water tank for the railroad and one was built in the river valley at what was to become the town of Aldrich. In the spring of 1886 a post office was established. It was named for the first conductor of the railroad. Everett Griffin, John Strain, Erith Coffman and Oliver Mitchell were other early officials of the post office. A Mr. Hensley opened a general store and other businesses soon followed. The two main streets were Commercial and Front Streets. By the beginning of the century Aldrich had a school, two churches, a depot, a section house, a hotel, a bank, several general stores, a mill, the stockyards and many homes. A fire had earlier burned the mill and the south part of Commercial Street. In 1909 there was a flood that caused considerable damage to the railroad tracks. Soon after the flood another fire destroyed part of the north section of Commercial Street. A few years later in 1914 a fire again burned the south part of Commercial Street, but this did not keep the town from moving forward. It became known as a major shipping center for livestock and grain products. This railroad town as well as other towns was soon effected by the automobile. In 1935 the railroad track was removed and the population of the town dwindled. The construction of Stockton Dam and Reservoir caused more problems for Aldrich as the residents learned they were to be in the flood plain and would have to give up their land. The town must be moved if it was to survive. It was moved to higher ground, leaving memories of a once thriving railroad town. It is now on the edge of Stockton Lake.

AMISH COMMUNITY

Located between Humansville and Dunnegan on Highway 123. This is an Amish community with many businesses ranging from

Front Street in old Aldrich in the 1960s.

Cordelia Burns Rymer and her son Edgar at their home at Bob Town.

William Douglas Crone and his hogs. Located southwest of the Old City Cemetery in Bolivar on land adjoining the Dunnegan Estate.

The new stucco passenger station of the Frisco Railroad in Bolivar.

a bakery to a harness shop. The women make breads, jams, jellies and many other goodies to be sold in the grocery store or bakery.

APPLEBY MILL

An early mill built on Sac River in the southwest part of the county. Tom Stokes ran the mill at one time. It was near what locals called the Appleby Hole. It was believed to have been owned by James Appleby.

BARKER MILL

See Cable Mill.

BEAR CREEK MILL

Located south of Fair Play on Bear Creek. The owner of the mill is unknown.

BOB TOWN

Located about two miles north of Pleasant Hope on the Pomme de Terre River. Robert Rymer was the proprietor of the store located there, hence the name Bob Town. Providence Missionary Baptist Church was just west of the store for many years in a concrete building of which part of the walls are still standing.

BOLIVAR

Located at Highway 13 and Highway 32 near the center of the county. There was a community here as early as 1834 according to state records with the first building being a log structure built about 1832. It wasn't long before other buildings followed and by the time the county was organized there were a number of dwellings in the little community which had still not been named.

The post office was opened on April 1, 1836 with Andrew W. Temple in charge and he served until July 12, 1837 when Nicholas McMinn took over the position. He was followed by Thomas Shannon. In 1839 Caleb and Joshua Jones had a hotel on the east side of the square. That same year Caleb Jones became the fourth postmaster of the Bolivar office and Israel Davis was clerk of the circuit court.

In 1840 Tilton and Sanders built a hotel on the south side of the square. The town had begun to grow with a variety of businesses.

By 1850 the grain that was grown in the area was taken to Boonville and cattle were driven to market in St. Louis to the nearest railroad.

In 1858 the Tilton and Sanders Hotel was purchased by Ahab Bowen. The Butterfield Stagecoach Line which began in 1858 had a stop at the hotel. The property changed ownership several times and became most well known as the Old Franklin House. It remained a stop on the Butterfield Line.

By 1860 Bolivar had a population of just more than 400 citizens and numerous business establishments, but threats of war were at hand. The years during the Civil War were hard on the businesses. Most of the churches and lodges disbanded as the men had gone to war and other family members moved to what they thought would be a safer place.

After the war had ended and families returned, the town took on a new growth period and continued to grow and become the largest town in Polk County.

The Republic of Venezuela gave the town of Bolivar a statue of Símon Bolívar in 1948. The White House was contacted and President Harry S. Truman agreed to be in Bolivar for the dedication of the statue. Venezuelan President Romulo Gallegos was also in attendance for the ceremony. It was a big and proud day for the city. It was a very hot day with temperatures more than 100 degrees, but that didnt stop the crouds from attending this much anticipated event which took place at Neuhart Park and Highway 13 a few blocks south of the Bolivar Square.

Adam Ricchetti was considered by many as Bolivar's most infamous character. He was involved in the kidnaping of county sheriff Jack Killingsworth who was taken to the Kansas City area and then released. After Ricchetti's death his body was taken to Bolivar for burial. He had family members who lived in the area at that time. For many years his grave was decorated regularly.

Mayors of the City of Bolivar from 1881-1999 were as follows: 1881-J. W. Ross, 1883-I. P. Warren, 1885-J. B. Upton, 1887-J. G. Simpson, 1889-John W. Ross, 1891-Frank W. Adams, 1893- R. M. Dysart, 1895-J. T. Standley, 1897-J. N. Sperry, 1899-H. B. Utley, 1901-J. M. Leavitt, 1903-J. A. Delaplain, 1905-J. M. Dunnegan, 1911-W.E. Martin, 1915-Frank Lightfoot, 1917-F. M. Shoffner, 1919-D. W. Puthuff, 1921-N. W. Maas, 1923-Dr. W. E. Rice, 1925-C. E. Elliston, 1927-C. K. Willis, 1929-T. H. B. Dunnegan, Jr., 1943-Dr. Doyle C. McCraw, 1949-Dr. C. H. Barnett, 1953-Winton Melton, 1954-Claude R. Blue, 1957-William H. Roberts, Sr., 1959-Jack Killingsworth, 1963-J. V. Wommack, 1965- Jack Killingsworth, 1973-Joe L. Lemmon, 1991-William R. Jones, 1993-Joe L. Lemmon, 1995-William R. Jones, 1997-Charles L. Ealy, 1999-Charles L. Ealy.

BOYD'S STORE

A post office and trading post ran by Hugh Boyd who was a very early resident of the area. Along with brothers Rodham K. and William M. Payne,he purchased the east half of Section 33, Township 32, Range 22 of Polk County. This plot includes what is now the town of Brighton and extends east to the section line near the Brighton Methodist Church. The men were able to purchase the land because of the Preempting Act of 1834 which indicates they had been on the land and made improvements to it prior to the land being surveyed in 1838. Hugh Boyd was the assignee of the two Payne brothers. He had arrived in the area by the time of the 1837 Polk County Tax Assessment List. The post office was in existence from May 12, 1838 to October 13, 1842 with Hugh Boyd as the only postmaster. The exact location is unknown, but if the store was on the property that was purchased in 1838, then it would have been located near the junctions of Highways 13 and 215 in Brighton. It was the third post office to be established in Polk County.

A man who called himself "Old Timer" wrote several articles for the Bolivar newspaper in 1887. He told about a trip he took from Greene County to the town of Bolivar in July of 1839. He said he passed Boyd's Store on the State Road on his way to Bolivar. He stopped to rest for a bit. He found Hugh Boyd as his own storekeeper with coffee, calico, wine and whiskey for sale.

Bolivar after a tornado. Hail can be seen on the ground. Taken in the mid 1930s.

Braithwait House on South Lillian after a tornado. Hail can be seen on the house and on the ground. Taken in the mid 1930s.

A mill was somewhere nearby and this may have been the same mill that stood just down the hill east of Brighton to the south of the present Highway 215. See Brighton.

BRADLEY'S MILL

An early mill in Green Township less than a mile from the Hickory County line. The site is now under water. In 1860 the mill was purchased by John Lightfoot. He operated the mill for 10 years. Francis Hatler and D.W. Rush were his partners for a short period of time.

BRIGHTON

Situated about 10 miles south of Bolivar on Highway 13 and five miles west of Pleasant Hope on Highway 215. It was named by settlers from their earlier residences in the Brighton, TN area. John T. and Mary Williams were very early settlers in what was to be Brighton. They settled there before the county was formed. After the government survey of land was made they purchased land one mile north of Brighton on which they resided. They also purchased land a mile west of the future town.

The Butterfield Overland Mail had a stagecoach stop nearby at the home of J.H.M. Smith. The county's first telegraph office was also nearby at the Malloy/Molley/Mulloy place south of Brighton. The line ran southwest from St. Louis and crossed the southern part of the county. It was constructed in 1859.

The post office was opened on May 7, 1852 with R. M. Barnes as postmaster. Other early postmasters were Calvin M. McDaniel, William Smith Woodard who was a Methodist Episcopal clergyman and James H. Smithson. A mill stood near the little branch on the east edge of town. A mill stone from the mill is on display at Edwards Mill on the campus of the College of the Ozarks in Hollister, MO. The first buildings in the new town were south of the present town at the bottom of the hill. Abandoned buildings in Brighton are reminders of a once busy village.

BUFFALO

This was the fifth post office to be established in Polk County with Samuel Williams in charge of the office. He assumed his duties on September 17, 1840. Archibald Cowen then took over the position on November 2, 1842. By that time the first division of Polk County had taken place and Buffalo became the county seat of the new county which was called Niangua. It was changed later to Dallas County.

BURNS

A community that was named for Thomas J. Burns. His son was Captain Joseph W. Burns who served in the Civil War with the 15th Missouri Cavalry. It is located six miles east of Bolivar and four miles west of Halfway at Highway 32 and Highway AA which goes north off of Highway 32. Pomme de Terre River is just to the west of the town. Before the Civil War a grist mill and a saw mill were located on the river north of town. The post office was opened on December 2, 1884 and closed in 1923 when the mail was sent to the Bolivar Post Office. Freeman Higginbotham was the first postmaster. He served until January 27, 1894 when he was replaced by Reuben Higginbotham. He was followed by Polk Cunningham. For many years there was a general store that housed the post office.

CABLE MILL

An early mill that might have been on Pomme de Terre River in the north part of the county. It was believed to have been started by a Mr. Barker, probably William Barker, and was the same as the Barker Mill or Kelly Mill. There was a mill south of Ingalls post office and it could possibly have been that mill.

CEDAR VISTA

Near Slagle on northbound Highway 13.

CLIFFORD

A store located about two miles northeast of Goodson. It was nicknamed Jim Town for Jimmy Warren who ran a store at Clifford. Highway P goes by the former site.

CLIQUOT

Cliquot was formed later than most towns in the county. It began in 1898 when the Frisco Railroad extended its High Line from Osceola to Bolivar. Mr. Ben Leonard gave the land for the town and named it for his race horse "Cliquot". In the earlier years it had several general stores, a doctor, a drug store, a blacksmith shop, a depot and the stock yards from which cattle were shipped out.

In a meadow behind the depot was a favorite spot for church and family gatherings. An artesian well formed a branch through the meadow which made it a favorite for swimmers. This was on the east side of the railroad tracks.

Like many other towns located on a railroad line, Cliquot suffered when the railroad discontinued service. The old businesses closed and there were no new businesses opened to replace them.

The post office was established on March 2, 1893 with James A. Jones as postmaster. He served in the position until July 23, 1903 when Oliver C. Scudder became the new postmaster. Thomas Phillips, George E. Worthan and Richard A. Baldwin were other early postmasters at Cliquot.

CLYDE

A post office in service from September 4, 1876 until April 11, 1878 with John R. Hargrave as postmaster. His family lived in Jackson Township near Eudora and the office was probably a few miles southwest of Eudora on the family farm.

COLEMAN STORE

Rose Coleman was the owner of a store at this location about two miles north of Bolivar.

CONCRETE

Very little is known of this post office other than the name of the two men who served the office. They were Martin V. Hurst who was appointed on December 19. 1894 and served until Robert J. Ross was appointed on July 16, 1895. The office was closed in July 1896 and the mail was sent to Goodnight. Mr. Hurst was later living at Red Top in Dallas County. A map of that time period shows the post office to have been located east of Rock Prairie near the Dallas County line. It is possible that it was in a concrete building that stood for many years in that location.

CRONJE

A name found on 1940 era maps northwest of Huron. There was not a post office there and nothing is known of the site.

DAVIS MILL

Located two miles west of Aldrich on the Little Sac River. It was probably owned by James Davis and his sons. For more information see Strain's Mill.

Heaston Home near Brighton. Left to right: Martha Ann Shaw Heaston holding, Walter, Lydia, Adeline, Hannah, Maria, Susie, Armilda, Celeste, Carilla and Enos Heaston about 1895.

Dewey

A small town and post office located about two and one-half miles southwest of Goodson where sections 17, 18, 19 and 20 connect. Abe Drake was the first postmaster. He served from June 1, 1898 until March 24, 1906 when James R. Rentfrow assumed the position. He served until September 29, 1906 when the office was closed and the mail was sent to Halfway. A Methodist Episcopal church was located there. Newell Fulbright ran a general store nearby. The town was named for Admiral George Dewey of the Spanish American War.

Dunnegan

The original name was Dunnegan Springs. It was named for the Dunnegan family who settled in Polk County just a few months after it was organized. A big spring was located nearby on Dunnegan property. It was called Big Springs at that time. The post office was not opened until March 12, 1886 with Henry M. Wollard as postmaster. He served for a year and then John Sprout was appointed to the office. The office is still in service. Dunnegan was considered a railroad town as the Leaky Roof line of the K.C.C. and S. Railroad ran through town. Because of the railroad, it was a busy and prosperous town for many years. The section hands and their families lived by the tracks in railroad cars that were somewhat like today's mobile homes. At different times in the past the town has had a bank, a roller mill, a flour mill, general stores, a millinery shop, a hardware store, a depot, a doctor's office and a garage. Some of the buildings were destroyed by fire many years ago. Francis Dunnegan built a wool-carding machine and a cotton gin which were perhaps the earliest in the country.

Dunnegan Springs

See Dunnegan

Dunnegan Mercantile Company/Hacket Store, about 1912.

Dunnegan Store owned by Jim Larew and Tom Holmes. Left to right: Jim Larew, Guy Burrell, Marion Gilpin.

Main Street of Dunnegan, date unknown.

ELKTON

A town with its beginnings in Polk County and the second post office to be opened in the county, but with the division of the county in 1845 it became part of Hickory County. Cyrus Arbuckle assumed the position of postmaster on April 16, 1838. He served until August 25, 1841 when William H. Ables assumed the position. Alexander Blue and Andrew Yoast served the position up until the time Hickory County was formed.

ERIE

Located two and one half miles northeast of Goodson between Lindley Creek Church and Carter School.

ERNA

A store and post office from 1898-1903 on the old Bolivar-Warsaw Road near the Hickory County line. The Butterfield Stage had used that same route in its day, but at that time there was no post office or store. The nearest stop was just over in Hickory County at the Yoast Station. In 1896 James H. Baldwin and his family settled on property on the old road. They had operated a store and post office in Colorado previously. A post office was opened July 1, 1898 and served the area until June 30, 1903. James H. Baldwin was the postmaster. Mr. Baldwin helped to organize the Farmers Mutual Fire and Lightening Insurance Company of Polk County and he became the secretary of the organization. In 1904 he was elected as presiding judge of the county court. He worked hard to get a bond issue passed that would supply funds to build a new courthouse. It had failed three times before he had taken office, but in 1905 the issue was successfully passed. For a few years the Erna community was busy, but when Flemington was founded on the railroad line it was the demise of Erna. A rural mail route was established out of Flemington post office and then the Erna office was closed and the mail was sent to Elkton in Hickory County. Mr. Baldwin moved to Louisiana. Union School was located near Erna. The store and post office was named for the youngest Baldwin daughter, Ernestine.

EUDORA

In 1884 a new feeder railroad line was built that would miss Orleans and Shady Grove. Business owners at Orleans were very concerned about the railroad bypassing them and feared for their businesses. They decided they would move those businesses to be near the railroad line. This was near the mineral springs called Eudora Springs. The resort was not yet in its heyday. The new little town was called Sharon. A post office was applied for and since Sharon was the name of another office they had to chose a new name. That name was Gulf with Samuel D. Strain, Jr. being appointed as postmaster on August 14, 1886.

The town depot still went by the name Sharon and the post office was Gulf. On July 17, 1900, a new post office was opened with the name Eudora and the Gulf post office was closed. John B. Gates served as the first postmaster. He was followed by Frank M. Davison. With the closing of the railroad and the building of Highway 123 missing the central section of town, Eudora businesses soon began closing. The post office remains open.

EUDORA SPRINGS

Located a mile east and a mile north of Eudora. The Osage Indians called it Walula, which meant "Medicine Water" because they felt it had healing powers. Above the first spring about 100 feet was a second spring which was named Congress Spring.

Before the Civil War, Mr. E. R. Davis of Bolivar had purchased the land on which the springs were situated. His plans were to build a health resort because of the mineral content of the springs. These plans went astray because of the war. When the war was over people once again would go to the springs for the healing power of the water. In 1899 the property was sold to C.L. Allen who made improvements to the resort and began advertising of its benefits. It was a busy place for many years with reunions and picnics, but the depression took its toll on the resort. There wasn't money or time for events of the past.

FAIR PLAY

In 1852 a man by the name of Owen was the proprietor of a store just to the south of the present site of Fair Play. He called it Oakland and applied for a post office, but he was told there was already an Oakland post office in the state of Missouri. Then Millard W. Easley and John Wakefield donated land just to the north of the store. It was decided to call the new site Fair Play. A post office was applied for and on July 20, 1852 the office was opened with J. W. Wakefield as postmaster. He served until January 16, 1855 when Millard W. Easley assumed that position. Mr. Wakefield assumed the position again in 1863 for just a year and Mr. Easley again took over the position for eight years. This was in the part of Fair Play that later became known as "Old Town". "New Town" was the part of town that came into being with the building of the railroad. Bolivar did not have a railroad for almost 15 years after Fair Play so the town was a major shipping point from the Bolivar area. Plans were discussed to build a branch line into Bolivar from Fair Play, but this was not done. In 1887 a fire almost destroyed all of the town, but it was rebuilt soon after.

The Ewart and Train Charcoal Company was a big industry for the town in the earlier days. It was established in 1880. Charcoal from the plant was shipped to the Kansas City Train Works in Argentine, KS. Other businesses were the stockyards, hotels, a bottling company, an opera house, a livery stable, several mercantile companies, a bank, doctors, a lumber company, a dry goods store and a hardware store.

In 1879 Fair Play had a new newspaper called *The Fair Play Advocate*. It served the community for many years.

J.W. "Bill" Akard was a Fair Play resident who became a legend with a gun, not as a "gun slinger" but as the best shot in the country. He worked for the Remington Arms Company and traveled for them doing advertising with his sharp shooting.

Hines Lodge No. 114, K. of P. was organized in 1887. Other lodges in Fair Play were Purity Rebekah, No 305; Fair Play Lodge, No. 55, IOOF; Hardwood Lodge, No. 57 and Fair Play A. F. and A. M., No. 44.

FLEMINGTON

Located just south of the Hickory County line and three miles east of Humansville. The town was built on the Frisco "High Line" when it was built north out of Bolivar. The land for the town was given by Robert L. Fleming and the town was named for him. It was a prosperous town at one time with a bank, hotel, school, churches, lumberyard and general stores. The post office was opened in 1898 and continues to the present time. John Reed was appointed as the first postmaster on June 25, 1898. On

Dr. Charles H. Brown in uniform from the Spanish American War. He served in the Missouri Volunteer Regiment U.S. Army. He is seen with his brothers and sisters, all from the Fair Play area

August 26, 1899 Ora E Reed was appointed to the position. William A. Mottesheard, Jerome T. Mottesheard and Dora Harrison were other early postal officials at Flemington. In 1910 cowboy star Tom Mix made a movie there. It was his first starring role. He was not a native of Polk County, having been born in Pennsylvania. He worked for the Will Dickey Wild West Circle D Show. The group spent some winters on a farm owned by Mr. Dickey near Buffalo in Dallas County. Members of the group who were in the movie boarded in homes at Flemington.

FLOWER'S MILL

Located near Adonis on the Pomme de Terre River near the Hickory County line. The first mill was built by William Luttrell and was only used to grind corn. The mill has gone by several names, including Simpson's Mill which was an earlier name, but is best known by Flower's Mill. In 1910 some scenes from a Tom Mix movie were shot at the mill. Tom Mix, who was playing the sheriff, was chasing rustlers who fled to the mill. He and his men surrounded the mill and he captured the rustlers who had not jumped into the river.

FRISCO

See Graydon Springs.

FUGATEVILLE

See Mission.

GOLD

A small village located just inside the county on the Dallas County line east of Pleasant Hope. There was a general store, a blacksmith shop and a steam mill located there. The name came about because the Spaniard's were supposed to have buried gold on at least one of the three mounds or knobs along one side or the other of Pomme de Terre River. The earliest names for the knobs were Bald Knob, Henley Knob and Cowden Knob. Bald Knob now goes by the name of Goodnight Knob and Cowden Knob is sometimes called Potter Knob or Lucas Knob. The post office was opened on December, 6, 1900 with Lorenzo W. Stewart as the postmaster. He served until January 28, 1903 when Luke W. Hilton filled the position. Other postmasters were George Sheetz, James W. Cowan, Wm M. Glover and John R. Champion. The office was closed in 1915 and the mail was sent to Red Top in Dallas County. Gold was sometimes called Klondike as a derogatory name.

GOODNIGHT

Located southeast of Pleasant Hope on the Pomme de Terre River. The site of the mill that now goes by Goodnight dates to about 1825. Hugh Boyd was the original owner of the land which he purchased soon after the government survey in 1844. He owned the mill for 10 years before selling to Peyton Keele. The earliest known name to be associated with the mill is Whelchel Mill in the 1830s. It isn't known how long he ran the mill and he may have not been the first to operate a mill at the site. He would have been a squatter since the land had not been

Square Deal Mercantile in Goodson owned by Francis Arthur Breshears

Will Slater standing in front of the Goodnight Mill.

Northeast side of Goodnight Mill from across the river.

surveyed at that time. Zach Skaggs was known to have been an early miller at the mill. He probably worked for several mill owners.

The mill was supposed to have burned during the Civil War. Nelson Goodnight bought the property in August 1870 from Rameys and Cavins. The deed does not state there was a mill at that time. Mr. Goodnight died in 1873. The estate settlement states that Abraham and Daniel Goodnight, sons of Nelson, had erected houses, saw and grist mills. The present structure was built in 1914 after the previous mill was washed out during a flood and it is believed to be at least the fifth building according to land and tax records. There were also a general merchandise store and a blacksmith shop.

The post office was opened on April 5, 1883 with John H. Goodnight as postmaster. He remained in that position until January 27, 1894 when John M. Goodnight became the postmaster. He served until the office was closed on May 14, 1906 and the mail was sent to Fair Grove in Greene County.

GOODSON

The town was established in 1870 and named for Samuel Goodson whose father was county assessor in the early years of the county. Emma D. High School was located there. Goodson is six miles north of Halfway. The first post office was opened on June 19, 1874 with James K.P. Jump in charge of the office. He served only until November 24, 1874 when James M. Powers assumed the position. Then on July 13, 1876, Louis Strafford was appointed to the position. He was followed by John Standley on July 23, 1877. The office was closed in 1883 and reopened again 1889.

General Store in Goodson, owner unknown.

Halfway MFA in January 1931. Left to right are employees: Ethel Smith, Edgar Austin, Arthur Roderick, Melvin Davison and Verla Locke. Next is a customer, Orville Redd, and a salesman.

GRAYDON/GRAYDON SPRINGS

A town that lived and died with the railroad. Frisco Railroad officials never intended for Graydon to be more than a stop for summer visitors on their way to and from the mineral springs. Area citizens, though, had hopes of having a depot where they could take the train to Bolivar or Springfield. They had visions of being able to load livestock to send to market. There was no place for local residents to purchase tickets. They had to go to a nearby town in order to purchase a ticket and this defeated the purpose of being able to take the train from near their homes. Visitors to the springs had round-trip tickets, so a depot was not a necessity for them. Anyone wanting to board the train could wait at the store of Dr. William Lemmon. A village began to grow around the Lemmon Store and Dr. Lemmon became the first postmaster on September 4, 1886, but the post office was called Frisco. In 1889 Samuel Crain was appointed as postmaster. In 1890 James Chittim was appointed as postmaster. At this time the name was changed to Graydon Springs. Shortly after the name change, Simpson Chittim became the postmaster. He was the father of James Chittim. Henry Watson became Graydon Springs' first ticket agent, but there was still no depot at this time. In 1909 the railroad had abandoned a building at Peculiar, MO and the residents thought this was a good chance to have their depot. They raised enough money to have the building moved to Graydon Springs. The name on the building was not changed. It still had PECULIAR painted on the front of the building. In 1915 Frisco Railroad erected a new building with the correct name. In later years the resort area became a private girl's camp.

GRESHAM

A post office from 1885-1900. It was named for Secretary of the Treasury Walter Q. Gresham in 1884 and located just one half mile north of the Greene County line in Section 7 of Township 22 and Range 31. James G. Sloan served as postmaster from December 20, 1890 until the mail was sent to Morrisville on August 5, 1900.

GULF

A post office opened in Gulf on August 4, 1886 with Samuel D. Strain as postmaster. He served until April 18, 1888 when William H. Gilliam took over the position and served until 1892. The office was in service until 1900. See Eudora.

GULICK

A post office was opened there on January 7, 1916 with John M. Crawford as postmaster. He served until July 23, 1917 when James P. Brock filled the position. On September 30, 1919 the office was closed and the mail was sent to Morrisville. See Morrisville Station.

HADLOCK

A post office in service from March 27, 1893 until January 6, 1894 with Henry C Guinn as postmaster. It was probably near Hadlock Springs southwest of Bolivar.

HALFWAY

The land which was to later become Halfway was first purchased from the government by John Vanderford in 1839. The first business was probably a blacksmith shop. Then Mr. Vanderford opened a general store. It wasn't long before other businesses were opened. There were several drug stores, physicians and a grist mill, which was operated with steam instead of being a water mill.

John Vanderford was also the first postmaster of the Halfway post office which opened on May 27, 1850. He served until July 3, 1863 when John M. Eagon took over the position. John Ashren assumed the position on February 4, 1869 and served until December 17, 1872 when Littleton I. Logan became the postmaster. Rural mail service did not come to the community until November 1904. The name for the town was said to have come into being because the town was halfway between Bolivar and Buffalo.

In later years Halfway had a creamery, a tomato canning factory, a turkey processing plant, a bank, a garage for automobile repairs, a photographer, a barbershop and a café. With the coming of the automobile it was easy to travel to bigger places and gradually the businesses began to close.

The town became an organized village in 1967 and has an active town council. In the past few years a few new businesses have opened up in or near the town. The school system has been in the same location for many years. It is the home of Morris Westfall who served both in the State Senate and as a State Representative for Polk County. He was the son of Johnny Westfall who also served as a state representive. Ken Legan, also from Halfway, followed Morris West fall as representative.

Hickory Point

Located one-half mile west of Slagle in a grove of hickory trees in the southwest corner of Three Mound Prairie. William Jamison was said to have had the first general store in the county there for a short while. He was the commissioner of the permanent seat of government for the county and was a member of the militia during the Indian troubles in the 1830s.

Huckaby

This was a small trading point in the far northeast part of the county. The post office opened in 1905 with Henry Huckaby as postmaster. The office only lasted for 10 years before being closed. The store remained open until the late 1950s.

Humansville

James G. Human arrived in 1833 in the area of what would later become a town named after him. The land had not been surveyed and very few people were in the area at that time. He had come with a friend from South Carolina. They found a clear creek and followed it to a large spring where Mr. Human would settle. He then went to Illinois and in 1834 returned to the spring and built a cabin. He named the spring Big Spring and from there Humansville came into being. The town was the first founded in Polk County. It was the fourth post office to be opened in the county which was on December 5, 1839 with James G. Human as postmaster. Mr. Human filled that position until July 3, 1863 when Levi B. Human became the new officer. In 1838 Mr. Human opened a mercantile store and from there the town grew into a prosperous business center with a variety of businesses through the years.

Another of Humansville's well-known names was that of actor Edgar Buchanan. He appeared in many movies and then spent several years acting on television. He appeared in "Petticoat Junction," "Cade's Country" and "Judge Roy Bean" as a regular cast member.

George Dimmitt Memorial Hospital was dedicated on November 21, 1929 and served the area for many years. It provided general nursing care, surgical procedures and delivery of babies. It is presently a nursing home facility.

Emanuel Chapter NO. 24, O. E. S. was formed in 1894 with Mary A. Tinker, Susan Barnett, Flora Griffen, Nettie Mitchell, Alice Heaton, Susan Wann, Lizzie Akin, Flora Tinker, Euphemia Fisher, Lenora Griffen, Sarah K. Dunnegan, Laura M. D. Brown, Catharine Watkins, Ann E. Mashburn, Flora B. Elliott, S. M. Tinker, J. B. Barnett, S. H. Griffen, A. W. Mitchell, J. B. Wann, J. D. Elliott, T. J. Akins, O. W. Fisher, J. H. Mashburn and Benton Heaton as organizing members.

In 1858 the first Masonic Lodge in Humansville was organized and lasted until 1861 and the beginning of the Civil War. The organizing members of that lodge were Lawrence Smith, R. A. Richardson, D. P. Harris, I. V. Hunt, R. G. Noland, R. G. Hall, Silas Hindman, T. D. Hall and J. J. Smith. It was called the Modern Lodge No. 184.

After the war the lodge was again organized and called Modern Lodge No. 144. Thomas B. Sutherland, Samuel M. Tinker, Andrew T. Rentfrow, Preston Richardson, John Starkey, L. B.Human, John M. French, Samuel G. Smith and Joshua Whitaker were the charter members for the new lodge.

Humansville I. O. O. F. Lodge No. 310 was granted a charter on May 21, 1894. John W. Ross, Thomas Durham, L. P. Crank, J. R. Allison, J. F. Beaty and P. W. Bufford were the charter members.

George Dimmitt Memorial Hospital

Paxton Springs

HURON

A settlement named for Huron, TN. It is located northwest of Bolivar and is now a residential community. The post office was opened on August 9, 1897 with William D. Wood as postmaster. He served until December 28, 1898 when William F. Warren assumed the position. William A Lively, John C. Franklin and Elbert W. Payne served after Mr. Warren. Then on June 13, 1918, the office was closed with the mail going to Bolivar.

INGALLS

Located in the far northeast part of the county where Sections 11, 12, 13 and 14 connect in Range 21 and Township 35. A brickyard was located less than a mile to the west of the post office. The first postmaster was Samuel H. Hamill who served from January 11, 1890 until December 16, 1895. William F. Hoppers then served the office until. October 13, 1900. He was replaced by George W. Dryer. This place was named for the Inglis family who settled in the area, but the name was misspelled and so the post office became Ingalls.

JOLLY MILL

Located on Piper Creek.

KARLIN

It was named after Karlin located in the country of Bohemia and it was originally called Three Mound Prairie. The post office was first called Tremont because of the three mounds. There was confusion with a post office called Fremont in another part of the state so in 1903 the name was changed to Karlin. The office was in operation until 1944. Joseph W. Dvorak was the first postmaster serving from April 2, 1903 until October 18, 1922 when Joseph Vodicka became an acting postmaster.

Because of the town being located on the railroad tracks it was a shipping point for cattle. The stock yards was located west of the railroad tracks. The church and cemetery sat on the east side of the tracks. See Tremont.

KELLY MILL

See Cable Mill

KLONDIKE

See Gold.

LAMARTINVILLE

A new town was to be created by this name and was to be located one or two miles northwest of Halfway. Dr. Perry B. Larimore divided land into lots in 1859 with the hopes of creating the town. He could not raise enough interest in his plan. Dr. Larimore died 10 years later and is buried in the Bolivar City Cemetery. He was a medical doctor and lived in Bolivar when he passed away.

LEMMON'S MILL

John S. Lemmon built the first saw mill in the county just a few months after the organization of the county in 1835. It was a water powered mill located almost two miles east of Graydon Springs, slightly more than one-half mile southwest of West Bend. Mr. Lemmon later added a grist mill, store and blacksmith shop. This is probably the same mill ran by Thomas B. Lemmon, son of John S. Lemmon. In 1975 the site of the wooden dam was located and timbers were recovered from the Little Sac River.

LICK SKILLET

A name sometimes associated with Pleasant Hope, possibly because of the church campground located there. Large skillets were used to cook food for those in attendance at camp meetings and tales are told of the large skillets being placed on the ground and licked clean by dogs.

LIGHTFOOT MILL

See Bradley's Mill.

LUTTRELL MILL

See Flowers Mill.

MISSION

A post office was opened there on August 1, 1899 with Lizzie Alexander in charge. On October 22, 1900 William H. Jenkins became the postmaster. The office was closed on May 15, 1905 with the mail being sent to Halfway. A Baptist church was located there in the early 1900s. A man from the state of Pennsylvania was said to have donated land for a church and a school. They were called Mission.

MOHAWK

Elias Wicker was the first postmaster beginning on June 29, 1899. The office was in his store. He served the office until B. F. Renfro assumed the position on February 5, 1900. The office may have been moved to a different location at that time. Charles Pitts assumed the position on March 5, 1901. The office was in service until August 31. 1916. After its closing the mail was sent to Polk. A telephone switchboard was at Mohawk for a while after the post office closed. It is also called Mohawk Junction.

Lovett's Garage in Morrisville–E. J. Lovett working on car at left, standing are Wendell Cunnyngham and Charlie Lovett

Polodna Home, built by Frank Polodna in 1910, near Karlin

Morganville

A post office which opened on February 19, 1891 with William P. Warford as postmaster. He served for just three weeks and William R. Highfill assumed the position on March 9, 1891. The office was closed on March 26, 1894 and the mail was sent to Halfway.

Morrisville

The town had its roots founded in 1833 about the time Greene County was formed and two years before Polk County came into existence. Benjamin Looney had settled nearby. In 1838 a Methodist church had been started about a mile east of the present town. The building was used as a school also and was considered one of the first schools in the new county. Sometime later a new building was to be built, but a mistake was made as to where the new logs were to be unloaded. It was decided to build the new building where the logs had been left. This was a mile west of the first church and where the town is now located.

A survey for a town plot was made in 1867. At that time a Mr. Langenburg and a Mr. Jordan showed interest in building a mercantile store in the town. By 1870 they had built their store and were open for business. A post office was opened on April 18, 1871 with the name of Pleasant Prairie and Morris Mitchell was appointed the postmaster. It was decided a name change should be made for the post office. On July 23, 1872, this office was discontinued and reopened as Morrisville, having been named for Morris Mitchell who had done so much for the community. He served for a total of 10 years as postmaster.

Morrisville had its own newspaper called the *Morrisville Journal* during the early part of the 20th century.

After the college closed the population of the town began to dwindle. On April 13, 1945, a tornado hit the town and destroyed a number of homes with two people being killed by the storm. Like many other small towns Morrisville also lost many of its businesses as the years went by. A senior housing unit was built in 1979 on the east side of town which is called Grant Manor. There is an active volunteer fire department.

Morrisville Lodge No. 261 was organized in December 1886. Charter members were B. H. Bond, J. M. Worden, George A. Hamilton, Dr. J. F. Lemmon, James Shelton, B. W. Mitchell, Dr. J. W. Miller, G. A. Palsten, H. R. Conethard and W. S. Woodward.

Pleasant Lodge No. 160 A. F. & A. M. organized in October 1866 at West Bend and later was moved into Morrisville. Charter members were C. L. Lane, Thomas W. Mitchell, G. M. Winton, John Appleby, B. H. Bond, W. B. Mitchell, T. W. Cunnyingham, Seth Walker, J. F. Ball, S. N. Jones, A. C. Mitchell and Dr. J. W. Miller.

The Modern Woodmen of America had a camp in Morrisville.

Morrisville Station

A railroad station located one and one-half miles north of Morrisville on the Frisco High Line. It was a busy station with lots of freight shipments. It had a siding with stock pens for buyers and shippers. There was a store, a blacksmith shop and a scale yard located there. The last post office to be established in Polk County was located there. It was called Gulick. It was only in service for three years during WWI. See Gulick

Mount Pleasant

See Morrisville

Mulloy's Station

South of Brighton It was a post office from December 12, 1859 until March 14, 1860 with Wayne H. Parsons as postmaster. He is buried in Goff Cemetery located northeast of Bolivar.

Murray Mill

East of Pleasant Hope on the Pomme de Terre River and north of the present Highway 215 bridge across the river. Caleb Murray established the mill on land he had settled before the official government survey, so according to the Pre-emption act of 1838, he was able to purchase that property. Not long after that, he went to Iowa to pre-empt land there. He had left the mill in the care of his sons. He was found dead in his cabin in Iowa. The Murray Mill was in use for just a few years.

New Market

Another early settlement and trading point in the southwest part of the county. It was planned by William Campbell. With Orleans being nearby and the leaving of Mr. Campbell for California in 1852, New Market soon became a memory.

Nox

A small village near the Dade County line and just a few miles east of Dadeville. The post office was in existence from February 2, 1901 when James R. Hays became postmaster and served until January 28, 1903 when William L. Wheeler took over the position. He served until May 18, 1906 when the office was discontinued and the mail sent to the Walnut Grove Post Office in Greene County. Mr. Wheeler was credited with naming the town. Nox means "night" in Latin. The town was near a large grove of oak trees that made a lot of shade.

Oakland

See Fair Play.

Oakville

A community about two miles west of Morrisville near the Little Sac River. Concord Church located nearby was built in 1873. Several years later a cemetery was started by the church.

Oakwood

This was a store located about two miles north of Bolivar on an east-west road between the present Highway 83 and Highway 13. It was just to the east of the present Highway 13.

Orleans

According to early state records, Orleans was founded in 1832 by Ransom Cates. The area was about four miles southeast of Aldrich near the Little Sac River. Early Greene County records show Orleans as an important trade center to the people of the northwest part of that county. It was a bustling village with general stores, blacksmith shops, boot makers, a tannery, a tin shop, a distillery, two schools, two churches, a tailor shop, three physicians and a post office. Nearby was the Orleans Mill, sometimes referred to as the Campbell and Cates Mill. Ezekial Madison Campbell built the first mill there on Little Sac River. He later sold the mill to Ransom Cates. In 1869 Samuel Strain and B.B. Rice purchased the mill and operated it for a number of years. The first person to serve as postmaster was Daniel Bradford who served July 21, 1846 until March 7, 1848 when William Hill took over the position. David M. Strain was the last postmaster to serve the post office. It was closed on November 27, 1895 and the mail was sent to the Aldrich post office. In 1885

Pleasant Hope Mill.

the new railroad missed Orleans and business went to Eudora and Aldrich. Gradually the town became a memory.

PAYNE'S PRAIRIE

This was more of a settlement than a town, but it did have a post office. It was located to the northwest of the town of Polk and named for the Payne family who settled there. The first postmaster was Alexander Barnes who held the position from May 8, 1872 until December 9, 1873. A.Y. Brandenburg, Elizabeth Brandenburg and Melinda M. Snapp also served in the position until the office was closed January 13, 1882.

PIN HOOK

An old nickname for Pleasant Hope which at one time was considered to be a derogatory name. See Pleasant Hope.

PIPER CREEK MILL

PLEASANT HOPE

This post office was first opened on December 3, 1851 with Robert D. Smith, discontinued in 1855 and reestablished on December 3, 1860 with Robert Cowden as postmaster. He served until January 13, 1865 when Willis J. Tiller filled the position. The above Mr. Smith and a Mr. Hedden opened the first general store in 1851. It was probably in the home or an outbuilding of Robert Smith with post office being located in the business. In 1853 Mr. Heddon sold his interest to a Mr. Kerr.

Robert D. and Eliza A. Smith arrived in the area of what is now Pleasant Hope by March 20, 1847, when they purchased land that would become part of the town. This was located north of the present day business section and was where the present high school property is situated. Mr. Smith served as pastor of the Cumberland Presbyterian Church located north of the town near the cemetery.

J.A. Cowden and his brother opened a business in 1855 and were in business until about the time of the beginning of the Civil War. In June 1857 Neil McKenzie, who had a business in Bolivar, also opened a business in Pleasant Hope according to an advertisement in the *Bolivar Weekly Courier*. Robert and Eliza Smith did not stay long in the area. They left to go back to Kentucky. There is very little information on the businesses during the Civil War. Just after the war McClure and Company opened for business. Massey and Patterson was a partnership business. In 1889 the village contained a general store, an implement store, a grocery store, a drug store, a blacksmith shop, a wagon maker shop and a flouring mill owned by Sallee and Cowden. In the early 1900s Pleasant Hope had a newspaper called *The Eclipse*.

The Pleasant Hope Lodge No. 8, I.O.O.F was organized in July 1886 with the following charter members: L. D. Burdett, L. C. Adams, J. M. Hearalson, Levi Boswell, J. J. F. Caldwell, Jesse Eagon and R. G. Wilkinson.

The Pleasant Hope Lodge No. 467, A. F. & A. M. was organized June 14, 1873 with the following charter members: E. S. Mason, E. W. Spence, Henry Gardner, J. H. Walker, I. O. Parrish, W. B. Cavin, Z. T. L. Burns, W. B. Patterson, J. W. Barr, J. A. Cowden, William Patterson and G. T. Patterson. This lodge is still active in the community.

At times a fight would break out when citizens of another town would call the town Pin Hook. That was considered a derogatory name. Some consider the name as an early name, but Pin Hook was probably a later name instead of an earlier name. Lick Skillet is also a name connected with Pleasant Hope.

PLEASANT PRAIRIE

A post office from 1871-1872. Morris Mitchell was appointed the postmaster on April 18, 1871. He served until July 23, 1872 when the office was closed. See Morrisville.

Men and their horses in Pleasant Hope.

Fishing Party near Pleasant Hope early in the morning of November 10, 1914.

Polk County Post Office

This was a small settlement four miles northeast of the Paynes Prairie Post Office.

Polk

Located 11 miles northeast of Bolivar on Highway D. John. M. Zumwalt was the first postmaster serving from April 23, 1880 until June 29, 1895. In its earlier days there was a tomato canning factory, a bank, a walnut processing plant, a mill, different general merchandise stores, service stations and the Farmers Exchange.

Polk Town

A store and post office established in 1879 by John M. Zumwalt. In about a year this office was closed and the Polk office was opened. See Polk.

Principia

Location unknown, but it was started as a Utopian Community in the 1890s by Mr. Alcander Langley. It was an unsuccessful attempt.

Rex

A post office from 1900-1906 with John T. Loftin serving as postmaster from April 14, 1900 until November 15, 1904 when Elijah W. Ross took over those duties. He served until the office was closed on October 30, 1906. It was located in Section 4, Range 21 and Township 32 south of Halfway. About 1930 a man named Dober Duke ran a store very near where the post office stood.

Rice's Mill

Located just below Aldrich on the Little Sac River and was named for B.B. Rice who at one time owned the mill. This may be the Shady Grove Mill which was run by a Mr. Rice. B. B. Rice was a partnership owner of the Orleans Mill for a period of time also.

Rimby

Located on Highway 64 just west of the Dallas County line. At one time it was a trading post. William H. Greer served as postmaster from July 2, 1897 until October 31, 1898. Samuel Anderson then served until February 13, 1906 when Mary M. Rimby took the post and served until the office closed on December 29, 1908 and the mail was sent to Goodson.

Rock Prairie

Located on Highway Z northeast of Pleasant Hope and two miles north of Tin Town. At one time there was a tomato canning factory and a general store. A Missionary Baptist church and cemetery are located there.

Rolla

A post office was opened there on January 12, 1858 with John B. Weaver in charge. It was closed on July 1, 1858. See Rondo.

Rondo

The first store was to the east of Highway 83 and the present Rondo. A Baptist church and cemetery are located there. It is 10 miles north of Bolivar on Highway 83. The Rondo post office was opened the same day the Rolla post office closed. John B. Weaver was the

County Store at Rondo, bought by Earl and Christena Blackwell in 1944 from Irene and Carl McBride. Blackwell operated store from 1944 to 1981 when the store was closed. Store was built by Carl and Sylvia Franklin in the late 1930's.

Robert Clave and his horses near Rock Prairie.

Berniece Zumwalt Sallee in 1935, postmistress of the Polk Post Office.

postmaster at both offices. He served until June 24, 1862 when William VanKannon filled the position. The office was closed on August 25, 1864 and re-established June 4, 1866 with Thomas Price as the postmaster. The office was closed in 1919.

SCHELL/SCHNELL

It was probably named for the Schnell Spur line which was located between Cliquot and Flemington on the railroad line. It was used to load cordwood for shipping.

SCHOFIELD

Located six miles southeast of Halfway on Highway EE. It was named for a Baptist minister. D.P.Brockus was appointed postmaster on February 26, 1887 and less than a month later on March 18, 1887, Wm T. Chittenden assumed the position.

SENTINEL PRAIRIE/SENTINEL

The first post office was opened on April 26, 1850 under the name of Sentinel Prairie with Avington Simpson as postmaster. He served until August 25, 1851 when the office was discontinued. It reopened on August 18, 1853 with Peter Burns as postmaster. On September 28, 1854 Reuben Simpson assumed the position. It was taken over by Henry Simpson on December 6, 1856. Samuel Little and Reuben Bean both served the office until it was again closed on July 21, 1863. It was closed for two years and was reopened on June 29, 1965 with Jeremiah Vaughn as the postmaster. Mr. Vaughn moved the office to his place of business which was four miles north of Sentinel Prairie at Sentinel on the south edge of Lindley Prairie, sometimes called Pitts Prairie which extended into Hickory County. Previous to the time of the Civil War there had been a Baptist church where the Mt. View Baptist Church at Polk is located. There was lots of distrust and strife among citizens of the area at that time so the church trustees sold the building to Jeremiah Vaughn. He tore down the building, hauled it to Sentinel and rebuilt it to house his place of business. During the Civil War a conflict took place near the store and two area young men were killed there. After that incident the place was sometimes called Vaughn's Stand. The post office still went by the name of Sentinel Prairie for almost 35 years after being moved to Sentinel and finally in 1899 the name was changed to Sentinel. At different times in its history the town has had general stores, a blacksmith shop, drug store, hotel, barber shop and a whiskey still.

SHADY GROVE

Located northwest of Aldrich and about a mile east of the Cedar County line. In the early 1870s Thomas B. Slagle built a shingle and saw mill, then added a carding mill and general store. One source says Shady Grove was not a water wheel mill. The mill also went by the name of Rice's Mill. The name came from a grove of shade trees. In 1885 W.D. Coats gave right-of-way through his property to the railroad. A post office was opened there on February 21, 1882 with George W. Griffin as postmaster. He served until September 11, 1884 when William J. Hensley took over the position and served until Thomas B. Slagle became the postmaster on November 11, 1886. Arthur Griffin and Armand Blair followed Mr. Slagle as officials at the office. In 1896 the office was closed and reopened under the name Shadygrove as one word. George W. Griffin and then James R. Johnson served the office under the new name. The reason for the name change is not known. This office was discontinued in 1905 with the mail being sent to Fair Play

Joe Overmeyer and Rena Slagle Boswell, employees of the Slagle Meat Market owned by Bud and Lucille Grider. Taken in the late 1960s.

SHANGHAI

Located about two miles northwest of Morrisville. This name is found in the Turnbo Manuscripts written by S. C. Turnbo. William and Easter Grider lived at Shanghai according to Mr. Turnbo in the early 1860s. Mr. Grider was a Methodist minister.

SHARON

See Eudora.

SHAVE TAIL

Old nickname for Morrisville.

SHEPPERDS GROVE

In July 1870 Rev. Frank P. Schofield gave a talk at Shepperds Grove in the extreme edge of Polk County seven miles west of Buffalo. He is buried in Schofield Cemetery.

SIMPSON'S MILL

See Flower's Mill

SKILLET

Located eight miles east of Pleasant Hope, four miles west of Elkland and 2 1/2 miles north of Greene County. It was an early place name and was located in what is now Dallas County near the junction of Highways 65 and 215.

SLAGLE

The Slagle Post Office was established on November 16, 1874 with Richard H. Fox as postmaster. Jesse H. Murray was appointed to the position on December 13, 1875. Edward H. Vincent took the postmaster position on August 24, 1877 and served until the office was discontinued on December 6, 1878, but on March 28, 1879 the office was again opened with Isaac J. Rains assuming the postmaster position. The office continued until 1905. The old building sat for many years just to the north of the Grider Meat Market which later became a mobile home dealership.

SLAGLE CREEK

This was an early settlement named after the Slagle family who came from Kentucky in the 1830s. James A. Slagle served as the postmaster at Slagle Creek from the opening of the office on May 12, 1852 until it was closed on February 21, 1853. The Slagle Creek Missionary Baptist Church is still active and the Slagle Cemetery is next to the church. The school building is now a residence. It is located south of Bolivar just to the west of Highway 13 and south of present day Slagle.

SMITH MILL

Located east of Pleasant Hope on Wilson Creek. It was owned and operated by Dick Smith. Timbers from the mill can still be seen along the creek bed.

SOCIALIST HALL

This was a meeting house for the Socialist Party located about two miles north of Bolivar and near Highway 13.

South Prairie
See Sentinel Prairie.

Star Ridge
Located just to the west of Rimby. There was a school, church and post office. The church still stands on the south side of Highway 64. The post office was served by Charles J. Ashworth from May 1, 1891 until May 4, 1893 with the mail going to Polk at the closing of the office. The office was reopened as Starridge instead of Star Ridge on October 24, 1894 and then closed exactly a year later.

Strain's Mill
In the early 1840s John Strain rebuilt the Davis Mill which was considered a very early mill in Polk County. His son Samuel helped him with the mill until Samuel enlisted for service in the Civil War. It is not known how long the mill was in existence. The mill was on Little Sac River west of Aldrich. Samuel Strain was a partnership owner of Orleans Mill after his return from the war.

Sunset
Located just over five miles north of Slagle and east of Highway 13 near Pomme de Terre River. A church is all that remains there. Before the turn of the century there was also a post office, store and school. James R. Salsman assumed the position of postmaster when the office was opened on May 23, 1888. He served until July 3, 1890 when James R. Fitzgerald became postmaster. The office served the community until it closed in 1900.

Tin Town
A village that sprang up after Gold ceased to exist. It is located four and one half miles east of Pleasant Hope and just west of where Gold was located on Highway 215. The name came about because of the tin used on the buildings. At one time there was a blacksmith shop, cheese factory, general store and upholstery shop. The Night Owl Theater was located in the old cheese factory. Live plays were performed there in the 1930s. This later became a church which is still there. The three knobs or mounds in the southeast part of the county can be seen from there.

Three Mound Prairie
See Karlin.

Tremont
There was a post office from 1889-1903. Because of the confusion with Fremont, MO, the name was changed to Karlin. John W. Hoaglin was the first postmaster beginning on October 14, 1889. See Karlin.

Union Grove
A community in the far southeast part of the county near Greene and Dallas Counties. A church and cemetery are still there. The first school building was located north of the church and west of the cemetery. Many new homes have been built there in recent years. Goodnight Mill is nearby to the northwest.

Unknown Mills
It is believed there were two mills southwest of Dunnegan on Spring Creek. One was located just before Spring Creek goes into Jump Off Creek. The other mill was closer to Dunnegan. Both mills may have been located on land owned by the Hopkins family. The dates are unknown.

Unknown Mill
On Bear Creek near the head waters of the creek.

Van
Located southwest of Halfway on Highway YY. It had its beginning in 1900 and grew to be a very busy town with several stores, blacksmith shops, doctor, drug store and mill. John Sanderson was the first settler there. Bud Brown settled there next and he built the first store building. It burned sometime later. Van Burns then built a concrete building which he used as both a hotel and a store, but it also burned. The town was named for Mr. Burns. Andy Davis built a blacksmith shop about that time. Van had its own doctor. He was Dr. Matthew Haralson who was located on the north side of the road running through town. The Van Post Office was opened on March 14, 1899 with William R. Brown as postmaster. He served in that position until June 19, 1901 when Walter W. Brown became the postmaster. Other early postmasters were Samuel Redd. Maner Clark, L.B. Parrish, Frank Botts, Asa Vanderford, Albert Woodmansee and Andrew Davis. The office was closed in 1934. Van is now a residential community.

Vaughn's Stand
See Sentinel Prairie.

Victor
Located in the far northeast part of the county on what is now Highway AC. It was also called Sugar Lip. There was a store and school there at one time. A Baptist church is still active just west of the site.

Violet
A trading post started somewhere around 1890. By the turn of the century it was a bustling town, but the loss of the post office caused the town to dwindle to nothing. At its busiest time there was a blacksmith shop, several stores, three grist mills and the post office. John Lyttle was the first postmaster and served from November 20, 1896 until September 9, 1898 when Amy White took over the position. She served until Joseph J. Hawkins assumed the position on October 16, 1899.

Wallula
An Indian name meaning *Medicine Water* because of the mineral content of the water. Mr. E. R. Davis bought the property to turn it into a health spa. The name was changed to Eudora Springs. The resort was never completed.

West Bend
This was a trading point near the Little Sac River about two miles southwest of Morrisville. Carroll Lemmon was the first postmaster beginning on May 22, 1855. William Lemmon took over the position on June 13, 1856 with the office being discontinued on May 21, 1857. It was re-established on May 30, 1860 with William Lemmon as postmaster. A month later Seth Walker took over the position and served until the office was permanently closed on November 21, 1865. Lemmon Mill was nearby.

Williamson Mill
This mill was built by James Williamson two miles below the Luttrell Mill on Pomme de Terre River.

Wishart
Like several other towns in Polk County, Wishart came into existence because of the railroad. A water tank was placed along side of the line at what would later become Wishart. This was on the property of Berry Scroggins. It was decided to build a depot and from there a town grew. It is located about 10 miles southwest of Bolivar at the end of Highway UU and was named for Mr. Dempster Wishart who was the passenger agent for the Frisco Lines when the line was built north into Bolivar. A post office was located there from 1884 until 1957. Jacob Kelly, Hugh L. Winton, William R. Brown and Bernard B. Haga served as early postmasters.

Charles U. Becker was a resident of Wishart after his retirement. He had been a reporter for newspapers in Kansas City and St. Louis. He was elected as a State Representative and then as Secretary of State in 1920. He was not born in Polk County, but he called it home and he was buried in the Morrisville Cemetery.

Ramsey Benson was another journalist that called Wishart his home. He lived there for many years after his career with newspapers in the state of Minnesota. He wrote articles for various magazines. Both of the above men were considered good citizens of the community.

The businesses are gone and the Methodist Church remains along with a number of homes.

Woodard Mill
An early mill on Little Sac River. It was built by Pitt Woodard in the 1830s. The mill and dam were washed away in 1864. The logs were salvaged and used to build a barn, then 30 years later the barn was demolished and the best logs were used to build a corn crib. Later the logs were used to set bee hives upon. This is near the site of the present day Brooks Sod Farm.

Xerxes
Located near Goodson. There was a post office there for three years with Sarah Dickey serving as postmistress from July 21, 1888 until February 6, 1891 when the post office was closed and the mail sent to the Goodson office.

Young Hickory
A post office in the northern part of the county and of which very little is known. It was opened on September 19, 1853 with William Ingles in charge and closed two months later.

Pleasant Hope Roller Mill

Fair Play Store

37

Polk County Churches Past and Present

Most of the earliest religious services in Polk County were not held in a church building. They were held in homes and campgrounds until a house of worship could be built. Sometimes it was years before a building was erected for services and then that building might be used for the local school. A school may have been used for worship services.

When families arrived in a new area there was not always a church of their denomination to worship in. It wasn't unusual for them to attend the closest available church service at least until a church of their own denomination was formed nearby.

Campgrounds were used especially by the Methodists and the Presbyterians. They might have had a shed or a brush arbor for worshiping and log cabins for people to stay in while they attended the services which could last for a few days or many days. It was common for many congregations to have their camp meeting in the fall of the year. People would attend from surrounding counties. They would take a milk cow and chickens with them to provide food for the family while in attendance at the meeting. Nearby residents would provide pasture for the cows. Some families even took their family dog on the trip with them.

In some cases the descriptions and locations of certain churches seemed to be that of another name or denomination. Some buildings were used by different denominations with certain Sundays set aside for each denomination. Land records show that some buildings were designated that way in the official county record. Some church land was never recorded as such and therefore it is hard to find a definite location or name. This is especially true of the very early county churches.

The location of some churches is given by using a legal discription. In this case S is for Section, T is for Township and R is for Range. In some cases only a name was known and not a location.

ABUNDANT LIFE ASSEMBLY OF GOD

ALDRICH CHRISTIAN
Organized in the early 1900s. The building was finished in 1906.

ALDRICH UNITED METHODIST
Organized about 1898 as a Methodist Episcopal Church.

ALLIANCE OF CHRISTIAN FELLOWSHIP
Bolivar

Bismont Missionary Baptist Church

Bolivar First Baptist Church and parsonage.

Baptist

Name unknown. S-36, T-34, R-21 east of Halfway.

Barren Creek Cumberland Presbyterian

Located between Bolivar and Fair Play.

Barren Creek Community

Located between Bolivar and Fair Play

Bethel Community

Located southwest of Fair Play on Highway 245

Bethel Presbyterian

Located in Bolivar. It was organized on April 15, 1879 with Reverend John McFarland as pastor. It dissolved on October 18, 1883.

Bismont Missionary Baptist

Located between Bolivar and Fair Play and north of Highway 32. On November 17, 1894 a council met at the home of Columbus Hopkins one-half mile south of the present site for the purpose of organizing a Baptist church. Members from Dunnegan Baptist and Salem Baptist Churches were there to help. Seigle Mead was the moderator and J.A. Hopper was the clerk. In 1898 a building committee was appointed. Bismonth was the name suggested. A few years later the "H" was dropped and the name became Bismont.

Bolivar Berean Baptist

Bolivar Church Of Christ

Bolivar Church Of Jesus Christ Of Latter-day Saints

Bolivar First Baptist

Organized in 1859. The first building was erected in 1861.

Bolivar First Christian

Organized 1852.

Bolivar First Church Of The Nazarene

Bolivar First Foursquare

Bolivar Maranatha Baptist

Bolivar Methodist Episcopal

This church was organized in 1840 and the first building was located on Lot No. 3 in Block 4 of "Old Town". The building was used as a court house until the county courthouse was built. In 1844 there was a division in the church. There was both a Northern and Southern branch. The ownership of the building went to the Southern congregation. During the Civil War both branches of the church suffered with attendance. Services were sporadic.

Bolivar Methodist Episcopal North

After the Civil War this branch of the church held their services in the old academy building where later the North Ward School was built. Services were held in the academy for a number of years and then in other buildings. In 1877 a new building was erected.

Bolivar Methodist Episcopal South

On the 14th day of November 1849 an indenture was made between Joseph L. Young, Stephen Mitchell and Wesley Mitchell as trustees of the Methodist Episcopal Church South of Bolivar and Lymon Beamon. The amount was for $200. The site was Lot No. 1 in Block 6 of the town of Bolivar. See Bolivar Methodist Episcopal.

Bolivar Pentecostal Church Of God

Bolivar Presbyterian

Organized May 27, 1883 by Rev. J. J. Marks. It was a member of the Northern Organization of the Presbyterian Church. The first elders were W.G. Drake, S.D. Strain, T. J. Poage and C.D. Lyman. A few months after the organization of the church a new building was started. It was two stories high of brick and stone. James Safferty was the first pastor beginning in November 1886. The building is still standing and has been used by a number of organizations through the years.

Bolivar Seventh Day Adventist

Bolivar United Methodist Church

Located on North Main. See Bolivar Methodist Episcopal.

Brighton Baptist

On northbound Highway 13 just to the south of the junction of Highway 13 and 215. It was organized as a Missionary Baptist. During the Civil War services were discontinued. In 1885 the church was reorganized. It is now a Southern Baptist Church.

Brighton Methodist

The church may have started in the 1840s. It is situated on land settled in 1843 by Jesse Mitchell who was a Methodist Episcopal minister. The first

College Hill Methodist Church in 1910

building was of logs. In 1882 a new building was erected which still stands next to the cemetery. Services are no longer held at the church.

Calvary Missionary Baptist
Bolivar

Campbell Grove Missionary Baptist
Originally called Campbell's Grove it was organized on July 20, 1879 at the Oak Grove School southwest of Bolivar.

Central Church Of Christ
Bolivar

Center Point Missionary Baptist
Organized on February 20, 1897. The church building was built after May 1897.

Christ Church
Near Humansville. S-34, T-35, R-24,

Church Growth Today
Bolivar

Church Of Christ
Located in Bolivar, but it is not the same as Bolivar Church of Christ.

Church Of Jesus Christ Of Latter Day Saints
Bolivar

Church Of The First Born
S-23, T-35, R-23

Church Of The Nazarene
Bolivar

College Hill Methodist
Three miles southeast of Fair Play. Services are no longer held there.

Community Of Christ
Humansville

Concord Missionary Baptist
See Oakville

Damascus Road United Pentecostal Church
Dunnegan Bible Baptist

Dunnegan First Baptist
Organized as a Missionary Baptist and now a member of the Southern Baptist Convention.

Dunnegan Christian Church
The building has been gone for many years.

Enon Missionary Baptist
Organized in 1841. The first building was log construction built in 1842. A new building was erected in 1884 and stood until it was destroyed by fire. Another new building was erected and it is used for regular services at the present.

Eudora Baptist
Originally called Sharon. It was organized on December 15, 1888.

Eudora Church Of God

Evangel Assembly Of God
Humansville

Exodus Ministry

Fair Play Assembly Of God

Fair Play Baptist
Organized on May 13, 1888 as a Missionary Baptist and is now a member of the Southern Baptist Convention.

Fair Play Christian
Organized on January 1, 1893. Years later the church attendance dropped and the church was abandoned. The building was rented to the Church of God. During the 1950s Christian Church members again used the building for bible study.

Fair Play Church Of God
The congregation used the Christian Church building after the Christian Church was abandoned.

Fair Play Free Methodist
In existence during the 1890s.

Fair Play Presbyterian
It was a stone building located on Walnut Street next to the school.

Fair Play United Methodist
Organized in 1864 as a Methodist Episcopal Church by Reverend Isaac Routh and Reverand William Denby. Shortly after a frame building was erected. In 1888 a new building was erected in the newer part of town.

Charles and Mattie Calhoun in front of Hickory Point Church on their 50th Anniversary.

Vere Miller, daughter of H.D. Miller at College Hill Church

Goodson Missionary Baptist Church

Fair View United Methodist
Located north of Bolivar on Highway D near Huron.

Fender Chapel
Organized in 1865 as Pleasant Hill Sabbath School of the Methodist doctrine. In 1962 it was voted that the church would be changed to the Baptist denomination because most of those attending were of the Baptist faith. It is located in the southern part of the county just to the east of Highway 13. Johnson/Gumbo School was just to the east of the church.

First Assembly Of God
Bolivar

Flemington Christian
Organized on December 18, 1910. The building was erected in 1911.

Flemington Methodist

Flemington Missionary Baptist
Organized in 1909 and a church was built in the following year.

Flemington Seventh Day Adventist

Freedom Fellowship
Bolivar

Freedom Missionary Baptist
Organized in 1845 as Freedom. It had previously been Bethel that was organized in 1842. Services were held in a log school west of Reed Cemetery until 1855 when the church purchased land located near the present Gordon Cemetery and built a new building. Services declined during the Civil War and in 1868 the church services were discontinued. This building may have also served as a school. This church may be the same as an unknown church and school building which was supposed to be located at the northeast corner of Reed Cemetery although it was thought to be a Methodist church. Possibly they were near to each other.

Friendship Missionary Baptist
Organized in 1843 on Upshaw/Upshur Prairie southeast of Pleasant Hope. A second building was erected in 1870. Exact location unknown.

Full Gospel Assembly Of God
It was organized in January of 1975. It is east of Halfway on Highway 32.

Goodson Missionary Baptist
Goodson

Grace Fellowship Baptist
Bolivar

Halfway Christian
The church first shared a building with the Halfway School system beginning in 1868. In 1897 the school voted to erect its own building. In 1903 the Halfway Academy used the church building for a few years. In later years the church moved into another building and no longer has services. See the Halfway Academy in the schools section.

Halfway Missionary Baptist
Located at the west edge of Halfway. See Mission Chapel Baptist.

Hardshell Baptist
Located north of Bolivar near Cooper School House.

Harvest Assembly
Fair Play

Herman Or Hermon Presbyterian
Organized in the 1830s. Reverend E. P. Noel was the first pastor. The church dissolved after just a few years. It was located south of Bolivar and north of Slagle.

Hickory Grove Methodist
Organized in 1837 at the home of Pitt Woodard. The present building was erected in 1868 at the Hickory Grove Cemetery. It is located south of Morrisville near the Greene County line. Decoration services are held there each year.

Hickory Point Church Of God
Southwest of Karlin. The building has been gone for a number of years. It stood across the road from the Hickory Point School House.

High Praise Assembly Of God
Bolivar

Highway Assembly Of God
Brighton

Hood's New Methodist Episcopal
Organized in 1868 in Green Township with the meetings being held in a school house. The church building was erected in 1885. No services are held there now.

Hopewell Missionary Baptist
Located in the northeast corner of the county. It was organized in 1855. The first pastor was William Spillman.

Fender Chapel Sunday School in 1918 or 1919. Reverend Billy Winton with the white beard, holding his bible. Others known to be in the picture were Edith Fender, Ethel Fender, Ola Scroggins, Relod Sallee, Jewel Blackburn, Tiny Bridges, Lucy Ball, Frances Owens, Lewis Tiller, Rosie Phillips, Cora Blackburn, Mrs. Whitman, Lula Presley, Olive Fisher and Leta Dickerson. Fender Chapel Sunday School in 1918 or 1919. Reverend Billy Winton with the white beard, holding his bible. Others known to be in the picture were Edith Fender, Ethel Fender, Ola Scroggins, Relod Sallee, Jewel Blackburn, Tiny Bridges, Lucy Ball, Frances Owens, Lewis Tiller, Rosie Phillips, Cora Blackburn, Mrs. Whitman, Lula Presley, Olive Fisher and Leta Dickerson.

Humansville Bible

Humansville Christian

Organized in 1877 and the building was erected in 1878.

Humansville First Baptist

Organized in June 1852. Except for four years during the Civil War the church has had regular services. It was originally called Senter Missionary Baptist.

Humansville Full Gospel

Humansville Methodist Episcopal

It was originally the Shady Grove Methodist Church and was moved into Humansville. See Humansville United Methodist.

Humansville Methodist Episcopal Colored

Building erected in 1892. See Humansville United Methodist.

Humansville Methodist Episcopal South

Organized in 1890. See Humansville United Methodist.

Humansville Reorganized Church Of Jesus Christ Of Latter Day Saints

Organized in 1955.

Humansville United Methodist

The Humansville M.E. Colored, Humansville M. E. South and Humansville Methodist (Old Shady Grove) formed into one church.

Ladd's Chapel

Located in the area of S-8 or 9, T-32, R-21, about two miles north of Pleasant Hope.

Liberty

Denomination unknown.

Lighthouse Assembly Of God
Humansville

Lighthouse Assembly Of God
Bolivar

Lighthouse Missionary Baptist
Bolivar

Lindley Creek Missionary Baptist

Hickory Grove Methodist Church and Cemetery near Walnut Grove, MO

Lindley Creek Church in 1924 as the new building is being built to the right.

The church was organized in 1884 and is still an active church which is located in the northeast corner of the county.

MARANATHA BAPTIST
Bolivar

METHODIST EPISCOPAL
Near the Dallas County line in S-13, T-34, R-21 east of Mission.

METHODIST EPISCOPAL
S-12, T-33, R-21 southeast of Halfway a mile from the Dallas County line near Knapp School.

MISSION BAPTIST
Located in S-14, T-34, R-21. See town of Mission

MISSION CHAPEL NO. 1
See Rondo Baptist

MISSION CHAPEL BAPTIST
It was organized on September 18, 1889 near the Dallas County line east of Halfway. The church moved to Halfway in 1907. In 1952 the church changed its name to Halfway Missionary Baptist. In 1960 a new building was erected at the west edge of Halfway.

MISSIONARY BAPTIST
Near Old Union

MITCHELL CAMPGROUND
On the 30th day of November 1839 Ransom and Edith Cates sold a parcel of land to A. Ewing, R. Stout, J. L. Minton,_____ Mitchell, M. Mitchell, S. Mitchell, W. Mitchell, M. R. Mitchell and M. Mitchell Jr "that they shall erect and build or cause to be erected or built thereon a house or place of worship for the use of the members of the Methodist Episcopal Church in the United State of America". It is located in S-6, T-32 and R-23 east of Aldrich on E 490th Road.

MORRISVILLE ASSEMBLY OF GOD
About 1933 the church was organized and they purchased the former cheese plant building to be remodeled for church services. A new building was erected on what is now Highway 215 at the east side of town.

MORRISVILLE FAITH BAPTIST
Organized on February 1, 1975, it is located on Highway 215 on the west edge of Morrisville.

MORRISVILLE FIRST BAPTIST
Organized on May 11, 1890 by members of the Polk County Baptist Association. After wind damage to the first building, the congregation moved to the Old Union site for a few years and then built a new building on the south edge of town.

MORRISVILLE UNITED METHODIST
On Highway 215 across the highway east of the school. In 1836 a Methodist Episcopal class was formed with Aaron and Elizabeth Ruyle, Samuel Mackey and wife, Benjamin Hancock and wife, Mrs. Elizbeth Powell and B. C Mitchell. They were later joined by Mrs. B. C. Mitchell and George Mitchell. In that same year a log building was built on Pleasant Prairie just east of the present Morrisville. This was the beginning of the Methodist Episcopal Church there. It is believed the first sermon preached in what is now Polk County was preached near there at the home of Aaron Ruyle. The church later became affiliated with the Methodist Episcopal Church South.

MT. BETHEL PRESBYTERIAN
Organized in August 1874 and discontinued in April 1889. It was located near Orleans.

MT. ETNA BAPTIST
Located on NN Highway

MT. GILEAD UNITED METHODIST
Located southeast of Bolivar.

MT. OLIVE BAPTIST
Organized in August 1869. North of Bolivar on Highway D.

MT. PISGAH
Located west of Bolivar in S-18, T-33, R-23

MT. TABOR CAMPBELLITE– CHRISTIAN
Located about two and one half miles east of Cliquot in T-34, R-23, S-15 near Highway 83.

MT. VIEW MISSIONARY BAPTIST
First organized in 1851, but dissolved after eight years. It was reorganized in 1868 as Mt. Moab. In 1871 the name was changed to Mt. View.

Mt. Olive Church in the mid 1920s. Row 2: Second from the right is George Moore. Row 3: Fourth from the right is Jessie Moore Phillips.

Mt. Zion Missionary Baptist

Located between Aldrich and Fair Play on Highway 123. It was organized in 1840 with Elder Daniel R. Murphy presiding over the organization. Organizing members were Ezekiel Madison Campbell, William P. Hughes, Pleasant Crain, Rutha Crain, Nathan W. Wilson and Sarah Wilson. The church was moved to a new site in 1968 when Lake Stockton took the land.

Mt. Zion Methodist

Near Dewey in the northeast corner of S-19, T-34, R-21.

Mt. Zoar Missionary Baptist

Organized about 1856 in the northeast part of the county. It is no longer in existence.

New Bethel Methodist

S-20, T-33, R-21

New Life Community

Bolivar

New Life Assembly

Halfway

Oak Grove Missionary Baptist

Located at Adonis. It was organized in 1867.

Oakville

It was originally Concord Missionary Baptist, but because of the nearby Oakville Cemetery and Oakville School it became known as Oakville. It was organized in 1873. Located about two miles west of Morrisville. The deed to the ground was conveyed in 1889 from Rolen C. Sell and his wife E. A.(Ezenith Ann) to the trustees: Samuel Griffen, G. W. Hamilton, Josiah Johnson and their successors in office.

Old Freedom Meeting House

Located north of Pleasant Hope on the north side of the Pomme de Terre River. It was used by Providence Missionary Baptist Church for a while.

Old Union Hardshell Baptist

Located near the Henegar Mitchell Spring and Old Union Cemetery. The first building was log and it was replaced by a brick building which in no longer standing. Josiah Conn was the pastor about 1845.

Open Bible Church Of God

Bolivar

Pentecostal Church Of God

Pentecostals Of Bolivar

Pleasant Grove Freewill Baptist

Located northeast of Brighton and west of Pleasant Hope. It was organized on September 18, 1886 by Elder John K. Noble and Elder John C. Thompson with 14 charter members. N. L. Crawley was elected deacon and John C. Thompson was the first pastor. The church was organized in the Pleasant Grove School House and work was started shortly

Cornerstone of the new Pleasant Hope United Methodist Church.

Pleasant Hope Cumberland Presbyterian Church

Old Rock Prairie Church just before demolition in late 1990.

after, but it was not finished for a few years. The building burned about 1910 and was not rebuilt.

Pleasant Hill Missionary Baptist

Located on Highway 32 between Bolivar and Burns.

Pleasant Hope Assembly Of God

South of Pleasant Hope on Highway H. Pleasant Grove School House and work was started shortly after, but it was not finished for a few years. The building burned about 1910 and was not rebuilt.

Pleasant Hope Cumberland Presbyterian Church

The Shiloh Cumberland Presbyterian Church was organized on July 15, 1837 just north of what is now Pleasant Hope. On March 2, 1841, the name was changed to Pomme de Terre Cumberland Presbyterian. On October 4, 1882, the name was changed to Pleasant Hope Cumberland Presbyterian. The local session had asked for a name change. This church dissolved in 1974 after 137 years. The church bell is now part of a monument on the Pleasant Hope High School campus.

Pleasant Hope First Baptist

Pleasant Hope Fundamental Baptist

Pleasant Hope United Methodist

Organized in 1895. Because of the condition of the original building, the church voted to build a new building. The basement part was finished first and used for a while until the upper floor could be finished.

Pleasant Ridge Missionary Baptist

Located in the southwest corner of the county just off Highway 123. It was organized on December 19, 1868. The first building was a log structure located across the road from the present church. Another building was built later and it burned. The present building was erected in the middle 1880s with two additions being added since that time. Regular services are still held at the church.

Pleasant View Missionary Baptist

Organized April 14, 1883 in the nearby Roberts School house. The first pastor was D.P. Brockus. It was relocated to its present location in 1933. The church still has regular services.

Polk Christian Church

Organized about 1870 and reorganized in 1888.

Providence Missionary Baptist

Organized on September 5, 1839 at the home of Cirus/Cyrus Patterson. It is the oldest Missionary Baptist Church in Polk County. The first services were held in homes of the members, Chittenden School House and at the Cumberland Campground at Pleasant Hope. In 1867 it was decided they needed a building and it was decided to meet in the Old Freedom Meeting Place which was an old log building on the north side of the Pomme de Terre River. In 1889 a concrete building was erected at Bob Town. Services were held there until services were moved to the old Providence School building and in 1983 plans were made for a new building to be erected next to the school house.

Rimby Assembly Of God

River Of Life Community

Bolivar

Rock Prairie Missionary Baptist

Organized on April 17, 1874 with 18 charter members. The first services were held in a building to the east of the present day site. In 1877 a new building was erected at the crossroads to the west of where the congregation first held. Then in 1990 a new brick building was erected next to the old building which was then torn down.

Rondo Baptist

Organized on March 4, 1872 on two and three-fourths acres of land purchased from Mr. and Mrs. Jesse Boon. The original name was Mission Chapel No. 1 as it was a mission of the Elkton Baptist Church.

Sacred Heart Roman Catholic

Bolivar

St. Alban's In The Ozarks Episcopal

Bolivar

St. Catherine Of Siena Catholic

Humansville

Building that was used first as Providence School and then later as the church after the school was closed. A corner of the new church can be seen on the far left.

Schofield Chapel Missionary Baptist Church-1926

ST. WENCESLAUS CATHOLIC

Located at Karlin. The first building burned in 1905. A brick church of the same style was built in its place. That building is no longer standing, but a monument was erected on the site of the church.

SALEM MISSIONARY BAPTIST

Organized in October 1888. Elder J.F. Hampton was the first pastor. A previous building stood where the present day Salem church stands and was burned about the time of the Civil War. The name of this church or its denomination have not been determined. Salem is still an active church.

SCHOFIELD CHAPEL MISSIONARY BAPTIST

In 1869 a Sunday School was started and preaching services were held in the nearby log school. On February 3, 1877 the church was officially organized. A new building was erected in 1928.

SENTER MISSIONARY BAPTIST

See Humansville Baptist

SENTINEL MISSIONARY BAPTIST

Organized on February 5, 1907 after a revival meeting at Rose Hill Schoolhouse. Noah Stinecipher was the first pastor.

SHADY GROVE BAPTIST

Located near the Shady Grove post office in western Polk County. It was probably a Missionary Baptist Church.

SHADY GROVE METHODIST

Organized before 1840. It was a Methodist Episcopal, located south of Humansville. It became part of the United Methodist Church at Humansville

SHARON MISSIONARY BAPTIST

See Eudora Baptist

SLAGLE CREEK MISSIONARY BAPTIST

Organized on December 15, 1850, the church is located south of Bolivar on Highway 13.

St. Wenceslaus Church

Salem Missionary Baptist Church

Shady Grove School at Cemetery, picture taken 1990

Music Class at Spring Creek Cumberland Presbyterian Church about 1917-18

Dinner on the ground at Spring Valley Church in the 1920s.

Southern Hills Baptist
Bolivar

Southside Missionary Baptist
Bolivar

Sovereign Grace Reformed
Fair Play

Spring Creek Cumberland Presbyterian
Dunnegan

Spring Valley Missionary Baptist
Located at the junction of Highway AA and 390th Road north of Violet. The church was begun in 1912 on land donated by John Kaudle. Services were held there until in the 1960s. The building has been converted into a hay barn.

Star Ridge Methodist Episcopal
S-28, T-35, R-21. One mile west of Rimby on Highway 64.

Tin Town Missionary Baptist
Located in the old cheese factory building at Tin Town.

Turkey Creek Methodist
Located by the Turkey Creek Cemetery and

Turkey Creek Missionary Baptist Church and Cemetery near Walnut Grove, MO. Picture taken 1990.

Slagle Creek Sunday School Classes

near the Baptist Church on Highway 123 near the Greene County line.

TURKEY CREEK MISSIONARY BAPTIST

Organized on July 25, 1841. It is in the far southwest corner of the county, just inside the county line on Highway 123 south of Eudora.

UNION GROVE

Organized in January 1867 northeast of Bolivar. It no longer has services.

UNION GROVE MISSIONARY BAPTIST

It was organized in 1879 as a Methodist Church with other denominations being able to have services also. After other denominations no longer had services, it was declared a Missionary Baptist Church by the county court and a new building was erected in 1959. Located south of Tin Town near the Greene County line.

UNKNOWN

Located near the northeast corner of Reed Cemetery south of Halfway and the William Clark home. Reverend Yeager was one of the pastors of the church which was probably a Methodist Church. A very early Polk County school was also held in this building about 1845. This may be the same as Freedom Missionary Baptist Church, although it was said to be to the west of the Reed Cemetery. Two denominations may have used the same building.

UNKNOWN

Located on the same spot as Salem Missionary Baptist. It burned about the time of the Civil War. The name of the church or its denomination is unknown.

UNKNOWN CHRISTIAN

Organized by Jeremiah Sloan about 1842 near the boundary line of what was then Jackson and Mooney Townships. It is possible there was never a building for the congregation and they met in the homes of the members.

UNKNOWN CHRISTIAN

About 1852 Reverend Peter Wright came from Kansas to preach and helped to organize a Christian Church in the home of David West four miles southwest of Bolivar. After 1855 church services were held in a nearby schoolhouse. David West owned land very near where Wishart would later be located and also acreage about two miles north from there.

UNKNOWN HARDSHELLED BAPTIST

Located near Millican Spring.

UNKNOWN MISSIONARY BAPTIST

Located south of Karlin. It was destroyed by a tornado and the members joined Enon and Campbell Grove Missionary Baptist Churches.

UNKNOWN METHODIST

Located near Polk Town in the 1840s.

WALNUT RIDGE MISSIONARY BAPTIST

Also known as Van or Van Town Church. A new building was recently erected at the same location.

WELLSPRING BAPTIST FELLOWSHIP
Bolivar

WISHART CHRISTIAN

WISHART SOUTHERN METHODIST

WORD OF GOD FELLOWSHIP
Bolivar

ZION LUTHERAN
Bolivar

Old Walnut Ridge Church at Van. It has been replaced with a new building.

The first Union Grove Church building about 1955, south of Tin Town

Cemeteries

Located By Range

The cemeteries can be located by using section, township and range numbers.

RANGE 21

Agee Farm—26-32-21
Armstrong Farm—20-33-21
Boone—5-33-21
Breshears—2-34-21
Bridges-Beem—4-34-21
Burdett-Cavin—4-31-21
Case—12-32-21
Church Of The First Born/Stoddard—23-35-21
Clark—13-33-21
Fouts-Ankrom—9-32-31
Glover—36-32-21
Gorden—14-33-21
Greer—35-35-21
Grove—26-34-21
Hopewell—1-35-21
Jackson—2-33-21
Jump—24-35-21
Kain—31-35-21
Lindley Creek—3-24-21
Martin—11-35-21
Mayfield—3-32-21
Mission—14-34-21
Mt. Zoar—8-34-21
New Bethel—20-33-21
New Life—22-32-21
Pleasant Hope—30-32-21
Pomme De Terre—17-32-21
Prock-Murray—27-32-21
Ragsdale—27-34-21
Reed—9-33-21
Rock Prairie—23-32-21
Sawyers—7-34-21
Schofield—26-33-21
Sentinel Church—18-35-21
Sentinel-Pitts Farm—18-35-21
Sentinel-Town—7-35-21
Sheridan—36-33-21
Star Ridge—28-35-21
Terrell—20-33-21
Tiller—32-32-21
Union Grove No. 1—12-31-21
Viles—33-33-21
Range 22
Acock–16-32-22
Adonis-Oak Grove—9-33-22
Bailey—29-35-22
Beckley—34-32-22
Bennett—4-34-22
Bewley-Finch—5-33-22
Botts-Higginbotham—3-33-22
Brighton—34-32-22
Brock-No.1—9-31-22
Brock No.2—22-32-22
Callaway—13-33-22
Chamberlain—13-35-22

Crestview Memorial Gardens—9-33-22
Dunnaway—29-34-22
Emmons—12-34-22
Goff—34-34-22
Graveyard Hill-Elliot—11-32-22
Hickory Grove—7-31-22
Keeling—21-33-22
McKinney—12-33-22
Meyer—25-32-22
Mound View-Mt. Zoab—35-35-22
Mt. Gilead—20-33-22
Mt. Olive—31-34-22
Owens—25-33-22
Payne—36-35-22
Pleasant Hill—2-33-22
Polk.Mt. View—1-34-22
Ruyle—19-32-22
Slagle—8-32-22
Spillman—13-35-22
Spring Valley—15-34-22
Wells—12-32-22
Wilcox-Wilson—24-33-22

RANGE 23

Appleby—25-32-23
Bolivar City—2-33-23
Booher—11-32-23
Campbell Grove—20-33-23
Chappell–31-32-23
Corben—9-31-23
Crain No. 2—11-33-23
Davis No. 2—12-32-23
Enon—9-32-23
Flemington—7-35-23
Greenwood—11-33-23
Hadlock—17-33-23
Hendrickson—13-33-23
Hensley-Kennon-Buck-Shannon-Lunceford-34-33-23
Heydon-Williams-Devin—32-34-23
Johnson—13-32-23
Karlin—25-33-23
Kelley—25-35-23
Kelly-Francka—12-34-23
Mitchell Campground—6-32-23
Moore—1-34-23
Morgan—2-34-23
Morrisville—23-32-23
Oakville—28-32-23
Old Union—35-32-23
Richardson-Gallivan-Elliot—24-34-23
Rondo No. 1—23-35-23
Rondo No. 2—27-35-23
Salem—12-34-23
Spencer-Hufford—19-33-23
Springer—19-33-23
Strepey—13-33-23
Taylor-Milliken—21-33-23
Union Grove No. 2—20-34-23
Vannice—15-33-23
White—27-34-23

Whittenberg—4-31-23
Williams—13-34-23
Worthan—19-34-23

RANGE 24

Akard No. 1—4-23-24
Akard No. 2—9-33-24
Anderson-McDaniel—7-33-24
Ashlock—23-34-24
Barren Creek—36-24-24
Brown-Blair-Courtney—31-33-24
Brush Grove-Potts—28-35-24
Bunch—25-33-24
Burros-Emberson—12-32-24
Chandler—25-33-24
Claypool—5-31-24
Coffman-Howe—23-33-24
Crain No. 1—27-33-24-relocated
Davis No. 1—28-33-24
Dotson-Dodson—35-23-24
Dunnegan—4-34-24
Eudora—26-32-24
Harper—19-32-24
Henderson—13-32-24
Hillbrant—11-33-24
Hopkins-Cave Springs—31-34-24
Hubbard—34-33-24-relocated
Humansville—15-35-24
King No. 1—32-32-24
King No. 2—31-32-24
Lemon-Lemmon—12-32-24
McMasters—11-31-24
Molder—6-35-24
Mt. Zion—27-33-24-relocated
Oak Grove—8-31-24
Pickel-Meade—23-34-24
Pleasant Ridge—9-32-24
Plum Grove—3-35-24
Richardson No. 1—12-35-24
Shady Grove No. 1—2-33-24
Shady Grove No. 2—22-35-24
Stockton—24-33-24
Sutherland—21-33-24
Tinker—31-35-24
Trimble—18-33-24
Turkey Creek—10-34-24
Welsh Slave—24-33-24
Wilson-Coats—1-31-24
Wollard—23-33-24

CEMETERIES WITH UNKNOWN NAMES OR LOCATIONS

Northwest Marion Township near Cooper School
Southwest Marion Township—7 or 9-33-23
Southwest Marion Township—22-33- 23
McKinley Township three-fourths mile east of Huron—4-34-22
McKinley Township one and one-half miles northeast of Violet—12-34-22
McKinley Township one-fourth mile south-

east of Sentinel–29-35-22

Union Township one mile north of Aldrich—27-33-24

North Benton Township three and one-fourth miles northwest of Burns—23-34-22

South Benton Township Near New Bethel Church–20-33-21

South Green Township One mile north of Goodson—5-34-21

West Looney Township–About three miles southwest of Morrisville

CIVIL WAR
About two miles northeast of Pleasant Hope.

INDIAN BURIAL SITE
About three miles northwest of Halfway.

POMME DE TERRE
North of Pleasant Hope, probably on the old Bridge Road.

UNKNOWN
About two miles west and south of Goodson. The burial places of John and Jane Zumwalt, possibly other burials.

UNKNOWN
West of Violet.

WEAVER
Eight miles north of Bolivar

Schools, Academies, Colleges And Institutes

On July 19, 1820, just a few months after the State of Missouri was formed, the state government stated "that section numbered sixteen in every township shall be granted to the state for use of the inhabitants of such townships for the use of schools." Proceeds from the rental of this land were used to provide funds for the local school districts. A commissioner was to oversee the use of the section of land to see that it was not damaged while being rented. A person could be fined if they destroyed the property. A tenant was not allowed to cut trees from the land unless they were to be used for his own personal use. He had to keep the fences in good condition.

An act was passed in 1831 to allow for the sale of school land if three fourths of the free white landowners signed a petition requesting the sale, but the law also stated that there must be 15 free white householders in the congressional township.

If the land was to be sold, it had to be posted and then sold at a public auction in one-half quarter sections of 80 acres at $1.25 per acre and nothing less would be accepted. This way of keeping up the schools was used for sometime in the beginning of the State of Missouri and each county. It was a controversial issue and many districts had trouble meeting the requirements set forth by the state.

The first schools in Polk County were subscription or private schools. Each family paid by the number of students from their family in attendance at the school. The buildings were built by the area families. At this time school was only in session for three months and usually during the winter months when there was not as much for children to do at home. If a teacher could not be found that lived nearby, then many times the teacher would board with the family of a student during the school term. The teacher was also the janitor at the school, being required to take care of the fire and the general cleaning of the building. Many students of that day had to cross a creek to get to school as the districts were quite large. Some students had to walk several miles to reach their school building.

In 1908 Mr. J.M. Zumwalt wrote a series of articles about his life for the *Bolivar Free Press* newspaper. He was born in 1841 in Polk County near Sentinel and lived his life in the county. The following is his recollection of the first school he attended.

" The first school I ever attended was a subscription school taught by George Jump. The whole school, teacher and all, are dead, so far as I know, except myself. The school house was a room about 18 feet square, built of round logs.

The fire-place consisted of a wall of stone built against the log wall on the inside of the house and was about 6 or 7 feet high by about 10 or 12 feet long. The stem of the chimney was built on a joist by placing one end of the stick of which it was made on the joist and the other end in a crack in the wall. It was directly over the center of the stone wall or fire-place, which had no jams. The seats were made of logs split open and the splinters scraped off with an ax. They had no back. They rested on four legs, which were made by boring holes in the slabs with a 2-inch auger and driving in legs made of stout sticks. They were generally too high for our feet to reach the ground (for the house had no floor) and our feet were generally swinging as regular as the pendulum of a clock. The teacher would go to the school house a little after sunrise and build a fire and as soon as any scholar came in he took up books. He gave recess in the forenoon, an hour playtime at noon and recess in the evening and would dismiss a little before sunset. We studied our lessons vocally, everyone spelling or reading in a medium tone of voice. We recited out lessons in the order we arrived at the school house, the first to arrive recited the first lesson. The door of the house was in the south side and the window was in the north side. It was made by cutting out a

County wide Eighth Grade Graduation held at the county courthouse in April 1928.

log as close to the wall at each end as possible, which left an opening from 10 to 12 inches wide. This had neither glass nor shutter, but stood wide open the year around. The writing desk was made by boring two auger holes in the wall under the window and driving into them two stout pieces and placing on them a slab. This we thought was all right. We learned to write after copies set by our teacher. We had two writing lessons a day, after which we would hang our copy books on the wall until the next day."

By the end of the Civil War most subscription schools had ended and county schools came into existence with exact districts set up. In many instances a student would attend school in a different county than the county of their residence.

In 1875 the General Assembly of Missouri provided for the public education of its young people of school age.

The first school attendance law was enacted by the Missouri General Assembly in 1905. It required attendance of children from ages eight through fourteen.

The location of some schools is described by using S for Section, T for Township and R for Range.

ALDRICH

The high school opened in 1910 with a two-year school program. The first graduating class was in 1912 with the following graduates: Jesse Box, Leland Courtney, Frank Davis, Ray Davis, Edith Hamby, Edna Harvey, Bess Hoodenpyle, Conrad Owens, Treacy Shuler, Trella Spinks and Anna Vermillion. The school burned in 1928 and the students were sent to Fair Play, Bolivar and Morrisville. A year later the school was reopened with a three-year school and later a fourth year was added. The school continued until 1949 with five students graduating. Students from the surrounding rural school districts attended high school in the Aldrich district.

ARMSTRONG

See Persimmon Grove.

BLACK OAK

S-35, T-32, R-21. The following students attended Black Oak School about one mile west of Tin Town in 1911 and are the students pictured above but not in order: Mack Nunn, Zella Choate, Bertha Glover, Leunna Fullerton, Loyd Glover, Effie Mayfield, Guy Cruz, Myrtle Choate, Frank Lewis, Carl Medley, Helen Culbertson, Ona Glover, May Mayfield, Ula Mayfield, Barny Culbertson, Vina Nunn, Lacy Nunn, Pearl Mayfield, Leon Matheny, Grace Choate, Helen Matheny, Don Edmonson, Zelma Mayfield, Lois Choate, Roy Fullerton, Claude Medley, Ava Mayfield, Dorothy Medley, Ralph Glover, Hattie Glover, Maud Fullerton, Joe Belt, Lucy Nunn, Luette Moore.

BLACK OAK

S-26, T-34, R-22. Located about one and one-half miles south of Violet. The first building was located about one-half mile west of the last building.

BLOOMER

S-35, T-34, R-21. East of Halfway near Highway 32.

Aldrich boys' basketball team 1928–1929

Aldrich girls' basketball 1940-1941. Left to right: Betty Mosier, Mary Young, Mary Curl, Florene Crain, Elizabeth Shuler, Mary Neil, Betty Tygart, Wanda Willey, Frances Tygart and Coach Emmitt Rodebush.

Black Oak School near Tin Town in 1911. Mamie Glover, left in the back row was the teacher.

BOLIVAR

An 1841 map of Bolivar shows a school house in the area of Broadway, West Chestnut and Pike Street. It was a log building that belonged to the Methodist church and court was also held in the building for a time. School was probably held there for several years. In later years the Cary Hotel was located at this site and then it became Hoffman Hall which was the men's dormitory of Southwest Baptist College.

In 1858 a plan for a new school was planned. On July 17, 1858, William R. Devin, Benjamin M. Jewett, Moses P. Hart, Thomas R. Blake and Perry Laremore leased the south half of lot 11 of the original plot of Bolivar for the purpose of building "A Male and Female Seminary of Learning." This was known as the Bolivar Academy and was located where North Ward School was later located and the museum of the Historical Society of Polk County is situated at the present time. The school received both public and private funding and was not considered a public school. School was discontinued at the time of the Civil War and there is no record that school was held during the war years.

In 1865 Reverend J. C. Nodurfth opened a private school in the old academy and classes were held there for several years. In 1866 a public school district was organized with three directors elected to the board. Judge T. H. B. Dunnegan and George W. Drake were two of

Brighton School, 1948-1949. Row 1: Jackie Slagle, Billy Boswell, J.W. Burk, Jackie McGuire, Donald Gene McGuire. Row 2: Colleen Looney, Katherine Sue Brazil, Barbara Burk, Mary Brazil, Wanda Stokes-teacher.

Bloomer School 1930-31. Starting on the left front, going to the back of the room and across to the right and to the front. Wayne Polly, Denzil Sergent, Warren Austin, Warren Shadwick, Mary Barnett (Teacher), Dean Short, Mary Eastburn, Virginia Polly, Victor Cowden, Lucille Cowden, behind Lucille is unknown boy and possibly Dwight Legan, Lavern Short, unknown girl, Leland Polly, Gene Sergent, Wanda Shadwick, _____Eastburn, Dean Polly, Marie Short, _____Shadwick, Minnie Eastburn.

Brooks School after it was moved to Highway P south of Goodson.

Thora Tolbert, daughter of John Tolbert of College Hill.

Carter School on October 17, 1938

the members. The new district had no money so they worked with the academy to continue school classes.

In 1870 a new state act was passed allowing for local school boards to organize a school district with six members to each board. In June of the next year the Bolivar district held an election for this purpose. They elected T. H. B. Dunnegan, John D. Abbe, John H. Oldham, Charles L. Dalrymple, John F. Shipley and T. G. Rechow as directors to the board. In 1875 John A. Cochran signed a contract with the school district to teach at the school for $140 per month, but out of that sum he was to pay two more teachers for a term of 10 months. Part of this salary would be paid by subscription. The school had three sections at that time which were Primary, Intermediate and Higher Education. The average daily attendance was 120.

Since that time the Bolivar school system has continued to grow with many smaller districts consolidating into the larger school. It is the largest school district in the county.

BRIGHTON

S-28, T-32, R-22. The school was located just to the north of Brighton on the west side of the road. The last graduating class was in 1935 when the high school was closed. The grade school continued through the 1948-49 school year with Wanda Stokes as teacher. The school consolidated with the Marion C. Early School. The building is now part of the Highway Assembly of God Church. The south half of the building had burned after W W II. It was being used for the grade school which then used the older section built about 1926 by B. A. Dickenson.

BROOKS

S-16, T-34, R-21. South of Goodson.

BRUSH CREEK

S-28, T-34, R-21. North and slightly east of Halfway.

CARTER

T-34, R-21, S-2. Northeast of Clifford near the Dallas County line.

CEDAR GROVE

S-27, T-35, R-22. Two miles south of Humansville.

CHAPEL

An early school located either in or near Fair Play. After its closing the school was held in the Methodist Church at Fair Play.

CHERRYVALE

S-15, T-33, R-22. Southwest of Burns.

CHITTENDEN

Located between Pleasant Hope and Halfway, with the exact location unknown. It is mentioned in Providence Church minutes as church services being held at Chittenden School.

CHURCH OF GOD BIBLE SCHOOL

At Eudora from 1959-1970

CLARK

S-20, T-34, R-21. Three miles south of Goodson

CLIQUOT

S-8, T-34, R-23.

COATS

A school near Orleans in the 1880s and may have been the same as the Orleans school.

COLLEGE HILL

S-14,T-33, R-24. Three miles southeast of Fair Play.

COLLINS

S-11, T-32, R-23. One mile north of Morrisville Station.

CONCORD

S-11, T-34, R-21.Two miles east and slightly south of Goodson. It may have been just over in S-2.

COOPER

S-14, T-34, R-23. Four miles north of Bolivar. The first frame building was erected about 1875 and may have been in S-15 instead of S-14.

COY

S-23, T-34, R-21. Located one and one-half miles from the Dallas County line northeast of Halfway. This school was known to have had three locations in the same area with all three locations adjoining Highway J.

DUNNEGAN

Dunnegan High School was located on the corner of Ranken and Hazel Streets. The

Cooper School–Christena Rowles, teacher 1927-1928

Collins School 1932-1933, 5th and 6th grades. William Lane, Willis Wilson, Howard Taylor.

Collins School 1932-1933, 7th and 8th grades. Stella Wilson, David Davis, Jewell Brown.

Coy School, 1934 Row 1: Roma Whitney, Thomas Dunaway, Leonard Davison, Grant Barham, Alfred Dunaway, Johnnie Davison, Milburn Erwin, Francis Hinkle and Leslie Short. Row 2: Beatrice Patten, Geneva Patten, Doris Long, Ivey Erwin, Thelma Long, June Jones, Opal Hinkle, Marie Long, Betty Long, Lawrence Lockhart and Gene Erwin. Row 3: Basil Fullerton, Frances Long, Verian Redd, Bertram Lemmons(teacher), Ruby Reedy, Willene Dunaway, Denzyl Redd, Pauline Erwin, Wilburn Erwin, Mildred Freeman.

building was struck by lightning in the 1940s and was destroyed by the resulting fire. It had started as a two-year high school and by the time the school was closed it had become a four-year high school. Nineteen thirty eight was the last year for a graduating class at Dunnegan High School with only seven students graduating. The district was divided with the students going to several of the surrounding school districts. A number of rural school districts were around Dunnegan and students from those schools who wanted to receive a higher education attended the Dunnegan High School.

EAGLE HILL

S-16, T-35, R-21. Just southwest of Huckaby and two miles north of Rimby.

EDGEWOOD

S-18, T-32, R-24. Near the Dade County line three miles southwest of Aldrich. On April 25, 1919 Vernon Pyland was the teacher. Edd Maxwell, John McClelland and Jack Cowan were the directors. The following were students for 1919: Elma Witt, Wilma Witt, Thea Rowan, Leslie Rowan, Bernice Maxwell, Arthur Maxwell, Glen Rowan, Mary Rowan, Golden Rowan, Ruth Owen, Edith Owen, Lawrence Owen, Lafayette Anderson, Maggie Cowan, Clara Cowan, Myrtle Cowan, Hugh Cowan, Lelah Cowan, Helen Stanley, Leota Stanley, Everette Cowan, Oscar Beal, Adrain Wright, Lawrence Cowan, Ruby Crane, Zulema McClelland, Goldena McClelland, Claud Cowan, Ralph McClelland, Joseph Landreth, Kenneth Landreth, James Landreth, Otis Anderson, Jewell Anderson, Ella Marie Cavender, Clarence Cavender, Bessie Taylor, Hazel Taylor, Earl Taylor, LaVerne Cowan, Heath Cowan and Finis Cowan.

EIDSON

S-21, T-34, R-22. Northeast of Bolivar.

ELM GROVE

S-18, T-35, R-24. Between Humansville and the Cedar County Line.

ELM GROVE

S-26, T-33, R-23. Just west of Karlin.

EMMA D HIGH

Located at Goodson the school was named by Mrs. Mary Hogg for her step daughter Emma D. Samples. It was not a county supported school, but was supported by the patrons of the district.

Emma D. High School

EUDORA

Grade school was held there until 1951 when the school was consolidated into the Marion C. Early district. The building became a community center.

FAIR PLAY

Chapel School may have been the beginning of the Fair Play School District. It was an early school in the county. After school had been discontinued at Chapel School, classes were held in the Methodist Church for a few years. Then a one-room frame building was erected just to the west of the church. Because of growth in the district a two-room house nearby was remodeled for a high school. Growth continued in the district and it was necessary to find more room. Again the Methodist Church was used for this purpose with some students attending class there. In 1889 it was decided the district needed another building to have room for more students so in 1890 another building was erected. This was a two-story building and was located where the present school system is located. In 1904 two additional rooms were added to the building. The school has a new modern school building. This was the result of bond issue that was passed by the patrons of the district.

FAIR VIEW

S-29, T-35, R-23. Three miles north of Rondo.

Emma D. High School Boys' Basketball team for 1937-38. Row 1: Garland Hale, Leon Meadows, Dewey Dryer, Jess Roberts. Row 2: Kenneth Morris, Glen Huckaby, Coach George Bobbit, Ed Ervin, Glen Breshears

FISHER CREEK

Located near Hopewell Baptist Church in northeast Polk County. Stella Pippen was a teacher there about 1916.

FLEMINGTON

S-7, T-35, R-23. The school opened in 1928 with a graduating class of 11 students. The school closed in 1943 with a graduating class of 11. Later the building was used as a community building.

FLINT

S-6, T-34, R-23. Located near what is now Cliquot. The first school was a log building erected in 1858. It was about 20 feet by 20 feet. The building was used as both a church and school. The deed for this school was recorded on March 20, 1858 from William Morrow and wife Ruth E. to Ezekiel Flint, James Hamilton and James B. Hicks who were trustees of District No. 1. On April 1, 1878 the district voted to build a new building, but it was not completed for a few years. The first teacher in the new building was George Meade who had taught two terms in the old building.

Fair Play School before the gymnasium was added. It was torn down in 2002.

2nd, 3rd and 4th grades at Fair Play in 1923

Goodson Grade School on October 17, 1938. Row 1: Billy Rodgers, L.J. Farmer, Dennis Wheeler, Janis Wheeler, _____ Vest, Lenna Keith, Erma Lee Farmer, Erma Dee Roundtree, Barbara Keith, Opal Jones. Row 2: Lowell Farmer, Nevin Breshears, Jess Fisher, Wilbur Breshears, Ella Mae Keith, Herbert Fisher, _____ Vest, Evelyn Breshears. Row 3: Don Breshears, David Breshears, Morse Fisher, Paul Keith, Bob Morris, Leona Richards(teacher), Emma Lou Rodgers, Emojean Farmer, Ruth Fisher, Roma Morris, Joe Ben Keith.

Fox School, Polk County, MO, 1939–Front row (L-R): Pete Mitchum, Jerry Griffin, Charlene Sawyer, Louise Smith, Anna Lee Combs, John Mitchum, Juanita Fleeman, Betty Friehedge and Gene Mitchum. Second row (L-R): Zelma Brown, Thomas Lewis Chastain, Neva Sawyer, Floretta Combs, Edna Jo Griffin, Etta Brown, Dessie Fern Manning and Jackson Griffin. Third row (L-R): Grant Chastain Gordon Sawyer, Junior Griffin, Fred Manning, Cletis Sawyer, Guy Sawyer, Luther Manning, Glen Sawyer and Ray Miller. Teacher: Helen Dickinson

Forest Grove
S 18, T 33, R 22. Southeast of Bolivar, east of Highway 13.

Fox
S 8, T 33, R 24. Southwest of Fair Play about two miles.

Goodson
Goodson Grade School was located at the west edge of the town. It was a separate school from the Emma D. High.

Green Grove
S-30, T-35, R-22. Three miles southwest of Adonis.

Green Leaf
S-5, T-34, R-22, Due west of Huron.

Green Mound
T-34, R-22, S-3. Located in the far southwest corner of S 3, southwest of Polk and southeast of Huron.

Gumbo
See Johnson School.

Forest Grove School in 1908. The only known person in this picture is Marie Arnold who is the first girl in the second row from the right, standing by the teacher.

Johnson/Gumbo School on September 26, 1913 Effie Brock was the teacher. Rows run left to right.
Row 1: Tome Bridges, Bill Fisher, Roland Dickinson, Emery Phillips, Esther Stokes, Lucy Ball, Floyd Boswell, William Whitman, Erma Buckle, Gladys Shuck, Bonnie Fender, Pauline Sallee, Ida Shuck, Paulene Tiller, Tommy Blackburn.
Row 2: Clyde Phillips, Lee Fender, Troy Tummons, Olive Fisher, Pearl Cross, ____Shuck, Lara Boswell, Alice Whitman, Fern Stokes, Frances Owens, Charles Bridges, Effie Brock, Thelma Ball, Florence Pierce,_____Shuck.
Row 3: Cecil Ball, Rob Presley, Earnest Cross, Edward Dickinson, Tene Bridges, Jewell Blackburn, Relod Sallee, Gusta Presley, Ola Scroggins, Monnie Fender, Ernest Bridges, Hazel Dickinson, Lula Presley, Bill Balwin, Walter Bridges.
Row 4: Grady Pierce, Charley Tuck, Leta Dickinson, Edith Fender, Ida Whitman, Robert Choate, Ida Cross, Louis Tiller, Opal Sallee, Gid Presley, Beach Sallee, Ethel Fender, Ressie Scroggins, Lynn Fisher, Lynn Stokes, Bryer Stokes, Guy Bridges.

Kinder School in 2002.

HALFWAY

On February 4, 1868 John Askren deeded one-fourth acre of land for use as a school and church. The church was the Halfway Christian Church. The trustees of this site were John W. Ratcliff, William F. Burns, C. B. Davison, John Askren and Jesse W. Eagon. A frame building was erected for this use. In 1897 this property was deeded back to the owner by school directors C. Cowden, J. C. Legan and J. B. M. Ramsey. That same year Mrs. M. E. Barham deeded one and one- half acres where the present school is located. It was a white frame building and was in use until 1911. Mabel Peterson Teters was the teacher. In 1900 the school district voted to build another building to house the grade school and a two year high school. The building was ready for the new school term in the fall of 1911. It was a brick building with the bricks being made in a kiln located where the Stewart Concrete Products is located now. After a few years the high school was discontinued. The building was then used only as a grade school.

The district did not have a high school again for a number of years. In 1924 a two-year high school was held in the Finly Creamery Building. Students soon nicknamed the school as

Heel String School on February 27, 1913. Ruby Ross was the teacher. It was her first school. Daisy Johnson was the school superintendent.

"The Buttermilk Academy". A year later the high school was moved to the old Masonic Lodge building. The school first used only the top floor of this building, but two years later the school had grown and began using all of the building for the school.

In 1929 five rural districts in the area voted to consolidate with Halfway School to furnish a better education for their children. They were Knapp, Bloomer, Ratcliff, Coy and Brush Creek. The Halfway School District has had a number of building additions since that time and continues with its education program to this time.

HALFWAY ACADEMY

Located in the Christian Church in Halfway. This academy began in 1903 with Mr. Ollie Hollingsworth as the instructor. It lasted only a few years and was discontinued.

HEEL STRING

S-11, T-32, R-23. South of Morrisville near the Greene County line.

HEYDON

S-2, T-34, R-23. South of Rondo.

HICKORY GROVE

S-12, T-31, R-23. South of Morrisville near the Greene County line.

HICKORY POINT

S-31, T-33, R-22. Southwest of Karlin. It was converted into a private home after school was discontinued there. The Hickory Point Church of God was across the road from the school.

HOPKINS

S-17 or 18, T-34, R-24. Southwest of Dunnegan near the Cedar County line. Jump Off School may have been an earlier school in the same location.

HUMANSVILLE

The first school began as a two-year high school in 1890. In 1902 it had become a four-year school. Only six years after being built the school was destroyed by fire. The site for the new school was moved and the new school was completed in 1898. It was similar to the previous building. Growth in the school continued and in 1934 a new building was constructed and the old building was torn down. The school continued to see a steady increase through the years.

INDEPENDENCE

S-8, T-34, R-21. Located about a mile northwest of Wishart.

INGLIS

S-25, T-35, R-22.. Located about one-half mile west of Mohawk. Also found as Ingles and Ingalls.

JOHNSON

S-9, T-31, R-22. Also known as Gumbo. Located near Fender Chapel Church. The building was erected about 1878. The building is no longer standing. The name is sometimes found as Johnston.

JUMP OFF

See Hopkins.

KINDER

S-26, T-33, R-24. Just northeast of Aldrich. Cornelia Saxby was the last teacher at Kinder.

KING

S-29, T-32, R-24. Just over three miles west of Eudora near Nox.

KNAPP

S-11, T-33, R-21. Two miles southeast of Halfway near the Dallas County line.

LEE

S-16, T-32, R-22. On the north side of Highway 13, two miles north of Brighton. The building was moved to the Dunnegan area and is now a private home.

LEITH

S-29, T-33, R-22. Southeast of Bolivar, east of Highway 13.

LIBERTY

S-32, T-34, R-22. East and slightly north of Bolivar. It was truly "The Little Red School House" as it was a small building and red in color.

MARION C. EARLY (MORRISVILLE)

This school had its beginnings in a log Methodist church building to the east of the location of the present day Morrisville. Later the church moved into town and the school was moved at the same time. The school began to grow so a new building was erected for the school which was for elementary grades. If a student wanted a higher education they could attend the institute. The first school building was destroyed by fire and a new building was erected in 1880. A high school was begun in one of the college buildings after the closing of the college in 1918.

Marion C. Early was a previous resident of Morrisville and was concerned for the town with the closing of the college. Mr. Early purchased all of the college facilities and presented it all free and clear to the community for a consolidated district. The district passed the issue in a special election in June of 1925. He also donated equipment and books for the school district. Because of this gift the school was named Marion C. Early Consolidated Schools. The high school building was struck by lightning in 1927 and a new building was constructed. Since that time the school has continued to grow and a number of additions have been made to the school campus.

MCKINNEY

S-12, T-33, R-22. Just southeast of Burns.

MISSION

S-13 or 14, T- 34, R- 21. Near the Mission Post Office and Mission Church, close to the Dallas County line.

MONTGOMERY

S-14, T-35, R-24. Two miles east of Humansville.

MOORE

S-1, T-34, R-23. Three miles southeast of Rondo.

MT. BETHEL

S-31, T-33, R-24. Three miles west of Aldrich near the Dade County line.

MT. ETNA

S-7, T-34, R-22. Southwest of Huron.

MT. HERMAN

S-1, T-34, R-24. Three miles northwest of Cliquot.

Leith School on August 23, 1939. Row 1: First five are unknown, ____Johnson, Robert Polodna, last two are unknown. Row 2: Mr. McGee, ____Shoffner, Ruth Bradford, unknown, Mary Edna Bradford, ____Shoffner, ____Shoffner, unknown.

NEW BETHEL
S-20, T-33, R-21. Three miles south of Halfway.

NEW HOME
S-10, T-34, R-24. Between Cliquot and Dunnegan.

NEW HOPE
S-13, T-34, R-24. Southwest of Cliquot.

NEW MARKET
One of the earliest schools in the county, it was located near Orleans.

OAK GROVE
S-9, T-35, R-22. North of Adonis

OAK GROVE
S-29, T-33, R-23. Four miles southwest of Bolivar.

OAK GROVE
S-5, T-31, R-24. In the far southwest corner of Polk County.

OAKVILLE
S-29, T-32, R-23. Southwest of Morrisville. Some of the known teachers were _____ Boyd, Eva Raines, Ebb Mitchell, Ada Woodard, Morris Dutch Grant, Fred Coble, Harley Bloomer,

Oakville School, November 16, 1904. Teacher is Ebb Mitchell. Row 1-Lora McKnight,_____Martin, Tina Grisham, Alberta Millican, Llano Hamilton, Andy Sell, Edgar McKnight, Leonard Lemmon, Leonard Cossin. Row 2-Ruby Hamilton, Claudia Grisham, _____Martin(in front), Ruby Lemmon, Ruth Hamilton, Zoe Lemmon, Flossie Cook, Ella Jones, _____Martin, Jessie Martin, Melissa Thompson, Bub Martin. Row 3-May Hamilton, Lucy Derossett, Jewell Jones, Nora Cossin, Ivey Sell, Ida Sell, Ina Sell, Ocie Palmer. Row 4-John Thompson, Julien Childress, Wade Derossett, Ruel Palmer, Leonard Hamilton, Jesse Thompson, Oren Cossin, Ottie Cossin.

Mt. Etna School, 1933-1934. Row 1: Latha Belle Blankenship, Robert Mainess, Earl Blankenship. Row 2: Trevie Gene Dryer, Avanelle Watson, Virginia Blankenship, Dorothy Eidson.

Persimmon Grove School in the 1920s. Row 1: James Laney, Bill Prater, Oscar McCurdy, Lee Mullings, Lester Patterson, Ernest Mullings, Max Prater. Row 2, which is a short row in the center: Edward Buckner, Carl Kelly, Art Kelly, Mable Buckner, Velda McCurdy. Row 3: Mylene Mullings, Frances Erwin, Mary Ervin, Helen Kelly, Wanda McCurdy, Wilma McCurdy, _____, Maxine Prater, Madge Buckner, _____. Row 5: Earl Buckner, Clesta Prater, Marie Buckner, Zora Laney, Ervin Buckner, Myra Shade, Harry Eddings, Avis prater, Jesse Prater, Herbert Wallis.

Mt. Etna School, 4 H Club preparing a hot lunch. Naomi Inglis, Marie Ikerd, Maxine Hawkins, Alverta Henson, Frances Ikerd, Anna Dean Eidson, Maxine Watson.

Letta Boyd, Jewel Watson, Mabel Edwards Rentfro, Maude Grant, Lois Sechler Slagle, Fay Bradford, Florence McCrory and Nora Brown.

ORLEANS
S-12, T-32, R-24. Southwest of Aldrich.

OZARK
S-27, T-34, R-23. North of Bolivar.

PERSIMMON GROVE
Located southeast of Pleasant Hope. After consolidation with the Pleasant Hope Schools the building was moved to Pleasant Hope and remodeled into a private dwelling. An earlier building was located near the Greene County line in S-10, T-31, R-21. It was also called Armstrong School.

PICKEL
S-26, T-34, R-24. Northeast of Fair Play. The building was used as a hay barn for sometime. It is still standing.

PLEASANT GROVE
S-26, T-32, R-22. North and east of Brighton, it was also called Frog Pond. Katie McArtor was a teacher there before her marriage to Willard Fullerton. The building was moved into Pleasant Hope and it is now a private home.

PLEASANT HOPE
On March 20, 1847 Reverend Robert D. Smith and his wife Eliza A. purchased land which would later become the Pleasant Hope School District. On October 3, 1851 Robert and Eliza deeded the property to the Pleasant Retreat Academy. Reverend Smith was a trustee. The deed states that this may also be used by the Pomme de Terre Presbyterians on the second and fourth Sundays of each month. Other denominations were to be able to use the academy on the remaining Sundays. This academy was closed in 1855.

In 1859 another minister arrived in town to start a high school. It was a subscription school, but was short lived as it only was in existence four months. Mr. A. C. Lemmon then conducted classes in the academy building. He was more successful with his school and it continued for a number of years.

In 1876 Pleasant Hope and Humansville were the only two county schools said to have a high school each.

In 1878 a public subscription school was organized on a two-acre plot. This lasted for about five years and again the school was closed, probably due to a lack of students. In 1883 another educator arrived in town to again start another term of school. By this time local civic leaders decided they needed to support a school so the Pleasant Hope Institute was organized just to the west of the previous location. This was a two-story brick building. It contained three rooms. It was ready for use in a 1885. The name was then changed to Pleasant Hope Normal Academy. This building was added onto in 1926, but just two years later the building burned to the ground. Immediately a school bond election was held and the citizens voted to build a new building. It was a large rock building. Several additions were made to this building through the years and in February 1979 the old section of the building was destroyed by fire. Again a bond issue was passed and the school was rebuilt. Pleasant Hope has a strong school system with an elementary building, a new middle school and the high school complex.

Pickle School building in 1985.

Pickle School building in 1985.

The man on the right is Professor Ziegel who taught at Pleasant Hope School. The other man is unknown.

Ruth Apperson and her horse Bird on the way to school at Providence around 1918.

PLEASANT RIDGE
Southwest of Aldrich.

PLEASANT VALE
S-11, T-33, R-23. Located on Highway T in the southwest corner of the Bolivar City Limits. Fern Needham was one of the last teachers at the school.

PLEASANT VALLEY
S-8, T-35, R-24. Between Humansville and the St. Clair County line.

PLUM GROVE
Four miles south and to the east of Humansville.

POLK
Located at the south edge of the town of Polk.

POLK COUNTY CHRISTIAN
Bolivar

POTTS
S-11, T-33, R-24. A. F. Hughes was the teacher at Potts in the spring of 1896. The following were students who attended school there at that time: Frank Hays, Clay Oringderff, Marion Holiday, Ora Quinn, Dona Potts, Lentie Potts, Bertha Smith, Jennie Eaves, Cora Wine, Oren McCrory, Richard Hays, Horace Evans, Wesley Manuel, Oma Manuel, Bertha Manuel, Cora Oringderff, Fannie Mead, Connie Mead, Rosa Wine, Cora Devin, Minnie Potts, Bertha Eaves, Golden Hays, Charley Manuel, Omer Smith, Mary Quinn, Laura Oringderff, Lonnie Glyspy, Mabel Pinkard, Cora Derossett, Walter Oringderff, Omer McCrory, Gertie Oder, Perl Holiday, Eva Landacer, Bob Oringderff, Ernest Stewart, Lulu Manuel, Dorcas Hays, Perl Landacer, Rena Holiday, Rosa Smith, Edith McCrory and Lucy McCrory.

PROVIDENCE
North of Pleasant Hope on Highway H. The school consolidated into Pleasant Hope. See Providence Church.

RATCLIFF
One mile west of Halfway. Boone Cemetery was next to the school.

RICE
S-2, T-31, R-24. Three miles south of Eudora and one mile northeast of Turkey Creek Church and Cemetery near the Greene County line. This was on or near the property of Jonathan Rice who settled there in 1843. A Civil War vigilante group held meetings in the school at one time. A storm cellar is all that remains.

ROBERTS
Just east of Violet.

ROCK
S-15, T-34, R-24. Two miles southeast of Dunnegan.

ROCK PRAIRIE
Located northeast of Pleasant Hope. The building is still standing. Miss Beulah Potter of Red Top was the teacher in 1932. Mrs. Lena Case was the District Clerk.

Pleasant Grove School, about 1888. The only person known in this picture is Nora Rymer, fourth from the right in the front row.

Old Pleasant Hope High School before addition was added to the building.

Rock Prairie School.

Last day of school at Ratcliff for 1931-1932. Mary Barnett, teacher.

Roberts School class for the year of 1947-1948. Row 1: Ronald McDowell, Kenneth Holt, Derrel Holt, Walter Holt, Dale Harmon, Lewis Harmon, Teddy McTosh, Eddie Harmon, Bobby Boren. Row 2: Joyce Cummings, Karen Holt, Sonja Wright, Shirley Standley, Della May Boren. Row 3: Erma Jean Hampton, Colleen Cummings, Florence Cheek, Ruby Ahart, Wilma Sanders, Ricena Blackman, Lucille Hampton, Joyce Standley, Barbara Standley, Marcia Blackman. To the left in the back is the teacher, Mrs. Dorothy Ragains.

Rosebud School

Schofield School on November 5, 1915. The teachers were L.C. Thompson and Clara LeJeune. Student names are unknown.

Recess time at Schofield School on November 5, 1915.

RONDO
One-half mile south of Rondo.

RONDO INSTITUTE
One mile north of Rondo. It was a two-story building with the first floor used by a church and the top story was used by the institute. The land was deeded to the Rondo Institute and trustees of the Methodist Episcopal and Cumberland Presbyterian Churches. It was used for about 50 years.

ROSEBUD
S 29, T 35, R 4. Rosebud is two miles south of Humansville. It is believed the building was built about 1886. It was consolidated into the Humansville R-IV district in the 1950s and school ended for Rosebud in the spring of 1954. The Rosebud Good Neighbor Club, organized by Mrs. Rolland Rains in 1941, organized a successful Rosebud Community effort in 1955 to purchased the landmark as a memento to the fastly disappearing one room schools and to use it as a community house for approved activities. The building is still used by the Rosebud quilting group. Their quilting is the means of keeping the building maintained.

ROSE HILL
T-5, R-22, S-12. West of Sentinel. It consolidated with the Bolivar R-1 School system.

RUNYAN
S-8, T-33, R-22. Four miles west of Bolivar on the south side of Highway 32.

SAND HILL
It was sometimes called the Graydon Springs School and was located southeast of

Eudora. Jesse Petiford, Mary Petiford, Glen Rummel, Ferne Rummel, Brent Rummel, Ruby Lemmon, Mary Frank, Irene Watson, Hoyt Watson, Etho Watson, Ralph Acuff, Pete Acuff, Gus Acuff, Don Lawrence, Dink Chitten, John Carter, Jessie Wiley, Brent Coble, Bob Rook and Ida Kensinger were some students that attended Sand Hill School in the early 1900s.

SCARRITT-MORRISVILLE COLLEGE

In 1871 the District Conference of the Methodist Episcopal held an educational conference and established a school at Pleasant Prairie. It was the Pleasant Prairie Institute and a building was to be erected for not less than $2000. About 30 years before an institute had been formed at Ebenezer Campground in Greene County. It closed at the time of the Civil War. Methodist officials were anxious to see another institution of higher learning where there was good support and so Pleasant Prairie was chosen because of the strong hold of Methodism in the area.

The first board of curators for the new institute were Morris Mitchell, Elisha Headlee, Benjamin Appleby, A. C. Montgomery and A. C. Mitchelll. Dr. W. M. Prottsman was the presiding elder.

In September 1872 the new building was ready for the opening of school. It was called Ebenezer Hall and had four classrooms and office space.

In 1889 the name was changed to Morrisville College. By this time the school had expanded its curriculum as the number of students continued to grow. By 1900 there was a strong athletic program with football, basketball and baseball. Because of an accident the football program was discontinued after about 10 years. In 1909 the Southwest Missouri Conference moved the Scarritt Institute from Neosho to Morrisville and it became known as the Scarritt-Morrisville College at that time. During this time span a number of new buildings were added to the campus.

Because of the lack of young men to attend the school during W W I it closed in 1919. The town decided it would use part of the facilities for a four-year high school, but in 1921 the college was reopened. Three years later the school was again closed for the last time and the property was sold.

SCHOFIELD

South of the Schofield Missionary Baptist Church and the Cemetery.

SCROUGE OUT

S-8, T-31, R-23. Southwest of Morrisville near the Greene County line. It consolidated with the Walnut Grove School District in 1949.

SHADY GROVE

S-20, T-33, R-24. One mile east of the Dade County line. *See picture on page 46.*

SLAGLE

Located just to the north of the Slagle Creek Church and Cemetery, it is now a private home.

This picture was taken in the Spring of 1925 - the last year of Scarritt Morrisville College.
Top Row, Left to Right: *(1)Gola Walker Blakey, (2)Winnie Blakey, (3)Georgia May Calhoun, (4)Freda Dodd, (5)Berniece Maxwell, (6)Esther Walker Maroney, (7)Esther Alexander Dixon, (8)Ruth O'Toole, (9)Blanche White, (10)Helen Gordon Klaus, (11)Edna Haden, (12)Ezenith White Dodd, (13)Geneva Becker, (14)Joanna McReynolds Jones, (15)Frances Neil Stone, (16)Lucy Lee Hinkle, (17)Lula Mitchell, (18)Cora Mackey Perryman, (19)Verna Brewer, (20)Annalee Rice, (21)Mabel Marshall, (22)Esther Nickerson Bowman, (23)Nora Moseley, (24)Berniece Burchell, (25)Delpha Briggs, (26)Olivia Rice, (27)Nanah Ezell Annyghan, (28)Beulah Parker, (29)Lovan Ezell, (30)Rex Murdock, (31)Helen Hayes Crawford.*
Second Row, Left to Right: *(1)Marlene Watson Klaus, (2)Ralph Rand, (3)Clarence Blakey, (4)Johnny Bond, (5)Paul Guthrie, (6)Loeda Kleeman Sims, (7)Wilma Dixon, (8)Golden Hood Schooley, (9)Bessie Phelps Hutchinson, (10)Marie Ross, (11)Pearl Williams, (12)Irene Williams, (13)Mary*

SOUTHWEST BAPTIST UNIVERSITY

It was originally known as Southwest Baptist College. The college moved to Bolivar from Lebanon in 1879. The first graduating class was in 1883. For many years it was a junior or two-year college. In 1981 it was granted university status. It has grown from a small school to a big university with students attending from all over the world.

STAR RIDGE

Located at the corner of S-21, 22, 7 and 28, T-35, R-21. Just to the west of Rimby.

SUGAR LIP

See Victor.

SUNSET

S-26, T-33, R-22. West of Sunset Church, east of the present Highway 13.

TILLERY

S-11, T-35, R-23. The following article is from the *Bolivar Free Press* in January 1932. It depicts early school life and an early school in Polk County.

"I began going to school when I was about six or seven years old in 1860 in what was then called the Tillery School District situated in the north side of Polk County just south of the county line between Polk and Hickory counties. About the time the Civil War started it was hard to hire a teacher; and for three or four years they did not hire anything but women teachers.

The first teacher I went to was Fanny Gray, the next one Anna Bradley, an old maid. About that time the war began and no money to hire teachers, so the parents that had children to go to school had to hire the teacher out of their own pockets and not much of that, for we had to go to what they called subscription school.

My next teacher was an Arkansas girl. Her name was Sophrona Netherton and she had twin sisters. Then they got what money was due our district, and hired Mrs. Burrell. Mr. Burrell had one girl he wanted to go to school.

This ended my career in school for a while until an old man called Colonel Graft began a subscription school in an old hull of what was intended to be a church. But the Civil War had begun in earnest by this time and it was no uncommon thing to see bunches of soldiers passing through the country. I went two or three terms to Colonel Graft during the first part of the Civil War.

Then came the readjustment of things in general, such as organizing the schools. The old Tillery district was divided and a new school house built farther east. The new house was built in the center of the eastern part of the new district on what was the Andy Yoast farm and just across the road on my father's farm was a good well of water which was a very necessary thing to have for a school. This school house was built of native lumber and donated labor.

The first man to teach our school was James Warren, an old Union soldier. He would drill the children in military factors. Then came three more teachers, all of whom went

Knight Thomson, (14)Inez Martin, (15)Leona Horn Clayton, (16)Doris Milligan, (17) unknown, (18)Rietha Raynolds Lee, (19)Ova Fowler, (20)Mayble Shooley Cole, (21)Nora Edwards Wilson, (22)Beulah Earley Bryant, (23)Elizabeth Mackey Fischer.
Bottom Row, Left to Right: (1)Ray Blakey, (2)Jesse Watson, (3)Ewell Euliss, (4)Ralf Woodward, (5)Marion Hutchinson, (6)Euel Alexander, (7)Herbert Dixon, (8)John Cowden, (9)Frank Copeland, (10)Newton Edwards, (11)Wilbur Fulbright, (12)Dick Jones, (13)Carl Sloan, (14)Paul McReynolds, (15)Glen Howerton, (16)Van Anderson, (17)Earl Noble, (18)Bill Eckerle, (19)Marvin Ross, (20)Otis Mackey, (21)John Mackey, (22)Bill Buchanon, (23)Farmer Sargent.
Students not present for the picture were: *James Becker, Mary Lou Bond, Dolly Marshall, Neil Neff & Ralph Sidebottom.*
Picture was the property of the late Marvin T. Ross.

Slagle School on November 20, 1890

Slagle School on October 5, 1922. Row 1: first three unknown, Ruth Slagle, unknown, Chloe Ella Slagle, unknown, Grace Slagle, next two unknown. Row 2: ____Herbert, Emma Slagle, ____Mitchell, Keith Slagle, Verna Slagle, ____Herbert, Lorayne Slagle, Dorothy Scroggins, Frank Slagle, Harley Boaz. Row 3: first four unknown, ____Mitchell, unknown, Henry Scroggins, Glen Scroggins, ____Pierce, unknown, the teacher is unknown. Row 4; first two unknown, Glen Slagle, Rena Slagle, Byon Slagle, Neta Slagle, unknown

Watson School 1936-37. Row 1: Ray Dale McCarty, Bobby Kadau, Iris Pursley. Row 2: Herbert Kadau, Harold Burks, Charles Barker, Mary Barnett (Teacher), Charlene Barker, Betty Barker.

Wells School as part of the Pleasant Hope First Baptist Church.

under the very common name of Smith, namely Alonzo, Stacy and their sister Cinderella, then Quince Keeling, then another Smith named Maggie.

There have been several new school houses built. The present one now stands just one-fourth mile east of my old home and what is now the Ray McCracken place. He lives in California, but his father and mother live on his place.

While writing this it made me think, his father, Marcus McCracken, and I are the only two living that used to go to school at the little old log school house in the old Tillery district. W. J. McCracken."

TUCK
S-29 or 30, T-32, R-22. Northwest of Brighton.

UNION
S-2, T-34, R-22. Two miles southwest of Polk.

UNION
S-11, T-35, R-23. Three miles east of Flemington.

UNION GROVE
S-20, T-34, R-23. South of Cliquot

UNION GROVE
Located in the far southeast corner of the county. The first school was a log building located just to the north of the church on adjoining property. It is part of a private home just south of the church and cemetery. A second building was erected about a mile west of the original school. It has been turned into a barn. The school consolidated into the Fair Grove School District in Greene County, but a few students opted to attend Pleasant Hope School.

UNION RIDGE
S-35, T-34, R-22. Near Goff Cemetery on Hominy Creek.

UNKNOWN
Located near the northeast corner of Reed Cemetery south of Halfway about 1845. Church services were held in the same building.

UNKNOWN
Just to the west of Reed Cemetery. It may be the same as the above.

UNKNOWN
S-5, T-34, R-24. Located near the railroad tracks in the northeast corner of S-5.

VAN
S-25, T-33, R-22.

VICTOR
S-11, T-35, R-21. It was also called Sugar Lip and located near the Hickory County line northeast of Hopewell Baptist Church.

WATSON
S-19, T-34, R-22. Northeast of Bolivar

WELLS
S-32, T-33, R-21. Between Halfway and Pleasant Hope. The building is now part of the Pleasant Hope First Baptist Church.

WEST
A very early school mentioned in connection with an early Christian Church in that area and also David West who lived two to four miles southwest of Bolivar near what later became Wishart. It may have been a private school in the West Home.

WEST UNION
S-27, T-34, R-23. Two miles northwest of Bolivar.

WILKINS
S-31, T-32, R-22. Just over two miles southeast of Morrisville.

WILMINGTON
S-3, T-33, R-22. West of Burns on the north side of Highway 32.

WILSON
S-11, T-32, R-22. Northwest of Pleasant Hope on Highway KK. It was a private home for many years.

WISHART
S-9, T-32, R-23. Located at Wishart.

WOODLAWN
East of Fair Play near Barren Creek Church and Cemetery. It is now used as a community building.

WORD OF GOD CHRISTIAN ACADEMY
111 N. Oakland, Bolivar.

Polk County Teachers, 1926-27.

Anna McCracken—County School Superintendent.
VICTOR–Mrs. Leona Richards, Urbana.
EAGLE HILL–Virgil Kee, Sentinel.
ROSE HILL–Georgia Miller, Bolivar.
UNION–Joe Allison, Flemington.
FLEMINGTON–Cecil Snow and 2 yet to be named.
MONTGOMERY–Ruth Hammond, Humansville.
ROSE BUD–Ida Martin, Bolivar.
CEDAR GROVE–Pearl Dungan, Humansville.
FAIR VIEW–Mrs. Martha Kearney, Flemington.
RONDO–Edith Stewart, Bolivar.
CARTER–Hamie Martin, Louisburg.

Wilson School, September 26, 1905.
Row 1: Troy Overcash, Edna Human, Mary Halla, Dot Hatler, Beulah Acock, Susie Acock, Lula Acock, Lela Allison, John Halla, George Overcash.
Row 2: Mary Smith, Myrtie Pake, Charlie Scroggins, Bessie Wilcox, Bessie Huff, Mattie Scroggins, Roy Overcash, Lumilla Rhuska, Frank Otradovec.
Row 3: Grace Whitman, Layle Vanzant, Ernie Schmick, Jessie Scroggins, Corry Wilson, Maggie Schmick, Josie Otradovec, Unknown visitor.
Row 4: Lee Wilson, Joe Otradovec, Tom Whitman, Paul Scroggins, Paul Ingram, Tillie Halla, Ethel Human, Nel Overcash, Christina Rhuska, Bell Acock, Carrie Whitman.
Row 5: Dave Whitman, Joe Schmick, Shelbern Wilson, Joe Allison, Clarence Wilson, Jess Polick, John Allison, Carl Wilson, Bill Human, Ben Whitman.

INDEPENDENCE–Opal Burks, Bolivar.
GREEN LEAF–Ray Vest, Polk and 1 yet to be named.
MOORE–Mrs. Lela Lunderman, Bolivar.
HEYDON–Julia Davison, Bolivar.
FLINT–Delsena Hobbs, Bolivar.
MT. HERMAN–Gladys Dorman, Flemington.
PLUM GROVE–Florence Stone, Humansville.
NEW HOME–Katherine Ellsworth.
NEW HOPE–Maude Ellsworth.
CLIQUOT–Mrs. Nellie Watkins.
UNION–Campbell Viles, Halfway.
GOODSON–J.B. Remington, Springfield and Blanche Fraser, Polk.
CONCORD–Mrs. Anna Meyer, Buffalo.
COY–Leda Chamberelin, Halfway.
BROOKS–Lowell Platt, Bolivar.
ROBERTS–Helen Miller, Bolivar.
EIDSON–Patsy Hutchison.
UNION GROVE–Ray Hubbard.
PICKEL–Millie Coffman.
WOODLAWN–Thera Cavender, Aldrich.
WEST UNION–Audrey Cooper, Bolivar.
OZARK–Rintha Robbins, Bolivar.
WATSON–Homer Weese, Bolivar.
BLACK OAK–Jerrell Craig, Halfway.
CLARK–Mrs. Olive Pritchard, Halfway.
BLOOMER–Audrey VanGilder, Buffalo.
HALFWAY–Amy Craig and Letha Rose also 1 yet to be named.
RATLIFF–Mrs. Pearl Herring, Halfway.
UNION RIDGE–J.B. Brock, Bolivar.
WILMINGTON–Opal Clingman.
LIBERTY–Bertha Burks.
RUNYAN–Mrs. Elva Stewart, Bolivar.
POTTS–Rebecca Cox.
FOX–Viva Utterback.
COLLEGE HILL–Anna Vermillion.
PLEASANT VALE–Albert McKinney.
FOREST GROVE–Mildred Bush, Bolivar.
CHERRYVALE–Edna Hood, Bolivar.
MCKINNEY–Grace Goldsberry.
KNAPP–Carl Angle.
SCHOFIELD–Hubert Curlin, Halfway.
NEW BETHEL–Cecil Peterson.
VAN–Delbert Hutcheson.
SUNSET–Charlotte Callaway, Bolivar.
LEITH–Lelia Murray.
ELM GROVE–Mrs. Alma Bacon.
OAK GROVE–2 to be named.
SHADY GROVE–Beatrice Martin, Bolivar.
MT. BETHEL–Mary Lee Miller, Aldrich.
HICKORY POINT–Mrs. Sabra Ruckman, Bolivar.
WELLS–Zona Hood, Bolivar.
ROCK PRAIRIE–Amy Gardner, Fair Grove.
WILSON–Mrs. Ethel Hook.
LEE–Will Mankin, Pleasant Hope.
COLLINS–Bernice Davis, Aldrich.
INDEPENDENCE–Lula Mitchell, Bolivar.
WISHART–Neal Neff.
ORLEANS–Reed Hurd, Morrisville.
PLEASANT RIDGE–Vera Cavender.
EDGEWOOD–Racheal Ross, Morrisville.
KING–Louise Neal and 1 yet to be named.
SAND HILL–Martha Wilson, Walnut Grove.
TUCK–Pauline Grant, Morrisville.
BRIGHTON–Mrs. Bessie Parrish.
BLACK OAK–Roy Lynn, Pleasant Hope.
PERSIMMON GROVE–Myra Shade, Fair Grove.
JOHNSTON–Frank Laney, Fair Grove.

Woodlawn School, February 10, 1911, Forrest Forsee, teacher.

SPRING HILL–Grace Alley, Pleasant Hope.
SCROUGE OUT–Gladys Sewell, Walnut Grove.
OAK GROVE–Mrs. Elizabeth Eaves, Walnut Grove.
BRUSH CREEK–Roscoe Ragsdale, Halfway.
GREEN MOUND–Mrs. Amy Harris, Polk.
DUNNEGAN–J. Fred Lawson, Daisy Vannoy and Daisy Lee.
EUDORA–Lois Baker, Aldrich and Anna Burros, Walnut Grove.
ALDRICH–Albert Godfrey, Grace Godfrey, Mrs. Christa Wainscott and Florence Mulanax.
PLEASANT HOPE–Ray Hailey and 4 yet to be named.
MORRISVILLE–Alfred N. Weiser, Osceola and 3 yet to be named. Also Iva McCrory (7&8), Verna Luncefore (5&6), Beulah Early (3&4), Bessie Jones (1&2).
FAIR PLAY–A.S. Bradbury, Edna Garner and l yet to be named. Also Mrs. Nina T. Ditmars (7&8), Nellie Scroggins (5&6), Georgia Campbell (3&4), Mrs. Fern McCrory (1&2).
HUMANSVILLE–G.C. Ely and 5 yet to be named.
BOLIVAR–John A. Doak, T.L.Yates, Ora E. Hughes, Clyde F. Whitman.

W. H. Hood—A Teacher's Story

Vocational Agriculture IV Class Constructing Terraces (L-R): Deab McCroskey, Chester Miller, Mr. Hood, Bob Wooten and Allen Gott

W. H. Hood is a prime example of how one person can influence a life. He, in fact, influenced many lives over the course of his eighty years. Although not a native of Polk County (he was born Dec. 30, 1919 in Miller, MO), he spent most of his life there and considered it his home.

Winfred Harold Hood, a novice school teacher, arrived in Pleasant Hope, MO in 1944. He took up residence at the Cochran Hotel, located a short distance from the high school where he taught vocational agriculture, never dreaming he would be doing it for the next 34 years. It didn't happen overnight, but when his confidence rose, he knew he'd found his true calling in life.

In 1945, he found another calling—"LOVE"—in the form of the beautiful Miss Rebecca Ann Lathem, daughter of Ralph and Stella Lathem of Pleasant Hope. Legend has it that when W. H. proposed, he threatened to throw himself in the river if Becky refused. "I didn't know he could swim," she later said with a smile.

Like many couples at the time, they eloped to Harrison, AR on Dec. 22, 1945, and Becky returned home to her parents with her secret intact. The newlyweds hoped to conceal their marriage until school was out for the year and avoid a major shivaree from the FFA boys.

Secrets as good as their were hard to keep, however. The word was soon out, and they proceeded to make a home together. Their "little secret" would go on to last 54 years and produce three children: Marilyn Hood Hayes (who currently resides on Indian Point, near Branson), Dennis (who is a Bolivar veterinarian as is his son Bruce), and Rita (who lives in Bolivar with her husband Greg Hill, another 'Pin Hooker').

With his home life on track, W. H. buckled down to teaching vocational agriculture, shop, and acting as FFA advisor to generations of students. "My boys," he affectionately called them—and they were.

"Papa Hood" they affectionately called him—and he was. He truly cared about them and tried to guide them in the right direction. He taught them the subject of 'life.' Pleasant Hope may have been a very small school, but W. H. believed the only limitations we have are those we put on ourselves. His vo-ag. department dreamed big, worked hard, and achieved much.

He furthered his own education by receiving a master's degree in dairy science. It would come in handy to the competitive-minded teacher for coaching decades of successful judging teams.

W. H. Hood was famous for his personal style of teaching, which included a wry sense of humor. Catching a student whispering a joke to another during class, he asked the student to "Come on up and share it with the rest of the class. We all want to hear it!" The student was undoubtedly too embarrassed to repeat that mistake. Hood's stories of classroom antics could fill volumes.

His FFA boys were "the best," and he was fortunate to coach many winning judging teams on local and state levels. However, the highlight of his career was having the world's number one dairy judging team for 1977, which was achieved at Wales in the United Kingdom.

Feeling that event was hard to top, he decided to retire in 1978 after 34 years of teaching. In return, the Pleasant Hope School system named its vocational agriculture building in his honor. His name would grace the place where he'd given so much time and energy to his "boys."

At his retirement reception, Mr. Hood took time to reflect on a career that spanned the educating of both fathers and their sons. "I can't think of a career more rewarding than teaching," he mused, "other than perhaps being a minister. Not financially rewarding, but personally rewarding."

Although he may have retired to farming, traveling with wife Becky, hanging out at the Stock Yards and the commodity market, and attending the occasional auction (which he loved), W. H. remained in contact with former students, the majority of whom still live in Polk County. He was always available to offer advice.

Also, through his lifetime, he was an active member of the First Baptist Church of Pleasant Hope as well as the Lion's Club, and during his tenure as Mayor of Pleasant Hope, the city water system was installed.

Members of the World Champion Dairy Judging Team with their instructor and his wife (L-R): Wayne Seitz, Kenneth Dillard, their instructor, W. H. Hood and his wife, and William Erwin. Photo Courtesy of Bolivar (Missouri) Herald-Free Press

He relished staying busy and did so until March 14, 2000, when a sudden heart attack struck. Before he was laid to rest in the Pleasant Hope Cemetery on March 17, 2000, a funeral was held in Bolivar that brought together many generations of 'Hood's boys.' Several former students, including Derald Isdell, Alvin Rohrs, and David Agee, shared amusing and warm reflections of their beloved teacher. David Agee presented the final analysis of Mr. Hood: "He may have been retired, but he never stopped teaching." For that, Polk County and Pleasant Hope in particularly are very grateful.

The Ballad of Papa Hood

In Polk County's teaching history, I confess,

One stands out above the rest.

"Do as I say, not as I do,"

Was Papa Hood's motto through and through.

But what he did, and we're not surprised,

Was make a difference in many lives.

When it came to vo-ag., he was 'the man,'

He thought every future farmer needed a 'plan.'

If there's a school in heaven, as I have my hunches,

You can bet he's teaching them that there are 'no free lunches.'

Thank you, Papa,

Thank you, Hood.

You did your best,

And that was good.

– MSH –

Businesses, Churches and Organizations

On left: Cyrus T. Ward, center: John William Atkinson in blacksmith shop of John Williams at Humansville, MO, early 1900's.

Churches

SOUTHERN HILLS BAPTIST CHURCH

In the spring of 1952 a group of Christians came together for worship and fellowship with the idea of forming a second Southern Baptist church in Bolivar. This group constituted as Second Baptist Church on May 23, 1952, with twenty-one charter members. Their meeting place was the basement of the Teegarden Building (now housing T M Clothing and Frogs N Friends) on the southwest corner of the square. Their first pastor was J. Austin Hook.

The young church purchased the former First Presbyterian Church building at 114 W. Walnut Street from the American Legion. The first worship services were held at that building on Dec. 20, 1953.

In January 1965 the church purchased a plot of three acres on S. Springfield Avenue, across from Southwest Baptist University. The first building was completed and occupied on March 20, 1966. At this time the congregation took a new name: Southern Hills Baptist Church. The parsonage, which is located on the east end of the land tract, was the second building and was completed in early 1970.

On Sept. 5, 1972, the church launched a Day Care ministry known as Creative Years Day Care Center. This ministry occupied the lower floor of the main building until a third building was completed in 1981. The "Annex" provided for the day care ministry as well as space for children and youth ministries. The Annex also housed the office of the Director of Missions of the Polk County Southern Baptist Association for several years. The Creative Years Day Care was closed in August 1998.

With increased attendance, particularly from SBU students, two morning worship services have been held various years.

As God blessed and attendance continued increasing there was a need for more Sunday School classrooms. The east class rooms, offices, fellowship hall and third floor (latest addition) were completed September 1995 with the help of several mission groups.

At the time this article is being submitted, there is a committee looking at present needs and possible expansion of the church facility. The church is blessed to be able to partnership with Southwest Baptist University students in ministry. This has allowed expanded ministry, rich blessings to the church, and development with students involved.

The church in 2001 developed a concise and precise mission statement which serves as guide for its programs and activities. This statement is as follows:

OUR MISSION STATEMENT

Southern Hills Baptist Church Exists for the Purpose Of:

Magnifying Jesus Christ through worship, the Word, fellowship and

Moving believers in Jesus Christ toward maturity, ministry, membership in His church and

Making Jesus Christ known to our neighbors and the nations.

The church has had eleven pastors:
J. A. Hook	6/52-2/58
David Caldwell	7/58-6/61
Hubert Fugitt	10/61-7/62
William Smith	12/62- 1/64
LeRoy Roberts	6/64-6/69
Bob Webb	1/70-/74
Dennis Betts	11/74-10/81
Glen McLaughlin	3/82-3/86
David Berryhill	4/86-9/91
Jim Tolliver	3/92-2/99
Gary Urich	12/2000-

1220 S. Springfield Ave.
Bolivar, MO 65613
Phone/fax 417-326-7474
website:shbcbolivar.org
e-mail: shbc@microcore.net

Current Building

First Baptist Church

Bolivar began as a hamlet in 1834 but had no organized churches until 1840. The Methodists were first followed by the Christian church in 1852 and the Baptists in 1859 when the population had grown to about 400. On September 3, elder William B. Senter called for a meeting at the courthouse to organize a Baptist church. The new church was organized with seven members and called "The United Baptist Church of Jesus Christ at Bolivar."

What the seven members lacked in number, they made up for in vision, because they voted in their second meeting to build a house of worship. Contributions were sought throughout the community with initial success and plans were made to start construction in 1860. The north half of the lot at the NW corner of Chestnut and Main Streets was purchased as a site. Things looked promising early in 1860, but payments on pledges lagged resulting in frequent work stoppages. At the first business meeting in 1861, it was borne out that the church treasury was depleted. The March business meeting was the last. After the session began it was immediately closed - there being no business brought before the house. The Civil War was about to erupt and the people were making preparations for their safety. The church had enrolled 21 members by that time.

After the war was over, there were only four members of the first congregation living in the community. There was no move to reactivate the group until 1866, when Elder D. R. Murphy, who was widely known in Missouri, came to Bolivar in March and called for meeting. Four women were carried over from the original church roll, while the only additions at that meeting were W. M. Delaplain and James Dalton, both joining by statement. Both had been strong supporters of the Union, and the first order of business was to pass a resolution which read, "We will not fellowship with those that have been in rebellion against the government of the United States, without evidence of repentance." Elder Murphy resigned the pastorate in 1868, and the church called J. M. Lappin, with the building still under construction. By August the structure was finished except for plastering the walls and a call went forth that the church would furnish plans to provide anyone who would build and donate pews. The first meetings were held before the pews were finished and kerosene lamps were installed for light.

Membership grew at about the same rate as payment on the debt; with 64 members in 1878, but only 47 "in good standing." Drastic change came when Southwest Baptist College was moved from Lebanon in 1880 and a revival held Jan. 15, 1880 to February 6 resulted in 55 additions to the congregation, 28 being baptized on February 8.

Sometime between 1884 and 1888, the name was changed to "First Baptist Church." The membership gradually increased as the town grew and plans were drawn up in 1889 to enlarge the church house. But before the project had gotten beyond that stage, it was postponed until financial affairs at the college could be settled. Six years later, plans were adopted for a new building with as estimated cost of $2,000. The first building was razed. The new building was built on the same spot and dedicated on Dec. 12, 1897, complete with baptistry and gravity furnace. Total cost with furnishings was $6,000.

In 1904, the church bought an adjacent dwelling and rented it to the pastor for $100 per year. By 1917 more Sunday School was needed and the parsonage was converted into educational space. Serious consideration was given in 1919 to erect a larger building but continual problems in meeting current expenses ruled out such an undertaking at that time. That situation was improved in 1921, after a newly appointed Finance Committee challenged the congregation with a budget goal of $3,600. An itemized budget was adopted for 1922 and a bolder emphasis on stewardship. Convinced that where was no choice but to build, the congregation approved a new set of plans for a much larger building with an estimated cost of $45,000. After a campaign was begun to finance the project, Mr. and Mrs. Zenas Hutcheson donated the north half of block #32, bordered by Main, Locust and Springfield Streets. When the new structure was occupied in January 1926 the cost including furnishings was $52,000. Dedication was postponed until the debt was paid on Nov. 28, 1943. The church continued to grow through depression and war years leading to purchase of the south half of the block and construction of an Educational Building in 1958.

Southwest Baptist College advanced to a four-year institution in the mid '60s and a more rapid increase in church membership was experienced. A long-range planning survey in 1972 developed into a building program which included a new auditorium with surrounding classrooms, administrative offices, and a recreation building with educational space. Over one million dollars was invested in the project.

In the 1980s the staff was increased to four Ministry Staff, and by 2002 to seven. Beginning in the '80s the church sponsored more national and international mission trips leading to about 200 members' participation. In 1988 the church launched Alpha House, a Crisis Pregnancy Resource Center which now functions with a board of directors from area churches. Church ministries by the 1990s included expanding Sunday School classes for all ages, choirs for pre-school thru adult, orchestra, traditional and contemporary worship services, mid-week youth led worship as part of the larger youth ministry, children's worship, missions groups for children and adults and special study groups.

Continued growth led to the razing of the 1926 building and construction of a 25,000 square foot Fellowship Hall and Educational Building in 1991. This additional space created a Sunday School capacity of about 800 and attendance averaged 750 in 2002. Two morning worship services were begun in 1995 to accommodate attendance and provide for growth. In 1998 the church purchased the Esquire Theater on Chestnut Street, and renovated the building. Wednesday evening worship services, which now average about 250, were begun at the Esquire utilizing multi-media and a contemporary-country music style. At this writing the church is seeking to make a decision on providing additional space for continued growth.

Summarized from writings of George Hooper, 1984.

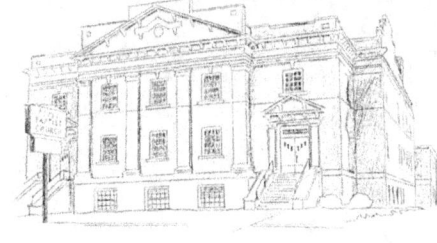

1926-1991

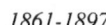

1861-1897   *1897-1926*   *1991-2004*

The First Baptist Church Of Fair Play

In 1885, with the disbandment of the Brushgrove Baptist Church north of Fair Play, some of its members came to Fair Play and organized the First Baptist Church. The first pastor was Rev. J. F. Hampton. For the first year, the services were held in the old Methodist church which stood on the hill north of the present building. This lot, on which the church is built, was purchased in 1886. Twenty-one persons constituted the membership of the original church. A fire destroyed the building on March 4, 1958.

A new church, 30 feet by 60 feet, was built and interim pastor Perry Cossins conducted the first worship service on March 12, 1959. The first pastor in the new building was Rev. Bill Moore. Since then the church has many additional additions and changes. In 1974 the church was incorporated on July 1, and a new sanctuary was built under the pastorate of Rev. Randall Terrill. In 1981 the debt was paid off and in 1983 a fellowship hall, 30 feet by 40 feet, was added under the ministry of Rev. Pete Dominguez. An extension, the same size, was begun in 1987 and completed in 1989 during the pastorate of Rev. Larry Graves. On July 3, 1994 a parsonage was purchased from Mr. and Mrs. Olan Hamlin. The home was located across the street from the church, on the west side of Walnut Street. The pastor at that time, Rev. Billy Joe Deer, and his family were the first to occupy the parsonage. The debt on the parsonage was paid in three years. The final payment was made on July 2, 1997. In 2001, under the pastorage of Bro. David Stunkel, the church voted to use the parsonage as a home for furloughed missionaries.

Above: First building used by Fair Play Baptist Church . *Below:* Current church building.

Fender Chapel Baptist Church

The history of Fender Chapel Baptist Church can be traced to 1875, when Christian Fender hauled lumber by oxen and wagon from Arkansas to construct a house of worship on a small plot of hillside land overlooking the Sac River near Brighton, MO. With the help of friends and neighbors, a small church building was erected and during its initial years was known as the Pleasant Hill Sabbath School.

In September 1878, the land on which the church was situated was deeded by Thomas and Eliza Johnson for the sum of $1.00 to George Griffin, Christian Fender, Asa Fender, Elijah Blackburn, and Jesse Fender to be "used, kept, maintained and disposed of as a place of Divine worship for the use of the ministry and membership of the Methodist Episcopal Church," but was, "to be free to all Evangelical Denominations to organize and hold church" when not in use by the Methodist membership. In 1881, the church was renamed Fender Chapel in honor of the man who had been the driving force in providing a place of worship for the community.

During the years between 1881 and 1936, Fender Chapel provided a place of worship for congregations of various denominations, and according to records, regular services were held each Sunday, weather permitting. In 1936, because the majority of the congregation was of the Baptist faith, it was decided to seek affiliation with the Southern Baptist Convention through the Greene County Baptist Association. Under the leadership of the Reverend Coy Dickey, Fender Chapel became a mission under the watch-care of Northwest Baptist Church, and on Sunday, May 9, 1937, with 11 founding members, was formally accepted into the Greene County Association.

Between 1937 and 1965, except for general maintenance, little was done to expand the church building. Then, in 1965, the Intermediate Sunday School Class, a group of young members taught by the Pastor, Wayne Presley, began a love offering to add classrooms to the church. When the class had accumulated $5.00, the church began a building fund. Grasping the vision, others began to contribute generously to the fund, until sufficient monies were available to not only build new classrooms, but to remodel the interior and exterior of the church. New carpeting, pews, central air and heat, steel siding and other improvements were made to the building. Later, inside restrooms, an additional classroom and a fellowship room were constructed.

Every October, a reunion is held at the church in honor of the Fender family, but it is agreed that Fender Chapel stands as a testimony, not only to the man for whom it is named, but also to the many pastors, deacons, teachers, and members who have dedicated themselves to serving God and caring for the spiritual needs of a community. Fender Chapel's rich history of service to God spans 127 years, and it is the sincere hope of the current congregation that such service and dedication will continue as we reach out in love to others.

Fender Chapel

First Christian Church (Disciples Of Christ)
Bolivar, Missouri

The religious movement known as the Christian Church (Disciples of Christ) was born on American soil shortly after the Revolutionary War. It was a blending of American idealism and New Testament Christianity and became a major religious force on the frontier. One movement led by Thomas and Alexander Campbell was called The Disciples of Christ. Another similar group was led by Barton W. Stone. In 1832, the two groups united near Lexington, KY, and both names were kept in the union.

The First Christian Church of Bolivar had its beginnings in the original courthouse on the square. Elder Buchanan held a meeting and several were added to the fold. In 1882, Morgan Morgans came and gave the church a more official beginning and it claimed 27 members at that time. The first church building was erected on the present lot donated by Mr. and Mrs. E.G. Lunceford in 1885. It was finished and dedicated in that same year.

The present building at 407 West Broadway was started in 1921. Funds ran short and discouragement set in. Default on the debt seemed imminent and so the women of the church began selling lunches at farm auctions. In the end, they and the sacrifice of some of the members saved the church. The building debt was not paid in full, however, until March 1, 1941 at a total cost of $55,000. Church membership grew from 27 to about 450 in the '40s and is presently about 300.

In the late '60s the parsonage, standing just to the north of the church, burned to the ground and was not replaced. A few years later the front steps of the church were remodeled and in 1978, a small memorial tower was built, in memory of James Rains, to house the church's bell, whose history goes back to the first church. The bell still tolls every Sunday morning at 10:20. A lot was acquired across Clark Street east and then another to the west of the church and these have been paved for parking lots. For 70 years members of the church dreamed of an elevator and more space. In 1999 that dream came true with the completion and the dedication of an addition that included not only an elevator, but new offices, a modern nursery, a new kitchen, an all-purpose room and gymnasium, new rest rooms and showers, a covered drive-thru entrance and a meeting place called the Upper Room. Decor reflects the present and the past with many antique pieces from the original church.

The Centennial Celebration of the church was held in 1982 with Harold E. Ball as pastor. The general chairman in charge of arrangements was Doris Blankenship and other chairmen were History, Latha Blankenship; Worship and Music, Nancy McMillin; Finance, David Scott; Hospitality, Marilyn Parrot; Publicity, Mark Stephens and Administrative Advisor, Mark Besser.

First Christian Church of Bolivar is affiliated with the Disciples of Christ. The area office is in Springfield, with a regional office in Jefferson City and international headquarters in Indianapolis, IN. The local church owns its own property, sets its own budget and program, and calls and dismisses its ministers. The present minister in the year 2002 is Rev. Jerry Book. The church board consists of Mike Stephens, President; Tim Scott, Vice President; Secretary, Courtney Welch; Treasurer, Synda Douglas and Financial Secretary, Nancy McMillin. Trustees are David Scott, Nick Maas and Tony Porter who replaced the late Kent Snodgrass.

The exact status of Morgan Morgans has been lost in the midst of time, but if one starts with him as the first full-time minister of the church, the current minister is the 37th in the near century and a half of the congregation's existence. Our doors swing on welcome hinges and we are always glad to greet old friends and to become acquainted with new people.

Zion Lutheran Church

Zion Lutheran Church—the first Lutheran church in Bolivar—currently located at 600 E. Aldrich Road, Bolivar, was organized in January 1974 after meetings with LCMS District President Dr. Shearer, Rev. C. W. Heileman and several members of Trinity Lutheran Church in Springfield. Following is a timeline of the history of this church.

February 1974 - Several meetings were held at the Selvey home to discuss plans for holding church services. Pruitts, Ankroms, Selveys, Griffin, Whites, Gabels and Pastor Heilman were the planners. Since no vacant buildings were available, services were held at the Selvey home.

March 17, 1974 - The first service was held at the Selvey home at 7:30 with Pastor C. W. Heilman serving us. There were 41 in attendance. Joe and Sharon Hackley, members of Trinity, were regular attendees at our worship services and were always around for our support.

April 25, 1975 - We moved to 1423 West Broadway, an older house which had been used as a church by another congregation. Frequent visitors to our Sunday night services were Tom and Erna Moore, K. C. who spent holidays and some weekends at their resort home on Pomme de Terre Lake.

Ron and Donna Selvey's home, our first meeting place in 1974.

June 29, 1975 - The Mission Board sent word that Pastor Schnelle of Springfield would be our new minister on a part time basis. He would live in Springfield and serve Faith, a Mission Congregation there.

Sept. 7, 1975 - Pastor Schnelle was installed at Faith to serve both congregations.

Oct. 23, 1975 - Fall was a busy time with meetings held to discuss future plans. The name Zion was picked for our church name. Temporary officers were elected to serve until the constitution was drawn up. Everett Purrington, President; Gene Ankrom, Vice-President; Mary Ankrom, Secretary; Ron Selvey, Treasurer; Roy Bruce, Charles Brooks and Arthur Heithold, elders; and Donna Selvey, evangelism and publicity.

March 14, 1976 - The constitution was approved by the voters.

March 17, 1976 - Charter members were Mr. and Mrs. Gene Ankrom, Janet and Roger; Mr. and Mrs. Charles Brooks; Mr. and Mrs. Roy Bruce; Mr. and Mrs. Delmar Gabel; Mrs. Jeannie Griffin and Bryan; Mr. and Mrs. Arthur Heithold and Kathy; Mr. and Mrs. Everett Purrington, Everett Jr., Cecil, Scott, Robyn, RayJean, Curtiss, Fred, and Mary; Mr. and Mrs. Ronald Selvey, Roger, Peggy and Cammie; Mr. and Mrs. Oscar Myers; and Mrs. Thomas South.

April 11, 1976- Emma and Donna Jacobs, twin infant daughters of Jake and Connie Jacobs, were the first babies baptized at Zion.

April 16, 1976 - Everett Purrington and Peggy Selvey were the first youth to be confirmed at Zion.

June 14, 1976 - Our first Vacation Bible School was held with Mary Ankrom as coordinator. Approximately 25 children attended.

June 20, 1976 - Mrs. Geneva Goins was the first adult to be baptized at Zion.

July 1977 - The purchase of property on Aldrich Road for $45,000 provided the location of our present church building.

January 1978 - At this time we had 70 baptized members and 50 Communicants.

Jan. 7, 1979 - Pastor Mark Stenbeck was installed at Faith, and on February 3 he was installed at Zion to serve both Congregations.

Oct. 17, 1979 - Pellham and Phillips of Springfield were selected as the architects for the new church building.

Feb. 3, 1980 — Rev. Clarence Stenbeck, a retired pastor, was installed as our first resident Pastor.

May 18, 1980— We held the groundbreaking service for our new church building.

Sept. 20, 1980 — Miss Janet Ankrom and Mr. Norman Nelson were the first to be married in our church.

Sept. 21, 1980— Our first church service was held in our new building.

Oct. 12, 1980 — Our first baptism in the new building, Kellie Sue Rader, daughter of Mr. and Mrs. Randall Rader, was celebrated. In November our second baptism was Todd Benjamin Black, son of Mr. and Mrs. Greg Black.

March 27, 1983 — Rev. Joseph Barbour was installed as our first full-time pastor.

April 10, 1987 — St. Andrew Lutheran Church of Stockton, MO, was established as a mission start from Zion.

Sept. 29, 1987 — Dual Parish agreement signed with St. Andrew of Stockton.

April 24, 1988 — Rev. Lloyd F. Groenke was installed as our pastor.

June 30, 1991 — Rev. Mark E. Lavrenz was installed as a dual pastor with our congregation and St. Andrew of Stockton.

Dec. 15, 1991 — A new mission was started in Hermitage, MO. Several families left Zion to attend there. They met at a local nursing home, and bought a building in April of 1992.

Sept. 12, 1999 — Zion dedicated a new fellowship hall and classroom addition named in memory of Alfred and Ruby Kelderhouse, members from 1980 until their death, who donated generously to the church.

Zion Lutheran Church–Church and 1999 Fellowship Hall addition.

History of Calvary Missionary Baptist Church

The thought of organizing a church had its beginning in the hearts and minds of a group of Baptists living in Bolivar, MO, who held church membership in rural churches near Bolivar. For a long period of time, this group met together in cottage prayer meetings, where they received many spiritual blessings. The church was organized on March 5, 1940 with thirteen charter members: Rev. J. A. Hook; Bernice Hook; Abe Waggoner; Hester Waggoner; Leo Smith (Deacon); Bess Smith; Harvey Edge; Helen Edge; Bill Radcliff; Lela Radcliff; Pat Jenkins; Berniece Jenkins; and Rev. Charley Russell. Two days later, Milford Hicks and Leona Hicks joined with the thirteen charter members. The membership continued to grow rapidly until by the end of the year of 1940, the church membership totaled 83. During the organization of the church, the name of CALVARY MISSIONARY BAPTIST CHURCH was chosen. The first officers were Rev. J. A. Hook, Pastor; Hester Waggoner, Church Clerk; Leo Smith, Treasurer. Bill Radcliff, Leo Smith, and Pat Jenkins were chosen to serve as trustees. The motive adopted by the church reads as follows:

We will strive to be a New Testament Church, and to see that the teaching and preaching shall be the same as that taught by John the Baptist and of Christ and His Apostles, that salvation comes only by conviction of sin by the Holy Spirit and Repentance, which is a work of the Holy Spirit. We do not believe Repentance is just a change of the natural mind, but that it is a change wrought in the Soul by the Spirit and brings the Soul where it can believe in Christ as his Savior and only those who have taken these steps have truly been born again.

A lot on Canton Avenue in the northwestern part of Bolivar, MO was purchased. Although the group had very limited personal finances, the building was begun. Many sister churches and friends helped financially, some anonymously, and the church has always been grateful for the help. After hard work by many volunteers, the building was completed. Dedication services were held on July 25, 1943. The membership was 158. It was a blessed day for the Church as they were free from debt, and the house was dedicated to God. A large crowd, many from sister churches, witnessed the dedication. During those early years, one of the charter members, Abe Waggoner, testified to his calling to the ministry and was ordained by the church.

In 1951, Bro. Clarence Salsman accepted the pastorate of the church. The church became a part of the Tri-County Association which is composed of churches that were separated from the Southern Baptist Convention. The division was brought about due to the differences in practice and belief of the churches regarding repentance. Calvary Missionary Baptist Church is a member of the Polk County Missionary Baptist Association.

Other pastors of the church have been Bro. Alpha Redford, Bro. Dennis Spear, Elder Keith Frieze, and Elder Stephen Skinner. The current pastor is Elder Douglas Skinner.

Deacons who have served the church are: Leo Smith, George Beason, T. S. Welsh, Carl Irby, W. R. Woodmansee, Charley Vincent, John Davison, Audie Turner, Clyde Ed Fish Sr., Walter Roberts, Hurshel Spencer, Roy C. McReynolds, Bill Strader, Russell Payne, Cletis Andrews, Lonnie Scurlock, Roy Phillips, Dee Ruyle, Standley Ross, Earl Campbell, Rob Scroggins, Carl Shuler, Bobby Miller, Lowell Hagerman, Morris Stephens. Current deacons are: Norman Hutchison, Ed Hagerman, Derrell Ashlock, Gerald Sergent, Larry Scroggins, Kyle Legan, James Shade and Mick Hood.

Currently, five ordained ministers are members of the church: Elder Ron Erven, Elder David Keith, Elder Aaron Hood, Elder Douglas Skinner and Elder Terry Nicodemus. Currently serving as trustees are: Pat Foster, Ed Hagerman, Kyle Legan, Larry Scroggins and Kelley Roberts.

As the membership increased through the years, the church increased the size of the auditorium, added Sunday School rooms, and purchased adjoining properties for parking needs. A sizable estate donation from a former member allowed purchase of two nearby homes, one of which is being used by the church school authorized by the membership. The school, named Grace Academy, began the first class of pre-schoolers in the fall of 2002.

Calvary Missionary Baptist Church has held many revivals, both planned and spontaneous. A week-long full church fellowship is held each summer as well as a youth weekend in the month of August. Fellowship trips have been made to sister churches in Tennessee, Indiana and other states. The church has been blessed in supporting God-called men who have the task of carrying the message to a lost and dying world. Other ministers who have been ordained by Calvary Missionary Baptist Church include: Elder Paul Cofer, Elder Aaron Hood, Elder Douglas Skinner and Elder Kent Welch. In addition, several young men have been licensed to preach by the church.

The Lord's Supper is observed on Saturday Evening two times a year with communion taken only by members of Calvary Missionary Baptist Church. Singing praises to God has always been important to the church. A ladies group of singers from the church membership called <u>Sisters in One a-Chord</u> have recorded gospel music with the church's support. Their music has been especially helpful to missionaries for their services out on the field.

As well as giving any needed aid to its own members, Calvary Missionary Baptist Church donates to the needs of sister churches, and gives a money donation yearly to the Polk County Community Center to be used for the needs of the community. The Church helps support several missionaries both in foreign countries and in the United States by sending the money directly to the missionary. Support has gone to Jamaica, West Indies, Japan, Mexico, Russia, Trinidad, Ghana, West Africa, Romania and several states.

Of the thirteen original members, there is one still living at the time of this writing; Berniece Jenkins, who is age 95. The oldest member of the church is Helen Phillips, age 104. They are both inspirations to the present congregation.

Calvary Missionary Baptist Church is thankful for God's leadership and His blessings, and for the many souls who have been saved and for all that has been added to the Church.

Calvary Missionary Baptist Church, 123 N. Canton Ave., Boliver, MO, 65613. Photo by Debbi Roberts-McGinnis

Methodist Episcopal Church

Early in the history of Polk County, MO, the Methodist Episcopal Church sent circuit riders and exhorters to any and every place where a few persons could be brought together for worship, meeting in open fields, private homes and school houses. According to tradition, the first sermon preached in Polk County was by the Methodist circuit rider, the Rev. W. Slavens, in 1832 at the residence of Aaron Ruyle in Looney Township. The early Methodist plan was to have a class or church every five miles, if persons were willing, even in the open country areas, so that no one would have to travel more than an hour by foot to attend worship and learn about God. ... There were many places to preach but very few Methodist Episcopal Churches at first. A church was chartered only after a Methodist Class had been established, the "scholars" discipled, and then, if in the judgment of the pastor, they were acceptable for membership in the Methodist Episcopal Church. Classes were begun in and around Bolivar as early as 1832, but it was 1840 before a congregation was organized into a church. Some of the classes in the area started churches earlier. Others, such as Stockton and Humansville would not be organized into a church for another thirty years...

Bolivar, as the new county seat of Polk County, was one of the many stopping points for the early circuit riders. It was not, however, seen as a promising site for a Methodist Church.... A Methodist Episcopal Church did come into being in 1840. Its first building was a log house, 20 feet by 24 feet, {that} stood on lot No. 3, block No. 4 of "Old Town," as the original town plot is sometimes called. The First Baptist Church of Bolivar now sits on this site. This building was also used as the County Courthouse before the Polk County Courthouse was erected.

Almost immediately, the congregation faced a divisive issue. There had been a growing debate within the Methodist Episcopal Church over the issues of slavery and state rights, and at the General Conference of 1844, there was a split in the denomination which led to the formation of the Methodist Episcopal Church, South. This split is often sited by historians as a major contributing factor in the War Between the States... The congregation in Bolivar sided with the southern church and the Methodist preachers, which were usually seen as representatives of the "northern" church, were often run out of town....

It is certain that there were pastors appointed from the Methodist Episcopal Church, South to the Bolivar Church from 1845 to 1865 and to another Methodist congregation in Bolivar until 1925. At that time, the membership of the south church joined with the north church in the present church building. Planning for the new building located at the corner of Main and Division streets was begun in 1920 and completed in 1922 free of debt. The building has undergone a complete renovation of the sanctuary and the addition of a new fellowship hall, offices, classrooms, and kitchen in 1988 and the early 1990s. *(Excerpts from <u>Celebrating 150 years of Faith: Bolivar United Methodist Church 1940-1990</u> by Nickolas J. Campbell, Tapestry Press, Ltd. Acton, MA 01720).*

The Catholic Church In Polk County

There have been three Catholic parishes in Polk County. The oldest was St. Wenceslaus Church at Karlin built in 1901. The second one, St. Catherine of Siena was established in Humansville in 1940 and the third, Sacred Heart, in Bolivar in 1946.

St. Wenceslaus

As far back as 1897 there were some families settled in the area called Tremont (because of three hills that mark the landscape). These were Irish settlers who were Catholic. The priest from Osceola, Father Clinton and later Father John W. Keyes would travel to Tremont to celebrate Mass for these Catholics in their homes. At the turn of the century Bohemian families arrived from Lawrence County, MO and from Nebraska, Iowa and Wisconsin. These families were interested principally in farming. The organization of this parish can be set on the 31st day of March 1901 with a meeting at the farm house of M. F. Divin, who was the first Bohemian to settle in Polk County. Within a short time a Church was built in honor of St. Wenceslaus, the patron saint of Bohemia and beloved saint of these newly arrived people.

The land for the church and adjacent cemetery was donated by the Frank Korn family who had come from Nebraska. The original Pastor was Fr. Keyes and the parish lay within the diocese of Kansas City. By 1904 a native son, C. J. Francka was ordained and remained to be Pastor for almost 50 years. The little community had faced setbacks when the first frame church was destroyed by fire in 1903 and the second church of brick sustained a wind that blew down the rafters and one wall before it was finished. Not daunted by these misfortunes, the Church was finished and served as the center of faith for 60 years. This community was renamed Karlin after a certain Karel (Charles) Andera,

St. Wenceslaus Church

Sacred Heart Parish in Bolivar

the head of an early family. He was known for his woodcarving skills. (Also it may have been named after a town of the same name in the old country).

In 1963 the parish was closed because of changes in demographics and members were encouraged to worship at Sacred Heart Church in Bolivar. The church building had to be taken down because vandals began to demolish it. The church cemetery is still in use and the location of the old church is marked with a special monument and the memories are held dear in the hearts of many. The statue of St. Wenceslaus and its beautiful wood carved niche were placed in Sacred Heart Church in Bolivar and the great bronze cast bell was moved to that new location. Its voice rings out as It did for many years in the past to announce the beginning of Mass.

SACRED HEART

Parish in Bolivar: founded 1946. Originally located on Main Street, it was dedicated by Bp. E. O'Hara of Kansas City, MO. During its first year Monsignor C. J. Francka, of Karlin, celebrated Mass there once a month. Thereafter, Fr. W. Curran of Osceola had its Mass twice a month. Then in 1949 Fr. Clem Ilmberger (assigned to be associate of St. Wenceslaus in Karlin) began to regularly have Sunday Mass. The little church grew over the coming years. Fr. John J. Rynish followed as Pastor. He was followed by Fr. Eugene Deragowski (a native son of Karlin). Ten acres on the west side of Bolivar were purchased and plans began to build a new church with rectory attached. The contract was awarded in November 1957 and was completed and dedicated on Aug. 31, 1958. The Archbishop of Chicago, William D. O'Brien officiated. Fr. James Seyer was pastor in 1960-61 and in 1961 Fr. Wm. Winkelmann became pastor. The following year quarters for a housekeeper were added (presently used as church offices). In 1986 a multipurpose building was built and named McKenna Hall in honor of Fr. James McKenna who served over ten years as Pastor. In 1996 plans were developed for a new rectory which was soon built. In 2004 discussion is underway for building a new church to house a growing congregation.

ST. CATHERINE

Mission in Humansvllle

As early as 1920 Mass was celebrated six to eight times a year in the homes of people from Humansville by Fr. C. F. Francka from St. Wenceslaus parish in Karlin. It was known as St. Jude Mission. In 1940 a Fr. Ronald F. O'Dwyer, the pastor of St. Catherine of Siena Parish in Osceola, MO was made the pastor of this mission church with about 35 members who gathered in the L. T. Heaton Building. In the following year St. Jude Mission moved into a larger building across the street with the help of Rev. Senan O'Connell, of Osceola. On Jan. 20, 1946 a new church was dedicated at the present location by Bp. Edwin V. O'Hara of Kansas City. It was renamed St. Catherine of Siena and it numbered mainly German and Irish Catholics. When the new Diocese of Springfield-Cape Girardeau was established on Aug. 24, 1956, the mission at Humansville fell under the auspices of the Pastor of El Dorado Springs. Later its care was transferred to the Pastor of Bolivar in 1984 and continues as such. Under the guidance of Fr. Gregory Zatina the church underwent extensive renovation. It counts 37 families in its membership at present.

St. Catherine Church

Businesses and Organizations

Mt. Gilead United Methodist

In the fall of 1853 a group of neighbors met and organized a Sunday School, meeting in a schoolhouse. On June 6, 1854 T. McAllister deeded 4.93 acres for a campground and place of religious worship. Later, 2.29 acres were purchased from the McAllister and Snodgrass families for $22. In about 1908 a frame building was constructed where the present church stands. This was destroyed by fire in August 1932. Services were held in the Forest Grove School until Christmas when the present church was completed. In 1958 a basement was dug and finished with kitchen and rest rooms. A nursery-classroom with rest room was built in 1997. Mt. Gilead church and cemetery is located two miles southeast of Bolivar at intersection of S. 145th Road and E. 464th Road. Services are at 11:00 every Sunday. Come worship with us!

Mt. Gilead United Methodist Church

Bank of Bolivar

Chartered in 1997, Bank of Bolivar opened its doors on April 16, 1997 with $3,000,000 in total assets, six full-time employees and one part-time employee. Projections indicate that in the first quarter of 2003 we will surpass $100,000,000 in total assets. We credit our philosophy of putting local money to work in the local economy for our exceptional growth.

Bank of Bolivar is owned by local stockholders dedicated to the prosperity of the local community. We refer to our bank as "A Real Community Bank," locally owned, locally operated, built with local money, and staffed by local employees.

April, 1997

September, 1997

Bolivar Herald–Free Press

We at the *Bolivar Herald-Free Press* are proud to be stewards of the oldest continuous business in Polk County. And we are careful to say it that way, because time has proven that regardless of the "legal ownership" of the publication throughout its many years, it has always belonged to its readers.

The "Free Press" part of our name can be traced to June 1868 when T.H.B. Dunnegan, who was also deputy sheriff and collector, saw a need for a newspaper here. All previous publications in the county had come and gone. As collector, he was well aware of the size of the delinquent tax list and of a law requiring that it be published in a county newspaper. Without a newspaper in the county, the list would need to be published in a newspaper in an adjoining county.

Mr. Dunnegan organized a company consisting of Capt. William M. Delaplain, John Watson, William J. Williams, W.L. Snodgrass and several others to start a newspaper. They counted on revenue from the publishing of the tax list to pay for their start-up.

The first office was set up on the second floor of a building on the south side of the public square and on June 4, 1868, the first issue of the *Bolivar Free Press* was published.

The newspaper stewards of that time proudly proclaimed the paper as the "Official Journal of the County" on its masthead. In addition to that, they also proclaimed it as "The Cheapest Radical (Republican) Newspaper in the State of Missouri. A Prospectus of Bolivar. The Free Press. A Weekly Paper Devoted to General News, Politics, Local Interests, Agriculture."

The newspaper came out solidly in support of U.S. Grant for president.

The *Bolivar Herald* was first published May 1, 1872, with its publishers, John W. Potter and W.J. Barton, formerly of the *Springfield Leader*, promising to be "as thoroughly Democratic as the case would allow."

Many editors and publishers of both publications would come and go over the next 96 years, and the political rhetoric back and forth was quite lively at times.

Ralph Stufflebam, general manager of KYTV at the time, and whose family had owned the *Bolivar Herald* on multiple occasions, assumed control of that publication in November 1967. On the same evening, he purchased the *Bolivar Free Press* from the Gravely family (owners since 1892) and the *Polk County Times* from Joe Mann and Doyle and Jerrie Keller, a publication that existed only from 1966 until that sale.

Two weeks after the purchase, the *Herald* and the *Free Press* were merged, first as the *Bolivar Free Press-Herald*, based on the predominance of Republicans here, even though its new direction would be void of partisan affiliation.

Jim Sterling was immediately hired to serve as general manager of the merged publications, and his first official act was to suggest a name reversal, "because it sounded better and Herald always came first in the names of merged newspapers."

Jac and Rheba Zimmerman bought the merged product from Mr. Stufflebam in March 1968 and kept Mr. Sterling as a general manager. The latter would acquire full ownership in October 1979. It was sold to Community Publishers of Missouri, Inc., in February 1999.

Its publisher, Dave Berry, has been with the publication since 1977 and its editor/general manager, Judy Kallenbach, came aboard in 1978. Jim Hamilton took over for Judy in 2004.

Again, legal ownership has changed over the years, but the management attitude remains the same: we don't mind at all that readers have a sense of ownership.

(Information for this includes research by Jim Sterling in 1962 and Martin E. McCullen in 1959. We also express renewed pride in Jim Sterling's coauthorship of the 1985 Sesquicentennial Photograph Album, "Polk County Classics.")

Bolivar Herald-Free Press

Southwest Baptist University

The University first opened its doors in 1878 in Lebanon, MO, as Southwest Baptist College. In 1879 the college was chartered by the state of Missouri and moved to Bolivar. Early writings recount a legacy of sacrificial giving and extraordinary efforts by Baptists in southwest Missouri to establish and maintain the college. The founders, James R. Maupin and Abner S. Ingman, faced many difficulties as they rode horseback seeking funds, students and an ideal college site.

The college faced many hardships in its early years and actually closed from 1908-13 to regain financial solvency and to recover from a devastating fire that destroyed the college's only building. The efforts and prayers of area supporters and Missouri Baptists brought results, and the college reopened in 1913 as a two-year junior college.

The University has maintained its strong Baptist heritage through its affiliation with the Missouri Baptist Convention, which provides some financial support for the University and elects the 25-member board of trustees, which governs the institution.

The Missouri Baptist Convention approved plans in 1964 for the college to become a senior liberal arts college. The first baccalaureate degrees were awarded in 1967. Bolivar citizens donated a 102-acre farm on the southern edge of the city that allowed the college to expand physically beyond the small 10-acre campus located near downtown as part of its growing academic expansion.

Another milestone occurred in 1981 when the college name was changed to Southwest Baptist University. In 1995 the University entered a joint nursing education agreement with St. John's Regional Medical Center in Springfield, MO, to form St. John's School of Nursing of Southwest Baptist University.

Today, SBU is a thriving higher education institution with more than 3,700 undergraduate and graduate students enrolled annually. The 152-acre main campus is located in the southern portion of Bolivar. There are 37 buildings on the main campus. The University has degree-granting centers in Mountain View, Salem and Springfield, MO.

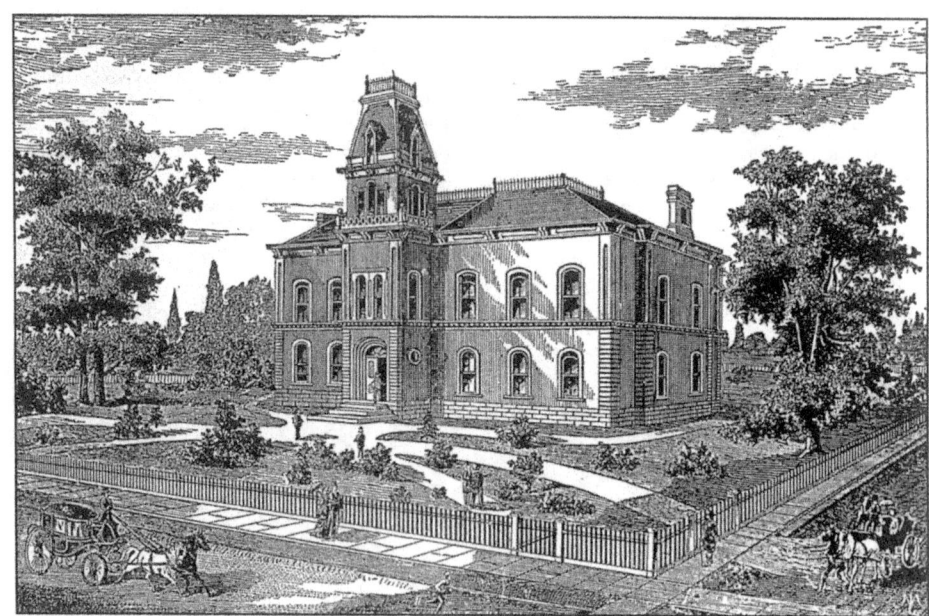

Southwest Baptist University 1892-93 Catalog

Southwest Baptist University Today

Mid-Missouri Bank
Committed To Our Past, Focused On Our Future

Since 1872, Mid-Missouri Bank has been a cornerstone of the Bolivar community and a pioneering partner in its growth and development. Surviving through the country's economic hardships, lifestyle and banking changes, and even the continuous evolution of money and the medium of exchange, the bank has served the public for 130 years.

Founded by T.H.B. Dunnegan, J.A. Tolfree and J.B. Kelsey with capital of $10,000, the bank was originally created for what *The Bolivar Free Press* described as "general banking and exchange." According to an article in the June 20, 1872 *Free Press,* the foundation of the new bank meant, "A secure place is thus afforded to farmers and others for the deposit of their spare funds until needed." A 20 by 50-foot corner of an existing business's storeroom served as the bank's original office. Cart and a team of 12 oxen from Springfield, MO, transported the first safe.

In 1877, the bank began using the name Polk County Bank, with T.H.B. Dunnegan serving as president. When Dunnegan passed away in 1934, he was the first and only president of the bank during his lifetime and the oldest banker with continuous service as bank president in the United States. The bank's current location was erected in 1892 and is still a local landmark on the square.

Polk County Bank officially became Mid-Missouri Bank in November 2002. With assets in excess of $300 million, the bank offers traditional banking products as well as investment, trust and insurance services.

Since its inception in 1872, Mid-Missouri Bank has focused on the needs of the Bolivar community. It has been an honor to serve you over the last generation, and we look forward to banking with you in the generations to come.

MID-MISSOURI BANK

This photo of the west side of the square shows the block of buildings from Mid-Missouri Bank south to the alley.

Left: *Children from North and South Ward schools parade at the new courthouse dedication in 1907.* **Right:** *This view from West Broadway shows Mid-Missouri Bank. The International automobile parked in front of the bank was one of the town's first two automobiles.*

Left: *Mid-Missouri Bank was once one of three banks that stood on all three corners of the northwest corner of the square. The building was completely remodeled in the 1950s.* **Right:** *A jeep-drawn float celebrating the 1948 visit of President Romulo Gallegos of Venezuela and President Harry S Truman passes Mid-Missouri Bank.*

Polk County Commission

Courts of Justice and County Officials

The first meeting of the county court was held on the 9th day of February, 1835, at the house of Daniel M. Stockton, at present the residence of James M. Henslee, Esq., five miles southwest of Bolivar, on the West Bend road. Jeremiah N. Sloan and Richard Saye constituted the Court; Joesph English was the Sheriff, and William Henry was appointed Clerk, pro tem, J. N. Sloan was the President of the Court, and E. M. Campbell was made county surveyor. The Court adjourned on the first day, to meet on the next at the house of William C. Campbell. At this court the county was divided into three Municipal Townships; the central portion was called Marion, the eastern part, Washington; and the western, Jackson.

The Polk County Commission oversees 850 miles of county roads, which includes seven Special Road Districts. Approximately 100 weight-limited bridges are inspected by the State but are cared for by the Commission. The Commission aggressively installs new culverts for drainage on county roads. The half-cent Capital Improvements Sales Tax has chipped and sealed 251 miles of rural roadways in the last seven years. The Commission endeavors to participate in the Federal Bridge replacement program for bridges over the Pomme de Terre and Sac Rivers.

A new E-911 Communications Center is a priority of the Commission to enhance emergency services to county residents. The Commission works hard to provide competitive wages and benefits for county employees for whom they are very proud to work with. Polk County is one of the fastest growing third class counties in Southern Missouri. The Commission hopes to continue the aggressive but conservative manner of spending county funds into the 21st Century.

The following is a list of the members of the County Court from the first organization to the present time:

Names	Elected	Term
J. N. Sloan	1835	
Richard Saye	1835	
Winfrey Owens	1835	
Thomas Martin	1836	
James G. Human	1836	
Wm. Fourshee	1836	
Isaae Ruth	1837	
Henry Akard	1837	
William Lunceford	1837	2 yrs
A. W. Temple	1838	4 mos.
Wm. Henry	1839	1 yr.
Winfrey Owens	1840	4 mos.
Thomas Rountree	1841	3 yrs.
Benjamin C. Mitchell	1844	8 yrs.
Francis Dunnegan	1844	2 yrs.
Caleb Luttrell	1844	5 yrs.
John Burns	1846	2 yrs.
Wm. R. Devin	1848	2 yrs.
Wm. H. Newland	1849	3 yrs.
Leander Wilson	1851	1 yr.
T. W. Cunningham	1852	4 yrs.
Wm. Lunceford	1852	4 yrs.
David M. McCluer	1853	8 yrs.
Wm. H. Lemmon	1856	4 yrs.
Moses P. Hart	1856	6 yrs.
Thos. D. Hall	1860	2 yrs.
James Jump	1862	2 yrs.
Moses L. Carter	1862	6 yrs.
James Potts	1862	4 yrs.
Thos. Higginbotham	1864	2 yrs.
Thos. Fox	1866	4 yrs.
Hiram Hopkins	1868	1 yr.
John W. Ratcliff	1868	1.5 yrs.
W. H. Branham	1870	6 mos.
Jesse H. Murray	1870	3 yrs.
J. B. Barnett	1870	3 yrs.
L. J. Mitchell	1872	8 mos.
Wm. McVanzandt	1873	2 yrs.
J. W. Farmer	1873	
Enoch Plumer	1873 re-elected	
Benj. Rodgers	1873	
Hiram Hopkins	1873 re-elected	
B. W. Appleby	1875	

L-R: Danny Barker, Roy Harms and Billy Dryer

Year	Office	Name of Officer	Politics	Town
1876	Presiding Judge County Court	B. W. Appleby		
	District Judge	Benjiman Rodgers		
	District Judge	Hiram Hopkins		
1877	Presiding Judge County Court	B. W. Appleby		
	District Judge	Benjiman Rodgers		
	District Judge	Hiram Hopkins		
1878	Presiding Judge County Court	B. W. Appleby		
	District Judge	T. H. B. Dunnegan		
	District Judge	Enoch Plummer		
1879	Presiding Judge County Court	B. W. Appleby		
	District Judge	T. H. B. Dunnegan		
	District Judge	Enoch Plummer		
1880	Presiding Judge County Court	B. W. Appleby		
	District Judge	T. H. B. Dunnegan		
	District Judge	S. A. Morgan		
1881	Presiding Judge County Court	B. W. Appleby		
	District Judge	T. H. B. Dunnegan		
	District Judge	Theodore G. Weatherby		
1882	Presiding Judge County Court	B. W. Appleby		
	District Judge	T. H. B. Dunnegan		
	District Judge	Theodore G. Weatherby		
1883	Presiding Judge County Court	James Rule		
	District Judge	John R. McDonald		
	District Judge	William McVanzandt		
1884	Presiding Judge County Court	James Rule		
	District Judge	John R. McDonald		
	District Judge	William McVanzandt		
1885	Presiding Judge County Court	James Rule		
	District Judge	James M. Zumwalt		
	District Judge	A. B. Hughes		
1886	Presiding Judge County Court	James Rule		
	District Judge	James M. Zumwalt		
	District Judge	A. B. Hughes		
1887	Presiding Judge County Court	James Rule		
	District Judge	John R. McDonald		
	District Judge	J. B. M. Ramsey		
1888	Presiding Judge County Court	James Rule		
	District Judge	John R. McDonald		
	District Judge	J. B. M. Ramsey		
1889	Presiding Judge County Court	James Rule		
	District Judge	T. H. B. Dunnegan		
	District Judge	James P. Slagle		
1890	Presiding Judge County Court	James Rule		
	District Judge	T. H. B. Dunnegan		
	District Judge	James P. Slagle		
1891	Presiding Judge County Court	Daniel P. Brockus		

Year	Office	Name of Officer	Politics	Town
	District Judge	T. H. B. Dunnegan		
	District Judge	W. B. Patterson		
1892	Presiding Judge County Court	Daniel P. Brockus		
	District Judge	T. H. B. Dunnegan		
	District Judge	W. B. Patterson		
1893	Presiding Judge County Court	Daniel P. Brockus		
	District Judge	T. H. B. Dunnegan		
	District Judge	W. B. Patterson		
1894	Presiding Judge County Court	Daniel P. Brockus		
	District Judge	J. F. Hopkins		
	District Judge	J. W. McCurry		
1895	Presiding Judge County Court	James Rule		
	District Judge	Ben Meyers		
	District Judge	Jesse Griffin		
1895-1896	Judge Circuit Court, East Dist.	Ben Meyers		
	Presiding Judge County Court	James Rule		
	Judge County Court, West Dist.	Jess Griffin		
1899-1900	Presiding Judge County Court	James J. Akard		
	Judge County Court, 1st Dist.	William W. Viles		
	Judge County Court, 2nd Dist.	Enoch B. Keeling		
1901-1902	Presiding Judge County Court	James J. Akard		
	Judge County Court, 1st Dist.	Samuel F. Arnold		
	Judge County Court, 2nd Dist.	Enoch B. Keeling		
1903-1904	Presiding Judge County Court	James H. Baldwin		
	Judge County Court, 1st Dist.	Samuel L. Brock		
	Judge County Court, 2nd Dist.	Daniel D. Fisher		
1905-1906	Presiding Judge County Court	James H. Baldwin		
	Judge County Court, 1st Dist.	Charles Grove		
	Judge County Court, 2nd Dist.	Daniel D. Fisher		
1907-1908	Presiding Judge Co. Court	Wm. C. Ditmars	Rep.	
	Judge Co. Court 1st District	Clarence E. Markey	Rep.	
	Judge Co. Court 2nd Dist.	Richard W. Hart	Rep.	
	Clerk, County Court	John T. Waddill	Rep.	
1913-1914	Presiding Judge Circuit	John I. Reed	Rep.	
	Judge Co. Court District 1	W. A. Gilmore	Dem.	
	Judge Co. Court District 2	A. F. Hughes	Dem.	
	Clerk, County Court	E. L. Hirst	Dem.	
1917-1918	Presiding Judge Co. Court	Joseph M. Dunnegan	Rep.	
	Judge Co. Court Eastern Dist.	C. B. Owen	Dem.	
	Judge Co. Court Western Dist.	J. A. Fox	Rep.	
	Clerk, County Court	Emmet L. Hirst	Dem.	
1921-1922	Presiding Judge Co. Court	E. C. Devin	Rep.	
	Judge Co. Court Eastern Dist.	Jno. W. Hook	Rep.	
	Judge Co. Court Western Dist.	Floyd R. Rees	Rep.	
	Clerk, County Court	J. F. Underwood	Rep.	
1923-1924	Presiding Judge Co. Court	E. C. Devin	Rep.	Bolivar
	Judge Co. Court Eastern Dist.	J. F. Hockenhull	Dem.	Polk
	Judge Co. Court Western Dist.	F. R. Rees	Rep.	Aldrich
	Clerk, County Court	Geo. Robertson	Rep.	Bolivar
1925-1926	Presiding Judge Co. Court	E. C. Devin	Rep.	Bolivar
	Judge Co. Court Western Dist.	F. R. Rees	Rep.	Aldrich
	Judge Co. Court Eastern Dist.	J. F. Hockenhull	Dem.	Polk
	Clerk, County Court	Geo. Robertson	Rep.	Bolivar
1927-1928	Presiding Judge Co. Court	F. R. Rees	Rep.	Aldrich
	Judge Co. Court Western Dist.	J. A. Pickering	Rep.	Cliquot
	Judge Co. Court Eastern Dist.	Thos. McArtor	Rep.	Brighton
	Clerk, County Court	J. E. Thomasson	Dem.	Bolivar
1929-1930	Presiding Judge Co. Court	F. R. Rees	Rep.	Aldrich
	Judge Co. Court Western Dist.	J. A. Pickering	Rep.	Cliquot
	Judge Co. Court Eastern Dist.	Thos. McArtor	Rep.	Brighton
	Clerk, County Court	J. E. Thomasson	Dem.	Bolivar
1931-1932	Presiding Judge Co. Court	F. R. Rees	Rep.	Aldrich
	Judge Co. Court Eastern Dist.	David M. Ingram	Dem.	Bolivar
	Judge Co. Court Western Dist.	J. A. Needham	Rep.	Aldrich
	Clerk, County Court	Baxter Lightfoot	Rep.	Bolivar
1937-1938	Presiding Judge Co. Court	W. E. Martin	Rep.	Bolivar
	Judge Co. Court Eastern Dist.	Troy Haralson	Dem.	Halfway
	Judge Co. Court Western Dist.	T. Y. Dickerson	Rep.	Aldrich
	Clerk, County Court	L. E. Emprey	Rep.	Bolivar
1939-1940	Presiding Judge Co. Court	Walter E. Martin	Rep.	Bolivar
	Judge Co. Court First Dist.	Floyd Owen	Rep.	Fair Play
	Judge Co. Court Second Dist.	Troy Haralson	Dem.	Halfway
	Clerk, County Court	Elmer Hicks	Rep.	Bolivar
1941-1942	Presiding Judge Co. Court	W. E. Martin	Rep.	Bolivar
	Judge Co. Court First Dist.	Floyd Owen	Rep.	Fair Play
	Judge Co. Court Second Dist.	Claude Crain	Rep.	Morrisville
	Clerk, County Court	Elmer Hicks	Rep.	Bolivar
1943-1944	Presiding Judge Co. Court	J. F. Owen	Rep.	Fair Play
	Judge Co. Court East Dist.	Claude Crain	Rep.	Morrisville
	Judge Co. Court West Dist.	Roy F. Beaman	Rep.	Bolivar
	Clerk, County Court	W. B. Alley	Rep.	Pleasant Hope
1945-1946	Presiding Judge Co. Court	J. F. Owen	Rep.	Fair Play
	Judge Co. Court East Dist.	Claudie O. Crain	Rep.	Morrisville
	Judge Co. Court West Dist.	T. Y. Dickerson	Rep.	Aldrich
	Clerk, County Court	W. B. Alley	Rep.	Bolivar
1949-1950	Presiding Judge Co. Court	T. Y. Dickerson	Rep.	Aldrich
	Judge Co. Court Eastern Dist.	Wm. J. McClain	Dem.	Halfway
	Judge Co. Court West Dist.	W. T. Flint	Rep.	Dunnegan
	Clerk, County Court	Francis H. Roberts	Rep.	Bolivar
1951-1952	Presiding Judge Co. Court	Claudie O. Crain	Rep.	Morrisville
	Judge Co. Court Eastern Dist.	Otis Hook	Rep.	Bolivar
	Judge Co. Court Western Dist.	W. T. Flint	Rep.	Dunnegan
	Clerk, County Court	Ray A. Pitner	Rep.	Bolivar
1953-1954	Presiding Judge Co. Court	Claudie O. Crain	Rep.	Morrisville
	Judge Co. Court North Dist.	W. T. Flint	Rep.	Bolivar
	Judge Co. Court South Dist.	Otis Hook	Rep.	Bolivar
	Clerk, County Court	Ray A. Pitner	Rep.	Bolivar
1955-1956	Presiding Judge Co. Court	Jim Bates	Rep.	Bolivar
	Judge Co. Court North Dist.	Merle Swingle	Rep.	Flemington
	Judge Co. Court South Dist.	Arthur Welsh	Rep.	Aldrich
	Clerk, County Court	Richard E. Lower	Rep.	Bolivar
1957-1958	Presiding Judge Co. Court	Jim Bates	Rep.	Bolivar
	Judge Co. Court North Dist.	Merle Swingle	Rep.	Flemington
	Judge Co. Court South Dist.	Arthur Welsh	Rep.	Aldrich
	Clerk, County Court	Richard E. Lower	Rep.	Bolivar
1959-1960	Presiding Judge Co. Court	Jim Bates	Rep.	Bolivar
	Judge Co. Court Northern Dist.	L. B. Pangborn	Rep.	Humansville
	Judge Co. Court Southern Dist.	E. D. Scorggins	Rep.	Morrisville
	Clerk, County Court	R. E. (Dick) Lower	Rep.	Bolivar
1961-1962	Presiding Judge Co. Court	Jim Bates	Rep.	Bolivar
	Judge Co. Court Northern Dist.	L. B. Pangborn	Rep.	Humansville
	Judge Co. Court Southern Dist.	E. D. Scorggins	Rep.	Morrisville
	Clerk, County Court	R. E. (Dick) Lower	Rep.	Bolivar
1965-1966	Presiding Judge Co. Court	Earl E. Ditmars	Rep.	Bolivar
	Judge Co. Court Northern Dist.	L. B. (Roy) Pangborn	Rep.	Humansville
	Judge Co. Court Southern Dist.	Albert Forgey	Rep.	Fair Play
	Clerk, County Court	R. E. (Dick) Lower	Rep.	Bolivar
1967-1968	Presiding Judge Co. Court	James A. Bates	Rep.	RFD 3 Bolivar
	Judge Co. Court Northern Dist.	LeRoy B. Pangborn	Rep.	Humansville
	Judge Co. Court Southern Dist.	James Albert Forgey	Rep.	Fair Play
	Clerk, County Court	R. E. (Dick) Lower	Rep.	Bolivar
1969-1970	Presiding Judge Co. Court	James A. Bates	Rep.	RFD 3 Bolivar
	Judge Co. Court Northern Dist.	LeRoy B. Pangborn	Rep.	Humansville
	Judge Co. Court Southern Dist.	James Albert Forgey	Rep.	Fair Play
	Clerk, County Court	Richard E. Lower	Rep.	Bolivar
1971-1972	Presiding Judge Co. Court	James A. Bates	Rep.	Rt 3 Bolivar
	Judge Co. Court Northern Dist.	L. B. Pangborn	Rep.	Humansville
	Judge Co. Court Southern Dist.	Albert Forgey	Rep.	Fair Play
	Clerk, County Court	Bill Bob Kallenbach	Rep.	Bolivar
1973-1974	Presiding Judge Co. Court	James A. Bates	Rep.	Rt 3 Bolivar
	Judge Co. Court Northern Dist.	Cecil Pitts	Rep.	R 1 Goodson
	Judge Co. Court Southern Dist.	Owen Kirby	Rep.	R 1 Aldrich
	Clerk, County Court	Bill Bob Kallenbach	Rep.	R 2 Bolivar
1975-1976	Presiding Judge Co. Court	Cecil O. Pitts	Rep.	R 1 Goodson
	Judge Co. Court Northern Dist.	Cecil N. Chaney	Dem.	Humansville
	Judge Co. Court Southern Dist.	Owen Kirby	Rep.	R 2 Aldrich
	Clerk, County Court	Bill Bob Kallenbach	Rep.	R 2 Bolivar
1985-1986	Presiding Commissioner	Howard B. Hayter	Rep.	Bolivar
	Comm. Northern District	Art Garretson	Rep.	Humansville
	Comm. Southern District	Gene Ankrom	Dem.	Bolivar
	Clerk, County Comm.	Bill Bob Kallenbach	Rep.	Bolivar
1987-1988	Presiding Commissioner	Howard B. Hayter	Rep.	Bolivar
	Comm. Northern District	Denzil Roberts	Rep.	Polk
	Comm. Southern District	Gene Ankrom	Dem.	Bolivar
1989-1990	Presiding Commissioner	Denzil Roberts	Rep.	Polk
	Comm. Northern District	Roy Harms	Rep.	Bolivar
	Comm. Southern District	Gene Ankrom	Dem.	Bolivar
	Clerk, County Comm.	R. King	Rep.	Bolivar
1997-2002	Presiding Commissioner	Denzil Roberts	Rep.	Polk
	Comm. Northern District	Roy Harms	Rep.	Bolivar
	Comm. Southern District	Billy Dryer	Dem.	Aldrich
	Clerk, County Comm.	Sue Entlicher	Rep.	Bolivar
2003-2004	Presiding Commissioner	Roy Harms	Rep.	Bolivar
	Comm. Northern District	Danny Barker	Dem.	Bolivar
	Comm. Southern District	Billy Dryer	Rep.	Aldrich
	Clerk, County Comm.	Sue Entlicher	Rep.	Bolivar

Family Institute Of The Ozarks

According to a title search, a certificate deposited in the General Land Office of Springfield indicated that Amos Richardson purchased 160 acres in Bolivar and this is the land that contains the Kemp Professional Building. This 160 acres was later sold to Edmond Keeling. This certificate was signed by James K. Polk on Sept. 1, 1848. The next records stated that "John H. Akard and Mary E. Akard, his wife of the County of Polk, in the state of Missouri, have this day for and in consideration of the sum of three hundred dollars to us, the said John H. Akard and Mary F. Akard in hand paid by George T. Kirby" purchased a portion of this acreage. This transaction took place on the "13th day of October in the year of our Lord, one thousand eight hundred and seventy-seven."

Other owners of this parcel of land have included Rufus A. and Nancy J. McClure, Buckingham and Susan B. Sturges, J.E. and Carrie W. Tolfree, Richard and Amanda Viles, Landon C. and Mayme F. Viles, Charles W. and Eunice E. Viles, Clara A. Drake, and Nellie N. and Kirk Hawkins. In 1938, a portion of this acreage was sold for twenty-six hundred and thirty and no dollars to the Polk County Bank. T.H.B. Dunnegan was the President of the bank at that time.

In 1933 part of this parcel of land was occupied by the Faulkner Lumber Company. In the 1940s it became the Cole Lumber Company. In June, 1954 Eunice Viles, the widow of C.W. Viles leased the property and the buildings to partners doing business under the firm name of the Bolivar Lumber Company. In 1965 part of the land was sold to Bolivar Farmer's Exchange, a corporation. In May of 1979 Orval M. Davis and Warren B. Davis became the owners of the properties. On the 8th day of April, 1994 some of the parcels of the original land were sold to Ronald Nuburn and Lou Thelen Kemp.

The picture above shows a two-story building which was the White Palace Livery Stable and was built by Charles Viles. It was called the "Waldorf-Astoria" of livery stables. The livery stables were like the rent-a-car places of today. They rented out teams and buggies to the people who came in on the train. Or, those leaving on the train could leave their horses and rigs there. The White Palace, one of several stables in town, was completed in 1910. It had an elevator that took the buggies to the second floor while the horses boarded on the first floor. The only bad part about this livery stable was that automobiles were starting to come in about the time it was built. In 1920 the state passed a bond issue to improve roads and the horse and buggy began to wane. The building, which later was used by the lumber companies was razed in 1996 to make way for the Kemp Professional Building. Dr. Ron Kemp, a licensed psychologist and his son, Dr. Wes Kemp, an optometrist occupied the new building. In 2002, another building was built upon a portion of the land originally owned by Amos Richardson and it now houses the Family Eye Care. The present building is now occupied by the Family Institute of the Ozarks. The services provided by the Family Institute of the Ozarks fall into three broad categories: counseling, education and training.

S & S Towing Service

In the summer of 2000, my wife Suzette and I decided to make our plans for an alternate income, should either of our jobs be moved to Mexico, like so many others in Springfield had been.

We bought our tow truck, originally, to go into business repossessing cars for a second party. Word of advice, when you enter into business with a second party, be SURE what the second party tells you about the business is, in fact, true. And that you will be able to keep your head above water, so to speak.

After using up all of the money we borrowed to run our business, plus most of our savings, it was time to part company, and do something else. After all, we still had a business loan to pay off. THANKS MOM!!, for instilling in me the financial discipline not to let your credit go bad. (See, I did listen to you sometimes.) Most people in our situation, in this day and age, would have let the bank have the truck. But, we're stubborn. Thanks again, Mom!

Aside from both of our full time jobs, we started towing cars for dealers in the area, plus both of us working for an auto auction, and towing for them as well.

I was born and raised in Polk County about ten miles southeast of Bolivar and attended Pleasant Hope Schools. Suzette was born in Monett, but lived in various places around Missouri, as her father was a minister and moved around preaching in different churches. We met in Springfield and got married about five years later, then moved to Willard and have been there ever since.

As we do live and work in Greene County, most of our towing does come from this area, but we have quite a volume of towing for dealers in Polk County and surrounding areas. We take towing jobs from Arkansas, Oklahoma, Kansas, Texas, Illinois and even spent one weekend towing a car to Indiana and it is difficult making that long a trip, then trying to get back home in time to go to our respective jobs, but so far we have managed. We get to see a lot of country that a desk job wouldn't allow us to see, and we both enjoy it.

We consider ourselves to be lucky getting into the business when we did. We've been lucky to get our truck paid off so early and are working toward buying a bigger, better one so we can haul one and tow another.

We have put our faith in God that we are making the right choices and thank Him for what we have already accomplished.

The only regrets that you will have in life are the risks that you didn't take. (I don't know who said that first but, I'm sure I didn't come up with it. I'm not that smart.)

Steve and Suzette Smith, S & S Towing

REASONABLE RATES/INSURED

S & S TOWING SERVICE

FAMILY OWNED & OPERATED (417) 839-6356
STEVE & SUZETTE SMITH (417) 838-9139

Bill Roberts Chevrolet Inc.

If one had to describe the Bill Roberts Chevrolet Pontiac Oldsmobile Buick dealership in Bolivar, perhaps "All in the Family" or "Family Affair" would be appropriate choices. For over 70 years the Roberts family has run a successful dealership in Polk County. From the end of the depression through World War II, through inflation and recessions, this family owned business has succeeded where others have failed.

The business truly began back in 1930 when Bill Roberts Sr. and his brother Luther opened a Chevy agency in Humansville on June 3 of that year. Soon their brother Harold joined the business.

Taking time away from work, Bill Sr. married Agnes Hammons; however, the ceremony was performed in a '31 Chevy Convertible, because the floor in the preacher's home was being repaired. From the start both were involved with the business, Bill Sr. selling and Agnes keeping the books.

The brothers decided to dissolve the business in 1936 and go their separate ways. After much influence from General Motors, Bill Sr. opened the Chevrolet dealership in Bolivar in 1937. At the time, Bill Roberts Chevrolet was located at the current site of the CMH training facility, two blocks east of the current location. As the business prospered, Bill Sr. moved the dealership to the current location and began carrying John Deere farm and tractor equipment.

Bill Sr. and Agnes had two boys, Bill Jr. and Lee. Both were involved with the business from an early age. In 1955 Bill Jr. returned from the University of Missouri to run the day-to-day operations. Shortly thereafter, he married his high school sweetheart, Carolyn Kilpatrick, although she was the daughter of Barney Kilpatrick, the competing Hudson-International dealer. Bill and Carolyn had six children, most of whom later work in the dealership.

In 1963 the dealership dropped the John Deere franchise and added Oldsmobile. Not long after, they added Pontiac. The Buick franchise was added in the early 1970s. These were record years for the car industry nationwide, and Lee and his wife Georgia moved and took over the Chevrolet dealership in Republic, MO. After selling his dealership, he returned to the Bolivar store in 1982 to help Bill Jr. with Finance and Insurance.

A major contributor to the success of Bill Roberts Chevrolet over the years has been hardworking, loyal, and honest employees. At the risk of leaving someone out, some of the salesmen include: Buck Seiner, Ralph Tillery, Roe Newsum, Dee Ruyle, King Wilhite, Paul Butler, Jimmy Moore, Reggie Taylor, Lindsay Taylor, and Brent Coleman. Some of the key employees in other departments include: Paul Roberts and David Grant in parts; Lev Simpson, Aley Smith, Leonard Mauck, Fred Latiker, Bobby Pearson, and Rick Hagar in service; George Rhoades and Keith Combs in the body shop; and Bob Hammons and Wylla Williamson in bookkeeping.

In 1984, Bill Sr. passed away. Agnes continued to maintain the bookkeeping and greet customers until she passed away in 1999. Bill Jr. remains active in the dealership, with Craig Preston, Bill's son-in-law, managing the day-to-day operations. Mark and Bill Roberts IV work in the business office.

For many residents of Polk county, "Roberts Chevy" is the place where they bought their first car, had their first (and only) job, or simply visit to drink coffee and talk. They continue to provide the residents of Polk County fair deals at honest prices and are committed to the GM slogan, "We'll be There."

Bill Jr. taking delivery of a fleet of driver's education cars, 1958

Western Auto Associate Store

Western Auto Associate Store in Bolivar, MO was started in 1935 on the southwest corner of the square by Mr. and Mrs. Homer Utley. In 1948, Walter and Osra Roweton purchased the store from the Utleys. The store had many selections—from Western Flyer bicycles to appliances—also batteries, tires, auto parts, televisions (when they came on the market), toys, tools, guns, sporting goods, lawn mowers—and the list goes on. The Rowetons' son, Max Roweton, age 13 when the Rowetons bought the store—helped out at the store when he could. Not long after purchasing the store the Rowetons moved a few doors south and it was at that location, in 1969, that the store burned to the ground one August Sunday evening. It was thought to be caused by an electrical surge of some sort. Saved were the records which were in metal safes and cabinets and some bikes and wagons in the basement and they were very wet. A new location was selected on the northeast corner of the square, part of which was built a short time later, as Jim Raney's filling station had previously been there before the Rowetons purchased it. Also Davis tire had occupied the north end of the store previously. Max Roweton, now married to Rose (Douglas) Roweton and the father of five children, had taken over the franchise at his parents' request in May 1969. The store never missed a weekly Western Auto truck—re-starting in a former beauty shop which is currently the housewares department of the store. Osra Roweton passed away in 1985—Walter Roweton in 1990. Max and Rose Roweton currently own the store which is still on the northeast corner of the public square. Several members of the family have and do work at the store, including son-in-law Steve McColm—manager for a few years, son Kelly Roweton—manager for 11 years, daughter-in-law Sue Roweton currently doing the warranty paper work, Synda Douglas—Rose's sister-in-law does general book work, and at times all the Roweton children and grandchildren have worked or filled in at the store. It truly is a family business. Also currently employed at the store are long-time employee Lula Kent, Ken Hatfield, and Bill Cook. Rose Roweton is the present manager of the store. With the exception of tires and auto parts, Western Auto Associate Store—also called Roweton's Western Auto—carries many of the same type items as it started with—but much updated—with the main emphasis on appliances and lawn and garden supplies. To supplement its merchandise so as to have a large variety for the public to choose from Western Auto is also a "Do It Best" dealer and deals with around 30 to 40 other suppliers. We at Western Auto are proud of our heritage, and strive to serve our customers with personal service, compassion, and appreciation for their many years of doing business with us. In January 2003 we will start to celebrate 55 years in business in the same family!

Recently, (December 2003), the Western Auto Supply Company announced that it will no longer supply merchandise and services to its network of independent Western Auto dealers because of changes to the dealer network. In the 1970s there were nearly 5000 dealers—and today there are 304. Roweton's Western Auto buys most of their merchandise form other suppliers, including "Do It Best Corp." of which they are a member, and they account for the large catalogue on their counter as well. So it will be "business as usual" for Roweton's—now named Roweton's Home Center. And they look forward to many more years of serving their customers in Bolivar and the surrounding area. They are at 56 years and counting in the same family!

Walter and Osra Roweton with son Max, shortly before they purchased the Western Auto store in Bolivar in 1948.

Max and Rose Roweton inside Western Auto Store as it appears today.

Western Auto Store as it appeared on the Northeast corner of Boliver Square.

Current day store

Wes Kemp O.D. Family Eye Care

Wes Kemp graduated from the Illinois College of Optometry in 1991 and established Family Eye Care in September 1991. During the first four and a half years, the practice was located at 213 East Broadway, on the east side of the Bolivar square. Wes Kemp, O.D. began the practice with one employee and within the first year employed two staff personnel. By April of 1996, Wes Kemp O.D. had outgrown their facility and moved into the front half of the Kemp Professional Building located at 315 South Main. At that time there were three full time employees. After six years at that location, Wes Kemp, O.D. Family Eye Care built their current building located at 325 South Main. This property was part of the original 160 acres purchased by Amos Richardson. A certificate deposited in the General Land Office of Springfield was signed by James K. Polk, Sept. 1, 1848.

There are now six full time employees and one part-time employee. Through the years, Wes and his wife, Marla Jo Roweton Kemp have loved being a part of the Bolivar community. They have three children, Tyler Don, Landon Holt and Rylee Lou.

The Country Hearth
The Tea Garden Cafe

Cindy Ussery Hood started her business in June of 1984 on Jackson Street with the intent to bring unusual and hand-crafted gifts and decorative accessories to this area. This business changed directions the following year when an opportunity to relocate to the Bolivar Square became available. The building that houses The Country Hearth and The Tea Garden Cafe was built in 1929 by Otis and Ethel Teegarden following a fire that burned the original frame structure to the ground. The Teegardens both had optical offices on the third floor of the building and the bottom was rented out.

The room that serves as the kitchen area was originally Dr. Harry McCracken's optical office in the early 1900s. Dr. McCracken also owned a men's clothing store located below in what is now known as the Olde Building. The north part of the building burned in 1928 and the roof fell in on McCrackens' Haberdashery. The Teegardens eventually owned all the buildings from the alley to Jackson Street and installed a sprinkler system from one end to the other. Quite a novelty for the era. Artifacts found during the construction of the Tea Garden Cafe are proudly displayed.

Cindy's business more than doubled due to the relocation and branched out to more gift ware due to being unable to find enough area artisans to meet the demand for the crafts. In 1988 after inviting a friend out to lunch and the 13 other eating establishments were full, The Tea Garden Cafe was established on the mezzanine of the Country Hearth Gift Shop. Since that day they have added on many times, and expanded their inventory and seating to meet the needs of their gracious customers. Today they have doubled the physical size of their business and added many more lines, including Merle Norman Cosmetics.

The Country Hearth and Tea Garden were chosen business of the year in 1988 and have been written up in *417 Magazine* and a St. Louis, MO publication.

Two significant women that helped the establishing and continued growth of this business are Dorothy Ussery and Cindy's sister, Janie Cooper.

Teters Florist Inc.

Founded in 1904 by Henry Clay Teters we will celebrate our Centennial Anniversary.

Henry moved here so his son, Roy, could attend college. At that time it was a nursery, only supplying trees, strawberries, grapes and shrubs. He peddled these items across Missouri.

In the early 1930s they bought a greenhouse from Ha Ha Tonka and hauled it to Bolivar. At that time they started the fresh flower business. They grew a lot of their flowers, but also purchased some flowers from outside sources. When his son was old enough, he became a partner in the business. Roy had seven children and was married to Mabel. Due to tuberculosis, Roy had only one arm. Mabel did most of the arranging and taught others.

Roy Jr. joined the business during World War II. Tiffin, Roy Jr.'s brother, bought into the business in the 1950s. At that same time they started Teters Floral Products. It was located in their basement.

Paul and Jim Davolt continued the business in the 1960s and 70s.

Don Woods Sr. was an owner and then Yvonne Hamlet and Lena Lipe bought the

business in 1984. Danny and Teresa Barker and family purchased the business on July 30, 1996 to the present time. Teters Florist is now silk arrangements and fresh flower arrangements for weddings, sympathy tributes, home styles, romance, friendship and all occasions.

We also have a large gift shop with candles, chocolates, gourmet fruit/snack baskets, crystal, stuffed animals and as always classic roses.

Teters Florist "When it has to be special."
404 W. South St., Bolivar, MO

Grandson, Peyton Barker

Teters new sign

Stephens Photography

Gerald and Helen Stephens moved to Bolivar in the summer of 1946 from Aurora, MO. After his services were no longer needed to defend America, Gerald attended photography school in Aurora, MO and worked for a studio in Mountain Grove, MO.

Upon encouragement from Betty and Herman Braithwait they moved to Bolivar. They established their photography studio over the Braithwait's Men's and Boy's Store on the southwest corner of the square.

In 1948 they leased the building and bought the equipment and business that had been established by Bettie and Marion Ross. This original building located at 211 W. Broadway Street was built by John Ross, the father of Bettie and Marion. This building housed his law practice and their photography studio with living quarters upstairs. Photography began to become prominent during the Civil War when Matthew Brady took black and white photos using "wet plates." After Bettie Ross died Marion Ross lived in a small cottage located behind Ray Blankenship's gas station. Gerald and Helen became the caretakers for Marion Ross and in the early 1960s purchased the building.

Gerald and Helen retired from their photography business in 1984 and the studio, photography business and living quarters is now in the hands of their son Mark David. Mark began to work at the studio in 1976 and eventually took over full production.

Some of the changes the Stephens have experienced during their years in the photography business is from black and white photos to the direct color photos, a revolutionary process. Helen went to school to learn to add oil coloring to the brown toned portraits.

Studio cameras used 4 x 5 film and now use smaller format cameras. The studio originally did their own processing for the black and white film. Commercial labs came into being when it became impractical for local studios to develop the color negatives. The Stephens installed a color processor printer to use after the color negatives were returned from the commercial labs.

The business and building established by the Ross Sisters and maintained by the Stephens, Gerald, Helen and Mark, will celebrate 100 years in 2004.

Douglas, Haun, Kirksey & Heidemann, P.C.

In 1912, Thomas H. "T.H." Douglas received his law degree from Missouri University Law School and opened a practice at 111 W. Broadway in Bolivar, MO. To date, nine direct descendants of T.H. have graduated from the UMC School of Law. T.H. practiced 52 years before he died in 1964. T.H. was quite active in Republican politics, and ran for Circuit Judge in the 1940s. His eldest son, Elvin S. Douglas Sr., joined his father's law practice in Bolivar in 1932 when the firm became known as Douglas & Douglas. Elvin practiced for 46 years until his sudden death in 1979. Kerry D. Douglas, Elvin's son, joined the firm in 1972 after graduating from UMC School of Law and serving two years in the US Army. Kerry is now the senior member of the firm.

Gary W. Lynch became the first non-Douglas attorney to work for the law firm after he joined the firm as an associate of Elvin Sr. and Kerry in 1976. Gary became a partner in 1979, when the name of the firm was changed to Douglas, Douglas and Lynch. Following Elvin's death in 1979, Kerry and Gary incorporated as Douglas, Douglas & Lynch, P.C. and began expanding the practice by the addition of associates. David R. Munton joined the firm as an associate in 1983 and became a shareholder in 1987. Verna Haun joined the firm in 1984 as an associate and became a shareholder in 1987. The firm name then became Douglas, Lynch, Munton & Haun, P.C. Jerry M. (Jay) Kirksey joined the firm as an associate in 1992 and became a shareholder in 1994. David R. Munton was elected to the office of Associate Circuit Judge of Dade County in 1995. The firm name was then changed to Douglas, Lynch, Haun & Kirksey, P.C. John Kallenbach joined the firm as an associate in 1994 and is currently working in an *Of Counsel* capacity. Craig Heidemann joined the firm in 1996 as an associate and became a shareholder in 2001. Kerry's son, K. Patrick ("Pat") Douglas, joined the firm in October 1999 as an associate and became a shareholder in 2002. Pat is the fourth generation to have the privilege of serving the residents of Bolivar, Polk County and Southwest Missouri as an attorney with the law firm. In 2002, Gary W. Lynch was elected to the office of Polk County Associate Circuit Judge and began his term in January 2003. As a result of his election to judgeship, the firm name was changed to Douglas, Haun, Kirksey & Heidemann, P.C. Richard D. Winders joined the firm as an associate in 2002 and John W. Forkner joined as an associate in 2003.

Since 1912, the law firm has maintained a general civil practice, with some criminal law practice. Currently, all shareholders and associates limit their practice to certain areas of the law in order to maintain a greater level of expertise in their areas than would be possible with a general practice. The firm provides legal services in most areas of civil law, with emphasis on estate planning and estate law, family law, employment law, real estate, small business law, personal injury and insurance claims, education law and municipal law. While the firm has always emphasized legal services to individuals, it also provides services to several area banks, a large number of area school districts, Southwest Baptist University, the City of Bolivar, the City of Hermitage and Southwest Electric Co-operative, in addition to numerous area businesses and institutions.

The lawyers of Douglas, Haun, Kirksey & Heidemann, P.C. are deeply involved in community and church activities, and spend thousands of *pro bono* hours each year working for community betterment and religious activities.

111 W. Broadway
Bolivar, MO 65613

Thomas Douglas, 1882-1964

Elvin Douglas, Sr., 1909-1979

Bill Grant Ford–Mercury, Inc.

On April 19, 1976 Ford Motor Company notified Bill and Eulala Grant that they had been accepted as the new Ford-Mercury dealer for the Bolivar, MO area. Previously the Grants were engaged in a dairy farming operation south of Bolivar for 21 years.

Initially, Bill and Eulala joined five new employees to clean and paint the old Ford building at 204 N Main utilizing 26 gallons of Ford blue paint in preparation for its opening. The first five employees were:

John Smith, Salesman
Cam Seiner, Salesman
Leamon W. Havens Jr., Service Manager
Eric Kirkland, Mechanic
Kenny Fleeman, Parts Manager

That original building had been the location of many previous Ford dealerships and is now a parking lot owned by the city of Bolivar.

The service department entrance opened directly onto Main Street on the west side of the building. Traffic usually had to be stopped to let cars and trucks in and out of that original service department.

The used car lot was across Main Street and the new cars were parked across Missouri between Main and the alley west of Main. That area is now developed retail space.

Bill Grant Ford-Mercury quickly caught on in Bolivar and new employees joined in:

Randy Keith, Prep & Cleanup
Joe Ivey, Mechanic
Martin Addison, Mechanic

Bill and Eulala purchased 14 acres of land on South Business Highway 13, now known as 3060 S. Springfield Ave., in 1977. By 1979 ground was broken for a new 15,000 sq. foot building where they remain today. The vehicles, parts, shop and office equipment were moved to the new building Thanksgiving weekend in 1979.

From 1980 until 1983 a satellite dealership in nearby Stockton was operated in the old Ford building on South Street. When that building was sold by its owner in 1983, the inventory was moved to Bolivar. Many long-time relationships were established during those "Stockton years."

By the mid-1980s Bill Grant Ford—Mercury employed 16 people. The parts, service, and body shop operations created a solid customer base for new Ford and Mercury vehicle sales. Repeat customers brought friends and neighbors into the "Ford Family." In 1987, Ford Motor Company created a new award for top 100 dealers ranked solely on customer satisfaction. Bill Grant Ford-Mercury was a "President's Award" winner that first year.

In the fall of 1987 Bill and Eulala's son, Kelly Grant, joined the firm. At age 29, he brought outside experience into the company. Previously employed with Martiz, Inc. in St. Louis, a national marketing company, Kelly gained valuable perspective on the "corporate" side of the automotive business as a creative supervisor. At a time when the information age was evolving, Kelly's experience with database management, communications, advertising, and marketing were important for the long-term growth of Bill Grant Ford-Mercury.

By the fall of 1993, the service department growth necessitated construction of a separate 5000 sq. ft. body shop facility east of the main facility. Polk County's first downdraft paint booth allowed Eddie Lamke's staff to repair vehicles better than new. They got a lot of practice that first year as the Ford Motor Company Owner Dialogue program repainted 350 Ford F-Series trucks as customer satisfaction initiative.

Starting in 1993, the dealership developed in-house software integrating service, parts, vehicle inventories, accounting, area sales history, Ford Motor Company interfaces, satellite and internet web technology. Complete conversion occurred in 1998. This database and programming project eliminated high-priced computer overhead required of Ford Dealers at that time thus reducing the cost of doing business. The customer website, www.billgrantford.com was one of the first in this area that really brought live inventory data to the customer without third-party programming.

In 2001, Bill Grant Ford-Mercury, Inc. celebrated 25 years as Bolivar's Ford dealer—longest time of any previous Ford dealer. An open house for the community was attended by hundreds of customers, friends, Chamber of Commerce members, representatives from Ford Motor Company and Ford Motor Credit. Mayor Charlie Ealy, a Ford car salesman in the mid-60's, cut the ribbon as onlookers cheered this 25 year milestone. Local radio KYOO broadcast live interviews with longtime customers, Ford Motor Company District Manager Molt Johnson, and Ford Credit Branch Operations Manager Phil Holcomb, Bill, Eulala, and Kelly, and Mayor Ealy. Photos of that day are on display in the showroom alongside advertisements and commemorative materials from 25 years of selling and servicing Ford vehicles in Bolivar.

In 2004, Bill Grant Ford-Mercury, Inc. employs 24 people. More than two million dollars annually are contributed to the local economy through payroll, goods and services purchased locally, and charitable activities. Ford cars and trucks from Bolivar can be found across the Cedar, Polk, Hickory, and Dallas County areas. Population growth projections for the Bolivar area create tremendous challenges for long-time Bolivar businesses and Bill Grant Ford-Mercury is no exception.

For 28 years, Bill and Eulala Grant overcame tremendous challenges to grow the business. By the fall of 2003, son Kelly Grant, now president and major stockholder, looked toward renewed challenges as newcomers to the Bolivar area expect more than ever before. Internet technology brings the showroom to the living room and the "remote control society" of 2004 wants the product, price and service at the click of a button.

Major facility expansion is on the horizon once again as Bill Grant Ford-Mercury looks forward to serving the Bolivar trade area with a complete line of automotive needs for more decades.

3-Jumps

Ronald Dean Jump was born March 29, 1948 in Bolivar, MO. After graduating from Bolivar High School he went to K.C. to work. There he met and married Sara L. Essex from Arkansas in 1971. Their daughter Rhonda Lynn was born Jan. 22, 1976. Ronald has had several businesses. His first business was a Skelly Service Station on West Broadway in 1970. This is now Eversoll's Station. He then located to a station on Market Street. This is now a carpet store. The next location was on East Broadway, a station he purchased from Jay Adams. This is now owned by Kelly McAtt and Ken Legan. In 1982 he purchased the Hite Oil Co., owned by Berkley and Martha Hite. Over the next few years he purchased four more oil companies, including the Joe Rayl Oil Co., in 1984. Today the Jump Oil Co. is still in business although he sold it in 1988. His hobbies include raising and selling Belgian horses, mammoth jacks, jennets, and mules. He also has cattle farms. Over the past 30 years he has been in several fairs, always showing in the Missouri State Fair in Sedalia, where he has won lots of ribbons and trophies. He has had the Grand Champion Jack and Jennet for several years. He was the wagon master of the Butterfield Wagon Train that left Blue Eye, MO and ended in Springfield in 1976, our Bicentennial year. He has sold animals all over the United States and three other countries. It has been recorded that he has the largest herd of jacks and jennets in the U.S.

3-Jumps
Reg. Belgians
Blacks & Sorrel - Jacks
Jennets - Mules
(417) 253-4244
Ronald Jump   Bolivar, Mo. 65613

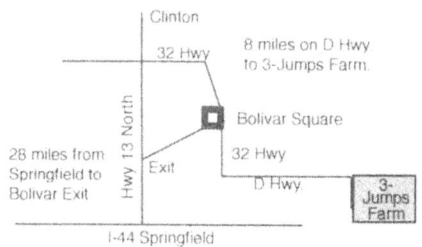

BUTLER FUNERAL HOME

In 1958, Butler Funeral Home began in Bolivar, MO, carrying on the tradition of the Walter S. White Undertaking Co. with its beginning in the late 1920s and followed by the Erwin-Blue Funeral Home, then the Willard B. Erwin Funeral Home, with its purchase in August 1958, by Paul D. Butler and Mary Lou Butler.

The original funeral home building was a three story, stucco with tile roof home built around 1909 by the Townsend Family, who donated the clock for the Polk County Court House and the house then served as a hospital for the late Dr. Gervais D. Smith and his wife Flossie Grace Baker Smith.

1969 saw a major expansion for the Butler Funeral Home with the building and opening of their new funeral home facilities for the convenience of all of their families. The ultra modern facility was built on one level with no steps even before Federal Law mandated such construction. 1971 also ended some services that most funeral homes in the area provided with the elimination of ambulance service. For many years, red 'Butler' ambulances were seen carrying the sick and injured to local Doctor's offices and hospitals in Springfield and Humansville.

In 1969, the Butlers' son, R. Stephen Butler, graduated from the Dallas Institute-Gupton-Jones College of Mortuary Science in Dallas, TX and returned to Bolivar to join his parents in the business.

After the death of Mary Lou Butler in 1988, Stephen's wife Jarolyn Stanfill Butler retired from a 20 year banking career and joined her husband and father-in-law in the funeral business. Butler's remains one of the many family owned funeral businesses in the country, and the oldest family owned funeral home in Polk County and Bolivar.

Now that the new century is upon us, the Butler Family will be carrying on the tradition of helping those in need for many more years, by offering the finest in professional services, facilities and quality of caskets, vaults, and other funeral merchandise. Be sure to visit our website at **www.butlerfuneralhome.com.**

Paul, Jarolyn and Stephen Butler

Butler Funeral Home

Countryside Veterinary Clinic

In 1994, Dr. Dennis Hood and Dr. Wendell Stewart opened Bolivar Veterinary Clinic in Bolivar, MO. These two classmates had just graduated from the University of Missouri in Columbia with Doctor of Veterinary Medicine degrees. After two years of business together, they decided to open their own individual practices. Dr. Stewart opened and still operates Animal Care Clinic in Bolivar.

Dr. W. Dennis Hood opened Countryside Veterinary Clinic in 1976, offering small and large animal services to Bolivar and the surrounding areas. The business, originally started in a remodeled hay barn, has grown extensively throughout the years. An additional clinic was eventually opened in Pleasant Hope and remains open today.

Large animal services represented about 95% of the business for several years, however percentages have changed dramatically over the past years with current numbers reflecting an approximate 50% large/50% small animal service practice. Many factors contributed to this change including the great reduction of dairy operations. Our small animal owner client base has grown significantly during this time as has the services these clients want.

Large animal services include, but are not limited to: dairy herd health, beef cattle vaccination programs, foot work, reproduction exams, OB's, breeding soundness evaluations, surgeries and much more. All types of equine reproduction work are offered including artificial insemination and ultrasounds, routine vaccinations, floating teeth, radiology, etc. Special events are held during the year, such as Bull Days featuring bull breeding soundness exams and deworming as well as Coggins Clinic's for horses.

Countryside Veterinary Clinic has been very supportive to the Polk County Humane Society since it was established. We offer feline and canine exams, in addition to spays and neuters at reduced prices and other services as needed.

Small animal services included, but are not limited to: wellness exams, routine vaccinations, canine and feline spays and neuters, artificial inseminations, surgical inseminations, exams for health papers, kennel inspections, a full range of surgical procedures, boarding, etc.

Many other veterinarians have been associated with Countryside Veterinary Clinic over the years before going on to open their own clinics or pursue other interests. These veterinarians include Dr. Rich Markham, Dr. Allan Honeycutt, Dr. Margaret Snyder, Dr. Leonard Martin, Dr. David Hutto, Dr. Bob Streeter, Dr. Craig Spence, Dr. John Mozier, Dr. Lee Hinson, Dr. Rick Elliott, Dr. Mark Hale, Dr. Bruce Hood, Dr. Franka Figari, Dr. Kim Ahlers, and others.

In May 2002, Dr. Dennis Hood sold the small animal services clinic to his son, Dr. Bruce Hood, who joined him at the clinic in 1994. Countryside Veterinary Small Animal Clinic, which is in the same location as always, now offers small animal services exclusively.

In October 2002, Dr. Dennis Hood opened a new Countryside Veterinary Clinic office next door to the existing clinic. This new clinic specializes in large animal services. The separation of large and small animal services enables both clinics to offer more and provide even better service for our clients. Both clinics offer 24-hour emergency care. Countryside Veterinary Clinic and Countryside Veterinary Small Animal Clinic are located at 4391 S. 95th Road in Bolivar. Regular business hours are 7:30 a.m.-5:30 p.m. Monday-Friday and 7:30 a.m.-4:00 p.m. on Saturday. Appointments for large animal services with Dr. Dennis Hood or Dr. Franka Figari may be scheduled at (417) 326-2992 in the Bolivar clinic or (417) 267-2273 at the Pleasant Hope clinic. Small animal service appointments may be scheduled with Dr. Bruce Hood by calling (417) 326-7297 (PAWS).

After over 26 years of providing quality services and products for large and small animals, we look forward to continuing this family tradition for years to come.

4391 S. 95th Rd.
Bolivar, MO 65613
PH (417) 326-2992
Fax (417) 777-3848

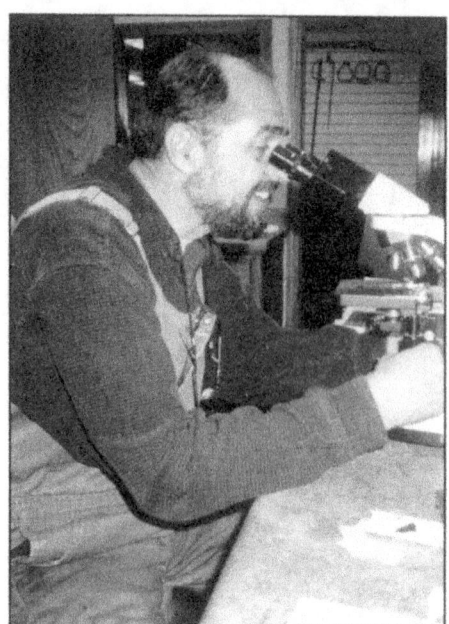

Dr. Dennis "Doc" Hood

Countryside Veterinary Small Animal Clinic (left) and Countryside Veterinary Clinic-Large Animal Services (right).

Animal Care Clinic

In May 1974, R. Wendell Stewart, D.V.M. and W. Dennis Hood, D.V.M. opened the Bolivar Veterinary Clinic. This clinic offered care to both large and small animals, and supplies to their owners. The clinic was located just east of Taco Bell.

In 1976 the present clinic facility at 2830 S. Springfield was built.

In 1984 a separate facility was added, just south of the clinic. This facility is used for pet boarding and grooming and also for retail sale of pet food and supplies.

The clinic offers surgery, medicine, preventative care, boarding and grooming for small animals. Also offered is small animal health related products including diets and grooming products.

Over the years, the clinic has evolved into primarily a small animal practice, both medical and surgical. They offer an extensive variety of small animal surgical procedures, x-ray capabilities and diagnostic laboratory procedures.

In the future, the clinic plans on an expansion of medical and surgical facilities, including an in-house laboratory service.

Boarding and Grooming Facility

Animal Care Clinic

Citizens Memorial Healthcare

Citizens Memorial Healthcare's 22-year Milestones

When it started in 1976, no one could believe that it would take more than six years to accomplish the task of developing and building a hospital for this community.

In fact, there weren't many back then who believed the job to ever be possible.

Perhaps one of the earliest moments in this thrust came when T.H.B. Dunnegan called a Blue Cross Hospital insurance representative, asking for a list of hospitals in Missouri. From that he developed a list of towns that were both smaller than and had less in bank deposits than Bolivar. Dunnegan was astounded that the total of towns smaller than Bolivar was 35 and those with less bank deposits neared 50.

One morning he put through a call to Jack Zimmerman and Jim Sterling of the Bolivar Herald-Free Press and the three men met in the upstairs of the Polk County Bank to go over figures. Dunnegan thought an editorial relating those numbers might be of interest to Polk Countians.

That editorial appeared in the August 12, 1976, editon. Later that year, after several meetings of interested citizens, the Bolivar Area Chamber of Commerce took the hospital project on as a goal.

Starting a Hospital

Tuned to the needs for local acute medical services by the death of his father, who might have lived had healthcare facilities been available in Polk County, Kerry Douglas has become a consistent and hard-working promoter of Citizens Memorial Hospital (CMH). His skills as an attorney helped guide the hospital through the early days and his administrative abilities serve him well as the only chairman of the CMH board to date.

For those dedicated to the project, no price would be too high for quality healthcare in this area. With the nearest hospital more than one-half hour from Bolivar and 45 minutes to one hour from other parts of the county, this area was desperately in need of a hospital.

And with the closing of the Polk Community Hospital in Humansville, more pressure was put on traveling the distance to Springfield. Also at that time in 1976, there were only three full-time physicians in the community, and prospects for gaining more hinged directly on having a hospital facility.

Opening the Hospital

When CMH opened in 1982, it housed 48 medical/surgical beds, four intensive care beds, four postpartum beds, six obstetric beds, emergency room, operating room, respiratory therapy, radiology, laboratory, pharmacy, physical therapy and an auxiliary. After two years of operation, the hospital district tax levy was suspended and the people of Polk County no longer funded the public hospital district—the not-for-profit organization was self-sustaining.

In 2004, Citizens Memorial Healthcare, as it is now called, supports a healthcare provider staff of nearly 80; hospital services such as: air ambulance; Level III Trauma Center/emergency room; ground ambulance services; Cardiovascular Center including catheterization lab; intensive care unit; the Birth Place with labor, delivery, recovery and postpartum birth suites; Parkview Wellness Center; home health services; hospice services; outpatient physician and surgical services; cardio-pulmonary rehabilitation; inpatient and outpatient rehabilitation services; hospitalist services; nutritional and catering services; radiology services including MRI, CT scan, nuclear medicine, mammography, foot and ankle center; pain management; filmless PACS system to view radiology images; surgical services; diabetes education; family practice and specialty clinic practices; sports medicine center, a sleep clinic and massage therapy.

Citizens Memorial Healthcare Foundation

As the hospital continued to grow and new services were added yearly, Citizens Memorial Hospital needed the flexibility to continue its growth pattern. Missouri law did not provide for the ownership of allied health facilities by a hospital district; therefore, in 1986, Citizens Memorial Healthcare Foundation was established as a sister entity to the hospital. This not-for-profit entity would assist the healthcare system by managing a new residential care facility, skilled nursing facility and a home medical equipment outlet. The foundation also was charged with developing and managing an endowment fund—the Medical Excellence Scholarship program—to assist individuals with medical training.

In 2004, the foundation owns and operates one residential care facility; five skilled nursing facilities; four senior/independent living communities; eight Home Medical Equipment satellite locations; Homemaker Plus services; Health Transit services; and the Medical Excellence Scholarship program.

Independent Living

Citizens Memorial Healthcare operates four independent living communities for senior adults who have an active lifestyle and would like to remain in a home of their own, yet close to healthcare professionals. These facilities are located near a skilled nursing facility, which allows individuals to join the facilities for meals, activities and outings. Arranged as duplex and triplex apartments, each are equipped with one or two bedrooms, one or two bathrooms, a full kitchen, living room, covered patio and garage.

Citizens Memorial Hospital Original Board of Directors, 1982.

Citizens Memorial Hospital, Front Entrance, 2004.

Residential Care

CMH operates one residential care facility that allows residents to remain independent in their own apartment style room, while having routine medical assistance 24 hours a day, a full activities program and prepared meals. CMH transports residents to and from local medical and rehabilitation appointments and takes care of laundry and maintenance.

Sub-acute Care / Short-term Care

CMH provides transitional care for short-term stays in its skilled nursing facilities. Short-term stays may be required after discharge from the hospital setting, when 24-hour care is needed for nursing and/or extensive rehabilitation. This transitional care may be referred to as sub-acute care.

Skilled Nursing Care

CMH offers skilled nursing facilities for short-term and long-term stays. Long-term stays may be necessary for those individuals needing routine or continual assistance. Facilities offer regular visits from physicians, dentists, podiatrists, eye care professionals and behavioral health professionals. Some of CMH's skilled facilities offer special care units for the care of patients with Alzheimer's Disease and other dementias.

Citizens Memorial Hospital Board of Directors, 2004.

InfoCare Expansion

CMH recently invested $5 million in a comprehensive upgrade of its technology infrastructure in order to provide better information to physicians at the point of care for their patients.

InfoCare (the name of the new computer system) provides additional patient safety measures by allowing physicians to directly order tests and procedures. "I remember when the hospital opened 22 years ago, we had three computer terminals for processing information on our main system," said Donald J. Babb, CMH CEO/executive director. "When InfoCare is completely implemented, we should see in excess of 400 personal computers linked through our facilities."

Citizens Memorial Healthcare Continues to Grow

In the 1970s, many Polk county residents thought the pipe dream of building a hospital would never become a reality. And many believed that the facility would and could be nothing more than an expanded version of a physician's office. Many rural hospitals throughout the nation and state were struggling to stay open.

Citizens Memorial Hospital beat the odds.

With the dedication and support of its growing community, CMH has continued to experience an unprecedented rate of growth not seen in some metropolitan areas, let alone a rural region. According to the Missouri Hospital Association, 22 hospitals closed in the 1980s and another 12 rural hospitals had to closed or reduced to clinic settings between the years of 1990 and 2001; many others only have been able to survive by joining larger healthcare systems or parent organizations.

But CMH's boards of directors, medical staff and administration have learned throughout the years that it is very important to be flexible and change as the needs of people change and as the regulations of government change. Three major universities recognized this philosophy in 1994 when CMH was named one of the top ten rural hospitals in the nation.

Expansions In CMH's Future

In its 22nd year in operation, CMH is planning its eighth major expansion to the current hospital facility and many additional expansions to its other properties.

The first phase of the hospital expansion included the radiology department, the laboratory and the emergency services department. This construction recently was concluded.

The radiology department saw growth in terms of size and technology. The newly constructed permanent Magnetic Resonance Imaging (MRI or MR) suite contains the most modern technology available. The expansion also included the addition of the new Picture Archival Communication System (PACS) for the storage of images. This web-based system allows images to be distributed throughout the facility within seconds, without the use of traditional film processing.

CMH emergency services also were included in the recent expansion. On May 1, 2004, CMH stepped into a new dimension in terms of emergency services when it partnered with St. John's Hospital in Springfield to base an air ambulance helicopter in Bolivar. The motivation was to place the helicopter closer to emergency patients "in the field," therefore reducing the time required to reach and treat a patient.

In addition to the new air ambulance service, CMH recently underwent a multi-million dollar expansion to its emergency room. The new facility features a streamlined patient triage system; a fast-tract "urgent" care area; 12 beds; designated cardiac, obstetric and orthopaedic rooms; a state-of-the-art nurses' station; and an enclosed garage to protect patients during the transfer process from ambulance to hospital. The emergency room garage also includes a HAZMAT decontamination area.

The laboratory department more than doubled in size during the expansion project. The space was needed to accommodate new technology and staff members. The new area now includes patient registration, a designated patient waiting room and a private phlebotomy room where a patient's blood can be drawn for laboratory tests. Due to the expansion of this department, more laboratory tests are being performed in-house.

In April of 2004, CMH also opened the new CMH Cardiovascular Center. This facility offers the latest technology available for cardiac and peripheral catheterizations. The equipment purchased for this center requires 70 percent less radiation than most catheterization labs and allows the physician to perform testing in an atmosphere that requires less recovery time for the patient.

The second phase of the hospital expansion will include a new four-story patient tower; additional operating room suites; new, all-private

Citizens Memorial Hospital Board of Directors and Officials at Grand Opening Ceremony, 1982.

patient rooms; enlarged intensive care unit; and other enhanced services. In addition, a cancer care center also is being planned for CMH.

"Twenty-two years ago, people had to drive from Hermitage to Springfield for emergency treatment," said CMH Chief Executive Officer/Executive Director Donald J. Babb. "This meant one and a half hours of driving to see a physician. Citizens Memorial's vision stemmed from wanting to treat people locally – and to do so with quality."

As a not-for-profit, public district hospital, CMH is financially is accountable to the people it serves. It always has been the vision of the board of directors to continue growth without asking the community for additional tax dollars to expand the hospital. The hospital suspended its original tax levy in 1984, two years into operation.

"The growth of CMH has been very calculated and planned," said Babb. "It has taken many small steps to reach this point. We just have reached another growth plateau and are busting at the seams with our current space." said Babb.

CMH currently is providing more than 16,000 emergency room visits each year and more than 215 inpatient and outpatient surgeries monthly.

"We continue to see an increase in services through our radiology (x-ray) department with mammograms and MRIs and in our outpatient department," said Babb.

The increase in hospital services directly is related to the increase in clinic visits that the CMH system has experienced. In September of 2001, CMH had 5,920 clinic visits. In fiscal year 2004, CMH clinics averaged 11,250 visits per month. Babb noted that the increase in hospital services also could be attributed additional primary care physicians, specialty physicians and the steady growth of the Bolivar Family Care Center and other independent physician clinics.

Within the past few years, CMH has built two new rural-certified physician clinics; one in Pleasant Hope and one in Greenfield.

The healthcare system also includes five long-term care facilities, one residential care facility and four independent living communities. Soon an expansion and renovation project will begin at Colonial Springs Healthcare facility in Buffalo. This 104-bed long-term care facility will expand to provide a total of 134 beds, including an enlarged Special Care Unit for those with Alzheimer's disease and other dementias. In addition, three tri-plex independent living units will be added, along with a new facility for inpatient and outpatient rehabilitation services for physical, occupational and speech therapy.

In 2002, CMH built a new medical complex in Ash Grove to replace an existing physician clinic and long-term care facility. The complex includes a new 78-bed long-term care center that encompasses sub-acute care, a special care unit and rehabilitation department. The complex also includes a new and expanded physician clinic, an independent living community and a local retail pharmacy.

Since opening in 1982, CMH has grown financially from a $3.6 million to a $130 million budget for both the hospital and foundation.

When CMH opened in 1982, there were 90 employees. "It started as a family," said Babb. "There are 37 original employees, board members and auxilians still with the CMH family today." Babb said that additional staffing will be needed to support the growing facility, raising the current number of employees from 1,400 to nearly 2,000, and growth to the medical staff will continue.

"Without the support of our community, boards of directors, medical staff and employees, this dream could have died," Babb said. "But the enduring spirit of so many have made it what it is today, and I'm proud to see us take healthcare to a new level."

In the Past 22 Years

In 1982, CMH's facilities totaled 45,072 square feet; the service population totaled 14,000; there were three physicians and 90 employees. In 2004, CMH's facilities total more than 600,000 square feet; the service population totals more than 90,000; there are more than 80 healthcare professionals on staff and more than 1,400 employees.

Air Ambulance, services added in 2004.

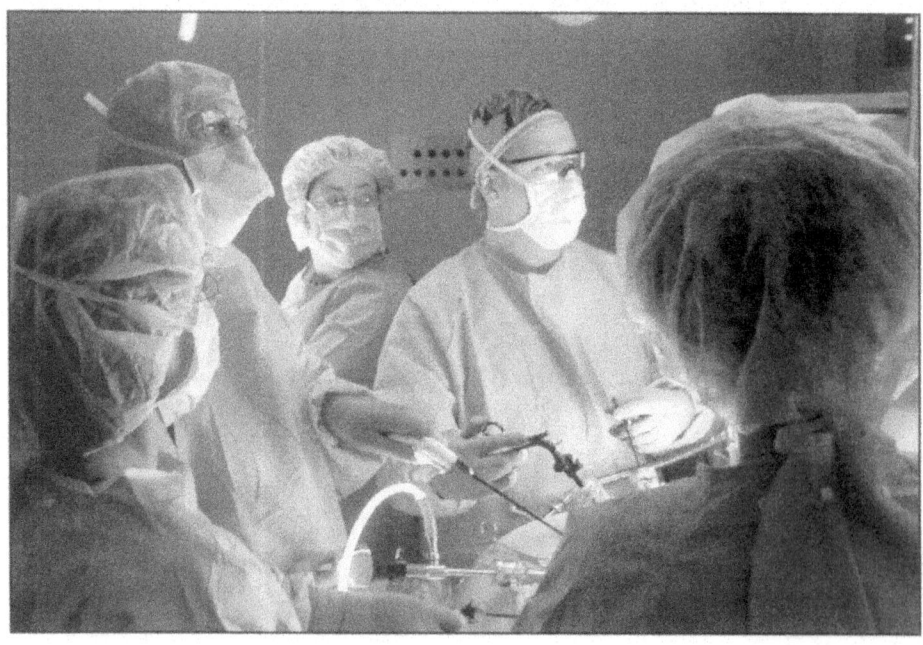

Laparoscopic surgical procedure being performed at CMH in 2004.

CMH Milestones

1976
- Concerned citizens and business leaders formed a committee to study the possibility of a community hospital.

1978
- The community approved and organized a public hospital district, formed the district's board of directors.

1982
- The hospital opens on September 28.
- ICU addition is complete.

1983
- First health fair held.
- Telemetry monitors used.
- Swing bed program added.

1984
- Accreditation received by JCAHO.
- Home Health and Home Medical Equipment added.
- Hospital district tax levy was suspended.

1985
- Approval given for two Advanced Life Support ambulances.
- Mammography services added.

1986
- Citizens Memorial Healthcare Foundation established.
- Hickory County ambulance services added.

1987
- Hospice program started.
- 8,000 square foot expansion for ICU/CCU.

1988
- Outpatient wing completed bringing the hospital to 76,000 square feet from 47,000 square feet originally.
- First phase of construction began on the Butterfield Residential Care Center.
- Purchased the Bolivar Nursing Home and renamed it Citizens Memorial Healthcare Facility.

1989
- Designated as a Level III trauma center.
- Acquired clinics in Stockton and Humansville.

1990
- Medical Excellence Fund established.
- Phase II of Butterfield Residential Care Center completed.
- Opened clinics in Hermitage and Butterfield Park Medical Center in Bolivar.

1991
- Dedicated the Birth Place and the Parkview Geriatric Wellness Center.
- In-Home Infusion Therapy added.
- Acquired the Parkview Bone and Joint and Surgical Services clinics.
- Phase III of construction for Butterfield Residential Care Center.

1992
- Celebration of CMH's 10-year anniversary.
- Acquired Dade County Family Medical Center in Greenfield.

1993
- Opened Parkview Healthcare Facility.
- Began behavioral health services in the clinic setting.

1994
- Citizens Advantage (HMO) began service.
- Started clinics in Ash Grove and Buffalo.
- CMH was named one of the top ten rural hospitals in the nation.

1995
- Added neurology services.
- CHART program established in Polk, Dallas, Dade and Hickory counties.
- Added OB/GYN clinic.

1996
- CMH became home for 9-1-1.
- Mobile MRI unit added to services.
- Acquired Colonial Springs Healthcare Center in Buffalo.

1997
- A corporate compliance plan was instituted.

1998
- Health Transit Services began.
- CMH Sports Medicine Center opened.
- Rural behavioral health services began.
- Added dialysis services in Bolivar.

1999
- Purchased Ash Grove Healthcare Facility.
- Opened clinic in Urbana.
- Occupational Health program created.
- Citizens Memorial Healthcare Facility was named the first skilled nursing facility in the nation to receive the OSHA VPP award.

2000
- Opened a clinic in Pleasant Hope.
- CMH launched its first Web site.
- CMH Administrative Center opened.
- A 3-year strategic plan was implemented.
- Parkview Senior Living Community opened in Bolivar.
- Miles for Smiles mobile dental unit added.

2001
- Expansion of the Cardio-Pulmonary Rehabilitation department.
- Screened over 10,000 children at area school health expos.
- Began partnerships with area businesses to build the CMH Senior Health Center.
- Opened the Butterfield Park Pediatric clinic.
- Addition of Parkview Physical Medicine and Rehabilitation.

2002
- Launched InfoCare computer technology upgrade.
- Purchased Community Springs Healthcare Facility in ElDorado Springs.
- Missouri Sleep institute added to CMH.
- Opened new location/retail facility for Home Medical Equipment in Bolivar.
- Opened the newly constructed Ash Grove Healthcare Facility, Ash Grove Senior Living Community and new facility for the Ash Grove Family Medical Center.
- Bolivar Medical Group established.
- Added a hospitalist in the hospital.

2003
- Built a new facility for the Dade County Family Medical Center in Greenfield.
- Added CMH Endocrinology Center.
- Added CMH Diabetes Education Center.
- Added Pain Management Clinic.
- Opened the CMH Eye Specialty Center.
- Added in-house MRI/MR services.
- Added independent living units in ElDorado Springs.

2004
- Expanded and remodeled the emergency room, radiology services and laboratory services at the hospital.
- Added the CMH Cardiovascular Center and cath lab procedures.
- Added the Women's Clinic of Bolivar.
- Opened the CMH Senior Health Center.
- Addition of air ambulance helicopter.
- Opened retail location for Home Medical Equipment in Buffalo.
- Created the CMH Ankle & Foot clinic.

Bolivar Masonic Bodies

The first Masonic Lodge (Ancient Free and Accepted Masons) in Bolivar was started in 1839 and was called Bolivar Lodge No. 41. In 1863 it surrendered its Charter and most of its records to the Grand Lodge of Missouri where they eventually were destroyed in a fire. The only remaining records of that Lodge is a treasurer's receipt book.

After the Civil War it was first proposed to have the Charter of Bolivar Lodge No. 41 restored, but since some of the original members had joined in the organization of other Lodges in the area it was decided to seek a Dispensation from the Grand Master to organize a new Lodge. The Dispensation was granted in January 1867 and in October of that year a Charter was granted by the Grand Lodge to Bolivar Lodge No. 195 which still exists today.

The first meetings were held on the second story of an old wood frame building on the southeast corner of the square known as Akard Bros. Store. In 1874 it moved to the northwest corner of the square on the second story of the old building that was where the First National Bank building stands which now is home to Dan and Stan's Pharmacy. For a time meetings were held in the building next door on the eastern part of where the First National Bank building now stands and for a while on the west side of the square on the second floor of the Rains Building.

About 1877 when Bolivar Chapter No. 5, Royal Arch Masons was organized, they met on the second story of a building on the Post Office Block on West Broadway.

In 1883 St. Elmo Commandary No. 43, Knights Templar was organized and met in the same building. In 1892 Mizpah Chapter No. 230, Order of the Eastern Star was formed. In 1950 The Social Order of the Beauceant was added.

In 1892, Bolivar Lodge No. 195, Bolivar Chapter No. 5, R. A. M., and St. Elmo Commandary No. 43 K. T., purchased the upstairs of the new brick building on the southeast corner of the square, which for many years had the Post Office and later the Sears Catalogue Store on the ground floor.

In 1987 it was decided that it would be better to have a building on ground level that was handicap accessible. With the location provided by the kindness of an Eastern Star Sister and the money from the wise investments of our predecessors, a new Masonic Temple was completed in 1988 on Killingsworth Avenue.

Over the years most of the other Masonic Lodges in the area have consolidated with Bolivar. They are: Cement Lodge from Halfway, Pleasant Lodge from Morrisville, Modern Lodge from Humansville, and Fair Play Lodge from Fair Play.

As the world's oldest fraternity we hope to continue far into the future.

Wommack Monument

The purpose of the business is still the same as it was when J.V. Wommack became a partner in 1954. That purpose is to turn out a monument for a person or a place that will last even longer than a memory.

The material is still the same, too, with nearly indestructible granite as the medium for the monuments.

But beyond that, Wommack Monument Co., based in Bolivar, is as different from its forebears as night from day.

J.V. Wommack became a partner with Bill Propp in what was then Bolivar Memorial Co. on Feb. 4, 1954, after buying out Propp's previous partner, Clint May.

"Mr. Propp was 54 and I was 23," Wommack says. "People thought it was an unusual partnership. A lot of people thought I just worked for him, but I was a full partner." The company itself probably dates back into the 'teens, Wommack says. At the time he joined it, the staff consisted of himself, Propp, and Albert Beason, who was 77 and worked only part time. Wommack became sole owner in 1961 when Propp retired and moved to North Carolina, where his widow Rachel, still lived in 1991.

Wommack's wife, Ruth, became active in the company in 1961, and now serves as corporate treasurer. The couple's older son, Joey, worked for the company until 1979 (he now lives with his family in Arlington, TX) and their younger son, Brad, became involved in 1977. The name change from Bolivar Memorial to Wommack Monument came in 1964, when the company acquired a second office in Osceola. There now are branches in Springfield, Monett, and Aurora as well. All told, Wommack Monument operates regularly in a 36-county area.

There have been other changes besides the name and the corporate structure.

"If we were still doing things like we did 20 years ago, no one could afford (our products)," says Brad Wommack. "The increasing technology has helped us be able to offer a wider variety. We've gone from a one-horse operation to modern technology."

Granite slabs come in precut to specifications from their origins in Missouri, Georgia, South Carolina, Oklahoma, Pennsylvania, Virginia, New York, Vermont, Minnesota, South Dakota, Wisconsin, California, Texas, Canada, India, Sweden, South Africa, Norway, "and on and on and on," says J. V. Wommack.

"The majority of our granite is domestically quarried, but certain colors are not available through domestic sources," he adds.

The design is transferred to the monument with the use of a rubber stencil, then mechanically and/or hand chiseled onto the granite. While some designs involve an overlay or dyeing, most color variations are achieved by "bruising" the stone's polished surface.

Much artistry and craftsmanship still is involved, the Wommacks stress. The tools of modern technology are simply that, tools. Such things as computer-aided stencil drawings, chiseling to pattern through sand-blasting, and even the copy machine that can reduce or enlarge patterns have allowed the business to extend its services and keep them affordable. Trucks with cranes for moving and setting the heavy monuments and pneumatic tools for helping to set footings are other modern helps.

But the custom touch is still much evident in the operation. Though it's the air-driven abrasives that shape the details, it's the hand of the craftsman that brings it to life. And though it's the computer that helps in cutting the stencil, it's the mind of the designer that brings to the monument the personality of the one to be remembered.

"One of the nicest compliments anyone can pay us is to say a monument looks just like an individual or a family," J.V. Wommack says.

Over the years, the company has done much unusual work. Some families ask for established symbols—the cultivated rose, a symbol of love; the dogwood, for Christ and the crucifixion; the oak leaf, for family character and strength; or the ivy, for faith and eternal life.

But other families want more personalized monuments. One featured an etching of the home in which the person lived, with a Navy plane flying over a field of Black Angus cattle. Once, J.V. Wommack recalls, a family asked for a scale model of the original Great Pyramid of Giza.

"I probably spent 120 hours myself on that one," he says. "The family gave me a book to study on the dimensions. Then they gave me false measurements when we got ready to build it, so they could see if I'd read the book."

The monument weighed some 15,000 pounds when it was completed, and included even scale etchings of the inner passageways. Wommack isn't telling in which cemetery the monument is located.

"This was something that had special symbolism for these people," he said. "It was not an ego trip. Their intent was to leave something permanent that was interesting enough to spark someone to go to the Bible and do some reading."

Besides tombstones, the company also does granite signs, such as the one at Baptist Bible College in Springfield, the memorial at the Harry Truman birthplace in Lamar, and the Jaycee plaque in Tulsa.

A recent unusual request was moving the bust of George Washington Carver at his monument near Diamond, MO.

"No one would touch that one," J.V. Wommack says of the complicated and tedious job. Because what is a commonplace job to them is a once-in-a-lifetime purchase for most families, the Wommacks say they feel a deep responsibility to their customers.

"Sometimes we see things in our own industry... sometimes we think they are getting less than they should receive," says Brad Wommack.

They say whether customers are buying a monument from them or another company, there are four main areas they should look for. Those areas are:

1. Choose a company that has a good reputation.
2. Look at the quality of granite which, like wood, comes in several grades.
3. Check the rendering of the artwork in monuments the company has done.
4. And most important, check the foundation. It's not uncommon for a large monument to use a full load of redi-mix concrete for a proper setting, the Wommacks say. A typical foundation should extend to the frost line, which can vary widely even among cemeteries in the same area.

1955

1966

1975

2004

Family Histories

November 26, 1950 at Republic, MO, home of W. W. Hughes Ross relatives

ABEL – Francis John Abel Sr. (born 1758) married Isabel O'Connor in 1783. Francis John Abel Jr. (born Aug. 26, 1793; died May 25, 1869) married Barbara Horner (born Sept. 8, 1788; died Sept. 3, 1877) on May 25, 1816.

Mary and Branson Able

Samuel Houston Abel (born Jan. 23, 1819; died Dec. 26, 1889) married Mary Polly Cox (born October 1821; died Feb. 21, 1901) on May 14, 1839.

Branson Abel (born Feb. 9, 1846; died Aug. 31, 1921) married Elizabeth Mahan (born circa 1844; died Feb. 11, 1875) on Oct. 8, 1865.

On Nov. 5, 1876, Branson married Mary Emiline Keynon (born Sept. 9, 1857; died July 19, 1939).

The Abel families came from Indiana in the 1800s. Samuel Houston Abel and wife, Mary Polly Cox, had 11 or 12 children. They traveled west with some of the younger ones and settled in Polk County, MO on the Hominy River east of Bolivar and northwest of Halfway.

Years later in the 1800s, their son Branson left Indiana with is first wife, Elizabeth Mahan, and children. He and Elizabeth had nine children but only seven lived to start the trip west. Names of those who went with them: Ike Isaac C.; Luella J.; Phoeba Helen; Lydia M.; Willard DeLoss; and Charley Preston. Elizabeth was pregnant at the start of the trip and she and the baby both died on the trip. Branson buried mother and child and then he turned around and took the other children back to Indiana.

Within a year or so, Branson married his second wife, Mary Emeline Keynon and they lived in Indiana a few years before heading to Missouri. They had nine children together. Some of the children who came with them to Polk County, MO were: Elvett T.; Lizzie Peal; Walter M.; Lawrence; Lora Elda; Belzona "Belle"; Lucy; Frank T.; and Fred Olin.

Arriving in Polk County, they settled close by Branson's parents on the Hominy River. They built a house and Mary Emeline made the shingles for it herself. This was a log house. Later they built a seven-room frame house. For furniture the men cut a large maple tree and sawed it into lumber at a neighbor's saw mill. The seats of the chairs were of strips of hickory bark woven into an artistic pattern – hard work for both husband and wife with the help of the children. Branson also made his ax, fork and plow handles and all the wooden framework of his farm tools mostly from tough, native hickory. This was cut, then hewed down to size with a drawing knife. Mary ran the spinning wheel, wove the carpets and did the knitting for home and family. She made their soap and this is the way she did it. They made an ash hopper in the shape of a "V" open box with the sharp point set in a trough made from a hollow log. In this big box all the ashes from the fireplace and stove were put. In those days, they burned nothing but wood to heat and cook. In the spring buckets of water were poured on the top of the ashes and these seeped through, removing the lye. This solution of lye was caught in a large 20-gallon kettle set at the open end of the trough. When the kettle was full, a fire was built under the kettle to bring the solution to boiling. Next the grease was added; this being scraps and refuse from hot killings, and the mixture was boiled until it was a thick soap. This is what they used to wash clothes.

They had animals that were tended by parents and children alike. The cows were milked by hand; chickens, ducks and geese fed in the open pasture by the house. There was time for hunting and fishing. There was time for the families to gather at each other's houses for a frolic. Usually straw would be put in a wagon, some quilts would be taken to cover with, and then they would drive the horses and go to square dances or a kitchen romp. They most always went to church and church functions. Attended school, usually for six months out of the year. Back then all the children of all ages went to school. Some were grown and even larger than their teacher was.

In the wintertime, the river would freeze over and the families would gather and go skating. A huge fire would be built and most would stay and enjoy the evenings.

At school in the winter they would help the teacher with the wood box, clean the schoolroom and even have parties like box suppers. Everyone would bring a box supper and these were put up for high bid with everyone bidding on the box they wanted and the boys hoped they would get the one their girlfriend brought.

The children all grew up, married, and had their own families. Branson and Mary moved into Bolivar and finished out their lives there. They were wonderful people. When Branson died he was past 75 years and Mary was 81 years, 9 months and 24 day when she died. *Submitted by Mrs. Vaden (nee Abel) Anderson*

ABLES – Isham Ables, born about 1800 in North Carolina and Janiza Lewisa Woodson, born about 1810 in Kentucky, were married on April 8, 1830 in Marion County, MO. They had nine children, all born in Missouri, the last seven born in Polk County. Isham died between 1860 and 1870 but no record of burial can be found – the same goes for Janiza.

Joseph Edward Ables, born Jan. 12, 1831, married Nancy Elizabeth Milliken on Dec. 16, 1855 in Polk County. They had two children: Susan C. (married Hudson C. Narcross, two children) and John William Ables (married Maria Irene Wells, three children). After Nancy's death in 1867, Joseph was remarried to Harriet Roberts on March 24, 1869 in Polk County. Joseph and Harriet had five children: Agnes Eliza Jane (married first, Dudley Roberts, one child; married second, Neal Wine, four children); Lilly Belle (married Leslie Fairfield Emmons); Mary Alice; Pearl (lived nine days, buried at Salem Cemetery); and Joseph Lewis (married Nellie Mary Chancellor, two children). Joseph, a Civil War veteran, died Feb. 27, 1882 in Polk County and was buried at White Cemetery, northwest of Bolivar.

Shadrach VanBuren Ables, born March 23, 1833, married Mrs. Catharine Moore in Polk County on Jan. 17, 1875. Shadrach was a Civil War veteran. He died April 15, 1888 in Texas, probably in Cooke County.

Jesse Woodson Ables, born Nov. 27, 1835, married Mrs. Mary Irene (Lockwood) Warren on March 5, 1863 in Polk County. They had three children: James Isham (married Nancy Anna Meade, four children); John Lewis (married Mrs. Margaret Isabelle Pickering White, four children); and Mary Caldona (married first, Guinn K. Yates, seven children; married second, Joseph A. Guinn). After Mary's death on April 16, 1869, Jesse was remarried to Paralee Caroline Jones on April 21, 1870 in Polk County. They had five children: Olla Florence (married William Merida Wells, seven children); Jesse C. (married Loretta A. Coberly, two children); Edward Marion (married Mrs. Zela G. Hood, no children) and twins Leander E. and Leroy Emmons. Jesse, a Civil War veteran, died July 18, 1900 in Cliquot and was buried at Salem Cemetery.

James Ables, born Feb. 1, 1838, married Isabella Caroline Morrow on March 17, 1869 in Polk County. They had two children: Margaret S. (married William H. Anderson) and John William Ables (possibly married Emma – last name unknown). James, a Civil War veteran, died Aug. 4, 1879 in Polk County and was buried at Salem Cemetery.

William A. Ables was born Jan. 14, 1840. He served during the Civil War – Union Army, Company C, First Battalion Nevada Cavalry (same as his brother Shadrach).

John David Ables was born July 27, 1842. He was last found on the census with his parents in 1860.

Drury Lewis Ables, born Oct. 14, 1846, married Laura Ann Jones on April 21, 1870 in Polk County. They had five children: William I. (died at age 11, buried in Salem Cemetery); Francis L. (married Mr. Williamson); Albert M. (died at age 18, buried in Salem Cemetery); Stella (married Mr. Carpenter); and Clara (married Mr. Bran). Drury died Feb. 8, 1892 in St. Clair County and was buried at Salem Cemetery in Polk County.

Alcy (or Elsa) Jane Ables, born May 13, 1849, married William M. Young on March 21, 1875 in Polk County. He was a widower with two children. Alcy and William had at least three children: Washington and two others whose names are unknown at this time. Alcy was last found living in 1900 in Polk County.

Martha Anna Ables, born March 30, 1854, married Josephus Mead on Sept. 10, 1874 in Polk County. They had eight children: John L. (lived three days, buried in Salem Cemetery); James William (married Sarah E. Gresham); an unnamed child (apparently died at birth); Isaac Jaron; Thomas M; Ira S.; and twins Rhoda and Rosa. Martha was last found in the 1900 census.

ABLES – Jesse Woodson Ables, born Nov. 27, 1835 in Polk County, married Mrs. Mary Irene (Lockwood) Warren on March 5, 1863 in Polk County. Mary was born Sept. 1, 1838 in Alabama or Arkansas. They had three children, all born in Polk County. After Mary's death on April 16, 1869, Jesse was remarried to Paralee Caroline Jones on April 21, 1870 in Polk County. They had five children, also born in Polk County. Jesse, a Civil War veteran, died July 18, 1900 in Cliquot and was buried at Salem Cemetery. Paralee died July 26, 1915 and is buried at Salem.

James Isham Ables (born Oct. 5, 1864; died April 13, 1948 and is buried at Forest Park Cemetery, Harper County, KS) married Nancy Anna Meade on March 6, 1887 in Polk County. They had four children: Henry (a WWI veteran), Jessie Pearl, Mildred and Charles W. James and family moved to Kansas in 1915.

John Lewis Ables (born March 4, 1867; died Nov. 19, 1952 and is buried at Salem Cemetery) married Mrs. Margaret Isabelle (Pickering) White on Dec. 14, 1890 in Polk County. Belle already had a son of her own, James Robert White and then she had four children with John Lewis Ables: Alma, Bertha, Otto and Pearlee. Mary Alma Ables (born Dec. 5, 1891; died July 3, 1973 and is buried at Greenwood Cemetery) married first, Hiram James Henson and had six children: Maggie Mae, Neta Wilma, Wauneta Faye, Emma Lorene, Oren Stanley and Thelma Jewell. Alma married second, Grant DeWitt. Bertha Annis Ables (born Dec. 25, 1896; died Nov. 10, 1976 and is buried at Salem Cemetery) married Charles Alvin Lawson and had five children: Harold Raymond, Bernice Isabel, Opal Marie, Hazel Annis and Lois Jean (died at age 5). Otto Francis Ables (born Sept. 6, 1901; died July 1, 1966 and is buried at Sunny Slopes Cemetery, Corona, Riverside County, CA) married Lena Davison and had three children: Wilma Jean, Shirley Marie and John Hamilton. Martha Pearlee Ables (born July 2, 1904; died May 4, 1955 and is buried at Glendale Cemetery, Louisville, Cass County, NE) married Charley Devin Hammons and had five children: Margaret Mabel, Maurice Bernard, Mary Louise, Charles Robert and John Myron. After Belle's death in 1941, John Lewis Ables was remarried to Mrs. Della (Crawford) Kennon in 1945.

Belle and John Ables; back row: Alma, Bertha, Pearlee and Otto, circa 1940-1941

Mary Caldona "Mollie" Ables (born April 5, 1869; died Oct. 26, 1930 and is buried at Greenwood Cemetery) married Guinn K. Yates on Dec. 2, 1888 in Polk County. They had seven children: Mima, Ella, Elsie, Inez, Cora, Jessie M. and Wesley R. In 1907, Guinn died and Mollie was remarried to Joseph A. Guinn on June 14, 1911 in Polk County.

Olla Florence Ables (born Aug. 20, 1872; died 1926 and is buried to Greenwood Cemetery) married William Merida Wells on Oct. 7, 1894 in Polk County. They had seven children: Florence Carolina (died at age 19 of influenza); Robert Wayne (died at age 15 of influenza, at same time as sister Florence during the great flu epidemic of 1918); Albert T. (died young); unnamed twin boys (died at birth) and two other children who lived to adulthood but whose names are unknown at this time.

Jesse C. Ables (born Sept. 1, 1875; died May 6, 1913 and is buried at Salem Cemetery) married Loretta A. Coberly on Sept. 17, 1905 in Polk County. They had two daughters, Lucia Belle and Jessie.

Edward Marion Ables (born Sept. 15, 1878; died Nov. 13, 1962 and is buried at Salem Cemetery) married Mrs. Zela G. Hood on Sept. 1, 1942 in Polk County. They had no children together; Zela already had one son named Carl from her previous marriage.

Twins Leander E. (born March 5, 1881; died Jan. 15, 1969) and Leroy Emmons (born March 5, 1881; died Jan. 24, 1962) never married and lived with each other all of their lives. They are buried next to each other at Salem Cemetery in the same plot with a double gravestone.

ADAMS – The history of the Adams and Belcher families is scattered throughout Cedar, Polk and Dade Counties and includes some of the following surnames: Warner, Tow, Stockton, Beck, Belcher and Stalcup.

Jesse Finas Adams (1855-1962), born in the Masters Community area in Cedar County, married Ada Mae Belcher (1890-1972) from the nearby town of Needmore near the Sac River. Jesse and Ada Adams met at the Fleeman Church and were married there in 1905. They had seven children: Wyvle, Clayton, Georgia, Earl, Margaret, Lois and Bobby.

Franklin Levi Adams and Nancy Jane Warner, grandparents of Jesse Adams, were the first of the Adams family to migrate to Madison Township in Cedar County in the 1860s from Macon County, TN. Levi Adams built a log house and later a clapboard house that was built very near the original log cabin. It was in this house that Jesse's parents, Noah "Node" Halbert Adams (1847-1920) and Martha Jane Tow (1853-1948) raised their family. Martha and Node Adams are buried in the Lindley Prairie Cemetery, Bear Creek, Cedar County, MO.

Martha Jane Tow's father, Mitchell Alexander Tow (1822-1895) moved to the Polk County area with his parents, Ruben Tow and Lurana Barclift Tow, and his brothers, Samuel and Jesse Tow. They settled in the Polk County area in the early 1840s. Mitchell Alexander Tow married Sarah Ann Stockton (1827-1895) in Polk County, MO in 1845. Their 11 children were all born in Bolivar. Sarah Stockton's family moved to the area in 1833 from Tennessee. Alexander and Sarah Tow are buried in Roach Cemetery, Barry County, MO.

Ada Belcher's family migrated from Virginia to Missouri during the 1840s and later on into Cedar, Polk and Dade Counties. Ada's parents, John William Belcher and Martha Jane Stalcup, were living in the Cane Hill area when they married and eventually settled in Needmore near the Sac River where they raised their children: Wilma, Itress, Alla, Della, Ada, Coy, Eddie and Chester. John William Belcher and Martha Jane Stalcup Belcher were both preachers and daughters Alla, Itress, Wilma and Ada sang as a quartet when their parents were preaching. Ada Belcher, a talented alto singer, also played music by ear and enjoyed playing the jew's harp and the pump organ.

In 1913 Jesse Adams and his brother-in-law, Albert Trimble, moved to Fergus County, MT to homestead. Ada, and daughter Wyvle, came the following year in 1914. Georgia, Earl, Margaret, Lois and Bobby were born after the family settled in Montana.

The family returned to Missouri in 1938 and lived on the Adams farm until 1962. Jesse and Ada Adams took great pride in their family and their farm. Jesse truly enjoyed working the land and taking care of stock, especially his horses. He worked very well with his hands and could do most anything that needed to be done on the farm. Ada was a wonderful cook and amazed her family and the many dinner guests she cooked for with her fried chicken dinner and fruit cobblers.

Jesse Finas Adams and Ada Mae Belcher Adams 50th Anniversary

Jesse Adams died in 1962 at which time Ada moved to Fair Play in Polk County and lived there for the next 10 years until her death in 1972. She and Jesse are buried in the Lindley Prairie Cemetery near Bear Creek, in Cedar County, MO.

The farm was eventually purchased by the Corp of Engineers and is now part of the Stockton Lake Park. *Submitted by Jeanelle Ash*

AGEE – Eugene "Gene" Agee and Emma Jean "Jeanie" Agee have lived six miles east of Bolivar, at Burns, for the past 51 years. The place was known as Gypsy Gardens. It was a type of resort in the 1930s with a café and swimming pool. Gypsy Gardens is still engraved on the rock gate entrance.

Gene was born March 28, 1924, near Schofield, MO to Ralph and Marie (Buck) Agee. Gene has two sisters, Dorothy Miller and her late husband, Bobby, of Bolivar, and Rowena Langston and her husband, Don, of Plano, TX. Gene passed away on June 28, 2003 and is buried at Pleasant Hill Cemetery east of Bolivar.

Ralph was the son of Isaac and Margaret (Brundridge) Agee, and one of 14 children. Ralph had five brothers: Lon, Walter, Oliver, Leonard and Lloyd; and eight sisters: Francis Brown, Florence Bills, Belle Wilson, Stella Atkinson, Effie Allen, Lula Agee, Lillie Atkinson and Flora Sharar. The lived near Foose, south of Buffalo, where all the children attended Foose Grade School, a one-room schoolhouse. Isaac's ancestors came from France to Virginia and Tennessee and then settled in Missouri.

Marie (Buck) Agee was the daughter of Leland and Florence (Edison) Buck. She had two sisters, Nellie (Buck) Francios and Juanita (Buck) Voris. They lived in the Halfway-Schofield area.

Eugene and Emma Jean Agee

Jeanie was born Jan. 31, 1931, near Adonis, MO to Ray and Veda (Capehart) Hobson. Jeanie had two brothers, Glenn and wife Gladys (Coffman) Hobson of Santa Paula, CA, and Larry and wife Juanita (Gile) Hobson of Bolivar, and one sister, Marjorie Brooks and husband Elmo of Oxnard, CA. Ray and Veda lived in Polk County most of their lives with a few years in California during WWII. In 1943, Ray's brother Virgil asked him to come to Santa Paula, CA, to help prune lemon trees, as so many of his crew had been called into the military service. Ray was 45 at the time and was too old to be drafted. The family moved back to the Huron area in 1947.

Ray was the son of Velza and Nancy (Huckaby) Hobson. They lived in the Urbana and Pittsburg area. Ray had three brothers: Virgil, Elgie and Arlie; and one sister, Myrtle (Hobson) Davis; and three half brothers: Willard, Clifford and Ralph.

Veda was the daughter of William and Rachel (Pope) Capehart. They lived in the Sentinel-Adonis area. Veda had three brothers: Glen, Herbert and Benjamin; and three sisters: Elsie Skinner, Tressie Crouch and Laura Morrow.

Jeanie went to Bolivar High School for her senior year, and graduated in 1948. A week after graduation her family moved back to Santa Paula, CA. She met Gene during the year she spent in Bolivar. He came to California in September 1948 and they were married Feb. 5, 1949 in Santa Paula. They moved back to Bolivar in June 1950.

Gene was a mechanic and gravel hauler and also spent some time in the US Marine Corps in 1945 to 1946, going to Japan. Jeanie was a bookkeeper in the early years but since then was a stay at home mother and kept the books for Gene's garages and gravel hauling business.

Gene and Jeanie have four children and six grandchildren: Gerald "Jerry" and wife Debbie (Batterson) Agee, who live south of Springfield, their children, Phillip and Courtney; Connie

(Agee) Helton and her husband, Vince, of Halfway, their children Kristopher and Kevin; Rhonda Agee, of Halfway; and Dale and Rhonda (Voris) Agee, of Halfway, and their children, Kody and Madison. *Submitted by Jeanie Agee*

AKARD – Jonas Akard was born in 1792 in North Carolina and Elizabeth (Hopkins) Akard was born South Carolina. Elizabeth was the daughter of Andrew Hopkins and Sarah (Dill) Hopkins of Henry County, TN.

Jonas and Elizabeth Akard settled in Missouri with her sister and brother-in-law, Margaret and William Davidson (Davison). Jonas' father immigrated to Maryland from an area on the German/Swiss border before the Revolutionary War. The first Missouri record of Jonas Akard is the 1833 Greene County tax list but little of their lives is known from other sources. In the *History of Polk County Baptist Association*, their daughter, Priscilla (Akard) Dunnegan, reported that she came to Missouri with her parents about 1831, "just after the Indians had ceded the southwest part of the state to the whites. Her parents made the first settlement on Bear Creek about two miles south of Fair Play. This was one of the first settlements made in what is now Polk County, and the date is a short time before Greene County was organized." An obituary for an Akard grandson, Judge J. M. Akard of Cedar County, states that "the family lived for months in their wagons until log cabins could be erected. Some of the Kickapoo Indians were yet here at the time, two Indian girls coming to the cabin to see their first white woman."

Jonas and Elizabeth had 10 children: Henry (born 1813; married Lavina Jones); Joseph Dill (born 1815; married Keziah Dunnegan); Priscilla (born 1816; married Matthew Dunnegan); Sarah N. (born 1818; married Elijah Fox); Martha A. (born 1822; married Silas Fox); Saphronia (born 1823; married Miller Woodson Easley); Andrew M. T. (born 1824; married Parthena); William C. C. (born 1826; married Sarah Bowen); Elizabeth P. (born 1830) and John H. (born 1832; married Mary E. Jackson).

Just 10 years after bringing his family to Polk County, Jonas died in 1841. His oldest sons, Henry and Joseph Dill Akard filled the void, but then Joseph died in 1846 and Henry died before 1850. Their wives, Lavina (Jones) Akard and Keziah (Dunnegan) Akard, without adult men in the family, were appointed administrators of the estates. Although Henry was only in his 30s when he died, he had served as Polk County Court Judge, Justice of the Peace and as an Elder in the Liberty Association of the Primitive Baptist Church. Joseph's estate papers reveal one of his occupations. They contained many receipts for volumes of whiskey. Genealogist Marsha Hoffman Rising comments, "Joseph, William and Andrew Akard were operating a whiskey still. It appears that half of the people in the county were purchasing whiskey from these brothers."

The 1844 Polk County Tax Book show the families living in a cluster south of the present town of Fair Play near the Akard Cemetery. In addition to pillars of the church and makers of whiskey, the Akard men built roller mills, bought and sold property and were often active in politics. The women of the family put their own stamp on the traditions of Polk County. They often named their offspring after famous people, attaching a string of initials to the names that are sometimes documented in the official record. William C. C. Akard was said to be William Christopher Columbus Akard. T. H. B. Dunnegan (son of Priscilla Akard and Matthew Dunnegan) was Thomas Hart Benton Dunnegan. William N. C. C. A. Fox (son of Martha Akard and Silas Fox) was also called "Alphabet Fox" was actually named William Napoleon Christopher Columbus Akard Fox.

Notables in the family include James Jasper Akard who was Captain of Company A, 8th Missouri State Militia Cavalry (1863); State Legislator (1866); Sheriff (1876-1880); Collector (1878-1880); and Clerk of County Court (1886-1888). Andrew M. T. Akard was a Polk County Commissioner. William C. C. Akard, a businessman and noted Confederate, left Polk County and started a Texas branch of the family after the Civil War. James M. Akard was a Cedar County Judge.

The fame of John William Akard seems to be known most widely. "Bill" Akard was a well-loved Shooting Champion of the World from 1905 to 1917. He is said to have practiced by shooting grasshoppers at the cemetery. Employed by the Remington Arms Company, he was an acquaintance of both Annie Oakley and Will Rogers. He owned an automobile dealership for a while but reportedly was not much interested in the business. From his inventive mind came modifications to Remington's 30-06 and other clever inventions, including the first power lawnmower for the cemetery. *Submitted by Janine (Davison) Hernbrode*

AKIN – Ray Lee Akin was born in Kansas City, KS on April 29, 1950. He was the only son of Roy Akin and Regina Frances "Toots" (Borushaski) Akin Ghan. Ray died Jan. 26, 2002 and is buried in Mt. Gilead Cemetery near Bolivar, MO. He was raised on a small dairy farm near Wheaton, MO. He graduated from Wheaton High School in 1968. Ray attended the University of Missouri from 1968-1972 where he graduated with a bachelor of science degree in agriculture sciences. He was employed by the University of Missouri in the dairy husbandry research laboratory while in college.

After Ray graduated from college in August 1972, he was employed by the Federal Land Bank as a loan officer, being assigned to the Springfield office. From 1973 to 1986 he was the branch manager of the Federal Land Bank in Lebanon, MO. In 1986, the Federal Land Bank merged with Farm Credit Services and he was transferred to Bolivar, MO. In 1992, Ray was an account executive for Wells Fargo Bank until his death.

Ray was married to Nyla M. Bartholomew on June 25, 1977 in the Muncie Methodist Church in Wheaton, MO. Nyla was born May 11, 1945 in Tecumseh, NE. She was the daughter of Loren E. and Ellyn Lennorah (Lawrence) Bartholomew. Nyla was employed by the state of Missouri as a social worker. After her retirement, Nyla enjoyed doing genealogy research.

Ray adopted his stepson, Edward Lee, in 1979. Edward was born on April 9, 1963 in Oklahoma City, OK. Both enjoyed a passion for aviation.

Ray was a member of the Fairview Methodist Church. Nyla was Catholic. *Submitted by Nyla M. Akin*

ALEXANDER – James Hullum Alexander, born November 1847 to Reuben and Eliza Jane Looney Alexander, married Nancy Ann Stretch about 1868, who was the daughter of John and Elizabeth Long Stretch from Illinois. She was born on Feb. 24, 1851. Hullum was a farmer in Polk County, according to the 1900 and 1910 census. He and his wife had 12 children: Willis F. (born Aug. 13, 1870; married May about 1896 or 1897); Mary Leona E. (born Feb. 16, 1873; married Henry Stokes on Sept. 14, 1892); William Benton (born May 21, 1880; married Amanda May Atwood); James Harvey, (born Aug. 7, 1882; died Dec. 8, 1974; married Mabel); Rosa A. (born September 1884; married George Cruse Sr. about 1903); John T. (born July 10, 1888; died May 16, 1924; married Edith Beland); Edward Atley (born September 1890; buried near Joplin, MO); Perry "Alda P." (born probably 1892, was a laborer in 1910, died young); George Calaway (born July 20, 1893; married Ola Choate whose father was Walter Choate whose father was Walter Choate. George died April 19, 1984; had 11 children); Elizabeth (died young); Matilda (died young); and Rebecca (died young).

James Hullum Alexander

Hullum has been spelled Hullem, Hulem, Hulum and HullamU As the picture shows, it was probably Hullum. Nancy is buried in Kelley Cemetery, northeast of Ash Grove as she was living with her son George at the time of her death on Jan. 2, 1931. Most of their lives were lived in Polk County as most of their children married Polk County people. *Submitted by Greg Dillard*

ALLEN – John Birdette "J. B." Allen was born on Sept. 27, 1850 in Missouri. John married Rachel Mahala Mead on Aug. 27, 1871 in Polk County, MO. Rachel was born on May 10, 1852 in Roane County, TN to John Luttrel and Amanda Caroline (Lysle) Mead. No information is known of John's parents, but family members say John was full-blooded Cherokee.

John and Rachel had nine children: Amanda "Florence" (Sudduth), James, LaVerne "Verne" Jane (Ashlock), Mary Belle (Wollard), Doriada, Surilda (Wine), Rhoda Alice, Clarence and Bertha. John owned 80 acres of land located at T34, R24, S23 in Polk County.

Surilda, Clarence and Rachel Allen about 1903-1904

John died Jan. 29, 1903 in Polk County. After John died, Rachel married James Alsbury Griffin on Oct. 5, 1904 in Polk County, MO. Rachel died in St. Louis, MO on Jan. 14, 1943. She is buried in New St. Marcus Cemetery in St. Louis, as is a son, Clarence Allen.

Verne Allen was born Aug. 23, 1876 in Dunnegan, MO. She married Obediah Ashlock in Dunnegan Springs, MO on Aug. 3, 1893. He was born on March 23, 1869 in Fair Play, MO. LaVerne and Obediah had two children, Elva and William Connie. LaVerne died on Feb. 22, 1904 in Fair Play, MO. After LaVerne died, Obediah married Margaret Vest on Feb. 22, 1905 in Polk County, MO and moved to Nebraska. Obediah died on Sept. 8, 1951 in Plattsmouth, NE.

Per Clarence Allen: Doriada, Rhoda, Bertha, LaVerne and John are buried in Barren Creek

Cemetery. Since many graves have unmarked stone markers or no markers at all, this fact can't be verified and according to the church caretaker, the church records were destroyed in a fire about 40 years ago.

William "Connie" Ashlock was born on Aug. 23, 1894. He married Pearl Tuttle on Oct. 19, 1919. He lived in California until his death on April 1, 1977. Both Connie and his father, Obediah, are buried in E Union Cemetery in Nebraska.

Elva Belle Ashlock was born on Dec. 24, 1896 in Cliquot, MO. She was born on Dec. 24, 1896. She married Ernest "Palmer" Crain on Dec. 19, 1920 in Aldrich, MO. Palmer was born on Aug. 24, 1890 in Aldrich, Polk County, MO to Nelson and Emily Louise (Rotrock) Crain. Elva and Palmer operated a restaurant in Aldrich, MO. They had two children, Richard and Edith "Florence." After Elva died on Jan. 12, 1929, Palmer and the children moved in with Emily and she helped raise the two small children. Palmer, Elva and Emily are buried in Pleasant Ridge Cemetery.

Richard Crain was born in Aldrich, MO and married Dorothy Bean, the daughter of Edwin and Lucille (Marshall) Bean. They had one daughter, Carmen. Richard also had a son, Richard Jr., by his second wife Ethel Maxine Street.

Florence Crain was born in Aldrich, MO and married Curtis "Mac" McDaniel, the son of Grover and Katie "Peters" McDaniel. They moved to the Kansas City area and had one daughter, Karen. *Submitted by Florence McDaniel*

AMMERMAN – Sanford Ammerman was born Aug. 12, 1815 in Bourbon County, KY, son of Isaac Ammerman and Jenny Johnston, daughter of Robert Johnston. Isaac was the son of Philip Ammerman and Mary Francis Hibler of New Jersey, Pennsylvania, Maryland and Kentucky.

About 1818, before Missouri became a state, Isaac and family moved from Kentucky to the area of Montgomery County that became Warren County.

By 1839 the family had crossed the Missouri River and were living in the area of Gasconade County that later was Osage and then Maries County. In Gasconade County on May 23, 1839, Sanford married Susan Aubrey. Their only child was Josephus. Susan died and about 1851, Sanford married Rebecca (Newberry) Ramsey. They had three daughters: Susan, Jane and Belle.

They came to Polk County about 1855 and settled in Marion Township, two miles east of Bolivar.

Sanford died Sept. 12, 1883 and was buried in Bolivar City Cemetery. Rebecca died Dec. 5, 1915, age 91, and was buried by Sanford.

Susan Parilee married Jehue Dean and died about two years later, in 1885.

Nancy Jane married Richard A. Baldwin. Children: Pearl E. (Barnett) and Chloe R. (Payne).

Pauline Belle married Marcus A. McCracken. Children: Allie L. (Tompkins), Joseph C., Neita (Pitts Long), S. Ray, Virgil S., Gladys M. (Squibb), infant son.

Josephus "Joe" Ammerman was born July 3, 1842 in Gasconade County. He served three years in Company A, 8th Regiment, State Militia Cavalry and was very active in the GAR. He was elected Bolivar's City Marshall in April 1881 and later served as police judge. He was a member of the last grand jury that met in the old courthouse about 1905.

Sometime after his death, T. H. B. Dunnegan wrote, "Since the death of Comrade Josephus Ammerman there is no one left who know who were soldiers of the Civil War and other wars buried in the city and Greenwood Cemeteries."

Josephus married Elizabeth J. Peters (born 1841; died Feb. 24, 1897), daughter of Volantine Peters and Mary Allison from Greene County, TN. They had six children.

Buenavista E. married Ottoman C. Odor and had Mattie (Brown).

Sanford Aubury married Sarah D. Lloyd and had William J., Phillip, Jesse Sanford, Rome, Robert, Iva E. (Reynolds), Beuanesta, Sarah (married Bonnie Pike), Ernest O. and Lloyd T.

Joseph Henry Ammerman (born Sept. 19, 1870; died March 21, 1925) married Emma Mae Sims (born May 6, 1871; died Oct. 22, 1958) daughter of Thomas A. Sims (d. 1890, buried Bolivar City Cemetery) and America McCammack. Their children were: Lucy and Mae, died single; Claude O. (married Maggie Summers); Joe F. (married Mae Vaughn); J. Henry (married Julia Brich); Bertie M. (married Millis Zidlicky); Emma M. (married Wayne Sterling); Ethel Mary (married Albert Griffin).

Susan M. married E. C. Snapp and moved away.

Elizabeth "Jennie" married Ernest O. Gill. They lived in Sterling, CO and had four children.

Clem B. married Harry S. Jones, also lived in Sterling and had two children.

Josephus married second. Louisa J. Mounce (born March 4, 1873; died Jan. 20, 1954). They had three children.

James B. married Winnie Waggoner. They had Irene (Westherwax), James D., Betty (Anderson), Billy, Gloria (Weatherwax) and Robert N.

Robert Todd married Alice May Sharp.

Augusta A. married Willard T. Wrinkle. Both are buried in Redding, CA. They had Dixie (Payne), Beryl G., Jack H., Shirley A. (Church), Norma L. (Culbertson), Willard T. and Sharron K. (Bradley).

Josephus died Feb. 7, 1922 and was buried in Greenwood Cemetery where five generations of the Ammerman family are buried. *Submitted by Jim A. Ammerman*

Bessie and Lloyd Anderson

ANDERSON – Bessie Coren Renfro was the first child of Thomas Asbury Renfro and Ellen Eliza Pierce Drake Renfro.

She was born Dec. 4, 1904 in Morrisville, MO and died on Sept. 26, 1973. She and her husband are both buried in Slagle Cemetery near Morrisville, MO.

She met and married Lloyd Arthyr Anderson in Bolivar, MO on Aug. 3, 1925. Lloyd is the son of David Anderson and Susan Cossins Anderson. He was born Sept. 23, 1903 and died Nov. 27, 1985. To this union two sons and one daughter were born. Lloyd Arthyr Anderson Jr., better known as "Windy," was their firstborn. He married Mary Cruso. They had one son, Ronald Owen. Windy married Frances Rife Dugan on July 3, 1953. She had a son, Larry Dugan, and a daughter, Patty Dugan. They loved each other very much and soon loved the stepchildren as their own. Windy was born Aug. 7, 1926 in Cheyenne Well, CO and died in Kansas City, MO on Feb. 13, 1982 and is buried in Pleasant Valley Cemetery in Stanley, KS. Francis was born Oct. 22, 1920 and passed away April 11, 1997, at Greenfield, MO. She is also buried at Stanley, KS beside her husband, Windy.

James Wilbert Anderson was born Sept. 9, 1929 and died Aug. 22, 1954. He is buried at Slagle Cemetery. He always enjoyed being around Uncle Joe (Steele) and would do anything to please him. Joe also liked Wilbert very much and would kid him a lot just to see him smile. When Wilbert was 5 years old in 1934, Lloyd and Bessie returned to Morrisville from Colorado. His lungs were full, like honeycomb with dust from Dust Bowl. He had a serious operation in the Humansville Hospital, taking half of his shoulder blade and injuring his spine. His mind was like a 7-year-old all the rest of his life. He loved chicken, toys and to build fences. We all loved him deeply.

Mary Ellen Anderson was their only daughter. She was born Sept. 1, 1934 in Cheyenne Wells, CO. She attended Raymore High School in Raymore, MO. She graduated in 1953; she was baptized at Stockton Lake, along with her children, in 1971.

Mary Ellen and J. T. Moore were married on Nov. 15, 1952 in Bentonville, AR. Bessie Anderson, Charles Moore and Jeanette Steele accompanied them and when they returned, Mary Steele had baked a cake for them and had a wedding gift waiting. She told them she had done this for a very special niece and told J. T. she and Joe were glad to have another nephew.

To this union four children were born: three sons and one daughter. Sharon Kay was their first child. She was married to James Edward Belcher and they had one son, Jeremy and one daughter, Kim. Danny Ray was married to Margarite Smith. They had one daughter, Steffeny and one son, Justin. David Lee is married to Betty Winkler. They had one son, Brandon and one daughter, Amy. Robert Jay is married to Connie Thomas. They had one daughter, Crystal and one son, Lance. Danny, David, Robert and J. T. have all served in the United States Army. *Submitted by Mary Ellen Anderson Moore*

ANDERSON – Jordan A. Anderson came to Polk County, MO with his father William Anderson and grandfather John Anderson, about 1837 from Memphis, TN, settling on Turnback Creek in what is now Dade County. Many of the children of John Anderson also came to Polk County with them.

The children of John Anderson and unknown wife were James (born Feb. 6, 1809); William (born April 19, 1811); Elizabeth (born Feb. 18, 1814); Mathew (born Jan. 24, 1816); Matilda (born Nov. 26, 1819); July (? Suly) (born Dec. 20, 1820); Andrew (born Sept. 11, 1822); Alexander (born Dec. 19, 1823) and Christopher (born Oct. 20, 1825).

John Anderson married Elizabeth Smith in Polk County on Oct. 28, 1840. It is not known what happened to John and Elizabeth after this.

Jordan A. and Mary Elizabeth Watkins Anderson taken in Polk County, MO in 1905

119

Various records for William, Elizabeth, Mathew and Matilda are found in Polk County.

William married Mary Coggins, place and date unknown. Their children were John Alexander (born about 1829); Jordan A. (born Sept. 15, 1832); Andrew Jackson "Jack" (born Dec. 25, 1839); and Robert Allen (born March 27, 1840). William died before Jan. 7, 1840, before Robert was born. Mary married Allen Berton or Burton, Dec. 20, 1845 in Polk County, MO. To this union were born Sarah M. (born about 1849); Susan (born about 1853); Elizabeth (born about 1856); Parthena (born about 1859). Mary later moved to Kansas where she died.

Jordan and his brother John went to California in 1850 to work in the gold fields. Their brothers Andrew "Jack" and Robert Allen went to Chico, CA in 1858 traveling by oxen team.

After returning to Missouri, Jordan married Mary Elizabeth Watkins Sept. 6, 1855 in Polk County. They homesteaded, raised their family and died in Madison Township, Polk County. Jordan and Mary had 15 children, all born in Polk County. They are Mary Elizabeth (married Robert J. Reeves); Robert A. (married Kisiarah J. Hensely, they lived in Polk County, MO); John Thomas (married Malissa A. Estes); Francis (born about 1860; deceased while young); Susan C. (married Henry Woods); William H. (married Mary R. Potts; she died in Polk County); James H. (married Jossie Burns and went to California); Nancy A. (married Marshall Wakefeld; Nancy died in Polk County); Phillip M. (went to California and married Laura); George W. (married Sarah F. Ware and lived one mile east of Fair Play, Polk County until he died; Sarah then married Oren Glispey and in 1916 went to Oklahoma, traveling in a covered wagon; they had four children: Lela, Cleta, Oral, all born in Fair Play, MO and Harrold, (who was born after they moved to Oklahoma); Charles W. (died in Polk County); Drewy (died in Polk County); Solly A. (lived in Polk County in 1917 and in 1936 he lived in Flint, MI); there were two unnamed children. *Submitted by William L. Anderson*

Front: Sue, Mary and Phyllis; Back: Eugenia, Virginia, Rolla, Sam, Marcene, and Irene.

ANDERSON – William Wilson Anderson and Martha Staples Anderson, with their family of small children, left Hart County, KY in October 1878, reaching Humansville after 30 days on the road. There were four wagons in the train; David Curtis Anderson and two of his sons each drove wagons. Foster Anderson, a half-brother of Wilson, came with the group on horseback.

Wilson and Martha settled near Humansville, north of what is now the racetrack. Not too long after they arrived, Wilson passed away and the mother was left with her family: Sally, Joe, Jack, Samuel and Fanny. They all lived near Humansville until they were grown, then drifted to other parts of the country.

Sam remained near town and took a keen interest in Humansville. He was a member of the IOOF earning his 50-year pin. He also served on the special road district as clerk and commissioner. The Reverend Lynch united him in marriage Feb. 10, 1962 at the Christian Church parsonage to Mary L. Purdin.

Mary came from north Missouri being born near Purdin, in Linn County, MO. Mary later moved to a farm just south of Humansville with her parents, C. O. Purdin and Iona Brown Purdin. The Purdins lived there until their deaths. They are buried in the Humansville City Cemetery.

Seven children were born to Samuel and Mary Anderson, one son and six daughters. Rolla E. served in Italy during WWII and was employed at the Humansville Post Office. He lived south of town with his wife Juanita Kester Anderson and their four children: Samuel David, Steven Rolla, Karla Kay and Brien Allan.

Virginia married Eldon Warren and lived near Polk, MO with their three children: Rex Eldon, Vanette Dee, and Cynthia Lee.

Eugenia, Virginia's identical twin, married L. D. Hale and they also lived near Polk with their four sons: David Lynn, Robert Eugene, Donald Ray and Joe Wayne.

Phyllis married Rolin Howard of Buffalo. They have one daughter, Cindy Sue, and made their home in Lee's Summit, MO.

Irene married Joe Tinsley and lived on a farm east of Humansville with their three daughters: Ella Jean, Vonna Marie and Kathryn Ann.

Marcene, Irene's fraternal twin sister, married Paul Steffens of Gaddes, SD. They lived on a farm east of Humansville with their six children: Paula Sue, Joseph Glenn, Debra Irene, Gary Jacob, Michael Eugene and Linda Kay.

Martha Sue married Allan Garretson. They lived near Humansville with their children: Edwin Dean, Judy Lynn and John Dale. Sue had a flower and gift ship in Humansville for some time. She now owns a flea market in Humansville.

The Anderson family had always been active in church and community affairs. They always try to work for the good of their town and community.

Samuel Anderson passed away July 14, 1953. After her husband's death, Mary lived with her son Rolla until her death on Feb. 18, 1982. Both Samuel and Mary are buried in the Humansville City Cemetery. *Submitted by Irene Tinsley*

Jerald, Jane and Cletis Andrews; Raymond Wilson (milkman)

ANDREWS – Cletis and Jane Andrews moved to a farm about five miles west of Bolivar when their child, Jerald was 2 years old. The place was the first road west of the "S" curve on Highway 32. It consisted of 220 acres that was one of the Ray Engledow places. The neighbors were Mr. Delaney, who had a wonderful grape vineyard and a cellar that was visited when it would storm; Mr. Dozer, who lived on the road by himself; and Stanley Salama, who lived with his sister Sophia Novak. Stanley and Sophia drove a 1926 Model T Ford, farmed with two horses and had no electricity.

When the folks moved there, Cletis started milking in a typical large hay barn and sold Grade C milk. Carl Sterling, the owner of the place, agreed to build a Grade A milk barn for a portion of the increased milk prices over the Grade C price. He sold milk to Houk Dairy and around 1960, Houk sold out and he bought a 400-gallon stainless steel Paul Mueller bulk tank and began selling to Daricraft. In the mid 1960s he bought a Surge pipeline milk. He worked long hours but never complained. He was named the Polk County Young Farmer of the Year in 1955.

Jane raised hundreds of chickens and would kill, dress and sell them. It was quite a sight to watch her lay a chicken on the ground, put its head under her foot and pull it off. The chicken would flop around, spraying blood everywhere until it bled to death. Jane also picked up walnuts every year. One year she sold enough to buy Jerald a Lionel train set for Christmas. When the garment factory opened in Bolivar she went to work there, as did many farm wives.

Trips to town were made every Saturday. Stops were made at MFA to pick up feed supplies, Houk Dairy to receive the milk check and to buy buttermilk, and various other places where business needed to be conducted prior to securing a parking place on the square where visiting Grandma Andrews would occur. A trip inside Rexall would result in a cherry coke. A visit to Blue's or Newport's dime stores would be the highlight of the trip. Much to Jane's disdain a walk up the street to one of the pool halls would take place to see Grandpa Andrews. The grocery store always required a visit on the way home so the ice cream would not melt.

Although long hours of work were put in daily, an entertainment trip consisted of going to the Lucky 13 Drive-In. The folks would dress Jerald in his pajamas, pop a tub of popcorn and arrive just before dusk. Jerald would often fall asleep shortly after the cartoon. A real treat would be a brief fishing trip on a day to wet too work in the fields. A favorite activity was to visit Mother's parents, Audie and Thelma Turner who lived on Morrisville Road. They had a great farm pond where fish were caught with a cane pole as fast as the hook could be baited.

Life for a young boy on a farm west of Bolivar seemed about perfect. It was a simpler time and a simpler way of life that was preparing children for a much more complex time and way of life. *Submitted by Jerald L. Andrews*

Back row: Carl, Vincent and Harold
Middle row: Pearl, Ray, John, Rolland and Joe
Front row: Roscoe, Mary and Martha, 1934

ANDREWS – The Ray Burnside Andrews and Josie Pearl Franklin family began with the marriage of Ray and "Pearl" (as she was known) on March 9, 1913. They were both natives of west of Urbana, MO, in Hickory County. Ray was the son of Mark L. and Mary P. "Mollie" French Andrews and brother of May Brunner (Wilber), Mary Brown (George), Amanda Holt (Lester), Zada Wilton (Justin), Emma Little (Andy), Lawton and William "Bill." Four siblings died in infancy. They are buried at Rondo Cemetery, Polk County, MO. Ray was born Feb. 19, 1889, west of Urbana in Hickory County.

Back row: Roscoe, Rolland, Joe, John and Vincent
Front row: Harold, Martha, Mary and Carl, 1977

Pearl was born March 4, 1894 to Benjamin Basil "Duke" and Amanda Carver Franklin in Hickory County, west of Urbana, MO. Her siblings were Grace L. Barnes (Kyle), Maude Richards (Jim) and Zelda Franklin (Ivor, __ Reagan, Ira Ezzell). Pearl died Jan. 1, 1975. Their first of nine children, Carl, was born Feb. 14, 1914 at Urbana; Harold (born 1916); Vincent (born 1918); John (born 1920); Joe (born 1923); Rolland (born 1925); Roscoe (born 1927) and twins, Mary and Martha (born 1931).

Ray and Pearl lived all of their married life in or near Flemington, MO, except about the first two years with Ray's parents west of Urbana, MO.

Ray was well known for his meticulous carpentry, concrete, stucco, and brickwork ability. Numerous structures and houses still stand strong and straight. Ray was a strict family disciplinarian with his family but was always ready to help a neighbor and always generous to those in need.

Peal was a hardworking, kind and loving mother who enjoyed visiting her neighbors. She would walk as much as two miles to visit. She always had a large garden. Canning and preserving in the summer and butchering hogs in the winter were ways to keep a large family fed. The summers were busy with putting hay in the barns, threshing grain crews going from farm to farm, neighbors helping neighbors, the women preparing the noon meals and sometimes supper. That is what they called the evening meal.

When the United States was forced to become involved in WWII that changed their family forever, as it did a lot of families in and around Flemington and the whole country. All of those sons of Ray and Pearl were at the right age to be called into service. Some had not completed their high school yet but soon would. It wasn't long before Ray and Pearl would have five sons in the military service all at one time. This was rather unique in itself. Vincent and Rolland served in the Navy; John as a sergeant in the Air Corps; Joe and Harold in the Army. They served their country proudly and well. Ray and Pearl were reminded everyday by the flag in the window with the five stars on it that their sons were in possible peril. WWII would change their lives in other ways, too. They would meet their companions in life. They married, making homes in New York, Iowa and California.

As this history is being written, three boys and two girls are still living; Martha being the only family member living in Missouri.

The early family history of Ray and Pearl can be traced back to 1600 and 1700. The Franklin family has been traced back to the Higginbotham and Graves family, early settlers in New England, coming to Missouri from Kentucky. The Andrews family arrived in Dallas County, MO around 1840 from Virginia. Ray and Pearl's marriage certificate is filed in Polk County, MO. They are buried at the Rondo Cemetery in Polk County, MO. *Submitted by Martha Andrews Morrison (Mrs. Kenneth)*

Apperson family in front of their house: Willie P., Richard holding Sarah E., Susan, Anna M., Ophelia, Nettie C., Florence, Della and in front Charles W. with the wagon.

APPERSON – Richard Benjamin Apperson was born on Nov. 24, 1855 in Tennessee. After the close of the Civil War, his parents moved to Slagle in Polk County, MO. They were Richard and Catherine Apperson. Richard Benjamin died on Aug. 21, 1936.

Susan Elizabeth Safrit was born on May 5, 1857 in North Carolina and died on June 4, 1947. Her parents were Moses Safrit and Christina Misenheimer Kluttz Safrit. Moses Safrit was a private in Company 16, 5th Regiment of the North Carolina Infantry. He was wounded at Gettysburg and died in the enemy hospital there on July 17, 1863. Christina later married Jacob Rymer and they also migrated to Polk County.

After their marriage, Richard Benjamin and Susan Elizabeth Apperson lived on their 300-acre farm three miles north of Pleasant Hope on the Pomme de Terre River. Their children were: Willie P., Sarah E., Anna M., Ophelia, Nettie C., Florence, Della, Charles W., Cora E and Ruth. Richard and Susan are buried in the Pleasant Hope Cemetery. *Submitted by Carolyn Peine*

James and Nancy (Lane) Appleby

APPLEBY – James Appleby and Nancy Lane Bond were married April 7, 1840 in Polk County, MO. James was born March 15, 1801 in Georgia and moved with his parents to Tennessee in 1810. He was the son of John Appleby (born Dec. 21, 1778; died April 6, 1863) and Sarah Bell (born June 8, 1772; died Dec. 8, 1852). They were married March 18, 1800 and are buried in Bethbirei Presbyterian Church Cemetery in Lewisburg, Marshall County, TN. Nancy was born Feb. 4, 1818 in Tennessee, the daughter of Tandy Lane, born April 18, 1788 and died Nov. 13, 1866. It is said Tandy fought at the battle of New Orleans as a major under Colonel Jackson. He is buried in the Appleby Cemetery near Morrisville, MO.

James' first marriage was to Syntha S. McMurray on Feb. 2, 1826. Syntha was born Jan. 16, 1804; died May 10, 1839 and is buried in the Appleby Cemetery. They had seven children. Nancy was married before to Amon Bond who died in a hunting accident. They had two daughters. James and Nancy had eight children, so between them they had 17 children. Their names are Andrew M., John B., Elizabeth C., Benjamin W., Samuel J., Sarah C., Eliza F., Elizabeth Jane Bond, Mary Emaline Bond, William Robert, Jemina E., Amanda M., James M., Nancy Josephine, Eagleton Argile, Margaret Isabell "Maggie" (born Jan. 29, 1855; died April 8, 1931) and Sintha O.

Margaret Isabell Appleby was Carol's great-grandmother. She married Marvel Preston Mitchell on Christmas Day 1881. He was from Everton, Dade County, MO and the son of James Cannon Mitchell and Matilda J. (Wickliff) Mitchell. Marvel was born Dec. 30, 1851 in Grainger County, TN and died Feb. 10, 1926 at Eureka, Greenwood County, KS. Margaret and Marvel had three children: Bell A. Mitchell, born 1884 near Everton, MO and died in 1902 of typhoid fever in Eureka, Greenwood County, KS; Cynthia Veda Mitchell, born Jan. 14, 1866 near Everton, MO and died Jan. 10, 1977 at Hamilton, Greenwood County, KS. She married Robert Stoker Ross in 1909 at Eureka, KS and they had one son, Robert M. Ross, born April 24, 1918 at Eminence, MO, died Aug. 20, 1995 at Hamilton, KS. Marvel and Margaret moved to Greenwood County, KS in 1886 and their third child, Carol's grandfather Benjamin Eugene Mitchell was born Oct. 24, 1888 and died Oct. 20, 1972. He married Ruby Irene Standiferd on Christmas Day 1923. She was born Aug. 23, 1891 and died Feb. 16, 1974, the daughter of David James Standiferd and Ida Augusta (Umdenstock) Standiferd.

They had three sons. Merle S. Mitchell was born March 19, 1926 and died July 28, 1996; married Eda F. Matlock and their children were Standiferd and Douglas.

Wilbur Eugene Mitchell was born July 4, 1927 and died July 13, 1970; married Beverly Lou Harvey and their children were Susan, Julie, Rebecca, and Carol's father, James Preston Mitchell, who was born Aug. 23, 1930; married Violet Beverly Tucker on June 20, 1952. Their children are Carol, Ray and Kenneth. James and Syntha Appleby and their family moved from Tennessee to Springfield, Greene County, MO in 1833 and he had a blacksmith shop on the square. Between 1836 and 1839 they moved to Polk County, MO. He also farmed and raised horses. Family legend says that in the Civil War when they heard either army was coming they would hide their silver under the stairs and all the good stock in the woods and let the armies take the old horses, chickens, cows, hogs, etc. James died Feb. 21, 1869 and is buried in the Appleby Cemetery near Morrisville, MO. Nancy came to live with her daughter, Maggie Mitchell, in Kansas in 1888. It is told she would ride a horse to town to sell eggs. She then went to live her daughter Amanda in Sedan, OK. She died April 15, 1909 and is buried in Elmwood, Kiowa County, OK Cemetery. Benjamin Appleby was a judge. Samuel died in a sawmill explosion. William Robert fought at Vicksburg under General Grant. After the war he became a doctor. He married Mary E. Wheeler Aug. 9, 1868. They had a daughter, Lulu. Mary died and he married Laura Emma Ross May 1, 1895. He is buried in Hamilton, Greenwood County, KS. Jemima married James Anderson. Amanda married W. N. C. Fox; they had a son, Bob. Argile lived to be 93 and died when his car pinned him against a wall in his garage. Carol's father remembers seeing him several times. *Submitted by Carol (Mitchell) Waterman*

APPLEBY – William Appleby was born about 1742 in Northern Ireland and died about 1807 in Williamson County, TN. William married Elizabeth McKeehan first and then his second wife was Nancy Agnes McCurdy, probably born in Pennsylvania. Children were David, Nancy, Samuel B., Mary "Polly," and Rebecca. The descending line is David Appleby, born Nov. 4, 1788 at Newville, Cumberland County, PA and died Oct. 15, 1867 in Springfield, Greene County, MO. He married Catherine Bell, Sept. 9, 1813 in Jackson County, GA. She was born Sept. 29, 1782 in North Carolina, and died Sept. 29, 1866 in Springfield, Greene County, MO. Both are buried in Bellview Cemetery in Greene County, MO. Their children were Ammanda Ann, William Alfred, Margaret Arminta "Minty," James Newton, Nancy M., Sarah M. "Sallie" and John Quincy Appleby. A biography of David in the Greene County, MO History says he was the first teacher in the rural Springfield, MO area and for 32 years he was an Elder in the Presbyterian Church. John Quincy Appleby was born July 9, 1825 in Bedford County, TN and died June 11, 1896 in Cedar Vale, KS. He married Margaret Jane McCracken June 17, 1847 and divorced about 1865. She was born May 26, 1824 in Williamson County, TN and died July 16, 1922 in Greene County, MO and was buried in Bellview Cemetery. Her parents were Thomas McCracken, 1778-1859, and Elizabeth Homes, 1788-1870. Their children were Albert Barnes, Thomas Newton, Margaret Matilda Ann, Samuel David and Robert Lyttle. John Quincy had a second spouse, Sarah Jane Wade.

Roscoe Ross Appleby and Ora Elizabeth Sneed, wedding picture 1909

Samuel David Appleby was born Sept. 16, 1855 in Greene County, MO and died Jan. 6, 1922 in Greene County, MO and is buried in Bellview. He married Sarah Elizabeth Kite, Jan. 24, 1877 in Greene County, MO. Sarah was born May 6, 1854. Her parents were Benjamin Kite (1822-1896) and Mary S. Gott (1830-1896), both born in Kentucky. Samuel and Sarah's children were John Benjamin, James Albert, Roscoe Ross, Ellen, Rhoda, Flossie, Lincoln, Mary, Clara, Samuel, Jane and Elsie.

Roscoe Ross Appleby was born Sept. 9, 1881 and died June 21, 1949. He married Ora Elizabeth Sneed, Aug. 25, 1909 in Greene County, MO. Her parents are Mollie Knox Sneed and Philip Sneed. She was born Aug. 6, 1888 and died March 3, 1971. They lived in Willard, MO. Their children were Roy Sneed, Joseph Lee, Rex Wilson, Sarah Marie, and Mary Jane.

Roy Sneed Appleby was born July 21, 1910 in Willard, Greene County, MO and died Jan. 9, 1993 in Bolivar, Polk County, MO. He married Iona Mae "Bobbie" Jarvis, daughter of Thomas Jefferson Jarvis and Mary Elizabeth Cody. Bobbie was born Oct. 31, 1911 in Sneedville, Hancock County, TN and died January 1988. They are both buried at Crestview Memorial Gardens in Polk County. Children are Robert Eugene, Anna Marie, Paul Thomas, Johnny Joe and Sherry Lynn.

Robert Eugene Appleby was born Oct. 18, 1930 in Ashland, Clark County, KS and died Sept. 14, 1973 in Bolivar, Polk County, MO and is buried in Crestview Memorial Gardens. He married Dolores Jean Ritter March 5, 1951 in Greensburg, KS, daughter of Miller Perryman Ritter and Anna Mae Crane. She was born Sept. 22, 1933. Children are Teresa Susan, Robert Roy and Dana Jean. *Submitted by Robert Appleby*

Landon S. and Victoria Josephine Headlee Parrish

ARMOUR – Washington Armour, born 1804 in Georgia, died Sept. 3, 1852, and is buried in Pleasant Hope Cemetery, married Nancy Scott Kerr, born Dec. 14, 1804 in North Carolina, died February 1893, and is buried on farm of son, Robert A. Armour. They married Jan. 25, 1827, probably Giles County, TN. Amour is on the 1840 census for Giles County, TN. He is in Greene County, MO for 1850 census, age 46, born in Georgia. They were living next door to their daughter, Caleb and Dovey Headlee.

Jane Katheryn, (born Dec. 12, 1827; died Aug. 19, 1910 in Pratt County, KS) married Thomas Patterson July 13, 1848 in Greene County, MO.

Dovey L. (born Jan. 9, 1830 in Giles County, TN) married July 12, 1849 in Greene County, MO to Dr. Caleb Nuton Headlee (born June 27, 1827 in Maury County, TN; died Aug. 22, 1898, buried in Nevada, MO). Caleb was the son of Caleb Headlee and Mary "Mollie" Steele.

Nancy Emily Louisa (born May 10, 1832; died April 12, 1917, in Greene County, MO) married Samuel W. Headlee May 2, 1855 in Polk County, MO. Samuel was a state representative.

Robert Alcorn (born March 12, 1834 in Tennessee; died Jan. 18, 1901) married Eunice Headlee April 22, 1856 in Greene County, MO.

Frances A. Martha (born Nov. 19, 1835) married Francis M. Shockley May 7, 1854 in Polk County, MO.

Rachel J. C. (born Sept. 27, 1838 in Tennessee; died Oct. 30, 1852) is buried in Pleasant Hope Cemetery.

Caleb studied medicine, then moved to Marion County, AR in 1859-1864/5. He is in the 1860 census in Arkansas. He returned to Springfield but after a short time moved to Pleasant Hope where he won an enviable reputation as a medical practitioner. In 1880 he began selling apothecary medicine. He and Dovey had eight children, three died young.

Nuton Jr. was born July 10, 1850 and died Oct. 24, 1863.

Victoria Josephine was born June 1, 1854 and died Jan. 4, 1908; buried Reed Cemetery, married Landon Sanders Parrish on Feb. 2, 1875.

Alice J. was born Sept. 27, 1856 and died Oct. 18, 1862.

Mary O. was born Feb. 5, 1859 and died March 2, 1893 in Greene County, MO and married Garry H. Hoobler.

Melville P. was born March 5, 1861 and married Mariah E. Kerr Nov. 9, 1894.

Emmet B. was born Nov. 24, 1863 and died Dec. 16, 1863.

Nancy Lulu was born Feb. 20, 1865 and married J. Frank Porter.

Arminios Elmer was born Oct. 10, 1871 and died Nov. 3, 1966 in Monte Vista, CO, and married Maude Tucker June 16, 1890.

Landon Sanders Parrish was born Aug. 18, 1850 in Polk County, MO, died Nov. 26, 1924, buried Reed Cemetery. His parents were Barnett P. Parrish and Emiline Wright. He was a farmer and very involved in the Masonic Lodge at Halfway. He married Victoria Headlee. Their children were Jessie Ophelia (born Jan. 17, 1878; died Jan. 12, 1950 in Polk County) married Edward Lewis Voris Dec. 27, 1896; Edna Louelle (born March 9, 1876; died Sept. 27, 1944) married Ernest Wolfe in 1899; and Bonnie (born Jan. 21, 1889; died Jan. 22, 1899 in Polk County).

Landon was a farmer. He lived with Jessie and Ed Voris family for more than 16 years after his wife died.

Children of Ed and Jessie Voris:

Guy (born Jan. 17, 1898; died Jan. 22, 1898) buried in Reed Cemetery;

Hazel L. (born Nov. 4, 1899; died Oct. 16, 1986 in Cedar County), married Ezra Towner "Dick" Walker Dec. 30, 1930 in Sidney, NE;

Morris (born March 25, 1903; died May 17, 1945 in Port Renfrew, British Columbia, Canada) married Dorothy Helen Walker Aug. 26, 1929 in Anaheim, CA and they had James Edward Hamilton and Julie Dorothy who married Wilf Hanshaw in 1958; they live in Campbell River, British Columbia, Canada;

Catherine (born Oct. 8, 1906; died Nov. 11, 1906);

John Mose (born Aug. 31, 1910; died Oct. 20, 1991 in Bolivar, MO) married Lillian McKinney July 16, 1932 and their children are Twyla who married Leland Stewart in 1954, Derrell who married Mary Jane Thomas, and Judy Johnson in 1999; they live in Springfield and Kenny who married Carol Wenman and Susan Lash in 1995; they live in Elkland, MO.

Wade Wallace (born July 30, 1914; died Oct. 25, 1996 in Greene County, MO) married Geneice Gorden on July 3, 1938. Wade and Geneice lived on a farm near Halfway and were married for 56 years. He enjoyed antique tractors and she had a reputation for making the best chocolate pies. Their children: Larry married Hazel Dulin in 1958, they have Voris Hydraulics, Inc. in Springfield; Jerry Wade married Linda Wagoner in 1971, he is retired from Ammco Oil and is Pastor of Discipleship at Evergreen Baptist Church in Tulsa, OK; Wilby Dean married Mary Ballew in 1970, he is a rural mail carrier, they live in Halfway on Gorden property. *Submitted by Wilby Dean Voris*

ARMSTRONG – James Armstrong was born Sept. 9, 1830 in Hawkins County, TN and died March 15, 1913 in Bolivar, Polk County, MO. He is buried at Union Grove Cemetery in Polk County, MO. James arrived in Polk County about 1850 from Knoxville, TN along with his parents, Samuel (born Aug. 12, 1792 – died March 12, 1867) and Margaret Armstrong (born Aug. 22, 1804-5; died Aug. 8, 1892). Both parents are buried in the Pleasant Hope Cemetery in Polk County, MO. They purchased land in the southeast part of Polk County, MO and owned slaves according to records. Other children

James Armstrong and Sarah Clementine Donnell Armstrong

of Samuel and Margaret were Abner, Hannibal, Margaret Jane (Gillenwaters), Sarah C. (Cowden), and Lydia Ann (Burns).

James Armstrong married first Mrs. Cynthia D. Wills on Sept. 20, 1855. She died Aug. 30, 1862. Two children were born to this union: Violey Victoria (born Oct. 5, 1859) and Margaret Jane (born Sept. 9, 1857—died 1919). Victoria Armstrong married first George W. Kepley on Jan. 4, 1883. One child was born to this union, Maud C. Kepley, born May 17, 1884. George W. Kepley was born Sept. 13, 1856 and died May 15, 1885. He is buried in the Union Grove Cemetery, near Pleasant Hope, MO. Victoria Armstrong Kepley married second. A. M. Vanderford on Oct. 12, 1892. One son was born, Jonah M. Vanderford. The family eventually moved to Kansas and are buried there. Margaret Jane Armstrong married first, John J. Goodnight (born Sept. 8, 1833—died Jan. 7, 1894). One son was born and died in infancy, James E. Goodnight. Margaret Armstrong Goodnight married second. Immanuel Clint Summers. Margaret died in 1919 and is buried in the Reed Cemetery. Halfway, MO.

James Armstrong married second. Sarah Clementine Donnell on July 28, 1863. Sarah Clementine was the daughter of John Donnell and a step-sister to Cynthia D. Wills. Sarah Clementine was born March 4, 1844 and died May 29, 1924 in the home of her son, Sterling. She was buried in the Union Grove Cemetery in Polk County, MO. There were five children born to this union: Marien (died young); Sterling Webster; Charles E. (died young); John William; Sarah Alice; and Mary Frances "Mae." James Armstrong was a farmer and raised horses.

He lived in the Pleasant Hope, Wishart and Bolivar communities. James served in the 26th Regiment, E. M. M. Company during the Civil War.

Sterling Webster Armstrong married Teresa "Ressie" Alice Vanderford on April 27, 1892. She was the daughter of John A. and Mary Woodle Vanderford. Ressie's parents lived southeast of Halfway when the couple married. Sterling, from the Pleasant Hope, MO area, had rented a farm just east of the Reed Cemetery and had his recently widowed half-sister, Victoria Armstrong Kepley, and her little girl keeping house for him. One day, while he was plowing in a field next to the road, he noticed that a young girl was having a difficult time with a run away mare. He ran out to the road and stopped the runaway. The girl was to be his bride one day. He often said, "He had to wait for Ressie to grow up old enough to be married." Later in the year of 1892, Ressie's brother, A. M. Vanderford, married Sterling's half-sister, Victoria Armstrong Kepley.

Sterling was born June 28, 1866 and died June 24, 1956. Ressie was born Feb. 8, 1874 and died Aug. 4, 1938. Both are buried in the Greenwood Cemetery in Bolivar, MO. Sterling and Ressie were Missionary Baptists. Sterling was ordained to be a deacon while he was a member of Campbell Missionary Baptist Church. His last membership was with Star Ridge Missionary Baptist Church in Van, MO. Sterling and Ressie were the parents of 13 children: G. A., James Paul, Mary Lucille, Raymond McClain, Leland Earl, Helen Marie, William Roy, Vera Berniece, Anna Mae, Ralph Glenwood, Lula Cornelia, Ada Clementine and Eva Mildred.

John William married first, Ella M. Keeling on Oct. 19, 1892 – three children: Glen O., Leo and Wilma (twins). This marriage ended in divorce. John William married second to Susie Marshall on Nov. 7, 1920. They were the parents of one son, John William Jr. John and Susie Armstrong are buried in Oklahoma.

Sarah A. Armstrong married John C. Mullings on Nov. 22, 1893; children were Olga, Don, Gaines, Sam, Jesse, Nora, Wayne and George. John and Sarah Mullings lived most of their married life in the Pleasant Hope, MO area. They are buried in the Union Grove Cemetery southeast of Pleasant Hope, MO.

The youngest daughter, Mary Frances "Mae" Armstrong, married Fred Byersdorf on July 3, 1900. They were the parents of one child, Donald L. Byersdorf (born 1903). Fred and Mae Byersdorf lived all of their married life in the state of Washington and are buried in that state. *Submitted by Berniece Armstrong Jenkins*

ARMSTRONG – The Samuel Armstrong family moved to Polk County in the 1850s. Samuel, Margaret and their children Abner, James, Sarah, Lydia Ann and Hannibal moved to Polk County from Tennessee.

Samuel and Margaret joined the Pleasant Hope Presbyterian Church on Sept. 26, 1856.

Their children married into families still known today in the Pleasant Hope area…Cowden, Burns and Mullings.

Abner married Mary Francis Karnes in 1860 in West Fork, AR. They hauled walnut lumber from Arkansas and built a new home on the farm southeast of Pleasant Hope near the Pomme De Terre River. Abner was instrumental in early development of the Pleasant Hope Schools.

Abner and Mary Francis had five children: James, Orville, Horace, Margaret and Ida. Horace married Ida Mae Wallis. Their children were Lon, Bernie and Hubert. Bernie farmed the original farm until his death in 1974. He had a dairy and grain farm. He also owned a threshing machine and did custom work for the neighbors, later buying a combine which made the work easier. He married Macie Isreal of the Hickory Barren community and they had six children: Horace, Kelly, Peggy, Patty, Sharon and Guy. The children all gradated from Pleasant Hope High School. *Submitted by Sharon Armstrong Nahon*

ATKINSON – Debbie Wilkerson is the submitter and great-granddaughter of John William (born March 27, 1875; died Sept. 21, 1952) and Hattie Belle (Ward) Atkinson (born June 23, 1881; died Nov. 18, 1940). They had two daughters, Lyndy (born June 18, 1899) and Ona Myrtle (born Sept. 8, 1906—died Feb. 20, 1968). The family descendants have just begun their research and don't know how they came to be in Humansville.

For years, the descendants have been told that in early 1900s, John William had a blacksmith shop in Humansville, thus the picture (shared by Luann) of what they believe to be the working blacksmith shop, with great-grandfather, John, his father-in-law or their great-great grandfather or father to Hattie Belle, Cyrus T. Ward and another man. Humansville historian Mary Owens told us that John William's blacksmith shop's location was about where Humansville's present-day liquor store and car wash are located.

Ona, Debbie's grandmother, was born in and graduated eighth grade in Humansville. She graduated May 24, 1921 at William Chrisman High School, Independence, MO.

Ona married Frank Everett and beget Aunt Frankie Belle (Everett) Snelling (born June 23, 1928—died Aug. 9, 1984) who married Virgil Snelling, children: Vickie, James David, Luann and Sharon Kay.

Also, Ona married Albert Edward Dike (born June 30, 1914—died Feb. 27, 1984) begetting Carol Irene (Dike) Carman (born Dec. 20, 1937—died November 1996). Carol first married Glen Wells, begetting Michael Albert, then married Robert Charles Carman Sr. (born Dec. 11, 1934—died October 1995). They beget Robert Charles Jr. and Buffy Rene. A son, Albert Edward Dike Jr. "Sonny Boy" (born April 3, 1940—died 1941) and Linda Lou (Dike) Stillwell Oldham Woods (born Feb. 23, 1941). Ona and Albert lived in Independence, MO and were divorced, each remarrying.

Debbie says, "now onto what we find to be an ironic part of our history, and we feel, we have been turned in part to our roots. Albert worked and then retired from Ford Motor Company and

Man on left is Cyrus T. Ward, man in middle is John William Atkinson in blacksmith shop of John Williams at Humansville, MO early 1900s.

in 1959 and went in search of lake property. We don't know why he located first renting, then purchasing our home place, by Inlet Village. After many summers and some Easters visiting the lake, in 1975, he retired and made his home here, just outside Humansville until his death. All of us kids have fond memories of going to the lake and having fun."

Their daughter, Linda Lou, first married Donald Owen Stillwell Sr., begetting four children: Debra Jean (born Sept. 29, 1956), Linda Sue (born Oct. 14, 1957), Donna Kay (born April 8, 1960) and Donald Jr. (born Aug. 27, 1961). Linda's second husband, William Edward Oldham (born May 13, 1934—died Oct. 13, 2002) beget Lawrence Edward (born March 30, 1968) and Linda inherited Gerald Lee Oldham (born Dec. 30, 1960), moved with William and the boys in 1975 to be just next-door to her father. All her girls followed. William Oldham remained in Humansville until his death. Linda's girls are still all in Polk County. Linda Sue, outside of Bolivar, will soon be a grandmother and daughter Melissa graduated from Humansville. Donna lives in Humansville and is married to Gary Parke with one son, Alex Wilson who will graduate Humansville High School, 2003.

Debbie, married to Kenneth Wilkerson, lives next door to Linda Lou, and daughter Angela Jean (Kirby) Campbell also graduated from Humansville and lives in Bolivar. Larry's in Independence, yet his daughter, Aleisha Marie is in Bolivar. Jerry's in Camdenton, MO and Donnie's in Tulsa, OK. Any family or friends with a story, pictures, or known dates are invited to contact us. *Submitted by Debbie Wilkerson*

AUSTIN – John Lowry Austin, born Feb. 14, 1874 and Nancy Elizabeth Rotrammel, born Feb. 23, 1873 were born and married Oct. 8, 1893, in Benton County, AR. In the year 1899, John L. and Elizabeth loaded their covered wagon with the few items they had room for and their three sons: James, age 6, Elmer Dee, age 4 and Lester, age 2. They hitched their team of oxen to the wagon and set out on the long journey from Benton County, AR to Polk County, MO.

John L. Austin and Vernie L. Austin

They were not complete strangers to Polk County, as they already had several kinfolk living in the county and had visited the area where they settled, near Pleasant Hope, Van and Burns, many times. The first in the family to be born in Missouri was Verba May in 1900, then Vernie Lee in 1902, Kathryn in 1905, Alfred in 1908, Viola in 1910 and Virgil in 1913. During the time between 1910 and the 1930s when the children were becoming adults, most of the farming was done by hand. The Austin young men were kept busy at this work. They helped other farmers in the area as needed.

Soon after WWI began in 1914, Elmer D. was called to serve in the Army. After his return in 1918 he married Ida Nora Hughes. Their children were Velda, Harriet, Harold and Hugh. Harold and Hugh served in the military during WWII, Hugh serving in US Air Force. Two other grandsons, Don Austin and Lowell Hargis, from Polk County would also serve in WWII. John L. also had two sons, Alfred and Virgil Austin, who served in WWII. Virgil saw action in the North African campaign and landed on the beach at Anzio, Italy, fighting up through Eastern Europe and into Germany.

Lester Austin married Lora Nell Overcash and they had a son named Don Lester. To a later marriage to Mabel, a daughter named Nona was born. Verba May Austin married Oran Hargis and their children are Lowell, June, Ruth, John Logan and Betty. Vernie L. Austin married Ethel M. Stewart and their children are Betty, Bobby, Joann, Sharon and Roy. Kathryn Austin married Alvie Barnes and they had a son named Dwayne Barnes. To a later marriage to William Conner, two sons Dwight and Gene Conner were born. Alfred Austin married Wilma and their children were Rex, Donna May, George, John L., Dezil, Randal, Nancy and Brenda. Viola Austin married Leonard Gist and they had a daughter named Joyce Gist.

Vernie Austin worked at the ice plant on South Springfield Street in Bolivar during the 1940s. His job was making the 300 lb. blocks of ice; a very important job during the early 1940s, when most of the homes had ice boxes. One summer day in the late 1940s a big rainstorm hit Bolivar. There was no wind and the rain just came straight down. It rained so hard one could barely see the house across the street. The railroad bridge on West Broadway Street had a high water mark of about four feet under it. Many businesses and homes were flooded. The ice plant was damaged so badly the owners decided not to build back. The demand for ice had dwindled off and most homes had refrigerators by then.

Bobby Austin was born in Bolivar, MO and went to school there. After leaving school, he served three years in the US Marines Corps. After returning he went to work for a major wholesale company in Kansas City. In 1957 he married Shirley Darlene Stovall, also from Polk County. They have three sons, Stephen, Richard and Gary. In the 1960s he began a career with the US Postal Service as a letter carrier in Independence, MO. After retiring from the postal service he returned to live in Polk County and the surrounding area. *Submitted by Bob Austin*

AUSTIN – Samuel Preston Austin, son of Justice of the Peace, Absolam Chrisfield and Nancy Gass Austin, was born Nov. 25, 1864 in Dallas County. Samuel married Joletha Eldelene Gott Feb. 7, 1866. Joletha was the oldest child of Richard and Sarah Jane Brockus Gott. Samuel and Joletha were blessed with 10 children between the years 1886-1911; Alta, Alva, Edgar, Nora, Delma, Ollie, Eunice, Gene, Opal and Alice. Alva and Delma were born in Dallas County, the rest were born in Polk County. The family bought a farm east and north of Halfway Jan. 15, 1903.

Alva Dred, born Feb. 11, 1889, married Martha Opal Moore, Aug. 12, 1914. Opal was a daughter of John and Tamsey Hoover Moore, born April 7, 1898. Alva bought a farm east and south of Halfway Feb. 25, 1916. They were blessed with eight children: John, Lawrence, Martha, Alvin, Gladys, Carolina, Tommy and Naomi.

Samuel and Joeletha Austin

The Lord took Martha at 3 days of age. John was taken as a teenager. Then Daddy was taken away Jan. 20, 1942, after cutting wood and having a tree fall on him. Opal still had more heartache as Lawrence was taken as a young man in September 1946. Carolina was taken Oct. 25, 1955, leaving four little children: Martha, Wanda, Darrell and Larry, and her husband Henry Todd. Opal passed away July 16, 1976; all are buried in Red Top Cemetery, except for Carolina who is in Oaklawn Cemetery in Buffalo.

Alvin Dee "Buck" was born Oct. 11, 1927 and married Betty Jane Smith, July 3, 1948. They have two children, Sherry and Steven. Buck worked for the Halfway State Highway Department.

Gladys Irene was born Nov. 8, 1930 and married Bert Summers May 14, 1949. They were blessed with six children: Charles, Gene, Jim, Berta, Victor and Kelly (stillborn). They lived on a farm south of Halfway.

Tommy Jr. was born April 14, 1937 and married Betty Jo Glass April 16, 1955. They have three children: Roberta, Martin and Michael. They live on a farm in Dallas County.

Naomi Jewell was born March 4, 1940 and married Doyle Claud Barham June 6, 1958. They were blessed with a son, Roy. They live on a farm north of Burns in Polk County. *Submitted by Gladys Summers*

BACON – Thomas Clark Bacon was born in Fayette County, KY on Nov. 13, 1835. He grew to be six foot, two inches with dark hair and hazel eyes. During the Civil War Thomas served in the First Regiment of Nebraska Veteran Volunteers Cavalry. After being discharged in 1866 he went to Polk County, MO. There he met and married Elizabeth Ann Slagle on Nov. 29, 1868.

Wedding Day Oct. 19, 1893 Dorithia "Dolly" Ann Bacon and Samuel Elijah Kennemer

Elizabeth Ann had deep roots in Polk County. Her great-great-grandfather, John Slagle Sr., was born about 1770 in Virginia and died in Polk County, MO in November 1841. He left a widow and 10 children. The second-born child was Jacob Slagle. He was born in Virginia on Nov. 7, 1794. Jacob married Frances Dunlap in Christian County, KY on Oct. 15, 1819 and settled in Polk County in 1832. Jacob and Frances had eight children; the oldest was John A. Slagle, born 1821. John A. married Rhoda Sears on March 6, 1842 in Polk County. Rhoda's parents, Abraham and Dorethia Simons Sears, were also early settlers of Polk County. John A. and Rhoda's daughter, Elizabeth Ann Slagle, was the bride of the tall, dark and handsome Thomas Clark Bacon. Elizabeth Ann was the fourth generation to have resided in Polk County.

Thomas and Elizabeth farmed in Marion Township and reared a family with nine known children: John A. (born October 1869), William M. (born May 25, 1871), Edmund (born Aug. 25, 1874), Dorithia Ann (born Aug. 22, 1875), James Preston (born Aug. 27, 1877), Rosa N. (born 1879), Joseph (born Oct. 29, 1882) and Charles (born July 22, 1883).

Elizabeth Ann died of pneumonia on Jan. 11, 1884 in Sunset, Marion Township, Polk County. The baby of the family was only 6 months old. Thomas never remarried and apparently, friends and family helped with the children. Daughter, Dorithia "Dolly" went to live with a family in Turner, Greene County, MO. There she met and married Samuel Elijah Kennemer.

For many years Polk County was home to this family. Through hard times and good times they helped to lay a foundation for the Polk County of today. *Submitted by Judith A. Wilkinson*

BAKER – Charles Michael Baker, son of Thomas and Mary Katharine (Worley) Baker, was born in Cedar County near Bear Creek, MO, Oct. 24, 1878 and passed away at his home in Bolivar, MO, Thursday, May 26, 1949, at the age of 70 years, 7 months, and 2 days. Funeral services were held at Lindley Prairie Church in Cedar County with the Rev. Joe F. Leith officiating with interment in the Lindley Prairie Cemetery under the direction of Erwin and Blue of Bolivar. He moved from Cedar County at the age of 10 with his mother to Polk County, near Dunnegan, MO, where he lived most of his life as a farmer, bottling and delivering milk to Humansville and taking great pride in raising mules.

Charles Baker married Daisy Grace Paul "Grace," Jan. 2, 1900 at Dunnegan Springs, MO by D. R. Jones, J. P. Daisy Grace, the daughter of Martha Jane Cooper Vannoy and John Paul, was born Dec. 10, 1879 in Dunnegan, MO, died Dec. 20, 1972 in St. John's Hospital, Springfield, MO. Her funeral was held in the Butler Chapel with the Rev. Harlan E. Spurgeon officiating with burial in the Lindley Prairie Cemetery. To this union were born three children: Tommie, George and Flossie Grace.

Charles Baker and family, 1918

Tommie Blanche Baker was born Nov. 27, 1900 in Polk County, MO, died Friday, Nov. 28, 1969 in Cox Medical Center, Springfield, MO. Funeral services were at the Butler Chapel with Rev. J. Leland Hall and the Rev. Lloyd E. Morgan officiating with burial in Greenwood Cemetery under the direction of the Butler Funeral Home of Bolivar. She married Harry Delbert Butler on Oct. 30, 1920 in Bolivar, MO. He was born Dec. 26, 1898 in Cedar County. Harry owned a general store in Dunnegan. They had two sons, Paul Delbert Butler, born Aug. 10, 1921, Dunnegan, MO and Charles Bob Butler, born June 29, 1923 in Dunnegan, MO.

George William Baker was born Sept. 26, 1906 in Dunnegan, MO. He died Nov. 23, 1979 at Cox Medical Center in Springfield, MO. George, a retired carpenter, was a longtime Dunnegan resident and 30-year Bolivar resident. He was buried at Greenwood Cemetery with Rev. Lloyd E. Morgan officiating. George Baker married Wilma Butler, Feb. 2, 1924 at Bolivar, MO. Wilma was the sister to his brother-in-law, Harry Delbert Butler. Wilma died at Bolivar, Thursday, May 18, 1989 and was buried beside her husband. They had no children.

"Grace" Flossie Grace Baker was born Dec. 29, 1916 in Dunnegan, Polk County, MO and attended the Dunnegan and Humansville schools. She married Dr. Gervais Dean Smith June 2, 1941 at Bolivar, MO. Dr. Smith was the son of Sarah M. Logan and Dr. Sterling B. Smith. He died Jan. 21, 1995 and was buried at Lindley Prairie Cemetery. He was born in St. Louis, MO and grew up in Walnut Grove. In 1922 he graduated from Washington University Medical School in St. Louis, MO. In 1924 he began his 66-year medical practice in Bolivar. *Submitted by Grace Baker Smith*

Silas A. Ballinger, wife Mary "Mollie," Mary E. Durham; children: Truman Silas Ballinger and Ressie Ballinger Dorman

BALLINGER – John Ballinger Sr. was born Jan. 1, 1802 in Tennessee. He married a woman by the name of Mary (last name unknown). She was born July 25, 1801 in Virginia. The couple had seven children: Elisa J., Martha, Eady, John Jr., Mary, Elizabeth and E. James "James." James married Elizabeth Jane Slagle, the daughter of Jacob and Francis (Dunlap) Slagle. Jacob was one of the founders of the town of Slagle. James and his father purchased land from the US Government. This land was on property that became part of the town of Slagle.

James and Elizabeth had seven children: Mary Frances, William Lafeyette, John Allen, James Henry, Martha Eliza, Jemema Ellen and Silas Arthur. Silas was born April 18, 1858. When James and Elizabeth died, their children sold their land to a Slagle relative.

Silas first married Nancy Conley. They had children together but later divorced. Some of the children of this marriage changed the spelling of the name Ballinger to Ballenger. Some of the descendants of this line live in Nebraska. Silas married a second time. He married Mary Martha Swadley, nicknamed "Mollie." Mollie was a half-Cherokee Indian. She was born in March of 1878. Mollie's parents were William Howard and Elizabeth Ann Brown. William was a German fur trapper. Elizabeth was a full-blooded Indian. Her Indian name is unknown. It is believed she came to Oklahoma with the Indians on the "Trail of Tears."

Silas and Mollie had seven children: Reuben Lewis, Ressie Bell, Roman Truman Silas, Mary Elizabeth, Esther, Logan and Jessie. Esther, Logan and Jessie died as small children. Mary Elizabeth was born in 1899; she married Walter Durham. *Submitted by Margie Barker*

BARCLAY – Robert Barclay is the son of Robert Barclay (Barkley) and Leah ___ of Rowan County, NC. He was born Jan. 3, 1772 in Rowan County, NC and died March 14, 1846 in Polk County, MO. He married Mary Hubbard, the daughter of Durret Hubbard and Susannah ___, March 3, 1802 in Louisiana, Spanish Territory. She was born April 22, 1785 in Madison County, KY and was buried June 1857 in Polk County, MO. Robert Barclay was given a grant or concession of 800 arpens of land situated in St. Louis County from the Spanish Government. The concession was dated 1802. He lived several places in Missouri before coming to Polk County. He acquired two tracts of land three and one-half miles west and about six miles north of Columbia, MO, on a creek named for him later and still bearing the name.

In 1834, Robert Barclay pre-empted land, Township 33, Range 21, Section 11, in Polk County, MO. This 80-acres certificate is dated Dec. 21, 1838. Robert Barclay was in the 1840 Federal Census of Polk County. Robert and Mary Barclay had 13 children: William (born Sept. 19, 1805, St. Louis County, MO, died Aug. 14, 1889, Lincoln County, OR); Elizabeth (born Feb. 7, 1807, Missouri, died about 1868, Polk County); Leah (born Oct. 13, 1808, Missouri); Robert (born Oct. 14, 1810, Boone County, MO, died 1841); Derrett Hubbard (born Feb. 12, 1812, Howard County, MO, died Nov. 7, 1900, Webster County, MO); Sarah (born Jan. 18, 1814, St. Louis County, MO); John (born Dec. 13, 1816, Howard County, MO); David D. (born May 26, 1818, Howard County, MO, died Sept. 11, 1900, Polk County, MO, buried New Life Cemetery, northeast of Pleasant Hope, MO); Daniel (born Dec. 23, 1820, Howard County, MO, died Oct. 13, 1865, Riverview Cemetery, Dallas County, MO); Lucy Ann (born Sept. 20, 1922, Boone County, MO, died Aug. 6, 1896, Polk County, MO, buried Goff Cemetery); Mary Francis (born Aug. 16, 1823, Boone County, MO, died Dec. 27, 1948, Polk County, MO, buried Mt. Zoar Cemetery, near Goodson); Margaret (born Feb. 15, 1825, Boone County, MO, died 1846); James Eusibius (born Aug. 4, 1827, Boone County, MO, died June 15, 1892, Monroe, Benton County, OR).

Several of the Barclay children were married in Polk County, MO. Elizabeth Barclay married Thomas McDearmon Davison on March 21, 1841; Derrett Hubbard Barclay married Lucretia Liencreacy Davison on April 15, 1841; Sarah Barclay married Jesse Sterling Brown on Nov. 27, 1835; David D. Barclay married Tabitha Stites on Nov. 12, 1840, second married to Charlotte Elender Ray on March 26, 1863; Daniel Barclay married Jane Stites in 1841 in Dallas County, MO; Lucy Ann Barclay married James Hardison Davison on March 24, 1844; Mary Francis Barclay married Francis Porter Ashlock Nov. 10, 1842. Many of the descendants of Robert Barclay and Mary Hubbard still live in Polk and Dallas Counties and southwest Missouri. *Submitted by Robert W. Barclay*

BARHAM – Joel Harrison Barham was born 1830 in Kentucky. His parents were James F. and Margaret Holbrook Barham. They moved to Missouri where Joel married Mary Ann Slagle Oct. 5, 1855 at Slagle, MO. They were the parents of Barbara, Thomas, Sarah, Susan, Prudence and Mary. Joel and Mary are buried in Rock Prairie Cemetery.

Thomas Jefferson Barham was born Aug. 3, 1857. He married Rebecca Hannah Felthoff Nov. 23, 1884. Rebecca was born Aug. 11, 1863 to Benjamin and Charlotte Bennett Felthoff of Indiana. They moved their family to Missouri when Rebecca was 18. She was one of 12 children.

Thomas and Rebecca lived on a farm south of Burns until they bought a farm Sept. 27, 1895, north of Burns along Pomme De Terre River, where they farmed, fished and hunted. Thomas was plowing corn barefooted when a small copperhead bit him. He killed the snake, split it open, and put it on the bite and continued plowing. Rebecca liked to carry two pocketbooks, one with her candy corn and money, the other one carried her corncob pipe and tobacco. They were members of Pleasant Hill Missionary Baptist Church.

First row: Claud, Rebecca and Myrtle; second row: Lottie, Roy, Emmett and Joel Barham

Thomas and Rebecca were blessed with six children: Roy Levi, Myrtle Almyra, Charles Emmett, Lottie Ann, Joel Benjamin and Claud Jessie. Thomas built a new home for his family, but didn't get the upstairs finished when they moved in. Thomas took the measles, then pneumonia and passed away April 3, 1913. Rebecca still lived on the farm with some of the children or grandchildren until she later went to live with her daughter Myrtle. She passed away April 2, 1949. They are buried in Pleasant Hill Cemetery.

Charles Emmett, born in 1891, paid the supreme sacrifice by giving his life for his country during WWI in France in 1918.

Claud Jessie was born Nov. 25, 1907. Claud married Wannah Nina Nasalroad June 8, 1935. Wannah was daughter of Joseph and Ada Hooper Nasalroad. Joe was an oil field worker; they moved around a lot. Wannah was born Nov. 2, 1916 in Shamrock, OK. Joe and Ada lived in Sentinel and Halfway where Joe had a blacksmith shop.

Claud and Wannah lived on a farm adjoining his parents' farm. Later they bought the home place. Claud had hounds and went fox and wolf hunting. He also liked to fish.

Claud and Wannah were blessed with a son, Doyle Claud, born April 26, 1936. Doyle farmed with his dad. They were the first to raise hybrid seed corn in Polk County. Doyle liked to go fishing with his uncles. They had a lot of good times together. Claud and Wannah are buried in Pleasant Hill Cemetery.

Doyle married Naomi Austin June 6, 1958. Naomi was born March 4, 1940 to Alva and Opal Moore Austin of Halfway. They moved into his grandparents' home and still live there. They did remodel the house some. Naomi worked at the garment factory for seven years. Doyle did farming and decided to milk cows. They were blessed with a son Roy Austin, born Feb. 22, 1969. They were dairy farmers for 33 years. Roy attended Halfway School and University of Missouri, at Columbia. Roy took up golf until he found a job with Mid-Am, later became D.F.A.

Roy married Tracy Silvey Oct. 24, 1998. Tracy was born May 25, 1972 to Ralph and Sharon Salzman Silvery of Tipton, MO.

Thomas and Rebecca's other children are in the following stories as they lived in Polk County. *Submitted by Naomi Austin Barham*

BARHAM – Roy Barham was the eldest son of Thomas and Rebecca Felthoff Barham. He was born in 1886. He grew up in the Burns area. He married Lee Parrish and they raised two sons, Clark and Grant. Roy and Lee always lived on the farm working and making the best of what God provided.

Roy was an avid fisherman all his life. His wife often said he would be found dead on a creek bank, but added that she didn't know any place he would rather be. He died on a cot in the front yard on a balmy June day in 1954; four months later his wife followed him in death. The farm had remained in the family, owned now by a grandson. They have five grandchildren, ten great-grandchildren and the list goes on.

Leota, Clark, Randell, Grant, Mary, Roy and Lee; grandchildren Doris, Kathy and Kay.

Clark grew up and married Leota Pritchard, and they raised two children, Randall and Doris. Their lives were also mostly spent in farming or related interest. Clark was killed in a highway accident in 1980. His children and descendants lived in Polk and adjoining counties.

Grant married Mary Miller, a Bolivar girl, while he was serving in the navy. His area of service was in the Pacific during the 1940s. After the war Grant and Mary settled in Ponca City, OK and had three children: Kathy, Kay and Kenny. Grant passed away with leukemia in 1959, leaving his wife and small children. Then they moved to Liberty, MO to be near her family. Mary passed away there in 1996.

So goes the family of Roy Barham leaving grandchildren, great-grandchildren and great-greats, to carry on the name and family traditions. *Submitted by Leota Barham*

BARHAM – Myrtle Barham was born Nov. 5, 1888, daughter of Thomas J. and Rebecca Felthoff Barham. She married Clarence B. Cunningham Nov. 18, 1924. Clarence was born March 5, 1874, and was the father of Myrtle's brother Joel's first wife Fleete. This marriage made the family's relations very complex. Carolyn (Barham) Wakefield, great-granddaughter of Clarence, one time as a small child, when asked what kin she was to Myrtle, said, "Aunt Myrtle is my grandma," which was correct. Audrey's son, when a young child, was asked what relation he was to some of the family members said, "I don't know, my mom can't even explain it."

Myrtle and Clarence Cunningham, Luther and Myrtle Cunningham, Joel and Fleete Barham, Audrey and Berton Cunningham, Max and Rex Barham and Luther and Boy W. B.

Daughter Audrey R. was born June 9, 1927, married J. Bueford Skidmore Nov. 18, 1956. They have one son, Brent J. Skidmore, born Feb. 2, 1959. He married Brenda G. Jackson, May 17, 1978. They have one son, Jesse J. Skidmore, born Oct. 16, 1987. Myrtle and Clarence had one son, Berton W. Cunningham, born Aug. 18, 1932, married Peggy Prater, June 17, 1960, no children.

Myrtle and Clarence lived on their farm north of Burns where they farmed all their lives. Their children grew up on the farm, which is owned by Audrey, and husband where they now live.

Audrey attended Union Ridge and Halfway Schools. She worked as a bookkeeper at the Bolivar Farmers Exchange for 44 years. Berton attended Union Ridge, McKinney and Halfway Schools. He worked as a driver's license examiner in Troop D Highway Patrol area.

Bueford and Burton served their country during the Korean Conflict.

Audrey's mother and father attended and were members of Pleasant Hill Missionary Baptist Church for many years. Her father died Aug. 9, 1956. Her mother died May 6, 1979. They are both buried in the Pleasant Hill Cemetery. *Submitted by Audrey R. Skidmore*

BARHAM – Lottie Ann Barham was born on June 30, 1894, south of Burns in Polk County, MO. She was the daughter of Thomas and Rebecca Barham. She had one sister, Myrtle, and four brothers: Roy Levi, Charles Emmett, Joel Benjamin and Claud Jessie. She attended school at Union Ridge. She was a member of the Pleasant Hill Missionary Baptist Church.

She was united in marriage to Andrew Jackson Redd on Oct. 7, 1923. Andrew or "Jonah" as his friends knew him, was born July 28, 1895, north of Halfway. His parents were Rufus and Belle Lewis Redd. He served in the military during WWI.

Fleete Cunningham and Lottie Barham, best friends, later became sisters-in-law.

To this union came four boys. They were living north of Burns when their first and second children were born. Hobert Andrew was born on Nov. 11, 1924 and Herbert Barm was born on Sept. 20, 1926. During the birth of Hobert, Andrew's mother, Belle, came to stay and help with the baby. Custom was to stay in bed for two weeks after giving birth. Lottie's bed was situated so the dinner table was in view. One evening when dinner was on, she asked Andrew for a biscuit. He calmly took the biscuit from the table and threw it to Lottie in the other room. Belle was not happy and commenced to tell him that Lottie was not a dog and not to throw her food.

Their third son, Ray Dean, was born on Aug. 20, 1932 after the family moved to a place of 117-acres northeast of Halfway. They then moved in with Lottie's parents and Tom R. was born on Sept. 12, 1936.

After living several different places, the finally settled northeast of Halfway on the "160." When the boys started getting married and the grandchildren came along, Lottie was known as "Mom Redd" and Andrew was known as "Papoo."

Lottie loved to tat, knit and crochet. She also quilted and once made a quilt with the down she collected from the geese she raised. She also had hens and chickens and helped milk the cows. She also loved to garden and had a huge strawberry patch.

Andrew purchased a house and some land in Halfway. He fixed up the house with running water and modern appliances. She said that she did not want to live in the "city." They moved in 1959 much to Lottie's dismay. She dug up some of her strawberries, replanted them, and eventually had a big garden at Halfway. There was also a nice cherry tree in front of the house.

On Aug. 9, 1966, at the age of 71, Papoo passed away with heart failure. He is buried at Reed Cemetery south of Halfway. Lottie lived for 18 years as a widow. She lived at the house in Halfway for some time. Finally, she moved to a small house next to her youngest son until her death on Dec. 6, 1984. She was 90 years old. She is also buried at Reed Cemetery. *Submitted by Shawna Redd Grisham*

BARHAM – Joel Benjamin Barham was born Dec. 26, 1896 to Thomas and Rebecca Felthoff Barham. Joel married Fleete Cunningham April 3, 1921. Fleete was the daughter of Clarence B. and Mary Catherine "Kate" Higginbotham Cunningham. Fleete was born July 15, 1896. Clarence was the son of Jim and California Wright Cunningham. Kate was the daughter of Gideon and Mary Agnes McKinney Higginbotham.

Joel and Fleete Barham

Joel and Fleete lived on a farm north of Burns on Hominy Creek. They were dairy farmers. They had three children: Max, Rex and Joan.

Max Berton was born Feb. 15, 1922. He married Floradelle Quick Sept. 7, 1946. Their children are Gary Wayne (born Sept. 27, 1947), Thomas Berton (born Feb. 23, 1950) and Beverly Jean (born March 25, 1953). Max and Floradelle had a meat packing plant in Slagle and then moved to a farm south of Burns.

Rex Emmaett was born April 1, 1924. He married Florine Hopkins April 24, 1943. They had one daughter, Carolyn, born Feb. 9, 1948. Rex and Florine board and train Fox-Trotter horses on a farm west of Burns.

Fleete Joan Barham was born July 31, 1935. She married J. C. Meador Feb. 16, 1952. J. C. and Joan had four children: Janell (born Sept. 23, 1952), Jeffrey Christopher (born Dec. 1, 1956), Jodie Gay (born June 26, 1962) and Jill Ann (born Dec. 3, 1964). J. C. and Joan owned and operated a fertilizer plant, fescue seed house and a farm implement company. They also continued to farm southeast and north of Bolivar. J. C., Joan and their children all live in this area.

Fleete took her grandchildren and neighbors to church. One of her favorite sayings was, "If you can't say anything good about someone, don't say anything." Fleete lived to be 102 years young.

Most all of Joel and Fleete's family are Missionary Baptist. Joel and Fleete are buried in Pleasant Hill Cemetery. *Submitted by Joan Meador*

BARHAM – These photos are of Dawn's great-grandmother, Almedia Barham Slagle. She was born Feb. 11, 1862 and died Feb. 3, 1931. Almedia, or "Medie" as she was called, was hired as a young girl to help care for W. L. and Emma Jane Slagle's children. After the death of Emma Jane, Almedia remained and later married W. L. Slagle. She cared for and helped raise the four children: Austin, Calvin, Ruby and Bill, from that first marriage and then W. L. and Almedia had two more daughters, Anna Lee and Rena Mae Slagle. W. L. and Almedia were lifelong residents of Polk County, MO and lived on a farm southwest of Bolivar near Morrisville. They are both buried in Slagle Cemetery, Polk County, MO as are all of their children.

Almedia said, "I love my grand babies," obviously enjoying her growing family. She also had letters from friends complimenting her on her fine cooking. The family has a "Grandmother's Flower Garden" quilt that Almedia was working on at the time of her passing. With the pieces that she had already cut

Almedia Barham late 1870s

and a few added in, the next four generations were working together to hand stitch her blocks and attempt to finish the five-generation quilt. It will be beautiful. Almedia passed the legacy of quilting to her daughter, Rena, who also made many beautiful quilts.

Almedia Barham Slagle in her cotton patch, 1925-30

The family still has many items of Almedia's including a bag of cotton that she raised in her last cotton patch and hand finished quilts she made for her family, a walking spinning wheel, sugar bowls, green mixing bowl and wooden spoons, skillets, oak dining table, trunk, and her mother's rocking chair.

Almedia's mothers name was Pheby Barham-Sherman, born Feb. 20, 1837, died March 1, 1906 and is buried in Brock Cemetery, Polk County, MO with her husband Charles W. Sherman, born April 21, 1823, died Sept. 23, 1903. Almedia was raised by Charles and Pheby in Polk County, MO. Pheby was Dawn's great-great grandmother. These stories and more were related to Dawn by her grandmother, Rena Mae Slagle Boswell and by her mother, Ginger Lea Boswell Wheeler. *Submitted by Dawn Wheeler*

BARHAM – James "Jim" Barham was born in Kentucky, Feb. 20, 1820, the son of James F. and Margaret Holbrook Barham and came to Polk County in early 1843. Jim's grandfather James Jr. was a veteran of the Revolutionary War and witnessed the surrender of Cornwallis at Yorktown in 1781.

Jim Barham and Maria Ellen Slagle were married June 20, 1847, and settled near Slagle. She was the daughter of Jacob and Francis Dunlap Slagle. They moved to a farm on the Pomme De Terre River near Sunset and reared a family of seven sons and two daughters.

Jim and oldest son Jacob fought for the Confederacy in the Civil War. Jim was shot and killed by bushwhackers near Fair Grove as he and Jacob returned from the war. Jacob was wounded but escaped by swimming a horse across the flooded Pomme De Terre River. During their absence Union forces raided the Barham homestead and shot and killed their 8-year-old son John as he and his 3-year-old brother played in the yard. The 3 year old Lafayette Young, "Dick" as he was called, lived with a bitter memory of this his entire life.

Lafayette Young Barham "Dick" was born April 15, 1861, and married Mary Eliza Teeter Callaway Jan. 2, 1889. "Molly," as she was known, was the widow of Charles Callaway and daughter of Jacob and Sarah Weeden Teeter, born Oct. 13, 1851 in McKinney, TX and moved with her family to Missouri in 1867. The teenaged girl and older brother drove a herd of mustangs to Missouri; this was the family's grubstake.

Dick and Molly made their home south of Halfway. Dick was a stock trader while Molly and a hired hand worked the farm. They took a firm interest in the community and Molly donated the land for a school -- land now occupied by the Halfway School District.

Left to right: Delbert, Dick, Mollie and Estella

127

They had two children, Estella Rebecca and Delbert Lloyd. Estella became a teacher and married Otho Davis of the Aldrich community. They homesteaded near Craig, CO. Delbert, born Oct. 14, 1892, farmed and dealt in livestock with his father.

On July 3, 1918, Delbert married Lina M. Porter, one of 12 children of James G. and Lena M. Slagle Porter of Schofield. July 5, 1918, Delbert was inducted in the US Army and served in France in WWI. He and Lina made their home on the family farm and were parents of Naomi and D. L. Naomi taught school and married Phillip Rea and they lived in California.

D. L., born July 13, 1921, entered the army in 1942 and served until 1946, seeing duty at the Normandy invasion "D-Day" through the Battle of the Bulge. He was awarded the Bronze Star and other medals and the Purple Heart for wounds in action.

He returned to the farm and on Jan. 1, 1951, he married Faye Robison in Springfield. She was the daughter of James M. and Grace Adams Robison of Sparta, MO. They made their home at Halfway and were active in their community and their church, where D. L. served as a deacon and Sunday school superintendent for a number of years. D. L. farmed and Faye was employed at the Halfway Post Office for 10 years and retired from the Polk County Bank in Bolivar after 22 years of employment there.

They were parents of a son, Jack, and daughter, Mary Ellen. Jack is a mail carrier out of the Halfway Post Office and farms. He and wife Peggy have three daughters and live in the original farmhouse built by Dick and Molly in 1894. Mary is a RN and lives with husband Mike Walker in Springfield. She has one son and two daughters and one granddaughter.

D. L. passed away April 22, 1999. Faye continues to live on the farm in the home they built in 1951. She continues to be active in her church and community. *Submitted by Faye Barham*

BARKER – Ellas Barker was born Feb. 17, 1800 in Madison County, KY and died Aug. 13, 1862. He married Elizabeth Warner Dec. 13, 1821 in Madison County. She was born in 1799 in Madison County, KY and died Feb. 18, 1885. Their children were William W., Anna, Stephen W., John W., Elizabeth, Sallie A. and James.

William W. Barker was born June 14, 1827 and died 1908. He married first an unknown woman, and second Purmellia Hatten Jan. 23, 1853, daughter of Joseph Hatten and Peggy Ashcraft. She was born Feb. 12, 1833 and died Nov. 9, 1896 and is buried at Star Ridge. William and his first wife had one child, Mary Ann. William and Purmellia's children were Marshall, Sarah Ann, Jennie, Joseph, Purmellia, Zachariah, Martin, Janes M., Fannie and William Jesse.

Joseph Barker was born Nov. 9, 1861 and died July 16, 1939. He married Phoebe Ellen Sawyers Oct. 16, 1884, daughter of Thomas Sawyers and Mary Warren. She was born Nov. 6, 1864 and died April 11, 1950. Children of Joseph and Phoebe were Arthur Wesley, James Montford, William Ellis, Frank Leslie, Walter, baby boy, Roy Jessie and Sylvia.

Arthur Wesley Barker was born Feb. 17, 1886 and died March 18, 1963. He married first Ora May Brooks March 25, 1906, daughter of Theo Brooks and Sara Harper. She was born June 23, 1879 and died May 11, 1943. He married second, Ina Ahart about 1947 in Polk County. She was born Dec. 9, 1912 and died Jan. 12, 1969. Arthur and Ora are buried at Polk Cemetery in Polk County. Arthur and Ora Brooks' children are Earnest Wilson, Lovell Carl, Mildred, Nellie Mae, Thomas Arthur, William Dwight and Joseph Guy. Arthur and Ina's child is Nancy Kay Barker.

William Dwight Barker was born Dec. 4, 1917 in Polk, MO. He married Mary Ethel Pridgen, daughter of William Jackson Pridgen and Eva Biggs. She was born June 26, 1921 in Willard, Greene County, MO and died June 1, 2002. William and Mary are buried in Greenwood Cemetery, Polk County. The children of William and Mary are Peggy Jean, Eileen Kay, Theodore Wayne, Carolyn Sue, William Kent and Danny Gene.

William, Curtis and Travis Barker "The Barker Boys"

Theodore Wayne Barker was born Nov. 3, 1943 in Goodson, Polk County, MO. He married Carolyn Anne Sawyer April 20, 1968 in Nativity Catholic Church in Independence, MO. She is the daughter of Kenneth Sawyer and Anne Ernst. She was born June 13, 1944 in Kansas City, MO. The children of Ted and Carolyn are John Theodore, Amy Suzanne and Jennifer Lynn.

Carolyn Sue Barker was born April 7, 1949. She married first, Stephen LeRoy Bruce, son of Roy Bruce and Betsy Taylor. She married second, Max Maloney. The children of Carolyn and Stephen are Michael Roy and Michelle Marie.

Danny Gene Barker was born Oct. 16, 1951 in Humansville, Polk County, MO. He married Teresa Susan Appleby July 2, 1971 in Bolivar, Polk County, MO. She is the daughter of Robert Eugene Appleby and Dolores Ritter. She was born July 22, 1952 in Ashland, Clark County, KS. The children of Danny and Teresa are Travis Aaron, Daniel Curtis and William Robert.

Daniel Curtis Barker was born Nov. 9, 1979 in Bolivar, MO. He married Heather Shadwick Oct. 17, 1998 in Fair Play, Polk County, MO. She was born Jan. 5, 1983. Child of Daniel Curtis and Heather is Peyton Daniel. *Submitted by Curtis Barker*

BARNES – Allen was born on May 4, 1848 in Jennings County, IN. His parents were Eliza (Graham) Barnes and John Andrew Barnes. Eliza died in 1855 when Allen was 7 years old and his siblings ranged in age from 15 years to 6 years. Allen and his siblings, Lucinda, Mary Jane, John, Willis, Anderson, James, Allen and Nancy remained in the home for several years. When the last sister married, his father broke up housekeeping and went to live with one of his daughters. Allen and his brother John lived together, and when John married, Allen lived with them.

Sophia Alice was born July 28, 1856 in Lexington, IN. Her parents were Elizabeth Jane (Hardy) Nickels and James Robert Nickels. Elizabeth's father, John Hershel Hardy was the seventh generation of Thomas Hardy who came to America from England around 1633. Elizabeth's mother, Minerva Boles came to America from Ireland in the 1800s. Not much is known of James Nickels as his mother died when he was young and his father did not raise him. Elizabeth and James are buried in the Plum Grove Cemetery in Polk County.

Allen and Alice were married Dec. 10, 1875 in Clark County, IN. They decided to move to Missouri in 1879 where Allen's sister lived. Alice's parents and siblings decided to come also. Fourteen of them left Indiana with six horses, two wagons, two saddle horses and two dogs. They left Indiana on Sept. 16, 1879 and arrived in Dunnegan on Oct. 13, 1879.

They lived in the area northeast of Dunnegan and farmed with her parents. They built a home on the prairie in 1880. In 1885 they bought an 80-acre farm about three-fourths of a mile east of Dunnegan. They built a house and lived and farmed there the rest of their lives. Part of their farm included what is now the Dunnegan Cemetery.

Allen Barnes and wife Alice and daughter Maude

Allen and Alice had five children. Frank Orlando and Maude Alene were born in Indiana, Prudie Irene was born in Dunnegan as were two sons, Freddie and Clemmie Herschel, who died as infants. Frank Orlando married Edna Summerhauser and moved to Colorado. Maude lived with her parents and never married. Prudie Irene married Jim Mitchem and lived nearby. One of Prudie's children always lived with Alice and Allen and helped care for them.

Allen was a very kind and honest man. While traveling to Missouri, a man refused to sell them some corn for their horses and Allen said he would let his team go hungry until the next day before he took any without their permission. He was very kind to his animals but stealing was something he couldn't do. He had a gray mare named Nellie, who balked on him one day when he was hauling wheat. He removed her harness and couldn't find anything wrong, but after putting the harness back on, she started right off. He thought there must have been a burr somewhere under the harness. He would not even think about whipping her to get her to move. It was the only time Nellie ever balked on him.

Allen and Alice were members of the Christian Church of Dunnegan, MO. Allen died on Oct. 10, 1931 at the age of 83. He told his family that when Alice died to have them bury her as close to him as they could. Alice died on March 17, 1937 at the age of 81. They are both buried in the Dunnegan Cemetery. *Submitted by Darlene Austin*

BARNES – Frank Orlando Barnes was born to Allen and Sophia Alice Barnes on March 28, 1877 in Madison, IN. In 1879, accompanied by his parents, he moved to Polk County, MO near Dunnegan. They were accompanied on this move by Alice's parents, Jim and Elizabeth Nickels, and some of her siblings. There were 14 people in all. They came in two wagons, with six horses, two saddle horses and two dogs. Frank attended elementary school with his two sisters, Maude Barnes and Prudie Barnes Mitchem, in Dunnegan, MO. Frank was known for his great sense of humor. In the spring of 1900, Frank moved to St. Joseph, MO and became a clerk at the Benton Club. While living in St. Joseph, he met and married Edna Sommerhauser. The Benton Club provided their place of residence, while Frank was managing the club. He left the Benton Club, to manage the Harvey Houses in New Mexico for the Fred Harvey Railroad Chain. In 1912, Frank and Edna moved and settled in Denver, CO, where, for almost six years, he worked for the George Sell Baking and Confectionery Company. He became the retail manager for Paramount Sales Company in the summer of 1916. In 1921, after the automobile became popular, he began work in the automobile sales business. June of 1922 brought the birth of their only child, a daughter, Virginia Marie. Frank continued to work in automobile sales until he fell on some ice and broke both hips in December of 1936. He had several operations, but never completely recovered after his accident, causing him to retire in 1937. In March of 1951, Frank Barnes died and was buried in Denver, CO.

Uncle Buff, Virginia and Aunt Edna

Virginia Marie Barnes was born June 14, 1922 in Denver, CO. She retired after working for the Civil Service for 42 years. She married William Goodsell in Denver, CO on July 3, 1947. In 1950, they had a daughter, Judith Marie. They moved to Colorado Springs, CO in 1953. In 1958, they had a daughter, Ginnette Kay.

Judith Marie Goodsell was born Dec. 15, 1950 in Denver, CO. She married Gary Arthur Miller in Colorado Springs, CO on July 3, 1972. On April 5, 1975, they had one son, William Arthur.

Ginnette Kay Goodsell was born April 12, 1958. She married Brian Sherwood Ritz in Colorado Springs, CO on Dec. 5, 1987. They had a son Scott Joseph Ritz, born Feb. 9, 1990 and a daughter Elizabeth Ashley Ritz, born Oct. 23, 1991. *Submitted by Virginia Barnes Goodsell*

Back row: Janet Skidmore, Doris Blankenship, Charles Barnhouse, Rose Matthews and Patsy Hood; Front row: Bob Barnhouse, Linda Benner, Allean and W. H. Barney Barnhouse and Bill Barnhouse.

BARNHOUSE – In 1925 the Commodore Perry Barnhouse and the Barnhouse-Fittro Trucking Company moved from Billings to Bolivar. Their business was on Springfield Avenue, where the Bolivar Herald-Free Press is now located. C. P. married Ada Rachel "Julie" Tabor and they had two children, Blanche and William. Blanche married Jack Fittro. They had one child, Virginia, before Jack died after his appendix ruptured on one of their trucking runs to southeast Missouri.

William Henry "Barney" Barnhouse married Allean "Pudder" Lunceford, daughter of George Lunceford of Karlin and Virgie Mae Hensley of Wishart, in 1929.

Barney and Pudder had eight children. Doris Blankenship, Pat Hood, and Charles, Bill and Bob Barnhouse still live in Bolivar; Rose Matthews, Janet Skidmore and Linda Benner have moved away but come back frequently to visit.

Rick says, "I barely remember Granddad Barney but the one thing I do remember is that I was over visiting one day and he told me, 'Always remember that your granddad loves you.' I always have."

Charles Barnhouse, Rick's dad, married June Mosier, the only child of Frank and Alta Mosier of Aldrich, in 1956. Rick had fond memories of growing up in Polk County with his brother Jeff (Greenfield) and sister Dagny Hall (Aldrich). They used to explore down by the old railroad tracks where they cross Locust while visiting family friends Bill and Georgine Jenkins; and the whole town of Aldrich was "our playground" when the city was moved to higher ground to make way for Stockton Lake. Rick would ride his bike three miles from his Granddad Frank's farm into town to Rice's Store for a bottle of Pommack or Nehi and then head back home or stop over at his Aunt Ruth's and Grandma Pauline Toalson's to play in the big flower garden or make taffy. There was plenty of work back on the farm as Rick learned to drive on the Ford tractor while he brush hogged or fed cattle. There was plenty of fun in the woods hunting and picking berries or all the things a boy can create in the old barn. Rick tells everyone, "I haven't gotten far in life but I traveled a lot of miles to get here." After living in Nixa for his high school years, six years in the navy and 15 years working in Kansas City, Rick finally found a way to get back home to Bolivar. On the way he was blessed to travel all over the world in the navy, marry his high school sweetheart (Debbie Baker of Nixa), and to make some good life-long friends. Debbie and Rick really enjoy being back close to family and having a safe and modern town to raise their three children, Kevin, Brian and Allison. They are in the Bolivar School System with their cousins and they are still able to get together every Christmas with all the "kids" of Barney and Pudder at one of the eight "kids" or 24 grandkids' houses. *Submitted by Rick Barnhouse*

BATTEN – "W. F. Batten Tells His Own Life Story": circa 1926 from a Bolivar newspaper.

He was born April 10, 1850, three miles northeast of where Goodson, MO now stands on land his father owned. There were 12 children in his family. Their father was a Methodist preacher and went far and wide to preach where he was wanted and never charged a cent. He was born in North Carolina and moved to Tennessee from there to Greene County, MO and in 1832 came to Polk County.

During the Civil War from 1861 to 1865 he had four brothers in the Southern Army. John Batten was killed down around Pittsburg, MO. David Batten was killed about one and one-half miles from where the family lived in 1926. William Batten went through the war without a scratch and Jim Batten was wounded while on the Missouri and Kansas line. After his brothers were killed, W. F. went into Minaffee's Company for protection, as he was a boy. He remembers that while they were stationed at the Polk County Courthouse, Ivan Wainscott and Jack Stewart rode through Bolivar with a 12-foot flag. There were 100 of them in the courthouse and no one fired a shot because they thought an entire army was following the two men. It turned out that there was no army following them and they rode through

Bolivar and burned the livery barn. The company followed them to Linn Creek Ford and they got up on a high cliff, fired a few shots down at them and that was the end of that.

In the fall of 1863 W. F. and two sisters, Mrs. Wilcox and Mrs. Curr, started for the south. Their husbands had both been killed. Curr had owned a tin shop and dwelling east of Babe Shoffner's old hardware stand. Wilcox owned a big ranch and store on Panther Creek near W. F. Batten's father's home. They met up with their parents in Carlton County, AR a few weeks later and moved on the Buffalo River.

W. F. Batten married at age 23 to Mary Margaret McReynolds. They paid $300.00 for a pair of mares, a wagon and a set of chain harness, some bacon, lard and some sheaf oats. They lived on the farm they purchased when first married for 26 years. All of his children were born there but one and she was born in sight of it.

He was converted 40 years prior and joined the Mt. Gilead Church. He always tried to do his bit for the church and always helped bury the dead. He raised 52 wheat crops in succession and was over 70 years old before he ever bought a pound of flour. He said he had bought only 55 cents worth of bacon in his life. At the time of this article he had been married 52 years and said he knew the last days of his life were drawing to a close as he had been confined to his room for five weeks now. He said, "There is just one thing to death, and that is being ready to go when you are called. If you are not, you have missed it all."

BAYS – John Franklin Fielding Bays was born 1770 in Maryland. He married Mary Ann Knight, born 1775 in Maryland. Their children: John, Thomas, William and Isaac. Three of the Bays brothers appeared in the Loop (Cabins of the Loop) West Virginia in 1830s, before the formation of Fayette County.

William married Louisa Stuart, the daughter of Henry and Mary Polly (Eagan) Stuart. William and Louisa built a cabin on the west side of Laurel Creek, on the Cassidy Branch (then labeled Bays Branch). Their children: Mary, Elizabeth, John, Sarah, James, George, Sabina, Eliza, Charles and Joseph.

James Louis was born Aug. 14, 1846. He married Leedona Dorsey who was born July 15, 1859. Enumerated in the 1900 Coldwater Township/ Drexel Village census Cass County, MO. Their children: John (farmer), Walter (Rondo store/post office), Gene, Joseph (railroad), Bertha (died at 14), Jesse (farmer, preacher), Frank (railroad) and Leonard (died at 17 months). James died in 1930 in Kansas. James, Leedona and son Joseph are all buried at Sharon Cemetery, Drexel, MO, Cass County. James is buried at Louisburg, KS. Walter is buried at Ronda, MO. Frank is buried at Mt. Vernon, MO.

Jesse was born Sept. 11, 1886. He married Carrie Adell Darmon on Sept. 21, 1908 in Bolivar, MO. Carrie was born Feb. 23, 1890 in Cabery, IL, the daughter of John and Anny (Conavle) Darmon. Their known children: Charlie, Ruby, Carrie and Cora. Jessie and Carrie were enumerated in the 1920 census, Cliquot Township, Polk County, MO.

Wedding Day 1908 in Bolivar, MO; Jesse Meloy Bays and Carrie Adell (Darmon)

Children were Florence, Effie, Annie, Charlie, Glen, Shirley, Nellie, Richard, Clarence and Earshell Lee. Jesse died March 19, 1963 in Kansas; burial was in Salem Cemetery, Cliquot. Carrie died Oct. 19, 1975 in Bolivar; burial in Greenwood Cemetery, Bolivar.

Family of Charlie Joseph and Myrtle Lorene (Seiner) Bays, front: Lorene, James David, Charlie, Sandra Sue, Bonnie and Jeanette; back: Harold, Ray, Charles and Lendville

Charlie was born Nov. 18, 1915 in Drexel, MO. He married Myrtle Lorene Seiner on April 19, 1941 in Bolivar. Lorene was born Dec. 6, 1919 in Polk County. (See Waggoner/ Seiner family by Ronda (Vote) Wood.) Charlie enlisted in the army serving from Nov. 12, 1942 until March 12, 1945; being honorably discharged in Colorado. Their children: Ray, Charles, Bonnie, Harold, Lendville, David and Sandy. Charlie died May 10, 1976, buried in Greenwood Cemetery in Bolivar.

Bonnie was born Jan. 26, 1946 near Huron. She attended Pleasant Hope and Morrisville Schools. She married John W. Vote Jr. (See Vote family by Lisa Ann Vote-Hickman.) They married Jan. 25, 1963 in Eudora, Polk County. Their children: Ronda Yvonne, Regina Jeanette, Melissa Ann and John Joseph. All of their children attended and graduated Morrisville, 1982, 1983, 1984 and 1986.

Ronda was born Dec. 11, 1963. She married David Butler on Dec. 27, 1983 at Bolivar. Their children: Heather Dawn and Brian Allen. They divorced and Ronda married Ray Wood in Peculiar, MO on Oct. 6, 2000. Ronda works for a real estate company.

Regina was born on Oct. 26, 1965. She married David Phillips on Jan. 19, 1985 in Aldrich, MO. Their children: Derrick Scott and Rachel Diane. Regina has worked at CMH Bolivar since the second year of operations. David works at Bolivar Sheet Metal.

Melissa "Lisa" was born on Feb. 28, 1966. She married Lullel Hickman in Morrisville. Their children: Logan Ryan and Lacy Diane. Lisa is a homemaker and a genealogist. Lullel works for Terry Rountree in Bolivar.

John was born May 10, 1968 and married Kim Bruebeck in Bolivar. They divorced and John and girlfriend Kelly Fargo of New York had a daughter McKenna Mae. John is a truck driver.

The Bays family has had six generations to live in Polk County, MO. *Submitted by Regina Jeanette (Vote) Phillips*

BEASON – Josiah Beason was born about 1837 in Jackson County, AL, the son of Henry Beason and Frances McKie. After 1843 Henry and Frances and nine of their ten children moved to Oregon County, MO. In the early 1850s Frances, a widow, and some of the children came to Dade County, MO.

Josiah married Aug. 30, 1855 in Polk County, Sarah Jane Blair, born circa 1839, daughter of Alexander Blair and Rebecca Brown. In 1857 Josiah and Sarah were living in Texas, probably Denton County, when their son Henry was born. They were back in Missouri when son John was born in 1858. It appears Sarah died not long after 1860.

In September 1862, Josiah enlisted in Company A, Shelby's Brigade, 3rd Missouri Cavalry, Confederate Army. He was probably in the Battle of Newtonia and later was in the Battle of Springfield, Jan. 8, 1863. He was so severely wounded that he was one of those left to be cared for by the Federals. He died in the Courthouse Hospital in Springfield, MO on Jan. 20, 1863.

The two young orphan boys, aged 4 and 5 years, lived mostly with their grandmother, Frances Beason. They both later lived many years in Polk County where they married and reared their families.

Henry A. Beason (born Jan. 24, 1857; died March 18, 1945, buried Pleasant Ridge Cemetery) married Melissa Emily O'Neal (born 1859; died 1892) the daughter of James W. O'Neal and Chloe Pyland. They had four children: James, Lula, Chloe and George.

James Albert (born Feb. 7, 1881; died Sept. 24, 1972) married Bessie J. Hagerman. He married second, Myrtle Tarter.

Lula Ann (born July 29, 1884; died March 2, 1966) married Jeddiah Wynkoop. Their children: Wilda A. (Carter) and John J.

Chloe (born April 11, 1886; died Sept. 25, 1974) married J. Marion Douglas.

George Washington (born Dec. 22, 1888; died Feb. 5, 1975) married Mollie Smith. Their children: Vera (Low Bath), Marjorie (Root Shiner), Thelma (May), Gaylord and Mary L. (Sikes).

Henry married second, Lura M. Coffman Smith. A daughter, Nola Pauline, born July 24, 1908 lived only 6 months.

Richard Jonathan "John " Beason (born Sept. 15, 1858; died March 18, 1834, buried Shady Grove Cemetery) married Rebecca Caroline Wright (born Nov. 14, 1857; died Sept. 14, 1906) daughter of Josiah A. Wright and Elizabeth J. Gothard. They had nine children (listed below):

Joseph Wiley (born Jan. 1, 1879; died Dec. 15, 1943; buried in Shady Grove Cemetery) married first, Lillian E. Stevens (born 1881; died 1902) and second, Ida Maud Jones (born 1884; died 1905). After Maud's death Wiley married her sister, Millie M. Jones (born 1878; died 1966). They had two children, C. Forrest and Fern (Coy.)

Mary Jane (born Jan. 24, 1881; died April 5, 1950) married John D. Castle. They had a daughter, Ruth C. (Tindle).

John Robert "Bob" (born May 17, 1885; died April 26, 1954; buried in Lindley Prairie Cemetery) married Amanda J. Smith and they had a son, Paul A.

Charles A. (born Jan. 2, 1887) was killed in a hunting accident Nov. 29, 1904.

Inis Bell (born June 5, 1888; died March 12, 1914) married Coy E. Smith, Amanda's brother. Their children were Shelton R. and John Henry.

Pearl Elizabeth "Dollie" (born Oct. 10, 1891; died Nov. 3, 1960) married Don S. Lyman. Their children were Paul M. and Calvin R.

Girtha Elmer, twin (born Oct. 10, 1891; died March 8, 1950; Visalia, CA) married Bessie L. Smith. Their children were John T., Lowell and Geraldine (Kelm Waller).

Golden Verna (born March 18, 1895; died March 30, 1969) married W. Franklin Reynolds. Their children were Luella (Anderson) and Anna (Carson).

Henry Mack (born Aug. 7, 1890; died Feb. 2, 1962, buried National Cemetery, Ft. Scott, KS) married V. Ruth Herman. Henry served in both WWI and WWII. Their children were Eugene M. and Robert G.

After Caroline died, John married her cousin, Amanda P. (born Jan. 10, 1867; died March 13, 1942) daughter of Louiza J. Wright and Armstead Owen. A daughter, Helen Dale, was born Jan. 4, 1910, and lived only a week.

Many members of the family lived and died and were buried in Polk County. Descendants still live here. *Submitted by Kay Ammerman Wilson*

BEERSMAN – On Feb. 14, 1964 Billy Lee and Wanda Lea Beersman moved to Polk County. They were both raised in Greene County near Springfield, MO. Billy was born on Oct. 23, 1928, the oldest child of William Gustaf Beersman and Gladys Lee (Hendricks) Beersman. Wanda was born on April 23, 1932, the youngest child of Benjamin Maxwell Edmondson and Grace Jurettea (Paul) Edmondson. They brought with them two children, Sandra Lynne, born June 30, 1954, who was 9 years old at the time and Wesley Gene, born June 6, 1957, who was 6 years old at the time. The family settled on a farm near Morrisville, which they purchased from Lora Grant, widow of Lester Grant. Here they established a large dairy farm along with Wanda's brother, Dale F. Edmondson and his wife, Mary.

Billy and Wanda were united in marriage on May 17, 1953 in the Oakland Methodist Church east of Springfield by the Reverend Guy Thompson, a Polk County native.

Wesley and Sheri Beersman, Wanda and Billy Beersman, Garry Jackson and Sandra (Beersman) Jackson.

Wanda attended Springfield Central High School and graduated from Southwest Missouri State College. She taught one year in Marshfield High school before marrying Billy. Billy attended Strafford High School and Business College before he joined the Marine Corps in 1950 during the Korean War. He spent two years at Camp Pendleton in California.

The Beersmans lived six years in western Greene County on a farm bought from Billy's grandparents, Lee and Margaret Hendricks (1958-1964). In 1970 Wanda became a teacher in Morrisville High School where she taught mathematics for 15 years.

Both Sandra and Wesley graduated from Morrisville's Marion C. Early High School. Sandra graduated in 1972 and Wesley graduated in 1975. Sandra graduated from Southwest Baptist University after marrying Gary Wayne Jackson on Aug. 11, 1973 with a degree in elementary education. Wesley graduated from the University of Missouri in Columbia with a degree in agriculture in 1979, then worked on a dairy farm in Lamonte, MO for two years. Following this time, he came home and joined the farm partnership in 1980. On June 20, 1992 he married Sheri Lynn Cable and became father to her two children.

Billy and Wanda have six grandchildren: Mark Allen Jackson (born Jan. 4, 1977); Jenny Ellen Jackson (born June 23, 1983); Holly Nicole Jackson (born Sept. 9, 1985); Christopher Ryan Cable (born March 21, 1987); Lauren Elizabeth Cable (born May 26, 1988) and Danielle Lynne Beersman (born May 20, 1994).

The farm partnership lasted until April of 2000 when it disbanded. Billy spends his time making toys and helps Wanda work in their life-long service to the United Methodist Church in Morrisville. *Submitted by Billy Beersman*

BELBACKS – The Belbacks came to Polk County sometime in the 1930s. Maeland "Bud" Belback, son of Harry and Cora Mae (Newman) Belback was born in Flint, MI on Aug. 20, 1914. He died in Kansas City, MO on June 10, 1969. He is buried in National Cemetery in Fort Leavenworth, KS. He was married on June 3, 1938 in Polk County to Pearl Willine Dunaway. She was born in Halfway, MO on Aug. 20, 1920, daughter of Elijah Alphred and Nina Pearl (Tucker) Dunaway. Willine died in Grants Pass, OR on Sept. 25, 1979. She is buried in Hillcrest Memorial Park Cemetery, in Grants Pass, OR. Two children were born to this union, Harriette Willine and Elijah Earnest "Buck." Bud and Willine divorced on May 14, 1956.

Harriette Willine Belback was born in Polk County on July 17, 1939. She married Jan. 25, 1957 to Kenneth Clayton Cole, born March 15, 1934 in Orange County, CA, son of Noble and Mable (Schoaley) Cole. They had three children.

Debra Lynn Cole was born Aug. 21, 1959 in Roark Springs, WY. Debbie had two children. Cassandra Cole Childers was born in Honolulu, HI on April 18, 1992 and Noah Paul Shepherd was born in Oklahoma City, OK on Sept. 24, 1998. Debbie was married on Jan. 21, 2001 to Michael New.

Kenneth Clayton Cole Jr. was born June 21, 1961 in Odgen, UT. Kenny and Nellie Lee Taylor's daughter Susan Ashley was born in New York state on May 16, 1990.

Allan Dale Cole was born in Independence, MO on Nov. 21, 1963. He was married on June 3, 2001 to Stephanie Wallace.

Kenneth and Harriette divorced on March 28, 1969.

Harriette's second marriage was on Oct. 10, 1969 to Jackie Lynn Cummings, son of J. C. and Nellie (Buchanon) Cummings. Jack was born in Clinton, MO on Nov. 27, 1939. He died Aug. 15, 1984 and is buried in Englewood Cemetery in Clinton, MO. They had one child.

Stephanie Rene Cummings was born in Independence, MO on Jan. 23, 1971. She was married on Oct. 9, 1987 to David Ben Carpenter, born in California on March 5, 1968. The have two children, Cody David, born Jan. 2, 1989 and Bethanie Rene, born May 14, 1992. They were both born in Independence, MO.

Jack and Harriette divorced on June 28, 1977.

Harriette's companion of 13 years, James Lee Miller Jr., was born in Orange County, CA on Nov. 24, 1946, son of James Lee Miller Sr. and Ruth (Faircloth) Miller. James and Harriette plan on returning to Polk County after retirement. *Submitted by Harriette Cummings*

BELBACK – Elijah Earnest Belback "Buck" son of Maeland and Pearl Willine (Dunaway) Belback was born in Polk County on Sept. 15, 1941. He was married on Dec. 26, 1961 to Charlesetta "Shorty" Willis, daughter of Leaford and Lottie (West) Willis, born on Dec. 18, 1943 in Strafford, MO. They had two children, Mark Eugene and Jeffrey Scott Belback.

Mark Eugene Belback was born at Wright Patterson Air Force Base in Dayton, OH on Dec. 3, 1962. He was married Feb. 9, 1980 to Mary Magdalene Gray, born in Iowa City, IA on Jan. 23, 1964. They had two children. They divorced on April 2, 1988.

Kellie Ra'Shea Belback was born in Phoenix, AZ on April 13, 1982 and was married on June 10, 2000 to Brandon Wesley Flack, son of Wesley and Rhonda (Fletcher) Flack, born on Feb. 7, 1983 in San Diego, CA. They divorced on May 29, 2001.

Krystal Re'Nea Belback was born in Phoenix, AZ on May 1, 1983.

Mark Eugene was married a second time on April 22, 1988 to Penny Diane (Griffith) Underwood, born in California on June 8, 1964. They had one child, Lacey Danielle, born on June 29, 1989. They were divorced on May 14, 1991.

Mark Eugene was married a third time on July 9, 1998 to Dalene Ann (Gabbert) Belle-Isle, born in Denver, CO on Dec. 5, 1954. Mark and Ann moved to Polk County in July of 1998.

Jeffrey Scott Belback was born in Independence, MO on April 18, 1964 and was married on Aug. 24, 1984 to Doris Mae (Carlson) White. She was born in California on June 8, 1957. They had one child, Faye Marie Belback, born on Jan. 27, 1985 in Phoenix, AZ. They separated in 1985. He plans to move to Polk County in the near future.

Buck left Polk County in 1959. After spending 15 years in Phoenix, AZ, they moved back in May of 1995 along with two of their granddaughters, Kellie Ra'Shea and Krystal Re'Nea. Kellie graduated from Fair Play High School in 2000. Krystal graduated from Fair Play High School in 2001.

Maeland "Bud" Belback was born on Aug. 30, 1914. He was married on June 4, 1964 to Virgie Smith. She was born on Sept. 7, 1924. They had one daughter, Judy Faye, born July 19, 1965.

Judy Faye Belback married Arlis Lee Gale on Feb. 14, 1984. He was born on March 27, 1921 and he died on April 27, 2002. They had two children, Matthew Artis, born Dec. 10, 1984 and Sarah, born on Sept. 4, 1994. *Submitted by Ernie Belback*

BENGE – George Washington Benge was the fifth child of James Almon and Mary Jane Utley Benge. His family left Tennessee in 1858 and was residing in Bolivar, MO when George was born on March 12, 1860. Later, his family lived about two miles southwest of Brighton near the main road to town at that time.

George Washington Benge about 1928 in Norman, OK, showing off the fruits of his labor.

When he was 11, his mother died and his father married the widow Woodard about a year later. They moved a mile southwest to the Woodard place; this was down in the valley almost directly north of the forks of Sac and Dry Sac Rivers and the ford across the river became known as "Benge Ford."

At the age of 14 George left home as a stowaway. He hid in the back of the wagon when his sister and her husband migrated to Texas. When he was discovered, they had traveled too far to turn back, so he was allowed to continue with them.

George remained in Texas for several years before returning to visit his father in Polk County in 1880. Leaving there, he traveled to Lake County, CO where he joined his brothers in a mining venture.

When his father died in 1882, George returned to Polk County and it was decided he would take his young siblings to Texas where most of the Benge children were residing in the Moody area. These children remained with family members until they married and began their own families. On Sept. 19, 1885, George married Fannie Witt in Moody, TX. She was the daughter of Francis Witt and Eliza Llewellen and was born on March 7, 1863 in Alabama. They had four children: Walter Lee (born Nov. 10, 1884; died Aug. 8, 1972); Mary Frances Benge (born April 28, 1887; died Feb. 8, 1970); Thomas Guy (born Jan. 19, 1890; died Aug. 25, 1984) and Ellie Ester (born March 23, 1892; died May 3, 1896).

George's half-sister, Virginia Stokes, reported that he helped obtain her first teaching position at Willow Springs School near Moody, TX in 1893. Fannie died March 1, 1894 and is buried in the Moody Cemetery; Ellie is buried beside her mother.

George and Ida Ann Newsom were married in Moody, TX on Dec. 23, 1895. She was born Aug. 4, 1867 in Clay County, AL to Joseph C. and Eliza Jane Goode. They had the following six children: Rudy (born Nov. 9, 1896; died Nov. 9, 1896); Utley Newson (born Oct. 31, 1897; died Oct. 22, 1966); Garland George (born Dec. 31, 1898; died July 6, 1967); Fred Sherman (born Jan. 7, 1901; died Nov. 4, 1977); Johnie Blain (born Dec. 18, 1902; died June 8, 1910) and Cecil Orville (born Feb. 22, 1905; died Jan. 15, 1981).

By 1897, they were living in Brandon, TX where all his sons were born. George had orchards of peaches and apples in addition to his farmland. With all these activities he found time in June of 1900 to help with the census enumeration in Hill County, TX.

Around 1910 they moved to Randlett, OK where Johnie Blain was killed in a tragic wagon accident and was buried in the Fairview Cemetery. The family remained there until about 1917 when they moved to Norman, OK.

His sons helped George establish a farm on the outskirts of Norman and later he acquired properties in town as well. The death of Johnie Blain had a devastating effect on the family and on Sept. 13, 1922, George and Ida filed for divorce in Norman, OK. The decree became effective six months later.

George suffered losses when the stock market crashed in 1929. His farm and other properties sustained his family during the years of depression and drought. George maintained his farm until his death on June 6, 1935. Ida died on May 26, 1945 and both are buried in the IOOF Cemetery in Norman, OK.

As a young man George loved adventure and travel; these traits carried him through life and provided him with a positive outlook to the very end. *Submitted by Syndi Austin Samsoe*

BENGE – James Almon Benge was born Dec. 18, 1828 in Tennessee. His father's name is unknown, but the 1880 census indicated he was born in Tennessee. Family members have maintained that his father died when James was about 4 years old and his mother, Mary Benge, took the children and returned to "her people" after her husband's death. It is not clear where she or "her people" were living at that time. Her granddaughter recorded that Mary's maiden name was Luttrell. Mary died in 1849 in Roane County, TN at the age of 40; she is reported to have been born in Kentucky. James had two sisters, Easter and Fanettie Benge. Fanettie died when she was about 15 years and Easter married Thomas Nelson on May 17, 1849 in Roane County, TN. Later, she married John Barton and according to surviving letters, lived in Nevada City, Nevada County, CA in 1855.

James Almon Benge married Mary Jane Utley

in Roane County, TN on Aug. 19, 1849. Mary Jane was born June 17, 1832 in either North Carolina or Tennessee. Her father is believed to be Henry Utley, residing near them in Roane County in 1850.

James and Mary began their journey from Tennessee to Polk County, MO in 1858 with their four small children. The only known family connection to the Benges in Polk County was James Utley, who was referred to as Mary Jane's "uncle" by her family.

In 1862, in accordance with General Order No. 3, a list of "Rebels of Polk County" was compiled, listing James A. Benge. However, the Enrolled Missouri Militia, Company F, Regiment 26 had James A. Benge enrolled and ordered in on Sept. 25, 1864 and relieved on Nov. 18, 1864 in Bolivar, MO. What his true convictions were during this time of civil war may never be known.

Virginia Stokes described her father as a man of medium height and build with light brown hair, fair complexion and deep blue eyes that looked upon life seriously.

The children of James Almon and Mary Jane Benge are, as follows: William Henry (born Jan. 13, 1851; died about 1905); Mary Elizabeth Ryan Spillman (born Feb. 16, 1853; died Aug. 9, 1918); Phoebe Jane Gent Kilman (born April 11, 1855; died July 3, 1938); John Thomas (born Sept. 19, 1857; died April 9, 1932); George Washington (born March 12, 1860; died June 6, 1935); Louisa Matilda Williams (born Dec. 22, 1863; died about 1944); James Wilson (born Jan. 9, 1866; died June 15, 1868); Lidda Ellen (born March 20, 1868; died April 13, 1868); Edward Monroe (born May 25, 1869; died Dec. 25, 1947); Easter Finettie Torrance (born May 25, 1869; died Dec. 10, 1934) and Eva Isabella (born Oct. 21, 1871; died Sept. 17, 1872).

Mary Jane died at the age of 39 from complications due to childbirth on Oct. 21, 1871. She was buried in Hickory Grove Cemetery near Brighton, MO.

Sept. 22, 1872, James Almon Benge married Martha Ann Bland Woodard. Martha was born in Humansville, MO, on Nov. 23, 1839, the daughter of Elliot Bland and widow of Hiram Monroe Woodard. On Aug. 18, 1873, Martha Virginia Benge was born to this union in Brighton, MO.

James Almon continued farming near Brighton until his death of a heart attack. On April 19, 1882, at the age of 53 he died in Morrisville, MO. He is buried beside Mary Jane and three of their children.

Virginia Benge Stokes described her father as, "an extremely energetic man, always in a hurry to be about his business." She recalled, "He had a nice habit of singing at his work." Virginia remembered, "Every evening before retiring, James called everyone together for a time of family worship." He'd been a member of Hickory Grove Methodist Church until his expulsion a year or so before his death. Summing up the event recorded by Virginia Stokes, he and his wife stood trial for breaking the Sabbath by working to repair a fence, a chore deemed non-essential by the church. Neither denied their guilt, but James refused to say he was sorry because he felt he'd done nothing wrong, so he was expelled from the church.

James Almon wrote a letter to one of his daughters in Texas on Aug. 26, 1879 and concluded with this statement, "I must come to a close by Saying to you when this you See remember me and Bear in mind a trusty friend to find." Today, he is remembered. *Submitted by Gayla Tarry Austin*

BENNETT – John Bryan Bennett was born on July 7, 1896 in Mt. Airy, NC. He was the third son of Lucinda (Hull) and James Martin Bennett. John's siblings were Sallie, Edward, Emma, Lee, Nettie, Celia and Jim.

James and Lucinda brought their eight children to Missouri in the early 1900s and settled on a farm between Cliquot and Flemington. In 1954 the eight Bennett siblings had a family reunion at Sallie Creed's home in North Carolina. At that time John's brother Lee and wife Lena lived in Rondo, MO. His brother Ed and family lived in Deepwater, MO. His brother Jim and family lived in California and his sister Nettie Edwards lived in Columbia, MO. John lived in Flemington with his sisters Emma and Celia. The oldest sister Sallie had returned to Mt. Airy, NC in 1904 where she married and had a family.

John married Ethel Fowler, daughter of Will and Alice (Bugher) Fowler on July 17, 1928. Ethel and their only child, a son, died in April of 1936 following flu complications. Her sister, Ova Whitlock and her new baby also died that spring with the same illness. John kept in close touch with Ethel's family in the following years. His mother-in-law was a special friend until her death in 1949. He also visited Ethel's brothers Grant and Frank and brother-in-law, Noel Whitlock and their families on a regular basis.

John and Esther Bennett

John was a veteran of the United States Army and he did farm work and cut wood in his younger years. He lived in a tent for about a year, while cutting wood with a friend. John also drove a school bus and later operated a gas station for several years in Flemington. He liked to fish and had many friends around the community.

John married the widow of Ray Stovall, Esther (Mitchem) in August of 1957 in Polk County, MO. He became "Papa John" to her seven grown children. He was proud to be "Grandpa" to 23 grandchildren and later several great-grandchildren. He was loved and respected by this ever-growing family. One of his grandchildren, Becky, named her son after him.

John and Esther moved to Fair Play in 1957 and operated the telephone switchboard until 1961. They then bought a place near Bear Creek and lived there for a few years before moving to Humansville. They enjoyed traveling together to visit relatives. They made a trip to Nevada and California to see relatives and also joined Lee and Lena on a trip to North Carolina.

John and Esther lived in Bolivar in their later years until his death on Nov. 24, 1977. Esther died on April 1, 1991. They are buried in the Dunnegan Cemetery. *Submitted by Becky Erickson*

BERRY – Hunter Dene Berry was born in Bolivar on Oct. 12, 2001, the first child of Heath Damon Berry and Patricia S. (Rice) Berry. His initials are from his father, grandfather, and great-great grandfather.

"Dene" is from the late Justin Dene Fulbright, lifelong friend of Hunter's father.

Heath is one of two sons of Harold Dave and Brenda K. (Steinshouer) Berry. He was born Nov. 6, 1978. His brother, Joshua David Berry, was born Feb. 20, 1982. Both are graduates of Bolivar High school (1997, 2000) where they were multi-sport lettermen. Heath is in management with Wal-Mart. Josh is a junior at Southwest Baptist University where he is a business major and a pitcher on the baseball team.

Patricia is the daughter of Marty and Susan Rice, also of Bolivar. She, too, is a graduate of Bolivar High School (1998).

Dave Berry was born in Aurora, MO on Aug. 2, 1953. He graduated from Aurora High School (1971) and Southwest Missouri State University (BA in English, minor in journalism, 1975). He moved to Bolivar in August 1977 to become editor of the *Bolivar Herald Free-Press*. He became publisher in 1986 and the title of executive vice president of Sterling Media Ltd. was added in 1989. That company owned newspapers in Bolivar, Buffalo and Stockton, in addition to Missouri ColorWeb Printers in Bolivar. James C. Sterling was president.

In 1999 the company was sold to Community Publishers of Missouri, Inc. Berry became vice president/publisher of that organization which soon grew to include newspapers in Marshfield, Rogersville/Fordland, Ozark and Nixa.

Dave is the 2003 president of the Missouri Press Association. He had served on the Bolivar Board of Aldermen and is past president of the Bolivar Rotary Club, the Bolivar Area Chamber of Commerce, the Missouri Advertising Mangers Association and Ozark Press Association.

He is the son of Helen M. Berry, now of Bolivar, and the late Ben Berry. Helen was a nurse's aide for almost 30 years in Aurora. Ben farmed, worked in orchards, built farm fences, sold firewood and peddled fruit and vegetables.

Brenda Berry was born Brenda Steinshouer on May 16, 1948. Her twin brother is Danny Steinshouer and their mother is Veta (Wells) Steinshouer. Brenda and Danny's father, Lester Steinshouer, was killed in a dynamite accident near Sunset, south of Bolivar in 1953. All are Polk County natives. Brenda and Danny graduated from Bolivar High School in 1966.

Brenda owns and operates Brenda's Café in downtown Bolivar, which she purchased from her brother in 1999. For 16 years prior to that she worked for Dr. R. Lane Nutt, local optometrist.

Veta bakes pies and tends the cash register at Brenda's Café. She had been a waitress for several cafes in and around Bolivar and also worked at Teters Floral Products for many years.

Dave and Brenda also owned Bolivar Bowl and Fantasy Island Arcade for three years, beginning in 1979. It was located alongside Springfield Avenue, north of the square. *Submitted by Dave Berry*

BEST – Mary Elizabeth Renfro Lovett Best was the daughter of Elizabeth Jane Tindle Renfro and Robert Renfro. Her brother was Thomas Asbury Renfro. It is believed that Robert Renfro died in the Rock Island prison in 1864 during the Civil War. Lizzie was born Nov. 26, 1864 and died April 20, 1944. She is buried at Enon Cemetery.

Mary Elizabeth and Joe Best

She first married James William Lovett and to this union two sons, Charlie and Walter, and two daughters, Della and Willy, were born. James died in 1891 and is buried in Enon Cemetery. Lizzie and Joe Best married in 1892 and moved to Iowa where their daughter Sally was born March 1894. Joe Best was born July 12, 1868 and died June 14, 1953. He is buried at Enon Cemetery. Her niece, Mary Elizabeth Renfro Steele was named after her. This made a special bond between the two of them. *Submitted by Janell Dyson Dennis*

BEWLEY – Francis Asbury Bewley was born in Greene County, TN, July 7, 1816, son of John G. Bewley, a local Methodist preacher, and Catherine Hunter. In the mid 1830s, after his father's death, Asbury went to Missouri. Others in his family found in Missouri include his mother, sister Catherine, brothers Isaac and Wells, and his brother, Anthony, the Methodist minister sometimes referred to as a martyr. His brother John continued on to the Oregon Trail.

On Aug. 1, 1837 in Polk County, Asbury married Clementine Winton, born Feb. 15, 1819 in Tennessee, the daughter of William Winton and Mary Mitchell who helped to form the Hickory Grove Methodist Church. Asbury and Clementine had four children: John Wesley, Sarah Jane, Athenias Beriah and James A. Sarah Jane died in 1841 in Lawrence County; the same year Asbury received a land patent in that county. Athenias died in 1861 in Polk County at age 19 and is buried in Hickory Grove Cemetery.

On Aug. 1, 1845, Asbury died at age 29 in Fannin County, Republic of Texas. There was no will, but probate records did include a list of his possessions. The administrator of his estate was William Degraffenreid. Two months after his death, Asbury's son James was born in Texas. By the 1850 census, Clementine and the children are found back in Polk County, MO, living with her parents. Clementine remarried on April 30, 1854 to John Cook and they had three children: Mary L., Martha J. and Sarah D. Clementine died July 14, 1910.

Asbury's brother Anthony, born May 22, 1804 in Tennessee, was a Methodist minister falsely accused of an abolitionist plot and was hung by a mob in Fort Worth on Sept. 13, 1860. Many articles have been written about this sad event. He was married to Jane Winton, Clementine's sister.

John Wesley Bewley, according to his pension file, was born May 28, 1838 in Polk County. In 1860 he was residing in Looney Township and on July 26, 1860 married Ruth Hathaway, who was born in Tennessee in June 1839. During the Civil War he served for the Union in the Enrolled Missouri Militia and in the 15 Regiment Cavalry Volunteers and was mustered out on July 1, 1865 in Springfield.

John Wesley and Ruth had five children: Rose (who died young); James Holbert; George Henry; John Asbury and Vinson Philo. The family moved to Texas around 1876 and John Wesley is said to have been a Methodist circuit preacher in Cooke and Fannin Counties. They were living in Cass County by 1900 where Ruth died in 1913. John Wesley Bewley died June 19, 1921 near Foss, OK age 83.

George Henry Bewley was born in Polk County in August 1864. He married Mary Evelyn "Eva" Gent around 1892 and they lived in the McLennan County, TX area. Eva was born June 1874 in Missouri, the daughter of William T. Gent and Phoebe Jane Benge. They had 10 children. George died in 1921 in Texas where many of his descendants still live today. Some are also found in Oklahoma and Arkansas. *Submitted by Oscar Bewley and Bertie Jo Bewley*

BEWLEY – From a newspaper article published in the *Bolivar Herald Free Press* on April 20, 1922.

CLICKS HIS HEELS AT 85

"Uncle Jesse" was 85 years old last Saturday. He can still jump up and crack his heels together. He says there are only five older men around Bolivar: J. W. Johnson, a month older; L. L. Stafford and W. J. Cox, a year older; and James T. Marshall and D. M. Northern, two years older.

Jesse Bewley was born April 15, 1837 on a farm 15 miles south of Glasgow, Barren County, KY. He was the sixth of eight children and the only one alive today. His father died at 61 and his mother at 55.

Jesse married at the age of 18 on Oct 18, 1855 to Mary J. Davis, a neighbor girl living five miles away. They, her father, John David, and his children arrived at the Grand River bottom in Henry County, MO on May 4, 1856. They spent the summer there and that fall they settled in the wood of Polk County, the Bewleys 10 miles north of Bolivar, one mile east of Pomme de Terre, and the Davises a short distance away.

Mr. Bewley started housekeeping on $30 (charged). He made some of his own furniture. Besides farming he did odd jobs, often mending shoes into the night after a hard day's work on the farm. His wife grew cotton and he had a cotton gin.

When the Civil War began he first enrolled in the Home Militia, was next in the post service under E. P. S. Roberts, then with the 7th Provisional Rangers under Colonel Allen, and finally served 20 months with the regular army. He was mustered out at Springfield in 1865. He went through the war uninjured.

His first wife died soon after the war. They had seven children, five of whom area still alive: Mrs. Nancy Franklin of Willard; John W. Bewley of R 5, Bolivar; James T. Bewley, near Louisburg; Mrs. Nancy I. Waggoner, near Hennessey, OK and Mrs. Belle Odom of Bolivar.

In 1872 he married Ada Spillman. One child survives this union, Mrs. Luther McPheeters of Lone Wolf, OK. His wife died about 1878.

Mr. Bewley's third wife was Mrs. Catherine Odom, whom he married in 1880. Their married life covered nearly 40 years until her death on March 19, 1919.

Mr. Bewley spent his first 30 years in Missouri on the old farm north of Bolivar. He went to Walnut Grove for five years, came back to the home place for a year and a half then moved to Bolivar, where he had lived 29 1/2 years. His two pet hobbies are the Bible and fishing. He was converted in 1872 in a Baptist meeting at Oak Grove conducted by Rev. Robertson and had worn out four Baptist Bibles since that time.

Jesse Bewley

He joined the Masonic Lodge at about the same time he joined the church. Since living in Bolivar, he has had leisure to fish a good deal. Fishermen of past years were never surprised to run across Uncle Jesse anywhere on Piper or Pomme de Terre, with his hook in the water, and his boast is that he always came home with fish. He is convinced that perch are the best eating yet. In recent years he has passed up the creek, for he is getting old and fishing in not what is used to be anyhow.

Mr. Bewley is in good health and spirits having survived two critical attacks of pneumonia many years' back. He is selling all his possessions and will visit among his children the balance of his life. He plans a trip to Lone Wolf and Hennessey, OK next fall to his two daughters there. *Submitted by Jim Phillips*

BLACK – James Black came to Polk County in the late 1830s from Kentucky with three sons, Joseph, Jeramiah and William. James bought and sold several farms in Polk County before moving to Pettis County. James is buried in the Hickory Point Cemetery.

Jeramiah was a member of the Turk-Hobbs circle during the Slicker War. For his duties performed in the Mexican War, President Buchanan awarded him 160 acres in Polk County on Nov. 7, 1852. He married Matilda Loyal, daughter of Andrew and Malita (Goodson) Loyal. Jeramiah and Matilda bought other farms. They had two son, John Andrew and James William. While sitting on a rail fence at his brother William's house, Jeramiah was shot by a bushwhacker and died that night, April 1864. He is buried in the Rondo Cemetery. Matilda died in 1884.

Molly (Franklin) Black and John Andrew Black

John Andrew was born Aug. 12, 1853 and married Eliza Austin in 1874. In 1880 he bought 80 acres in Green Township. Their children were: William, Elbert, Elizabeth, Isaac and Eliza. In 1887 Eliza died and John married Molly McGuligan Franklin on Oct. 3, 1888. She was the daughter of Henry and Josephine (Bridges) Franklin. Henry and brother Anthony left Kentucky with their families and a Negro named Mammie in the spring of 1881 and came to Polk County. John and Molly's children were Frona, Henry, Myrtle, Meggie, Cecil, Mire and Orpha. They homesteaded 80 acres besides his first 80 acres. Here they built a log one-room home with an upstairs. Soon after they added two rooms with two upstairs onto the log rooms; these new rooms were not made of logs. They also added a front and back porch. John made and fired the bricks for the fireplace. They bought several other farms, all but a few years they lived on the first homeplace. John enjoyed trading and buying horses. John died Nov. 18, 1926 and Molly then made her home with Cecil, where she died July 1, 1950. John, Eliza and Molly are buried in the Lindley Creek Cemetery.

Clarence Cecil was born April 1, 1898 in the

Clarence, VaNita, Kenneth Black, Doris Crawford and Buford Black

Caroline (Shoman) Black and Clarence Cecil Black

Back row: Lee, James III and Doris Crawford and Robert Boyd; front row: Thomas, Vanessa LeBow, Trina Crawford, Tamaira LeBow and Samantha Boyd

home his folks had built. He enjoyed hunting and fishing. As a young man, he and two friends drove to California to work where they picked peaches, figs and melons. Returning home, he married Caroline Wilda Shoman on Jan. 1, 1927, the daughter of George and Ola (Harmon) Shoman. Their children were John Kenneth, Doris Evelyn, George Clarence, Buford DuVane and Dorothy VaNita, all born in the same room as their father. Cecil was a member of the Star Ridge School Board; as a youngster he had gone to school there. Later all five of his children walked the same path to school. In November of 1943, the family moved to a farm joining the Carter School. Cecil was also a member of their school board. Cecil died March 26, 1976, Caroline died July 24, 1981 and both are buried in upper Lindley Creek Cemetery.

Doris Evelyn was born March 8, 1929 and married James Ralph Crawford. Their children were

Back row: Rosetta Bolling, Kay Crawford and Lois LeBow; front row: James, Doris and James II Crawford

Molly Rosetta (Boyd) Bolling, Lois Evelyn LeBow, James Ralph III and Marilyn Kay Crawford. Their grandchildren are Robert Boyd, Samantha Mathew, Thomas, Tamaira and Vanessa LeBow, James Lee and Trina Crawford. *Submitted by Doris Crawford*

BLACKBURN – Neva's great grandfather, Jesse Blackburn was born in Blackburn, England UK, and died 1860 in Rochester, Racing County, WI from a logging accident. He married Cornelius Fields who was born April 13, 1883 and died Sept. 19, 1915. Their children were John Alexander (born Jan. 14, 1852; died May 30, 1938) Frank (born Feb. 8, 1857; married Charlotte McCutcheon); and Lillian J. (married O. Rigby Strong).

John Alexander married Loretta Eliena Davis (born June 28, 1859) on Feb. 20, 1879 in Cordon, Wayne County, WI. He died Feb. 13, 1956 in Bolivar, Polk County, MO and was buried at Greenwood Cemetery in Bolivar, Polk County, MO. Their children: Nellie Mae (born Dec. 13, 1880; died Sept. 18, 1968) married William Henry Wenzel (born March 11, 1869; died Nov. 2, 1956) both are buried in Greenwood Cemetery; Arthur John (born Oct. 17, 1883; died June 10, 1946) married Cora B. Bradford (born 1885; died March 2, 1939) both are buried in Greenwood Cemetery; and Jesse Matthew (born Oct. 1, 1887; died April 10, 1965) married Elmeda Helen Carey (born March 25, 1892; died June 28, 1952).

Loretta E. Blackburn came to Polk County with her daughter Nellie Mae and William Henry Wenzel from Mabel, Daviess County, MO in 1913 or 1914. They bought a farm in the Pleasant Vale School District just west of Bolivar where they built a home, drilled a well and installed a windmill. Will farmed and raised cattle and hogs. Some years later the Polk County Court asks them to manage the "Poor Farm" that joined their property. Neva can remember as a child that the living quarters were on the second floor of the brick, two-story house. The women also had rooms on the second floor, with the men on the first floor and the kitchen and dining room. Some of the patients, Derby and Ward, who was a deaf mute, shared a room. Alice had a doll collection and would let Neva play with some of them under her supervision when Neva would visit. Those who were able would help with the gardening and chores and other farming projects. The extra garden yield was canned. Uncle Will would butcher and cure the meats for future use. The Polk County Youth Building is located on the site just south of Highway T.

Arthur and Cora Blackburn came to Polk County from Mabel, Daviess County, MO around 1918 and settled in the Union District. He was a skilled carpenter. Their home is still standing on West Austin Street in Bolivar, MO.

Jesse Matthew and Elmeda "Meda" and daughter Neva Mae came to Polk County in 1921 by rail, from Mabel, Daviess County, MO with all of their household and livestock to settle on 40 acres west of Bolivar, MO. Jesse would later trade it for property on East Locust Street in Bolivar, Polk County, MO. Here their second daughter was born, LaurNell Jessie, on Dec. 23, 1926. They both attended grade and high school in Bolivar, MO. Neva Mae married John Charles Titus (born July 12, 1900; died Feb. 14, 1982) on Aug. 12, 1930. Their daughter, Neva Charlene was born at her Uncle Arthur's home on Aug. 14, 1934. LaurNell married John Edward Strack (born May 11, 1924) on June 16, 1943. Their two children are Helen Ann (born April 1, 1952) and Jesse Christopher (born July 8, 1956). *Submitted by Neva Mae Titus*

BLACKWELL – Christena Blackwell, a third generation resident of Polk County, descended from John and Debora Christena Rowels and Marion and Elizabeth "Lizzie" Rowels. Christena married Earl "Pick" Blackwell. Their first two children, Betty Jean and Gerald Wayne, died at a very early age in the early 1930s. In 1935, they had another child, Patricia Louise.

At age 9, "Patty Lou" and parents moved to Rondo to run a store selling food and novelties. Pat, as she was later called, grew up with many friends and neighbors. In 1957 in Oakland, CA, Pat married Navy man Edward Shoemake, son of Audrey and Glen Shoemake. In 1959, she gave birth to Christy Faye. By 1961, "Eddie" was on the Kansas City police force, and Pat gave birth to Deborah Kaye "Debbie." Eddie had spent time in Polk County, attending school in Humansville.

The Shoemakes spent seven years in Kansas and often made trips "home" to Polk County, often to attend reunions in Dunnegan Park. In 1968, Eddie rejoined the navy and was sent in 1969 to Vietnam. Pat and the girls stayed in California. In 1971, the family moved to Midway Island.

On a trip home to Rondo, Eddie was visiting with Pat's Uncle Colonel Arnold, brother of Earl. They negotiated for Eddie and Pat to buy land next to Rondo property owned by him and wife Elva. This was a place where they sat two mobile homes over time. They put a nice pond on the property, and Christy and Debbie enjoyed going there for walks and to fish or interact with nature.

Back row: Todd Hoffren, Kimberly Johnson, Edward Shoemake and Tom Johnson; Front row: Deborah Hoffren, Patricia Shoemake, Janet Johnson, Christy and Denise Johnson, 2003

In the 1970s, Christy and Debbie spent time fishing for catfish at Arnold and Elva's pond and visiting their home.

Christy and Debbie visited around Rondo as kids and teens. They walked to the church to play the piano and to visit neighbors like Ada French and her dog, Pug and also Mildred Campbell. For years, they would go with their grandfather to the stockyard, to deliver feed or to feed hogs. They looked forward to times at their grandparents' store where they were given candy and soda. Sometimes they would slice meat, pump gas sell groceries and novelties just to be with their grandparents and visit with local residents.

Christy and Debbie would help clean fish caught at their uncle's pond, and Debbie developed a passion for cooking the country foods she learned to make at her grandmother's hand. Both girls learned crafts here. Debbie has fond memories of eating melons with their grandfather.

The girls and parents moved around with the military. Both went back to Polk County. Christy was in college at Bolivar in 1978 and Debbie was in high school at Humansville, graduating in 1979. The girls previously attended high school in California and Guam.

Both girls were married at Rondo Baptist Church. Christy remains married to her husband, Tom and has three teenaged daughters: Janet, Denise and Kimberly. Debbie is remarried to Todd and lives happily in south Texas. Neither could live without memories of their time in Rondo. *Submitted by Deborah (Shoemake) Hoffren*

BLACKWELL – Christy Johnson is the daughter of Edward and Patricia Shoemake and also the granddaughter of Earl and Christena Blackwell. She now resides in southeast Missouri with her husband Tom and her three daughters, Janet, Denise and Kimberly. Her connection with Polk County dates back the early 1960s. As a child Christy lived a good portion of the time in Edgerton, KS, and many a weekend was spent loading up the Plymouth or Buick or whatever her parents happened to own at the time and traveling to her grandparents' house located out on Highway 83, 12 miles north of Bolivar.

Christy's grandma and grandpa owned the Blackwell Feed and Grocery Store. During about every visit her grandma offered her and her sister Debbie one of every delectable treat available; a candy bar, a bottle of Vess soda pop, a push-up or ice cream sandwich and a bag of Guys potato chips. Those were truly great days for the Shoemake sisters. Their grandma and grandpa had one staunch rule, and that was that they couldn't sit on the pop boxes, which was of course, in an excellent location for sitting. Christy and Debbie always found it tempting. Christy and her sister would also get to help wait on customers and help put coins in little stacks at the end of the day. Christy still enjoys counting money.

During the visits to Grandma and Grandpa's house, Grandpa would sometimes take the girls in his truck a short distance down the road to help feed the pigs or to get buckets of water from a well to haul back to the house. Grandpa Blackwell had quite a sense of humor and would sometimes chase Christy's sister, Debbie, around the house with his false teeth. On Sunday, the family would attend church at the Rondo Baptist Church, Grandma Blackwell would teach Sunday school class, something that she was quite good at. In later years, Christy and Debbie each had the pleasure of accompanying Grandpa Blackwell on a cattle hauling trip to Kansas City in his big truck. All of these were terrific experiences for Christy and her sister.

In later growing up years, Christy's family moved around a lot because of her dad being in the navy. Trips back to Polk County were still managed and in 1977 Christy and her parents decided that she would attend Southwest Baptist University. She loved the professors and the friendly atmosphere there and would choose it again in a heartbeat. This was also where she met her future husband, Tom. Christy and Tom had many fun exciting times visiting the Pomme de Terre Lake, waling to the Pomme de Terre River and taking occasional trips to Springfield. They also attended the Rondo Baptist Church, where they were active in Sunday school. Sundays were always spent at Grandma Blackwell's house eating fried chicken and mashed potatoes.

Christy and her family still make occasional trips back to Polk County to visit Christy's mother, Patricia, and Tom's parents, Charlie and Loretta Johnson. They always have a great time. *Submitted by Christy (Shoemake) Johnson*

BLAND – Elliot Bland was born in Shackleford, VA on Oct. 3, 1813 and died on July 4, 1898. The family farm was two miles from Shackleford and five miles from West Point. He was the youngest of 10 children and was only 8 days old when his mother died. He was raised and nursed by "Black Sadie." He was named Elliot after a Captain Elliot who commanded one of Perry's fleets. At the age of about 14, he was "bound out to a shoemaker" in Richmond to learn the trade. When he became 21, he was given a horse, bridle, saddle and a tool kit. At that time he journeyed to Sumner County, TN to join his brother Isaac. The both of them were enrolled and were veterans of the Seminole Indian War for which he received a land grant. He was married to Virginia Adeline Clay in Sumner County, TN on Dec. 4, 1835. There, his eldest son was born and in 1838 he was notified that his father in Shackleford was dying. He and his brother Isaac returned to Virginia and were there when their father died. Elliot received as his inheritance: four oxen, three slaves, Ephraim, Mandy and their child Ellen, and a wagonload of household and miscellaneous items. He returned to Tennessee, loaded up his wife and son and came to Polk County, MO in 1838. He exercised his land grant rights and selected a homestead southwest of Humansville. This homestead was located just north of the salvage yard southwest of Humansville. Elliot and his wife Virginia Adeline Clay had a total of 10 children but only the four older girls survived to become adults. The younger children died and were buried on the farm. Typhoid fever was the probable cause from drinking spring water.

At the onset of the Civil War, Elliot had a prosperous operation there. He had bought additional land. His wife also had her personal slave she brought from Tennessee, as well as other property. Her sisters and husbands also joined Elliot's group coming to Missouri. Knowing that hard times were ahead, Elliot sent his slaves south with a neighbor to be sold. He never heard from that neighbor or the slaves.

When General Fremont gave his orders that all Southern sympathizers were to be deprived of their property, Elliot was given 10 days to vacate his homestead. Meanwhile, his wife died and is buried on the farm as well as the five younger children. After the war was over, he came back to the farm but failed to locate the grave of his wife and children. Elliot took his eldest son and three daughters to Callaway County, MO for the duration of the war. His son Jonathon died in Callaway County.

Elliot made three trips to California, the first from 1850-1953, the second from 1876-1880 and the third from 1888-1890. On his first trip, he was so much in demand as a shoemaker that he had to hire a driver and he worked in the wagon en route making shoes for the other travelers. It is worth mentioning that two of the four oxen on the trip west were the same two he had driven from Virginia. Driving the oxen from Virginia to California was a considerable feat in itself. After filing his first claim and working it for a while, he sold it and set himself up as a shoemaker, a much more profitable line of work. When Elliot left San Francisco by boat to sail home, he left a friend, the son-in-law of Ezekial Campbell who wanted to come with him, but wanted to wait until he sold his claim. I believe Ezekial Campbell ran the Orleans Mill near Aldrich, MO. Elliot's ship was becalmed for a while and it finally docked at New Orleans. He came up the Mississippi on a flat boat with three Spanish horses (Arabian) he had bought while they were being unloaded from a ship. They were palomino in color, a stallion and two mares. When he got back to Missouri, he made a trip to see the Campbell family and was surprised to find the son-in-law had arrived three days earlier, having ridden a mule from California in 67 days. On his later trips to California, he stayed with two of his daughters who now lived there. After his last trip, he came to live with his daughter, Martha Ann who had been married to Hiram Monroe Woodard, a schoolteacher in Humansville. When Elliot was forced to leave the

Christena and Earl Blackwell Country Store at Rondo

farm and go to Callaway County, Martha Ann and her husband returned to the Woodard farm and mill at the forks of the Sac River west of Brighton where the sod farm is located today. Hiram inherited the farm from his father and when Hiram died the property title fell to Martha Anna Bland Woodard. She was left a widow with two small daughters and became the wife of James Almon Benge, who had a number of children of his own. Elliot came to live with Martha Ann in 1880 and lived there until he died. He did make one more trip to California to see his daughters.

Most of this history of Elliot Bland came from Norris' grandmother Martha Virginia Benge who lived in the same house with her Grandfather Elliot from the time she was a small girl until he died. Martha Virginia Benge married John R. Stokes, their oldest daughter is the mother of Norris B. Tummons. *Submitted by Norris B. Tummons*

BLAZER – John Wesley Blazer was born May 14, 1926 in Marshfield, MO, the fifth of 11 children born to Harvey and Samantha Elizabeth Dalton Blazer. John's grandmother was Lydia Isabel Wilson Dalton, granddaughter of Isaac and Nancy Bolton Wilson who settled in Polk County about 1850 and are buried in the Brighton Cemetery.

John and JoAnn Blazer family June 1969

John attended Plank Rural School in Webster County. In 1950 he married JoAnn Elizabeth Pettit, daughter of Ivan and Dorothy Elizabeth Charleston Pettit. John and JoAnn lived in and around Marshfield for about 10 years, where John worked for various farmers. During these years Larry Dale, John Wesley Jr., Thomas Eugene, Michael Wayne and Rebecca Ann were born. In 1959 they moved to Polk County where Mary Janette was born in 1961 and Susan Jo in 1964.

John worked for Townsend Tree Service and Polk County Concrete. He was also a farm laborer and worked for Dunnegan Park in Bolivar. In 1970 John and JoAnn moved southwest to Bolivar and in 1971 the separated. John and the four youngest children Mike, Rebecca, Mary and Susan moved into Bolivar. Four of John and JoAnn's children graduated from Bolivar High School: Larry, John Jr., Mary and Susan. Later John married Irene Bridges and JoAnn married Fritz Standgard. John Wesley Jr. went into the army and served our country for seven years. Michael Wayne went into the army and served for three years. Joann moved out of state for about 14 years. She moved back to Bolivar in 1985. John died of lung cancer Aug. 19, 1981 and is buried at Polk, MO.

John and JoAnn were very proud of their children and their accomplishments. The oldest, Larry married Emma Bonner and later married Debra Jump Patrick. He has a daughter, Jessica Rose Blazer. He resides in Bolivar and works at Jim Rush. John Wesley Jr. resides in Bolivar and works at Thomas RV in Springfield. Thomas Eugene married Nancy Vest and they have two children, Eric Eugene and Aaron O. and they reside in Bolivar. Thomas works for the Bolivar Bus Barn. Michael Wayne resides with his wife and three children, Kyle, Christopher and Katie in LaGrange, KY. Rebecca Ann married Junior Vest and later Tim Winfrey. She had three children, Jamie, Crystal and Brandon. She resides in Pleasant Hill, MO. Mary Jeanette married John Lentz. They have three children, Janetta, John Jr. and Keith Allen. They reside in Springfield, MO. Mary works at Name Brand Clothing in Springfield. Susan Jo married Robert Appleby and later Joe West. Susan and Joe have a daughter Jennifer. Susan lives in Hollister, MO and works in Branson. JoAnn died Sept. 26, 1999 of a lengthy illness. She is buried in Hillcrest Memory Garden Cemetery in Washington, IL. The children have fond memories of their childhood and precious memories of their parents. *Submitted by John Wesley Blazer Jr. and Mary Blazer Lentz*

BLOOMER – John Baxter (1849) and Ellen Wallen Bloomer (1844) are listed in the 1870 census of Scott County, TN. He was the son of Joseph (1807) and Suzannah Roberts Bloomer (1810, married 1827). Two years later they moved to Linden, Christian County, MO for six years prior to moving to Walnut Grove, Greene County, MO.

Their children are Thomas Jefferson, born Feb. 2, 1867; Tivis, born Oct. 15, 1868; and William, born in September 1870. Thomas Jefferson married Josie Wells and died May 13, 1922. She is listed in the *Bloomer Family Book* by Robert J. Bloomer in 1988. Cordie lists his wife as Meg Anderson with the marriage date as March 17, 1898. Tivis married Harriet Jones Aug. 26, 1886 and died December 1923. William married Alice Hayter. A daughter is said to have died as a child.

Tivis and Harriet "Mayme" are Kathy's direct line. Tivis and Harriet lived on the Dade-Polk County line. Their address was Walnut Grove but their store was in Dadeville. The first store burned. They rebuilt a concrete store. It is still standing. The original grocery counter has been divided into three sections and a third is in Kathy's possession.

Their home burned three times. The final concrete home still stands.

Tivis and Harriet had only one living child, Sherman Leonard, born April 14, 1892. He married Sarah May Trost in 1909 in a buggy at the Oak Grove Church. They had two children, Cordie Evelyn born 1910, who married Wayne Davis of Aldrich. She died in 2002. Aaron was born in 1913, marrying June Duffy.

Wedding photo of Sherman and May Trost, July 11, 1909

Cordie and Aaron had two sets of Bloomer grandparents. They called Tivis "Dad" and Harriet "Mayme." Tivis died of appendicitis. Sherman died of appendicitis in 1944. In 1974, Aaron almost died of a gangrenous appendix.

The Bloomer men were tall and large-framed. Sherman loved sports. Aaron and Cordie remember going to bed on someone else's bed many times as the men played croquet. The lighted field allowed the men to play all night at Nox.

Sherman loved to tease and joke. He also loved music and played the guitar. Sherman and May would go to dance parties in the neighborhood.

Although earlier generations were active in the Baptist Church, Sherman did not make a profession of faith in Jesus Christ until Aaron was a young man. He and Aaron both were saved in a brush arbor meeting. Although active for many years in the Oak Grove church, we have no record that he ever joined this church. A handwritten obituary of Tivis states he professed Christ 16 years prior to his death.

The Bloomer farm in Walnut Grove is still owned by Aaron. May helped mix concrete for the last house. As they worked on the house they kept Aaron in a barrel or tub so he wouldn't stray.

Across the road is land they called "Poor Loney," named after some distant kin. Family say they had a mining operation there, as a front for bootlegging.

Tivis, Harriet, Sherman and Mary are all buried in the Oak Grove Cemetery, Polk County, in the Bloomer Plot. *Submitted by Kathy Bloomer*

BOND – Henry Bond was born April 4, 1872 in Maryland. He married Charlotte Lee, born Dec. 6, 1791 in North Carolina. Henry and Charlotte were the parents of three children, all born in Tennessee: Elizabeth (born Oct. 9, 1809); Anne (born Oct. 3, 1812) and Benjamin (born Dec. 29, 1814).

Holbert McClure Bond

All three married in Blount County, TN. Elizabeth to Joseph Tuck Jan. 13, 1825; Anne to Joseph's brother, William Tuck in 1828; and Benjamin to Martha McClure July 14, 1833. Martha, born July 12, 1815 in Tennessee, was the daughter of Holbert and Elizabeth McClure.

Benjamin and Martha had three children, the first of whom died in infancy: Holbert McClure (born June 14, 1835). Benjamin died in Tennessee shortly before his last child, Benjamin H., was born on April 23, 1837. In 1835 the Henry Bond and Tuck families moved to McMinn County, TN, remaining there until 1837 when they moved to Polk County, MO. Martha and her two sons moved with Henry and Charlotte. Upon settling in Polk County, Benjamin's widow, Martha, married Stephen Mitchell. Henry and Charlotte raised the two boys, Holbert McClure and Benjamin H.

Holbert McClure Bond married Corena Lemmon Jan. 12, 1854. Corena was born Sept. 14, 1830, the daughter of John Smith Lemmon and Parmelia Wallace/Wallis. Holbert's brother, Benjamin, married Sarah Mitchell in December of the same year. It is interesting to note that while Holbert fought as a Confederate soldier during the Civil War his brother Benjamin served in the Union Army; years later, the 1880 Census indicates they were living together under the same roof. Henry Bond died July 8, 1855 and his estate was entered into probate Aug. 7, 1855. The court appointed his son-in-law, Joseph Tuck, to be administrator of Henry's estate. Charlotte died in 1857. Henry and Charlotte are buried in Hickory Grove Cemetery, Polk County, MO.

Holbert and Corena were the parents of six children, all born in Polk County. Their fifth child, William Benjamin, was born Nov. 15, 1859, married Jan. 15, 1885 in Polk County, MO to Louisa

Adelvia Willey. Louisa was born Feb. 10, 1860 in Delaware County, OH, the daughter of Henry Willey and Caroline Miller. The Henry Willey family moved from Ohio to Greene County, MO in 1868. Holbert died June 15, 1909 and Corena died June 9, 1878. Both are buried in Hickory Grove Cemetery, Polk County, MO.

William Benjamin "Ben" and Louisa settled on a farm just south of Morrisville, Polk County, MO and were the parents of six children: Corena, Mary Charlotte, Agnes Louise, William Henry, Charles Holbert and Benjamin Roy. Louisa Willey Bond died March 3, 1935 and William Benjamin died Feb. 19, 1939. Both are buried in Wesley Chapel, Greene County, MO.

William Benjamin and Louisa's son Charles was born Sept. 9, 1895, in Polk County, MO. On Dec. 13, 1914 he married Lora Murel McKnight, the daughter of George Donald McKnight and Clara Eldora Sell. Lora was born in Polk County, MO on March 15, 1897. Like his Polk County ancestors before him, Charles farmed. In the late 1920s and early 1930s Charles owned Hillside Kennels, where he bred coon/hunting dogs that were shipped all over the Midwest. Charles and Lora were the parents of five children, all born in Polk County. Charles died March 29, 1949, in Springfield, Greene County, MO and is buried in Wesley Chapel Cemetery. Lora later remarried to Roy Scott. After his death in 1970, Lora moved into Morrisville, where she was living at the time of her death, March 24, 1983. She is buried beside her first husband, Charles, in the Wesley Chapel Cemetery. *Submitted by Junior Bond*

BOND – The great-grandfather of Lero Robertson Tinsley Frazier (born Jan. 12, 1915), John Wesley Bond (born March 25, 1834; died 1911) was born in Simpson County, KY. His grandfather emigrated from Ireland. On Jan. 10, 1861, John married Evaline Ligon (born Dec. 11, 1835; died June 2, 1888), a descendant of President Harrison. They had six children, of whom four daughters survived. John Wesley was a Methodist minister circuit rider, and Lero has his Bible, which has water stains from getting wet in his saddlebags. A family story has it that a Quantrill outlaw was saved under John Wesley's preaching.

One day John Wesley and Mary Adeline "Addie" (born Oct. 9, 1861; died Feb. 27, 1948) set out to pick gooseberries and a handsome young man on a fine horse came riding along. Preacher Bond knew the young Ben Williams and introduced him to Addie, who was extremely embarrassed to be caught wearing her old gloves and sunbonnet. However, Ben began courting Addie, and they were married on Sept. 9, 1880.

Ben F. and Mary Williams with Mabel and Lee circa 1895

Addie and Benjamin Franklin Williams (born March 13, 1855; died Jan. 27, 1932) set up housekeeping in a one-room log cabin where Addie papered the walls with newspapers. Ben rode horseback five miles to teach in a rural school. Their first child, Stella, was born on July 2, 1881, the day President Garfield was shot. As time went on, Eva, Ethel, Alice, Mabel, Lee and Irene were added to the family circle.

Stella left as a missionary to Mexico around 1901. Eva taught three years and then married. Shortly before her marriage, a call came offering Eva another teaching position. Ethel answered the phone and said that Eva was to be married, but that she would teach for them. They accepted, and Ethel began her teaching career.

Ethel and her sisters enjoyed "literary" meetings; programs of singing, reading, jokes, ciphering and spelling matches held at rural schools. They walked and others joined along the way. The weather never kept them at home, though crossing swollen streams on a foot log was sometimes treacherous! Ethel played the organ or piano, while Ike Robertson added his booming bass to the program.

On Sept. 29, 1913 Ethel (born Dec. 27, 1884; died April 29, 1926) and Isaac Benjamin "Ike" Robertson (born May 1, 1885; died April 12, 1949) were married. Lero Irene was born Jan. 12, 1915, and Lucy Pauline (born May 25, 1919; died May 16, 1990) arrived four years later. Her mother told Lero that

Ethel (Williams) Robertson, Lero and Pauline

once when she and her sisters were thinking up names for children, Aunt Mabel came up with the name "Lero." The name seems to be unique; so far as she knows, Lero has exclusive rights!

When Lero was 3, her mother went back to teaching, riding horseback to the New Hope School with Lero on behind her. Aunt Irene used to tell how she enjoyed visiting the school and watching Lero sometimes answer questions and spell words the older kids didn't know. However, she said Ethel, the teacher, thinking of her students' feelings, never encouraged Lero in showing up the other kids.

Ethel and Ike bought a farm near Cliquot, MO in 1920. They took Pauline and Lero down the hill to Salem Church, where Ike sang in the church choir and Ethel played the organ. On April 29 after Lero's 11th birthday, great sadness entered the home when their beloved mother died of complications following a case of influenza. Ethel was buried at Salem and her young daughters often gathered wild flowers to place on her grave. *Submitted by Lero Robertson Tinsley Frazier*

BOSWELL – Drue L. Boswell was born Sept. 24, 1897 to Levi Boswell III and Bertha Agnes Boswell. Bertha Agnes' maiden name was Cribbs. Levi and Drue first bought a grocery store in Springfield, MO at the corner of National and Commercial Streets. The family sold the store there and would later move to Brighton, MO in Polk County where Levi would buy another grocery store and Drue would buy a restaurant. Levi also bought the gas station on north Highway 13 and 25. This is the picture of the gas station back then. It is not known the exact year this all took place but it was after 1920.

The man and his wife in the picture were the people who ran the gas station for Levi. Agnes knows only that the man's name was Shorty. Levi died of heart disease on March 11, 1943. Levi and Bertha Agnes are buried at the Pleasant Hope Cemetery.

Drue L. Boswell married his first wife Ona Bingaman May 17, 1918. They had a daughter that was stillborn on June 28, 1920, and then Ona died the next day. Ona and the baby are buried together at East Lawn Cemetery in Springfield, MO. Drue then married Zelma Mae Johnson. Drue and Zelma had two daughters, Agnes Mae and Peggy June. Agnes Mae married Marshel Ray Choate Sept. 18, 1943. Marshel was the son of Boyd and Flora Choate. Boyd, Flora and Marshel also lived in Brighton, MO for a while then they all moved to Willard, MO where Agnes still lives. Marshel and Agnes have eight children. They are Zelma, Ray, Velma, Ann, Susie, Carlyon, Liz and Dennis.

Boswell Grocery Store at North Highway 13 and 215 in Brighton, MO

Drue sold the restaurant about 1928 and went to work for Levi at the grocery store. Drue then married Dazel McKnight. They had a son together, Bill Lee Boswell. Drue and Dazel ran the store together until Drue got sick, then Drue hired Orpha Crosswhite; that was in 1954. Later Bill took over the store until he went to the service, then the store went out of business. There is a gas station there today at the top of Brighton Hill but looks nothing like the picture that has been handed down to Agnes. The old grocery store of Drue's is still standing as of today, July 2002. There is talk of tearing is down this fall. Agnes has no picture of the store from back then, but only the ones she has taken the last few years. "Oh, what great stories my mother Agnes can tell of the grocery store and the people that lived in the little town of Brighton, MO. I can almost see them laughing and having a good time back then," said Agnes. *Submitted by Agnes Choate and Liz Pratt*

BOSWELL – Sandra Boswell's heritage begins with, Thomas Boswell, Virginia 1675; George Boswell, North Carolina 1710; Isaac Boswell, Perquimans County, NC, July 5, 1736; Barnabas Boswell, Perquimans County, NC, July 21, 1765; Levi Walter Boswell Sr., Pasquotank County, NC, Jan. 31, 1787 and Levi Boswell Jr., Taney County, MO, Nov. 28, 1840.

Levi Boswell Sr. and Jr. moved from Taney County to Greene and Polk Counties and back for business, political and family reasons. Excluding a great deal of history, this account begins with Levi Jr. and his third wife, Annie Eliza McKinney, from Kentucky. They were married on Sept. 27, 1866 in Bolivar, MO. They had eight children identified as Royal Grant, Clarissa D., Laura Ann, Levi, Martha Ellen, Minnie, Harrison and Boone. Their family was raised in the Pleasant Hope area of Polk County. Levi Jr. and Annie Eliza are buried in Slagle Cemetery.

Harrison "Harry" Boswell (born Jan. 13, 1880) married Ina Inez Griffitts on Oct. 16, 1904. Ina was born March 22, 1885 to a long line of Griffitts that resided in Polk County. She died Jan. 26, 1972 and rests in Slagle Cemetery with her husband and family.

Harry and Ina had eight children identified as Laura Francis, Floyd Weldon, Ruby Edna, George Efton, Harry Lester, Lester Ray, Daisy Pearl, all deceased and buried at Slagle Cemetery. Eunice Maxine is still with us, living in California.

Floyd Weldon Boswell (born Nov. 28, 1907) married Rena Mae Slagle on Dec. 14, 1933. Rena Mae was born May 16, 1908 in Polk County. Both are buried in Slagle Cemetery with their ancestors and their stillborn son, born and died Nov. 2, 1942. Their two surviving children are Charles Floyd (born Aug. 25, 1936) and Ginger Lea Boswell Wheeler (born April 11, 1944).

Ginger married Bruce Wheeler from Wisconsin on Aug. 19, 1962 at Morrisville, MO. Their families live in other counties and states. Regardless, they are all descendants to the farmers, teachers, bankers, carpenters and well drillers that were Polk County pioneers. *Submitted by Sandra Wheeler Lininger*

BOWMAN – James Madison "Matt" Bowman was born to Rice Duncan Bowman and Mary C. Eidson in northeast Tennessee (Hancock County) on Feb. 22, 1846. After the death of his mother, before 1850, Matt was raised by his grandparents Creighton (1811-1890) and Isabel Davis (1812-1875) Eidson in Hancock County, TN.

Family lore states Matt married Malinda Wallen (1842-1929), the daughter of William "Big Sandy" Wallen and Jane Banks circa 1860 in the Cumberland Gap near Kyles Ford, TN. In 1861 Matt and his brother John C. Bowman were conscripted to serve with the Confederate Army, each serving a year or less. One story from the days of the Civil War told of Confederate soldiers coming to Matt's farm presumably in Tennessee) where they first looted the farm, then prepared to hang Matt, only to be interrupted and run off by Union soldiers. Another story told of Malinda removing clothing and bed linen from a safe storage area under the floor of their home to air on a sunny day only to have them pulled from the clothesline by Confederate soldiers and trampled by their horses. Livestock was then released to eat or destroy the crops in the fields.

After the birth of his son Ellis on March 21, 1863, Matt and Malinda relocated their family through Kentucky to Polk County arriving in the area about 1866. Matt was a farmer, but also worked for Polk County constructing highways and other community projects. Matt and Malinda had 12 children: Joanie (infant death); Ellie (born 1863; died 1936; married Elizabeth Jane Hayter in 1884); Mary (born 1866; died 1949; married James Monroe O'Kelley in 1886); Sarah (born 1867; died 1942; married Leonidus E. "Onnie" Looney in 1892, Dade County, MO); Orlena "Lena" (born 1869; died 1941; married James Walter Parker in 1892); William (infant death); Louisa (born 1872; died 1931; married Jesse Lee Claypool in 1893); Edna (born 1874; d. 1903); Ethel (infant death); Martha "Mattie" (b. 1876; died 1951; married Samuel Glover Williams in 1893); John (born 1878; died 1921; married Tella Finney in 1899) and Rachel Susan "Dolly" (born 1880; died 1961; married first, Traverse Neodesha Tyler in 1902, then second, Coy E. Smith in 1923). All marriages, except for Sarah's, took place in Polk County.

Matt died Feb. 4, 1906 in Walnut Grove, MO, after which Malinda began to move from home to home living with each of her children for six months at a time until her death in Randlett, OK on Oct. 21, 1929. Matt and Malinda are buried in Turkey Creek Cemetery near Walnut Grove, MO.

Matt and Malinda Bowman

Mary, Edna, Mattie, John and Dolly remained in southwest Missouri (Polk, Lawrence and Hickory Counties) where they worked and raised their families. In the early 1900s, Ellis, Sarah and Lena moved with their families to the Oklahoma Territory. Edna became ill after a visit to the 1900 World's Fair in St. Louis and died Nov. 7, 1903; she is buried with her parents in Turkey Creek Cemetery. John was killed by lightning Aug. 26, 1921 while caring for livestock on his farm near Walnut Creek, MO. Both John and Dolly's family are buried in Oak Grove Cemetry in Walnut Grove, MO, while Mary's family is buried in Maple Park Cemetery (Aurora, MO). Matt's grandparents, Creighton and Isabel Eidson migrated to Polk County between 1865 and 1870 and are buried in McMasters Cemetery near Walnut Grove. Many other Eidsons can be found in Polk County; they are descendants of Edward Gaines Eidson (born 1839; died 1874), son of Creighton and Isabel. *Submitted by Judy Millsap*

BOX – Daniel R. Box was born Oct. 9, 1821 in Jefferson County, TN. His parents were Samuel Box Jr. and Jemima Murphy. Daniel married Parthenia McGee in Jefferson County, TN in 1838.

Daniel's parents and some siblings moved to Missouri in the early 1840s, but Daniel and his family didn't make the move until 1858. Daniel lived near the town of Orleans, close to present-day Eudora and Eudora Springs. Daniel served as Polk County Justice of the Peace and was postmaster in Eudora at one time.

Daniel and Parthenia were the parents of 10 children, all born in Tennessee. They were James Clayborn, Josiah, George Washington, Mary Jane, William Riley, Franklin Murphy, Andrew Jackson, Rhoda Adeline, John and Hannah. Parthenia died Oct. 19, 1861 and is buried in the Mitchell Campground Cemetery, east of Aldrich, Polk County, MO.

Early in 1862, Daniel married Sarah Griffin and they had three children: Samuel (born Nov. 16, 1862); Mandelia Caroline (born Feb. 7, 1864) and Thomas (born Nov. 29, 1865). Sarah died Oct. 20, 1867, and, like her predecessor, is buried in Mitchell Campground Cemetery.

Widow Sarah (Chesser) Moore became Daniel's third wife on Sept. 9, 1873. They had one child, Ara Belle. Daniel R. Box died Jan. 14, 1909 at the age of 87 in Eudora and is buried in Mitchell Campground Cemetery by all three of his wives.

Samuel Box married Annie Rhoda Looney May 17, 1885 in Polk County. Annie was born Dec. 29, 1863 in Buckley, Greene County, MO, the daughter of David R. Looney and Mary Eliza Simpson. Samuel and Annie had 12 children: Iona, Franklin Pierce, Virgil Daniel Renfro, Dely, Margaret Eugenia, Jessie May, Jennie Lula, Lillian Belle, Walter Ray, Samuel Carl, William Wesley and Homer Dolen. Samuel died April 22, 1942, having lived his entire life in Polk County. In her later years, Annie lived with sons Homer and Wesley. She died April 3, 1952 and was buried next to Samuel in Mitchell Campground Cemetery.

Daniel Box's granddaughter, Sam and Annie's daughter, Jennie Lula was born May 27, 1895. On Dec. 3, 1916 in Aldrich, MO, Lula married Homer Clinton Ketchum, son of Everett Eugene Ketchum and Sarah Jane Taylor. Homer was born Sept. 25, 1892 in Taney County, MO. Lula and Homer were the parents of three children, all born in Polk County: Carl Eugene (born Aug. 29, 1917) married Estalee Wallis and were the parents of Carla Kay and Virginia Lee; Wilma Faye (born June 5, 1921) married Orval Eugene Creed and were the parents of Donald Gene, James Allen and Phyllis Ann; and Harold Dean (born Sept. 14, 1926; died Dec. 7, 1997). Harold married Freda Keeney in Springfield, Greene County, MO on Feb. 21, 1947. Freda was born Jan. 17, 1927 in Phelps County, MO, the oldest of five children born to Melvin Eddie Keeney and Ida Lee Lanning. Harold and Freda were the parents of two chil-

Samuel and Annie R. (Looney) Box family reunion August 1908
Seated: Samuel holding Wesley, Annie holding Homer, Walter standing between Samuel and Annie; others left to right: Margaret, Lillian, Jessie, Virgle, Jennie, Franklin and Iona.

Malinda Bowman and children

dren, both born in Springfield, MO, Donna Sue and Sarah Jane. Jennie Lula died Dec. 19, 1976, having lived her entire life in Polk County. Homer died Aug. 25, 1979 and both are buried in Pleasant Ridge Cemetery, Polk County, MO. *Submitted by Donna Sue Ketchum Bond*

David Brockus   Elizabeth Ann Box Brockus

BOX – Elizabeth Ann Box married David Brockus March 28, 1841 in Polk County shortly after her family's arrival from Tennessee. The Brockus family came in 1835 from Jefferson County, TN. It is very probable that these young people had not seen each other for six years. Elizabeth Ann was born April 16, 1820 in Tennessee and died Aug. 2, 1888. David Brockus was born Oct. 17, 1816 in Grainger County, TN and died Jan. 23, 1889 and is buried in Schofield Cemetery.

Her father was Samuel Box, born Aug. 18, 1789 in North Carolina and died Feb. 19, 1873 in Polk County, MO. He was the son of Samuel Box (born 1745; died before 1836 in Jefferson County, TN) who was a Revolutionary War Veteran, S3015. Samuel married Jemima Murphy (born 1797 in Tennessee; died July 12, 1869; and buried at Mt. Gilead Cemetery) on June 9, 1814 in Grainger County, TN.

They had Pleasant M. Box (who was in Polk County in 1840), Elizabeth Ann, Daniel Renfro, William Pickney, Nancy, Jane and Margaret Adeline.

Jemima was the daughter of William Murphy (born March 31, 1760 in Anson County, NC; died Aug. 16, 1850; buried Enon Cemetery) and Nancy Hornbeak (born Feb. 28, 1765 in Anson County, NC; died March 10, 1833 in Jefferson County, TN). Samuel was the guardian for his father-in-law, William Murphy, who was in the Revolutionary War, S16986, and came with them.

David Brockus was the son of John Brockus (born circa 1747 in Virginia; died April 14, 1824 in Grainger County, TN). His wife was Mary Smith (born 1765). This was probably a second marriage because his will mentions a son, William, along with John, David and Betsy. John's Revolutionary War File is S39224. David and Elizabeth Ann had 10 children: four died young, Samuel, Elizabeth, Caroline and David. Their only surviving son was a prominent Polk County minister, Daniel P. Brockus (born Feb. 24, 1842; died Dec. 19, 1917). Five daughters were Mary, Sarah Jane, Jemima, Margaret A. and Artemisee.

Sarah Jane Brockus (born July 6, 1846; died Feb. 7, 1929) married Richard Gott on Dec. 21, 1865 in Polk County. Richard was born Feb. 18, 1842 in Warren County, KY and died Jan. 20, 1921 in Polk County. He was the son of Thomas J. Gott born 1800/1803, Kentucky and died after the 1870 census, and was married three times. Richard's mother was Rachel Shipley born circa 1800 and died before 1848 in Kentucky. The Gott family came to Missouri about 1851 or 1852. Richard was about 9 years old when they got to Missouri.

Richard and Sarah Jane Brockus Gott

Sarah Jane and Richard had 10 children, all born in Dallas County. They are Joletha Eldeline, Cora Bell, Mary Ellen, Susan Margaret, Corbia Valentine, Ursula Jane, Rachel Elizabeth, Claude Robert, David Corry and Daniel Richard. They moved in with Sarah's aged parents in the late 1880s, so they could take care of them.

Joletha Gott, born March 15, 1867, died April 2, 1960, buried Reed Cemetery, married Samuel Preston Austin Feb. 7, 1886 in Dallas County. Samuel was born Nov. 25, 1864 in Dallas County and died Aug. 4, 1941 in Polk County. He was a farmer. He was the son of Absalom Chrisfield Austin Sr. who moved to Missouri in 1841 from Burke County, NC and second wife Nancy Gass of Franklin County, TN.

Joletha and Samuel Austin had 10 children: Alta Zora, Alva Dred, William Edgar, Nora Edna, Iva Delma, Ollie May, Eunice Xerritta, Herman Eugene, Mary Opal and Alice Eldelene. Alta married Ed Moore, Alva married Martha Opal Moore, Edgar married Alpha Ragsdale, Nora married James Randleman, Delma married Cecil Cates, Ollie married Archie Day, Eunice married Virgil Dulin, Gene married Sarah Cusanbury, Opal married Loren Jones and Alice married William Self and Maxwell "Mac" Bellamy. *Submitted by Hazel Dulin Voris*

Samuel P. and Joletha Gott Austin

BOYCE – George W. Boyce was born March 4, 1864 in Doddridge County, VA. He married Orpha Jane Smith on Dec. 10, 1885. Orpha was half-Cherokee Indian. Orpha was born Feb. 29, 1864 in Ohio. Orpha's parents were John George Smith and Jane Baucam. George and Orpha had six children: Harry, Myrtle, Jesse, Launia, Della and Teddy Roosevelt.

Jesse Elmer was born Sept. 29, 1890 in Bull Run, WV in Doddridge County. Launia was born Dec. 10, 1892 in Doddridge County, WV. Della was born Nov. 7, 1900 in White County, AR. Teddy Roosevelt was born in 1905 in White County, AR. George died Aug. 16, 1947. Orpha died April 30, 1948. Both are buried in Pleasant Hill Cemetery at Burns in Polk County.

Katie and Jesse Boyce

Jesse Elmer was a WWI veteran. Jesse married Katie Lee Shay on Nov. 19, 1918. Katie was born Aug. 11, 1892. Katie's parents were Ben Shay and Jane Stewart Shay. Ben was born on Jan. 10, 1847 in Wisconsin and died Oct. 27, 1943. Jane was born Nov. 30, 1863 and died Jan. 13, 1949. Both of them are buried at Bolivar City Cemetery, Bolivar, MO. Jesse died June 8, 1965 and Katie died March 17, 1968. Both are buried at Greenwood Cemetery, Bolivar, MO. Jesse and Katie had six children. Lillian Jane was born June 7, 1920 and married Glenn Thompson; they had no children. She died Aug. 24, 1967 and they are both buried in Greenwood Cemetery, Bolivar, MO. Pearl Pansey was born March 22, 1922 and married Charles Dailey on April 22, 1945. Charles died April 25, 1998 and Pearl died July 7, 1999; they had no children. They are both buried in Memory Garden, Richmond, MO. Carl William was born Nov. 4, 1923 and married Patty Due in July of 1950. Patty died Dec. 19, 1962. They had two children, LaDonna and Terri. Carl died Feb. 11, 1988 and they are both buried in Memory Garden, Richmond, MO. Wayne Benjamin was born April 27, 1926 and married Laverne Stewart; they had no children. She died on July 13, 1964 and is buried at Greenwood Cemetery, Bolivar, MO. Wayne married Bernice Clark Waller and had no children. Wayne died May 31, 1991 and is buried in Bradshaw Cemetery, Lebanon, MO. Betty Jean was born Nov. 26, 1928 and married Leonard Jump. She lived in Kansas City, MO and then in California for 32 years. They had seven children: Sylvia, Carolyn, Sandy, Larry, Gary, Mark and Tarma. Betty died on Feb. 20, 1993 and is buried in Greenwood Cemetery, Bolivar, MO. Herby Franklin was born Sept. 5, 1934 in Bolivar, and after high school he moved to Kansas City and Richmond area. Herby married Roseann Davison on Nov. 21, 1964 and they have two sons, Jeffrey Franklin and Rodney Conrad. Herby had two children by a previous marriage, Herby Jr. and Kathy Ann. Herby and Roseann moved back to Bolivar in 1969 and bought a farm where they live today.

Launia A. Boyce was born Dec. 10, 1892. She married Daniel Rhodes and their children were Orpha, Orlay, Blanch, Katherin, Danny and Glenn. Daniel died and Launia married George Thompson in 1940; they had no children. Launia died July 5, 1975. George was born Aug. 27, 1886 and died Jan. 15, 1977; they are buried in Pleasant Hill Cemetery.

Della Boyce was born Nov. 7, 1900 in White County, AR. She married John Sanders on July 1, 1916. John was born Dec. 7, 1889. They had 11 children: Harry, Jesse, Floyd, Balance, John Leonard, Sidney, Lavinie, George, Mildred and Robert. John died Dec. 4, 1975 and Della died March 19, 1991 and they are buried at Pleasant Hill Cemetery.

Teddy Roosevelt Boyce was born in 1905 in White County, AR. Teddy Roosevelt married Elsie Stewart on June 2, 1922 in Arkansas and they had one son Ralph. *Submitted by Rodney Boyce*

BRADFORD – John Bradford is listed as the great-grandson of Governor Bradford of the Mayflower fame. John's son Joseph Bennet Bradford, born in 1738 in Prince William County, VA, married Lucretia Tipton in 1766. Joseph's son Colonel Henry Bradford, born in 1766 in Jefferson County, TN married Rachel McFarland in 1799 in Jefferson County, TN. Henry's son Dr. Hamilton Bradford, born May 31, 1801, married Margaret Wilson in Monroe County, TN. Dr. Hamilton is mentioned in a sketch of prominent men in Tennessee. Dr. Hamilton's children were: Jonathan Tipton, Henry Ford, Edmond, Maldarena C., Asbury C., Lavina W., Rachael Ellen and Mary.

The earliest settlers of Polk County lived on claims. Looney Township was the first part of the county settled. Benjamin Looney, for whom it was named, located there in 1833. The government lands were first opened to entry in fall 1837. Dr. Hamilton was among the earliest settlers in Looney Township. His son's township listed as "Jonathan T. Bradford-Public land entry- 1837 Looney Township 33 Range 21."

John Hamilton, Adrian Agustus Bradford, James Bradford Hoodenpile and Reva Flo Hoodenpile

Dr. Hamilton's son Henry Ford, born in Athens, TN on Feb. 2, 1826, married Sarafine Jane "Sara" Lusk in Polk County, MO in 1847. They are buried in Polk County, MO at Slagle Creek Cemetery. Henry's children are John Hamilton, Lucretia J. (Crees), Rebecca L., James Augustin, Virginia T. and Mary T. Henry's son John Hamilton, born Aug. 20, 1850, married Mary Margarett Utley. John's children are Adrian Augustus "A. A.," Benjamin Wiley, Mary May and Earl. John later married Eda Frances Ballinger. Their children were Eula, Faye, Henry F., Herbert and James Bean "Jim."

Adrian "A. A." was born Oct. 3, 1875 at Slagle, MO, and married Anna Pauline Apperson in 1895. Their children were Reva Flo, John Ford and Anna Athelyne. After Anna's death Adrian married Eunice Katherine "Kate" Ruyle, born April 11, 1890. Their daughters were Helen Virginia, Mary Edna and Ruth Lucille.

Adrian Bradford, Ruth's dad, was blind most her life. Ruth says, "Although my father was blind he could still work on your bailer if it broke down." He was a farmer. After they moved to Pleasant Hope they would take him down town to visit and he would walk home by himself.

Ollie Bert Miller, Cora Spillman, Maude E. DeGraffenreid, Nanny May Lunsford-Lindsey, Jack Ruyle and Eunice Katherine Bradford

Kate Ruyle's great-grandfather, Aaron Ruyle, born in 1781 in Hampshire County, VA, married Elizabeth Adams, born in Virginia. Aaron's son Alvis Ruyle, born in 1825, married Susanna Ellen "Susan" Casey. Alvis' next to the youngest son, John Casey, was born in 1850 and married Mary Francis Fletcher in 1877. John's children were Ollie Bert, B. B., Nannie May, Maude E., Cora, Eunice Katherine "Kate" and Jack.

Kate Bradford was thought to be the first woman driver in Polk County, MO. She liked to do several kinds of handwork. She carded cotton and spun thread for weaving, crochets rugs out of old socks, and made quilts which Ruth and her sisters still have.

Ruth and her family lived southwest of Bolivar on a farm in a two-story house with a fireplace on both ends. They carried water from a spring for house use and laundry. Ruth and her sisters attended Leith School where the first, third, fifth and seventh grades were taught one year and second, fourth, sixth and eighth grades the next. In 1939, they moved to Pleasant Hope where they lived until after both parents died. Virginia graduated from Pleasant Hope High School. Mary Edna and Ruth went to Shidler, OK to live with their half-brother and his wife, Ford and Ina, where Mary Edna graduated. Then Ruth returned to Pleasant Hope where she graduated. Although they have all moved to other places they still have lost of memories of Polk County. *Submitted by Ruth Bradford Long*

BRAITHWAIT – John Vance Braithwaite was born Jan. 18, 1873 in Bentonville, AR and died July 3, 1935 in Bolivar, MO. He married Mary Alma Polson in Southwest City, MO. Alma was born Sept. 10, 1880 and died June 9, 1966. Her mother was M. Henrietta Stevenson, who was born Oct. 27, 1851 and died Jan. 16, 1901. Her father, James Norwood Polson was born Aug. 10, 1845 and died Aug. 24, 1894. John Vance dropped the "e" from Braithwaite when he moved to Bolivar.

John and Alma had three sons. Alfred Emil was born in 1902 in Southwest City, MO; died Dec. 5, 1963 and married Mary Elizabeth Carpenter who was born June 10, 1905 and died Dec. 10, 1954. John Ralph was born July 17, 1905; died Oct. 11, 1950 and married Rena Ann Lee who was born Dec. 31, 1908 and died May 18, 1947. Herman Evan was born Dec. 18, 1912 in Grove, OK; died May 15, 1989 and married Betty Jean Mathias who was born March 6, 1921 and died Feb. 21, 1995.

Alfred and Mary also had three sons; John Alfred Braithwait (born Dec. 31, 1926; died Nov. 4, 1996); Charles Edwin Braithwait (born July 31, 1931) and David Vance Braithwait (born Oct. 9, 1940; died Aug. 28, 1965).

Ralph and Rena's children were Barbara Ann Braithwait (born Aug. 14, 1928) at Osowatomie, KS; William "Bill" Vance Braithwait (born July 1, 1932; died Dec. 13, 1995 in Tulsa, OK); Janet Lee Braithwait (born Dec. 19, 1935; died Jan. 19, 1936) and Judith "Judy" Kay Braithwait (born Sept. 24, 1939).

Herman and Betty had no children but most of the nieces and nephews lived with them at one time or another.

The Braithwait Store was on the southwest section of the square. Founder, John Braithwait, moved to Bolivar from Southwest City, MO in 1906 and began working at F. M. Shoffner Hardware. With a few years of business experience behind him, John and his brother-in-law, Herman Polson, bought out a grocery store. This was the first step into the Braithwait era of business in Bolivar.

In 1918, from the original store on the southwest corner of the square, the partners began to expand northward. They first purchased a dry goods store. In 1922 Braithwait bought out his brother-in-law's share and expanded another 20 feet north. He added men and women's clothing and shoes.

John and his sons were sportsmen and in 1935 John and friends were building a fishing cabin at the Lake of the Ozarks where he was bitten by a tick and soon died of Rocky Mountain Fever.

His wife and three sons then became owners of the store. The oldest brother, Alfred, was the general manager of the store called Braithwait & Co. They expanded one more store to the north. It was strictly men's clothing and was run by Ralph.

The store was a family affair with every member working there as soon as they were old enough to help in any way.

In 1941, when Herman went into the army, the grocery store of which he had been in charge was sold to the Frasers. After Rena's death, Alfred and Herman bought out Ralph's share in 1948 when he moved his family to Colorado. In 1952 they bought their mother's share. In 1960, men and boy's clothing became the only focus of the store when Herman and his wife, Betty, bought out Alfred and became the sole owners. When they sold the store in 1974, it was the end of over 60 years of Braithwait & Co. on the Bolivar square.

All children and grandchildren of John and Alma graduated from Bolivar High School, except Bill who left his junior year. They were involved in music and athletics and are a proud part of the history of the school. Also, several members attended SWBC.

The Braithwait family were all members of the Methodist Church in Bolivar. They were very active in their membership and held many positions: superintendent of Sunday school, teachers, choir members, Ladies Aid Society, youth group, and others. When Herman married Betty, he became active in the First Christian Church.

The family was very civic minded, participating in all projects and activities to help Bolivar grow and be a great place to live. *Submitted by Judy Braithwait Wood*

BRADLEY - Edward R. Blevins, commonly known as "Uncle Ed," a well-respected citizen of Polk County, a farmer and wool mill worker, lived three and one-half miles northwest of Bolivar. He was born May 8, 1832 in Kentucky and died Feb. 24, 1901 in Bolivar at age 68, and was buried in City Cemetery, Bolivar, MO.

Edward married Lucretia Ackers about 1858. Lucretia was born about 1839 and died at age 28 in 1867. They had four children: Elisha, Susan Ann, Mary Ann and Stephen.

Edward then married Mary Ann Jones (born Nov. 29, 1837; died Aug. 10, 1910) on July 20, 1871 in Henry County. They had five children: Edward A., Frankie, Edgar, Charles, and Arthur.

Susan Ann Blevins was born Dec. 18, 1861 in Johnson County, MO. The 1880 census, Hendricks Addition, Bolivar, MO, lists Susan Ann as age 18. Stephen Blevins, uncle of Susan Ann, was a 60-year-old physician (born Feb. 8, 1815 in Whitley County, KY and prominent citizen of Bolivar who died March 4, 1902 in Polk County. The same 1880 census also lists a David Ligora Bradley, white male, age 35, living in the house of Dr. Stephen Blevins.

David L. Bradley, son of Levin Granger Bradley and Luellen Findley, was born April 14, 1845 in Kentucky and came to Missouri in 1861.

He worked many years as a thresher and sawyer in Dallas County, MO.

Levin Grainger Bradley was born Sept. 22, 1807 in Sumner County, TN. He is buried in Prairie Grove Cemetery in Dallas County.

Susan Ann Blevins and David L. Bradley were married in 1882 and had three children: Eugene Drake, a sawyer (born Oct. 11, 1882; died Jan. 7, 1977), Lu Ellen (born May 17, 1887; died May 25, 1974) and Wilford, sawyer and thresher (born Sept. 27, 1889; died May 31, 1964).

Susan Ann Blevin's family: seated, David Ligora Bradley and Susan Ann Blevins Bradley; standing left to right, Eugene David, Lu Ellen and Wilford

Susan and David probably lived in Bolivar area in 1895 because they purchased a kitchen clock that year in Bolivar. The eight-day desktop pendulum clock was owned by their daughter Lu Ellen Bradley Slack who gave it to her son Herbert Slack. The clock is now in the possession of Susan and David' s great-grandson, Don Slack of Springfield, MO.

Lu Ellen Bradley married Lewis Allen Slack Dec. 17, 1905 in Dallas County, near Long Lane, MO. Lewis Slack (born Nov. 4, 18871; died March 4, 1968) was the son of John Daniel Slack (born Oct. 27, 1853)and Livona Hill (born April 9, 1856; died Aug. 17, 1924). Lu and Lewis had nine children: Claude, Herbert, Glendon, Lendol, Marjorie, Anna, Almon, Norma and Dale.

David L. Bradley died March 15, 1920 at their home near Long Lane and Susan lived alone for a while. When her son Gene's wife died, Susan lived with them for some time to take care of her grandchildren. Susan remarried in 1928 to John Daniel Slack, the father-in-law of her daughter Lu Ellen Bradley Slack. Lu Ellen did not approve of the marriage, saying, "it was not right." They were married about one year when John Daniel died July 1, 1929 from injuries received after falling off a wagonload of mowed oats at their farm near Long Lane.

Great-Grandma Susan lived many years with her daughter and son-in-law. She loved her many grandchildren and great-grandchildren. She was bed-ridden her last few years and was cared for by her daughter Lu Ellen. Susan Ann Blevins Bradley passed away Jan. 20, 1955, at age 93, and was buried next to David L. Bradley in Hill Cemetery near Long Lane. *Submitted by Donald B. Slack*

BRESHEARS – Francis Arthur Breshears, as stated elsewhere, was a descendant of John Quincy and Naoma Ann Hogg Breshears through their son William A. Breshears and his son John Morrison Link Breshears.

"F. A." married Nancy Helen Carter (buried in Breshears Cemetery) on Oct. 16, 1907 in Clifford. Their union produced Lela Veneta, Voyne Leland, Orlena Mable, Kenneth Arthur and Forrest Wayne.

Lela (buried in Payne Cemetery) married Jesse William House (buried in Payne Cemetery) on Sept. 6, 1931 in Hermitage, MO. Jesse's parents were Joseph Patton House and Annie Elizabeth Payne. Lela and Jesse owned a store in Bolivar and were cooks for Polk County Schools. They had four children: Donald Lee (graduated from SBU) ; Patsy Lou (graduated SBU); Willodean (graduated SBU) and Deryll William. Donald (buried in Payne Cemetery) and Deryll (buried at Payne Cemetery) both died without marrying. Willodean (St. Clair, MO) married Leon Estle Gullet with no children. Patsy married Dr. Harold Paul Pottenger (SBU staff) and both are buried in Springfield National Cemetery. Their children were Diane Elizabeth and Veneta Kathleen.

Francis Arthur Breshears, Lela (Breshears) House, Voyne Leland Breshears, Nancy Helen (Carter) Breshears and Orlena (Breshears) Woodruff in front

Diane Elizabeth (graduated SBU) married David Lynn Watson (graduated SBU), bearing Rachel Leigh, Jessie Nicole, Hannah Kathleen and Joseph Paul. Veneta Kathleen (gradated SBU) married Kenneth Ray Herman Jr., bearing Samantha Rose and Abigail Hope.

Voyne (buried Mt. Gilead Cemetery) married Virginia Helen Cunnyngham on March 24, 1940 in Bolivar. Helen's parents were James William Cunnyngham and Mattie Chloe Johnson. They had two children, Nancy Kay and William Arthur. Voyne was a farmer and postal carrier in Bolivar.

Nancy (Platte City) married Jay W. Amos on Jan. 31, 1973 in Platte City. They had twins, Jason Vance (Platte City) and Joylyn Vinitia. Joylyn married Darryl Liberty, having one daughter, Taylor Nicole.

Bill married Pearlene Brumfield (currently SBU staff) on Nov. 10, 1973. Pearlene's parents are Ottis Thomas Brumfield and Bonnie Fay Hively. They had two children, Reggie Lee (graduated SBU) and Cherita Kay (graduated SBU), both of whom married in June of 2001. Reggie Lee married Andrea Celeste Swearington and Cherita Kay married Michael Brandon Heller. Bill works for the *Bolivar Herald-Free Press*.

Orlena (graduated SBU) moved to California where she met and married Everitt Stilson Woodruff (both buried in Greenlawn North, Bakersfield, CA) on April 3, 1948 in Las Vegas, NV. They had no children. Everitt was a widower with one daughter, Barbara Jean. Barbara married Herbert Clay Foster, producing Danny Everett and Lorraine Gay. Orlena took the role of grandmother very seriously and loved her stepfamily.

Kenneth (buried DFW National Cemetery) married W. Faqueta Blackwell (buried DFW National Cemetery) on Feb. 10, 1945 in Williamsville, NY. Faye's parents were William Clarence Blackwell and Ruby Willie Gantt. They had one daughter, Janet Sue, who married Darwin LaVerne Thomas (Seale-Round Prairie, TX) on Jan. 15, 1971. They had no children. Since leaving for WWII, Kenneth and his family have not lived in Polk County.

Forrest was born on Nov. 28, 1927 and died six days later. Helen Carter Breshears' death on Jan. 4, 1929 was as a result of the birth of Forrest.

F. A. married Minnie Lee Brooks Holt on July 24, 1930 in Stockton. At the time of their marriage, Minnie was a cook in a hotel in Bolivar, working to provide for her three daughters, Fern, Bryl and Jewell, after the death of their father, Noble Mason Holt, on Aug. 12, 1921. At the time of Mr. Holt's death, Minnie was pregnant with her fourth daughter, Beatice M. (buried in Goff), who was born on Oct. 4, 1921 and died on March 27, 1924.

Because of the death of Kenneth's mother, Minnie became the mother he would not have had. She also became the grandmother of the grandchildren she would never have had. Minnie was greatly loved by all members of the family. *Submitted by Janet Sue Breshears Thomas*

BRESHEARS – John Quincy Breshears was born March 16, 1793 in South Carolina. His parents were Henry Breshears and Eleanor Hardin. John married Naomi Ann "Oma" Hogg in Lawrence County, TN on March 1, 1821. Naomi was the daughter of Reuben Hogg and Mary Wisdom. She was born in Lexington, KY on June 17, 1804.

John Breshears

John and Naomi moved to Polk County, MO between 1837 and 1840 as they were enumerated on the 1840 Polk County federal census, but John is not listed on the 1837 Polk County tax list. John and Naomi were the parents of 17 children. They were Mary, Henry Hardin, Reuben Dobbin, William Arthur, Sarah P., Jesse Carroll, Susan, Nancy G., John W., Margaret "Peggy," Joseph W., Ozais Martin "Mark," James Knox Polk, Thomas Hart Benton, Andrew Jackson and two who died in infancy. John and Naomi are buried in Breshears Cemetery in northeast Polk County.

Naomi (Hogg) Breshears

Jesse Carroll Breshears was born Dec. 17, 1830 in Lawrence County, TN. On Feb. 1, 1855 he married Rhoda Catherine Jump, who was born Dec. 22, 1836 in St. Louis, MO.

Rhoda was the daughter of James Jump and Eulila Palmer who moved to Polk County about 1838. In addition to Rhoda, they were the parents of Peter, William Kincaid, Lucinda, Joseph Henry and James Knox Polk Jump. James and Eulila are buried in Lindley Creek Cemetery in northeast Polk County.

Jesse and Rhoda Breshears were the parents of James Knox Polk, John Henry, Naomi Elizabeth, Joseph Carroll, Sophronia Angeline, Mary Lucinda, George Washington, Missouri Belle, Jesse Simon, Matoke Erickson and Lewis Hardin. Mary Lucinda married Charles Leslie Gladden.

Leslie and Mary were the parents of Florence Elnora "Nora" and Pelura Elizabeth "Lura." Nora was just 3 years old when her father died. It was decided that Mary and her two daughters would live with her parents Jesse and Rhoda. By this time Grandpa John Breshears had died and Grandma Naomi was living with Jesse and Rhoda in their home also. Nora told how she could remember her Great-Grandmother Naomi sitting in a chair piecing quilts or doing the mending. She cut the threads with a small pocketknife. That knife was given to Nora after Naomi died. Larry Fowler, son of Carl and Minnie McGee Fowler and grandson of W. K. and Nora McGee, is now in possession of the knife. The tips are broken off both blades. Larry is the brother of Linda Fowler Crawford. Along with Sandra and Brenda, they are the children of Carl and Minnie McGee Fowler who spent their last few years living at Pleasant Hope in Polk County. Linda and her husband Jack Crawford have lived in Polk County since 1961. Their daughters Julie Graves and Jeannie Cook grew up in Polk County and attended school in Pleasant Hope as did the sons of Ray and Julie Graves. They are Matthew and Andrew Graves.

Beginning with John and Naomi and ending with Matthew and Andrew, all eight generations have lived all or part of their lives in Polk County, MO. *Submitted by Linda Fowler Crawford*

BRESHEARS – Like Linda Fowler Crawford, William's branch of the Breshears family is descended from John Quincy and Naoma Ann Hogg Breshears through their son William A. Breshears, born in 1827 in Lawrence County, TN.

William married Abigail J. Batten on March 19, 1850 in Bolivar. Abigail's parents were John and Emily Batten. William and Abigail had nine children: John Morrison Link, Mary E., Susan Ellen, Sarah M., Reuben Joseph, Margaret Priscilla, Andrew Jackson, Eva Avya and Henry M. William and Abigail along with five of their children and their spouses are buried in Breshears Cemetery along with his parents, John and Naomi.

William Arthur Breshears

John M. L. was born Dec. 23, 1850 in Missouri and passed away in Portales, NM, burial local. He married Safrona "Frona" Bashaba Tuckness on Dec. 18, 1879. Safrona's parents were Francis Asbury Tuckness and Charlotte Keith. They had three sons: James Henry (buried in New Mexico), Charles William (buried in New Mexico) and Francis Arthur (buried in Breshears Cemetery). After the death of Safrona in 1888 (buried in Lindley Creek), John M. L. married Laura Engle (buried in Lindley Creek) on Sept. 16, 1890 producing James Edgar (buried in Reynolds Chapel) and Fred Vail (buried in Lindley Creek).

John Link Breshears and his grandson, Kenneth Arthur Breshears

F. A. married Nancy Helen Carter (buried in Breshears) on Oct. 16, 1907 in Cifford. Helen's parents were James Trousdale Carter and Harriet L. Arnold (both buried in Mission). Their union produced five children: Lela Veneta (buried in Payne Cemetery), Voyne Leland (buried in Mt. Gilead Methodist), Orlena Mable (buried in Greenlawn North, Bakersfield, CA), Kenneth Arthur and Forrest Wayne (buried in Breshears). After Helen died, F. A. married Minnie Lee Brooks (buried in Goff) widow of Noble Mason Holt (buried in Goff) with three daughters: Fern, Bryl and Jewell.

To quote Orlena's writing in later years, "Then we built a house with nine rooms in all. We moved into this mansion late in the fall. Grandma Carter, now a widow, came to live with us, too. Grandpa Breshears also came, now we were six plus two."

The house described here is where Kenneth was born. Orlena continues, "Dad farmed for a while, then trucked to make more money. Later bought a small house in Goodson, sounds rather funny. We did not have two extra bedrooms to spare, so the grandparents had to find homes elsewhere. Then Dad bought the store he had been trucking for. Another small house went with the store. Later, when Rural Electrification came our way, the old house was no good for wiring, some did say. So we built a big barn to house car, truck and bus and it housed all our furniture and it also housed us. Then Dad built his last house, it was a sight to behold! It had three bedrooms, a bath but only four in the fold."

The house described here is the house moved to Bolivar in later years.

F. A. owned the Square Deal Mercantile Company store in Goodson from the 1920s until the late 1950s. They sold the property in Goodson by auction. The house was moved to Bolivar by cutting it in half. F. A. and Minnie spent their first night in Bolivar sleeping in half of the house on the street. The house was moved onto the foundation the next day. The house still stands on Chestnut Street.

Researchers who contributed to this article are Voyne Breshears, Faye Blackwell Breshears and Orlena Breshears. *Submitted by William Arthur Breshears*

BRESHEARS – John and Naomi (Hogg) Breshears had 17 children. One of those was William Arthur Breshears. William was born Sept. 7, 1827 in Lawrenceburg, TN before the family moved to Missouri in the late 1840s. On March 16, 1850, William married Abigail Jane Batten here in Polk County. Abigail's parents were John Batten and Emily King from Tennessee. Abigail was born March 30, 1832 in Carroll County, TN. William and Abigail had nine children. The children included: John M., who married Safrona Tuckness; Mary E., who married Marion Bridges; Henry, who married Rebecca J.; Susan F., who married Joseph Anderson; Sarah Nancy, who married John Anderson Tuckness; Rhuben Joseph; Margaret Priscilla, who married Ira "Bud" Patison; Andrew Jackson, who married Rosella Turner and Ava A., whose husband was Joe Richards.

Rueben and Margaret (Buckles) Breshears family; left to right: Jack, R. J., Ed, Mary, Meg and Tom

Rhuben Joseph Breshears married Margaret Cena Buckles Sept. 7, 1885 in Dallas County, MO. Margaret was the daughter of Tennessee Nave Buckles and Margaret J. Pierce from Carter County, TN. Margaret was born April 18, 1867 in Butler, Bates County, MO. Rhuben was born in Polk County June 30, 1864. They ran the R. J. Breshears store in Goodson for many years. R. J. and Meg, as they were known, had seven children. They were Edward Linville; William Jackson; Thomas Mitchell; Mary Ann, who passed on at age 4; Elmer Claud, whose wives include Enda Mabel Morris and Lola Coonis; Homer Merritt, who married Hazel Mary Warren; Rueben Alden "Buster" who married Velma Farmer.

William Jackson "Jack" Breshears, a postman, married Minnie Lois Brooks or Lois as she was known. Her parents were Theophilus Brooks and Sarah Jane Harper. Jack and Lois were married Nov. 19, 1910. Lois was born April 23, 1892 and Jack was born Aug. 27, 1889; both were born near Goodson. They had 12 children, including one set of twins. Their children include Violet, who first married Earl Angle; Pansy, who married Wayne Angle; Rose, who married Ray Abel; Lily,

Kenneth A. Breshears' maternal grandparents, James Trousel Carter and Harriet Arnold Carter

who married Dwight Farmer; Glen; R. T., who married Rozella Stoner; Nevin, who married Betty Lane; David, who married Peggy Lane; Don, who married Emma Payne; Adrian, who married Irene Needham; and Jerroll, who married Maureen Stack. Jerroll, or Jerry, had a twin brother Deryll who died in infancy.

Glen married Pat Love, daughter of Robert Love and Hetty Gowin. They had five children including a set of twins. Their children are Patty, who married Gary Warren; Randy, who married Janice Short; Jane, who married Frank Stoner; Terry, who married Tina Woodham. Terry's twin, Kerry died in infancy. They have nine grandchildren: Suzanne Warren Mayfield, Todd Warren, Lynn Breshears Quennoz, Brent Breshears, Ashley Stoner, Alison Stoner, Jeffrey Stoner, Valerie Breshears and Kerry Breshears. Glen and Pat have two great-granddaughters, Maddison and Brooke. Most of this family has spent most of their lives in Polk County, MO. *Submitted by Glen Breshears*

BREWER – Benjamin Brewer was born May 8, 1817 in Frankfurt, Germany. His parents were Samuel Brewer and Margaret Moore. He married Nancy Edge Jan. 28, 1848, Minerva McMillen Sept. 4, 1866 and Salena McMillen Dec. 13, 1871.

Benjamin and Nancy had eight children: Martin, Samuel, John, Hannah, William, David, Sarah and Robert. He and Salena had one daughter, Margaret.

Martin was born Nov. 18, 1847 in Dade County. He married Mary Davis, (born March 29, 1879).

Martin and Mary had three daughters: Ruth, Nellie and Gladys. Martin was a doctor in Fair Play, MO for several years; he specialized in skin diseases and typhoid fever.

Samuel was born Feb. 20, 1850 and died Jan. 5, 1854.

John was born May 25, 1852 in Dade County. He married first, Beulah Perry, second, Ida Bell Russell-Hamlet, and third, Janet Lucy Miller-Curtis. John and Beulah had two children: Benjamin and Minnie. John and Ida had four children: William, Lewis, Robert and Ruby. John and Janet had one son, Bill. John and his wife operated a drug and sundries store in Fair Play, MO for 37 years; the store was organized by Martin. They also operated the Fair Play Bottling Works.

Hannah was born Oct. 20, 1854 and died Sept. 23, 1867.

William was born Dec. 12, 1856. He married first, Florence Oldham and second, Terusha. William and Florence had two children, Homer and Jessica. William was a doctor in Fair Play, MO also and was in practice with his brother Martin.

David was born Nov. 2, 1858. He married Nancy Potts, daughter of Henry Potts and Margaret Worthan. David and Nancy had nine children: Beulah, Carl, Clarence, Margaret, Ben, Sarah, Zina, Lonabell and Edith. David was a clerk in a dry goods store, and he drove the delivery wagon for the Fair Play Bottling Company.

David Rice Brewer

Sarah was born Nov. 17, 1860 and married Siegel Coats.

Robert was born April 26, 1863.

Henry Potts was born Jan. 14, 1836, son of James Potts and Rebecca Fox. He married Margaret Worthan born 1850. She was the daughter of Richard Worthan and Mary Abbott. Henry and Margaret had three children: Nancy (born June 25, 1868), James (born Jan. 28, 1871) and William (born Dec. 20, 1875; married Della Manuel). William and Della had seven children. William was a partner in the Fox, Potts and Company, which was changed to Fair Play Mercantile Company. The company did a very good business because of their fair dealing and prompt attention to the patrons, and from the fact they were pleasant social gentlemen to deal with. The Brewers, Potts, Foxes and Bakers and several generations lived in or around Polk County and were very active in the community. *Submitted by Wilma Hurlbert*

BREWER – The family's first known Brewer ancestor, Sackfield Brewer (born about 1632; died after 1699) was born in England, and came to Virginia in about 1655. He and his family lived and died there.

In the late 1700s, a sixth-generation Brewer, Samuel (born 1773; died 1844), migrated to Green County, TN. In 1800, he married Margaret Moore (born about 1780; died 1842). They lived there and reared eight children, as he worked in buying and selling land.

In 1842, the family decided to move to Missouri. They chose Dade County, for they had relatives of the Rice family there. Most of the children and their spouses moved with them.

On their journey to Missouri, Margaret died and was buried along the way. Samuel died in 1844 and was buried in Dade County.

Benjamin Sackville, Samuel's sixth child, married Nancy Edge (born 1824; died 1863). They had eight children, and Nancy died at childbirth. She was buried at the Rice Cemetery. Benjamin and his family moved to Fair Play, perhaps to be closer to his brother-in-law, John A. Strain, who had bought the Old Davis Mill and rebuilt it.

David Rice Brewer and Nancy Elizabeth (Potts) Brewer and their daughter Beulah.

Benjamin's children married and earned their livelihood in Fair Play. His first son, Martin Dickerson (born 1847; died 1912), went to medical school and received a MD degree. He practiced medicine in Fair Play and was at one time president of the Polk County Medical Association.

Benjamin's second son, Samuel, was born in 1850 and died in 1854.

His third son, John Henry (born 1852; died 1929) spent some time in Arizona, then owned and operated a drug store and the Fair Play Bottling Works.

The fourth child, Hannah, was born in 1854 and died in 1867.

Benjamin's fifth child was William Philip (born 1856; died 1943), known as "P." He was a doctor and a dentist.

The sixth child was David Rice, named for his uncle, Colonel David Rice of Tennessee. David Rice Brewer (born 1858; died 1951) and his wife, Nancy Elizabeth Potts (born 1868; died 1950) went to Arizona in the 1880s, where he was a stagecoach driver. They later returned to Fair Play, where he was a clerk in John's drugstore and worked in the bottling works.

The seventh child was Sarah Margaret (born 1860; died 1945). She married F. Segel Coats and later Stephen Gray.

The last child was Robert Caldwell (born 1863; died 1943). He was partly reared by relatives, who cared for him after his mother died at his birth. He remained a bachelor.

Benjamin served as Fair Play postmaster during part of the 1880s.

Most of Benjamin's children were laid to rest in Polk County. Martin, John and William P. were buried at Akard Cemetery near Fair Play; David was buried at Brush Grove; and Sarah and Robert were buried at Oak Grove. Benjamin was buried at Rice Cemetery, near his wife, siblings and near his father and the two children who died young. *Submitted by Dorothy (Brewer) (Burchett) Hopkins*

Milos and Mary Svoboda Brich family about 1918; Standing: Laura, Clara, Paul, Julia (Ammerman) and Lena; Sitting: Emma (Renken), Milos (father), Bertha, Mary (mother), Eva, Betty (Harbutt) and Ted

BRICH – Milos and Mary (Svoboda) Brich moved from Verdigre, NE to Polk County, MO in 1908. They settled near Cliquot with their five children: Emma, Paul, Clara, Julia and Laura. They lived the remainder of their lives on the family farm. Eleven girls and four boys were born to them. A baby boy, Frank, died in Nebraska. Six-year-old Bertha and two-year-old Eva died of diphtheria on the same day in 1915. Another daughter, Lena, was struck and killed by lightning when she was 18.

The children attended Heydon School seven miles north of Bolivar. The younger children attended Bolivar High School. Their favorite gathering place was a swimming hole beneath the Francka Bridge.

Although the children scattered across the country, their roots and ties to Polk County brought them home often.

Paul moved to Nebraska for a time, married Emma Winchell and returned to Polk County in 1935. They raised five children: Doris, Dwayne, Deloris, Cameron and Judy. He lived on his farm near Halfway, MO until his death in 1975.

Fred stayed on the family farm. He and his wife, Jean, raised two sons, Garland and Robert.

Clara and Alberta returned to Bolivar to spend the last years of their lives.

Betty went to England during WWII, married an Englishman, Jack Harbutt, and raised her family (Terry, Carol and Connie) in England.

Fred and Marion both served in WWII.

Emma lived and worked in Chicago. She married Rudi Renken but had no children. Alberta lived in Chicago, married Jerry Whalen and had two children, Lynn and Rodger.

Julia spent most of her life in Kansas City. She married Henry Ammerman from Bolivar and had two children, Charlene and Henry Jr.

Ted was an avid hunter. He lived in Colorado where he loved to hunt deer and elk in the mountains. He and his wife, Marge, had two children, David and Matilda.

Mary married Albert French and moved to Memphis, TN. They had three daughters: Roberta, Deena and Janyth.

Marion is the only surviving child of Milos and Mary Brich. He married Betty Sue Ashlock from Bolivar and lives in California. They have one daughter, Mary Lynn.

A cousin reunion brought 11 of the 21 living offspring to Bolivar in 1999. Betty's son, Terry, came from England to meet his American cousins for the first time.

Betty's daughter, Carol, was on a worldwide yacht race in 2000. She took advantage of a stop-over in Boston, MA to come to Bolivar and see her mother's birthplace.

Cousins' visits always include a tour to the family cemetery in Cliquot, MO where they can visit their grandparents' graves. The Francka Bridge is also a favorite attraction. No cousin's visit is complete without going there. The cousins share a magic feeling on the bridge. Their parents can almost be seen and hear splashing and laughing in the old swimming hole below.

Seven Brich descendants live in Polk County including two great-great-grandchildren.

A poem written by Milos Brich to his family when he was sick and in the hospital in 1946:

My radio I hated to hear
The newspaper I detest
For my heart was troubled greatly
And my soul could not rest
A letter from my beloved came
Like sunshine in dark storm
It made me happy as a lark
In bright and shining morn
My family to, their far away
Gave aid and comfort without delay
That I could enjoy and say with pride
Never I had such happy ride!
With compliments to my wife and family, Dad, M. I. Brich" Submitted by Deloris Brich Presley

BRICH - Eleven of the 21 grandchildren of the late Milos and Mary Brich gathered in Bolivar in October 1999 for a cousin reunion.

A special treat for the cousins was meeting their cousin, Terry Harbutt, for the first time. He came from near London, England to meet his American cousins and to visit his mother's Betty Brich Harbutt homeland.

Cameron Brich and Deloris (Brich) Presley, whose father was Paul Brich and Garland Brich, whose father was Fred Brich, were born and raised and still live in Polk County, MO.

Henry Ammerman Jr. came from Camdenton, MO and Charlene (Ammerman) Murphy came from California. Their mother was Julia (Brich) Ammerman. Doris (Brich) Meadows came from Florida and Judy (Brich) Musser came from Texas. Their father was Paul Brich. Lynn (Whalen) Pottebaum came from Illinois. Her mother was Alberta (Brich) Whalen. Janyth (French) Goodwin came from Tennessee. Her mother was Mary (Brich) French. Mary Lynn (Brich) Rueb came from California. Her father is Marion Brich.

The old swimming hole, Francka Bridge Oct. 2000

After a luncheon at Simon B's in Bolivar the cousins went on a family tour. First, they visited the graves of their grandparents in Salem Cemetery, Cliquot. Next, a visit to the old home place where their parents grew up on a farm near Cliquot. Then, off to a very special place at the Francka Bridge over the old swimming hole where their parents spent many happy hours.

The cousins share a magic feeling standing on the bridge. They can almost see and hear their parents laughing and swimming below.

Betty's daughter, Carol Redgrave, came to Polk County a year later. She was on a worldwide yacht race in October 2000. She took advantage of a stopover in Boston, MA to come to Bolivar to visit her mother's birthplace and to meet her American cousins. Carol was treated to a luncheon at Simon B's with her Missouri cousins. She also had a family tour to the home place, cemetery and Francka Bridge. Deloris (Brich) Presley wrote a poem in honor of her "faraway cousins."

"Those Faraway Cousins"
We have first cousins from afar
Oh, how wonderful they are...
When they come - but when they go
They leave our lives with a gaping hole.

Their mother was my father's little sister
She went to England and how he missed her!
Her memory stayed always with my dad
And mom shared with us the ones she had.
Leaving us years and years to ponder and think
And wonder about our missing link.

Now, our cousins have come across the sea,
Their mother's homeland they're longing to see.
They want to visit the old home site...
It's gone now, progress has been its plight.
We visit our grandparents' cemetery plot
And then we're off to a wonderful spot.
There's a special place where we always go
To the Francka Bridge o'er the old swimming hole.

A place on the map that's merely a dot,
Yet on our hearts leaves an indelible mark.
The feeling we get is a weird mystery
A strange connection to our ancestry.
As we look over the edge we almost can see
Our parents swim and laugh and shout with glee.
Oh! What fun they must have had!
These aunts and uncles and my dad.

So, our cousins have come to their mom's homeland,
How wonderful to meet them, and we offer a hand
Of love and kinship and hope that they see
They're as welcome as welcome can possibly be!

We have mores cousins across the U.S.A.
It's so wonderful when they stop our way!
And we throw open our door and invite them in
With a "So glad you're here!" and a big country grin.
We so blessed to have them - our cousins - our kin!
Written by Deloris L (Brich) Presley *Submitted by Janet (Presley) Good*

BRIDGES – By the time the 1850 census was taken in Polk County, MO, several families with the name of Bridges had settled there. Among them were William G. and Nancy Greer Bridges, Joseph and Sally Hogg Bridges ad Benjamin and Mary Satterfield Bridges. All of the adults and many of their children had been born in Kentucky. Without specific written records, it can only be assumed that they entered Missouri in the late 1840s. They were all concentrated in the northeast part of the county, around Goodson. Land books also indicate that all of them owned farm acreage as early as 1846. All seem to have been farmers; no other occupations are listed.

These families came to light when a California descendant, Bill McPheeters, began doing genealogy about 12 years ago. Bill turned up another California descendant, cousin, Jackie Mattison, who subsequently joined him in his family search. Bill and Jackie found that they shared several Bridges ancestors. William G. and Nancy Greer produced Haseltine Bridges who married Samuel Bridges, son of Samuel and Lucy Cowden Bridges. Their son, Thomas Fletcher Bridges, is Jackie's grandfather and their daughter, Maude Bridges, is Bill's grandmother. Benjamin and Mary Satterfield produced Thomas J. Bridges, whose first two marriages produced Jackie's great-grandmother, Mary Narcissus, and Bill's great-grandfather, William Thomas.

Jackie and Bill tracked down many other Missouri ancestors, reaching back to the late 1700s. These earlier ancestors came to Missouri from Kentucky and Jackie and Bill speculate that they came to Kentucky from Virginia and North Carolina. Some of the other families that married the Bridges progeny were Pitts, Brannon, Diamond, Cowden, Williams, Greer, Beavers, and of course, McPheeters. It appears from census records that most of these early Bridges stayed in Missouri. However, in the early part of the 20th century some of them started moving west. Jackie's grandfather, Thomas and his wife, Stella Diamond, and

Left to right: Henry Ammerman Jr., Charlene (Ammerman) Murphy, Doris (Brich) Meadows, Deloris (Brich) Presley, Judy (Brich) Musser, Cameron Brich, Lynn (Whalen) Pottebaum, Terry Harbutt, Garland Brich, Mary Lynn (Brich) Rueb and Janyth (French) Goodwin; Oct. 2, 1999

family first went to Arizona where their last child was born in 1917. The older ones were born in Missouri including Jackie's mother, Lora Bridges. William Wesley (grandson of Thomas J. and Martha Hogg) and his wife Maude Bridges also went to Arizona where their youngest child, Emma Bondena Bridges, Bill's mother, was born in 1917. Some of Thomas and Maude's other siblings also came to California including Clarence and Bert. They moved back and forth several times. It has been said that Bill's Grandma Maude was ready to go if she heard the car start.

Thomas and Stella subsequently settled in Sanger, Fresno County, CA while Bill's grandparents returned at least once to Missouri. When they lived in California, they lived in Santa Paula, Ventura County. Many folks from Polk County have settled in Santa Paula earning it the nickname of "Little Bolivar." In California, Jackie and Bill's families worked in agriculture.

Both Jackie and Bill were born in California. Jackie's first trip to Missouri was about 10 years ago. Since then, both Jackie and Bill have returned to Missouri and gotten acquainted with family members and other new friends. They have also worked on furthering their knowledge about their Missouri ancestors. Counted among their extended family are Dudley and Christina Huckaby, Elza and Genevieve Bridges, Alvie Watkins and Leona Scurlock. Of great help in making these connections has been Lorraine Kincaid. Leo Pitts was also a serendipitous find who introduced them to the Pitts family connection.

Jackie and Bill have submitted this entry for the Polk County book in order to record a small history of the Bridges family. There is much that they will never learn about their ancestors but cherish what they have discovered. One of those discoveries is that Jackie and Bill are related to many people in both Polk County and Ventura County. They will never meet all of them but they know their Bridges family is widespread and doing well. *Submitted by Jackie Mattison and Bill McPheeters*

BRIDGES – Many Polk County families with the surname of Bridges and related families can trace their lineage back to Joseph and Martha Bridges who settled on Canoe Creek in Barren County, KY about 1800. Previously they had lived in North Carolina and South Carolina. Joseph died in 1805 but Martha recorded the 250-acre farm in her name, paid the taxes and supported her 11 children. She died in 1856 in Barren County, still possessing the farm, 51 years after the death of Joseph.

Two of their sons, Benjamin and Joseph, were in Polk County by 1850. Joseph married Sally Hogg, July 29, 1825 in Barren County. He was living when his mother's estate was probated in 1856. Benjamin died in Polk County sometime between 1850 and 1856.

Several of Joseph and Martha's grandchildren moved to Polk County. Among the surnames added through marriage are Edwin, Sawyers, Schwarting, Watkins, Black, Martin, Richards and Huckaby. Most settled in the northeast corner of the county.

Josephine, a great granddaughter of Joseph and Martha, did credit to Martha's grit and tenacity. She was born on a tobacco plantation in Barren County, KY in 1840, the sixth of seven children born to Samuel and Lucy D. (Cowden) Bridges.

Josephine (Bridges) Franklin

About 1860 Josephine married Henry M. Franklin, shortly before the beginning of the Civil War. The newly married couple assumed the management of the Franklin tobacco plantation where seven of her eight children were born.

Even though it was war and reconstruction times and everyone had to work hard both indoors and out, she believed in "keeping up appearances." Josephine was a beautiful, daring girl with long brown hair and dark brown eyes as well as every ounce a lady. A lady's skin should be white, so she always wore a bonnet and gloves when working outside and taught her daughters to do so. Josephine loved stylish clothes. As a young woman her gowns were colorful, off the shoulder, skirts long and full, worn with necklaces, dangling earring and other jewelry.

Early spring of 1881 they sold the plantation and started for Polk County, along with other families. Fredrick, the then youngest child, had a Negro mammy who traveled with them. They camped beside the Mississippi River until the spring floodwater receded enough for them to cross over. May 20, 1881 they were in Buffalo; Frederick's birthday. They traveled on to Hickory County where they purchased a farm and the youngest son Henry "Babe" was born. Later they bought a farm in Polk County. The Hopewell Church has the record book where Josephine signed her name when she joined.

Josephine was a strong lady, both mentally and physically. She taught her children to work hard and to be independent. Among her descendants are farmers, educators, merchants, financial and political figures. Some of her grandchildren worked in the war effort building ships in California during WWII. One granddaughter, Garnet Franklin, owned and operated a tavern in Urbana. Doris Crawford remembers as a child going into the tavern with her father. Garnet served her a "plum beer" in a real beer glass.

Josephine's husband Henry M. died in 1905. About 1909 she married Mike Hopper, a Civil War veteran. For a wedding gift Mike gave her an organ, buggy and a gray horse.

Josephine saw all her children married except Thomas. Thomas was lost when a young man. She had her picture made with her great-great-grandson Conley Crain, grandson of Frona Black Crain. Josephine died June 1, 1930, age 91, and is buried in Hopewell Cemetery beside her first husband, Henry M. Franklin. *Submitted by Dorothy V. Black*

BROOKS – Thomas and Louisa Brooks came to Polk County in 1857. They came originally from Hart County, KY, but had spent several years in Harrison County, MO first. Thomas's parents were John Brooks and Betsy Courts. Louisa's parents were Hiram Harper and Nancy Locke. Thomas was born Dec. 16, 1821 and Louisa was born April 4, 1830. Thomas and Louisa were married in Hart County, KY, April 16, 1847. Upon coming to Polk County, they were leaders in establishing the Mt. Zoar Baptist Church near Goodson. The church lasted slightly longer than Thomas, who passed on in 1859. Thomas and Louisa had four children: John, Theophilus, Peter, who married Susan Duncan and Lucy, who married John Hart. Louisa later remarried. She married George Jenkins. They had one daughter Elizabeth.

Theophilus married Sarah Jane Harper, daughter of James Riley Harper and Rebecca Graham Russell, on Sept. 28, 1873 in Dallas County, MO. Theo was born Aug. 31, 1851 and Sarah was born Aug. 26, 1856. They made their home on Thomas and Louisa's place a couple of miles west of Goodson. They ran a store nearby. Theo and Sarah had seven children. The children were Tom; Charles Albert, who married Jessie Summerlott; Ora, who married Arthur Barker; Della, whose husbands include John S. Garrison; Mary Addie, who married Jess Morris; Minnie Lois; and William Lee, who married Rhua Fuller.

Theophilus and Sarah Jane (Harper) Brooks

Minnie Lois, or Lois as she was known, married William Jackson "Jack" Breshears, a postman. His parents were Rhuben Breshears and Margaret Cena Buckles. Jack and Lois were married Nov. 19, 1910. Lois was born April 23, 1892 and Jack was born Aug. 27, 1889; both were born near Goodson. They made their home on Thomas and Louisa's place. They had 12 children, including one set of twins. Their children include Violet, who first married Earl Angle; Pansy,

145

who married Wayne Angle; Rose, who married Ray Able; Lily, who married Dwight Farmer; Glen; R. T., who married Rozella Stoner; Nevin, who married Betty Lane; David, who married Peggy Lane; Don, who married Emma Payne; Adrian, who married Irene Needham; and Jerroll, who married Maureen Stack. Jerroll, or Jerry, had a twin brother Deryll who died in infancy. Jerry' son Mike lives today on the place started by Thomas and Louisa.

Glen married Pat Love, daughter of Robert Love and Hetty Gowin. They had five children including a set of twins. Their children are Patty, who married Gary Warren; Randy, who married Janice Short; Jane, who married Frank Stoner; Terry, who married Tina Woodham. Terry's twin, Kerry died in infancy. They have nine grandchildren: Suzanne Warren Mayfield, Todd Warren, Lynn Breshears Quennoz, Brent Breshears, Ashley Stoner, Alison Stoner, Jeffrey Stoner, Valerie Breshears and Kerry Breshears. Glen and Pat have two great-granddaughters, Maddison and Brooke. Most of the family has spent most of their lives in Polk County, MO. *Submitted by Patty Warren*

BROWN – Alexander Brown, of Cherokee heritage, owned land in Virginia and Tennessee. His father, mother and birth place is unknown. He married Violet Barton, daughter of Bur Barton, Feb. 25, 1797 in Bedford County, VA. All children were born in Virginia: Thomas, married Mary Turner; Annis, married Robert T. Pace; Sarah, married Elijah Hambelton; Dicey, married Daniel Alexander Fender; Isom Alexander, married Matilda Tindall; John Burrell, married Nancy K. Proctor; Zachariah (James), married Matilda unknown; Violet, married Levin Routh; Susannah married Moses Proctor; and Mary Elizabeth, married Hugh C. Routh.

In 1802 Bedford County, VA Alexander signed land deeds using his Indian name "Swaney" Brown. Alexander and Violet Brown both signed no marks. These signatures were written in same handwriting as that of the deed description itself, therefore, probably not their true signatures.

Alexander moved to McMinn County, TN. On Dec. 27, 1826 he purchased 40 acres then another 120 acres March 15, 1827. In 1835 Alexander's family left for Missouri with James Proctor, Daniel and Christian Fender, wintering in St. Clair County, IL where James Proctor died, arriving in the summer of 1836 in Brighton, Polk County, MO.

On Sept. 17, 1837 Alexander died and was buried in Brock Cemetery, Brighton, MO. Judy Fortner attended a Cherokee Memorial Ceremony in Brock Cemetery for Alexander about 1999.

Oct. 12, 1837, *Polk County, MO Missouri Book A*, "I Thomas Brown Do affirm that to the best of my knowledge the following is the names and Residences of the heirs of Alexander Brown deceased, Thomas Brown, Polk County; Mrs. Elijah Hamilton, Polk County; Robert Pace, Greene County; Mrs. Daniel Fender, Polk County; Isham Brown, Polk County; John Brown, Polk County; James Brown, Sinclair County, IL; Vilety Brown, Polk County; Susanna Brown, Polk County; Elizabeth Brown, Polk County. His mark Thomas Brown."

In 1906-1910, 271 applications to the Guion Miller Cherokee Rolls were filed, claiming to be Alexander's descendants, all were rejected. Grandson Michael Alexander Fender's application stated: Alexander was tall, slim, high cheekbones, dark complexion, black hair and eyes. Acquaintances who knew Alexander made affidavits stating he told them he was half-Cherokee Indian and had papers, however these papers were never found. John Thomas Brown, son of Isom Alexander, grandson of Alexander, from Braggs, OK Jan. 1, 1908, wrote to Guion Miller Commission to answer the question, "Who are your grandparents?" He states that Isom Brown's father was Alexander Brown and Isom's mother was Sarah Canoe, a full-blooded Cherokee. This is incorrect, Violet Barton was Alexander's wife.

Some researchers have Alexander Brown's father as Alexander Brown Sr., who married Sarah Canoe, daughter of Dragging Canoe, famous Cherokee Chief. Cherokee history and Cherokee researchers have not listed a daughter for Dragging Canoe. *Reference History of Hamilton County, TN,* by Zella Armstrong, *Heart of the Eagle* by Brent Cox, and *Nancy Ward and Dragging Canoe* by Pat Alderman.

Judy Fortner's third great-grandmother was Sarah Brown, born June 20, 1802 in Virginia; died 1863; married Jan. 4, 1820 to Elijah Hambleton, born 1796 in Virginia; died 1864. They are buried on Jacob Hinkle's farm, Morrisville, MO. Martha Dove Hambelton born Dec. 7, 1822 Tennessee; died March 23, 1900, the second of eight children was Judy's second great-grandmother. She married Vincent Harralson (born Dec. 3, 1817; died Aug. 20, 1862) on Dec. 7, 1843, both buried in Hickory Grove Cemetery, Polk County, MO. One of their 10 children, Lorinda Vashti Harralson was Judy Fortner's great-grandmother. She married Jonathan Albert Hicks. (See Hicks-Harralson). Ernest and Jerlie Stepp-Hicks were Judy's grandparents; they lived all their lives around Walnut Grove, MO. *Submitted by Judy Fortner*

BROWN – Cyrus "Cy" Field Brown was born at Louisburg, MO Jan. 8, 1863, the son of Ezekial Dudley and Sarah Jenkins Brown. He had two brothers, Edward E. (born 1858) and Jesse W. (born 1871). He also had two sisters, Mary Emily "Mollie" (born 1867) and Minnie (birth date unknown). Their parents died when the children were small (approximately 1874) and they were cared for by relatives.

Cyrus F. and Alice Elizabeth Brown, Cyrus is in IOOF (Odd Fellow) uniform, 1910

As a young man Cyrus moved to Joplin to work in the lead and zinc mines. He married Alice Elizabeth Schell June 30, 1886. Alice was born March 25, 1869 in McDonald County, daughter of Fredrick and Polly Johnston Schell. Alice had a brother, Thomas, and a sister, Sophie Belle.

Cyrus was proud of his 31-year membership in the Joplin IOOF, the Independent Order of Odd Fellows.

Cyrus and Alice were the parents of Lillian Belle (born Dec. 7, 1890) and Fred Dudley (born Aug. 1, 1895). Lillian and Fred attended Joplin schools.

When Fred was a young schoolboy, his mother decided he needed violin lessons. One day a neighbor boy came to visit, but Fred didn't want to play with him. He told his mother to tell his friend that he wasn't home. Then he ran and jumped into a closed to hide, forgetting the violin was on the closet floor. Alas! Sad end of the fiddle and happy ending of the lessons!

The family moved to Polk County in 1912, first to a farm on the Sac River near Aldrich, then later to a farm northwest of Cliquot near Flint school. Lillian was a teacher for many years in Polk County schools. Fred was a carpenter by trade.

Lillian married Mark R. Winton Dec. 12, 1924. Mark was born Dec. 13, 1888, son of William C. and Ofena Winton of Fair Play. Mark was a WWI veteran with service in France. He was elected sheriff of Polk County 1925-1929. Their son, Mark Frederick, was born Dec. 21, 1925, while they were in residence at the county jail.

Fred Brown met Cora H. Flint during her first year of teaching at Flint school. Cyrus was on the school board. Cora (born March 21, 1907) was the daughter of R. A. "Bert" and Ona Flint. Cora had attended first grade at Flint school. Fred and Cora were married May 1, 1927. Their daughter, Helen L., was born April 17, 1930. Helen also went to first grade at Flint school.

Cyrus F. Brown passed away June 12, 1932 and Alice on June 24, 1956. Both are buried at Pleasant Ridge Cemetery. Cy's brothers, Ed and Jesse, never married. His sister Mollie married Frank M. Davison, a long-time Eudora merchant. They are all buried at Pleasant Ridge. Sister Minnie married a McGhee and lived in Coalgate, OK. She is buried there.

Cyrus's son Fred and his family moved to Mesa, AZ in the 1940s, where Fred worked as a carpenter until retirement. He died May 20, 1970. Cora returned to Missouri in 1992 where she resided with her daughter until her death on March 19, 2000. Fred and Cora are buried at East Resthaven Cemetery, Phoenix, AZ.

Helen L. Brown married Gordon D. Pierce (from Pennsylvania) in Mesa, AZ Dec. 23, 1950. They had two sons, Daniel R. (married Jennifer Wallen) and Scott P. Pierce. Following Gordon's death in 1965, Helen married a childhood schoolmate, Donald H. Nottingham, and returned to Missouri where they lived on Don's farm north of Fair Play.

Don was a Marine veteran and served in the Korean Conflict. They had one son, Joe Donald Nottingham, who resides on the farm. Don was injured in a farm accident resulting in his death Feb. 4, 1988. He is buried at Dunnegan Cemetery. Helen resides in Fair Play. She has three grandchildren, Amy and Emily Pierce in Moscow, ID and Kyle Don Nottingham in Fair Play, MO.

Cyrus's daughter Lillian B. and husband Mark R. Winton lived on a farm northwest of Cliquot and later moved north of Fair Play. Mark died Jan. 13, 1970 and Lillian on May 10, 1982. Both are buried at Pleasant Ridge Cemetery. Their son, Mark Fredrick, was an Army veteran and had been stationed in Germany. He married Amelia Lois Ballard of Dunnegan, MO on Nov. 28, 1953. Mark was an engineer for Texaco Oil Company, first working in Illinois and later transferred to Metairie, LA. Mark and Lois had one son, Mark Thomas, and two daughters, Alice (married Art Johnson) and Carol (married Stephen Harlan). They had three grandchildren, Matthew and Kevin Harlan, and Emily Johnson. Mark Frederick Winton died of multiple myeloma Jan. 16, 2001. He is buried at Dunnegan Cemetery. Lois resides in Metairie, LA. *Submitted by Helen (Brown) Nottingham*

BROWN - The son of Athel Brown and Winnie Barker, Harold Raymond (H.R.) Brown was born Nov. 28, 1921 in Polk County, MO about two miles south of Fair Play, MO.

He attended nine years of schooling at a country school called Fox School, just a short distance from where he was born. He was the second of eight children, two of whom died at birth. He had a brother John Grant Brown (married Marjorie) and four sisters: Nannie Mae (Brown) Combs, wife of Robert Combs; Wilma Elizabeth (Brown) Combs, wife of Lawrence Combs; Shirley Etta (Brown) Stewart, wife of James Stewart: and last but not least, Zelma Lois (Brown) Chastain, wife of Grant Chastain.

On July 13, 1941, he was joined in marriage to Miss Gladys Mae Mitchell, the daughter of Harry Gerald Mitchell and Dona Ellen B. Stacy and granddaughter of David M. Mitchell and Dora Clementine Davidson (or Davison) of Polk County, MO.

Harold Raymond and Gladys Mae were the parents of five children, four daughters and a son. Their children are Lois Arlette, Joann Ellen, Raymond Leon, Carol Ann and Linda Mae. They are grandparents of 13 grandchildren and 20 great-grandchildren. They lived in Polk County for several years, then moved to Cedar County. They moved back to Polk County in September of 2002 to an address in Fair Play. The two oldest children were born in Polk County. Lois and Joann died in Kansas City.

The Brown children's spouses were, as follows: Lois Arlette married James Leroy Larcom of Humansville, MO; Joann Ellen married John Wesley Boone; Raymond Leon married Kathern; Carol Ann married Gary Poppe who is now deceased and Linda Mae married Jerry Taylor. *Submitted by Gladys Brown*

Johnathan Albert and Lorinda Vashti (Harrelson) Hicks

BROWN - As he and his Cherokee family left the campsite near what is now Highway 13 and Kearney Street in Springfield and journeyed north and settled in the Little Sac River bottom, he was not the first settler in Polk County; however, he was one of the first.

Isham Alexander Brown, whose Indian name was Sawney, was the son of Sarah Canoe, who was the daughter of Dragging Canoe, who was the son of Attakullakulla. Dragging Canoe was a rather famous Cherokee war chief and Attakullakulla was famous for being one of the Cherokee chiefs taken to England in 1730 to be presented to royalty.

Sawney, who lived in Cherokee Indian lands in southeast Tennessee, sensed big trouble ahead for the Cherokee. So, in the summer of 1835 he packed up his family and belongings, and along with five other related families; set out west. The group arrived just east of St. Louis in the late fall of 1835. They wintered just east of the "great river" and in the spring of 1836 crossed the river and made their way southwest, finally camping in what is now Springfield.

The guide for the Indian families was a white man named Stokes. His nephew lived near what is now Brighton and traveled to Springfield to visit his uncle. While there he convinced Sawney, or Alexander Brown, that there was good land on the Little Sac River. Alexander and his family turned north and settled on the Little Sac near what is now the Polk-Greene County line. The actual site was likely just north across the river from the Snow Bluff Recreation Area.

Alexander lived on this site until October of 1837 when he died rather suddenly. He was buried on a small knoll just north of the river bottom and became the first person to be buried in what is now known as the Brock Family Cemetery. However, his 10 children married and settled in the area and provided the ancestral lineage for literally hundreds of residents in Polk and Greene County. Many of these families aren't even aware of their common grandfather of several generations ago.

The DNA of Sawney may be found in individuals with the following family names: Brown, Doke, Fender, Hambleton, Harrelson, Hicks, Hinkle, Matthews, McNutt, Proctor, Shelton, Tummons and many, many others. When you consider all the other families that have become linked to these families by marriage, you realize that when Sawney, or Alexander Brown, settled on the Little Sac, he provided the basis for the continued settling of Polk County and for Polk County population today. *Submitted by Joe B. Shelton*

BROWN – Samuel Bruce Brown was born in Ash Grove, MO on Oct. 3, 1888. His father attended the University of Michigan in 1910 and 1911, studying to be an electrical engineer. His brother-in-law Milton Kirby has a hardware and grocery store on the north side of the Bolivar square. Bruce was in Germantown, PA in the summer of 1911 when his sister wired him to come home and close out the store as her husband was dying. He lived but could not come to work for over a year. He made Bruce a proposition to go into partnership with him, which he did. The store was later sold several times.

Andre Pearl Galbraith was born in Cedar County, MO on Nov. 30, 1889. Her father died three and one half months before she was born. Her mother bought a home in Fair Play, MO and worked as a seamstress. When Pearl finished school they bought a home three blocks north of the Bolivar square and Pearl went to work at the First National Bank of Bolivar. She and Bruce were married July 6, 1915. They had one son, Samuel Bruce Brown born Nov. 29, 1922. In 1922 they bought Charley Elliston's grocery store in the East building on the north side of the square. They closed it out and put in a hardware store, which later became more of a gift shop.

After Bruce died in 1953, the store was closed out in 1966 and Samuel Bruce Brown went to work for the city of Bolivar. He retired after 26 years. He was city clerk, city water collector, clerk of the Bolivar police court and Sunday dispatcher for the Bolivar police and fire departments. He now resides in Bolivar with his caregiver Michael Wright and family. *Submitted by Samuel Brown*

BROWN - Early one morning in the spring of 1969 a call came to the apartment of Rex and Ann Brown in Fayetteville, AR. The caller identified himself as Dr. Tom Padgett, Academic Dean of Southwest Baptist College in Bolivar, MO. He explained that he was looking for someone to fill a position at Southwest Baptist College in the teaching area, which Rex was studying at the University of Arkansas. Since Rex was not familiar with the college or Bolivar, it took several conversations and visits to Bolivar before he accepted the position. On July 1, 1969 Rex, Ann and 5-year-old Kyle Brown became residents of Bolivar and Polk County. In discussing the move with his father, Rex was told that he might expect to find some relatives in Bolivar. He was informed that his grandfather and great grandfather had moved to Arkansas from Bolivar, MO.

As Rex began to look for records of his relatives he found the first member of the Brown family to live in Polk County came in the early 1830s. Richard Brown was born in North Carolina in 1785 (died Sept. 16, 1850 in Polk County) and came to Polk County from White County, Tennessee. He obtained land (240 acres) in southeast Polk County (Section 10, Township 33, Range 21) and lived there until his death. His first wife was Margaret. After her death he married Jemimah Turner on Feb. 9, 1834 in Franklin County (Book A). On June 26, 1849 he paid her $400 for a divorce. Richard's children were Sterling, married Sarah Barclay Nov. 27, 1835, Polk County; Mary, married William Barclay; Elizabeth, married William Jenkins; James Richard Jr., lived in Hickory County; Rebecca Ann, married Benjamin Franklin Gordon; Margaret, married Perry Viles. Richard was living with Rebecca and Benjamin F. Gordon when he died. It has not been determined where Richard is buried or who his ancestors were or where in Tennessee they lived.

Next in the line of ancestors was Richard's oldest son, Sterling. He was born in 1813-14 in Tennessee; died March 7, 1853; married Sarah Barclay on Nov. 27, 1835. Sarah was the daughter of Robert Barclay and Mary Hubbard. Children of Sterling and Sarah were Margaret, born 1837, married Reuben McKinney; Elizabeth. born 1838, married John Payne; James Henry, born April 10, 1840, died Sept. 3, 1898 in Bruno, AR, married Jan. 30, 1862 to Hannah Rebecca Ragsdale, born Jan. 15, 1840, died 1918-1920 in Laverne, OK (she was the daughter of Joel Ragsdale and Jain Allred); Richard, born 1844, died 1928-1930 in California, married Phyllis; Robert, born 1847; George, born 1849, killed in a land slide in California; Daniel, born 1851, died 1935, married 1871, Nancy.

Sterling's son, James Henry, was great-grandfather to Rex. He and Hannah Rebecca Ragsdale had four children, all born in Polk County. Joel Sterling, born 1867, married Wilda Elease Ogden; William Wesley, born June 14, 1868, died Dec. 23, 1918, married Martha Ann Ezell; Sarah Jane, born 1863, died May 6, 1937, married Henry Price Ogden; and Mary Susan, born 1872, died 1963, married John Wesley Coleman in 1902. During the Civil War several skirmishes occurred near where they lived and her father, Joel Ragsdale, was wounded in one skirmish by bushwhackers and a Union General who was riding in his buggy was killed. A short time after the war James Henry and Hannah Rebecca moved to Marion County, AR with their family.

William Wesley, who was Rex's grandfather, earned his living by driving a mule team with a wagonload of freight from Yellville, AR to Springfield, MO. When he arrived in Springfield he would leave the wagon to be unloaded of the Arkansas produce and loaded with merchandise for the return trip. He would rent a horse and ride to Bolivar or Halfway to visit with relatives. In good weather the trip took between seven and 10 days.

What seemed at first to be a move to an unfamiliar place for Rex, Ann and Kyle Brown turned out to take them to the home of ancestors and distant cousins. A second son, Scott, was born in Bolivar on May 4, 1971. *Submitted by Rex B. Brown*

BUCKLE – Mathias "Matt" G. Buckle was born Oct. 5, 1839 in Cincinnati, Hamilton County, OH, the son of David Buckle and Catherina Felix of Barbria, Germany. Matt enlisted in the Union Army, Company K, 26 Regiment Indiana Volunteer Infantry as a private at Manchester, IN on Aug. 6, 1861. He was described at age 22 as standing five feet, ten and one-half inches tall with a ruddy complexion, gray eyes and light hair. He was in battles in Prairie Grove, AR; Brownsville, TX; Spanish Fort, AL; and the siege at Vicksburg. He was in several skirmishes in the Brighton-Bolivar area. One such skirmish took place at the Brighton Spring, another took place at Bolivar and a third took place one and one-half miles north of Brighton at a hotel-stage shop stop on the Butterfield Overland Trail. He liked the Brighton area and wished to settle there someday. Matt was discharged Jan. 15, 1866.

The Mathias and Maggie Buckle family

On Oct. 19, 1868 Matt married Margaret Rebecca Gumbert in Cincinnati, OH. Maggie was born May 5, 1845 in Germany. Around the age of 6, Maggie's family came to America. It is believed that her father died on the voyage and was buried at sea. She told stories of seeing bodies wrapped in canvas and dropped in the sea. Maggie could not write in English and barely spoke the language.

While living in Dearborn County, IN, they had four daughters. Magdalena was born Aug. 15, 1869 and, according to the family Bible, died in 1870. Kate Buckle was born Aug. 19, 1871. She married William McGuire and moved to Crescent, OK. Kate died June 17, 1953. Alice Kathryn Buckle was born April 17, 1873. She married Luther Charles Fisher. Alice Kathryn died Oct. 12, 1952 and both are buried at the Brighton Cemetery. Clara was born Nov. 10, 1874. She was married first to Yancy McGuire and then to Nimrod King. Clara died July 25, 1904 and is buried in the Brighton Cemetery.

Mathias and Maggie then moved their family to Harvey County, KS. Delia was born Dec. 10, 1880 in Harvey County. She married James Austin Brown. She died March 27, 1947 in Fame, OK. Susan Mary Ann was born March 10, 1882, also in Kansas. She married Mark Lillard in Polk County. She died Oct. 19, 1961 in Springfield, MO. Hattie May was born Aug. 7, 1884 in Iola, KS. She married Fred Winton in Polk County. She died Dec. 27, 1938. Mathias H. Buckle Jr. was born Feb. 3, 1887 in Halsted, KS. He married Myrtle Howard.

In 1890, Matt Sr. and Maggie moved their family by covered wagon to Brighton, MO. Their youngest daughter, Edna Viola Frances, was born Oct. 12, 1890 in Brighton. She married Leta Gay Proctor.

Matt chose a farm and built his house about one mile north of Tingler Hill in Polk County. They attended the Methodist Church in Brighton. Matt died Dec. 1, 1896 and Margaret died March 10, 1916. They are buried in the Brighton Cemetery. *Submitted by Tammy Hicklin Groves*

BUNCH – Karen's great-great grandfather was John William Bunch. He mostly went by "William." He moved to Polk County from Indiana, shortly after the Civil War was over, 1865. His wife was Eliza Demaree, and she died near Bolivar in 1866, a few months after childbirth. They had seven children. Eliza's family, James and Mary Demaree, also moved from Indiana with

John William Bunch

the Bunch family. That Demaree family married into the Polk County Shellenberger family at Bolivar.

John William Bunch then married his second wife, Mary C. Box, in 1868, at Polk County. They had three children. She had more Box family there near Aldrich. She and John Bunch moved over to Taney County about 1870.

Karen had not been able to connect John William Bunch to other Bunch families in Polk County, but truly feels there is a connection, for him to choose that area. He died approximately 1907 in Taney County and is buried with his second wife Mary C. Box in the Helphrey Cemetery in Tanneyville, MO. They have many descendants scattered around, mostly in Missouri and Oklahoma. *Submitted by Karen Rogers*

BURDETT – William "Buck" Burdett Jr. married Sarah Jane Lowe in Tennessee. Four of their nine children moved to the Missouri Ozarks. They were Patience Delacy Burdett, Kenneth Louis Burdett, Sarah Jane Burdett, and Dr. Samuel Stewart Burdett.

Patience Delacy Burdett (born Jan. 14, 1818; died May 10, 1860) married William Clinton Cavin in 1836. They moved to Polk County, MO and are buried at Burdett-Cavin Cemetery, Polk County, MO.

Kenneth Louis Burdett (born Aug. 13, 1833; died Aug. 12, 1903) married Nancy Elizabeth Ramey. After practicing medicine at Forsyth, MO from 1856 until 1889, they moved to Ava, MO. He is buried in a family cemetery northwest of Ava, Douglas County, MO.

Sarah Jane Burdett (born Aug. 20, 1835; died Jan. 10, 1858) in 1856, moved with her mother and siblings and settled in Fair Grove, MO. She is buried in the Burdett-Cavin Cemetery, Polk County, MO. She never married.

Dr. Samuel Stewart Burdett Sr. (born July 26, 1823, Bedford County, TN; died Jan. 10, 1877) graduated from medical college in Nashville, TN; then married first, Polly Cavin (born Nov. 15, 1825; died July 26, 1846) and moved to Polk County, outside of Pleasant Hope.

Children of Dr. Samuel S. Burdett and Polly Cavin were William Joseph Burdett (born 1844; died 1898) and Sarah Roxanna Burdett (born and died July 4, 1846).

Polly died about three weeks after the birth of her daughter Sarah. Samuel married Polly's sister, Sarah Ann Elizabeth Cavin (born Sept. 27, 1833; died Sept. 22, 1899). Both Cavin girls were daughters of Joseph Cavin and Hannah Keele and are buried in the Burdett-Cavin Cemetery, Polk County, MO.

Samuel Sr. and Sarah had George Washington Burdett (born 1848; died 1937); Samuel Stewart Burdett (born 1850; died 1881); Orville Marion Burdett (born 1853; died 1853); Columbus "Lum" Marion Burdett (born 1854; died 1920s); Kenneth Louis Burdett (born 1856; died 1903); Sarah J. H. M. E. L. Burdett (born 1859; died 1866); Giles Hampton "Bud" Burdett (born 1861); Asbury Price Burdett (born 1866; died 1920); Cora Bell Burdett (born 1868; died 1949) and Frank Hochdorffer Burdett (born 1870; died 1894).

Samuel practiced medicine in Polk County until 1875. When his health failed, he moved to Forsyth, MO to be close to his brother, Dr. Kenneth Burdett and his family. Samuel died Jan. 10, 1877 in Forsyth. He is buried in the Burdett-Cavin Cemetery, Polk County, MO.

Sam Sr.'s son, Samuel Stewart Burdett Jr. (born 1850; died 1881) married Caroline Williams (born 1852; died 1909) and they moved to Missouri by covered wagon when daughter Allie was an infant. He is buried at Burdett-Cavin Cemetery in Polk County, MO.

Allie Burdett Chapman with grandson, John Miller 1952

Samuel Jr. and Sarah had William S. Burdett (born 1874; died 1892); Charlie Burdett (born 1875) buried at Burdett-Cavin Cemetery, Polk County, MO; Allie Sarah Burdett (born 1876; died 1970) married John Partee Chapman (see John P. and Allie Burdett Chapman article); Retta Burdett (born 1878; died 1952) married Charles "Charlie" Self; and George Edward Burdett (born 1880) married Evelyn B. Keeling. *Submitted by Velma Miller Stevens*

BURKHART – Judy Lorene Burkhart was born Sept. 17, 1957 at Osceola, St. Clair County, MO in the Osceola Hospital and spent her childhood in St. Clair County, graduating from Osceola High School in 1975. She was the youngest child of "Ted" Archie Van Buren Burkhart and Loga Lorene (Culbertson, Allen) Burkhart. Her six siblings, Roy Lee Allen, Alice Bea Allen (Williams, Carter), Phillis Darlene Allen (Moore, Fricke), "Jane" Wanda Jane Burkhart (Volkart), Peggy Jewel Burkhart (Laswell, Pelz) and Joyce Kay Burkhart welcomed her home. At the age of just a few months Judy became ill, nearly dying and was treated at Children Mercy's Hospital in Kansas City. Her father kept the tiny bracelet from her hospital visit.

Judy married Charles "David" Welch of Vista, MO on Feb. 27, 1975 in Osceola at the home of and by Jackson Kiefer, Baptist Minister. They lived at Vista, Urich, Bolivar, and then Cliquot, MO. David was born Feb. 27, 1953 in Wheatland, the son of Opal Ruth Quick and "Jay" John William Welch. They had two children, Daniel Jay Welch, born June 25, 1975 in Wetzel Hospital, Clinton, MO and Sarah June Welch, born July 30, 1981, in St. John's Hospital, Springfield, MO before divorcing in June 1982.

At Bolivar, on April 13, 1984, Judy married "Ted" James Edward Williamson. Ted, the son of Fern Margaret (Slagle) and "Jay" Rolland Jay Williamson, was born April 16, 1951 in Butler, MO. He drove for the Associated Grocers of Springfield, starting his career in 1974 and making frequent runs to Arkansas and St. Louis, MO. To this union was born one son, Jeremiah Edward Williamson, Dec. 12, 1984 in St. John's Hospital in Springfield, MO.

Ted's father, Jay, who was living with them, was in a serious motor vehicle accident in Polk County Sept. 25, 1987. He died at St. John's Hospital in Springfield from the resulting injuries. Judy helped care for her parents, Ted (born March 1, 1912; died Jan. 14, 1995) and Loga (born April 4, 1918; died July 29, 1994) Burkhart, who lived in Bolivar with her sister, Joyce Burkhart. Her parents died in the Citizens Memorial Hospital in Bolivar and were buried in the Freeman Holsapple Cemetery in St. Clair County, MO.

From 1979, Judy and family lived in Cliquot, MO and had a Dunnegan address, Bolivar phone number, and the children attended the Bolivar school system. Sarah Welch was the 1999 Bolivar graduating class valedictorian and attended Truman University in Kirksville, MO. In 1990 Judy started work as a rural postal carrier for the Humansville post office. Her route included about 100 miles of rural county roads. Judy and family would often visit the local coffee shop Country House when it was open, purchasing gas at Hill Top Service Station and later frequented the Country Kitchen restaurant.

The family would ride horses on weekend camping trips, taking along granddaughter, Taylor Jay Welch as well as taking weeklong camping trips to Wyoming and Colorado. Taylor, the daughter of Daniel Welch, was born Jan. 18, 1993 at Citizens Memorial Hospital in Bolivar, MO. Taylor was the elementary queen of the Fair Play PTO Carnival in October 1999 and competed at the Diamond S Arena to become the 2002 Country Days Rodeo Queen. *Submitted by Peggy (Burkhart) Pelz*

Jeremiah Edward Williamson, Daniel Jay Welch and Sarah June Welch, January 2001

Caleb Butler

BUTLER – Caleb Butler, the son of Jacob Butler and Martha Manley Butler, was born Aug. 30, 1809 in Tennessee and there he married Elizabeth Carneal. Elizabeth was born Oct. 11, 1809. They moved to Polk County from Anderson County, TN in 1850 or 1851. In November of 1851 he bought 200 acres of land two miles west of Rondo for $700.

Caleb was a farmer who owned 511 acres in 1861 according to the 1861 Polk County tax assessment book. His father, Jacob Butler, was a planter and slave owner in Tennessee. Though Caleb was listed in the 1861 assessor's book as owning two slaves, he, son Thomas, daughter Martha J. Ashlock and husband Obediah and Elizabeth Butler (either Caleb's or Tom's wife) signed an oath of allegiance to the Union in Bolivar in 1861 or 1862.

On Sept. 5, 1871, Caleb Butler joined Mission Chapel Church (later Rondo Baptist Church), thereby being one of the earliest members. Orlena Ann "Lena" Butler Emmett, a granddaughter, wrote in 1941, "There was another sacred, dear soul Grandfather Butler. I have nothing to fear about his soul. He was a quite up right Father, neighbor, never said an ugly word, no place. (He was) a great hand to talk. I can see him laugh. (He) gave me money, take me places where I never would have gotten to go, let me have a horse to ride."

Lena wrote about her grandparents, "(Grandma) got me to take her to see (the home place they had sold). She had me ride in the saddle and she rode back behind me. Grandfather had three beautiful bay mares. They would get on those mares and go to church or anywhere, stay all nite or for a while."

Caleb and Elizabeth Butler were the parents of at least 10 children.

Leah Eleanor Butler was born Sept. 28, 1829 and died Jan. 26, 1919. She married Thomas Berry Hudson March 4, 1845 in Anderson County, TN. They moved to Missouri about the same time as her parents and later to Arkansas where Thomas died. When she got older, Leah returned to Missouri to live with one of her children, Frances Flint. Leah is buried at Rondo Cemetery.

Jacob Washington Butler was born July 12, 1831 and died Nov. 18, 1920 at Buffalo, MO. He married Lucy Ann Gammon July 3, 1851 in Tennessee. Jacob served in the Union Army in the 8th Missouri S. M. Cavalry. After Lucy died in 1875, he married Eliza Cofland Jan. 2, 1876 in Dallas County, MO.

Nancy C. Butler was born July 10, 1833 and died Aug. 7, 1879. She married John Robinson Gammon Aug. 20, 1851 in Anderson County, TN. Nancy is buried at Rondo Cemetery.

Martha Jane Butler was born Aug. 4, 1835 and died May 8, 1909. She married Obediah Ashlock Dec. 28, 1852 in Polk County. Martha and Obediah are buried in Brush Grove (Potts) Cemetery in Polk County.

An unnamed child who died in Anderson County, TN.

Sarah "Sary" Butler was born in 1844. She married Francis "Frank" Whitten Oct. 15, 1857 in Polk County.

Thomas Henry Butler was born Jan. 15, 1846 in Anderson County and died Oct. 2, 1924. He married Hannah Elizabeth Flint Nov. 9, 1862 in Polk County and they had six children: Louisa J. (married Amos Zimmerman), Orlena Ann "Lena" (married Hiram Wills Emmett), Alice M. (married first, Theophilus Pope McCracken and second, Carlos Palmer), William Jasper, Jacob Washington (married Lora) and Daisy Bell (married a Mr. Workman). Thomas and Elizabeth are buried at Rondo Cemetery.

Eliza L. Butler was born in 1848 and married John A. F. Israel Sept. 25, 1866 in Polk County.

Rebecca Ann Butler was born May 21, 1850 in Tennessee and died Feb. 10, 1929. She married James D. Skaggs Jan. 24, 1867 and they had 12 children: Martha Allie (married Richard Worthan), Mary Ellen (married William Franklin Carneal), Obediah D. Dennis, Caleb Butler, Letha Jane (married Oscar L. Forgey), William Franklin, Walter Jameson, Stella May (married James Allen Nickels), Myrtle Ann (married J. E. Hale) and an infant son. Rebecca, James and the infant are buried at Salem Cemetery.

Charlotte Malinda Butler was born July 1857 in Polk County. She married Robert Enos Holmes Oct. 15, 1874 in Polk County. On Jan. 27, 1907, she married John M. Northern.

Elizabeth Butler died on Feb. 26, 1887. Twelve years later Caleb died on May 26, 1898. Both were buried in Rondo Cemetery near the church where they regularly worshipped. *Submitted by Rhonda Jean Downs Hughes, Caleb and Elizabeth's great-great-great granddaughter*

BUTLER – James Robert Butler was born May 10, 1892 in Huron, MO, the son of William H. Butler (born 1852 in Tennessee; died 1940) and Joann Miller Butler (born 1858 in Missouri; died 1906). Paternal grandparents were William J. Butler (born 1826, place unknown; died 1878) and Martha Jane Hudson Butler (born 1827, place unknown; died 1911). Maternal grandparents were Boyd Miller (born 1836 in Missouri; died 1905) and Nancy G. Bridges Miller (born 1835 in Kentucky; died 1914).

Chole Leona Edna Ingram was born Dec. 26, 1894 in Bolivar, MO, the daughter of Samuel Wesley Ingram (born 1871 in Georgia; died 1940) and Dora Ann Cloyed Ingram (born 1867 in Tennessee; died 1944). Paternal grandparents were J. Ingram of Georgia (dates unknown) and K. Ingram of Georgia (dates unknown). Maternal grandparents were James P. Cloyed of Tennessee (dates unknown) and Mary Jane Cloyed (born 1836 in Tennessee; died 1914).

James and Leona's story began in 1908. When Leona was 13 years old, she was called upon to take a pitchfork out to the field. As she leaned the pitchfork against the fence, she unexpectedly met, face-to-face, 15-year-old James, the boy she would marry.

James visited Leona on occasion until he decided they should have their first date; the Louisburg picnic on July 24, 1908. After courting for a couple of years, James decided to propose and Leona accepted. At the ages of 15 and 17, their fathers had to give consent, so arrangements were made for the trip into Bolivar for the marriage license.

James and his father drove up to Leona's house but in the anticipation of the event to take place, James didn't think to bring a buggy big enough to accommodate everyone. The only horse in the barn had not been broken, but the situation required he be ridden sooner than planned. With Leona's father in the saddle, the only conversation heard on the road to town was "Whoa horse, Whoa!" Fifteen miles later and with an investment of $1.50 the license was obtained.

James R. Butler and Leona E. Ingram Butler March 27, 1960, 50th wedding anniversary

Although rain ushered in on March 29, 1910, James hitched the buggy, went and claimed Leona, and they started the two-mile drive to Mohawk to be wed. Due to the rain and mud, James drove the buggy directly up to the front porch of the justice of the peace, Mr. C. C. Pitts. Two witnesses, Sarah Fellows and Ollie Pitts, stepped out on the front porch and with James and Leona in the buggy, a brief ceremony took place. Congratulations were quickly exchanged and with a chair, a table and $5, they started their married life together.

They moved from Polk County to California in 1912 but returned to Bolivar in 1914 when they acquired ownership of the Hotel Ozark. The sign on the front read: singles $1; doubles $1.50; meals a quarter. A lot of hard work went into the preparation of the meals and the upkeep of the hotel. To help with the serving, a girl was hired at $4 a week. Their day began at five a.m. and after breakfast, pies were baked and the dishes and laundry were washed by hand in wooden drums. After a couple of years, they moved to Iowa.

Nine years later they decided there would be no more Iowa winters and moved to northern California, where James worked as a farmer. In 1927, James, Leona and their five children moved to Ventura County, CA where they worked in the agricultural industry until they retired.

James and Leona celebrated their 50th anniversary in 1960. They went on to have a 75th anniversary and were married for 76 years until the death of Leona.

Chole Leona Edna Ingram Butler died Feb. 29, 1984 at the age of 89. James Robert Butler died Jan. 9, 1991 at the age of 98. James and Leona chose their final resting place to be the Payne Cemetery in Polk County, MO. *Submitted by Marie D. Figueroa*

CADDELL-COPELAND – Perrine S. and Blanche Lena (Darrow) Caddell were married Aug. 26,

1924 in Richland Center, Richland County, WI. The couple drove to Michigan in a Model T Ford for their honeymoon. They had a daughter, Mariam Louise Caddell, born on July 27, 1929 near Lucas, Missaukee County, MI. In 1930, the Caddell family moved to a farm south of Cadillac, MI and later bought a farm several miles west. They owned and operated Caddell's Guernsey Dairy and did general farming. A son, Ronald Perrine Caddell, was born. Blanche was active in home economics extension work and farm-women's work at Michigan State University. Perrine and Blanche are buried in Stotts City, MO.

Mariam's schooling included 12 years of grade and high school at Cadillac Public Schools and college works at Big Rapids, MI. She had worked since the age of 12 doing clerical work at the post office and during WWII she and her friends worked Saturdays, some evenings and summers at grocery stores or J.C. Penny stores. Mariam recalls that The Shopping Basket in Cadillac, MI was the first store to have carts for customers to serve themselves. In the summer of 1950 in Lawrence County, MO, Mariam worked in a rural store where she pumped gas, candled eggs, sold coal oil (kerosene) and had cheese and lunch meat available for the hay crews as they stopped in to eat and have a soda pop. The latter was 5 cents and the gasoline was 16 cents a gallon. Mariam married Van Osburn Copeland, a descendent of full-blooded Cherokees, on Aug. 15, 1953 and their daughter Candace Perrine Copeland was born in Dade County, MO on April 22, 1960. When Mariam was a freshman in college she worked at a soda fountain and did bookkeeping in the office of a 5 & 10 Store and was always available to type for people. Mariam graduated from Drury College in 1969, then earned a master's degree in 1965. She taught school from 1949 to 1972 and was involved in 4-H work and she encouraged her pupils in their 4-H projects. She has lived in Bolivar since January of 1998. Van Copeland served in WWII and he passed away on May 24, 1966 and he was buried with military honors in Shiloh Cemetery in Dade County. Mariam recalls a story about Van's dog "Old Shep" who had been with the family since WWII. Shep never adjusted to a move the family made three-fourths of a mile away to the Lawrence-Dade County line and every night he went back to the old farm. Shep lived to be 22 years old.

Candace graduated from Greenfield High School in 1978. She graduated from Drury College in 1982 with a major in music and education. She was a band teacher in Mt. Vernon, MO from 1982 to 1985. She was united in marriage to Melvin Lee Blankenship and they currently reside in Marshfield, MO where they raise fox-trotter horses and are employed in Springfield, MO.

Ronald Perrine Caddell lives in the Trinity Lutheran Church Community of Freistatt, MO. His children are Nicholas Lee Caddell, Michael A. Caddell and Christy L. (Mrs. Clifford) Rice. *Submitted by Mariam Louise Caddell Copeland*

CALDWELL - John Caldwell was born in Guilford County, NC on Dec. 17, 1823 to Joseph and Sarah Woody Caldwell of Orange County, NC. During 1824 John Caldwell's parents moved to Lawrence County, IN. Moving with them from North Carolina were Joseph's brother, William Caldwell and his wife Jane. The brothers, Joseph Caldwell and William Caldwell, obtained 80 acres each adjacent to one another on the eastern outskirts of Bedford. These Caldwell families were a part of a large migration from Orange County, NC to Lawrence County, IN, during the early 1800s. Some of the family names were: Woody, Box, Day, Crawford, Ray, Finger, Fender, Whitted and Allen. Descendants of a few of these families later moved to Polk County, MO during the mid-1800s.

John Caldwell married Amanda Freeman on July 12, 1844 in Bedford, Lawrence County, IN and moved to neighboring Martin County where they farmed for almost 10 years before moving back to Lawrence County. To this union were born six children: Sarah Elizabeth, Alexander Wesley, Mary E., Eliza Elender, Joseph Alonzo and Amanda Victoria. Amanda Freeman Caldwell died on June 13, 1859 in childbirth with their daughter, Amanda V. Caldwell. A year later, John Caldwell married Jane "Jennie" Whitted Box Ross on June 10, 1860 in Lawrence County, IN. No children were born to this marriage. They divorced sometime before 1869.

On Aug. 15, 1862, John Caldwell enlisted for three years as a private at Edwardsport, Knox County, IN for duty with Company C, 80th Infantry Regiment, Indiana. This regiment was engaged in war operations in Kentucky, Tennessee, Georgia, South Carolina, North Carolina and Washington, DC. During the winter of 1864-65 while his unit was encamped on the Mall in Washington, D.C., John was seriously injured when thrown by a mule that he was breaking. A few months later, he mustered out at Salisbury, NC on June 22, 1865.

After the war, John Caldwell returned to Lawrence County, IN where his children had stayed during the war. On Oct. 7, 1869, in Lawrence County, John Caldwell married Eliza Jane Beasley Fielder. She was born Sept. 2, 1839 in Lawrence County, to William and Elizabeth Reynolds Beasley. The Beasleys and Reynolds were from Tennessee and were early pioneers into Lawrence County. Eliza Jane Beasley was the widow of Nelson S. Fielder who was killed Oct. 12, 1864 near Morganza, LA as a soldier in the Union Army. Eliza had four children with Nelson Fielder: Andrew C., Joseph S., George and Sarah Jane. George died as an infant. Subsequently, Eliza and John Caldwell parented Ellsworth, Antoinette "Nettie," Oliver Porter, Minnie Isis and William Jason. All of the Fielder and Caldwell children were born in Indiana except for William Jason Caldwell who was born in Polk County.

During April of 1880, John and Eliza Jane Beasley Caldwell, along with their children and the Fielder children, moved to Polk County by covered wagon. They traveled on the road that essentially traces along what is now US Highway 50, crossed the Mississippi River on a ferry barge to St. Louis, continued to near Boonville, then traveled south to Bolivar and out to the Halfway Community. While waiting to obtain possession of their farm land, they camped about five miles west of Halfway near a large spring that today is adjacent to Highway 32 on the north side. During their time there, two of the children, Ellsworth and Nettie, became ill with typhoid fever. Ellsworth died but Nettie survived, albeit with severe brain damage that left her permanently an invalid.

In July 1880, John Caldwell obtained 80 acres located in North Benton Township near two of his cousins who had moved to Polk County from Lawrence County, IN several years earlier. These cousins were Joseph A. Caldwell and his younger brother John Caldwell. They were the sons of the earlier mentioned William and Jane Caldwell of Orange County, NC and Lawrence County, IN.

John Caldwell died May 24, 1893 and is buried in the Ragsdale Cemetery next to his son Ellsworth. Six years later, on Sept. 16, 1899, Eliza Jane Beasley Fielder Caldwell married Francis M. Clayton, who was a widowed neighbor. Eliza Jane died Jan. 22, 1933 and is buried in Reynolds Chapel Cemetery between her daughter Antoinette "Nettie" and her last husband, Francis M. Clayton, who died in 1915.

For six generations, descendants of John and Eliza Jane Beasley Caldwell have continued to live in and around Polk County. *Submitted by Mrs. Wilma Caldwell Davison*

CALDWELL – Levi William and Mary (Bashor) Caldwell arrived in Bolivar with their 10 children by train, in 1875. It took them eight days to travel from Tennessee. Levi was born April 18, 1836 in Hardy County, WV. His parents were Ferguson Caldwell (born 1799; died 1845) and Lydia Shireman (born 1805; died 1864). At 46 years of age Ferguson was plowing his hilly West Virginia farm when his horse bolted and dragged him to death. He was the father of six children. Levi W. was one of them. He married Mary Bashor Aug. 21, 1856 (born 1837). She was the daughter of Benjamin Bashor and Mary Sager.

Benjamin was born in Pennsylvania in 1797. Mary was born in 1800 in West Virginia. Levi W. and Mary moved their family first to Tennessee and then later to Bolivar, MO. They bought 94 acres four and one-half miles south of Bolivar. The house and barn are still there in good shape. Levi built the barn with wood pegs and it still stands straight. Three more children were born to them in Bolivar, including Arthur's grandfather, Levi Benjamin, born May 12, 1876. He married Arzetta Jane Heydon Feb. 22, 1899 in Polk County. She was born Jan. 19, 1874 in Bolivar. The Bolivar Free Press described the bride as "one of Polk County's successful teachers" and the groom as "a prosperous young farmer." It also said, "A number of friends were present to wish them Godspeed and partake of that bounteous repast so lavishly spread."

Back row- Levi, Ben, Lorenzo, Clyde, Bill and Jimmie; Front row- Jewell, Arzetta, Hazel and Zela, 1918

Arzetta was the daughter of James Clayton Heydon and Salatia Jane Lower. James was born Nov. 28, 1849 in Polk County, MO. He said he was 18 years old when he only 15 years old in order to fight in the Civil War. However, he was hospitalized in his last years suffering from flashbacks of the war. Salatia was born Feb. 7, 1848 in Roane County, TN. She and James were married Sept. 20, 1868. Her father was George Washington Lower (born 1813; died 1853) and her mother was Elvira Carter (born 1818; died 1897). Both of them were born in Tennessee. Salatia had a brother, Andrew Lower, who was crippled. He got around in a little cart when a child and grew up to be a judge. His name is on many legal documents in Bolivar during that era. Levi B. Caldwell was a staunch Republican. He and Arzetta were Baptist and active in the Lodge (Odd Fellows and Eastern Star). They had nine children, and one of them was Arthur's father, Clyde C. Caldwell. The others were Lorenzo, James, Benjamin, Zela, William, Hazel, Jewell and Mary (died an infant). They were raised in Bolivar in the house Arthur's grandfather, Levi B. built at 1105 South Lillian. Their playmates were the Teeters children just up the road. Grandpa had a huge garden, an orchard and grape vineyard. Arzetta died in 1952 and Levi in 1960. Arthur always enjoyed visiting his grandparents. Arthur says, "Although as a small boy, I couldn't understand why I had to kiss everybody. Ha!" *Submitted by Arthur Caldwell*

CALLAWAY - The Callaways were one of the earliest families to settle in Polk County, MO. The Reverend Joseph R. Callaway was born in Knox County, TN on July 11, 1811. At about the age of 25 he married Mary M. Wilson. In March of 1839 they moved to Polk County. Joseph came to Missouri as a Baptist preacher. In those days preaching was not a paying profession, but his preaching was so enjoyed by the people he was often given money by individuals in their appreciation. He was over six feet tall and had great physical strength. Because of this size, he was often a "peacemaker" at community gatherings when tempers flared.

Joseph and Mary, who was also known as Polly, had four children: James Ragan, born in 1837; John Farrar, born in 1840; Benjamin Hardin, born in 1845; and Mary Florence, born in 1854. Each of these children married and had children of their own. Only John Farrar does not have any living descendants, as his two children died in infancy. Mary died in 1871. Joseph married again in 1873 to Lillis Beckley. There were no children from that marriage. Joseph died in 1891 after living to be 80 years old. Lillis died in 1903.

James Ragan, the eldest son, is the individual through which Charles Lee Callaway's family descended. James married Mary Elizabeth Brown, who was also called Molly, on June 2, 1867. They had nine children: Flora Gertrude, born in 1869 and died at the age of 16 in 1885; Charles Lee, born in 1872; Mary Marget, born in 1874 and died at the age of 2 in 1877; Maudie Mae, born in 1878 and died at age 1 in 1880; Ada Florence, born in 1881, married Jay Davis in 1906 and died in 1973; John Joseph, born in 1884 and died in 1961, never marrying; the seventh child was a son who died at birth sometime between 1884 and 1887, never being named with his birth not being recorded; James Leroy, known as Roy, born in 1887, married Myrtle M. Pack in 1911, and died in 1955; Winnie Fay, born in 1893, married Eugene "Gene" Brown in 1916 and died in 1968.

James and Mary lived in Polk County until the Civil War. In November 1862 he began the first of two 90-day periods of active service with the Missouri Militia in Company F of the 26th Regiment. James was relieved of duty in March of 1863. He and his family moved further north to Roanoke, MO because he was a slaveholder. James served his second 90-day period there in 1865. His grandchildren remember his complaint about being marched to Springfield, "Dad burn em, dad burn em, they marched us to Springfield on the hottest day of the year." James was the son of a preacher and that was as close as he came to cussing. Mary died in 1913, with James following in 1922.

Charles Lee was the oldest living child of James Ragan and Mary Elizabeth Callaway. Charlie married Persis Cora Eagon in 1904. They had two children: Ramon Clifford, born in November of 1905 and Kenneth Charles, born in December of 1906. They lived on a farm in Bolivar where Persis taught school. Persis was known to be a strict, Victorian disciplinarian both at school and with her boys at home.

Recently her granddaughter Dorothy was told by someone about how strict her grandmother was as a teacher. She said, "Yes she was strict, but she called me Precious. She called all of her grandchildren Precious, but her grandson Charles was her favorite. She always did like the boys best."

Charlie was a dairy farmer. Every morning after milking the cows he took his milk to the cheese factory in Bolivar. There the cans were taken into the factory and emptied. They were then rinsed and returned on a conveyer system. It was the delight of his grandchildren to go with him and wait for the milk cans to come out and be loaded to go back home. Everyone's cans were marked with different numbers so that they could be identified from the many others that were also going through the same process. Today the cheese factory is gone, but the memories remain.

Persis liked to garden and she raised beautiful flowers. Several of her grandchildren today raise certain flowers because Grandmother Persis had those in her garden: hollyhocks to tiger lilies to sweet peas on the fence. Her flowers were a memorable sight.

Candy then was not as readily available as it is today, but Persis always had brown sugar and thick, heavy cream from the cows they milked. As treats for her grandchildren she made brown sugar sandwiches; thick cream and brown sugar mixed into a paste and spread on two slices of bread to make a sandwich. You don't know how good these tasted on a hot summer afternoon, sitting on a swing on your grandmother's porch at the age of 5 or 6.

W. A. Eagon, father of Persis Eagon Callaway, horses names, Ben and Prince

Charlie and Persis had a catalpa tree at the side of the driveway. This was the tree the grandchildren played in. They climbed to the top and would swing on the branches. The limb they used to pull themselves into the tree was polished like a fine piece of furniture. That tree gave many hours of pleasure as it took many years of wear and tear from children playing in its branches.

After Ramon and Kenneth finished high school in Bolivar they went to the University of Missouri. Both graduated with degrees in agriculture. Ramon taught high school agriculture and Kenneth went into business and worked for the Farmers Home Administration. Persis died in 1957 and Charlie died at the age of 97 in 1969. They were married for 53 years.

After teaching agriculture in several school districts, Ramon moved back to Bolivar where he taught agriculture until 1948. He also farmed during and after that time. He married Florine Ball on June 12, 1935. They had one daughter, Dorothy Ann, born January of 1939.

As a child Dorothy had a pet goat. One day someone left the garage door open. The garage was in the basement of the house. The goat came in the basement, up the stairs, through the kitchen, and into the living room where Florine was having bridge club. The goat went to market the next day.

In 1952 Ramon was diagnosed with a tumor on the pituitary gland. He had suffered for years from symptoms that ranged from severe headaches to blindness in one eye. A doctor in a new medical field, neurology, recommended he be seen for further testing at Barnes Hospital in St. Louis. There the tumor was diagnosed and he underwent revolutionary neurosurgery to remove a grapefruit sized tumor, which he survived. Ramon died in 1970 and Florine later died in 1974.

Dorothy attended school in Bolivar and graduated in 1956. She married Derald Isdell in December of 1956. Dorothy worked for Smith-Glenn-Callaway Clinic in Springfield, while Derald began a career in the lumber business working for Stockton Lumber Company. In 1968 together they opened the Town and Country Building Supply in Bolivar. They built their lumber business to include several stores in other communities. When Derald died in June of 2002, he had been in the lumber business for 49 years. Dorothy and Derald have two boys, Bradley, born in 1970 and Barry, born in 1974. Brad married Jennifer Allen in September of 1995 and they are expecting their first child in December of 2002.

Brad and Barry both graduated from Bolivar High School. Both have degrees from the University of Missouri; Brad majoring in agriculture economics and Barry majoring in political science. Brad's wife Jennifer is also a graduate of the University of Missouri, with a degree in recreational therapy. Brad and his wife managed the Town and Country Building Supply in Clinton, MO until they bought their own lumber company in Higginsville, MO where they now live. Barry had taken over the management of the Town and Country Supply in Bolivar. Dorothy has officially retired to the lake and is looking forward to doing "grandmother things."

LaVeda Fay Donaldson went to work as a secretary for Farmers Home Administration in 1935. Her boss, Kenneth Callaway, decided she was the one for him. On April 11, 1936 Kenneth married LaVeda. She was born in Puxico, MO on Sept. 28, 1915. They had three children: Kenneth Charles Jr., born April 3, 1937, while they lived in Marble Hill, MO; Rosemary, born Feb. 14, 1939, while they lived in Ellington, MO; and Evelyn Fay, born Dec. 20, 1940, while they lived in Sikeston, MO. They lived in 14 different places before moving to Bolivar in 1948. They remained in Bolivar the rest of their married life. While in Bolivar Kenneth was a dairy farmer and taught WWII veterans farming techniques. LaVeda worked as a bookkeeper for Delarue's and as the assistant manager of the office of the Federal Land Bank. She also was a caseworker for the State Division of Welfare in Polk County until she retired in 1977. When Kenneth died in 1991 they had been married 55 years. LaVeda still lives in Bolivar and is 86 years old.

All three of their children graduated from Bolivar High School. When Evelyn finished the seventh grade, Mamie Allen, a long-time teacher in the Bolivar schools stated that she had taught both Ramon and Kenneth, and all their children. Charles, following in the family tradition, graduated from the University of Missouri with a degree in chemistry. Rosemary started a new tradition in 1956 and went to Southwest Missouri State College. She graduated with a BS degree in education, with a major in vocational home economics. Rosemary also received a master of science in clothing and textiles from Kansas State University. Evelyn went to Burge School of Nursing and became a registered nurse. She went on to Drury College to get her BS degree in nursing.

After finishing college Charles worked as a chemist for the Frisco Railroad, Burlington Northern Railroad, and several independent laboratories. For 36 years he worked in the same little, yellow, brick building, doing the same job for who ever owned the lab at the time. He also ran an appliance repair service for washers and dryers. This he did to keep himself busy and out of trouble.

If you went to high school with Charles you should understand what that means. Kenneth Charles Jr. was always called Charles because two Kenneths in one family was too many.

Charles married Glenda Adams in 1958. Both Charles and Glenda received the Silver Beaver Scouting award for outstanding service to scouting during their marriage. They had five children: Jaquelyn Fay, born on Oct. 28, 1959; James Charles, born on Aug. 6 1961; Kenneth Lee, born on Nov. 25, 1962; John Russell, born on Feb. 22, 1968; and Mary Ann, born on Jan. 19, 1970. All of Charles and Glenda's five children graduated from Bolivar High School. Jackie and Mary Ann were both salutatorians of their graduating classes. All three of Charles and Glenda's sons are Eagle Scouts. Charles died on Jan. 6, 2000.

Jackie graduated from Drury College with a degree in accounting and business administration. Today she works as a CPA for the state of Missouri. Jackie married Patrick Odell and they have two children, Kevin and Megan. They live outside Jefferson City in Tebbetts, MO. Pat is a graduate of the University of Missouri and has a degree in accounting. He works for Midwest Independent Bank as a financial accountant.

James lives in Huron, MO just north of Bolivar and is a lineman for Southwest Electric. He attended Southwest Missouri State University. James' wife is the former Karen Greer. They have three children: Amanda, Samantha and Thomas. Mandy is a graduate of Bolivar High School. She is married to Ryan Bybee and they have one daughter, Hailey.

Kenny is a graduate of the University of Missouri with a degree in agricultural mechanization. He works for Dura Automotive. Kenny is married to the former Pamela Kell, who teaches preschool in Brunswick, MO. They have two children, Eric and Kenna, the light of her father's life. They live in Salisbury, MO.

John is a lineman for Parr Electric Company. He is a graduate of Central Methodist College with a degree in accounting. He is married to the former Pamela Sikes who is a letter carrier for the US Postal Service. They have four children: Jill, Levi, Jade and Luke. They live in Nixa, MO.

Mary Ann is a graduate of Central Methodist College with a double major in accounting and mathematics. She works for Citizens Memorial Health Care. Mary Ann has three children: Jacob, by her former marriage to Shannon Neal; and Joshua and Charlotte, by her former marriage to John Waddelow. Charles and Glenda's progeny has reached 14 grandchildren, and one great-grandchild.

Rosemary started her teaching career in Tuscumbia, MO. In 1960 she married Sandy Sutton. Their first son Ray Sandy Jr. was born on Sept. 12, 1960. She taught for several years in Kansas while her husband was in the army at Fort Riley and then while he attended law school in Topeka. Their second son, Stuart Andrew, was born March 11, 1968. Following their divorce in 1972 Rosemary went to work at St. Luke's Hospital in Kansas City, MO as a dialysis technologist. After 23 years, she decided to return to teaching. During her time at St. Luke's Rosemary attended the University of Missouri, Kansas City and majored in history, after developing a profound interest in the past. She was able to complete the necessary requirements to teach high school social studies. Upon her decision to return to teaching she was able to find a school where she could teach both home economics and social studies. Today Rosemary is retired to Raytown, MO and to keeping her son Stuart's children. She has four grandchildren.

Ray graduated from Grandview High School. He was also the youngest Eagle Scout in the history of the Heart of America Council in Kansas City. Ray followed the family tradition of his parents and attended SMSU. He nearly completed his degree in communications. For a number of years he had a construction company in Branson, MO. He had returned to Kansas City and was working in construction when he was killed at the St. Patrick's Day Celebration in 1996. He has one daughter, Acacia Ann. Acacia graduated from Raytown South High School. She, too, following the family tradition and attends SMSU where she is majoring in creative writing. Acacia is the proud parent of a seven and one-half foot red-tailed boa constrictor named Baby.

Stuart also is an Eagle Scout. He graduated from Center High School and has a degree in business management from Friends University. Stuart currently works for Greenleaf Auto Recycling, a division of the Ford Motor Company. He is married to the former Michele Fielding who graduated from Shawnee Mission South. Michele is a graduate with honors from the University of Kansas with a double major in business and economics. She has an MBA from the University of Missouri, Kansas City and will be attending law school there this fall. For a number of years Michele worked in management at several printing companies. They have three boys: Quintin, Taylor and Ian and live in Overland Park, Kansas.

Evelyn worked as a nurse at Cox Medical Center while obtaining her BS in nursing at Drury. She returned to Burge School of Nursing where she taught pediatric nursing. In 1962 she married Don Fullerton. They have five children: Jane Ellen, born on Dec. 19, 1962; Leslie Fay, born on July 31, 1965; Betsy Ann, born on May 25, 1968; and on Nov. 21, 1969 the twins, Jeffrey Donald and Jennifer Lynn, were born. Evelyn and Don were divorced in 1992. As Evelyn's family grew she moved closer to home and became the school nurse for the Bolivar School District. It has taken her many years, but she has developed the school nurse position to include several nurses and has taken on many other responsibilities. Those of you who have children in the Bolivar Schools are well aware of her excellent work and accomplishments.

Evelyn's oldest lives in Bristow, VA with her husband Terry Lemons and their two children Benjamin and Sarah. Jane graduated from Bolivar High School as valedictorian of her class. She is a graduate with honors from the University of Missouri with a degree in agricultural journalism. Jane has worked as a journalist for several newspapers, including the *Springfield News-Leader*. While working for them, she received a Pulitzer nomination. Her husband, Terry, is also a graduate of the University of Missouri with a degree in journalism. Jane and Terry both worked in Washington, D.C. for the *Arkansas Democrat/Gazette* as journalists covering the Clinton administration. Jane's Aunt Rosemary once found her picture in a political science textbook for one of her classes at UMKC. Jane was at a presidential press conference. Her aunt was impressed. Today Jane is the Washington editor for the *Farm Journal*. Her husband Terry has worked with her as a journalist and editor. Today he is in a new field of work. He works where he is greatly needed as the public relations specialist for the IRS.

Leslie graduated from Bolivar High School as salutatorian of her class. She is also a graduate of the University of Missouri where she graduated cum laude. She is a vice-president and partner of the Noble and Associates advertising firm. She is married to Jimmy Hutter, PhD. Jimmy is a professor of agriculture education at SMSU. He has a degree from SMSU in agriculture education, a masters from the University of Missouri, and a doctorate from the University of Minnesota. They have twin boys, Tate and Hayes. They live on a farm in Republic, MO.

Betsy is also a graduate of Bolivar High School. She lives in a small town outside London, England. Betsy is married to Stewart Eckols. He works for the US Government in the area of national security. They have two children, Alexandra "Alex" and Blace.

Jeff and his wife Tommi Mallernee live in Buffalo, MO. He graduated from Bolivar High School. Jeff works for D & J Automatic. Tommi is a glutton for punishment. She works with her mother-in-law in the nurse's office of the elementary school in Bolivar. They have one daughter, Logan. Tommi is going to have twin boys in early August of 2002. Twins seem to run in this family. LaVeda's mother Lottie Donaldson was a twin and had a twin brother named Ottie.

Jenny, the female half of Evelyn's twins, lives in Bedford, IA. She is a Bolivar High School graduate also. Jenny is married to Jim Ernst. Jenny and Jim live on a farm where Jim farms with his father. She works as a dental website programmer. Jenny attended the University of Missouri.

Evelyn, who for years was almost out of the grandchildren race with only one granddaughter, has really gotten back into it. She has done it two at a time. Right now Evelyn has seven grandchildren and the first part of August 2002 she will have two more.

In January of 1970 Kenneth and LaVeda had their 12th and last grandchild. Each one was born in a different month until the twins were born. That put three in the month of November. They have no grandchildren born in April or June. The number of Kenneth and LaVeda's great-grandchildren has grown to 25 with two more expected in August of 2002. They have one great-great granddaughter.

When the last of the three babies is born in 2002, Persis and Charlie will have 49 direct descendants. If descendants had been counted back to Joseph and Mary in 1839, and they had all remained in Polk County, there would be almost enough to populate the entire county. Persis and Charlie are gone now, but they left many descendants and pleasant memories behind.

From the *Bolivar Herald-Free Press* article by Jean Pufahl Vincent, dated January 2000.

My daughter, Lori, recently called me to tell me of Charles Callaway's passing, and I was very sorry to hear about that. There are people and families with whom we share a connection throughout our lives, and the Callaway-Pufahl connection is one that my brother and I grew up with and enjoyed.

I'm sure the association goes back further than I remember, but my own memories of Charles and his family begin at the Christian Church. I remember Charles' father, Kenneth, and Kenneth's brother, Ramon and their families attending services and being involved in dinners, holiday celebrations and all the events that occur in a church family.

My dad sponsored the youth group at the Christian Church then, and my memories of the Callaway kids: Evelyn, Rosemary, Charles and their cousin, Dorothy, began during that time.

Two of my most vivid memories of that time are of a dance at what is now the "Over 50 Club" building and a yard party my folks had for the youth group one summer. A Virginia Reel stands out in my memory of the dance. Those teenagers were always nice enough to include me, and when it was my turn to help make the "bridge" for the others to go under, they got me a stepladder to stand on. The yard party included lanterns and tables all over the yard, and

I was extremely annoyed when I had to go to bed before the party ended.

When Mother went to work at what we then called the "Welfare Office," one of her coworkers was Charles' mother, LaVeda. When my Dad died, Kenneth Callaway took my brother under his wing. He kept John busy doing farm work and became the male figure that John needed at that time. By then Charles had children of his own, and John would regale me with stories about their escapades.

Charles fixed just about every appliance I ever owned while I lived in Polk County. It was always a real relief to see that big yellow utility truck pull up in my driveway when something was broken. I'll never forget the time when the washer wasn't working, well, it was working, but it was definitely working in an extremely strange manner. It would wash the clothes, but then all the "unmentionables" would disappear.

Charles solved the mystery. My mother taught me to do washing with a wringer washer. We always washed the dirtiest stuff last. By the time this incident occurred, I had an automatic washer, but was still doing the laundry in the "old sequence," blue jeans last.

At that time, the jeans had a lot of powdered cement in them from the ready mix plant. When Charles discovered what was ailing the washer, I heard whoops of laughter coming from the utility room. Charles stuck his head around the corner and asked me if I happened to own a Phillips-head screwdriver, to get it, bring it to him, and he'd show me how to fix the washer.

All of the little holes in the tub were set up solid with cement, and all the water was going over the top of the tub, taking the lighter stuff with it. All I had to do was poke the screwdriver in the holes, clean out the cement, and the washer worked just fine!

Charles and I laughed about that one for years. During my years as a teacher, Charles' sister, Evelyn Fullerton, and I worked together. Charles' daughter, Mary Ann, had to suffer through my American History class. My daughter, Lori, and Charles' son, Kenneth Lee, were classmates and always have been friends.

My brother's close association to the Callaways continued throughout his lifetime, and when he and my mother died within five months of each other, it was the Callaways that Sue (John's wife) and I always went to when we needed help.

Once again, that yellow utility truck, filled with willing helpers, was a welcome sight when we needed furniture, refrigerators and other miscellaneous items moved.

Jean Pufahl Vincent

Now, when I pay my Polk County taxes, I always get a clever note stuck on the receipt from Charles' wife, Glenda. This year she thanked me for my "contribution to Polk County," and added a few other remarks, which make me laugh every time I think about them. I can honestly say that those receipts are the only ones I ever look forward to receiving.

Some Native Americans believe that death is only the end of a circle, and the beginning of something new. Now Charles has come to the end of his circle here. He was truly one of the good people of this earth, and I, for one, will miss him. I feel very blessed because Charles was one of those people with whom I've shared a life-long acquaintance.

May God bless you, Charles Callaway, for just being you.

Jean Pufahl Vincent now lives in Greenbelt, Md.

CAMPBELL – Carolyn's great-great-great-grandfather was Ezekial Madison Campbell, the son of John and Matilda Golden Polk Campbell. He was born July 21, 1802 in Mecklenburg County, NC. He died on Sept. 20, 1873 in Polk County, MO. On Jan. 10, 1821 he married Rebecca Patton Adkins in Maury County, TN. Rebecca was the daughter of William and Jane Patton Adkins. They moved to the area that later became Polk County, MO in 1832 and were among the first settlers here. E.M. was very involved in the organization of Polk County and the city of Bolivar. Polk County was named after his grandfather, Ezekial Polk and Bolivar was the name of the town that his grandfather had organized in western Tennessee. Polk was an admirer of Simón Bolívar of Venezuela

There were 10 children born to this couple. They are William Adkins (born Dec. 14, 1821; died Feb. 4, 1903); John Polk (born Sept. 4, 1823; died Dec. 27, 1900); Eliza Jane (born May 27, 1826; died Jan. 29, 1859); Ophelia Caroline (born July 27, 1828; died Dec. 25, 1891); Margaret Eugenia (born July 11, 1830; died July 16, 1859); Matilda Golden (born July 9, 1832; died March 6, 1918); Rebecca Patton (born November 1834; died June 27, 1868); James Madison (born Jan. 27, 1836; died Nov. 5, 1901); Mary Wilson (born June 27, 1840; died March 23, 1906) and Robert Bruce (born Aug. 28, 1843; died in service in Civil War).

Of these 10 children, John Polk, Ophelia Caroline, Margaret Eugenia, James Madison and Mary Wilson all died in Polk County, MO. Carolyn is descended from Ophelia Caroline who married David Simpson Clark, who was born Dec. 26, 1824 and died June 5, 1904. Their daughter Rebecca Patton Clark married James McGarity Sims. Their daughter Caroline "Carrie" Elizabeth Sims married Austin Oliver Keeling. Carolyn's mother was their fourth child, Ruth Elizabeth. Their other children were Howard Simpson Keeling, Grace Marie Keeling Wimberly and Robert Benton Keeling. *Submitted by Carolyn Mustain Mott*

CANTRELL – Horace Lando Cantrell, the oldest of five children, was born June 17, 1872 at Dadeville, MO to James T. and Emily Carolina Cantrell. Lando married Cora Miller on Oct. 14, 1896. Cora was born Nov. 2, 1882 near Fair Play, MO to John C. Miller and Louisa Crain. Lando and Cora lived several years near Dadeville, MO, but spent most of their lives farming in the Shady Grove Community. In their retirement years, they moved to Aldrich, MO. Cora passed away June 7, 1962 and Lando passed away 10 days later on June 17, 1962, on his 90th birthday. They are buried in the Shady Grove Cemetery. They had one daughter, Bessie Jane, born Jan. 11, 1909 at Dadeville, MO.

Bessie married Ray Williams July 7, 1934, son of Cliften Williams and Bertha Smith. They lived at Morrisville, MO, but later moved to the Shady Grove Community where they farmed. They had two daughters, Norma Jean and Judy Ann. Ray passed away June 6, 1975 and Bessie passed away Dec. 19, 1986. They are buried at Pleasant Ridge Cemetery, southwest of Aldrich, MO.

Norma married Don Leetch Sept. 9, 1961 at Fair Play, MO. They have two sons, Michael and Mark.

Michael is married to Kelly Piper and they have two children, Jacob and Meghan and live in Florida. Mark is married to Christine Santamaria and they have two daughters, Taylor and Summer and live in Kansas.

Ray and Bessie Williams, Lando and Cora Cantrell, child, Norma Jean Williams; picture taken on Lando and Cora's 50th wedding anniversary.

Judy married Leonard Davis in March of 1966. They had three daughters: Donna, Lynn and Lavern. Donna married Dennis Noblitt and they have three children: Ashley, David and Jonathan. Lynn is married and lives in California. Lavern has two daughters, Tasha and Allissa and live in Colorado. *Submitted by Norma J. Leetch*

CAREY – Peter Carey was born Nov. 18, 1812 in Sussex County, England, UK and died Aug. 15, 1864. His son, John, was born Dec. 12, 1833 in England, UK and died June 17, 1917 in Winston, Daviess County, MO. He married Ida Heldenbrand who was born Feb. 21, 1856 and died Jan. 27, 1918. Their children were Elmeda Helen who was born March 15, 1892 in Winston, Daviess County, MO, died June 28, 1952 in Bolivar, Polk County, MO and is buried in Greenwood Cemetery, Bolivar, MO; Charles Emmet and Lester.

Elmeda "Meda" married Jesse Matthew Blackburn Jan. 19, 1910 in Winston, Daviess County, MO. He was born in Mabel, Daviess County, MO on Oct. 1, 1887; died April 10, 1965 and is buried in Greenwood Cemetery. They had two children, Neva Mae (born March 12, 1911) and LaurNell Jessie (born Dec. 13, 1926; married John Edward Strack June 16, 1943; born May 11, 1924). Their two children are Helen Ann (born April 1, 1952) and Jesse Christopher (born July 8, 1956).

Jesse and Elmeda moved their livestock and household goods to Bolivar from Mabel, Daviess County, MO by rail and settled on 40 acres west of Bolivar on Highway T. In 1921, he decided that he could not make a living on the farm and started to work for the MFA as a shipping manager. He would take a load of livestock by rail to St. Louis market weekly. They traded the farm for house and land on East Locust Street in Bolivar. He worked for the Ozark Utilities Company and helped construct the high line between Bolivar and Buffalo, MO, and later in Southeast Missouri. In 1930 he became Bolivar's night watchman for several years. He also was a deputy sheriff under Jack Killingsworth. Neva attended grade, high school and college in Bolivar, graduating from high school in 1929. She taught at Ozark, a rural school, which was north of Bolivar, MO.

She married John Charles Titus Aug. 12, 1930 in Bolivar, Polk County, MO; he was born July 12, 1900 and died Feb. 14, 1982. They had a daughter, Neva Charlene, born Aug. 14, 1934. She attended grade, high school and college in Bolivar, MO. She married Arthur Stewart Gardner on Feb. 1, 1953, who was born Feb. 27, 1931, died May 15, 1980, and was buried in Greenwood Cemetery in Bolivar, MO. Stewart worked with

Charles and added appliances, electronics, furniture as well as carpet to establish the Titus Furniture and Appliances Store. They moved from the Locust Street location to the Plaza Shopping Center when it was built. That location is just east of the Simón Bolívar Statue on South Springfield Avenue. The site for the Plaza had been Smith Hatchery for several years.

They had one son, John Kemp, born Aug. 13, 1968. Including John Kemp, there has been five generations who have belonged to the Methodist Church in Bolivar, Polk County, MO. *Submitted by LaurNell Strack*

Elijah Carneal

CARNEAL - Elijah Leander Carneal was born March 8, 1844, Logan County, KY, the son of Littleton Carneal and Elizabeth Matilda "Betsy" Carneal. Elijah disliked his middle name so much that he had it shortened to "Lee."

He first married Adeline Artemissa Holmes, July 29, 1866 in Polk County. Thomas Fox, Justice of the Peace, performed the marriage rites.

Adeline was born Aug. 13, 1847 in Arkansas, the daughter of Robert Holmes and his third wife, Rachel Emeline Latta.

To this union were born six children: William Franklin Carneal, born May 9, 1867; Mary Lavine Carneal, born Oct. 5, 1869; Edward J. Carneal, born September 27, 1875; James Carneal, born Oct. 10, 1878; Minnie Lee Carneal, born May 3, 1881 and Ora Emeline Carneal, born Aug. 7, 1886, all born in Polk County.

Adeline passed away June 30, 1900, just four years after her last child was born. She was interred in Salem Cemetery near Cliquot in Polk County.

Elijah remarried Oct. 21, 1901 in Polk County to Laverna Catherine "Cassie" Nottingham.

Cassie was born Jan. 29, 1861, Richland County, IL the daughter of Benjamin and Mary Nottingham. At the age of 12 she came to Missouri with her parents, locating in Cedar County and later removing to Polk County.

Two children were born to this union, Orba Carneal, born Nov. 17, 1903 and Delphia Carneal, born Jan. 15, 1905.

Elijah died Jan. 16, 1922 at his home between Dunnegan and Cliquot. He never survived the operation on his appendix.

Cassie passed away Jan. 25, 1950 and is buried in the Dunnegan Cemetery.

All dates used in this reference came from Elijah's personal Bible in which he kept a meticulous family record.

In 1857 Elijah came to Polk County from Logan County, KY with his parents and brothers, Thomas Jefferson, William Washington and John Goodler and one sister, Mary. The family settled on a farm located near Humansville.

In 1858 Littleton moved his family to Bourbon County, KS where he died the same year. After his death in 1859, Betsy moved the family back to Polk County locating on a farm just south of Humansville where she died in October of that same year.

Elijah continued to reside with his brothers and sister until Oct. 1, 1863 when he enlisted in Company B, Second Kansas Cavalry, Civil War, at the age of 18. He was five feet, eight inches tall with brown, hair and gray eyes.

During his one and a half years of service he used his own horse in the cavalry for which the United States Government reimbursed him $23.00. He was discharged June 22, 1865 at Fort Gibson, Cherokee Nation.

Son William Franklin Carneal married Mary Ellen Skaggs, the daughter of James and Rebecca Skaggs and had four children: Elijah Carneal, Charles Carneal, Homer Carneal and Zula Carneal.

Daughter Mary "Sissie" Carneal married Alfred Frieze, the son of John and Elisabeth Frieze and had five children: Arthur Frieze, Alfred Frieze, John Frieze, Mabel Frieze and Addie Frieze.

Son Edward Carneal married Effie Dean Nickels, the daughter of William Perry Nickels and Charity Adeline Carroll. They had 11 children: Reba "Bob" Carneal, Clem "Razz" Carneal, Lola "Toad" Carneal, Fred "Hen" Carneal, Arnold "Man" Carneal, Donald "Pink" Carneal, a twin to Arnold, Audrey "Toot" Carneal, Glen "John" Carneal, Willis "Wick" Carneal, Lillis "Toby" Carneal—twin to Willis and Noel "Mack" Carneal.

Son James Carneal married Jessie Emmett and they had one child, Vestel "Buster" Carneal.

Daughter Minnie Lee Carneal married Charles Berchal Hammons and they had six children: Connie Lee Hammons, Dora Jewel Hammons, Gladys Armitta Hammons, Velma Beatrice Hammons, Harold Ellis Hammons and Finis Eugene Hammons.

Charles Berchal had first married Cora Mabel Devin, the daughter of Glaves Alexander Devin and Lucy Brown. They had three children: Charles Devin Hammons, Eunice May Hammons and Virgil Hammons. Cora died when Virgil was born and Bert remarried to Minnie Lee and together they raised both families of children.

Daughter Ora Emeline Carneal married John "Jim" Jones and they had two daughters, Zelma "Tooty" Jones and Ruby Jones.

Daughter Orba Carneal married Verner Ball and had six children: Laverna Ball, Marjorie Ball, Janice Ball, Wilma Ball, Wilburn Ball and Robert Ball.

Daughter Delphia Carneal married German A. "Jerd" Armstrong and had two children, Evelyn Armstrong and William Armstrong. *Submitted by Marie Hammons*

CARNS - Robert H. Carns was born March 13, 1910 in Dade County, MO to John Carns and Clossie Baker Carns. He married Mary Elizabeth King on June 6, 1954 in Bolivar, MO. She was born Aug. 20, 1921 in Dade County, MO to Horton King and Ruth Sunderland King.

Back: Gina, Berta and Becky Carns, Mary and Bob Carns, 1975

The early years of marriage for Robert and Mary were spent on the family farm in Dade County. During this time three daughters were born: Roberta Ann, Rebecca Lee and Regina Kay.

In about 1958 Robert opened a barbershop in Bolivar. It was known as Bob's Barber Shop and was on North Main Street. He worked there until his retirement in the 1980s.

In 1965 the Stockton Lake was being formed and the Carns family moved from the family farm to Bolivar.

In the fall of 1966 Mary started teaching for the Bolivar school system. During her 18 years with the system she taught second grade and remedial reading. She retired in May 1985.

Bob and Mary were blessed with eight grandchildren. They are Scott and Brad McReynolds, Lonnie, Bryan and Lisa Hensley, Christopher and Kyle Swinney, and Hal Reynolds. Some of these grandchildren are Polk County residents.

Mary died on April 16, 1991. Bob then married Verda Fulbright Walker on Jan. 30, 1999. Bob died on Aug. 11, 2001. Both Bob and Mary are buried in the Bona Cemetery in Dade County, MO. *Submitted by Roberta McReynolds*

CARTER - Joseph Carter (born 1816; died unknown) and wife Locky Luttrell (born 1813; died 1882) came to Polk County around 1852. They brought eight children with them and had one more born in Polk County. This family was from Roane County, TN. Joseph was the son of John and Jane McCarroll Carter. Locky was the daughter of Silas Luttrell. A brother, Moses Loony Carter, and his family arrived in Polk County in 1843. A sister, Elvira Carter Lower, and her husband George Lower arrived shortly after Joseph. Two sons of Joseph and Locky, William and Christopher joined Company E, Eighth Missouri Cavalry during the Civil War. Christopher died "of disease," family thinks typhoid, in Lebanon, MO. William and four others were caught by Rebels and hung near Stockton in 1863. Joseph and son Joseph M. brought the body back home

Joseph and Locky lived near Fair Play, MO. Carrol's ancestor was the seventh child, Joseph McCarroll, a.k.a. "Mack" Carter. He married America Elizabeth Stone, 1850-1901, in 1867. They had 11 children: Joseph, 1868-1951, Locky, 1870-1910, Viola, 1872-1957, Minnie, 1874-1947, Sarah, 1876-1954, Albert, 1878-1946, Eva, 1881-1948, Homer, 1886-1964, Henry Emmitt, 1888-1965, Ida, 1891-1962 and Ira, 1891-1964.

Joseph "Mack" and son Albert taught singing at various places in Missouri. The family called them "singing schools." They also farmed.

Many of the children wound up in California. The few that stayed in Polk County were Viola, who married Elmer Buchanan. They had four children: Guy, 1892-1971, Roy, 1895-1959, Ada, 1896-1978 and Don, 1902-1978. Sarah Annie married Charlie Ware and had 11 children: Hiram, 1895-1989, Otis, 1897-1964, Ethel, 1899-1960, Oma, 1901-1990, Lena, 1903-1913, Archie, 1904-1986, Henry, 1906-1991, Orpha, 1908-, Orie, 1910-1986, Frances, 1914-unknown and Minnie Gladys, 1916-unknown. Albert married Emma Neuhart and had four: Ernest, 1906-1983, Eldie, 1908-1974, Nellie, 1911-unknown, Victor, 1918-unknown. Ethel, daughter of Charlie and Sarah married Wilburn Allen. They were caretakers for many years at Dunnegan Park. When he passed away, Archie, or "Dutch" as he was known, took over for several years.

Moses Loony Carter, 1814-1883, married Cynthia McCarroll in 1831 in Tennessee. They had 13 children: James, 1832-unknown, Sarah Jane, 1835-unknown, John, 1836-unknown, Joseph McCarroll, 1838-unknown, Mary, 1840-unknown, Elvira, 1841-1913, Julia Ann, 1843-1870, Margaret, 1845-unknown, Amanda Caroline, 1847-1925, Elizabeth, 1849-unknown, Moses L. Jr., 1851-unknown, Cynthia, 1853-unknown, and Delila, 1855-unknown.

George and Elvira Carter Lower had eight children: John, 1839-1922, Andrew, 1846-1881, William, 1842-1939, Emaline, 1846-1910, Jane,

1848-1928, Elizabeth, 1850-unknown, Caroline, 1852-unknown. William was also in the Civil War and saw much action, among Gettysburg.

You will notice there are a lot of given names that are the same for these families. It makes it interesting when you are trying to sort them out. The family was closely associated with Stone, Hash, Luttrell and Ware families.

The first Carters in Polk County came there because of the unrest due to the slavery situation. Their children served in the Union Army. Some of the family that was left in Tennessee were southern sympathizers. John Carter was married three times and had 25 children. *Submitted by Carrol Dake*

Grandpa and Grandma J. T. and Harriet Carter, circa 1914

CARTER - James T. Carter was born April 8, 1853 in Pleasant Hill, Cass County, MO. James T. was the third child of James E. Carter, MD (born 1826; died 1899) and Mary A. McNair (born 1830, died 1908). His siblings were Columbus "Lum," Mary A. E., Oliver B., Charles L., William L., James E., Jack W. and Nancy Carter. His parents, along with three siblings, Columbus, Jack and Nancy, were buried at the Louisburg, MO. Cemetery. James T. married Harriet L. Arnold (born Oct. 12, 1849 in Knoxville, TN; died Feb. 13, 1933), the daughter of Nancy and William L. Gallaher. James and Harriet were married in Louisburg, Dallas County, MO in March 1876 and moved to Polk County, MO. To James T. and Harriet were born Sarah A., who married Jesse Mashburn; James, who died as an infant; George L., who married Viola Breshears; Edwin C. "Crum," who married Bessie L. White; and William M., who married Lenora May. James T., Harriet and William M. are buried Mission Cemetery in Halfway, MO.

Edwin C. and Bessie L. White had five children: Mildred L., who married Gorden Ellsworth; James A., who married May, unknown; Edwin W., who married Georgia Wimmer; a son who died in infancy and Lovell N., who married Merle Appling. Bessie L. died in 1928. In January 1929, Edwin C. married Bessie F. Erven, widow of Homer Erven, the daughter of Alma Starkey and Lon Nasalroad. Bessie F. Erven had four children: Mildred, who married Reynold Fittroff; J. Orel, who married Virginia Provolt; Edwin A., who married Helen Farmer; and Wanda, who married John Stuckey.

Edwin C. and Bessie F. had three children: Willa M., born on Nov. 13, 1930 (Edwin C.'s birthday) married Paul Strader March 19, 1948; Monford C. married Nelda Harris; and Vernon A. married Elma Jean McColm.

Willa has been a licensed cosmetologist for 32 years with a beauty shop in her home. Paul Strader was born May 8, 1920 in Aldrich, MO; served in the Army in WWII, tour of duty in Africa, Sicily, France, Italy and Germany; worked at Southwest Electric Cooperative for 38 years. Willa and Paul have three children: Jimmy, who married Adell "Dell" Williams, Donny, who married Cameron "Camy" Williams and Brent, who is single. Jimmy is retired from the Missouri Telephone Company, worked at Citizens Memorial Hospital and is now farming. Dell is a registered nurse. Donny is a licensed commercial electrician for Frymire Electric in Dallas, TX. Camy is a supervisor at Vinylx Corporation in Carrollton, TX. Brent is a systems administrator for the United States Bankrupt Court, Northern District of Texas. Jimmy and Dell have two children: Jeffrey and Joani. Joani married Trent Coble and they have three children: Memphis, Eian and Karissa. Donny and Camy have two children: Megan and Kyle. *Submitted by Willa Carter Strader*

CARTER – Moses Looney Carter, the oldest son of John P. or B. Carter and his first wife Jane McCarroll, was born on March 20, 1814 in Roane County, TN.

Moses L. Carter was apparently named in honor of east Tennessee pioneer Moses Looney, who was a neighbor of the family there.

On Oct. 26, 1831 Moses L. Carter married Cynthia McCarroll, the daughter of William McCarroll and Betsy White, in Roane County, TN.

In approximately 1842 Cynthia and Moses L. Carter moved to Polk County, MO.

The families of the widowed Elvira (Carter) Lower, Joseph and Locky (Luttrell) Carter and Samual and Elizabeth (Coker) Carter all eventually joined their older brother Moses L. Carter and his family in Polk County. Sometime between 1830 and 1850 their aunt Susannah (Carter) McDaniel also came to Polk County, since she was enumerated on the 1850 Census in the household of M. L. and Cynthia Carter.

Moses L. and Cynthia Carter had 12 children.

Jefferson, born Nov. 11, 1832 in Roane County, TN, married Emmaline Williams.

Sarah Jane, born March 15, 1835 in Roane County, TN, married Enoch F. Williams May 18, 1854, Polk County, MO.

John W., born Dec. 13, 1836 in Roane County, TN, died April 13, 1891 in Stone County, AR. He married Lenorah Jane Brackville on Oct. 3, 1874 in St. Louis, MO.

Joseph McCarroll, born March 25, 1838 in Lenoir City, TN, married Eliza M. Williams on March 10, 1859. [Note: Both Moses L. Carter and his brother Joseph had sons named Joseph McCarroll Carter.] By the 1870 Census, the family of Joseph M. and Eliza Carter can be found living in Johnson County, AR with five children: Mary J., Lovey J., Frederick A., Henry L. and Joseph H.

Mary was born Jan. 3, 1840 in Roane County, TN.

Elvira, born March 31, 1841 in Roane County, TN, died Feb. 8, 1913 in Polk County, MO and married Henry S. Hillbrandt, who died in 1864. They had two children, Willie and Henrietta. The widowed Elvira married second, William Lower, son of her Aunt Elvira Carter and George Washington Lower, on Jan. 1, 1867. Elvira and William Lower had 11 children together.

Julia Ann, born Feb. 7, 1843 in Polk County, MO, died Aug. 22, 1870 in Missouri and married Osman Gunn on Nov. 17, 1861. A daughter Sarah D. Gunn was born Oct. 18, 1862 and died Feb. 19, 1863. Their daughter Sintha A. Gunn was born April 25, 1870 and died Aug. 23 or 29, 1870. Their daughter Ida Gunn married William F. Cantrell on July 9, 1882. Their son William Osman was born Sept. 16, 1866; died May 16, 1911 and married Maggie Mosier Dec. 31, 1890.

Margaret Melinda, born April 18, 1845 in Polk County, MO, married Samuel M. Wykle or Wikle. They can be found living next door to Moses L. and Cynthia Carter on the 1880 Polk County census, with three children: Lenna E., John H. and Esley.

Nancy Amanda, born Dec. 27, 1847 in Polk County, died 1925 in Cedar County, MO and married James M. Akard on June 8, 1871 in Polk County.

Adaline, born April 28, 1849 in Missouri, died Feb. 24, 1884 in Bates County, MO; married George Washington Keirsey on March 2, 1873. Their children included Landon Simpson, James Fredrick, Agnes May, Henry Franklin, Carl George, Eugene Benedict and Adeline Mabel.

Moses Looney, born July 21, 1851, Polk County, died Aug. 17, 1878 in Cedar County, MO.

Cynthia Isabelah, born Jan. 6, 1853, was buried in Enon Cemetery.

Delilah Louisa, born June 28, 1855, married F. C. Lee on Feb. 8, 1877.

Moses L. Carter Sr. was a county judge and well known in the community. He died on July 21, 1883 on his farm in Polk County. He is buried in the Barren Creek Cemetery at Fair Play.

The probate inventory for Moses L. Carter lists an estate that was quite extensive, including real estate, livestock, horses, buggies, wagons, and equipment to distill fruit brandies.

His widow Cynthia died in Cedar County, MO on Oct. 22, 1892. She is buried next to her son Moses L. Cater Jr. in the Lindley Prairie Cemetery in Bear Creek, MO. *Submitted by Marcy L. Carter-Lovick*

CARTER – John Wesley Carter was born on Dec. 13, 1836 in Roane County, TN to Cynthia and Moses L. Carter. He moved to Polk County, MO with his parents in the early 1840s.

John W. Carter married Lenorah Jane Brackville on Oct. 3, 1874 in St. Louis, MO. Lenorah, who was born in 1852 in Pulaski County, AR, was the daughter of Dr. John P. Brackville and Jane Caroline Campbell. Lenorah left her parents' home in Arkansas about the time the Civil War ended and traveled to St. Louis, MO.

John W. is listed with his parents on the 1850 and 1870 Polk County census, but is not listed with them on the 1860 census. The census records corroborate the account of his early years, as told by his widow, to their children.

Lenorah told her children that John W. caught a wagon train at St. Joe, MO (which would have been about 170 miles from where his family was living at the time near Bolivar) when he was 13 years old, and traveled to California shortly after the gold rush of 1849. Since John W. appears on the 1850 census with the family in Polk County, it is possible that he didn't actually leave until he was 14 years old. Another possible explanation could be that John's parents considered their 13-year-old son as still making his primary residence in their home, even if he were en route to California at the time of the enumeration.

Lenorah Jane (Brackville) Carter

John W. Carter

At the end of the 13-year stay in California, John W. traveled by ship down the west coast of Mexico to the Isthmus of Panama, where he walked over-land to the East Coast. There he boarded another ship, which brought him to the port of New Orleans. He then traveled up the Mississippi River to St. Louis, MO. Although he can be found living in his parents' home in Polk County in 1870, he lived for at least part of the time between approximately 1864 and 1880 in St. Louis, where he earned a living by cutting and selling ice from the Mississippi River.

After his marriage to Lenorah in 1874, they returned to Polk County some time before 1880, when they were listed in the household of his parents, Moses L. and Cynthia Carter, on the 1880 Federal Census. They had established their own household by at least 1883, though, when John's father Moses L. died, since his obituary notes that the senior Carters were living alone on their farm at the time of his death.

Lenorah and John W. Carter had five children. The first four children were born in Missouri, while the fifth child was born en route to Stone County, AR, where John W. and Lenorah established a homestead.

William S. (born in 1876) is found with his parents on the 1880 Polk County census as a child of 4 years old. William S., who never married, disappeared about 1924.

Callie (born June 22, 1878; died June 5, 1966) married Beecher Hobbs. Their children include Bessie, Oscar, Maurie, Larcie and Elsie.

Howard L. (born about 1881) married Charity Hobbs. They had four children, including Enoch Lee, Winnie, Thelma and Wesley.

Amanda (born July 14, 1883; died Aug. 6, 1946) married James Frank George on March 6, 1897. Their children were Elisabeth, William P., Ossie R., Essie M., Ruby J., Dovie, Barbra, Raymon, Maggie, Eva and Glenn.

Nod (born Feb. 14, 1885 near Guion, AR; died Sept. 2, 1963) married Fannie Mae Jones on June 1, 1913. They had 10 children: Effie, Opal, Lois, Oran M., Ava Faye, Clayton, Dale, Odell, Doyle Ray and Noble.

John Wesley Carter died on April 13, 1891 in Stone County, AR at the age of 55. His widow Lenorah was left to raise the five children alone, the youngest of whom was only 6 years old at the time. She died on July 12, 1938 on the land they had homesteaded together. *Submitted by Marcy L. Cater-Lovick*

CASS - Norman Elbert Cass was born to Elbert D. Cass and Georgia (Myers) Cass on Sept. 12, 1923 in Webster County, MO. He married Betty E. Mobley, daughter of Jim Mobley and Beulah (Killian) Mobley of Springfield, in Spokane, WA, July 17, 1943, while awaiting orders to join the cruiser *St. Louis* in the Pacific theater of WWII. Norman, served as an electrician's mate on the *St. Louis* until after the Japanese surrendered. On several occasions this ship sustained severe damage from combat, but was returned to battle time and time again.

After the war Norman and Betty joined Norman's father on the family farm at Fordland, MO. It was here their first daughter Majuana, was born on Oct. 20, 1946. In 1948, they moved to Polk County where they purchased a farm northeast of Pleasant Hope on the Pomme De Terre River. After constructing the first "herringbone" style milk-barn in Polk County, they maintained a successful dairy operation for several years. In the drought of the 1950s, Norman installed one of the few irrigation systems in the county in order to sustain the row-crops in the bottom fields of the farm. At Pleasant Hope, they lost a son Roger at birth on Aug. 14, 1949. On Sept. 11, 1951 a daughter Sharon was born.

Norman and Betty Cass

In 1960 they sold the farm at Pleasant Hope and purchased a farm southeast of Halfway on Hominy Creek. On this farm Norman not only maintained a herd of beef cows but also became a respected trader of quality dairy heifers. A great portion of this farm was suited to row-crop and as a result many bushels of corn were harvested. It was there that Norman started a life long career as a gospel preacher, serving in several of the area Churches of Christ. All the while, Betty drove many miles to Springfield working for the St. Louis - San Francisco Railway. It was at Halfway that Majuana and Sharon completed their high school education. In 1964, Majuana married Dwight Kibby of Halfway, and in 1969 Sharon married Larry Corum of Willard. At Halfway, a third daughter Robin, joined the family on July 11, 1969.

After a time Norman and Betty sold the farm at Half Way, moving back to Webster County. There Norman established an Electro-plating business and continued to preach the gospel. After their move Robin married Rob Buttry of Marshfield. After retirement from the business, Norman once again returned to the farm in Webster County and maintained a beef-herd until his death on Feb. 19, 1999. At this writing Betty lives in their home in Marshfield, MO.

Grandchildren of Norman and Betty are Curtis Corum, Sonja (Kibby) Jacobson, Cassie (Corum) Harper, Nelson Kibby, Coby Corum and Nathan Buttry. *Submitted by Majuana Kibby*

CASTLEMAN - Hans-Dietrich Casselman (born Nov. 13, 1662, Germany; died between 1729 and 1732, New York) and wife Anna Rinder (born between 1660-1670, Germany; died after 1711, New York) and children arrived in America from Germany on June 14, 1710 on the ship *Midfort*.

One son, Andreas-Ludwig Casselman (born Nov. 6, 1698, Germany; died 1789, Pennsylvania) married Margaretha-Elisabetha Schafer (born between February 1698 and 1699, Germany; died between 1744-1761, Virginia) and one of their children was Jacob Casselman Sr. (born 1728, New York; died August 1803, Tennessee) who married Patience.

Benjamin Casselman (born about 1760: Hampshire County, VA; died 1825 or 1826, Davidson County, TN), son of Andreas-Ludwig and Margaretha-Elisabetha, wrote his will on Sept. 27, 1824, and added to it on Aug. 27, 1825. Benjamin named his wife, Amelia "Milly" (born about 1775, North Carolina) and children in the will. The inventory was taken Jan. 26, 1826 and his will was recorded March 6, 1826.

Abraham Castleman was the son of Benjamin Casselman (born about 1760, Hampshire County, VA) and Amelia "Milly" (born about 1775 in North Carolina).

Abraham Castleman (born 1802, Davidson County, TN; died 1888) and Elizabeth "Eliza" Jones (born 1805, Tennessee) were married Jan. 20, 1821 in Davidson County, TN. In 1830, Abraham and family were in Cooper County, MO, in 1836, Abraham bought land in Miller County, MO. On June 22, 1837, Abraham Castleman was a member of the first grand jury in Miller County, MO. In 1838, Abraham sold his interest in his father Benjamin's farm in Davidson County, TN. In 1840 and 1850, Abraham and family are in Miller County, MO.

In 1880, Abraham is living in Polk County with his son Benjamin F.

Children of Abraham and Elizabeth "Eliza" (Jones) Castleman: Mary Ann Castleman, (born between 1822 and 1824 in Davidson County, TN); Caroline Castleman, (born 1826, Davidson County, TN); Millie Catherine Castleman (born 1831, Missouri; died Dec. 24, 1912, Kansas City, MO) married to Samuel Caulk (born 1821, Tennessee; died Oct. 21, 1907, Springfield, MO) [see chapter on Caulk family for their children]; Elizabeth Castleman (born 1835, Missouri); Eliza Castleman (born 1837, Missouri); Nancy M. Castleman (born 1840, Missouri); Benjamin F. Castleman (born 1842, Missouri) married in Miller County, MO on April 9, 1863 to Minerva J. Hoskins. On June 23, 1884, Marion Township, Polk County, MO, Alfetta Castleman (female) was the seventh child of Benjamin F. Castleman and Nancy C. Breech (age 40).

Samuel Caulk, Millie Catherine Castleman

CATES - Ralph James Cates was born April 23, 1922 in Polk County, MO. He married Myrtle Marie Farmer on Dec. 24, 1945 in Columbus, KS.

She was born Oct. 26, 1926 in Polk County, MO. They had four children: James Milford (born Dec. 31, 1946), Johnny Lee (born May 30, 1949), Beverly Sue (born March 23, 1953) and Delsia Marie (born Feb. 14, 1955). Beverly Sue died Dec. 27, 1999. Ralph James died June 27, 1957 after being struck by lightning.

James Milford attended Hillcrest High School in Springfield, MO until entering the military in 1964. He married Wilma Lee Crowe at Southside Baptist Church on May 14, 1966. Shortly thereafter they moved to Kankakee, IL. They had two children, James Lee (born June 4, 1968) and Johnny Ray (born May 15, 1970). James worked for a company that made submarine batteries (Gould Battery) while living in Illinois and Wilma was a homemaker. In 1973 they returned to Missouri with their two sons and settled in Polk County where James' ancestors are originally from. Today they own and operate Hilltop Service Station in Bolivar, MO.

Both sons graduated from Fair Play High School. James Lee married Trudy Lynn Walker on Dec. 16, 1988. Trudy was born Oct. 3, 1967. They have one daughter, Abbey Jorden (born June 13, 1989). Johnny Ray married Carol Sue Cunningham on June 9, 1989. Carol was born May 17, 1970. They have three children: Margaret "Maggie" Lee (born Aug. 17, 1994), John Michael (born July 13, 1997) and Carol Olivia (born Jan. 10, 1999).

Wilma Lee Crowe was born Nov. 4, 1950 in Bernie, MO in the back room of her father's store. Her father Raymond Crow (born Jan. 16, 1909) and Virginia Lenora Sisk Crow (born May 6, 1928) were married April 19, 1944. Raymond was a jeweler by trade and her mother was a homemaker. She had two brothers, Donald Ray (born Nov. 1, 1944) and Robert Lawerence (born June 30, 1947) and one sister Carolyn Mae (born March 21, 1951). Wilma's father died Sept. 26, 1954. Shortly thereafter her mother was diagnosed with tuberculosis and had to enter the hospital. She was there for four years. During this time Wilma and her siblings were placed in foster care around the state. After Virginia was released from the hospital she settled in Springfield, MO with her children. *Submitted by Wilma Cates*

CAULK - Samuel Caulk (born 1821, Tennessee; died Oct. 21, 1907, Springfield, MO) and Millie Catherine Castleman (born 1831; died Dec. 24, 1912, in Kansas City, MO) were married on July 23, 1846, Miller County, MO. Samuel's father was James Caulk. Millie Catherine was the daughter of Abraham and Elizabeth "Eliza" (Jones) Castleman. Samuel was a blacksmith. Samuel and Millie are buried in lot 262, Hazelwood Cemetery, Springfield, Greene County, MO.

Eliza Catherine "Belle" Caulk

Children of Samuel and Millie Catherine were:

Benjamin Caulk (born 1849 or 1850, Miller County, MO; dead by 1860 census).

John A. Caulk (born July 1853, died May 23, 1945) married on Oct. 10, 1875, Polk County to Martha E. Wood. They had six children. John was a blacksmith.

William T. Caulk (born 1856, Missouri; died May 23, 1945; buried at Greenwood Cemetery, Polk County, MO) married on Sept. 24, 1881 to Adeline Evans. William was a blacksmith. It is possible William T. Caulk married second to Katie Stiles on May 17, 1884. Katie (born 1865; died April 26, 1941; and is buried at Greenwood Cemetery). William had a son named Augusta Grover Clark (born June 14, 1885) who married Blanche.

Henry T. Caulk (born 1859, Missouri) married Ms. Ross.

Lee Longstreet Caulk (born Jan. 1, 1863, Missouri; died Jan. 18, 1953; buried at Veterans Cemetery, Springfield, MO), was a blacksmith. Lee never married.

Eliza Catherine "Belle" Caulk (born Oct. 20, 1868, Missouri, died Jan. 13, 1953, Kansas City, MO) married to John Henry Forgey. Their children were: Juanita Belle Forgey (born Dec. 10, 1892; died August 1962; buried Kansas City, MO); Millie Wenonah Ruth Forgey (born May 8, 1901, Springfield, MO; died March 1965, Kansas City, MO); Hughetta "Teddy" Lee (born Aug. 1, 1907; died 1993 or 1994); and Robert "Little Bob" Forgey who died about age 3.

CAVINESS – Frank B. Caviness, his wife and two daughters moved to Bolivar, MO in September 1931 from Okmulgee, OK to attend college. They stayed. He was a builder and house mover. He is a direct descendent of Henri Cabanis I, a French Huguenot, who immigrated to Jamestown, VA on July 31, 1700 on the ship *Mary Ann*.

Andre Cabanis residence LaSalle, Grad, France.

Pierre Cabanis was born Aug. 16, 1628 in France and married Ann Soultiere.

Henri Cabanis I was born December 1665 in France; immigrated July 31, 1700 to Jamestown, VA; died 1720 in Westover Parish, VA; arrived with his wife Marie and son.

Henri Cabanis II was born 1699 in France. He married Jane Allen, daughter of William Allen. He died 1771 in Mecklenburg County, VA. Upon entering the colonies, the spelling of the name was changed to Caviness.

Matthew Caviness was born in 1740 in Petersburg, Prince George County, VA. He died in 1807.

Robert Caviness was born 1784 in Petersburg, Prince George County, VA. His wife was Ann Clark.

Edward Clark Caviness was born 1805 in Mecklenburg County, VA. On March 11, 1827 he married Lovina "Lovie" J. Cravens in Randolph County, NC. He died in 1865 in Texas County, MO.

William Frank Caviness was born Aug. 4, 1832 in Randolph County, NC. He died Jan. 3, 1901 in Licking, MO and is buried in Van Cleve Cemetery, Texas County, MO. He married Martha Ward July 31, 1853 in Gillbert County, NC.

Thomas Matthew Caviness was born March 26, 1854 in Randolph County, NC. He married Mary P. Carney of Hurse Hill, Dent County, MO on Aug. 2, 1874. He died June 1, 1919 in Success, MO and is buried in Caviness Cemetery.

John Frank Caviness was born Aug. 27, 1875 in Texas County, MO. On Aug. 24, 1899 he married Emma M. Barton in Bourbon, MO. He died Aug. 27, 1953 in Spokane, WA. He and his wife are buried in Pleasant Grove Cemetery in Sleeper, Laclede County, MO. He moved his family to Indian Territory (Oklahoma).

Frank B. Caviness was born July 5, 1902 in Henryetta, Indian Territory. On Aug. 10, 1925 he married Ruby Kinney. He died Oct. 8, 1977 in Bolivar, MO and is buried in Greenwood Cemetery, Bolivar, MO. His daughter, Dorothy Lee, was born April 22, 1929 and died Dec. 25, 1938. His widow, Ruby, still lives in Bolivar with her daughter.

Betty Jean Caviness Smith was born March 11, 1931 in Okmulgee, OK. She married Levi Ray Smith Nov. 20, 1950. They divorced in 1958.

Trudy Lynn Smith was born April 4, 1956 in Springfield, MO. She married Roy Lee Pischer on Dec. 23, 1989 and currently lives in Willard, MO.

Betty Jean Caviness Smith's grandmother Emma Magdalina Barton, mother of Frank B. Caviness was a descendant of John Barton, who immigrated to Jamestown, VA from England before 1700.

Thomas Barton Sr. was born June 12, 1727 and served in the Revolutionary War.

David Barton was born Dec. 27, 1752 and was a militiaman during the Revolutionary War. Connected with the trail of Benedict Arnold and the execution of Major Andre. He married Nancy Barrett on March 11, 1777 and died July 4, 1838. He and his wife are both buried in Tigerville, SC.

Thomas Barton II was born 1777 and died in 1862 in North Carolina.

John Barton II was born prior to 1831 and died prior to 1865.

Francis Marion Barton was born Feb. 4, 1845 and died Feb. 16, 1929 and is the father of Emma Magdalina Barton. *Submitted by Betty Jean Cavines Smith*

CHANEY - John Calvin Chaney was born in Ohio, Oct. 9, 1832. His parents were David Chaney and Mary Ann Greer Chaney who were married in Greene County, OH Dec. 15, 1831. His grandparents were Thomas F. Chaney and Mary Wishart Chaney. His great-grandparents were John and Elizabeth (Fenner) Chaney.

John Calvin and Esther Miller were married Jan. 12, 1854 in Huntington County, IN. Esther's parents were Jacob and Ann Miller. The Millers moved from Indiana to Daviess County, MO in the 1850s.

John Calvin and Esther Chaney, 1890s

Land records show that John Calvin and Esther were living in Warren County, IA Sept. 5, 1860, when they sold 85 acres of land in Daviess County, MO. It is believed that John Calvin and wife Esther; his brother Thomas J. and wife Eve, and father-in-law and mother-in-law, Jacob and Ann Miller, lived in Daviess and Harrison Counties in Missouri during the Civil War. It is believed that both John Calvin and his brother, Thomas J. Chaney, fought in the Civil War.

John Calvin Chaney and family were listed in the 1870 Federal Census of Cherokee County, KS. The family moved to Bourbon County, KS and then to Polk County, MO. In 1884, they bought land in Cedar County, MO, near the Polk County line and remained here until their deaths. Many of their descendants have resided in Polk County.

The children of John Calvin and Esther Miller Chaney were, as follows. (Some birth dates were determined by the Federal Census and may not be entirely accurate.)

Peter Jefferson, (born May 4, 1855, died March 8, 1877) married Tabitha Orlina Josephina Hopper Nov. 19, 1876.

Allen, (born Sept. 4, 1856, died Jan. 18, 1915) married Nancy Jane Rains, Aug. 10, 1879.

Eva Jane, (born March 27, 1857, died Sept. 18, 1944) married Harvey Endicott, March 26, 1876.

George, (born Aug. 15, 1861, died Jan. 19, 1941) married Nancy Ann Beaty Sept. 17, 1886. She died Jan. 26, 1894, he then married Sarah Emmaline Vickers Feb. 13, 1895 and their children were Bertha, Minerva, Iza, Delphia and Rhoda.

Martha Ann was born about 1862; her death date is unknown. She married Joseph Harper Nov. 14, 1877.

Maretta was born 1865; death date unknown.

Rosetta "Doll" was born in May 1863. Her death date is unknown. She married Nathan Endicott Feb. 3, 1880.

Matilda "Til" (born Sept. 30, 1865, died April 27, 1933) married Richard Sayres, date unknown.

Della was born about 1866, death date unknown. She married James H. Scribner March 6, 1888.

Malinda "Nin" was born March 1868, death date unknown. She married first, William Esicks Dec. 30, 1886; second, Willie H. Walker April 23, 1895; and third, Hugh Hopper July 24, 1911.

John Calvin Chaney died March 2, 1912. Esther (Miller) Chaney died March 4, 1903. Both are buried in Tinker Cemetery in Polk County, MO. *Submitted by Murle Phipps*

CHAPMAN – John Partee Chapman's father, William Franklin Chapman, was born June 30, 1838 in Wilkes County, NC, the son of Elisha Chapman (born Dec. 15, 1807 at Three Forks, Wilkes County, NC; died Dec. 31, 1887) and Sally or Sarah Jane Deal (born Jan. 27, 1815 in Wilkes County, NC; died Nov. 26, 1905).

John Partee Chapman, Allie Burdett Chapman, Georgia Chapman Miller and Raymond Chapman, around 1926

William Franklin Chapman married Ann "Annie" Goodnight, daughter of Nelson Goodnight and Mary Hoffman. Annie was born Jan. 20, 1836 or 1840 in Taylorsville, Alexander County, NC. William F. and Annie had at least six children: Julie Chapman, William Chapman, Silas Chapman, John Partee Chapman, Martha Jane Chapman and Sara Ellen Chapman.

William and Annie's son, John Partee Chapman, was born Feb. 16, 1870 and married Allie S. Burdett (born Oct. 30, 1876; died Jan. 22, 1970), daughter of Samuel Stewart Burdett Jr. (born Dec. 27, 1850; died Dec. 25, 1881) and Caroline Williams (born Sept. 2, 1852; died June 11, 1909).

John and Allie settled at Rock Prairie, Polk County, MO and to this union three children were born: Ava May Chapman (born Aug. 1, 1910; died Aug. 17, 1910 with croup), she is buried at Rock Prairie Cemetery next to her parents; Georgia Marie Chapman (born March 3, 1912; died Jan. 3, 2002) and she married John Horace Miller on March 17, 1928 (see Horace and Georgia Chapman Miller article); and Johnny Raymond Chapman (born Feb. 10, 1917), he married Wilma Nadine Highfill on June 1, 1940. Wilma was born on Jan. 2, 1920 and died in January 1999. She is buried at Joplin, MO. Raymond and Wilma have two children, Ramona "Mona" Fay Chapman Miller and Shirley Mae Chapman Wynn.

John Partee Chapman died on March 9, 1948. Allie Burdett Chapman died on Jan. 22, 1970, after a lengthy illness. Both are buried at Rock Prairie Cemetery, Polk County, MO. *Submitted by Chester L. Miller*

CHOATE - It is thought by most that Choate is a French name and that the Choate family immigrated to Brahant, Holland from France. Sometime in the 16th century the family moved from Holland into the eastern part of England, near the boundary in Essex and Suffolk Counties.

In Holland the family used the name Van-Choate, but because of the prejudice of the English against the Dutch immigrants they dropped the Van from the name upon coming to England.

It appears, from all research of Colonial records, that only three men by the name of Choate immigrated to America in the 17th century. Thomas Choate, the earliest immigrant, arrived in Charles City, VA in 1635. John Choate, the next immigrant, came to America from England in 1643. Christopher Choate landed in Maryland in 1676. It is believed that with much research that Jean Farmer Choate's husband's family descended from Christopher Choate. The family was adventurous, as a result they can be found among the first to settle many parts of America. Their migration started from Maryland to Virginia and from there spread throughout the south and southwest. The name Choate can be found among the early records of Virginia, Tennessee, North Carolina, South Carolina, Alabama, Mississippi, Arkansas, Louisiana, Missouri and Texas.

John A. Choate was Jean's husband's grandfather. He married Barbara Miller in Monroe County, TN on July 16, 1858. To this union eight children were born. They were John, Thomas, Martha, James, Sarah Tennie, David M., Mack Menn and Elias. Elias died at the age of 4. Three of the children were born in Tennessee, two in Indiana and then in Missouri.

John A. and his brother Thomas bought a farm in Polk County about five miles northeast of Pleasant Hope in the year 1874. Three of John's children were born on this farm. One of the children was Jean's husband Willard's dad, Mack Menn. He was born in 1877. When he became a young man he married Edith Gertrude Clave on Dec. 21, 1910. They bought part of the farm and raised five children. They were: Wilford, Thelma, Elsie, Novie and Willard.

Front: Mack, Willard and Gertie Choate; Middle: Elsie, Novie and Arcie Sallee, Wilford Choate; Back: Irene, Thelma and Ruth Choate.

Wilford married Ruth Cates in 1933. To this union four sons were born: Junior, Vester, Delbert and Edward.

Thelma married Arcie Sallee in 1932. They had a foster daughter named Carolyn.

Elsie married Fred Gaynor in 1945. To this union a daughter was born. She was named Madeline; also a son named Gaylord was born to them.

Novie married Irene Brakebill in 1939. They had a daughter named Loretta.

Willard married Jean Farmer in 1950. They have three sons: Kenneth, Ronnie and Mike.

Willard's parents Mack and Gertie lived on this farm until 1961. At this time they moved to the town of Pleasant Hope and sold the farm to Willard and Jean who had been living in a little house down in the field after they married. Willard was born on this farm and has never lived anywhere else. He is now 78. He and Jean have been married 52 years.

They are members of the Rock Prairie Missionary Baptist Church, which is located a little over one mile from their home. Much of the Choate family has gone to church there down through the years. *Submitted by Jean Farmer Choate*

CHOATE – Linda Morris's dad was born to Wilson Thomas Choate and Sarepta Dora Caroline Choate (Cook) on Aug. 5, 1911. Linda's Grandpa Choate's descendants came from Sweet Water, TN. At that time two brothers and a cousin came to the Polk County area and settled. Her great-grandpa was Thomas John Houston. Her Grandpa Choate, "Wilce" as most people called him, was a kind and gentle man who was extremely religious. He was the best grandpa in the world. Her Uncle Willie and Aunt Berniece had five kids and her parents, Sam and Reva Choate (Hoover) have three kids. Grandpa was equally great to all of his grandchildren. Grandpa Choate was legally blind, however he could see somewhat. He taught Linda and her sister to do all kinds of things. On Sunday they would go to the wood lot and catch a chicken and help grandpa chop its head off; then they would help Grandma Choate scald the feathers off and learn to pluck it. This may seem awful to people today, but it taught them life lessons. In those days people raised what they ate and processed it as they needed it. Linda and her sister spent a lot of time with their grandparents and they were wonderful. What they didn't have in money, they made

Samuel Paul Choate WWII picture

up for in love. They spent time with the girls and took time to play with them. They did all kinds of things together; they sat on the front porch and played with natural toys like butterflies or June bugs. Grandpa and Grandma taught them to tie strings to June bugs legs and fly them around. This was great fun for two little girls. They lost their grandma way too early; Linda was only 9 years old. Grandpa came to live with them and was still a great influence on them. He would encourage them in things that they wanted to do. Grandpa taught them patience, to be honest, to have compassion, to be trustworthy, and to trust in God. He took them to Hickory Point Church sometimes. As a young girl Linda learned about who she was and more importantly, what kind of person she wanted to be from her parents and grandparents.

Samuel and Reva Choate

Linda's dad married her mom after he returned from WWII. Daddy told them "war stories" as they grew up. So WWII was just part of their lives since they were born. He would show them his medals and patches; they didn't realize that they were looking at a part of history. Linda had one brother, Paul Wayne Choate and one sister, Paula Mae Choate. Linda's brother was older so it seemed like he was always gone somewhere with friends. Both of her parents spent lots of time with them doing things they were interested in. Daddy would lead Linda and her sister on their horse when they were 3 and 4 years old. He would spend half a day on Saturday just walking and leading that horse for them. We have always loved horses and continue to ride. Instead of griping or refusing to walk that much, Daddy wanted them to enjoy their lives and still be safe, so he spent time making it was possible for them to do that. They liked to go for walks, of course little girls thought they needed to take their puppies, whom would get tired halfway through the walk and have to be carried. Daddy never said, "I told you so" instead he just picked the puppy up and carried it the rest of the way. Mom was also extremely good to them. She took them swimming at the creek and took picnic lunches for them. Even though she wouldn't swim, she would take the time to meet Linda's aunt and her kids (who could swim) and allow Linda and her sister to learn to swim. Linda learned from both of her parents to try to do better for your kids than you had.

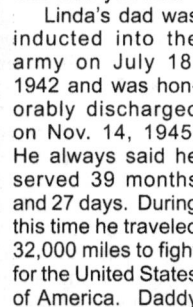
Wilson Thomas Choate and Sarepta Caroline (Cook) Choate

Linda's dad was inducted into the army on July 18, 1942 and was honorably discharged on Nov. 14, 1945. He always said he served 39 months and 27 days. During this time he traveled 32,000 miles to fight for the United States of America. Daddy told Linda on one occasion a bomb hit his individual bunk that he slept in and took it 60 feet in the ground. He was gone on duty when it happened. Another time he was held up on the road (he was hauling ammunition to the front line) and in just a few minutes the Germans blew that road completely out. On three different occasions he just barely missed death. Yet he survived all that and came home to have and raise a family of three children: Wayne, Paula and Linda. Wayne's children are Wanita Watts and Wesley Choate. Paula's daughter is Niki Odell. Linda's son is Thomas Morris. Great-grandchildren include Justin Watts, Jake Choate, Camary Choate, Tyler Morris and Kendall Morris. Linda's brother's wife is Alice Mathis, Linda's husband is Lendell Morris. Her dad passed away on May 10, 2002. He was 90 years old. Her mother continues to keep the family close and is still teaching them life lessons. *Submitted by Linda Morris*

CHOATE - Thomas J. H. Choate was born March 22, 1853 in Sweet Water, TN and died Oct. 30, 1928. He came to Polk County, MO in the 1870s along with a brother and an uncle as told by a relative. They came by way of covered wagon pulled by horses. It took several months to reach their destination.

Thomas met Rebecca Susan Bryan, whom he married on Jan. 16, 1878 in Polk County. She was born Feb. 19, 1854 and died July 25, 1935. They are buried in Brighton Cemetery, Polk County, MO. They had nine children.

Thomas John Huston and Rebecka Choate Susan

Wilson Thomas was born May 28, 1877 in Pleasant Hope and died April 26, 1970. He married Sareptia Dora Cook, born Aug. 24, 1885 and died Oct. 18, 1963.

Bertie Luella was born March 31, 1879 in Pleasant Hope and died July 29, 1953. She is buried in Brighton Cemetery. She had measles at about age 5 and was left blind. She never married.

Virginia was born March 9, 1881 in Pleasant Hope and died Jan. 1, 1964. She married first, W. Thomas Sinclair, born May 8, 1872, died Nov. 18, 1913. She married second, Mike Conley, born in 1895, died in 1971. All are buried at Brighton Cemetery.

Rose Etta was born Aug. 14, 1883 in Pleasant Hope and died Aug. 12, 1946. She married Tipton Monroe Johnston, born April 8, 1873, died Dec. 7, 1958. They are buried in Hickory Grove Cemetery, Brighton, MO.

John A. Logan was born Aug. 3, 1886 in Pleasant Hope and died July 2, 1927. He is buried in Brighton Cemetery. He never married.

Arlia Golden was born Jan. 31, 1889 in Pleasant Hope and died March 30, 1953. She married Festus Newton Conley, born Aug. 22, 1883 and died Sept. 5, 1945. They are buried in Brighton Cemetery.

Morlia May was born March 11, 1891 in Pleasant Hope and died April 9, 1987. She married Horace Willard Baker, born Dec. 13, 1879, died May 25, 1955. They are buried in Springfield, Greene County, MO.

Rosco Ray was born Dec. 4, 1894 in Pleasant Hope and died unknown. Rosco left Missouri to travel to Kansas. He sent a niece a birthday card and not thinking anything about the return postage the family threw it away. This was the last contact the family had with him. He was never heard from again. There were stories that reached the family but none were ever proven.

Elias Frances was born Nov. 6, 1897 in Pleasant Hope and died Dec. 6, 1980. He married Flora Elizabeth Clark Dec. 18, 1920. She was born May 18, 1901, died Oct. 17, 1981. They are buried in Brighton Cemetery. To this marriage eight children were born.

Hershel Leo was born Oct. 7, 1921.

Marshal Ray was born March 8, 1923, died February 17, 1988. He married Agnes Mae Boswell on Sept. 18, 1943 in Brighton. They were married by J. H. "Jim" Phillips who was the justice of peace in Brighton. Eight children were born to this marriage: Zelma Mae (born Oct. 15, 1944); Ray Gene (born Jan. 27, 1945); Velma Marie (born Sept. 24, 1947); Anna Louis (born Nov. 10, 1949); Flora Susan (born May 24, 1951); Carolyn Kay (born Aug. 20, 1954); Elizabeth Irene (born Dec. 20, 1957); and Dennis Dwayne (born Dec. 20, 1967).

Bonnie Arelin was born Nov. 9, 1924.
Baby boy was born and died May 7, 1929.
Bobby Paul was born Sept. 4, 1930.
Reva Elizabeth was born Aug. 3, 1932.
Baby girl was born and died May 12, 1934.
Verba Lee was born June 20, 1936.

Elias Frances did not like the name given to him at birth, so he changed it to Boyd. A record concerning this has not been found, but this could have been done without going through the legal process. Relatives said as a lad he always had his britches torn so one sister called him "ragged a Bob." This may have stuck with him as Boyd is very close to Bob. Grandpa Boyd was a farmer as most were; raised his own food and also milked cows. The grandkids liked to help Grandma churn butter. She would fill a half gallon jar about three-fourths full of fresh milk and it seemed like it took forever to get butter.

Here is a story about the watermelon patch. Frankie Walters hauled milk back then. Most times his wife Norma would be on his truck with him when he came to pick up milk at Grandpa and Grandma's house. Lee Johnston told Frankie to ask Grandpa if he had a watermelon patch next time he went to collect the milk. Frankie asked next time he went, and Grandpa asked, "Who wants to know?" Frankie told him Lee Johnston. Grandpa told Frankie to tell that ornery Lee that he had shot dogs, cats, snakes and a little bit of everything except a jack ass that he had caught in his watermelon patch. Frankie repeated this to Lee next time he talked to him. Sounds like Lee had thoughts about visiting the watermelon patch. Seems that Lee never did visit the patch; course Grandpa would have given anybody who passed a melon. Lee never forgot this about Grandpa. *Submitted by Carolyn Mitchell*

CLARK - James Clark was born Dec. 2, 1824 in Ross County, OH. His parents were William and Rachel (Sarkey) Clark and came to Ohio from Virginia. James was their second child born of 11 children. After James' mother Rachel's death, William and James moved to Missouri and both of their names appear on the 1840 census. William returned to Ohio but James settled north of Halfway and near the Joel Ragsdale homestead.

Martha J. Ragsdale was born May 13, 1835, daughter of Joel Ragsdale and Jane (Alred) Ragsdale. James and Martha (Ragsdale) Clark were married Sept. 9, 1852 and were the parents of 13 children.

He was a farmer all his life and deeply interested in church matters. They had church services in their home and a Methodist Church was organized there. Later the Mt. Zion Methodist Church was built, where many of their descendants were saved and became members.

He also was active in organizing the Clark school and donated the land that it was built on. The Clark school was where not only his children received their education, but many of his descendants. Three of his descendants, Roseann (Davison) Boyce, J. C. Davison and Eugene Quick were the fourth generation and were in attendance at Clark the last year it had classes. It was a one-room school and all eight grades were taught by the same teacher. The

Back row: Rachel Vanderford, Mary Jane Rimby, Thomas Jefferson Clark, William James Clark, John Wesly Clark and Sarah Ellen Slate; Second row: Hannah Rebecca Davison, Susan Virginia Freeman, Martha and James Clark, Anna Burlinda Quick and Martha Melissa Baltz; Bottom row: Hester M. Ardrey, Rosa Lavina and Margaret Adela.

Clark school closed in 1950 and was consolidated into the Halfway School District.

Each of the 13 children was deeded 40 acres of land at the time of James Clark's death. He died Nov. 14, 1899.

Rachel Vanderford was born May 16, 1869. Hannah Davison was born May 6, 1865. William J. was born Nov. 16, 1860. John W. was born Dec. 7, 1862. Thomas was born Aug. 14, 1857. Susan Freeman was born Nov. 29, 1866. Martha Baltz was born Oct. 11, 1871. Mary Rimby was born June 25, 1855. Martha and James Clark. Anna Quick was born Feb. 13, 1854. Sarah E. Slate was born Jan. 23, 1859. Hester Ardrey was born Nov. 8, 1873. Rosie Knight was born March 23, 1876. Adellia Standley was born April 9, 1878.

Submitted by Irene Quick Mayfield

CLIQUOT – Cliquot was the hometown of Lero Robertson Tinsley Frazier from 1920 until she married in 1933. She was 5 when her parents bought their farm north of Salem Church. Sometimes Lero and her sister, Pauline, walked with their mother, Ethel, to Cliquot. They walked on a foot log across the west creek before it emptied into the larger branch of Dry Fork. Her mother usually carried a basket of eggs, which she traded for a few groceries, and then they would stop by to visit "Aunt" Addie Gunn. Cliquot had several houses then, with a population of about a hundred.

Salem Cemetery 1988, Robertson sisters, Pauline Morris and Lero Frazier

Lero's dad, Ike, hitched his mules, Beck and Dutch, to his iron-wheeled wagon to go after chicken and cattle feed. When the neighbor boys heard the wagon, they often ran to jump on. Sometimes Ike let them drive the team. The road didn't go straight south from Salem Church to Cliquot. They went under the railroad-bridge to the east and followed the road around. Finally, they turned west and crossed a low water bridge, then the railroad track, and there was Cliquot. It was much handier for them when a bridge was built so the road went straight into Cliquot.

Like most, the school at Cliquot held pie suppers as fundraisers. At one time Mrs. Nellie Watkins was the teacher. One year at the pie supper her rather "rounded" look was noticeable, but she directed the students in an ambitious program lasting almost two hours, with the pies being auctioned after that. Her duties done, Mrs. Nellie Watkins went home and had her baby that same night!

There was a railroad track to the east of the Robertson farm. One day Pauline and Lero were crossing the big railroad-bridge high above a deep pool of water, where Salem Church held their baptismal services. They saw a family with several children down below swimming. The mother had long hair. She was washing her hair, and the girls were fascinated by how she dipped her hair into the creek to rinse it.

Sometimes after a heavy rain, the creek would flood. Once a neighbor, "Uncle" Cy Brown, had his can of cream behind his buggy seat, taking it to Cliquot to send to a creamery in Iowa. When he drove into the swollen creek, the can of cream floated away! When Lero was around 12 her dad sometimes had her take their can of cream by horseback. He tied the can on one side of the saddle horn, and Lero stood in the stirrup on the other side to balance it.

People drove their animals to the stockyard in Cliquot to be shipped to market by rail. The spring provided water for a big tank used for the huge train engine, which let off steam as it was being filled up. Cliquot had three stores, two in serious competition with the rivals engaging in a fistfight over pricing on one occasion! One store offered homemade ice cream on Saturdays and sold it for about five cents a dish, to draw customers. Until the 1950s when trains were taken off the Frisco Line, people could make a round-way trip to Bolivar in one day. After the post office closed, a mail route from Dunnegan came through Cliquot.

The loss of the trains and post office hurt Cliquot's business. As more people got cars, they went to Bolivar to trade. The last store closed about 1970. *Submitted by June Tinsley Seat*

CLOYDE – James Polk Cloyde was born March 27, 1845 in Tennessee. Sarah Elizabeth Bayless was born Jan. 29, 1844 on a tobacco plantation in Washington County, TN. Her mother passed away when Sarah was a child. She spent her time playing with her mammy's children who lived in a house behind the main house. Her father, Barton Bayless, remarried during her childhood. James Cloyde was a Confederate soldier in the beginning of the Civil War and changed to the Union side later. He and Sarah married on Jan. 31, 1866. They lived on the plantation in her father's home. By then Sarah's mammy had been freed but continued to live on the plantation. She helped with James and Sarah's children. Because of hard feelings over the war, James and Sarah decided to go west in 1876. Sarah asked to take her mammy, who was very dear to her, with them when they left, but her father refused the request.

James Polk Cloyde and Sarah Elizabeth Bayless Cloyde

James was considered a traitor to the Confederacy.

James and Sarah's daughter, Martha, remembered leaving the house and the mammy carrying her down the stairs and the many tears with their parting. The family settled near Morrisville in Polk County, MO. Barton Bayless sent his daughter a letter of apology, but she did not reply to his letter. She put the letter in the family Bible and never had contact with her father again. The Bible and letter are presently in possession of a family member.

James Cloyde died on May 8, 1929. Sarah died on July 14, 1921. They are buried in Slagle Cemetery. *Submitted by Cindy Orrell*

CLOYED – Sometime in the late 1860s James and Mary (Barnes) Cloyed left Tennessee for Polk County in a covered wagon. It is believed they planned to join other Barneses already living south of Adonis. Mary may have been a sister to Elic Barnes (1843-1892) who married Eliza Hart (1851-1887).

James died en route and George Washington "G. W." Cloyed, oldest of the six children, took charge of the trip. Near Warsaw the family met James M. Zumwalt, owner of a store at Polk. Mr. Zumwalt made weekly trips for fresh produce and other supplies from the train going through Warsaw. He made room for the Cloyed women to ride on his wagon. Two generations later these two pioneer families would be joined by the marriage of Laura Elizabeth Zumwalt and Frederick Earl Cloyed.

G. W.'s siblings were Dora who married Sam Ingram. Dora was a very religious woman and wrote a book, *Sin, Satan, Righteousness*. She and Sam lived on a farm adjoining G. W.'s. Later their son, Wesley, and his wife, Ruby, lived there. Their son Junior Freeman Ingram preached to hundreds in this area. Ellen married John W. Frank. Elizabeth married John Bennett. John married Amanda Bennett. Frank was a bachelor. (John Bennett and Amanda Bennett were siblings.) One or two of these siblings may have moved to Kansas. G. W.'s grandson, Ed Cloyd, remembers reunions somewhere in Kansas.

G. W. became a blacksmith, farmer and wheelwright. The anvil used to form the metal wheel ring is still in the family. G.W. (born June 7, 1854; died July 31, 1932) homesteaded northwest of Polk. He married Martha Stewart (born May 9, 1863; died Aug. 19, 1896) and they had five children.

Earl Avery (born Jan. 30, 1886; died Jan. 7, 1971) married Coessie Antha Thomas (born Dec. 16, 1889; died March 27, 1983) on Dec. 10, 1905. Ivy married Dick Overshiner. They had a store at Huron for several years. Bertha married Emmett Coonis. Della married John Butler. The Coonis and Butler families lived in California. Cortna married Letha Pitts who died a few months after their son, Leland Francis, was born.

Later Cortna married Fern Noblett. They had

six children: Gwendolyn, Shirley, Evelyn, Geroldene, Hildreth and Linford. Fern was an early switchboard operator at Polk, Pleasant Hope and Fair Grove. Earl and Cortna learned to blacksmith and Cortna had a shop in Polk at one time. Cortna made a walnut cracker for E. C. "Bud" Zumwalt that is still used by their descendants.

Earl and Coessie bought a farm near G. W. and had three children. Hattie Naomi (born July 23, 1907; died Jan. 20, 1968) married Alfred Emory on Sept. 22, 1923. He played the fiddle and guitar and she played the piano and organ. They were popular guests at parties. (Coessie was related to Buster Fellows who played on the TV shows out of Springfield in the early 1950s. He, Alfred and Earl could liven up a festivity.) Alfred and Naomi soon moved to St. Louis and had two sons, Donald and Gayle. Frederick Earl (born March 28, 1913; died Aug. 8, 1980) married Laura Elizabeth Zumwalt (born Sept. 21, 1911) on June 25, 1941. They eventually bought a farm adjoining Earl and Coessie. Their children are Jerry Lee and Joan Kay. George Edward "Ed" Cloyd (born April 10, 1915) married Florence Degraffenreid on Dec. 10, 1935. They operated the Bolivar Hotel for a few years. Their children are Gary and Derral.

Front: Coessie and Earl; Back: Ed, Fred and Naomi, the Earl Cloyed family

Earl and Coessie spent several years in California on a ranch. This was during the 1920s. So many Polk County people were living around Santa Paula that it was called "Little Bolivar!" Earl was a blacksmith and Coessie was nanny and housekeeper for the owners. Surprisingly, she made more money than he. They sent farm payments back and the farm was paid for when they returned to Missouri about 1930. They also had money to buy good stock at Depression prices. Good Jersey milk cows were $30 each. They could "live off the land," increase their herds and wait it out till prices started to climb again. Finally, in 1958 they sold the farm and retired to Bolivar. *Submitted by Jerry Cloyed*

COOPER - Written on the plane coming from Phoenix to Missouri for his grandmother's funeral and read at Cuba Gothard Cooper's funeral by Randy Cooper.

"As I sat in my soft chair watching TV, I got a phone call from someone back home. I could tell it was going to be the phone call I had been waiting for but didn't want to get. It was news that my grandmother had passed away. Saddened by the news I started making plans for my trip back home. I

Cuba Cooper and grandson Randy Cooper, 1983

had to call my boss to tell him I would have to miss some work. I explained to him that my grandmother had passed away. Knowing that the company gave time off for grandparents who helped raise you, my boss asked me 'Who was she to you?' At that moment I slipped back into time and my eyes began to tear. I could not answer right away, these thoughts went through my mind...

She was a big broad country girl that had a twinkle in her eye and a coy little smile. I saw this in a picture album she kept in her spare bedroom.

She was the woman that married my granddad and gave birth to my dad and two aunts.

She was the woman that worked on the farm doing the work of a farm hand, cook, dishwasher and mother.

She was the woman who would sell eggs, cut wood or whatever it took to buy her son a letter jacket.

She was the woman that other farmers in the area used as an alarm clock when she'd call for the cows.

She was the same woman a person could hear singing some old gospel song while she drove posts in the ground with an old post maul.

She was the woman that could eat watermelon over and over again.

She was the woman who lived over a garage with a man that would never leave her heart.

She was the woman that had to make a living and raise a young child after that man died.

She was the woman that fed anyone that was hungry that came to the back of an old cafe on 24 Highway.

She was the woman that called her grandkids funny names like Raggy, Robby or Greggy and Dougy.

She was always referring to kids over six-foot-tall as "poor little ole Gerald or poor little ole Richard."

She was the woman that could make food from nothing and make it look like more than you could eat.

She was the woman who always had beans in the refrigerator and cobbler on the stove no matter when you came to her house.

She was the woman that sent me a birthday card with money until I was 30.

She was the woman whose voice would get higher the more excited she got.

She was the woman that guided me spiritually along with everyone that knew her.

She was the woman in the wheel chair in church with that unmistakable smile.

She was the woman that answered her phone on the first ring.

She was the woman that prayed for me and everyone all her life.

She was a woman that thought God had the answers for anything.

She was the woman known as Maw, Mom, Mother, Sister, Granny, Sis, Cuba, Cuby, Miss Cooper, and the lady that had flowers in her yard.

All these things flashed through my mind as my boss waited for an answer from me. With tears in my eyes and a rattled voice I told my boss, 'She was my Granny.'

"Who was she to me, She was my Granny." *Submitted by Randy Scott Cooper*

COOPER - Coy Jr. was born Sept. 19, 1928 to Coy Sr. and Bessie (Gothard). Coy Jr. married Donna Lee Fisher, daughter of Athel and Velma (Sawyer) Fisher, on Nov. 22, 1949. Both Coy and Donna were born a few miles west of Fair Play in Cedar County.

In the 1940s and 1950s, going to Fair Play on Saturday nights was the highlight of the week. There was usually someone singing and playing country music on a wooden platform in the middle of the street. It was not always easy to find a parking spot in this bustling town.

Coy and Donna lived south of Stockton for seven years. During this time, Rickey Darrell was born in 1951 and Kathy Michelle was born in 1956. In September of 1957 the family moved to Benton, KS. At this time, Coy worked for Boeing. In addition, he farmed during the next 14 years. April 1959 added Jeffrey Kirk to the family, and then in 1963, Lesa Ann came along. Donna spent those 14 years helping with the farm, developing a huge garden and raising a family.

In 1969 Coy was badly injured in a tractor accident. Doctors were afraid he would lose his leg, but with the help of very good doctors and many people praying, they were able to save his leg. Coy had numerous surgeries and spent the next 11 months in a cast. It was another four months before he had full use of this leg.

In 1971 they decided they wanted to move home to Missouri to buy a farm on Piper Creek north of Bolivar, which is where they have lived for 31 years.

In 1969, son Rickey graduated from Circle High School and then spent some time in the Army National Guard in the early 1970s. In 1971 Rick married Della Bowlin. Together they have three children: Julie Scott of El Dorado, KS (husband George and sons Logan and Lucas); Kristi Cooper of Potwin, KS (son Trenton) and Jacob Cooper of El Dorado, KS (wife Tonya and daughter Trinity). Rick works for Furley Elevator in Furley, KS.

Kathy graduated from Bolivar High School in 1974. After business college, she married Dennis Williams in 1976. Together they have three sons: Curtis (a student at Pittsburg State University), Phillip and Jonathon. Dennis and Kathy spent eight years in El Dorado, KS and then moved to Strafford, MO. They have been there for 13 years. Kathy works in the insurance business in Springfield.

Jeff graduated Bolivar High School in 1977 and in June of 1982 he married Geni Siscoe. Jeff graduated Washburn Law School in 1985 and has an office in Topeka, KS. Together, he and Geni have three children: Jordan, Jessica and Jarod. Jeff has another son, Jason, from a previous marriage. They make their home in Berryton, KS.

Lesa graduated Bolivar High School in 1982. In June of 1984 she married Eddie Crain. Lesa graduated from Wichita State University in 1988. That same year, their oldest son, Scott, was born and they moved back to Bolivar. Their family grew rather fast in 1991 when twins Bethany and Bradley joined their family. They make their home on part of the original farm north of Bolivar. Lesa works at Citizens Memorial Hospital in Bolivar.

Coy and Donna are active members of Mt. Olive Baptist Church, where they have been members for 30 years. They spend many hours on the road to various activities in which their grandchildren are involved. No matter what state, if one of the grandkids is involved in something, they are there to support and cheer them on. *Submitted by Donna L. Cooper*

COOPER - Alta Marie Cooper, daughter of Henry R. and Cuba Dee (Gothard) Cooper, was born the day after Thanksgiving on Dec. 1, 1933. At the time, the Coopers were living on the Cave Springs Road about halfway between Fair Play and Bear Creek in Polk County.

By 1936 they had moved to the Bear Creek bottoms in Cedar County. It was here in a two-room log house that Marie welcomed a brother, Charles Kenneth "Kenny," on May 19, 1938.

Alta Marie started to school at age 5 at Bear Creek School. By third grade the family had

H. L. and Marie Lane and grandchildren: Cody, Zack and Greg Lane Jr., Jason Swartwood, Ethan Lane, Sara Lane, Hannah Swartwood, Steve and Amy (Swartwood) Felix.

moved to the Fair Play area and Marie walked over a mile to Fox School; it was a one-room school with eight grades. She remembers when hot lunches started. Mrs. Lois Hutchins was the teacher and she would bring stew or soup and cook it on the wood-heating stove in the middle of the room. The water came from a pump and there was an outdoor toilet. In fifth grade, due to consolidation, Marie changed to the Fair Play Schools where she graduated in 1951. After graduation Marie worked for the Citizens State Bank for one and a half years.

In 1943, the Cooper family moved to a farm located on the Cedar/Polk County line. The youngest child, Shirley Louise, was born there on May 3, 1946.

Marie remembers Fair Play when it was thriving. On Saturday night the town was a busy place. One couldn't find a place to park on the main streets many times. The men would gather and talk while the women sat on the benches and visited. As a kid, Saturday night was the big deal of the week. You got dressed up and went to town. The young girls would walk around watching the young guys drive up the street and turn around at the Methodist Church and drive down the street and do it over and over.

In 1952, Marie moved with her family to their farm in Cedar County. In early 1953 she went to visit her cousin, Betty Cusick, and family in Groom, TX. While there, she met H. L. Lane and on June 24, 1953, they were married in Groom, TX in Carson County.

Henry Layton was born March 19, 1921, the son of Martin Elmo Lane and Jessie Lois Colvin Lane, in Clarendon, TX, in Donley County. His ancestors left Tennessee and settled in Texas in the 1840s and 1850s, while it was still a wild frontier.

Shortly after their marriage, they moved to Independence, MO where Marie resumed her banking career and H. L. went to work for Ford Motor Co.

In the fall of 1955 they purchased a home in Independence, where they presently reside.

They had three children, all born in Independence, Jackson County, MO: Terri Genece (born July 13, 1955) married Dale Swartwood and they had two children; Amy Marie (born June 1, 1979) married Steve Felix Oct. 16, 1999, Amy has one child Hannah Marie Swartwood, born Nov. 26, 1995; Jason Lane (born June 30, 1981).

Gregory Layton (born March 3, 1957) married Rebecca Jo "Becky" Pine and they have two children: Gregory Layton Jr. (born July 31, 1979) and Sara Beth (born Feb. 5, 1981).

Douglas Richard (born July 24, 1959) married Joy Michelle Johnson and they had three children: Zackary Douglas (born April 30, 1985); Cody Daniel (born May 23, 1988) and Ethan Donald (born Oct. 6, 1992).

H. L. and Marie were both raised in the Baptist Church. Marie was a long time member of the Oak Grove Baptist, located near Masters, in Cedar County. At the present time H.L. and Marie are members of Reach Out Missionary Baptist Church in Blue Springs, MO.

H.L. retired from Ford Motor Co. in 1983 and Marie retired in 2001. *Submitted by Terri Swartwood*

COOPER - Henry Richard Cooper, son of Charley and Frances Corda (Simmons) Cooper, and Cuba Dee Gothard, daughter of George Sigel and Arminta Jane (Harmon) Gothard, were secretly married on Jan. 2, 1932 in Bolivar, Polk County, MO.

Henry, Cuba, Marie, Kenny and Shirley

Henry was born Feb. 21, 1904 near Needmore in Cedar County, MO. He was the seventh known child born to Charley and Corda and the third that lived. He had two brothers Coy (born July 7, 1894) and Merit Philip (born Nov. 8, 1889). On Aug. 25, 1905, Corda died in childbirth. Coy quit school to take care of Henry, while Merit helped his father make a living. When Henry started first grade at the Eldorado School, Coy, age 16, returned to school. Charley was a farmer and operated an old time hay baler and carried the mail between Needmore and Fair Play.

On Sept. 2, 1911, Charley married Pearl Blevins Hamilton, a widow with three small children. Charley and Pearl had one daughter, Jerlie Ethel, (born Sept. 6, 1914). On Feb. 27, 1915, Charley died from appendicitis. He is buried at Lindley Prairie Cemetery, near Bear Creek beside Corda and her baby that was buried with her.

Pearl and children moved to north Missouri. Merit married and Coy moved to California. Henry went to live with Merit in Cedar County.

Henry was unhappy and lived with different relatives. Later, he enjoyed a carefree life for some years, following the wheat harvesters in Kansas.

Cuba was born near Needmore on July 12, 1908, the seventh daughter of George and "Mint" Gothard. She was a fun-loving, mischievous child who loved school, singing and church. She attended the Needmore Church and the Eldorado School.

As a young woman, Cuba worked as a practical nurse, assisting in the birth of many area children. While helping her sister Bess, after Coy Jr. was born, Cuba got to know Bess's brother-in-law, Henry. They began corresponding and dated off and on for the next four years.

On Jan. 2, 1932 they married in Bolivar, MO and settled near Greenfield, MO. In early 1933 Cuba and Henry moved to a farm between Fair Play and Bear Creek in Polk County, on the Cave Springs Road. Alta Marie was born there on Dec. 1, 1933. A couple of years later they moved nearer to Bear Creek to a farm known as the Martha Fox place. Charles Kenneth "Kenny" was born there on May 19, 1938.

While living there, Henry and Cuba went to a little Baptist Church with services held in the Mountain Grove schoolhouse north of their home. They joined there and were baptized in Bear Creek River by Arthur Wynes. Around the regular roads it was quite a distance to church and times were hard and there was no gas money. So they walked, crossing the river of a foot log with Marie on Dad's shoulders and climbed the bluff to the schoolhouse. Through their lifetime they remained devout members of the Missionary Baptist Church and had a deep trust in God.

In 1941 the Coopers moved to a farm northwest of Fair Play, known as the Paynter place. Times were better. They joined Oak Grove Baptist Church.

In 1943 they moved west, across the fields to the Barker place where Shirley Louise was born on May 3, 1946.

In 1951 Henry and Cuba bought a farm near Bear Creek and lived there until 1956 when they moved to Independence, MO planning to return to the farm and retire.

On Feb. 3, 1960, Henry died suddenly of a heart attack. He was returned to Cedar County and buried on February 7 at Lindley Prairie. Cuba remained in Independence and raised Shirley. In 1963 they became charter members of Charity Missionary Baptist Church in Kansas City, where Cuba remained a member until August 1993 when she joined Reach Out Missionary Baptist Church.

She sold the farm in 1969 and bought a home in Independence. After retiring in 1972, she continued to be an inspiration and joy to her children and grandchildren.

On Sept. 10, 1980, Kenny was killed in a traffic accident in northwestern Missouri. He left his wife, Edna and six children.

On Dec. 7, 1993, Cuba died suddenly at her home of a burst aneurysm, with Shirley at her side. Her funeral was held at Jericho Church in Independence, with graveside services at Lindley Prairie Cemetery, where she was laid to rest between her beloved husband and son.

The Coopers were average people whose home was open to everyone. You were always greeted with a smile and open arms. *Submitted by Marie Lane*

COOPER - Charles Kenneth "Kenny" Cooper, son of Henry Richard and Cuba D. Gothard Cooper was born May 19, 1938, in a two-room log house, which sat above the Bear Creek bottoms, two miles northeast of Bear Creek in Cedar County. A 4-year-old sister, Alta Marie, welcomed baby brother.

Charles Kenneth Cooper, 1956

A couple of years after Kenny's birth, the Coopers moved to a farm southwest of Fair Play in Polk County. Within three years they moved west, across the fields to a house on the Cedar/Polk County line. It was here that his sister Shirley was born on May 3, 1946. Kenny attended Fair Play Schools from 1943 to 1952. His parents bought a farm near Bear Creek and moved in the spring of 1952. He attended Stockton High School, where he played football and raised prize winning Chester White hogs, graduating in May 1956. In the early spring of 1956 Kenny married Pauline Nichols. After graduation, they moved to Independence, MO, in Jackson County where their two children were born. In the summer of 1959 Kenny and Pauline were divorced.

On Feb. 3, 1960, Kenny lost his dad to a sudden heart attack and that summer he moved with Pauline and his babies to Phoenix, AZ, in a final attempt to reconcile their marriage. The reconciliation was short-lived but Kenny remained in Phoenix.

While attending the Sunny Slope Church of God near Phoenix, he met Edna Laverne Bucher and on May 28, 1961, they were married in Winter Haven, CA. Shortly after their marriage, they moved to Pueblo, CO, where their three children were born.

In November 1967 the Coopers moved to Independence, MO where Kenny spent the rest of his life. They spent a lot of time with his mother and family. He enjoyed hunting and fishing with his children and loved to watch his children play ball games.

Kenny was saved in 1950 and joined Oak Grove Baptist Church. He remained a member there until 1976, when he joined Jericho Missionary Baptist Church in Independence, MO, where he found great joy and peace and loved attending church with his family. He drove a truck for A. Reich & Sons delivering produce throughout Missouri, driving 300 to 500 miles a day. With his friendly manner and big smile, he made many friends on his daily routes.

On a beautiful fall day, Sept. 10, 1980, Kenny was killed when his truck and another truck collided about 150 miles north of Kansas City, near Milan, MO, in Sullivan County. He is buried beside his parents in Lindley Prairie Cemetery in Cedar County.

Eight years after Kenny's death, a young woman, Jane Smith Bartholomew, born Feb. 1, 1961, and adopted at birth, contacted Kenny's mother, searching for her birth father, Kenneth Cooper. She could not meet her father but she found a grandmother who welcomed her with kindness and love. They were a joy to each other until Cuba's death in 1993.

Kenny's children: Randy Scott, born Dec. 11, 1956, married Kim Keisling, March 15, 1980; two children, Jonathan Wayne, born July 4, 1982, and Amber Christine, born January 24, 1984. Divorced September 13, 1989 and married Terri Hicks, Feb. 14, 1995; one child, Garrett Scott, born Nov. 7, 1996.

Robin Lynn, born June 24, 1958, married Scott Keene Nov. 14, 1981; one child, William Cody Kenneth, born Dec. 16, 1983.

Jane Lindell, born Feb. 1, 1961, married Richard Bartholomew July 11, 1987.

Timothy Lane, born Aug. 2, 1962, married Shannon Renee Dohle June 20, 1981. One child, Nathaniel Quinn, born June 19, 2000.

Kenneth Richard, born Feb. 14, 1965, married Krista Bookout Oct. 1, 1994; two children, Chelsea Alexandra, born Feb. 13, 1996, and Kenneth Devon, born June 2, 1997.

Rebecca Dawn, born Sept. 20, 1967, married Watson Bond Dec. 7, 1996; three children: Charles Lester, born Dec. 25, 1988, David Ibrey, born June 10, 1997 and Brittany Alexandria, born Dec. 20, 1999. *Submitted by Robin Keene*

COOPER - Charley Cooper was born in Columbia County, PA on Jan. 30, 1863. His parents were Phillip and Lavina (Nagles) Cooper. The family moved to Cedar County, MO around 1869 and was listed in the 1870 Cedar County census in Madison Township.

Frances Corda Simmons was born Jan. 22, 1870 in Polk County, MO. Her parents were Merritt and Esther (Phipps) Simmons. Sometime between 1875 and 1879, Esther, her mother, died and is buried at Gum Springs Cemetery with her youngest son, Richard Simmons, 1875-1928, buried beside her.

Charley Cooper married Corda Simmons on March 12, 1888 at the home of her father in Bear Creek, MO. They made their home west of Needmore, near the Little Sac River bottoms. By the 1900 census, Corda had given birth to six babies and only two sons had lived. By Dr. Alder's records, she gave birth to a baby girl on April 16, 1896. On Feb. 21, 1904, their youngest child, Henry, was born. On Aug. 25, 1905, Corda died in childbirth. The baby also died and is buried with her, beside the other babies, in Lindley Prairie Cemetery. Corda's stepsister, Sultana Agnew, who died in 1897, is buried a few feet west of her. Corda's weathered tombstone reads: " Frances Corda Cooper Wife of Charley Cooper Born Jan. 22, 1870- died Aug. 25, 1905 A loving wife, a mother dear A faithful friend is buried here."

Standing at Lindley Prairie looking at her grave beside those little nameless markers, you can almost feel the total sorrow Charley must have felt as he left his wife and baby there. At their mother's death, Merit was 16, Coy was 11 and Henry was 18 months. Coy took care of Henry, while Merit helped Charley make a living. Charley was a farmer and operated an old time hay baler, powered by horses. He also carried the mail between Needmore and Fair Play for a while.

On Sept. 12, 1911, Charley married Pearl Blevens Hamilton, a widow with three young children. The two families merged and were very happy together. Pearl was a warm, loving stepmother to the Cooper boys. A daughter, Jerlie Ethel, was born on Sept. 6, 1914. Pearl cared for Henry until the family was separated by the death of Charley on Feb. 27, 1915. Charley is buried beside his first wife, Corda and their babies at Lindley Prairie Cemetery in Polk County. Twin sons of Merit and Cora Cooper are also buried beside them.

After Charley died Pearl took her three children and moved to north Missouri. Cedar County court records document that Merit acted as Henry's guardian so Henry went to live with Merit. Coy moved to California. Henry wanted to be with Pearl and family, so he walked from Cedar County to Norborne, MO where Pearl was living. Pearl would tell of him being half-starved and cold when he arrived. Merit traveled to north Missouri and took Henry back to Cedar County.

Merritt, Coy, Jerlie and Henry Cooper

At Charley and Corda's graves, looking southeast across the cemetery, you can see the graves of two of their sons, Henry and Coy. Nearby are buried four of their sons.

Children of Charley Cooper:

Merit Phillip, born Nov. 8, 1889, died Oct. 10, 1958 in Exeter, CA, buried in Deep Creek Cemetery, Farmersville, CA. Married Cora Chism Oct. 7, 1910; four sons: Uel C., Lloyd L., twin sons died at birth.

Coy, born July 7, 1894, died March 20, 1971, Polk County, MO, buried Lindley Prairie Cemetery, married Blanche Ingerham May 17, 1919 (died 1923). Married Bessie Gothard April 16, 1926; five sons: Coy Jr., Jack P., Joe K., Bobby K. and Gary D.

Henry Richard, born Feb. 21, 1904, died Feb. 3, 1960 in Independence, MO, buried Lindley Prairie. Married Cuba Gothard Jan. 2, 1932; three children: Marie Lane, Charles Kenneth and Shirley Moss.

Jerlie Ethel, born Sept. 6, 1914, died March 11, 1980 in Liberty, MO; married Chas Harrison Sept. 23, 1934 (1907-1970). Married Thorvald Damker Jan. 6, 1973; three sons: Charles L., James R. and Joseph D. Harrison. *Submitted by Amy Felix*

COVERT - George W. Covert was born in 1857 to L. B. Covert and Elsie Douglas. George had been a resident of Collin County, TX. For some unknown reason, George traveled to Polk County, MO where he met and married his bride, Amanda Angeline Hook, on Feb. 10, 1878. She was the daughter of Robert R. and Susan Hook.

George and Amanda had two children: Robert Luke Covert, born Jan. 21, 1879 in Polk County, MO and Ernest Edward Gibson Covert, born Nov. 21, 1880 in Collin County, TX. Shortly after Ernest was born the Coverts moved back to Polk County, MO. George unexpectedly died in 1882 and is buried at Enon Cemetery in Polk County, MO.

Ernest Edward Gibson Covert and Jesse Vinson (Brown) Covert

Amanda Covert then married Liberty Copeland in 1883 after both had lost their first spouses. Liberty had four children from his previous marriage. They added to their growing family by having eight more children, for a total of 14 children between them. Liberty and Amanda's children were Sarah A. (born 1884); Alta Mae (born 1887); Rhoda Ella (born 1891); Albert (born 1892); Leonard (FL) (born 1892): Jessie Jewell (born 1895); Addie Elizabeth (born 1896) and Everett E. (born 1900).

George and Amanda Covert's oldest son Robert married Mamie Thompson. They had one son, Leland Covert, born Oct. 3, 1908 in Polk County, MO. Robert died Feb. 27, 1959 and is buried in the Shady Grove Cemetery.

Ernest E. Covert, George and Amanda's youngest son, married Jesse Vinson Brown on March 17, 1912 at the bride's residence in Polk County, MO. She was the daughter of Jeremiah Vinson Brown and Mary Jane Hensley. Ernest was a farmer in Polk County and Jesse, a homemaker. They had six children: Wanda Lucille (born 1914); Allen Brown (born 1916); Helen Evelyn (born 1919); Mary Angeline (born 1920); George Vinson (born 1925); and Gerald Dean (born 1929). Jesse (Brown) Covert died Feb. 7, 1955 and Ernest E. Covert died March 16, 1965. Both are buried in Pleasant Ridge Cemetery in Polk County, MO.

Wanda Lucille Covert, the oldest child of Ernest and Jesse, married Lonnie Wesley Scurlock in 1936. To this union, two children were born: Shirley Jean in 1936 and Sharron Kay in 1945. Shirley married Loren Laird in 1956 and Sharron married Lyle Garretson in 1966. Lucille (Covert) Scurlock died Sept. 9, 1995. Lonnie Scurlock died Aug. 21, 1998. Both are buried in Greenwood Cemetery in Bolivar, MO.

Allen Brown Covert married Wilma Lea Dodd. To this union, four children were born: Jerry Allen (born 1940), Judy Lea (born 1944), Rita Jane (born 1945) and Becky June (born 1952). Allen died in 1985 and Wilma in 1991. Both are laid to rest at Pleasant Hope Cemetery in Polk County, MO.

Helen Evelyn Covert married James Lester Brakebill in 1940. They had two daughters: Beverly Kay (born 1942) and Linda Sue (born 1947). James Brakebill died in 1991.

Mary Angeline Covert first married Lloyd Combs in 1961. He died in 1990 and she next married Howard Griffin in 1992. Mary did not have any children but enjoyed spending time with her nieces and nephews. Mary passed away in 1995.

George Vinson Covert first married Marilyn Burchett in 1947. They had two daughters: Cheryl Ann (born 1948) and Carol Jeanne (born 1950). George then married Doris Highfill in 1951. George and Doris had four children: Patricia Irene (born 1952); Joyce Fern (born 1954); Milos Lee (born 1956) and George Steve (born 1958).

George passed away and was buried at Pleasant Ridge Cemetery in Polk County, MO in 1970.

Gerald Dean Covert married Shirley Parscall in 1953. To this union three children were born: Charlotte Ann (born 1955), Wayne Edward (born 1956) and Eddie Dean (born 1964). Dean Covert died in April of 1991. *Submitted by Sharron (Scurlock) Garretson*

Children of Charley and Mary (Cates) Cowden, Oren, Coy, Irene, Lonnie, Bertis, Otis, Arthur and Gladys

COWDEN – The name Cowden came from Ireland. The name originally started out as McCowden. When the families came to America, the spelling of the last name changed and various spellings of the name started. Cowdin, Cowdon, Cowen, Cowin and Cowan are variations of the name Cowden.

J. L. (believed to be John) was born in 1832 in Tennessee. In the 1880 census records of Dallas County, J. L. was listed with a spouse and six children. No marriage records have been found for his marriage to this spouse. Her name was Sarah, maiden name being Potts. She was born in 1836 in Missouri. The children listed with them are James H., George W., Margaret J., Mary E., William "Willie" or "Bill" and Charles A. "Charley." Charley was born July 7, 1873 in Buffalo, MO. He married Mary Cates. Her parents were Charlie (a Baptist minister) and Martha (Needham) Cates. J. L. and Sarah are buried at Shady Grove Cemetery. They both died in 1912. They share a cemetery stone.

Charley and Mary moved around a lot due to a doctor's order that Mary live outdoors in the country. The family mainly lived in very remote areas of Polk County. They spent most of their lives in Aldrich. They had nine children. Tommy married Willia Hutcheson. They raised their family in Iowa. Lonnie married Ruby Palmer. They also raised their family in Iowa. Bertis married Olie (Price) Wilson. He never had children of his own, but he raised Olie's children as his own. The family lived in Bolivar. Coy married Blanche West. They raised their family in Kansas. Arthur married Christine Sawyer. They raised their family in Kansas City and Polk County. Gladys first married Ernest Diass; after he died she married Ray Norris. She could never have children of her own, so she spoiled everyone else's children. She lived in several states but in the late 1960s she and her second husband Ray moved to Bolivar. Irene married Orville Gregg. They raised their family in Washington. Oren married Ruby Stanley. The family lived most of their early years in Kansas City. Sometime around the late 1960s the family settled in Polk County. They lived most of that time in Bolivar. Oren was a Baptist minister. He presided at the wedding of his twin brother, Otis. Otis married Gertrude Cowden. The family moved around a lot in the early years. In the late 1950s the family settled in Bolivar to stay. Otis made his living mainly painting houses. Otis had the gift of gab; he never met a stranger. He always had a story to tell or a bargain to sell.

The children of Charley and Mary would always have big family get-togethers. The last big family get-together that took place before they all passed away was in the early 1970s. Their favorite thing to do was play "Pitch," a card game. Some of the games would get really intense. They taught their children to play and today the game is still played. We all remember the old time players; we can still see them in our minds today. *Submitted by Beverly (Cowden) Manes*

COWDEN – Otis Cowden was born March 13, 1912 around Aldrich, MO. He was one of nine children born to Charley and Mary (Cates) Cowden.

In 1938 Otis was told to go to Abe and Hester Waggoner's house. There was a girl there that was helping care for their son that Otis should meet. So, Otis made an excuse to go to the Waggoner home. There he met Gertrude Durham. She told him she couldn't date at that time. He said, "Don't forget me!"

A year later they met again. Both attended a church revival being held by sisters Nora and Lela Seiner at the Assembly of God Church located off the Bolivar square. After church Otis asked if he could walk Gertrude home. He returned to her home the next evening to ask her out. She said she had to ask her father because of her age. Gertrude Durham was born Nov. 21, 1924. She was the daughter of Walter and Mary (Ballinger) Durham. Walter approved of the courtship. Otis had no driver's license so he had his brother Arthur take him to see Gertrude. After only a courtship of four weeks Otis and Gertrude married on Sept. 9, 1939. Otis's twin brother, Oren, a Baptist preacher, married the couple at the Durham home.

In the early years of his life Otis broke horses for people in the area. He also worked for REA, Bill Roberts Chevrolet, and the city. He did odd jobs painting houses that eventually led to having his own business. He had a license to preach but never did.

Gertrude held a few jobs. She worked at the old garment factory, the Nifty Café and the Red Cedar Motel.

Otis and Gertrude had eight children. Lela was born in Fair Play, MO. Ronnie was born in Lakewood, CA. Jane was born in Kansas City, KS. Beverly was born in Bolivar. Margie was born in Kansas City, MO. Janett was born in Bolivar. Connie and Ronda were born in Humansville, MO. All of the Cowden children attended Bolivar schools at one time or another.

Otis had several hobbies. He liked to fish, hunt and go to garage sales. He also made marbles from rocks. Some of his rock marbles are on display at the North Ward Museum.

Gertrude's hobbies included making clothes for her family. She would look at a picture and make her own pattern from newspapers. She also liked to make dolls, quilts and crocheted rugs for the family.

Descendants of Charley and Mary Cates Cowden, The Otis and Gertrude Cowden family

Along with their children and their spouses, the Cowdens have 25 grandchildren and 15 great-grandchildren. One of their grandsons is enlisted in the army. Their daughter Ronda and her husband Terry Mitchell, along with their children, received the first home built by "Habitat for Humanity" in Bolivar in 2002.

The family is still very close; most live in Polk County. Christmas is still spent at the Cowden home. Most of the time it's standing room only!

This article is in memory of Otis Cowden who passed away Dec. 6, 1995 and three grandchildren: Mike Cates (son of Lela and Lloyd Cates) who passed away in 1997; Tammy, who passed away in 1964 and Kevin in 1986, both children of Jane (Cowden) Sanders. *Submitted by Jane (Cowden) Sanders*

COWEN - The oldest known ancestor of the Cowen family was Peter who was born between 1770 and 1775. Records indicate he was in Logan County, KY in 1805 and possibly as early as 1799. Peter and his wife, Mary "Polly," born 1789 in North Carolina, had 12 children, all born in Kentucky: Elizabeth, Jane, Nancy, Sarah, Ann, Margaret (probably died young), Henry P., Margaret "Peggy," Mary "Polly," John Quincy Adams, Louisa Caroline and Peter Marion. They resided in Simpson County, KY, which was formed in 1819 from parts of Logan, Warren and Allen Counties.

Peter died in Kentucky about 1837. His wife Mary and children, Sarah, Henry P., Margaret, Mary, John, Louisa and Peter migrated to Polk County, MO in 1842, settling in the area which later became part of Hickory County. It is possible they came with daughter, Jane and her husband Michael Holland. Michael was from nearby

Warren County, KY. He was related to the Hollands who settled in Polk, Hickory and Benton Counties. It is unknown if the older daughters, Elizabeth and Nancy, remained in Kentucky or came to Missouri. Ann married Erasmus Bunch in 1841, raised a family and remained in Simpson County until her death in 1897.

Sarah Cowen married Jordan Mashburn in Polk County, MO, November 1842. Mary married first, Chesley C. Pierce and second, Daniel Bartsche. Henry P., born in 1821, married Elizabeth Massey in 1850. Elizabeth was born in 1827 in Tennessee. Margaret and John Q. A. apparently did not marry. Peter M. married Nancy Bradshaw and later moved to Madison County, AR.

Henry P. and Elizabeth Cowen

Henry P. and Elizabeth Massey Cowen were parents of Mary Frances, wife of Francis Parsons; John Henry, husband of Lucinda Williams; Peter Marion, husband of first, Allie M. Langford and second, Nancy Luella Carley; Joshua Luster, husband of Amanda J. Mason; Nancy Jane wife of John A. Williams; Margaret Ann, wife of Lafayette B. Dooley; America Elizabeth, wife of first, Allen Harman Ward and second, Burrell Boone Pitts; Sherman Alexander, husband of Nancy J. King; and Andrew Franklin, husband of Irene Hollingsworth. Most of this generation remained in Hickory County with the exception of America who moved to Oklahoma and Andrew who, along with his children and their families, homesteaded in Sedan, Union County, NM in 1911.

Henry P. and Elizabeth Cowen celebrated their 50th wedding anniversary in 1900 surrounded by 300 guests. Henry died March 4, 1901 and Elizabeth followed Aug. 29, 1901. In part, Henry's obituary reads: "Uncle Henry was a faithful husband, good father, a precious grandfather, a good neighbor, a good, quiet and law abiding citizen, a good and faithful member of the Baptist church for about 40 years."

The original Cowen property is now beneath Pomme de Terre Lake near Galmey, MO. Many of the first three generations of this family are buried at Dooly Bend Cemetery in Hickory County. *Submitted by Sharon Cowen*

CRAIN - Charles and Abigail Crain were from the Greenville, SC region; both were probably born in that vicinity circa 1770-1780. They migrated with their children to Grainger County, TN circa 1810. They lived there for approximately 20 years. Several of their sons were married in Grainger County including Charles Jr., who married Mary Wright; John, who married Elizabeth Simmons and Pleasant, who married Ruth. There was probably another son named Davis.

This extended family moved on to Polk County, MO in the late 1830s. They were enumerated here in the 1840 census. They settled on land between Aldrich and Fair Play, homesteading on several acres. Charles died between 1840 and 1850. Abigail then lived with Charles Jr.'s family.

Pleasant and Ruthey's children were Mary, Abigail, Charles Nelson, Archibald, Mahala, Sarah J., Pamela, Pleasant A. Jr., William H. and Daniel R. Pleasant and Ruthey were charter members of the Mt. Zion Baptist Church where many of the Crains were active members. See the history of Polk County Missionary Baptist.

This writer's great-grandfather, Nelson Crain, married Ruth Sophia Abbott. They were the parents of William Franklin "Pap," Susan Elaine, James Hardin, Henry Newton, Rhoda, Margaret, Orlena, Samuel, Joseph, Annie, Thomas Jasper, and Farmer Edgar. For a comprehensive genealogy of Nelson and Ruth (Abbott) Crain, see *The Descendants of Joseph and Keziah N. Abbott* by Noble G. Abbott.

William Franklin "Pap" married Mary Jane Sutherlin/Sutherland. They were the parents of Allen Lonzo, Elbert Richard, Fannie Elizabeth, twins William Nelson "Bill" and Belle, Lilly May and Aurelia. William Nelson married Margaret May (Taylor) Phipps and were the parents of Murtes William and Bernis Lucille.

Several of the Crains served and were killed during the Civil War. They were also active in Polk County politics, holding several different offices. This was a large, prolific family that married with other Polk County families, which is where several still make their home. The progeny of the Crain family is far reaching in Polk County. *Submitted by Bernis Lucille (Crain) Shay*

CRAIN - Clay Stanley Crain was born April 3, 1894 near Fair Play, Polk County, MO. He is the son of Thomas Jasper "Whitey" and Martha Drusilla Harrison Crain.

In 1900 when Clay was 4 years old he, along with his two sisters and mother, lived in Madison Township in the Lewis Harrison household.

Clay Crain, Ada (Wilson) Crain, Genieve, Wilson and Betty Sue

Clay married Minnie Ada Wilson March 5, 1916 at the home of A. W. Slater in Wishart, MO. Ada was born Feb. 12, 1898 in Polk County. She was the daughter of Rufus K. and Clarrisa C. Davis Wilson.

On Jan. 22, 1918 Clay received classification of 4A for the draft of the United States Army. He was 22 years old, married, and had one baby. He was never drafted.

Clay and Ada had three children. Gladys Geneive "Jennie" was born March 1, 1917. Wilson Stanley "Buddy" was born Aug. 27, 1927. Betty Sue was born April 3, 1936. Clay was very excited that his second daughter was born on his birthday.

Jennie married Harold Clark and has a daughter, Sandra Kay, born in 1944. They have lived in Harrison, AR since 1957. Jennie was a bookkeeper and has been retired since she was 68 years old.

Buddy married Doris Dodson from the Eudora area. They had four children. Jimmy Dean was born in 1950. Linda Karol was born in 1953. David Allen was born in 1960. Dwight Gene was born in 1967. Buddy and Doris moved to Belen, NM in 1952. Buddy retired as parts manager of an auto dealership. He died Dec. 11, 1993 and Doris died Jan. 15, 1997. They are buried in Belen.

Sue married Joe McDonald from Springfield, MO. They had three daughters: Joni Belen, born in 1960; Lesli Denise, born in 1961 and Kari Linn, born in 1962. Sue works in their accounting office in Springfield.

Clay managed the Farmers Exchange in Eudora, Walnut Grove and Wishart. Ada was taught how to do the bookkeeping. She passed this knowledge on to Jennie so she could help out when the other children were born.

Clay and his family were members of the Enon Baptist Church. They were very active in the church. One Sunday the preacher said he would be over for fried chicken and some of Ada's delicious pies. You see Clay always played baseball on Sunday afternoon. But this Sunday Clay sat on the porch with the preacher. The preacher took a little nap and Clay thought this would be a good time to go to the ballgame. Sunday night in church the preacher told what Brother Clay had done. The next Sunday in church Brother Clay had a few words to share. He said the preacher was welcome any Sunday for dinner, but if there was a baseball game that would be where he would be found. Clay was a man of few words.

Clay and Ada lived on a farm and grew a garden. Clay always stayed in trouble when it came plowing time. He would always let the horse step on the plants. They also grew corn and a little wheat. They milked cows and sold cream. Later when the milk routes were started, they sold milk. Times were hard and eventually they moved off the farm to a house with a few acres. Rural electric was coming to the Wishart area around 1950. This house was wired for electricity. One afternoon there was a short in the wiring and the house burned completely down. After the house fire Clay and his family moved north of Bolivar. Ada died on Aug. 28, 1950 at age 52 of a cerebral hemorrhage.

In 1954 Clay married Myrtle Hocker of Bolivar. She had one daughter, Wanda. Clay worked for Teters Nursery in Bolivar. On Jan. 22, 1958 while delivering flowers for the nursery to a funeral on ice slick roads he was injured in an auto accident. Clay was in a Springfield, MO hospital for a time. While there, Myrtle kept a constant bedside vigil. He never regained consciousness and died Aug. 6, 1960 in the hospital at Nevada, MO. He and Ada are buried in the Enon Cemetery near Wishart. *Submitted by G. G. "Jennie" Crain Clark*

CRAIN - Thomas Jasper "Whitey" Crain was born near Fair Play, Polk County, MO on March 18, 1872. He was the son of Nelson Crain, born May 6, 1836 in Grainger County, TN and Ruth Abbott Crain, born in 1834 in North Carolina. Nelson and Ruth had married Jan. 24, 1853 in Polk County, MO.

On Dec. 9, 1888 Jasper married Martha Drusilla Harrison. Martha was the daughter of William Lewis and Jane Wilson Harrison. She was born May 3, 1875.

To Jasper and Mattie, as her family and friends called her, three children were born. Bertha B. was born in December 1890. Their son, Clay Stanley, was born April 3, 1894. Clara S. was born April 11, 1895.

Bertha died young. She is buried in Enon Cemetery near Wishart, Polk County, MO. Kay has no records of Clara.

Jasper and Mattie divorced in the early 1900s. Jasper moved to Kansas and married Janet Davey on Feb. 28, 1909. Mattie stayed in the Polk County area and married Thomas Asberry Hawkins.

Clay married Minnie Ada Wilson, the daughter of Rufus and Clarissa Davis Wilson, March 5, 1916 in Polk County, MO. To this union three children were born: Gladys Genieve "Jennie," born March 1, 1917; Wilson Stanley "Buddy," born Aug. 27, 1927 and died Dec. 11, 1993 in Belen, NM and Betty Sue, born April 3, 1936.

Ada died Aug. 24, 1950 at their home in Bolivar, MO. Clay died Aug. 6, 1960 as the result of an auto accident on Jan. 22, 1958.

Jasper and his second wife, Janet, had four children: one daughter and three sons.

Jasper died Feb. 11, 1958 in Monrovia, CA. He is buried in the Mt. Olive Cemetery in Pittsburg, KS along with his second wife. *Submitted by Kay Webb*

Richard and Ethel Cravens

CRAVENS - Richard Clay Cravens and wife, Ethel F. Hill, moved to Polk County in September 1993 from Camden County, MO. Richard grew up in Wright County, MO; Ethel grew up in Camden County. Both attended Southwest Baptist College before meeting there and their marriage Sept. 30, 1950. Ethel holds a BS degree in social science and elementary education (1964) from Drury. Richard holds a BS degree in elementary education from SMS (1959), a master's degree in elementary school administration from Drury (1963) and educational specialists in school administration degree from MU (1978). They have three children: Sara L. Stock, of Jefferson City, MO; Richard D. Cravens, of Columbia, MO; and Roxy Jo Hudson of Bolivar. Sara married Ed Stock and has children Jennifer and Anna. Roxy married first, Tom Stanford and has children JoBeth Ann and Katelyn, married second, Kevin Hudson. The family lived on the original homestead of James Cannon Claxton until 1965 when they moved to Boonville, MO. In 1979 they moved to Glasgow, MO and retired from there.

Kevin and Roxy Hudson with daughters JoBeth and Katy Stanford

Richard's ancestors traveled from Randolph County, NC through Tennessee to Ray County, MO about 1830. About 1890 Richard's paternal grandparents, Riley B. and Sylvia A. (Wyman) Cravens, moved to Wright County, MO. His grandparents farmed and operated small country stores at Excelsior Springs, Old Mint and near Grove Springs, MO during the late 1800s and early 1900s.

Richard and Ethel both attended SBC, SMS, Drury and MU, both certifying for teaching in Missouri schools, (Richard, 36 years, Ethel, 31 years.) Starting in one-room schools of Laclede and Wright Counties, they worked several years in Boonville, Fayette and retired from Glasgow, MO schools in 1982 (Ethel); 1984 (Richard).

Richard's mother, Sarah E. Claxton, was the daughter of James Cannon and Jeritha L. (Baker) (Rodgers) Claxton, early settlers in Wright County, MO (1850s).

John Hill (about 1810-1850), Ethel's ancestor, traveled from Scotland and England through the eastern US to Moniteau County, MO. Descendant James Arthur Hill married Ethel T. Jackson, who had a common ancestor (Anthony Jackson born in England, 1599-1666) with President Andrew Jackson and Stonewall Jackson, a famous general.

The Hills, since the early 1800s, lived in Moniteau, Camden, Pettis and Stoddard Counties in Missouri.

Ethel (Hill) Cravens' mother was Roxie F. Eidson, daughter of B. N. Eidson and Rebecca M. (Nations) Eidson of Camden County, MO. The Eidsons are traceable to Virginia and are English in origin. *Submitted by Richard Cravens*

Robert, Elmer and Arizona (Gladden-Harris) Crawford

CRAWFORD - Elisha Crawford was born 1820 in Virginia, the son of Moses and Nancy Chlorsey Crawford. He was married in 1842 to Leutila Sheet in Indiana. They had a son Henry. Elisha married Hannah Peterson in 1847 in Illinois and had five children: Sarah, Abraham, Josiah, Vinton and Riley. They moved to Polk County in 1858 and bought 228 acres. They brought two Negro slaves with them. These slaves stayed with Elisha and were buried on the farm. Mary, Martha, Dulcina, James and Robert were born in Polk County. Elisha died in 1872. Hannah married Patrick Rogers in 1875.

Back: Arizona (Gladden Harris) Crawford and Otis Crawford; Front: James, Fannie, Rosa Mae (Myres), Elmer, Ruby and Junior Crawford

Robert Lonzo was born in 1869. He spent most of his childhood in Riley's household. Robert remembers one day some Indians came and told Riley that the chief had died and they were there to give them the Crawford's inheritance. Riley asked them to leave, stating they had no Indian blood in them. Time has passed and now it has been found that Nancy was a Cherokee Indian. In 1890 Robert married Elizabeth Snipes; their children were Ellie, James, Henry and Mattie. In about 1897, Robert, master of the wagon train, took his family and Hannah and Patrick to Union County, OR. In 1898 Elizabeth died and was bur-

Back: James Ralph II, Marilyn Kay and Doris Evelyn Crawford; Front: James Ralph Crawford, Lois Evelyn LeBow and Mally Rosetta Bolling

ied in Elgin, OR. In 1906, Robert married Arizonia (Gladden) Harris. Their children were Elmer and Addie (twins). Robert hauled logs and worked with the lumber mill. Arizonia worked for a doctor. She told that she gave out a lot of small, white bags of baking soda to the rich ladies of the town. With his family, Robert came to Polk County in 1910. They stayed a short time, moved to Ozark County and a child Edna was born in 1912. Robert was a truck farmer and, with his wagon and tram, had a freight line from Theodosia, MO to Springfield, MO and back. This he ran until the early 1930s; the Depression hit hard and they moved to Polk County on their farm with the Breshears Cemetery on it. Robert died in 1950, Arizonia died in 1953 and both are buried at Breshears Cemetery.

Back: Junior Crawford, Billy John Hampton, Ruby Peterson, Otis Crawford, James Crawford and Kreta Chaney; Middle: Rhonda Kerr, Fannie Hamilton, Dedia Marris, Ethel Fisher and John Shryer; Front row: Willa Thomas, Blanch (Friend Hampton) Crawford and Linda Jordan

William Elmer was born in 1909 in Oregon. His childhood was spent on his father's farm. As a young man he taught school. In 1928 he married Rosa Myers. They bought a farm by his father's farm. Their children were: James, Otis, Fannie, Junior, Ruby and Maxine. Rosa died in 1940. Elmer married Blanch Hampton in 1944. Blanch had five children. In 1947, Elmer, with his family, moved to Elkton, MO on their farm and Dedia, Kreta, Joan and Linda were born here. They bought and sold several places; twice went to California to work in the fruit harvest and cannery. Elmer died in 1983 and Blanch died in 1994.

James Ralph was born May 18, 1929. Growing up on a farm, James helped his father cut posts and firewood for sale. One summer with his Aunt Addie, another summer with Aunt Edna, he went to California to work the fruit harvest. In 1949 he married Doris Black and their children were Molly Rosetta (Boyd) Bolling, Lois Evelyn LeBow, James Ralph and Marilyn Kay Crawford, all born in California. Their grandchildren are Robert Boyd, Samantha Boyd, Thomas, Tamanaira and Vanessa LeBow, James III, Lee and Trina Crawford. *Submitted by Thomas F. LeBow II*

Francis Monroe and Nora May (Creed) Ross and their 5 daughters (left and right) Opal, Pauline, Virginia, Wilma and Delta

CREED - Nora May Creed (born Sept. 22, 1889; died March 25, 1969) was the fifth child of Sarah and John Creed. She was born and raised in Polk County, near Morrisville. She had six brothers and sisters: Arthur, Jim, Delie (a girl), Janie, Goldie and Luther Creed. All of them lived in Polk County for a part of their lives.

Nora May Creed married Francis Monroe Ross (born Sept. 4, 1891; died Sept. 26, 1956) on March 1, 1913 at Bolivar, MO. Monroe was the oldest of 10 children. His parents lived on a farm about two miles south of Morrisville. His parents were Thomas Francis and Eulalia Monroe (Woodard) Ross.

Monroe and Nora lived on his parents' farm a few years before buying a farm north of where the Morrisville Railroad Station used to be. They lived there until October of 1922. They then bought a farm in Greene County near Walnut Grove. They had seven children.

Twins, Velma and Leland Ross, born Dec. 30, 1913. Leland died at birth. Velma died Jan. 23, 1923. They are buried at the Morrisville Cemetery.

Wilma Francis Ross was born Dec. 1, 1917 on the Ross farm south of Morrisville. There were four houses on the Ross farm. One house was called the "weaning house." When one of the children married they could live there until they chose to move elsewhere. Monroe and Nora were the first to live in the "weaning house." Later, George Edward and Ruby Ross Booher also lived there. Wilma was born in the "weaning house" and she married Walter Marion Parrish (born July 18, 1916; died Sept. 27, 1984) on Nov. 27, 1937. His parents were William S. and Minnie Abbott Parrish. Wilma and Marion had three children: George Edward Parrish (born Sept. 17, 1938; died Oct. 17, 1939); Larry Dean Parrish (born Jan. 4, 1941) and Jerry Lynn Parrish (born July 1, 1946).

Delta Lee Ross was born Aug. 12, 1919 near Morrisville. She married William Thomas and they had two children: Billy and Cheryl Thomas.

Goldie Virginia Ross was born Dec. 27, 1922 north of Morrisville. Their farm was just north of the Morrisville Railroad Station. She married Andy Haze and they had one son, Rickey Dean Haze.

Opal Irene Ross was born Nov. 7, 1924 at their farm near Walnut Grove. She married Chris Christensen and they had no children.

Gladys Pauline Ross was born May 20, 1927 near Walnut Grove. She married Chester King on Feb. 14, 1941; they immediately got on a train and went to San Diego, CA and they built a new house to live in. They had two children: Steven Ross King and Cynthia King. *Submitted by Wilma Parrish*

CRIPPIN – Dr. Richard Eugene Crippin and Mary Ellen Schiltz Crippin became residence of Bolivar, MO in June of 1965. They were originally from Marceline and Wien, MO.

Dr. Crippin had just graduated from Chiropractic College and they picked Bolivar for their new home.

Their chiropractic office was set up at West Highway 32 across from the state Highway Building.

Richard was 22 and Mary Ellen was 20. They lived at Gothard Apartments for six months and then moved next to the chiropractic office on West Highway 32. During the four years they lived there, Connie Leann (born 1967) and Tricia Lynn (born 1969) were born.

Mary Ellen, Connie, Richard and Tricia Crippin

In May of 1969 the family purchased a home in Russell Addition at 1511 West Olive, northwest of the Sacred Heart Catholic Church where they were active members. There was no road north of the church (Locust Street), only a dirt path. George and Lucille Shuler were their only neighbors to the south.

Richard was active in Missouri State Chiropractic Association. He was on the State Board and named Doctor of the Year in 1995. He was a golfer and on the golf board, quail hunter, tennis player and director of the Jr. Tennis Association for a number of years.

Mary Ellen was a church organist for 35 years, sang with Sweet Adeline's, active in Polk County Christian Social Ministries and Share Your Christmas.

Connie and Tricia attended Bolivar Public School and took piano lessons from Mary Dean. They both played on the Bolivar tennis team. Tricia played the saxophone and was a cheerleader.

Connie and Tricia graduated from the University of Missouri in Columbia.

Connie became an x-ray tech and now works as a mammographer for St. John's Hospital in Springfield, MO.

Tricia married Donald Wayne Vogt from St. Genevieve, MO in 1991 and lives in Columbia, MO.

Dr. Crippin retired from his chiropractic practice May 2000 after 35 years of practice.

Richard and Mary Ellen moved to Marceline, MO to be with their aging mothers in May of 2002. It was a very hard decision. *Submitted by Richard Crippin*

CROCKETT - David Grandison Crockett (born May 12, 1809; died Aug. 1, 1862) was a minister and came to Polk County from Giles County, TN around the time of the Civil War. His father was Robert, whose brother was John, who was the father of the Davy Crockett of the Alamo. David Grandison and Davy were cousins. David Grandison married Martha Lois Andrews of Tennessee, April 6, 1843. They had five children, all born in Tennessee, including Robert Cephas Crockett (born July 19, 1850; died Jan. 2, 1916) who married Ruth Jane Raper from Monroe, TN on Oct. 7, 1873 in Polk County. She came across the Mississippi River on a raft to marry Robert Cephas, a farmer in Missouri. Robert Cephas had two children: Louetta Crockett Pike and John Andrew Crockett (born Feb. 19, 1878;died April 26, 1933). John Andrew married Nettie Elizabeth Prater Dec. 27, 1903. John was a farmer, photographer and postmaster at Pleasant Hope from 1921-1933. John and Nettie had five children, all born in Pleasant Hope. They were David Frank Crockett (born Nov. 16, 1905; died Sept. 8, 1987), Agnes Marie Crockett (born Dec. 3, 1907; died March 17, 1926), Thelma Ruth Crockett (born Feb. 18, 1910; died Aug. 6, 1919), Robert Ray Crockett (born Dec. 10, 1915), Mary Lorene Crockett Secrest (born Nov. 25, 1917; died Sept. 27, 1999). All of the above except Robert Ray, who is living in Springfield, MO, are buried in the Pleasant Hope Cemetery.

David Frank Crockett married Maxine Kibby May 24, 1931, and they had one daughter, Carole LaVaughn Crockett Beauchamp (born Aug. 10, 1933). She married Glen Dale Beauchamp Aug. 16, 1952 and they now live in Belton, TX. They had three children and seven grandchildren. David Frank moved to California and then to Texas, but loved the Polk County area, and made many visits back "home" and then insisted on being buried there. Robert Ray Crockett married Katheryn Lee Johnson Aug. 3, 1941 and lives in Springfield, MO. They have four children: David Allen Crockett (born May 27, 1943) an instructor at SMSU; Barbara Ann Crockett James (born Dec. 13, l944); Elisabeth Kay Crockett Stevens (born April 24, 1951) and Roberta Diane Crockett Tharp (born June 16, 1954). David Allen married Judith Ann Skelton, lives in Marionville, MO and has three children and six grandchildren. Barbara Ann married Ronald James and lives in Norman, OK. Barbara Ann has two children and five grandchildren. Elisabeth Kay married Jerry Stevens, lives in Richmond, VA and has two children. Roberta Diane is married to James Mark Tharp and lives in Springfield, MO. They have two children.

Mary Lorene Crockett married John T. Secrest, Sept. 24, 1948. They had three children: Mary Lois Secrest Chapin (born Sept. 13, 1950), Martha Elizabeth Secrest Mellentine (born Dec. 19, 1952) and John Andrew Secrest (born Dec. 24, 1955). Mary Lois married David Chapin; they have seven children and live in Kings Mountain, NC. Martha Elizabeth married Mark Mellentine, lives in Shelby, NC and has six children. John Andrew lives in Waukegan, IL and has two children and two grandchildren. *Submitted by Robert R. Crockett*

Thomas Jefferson Crook

CROOK - Thomas Jefferson Crook was born May 13, 1856 in Missouri. His parents were Cincinnatus Berry and Elvira Crook. Tom was one of six children: his siblings being Martha Jane Crook Kuykendall, Josh Crook, Susan Rebecca Crook Blythe / Holland, Mary Ellen Crook Blythe / Holland and Francis Americus Crook Anderson. His father, C. B. Crook, was an attorney and sometime schoolteacher.

Tom grew to manhood in the Benton County, AR area. Tom was described as being five feet, 11 and 1/2 inches with dark hair, gray eyes and wore a mustache. Tom considered himself to be a Baptist. In his early years, he was a farmer but later became a barber.

Sometime before 1875, Tom made his way to Missouri. He married Laura Elizabeth Smith in Dallas County, MO on Oct. 21, 1875. The couple eventually settled in Polk County where they appear on the 1880 census in Mooney Township.

Laura and Tom were the parents of eight children: Cincinnatus Bethule Crook, Thomas Bedford Crook, Myrtle Cordelia Crook Latimer, Price Crook, John William Crook, Edward Dwight Crook, Fred Crook and Eva Mae Crook

Gilmore. Fred and Edward Dwight Crook were twins. At least one son, Price Crook, was born at Pleasant Hope, Polk County, MO on June 6, 1884. Most of the other children were also probably born in Polk County, MO.

On Jan. 25, 1900, Laura Crook was granted a divorce from Tom. He remarried sometime between 1902 and 1904 to Lula B. Hedrick. Lula and Tom had two children: Ethus O. "Edward" Crook and Etha O. Crook Hicks. In 1920, Tom and his family were living in Vera, OK. They later moved to Glendale, CA where Tom died on Dec. 23, 1944. He is buried at Forest Lawn Memorial Park Cemetery in Covina, CA. *Submitted by Sharon Hamilton*

Andrew Jackson "Jack" Crow Sr. and wife Mary, taken in Missouri around 1900

CROW – Andrew Jackson "Jack" Crow was born Jan. 5, 1837 in Jefferson County, TN. Parents' names unknown. Other known siblings are William Crow (born 1829), Kate Crow, John Wesley Crow (born 1833). About 1859 he married Mary Ann (unknown). According to census records they lived in Perry County, MO in 1860, Polk County in 1880 and 1900. Andrew was a farmer. He served in the Civil War in the Missouri 78 Regiment Enrolled Missouri Militia Company D. Entered as a private and left as a corporal. Andrew and Mary had 12 children.

They are Mary Ellen Crow, born 1861 and died 1934. She married John Bullin, James W. Kennon and Thomas C. Capleton. She and James had three children: Emma, Oleaf and unknown.

John Wesley Crow was born 1866 and died 1927.

Henrietta was born Nov. 30, 1867 died 1886.

Andrew Jackson Crow Jr. was born October 1869. He married Mary Emma (unknown). They had six children: James, Mary, Henry and the other three names unknown.

Francis Catherine Crow was born Aug. 12, 1870 and died 1941. She married Charles Robert Reeves Oct. 9, 1895. They had seven children: William Oscar, Mary, Robert, Charles, Roy, Rosie and Dorthey.

William Henry Crow was born March 12, 1873 and died 1959. He married Alice Arizona Gilpin, on March 17, 1895. They had eight children: Marion, Portia, Ralph, Arizona, Willie, Mariam and two names unknown.

Sarah Aggie Crow was born 1875. She married Amos Rinks. They had two children, Oscar and Emma.

Rosa A. Crow was born 1876. She married Dal Hopper. They had six children: Stella, Nellie, Jack, Lee, Glydas and unknown.

Jennie Elvira Crow was born Oct. 8, 1878, died May 18, 1961. She married Albert Ira (Michem) Meacham. They had five children: Winnie, Lilly, Ruby, Emmett and unknown.

Issac Leonard (Harley) Crow was born March 26, 1880, died Oct. 29, 1940. He married Elsie Katherine Gilpin Sept. 24, 1903. They had seven children: Ina, Harley, Elzy, Burley, Lola, Velda and Alice.

An unknown child.

An unknown child.

Andrew and his wife both died in June of 1910 at Spurgeon, MO and were buried at Racine, MO near Spurgeon. *Submitted by Therese (Holland) Kruger*

CUNNINGHAM - The spring of 1964 a young lady from Slater, MO became engaged upon her graduation from high school. As spring faded into summer she became more and more unsettled at the prospect of spending the rest of her life with this young man. The engagement was called off. This same young lady had also considered attending a two-year college in Bolivar, MO, but had never sent in her application. With the engagement dissolved, she was told by her father to either go to college or get a job. She promptly sent in the application, was accepted and enrolled in Southwest Baptist College that fall.

A young man from Tulsa, OK hitchhiked to Bolivar that same fall for his second semester as a ministerial student at SWBC. During the first week, at one of the family style meals, the young man from Tulsa made a bet with his friends that if the invitation was given for the young lady from Slater and her friends to sit with them, that "she" would sit by "him." The invitation was given and the bet won by the young man from Tulsa.

After a brief courtship, this young man, Cleo Cunningham, and this young lady, Mary Beeler, were married Jan. 31, 1965 in Slater, MO. They spent that spring and summer in Tulsa, returning to Bolivar in the fall to continue their studies. His first job was with Truck Harbor on South Highway 13. She worked as a receptionist at SWBC maintenance office and at the SWBC bookstore.

Mary and Cleo Cunningham

Cleo graduated from SWBC in the summer of 1970. By this time two little girls had been added to the family, Margaret Arvona on Aug. 9, 1967 and Carol Sue on May 17, 1970. Bolivar was a nice place to live and about halfway between the two hometowns, so they settled in to raise their family. Two little boys eventually joined the family: Matthew Joseph on Nov. 17, 1973 and Curtis James on Aug. 28, 1978.

Margaret married Jeffery Mark Murray of Bolivar on June 6, 1986. They have three children: Megan Arvona (born Nov. 8, 1989), Joshua Mark (born July 29, 1993) and Meleah Annamarie (born Feb. 10, 1999). Carol married Johnny Ray Cates of Fair Play, MO on June 9, 1989. They have three children: Margaret Lee "Maggie" (born Aug. 17, 1994), John Michael (born July 13, 1997) and Carol Olivia (born Jan. 10, 1999). Curtis married Amanda Wedgeworth of Atlanta, GA, July 28, 2001.

Cleo pastored several small churches around the area in the early years of marriage. He also worked at Foremost Dairy, drove a school bus and a trash truck, ran a welding business and now has a small trucking company. After their first child was born, Mary was blessed to stay home, be a homemaker, and keep books for their business. She worked for a couple of years at Southwest Bank in Bolivar.

The family belonged to, supported and were active in First Baptist Church of Bolivar during the growing up years of the children. They have since joined fellowship with and are active in other churches in the area.

Cleo's parents, Clem and Gerti Cunningham, moved to Bolivar in 1981. His sister and brother-in-law, Larry and Katherine Dodson, came to Bolivar from Florida in 1995.

Cleo's father was raised around Carthage, MO and his mother around the Ritchey and Wentworth, MO area.

Mary's maternal grandparents, William R. and Elsie (Huckaby) Fisher, were married at Sentinel in Polk County in 1902 before moving their young family to Saline County sometime between 1913 and 1916. *Submitted by Mary Cunningham*

CUNNINGHAM - John Newton Cunningham was born Dec. 4, 1840 in Kentucky and died Aug. 4, 1906 in Polk County, MO. He was married on June 1, 1862 Martha Jane Hutcheson. She was born Nov. 23, 1840 in Tishomingo County, MS and died on Aug. 6, 1905. They are buried at Mt. Olive Cemetery near her parents, Charles and Elizabeth Bird Hutcheson. Charles was born Dec. 21, 1796 and died July 20, 1868. Elizabeth was born April 15, 1796 and died Sept. 23, 1874.

John Newton and Martha Jane had nine children.

Jemima Frances, born June 19, 1863 in Tennessee, was married in about 1889 to Charles Engledow of Polk County. Charles was born March 4, 1858 and died May 28, 1921.

Elizabeth Josephine was born May 6, 1865 and died Aug. 13, 1857. She married John Harvey Horn on Aug. 17, 1890. John was born Nov. 25, 1870 and died June 8, 1921.

Charles Grant was born Aug. 5, 1866 and was blinded at 4 years of age. He died July 26, 1950. He married Mary (Teague) Baldwin, who was born in 1877 and died in 1945.

Sarah Adeline "Addie" was born May 1, 1868 and died December 2, 1893 of typhoid.

William Bailey was born Sept. 15, 1869 and died May 30, 1936. He married Frances Jane McSwain in 1895. Frances was born in January of 1873 and died Aug. 11, 1936 in a car accident.

Amanda Eveline "Mandy" was born July 9, 1871 and died Nov. 16, 1955. She married Albert

Front row: Elizabeth, John N., Martha and Adeline; Back row: Molly, Emma, Charles, George, William Bailey and Amanda

Bowman in 1902; her second husband was Bill Young and her third husband was Fred Slagle.

George Long was born May 7, 1873 and died Oct. 6, 1975. He married Sarah Belle Weese on Nov. 24, 1906. Sarah was born Sept. 3, 1883 and died May 23, 1947.

Emma Susan "Emmy" was born March 9, 1877 and died Sept. 6, 1951. She married John Henry Eagon on Nov. 24, 1906. John was born Dec. 21, 1858 and died April 25, 1937.

Mary Lucinda "Molly" was born June 25, 1880 and died Sept. 30, 1958. She married John Milton Davison on Dec. 26, 1897. John was born Aug. 31, 1876 and died Jan. 18, 1958. Emogene Engle Conrad's grandparents were John Henry and Emma Susan Cunningham Eagon. They are buried at Mt. Olive Cemetery with many members, including her parents and grandparents. *Submitted by Emogene Engle Conrad*

Robert W., John M., Thomas W., three sons of Thomas W. and wife Disa Cunnyngham

CUNNYNGHAM – The Cunnynghams, with "y" are of Scotch descent. Originally it was "Conyngham" meaning home of the Conyngs. Their pedigree dates back to King David.

The ancestors of the Polk County Cunnynghams were natives of Ulster, Ireland. In 1769, James and his wife, Arabella Good Cunnyngham, with two sons James and William, moved from Ireland (because of fighting there) to Shenandoah County, VA. Sixteen years later, after the death of her husband, Arabella and the children moved to Taylor Bend, TN. Her son, James, tried to protect a lady and her son from Cherokee Indians, but the three were killed and buried in the same grave.

William Cunnyngham married a Miss Lewis in Sevier County, TN. One of their eight children was Thomas Wilkerson Cunnyngham who married Miss Disy Willson. They moved their family to a farm in Polk County, near Morrisville in 1850. Their children were James H. W., Robert Winton, John M. and Thomas W.

During the war Thomas W. Cunnyngham was Lieutenant Colonel in the Regiment of Missouri Home Guards. After the war, he served as surveyor, represented Polk County in the Legislature, and served as county clerk and recorder. From 1852 to 1856 he was the county judge. He was a prominent man and a loyal representative of the citizens of Polk County.

James H. W. was a hardware merchant in Morrisville. He married the daughter of Gideon Ruyle. Their children were Disa, Albert, Thomas and Sally. He was a very successful businessman and farmer.

Robert Winton "Bob" Cunnyngham served with the Missouri Cavalry during the war. He once rode a horse to Tennessee and brought back seed for the farm. Bob married Mary Florence Callaway April 18, 1868. They were parents of Dicy, who died young; Ben (married Fannie Weinberg); Etta (married Heth Hart); Altha (married Alex Farris); Anna (married Lon Batten); and Will (married Mattie Johnson). They are all Polk Countians and are buried in the Mt. Gilead Cemetery. On Easter 1916, Bob joined the Mt. Gilead Methodist Church and was a faithful member until death. Bob was instrumental in organizing the annual Decoration Service at Mt Gilead Church in May 1900 because he believed that a day should be set to put flowers on the graves of friends and loved ones. He served as president until his death 27 years later.

Bob's home was six miles east of Bolivar. The "old fishin' hole" on his farm was the gathering for their first annual July 4th celebration. All the neighbors, friends and friends were welcomed to a very enjoyable picnic with dinner "on the ground." Fifty-pound blocks of ice from the Nick Maas ice plant were chipped with ice picks for ice cubes and freezing ice cream. Fishing (noodling), swimming, frying the fish, eating and visiting were enjoyed by all. There were no political speeches or fireworks, but in those days everyone had to go home and do the chores. Many Polk Countians today are descendants of these early families. *Submitted by Helen Cunnyngham Breshears*

DAVIS - The Davis name originally came from Wales.

John Davis was born in 1760 in South Carolina and died in 1840 in Polk County, MO. He married Rachel. They had James, John, Clarinda, Clarissa, Melissa and Mary "Polly."

James was born in 1780 in South Carolina and died 1866 in Polk County, MO. He married Nancy. They had William, John, Elizabeth, Archibald, Anderson, Nancy, Tempey, Wesley and T. Green. They were among the early settlers in Madison Township of Polk County, MO. Acquiring 40 acres of land in the southeast quarter of northwest quarter, Section 19, Township 33, Range 24 on July 29, 1848 and another 40 acres in the southeast quarter of southwest quarter of Section 29, Township 33, Range 24 on July 9, 1851.

William was born April 8, 1810 in Knox County, TN. He died April 3, 1898 in Polk County, MO; buried in Trimble Cemetery, southwest of Fair Play. He married Susanna Groves (born March 3, 1809) on Dec. 11, 1832 in Knox County, TN. She died April 14, 1895 in Polk County, MO. They had infant daughter, Sarah, James Willis, Stephen Ducater, George Groves, Calloway, Joseph Henson, William Anderson, Dr. Jackson, Nancy Melvina, Benjamin Franklin, Adonixam Judson, Brantly Nehri and Green Wesley.

William Anderson was born Feb. 10, 1844 in Missouri and died April 11, 1929 in Missouri. He is buried in Bethel Cemetery. He married Mary Elizabeth Moore (born Feb. 15, 1854 in Tennessee) on March 7, 1875. She died Feb. 29, 1928 in Missouri and is buried in Bethel Cemetery. They had Myrtie, Almeda, Jonah, Earldon, William Coy, Rennie Reed and Lennie Lloyd.

William Coy was born Feb. 11, 1888 and died March 20, 1940. Buried in Pleasant Ridge Cemetery in Polk County, MO. He married Nora G. Hunt (born Dec. 16, 1888) on Dec. 28, 1910. She was the daughter of William F. Hunt and Anna Neil. She died July 14, 1972. They had Loren E., Finley Jackson and Lowell B.

Davis Family, Loren E. holding Wilma, Sina holding George Sr.

Loren E. was born Aug. 21, 1912 at Fair Play, MO and died March 23, 1977. Buried at Shady Grove Cemetery. He married Sina Katheryn Miller (born Dec. 17, 1917) in Cedar County, MO on Dec. 23, 1940. She is the daughter of George Miller and Eliza B. O'Dell. They had Lanora (died young), George William, Wilma, Loren Eldon, Bernard L., Mary L. and Martha Sue.

George William was born Nov. 12, 1941 at Fair Play, MO. He married Helen Delameter, born May 6, 1919 in Kansas City, MO on June 1, 1970 in Miami, OK. They had George Jr., Franklin L. and Wesley E.

George Jr. was born June 30, 1971 in Springfield, MO. He married Cara (Wellington) Allen on Nov. 9, 2000. She was born July 12, 1971 in Joplin, MO. They have Kevin Craig, born April 24, 2000 in Joplin, MO. She had Stephen, born Aug. 2, 1992 and Geoffrie, born Aug. 8, 1995, both in Joplin, MO from a previous marriage. George, George Jr. and Frank were in the navy. *Submitted by Helen Davis*

Everett Raymond Davis

DAVIS - This is a story of the life of Mary Ann's dad, Everett Raymond Davis, born Nov. 11, 1898 in Shady Grove, MO. He passed away on Aug. 3, 1971 in Avant, OK. He is buried at Hillside Cemetery just north of Skiatook. He was the son of George and Mary Ann (Roderick) Davis. George's parents were Ben Davis, who was born in North Carolina of English descent and Abigail (Crain) Davis, who was born in Tennessee. Ben's parents were John and Margrete Davis and Abigail's parents were Pleasant and Ruth Crain, pioneers of Polk County, MO. They were charter members of the Mount Zion Church. John and Margrete are buried in New Hope Cemetery in Greene County, MO. Pleasant and Ruth Crain are buried in Trimble Cemetery in Polk County, MO. Mary Ann's parents were Daniel and Rebecca (Prater) Rotrock; they are buried at Trimble Cemetery. Nelson Crain was a brother to Abigail. His second wife, Emma, was a sister to Mary Ann. Daniel and Rebecca's family were Henry, Melda (S. M. Lewis); Meg married Stanford Phipps; Emma married Nelson Crain; Laura married Ike Davis; Teresa married a Kirkendall; Sike married Josie Davis; Sophia married Robert Karr. George Davis was a blacksmith and he and Mary Ann moved quite often. Their children usually lived nearby. They were Alta, who married Elsie Cantrell; Lula, who married Will Hollister; Laura, who married Bob Lindsay; Dee, who married Rosa; Everett, who married Vivian Henry; and Merle, who married Dallas Cunningham. They left Missouri for Oklahoma in 1900. They lived in Kansas, Missouri and Oklahoma at different times. They later returned to Shady Grove and Bona, MO area when Everett was 12 years old. George was a strong man, six feet four inches and weighed 205 pounds. He was called on to assist in emergencies there in Missouri, sometimes diving into the Sac River to bring up drowning victims. George was always seeking new adventures. He sunk a shaft on the Leo Williams place near Shady Grove and found traces of copper. The Davis family moved to Avant, OK in 1916. George set up a blacksmith shop in the oil boom days. George died in 1922 and Mary Ann died in 1929. They are buried in Avant Cemetery. Mary Ann's dad Everett became an engineer for W. C. McBride Oil Company near

169

Avant where they processed gasoline. Her mother died at age 30 when Mary Ann was 5 years old and Mary Ann's dad raised her alone with lots of help from his sister Lula and Mary Ann's Grandmother Henry. *Submitted by Mary Ann (Davisf) Hayes*

DAVIS - John Davis was born in 1760 in South Carolina and died in October of 1840 in Polk County. His name was found among petitioners that worked very diligently in dividing Knox County, TN. Most of his six children were born in Grainger County, TN. He was thought to have had three wives. He came to Polk County in the 1830s where he was deeded land (120 acres) December of 1838.

John's son James was among the early settlers in Madison Township in 1866. He acquired 40 acres in Polk County in July of 1848 and another 40 acres in July of 1851. He and his wife Nancy had nine children, born in Tennessee and Alabama.

James' son William was born April 8, 1810 in Knox County, TN and died on April 3, 1898 and is buried in Trimble Cemetery (north of Shady Grove). He married Susannah Groves on Dec. 11, 1832 and they had 14 children. In the late 1830s with their first six children, they loaded meager possessions in a covered wagon, left their small cabin in Tennessee and settled in Cedar County, where they acquired land. All the children learned to read, but it is said that most of the boys never learned to write.

William's son William Anderson was born on Feb. 10, 1844 in Missouri. He is buried in Bethel Cemetery. He married Elizabeth Moore on March 7, 1875. They had seven children. When William Anderson was a boy, along with some of his brothers, they hooked a team of oxen to a wagon and headed to the mill at Shady Grove to grind grain into meal and flour. The line was very long. By the time their turn came it was quite dark, so they tethered their oxen to a log in the mill and decided to spend the night. Some stray, wild cattle wandered into the area where a fight quickly ensued with the Davis oxen. As a result, the log was damaged and caused further delay in grinding.

William Anderson's son William Coy was born Feb. 11, 1888 and died March 20, 1940 and is buried at Pleasant Ridge, all in Polk County. He married Nora Hunt on Dec. 28, 1910. They had three sons: Loren, Jack and Lowell. When Coy was a boy, he and his brother went fishing. They crossed the Sac River somewhere close to Wright and Brown Cemetery. It was about 10:00 a.m. and it began to rain. They found shelter in an old log house. There was a terrible flood. They stayed with the Thompson brothers for about a week until the flood receded. Their folks thought they were washed away. Sure was a happy homecoming!

Sons of William Anderson Davis: Earl, Jonah, Lloyd, Ren and Coy, 1905

Coy's son Loren was born Aug. 21, 1912 at Fair Play and died March 23, 1977. He is buried Shady Grove Cemetery where his father was caretaker for many years and they dug a lot of the graves there. Loren married Sina Miller on Dec. 23, 1940. They had seven children: George, Lenora (stillborn), Wilma, Eldon, Bernard, Mary and Martha. After Loren returned home from the war, they rented a farm in Cedar County. In 1949 they bought about 400 acres on the Polk and Cedar County line, west of Fair Play.

Wilma (Mead) Fisher, daughter of Loren and Sina, was born Feb. 20, 1943 in Polk County. She married Rex Mead on July 16, 1967 and they had three children: Kristie, Robby and Katie. They bought 260 acres southeast of Bolivar. Rex passed away of a massive heart attack on Nov. 13, 1996. Wilma married Wendell Fisher on June 14, 1999. They still live on the same land. *Submitted by Wilma Mead Fisher*

DAVIS - Lewis Davis was born Aug. 6, 1790 in the Territory of Tennessee and married Nancy McHenry in Knox County, TN, on July 11, 1815. Lewis and Nancy were the parents of two sons, both born in Tennessee: Alexander Lewis, born Sept. 25, 1817, and Robert, born in 1820.

It is believed that Lewis Davis moved to Missouri in the 1850s. By 1860 he lived in Polk County, MO; his name is found in numerous Polk County, MO deed records. Lewis married three times. His obituary says he married his first wife in Kentucky. However, there is record of a marriage of Lewis Davis and Nancy McHenry, Jan. 11, 1815 in Knox County, TN. His second wife, Abigail, was divorced with a daughter by her first marriage, Levina Jane Baker. Lewis and Abigale had four children: Marshall, William Yearwood, Alphia and Ellison. Lewis married a third time on Jan. 8, 1866 to Edith Atchley Ryder. Lewis is buried in the Lebanon Cemetery, Lebanon, MO next to James W. Ryder, Edith's first husband. Lewis has no stone.

An article in a Lebanon, MO newspaper noted: "Lewis Davis was born on the 6th day of August 1790, in the territory now embraced in the State of Tennessee, where he remained with his parents until the breaking out of the War of 1812, when he enlisted as a private in Capt. Walker's Company in the 39th US Infantry. During that struggle he took part in the battle known as the Miami, also in that memorable contest known in history as Dudley's defeat, in which Col. Dudley and his gallant command of patriots were captured by the British and Indians. After the capitulation, Davis with a number of his comrades were made to run the gauntlet, and being stout and fleet footed, he made his way safely through while many of the prisoners fell victims to the Indian tomahawks. After being discharged from the company and returning home, he re-enlisted in the Army, serving under Thos. H. Benton in the war with the Seminole Indians. He was an orderly for Col. Benton. He was intimately acquainted with Andrew Jackson."

Lewis's son Alexander Lewis "Pappy" was born Sept. 25, 1817 in Tennessee. He married Levina Jane Baker Sept. 12, 1839 in Monroe County, TN. Levina was the daughter of Abigale Baker and stepdaughter of Lewis Davis. Alexander and Levina had 13 children. Their first four children were born in Tennessee: James Huston, Sophronia, Julia Ann Elizabeth and Mary Elizabeth. After moving to Greene County, MO they had Alpha Caroline and Guin "Guy" Alexander. Lewis Bryant, Florence Haseltine, Allison, Frances Isaline, Paralie Parthenia, John Marshall Clay and Laura Neal were born in Polk County.

Plats of original land, entries for Polk County, MO, reveals that in January of 1859 Alexander Davis owned the "land" that would later be the site of the Pleasant Ridge Cemetery. Deed records also show that Alexander Davis purchased land from Andrew Blair, which is where the original church is believed to have stood. In 1870, Thomas N. Childers sold or gave land to the Pleasant Ridge Baptist Church. Alexander Davis died Feb. 12, 1893 in Dade County, MO and sometime between 1895 and 1898; his heirs sold portions of their land to John Belleman, who deeded over the land to the Trustees of Pleasant Ridge Baptist Church in 1909-10. This land is where the Pleasant Ridge Cemetery and Church are now located. Alexander is buried in Pleasant Ridge cemetery beside his wife Levina, who died May 23, 1887 in Polk County.

Alexander's 12th child, John Marshall Clay Davis, was born March 12, 1864 in Aldrich, Polk County, MO. On Sept. 6, 1885 in Greene County, MO, he married Joanna Kirby, born Oct. 2, 1864, in Dade County, MO. Joanna was the daughter of Solomon P. "Sharp" Kirby and Minerva Hayter. John and Joanna were the parents of 11 children, all born in Polk County: Otho Lauren, Ralph Kirby, Clara, Rose, Ray York, Earl Marshall, Frank Ada, Gene, John Paul, Lucile Geneuve and Victor Kenneth. John Marshall died Dec. 23, 1930 in Aldrich. On July 30, 1945 Joanna died and both are buried in Pleasant Ridge Cemetery.

Lucile Geneuve Davis was born March 7, 1906 in Aldrich. In Bolivar on Aug. 4, 1923, Lucile married George Lindsey Shuler, born March 29, 1898 in Aldrich. George was the son of George H. Shuler and Louisa Crone. Lucile and George settled on part of the family farm that George's father had acquired when he moved to Polk County from Morgan County, IN shortly before George's birth. Lucile and George were the parents of five children, all born on the family farm not far from Aldrich: Elizabeth Marian, Victor Crone "Bill," Kelton Rodgers, George Marshall and Linda Marie.

Lucile died Sept. 9, 1980 in Springfield, Greene County, MO and is buried in Pleasant Ridge Cemetery. George died Nov. 12, 1987 and is buried beside his wife. *Submitted by Laura Elizabeth Bond*

DAVIS - It was Oct. 15, 1888, near Aldrich, MO, in Polk County, when Thomas Fletcher Davis was born. He was the son of Archibald P. and Eliza "Liza" Jane (Wright) Davis. His grandparents, Josiah and Elizabeth Jane (Gothard) Wright, the Davis family were early settlers of Polk County.

Fletch matured into manhood and married Elizabeth Virginia "Jenny" Young. She was the daughter of John and Mary (Needham) Young. They lived near Aldrich and became the parents of two children, a son, Leotis, born July 31, 1911 and a daughter, Robbie Allene, born Aug. 27, 1913. On Nov. 24, 1915, a tragedy happened that would forever affect their lives. Their young son, Leotis, died.

After his son's death, Fletch surrendered to the calling from God to preach the gospel. He was a Baptist preacher and became a great evangelist. Over the next 40 years, he held hundreds of revivals and saw as many as 40 to 50 people saved in some of them. His revivals brought different denominations together, in the service of God. He preached a "born again" salvation.

On Nov. 7, 1948, Jenny Davis died after a lengthy illness. Fletch later married Eunice Hood. He lived the rest of his days in Aldrich, MO. Fletch departed this world on Nov. 15, 1965, following a long battle with emphysema. Fletch, Jenny and little Leotis are all buried at Shady Grove Cemetery in Polk County, MO.

Children born were Leotis Davis (born July 31,

1911; died Nov. 24, 1915); Robbie Allene (born Aug. 27, 1913; died Nov. 10, 1985 in Doniphan, MO and married Howard O'Neal).

Grandchildren were Georgia O'Neal (born 1930) married Lee Kibey, two children; Bob O'Neal (born 1936) married Elaine Tygart, two children; Janet O'Neal (born 1947) married Aaron Howard, two children; Eugene O'Neal (born 1952) married Pamela Holland, one child. *Submitted by J. W. Moss*

Aaron, Bessie, Verda, Vera, Donald and Lendell Fulbright

DAVISON - Bessie Jane was born to Hannah and Daniel Davison on July 13, 1896. She married Charles Aaron Fulbright on Jan. 1, 1923. Aaron died Feb. 20, 1963 and Bessie died Sept. 18, 1967. They are both buried in Pleasant Hill Cemetery. Bessie and Aaron Fulbright had four children.

Verda Oneta Fulbright was born April 25, 1924. She married John Clater Walker on Sept. 22, 1956. John died Sept. 25, 1985 and is buried in Pleasant Hill Cemetery.

Verda and John had one son, Charles Benton Walker, who was born Aug. 4, 1959. Charles married Deborah Ilene Mitchell on Oct. 12, 1985. Charles and Debbie have two sons, Gregory Allan, born April 1, 1990 and Kyle Andrew, born June 17, 1992.

Verda married Robert Herbert Lee Carns on Jan. 30, 1999. Bob died Aug. 11, 2001 and is buried in Bona Cemetery.

Charles Lendell Fulbright was born Feb. 5, 1927 and married Sibyl Iliene Ruark. Sibyl and Lendell had six children. Sibyl and Lendell are divorced.

Charles Edward Fulbright was born June 8, 1953 and he married Lois Jean Cleavenger on Jan. 10, 1975. They have two daughters, Virginia Elain, born on Sept. 24, 1975 and Joanie Michelle, born on May 12, 1978.

Thomas Wayne Fulbright was born May 12, 1956. Thomas married Mary Rutledge Johnson. Thomas and Mary have six children: Paula Sims was born Sept. 3, 1983; Thomas Wayne was born Nov. 17, 1984; Robert Curry was born Jan. 1, 1986; James Rutledge was born July 26, 1988; Julia was born Aug. 21, 1990 and David was born Sept. 18, 1994.

Jimmy Ray Fulbright was born Oct. 14, 1959.

Linda Kay Fulbright was born Feb. 5, 1962. Linda married Jonathon Lynn Clark on Oct. 2, 1982. They have two children, Jason Levi, born Sept. 6, 1983 and Janna Lynn, born July 17, 1984.

Randy Allen Fulbright was born June 18, 1963.

Deborah Sue Fulbright was born May 12, 1964 and she married Timothy Hugh Stacy on Feb. 14, 1985 and they have two daughters.

Vera Ann was born Sept. 21, 1928. She married Lovell Dale Ashlock on June 18, 1953. Vera and Lovell had three children.

Karen Sue Ashlock was born July 27, 1954, married Anthony Shimkuss and they have a daughter Christina Marie, who was born June 30, 1981. Christina married David N. Blevins on Aug. 24, 2002.

Roger Dale Ashlock was born Aug. 28, 1954. Roger died Dec. 26, 1996. He is buried in Reed Cemetery.

Dennis Lynn Ashlock was born April 1, 1962. Dennis married Martha Noland and they have two sons, Ryan Lee, who was born Feb. 29, 1981 and Daniel Ray, who was born Sept. 27, 1982. Dennis and Martha are divorced. Dennis married Nina Phillips and they have two children, Nicole, who was born May 29, 1992 and Trevor, who was born Oct. 11, 1995.

Donald Dene Fulbright was born Sept. 27, 1930 and married Doris Jean Ingles on Oct. 15, 1950. They had two children.

Donna Jean Fulbright was born Aug. 8, 1952 and she married Randy Jones on June 1, 1974.

Gary Dene Fulbright was born Oct. 13, 1956. He married Jolene Appleby on May 23, 1975. They had three children: Sarah Jo, born Feb. 13, 1977; Justin Dene, born Nov. 10, 1978; and Mariah Elizabeth, born June 19, 1992. Justin died September 18, 1997 and is buried in Mt. View Cemetery. *Submitted by Jeffrey Boyce*

DAVISON – James Hardison Davison was born Jan. 28, 1825 in Maury County, TN, probably on the family farm on Duck River. James was about 12 years old when the family came to live in Polk County, southeast of Halfway, MO.

When James was 19 he married Lucy Ann Barclay, daughter of Robert Barclay and Mary Hubbard. Lucy was born Sept. 20, 1822. Lucy and James had 11 children. They bought land and moved to Marion Township, north of Halfway. They are both buried in Goff Cemetery.

Daniel Thomas was born to Lucy and James Davison on Nov. 5, 1858 in Polk County. He married Hannah R. Clark on Dec. 18, 1887. She was the daughter of Martha and James Clark. Hannah was born May 6, 1865. Daniel died on Dec. 8, 1911 and Hannah died on Dec. 11, 1939 and both are buried in Goff Cemetery.

Daniel Tomas, Hannah Rebecca, and children: Clarence C., James Allen and Bessie Jane Davison

Hannah and Daniel's children were as follows.

Lelah Davison was born on Oct. 7, 1883, died on May 19, 1886 and is buried in Goff Cemetery.

Clarence C. Davison was born Dec. 10, 1885 and married Lucy Vincent on May 31, 1937. He died on Aug. 16, 1946 and both are buried in Ragsdale Cemetery.

James Allen Davison was born July 28, 1890 and married Bertha Ella Fuller on Feb. 12, 1930. James died on June 26, 1939 and is buried in Goff Cemetery. Bertha and Allen had two children.

Roseann Davison was born Dec. 29, 1936. She married Herby F. Boyce on Nov. 21, 1964. Roseann and Herby had two sons, Jeffrey Franklin Boyce, born July 24, 1965 and Rodney Conrad Boyce, born Sept. 3, 1969. Jeffrey married Janet Elaine Noel Fisher on Jan. 19, 2001. She has two children, Brian Jeffrey Fisher, born Dec. 22, 1982 and Nicole Marie Fisher, born March 22, 1990. Rodney married Rachel Ann Wilson on Oct. 24, 1997.

Bertha and Allen's other child was James Clark Davison, was born Oct. 10, 1938. He married Neta Joyce Barker on Sept. 16, 1960. They had two sons, Gregory Allen Davison, born on Aug. 12, 1961 and Paul Davison, born on Oct. 12, 1962. Greg and Terrie were married on June 14, 1986. They have two children, Joshua and Jorden. Paul married Terrie on May 11, 1996; she had a son Chase. Terrie and Paul have a child, James Allan.

Bessie Jane Davison was born to Hannah and Daniel on July 13, 1896.

There are still lots of Davisons in Polk County. *Submitted by Bertha Davison*

DAVISON - Brackett Davison was born Nov. 17, 1796 in Prince Edward County, VA as the second son to George and Lucretia McDearmon Davison. His given name was the family name of his great-grandmother, Phoebe Brackett, who married John Owen in Prince Edward County, VA. Sometime between 1811 and 1814, George and Lucretia Davison moved with their family from Virginia to Maury County, TN, where they settled on land purchased from Samuel Polk, father of President James Knox Polk.

On Sept. 28, 1814, Brackett and his older brother, Joshua Davison, enlisted for six months as privates in Captain James McMahan's Mounted Gunmen Company, First Regiment Tennessee Volunteers, for duty in the War of 1812. A few months later on Dec. 23, 1814, Brackett was wounded during a night battle with the British Army near Chalmette, LA. Although his wound, from a musket ball, resulted in the loss of his index finger and part of his left hand, he remained with his unit for the main Battle of New Orleans. Brackett Davison was honorably discharged in Nashville, TN on April 27, 1815.

Jacob Scott, Justice of the Peace, Franklin, TN, married Brackett Davison and Delila Hardison on Aug. 3, 1817. She was the daughter of James and Mary Roberson Hardison who, about 1812, had moved to Maury County from Martin County, NC.

Brackett and Delila Davison farmed in the northeastern part of Maury County, near their parents, until 1838 when they moved their family and their slaves to Polk County, MO. However, according to family history passed down by his descendants, Brackett Davison first came to Greene County, the part that became Polk County, temporarily in 1833, where he bought land from Mark Reynolds several miles north of Blue Mound. Earlier, his older brother Joshua Davison also moved to what became Benton Township, Polk County sometime before March 1833. In addition to Brackett and Joshua, several other Davison family members moved from Maury County, TN to Polk County between 1833 and 1843. These additional family members were their sister Susan Davison Johnson and her family, a nephew Miles Davison and his family, another sister Mary Davison, their mother Lucretia McDearmon Davison, and the children of their sister Nancy Davison Lawrence.

Twelve of Brackett and Delila's 14 children were born in Maury County, TN. The youngest two were born in Polk County. Their children and spouses were Thomas McDearmon Davison, who married Elizabeth Barclay; George Davison, who married Elizabeth Wollard; Fanny Manerva, who died as a teenager; Lucrecia Davison, who married Durrett Hubbard Barclay; James Hardison Davison, who married Lucy Ann Barclay; Milton McMacklin Davison, who married Rosa Caroline Glover; Margaret Catherine Davison, who married Joseph Stuart; Calvin Brackett Davison, who married Matilda Jane Glover; William H. Davison, who married Sarah Jane Davis; Sarah Elizabeth Davison, who married John R. Glover; Joshua Davison, who married Harriett Bennett; Mary Jane Davison, who married William Kennedy Atteberry; John Humphrey Davison, who married Susan Virginia Ragsdale; and Charles Isom Joel Davison, who died when about 2 years old.

While in Tennessee, Brackett farmed and bought and sold several parcels of land. However, during his years in Maury County, all of his wealth and business activities were not in real estate. He owned, bought and sold slaves, and at one time reportedly owned 33. Nonetheless, by 1840, his slave holdings were reduced to 11 and only increased or decreased by a few additional over the ensuing 20 years. In contrast, it should be noted that none of Brackett's children owned slaves and that they supported the Union during the Civil War. It is difficult to understand the troubles of the Civil War days and Brackett's reconciliation of his practice of slavery with his Christian beliefs. Brackett and Delila Davison were deeply religious and belonged to the Christian Church in Tennessee and in Missouri.

Although he continued to deal in Polk County land until 1854, Brackett actually moved to another farm that he owned about one and one-half miles south of Charity, Dallas County, MO, sometime between 1846 and 1849. It is believed that his ownership of slaves contributed to his decision to make this move so that he would be living in a community where slavery was more acceptable than it was in Benton Township of Polk County.

Brackett Davison died during the early evening of Sept. 29, 1863. According to family oral history, he had been out checking cattle on horseback and, upon returning to his front yard, he gave his horse's reins to one of his slaves, walked into the house, laid down on a couch and within a few minutes was dead. He is buried in the Attebury-Shed Cemetery, about a mile and a quarter northeast of March, Dallas County. His wife, Delila Hardison Davison, passed away almost 21 years later on Jan. 30, 1884 and is buried next to her husband in the Attebury-Shed Cemetery. Brackett's mother, Lucretia McDearmon Davison, born about 1769 in Prince Edward County, VA, died sometime between 1851 and 1859 and was thought to be buried in a cemetery near Halfway, Polk County that was bulldozed out when present-day Highway 32 was constructed. Her husband, George Davison, died in 1838, and is buried in Maury County, TN.

In conclusion, the Davisons were among the earliest settlers of Polk County, about 170 years ago. They came to Missouri from Virginia through Tennessee and today have numerous descendants who continue to reside in Polk and surrounding counties. *Submitted by Hollis Davison*

DAVISON - James Hardison Davison was born Jan. 28, 1825 in Duck River, Maury County, TN.

Jesse Lee and Maude Eunis (Black) Davison, November 1908 just after their wedding

His parents were Bracket Davidson/Davison and Delilah Hardison. Bracket served in the War of 1812 and fought in the Battle of New Orleans. They came to Polk County, MO in 1833 and bought land north of Blue Mound. They lived there until 1851 when they bought a farm near Charity, MO living there until his death. James married Lucy Ann Barclay on March 24, 1844 in Polk County, MO. Lucy was born Sept. 20, 1822 in Polk County. She was the daughter of Robert Barclay and Mary Hubbard who lived in Polk County, MO.

James and Lucy were the second great-grandparents of Nadine and Terry. They were the parents of 12 children. They were Delia, Stacy Leah Rebecca, Delilah, Mary, Sarah, David, Margaret, William, John Melton, Lucy, Daniel and George. James was in the Union Army during the Civil War. He was a private in Company K of the 26th Regiment of Enrolled Missouri Militia Volunteers and died during the war. They are buried at the Goff Cemetery northeast of Bolivar, MO. They are listed in 1860 Census of Polk County. All the children were born in Polk County, MO. James was a farmer.

Nadine and Terry's great-grandparents were John Melton and Lula Belle (Woodin) Davison. He was born Sept. 10, 1855 in Halfway, MO and

John Melton Davison and Lula Belle (Woodin) Davison parents of Jesse Lee Davison about 1914

Back row: Julia, John and Edath; Front row: Monroe, Jim, Roy and Nettie holding Lola about 1912 The Blacks

she was born Feb. 26, 1870 in Mt. Pleasant, MI. They were married Oct. 17, 1888 in Polk County, MO. They had eight children. They were Jesse Lee, Vernia May, Ernest Daniel, Lucy Bell, Ferry Avis, Ella Mable, Russell Orville and Gertrude. The family lived in Goodson and Louisburg, MO. John was a farmer. Lula died in 1915 and is buried in Bazine, KS. John moved to Santa Paula, CA in 1929 with his son and lived there until his death March 31, 1934. Lula (Woodin) Davison's parents were Llewellyn and Huldah Cmira (Schooley) Woodin. They had 13 children. In 1885 they moved to Goodson, MO. They are listed on the 1900 Census of Polk County. Llewellyn served in the Civil War for the Union Army in the Battles of Gettysburg and Spotsylvania. He was a private in Company E, 145th Infantry Pennsylvania Volunteers. They moved to Withrow, WA in 1908 and lived there until his death.

Nadine and Terry's grandparents were Jesse Lee and Maude Eunis (Black) Davison. He was born Nov. 27, 1889 in Goodson, MO. His parents

Back row: Marie, Gussie, Lindy, Dorthy, Lee and Maude; Front row: Jesse, Dean, Gearl and Bill about 1934

were John Melton and Lula Bell (Woodin) Davison. Maude was born Sept. 6, 1893 in Polk County, MO. They were married Nov. 29, 1908 near Goodson, MO. Lee was a farmer all of his life. They had 11 children. They are Perry Lee, Oscar Nolan, Ralph Glen, Gussie Opal, Leah Marie, Lindel Loyd, Dorothy Pauline, Jesse Hearld, Dean Elden, Gearl Eugene and William Melton. All but Glen, Marie and William were born in Polk County, MO. The family moved to Santa Paula, CA in 1929. This town was known as "Little Bolivar" due to most of the residents migrating from Bolivar, MO. They lived there until their deaths. Two of their sons returned to Missouri. Glen moved to Springfield, MO and lives there now and Oscar moved to Polk, MO. He was a dairy farmer until he retired. He married Wava Hood, who was born in Rimby, MO. Their son, Vernon Davison and his two daughters live in Bolivar today. Both Lee and Maude are buried at Ivy Lawn Cemetery in Ventura, CA. Sons Glen, Lindel, Jesse and Dean served in WWII, son Bill served in the Korean War and son Gearl served during peacetime.

James Marcus Carter

Caroline Carter

Maude's parents were James William and Marena Jnettie (Carter) Black. Jim was born Dec. 12, 1854 in Rondo, MO and Nettie was born Sept. 6, 1875 in Urbana, MO. They had eight children. Parents of James were Jeremiah B. and Matilda (Loyal) Black. They married Nov. 7, 1852 in Polk County, MO. Nettie's parents were James Marcus and Caroline (Moore) Carter, married Nov. 22, 1874 in Hickory County, MO. Caroline was full-blooded Cherokee Indian.

Parents of Nadine Evans were Leah Marie (Davison) and Gilbert Lesley Evans.

Parents of Terry Dean Davison were Lindel Loyd and Pauline (Ahart) Davison. *Submitted by Nadine (Evans) Ford and Terry Davison.*

DAVISON – James Hardison Davison was born Jan. 28, 1825 in Maury County, TN, the son of Brackett and Delila Hardison Davison. Brackett was the member of the family that came to Polk County in 1833 and bought land from Mark Reynolds, north of Blue Mound (south of Halfway, MO). He was given land for his service in the War of 1812 to which he later moved. Brackett and most of his family is buried in the Attebery Shed Cemetery, near Charity, MO. James was the fifth child of 14.

James would have been about 12 years old when the family moved here from their farm on Duck River in Maury County, TN. He married March 24, 1844, Polk County, Lucy Ann Barclay, born Sept. 20, 1822, the daughter of Robert and Mary (Hubbard) Barclay. They purchased land in Marion Township after their marriage, then in July 1862 he enlisted in the Union Army as a private in Company E of the 36th Regiment of Enrolled Missouri Militia Volunteers. He died March 1, 1863 at Halfway, MO of congestion while in the service. He was buried in the Goff Cemetery beside other members of his family. The family farm was sold and Lucy bought land five miles east of Goodson, MO. She later gave this to her son George for keeping her until she died, but she and George's wife didn't get along too well, so she went to live with her son Daniel and his family. Lucy died Aug. 7, 1898 and is buried in Goff Cemetery. James and Lucy's children: Leah (born circa 1845, died young); Delilah Jane "Lollie" (born 1846); Mary L. (born circa 1848, died young); Sarah Elizabeth (born circa 1849); David Brackett (born 1850); Margaret (born 1852); James William (born 1852); John Melton (born 1855); Lucy Ann (born 1858); Daniel Thomas (born 1858) and George Hubbard (born 1861).

James Wiliam Davison was born Nov. 24, 1853 at home in Marion County, MO. He married Nov. 4, 1880 in Polk County, Mariah Ellen Tarbert, born Nov. 15, 1864, Columbia, PA, the daughter of David F. and Maria (Broome) Tarbet. When Mariah's mother died, her father came to Missouri with the rest of his young children. David then let Mariah stay with the Nicholas Fairlamb family to raise as their own. James bought some farmland just one mile from his mother east of Goodson and remained there until his death April 29, 1923. Mariah died Nov. 29, 1934 at the home of daughter Maley in Santa Paula, CA but was returned to Missouri for burial beside James in Reynolds Chapel Church Cemetery. James William and Mariah Davison's children are as listed below.

James Ivan, born Oct. 22, 1882 near Goodson, married Myrtle Fugate (1889-1959) daughter of John Edward and Ida (Anderson) Fugate. Ivan died June 20, 1968. Both buried Oak Lawn Cemetery Buffalo, MO. Their children were Thelma Marie, married Raymond Marsh; Wilma Lois, married John Austin; Erma Adella, married Glen Harris and Lawrence Eugene, married Carolyn Harmon.

John Frank born March 6, 1885, married 1906 Edith Holt (1890-1933) of Louisburg, MO. Both died Sept. 1, 1933 and are buried in Louisburg Cemetery. Children were Permealia Elsie, married Leon Walker; Florence Edna, married Alpha T. Fisher; Ressie Unina "Nina," married Bob Booth; Jesse Owen, married Wilma Caldwell, Auda Ireen, married Glenn Merrifield; Glenn Ivan, married Clara McHaffey.

Nellie Ethel, born April 12, 1887, died March 16, 1965, married 1905 Charles O. Jones (1884-1935), both buried in Lindley Creek Church Cemetery. Children were Opal, married Glen Carter; Bessie Pearl married Buel Walker; Elgie Lloyd, never married; Gladys Okla, married Lowell Parscale and Archie Lovel, married Myrtle (Miller) Reed.

James W. and Mariah Davison

Alvin, born July 1, 1889, died Aug. 28, 1974, married 1912 Minnie Quick (1893-1979), both buried in Reynolds Chapel Cemetery. Children were Phyllis, married Harold Saxbury; Leon Lewis, died young and Gerald, married Bonnie Glover.

Dora May, born July 11, 1891, died Oct. 29, 1945, married 1920 John Russell Smith (died 1929). Both buried Reed Cemetery. Children were Ruth (step), married Fred Hendershot; Kathleen (step), married Eugene Able; Willa Mae, married Orvis Witt; Maley June, married Wilbur "Bill" Irelan; Russell Andrew, married Bertha Campbell; Bonny, married Dorothy White; William, married Phyllis Payne; Paul, married Treava.

George Claude, born May 22, 1893, died Feb. 8, 1975, married Flora Norman (1896-1982). Both buried Reynolds Chapel. Children were Ruby, married Ivan Sharp; Leonard Alvin, married Louise Botson; John Claude, married Ruby Hull and William Howard, died young.

William Harvey, born May 23, 1895, died July 10, 1969 Scottsdale, AR. Buried Collidge, married Helen. Children were Harvey Jr.; Mrs. Rosemary Taylor; Mrs. Margaret Lawrence and Mrs. Jo Anne Ford.

Maley Mable, born Sept. 28, 1897, died March 10, 1994, married 1928 William Forster (1901-1994), both buried Santa Paula, CA. Children were Kenneth E., married Jo May Mickel and Early Wayne, born and died.

Charles William, born June 9, 1899, died Aug. 12, 1984, married 1919 Grace Holloway (1902-2001), both buried Ivy Lawn Cemetery, Santa Paula, CA. Children were Wilda Gladys, married Lyndel Holt; Nellie Fern, married Johnny George.

Jessie Edna, born Sept. 15, 1902, died March 16, 1986, married Floyd Walter Ragsdale. Both buried Ivy Lawn Cemetery, Santa Paula, CA. Child was Lila Violet, married Kenneth Edwards.

A daughter born and died March 8, 1905.

Jewel, born March 31, 1907, died Jan. 4, 1908. (The last daughter and Jewel are buried across the road from home, Mission Cemetery). *Submitted by Shirley (Parscale) Covert*

DAVIDSON - William Davidson (Davison) (born about 1784, North Carolina) and Margaret (Hopkins) Davidson (born about, 1780, North Carolina). Margaret was the daughter of Andrew Hopkins and Sarah (Dill) Hopkins of Henry County, TN.

According to family tradition, the Davidson/Davison family came to America from Ireland before the Revolutionary War. Missouri immigrants William and Margaret Davidson moved from Tennessee and Illinois, joining her sister and brother-in-law, Elizabeth (Hopkins) and Jonas Akard, in a settlement along the Sac River. Their names appear on the 1833 Greene County Tax List. William Davison is listed by Goodspeed as one of the first settlers in Madison Township when the new Polk County was formed. When the townships were further divided and William's house fell into Jackson Township, it was designated as the polling place. He filed for 160 acres just south of the present town of Fair Play at the US Land Office in Springfield in 1837. The Polk County Assessors Book for 1841 taxes William for two very highly valued horses matched in value by only one other county resident's stock. He apparently died before 1844, the next surviving tax list, where his son Armstrong T. Davison appears to head the household.

William and Margaret Davidson had eight children: Mary Davidson, born 1809, married James M. Colston and moved to Douglas County, MO; Armstrong Tilford Davison, born 1811, married Hannah Haron Kennedy; Elizabeth Davidson, born 1813, married Andrew Hays and Samuel R. Rumley; John Stockard Davidson, born 1818, married Rodah Dunnegan; Elias Davison, born 1821, married Martha W. Lenox; Enoch Davison, born 1823, married Emily Josephine Lynd; Amzi A. Davidson/Davison, born 1825, married Louisa Jane Arkard; and Eliza Davison, born 1829, married John Pollard and William Eldridge.

William Henry Davidson, whose father Amzi A. Davison was killed while he was guarding the Polk County Courthouse, is shown here with his family in about 1902. Top row: Benton Franklin Davison, William Arthur Davison, Minnie Ardella Davison (later Tow). Middle row: William Henry Davidson, Mary Elizabeth (Neil) Davison, James Ora Davison. Front row: Lula Elizabeth Davison (later Maddox).

The land records of both Polk and Cedar Counties reveal that the sons of William Davidson speculated on land. Although early in their lives they were farmers, they also bought and sold a large number of properties. Later they all were owners of dry goods stores so the family record has been passed down in a ledger book by Andrew Jackson Davison. John Stockard Davison, who married Rodah Dunnegan, was the uncle of T. H. B. Dunnegan (the elder) and owned a corner store on the square in Bolivar where "Uncle Stock" taught his nephew the dry goods business. In 1863, Elias Davison served as Cedar County Court Judge. Armstrong T. Davison was a farmer, stonemason and storeowner who gave the property for the Brush Grove Church and Cemetery at the edge of his farm for a cost of $1. During the Civil War, his son William Thomas Davison was wounded in the battle for control of the Stockton courthouse (1863) and died three days later. William T. is buried in Brush Grove Cemetery.

There were other Davison casualties from the Civil War. Amzi Davison was a member of Company D, Polk County, Missouri Home Guards. While they were guarding the courthouse in Bolivar in 1861, Amzi was wounded accidentally when a gun leaning against a tree fell and discharged, the bullet hitting him in the ankle. He died 10 days later, leaving a pregnant widow, Louisa Jane (Akard) Davison and five other children. Eliza (Davison) Pollard's husband, John

Pollard, was a member of the Eighth Missouri Cavalry, Company L and died in the service in 1863.

Throughout the Davison family history they have been primarily independent owners of small businesses. The Davison Polk County forebears started out owning stores, hotels and boarding houses but they seemed to have survived the ups and downs of a frontier economy by doing a wide variety of things. While the women ran the stores and boarding houses, the men cleared land, had sawmills, farmed, laid stone, bought and sold livestock and property, and were active in politics. The merchants and traders of the past are reflected in today's Davison family, along with educators, engineers and computer specialists. *Submitted by Robert Hernborde*

James and Sarah DeGraffenreid

DEGRAFFENREID - James Degraffenreid, a descendent of Anton de Graffenreid and Catherine Henner of Switzerland, was of Huguenot background. They went from Switzerland to England. In England the Queen gave them a ship to bring settlers to the New World, where they first settled in Tennessee and North Carolina. A brother of James, Baron Christopher de Graffenreid, founded the town of New Bern, NC, taking the name from Berne, Switzerland.

James DeGraffenreid was born in Tennessee on Dec. 26, 1826. As a young man he moved to Polk County, MO, where he married Sarah "Sally" Grider Nov. 5, 1846. "Sally" was the sister of William T. Grider, a Southern Methodist preacher in Bolivar. On his way home one Sunday he was stopped by Union sympathizers near Slagle Creek. When he refused to promise to change his preaching or go back to Bolivar with them, he was killed, becoming the first casualty of the Civil War in Polk County.

They were pioneers in the Oakville Community near Morrisville, a "God loving, God fearing" community. When he first arrived there were still a few Indians to either fight or make peace with. He tried to make peace. James was a blacksmith by trade and had shops at Brighton and Slagle. "Sally" wove wool carpets.

James and "Sally" had 11 children: Isabella Elizabeth, (born 1847; died 1907), who married John A. Ballinger Oct. 18, 1879; William Charner, (born Dec. 5, 1848; died Jan. 1, 1907), who married Julia A. House Nov. 2, 1873; Mary Rebecca, (born Dec. 1, 1849; died Dec. 1, 1936), who married Mr. Scroggins; John Petty, (born 1851; died 1857), who died at about 6 years of age; Massie Ann, (born 1852; died 1942), who married L. R. Roark April 28, 1895; James Vincent Charner, (born March 15, 1855; died Nov. 4, 1910), who married Mary E. Tindle April 25, 1878; Sarah Jane, (born March 20, 1857; died Aug. 15, 1932), who married Richard Thomas Cossins (born Oct. 3, 1888); Joseph M., (born 1859; died 1935), who married Martha Griffin Oct. 24, 1880; Frances, (born Sept. 11, 1861; died May 6, 1945), who never married; Thomas, (born 1864; died 1940), who married Betty Gouty Jan. 13, 1884; and Henry M., (born 1867; died 1955), who married Annie Butcher June 9, 1887.

James served in Company F, Regiment 26, Missouri Enrolled Militia from Sept. 27, 1862 to March 31, 1863 during the Civil War. He never left home. He just served guarding his home area.

James and "Sally" built a "weaning house" on the property they owned and as the children got married, they moved into that house until they could get a place of their own.

Frances, who never married, lived with her parents and helped take care of the house. After supper, James and "Sally" would sit down in front of the fireplace and smoke their corncob pipes.

James and Sarah "Sally" DeGraffenreid and most of their children are buried at Oakville Cemetery near Morrisville, MO.

In memory of James DeGraffenreid, Dec. 26, 1826-Feb. 13, 1916, and Sarah "Sally" (Grider) DeGraffenreid, 1827-1909. *Submitted by Lola Mae Schleifer*

DENNEN – John W. Dennen was born in 1813 in Tennessee. His father may have been Robert Dennen (Blount County, TN). It was recorded on May 29, 1805 that he was granted petition for naturalization. The family has been told from relatives that the Dennens were from Ireland.

John married Elizabeth Daniel (June 25, 1834, Rhea County, TN). Elizabeth was the daughter of Plummer Daniel. Elizabeth was born in 1817 in North Carolina. She had a twin sister named Nancy, who married John Brady. Nancy and John Brady moved from Tennessee to Missouri about 1840.

The 1850 Census of Bedford County, TN list John W. and Elizabeth Dennen. (Their children: Harrison, 15; John, 13; Charlotte, 11; Plummer, 9; Robert, 7; Thomas, 5; Nancy, 3; Sarah, 1.) John W. and Elizabeth Dennen were Kathryn's great-great-grandparents.

Sometime between 1850 and 1855, the Dennens moved to Polk County, MO, perhaps to be close to Elizabeth's sister Nancy and her family. They settled in Jackson Township, near the town of Orleans on the Sac River.

The 1860 Census of Polk County lists only Elizabeth and her children. John W. Dennen and son John are not listed. It is believed they died before the others came to Missouri.

Kathryn's great-grandfather was Harrison Dennen. He married Frances Mitchell (June 16, 1858; Polk County, MO). Kathryn hasn't been able to determine who Frances' parents were, but Kathryn knows Frances was related to the Mitchells in that area. She was born in Missouri and lived close to Mitchell Campground. Harrison and his brother Robert were enrolled in the 15th Regiment of the Missouri Cavalry Volunteers, Company F under Captain Lafayatt J. Mitchell during the Civil War. Harrison's description reads as follows: "He was 39 years of age, 5' 9' high, fair complexion, blue eyes, light hair, and a farmer by occupation." This information is treasured, because Kathryn doesn't have any pictures of him.

Harrison and Frances Dennen had eight children: John W., Sarah, John, Robert, James, twin sister Amanda and Nancy. After the war, the entire family, including Elizabeth and children, moved to Newton County, MO. This is where Kathryn's grandfather James Madison was born. After Harrison died in 1887, Frances, her two sons, John and James, and their sister Nancy moved back to Polk County near Gresham, MO where they cared for their mother. John died in 1902 and Great-Grandma Frances died in 1905. They are buried at Hickory Grove Cemetery in Polk County. James Dennen married Mary Katherine Neff of Cave Springs, MO in 1910. Their children were Mary Elizabeth, James Neff and Frances Louise. Kathryn's father was James Neff Dennen, who married Frances Lucille Miller from Astoria, IL on Dec. 24, 1941. Kathryn's father was in the army and was stationed in the Philippines with the 863rd Aviation Engineer Battalion, Company C, during WWII.

James N. Dennen and Frances L. Dennen wedding picture Dec. 24, 1941

Kathryn's brother Robert married Pat Moody. They have three children and two grandchildren: Lisa, Krista, Jason and Zachary and Preston Dennen. Kathryn's sister married Robert Mayes. She has one daughter, Elizabeth Mayes.

Kathryn was married to Holace F. Breithaupt, whose maternal ancestors, the Higginbothams, have a long history in Polk County. Her children are Danny (married to Kathy Stewart of Pleasant Hope, MO), Kelly (married to Vince Dotson) and Frank Breithaupt. Her grandchildren are Sarah and Nick Dotson, and Staci and Tana Snyder. *Submitted by Kathryn Dennen Breithaupt*

Left to right, back row: Wade and Maude Derrossett, C. A. (Clois) and Lucy Robertson, Clinton Mervey and Alice Derrossett, Will and Flora Fugate, Dave and Slona Raney. Seated are James H. and Margaret Derrossett. James is holding Chester Fugate and Margaret is holding Raymond Robertson. Lee Allen Robertson is to the left of James H. and Jessie Robertson is to the right of Margaret. Front row on the left is James Robertson. (not sure who the girl next to James is) The two girls behind James H. are thought to be Alaine and Verba Lee Fugate, daughters of Will and Flora.

DEROSSETT – Wayne's great-grandfather was James H. Derrossett, born Feb. 13, 1855 in Polk County, MO. He was the son of William Daniel Derossett, born 1830 in Tennessee and Elizabeth Ann Hickman, born about 1835, also in Tennessee. He was the grandson of John Derossett and Martha "Patsy" Pritchett, born in Virginia and North Carolina, respectively.

James H. was the second child of William and Elizabeth, and of their five children, he was the only son. On Dec. 17, 1876, in Greene County, MO, he married Margaret E. Clark who was the daughter of Alexander H. Clark and Amelia Sarah Lane.

James H. lived in Morrisville, MO and was a farmer by occupation. He and his wife had seven children: Flora Ellen, Mervey Clinton, William Leonard, Slona E., Ray Nora, Lucy

Mabel and Wade Hampton. Of these, William Leonard was Wayne's grandfather.

On Sept. 17, 1913, William Leonard married Alice Jane Grant who was the daughter of John Caswell Grant and Sarah Belle Gilmore. To this union, five children were born: John Wilbur, who died the next day after his birth; Harold Leroy, Wayne's father; Elva Ruth; Bonnie Athelyen and William Leon.

Wayne never got to see his grandfather. He and his family lived first near Brighton, MO, then they moved to a farm on the Sac River and then to Phenix, MO, near Walnut Grove, MO. He had a job with the railroad repair crew in which they traveled the rails on a hand car making necessary repairs. He then went to work for the Phenix Marble Company. On Friday, April 17, 1925, soon after the 8:00 a.m. whistle had blown for the men to report to work, he was down in the bottom of the quarry when he told some of the men to help him get out because he wasn't feeling well. He died before they could get him to the top from apparent heart failure. He is buried in the Slagle Cemetery.

Wayne's grandmother, Alice, took her family and moved in with her parents on the Grant farm about two and one-half miles east of Morrisville. Later, she bought the house that James H. lived in at Morrisville. She and her children would live there in the wintertime and then go to the Grant farm in the summertime and put out a garden and pick berries to have food for the winter.

When Wayne was 10 or 11 years old, his great-uncle Mervey came to live with them for a short time. He brought a box of tools with him and in it was a small hammer with an iron handle. Wayne asked him about it and he said that it was the kingpin from the wagon that their ancestors used to make the trip to Polk County from Tennessee. The DeRossetts came to Missouri in 1841. Unfortunately, Wayne did not know what became of the pin. Wayne says, "I wish that I had that little part of history and could show it to my grandchildren as a keepsake." *Submitted by Wayne DeRossett*

DEROSSETT – Athelyene's mother was Alice Grant, daughter of John and Sarah Belle, better known as Uncle John and Aunt Belle. While the Grant family believes they are more Scottish than anything else is, there is evidence that the name originated in France, derived from the name "le grande." The name is said to have been established in several New England Colonies in 1657. Some Grant names carried over into the early history of North Carolina. Athelyene's grandfather's family came to Missouri from Tennessee.

Her father, Leonard Derossett, died at the age of 46 leaving her mother with four small children. She moved back to the home of her parents for a time, then bought a house in Morrisville where the family lived during the school terms, then back to the farm in the summer to plant the gardens. The gardens! Ah, the gardens! Large and generous, both food for the body and food for the soul. Althelyene's first love was her grandmother's flowers, a true garden, with always enough flowers for a visitor to take home a bouquet of "Aunt Belle's flowers." Some distance from the house the "old garden" grew the root crops, corn and melons in variety. The kitchen garden, a few steps from the house, provided much of the daily fare. Next came the "new" orchard with varieties of fruit and berries.

The children, with cousins, played in the stream in the pasture and carved their initials in the young sycamores, giving them a touch of immortality. They made many of their toys; a squirt gun made from elder branches with the pith removed and their accuracy was nothing short of amazing, as the target of a wet paper-wad could tell you. All boys had a bean flip: a Y shaped stick, two narrow strips of inner tube and an oval piece of leather in which a small stone was placed. Pull back on the stone, release, and it went flying through the air with a force that could slay a rabbit, if you could hit it. Her brother Harold and his friends contrived a contraption consisting of a wooden plank secured to two buggy wheels and a rope to guide it. As many children as could squeeze on the plank piled on, and then they went flying down the hill, hopefully to stop before they went into the branch. A small red wagon served the same purpose but often overturned, spilling children down the hill.

A rainy day was a time for investigating the cellar loft where wonderful junk was stored. This was a day for mom to bake and they were lured back by the scent of delicate custard and simmering raisins ready to be baked into pies.

Rozets, de Rosset, Derrossett, DeRossett: many spellings but the same name. The small "de" meant the house of Rosset. The spelling seemed to be changed at will. The Huguenots were members of the Protestant political faction in France in 1560. The leaders were French exiles in Switzerland, but later were trained as missionary pastors and sent back to their homeland where they established local churches that soon covered much of the nation. A Roman Catholic faction was determined to prevent any form of non-Catholic worship in France or the accession to power of any Protestant. This led to massacres and on the day of the Feast of Bartholomew, Catholic mobs killed seventy thousand Protestants in that one day. As far as can be ascertained Captain Louis DeRossett and his family were the only survivors of the French of that name. His son, Armand DeRossett was the Huguenot immigrant and founder of the American family of his name. He came to America in the 1740s where he and his family settled in New Hanover and Anson Counties, then joined the Cape Fear Colony in North Carolina. Armand was a physician and there was an unbroken succession of doctors for 186 years.

Though every DeRossett in the United States has descended from this one man, two brothers, one in the north, and the other in the south, fell out during the Civil War and some have not claimed kin since. *Submitted by Athelyene (DeRossett) Phillips*

DEVIN - Clayton Devin, born July 11, 1793 in Danville, Pittsylvania County, VA, and Margaret West, born Nov. 24, 1803 in North Carolina, were married on March 17, 1820 in Lincoln County, TN. They had 13 children, six born in Tennessee and the rest in Missouri. All of the children except Anna had red hair. They arrived in Polk County between 1833 and 1836, where all of the children were later married. Clayton, a War of 1812 veteran, was granted land (located near Bolivar) for military service. Clayton died Nov. 24, 1868; Margaret died June 5, 1888; both buried in the family cemetery (called Heydon-Williams-Devin) on their land.

Martha Mitchell Devin, born March 12, 1822, married William Heydon on Feb. 20, 1849 and had seven children: James Clayton, Joseph Henry, William Thomas, Nancy Jane, George Washington (died at age 1), John Smith and Leonard Leachman. Martha died Aug. 2, 1883 and is buried in the family cemetery.

William Marion Devin, born Feb. 26, 1823, married Judith Gunn on June 19, 1853 and had one daughter, Arvilla. He died circa 1870, last found in Fulton Hospital, Callaway County.

James Devin, twin of William, died Feb. 26, 1823 in Lincoln County, TN.

Clayton Smith Devin, born Dec. 22, 1825, married Nancy Rebecca Williams on April 19, 1849 and had seven children: Margaret Matilda, Elijah Clayton, Franklin Pierce, Martha Anne Eliza, Thomas Joseph, Sarah Malinda, Leota Rebecca. Smith, a Civil War veteran, died Oct. 6, 1887 and is buried at Barren Creek Cemetery.

Anna Sanders Devin, born Jan. 22, 1827, married Richard Carlyle Wilson on July 2, 1867 and had one daughter (died at birth). Annie raised Richard's other three children as her own. Annie died Jan. 17, 1916 and is buried at Greenwood Cemetery.

Sarah Jane Devin, born Oct. 14, 1828, married Hiram Thompson on Jan. 21, 1863 and had two children: George Washington and Hiram Alexander. Sarah helped to raise Hiram's other six children. Sarah was buried at Greenwood, her death date unknown.

Mary Elizabeth Devin, born April 23, 1832, married Enos Pickering on Feb. 23, 1854 and had four children: Martha Ann, Margaret Isabelle, Mary Frances and James Alexander. Mary died Sept. 18, 1909 and is buried at Salem Cemetery.

Joseph Benton Devin, born Aug. 27, 1835, married Elvira Pickel on Feb. 4, 1859 and had 12 children: Nathaniel Madison, Mifflin Jay, Catherine Florence, Margaret Delila, Smith Pickel, Irene Isabella, Elvira Argussa, unnamed daughter (lived one day), Letha May (died at 2 months), unnamed daughter (stillborn), Joseph Charley and Eunice Ursula (died at 7 months). Elvira died at Eunice's birth and Joseph was remarried to Belle Wall on Oct. 10, 1882. They had two children: Stella Ophelia and James Benton. Joseph, a Civil War veteran, died June 14, 1887 in Morrow County, OR.

Margaret Adeline Devin, born March 17, 1837, married first, Anderson Samuel Chitty on Sept. 2, 1857 and had six children: Belvina, Vanda, John, Benton, Zena and James C. Margaret married second, Phineas William Judd on Sept. 20, 1874 in Missouri and had two children: Martha J. and Margarett Rena. Margaret died July 20, 1893 in Missouri.

Patton Mack Devin, born Feb. 10, 1839, died of scarlet fever sometime before 1850 in Polk County.

Alfred Harrison Devin, born Sept. 20, 1840, married Mary Agnes Campbell on Jan. 29, 1861 and had five children: Margaret Parthenia, Glaves Alexander, Columbus Sanders (died at age 26), Sarah Agnes and Minerva Elizabeth. Alfred, a Civil War veteran, died Jan. 27, 1914 and is buried at Dunnegan Cemetery.

Massa Louisa Devin, born Feb. 23, 1844, married Abner Benton Hughes on Oct. 23, 1862 and had eight children: Alfred Benton West, Jessie Parthenia, Ella Louise, Delila Jane, Albert Franklin, Joseph Leander, Oma Clayton and Anna Marie (died as an infant). Massa died Aug. 28, 1925 in Riverside, CA and is buried at Evergreen Cemetery in Riverside.

Parthenia Tennessee Devin, born March 7, 1845 or 1846, married Leander Wilson Frieze on Dec. 16, 1866 and had six children: Margaret Elizabeth (died at age 3), Parthenia Jane, Louise Adeline, Wesley Marcellus (died at age 1 week), Alfred Smith and Benton Woodford. Parthenia died Dec. 5, 1901 in Fossil, OR. *Submitted by Doris Wilson*

DICKERSON – Albert B. Dickerson, 1790/1800, South Carolina and Louisa, 1808, South Carolina, came to Kentucky where all their children were born. In 1850 census Louisa and five of their nine children came to Missouri with several other family members. Children, viz: Nathaniel M., 1827, William, 1834, Mary, 1838, Thomas, 1840, John H., 1843. In 1860 census Louisa,

Nathaniel and John lived in Polk County, Green Township, later moving to Jackson Township buying land on the Sac River southwest of Aldrich, MO. John H. Dickerson, born June 25, 1843 in Warren County, KY died Jan. 7, 1916, married Hannah E. Thompson Feb. 4, 1866 in Aldrich, MO, daughter of Young William Thompson and Eliza Stevens. She was born July 24, 1846 in Polk County, died April 9, 1928, burial in Pleasant Ridge Cemetery, Aldrich, MO. Children viz: Rachel "Annie," born Nov. 9, 1866, died April 26, 1886; Mary S., born Dec. 9, 1867, died Oct. 5, 1883; Martha L., born Dec. 30, 1869, died April 22, 1870; John Albert, 1872-1947 married Sarah (Clemmie), 1872-1955; Thomas Young "T. Y.," born Feb. 1, 1879, Aldrich, MO, died Sept. 2, 1960, Springfield, MO, married Bertie Ann Hensley, Feb. 27, 1898, Polk County, MO. She was the daughter of James Andrew and Mary E. Hensley, born Jan. 17, 1883, died Jan. 5, 1957, burial in Pleasant Ridge Cemetery, Aldrich, MO. Children viz: Earnest Earl, born Oct. 26, 1904, died Sept. 13, 1968 in Polk County, MO, married Anna Lee Hughes, daughter of Albert Franklin Hughes and Alice (Edna) Wollard, born Sept. 1, 1905, Polk County, MO, died April 9, 1991. Children viz: Frank Thomas, born Dec. 21, 1930, Polk County, MO, married Cora Sue Ragsdale Sept. 12, 1954 in Halfway, MO, born April 3, 1932, died Jan. 16, 2002, Polk County, MO, daughter of Wayne Ragsdale and Helene Brown. Children viz: Russell Lee, born Oct. 27, 1955, married Deborah Sue Hoover Nov. 24, 1972, Polk County, MO; Dee Ann, born July 30, 1967, married Daniel Robinson. Children of Russell: Dustin Lee and Ryan Lee. Dustin Lee, born April 27, 1977, married Jennifer Black, children viz: Devin Lee, born May 26, 1998, Anthony Ward, born Aug. 19, 1996. Dee Ann's children: Denae Lynn, born Sept. 5, 1997, Dylan Ward, born Sept. 21, 1999.

Tom and Bertie Dickerson, 1898

The Dickersons came to Polk County in 1856. John H. was a Corporal in Company D, Sixth Missouri Cavalry from July 5, 1861 to July 10, 1864 in the Union Army. After getting out he married his childhood friend and became a farmer like his father. His son T.Y. was also a farmer as his son being raised on the same farm as their father. Earl sold the farm and moved to a new place about 15 miles away and with his son Frank raised and bought horses and mules to ship to the southern states for farming. They also had a dairy farm and sold milk and cream. At the age of 37 Frank farmed part time and drove a truck over the road until he retired. He was in the Korean War 1952-1954. *Submitted by Frank Dickerson*

DIXON - Michael "Mike" Dixon, son of Samuel Winter Dixon and Jane Hammill, was born in east Tennessee in 1833. The family settled in McMinn County, TN where Michael worked as a laborer on the farm of Moses Cunningham (1850). Frederick Hale Jr., his wife Sally Barnett and daughter Martha (born Dec. 25, 1837) were also living in McMinn County at that time. Frederick's grandfather's surname was Cunningham, which suggests that Michael and Martha probably met and married in McMinn County, TN.

In the early 1850s the Frederick Hale and Michael Dixon families began their migration to the west. A son, John Thomas Dixon (born March 30, 1855; died Aug. 14, 1936, married first, Ida Gardner about 1878, and second, Laura E. Bates about 1896), was born in Texas County, MO. By 1860 the families had completed their move to Polk County, MO settling on farms northeast of Brighton, MO.

The names Michael Dixon and Frederick Hale appear in *"A List of the Names of the Rebels of Polk County. . . in accordance with General Order (No. 3) dated Headquarters St. Louis, June 23, 1862."* Confederate Army War Records show that Michael enlisted in Company G, 11th Missouri Infantry and fought in battles from Arkansas to Louisiana. The unit was surrendered by General E. K. Smith, CSA to Major General E. R. S. Canby, USA on May 26, 1865 in New Orleans, LA. Michael Dixon's name appears on the prisoner's list for Alexandria, LA on June 7, 1865 where he was paroled.

Martha A. Hale Dixon, born Dec. 25, 1837 and died Nov. 7, 1921, wife of Michael Dixon, born 1833, died 1878

While living in Polk County Michael and Martha had six children: George B. (1857—unknown); Samuel C. (April 30, 1858-Jan. 18, 1927, married first, Laura J. Wilhite in 1887, and second, Mary Francis Stidham in 1897, and third, Artimisha Elizabeth Grabner in 1925); Margaret (February 1860- before 1878); Elizabeth Jane (Feb. 17, 1861-Sept. 5, 1940, married first, Mr. Hulen about 1888, second, William E. Caldwell in 1892); Frederick C. (April 9, 1866-Jan. 21, 1941 married Annie P. Caldwell in 1897) and William M. (Dec. 2, 1866-Aug. 14, 1922, married Mary Elizabeth Wilhite-Long in 1902).

About 1870 Michael relocated his family to a farm northwest of Columbia, Boone County, MO. The family continued to grow in size with the birth of Mary S. (1870-unknown), Sarah A. (1871-unknown) and Charles M. (July 14, 1873- Nov. 11, 1875). Michael died March 21, 1878 and was buried in the Bethlehem Church Cemetery near their Boone County farm. Martha lived with her son Samuel until about 1918 before moving in with her son Frederick with whom she lived until her death. She died Nov. 7, 1921 in Boone County and is buried with her husband Michael in the Bethlehem Cemetery.

Michael's son Samuel Carrick Dixon returned to the Hickory-Polk County area about 1911. He purchased property on State Road 123 between Humansville and Weaubleau, MO from Samuel Glover Williams. About 1920 Samuel Dixon sold all of his Hickory County properties and moved to land near Humansville. He and his wife Mary Francis (Stidham) Dixon remained in Polk County for several years before returning to Boone County. Samuel died Jan. 18, 1927 and was buried in the Bethlehem Church Cemetery next to his first wife Laura J. (Wilhite) Dixon (1868-1894). Samuel's second wife Mary Francis (Stidham) Dixon, (Sept. 21, 1842- Feb. 17, 1925) is buried in the Harrisburg Cemetery, Harrisburg, Boone County, MO. *Submitted by Donald J. Dixon*

DODD - James Dodd married Nancy Banta Oct. 16, 1824. Nancy was born in Kentucky. They came to Polk County in 1842. Their children were Keziak, Nancy, Martha, Margaret, Henry, Moses, John and Sarah Jane. All were born in Indiana except Sarah Jane, who was born in Missouri in Polk County. Keziak married Richard Wilkinson in 1846. Nancy married John Cantwell in 1847. Martha married Eli Henson in 1855. Margaret married Issec Cross in 1847. Henry married Martha Lusk in 1857. Moses married Nancy Tucknuss. John married Nancy Oglesby in 1870. Sarah Jane married Jacob Oglesby in 1870. James died in 1845 and Nancy died about 1882. Nancy Banta's two sisters, Martha Viles and Keziak Voris, came to Polk County sometime after Nancy did.

The cemetery James and Nancy were buried in has been bulldozed and there is no sign of it now.

The family had settled in the Providence area, the boys staying there. Moses was in the Civil War at Wilson Creek and into Mississippi. Leo served in WWII in Europe. David served in the Vietnam War.

Henry's great-great-grandson Tony Gott owns his farm, which makes it a Century Farm. Leo Dodd has a Century Farm. Part of it came through Great-Great-Grandfather Self, who bought the land from the government. Moses helped organize the Old Time Singing held at Red Top in Dallas County. He and Leo's grandmother Mary sang the old time songs. So did Leo's father, Oscar Dodd. They still have the singing, but they do not sing the old time songs.

Oscar was an ordained minister. The family was Oscar and Estella "Bills." Their children were Ines Agee, Opal Gott, Leo and Leonard "Shorty." Leo also has a grandson who lives in Polk County. His name is Jason Coy Dodd. He has a son named Jackson Clay Dodd. *Submitted by Leo M. Dodd*

DOHLE - Johann "John" Jacob Dohle was the seventh son of Ludwig and Barbara (Neher) Dohle, born May 3, 1859 in Huntington, IN and baptized at St. Peter Lutheran Church. John was a farmer, and was a member of St. Peter Lutheran Church in Huntington. In later years he was known to faithfully attend Providence Missionary Baptist Church of Polk County, MO.

John's father Ludwig was born in 1815 in Tichlen Hesse Kreis, Wurttenburg and Barbara was born in 1823 in Memmingen, Bavaria. Ludwig was a woodworker by trade, and both parents were active members of their church. Ludwig and Barbara's marriage (1849) was the first performed in St. Peter Church after it was built.

John Jacob and Mary Ellen (Dodd) Dohle with her son Pierce Dodd, circa 1911

John Jacob's siblings were Carl Saloman, who was adopted by Ludwig and Barbara, born in 1850, attended school at St. Peter's and died at an early age; Georg David Ludwig, born in 1851, died at 3 months and had a stillborn twin sister;

Christian Daniel, born in 1852, attended school at St. Peter's, married and had children and died at 22 years; Carl Ludwig, born in 1854, died at 20 months; Maria Margaretha, born in 1857, married David Hitzfield, had nine children, and died at 37; Johannes "John" Friedrich was born in 1862; David Friedrich, born in 1866, died single at age 22. Christian and both parents died of consumption. All children were born in Huntington, IN and all except the two stillborn were baptized at St. Peter's.

John Jacob Dohle married three times. His first marriage was to Euphrasine "Rosa" Recklyle, the daughter of Johann and Rosine (Gurthler) Rechlau, on April 25, 1882. Their children were Henry, Rosa B. and Mary who died in infancy. Euphrasine "Rosa" Dohle died in 1888.

Henry Dohle was born in 1883 and married Easter Beatley. They had the following children: Helen S., John W., Francis E., Esther L. and Glen H. Henry died in 1959 in Tampa, FL.

Rosa B. Dohle was born in 1885 and married William R. Minglin in 1906. They had the following children: Ruth B., Margaret, Charles D., Glen L. and Robert J. Minglin. Rosa B. Minglin died in 1969 in South Bend, IN.

John Jacob married Susan (Keeport) Buchman, the daughter of David and Susan (Book) Keeport, on Feb. 9, 1889. There are no known children from this union, though Susan had children from her previous marriage. Susan Dohle died in 1914 in Logansport, IN.

John moved to Oklahoma Territory with his two children sometime before August 1904 and established a 160-acre homestead. About 1910, John moved from Oklahoma to Polk County, MO, sold his Oklahoma homestead and married Mary Ellen Dodd, the daughter of Henry D. and Martha J. (Lusk) Dodd, in 1911. In 1915 they purchased 100 acres in Polk County and built a life together. They had the following children: Ralph D., Henry L. "Bill" and Mary E. "Mattie." On March 12, 1924, John Jacob Dohle died leaving his wife Mary to raise their three children alone. *Submitted by Shannon Renee (Dohle) Cooper*

DONNELL - Among the earliest settlers of what is now Polk County was the Donnell family from Tennessee. James M. Donnell, his second wife, Margaret, and family arrived in the Union Grove area about 1832. It is written that James and his wife brought the first stove to Greene County (which included the southeast part of what is now Polk County). Children making the journey from Tennessee were James' eldest son, John Marcellous Donnell, his wife, Jane McClain Donnell and children, James Monroe and Mary Ann. Also part of the family migration was Martha Donnell and her husband Robert B. Small; Mary Donnell, who married Thomas Glanville after coming to Missouri; William Pinkney Donnell; Archibald Madison Donnell; Robert W. Donnell, who later married Elizabeth Pipkin.

The Donnells were prosperous farmers and stock traders. Annual trips were made to New Orleans to sell mules. John Marcellous and Jane (McClain) Donnell were the parents of several children: James Monroe, Mary Ann, George Washington, Margaret R., William Maxwell, John Martin (who died as a young child), Robert D., Frances Jane, Nancy Caroline, Sarah Clementine (married James Armstrong), Columbus Williamson and Francis Marion. John's wife, Jane, died in 1847 and he married a widow, Jane Wills, who brought four children to the home. They had one son, Winfield Scott Donnell. There could have been 15 or more persons living in the John Donnell household at one time. John Marcellous died Jan. 8, 1860 and was buried in Union Grove Cemetery. One of the first graves in the cemetery, originally on the Donnell farm, was that of the young John Martin who died in 1840.

In 1863, John's daughter, Sarah Clementine, married a widower, James Armstrong, son of Samuel Armstrong, whose farm joined her father's. Sarah and James had six children: Marien (who died as a young child), Sterling Webster, Charles E., John William, Sarah Alice and Mary Frances. Sarah and James Armstrong were prosperous farmers and when they retired, they moved to Bolivar. Following the death of James in 1913, Sarah lived with her surviving children, as was the custom. Sarah was a petite, fair-skinned woman with a quiet demeanor. As did many ladies of that time, Sarah smoked a clay pipe. After each meal while living with her son, Sterling W., they would each fill their pipes with Bull Durham tobacco from a sack and smoke their pipes. Sarah wore a little cloth bag called an "asafetida" filled with herbs, etc. around her neck at all times. The bag was filled with a foul-smelling concoction, which reportedly warded off germs. While visiting her daughter, Mary Frances "Aunt May" Beyersdorf in Spokane, WA, her daughter bought Sarah an elegant, black taffeta dress which Sarah wore for a photo. Later, the dress was used for her burial.

Sarah grew increasingly weak in the spring of 1924 until she was bedfast. On May 29, 1924, Sarah called for her son, S. W. When he came to her room, she asked for a drink of water. Sterling raised her up to give her the water but Sarah passed away in his arms. A kind neighbor, Mrs. Schuler, prepared the black taffeta dress for Sarah's burial and fashioned a matching cap. The undertaker was W. S. White, who had his mortuary on the square in Bolivar. The long journey of the ornate metal white hearse was made from the S. W. Armstrong home west of Bolivar to the church at Union Grove where the service was to be held. The creek near the church was up due to recent rains; the hearse became stuck and nearby farmers brought horses to pull the hearse up the hill. At the funeral service, one of the songs sung by the congregation was The Home Over There. Laid to rest near her husband, Sarah Clementine Donnell Armstrong came full circle to the land where she was born so many years ago on March 4, 1844. *Submitted by Lula Armstrong Kinslow*

Sarah Clementine (Donnell) Armstrong

DOUGLAS - Thomas H. Douglass was born February 1785 and died January 1847 and is buried in the still-existing family cemetery he established on land between Sibley and Buckner, MO in Jackson County, MO. A portion of this land remains in the possession of a descendant. He married first, Anna McCord in 1809 and at least one daughter was born to them, Ann McCord Douglass, in 1810. They were living at that time in Madison County, KY.

After the death of his first wife, Thomas H. Douglass married Myrum Terrill, Sept. 12, 1815 in Garrard County, KY. Myrum's parents were Edmund and Mary Jane (Maxwell) Terrill. Thomas and Myrum had 12 children. Rose descends through the 10th of those, Sidney Albert Douglas, born May 6, 1836, the same year the family moved from Kentucky to Jackson County, MO. What a sight that family entourage must have presented on their journey of between 500 and 600 miles.

Sidney Albert Douglass was a minor at the time of his parents' deaths (1847 for Thomas and 1849 for Myrum). A guardian was appointed for him. Sidney later joined the Confederate Army. In December 1865 he married Melinda J. Graham, born March 4, 1844 in Lexington, MO, the daughter of James Hunter Graham and Elizabeth C. (Harrelson) Graham. They lived in Jackson County, MO and were members of the Six Mile Baptist Church near Sibley for a time, but the family is recorded on the Bates County, MO 1880 census where Sidney became recorder of deeds in 1890.

Sidney and Melinda had seven children. Rose's grandfather, Thomas Harrelson Douglas, was the sixth child and was born Aug. 27, 1882. He married Adelia Culp on Aug. 12, 1908. He received his law degree from Missouri University in 1909 and began practice in Bolivar, Polk County, MO. He was prosecuting attorney of that county from 1914 through 1918 and served several terms as city attorney and in 1928 he was appointed reporter for Springfield, MO Court of Appeals.

Thomas and Adelia had seven children. Rose's father, Elvin Sidney Douglas, was the eldest and was born July 10, 1909. His brothers and sisters were Howard Culp Douglas, born 1911; Thomas Harrelson Douglas Jr., born 1912; Herbert Hinton Douglas, born 1914; Delma (Douglas) Burhans, born 1916; Marjorie (Douglas) Olive, born 1917 and Garland Duane Douglas, born 1924. As of 2002, only Marjorie survives.

Elvin Sidney Douglas received his law degree from University of Missouri in 1932 and that same year he married Florence DeLisle, born July 31, 1909. They had three children, Rose and her two brothers. Ellen Rose Douglas Roweton was born April 2, 1937. Her brothers are Elvin Sidney Douglas Jr., born 1933 and Kerry DeLisle Douglas, born 1946. Both are attorneys. Their parents died nine days apart in 1979.

Elvin S. Douglas family, 1952

On Aug. 16, 1959, Rose married Doran Max "Buck" Roweton. They own the Western Auto Store in Bolivar and have a farming operation. They have five children: Vicki Roweton Morgan, born 1960, married to Bruce Morgan; Kendal Allen Roweton, born 1961; Denni Roweton McColm, born 1962, married to Steve McColm; Marla Roweton Kemp, born 1964, married to Wesley Kemp; and Kelly Doran Roweton, born 1965, married to Susan Casanova Roweton. Rose and Max have 17 grandchildren. *Submitted by E. Rose Roweton*

DUNAWAY – Elijah Alphred Dunaway was born in Polk County on May 18, 1857, son of Thomas and Catherine (Justice) Dunaway. He died June 15, 1943. He was married on Oct. 28, 1877 to Delilah P. McSwain, born April 17, 1857 in Polk County. She died on Dec. 9, 1917. E. A. and Delilah are buried in the old Dunaway family cemetery near Bolivar, MO. E. A. and Delilah had eight children.

Catherine, born Sept. 1, 1881, died on Sept. 21, 1885. Orlena Delilah, born Aug. 12, 1884, was a twin. Seven of these children are buried in the old Dunaway family cemetery. Field rocks are marking their graves.

Their daughter Orlena Delilah Dunaway was born in Polk County on Aug. 12, 1884. She died Dec. 10, 1942. She was married March 3, 1912 to Luther Hanson Standley, born Oct. 31, 1882. He died March 17, 1950. Luther and Lena are buried in Mount Olive Cemetery near Bolivar, MO. They had 10 children: Beulah (born Nov. 29, 1913); twins; Bretha (born 1917; died 1917); Luther L. (born Sept. 20, 1920; died July 26, 1999); Ruby (born March 6, 1922; died Nov. 3, 1998); Robert Elijah (born Dec. 30, 1923; deceased); James Morris (born Feb. 15, 1927); Betty (born April 10, 1929); and Mary (born Aug. 17, 1930).

E. A. Dunaway was married on Aug. 31, 1919 to Nina Pearl (Tucker) Dickerson, daughter of John Anthony and Susan (Standly) Tucker. She was born in Fristoe, Benton County, MO on Jan. 11, 1888. She died in Fordland, MO on Nov. 15, 1964. She's buried in Humansville, MO. They had three children: Pearl Willine, Alphred Orlean and Thomas Paul.

Pearl Willine was born Aug. 20, 1920 in Halfway, MO. (See Belbacks) Willine was married on July 25, 1957 to Timothy Winton Reaves, son of Araham and Nancy (Bell) Reaves. He was born in Webster County, MO on Jan. 27, 1905 and died in Grants Pass, OR on Feb. 13, 1977. They're buried in Memorial Park Cemetery in Grants Pass, OR.

Alphred Orlean Dunaway was born in Halfway, MO on Dec. 3, 1921; married on Oct. 11, 1941 to Nellie Marie Syphert, born in Osceola, MO on Jan. 4, 1923, daughter of Samuel and Helen (Tidwell) Syphert. Nellie died on Dec. 14, 2001 in Springfield, MO. They had three children.

Alphred Elijah, born July 14, 1942 in Polk County, married Feb. 16, 1968 to Judy Stevens. She was born on Nov. 19, 1946. They had two children, Stacy Paulette, born on May 3, 1970 and Tracey Lynn, born on July 27, 1971.

Helen Marie Dunaway, born in Polk County on Sept. 27, 1947; married Dec. 23, 1965 to Richard T. Porter, born Nov. 15, 1945. They had two children, Susan Michelle, born April 17, 1971 and John Alphred, born April 13, 1974. Helen Marie married Robert Kenchloe.

Sherry Ann Dunaway, born in Springfield, MO on Aug. 11, 1954, married Oct. 6, 1972 to Timothy Lovett, born May 1, 1954. They had two children, Angela, born April 21, 1973 and Brian, born Dec. 14, 1977.

Thomas Paul Dunaway, born in Polk County, MO on April 28, 1924, died in Ocean Springs, MS on Aug. 24, 1991, buried in National Cemetery (Springfield, MO); married in April 1961 to Evelyn Syphert, born May 28, 1948, daughter of Sherman and Edith Syphert. Tom and Evelyn divorced in 1964. *Submitted by Alphred Dunaway*

DUNN - Riley Benson Dunn, the third of five children, was born Jan. 28, 1883 in Daviess County, KY to Henry Crittendon Dunn and Susan Hill. Riley's family moved to Charleston, MO in 1890 by way of wagon. He worked for a newspaper company in Charleston as a young man. Riley first married Maud Mercer in Charleston, MO on Dec. 24, 1906. They had three children: Earlene Dunn, born in 1910, William Dunn, born in 1911 and Richard Dunn, born in 1912. Riley and Maud lived in Marmaduke, AR with the children until 1916. After Maud died, Riley and the children moved back to Missouri. Earlene Dunn was last known to be living in California. William Dunn died in 1925 at the age of 14 and Richard Dunn died in 1932 at the age of 20.

Riley then met and married Louie Alice Coldsmith Maupin at Harrisonville, MO on May 18, 1918. She was the daughter of Samuel Coldsmith and Frances Suddarth. Alice Maupin had two children from a previous marriage, Lyle Maupin and Louis Maupin. Riley and Alice added five more children to their growing family to total 10 children. Their children together were Louella May Dunn, born in 1919; Mary Lee Dunn, born in 1921; Riley Benson Dunn Jr., born in 1922; Charles Carney Dunn, born in 1924 and James Russell Dunn, born in 1925.

Riley started to work for the St. Louis - San Francisco Railway (Frisco) in Blairstown, MO. Riley and his family moved to Polk County, MO in August of 1932. They lived in the "section" house next to the railroad in Cliquot. This house was fully furnished by Frisco. While living in Cliquot, Riley pumped water for the steam engines at Wishart, Cliquot, Gerster and Osceola, MO. His whole family was provided with free passes to ride the trains. Alice Dunn took a job as postmaster at the Cliquot Post Office for seven years. In 1943, Riley and Alice's daughter, Mary, was appointed the postmaster job in Cliquot until the post office closed in 1957. Riley and Alice moved around for a while with the railroad until Riley retired in 1955 in Dixon, MO. He died Nov. 12, 1958 at the age of 75. Alice Dunn moved back to Bolivar, MO in 1960 to be near her daughters. Alice died in Bolivar on April 11, 1978 at the age of 95.

Riley and Alice Dunn's two oldest daughters stayed in Polk County, MO. Louella May Dunn married Elrie Healey on Feb. 28, 1949. They had one daughter, Patricia Lou Healey, born Sept. 2, 1957 in Illinois. Patti attended school in Bolivar and graduated from BHS in 1975. Patti then attended SMSU and St. John's School of Nursing. She married Tom Cox and now teaches classes at the Missouri School of Nursing in Rolla, MO. Patti and Tom also own a shoe store in St. James, MO. They have two children: Brandon Cox and Derrick Cox. After Elrie died, Louella moved to St. James to be near her daughter and grandchildren.

Riley and Alice Dunn

Mary Lee Dunn married Harold L. Garretson of Polk County on Jan. 8, 1938 in Osceola, MO. He was the son of Isaac M. Garretson and Clara Louise Collier. Harold and Mary lived in Cliquot, where Mary worked as the postmaster for 14 years. Harold worked different jobs for several years, but in 1958, Harold and Mary moved to Bolivar where they owned and operated Garretson's Trash Service for 12 years. Harold and Mary had four children: Mildred Ethel Garretson, born Oct. 29, 1938; Lyle Lee Garretson, born Sept. 16, 1946; Fred Earl Garretson, born May 1, 1942; and Harold James Garretson, born Sept. 18, 1944. Mildred and her husband, Bob are now retired and reside at Lake of the Ozarks. Lyle "Buster" and his wife, Kay, have owned and operated Garretson's Trash Service for 33 years. Fred "Bud" is now retired and spends some of his time in Kansas City and the rest at his cabin on Lake Pomme De Terre. After Harold J. "Jim" retired, he and his wife Sharon moved back to Polk County to work on the farm until his death in 1999. Sharon continues to live here and work at SBU.

Riley Dunn Jr. married Lois F. Adams on Dec. 6, 1941 in Bolivar, MO. She was the daughter of Jason and Clara Adams. Riley Jr. and Lois had three children: Janice Brix, Evelyn Hicks and Richard Dunn. Riley Dunn Jr. died Oct. 19, 1973 in Decatur, IL.

Charles C. Dunn married Geneva Hornbeek on March 22, 1943 in Stockton, MO. She was the daughter of Charles Hornbeek and Zelia Parrott. Carney and Geneva had four children: Dale, Gene and Ronnie Dunn, and Carol Force. Charles Dunn died Aug. 19, 1994 in St. Joseph, MO.

James R. Dunn married Pauline Helms. James and Pauline had four children: James, Thomas, Charles and Mark Dunn. James R. Dunn died Dec. 19, 1976 in Pacific, MO. *Submitted by Mary (Dunn) Engleman*

Dick and Val Dunagan of Wisconsin on the "Dunnagan Trail" in the Eno River State Park near Durham in North Carolina

DUNNEGAN - Finding Dunnegans of various spellings in Orange County, NC, Hall County, GA, Gentry County, MO and in Polk County, MO were key steps in the early 1990s for this retired history teacher asking, "Where did my Indiana Dunagans come from and where did they go?"

The Irish or Scotch-Irish background is still somewhat unclear. Among Dunnegan researchers there is still a lack of agreement about whether we trace from the "Dunnage" surname of colonial Virginia in the 1630s, the surname recorded as "Dunningham" in Virginia in 1738, or some other early arrival group. Varieties of spelling used by careless clerks and independent thinking relatives continue to provide research difficulties to this day.

The solid evidence shows that a variety of "Dunnagans" settled in the valleys of the Little River, Eno River and Yadkin River of North Carolina in the mid 1700s. Some of their descendants are still there.

By the late 1760s one of the Thomas Dunnagans left his land on "Tom's Creek" in North Carolina to claim land in southeast Georgia at the London Bluff location on the Savannah River near Spirit Creek and near Fort Augusta. Later he moved his family to the north fork (another "Tom's Creek") of the Broad River of northeast Georgia. Other Dunnagans moved into the north Georgia frontier area and were part of the militia defensive system. Captain John Lain's military report said, "Joseph Dunagan Hath Bilt the block hous agreable to the with in dementions - Certified this 8th day of March 1794. [sic]" It was built on land owned by Thomas Dunnagan. Joseph was paid and the event was recorded. In modern times, it was Jimmy Dunagan of Sharpsburg, GA who dug this story from the Georgia archives.

Several Dunnagans and neighbors complained that the surveyed line for the Cherokee treaty in Georgia unfairly and mistakenly indicated them on the Indian side of the line. They petitioned for negotiation of a new treaty. President Jefferson told his Secretary of State to straighten out the problems when the white settlers claimed the line was wrong and the Cherokee nation claimed they had not been paid.

Although mainly in three different colonies, North Carolina, South Carolina and Georgia, many of the Dunnagans of the colonial frontier still lived somewhat close to each other. Some probably raised livestock in north Georgia and then drove them to the meadow holding area of South Carolina "cow pens" before going to market. The "Battle of Cowpens [sic]" in the Revolutionary War was a few days after the more famous "Battle of Kings Mountain" that was nearby. Because of the family tradition of supporting the militia, it is likely that some of the local Dunagans may have been involved in these battles.

Some Dunagans stayed in this three-state area. Some went to northern Alabama and northern Mississippi. Abner Dunagan took his family on the trails (too early for most roads) to the frontier in southwest Georgia. Solomon Dunagan Sr., Dick's great-great-grandfather, migrated to Kentucky by 1800, to Indiana by 1822, and to Missouri by 1838. Solomon's brother, Isaac Dunagan, settled in southern Kentucky but many of Isaac's children went west. Although Solomon died in 1846 in Andrew County MO, his nine children by his first wife and nine children by his second wife were in several states.

Meanwhile, by 1804 three adult Dunnagans from North Carolina settled in Dickson County, TN. Naming the new Tennessee village "Eno" suggests that they came from the settlement of Dunnagans in the Eno River Valley of Orange County, NC. Over time some of them adopted the "Donnegan" and "Dunnegan" spellings. Many of the descendants went west, including some who went to Polk County, MO.

Many of the scattered Dunagans do not know these details, but do trace their family lines back to "Old Zeke," to Ezekiel Dunagan of north Georgia. Starting in the 1790s, Ezekiel's home was in Franklin County, then Jackson County, and eventually in the northeast corner of Hall County (the same house, but different county lines). With 13 children by his first wife and six children by his second wife there are many descendants with a north Georgia connection. The web site about the Dunagan Methodist Chapel in Hall County, GA is a good way to start exploring this background.

Although not among the very first explorers or the richest of the land-hungry settlers, there were many Dunagans of various spellings involved in the westward movement.

There was one, Joseph, signing the Cumberland Compact at the site of the future Nashville in 1780, but he apparently returned to Georgia. Another one, Francis, sold land west of the Mississippi River, near St. Louis, to Meriwether Lewis soon after the Lewis and Clark expedition returned to St. Louis. Villages, cemeteries, a lake, and a mountain named Dunnegan (in one spelling or another) appeared in Missouri, Kansas, Minnesota, Texas, Montana and California. A Kentucky-born Isaac Dunagan settled in the Republic of Texas before it became a part of the United States. At least one Dunagan went with McCloskey to California via the Panama route in the California gold rush and then returned to Georgia with his gold. The Arkansas farmhouse of Rev. Jasper Dunagin was burned when his farm became the site of the "Battle of Dunagin's Farm;" a preliminary skirmish of the Civil War's "Battle of Pea Ridge."

Dunagans from 14 or more states fought on both sides of the Civil War; but mostly for the South. The 1985 book, *Dunnagans in Dixie*, by Martha Gujda of California, reports on some of the families. Dunigans who went northwest from North Carolina to Ohio and other points west had more relatives in the Union Army.

A second wave of immigration from Ireland to America, starting in the famine years of the 1840s, brought more Dunnigans of various spellings. Very few of them, however, had any evidence or oral history to help remember their possible relationship with the earlier Dunagans of the 1700s.

The Primary Evidence memoirs of Thomas Hart Benton Dunnegan of Polk County, MO helps to confirm the facts and the feelings of an important part of the DOAS western migration and settlement. They look forward to learning more of his relationship to the Dunnagans and Bentons of North Carolina.

By 2002 the two states with the most Dunagans are Texas and California. The scattered Dunagans are learning to improve the process of sharing information with key books (such as this one), with the Internet, and with the *Dunnagans of All Spellings* (DOAS) newsletter.

Key sources for this article were Sybil McRay and George J. Dunagan of Hall County, GA; Jimmy Dunagan of Sharpsburg, GA; the North Carolina archives; the Georgia archives; Duston Stout of Oklahoma; Peggy Riviere of Washington; Carllene Marek and Martha Gujda of California; as well as the memoirs of T. H. B. Dunnegan of Polk County, MO. *Submitted by Dick Dunagan*

DUNNEGAN - Most of the information in this article comes directly from memoirs written in 1903 by William Dunnegan's grandson, Thomas Hart Benton Dunnegan. A copy of these memoirs is in the Bolivar Historical Museum.

William Dunnegan and Rodah Griffin were married Feb. 16, 1804 in Surry County, NC. Bondsman was listed as John Dunnegan, presumably William's father.

William and Rodah were the parents of nine children; most of whom were born after the family moved to Tennessee. Around 1831, with nearly all of their children grown, the family, apparently with all but two of their children, moved to Missouri, first to St. Francois and Morgan Counties and then to Polk County by 1835.

The remainder of this article will center on a

Front: Olive, Bess, Dorothy, Grace and T. H. B. Jr., Back row: Willard, T. H. B. Sr., Matt and John

son and a grandson of William, both of whom were prominent citizens of Polk County.

The son, Francis, was born Feb. 18, 1805 in North Carolina. Around 1831 he married Nancy Lenox and they settled in Missouri at Big Spring, which later became known as Dunnegan Springs. They were the parents of eight (or perhaps nine) children who lived to adulthood, but three sons died fighting for the Confederacy.

According to the memoirs, Francis built a gristmill, sawmill and one of the first wool-carding machines in this part of the country. Later he built a large flouring mill on Big Sac River in Cedar County near Stockton, where the family moved in 1856. While still in Polk County, he built mills for others all over southwest Missouri. He was a member of the old Bolivar Lodge, No. 41, and served as county judge in both counties. Francis died in 1877 and Nancy in 1882. Both are buried in Lindley Prairie.

Thomas Hart Benton Dunnegan, known simply as T. H. B., is the author of the memoirs mentioned at the beginning. He is William's grandson and his story needs to be included in this book.

T. H. B. was born to William Dunnegan's son, Matthew and his wife, Priscilla Akard, on April 1, 1842 in Lawrence County. During T. H. B.'s childhood, his family lived in a number of Missouri counties: Polk, Lawrence, Jasper, Dade and back to Polk.

After serving in the Union Army, he returned to Bolivar where he married Sally Beggs in 1866, by whom he had four sons. After Sally's death in 1876, he married Ella Carothers, and there were six children from this marriage.

T. H. B. acquired another title, "The Judge," after serving several years as a judge and also as sheriff and collector. Then in 1872 he helped organize a new bank called Tolfree, Dunnegan and Company (later Polk County Bank) and became bank president.

T. H. B. had many interests: literature, art, architecture, roses, music, education, etc. The bank was almost like a museum with many paintings, artifacts and rare books. During his long life, he was a major benefactor for the town of Bolivar, donating land or funds for many innovative ventures, including a memorial park, cemetery, library, the Methodist Church and Southwest Baptist College. He continued as bank president until his death in 1934 at age 92.

At that time, two unmarried sons from his second marriage, Thomas Hart Benton Dunnegan Jr. and John (known as Mr. Benton and Mr. John) took over the management of the bank, Mr. Benton as president and Mr. John as cashier. Bolivar continued to benefit from their generosity with the formation of the Community Concert Association and the Dunnegan Art Museum, named for their mother, Ella Carothers Dunnegan. The two sons served as bank officials until their deaths in 1983 and 1985 (ages 90 and 91). *Submitted by Peggy Culbertson*

Seated: Samuel Issac Durham and spouse Nora Bell Durham holding son, Ulysses, girl in back is household helper, Lisa Vest

DURHAM – The history of the Durham family shows many Durhams marrying Durham relatives. It was told that the family had money and wanted to keep it within the family. Coleman Durham married Lucretia Nancy Durham. They had seven children. Their son Benjamin Franklin, born Feb. 6, 1849 in Jacksonville, Randolph County, MO, married Mary Catherine Durham. Mary Catherine was born March 16, 1856 in Casey County, KY. Her parents were James "Kentucky Jim" Durham and Jane Coleman Durham. Benjamin and Mary had five children: George, Lucretia, Frank, Audra and Samuel Isaac, born Jan. 8, 1870 in Randolph County. Benjamin and Mary moved to Bolivar, MO about 1877. The couple later divorced, each remarried. Benjamin married Emma Hocker and Mary married Zackary Taylor Durham (an uncle to Benjamin). Samuel Issac married Nora Belle Durham born March 9, 1869. Samuel and Nora had seven children: Ulysses, Izare, Loder May, Dorothy, Horace, Clifford and Walter Franklin, born Sept. 18, 1894. Samuel made his living making monument headstones. He conducted his business in Polk County for many years. Some of the headstones he made are still standing today. He died in 1945 from an explosion from a coal oil stove. Samuel and Nora's son Walter married Mary Elizabeth Ballinger on Aug. 2, 1919. Mary was born in 1899. Walter spent most of his life as a carpenter and painter. Mary did a lot of sewing, always singing as she worked. She also had much musical talent playing instruments. Walter and Mary had six children: Willard (Franklin), born Oct. 11, 1920; Helen Pauline, born March 16, 1923; Clifford Truman "Buck," born June 26, 1927; Walter (Almas), born Dec. 24, 1929; Marcella Geneva, born April 4, 1932; and Gertrude Elizabeth, born Nov. 21, 1924 who married Otis Cowden. The three sons Franklin, Clifford and Almas all served in the United States Army during WWII. Franklin and Clifford were reported as MIAs during the same time. Franklin spent time on an island inhabited by cannibals. Clifford and Almas also served in the Korean War. All returned home safely. Mary died in 1934, leaving Walter to raise six young children. Walter married a widow also with young children to raise, Ruby "Gladys" Hembree Blacketer. Together Walter and Gladys raised their large family, later adding two of their own to the fold. They had two daughters, Lois Vivian, born July 28, 1939 and Shirley Ann, born Feb. 12, 1938. While the girls were young, Gladys developed an illness that left her bedridden for the rest of her life. Her illness didn't keep the family from fun times. Walter would load up the family, Gladys included, and took many family trips, some as far away as California. *Submitted by Gertrude (Durham) Cowden*

DYE - David A. Dye and Terri L. Dye met in the little town of Sebastian, FL in the spring of 1985. By the time autumn of the same year rolled around they were married and making their home in the Ozarks where he had always wanted to settle and raise a family.

David Alan was born in Lee's Summit, MO to William "Bill" Newton Dye and Zola Pearl (Davis) Dye on July 29, 1955. He has two older sisters Sheryl Jan (Dye) Pulse of Oldfield, MO and Phyllis Janette Dye of Billings, MO. David grew up northwest of Springfield. His parents were well rooted here in the Ozarks as well. His dad was from South Greenfield and his mother was from Dadeville. They passed away when David was a young man. They are buried in Penesboro Cemetery near Greenfield, MO. Also in Penesboro are David George Dye who is David's great-great-grandfather, lovingly known as "Pap," along with his first wife Nellie and some of his children. When David was a young man he joined the Marines. After serving four years he entered the work force. David found that sales was something that suited his personality and kept him challenged; although he does have quite an entrepreneurial spirit which has led him to many small business ventures throughout his sales career.

Terri Lee was born in Plymouth, MA to John Maki and Leah (Field) Maki on July 13, 1962. Her mother divorced when she was young and remarried Wendell Colburn Bassett. She was raised by her grandparents, George Carter and Lois Bessie (Snowdale) Field until they moved to Florida in 1971. Then she moved in with her mom and step-dad. Terri spent her childhood playing on the beaches, clamming, swimming, and collecting treasures from the shoreline, especially after a storm. Her interests were art, reading and craft making. Terri's family roots run deep in New England, specifically in the Plymouth, Cape Cod and Nantucket area.

David and Terri now have four children: Megan Elizabeth Dye, born on July 27, 1986 in Springfield, MO; Katherine Pearl Dye, born on March 25, 1988 in Vero Beach, FL; Michael Riley Dye, born on Oct. 22, 1993 in Bolivar, MO and lastly, but certainly not least William Jacob Dye, born on Dec. 14, 1995 in Bolivar, MO.

They live on 10 acres in Humansville, MO where they homeschool their children. *Submitted by Terri Dye*

Joseph A. Eagon, 1890 to 1976

EAGON - The impact of the development of the free rural mail delivery system initiated in 1902 by the US Postal system and becoming operational in Halfway by 1908 had a lasting effect on the Eagon family.

Burdette's father Joseph Arthur Eagon (1890-1976) was the mail carrier in 1908. He made frequent deliveries to the McLellan household. Burdette's mother, then a young lady from Wisconsin, Belle Stutzman (1892-1982), a relative of the McLellans visited in the summer of 1908, 1909, and again in 1910. Each summer she

Jessie and Joseph Eagon, 1909

was attended to by her older sister, Elizabeth. Eventually a romantic relationship developed between Belle and Joe during the course of the daily mail delivery. When Belle returned to Halfway in 1910, Joe and Belle were married in Bolivar, MO on Nov. 5, 1910.

Burdette's grandfather John Thomas Eagon was the sheriff of Polk County in 1910. Sheriff John Eagon's Colt 45 revolver was given to the Polk County Historical Society in 1994. The marriage of Joe and Belle took place at the County Jailhouse in Bolivar. Belle and Joe often joked about being married in jail. After the wedding they made the move to Belle's family homestead near Winneconne, WI. Three children were born: Beatrice in 1916, Bernece in 1918 and their only son Burdette in 1919.

Each summer from the time the kids can remember, they traveled back to Halfway, MO to visit their Great Grandmother Hadlock and Grandma Mary Eagon, their cousins the Glovers and Tafts. (Aunt Lily, Uncle George, Cousins Marjorie, Amy and Willie) They also visited Uncle OL and Aunt Amy Red.

Burdette especially remembers Grandma's house, east of Halfway, the first road to the right and up the rocky hill. He can still see the front porch swing and rocking chair, the old round barn, the fenced yard with chickens, a cow, a mule and a few pigs. They swam in the creek a short distance from the house.

Upon arriving Burdette's dad would stop the car in front of the house. His dad would always send one of the children to the door for something, fill a water jug, buy eggs, or ask for directions. Then he would appear and surprise Grandma.

Traveling was always great fun. They would always pitch a tent and sleep on cots with the smaller kids on the running boards of the car. The big trunk was anchored on the back of the car. It carried the tent, a little stove, food, and extra clothes. Over the years the travel time improved from

Great-Grandmother Hadlock

five to two days on the road. (From a Model T, a Chevrolet, to a Pontiac of the 1930s.) In those days small streams were crossed on roads simply by driving through them, however Burdette remembers the perilous travel after a flood one year when they were forced to cross a bridge near Lebanon, MO that had only two narrow planks to drive on. These visits to Halfway were always the highlight of the year and dearly remembered by all.

Burdette's father and mother made it a point to return to Halfway every year, if only to pass through or visit the cemetery. They enjoyed their reminiscences of meeting in Halfway and their life-long relationship. *Submitted by Burdette W. Eagon*

EAGON – Jesse Eagon Sr., born April 23, 1801 and his wife Elizabeth (Morris) Eagon, born May 2, 1799, came from Vinton County, OH circa 1853 to Halfway, MO along with their extended family. Jesse and Elizabeth were born in Waynesburg, Greene County, PA and were married June 28, 1821. They settled southeast of Halfway near Blue Mounds. A descendant has a large chest of drawers that Jesse made and brought in the covered wagon from Ohio. Jesse later built a top cabinet for it from packing cases with "Halfway" printed on the back. He died on a trip to north Missouri Oct. 15, 1865 and was buried there. Elizabeth died March 25, 1881, buried at Reed Cemetery. (Dates from family Bible.)

Jesse Eagon born ca. 1801

Jesse's father Barnet and his grandfather James (born circa 1740, Virginia) were both Revolutionary War soldiers in Captain James Archer's militia from Washington County, PA. Barnet married Hannah Wood, later moving to Guernsey County, OH where he died circa 1833.

The children of Jesse Sr. and Elizabeth Morris Eagon and their spouses were Hannah, born 1822 (married William Messer); Rebecca, born 1824, died 1825; Barnard, born 1826 (married first, Amy Clark, second, Lucinda Long, and third, Sallie Ann Gray); Mary, born 1828 (married Richard Ankrom); John Morris, born 1830 (married Mary Ratcliff); Jesse W., born 1835 (married Elizabeth Ann Boren); and James L., born 1838 (married Araminta Vanderford). Jesse W. is the one often mistaken for his father, Jesse Sr.

Linda's line descends from Jesse Sr.'s son Barnard and second wife Lucinda Long, born 1836 Bedford County, TN, died circa 1870. Barnard served as a corporal in the 26th Regiment, Company K, Missouri Militia of the Civil War.

Barnard and Lucinda's son John Henry Eagon, born Dec. 21, 1858 in Bolivar, died April 25, 1937, was a minister of the Christian Church and operated a small store. A family member has candy scales from that store. He married Emma Cunningham, born March 9, 1877, died Sept. 6, 1951. Her parents were John and Martha Jane Hutcheson Cunningham. John and Emma are buried at Mt. Olive.

John and Emma Eagon's children were Bertha, born Aug. 28, 1907, died Oct. 24, 1981 and Barnard Pearl, born March 11, 1911, died May 19, 1983. Bertha married Fred Engle, born March 9, 1907, died Sept. 12, 1968. Fred was the Sinclair Oil bulk dealer in the 1930s in Bolivar and was the Ford Automobile and Tractor Dealer there in the 1940s. Fred and Bertha are buried in Aurora, MO where he had the Chevrolet Dealership. Their children are

Bertha and Barney Eagon, 1911

1928 John H. Eagan & Emma (Cunninghham) Eagan. Granddaughter Emogene (Engle) Conrad

Emogene, married John Conrad; and Fred Earl Jr., married Kay Goodridge.

Barnard Pearl "Barney" Eagon married Hallie Day, lived in Lamar, MO was Phillips 66 Oil Dealer and owned Blue Top Restaurant there. Their children are Mike and Patricia.

John and Emma Eagon's home was featured in the 1976 booklet *A Driving Tour of Bolivar's Historic Homes*. It still stands today at 919 West Fair Play Street in Bolivar. *Submitted by Linda Conrad Hileman*

EALY - Pleasant Layfette Ealy was born Feb. 10, 1861 to James Robert and Elveria Greenlee Ealy near Greenville, TN but moved with his parents to Belle Plain, IA at the age of 4. P. L. and Minnie (Bricker) Ealy were childhood sweethearts, both growing up in Belle Plain, IA. They were very young when they married and P. L. worked for the railroad. Shortly after their wedding P. L. was transferred to Douglas, WY on September 1, 1886 to operate the roundhouse for FEMV Railroad, at what was then the "end of the line." While living there, three children were born to them, one being a baby girl who died shortly after birth and is buried in the Pioneer Cemetery in Douglas. P. L. and Minnie then moved back to Belle Plain for a few more years where two more children were born to them.

P. L. and Charles Ealy

They read about Polk County, MO where the trees, grass, and water were plentiful and the land was cheap. So, about 1895, they packed all their belongings in two wagons and, along with their children and livestock, set out to travel approximately 350 miles to what was going to be their home for the rest of their lives. They camped at night beside the trail where Minnie cooked their meals over a campfire and P. L. bought feed for the livestock from farmers along the way. They camped their final night on a farm between Wheatland and Elkton and arrived the next day at their farm, which was located two miles south of Adonis. The couple acquired almost an entire section of land and the homestead was just south of what was later to be called the Ealy Bluff overlooking the Pomme de Terre River. Over the next few years five more children were born. Eight children grew to adulthood. Those children are known as: Frank Ealy,

Clark Ealy, Elsie Ealy Borneman, Earl Ealy, Mae Ealy Walden, Charley Ealy, Arthur Ealy and Ethel Ealy Blanton.

Minnie Ealy was a true pioneer woman. Many times she would be called on in the neighborhood to deliver a baby or render a home remedy for someone who was ill. As the children grew up they all moved away, except Earl and Charley who stayed on the family farm all of their lives.

Charley married Opal Sullivan, daughter of Charley Sullivan and granddaughter of Jacob Bishop of Halfway. They had three children: Charles L., Dorothy and Mary. Charles married Shirley Newland, daughter of Arthur and Thelma (Ashlock) Newland. Charles and Shirley had three children: Danny, Judy and Barbara. Danny is the only Ealy great-grandson and Jeremy Ealy, Danny's son, is the only Ealy great-great-grandson.

When P. L. and Minnie moved to Adonis, it had several stores, a post office, a school and a church; all of which are gone except the church, which still has regular services. P. L. and Minnie, along with other family members, are buried in the Adonis Cemetery.

Charles L. Ealy was elected Mayor of Bolivar, MO on April 6, 1997.

EMMETT - Albert Emmett was born Dec. 11, 1814 in Carter County, TN to Lucas and Mary (Kelley) Emmett. He served six weeks in the First Regiment of Tennessee Volunteers in June/July 1838 when he rounded up or guarded Cherokee Indians for what became known as the Trail of Tears.

In Tennessee he married a young widow Elizabeth J. (Wininger) Haggard, born Jan. 22, 1827. Elizabeth had one daughter, Nancy J. Haggard.

Albert and Elizabeth's eight children were born in Hawkins County, TN and it was from there in October 1871 they moved their family, ages 20 to 5 months, to Polk County. (Nancy Haggard had married John B. Rodgers on Aug. 4, 1867 in Hawkins County and they moved, too.)

Flora Agnes Earp, Albert and Elizabeth's granddaughter wrote that they made the journey in a covered wagon, "camping at night wherever they happened to be at that time." Another granddaughter, Vera Emmett Dorman, inherited "the clever round kettle they cooked in during the move. It was hung under the wagon when they traveled."

Flora Earp remembered her mother, Mary Frances, telling her "they met some people who were also traveling in a covered wagon. They asked my Grandfather where they were going. He told them to Polk County, MO. The man said, 'We have been there and we didn't like it. Now we are going back home and you folks will come poking back, too!'"

On the trip with the Emmetts was the Jacob and Nancy Stokes family, including their son, John, age 11. In 1999 Chester Stokes, John's son, said they had split horseshoes and shod the cows' hooves for the overland journey.

Vera Emmett Dorman wrote, "Albert Emmett was a man of few words," but his son, her father Hiram, "was a talkative, devilish child who always saw everything." She said members of the Stokes family told about how entertaining Hiram was and how Hiram, age 5, liked to sit on the men's laps during the journey.

Albert Emmett and his family didn't go "poking back" to Tennessee but stayed in Polk County where most spent the rest of their lives.

James L. Emmett was born about 1850 and married Julia L. Arnold on April 8, 1875 in Polk County. He died in Prescott, AR about 1917. Julia died Dec. 28, 1928 in Whitesboro, TX.

Mary Frances Emmett was born June 12, 1853 and died Jan. 12, 1924. She married Solomon Martin Earp on March 20, 1884 in Polk County.

They had one daughter, Flora Agnes. Mary Frances and Solomon are buried in Rondo Cemetery.

John Vincent Emmett was born Aug. 4, 1856 and died June 12, 1933. He married Mandia J. Chapman on June 28, 1874 and they had five children who all died before their parents: Mary F. "Mollie" married first, Lewis Curtis Crawford, married second, Lewis C. Lunceford; Julie M.; William F.; Edward F. married Stella Crawford; and Jessie L. married James Carneal. John and Amanda are buried in Salem Cemetery.

Samuel Fred Emmett was born Feb. 25, 1859 and died Nov. 10, 1936. He married Florence Clementine Ralph Nov. 7, 1892 and they had one son, Leslie Fred who married Mattie Vest. They are buried in Rondo Cemetery.

Sarah A. Emmett was born July 4, 1861 and died March 14, 1908. She married Lafayette Wells Sept. 22, 1892. After his 1899 death she married George Washington Dunivant Sept. 17, 1900 and they had one daughter, Geneva Vivian "Neva" married George Vernon Holt. Sarah and George are buried in Tillery Cemetery.

Hiram Wills Emmett and Orleana Ann Butler, Oct. 20, 1889 wedding photo

William Emmett was born Sept. 20, 1863, died Jan. 23, 1916 and was buried at Rondo Cemetery.

Hiram Wills Emmett was born April 12, 1866 and died Nov. 24, 1934. (A neighbor of Albert and Elizabeth's in Hawkins County was Hiram Wills.) He married Orlena Ann "Lena" Butler Oct. 20, 1889 in Bolivar and they had eight children: Euliah, born Oct. 29, 1890, died Dec. 13, 1890, buried Rondo; Vera, born March 30, 1894, died Sept. 2, 1970. Vera married Rev. Clarence Wilbur Dorman Jan. 23, 1917 and they had one daughter, Vera Doris. Maybelle, born Oct. 17, 1896, died Feb. 14, 1946. Maybelle married Victor Nels Johnson July 18, 1931 and they adopted one son Richard Dean. Twin daughters born and died 1898, buried Rondo. Ruby Marie born Aug. 17, 1901, died Jan. 19, 1984. Ruby married Daniel Raymond Thatch March 15, 1924 and they had one daughter, Nancy Ruth. Thomas Ralph, born Jan. 17, 1905, died Feb. 1, 1994. Ralph married Mary Louise Garretson April 5, 1930 and they had seven children: Clara Louise, Mary Margaret, Frances Waneta, Thomas Ralph Jr., Dorothy Carol, John Robert, James William. After Mary's death Ralph married Ruth Andrews Marsh, Mary Neff, and Marjorie Leazer. Edith Elizabeth, born May 6, 1907 and died Oct. 1, 1984. Edith married Dale Yeager Sept. 6, 1924. Dale, son of Homer Elbert and Mollie Viola (Walker) Yeager, was born Dec. 2, 1902 and died Sept. 14, 1946. They had three children: Lena Maybelle (born May 19, 1925, died June 13, 2002), Robbie Jean and Edwin Dale. After Dale's death, Edith married Orla Emerson Cooper March 11, 1949. Hiram and Lena Emmett are buried in Rondo Cemetery.

Clara Medora "Dora" Emmett was born Nov. 20, 1869 and died May 3, 1929. She married William Alexander Ralph Nov. 13, 1889 and they had four children: Meta (married Eric A. Kuechel), Neva (married George F. Bandick), Jewell E. (married Elmer R. Gulledge) and Esther Mae (married Carl Otis Miller). Dora and Alex died in California where their last two children were born.

Elizabeth died March 15, 1898. Albert died June 17, 1901 in Humansville. Even though in 1892 at Bolivar, Albert had signed his Indian Wars pension application "Albert Emmert," he and Elizabeth were buried in Rondo Cemetery beside a tombstone inscribed "Emett." They and their children spelled their name without the "r" and with an added "t" after moving to Polk County, MO. *Submitted by Ruby Sharon Downs*

ERVEN - Marinell Rayfield got her first glimpse of Bolivar and Polk County on a Sunday afternoon in 1964. She was arriving at the campus of (then) Southwest Baptist College. After moving into Memorial Hall and getting settled, she started attending college functions. At one of these, she spotted a handsome young man, also a freshman, and she was smitten.

However, she never saw the young man again until the second semester, when they were both enrolled in Harlie Gallatin's political science classes. The rest is history.

The young man was Ron Erven, and although she hadn't seen him again, he had seen her cheerleading at SBU basketball games. Marinell hadn't seen him on campus because he was a local student who lived at home and worked part-time, so he didn't spend a lot of time on campus.

They married in 1966 and both got teaching degrees from SMSU. They taught in southeast Missouri for three years before returning to Bolivar in 1973, when Ron went to work for Teters Floral Products Co. He started as assistant manufacturing manager and later set up the human resources department. He retired in 2000 as vice president of human resources.

Marinell taught in Halfway, Stockton, and Bolivar. After having earned her MS degree, she was an elementary administrator in Bolivar, Humansville and Stockton. She taught one year at SBU before re-starting the Polk County Christian School as teacher/administrator. She retired from there in 2001. In 2002, she was one of nine Republicans vying for the newly created Recorder of Deeds position. Even though she wasn't elected, she met hundreds of wonderful Polk Countians whom she never would have met otherwise.

Marinell has been involved in numerous educational organizations, including Phi Delta Kappa and Delta Kappa Pi, honorary fraternities. She is on the Board of Directors for the Polk County Chapter of Habitat for Humanity and is a Sunday School teacher. She has served for many years on the Viewers Advisory Council of KOZK, public television. She is past president of GFWC Fidelis Club and is presently its reporter. Her hobbies are decorating, reading and writing.

Ron is a Mason and a member of the Bolivar Optimist club, having served that organization as president at one time. He is a past member of the Chamber of Commerce Board of Directors, and has pastored several Missionary Baptist Churches, including Adonis, Elkton, Halfway, Salem and presently, Pleasant View.

Ron and Marinell Erven 2002

The couple has two grown children: Tiffany Goff, born in 1970, an RN with CMH Home Health Care; Derek, born in 1972, a graduate of Missouri Southern State College, is a senior correctional officer at the Federal Medical Center in Springfield. The Ervens have three grandchildren: Alexandra Hunter, age 5, and Zane Christian, age 1, children of Derek and Julie Erven of Springfield and Cannyon Nicole, daughter of James and Tiffany Goff of Bolivar.

ERWIN - George C. Erwin was born March 19, 1829. His wife, Winnie Lane Bowman Erwin, was born March 10, 1833. They were married March 19, 1856. Their children were Clarence M., William A., Austin M., Lizzie C. and Nancy L.

Seated: George C. Erwin and Winnie Lane Bowman Erwin; Standing: Lizzie C., Clarence M., William A., Austin M. and Nancy L. Erwin

In the winter of 1883 and 1884, George and Winnie sold their farm at Hamilton, MO and moved to Polk County. They bought the Walnut Hill Farm of 560 acres which was located nine miles southeast of Bolivar.

The family had shipped some of their household furnishings by rail. The nearest railroad station to them at the time was at Ash Grove in Greene County. They took a covered wagon to pick up the furnishings which included a rosewood square grand piano. When they arrived at the railway station they could hear someone banging on a piano. When they went inside they realized it was their own piano. Two boys had decided to entertain themselves with the instrument. Pianos were a highly cherished item in those days and not to be banged on. The piano was so big it filled the wagon and took several hands to move it. They wrapped it in quilts for the journey home.

In the fall of 1896 George and Winnie moved to Bolivar. They lived there until George's death on April 4, 1901. Winnie then moved to Pleasant Hope to be near one of her sons. She died on May 3, 1912. They are buried in the Greenwood Cemetery in Bolivar. *Submitted by Michael A. Erwin*

ERWIN - About 1867, at the age of 23, George Washington Erwin came to Missouri from Monroe County, TN around the community of Tellico Plains and settled on the Sac River near the Greene/ Polk County line. All of his brothers and sisters except the youngest, Jefferson Davis, had come to Missouri earlier and probably at the same time. He was joined by his father and mother, John A. and Nancy Aikens (Hammontree) Erwin, and younger brother sometime after 1886. In addition to Jefferson Davis, his siblings were: Jacob, Elizabeth H., Stephen, Martha, Jane, Robert Wilson and John T. While in Tennessee, G. W. Erwin served as a private in the Third Regiment, Tennessee Mounted Infantry, Union Army. He later served for a brief period of time with the Seventh Regiment, Tennessee Mounted Infantry. He was a proud member of the Grand Army of the Republic (GAR).

Seated left to right: George Washington Erwin and Alie Lucinda Gent; Standing left to right: Ailie, Perry, John Lafayette and Nancy Elizabeth

After his children were grown, G. W. Erwin moved to Bolivar and later to the Burns community near Halfway. He later returned to Bolivar, residing on South Lillian where his wife died. His final home was to a small farm west of Bolivar. He was united in marriage to Alie Lucinda Gent, Sept. 16, 1869 in Polk County, MO. Her parents were Josiah S. and Mary Rutherford Gent.

G. W. and Alie Erwin were the parents of nine children, only four of whom lived to adulthood. Three died in infancy, one of who was Dale Gent. Mary E. and Lucy Jane died as children. The adult children include Nancy Elizabeth, who married George Washington Mackey; John Lafayette, who married Sarah Gertrude Reeves; Ailie, who married William Rasey Sullins and lived in New Braunfels, TX and Perry, who never married. He was a 1904 graduate of Southwest Baptist College and a member of the Osage Lodge No. 61, IOOF elected to Noble Grand a few weeks prior to his death. He was elected as Polk County Surveyor in 1906.

Nancy and G. W. Mackey had six children. Charles Ray married Hazel Ford and lived in California. Vera died as a young girl. Guy Erwin married Dorotha Lee Acuff, daughter of James Chester "Pete" and Goldie Omega (Dixon) Acuff of the Graydon Springs community. Before moving to Texas, he managed the Eudora Farmers Exchange. Mary Ester married Haward Roland Barnett of Bolivar. He was the son of Victor and Della Barnett. Victor came to Bolivar from West Plains in Howell County to work at Southwest Baptist College. Haward was a mechanic for the Barnett Chevrolet Company in Bolivar. He served as a city councilman. Troy Walter married Wilma Foster from the Fair Play area. He moved to California for a period of time but was residing in Bolivar at the time of his death. Ailie Lucinda married Dave Keefe.

Hickory Grove Cemetery was the burial ground for many of the descendants of John A. and Nancy Irwin. *Submitted by LeRoy Mackey*

EULISS – Phillipe Euliss was born between 1740 and 1750 in England and died in 1813 in Orange County, NC. He married Elizabeth Abt (born in England) in 1765 in Germany.

Henry Euliss was born Dec. 5, 1830 and died May 18, 1874. He married Melanie Jane Shofner (born Dec. 1, 1835; died April 6, 1908). They had 11 children: Henry Shofner, born June 23, 1852; Peter Monroe, born April 9, 1854, died Sept. 5, 1855; John Quincy Adams, born June 24, 1856, died June 4, 1946 in Sandy Grove, NC; Dora Ann Isabel (Scroggins), born Jan. 7, 1839 and died Oct. 6, 1931; William Henry Harrison, born Jan. 1, 1862 in Chatham County, NC, died Jan. 20, 1953 in Wishart, MO; James Randolph, born July 5, 1865 and died Nov. 23, 1915; Flora Ann Jermima (Derossett), born Dec. 25, 1867 in North Carolina, died Jan. 26, 1926; Marion Jackson, born March 26, 1873 in Brighton, MO, died Jan. 12, 1960; James Monroe, born Jan. 25, 1840, died Aug. 3, 1918; and Edward L., born Jan. 5, 1877, died March 9, 1969.

At the age of 8 William Henry Harrison and his family loaded up a covered wagon and began the three-year trip to Polk County. They settled south of Highway 215 between Brighton and Morrisville. On Aug. 9, 1883 he married Jermina Ellen Ballinger (born Dec. 16, 1861; died March 27, 1889). They had three children: Ida Bell, born and died March 27, 1899; James Floyd, born Nov. 1, 1886, died Feb. 5, 1969; and Gertie May, born March 5, 1897, died April 4, 1919. Will married Nora L. Hensley on Aug. 20, 1899. Nora, born April 18, 1881, died Dec. 24, 1948, was the daughter of Fielden and Tina Hensley. The day after Nora's wedding she washed 46 "ditties" (diapers).

Will and Nora raised their family on a small farm north of Wishart, MO. They walked many miles to and from their church at Enon Baptist. The children attended the one-room school at Independence. Nora and Will had eight more children: Voyd, died in infancy; Ernest Allie, born Dec. 12, 1901; Zelma (Murray), born Oct. 5, 1905, died Feb. 12, 1999; William Leonard, born Jan. 9, 1908, died May 29, 1993; Tina Bell (Murray), born Nov. 15, 1910, died March 12, 1974; Ina (Ahart), born April 5, 1914; Inez (Wilson), born April 5, 1914, died Jan. 16, 2000; and Pauline (Hensley), born Jan. 22, 1920.

Their small house burned in 1930 but they were able to re-build in the same location in 1931 at a cost of $800. Will cut his own logs and took them to the sawmill. They built a four-room house with a porch all across the front. Daisy, the horse, and a one-horse wagon made many trips to haul water from Enon Springs, until Leonard drilled a well for them. Nora would go to get a fresh cold drink from that well many times.

In 1928, their family increased by two granddaughters, one a 3-day-old baby, who came to live with them after the death of their mother. It was said of Will that he was a man of great patience and she, Nora, was just a half step behind him.

On Nov. 14, 1931, William Leonard married Catherine Marcella Francka, born June 24, 1908, died Aug. 13, 1987. Leonard was a person like his father, Will; they were both very good with their hands and could fix just about anything. Marcella was a nurse at St. John's and enjoyed working in the nursery. Leonard and Marcella lived north of Morrisville, MO and raised three children: Majorie Jean (Reser), born Jan. 12, 1932, Leonard Dean, born July 9, 1936 and Betty Louise (Graves), born Oct. 23, 1940. The children attended Collins and Morrisville Schools. Leonard drilled many wells in the area, including three artesian wells. In 1948 when REA came to the county he wired lots of homes around the Collins School.

Will and Nora Euliss family picture, Back row: William Leonard and Zelma; Second row: Tina, Pauline, Ina and Inez; Front row: Floyd, Will, Nora and Ernest

Leonard and Marcella moved to Bolivar in 1969. Leonard worked for the City of Bolivar for 18 years. He, like his dad and brothers, enjoyed fishing and telling great stories. Marcella did some part-time waitressing for a while at the Highway just off the Bolivar square. They both enjoyed being grandparents to their six grandchildren. *Submitted by Marjorie Reser*

EVANS – Benjamin Franklin Evans was born Oct. 27, 1846 in North Carolina. His parents were Thomas and Sarah C. Evans. Their other children were Sarah Elizabeth, Margaret Ann, William Conley and Martha Ella Evans. They moved to Moniteau County in 1858 when Benjamin was 10 years old and later to Polk County. Benjamin married Margaret E. Guinn from Greene County on Aug. 19, 1869. They homesteaded their acreage under Ulysses S. Grant on April 10, 1874. They were the parents of 11 children: Sarah C., Mary E., William D., Rose J., Ruth, Bessie Viola, James Blaine, Benjamin Harrison, Marion, Lewis and Nellie Evans. Margaret expired Jan. 11, 1914. Benjamin married Edna A. Slagle on Oct. 6, 1917. Benjamin expired May 31, 1935.

Donna descended through James Blaine, who was born Sept. 25, 1886. He married Maude Mae Perry, who was born March 23, 1891. They had nine children: Lloyd, Floyd, Goldie, Eugene, Cleo, Wayne, Alice, Evelyn and Viola Evans. Maude expired in 1964, and James "Jim" expired Dec. 12, 1965. Both great-grandparents and grandparents were buried in Salem Cemetery. On their way home from Mt. Herman School, Donna and her brothers always enjoyed biscuits and jelly or tarts grandma had prepared for them.

Sitting: Jim and Maude Evans; Standing: Lloyd, Wayne, Evelyn, Viola, Goldie, Eugene, Cleo and Floyd

Floyd was Donna's father. He was born Sept. 2, 1911. He married Lillian May Bays May 20, 1933. She was born Feb. 19, 1916 in Rosedale, KS. Her parents were Frank J. Bays and Irene Frances Casey Bays. Her grandparents were James and Ledona Dorsey Bays of Drexel, MO. Her great-grandparents were William Bays and Louise Stewart Bays. Floyd and Lillian were the parents of Donna Carol, Frank Edwin and Floyd Chester Evans Jr. Floyd expired June 23, 1976, with burial in Salem Cemetery. Lillian married James E. Dake on June 27, 1981. He expired April 17, 2001.

Donna Carol was born March 13, 1938. She was married to Donald L. Smith in Springfield, MO on July 1, 1960. Donald was born April 18, 1939. Donald and Donna are the parents of Karla Kay, Janet Lee and Lori Ann Smith. Karla Kay was born Sept. 24, 1961. She married Darrel Stephen Moore on June 6, 1981. Darrel was born July 19, 1960. Blake Adam was born June 20, 1989 and Brett Allen Moore was born Aug. 12, 1992. Janet Lee was born July 22, 1964. She was married to Quentin "Splinter" Dwaine Middleton from April 22, 1989 to April 14, 2002. Chelsey Dawn was born April 16, 1993 and Logan Andrew Middleton was born Aug. 31, 1995. Lori Ann was born Oct. 25, 1969. She married Stephen Lee Comer on June 6, 1992. Stephen was born May 11, 1968. Nathanael Stephen was born April 14, 1994, Kaylee Ann was born Jan. 15, 1997 and Jacob Evan Comer was born June 8, 2001.

Frank Edwin was born Oct. 16, 1940. He married Evelyn Jo Jones Sept. 1, 1962 in Kansas City, MO. They are the parents of Jeffrey Wayne and Gregory Edwin Evans. Jeffrey was born May 30, 1963 and was married to Cindy Hewitt May 22, 1991-November 1999. Lia Raechel was born Feb. 2, 1992 and Spencer Cole Evans was born June 17, 1999. Gregory Edwin was born May 16, 1966. He married Leslie Anne Eveloff on Sept. 22, 1990. Leslie was born April 22, 1967. MacKenzie Faye was born June 9, 1993 and Skyler Reid Evans was born May 1, 1996.

Floyd Chester Evans Jr. was born Oct. 25, 1944. He married Peggy Sue Farris on Aug. 31, 1963. They are the parents of Tracy Lynn and Tisha Lee Evans. Tracy was born Sept. 12, 1970. She was married to Tony Jones from Feb. 18, 1989 to Feb. 27, 2001. Travis Wade was born August 10, 1989 and Aundrea Nicole was born Dec. 3, 1991. Tisha was born July 20, 1973 and was married to Arley Allen Jasper Jan. 9, 1995 to May 21, 2002. Vincent Allen was born Dec. 19, 1994 and Lillian Blaine was born June 12, 2001. *Submitted by Donna Carol (Evans) Smith*

The Evans family

EVANS - Robert Lee Evans was born Dec. 22, 1940 to Katie Alma Moore and Mark Lee Evans. Their home was located between Cliquot and Humansville, MO. Mark Lee Evans was born Jan. 2, 1898 and died Nov. 13, 1967. Robert's paternal grandparents were Thad S. Evans and Zona May Cox. Thad was born July 20, 1866 and died Dec. 16, 1933. Zona May was born Dec. 27, 1867 and died Oct. 9, 1951. Robert's paternal great-grandparents were T. H. B. Evans and Margaret J. Maddox. T. H. B. Evans was born Jan. 22, 1841 and died Nov. 17, 1918. Margaret was born Oct. 27, 1840 and died Jan. 21, 1914. Robert's maternal grandparents were George T. Moore and Mollie L. Roach. George was born Jan. 27, 1872 and died July 13, 1941. He was a life-long resident of Polk County, being born and reared on the same farm where he died, the old home place near Center Point. Mr. Moore was married Aug. 26, 1900 to Mollie Roach of Windsor, MO. She was born in Henry County on July 29, 1881 and departed this life on Jan. 30, 1951. To this union was born one son, Guy Moore of Bolivar, MO and three daughters: Miss Susie Moore, Mrs. Katie Evans and Mrs. Helen Earhart. The maternal great-grandparents were A. G. Moore, born Aug. 25, 1821 and died Nov. 28, 1893. His wife was Ruth A. Williams who was born Jan. 11, 1831 and died Jan. 17, 1899. Katie Alma was the daughter of George Thomas and Mollie Roach Moore. She was married to Matthew Cook and to this union one daughter and one son were born. Later she was married to Mark L. Evans and to this union

three sons and a daughter were born. Their daughter Thadda Mae was born Feb. 8, 1934 and died July 25, 1935 at the age of 18 months, at the home of her parents in Halfway, MO. Jesse John Evans was born July 26, 1936 and married Glenda Agee on May 11, 1957. To this union two daughters and one son were born: Karen Kay Evans married John P. McGee on June 16, 1983; Donna Sue Evans married Albert C. Engelbret June 8, 1985; David Allen Evans married Christie D. Durham July 16, 1996. Jesse and Glenda's grandchildren are Albert Charles and Sean Michael Engelbret, Trevor Lane and Jessica Elizabeth Evans.

The second son, Robert, met his wife Teresa through a mutual friend. They both lived on the same street but had never met before. Teresa was born on May 13, 1954 in East Chicago, IN. Robert and Teresa were united in marriage on May 30, 2000 at Mt. Gilead gazebo in Bolivar, MO. Robert's rural schooling was at Adonis, Inglis, Polk, Halfway and South Ward Schools, of which he and brother Jesse walked many miles and crossed many creeks. Robert graduated from the old Bolivar High School in 1960. He started work at First Baptist Church in 1961 as a caretaker for 18 1/2 years. He worked for the Polk County Bank and the Dunnegan Estates beginning on May 14, 1979. He continues to work for the Dunnegan Estates. He is a member of the OATS and is chaplain for this Lake Stockton Council for the Blind. Teresa and Robert reside in Bolivar with their poodles Outee and ChaChi, raising a calf, Teresa Pauline, and a fish named Silo.

Mark and Katie's third son was William Clifford, born April 26, 1947. He resides in Fair Play, MO. *Submitted by Robert Evans*

Old Everly home, southwest of Halfway, Clara Everly Penninger, Myrtle Everly Wilcox and Stella Everly Brown

EVERLY – The earliest family member in Polk County was Nancey Stanley Tuck (Cary Tuck), who had moved from Halifax County, VA via Blount County, TN and Lincoln County, MO, where her husband Cary passed away in 1836. In 1838 she moved to the Morrisville area to be with her son Joseph and his family. Nancey died in December 1855 and was buried in the Lemon Cemetery.

Their son Hiram married Mary "Polly" Russell in March 1841 in Polk County. Their children were Minerva (William "Billy" Ryan); Nancy Jane (Tom McGuire); Elender "Ellen" (Frederick Everly); Sarah (James Ryan); Joseph (Polly Annie Crosswhite); Mary Elizabeth (John David Everly); William and Martha.

David and Elizabeth Everly moved to Polk County with their family and David's brother Frederick, his first wife, Lucinda (Elizabeth's sister) and their family, from Illinois, sometime before 1870. They appear on the 1870 Polk County census. David and Elizabeth's children were Sarah Jane (George Enyart); Elizabeth; John David (Mary Elizabeth Tuck); James (Cynthia Wells); Sherman; Josephine (James Stewart); William J., and Sam L., all of Polk County.

Bev's great-grandparents were John David Everly and Mary Elizabeth Tuck. They lived southwest of Halfway in the area, known as Van. Although there were 11 children born to them, only five survived infancy. Myrtle Mae (Henry Wilcox); Elmer (Gladys McIntosh); Clara (John Penninger); Stella (Pleasant Brown); and Walter Arvil. Mary died in August 1898 and John remarried in 1913 to Mary Oldham Hale. He died in 1920. Elmer and Stella raised their families in the Polk County area while Myrtle, Bev's grandmother, moved by covered wagon to northern Alberta, Canada where she and husband Henry homesteaded and raised 11 children. Clara moved to Idaho with her family and Arvil was in the US Army and died in Denver, CO.

John's father David died in Ash Grove in November 1911 as a result of being run over by a train. He was a soldier in the Union Army during the Civil War, belonging to an Illinois regiment and was wounded in battle in Atlanta, GA, receiving an honorable discharge. He was a charter member of the New Bethel Methodist Protestant Church.

One of Elmer Everly's daughters, Bertha Lamar, of Springfield, remembers visiting the Everly farm as a young child. Fresh strawberry shortcake is a fond memory as well as her grandfather, John, being a deeply religious man. He was known in the area as John Everly, the good man. Bertha was the last Everly born in the one-room, 12 foot square cabin where her father and his siblings were born, the old Everly homeplace.

A family scattered far and wide, their roots are in Polk County. *Submitted by Bev Allen*

EVERSOLL - Harold E. and Mildred M. Eversoll moved to Polk County in 1954. Harold came to Bolivar in the summer of 1954 as an artificial inseminator for Curtiss Candy Company. He bred cattle and later turkeys in this area. Mildred (Millie) and N. Lee, who were staying with Harold's parents in Lamar, MO, moved to Bolivar on Nov. 1, 1954. Ronald E. was born on Nov. 29, 1954 in Dr. Charles Barnett's office on South Main Street. Harold went to work on towboats on the Mississippi River in 1955 and worked for several different companies, the longest being Cargill Grain Company. Harold worked the length of the Mississippi, Ohio and Illinois Rivers and up and down both canals in Chicago. He also worked as far over as Chattanooga on the Tennessee River. He retired from the river in 1983 after 28 years.

David R. was born March 3, 1956, also in Dr. Barnett's office. The three sons attended school in Fair Play, MO for several years, moving to Bolivar school district when Lee was in sixth grade. Becky was born April 14, 1961. All children graduated from school in Bolivar, except David who joined the army and graduated in Colorado Springs, CO.

The Eversolls have owned a service station in Bolivar for almost 20 years, being mostly a car detail shop for some time, due to Harold's health. *Submitted by Harold and Millie Eversoll*

EWING – Arthur Ewing, born July 2, 1802, died Feb. 13, 1869, the census says born in Virginia, purchased land from the US Land Office located in Section 26 and 33, Township 32, Range 23 of

Polk County as listed in Volume 5, 1838-39 of the US Land Records.

Arthur came from Roane County, TN with a group of people, with some of the group settling in Webster County. Arthur settled in Polk County south of Morrisville and some settled near Carthage. Joseph Ewing, a brother, was already in Webster County.

Genealogy yields some interesting bits of information. Joseph, Arthur and Winston Ewing's wife's great-great-grandfather were living less than five miles apart in Roane County in 1826. One hundred and thirty-four years later a great-grand and a great-great-grand joined the two families together.

Arthur married Sallie Mitchell, a daughter of Rev. James Mitchell in Polk County on Oct. 17, 1840. To this union four sons were born.

James A. was born in 1842. He died at Reinzi, MS in 1862 fighting for the Confederacy.

Wesley M. was born Aug. 4, 1846, and married Rose Caplin Dec. 4, 1878. She died in childbirth with the baby dying a few days later. He lived on the home place, never remarrying and passed away June 1, 1886 in Polk County.

Jacob L. was born Dec. 2, 1848, died 1924, lived on the home place and never married.

Rev. Morris Ashley was born Sept. 2, 1851, married Rebecca Jane Hall Sept. 1, 1878 in Carthage. He passed away April 26, 1922 in Polk County.

Rev. Morris was the first graduate of the Methodist College at Morrisville in 1876, Morris and Rebecca had eight youngsters. Rev. Morris pastored several local Methodist Churches in the Polk County area.

Sallie Jane was born Sept. 25, 1879, died May 1, 1940, and never married. She stayed home and took care of the old folks and other family members.

Arthur Winston, Winston's father, was born Feb. 4, 1882. He married Emma May Briley in Shreveport, LA on Dec. 15, 1920. He practiced vet medicine mostly in southwest Missouri, until his death Sept. 13, 1957. Two boys were born to this marriage. Arthur Winston Jr., born Dec. 25, 1924 and Morris Briley, born May 25, 1926.

Alice Eunice was born Aug. 25, 1884, never married and taught school most of her life in northeast Oklahoma and southwest Missouri. Her last teaching position was at Goodson, MO. Eunice passed away Sept. 5, 1953 at Morrisville.

Mary Rebecca, born April 10, 1887, also became a schoolteacher. While teaching in the Texas Panhandle area, she met a school board member who became her husband, ending her teaching career. She and J. W. Houston, also a former Missourian, had two children, Robert and Ruth. Mary passed away Dec. 29, 1969 at Lubbock, TX.

Thomas Asbury, known to many as "Bill," was born Sept. 12, 1889. He was a graduate of Missouri University. Bill spent a lifetime as a county agent, Boone and Greene Counties, and as a livestock specialist. He married Mrs. Glenn Edith Miller, the widow of Dr. Glenn Miller Sept. 1, 1925. He was one of three doctors at Morrisville who were victims of the 1918 flu epidemic. After Edith's death, he married Mildred Henderson, a teacher of both the Springfield secondary school system and at SMS. He died Dec. 30, 1970 in Springfield.

Ruth Hall Ewing, the sixth child, was born Oct. 5, 1892 and passed away on her birthday, Oct. 5, 1905 in Polk County.

Morris Edward "Ed" Ewing was born March 1, 1895. He was a graduate of Missouri University and served as a captain and instructor of artillery in WWI. He also taught veteran's classes after WWI, WWII, and the Korean War. Morris was very active in the Masonic Lodge and Knight's Temple work. He served as Master of the Grand Lodge of Missouri and as a talented instructor in the Lodge work. He married Ruth Hines, a schoolteacher, May 1, 1925. He and Ruth had one son, Joseph Edward, whom most of us call Joe.

The youngest child of Morris and Rebecca was Helen, born Sept. 24, 1897. She followed in the footsteps of her siblings, teaching at Fargo, ND and Iowa State University. There she met her husband Richard Warner, a teacher in the math department, who she married Dec. 24, 1933. One son, Richard Ewing Warner, was born to this union. Helen died in California on Dec. 8, 1947.

Arthur Ewing's four children gave him and Sallie nine grandchildren. The nine were the parents of six great-grandchildren, four of which are still living in 2002.

Rebecca Jane Hall, Morris Ashley's wife, was the daughter of Winston Hall and granddaughter of Clisby Roberson. Both Winston and Clisby were murdered in southwest Missouri during the Civil War. Jane Hall took herself and her siblings to Round Rock, TX to escape the terror in southwest Missouri. Rebecca Jane and her brother William came back to Missouri.

Two of Arthur Ewing's sisters married brothers to Sallie Mitchell, his wife. One married a nephew of this Mitchell group.

This article except for announcing the great-grandchildren of Arthur Ewing does not discuss them or the two generations after them. Seven generations including Alexander Ewing born in 1733 or 1734 to Winston's oldest son Michael Bruce, now 41, covers 301 or 302 years. Alex Ewing was Winston's great-great-great grandfather. *Submitted by Winston Ewing*

William and Mary Faulkner family

FAULKNER - Charles B. Faulkner was born Nov. 13, 1837 in Trigg County, KY and came to Cedar County, MO before 1868 and to Polk County before 1880. He met Mary Ellen Jones, who was born in Virginia on April 27, 1830, while he lived in Trigg County. They were married in neighboring Montgomery County, TN on Aug. 5, 1856. Charles was a Confederate soldier in the Kentucky Infantry from November 1861 – January 1865. Charles and Mary had four children born in Kentucky. They were William A. Faulkner, born April 3, 1859, died Sept. 5, 1931, married Mary Louise Renfro on Aug. 10, 1882; Samuel J. Faulkner, born Jan. 19, 1862, died Feb. 7, 1939, married Avrilla Parrish on Sept. 2, 1880; Eli T. Faulkner, born 1864, died June 28, 1884; Letitia W. Faulkner, born Feb. 7, 1866, died Dec. 4, 1951, married Walter F. Pollock on Sept. 30, 1883. Two children were born in Missouri: Fanny F. Faulkner, born 1868; Johnie J. Faulkner, born Oct. 13, 1870, died Dec. 28, 1926, married Alameda Parrish on Nov. 30, 1892.

Shelby's great-grandparents were William A. and Mary Louise (Renfro) Faulkner who were married in Benton County, Arkansas. Mary Louise was the daughter of Thomas J. and Catherine (Wyrick) Renfro who lived in Benton County, Arkansas. The story of how the Faulkner family came to be in Arkansas has been passed down in the family and goes something like this. In the early 1880s Charles apparently traded his farm in Polk County for a hotel in northern Arkansas, however, upon arrival in Arkansas either there was no hotel or it was in terrible condition and not operational. They soon returned to Polk County where they lived the remainder of their lives. Mary Ellen, wife of Charles, died Jan. 27, 1905 and Charles died Oct. 24, 1917. Both are buried in the New Bethel Methodist Church Cemetery south of Halfway.

William and Mary Louise (Renfro) Faulkner's first child was born in Arkansas; however they were living in Polk County where their second child Dessie, Shelby's grandmother, was born in 1885. They lived on a farm south of Schofield most of their married life. Their children were Thomas Jefferson Faulkner, born July 3, 1883, died April 1, 1956, married Ida Bucholz on July 23, 1911; Dessie Dell Faulkner, born Sept. 28, 1885, died Sept. 17, 1966, married John Calvin Jones on Feb. 16, 1902; S. Leroy Faulkner, born Feb. 29, 1888, died Dec. 10, 1932, married Mary Tabitha "Mamie" Jones on May 19, 1916; Walter A. Faulkner, May 5, 1890, died Feb. 1, 1955, married first, Josie Jennings in May 1911, married second, Betty Sanders; Ira Nolin Faulkner, born Oct. 12, 1892, died Jan. 16, 1949, married Gladys Anglin on Nov. 1, 1938; Chloe Edna Faulkner, born Oct. 11, 1895, died June 21, 1980, married Frankie LeJuene on Feb. 25, 1915; Jessie E. Faulkner, born June 4, 1903, died July 1900, married Clifford Manes on April 16, 1922.

Dessie Faulkner and Calvin Jones, Shelby's grandparents, lived and reared their family in Polk County. Also, Thomas, Leroy, Walter and Ira lived in Polk County. Chloe had one child in Polk County but later moved to California. Jessie lived in Dallas County, MO and California. Mary Louise Faulkner died July 10, 1947 and both she and William, who died Sept. 5, 1931, are buried in the Pleasant Hill Cemetery. *Submitted by Shelby Jones*

FISHER - George Nicholas Fisher and Marie Wilmes Fisher came to Sunset in Polk County as newlyweds in 1895. George Nicholas Fisher was born in Bonhomme, St. Louis County, MO on March 12, 1862. He was the son of Samuel M. and Lucy Long Fisher. Lucy was the daughter of Nicholas Long and Elizabeth Stephenson. She was the granddaughter of James Long and Leah Fitzwater. Lucy's grandfather, James Long, was born Oct. 29, 1789 near Monticello, St. Anne Parrish, Albemarle County, VA. He was a volunteer soldier with Gen. McNair in 1814 at Cape au Gris, Fort Madison, Leutre Island, near St. Louis and with Col. Boone in his defense of Boonslick Settlement near Boonville, MO. His wife, Leah Fitzwater, was born in Kentucky Jan. 12, 1793. Leah was a descendant of Thomas Fitzwater, who, on Aug. 30, 1682, with his wife and four children sailed from England for Philadelphia in the company of William Penn onboard the ship *Welcome*.

Lucy Long was the great-granddaughter of Laurence Long and Priscilla Cogswell. Her great-grandfather, Laurence, was born May 10, 1756 in Culpepper County, VA. He served as Sergeant in the 14th Virginia Regiment during the Revolutionary War. He was with Gen. Washington at the surrender of Cornwallis at Yorktown. Laurence Long came to Missouri from Virginia in 1796. He settled on a Spanish grant of one thousand arpens, which included the site of Chesterfield.

Samuel M. Fisher was the son of George W. Fisher, a Methodist minister. Samuel was a Justice of the Peace in St. Louis County and owned land near where the Chesterfield Mall now stands before moving with his family to Springfield, MO in the late 1880s. He owned a Grocery and Mercantile on "Old Commercial Street" in Springfield, where his son George Nicholas was a clerk. George Nicholas was the direct descendant of two Revolutionary War veterans: Sgt. Laurence Long, see above, and Ens. Marcus Stephenson. George Nicholas married Marie Wilmes on May 9, 1895 in Lebanon, MO.

Marie Wilmes was born in Carrolton, IL on Nov. 22, 1863. She was the daughter of Theodore Wilmes and Emma Handwerker-Wilmes. Theodore Wilmes and Emma Handwerker were born in the small village of Lennep, in the Ruhr Valley in northern Germany where the landscape is patterned by hills, forests, meadows and rivers. Theodore Wilmes was a soldier in his time, having served three years in the Prussian Army, three years in the United States Regular Army and four years in the Union Army during the Civil War. He came to this country in 1852 from Lennep, Germany.

Fred, Marie (Wilmes), George Nicholas, John Theodore Fisher about 1919

George Nicholas and Marie (Wilmes) Fisher moved to "Sunset" in Polk County after their marriage in 1895. How sad it must have been to lose their first son at the early age of 18 months. A few days after their son Fred was born in February 1901 the temperature was -20F. They had to carry water from the spring quite some distance away from the house. George and Marie were the parents of four sons, two of whom died in infancy. Their sons, Fred and John, grew up at Sunset and lived their entire lives there attending the one-room Sunset School. John married Wilma Wayne Overcash in 1925 and Fred married Bertha J. Harper-Laster in 1944. Christine's father, Fred, was a kind and gentle man who went quietly in the way he should go and was loved by all who knew him. His citizenship is noted for its efficiency, integrity and its humble and quiet contentment. His friendship was constant and invaluable. Christine left Sunset in Polk County in 1964 and married Gerald (Jerry) R. Thiessen in 1966. Jerry retired from the US Army as a colonel in 1995 and they returned to the "Old Fisher Farm" at Sunset. *Submitted by Christine Fisher Thiessen*

James T. and Malinda (Moss) Fisher family. Back row: M. Helen, Joe, John, Hollie, Walter, Emma. Front row: James T., Malinda, Amanda, Dora, and William R., ca. 1900

FISHER - James Tyre/Tirey Fisher was born in 1846 in Barren County, KY. His parents were John Thomas Fisher Sr. and Emily Meador. James married Malinda Catherine Moss in Polk County on Dec. 24, 1868. Malinda, or Lindy as she was called, was the daughter of Matthew Moss and Margaret Dyer. She was born in Lincoln County, TN on Oct. 10, 1849.

James and Malinda were Charla's second great-grandparents. James' parents, John T. and Emily Fisher, were married in Barren County, KY on Dec. 26, 1844 and moved their family from that area to Polk County, MO about 1854. They were enumerated on the 1860 census in Green Township with their six children: James T., John, Woodford, George, Louisa and Nehemiah. After the death of Emily in 1861, John married her cousin Milly Meador on June 19, 1862 in Polk County. They were the parents of eight children: Robert S., Charles H., Rebecca Jane, Sarah L., Henry, Oliver P., Jahu and Burl. Malinda came to Polk County from Lincoln County, TN in 1856, when she was 7 years old, with her parents Matthew and Margaret Moss. Her father must have died shortly after arriving in Polk County as Margaret is shown as the head of the household in the 1860 census. They were the parents of 11 children: Jonathan, Sarah Ann, William W., Martha J., Mary M., Louisa E., Malinda C., Nancy, Margaret E., James, and Cinthia.

Charla is descended through the first-born child of James Tyre/Tirey and Malinda C. Fisher, William Radford Fisher, who was born Dec. 23, 1868 in Polk County. Their other children were Amanda Catherine, Lou Emma, Walter, Minerva Helen, Joe Berry, Dora Ellen, John Hollie and another who died in infancy. Seven of their nine children were born in Polk County. Their son Joe Berry was born in Hickory County in 1881 and their daughter Dora Ellen was born in 1883 at Page County, IA where they lived for about four years before returning to Polk County. James spent his life in Polk County as a farmer and raised prize mules, while Malinda kept house and cared for the children.

James also served in Company C, Eighth Missouri State Militia Cavalry, and Company I, 16th Missouri Volunteer Cavalry from 1862 to 1864.

James Tirey Fisher died on July 2, 1907 near Rondo at the age of 61. Malinda spent the remainder of her years at the home of her son and daughter-in-law, John Hollie and Jenny Wheeler Fisher. She died in Humansville on Jan. 13, 1936 at the age of 87 years. Both James and Malinda are buried at Adonis in Oak Grove Cemetery.

Charla's grandfather, Everett Earl Fisher, was born in Flemington to William Radford Fisher and Mary Lucinda Jane Dunaway. They raised seven children in both Polk and Hickory Counties before moving to Clinton, MO where they both are buried at Englewood Cemetery. Many of the descendants of the Fisher family still reside in the Polk County area. *Submitted by Charla J. Petelin*

FISHER – John Thomas Fisher Jr. was born Jan. 2, 1848, Barren County, KY, the son of John Thomas and Emily Meador Fisher. This family of Fishers have been traced back to a John Fisher, born about 1756, Lunenberg County, VA. His son was James W. Fisher who married Sally Bush of Lunenberg County, VA and are buried Barren County. Children of James W. and Sally: Rebecca, Woodford, Thomas, Washington, David Bush (Thompson Jones married his daughter, Eliza), William, Henry, James Radford, Oliver Perry, John Thomas Sr., Sarah Jane, Mary E. and Elizabeth Ann. John Thomas Sr. married Emily Meador and had several children. The family does not know where John, Emily or John's second wife, Milly, were buried. All the rest are buried in Hopewell Church Cemetery. Their story goes that when John Jr. was 7 years old, he and his family made the trip from Barren County, KY to Missouri in a covered wagon. He started the trip with a new pair of shoes, but when they got to Missouri, they were worn out. Several other families came with them. The old homestead was reported to be on the Polk-Hickory county line, close to Rimby.

John Thomas Fisher Jr. married 1868, Polk County, MO, Martha Elizabeth Jones, daughter of Thompson and Eliza (Fisher) Jones. She was born Sept. 22, 1846 in Barren County and died April 18, 1902. John Jr. and Martha and most of their children are all buried Hopewell Cemetery. Their children:

James Thomas (born Jan. 11, 1869, died April 23, 1938) married Mary A. Huckaby (1871-1936). Children: Clarence married Letha Breshears with children Dean, Roy, Ralph, Mary Lou, Jesse, Herbert Lee, Morse T., Ruth M. and Letha Aliene (died young); Iva married Mr. Rush; Velza died 1946, buried Greenwood Cemetery, Bolivar.

Eliza E. (born Sept. 2, 1870, died March 20, 1936) married second, Walter Foster (1872-1949) with child Roy Foster.

Henderson T. "Hence" was born July 27, 1873, married first, Mintie Bonds who died 1897, Iowa, and had Harmon Ancel. Hence married second, Missouri Key (1878-1909) with children Erma, Holbert, Orvil and Howard.

Wallas E. was born June 10, 1877, died Sept. 18, 1952, married first, 1899 Myrtle O. Hayes (1880-1901) with children: Walter Ray married Eva Mae Hill and had Robert Ray, Ruth Elaine, Darrell Eugene, Glenn Leon and Rita June. Wallace married second, Mary A. Schoff and had Alpha T. who married Florence Edna Davison and had Glenda Irene; John (died young); Rich (died young); Carrie married ? Foster of California.

Mary A. was born June 18, 1878, died young.

Joseph S. was born March 30, 1884, died Oct. 25, 1902.

Zelda May Bell was born Jan. 15, 1887, died 1961, married H. Everett Moore (1881-1965) and had children: Ruah Gladys married Clifford Hawkins and had Oma Jewel; Ressie Ellen married first, Noah Everett Attebury, married second, Lewis LeRoy Cline; Dorothy Jewel married Henderson Andrews and had Dorothy June; Henry Dale married Clara Evelyn Bruner and had Ralph, Joseph, James Henderson, John Everett; Lorene Elizabeth married Robert F. Kerrick and had Lorenda Morene.

William Irvin was born June 25, 1889, died young.

Omer S. was born Feb. 27, 1893, died Nov. 21, 1932. *Submitted by Glenda Fisher*

FLEEMAN – The Fleeman family can be traced back to Thomas Fleeman, born 1730 in Louisa County, VA.

Thomas Jefferson Fleeman was born 1753, Stafford County, VA. He served two years in the Revolutionary War. He was in the Battle of Germantown.

George Fleeman was born 1792, Henry County, VA. He served in the War of 1812. He brought his family to Missouri in 1842. He and a son homesteaded land just southwest of Fair Play.

George Collin Fleeman was born 1837, died 1891. He married Mary Patterson in 1856. He served in the Union Army during the Civil War and was a county judge in Cedar County.

William Thomas Fleeman, Ray's great-grandfather, was born 1860, died 1940. Married Rebecca Adeline Erwin, born in 1860, died 1952. They lived in Cedar and Polk Counties all of their lives. Grandma Becky could bake chocolate cakes that melted in your mouth. If she didn't have cake, she had a lump of brown sugar for each kid. They were parents of eight children: Charles, Earl, Ed, Fred, Lula, Fanny, Tressie and Ida.

Charles (Charley) was Ray's grandfather. He was born in September 1892, died October 1968, married Mary Magdalene (Maggie) Phillips in September 1905. She was born 1889, died September 1969. They operated a Phillips 66 service station in Fair Play for over 30 years. Ray remembers him being generous with nickels for ice cream cones. They had three children: Clyde, Naomi and Nora.

Clyde, Ray's father, was born in August 1906, died in June 1993. He married Mary Lela Butler, August 1926. She was born in January 1909, died in September 1987. Shortly after they were married, they moved to a farm on Little Sac River. Dad said he planted crops two years and the river got each of them. Ray's brother, Ezra, was born during the time they lived on the farm. They moved into Fair Play one day and Ray was born the next, Feb. 22, 1929. Ray's sister, Mary Lou, was born Feb. 23, 1931. Ray's dad worked for the MFA until he and his wife went into the grocery business. They later moved to the farm. Dad was drafted into the Navy in 1943, serving in the South Pacific, New Guinea and the Philippines. Ray's parents moved to Dunnegan. They managed Fair Play and Dunnegan MFA Exchanges.

Ezra was in the Army in Korea at the same time Dad served.

Pauline Phipps and Ray were married in 1946. They lived briefly in Fair Play before moving away, returning to Bolivar in 1979. Ray was in the Navy four years, in Korea, Japan and aboard ships. Their daughter, Sue Ellen, was born in 1955 and their son, Scott, in 1958. Ray was a city letter carrier in Springfield from 1960 until becoming Postmaster at Fair Play in 1974.

Both of Ray and Pauline's children live in Missouri. Ray's brother lives in Kansas City and Ray's sister lives in the Fair Play area. *Submitted by Ray Fleeman*

FLEENOR – On Aug. 19, 1939, the Paul and Nora Fleenor family moved to a farm in the Humansville area. It was purchased from C. D. Tharp of Humansville. It was about two miles from town. Sons, Ralph, John and daughter Mary enrolled in the Humansville School in the fall. In 1939, there wasn't electricity or telephones in the area, no running water or inside toilets. One reason they moved to Humansville was Paul's uncle and aunt lived there. Aunt Maude and her husband, Dr. Preston Sterrett, had a general practice in their home in Humansville. Dr. Sterrett had been on the staff at Bethany Hospital in Kansas City, KS for 50 years; he was one of the founders. He could sing in three languages, French, German and Italian. He would also visit patients in their homes. He had a 1934 Plymouth coupe he used in his practice. He was at that time in his late 80s. He

practiced there until the end of WWII and the military doctors came home from the war.

The Paul Fleenor family also had relatives in the Morrisville area – the George Booher family. They were school teachers. They taught in local country schools all of their lives. Another family of the Boohers, John, Mary, Carrie and Susie Booher, lived on their farm about one and one-half miles north of Morrisville, MO.

In 1942, Paul enlisted in the Army Signal Corps and son Ralph enlisted in the Army Air Corps. After becoming a pilot, Ralph became a flight instructor for the Army Air Corps.

Ralph married Blanche Chitwood, a Humansville High School sweetheart, in 1943 and they had a son, Robert, later that year. They separated and divorced in 1945. In 1950, while in the Army stationed in Germany, Ralph met and married Sonja, a German girl, and moved to California. Sonja had a 9-year-old son Reiner "Ray" from a previous marriage. Ralph came to love him as his own son. Ralph and Sonja were married 50 years. Ralph died on April 3, 2002.

The rest of the family moved from Humansville to work in the War Defense plants in California. Son John enlisted in the Maritime Service on his 17th birthday and went to the South Pacific on a "T2" Oil Tanker and was in Letye Gulf in the Philippines when Japan surrendered in August 1945.

In 1947 John, while on his ship in Sweden, met Anita Grandstrom, a Swedish girl. He brought her to the United States, married her and they had two girls, Frances and Janice. After 27 years of marriage, they separated and were divorced. John then met and married a Mexican lady, Sally Lujan and they have been married 26 years.

John's older daughter, Francis, is a real estate appraiser in Kansas City and Janice is a registered nurse and lives in Glendale, CA. *Submitted by John Fleenor*

Rufus Albert "Bert" Flint and Ona Flint, wedding photo, Feb. 28, 1905

FLINT - Rufus Albert Flint was born July 28, 1881, northwest of Cliquot in Polk County. He was the third child of William Jasper and Sarah Alice (Irwin) Flint. Bert and his brothers, Wm. T. and Caddo, had auburn hair. He also had sisters, Ida and Clara.

Bert and Carrie Cleona Drake married Feb. 28, 1905. Professor Bull officiated at the Bolivar Methodist parsonage ceremony. "Ona" was the daughter of David Henry Drake and Margaret Jennie (Gage) Drake. She was born April 7, 1886 in LaCygne, KS. Her family moved to Nebraska and then to Cliquot, MO in 1904.

Bert and Ona were parents of six children: Bernice Georgia, born Jan. 20, 1906; Cora Helen, born March 21, 1907; Lela Bert, born Jan. 4, 1909; Jennie Alice, born Feb. 10, 1911; Hobert Drake, born March 26, 1913; and Leon William, born Jan. 2, 1916. The girls were born near Cliquot and the boys south of Rondo on Dry Fork Creek.

Bert was a farmer and stockman. Life wasn't easy at times, but he and Ona worked hard to raise a good family.

When Bernice was 12, she had to have her appendix removed. The doctor used the kitchen table for operating. Later, sister Lela, 16, became ill, also requiring an emergency appendectomy, again on a kitchen table. Recovery was very slow under those conditions.

Once, while attending Rondo school, Cora went to pump a bucket of water on a frosty morning. Thick frost on the pump handle looked so inviting, so she tried to take a lick of it (very painful to get loose).

When Jennie was a toddler, her mother was ironing (irons heated on the stove). Jennie grew tired and decided to rest—to sit on a crockery jar and became stuck. Mother Ona broke the jar with an iron to free her.

R. A. Flint passed away Aug. 31, 1969 and Ona on June 4, 1974. Both are buried in Crutsinger Cemetery, Hickory County.

Bernice Flint married Roy Cecil Stokes May 1, 1924. Bernice passed away April 1, 1999 and Roy, March 27, 2000. Both are buried in Durnell Chapel Cemetery, Hickory County. Their children are Lela Fern, born Aug. 11, 1925 (married James L. Phillips Jan. 24, 1948). Jim died Sept. 13, 1998. He is buried at Humansville Cemetery. Oscar B. Stokes, born March 3, 1927 (married Edith Lindley May 20, 1955). One daughter, Jennifer, born Nov. 5, 1960 (married Steven Periman July 6, 1991). Jennifer and Steven have a daughter, Audrey Jo, born Sept. 17, 1996. Trixie Arlene, born Sept. 14, 1930 (married Gerald Vanderford Sept. 16, 1950). Vanderfords have a daughter, Ginger Arlene, born Sept. 24, 1966 (married Kendal A. Roweton Sept. 6, 1987—later divorced). Vanderfords also have a son, Michael Kent, born Dec. 3, 1967. Roweton's children are Mykal Ann and Keli Jo, born Sept. 21, 1988, Luther Lee, born March 22, 1990, Levin Eli, born March 12, 1992, Bethany Noell, born Sept. 7, 1993, Cherith Brook, born April 20, 1995 and Mattea Allene, born Oct. 17, 1996.

Cora Flint married Fred D. Brown May 1, 1927. They had one daughter, Helen L., born April 17, 1930 (married first, Gordon D. Pierce). Pierces had two sons, Daniel R., born March 6, 1953 and Scott P. Pierce, born March 17, 1963. Helen married second, Donald H. Nottingham—one son, Joe Donald, born Aug. 6, 1968. Daniel R. Pierce (married Jennifer Wallen), two daughters, Amy Lynn, born Sept. 23, 1982 and Emily Ann, born Dec. 16, 1985. Joe Donald Nottingham (married first, Karen Sawyer, 1990) (married second, Christina Pratt, 1996), one son, Kyle Don Nottingham, born Nov. 1, 1996. Fred Brown died May 20, 1970. Cora died March 19, 2000. Both are buried in E. Resthaven Cemetery, Phoenix, AZ.

Lela Flint married J. C. "Carmel" Franklin, March 14, 1930. They had one daughter, Janice Carrie, born Oct. 26, 1945. J. C. died Feb. 10, 1993 and is buried in Greenwood Cemetery. Lela resides north of Bolivar with her daughter.

Jennie Flint married J. Vernon Bigler July 4, 1933. One daughter, Barbara Ann, born Dec. 18,

1936 (married first, Ronald Harlow, Nov. 4, 1955). They had two sons, Eric, born Sept. 29, 1958 (married Judy Voelker) and Greg, born Feb. 20, 1961 (married Susan Halbert). Greg and Susan have son Talan, born Feb. 5, 1991 and daughter Astin Bria, born March 14, 1997.

Barbara married second, Ed Nielson, October 1990. Vernon Bigler died March 25, 1981 and Jennie on June 22, 1997. Both are buried in Greenwood Cemetery.

Hobert D. Flint married Ina Fay Walker Dec. 26, 1993. They had a daughter, Phyllis Jo, born April 26, 1939 and a son, Bill, born Feb. 11, 1944. Phyllis married Charles F. Price Dec. 12, 1955. Children: Tonjia Kay, born Nov. 18, 1956; Charles J. Jr. "Bud," born March 27, 1958; Tinia Jo, born Jan. 16, 1960; and Tarmia Lee, born Aug. 24, 1961. "Bud" died in a mobile home fire July 3, 1981. Phyllis married second, Gary Weatherly.

Bill Flint married Jolene Foster Sept. 25, 1967. They have one daughter, Terrie, born July 31, 1970 (married Kenneth Reed). Terrie and Kenny have a son, Jeffrey, born Aug. 25, 1994.

Hobert D. Flint married second, Ruby Moore. Ina Fay Flint married second, Mr. Elliott. Hobert died May 15, 1976, buried Greenwood. Ina Fay died July 13, 1999, buried Salem Cemetery.

Leon William Flint, born Jan. 2, 1916, died Aug. 16, 1936 of a ruptured appendix, at rest in Crutsinger Cemetery, Hickory County. *Submitted by Scott P. Pierce*

FLINT - Ezekiel Flint and Mary Jane Hamilton Flint were early settlers of Polk County, having come from Rockbridge County, VA in time to be recorded in the 1840 census. Ezekiel was born in Virginia, Jan. 31, 1807. His son by a first wife, John M., born Sept.. 26, 1829, came with him to Missouri. Mary Jane Hamilton was born Aug. 8, 1820 in Rockbridge County, VA and there she married Ezekiel Flint. They settled a homestead in Jefferson Township north of Cliquot. Today, Highway O passes by the site of the Flint Schoolhouse and over Flint Creek, near where their house probably stood, as the highway bisects Ezekiel's land.

In 1940 their granddaughter, Orlena Ann "Lena" Butler Emmett, related stories told to her of how they came to Polk County "in two covered wagons. The one she drove was [a] boat shaped wagon. [A tradition in another branch of the family says Ezekiel walked beside an ox cart while Mary Jane drove the covered wagon.] They lived in these wagons until he could build a house. He cut logs, made boards, split logs for floor. ... Later [they] built another house, a little way from the first, ... with a porch .... That was their living room, the other one was their kitchen. In the summer, [Grandmother would] cook and carry it up to the table that sat on the porch, then in the winter she cooked on the fire and such good biscuits she made and baked in a baker, put coals of fire under it, a lid over it covered with coals, and had the table in the house. Three beds, a pretty smooth floor, never had a carpet. ... She told me when Pa went to mill at Warsaw or Boonville [and] would be gone for several days and nights, the wolves would come right up to the door [and] howl, [with] just a quilt up for a door. Poor little John how his eyes would bug out, the wolves would howl and talk like people."

Mary Jane and Ezekiel prospered in fortune and family in Polk County. In the 1880 Agriculture census he reported owning 1635 acres of land valued at $8000. Seven children were born to them in Polk County.

Ezekiel died June 22, 1886. From the *Bolivar Free Press*, Cliquot, Feb. 16, 1905:

"Grandma Flint died Tuesday [Feb. 14] morning at 8:45 o'clock after an illness of several months. She was 84 years old and leaves children, grand children, and great grand children to mourn her death. She will be buried at Humansville beside her husband. Hers has been a long and useful life and she carries into the world beyond the love and respect of all who knew her."

Their oldest child, Samuel Hamilton Flint, was born Dec. 3, 1841. At his death Feb. 16, 1928 he was "Polk County's oldest native born" resident, according to a newspaper account. Samuel fought with the 15th Missouri Cavalry at the Battle of Humansville during the Civil War. He married Frances Elizabeth Hudson Nov. 3, 1867 and had eight children: Mary Elenore (married first, Jesse Railey, married second, Frank Ashlock); Minerva Ann (married first, John Wortham, married second, George Coberly) Ezekiel; William Thomas; John Taylor (married Verna ?); Charles Jones; Fred Wesley (married Jessie Nickels) and Annis Flint (married Frank Wilson). Sam and Fanny are buried in Salem Cemetery.

William Jasper Flint was born Feb. 27, 1844 and died Feb. 18, 1919. He married Alice Sarah Irwin April 15, 1875 and they had six children: Albert F.; Ida Bell (married George Troyer); Rufus Albert (married Ona Drake); William Thomas (married first, Goldie Ireland, married second, Mary Christina Hahn); Jones Caddo (married Bessie ?, married second, Cora Drake), Clara Minerva (married first, Dr. Charles Hahn, married second, William Mulvey, married third, Kenneth Scott). William J., a Civil War soldier also with the 15th Missouri Cavalry, and Alice are buried in Salem Cemetery.

Hannah Elizabeth Flint was born Dec. 30, 1846 and died Aug. 2, 1924. She married Thomas Henry Butler Nov. 9, 1862 and had six children: Lousia J. (married Amos Zimmerman); Orlena Ann (married Hiram Wills Emmett); Alice M. (married first, T. P. McCracken, married second, Carlos Palmer); William Jasper; Jacob Washington (married Lora ?); Daisy Bell (married ? Workman). Elizabeth and Tom are buried at Rondo Cemetery.

Zachariah Taylor Flint was born September 1848 and died May 4, 1920. He married Mary E. Minner Dec. 14, 1876 and they had two sons, William Ezekiel and James.

Minerva A. Flint was born in 1853 and died after 1928, probably in California. She married James A. Minner Jan. 16, 1873 in Polk County and had three children: Letha J., William and an unnamed child.

Thomas Alexander Flint was born Jan. 27, 1855 and died July 24, 1861. Alex is buried in Humansville Cemetery.

Sarah S. Flint was born July 14, 1859. She married William Henson June 14, 1878. She and their child died in childbirth Aug. 28, 1879 and were buried in Humansville Cemetery.

Ezekiel's son, John M. Flint, married Lovina Russell in Platte County, MO Dec. 18, 1851. He and Vina had four children: Jones (married Martha Wilson); Amanda Jane (married John Higgins); William Cadow (married Medora Rich); John Russell (married Matilda Parker.) John died July 6 or 7, 1862. One family tradition is that he was shot and killed for being anti-slavery on Bee Creek in Platte County. Another is that he was drowned crossing the Missouri River. *Submitted by Ezekiel & Mary Jane Flint's great-great-granddaughter, Robbie Jean Yeager Ash*

Betty and Lee Hampton

FLY-HAMPTON - Betty Hampton relocated to Bolivar July 1, 2002. She had lived in Independence, MO over 40 years.

Betty graduated from Pleasant Hope High School. Her siblings attended school there also.

Betty's father, Fred William Fly, was wounded and gassed during WWI and received the Purple Heart. He sometimes wore his uniform and medals and spoke about the war in schools. He was an ordained minister and held many evangelistic meetings. He was a barber at Pleasant Hope and Morrisville along with several other places as well.

Fred's wife, Elsie Adams Fly, from Christian County, MO, was a musician and teacher, having taught at Wishart and Halfway. She played the piano for silent movies, sang on radio stations WIBM and KGBX with Mattie Dean Campbell as "Elsie and Mattie."

Fred and Elsie had eight children: Ercel Eudel, who died in infancy; Lotha; Dwight William, who also died in infancy; Thetis Eugene, known as "Cotton;" Betty; Bill; Patty; and Dean.

One of the musical "Fly Family," Betty sang on the Alpen Brau program over KWTO with the Weaver Brothers, Bill Ring, "Goo Goo" Rutledge, Lenny Ailshire and others. She sang with the Fly Family at revivals and political meetings and over KOAM in Pittsburg, KS.

During WWII Betty went to Fayetteville, NC to be near her brother "Cotton" who was in the Air Force, stationed at Fort Bragg, NC. While there she sang on the village Barndance on station WFNC. In 1945, Betty sang with her sister Patty as "Betty and Pat" on the Renfro Valley Barndance in Kentucky, broadcast over WHAB.

Lee Hampton served in the Army Air Force during WWII as a radio operator in the 492nd Bomber Group, based in England. After several missions their B24 Liberator was hit by anti-aircraft fire and blown in half over Brussels, Belgium. Lee and the engineer were the only survivors. They bailed out, were captured immediately, and spent 11 months in Stalag IV prison camp.

Fly family – front: Billy, Patty, Betty. Back row – Elsie, Fred and Rev. Fulkerson

As the war ended, Betty and Lee hitch-hiked to Bolivar to get their marriage license. Betty's father performed the ceremony in the family home.

Betty and Lee (called Bob) who also sang and played the guitar well, joined Patty Fly, Zig Dillon and Jackie Phelps, broadcasting on KGBX, a program also heard over the Armed Forces network.

Betty and Bob had three children. Patricia attended SBU, as did her grandmother Elsie Adams Fly. She married and had two children, Jerry and Tricia. She is an import and export broker and lives in Blue Springs with her husband, Steve Ramsey.

Anita Jean was top virtuoso pianist at MAMA competition in the Middle West. She has three children, Kathryn McConnell and identical twin boys, Conner and Caleb Jonas. They live in Raytown, MO.

Robert Hampton and wife, Joell, have two children, Christopher and Shannah. Robert carries on the furniture business his father began almost 50 years ago in Independence, MO.

Through the years Betty became a very good artist with many lovely paintings. She has been active in music, and the last few years planned the Senior Activities at her church.

Lee passed away in 1996, the same year the Belgian people erected a monument at the site of the plane crash, honoring all of the crew members who died, as well as the two who survived.

Betty enjoys living in Bolivar, her church, the new Senior Center, and her new and old friends. *Submitted by Betty Jo Hampton*

FLY-PEAVEY - Ralph and Patty Peavey moved to Polk County in 1993 from Springfield, MO. Patty had ties to Polk County, attending Pleasant Hope school as did her brothers and sisters. A cousin, Carl Henderson, had been superintendent in earlier years, when an older sister, Lotha, had attended there. Lotha's son, John R. M. Nelson has been Polk County surveyor since 1989. Patty's father, Fred William Fly, was of Chickamauga Cherokee lineage, from Barry County, MO. He was wounded and gassed at St. Mihiel in France during WWI, receiving the Purple Heart. Fred was an ordained minister, avid Bible reader, and held many brush arbor meetings. Pleasant Hope and Morrisville were among the several places he was a barber. Fred's wife Elsie (Adams) Fly, from Christian County, MO, was a musician and teacher, having taught at Wishart and Halfway. She played the piano for silent movies in Springfield, sang on radio station WIBM and KGBX as a duet with Mattie Dean as "Elsie and Mattie." They were one of the earliest female harmony teams on radio.

Fred and Elsie had eight children: Ercel Eudel, who died in infancy; Lotha; Dwight William, who died in infancy; Thetis Eugene, known as "Cotton;" Betty; Bill; Patty; and Dean.

Patty began performing at age 6, singing and playing her accordion. Billy was playing guitar at an early age and, along with Betty and their parents, they performed as the "Fly Family."

Patty's music took her from the Ozarks to the Renfro Valley Barn Dance in Kentucky. With her sister, Betty, they were on radio station WHAS in Louisville, KY (broadcasting with 50,000 watts) known as "Betty and Pat." Patty went on to KFAB radio in Lincoln, NE, another 50,000 watt station, to perform with the western swing band "Radio Rangers" with Johnny Carson as the announcer. She also performed with Brush Creek Follies in Kansas City, and on the "Ozark Jubilee" when it began on KYTV and on to the Jewell Theater in Springfield.

Patty met and married Ralph Peavey while performing in Kentucky. He is of Chickamauga - Cherokee lineage, from Casey County, KY. During WWII, Ralph was assigned to the 82nd Airborne Division. He served as a member of Company B of the 517th Parachute Battalion as an infantryman. He served in Rome-Arno, Ardennes, Rhineland and Central Europe.

"Ozark Jubilee" Jewell Theatre 1954. Band: "Buster" Fellows, Zed Tennis, "Doc" Martin. Back – George Rhodes, Bob White

Patty and Ralph moved to Springfield when Ralph went to work for the Frisco Railroad. After 30 years with them and four years with Burlington Northern Railroad, he retired.

Their children are Pamela, married to Don Coones, Chief of the Chickamauga-Cherokee– lives in Fair Play; James Edward, formerly with IBM, now with Hammons Products Co. in nearby Stockton; Fred, retired from Frisco RR and lives in Kentucky; Joy Patrice, married to Ted Shrader, is a certified piano teacher in Tulsa, OK; and Alan, who lives near Springfield and works for Ozarks Technical Community College as web developer and adjunct instructor. All three sons served in the US Navy.

In July 2002 Betty Hampton moved to Bolivar to be close to sisters, Lotha and Patty, and brother Dean of Stockton. *Submitted by Pam Coones*

FORGEY - There were so many O'Neils in Ireland that when more O'Neils immigrated from Scotland and Wales, the O'Neil clan was so large one branch became known as the "Forgey" clan.

John H. Forgey (Feb. 12, 1809-March 30, 1886) and Matilda Eliza Holmes (May 12, 1821-Jan. 13, 1892) were married Sept. 28, 1837 in Maury County, TN. John and Matilda are buried at Salem Cemetery. Known children:

Robert J. Forgey (Aug. 17, 1838, Tennessee– Oct. 14, 1900) married first,to Julia M. Hendricks who died about 1869. Their children: Florence Matilda Forgey (1864–1959, buried Barren Creek Cemetery, Polk County) married in Polk County July 14, 1883 to Allen Phillips (age 25 in 1884). John "Henry" Forgey (1867–April 6, 1942, buried at Kansas City,, MO) married Eliza Catherine "Belle" Caulk (Oct. 20, 1868–Jan. 13, 1953). Children of John "Henry" and "Belle:" Juanita Belle Forgey (Dec. 10, 1892–August 1962); Millie Wenonah Ruth Forgey (May 8, 1901–March 1965); Hughetta "Teddy" Lee (Aug. 1, 1907–1993/ 1994); and Robert "Little Bob" Forgey (died about age 3).

Robert Forgey married second,Feb. 16, 1871 in Polk County to Lucinda J. Hinkle (born Oct. 3, 1852). Their son died at birth, Jan. 16, 1872.

Robert married third, Aug. 30, 1878 in Polk County to Charity A. E. (Dysart) Wortham (born 1843 in Missouri). Their son, Thomas Olevin "Ola" Forgey was married Sept. 11, 1903 in Polk County to S. L. Thruston/Thurston.

Nancy Jane Forgey (Jan. 17, 1840, Missouri– Feb. 12. 1923) married Dec. 10, 1858 in Polk County to John T. Watkins (April 23, 1836, Summer County, TN–July 25, 1878). Nancy and John are buried at Brush Grove Cemetery, Polk County. Known children: William C. Watkins (born 1860); Mary Jane Watkins (born 1862); James H. (born 1863); James T. Watkins (Dec. 18, 1866–1960, buried Salem Cemetery); Venny (female) (born 1870) and Amanda Laverne (Aug. 30, 1872).

Mary F. Forgey (Oct. 18, 1842, Arkansas-June 2, 1914) married to Thomas H. Ashlock (May 10, 1830-Nov. 26, Nov. 1901). Both buried Salem Cemetery. Children: Sarah A. Ashlock, born 1860; John F. Ashlock, (1861-1948; listed as William J. on 1880 census); Thomas J. Ashlock, (Jan. 17, 1864–April 4, 1893); Mary E. Ashlock (born 1871).

Andrew H. Forgey (Sept. 10, 1845-Jan. 15, 1865, Civil War–Co. L 15th Missouri Cavalry) (listed as Samuel L. on 1850 Arkansas census).

Marinda Forgey (born 1846, Tennessee).

Amanda M. Forgey (March 15, 1848–1921) married Jan. 1, 1871 to John Crawford (1844– 1915). Both buried at Salem Cemetery. Known children: Julia Crawford (Oct. 13, 1871–Nov. 20, 1872); Mary Frances Crawford (born Sept. 22, 1872); Lewis Curtis Crawford (1875–1902); Letha Belle Crawford (born 1877); Myrta (Mirtle) E. Crawford (Dec. 17, 1879–Dec. 31, 1892); Ella M. Crawford (June 1, 1883–April 10, 1903); female Forgey (born Oct. 13, 1885).

Margaret L. Forgey (Nov. 16, 1851-Feb. 22, 1887) married April 21, 1870 in Polk County to John Thomas Butler (June 3, 1851-May 28, 1921). Both buried at Salem Cemetery.

John Thomas Forgey (April 30, 1862–Sept. 29, 1935) married Aug. 5, 1883 to Margaret Isabelle Pickering (January, 1868–1961). Known children: Alonzo "Lon" M. Forgey (July 1, 1885) married Aug. 2, 1914 to Alta May Evans; Homer Conway Forgey (Aug. 27, 1890–June 6, 1919); Grace Leota Forgey (March 22, 1894); George Nelson Forgey (Aug. 12, 1897); Jessie May Forgey (May 24, 1901–Jan. 2, 1906, burned and died). *Submitted by Bonnie Forgey*

John "Henry" Forgey

FORGEY - Samuel S. Forgey (June 30, 1814-Nov. 13, 1884,) and Martha G. (May 2, 1819-

Fly family circa 1945, Billy, Elsie, Betty and Patty

April 25, 1850) were in Polk County by 1850, as listed on the census. Their children were Mary E. Forgey (May 26, 1839 – Nov. 10, 1846), buried at Dunnegan Cemetery.

Thomas N Forgey (Sept. 14, 1841, Arkansas – Nov. 5, 1913,) married on Dec. 18, 1864 at Polk County, MO to Elizabeth Jane Reeves (March 12, 1843, Tennessee – Oct. 15, 1903, buried at Dunnegan Cemetery). Their children: Coque Forgey (Jan. 15, 1866 – Sept. 21, 1868), her name had been listed as Connie in earlier records. Robert Lafayette Forgey (1868 – 1945, buried at Barren Creek Cemetery) married on July 18, 1892 to Minnie Florence Mead (1874 – 1959). Children: Albert Forgey; Harry Edgar Forgey; Mary Mattie (Forgey) Rice; and Benjamin Harry Forgey (Dec. 21, 1907 – Dec. 16, 1998, buried at Barren Creek Cemetery) married to Gladys Jewell Grant (died Jan. 24, 2000). Charles H. Forgey (Nov. 18, 1869 –Aug. 31, 1910, buried at Dunnegan Cemetery) married Dec. 22, 1891 to Annie Noblitt. Christiana E. Forgey (June 11, 1872–July 24, 1918), buried at Dunnegan Cemetery, is also listed as wife of Charles H. Oscar L. Forgey (1872, Missouri–Aug. 16, 1895, Bolivar) married first,on Aug. 21, 1895 to Bettie E. Holmes (Nov. 6, 1876 – March 8, 1899); married second on April 11, 1901 in Polk County, MO to Letha J. Skaggs. Oscar and Bettie buried at Dunnegan Cemetery. Martha E. Forgey (born 1879, MO) and Millie A. Forgey (born April 4, 1884, Bolivar, Polk County, MO).

James L. Forgey (born 1847, MO).

Sarah E. Forgey (born Jan. 15, 1850, Missouri) married June 13, 1872 to Charles Julius Hahn (Sept. 16, 1848, Lundenburg, Austria–Feb. 25, 1935). Both buried at Salem Cemetery. Children: William T. Hahn (died March 8, 1874, age 10 months); on Dec. 22, 1884, a female Hahn child was born to Charles J. Hahn (age 36, Dutch) and Sarah S. Forgey (age 35, born in Missouri, heritage was Ireland). This was their third child; and Ernest Hahn (Jan. 9, 1888–Aug. 19, 1911, buried at Salem Cemetery).

Samuel, Martha G., Mary E., Thomas N., were buried at Dunnegan. Cemetery records also list Elizabeth M. Reaves, (Sept. 14, 1812, Tennessee–May 12, 1906), as the third wife of Samuel. Samuel and Elizabeth were married Sept. 13, 1855 in Polk County, MO.

Wayne H. and Lavonne Foster, 2002

FOSTER – In May 1971, Wayne and Lavonne moved to a farm in southern Polk County. Both had been teachers in Billings and Marionville, MO. The farm they bought had been owned for several years by Roy Davis. No one had lived on it for some time, but there was a four-room house. Wayne's dad was a carpenter, so he batched for several weeks in the little house while he remodeled it and added on rooms and a bathroom and kitchen. In 1995 Wayne and Lavonne remodeled and added to it again, so the little four rooms are still a part of the house. Lavonne taught English at Morrisville during the 1971-72 school year and again during 1981-84. Wayne taught industrial arts at Walnut Grove during those same years.

Their son, Jason Todd Foster, was born in 1975. In 1998 he married Kimberly Carter, daughter of Michael and Rhonda Carter of Ha1fway. They live around the hill from Wayne and Lavonne. Where they live, there is a big barn built of the worm-eaten rock which can be found around there. Some of the rocks in the barn are as large as a table top. They often wonder what system was used to move those huge rocks into place and align them perfectly in the wall as it was built.

Wayne is an auctioneer and has held many auctions in and around Polk County for many years. He is well known in the area.

Wayne and Lavonne also raise beef cows and registered quarter horses here.

Lavonne runs Hooked on Books in Springfield.

There is a rock fence on this farm which has apparently been here since shortly after the Civil War. Wayne and Lavonne have been told that soldiers returning from the Civil War were put up over the winter in exchange for building the fence. They have tried to get it on a historical registry but have had no luck since it is not a building. It is a lot of work keeping it repaired, but they hate to remove it since it has such a history. It is mentioned in their abstract as the B.W. Mitchell fence in 1889, apparently a well known landmark at that time.

Frank and Nola Fowler

FOWLER – Frank Willard Fowler and Nola Frances Johnson were married in October of 1922 in Polk County, MO. Frank was born on Aug. 26, 1902 in McDonald County, MO, the oldest son of William Abner and Alice Lydia (Bugher) Fowler. He had one brother, Grant and two sisters, Ova and Ethel. In the spring of 1936 the two sisters, Ethel Bennett and Ova Whitlock, and their newborn babies died following flu complications.

Nola was born July 17, 1906 to John Wesley and Maggie Myrtle (Jones) Johnson. Her parents were both so small in stature that friends sometimes referred to them as "Mr. and Mrs. Tom Thumb." Her parents had 12 children, with only four reaching adulthood. They were Clarence, Nola, Lula and Minnie. Her father was a chairmaker.

Frank and Nola Fowler had seven sons: Willard, Carl, Jack, Bob, Donnie, Ted and Rex, in that order. They lived in the Humansville and Dunnegan area and attended several different country schools.

Times were hard during those depression years for most families. Frank did general farm work and the boys worked as soon as they were old enough. Nola sewed their shirts and overalls on her sewing machine. She made gardens, canned the extra food, cooked lots of dry beans, and made hundred of biscuits through those years for her growing family. They had many good friends in the area. They told of going to a neighborhood party one Halloween and an early snowstorm swept in and no one was able to get home that night.

Six of the seven Fowler sons were in the armed services; three served during WWII. Willard joined the US Coast Guard and Carl and Jack went into the Army. Carl saw action in the Philippines and was in Japan for the occupation. In the following years, Bob, Don and Ted joined the Army. Four of the Fowler grandsons have also served in the armed services.

All of their sons married and had families. Willard lived in Gloucester, MA and Jack in Fresno, CA for several years. Carl stayed in Polk County and the other boys lived in Kansas City, KS and Arkansas for a few years. Bob was killed in a car accident on June 20, 1959. Willard later returned to Missouri, as did Don and Rex.

Frank and Nola moved to Bolivar around 1948 and Frank began working in a tire shop. On June 18, 1963, Frank was killed instantly on the job in a shop accident. He was 62 and is buried at Greenwood Cemetery. Nola died 16 years later on June 27, 1979 and is also buried at Greenwood Cemetery.

They were a devoted couple and enjoyed their family and friends. *Submitted by Will Fowler*

FOX-WALTON - In 1877 he came for a visit to Humansville, MO, where she had grown up. They courted, married and made Humansville their home until 1884. William Jasper Walton, or Will, was born to Goldsmith Chandlee Walton and Sarah Halterman in Rosewood, OH on Dec. 3, 1854. Will was the third of nine children with six half-brothers and sisters. The family left Ohio in search of fertile land in wide-open Kansas. Will's parents valued education. They knew southern Kansas had no schools, so books were a priority in the wagon shared by the 11 family members. They traveled a route roughly parallel to US Highway 54 from Hannibal, MO to Humboldt, KS. Will's oldest half-sister and her husband, Sarah and Hiram Martin, left the group near Humansville, MO and settled on a farm there. This connection to the Humansville area would bring Will and brother, Joseph, back for visits, which ultimately lead to wives for each. The Waltons finally settled near the Ninnescah River in Sumner County, KS after arriving in Wichita, KS on July 4, 1870. Following their father's stroke and a couple of difficult farming seasons, Will and brother Lon left school to work cattle on the Chisholm Trail. Periodically they rode home to wash self and clothes for the first time since leaving home. A few days before the banknote was due on the family homestead they arrived home with the required amount in cowhand wages.

Francis Tranquilla Fox, or Fanny, was born Aug. 22, 1852 in Polk County, MO, the eighth of 12 children of Thomas Fox and Delila Jane Walker. Thomas and Delila moved to Polk County in about 1851 from Williamson County, TN. Between 1860 — 1870 Thomas became a judge in Polk County as his occupation in the 1870 census was listed as "County Judge." Judge Fox died Jan. 20, 1876 and is buried in the Plum Grove Cemetery, Dunnegan, MO.

In 1877 Will traveled to Humansville, MO, to visit his half-sister's family. He met and subsequently married Fanny Fox. On Dec. 21, 1879 they were wed at the bride's mother's residence in Polk County. They remained in Humansville until returning to Kansas in 1884. They had three children: Lora Elsie, born April 25, 1883 in Humansville, MO, Lulu May, born April 2, 1886 and Frederick Jasper, born April 15, 1890, both in Kansas. Family stories didn't carry forward any other children but the obituaries of each parent indicate that two other children died in infancy, "one for whom Fanny gave her life and was buried with her." Fanny died Oct. 3, 1901, probably resulting from childbirth complications. She is buried in the Council Hill Cemetery about one mile from the old Walton homestead in Sumner County, KS.

Will and Fanny were married almost 22 years at her untimely death. Even though Will was only 46 years old when Fanny died, he never remarried. This may attest to their commitment to each other. Will continued his enjoyment of horses and

Will Walton and grandchildren – front: Velma Walton, Marvin Walton, Loran Guinn, Rita Guinn, Will Walton, Max Walton and Elsie Guinn. Back: Ivan Guinn, Melba Guinn, Eloise Guinn, Merle Guinn, George Willey, Ralph Willey, Cecil Guinn, Charlie Guinn and Louis Willey. Picture taken about 1921 or 1922 in Wichita, KS

worked in livery stables in the area while raising his family. He enjoyed singing, playing the harmonica, a jew's harp, and made willow whistles for all the children. In his final years he lived four months a year in each of his children's homes. He died at his son's home July 27, 1927.

Not much information about Fanny has survived. Current generations would love to learn more about her early life, see pictures, or meet Fox descendants, Included here is a picture of Will with his grandchildren taken in about 1922. Obviously Fanny and Will passed on to their children a love of family. Now over 100 years after Fanny's death and at least six generations after her Humansville wedding to this Kansas horseman, their love of family continues to grow through 340 descendants. *Submitted by Janet Griffith, great granddaughter*

FRANCKA – James Procop Francka, the oldest son of Tracy Frances (Ruzicka) and James Thomas Francka was born April 26, 1936 in Polk County, MO. James died April 25, 2001 at St. John's Hospital, Springfield, MO and was buried at Karlin Cemetery, Polk County, MO. Jim, as he was known, grew up in the Bolivar area with many Bohemian relatives. He attended Wilson Elementary School with his siblings Evelyn, Jerry, Rosemary and Dorothy and then graduated from Pleasant Hope High School. He served in the military in Battery B. He was a member of the Pleasant Hope Lion's Club and officiated in numerous softball and baseball games.

His maternal grandparents Magdalene Sophie (Hruska) and James John Ruzicka and his paternal grandmother Kate Francka were present when Father Helfrick performed the marriage of James Francka to Carolyn Sue Jones Aug. 29, 1959 at St. Agnes Cathedral in Springfield. Jim's maternal grandfather, Jacob Francka, had died in 1949. Carolyn was the only child of Alice Anne (Stockton) and Lester Jones. Carolyn's mother died May 11, 1965 and was buried at White Chapel Cemetery in Springfield, MO. Her father then married Ruth Stafford on May 18, 1967. Carolyn's father was manager of Springfield airport. James and Carolyn met each other while Carolyn was attending Southwest Missouri State College. Her father died Dec. 27, 1972 at Springfield and was buried at White Chapel Cemetery.

James and Carolyn began their married life in the Bolivar area. With the help of wife and children he worked his own dairy farm near Bolivar. They milked up to 165 cows and farmed. James worked out at the Ozark Packing Plant in Pleasant Hope and later the Ace Packing Plant in Buffalo. In later years they moved to the Wilson schoolhouse with their grown children living in the neighborhood. With all the work to be done they took time for picnics at the Francka Bridge and hog shows at the Ozark Empire Fair. There was even time for raccoon and coyote hunting. Jim and Carolyn's CB handles were Playboy and Honey Bunny.

Carolyn began working at Citizens Memorial Hospital as a telephone (PBX) operator in March 1990 and received the 2002 CMH Customer Service Award. The plaque was presented by 2001 Customer Service Award winner, Donald Babb, CMH chief executive officer.

James and Carolyn Francka had four children: Gerald, Barbara, Jeffrey and Theresa.. Gerald James Francka was born March 2, 1962 at Humansville, MO. He married Tommie Jo Loring on Dec. 3, 1988 at Springfield. They had two children, Savannah Jo and Kyle Gerald Francka. Barbara Francka was born Feb. 6, 1964 at Humansville, MO. She attended Central Missouri State University in Warrensburg, MO. Barbara married Scott Allen Young on Aug. 11, 1989 at Springfield. They had one son, Daily Scott Young. Jeffrey Francka was born April 1, 1966 at Humansville. He married Deanna Kay Garzee July 1984 at Aldrich. MO. They had two children, Heather La'Michelle and Justin Heath Francka before divorcing. Theresa Francka was born July 31, 1968 in Bolivar and had one daughter, Kayla Nicole Francka. *Submitted by Carolyn Francka*

FRANCKA – During the 19th century, thousands of Czechs immigrated to the United States in search of freedom and progress. One of the first Missouri settlements to attract these hard working farmers was Verona, a small town in southern Lawrence County on the Spring River. The census from 1900 of Lawrence County shows that some Franckas came to the US in 1868 and 1874.

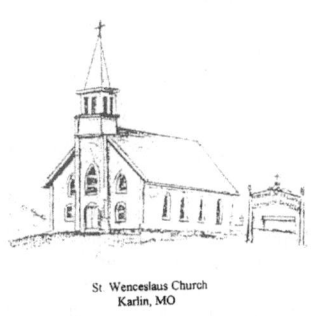

St. Wenceslaus Church, Karlin, MO

Matej and Marie (Leffleman) Francka, our beginning ancestors, and their family arrived during this time period. The Catholic Church in Verona was mostly German and the Bohemian parishioners felt awkward when they went to confession and had to use an interpreter for the German priest. So, at the turn of the century, about half of the Bohemian families moved to Polk County where a small Czech community called Tremont was already forming. Vaclav (James J.) Francka was among that group. He stated that his six brothers and one sister were also moving into the community. Most arrived in 1900 and 1901. Matej and daughter Mary died while living at Verona and are buried there.

Tremont, French for Three Mounds, was a railroad station and general store about four miles south of Bolivar. Postmaster Joseph Dvorak changed the name of the village to Karlin when the post office kept confusing the name Tremont with Fremont. The original Karlin was a suburb of the Czechoslovakian capital, Prague. It was, therefore, an appropriate name for this small community of Bohemian Czechs settling on the Three Mound Prairie.

One of the first orders of business for Vaclav (James J.) Francka and William Joseph Francka was to attend a meeting at the home of Michael F. Divin. Mr. Divin was a Czech Catholic who had moved from Novohrad, TX and settled in Polk County, in hope of finding good farmland. A meeting was called to discuss building a Catholic Church for the growing and thriving Bohemian community. A church was built and many other Czech families joined this community. Some well-known names are Ruzicka, Kroutil, Stanek, Divin, Dvorak, Pfitzner, Vodicka, Skalicky, Otradovec, Polodna, Skopec and Korn. Many descendants of these families remain around Bolivar. Several of Matej's great and great-great-grandsons continue to farm the area, following in their family's tradition.

Born to the marriage of Matej and Marie were William Joseph, Katerina, John, Frank, Mary (died as an infant), Matthew, Vaclav James, Thomas and Jacob. The daughter married and had two children, two sons were single and five sons married and had large families. The Francka family has a registry of all the descendents of Matej and Marie. The oldest son of the oldest son was Father Charles J. Francka, who was the priest at Karlin Church for 49 years. A family reunion was held in Bolivar, MO twice during the past ten years with approximately 300 people attending. This was written by Bernard Francka Sr., grandson of William Joseph Francka, and the great-grandson of Matej. Bernard Jr. lives on the farm his grandparents purchased in 1899 south of Bolivar. *Submitted by Bernard Francka Jr.*

FRANCKA – Father Francka was born at Verona, MO in 1880, the son of Bohemian immigrants. His father, Joseph Francka, left the Austria-Hungarian Empire at the age of 16 to escape conscription into the Austro-Hungarian army, and settled near Verona, MO. Father Francka received his elementary education in the public schools at Verona and then attended the Catholic School for Boys at Conception, MO, now a Catholic seminary. He then attended college at St. Minerad, IN and Kendrick Seminary in St. Louis, MO. When he completed his studies the St. Wenceslaus Church at Karlin, MO, which had been established as a mission, was in need of a pastor who could speak Bohemian.

Fr. Francka's parents moved to Karlin, MO which is south of Bolivar about 1901. Since Father Francka could speak Bohemian, he was selected to become the first pastor of St. Wenceslaus Church. He was ordained June 14, 1904. He never held any other pastorate and never aspired to leave the people he knew and loved so well. For many years he also served as pastor of Catholic missions at Osceola and Greenfield. He made the rounds to his missions by train. An excellent conversationalist, Father Francka became fast friends with every trainman on the route. It was a sad day in his life when the Frisco discontinued the Karlin stop in 1947.

The Karlin community had grown to include many Bohemian immigrants. Father Francka performed many baptisms, weddings and funerals for the parish.

In 1929, Father Francka celebrated his silver anniversary as pastor of the Karlin Church. Shortly after this anniversary, Fr. Francka took his only extended vacation in 29 years. In September 1929 he sailed for Europe where he visited the Vatican and had an audience with Pope Pius XI. Before he

Monsignor Charles J. Francka

returned home, he toured Czechoslovakia and visited his parents' birthplace in Bohemia. He was raised to the status of Monsignor in September 1944.

The portly priest, with his big cigar and dry humor, had wide and varied interests. He was an avid baseball fan, and followed the fortunes of the St. Louis Cardinals almost as closely as he followed the Democratic election returns. He counted many close friends among the ministers and laymen of protestant faiths. Father Francka established the Karlin Picnic which was conducted every Labor Day at the church grounds.

Father Francka had entered the hospital supposedly for a physical check-up. He died as he was preparing for morning mass in the hospital chapel. The hospital chaplain, who was waiting for Father Francka to begin the Mass, went to his room when he did not appear at about seven o'clock Saturday morning. He found Father Francka's body lying on the floor of his room. Monsignor Francka, pastor for 49 years at Karlin, died on July 25, 1953. *Submitted by Barbara Francka*

Charles, William, Agnes, William Joseph and Anna

FRANCKA - William Joseph Francka was born Jan. 30, 1852 in Prague, Czechoslovakia. He is one of nine children born to Matej Joseph and Marie (Leffleman) Francka. Matej and family immigrated to the U. S. in search of freedom and progress about 1868. Joseph Francka left the Austria-Hungarian empire at the age of 16 to escape conscription into the Austro-Hungarian army. They settled in Verona, MO. The children of Matej and Marie were Joseph, Katerina, John, Frank, Mary, who died in infancy and is buried at Verona, Matthew, Vaclav James, Thomas and Jacobus, all born in Czechoslovakia. Matej died Feb. 7, 1894 and is also buried at Verona.

Joseph married Anna Strobel in 1878. She was from Spillville, IA. Most of the Franckas moved from Verona, MO to Karlin, MO, south of Bolivar, where a Czech settlement was forming, about 1898 to 1901. They left Verona because it was a German town and the Bohemian speaking people could not understand the German language spoken at the Catholic Church. The first order of business after they arrived at Karlin was the building of a church.

Joseph and Anna purchased land south of Bolivar in 1899 and were the last to move from Verona. Grandson Bernard Francka lives and farms this land. Joseph and Anna had eight children: Charles, who became a priest and served at St. Wenceslaus Church for 49 years; William, who married Anna Ruzicka; Agnes, who married Benjamin Korn; Ida, who died in infancy; Maria, who married James W. Otradovec; Benjamin, who married Mary Ann Stanek and are Bernard Francka's parents; Wenceslaus (James), who married Margaret Scheer and was a doctor in Hannibal, MO until his death in 1972.

William had seven children, Agnes Korn had six children, Maria (Mayme) Otradovec had eight children, Ben and Mary had four children, and James and Margaret had two children.

Joseph died in 1914 and Anna died in 1948. Both are buried in St. Wenceslaus Cemetery, south of Bolivar. *Submitted by Daniel Francka*

FRANKLIN – Early members of the Franklin family can be documented in Polk County as early as the late 1830s.

In 1837, Alexander Moore came from Hawkins County, TN; it is likely he arrived with Ewell Moore, a man believed to be his father. The 1840 census documents Ewell with a son Alexander's age in the same place Alexander lives all his life. In 1846, nearly a decade after his arrival in Polk County, Alexander enlisted to fight in the Mexican War. Two years later, Alexander goes to Springfield Land Office to prove land in Polk County in the Center Point area. Then, on Sept. 3, 1851 Alexander and Ruth Williams, a young lady who also migrated with her family from Hawkins County, TN, were wed. Thus began the life of a family in the new and untamed Polk County.

On Nov. 4, 1854, John Alexander Moore was born to this union, the second of 10 children.

On Jan. 14, 1878 John Alexander Moore weds Sarah Ann Bewley, whose parents, Jesse H. Bewley and Mary J. Davis, had migrated to Polk County in 1856 from Barren County, KY. On Dec. 5, 1879 Katherine Elizabeth Moore was born to this union as the first of four children. She was raised in the Centerpoint area, where her grandfather, Alexander Moore, had homesteaded in the 1840s.

On Jan. 19, 1898 James Evert Franklin married Katherine Elizabeth Moore. James was born Aug. 29, 1860, in Barren County, KY where he was raised on a tobacco plantation. He had moved to Polk County in the 1890s where he acquired a farm north of Bolivar adjacent to Dry Fork Creek. James Franklin farmed this land and ran a country store at Rondo. To this union were born five sons and one daughter: Claude, JC, an infant son who died at birth, Carl, Dee and Willa. On May 19, 1935, Carl, the middle son, married Sylvia Loy of Flemington, MO. Carl and Sylvia lived in Polk County most of their lives. Sylvia taught school at many one-room schools throughout the county and still resides in Polk County. Carl was a farmer and country store operator; like his father he also ran a country store at Rondo. Carl and Sylvia raised two sons, Ben and Bob, who both reside in Polk County. On March 14, 1974 Bob Franklin married Barbara Dougherty, a California native. Bob is an electrician and Barbara, a medical transcriber; the two have one daughter, Jessica. Ben and his wife, Emma, reside in Bolivar and he has worked as an educator for the majority of his career. Ben has one son, Chris, who resides in Lexington, KY and is the father of one daughter, Elizabeth and one son, Alexander.

Interestingly, this family tree began with Alexander and ends with Alexander! As a member of a family whose Polk County history extends for eight generations, Bob is very proud of this county and his deep roots here! *Submitted by Bob Franklin*

FRANKLIN – Henry M. Franklin, son of Henry T. and Sally (Bridges) Franklin, lived and traded in Scottsville, Allen County, KY where he logged and farmed. In the early spring of 1881 he and his brother Anthony W. started for Polk County. With them were their families, a black mammy, and Elizabeth Tirey, whose husband Gorden had died in Kentucky.

Mally (Franklin) Black and Mally Rosetta (Crawford) Bolling

When they got to the Mississippi River it was overflowing from the spring rains. They camped there for several days; then, everything except the livestock was floated across on a raft. May 19 they camped west of Goodson, MO beside a spring, under a large cottonwood tree.

Anthony and some kinfolks came to Polk County in the late 1850s. He married Mary Tirey April 7, 1861. Their son William was born in 1862. Anthony and family, Mary's parents - Gorden and Elizabeth Tirey, moved back to Barren County, KY in the 1860s. Anthony was born April 22, 1835 in Barren County, KY and died June 3, 1898, Polk County, buried in the Hopewell Cemetery. Mary (called Aunt Molly) was born Sept. 23, 1846, Polk County, died June 26, 1926, Polk County and is buried by Anthony.

Henry M. married Josephine Bridges, daughter of Samuel and Lucy (Cowden) Bridges in 1857 in Barren County, KY. Their children were born on a tobacco plantation: James Grundy, Mally MacGuligan, Benjamin Basil, Cora Anna, Thomas H., Coatney Myrtle, Fredrick Oval and Henry Reeves (Babe). Henry M. bought a farm in Hickory County and later one in Polk County. He was born 1830 in Kentucky and died in 1905 in Polk County and is buried in Hopewell Cemetery. Josephine second married Michael Hopper. She was born in 1840 in Kentucky, died Jan. 6, 1931 and is buried by Henry M. using the Franklin surname.

Back row – Kenneth and Doris Black. Middle – Clarence Black, Mally MacGuligan (Franklin) Black and Buford Black. On lap is Dorothy Venita Black

Mally MacGuligan was born May 31, 1863 in Barren County, KY. As a young girl she worked in the tobacco fields picking tobacco worms off the plants. She pinched off bits of tobacco leaf to chew to help quench her thirst and chewed it until the day she died. She didn't want to leave Kentucky and her friends. She was so angry she walked "every step of the way to Missouri."

Oct. 3, 1888 Mally married John Andrew Black in Hickory County. This was John's second marriage. He had three children, William, Elbert and Elizabeth. John and Mally's children are Frona,

Katie and James Franklin wedding photo

Henry, Myrtle, Maggie, Cecil, Mirl and Orpha. John and Mally homesteaded 80 acres beside the land John had purchased in Polk County where they raised horses and did general farming. They built a two-story, six-room house, with a roofed back porch and a concrete front porch, and a walkway constructed from brick made by John and his sons. Later he bought a farm beside the Star Ridge School. They lived there a short time and moved back to the home place.

John stayed on the home place until his death, Nov. 18, 1926. He was buried in Lindley Creek Cemetery beside his first wife Eliza. Mally kept busy spinning, weaving blankets, knitting, and making quilts, in addition to visiting in the homes of her children. She took a trip by train to California to see her two sisters. She helped her grandchildren with reading, games, etc. She was a loving grandmother. In 1937 kinfolks and friends made her a friendship quilt. Her great granddaughter, Mally Rosetta, has it now. Mally continued to live on the home place with her son Cecil and his family until November 1943 when she moved with them to their new farm near Louisburg. Mally died July 1, 1951 and is buried beside Eliza and John. *Submitted by Mally Bolling*

Vesta Ross, our beloved "Nanny"

FRANZ – Debbie Sawyer Franz has many fond memories of Polk County. As a young girl in the 1960s, her mother Leota Ross Sawyer would allow Debbie and her sisters Bunny and Sherri to spend a few weeks with their grandmother, Vesta Ross, at her home in Cliquot, MO. The girls always called their grandmother Nanny and loved her dearly. The girls lived in Johnson County, KS, so they thought that the three to four hour drive home with Nanny was quite an adventure. On the way to Missouri, Nanny would always stop for lunch along Highway 13 and buy the girls and herself each a hamburger and malt at the local "drive-in." Highway 13 was then called "Bloody 13" due to so many car wrecks and was only two narrow lanes back then; now is almost all four wide lanes, quite an improvement!

Nanny had a rope swing in her backyard, which they always enjoyed playing on. She would take the girls to the Dunnegan Memorial Park in Bolivar, where they loved watching the swans and peacocks. On Friday nights after Nanny had worked all week in the hot garment factory in Bolivar, she would come home and take the girls to see movies at the Lucky 13 Drive-In. Debbie remembers that it would be "buck night" and they all four got in for only one dollar. The girls remember going across the road to visit Hoback's Grocery Store. Since they lived in "the big city" they had never seen a grocery store with wooden floors. They had saved their allowances and would make many trips across the road to buy candy bars and soda pop out of his pop machine. You would simply reach into the big red Coca-Cola rectangle box of ice and water and choose the glass bottle of pop that you preferred—another unusual experience for "city" girls. On Sunday mornings the girls and Nanny would walk over the hill to the quaint little church. It was Salem Church. There was a cemetery beside the church that was fascinating to read all of the dates and names because they seemed to be so "old."

Nanny lived on the corner; her house had originally been the old post office. Down the road to the east was the railroad tracks and just beyond them was the creek the girls claimed as their "swimming hole." They would go down and wade around to cool off on hot summer days. Nanny was an excellent cook and Debbie fondly remembers her cooking new potatoes and green beans for dinner, no others have ever compared.

When Debbie was a young adult she married Robert John Franz II in Shawnee, KS. They had two children, Megan Elizabeth and Jeremy John. The first trip Debbie and Bob took their new family on was to see their great-grandmother Vesta or Nanny as they later knew her.

In 1981 Debbie's sister Bunny and her husband Mike, along with their two children Michael and Angela, moved from Overland Park, KS to Bolivar, where the Franz family visited them often. In 1985, Nanny had moved to the Jones' farm and each time the Franzes visited Polk County, they got to see both the Jones family and their beloved Nanny. They lost their most wonderful grandmother in July 1991. Debbie and Bob's children are grown and married now, but still remember their Nanny fondly.

The Franz family comes back to Polk County from Colorado to visit and it has changed quite a bit. The gravel road to Bunny and Mike's farm is now paved, a big improvement! They still enjoy the last few miles before their arrival. Debbie is very proud that her sister Bunny Sawyer Jones chose to compile this history book on Polk County. She thinks that as we all look back we can learn a lot from our history. She loves the many memories of the simpler times. *Submitted by Debbie Sawyer Franz*

FRASER – Thomas G. Fraser, a prosperous Polk County farmer, was born in 1826 and came to the US from Glasgow, Scotland about 1847. The year of his death is uncertain, but he was still alive in 1900 as listed in the Polk County census. Thomas settled on a farm in Polk and in 1857 married Delphia Steel, daughter of Ninnian and Anna Steel, from Tennessee. Delphia was born in 1832 and her known siblings were Robert, Susanah, Sarah, William, Isaac and Ninnian George. Delphia's father died at the age of 84 and her mother lived from 1811 till 1880.

Thomas and Delphia had 10 children: twins, Napolean B. and Isaac; Thomas; Ann; Christina; Sarah; Ninnian Steele; and James, and two who died as infants. Thomas served nearly three years during the Civil War and was in the Missouri Home Guard.

Ninnian Steele Fraser (1869-1908) married Mary Ellen (Mollie) Pope (1873-1958) in 1893 in Polk. Mollie was the daughter of John William Pope (1847-1923) and Frances (Creed) Pope (1847-1938) and the granddaughter of Gideon (1817-1877) and Eucebia (1817-1910) Creed, who came to Missouri about 1840. Mollie's siblings were Thomas Edgar (1869-1945); Mittie (Pope) Pitts (1871-1960); Effie (Pope) Payne

Elpha, Charles and Elgie Fraser

(1875-1964); and Russell (1877-1961). John William Pope, who was the president of the Polk Bank, was the son of John C. and Sarah (Lightfoot) Pope of Kentucky.

Ninnian and Mollie's children were Elgie Ruel (1894-1986); Effie Grace (Fraser) Payne (1896-1918); Jessie (Fraser) Fowler (1902-1997); Thomas Willard (1905-1995) and Blance Ellen (Fraser) Remington (1907-1997). Ninnian and Mollie ran a general merchandise store in Polk, and after Ninnian died at age 39 of typhoid, Mollie ran the store alone. Their youngest child was only 20 months old.

Ryan, Elgie, Elpha, Charles, Jarrett, Georgia, Larry, Patton, Penny, Rob, Linda and Mike Fraser

Elgie married Elpha May Hood in 1914, and had one son, Charles Ruel Fraser, in 1919. They were in the grocery business for 76 years. Elpha (1895-1982) was the daughter of Charles and Stella (Rush) Hood of Fair Grove.

Charles Ruel Fraser married Georgia Lee Marsh in 1942 and had sons, Charles Michael in 1945, and Patton Marsh in 1948. Georgia was the daughter of Clyde and Maude (Atchley) Marsh.

Mike has two sons, Robert Graham and Ryan Michael, and Pat has three sons, Larry Michael, Jarrett Byron and Justin Morgan.

Charles Fraser was named president, CEO, and chairman of the board of the Farmers and Merchant's Bank in 1961. He retired in 1984 from the bank, now known as Commerce Bank of Bolivar, and continues to be active in community affairs. *Submitted by Chas. R. Fraser*

FRIEZE - The Frieze family history goes back to Jacob and Mary (Milburn) Frieze who moved to the Dunnegan area, along with their children, from Tennessee around 1832. Their oldest son, Alfred M., was a Baptist minister and farmer. He was married to Amanda Ann (Campbell) and they had eight children. After Amanda's death he married Mary Eliza (Worthan), age 16 — he was 55 years old. With Eliza he had six more children. He is listed in the 1860 census as having $5000 worth of real estate and $5000 worth of personal property.

Alfred Richard, the eldest son of Alfred M. and Eliza, married Mary (Carneal), Dec. 22, 1892. They were referred to as "Uncle Alf and Aunt Sis." They continued to farm 200 acres of the farm that Alfred M. settled. Uncle Alf and Aunt Sis had five children: James Arthur, Addie May, Alfred Otis, Mable Minnie and John Richard. J. Arthur married Vera Theda (Patterson), March 16, 1916. J. Arthur was known as "Pood" and was constable of Marion Township and is rumored to have chased Pretty Boy Floyd at one time. He was a veterinarian for all of Polk County for 16 years. Pood and Vera lived on North Main in Bolivar until their deaths five months apart in 1943. They had six children: Leonia Laverne "Lavine" (deceased); Lula Mae (deceased); Albert "Ralph" (deceased); Vera "Frances;" James Arthur II; and Mary Ann. Lavine married Vernon Orville Burgess Jr. (deceased). Vernon was a veteran of WWII.

193

Left to right, front row: Jim Davison, Rex Williams, James Frieze, Mary Ann Frieze Stoops, Alfred, Mary Frieze, Wayne Frieze. Second row: Raymond McCracken, Velbert Frieze, Frances Frieze Cornelius. Third row: Ralph Frieze, Lavine Frieze Burgess, Addia McCracken, Arthur Pood Frieze, Homer Williams, Mable Frieze Williams, Vera Frieze, Dorthy Frieze. Fourth row: Lula Frieze Davison holding Richard Davison, John Davison, Harry McCracken, Otis Frieze, Grace Frieze, John Frieze. Taken December 1942, Fiftieth Anniversary of Alfred and Mary Frieze.

They lived in Little Rock, AR for a number of years before moving to Springfield, MO to be close to family. They never had children, but raised James Arthur and Mary Ann after their parents' deaths. Lula married John Milton Davison (deceased), July 18, 1939. They had five sons: Jim, Richard, Bill, Mike and Bob (deceased). Ralph married Mary Alice Bashford, Sept. 24. 1949. They had four children: George, Jim, Tom and Susan. Mary Alice lives in California. Frances married Daniel Edward Cornelius, June 1, 1947. They had three children: Ed, Vera and Ron (deceased). Frances, Dan, Ed and Vera live on the Cornelius farm in Halfway, MO and Ron's widow and two children also live on the farm. James II married Linda Louise Burns of Pleasant Hope, Dec. 20, 1959. They had four children: James III, Rex, Ron and Melinda. Jim owns 80 acres southeast of Fair Play, about five miles from the family farm, but lives in Willard. Mary Ann married Charles Letterman. They had one daughter, Luann. After their divorce, Mary Ann married Oral Stoops, Dec. 31, 1968. They live in Springfield. Mable Minnie Frieze married Homer James Williams, Feb. 8, 1931. They had one son, Rex Williams who lives on the Williams farm near Fair Play with his wife, Deana Louise (Gladden). They had three children: Kimberly, Deana Kay and Jimmy, who continues to live in the area. Every year, around the end of September, the Friezes hold a family reunion at Dunnegan Memorial Park. All family and friends are welcome to attend.

Alfred and Arthur Frieze were both Masons until their deaths. Vera Frieze was an Eastern Star until her death and had Masonic services at both funerals. Francis is a member of Eastern Star at Buffalo. *Submitted by Melinda (Frieze) Kopfer*

Jim and Emily Frost

FROST – Jim and Emily Frost moved to Bolivar in June 1987 for Jim to teach at Southwest Baptist University. They came with their three children, John (15 years), Brian (14 years) and Amy (8 years) from southern California. In California they had lived in Riverside while Jim taught at California Baptist College, and later they lived in Valencia where they started a new church called Faith Community Church.

In 1988, the Frosts with Bob and Patty Ingold, Drew and Sherry Shoemaker, and Lou and Shelley Harris began a new youth ministry called Chi Alpha. Up to 80 high schoolers gathered every Wednesday night at the Frost home on Woodland Circle to play sports, to hear students share their spiritual stories, to have lots of good clean fun, and to build meaningful relationships. Some unforgettable Chi Alpha activities were Christmas Yule banquets, "cow-tongue" football, camping and rappelling trip to Arkansas, jello wars and water skiing.

John Frost met Carolynn Katrosh, daughter of John and Judy, at Chi Alpha. They both graduated from Bolivar High School and married in 1993. They attended New Tribes Bible Institute and have served as missionaries in Papua New Guinea. They have four sons at this writing—Jonathan, Jordan, Aaron and Andrew.

Brian graduated from Bolivar High and Southwest Baptist University where he also participated in several mission trips to Africa. In 1997, he married Tabatha Goss, a Georgia girl. Presently he serves as a pastor in Raleigh, NC. They have two sons, Josiah and Caleb and are expecting a third child.

Amy also graduated from Bolivar High and at this writing is almost ready to graduate from Southwest Baptist University. While in college, she has worked in numerous jobs: Bass Pro, O'Reilley Automotive, First Baptist Recreation Center, Kanakuk Kamps and the University. She serves Bolivar youth through a program called Youth Life.

Emily has become an artist since coming to Bolivar Her primary media are oil painting and collage through which she loves to express her ideas and her perspective on life.

Jim and Emily have been very active in First Baptist Church, Bolivar. Jim has pioneered a new academic program at the University called the Intercultural Studies major which aims to train students for cross-cultural service around the world. Children, grandchildren and college students remain the focus and love their lives. *Submitted by Emily Frost*

FULBRIGHT – Ancestors of Verda Walker Carns date back to 1597, living in Prussia. Johann Wilhelm Volprecht and wife Christine (Halstead) came to the United States in 1737, landing in Pennsylvania from Germany. He changed his name to John William Fulbright. They had five sons who moved to different states, Georgia, Tennessee and the Carolinas.

Verda's great-grandfather Jason Franklin Fulbright was born in North Carolina in 1827, moving to Missouri later. He died in Springfield, MO and is buried in Pleasant Hill Cemetery east of Bolivar, MO. Verda's grandfather, Leander Ellis Fulbright, was born in Georgia in 1850. He married Minerva Ann Dean in 1877. She was born in 1857 in Tennessee, moving to Missouri with her parents at the age of 12. They were the parents of eight children. She passed away in September 1923. Minerva was a member of Pleasant Hill Baptist Church, being saved at the age of 12. Leander was saved at the age of 70. Leander married Emma Ross in September 1925. She passed away in February 1937. Leander and Minerva Ann are buried in Pleasant Hill Cemetery.

Verda's father Aaron was born Feb. 13, 1894. He was the youngest of the family living, as the younger baby died in infancy. He was married to Georgia Batterall in December 1916. They had two children, Ella Jewell (Fulbright) Morris and Weldon Rogers Fulbright.

Aaron and Bessie Jane Davison were married on Jan. 28, 1923. They were the parents of four children: Verda, Lendel, Vera Ann and Donald Dean. They lived on a small farm one and one-fourth miles east of the Bolivar square. The children walked one and one-fourth miles to Forest Grove (a one-room school having eight grades). Aaron rented farmland from the neighbors to raise crops. He also did a lot of custom work. He and his parents had always planted sorghum cane. All the family helped when the cane was harvested in the fall to make the molasses. It was used to eat with hot biscuits and in making cakes and candy. If it was a good crop, some was sold to help out with expenses.

Bessie planted an orchard with fruit trees and a blackberry patch. With the large garden, most of the food was produced on the farm. The family had cows for milk, chickens for eggs and hogs for meat. It was a busy time with no modern conveniences.

In the summer on Sunday afternoons, Aaron would go the Maas Ice Plant in Bolivar, bringing home a big chunk of ice, which was crushed to make homemade ice cream. They would take turns turning the crank of the freezer. This was a very special treat. Aaron passed away on Feb. 20, 1963 and Bessie passed away on Sept. 18, 1967 and are both buried at Pleasant Hill Cemetery.

Verda married John Walker on Sept. 27, 1956. He passed away on Sept. 25, 1985. They had one son Charles, who with his wife Debbie and their sons Greg and Kyle, live on the home place. Verda then married Robert Cams in January 1999 and he passed away on Aug. 11, 2001.

Vera married Lovell Ashlock on June 18, 1953. They live on a farm in the Halfway community. They have three children: Karen Shimkus of Springfield, MO; Roger, who passed away on Dec. 26, 1996; and Dennis, who lives near Kansas City, MO.

Lendel, a Korean War veteran, married Sibyl Rouark on Feb. 23, 1952. They moved to Pittsburg, KS in 1963. There they raised their family of six children: Charles Edward, Tommy Wayne, Jimmy Ray, Linda Kay, Randy Allen and Debbie Sue. Lendel was a truck driver, traveling in several states, and is now a resident of a nursing home in Quapaw, OK.

Donald married Doris Inglis on Oct. 15, 1950. They were the parents of a daughter, Donna Jones, and a son, Gary, both of Bolivar. Donald was a farmer. He worked for the State Highway Department and Bolivar MFA. He also did custom tractor work. He was a Missionary Baptist preacher, holding many revival meetings and was the pastor of Forest Home Missionary Baptist Church at the time of his death on July 19, 1994. He is buried in Pleasant Hill Cemetery.

In the year of 1991, there was a reunion of over 250 Fulbrights in Springfield, MO with descendants attending from several states. *Submitted by Verda Walker Carns*

FULLER – John Amos Fuller was born March 15, 1861 to Elizabeth and Daniel Fuller. Flora Ann Baumgartner was born July 29, 1862 in La Grange, IN. With the consent of her parents, Charlotte (Ryason) and Benjamin Baumgartner, Flora Ann married John Amos Fuller on Dec. 17, 1879 in Peoria, IL. Flora and John had 10 children. The youngest daughter, Bertha Ella, was born May 12, 1902 in Parnell, MO. Flora and John moved to Halfway, MO on a farm in 1910. Their home was destroyed by fire and all their family records were burned.

Bertha Ella Fuller and James Allen Davison, married Feb. 12, 1930

Bertha Ella Fuller married James Allen Davison on Feb. 12, 1930 in Buffalo, MO. Allen was born July 26, 1890, north of Halfway, MO to Hannah R. (Clark) and Daniel Thomas Davison. Bertha and Allen lived on a farm northeast of Halfway, MO. Then, just nine years after their marriage, Allen died on June 26, 1939 at the age of 49 and was buried in Goff Cemetery. Bertha and her family moved in with her parents. John Amos Fuller died April 29, 1953 at the age of 92. Flora Ann Fuller died June 23, 1954 at the age of 92. Both are buried at Goff Cemetery.

Bertha had three children: Junior Fuller and wife Marcene, of Kansas City, MO; Roseann Boyce and husband Herb of Bolivar, MO and James Clark Davison and wife Neta of Independence, MO. Six grandsons: Bruce Fuller and wife Cecilia; Curtis Fuller; Greg Davison and wife Terrie; Paul Davison and wife Terrie; Jeffrey Boyce and wife Janet; and Rodney Boyce and wife Rachel. Seven great-grandchildren, three step-great-grandchildren and two great-great-granddaughters.

Bertha lived north of Halfway, MO on a family farm until 1964. She moved to Bolivar, MO. She moved to Parkview Health Care Facility on May 11, 1998.

There is no place like Polk County. *Submitted by Roseann Boyce*

FULLERTONS – The Polk County history of the Fullertons of Pleasant Hope dates from 1837, with the emigration of Robert Lucky Fullerton (1795 — 1873) from Tennessee. His father was Adam (1771 — 1836) and his grandfather, James Alexander (1746 — 1778), who left Scotland for Northern Ireland and arrived in Philadelphia in 1768. Among Robert Lucky's descendants were Robert Franklin (1837 — 1920), Robert Edmond (1876 — l945) and Willard James (1907 — 1976). In 1928, Willard married Katie Mae McArtor, who is now 96 and living in Springfield. They had four children: Robert James (1937), twins Roy Edmond and Ray Thomas (1940; Tom died in 1 994) and Rosemary (1946).

The Fullertons acquired substantial acreage, but the only part of the original holding that remained, inherited by Robert Edmond and subsequently by Willard James, was just under 80 acres and located about three miles southeast of Pleasant Hope on what is now Polk County AB. An additional 80 acres about three-fourths of a mile south on the Greene/Polk County line, was purchased in 1917. Katie sold the property in 1988, although she remained on the farm until her move to Springfield in 1994. Records show that besides agriculture, various family members engaged in local business ventures, law and surveying. Robert Franklin was 1900 census head in Mooney Township.

Involvement in churches, lodges and especially education was characteristic of the Fullertons. Several Fullertons were among the founders of the Pleasant Hope Normal Academy in the 1880s. Katie and Willard graduated from Pleasant Hope High School and Katie attended college, teaching elementary school a total of nine years in the 1920s and 1930s at Pleasant Grove (Frog Pond), Eidson, Persimmon Grove, Providence and Pleasant Hope. She and Willard were made life members of the Pleasant Hope Parent Teachers Association for their years of dedicated service. Willard served on the Pleasant Hope school board for more than a decade and on the Polk County school board, which was phased out as the one-room schools became part of larger districts. He also served on the regional library board. Willard read almost every night that he didn't have a community obligation or work. He had an extensive personal library but obtained many of the books he read from the Springfield library. He enjoyed playing educational games with his children, like dictionary and spelling games and quoted poetry to them while they worked. Due in part to Katie and Willard's interest in learning, three of their children chose education as a profession. Rosemary became a teacher and librarian, Ed a teacher and Tom, a professor.

The period of the 1940s and 1950s was a time of transition on the Fullerton farm. Electricity came to the farm through the Rural Electrification Administration in the early 1940s, instigating a change from kerosene lanterns and lamps to electric lighting, from hand milking to machines, from hand-pumped water to electric pumps, from stock-tank cooled milk to refrigerated coolers,

Fullertons in 1948; Willard, Katie and Maud (Willard's mother). Front: Bob, Rosemary, Tom and Ed

from a washboard to an electric agitator-wringer washing machine, from ice boxes to refrigerators, from curing meat to freezing and storing it in the local locker, and from hand tools to power tools. In the mid-1940s, Willard replaced bulls with artificial insemination and became a member of the Dairy Herd Improvement Association as he developed a top herd of Jersey cows. In the late 1940s, milking moved from the shed in the hay barn to a modern milking barn. Farmers increasingly specialized and the Fullertons eventually depended entirely on their dairy herd, no longer raising chickens and hogs. Tractors completed their takeover from horses, and threshing and silo crews were almost gone by 1960. Along with many other farmers, the Fullertons stopped growing grain, buying from feed companies instead, while concentrating on grass and hay crops. A chemical revolution was occurring as well, with Willard quick to adopt pesticides and herbicides to fight bugs and to control weeds and shrubs in fields and fencerows. Communication remained poor until the late 1950s, when hand-crank phones were replaced by a modern dialing system. The gravel road by the farm, which had been so muddy at times that vehicles became stuck, was gradually improved and was paved about 1960.

Rural life is sometimes idealized and many things about it were rewarding, but no matter what the changes, life was always hard on the farm. Low prices for products, drought or excessive rain, infestations of insects and other pests, and the never-ending work were a challenge, so many farmers left the land. Katie and Willard persevered, milking until 1972 and eventually renting the land to a neighbor. With all of the Fullerton children living elsewhere and none interested in staying on the land, the history of the Pleasant Hope Fullertons concluded with the sale of the property and Katie's move to Springfield. The work ethnic, integrity and commitment to public service represented by their lives provide a positive legacy for the family and for the larger Pleasant Hope community. *Submitted by Roy Edmond Fullerton*

GALLATINS – Harlie Kay Gallatin grew up on a farm near Meadville, MO in Linn County. Nancy Mae Morgan Gallatin was born and raised on a farm near Downing, MO in Schuyler County. Harlie and Nancy met at Hannibal LaGrange College, Hannibal, MO where they fell in love. They were married Aug. 5, 1954 in the Downing Baptist Church and began their married life in Liberty, MO. While Harlie attended William Jewel College, Nancy taught second grade at Englewood School. On weekends they drove to Linn County where Harlie pastored two country churches.

After Harlie graduated they moved to North Kansas City in the fall of 1955 so Nancy would be closer to her school and Harlie started attending Central Baptist Theological Seminary in Kansas City, KS. Their daughter, Kaylene Louise, was born April 6, 1957 and Nancy became a full-time mom and housewife. Rhonda Lee joined their happy family on Feb. 12, 1959. Harlie graduated from seminary in May 1959 and the family moved to Warrensburg, MO for him to attend Central Missouri State University. The history faculty of CMSU recruited Harlie as a teaching assistant. This allowed him to pursue a master's degree in history full time, graduating in May 1961.

Those years at Warrensburg were difficult. Harlie was also pastoring a small county church in Lafayette County. On Feb. 22, 1960, their son Morgan Dean was born and that winter both girls had pneumonia. A fellow pastor, Rev. C.J. Ford, who was a member of the board of trustees at Southwest Baptist College made inquiry and Harlie was hired to teach history at Southwest Baptist College. The Gallatin family moved to Bolivar, MO, August 1961. They remember well the call in 1962 that Pike Auditorium was on fire. Harlie went to the campus while Nancy watched the blaze from the front door of their home on West Madison. The Gallatins lived in Urbana, IL, for three years while Harlie completed residency for his PhD at the University of Illinois. Back at SWBC Harlie became chairman of the Department of History and Political Science in 1970 while completing his PhD requirements by 1972. Harlie

Left to right: Harlie holding Morgan, Kaylene, Nancy holding Rhonda, Christmas 1960

retired from SBU in August 2001, but still teaches his favorite course, "History of Christianity."

Nancy completed her bachelor's degree in 1970 after Southwest became a senior college. That fall she began teaching at Fair Play Elementary School. In 1977 she moved to the Bolivar R1 school system where she taught until her retirement in 1999. The family has been active in First Baptist Church. Harlie teaches an adult men's Sunday School class and Nancy teaches in the kindergarten Sunday School department.

Sitting: Alyssa and Andrew. Second row: Aaron, Harlie, Isaac, Nancy. Back row: Rhonda, David, Mark, Kaylene and Morgan.

Each of their children graduated from Bolivar High School and Southwest Baptist University. Kaylene married J. Mark Cox and they have three children: Andrew, Alyssa and Aaron. They live in Clear Lake City, TX. Andrew enrolled as a freshman at SBU in 2002. Rhonda married David L. Proffitt and they have a son, Isaac. They live in Owasso, OK. Morgan lives in Warrensburg, MO where he is director of the Art Center Gallery and adjunct instructor of art at Central Missouri State University.

Nancy's parents, Russell and Louise Morgan, retired and moved to Bolivar in 1978. Russell was a member of the Bolivar Saddle Club and a deacon at First Baptist Church. Louise loved to quilt with the ladies at First Baptist Church. Russell died February 1986 and Louise, March 1997. *Submitted by Harlie Gallatin*

Jimmy, Aimee, Caleb and Ryan Gallivan

GALLIVAN – Although Aimee is not originally from the Polk County area, her husband and his family have strong ties to the community. Jimmy and Aimee met in the summer of 1995 and were married two years later on Oct. 18, 1997. They have two handsome boys, Caleb David, born on Sept. 13, 1999 and Ryan Landis, born on Feb. 14, 2001. They reside just outside Halfway, MO on a family owned and operated dairy farm. Aimee worked outside the home up until she had Ryan and now enjoys staying at home raising the boys. Jimmy has worked for his family now for almost eight years. Jimmy's grandfather, David Gallivan, started the dairy in the 1940s which now has grown to a 500-cow dairy.

David married Ruth (Voris) on Dec. 25, 1941. They have three children; Jerry, Robert and Nancy. Together, David, Jerry, Jimmy, Robert and Robert's son, Steven, all manage and run the family dairy.

Jimmy's dad, Jerry, married Jeanette Shackelton on July 17, 1970. They have three children; Janelle, Jimmy and Jay. Jerry has his own trucking business in Bolivar as well as playing a large role in the family dairy. Jeanette worked as a secretary at Halfway schools for close to 16 years before she made the decision to stay home and help Jerry with his business, as well as taking care of her first grandbaby. Janelle works in Springfield at Queen City Warehouse. Jay lives in Ozark and works in Branson and is engaged to be married in May of 2003. Jeanette is the daughter of Clyde and Marcella (Sampson). Clyde and Marcella were married on Dec. 11, 1945. Clyde and Marcella lived on a farm just outside Halfway where they raised both Jeanette and her brother Tony. Clyde farmed and carried the mail for over 20 years in Halfway. Tony resides in Springfield with his wife Karen. They have three children; Mandy, Cody and Lacy. Clyde passed away on Oct. 31, 2000.

Aimee was raised on a stock farm that her parents, Brent and Helen, worked hard for and her roots are strongly attached to the farm life. She loves being outdoors and watching the boys run and play and to someday learn the values that their families have passed down through generation after generation. Although Aimee misses living near her family, she wouldn't want to raise her boys anywhere other than Halfway, MO. While she is a Lawrence County native, she has always had strong ties to Polk County. She is the oldest great-grandchild of Jones P. and Jewel Holman Campbell and visited them often as a child up until their deaths. Aimee and Jimmy's sons are sixth in line descendants of Ezekiel M. Campbell, early pioneer settler of Polk and Greene Counties. Their family can be extremely proud of their Gallivan, Shackelton and Campbell heritages. *Submitted by Aimee Hurst Gallivan*

GALLIVAN – Jeremiah Gallivan was born circa 1814 and immigrated to America from Ireland from probably County Kerry about 1848. He went to work for one of the various railroads that traversed the area through Illinois and into Missouri. During a stop in Coles County, IL, he met Catherine O'Sullivan, who was also born in Ireland in November of 1832. Within a short period of time, Jeremiah convinced her to marry him. Their marriage license was dated Sept. 11, 1854.

They set up housekeeping in Pettis County, MO where three of their sons, Daniel, Jerry and John, were born. Sometime between 1860 and 1863 they moved to Polk County, MO where Eugene, Michael L., Mary A., James and Lily were born. Jeremiah was a hard-working farmer, a deeply religious man and liked by all who knew him. In his obituary he was called "Uncle Jerry." Jeremiah died March 14, 1908 and Catherine, died July 13, 1918. Both are buried in the Gallivan Cemetery.

Daniel married first, Bettie Haden, had seven children, second, Lavina Griggs. Jerry and Eugene never married. Michael married Mary Erwin, had five children; Mary married Frank Elliott, had eight children and James married Clara Bowen, had six children. John and Lily died young.

Just up the road was the farm of Charlie T. Hutcheson who was born Dec. 21, 1796 in East Tennessee, died July 21, 1868 in Polk County. He married Elizabeth Ann (surname unproven), born April 15, 1798 also in East Tennessee, died July 23, 1874 in Polk County. Both are buried in Mt. Olive Cemetery.

They had a large family consisting of 14 children. They were Margaret, William H., Sarah, Nicodemus D., John Grayson, James Henry, Jefferson, Sargent Wisdom, Charles Henderson, Elizabeth, Shelby Usery, Martha J., Emma and Mattie. Charlie T. and Elizabeth moved several times between 1830 and 1860. They moved from Monroe County, TN to McNairy County, TN, then to Tishomingo County, MS and to Carroll County, AR before their final move to Polk County, MO about 1861.

They also were hard working farmers, and three sons and four sons-in-law served in the Civil War. The sons that served were Nicodemus, Shelby Usery and Sargent Wisdom.

Margaret married William Wyatt and had two children; William H. married Elizabeth Jones, had nine children; Sarah married T.B. Youngblood, had 10 children; Nicodemus married Mary Elizabeth Gaustin, had six children; John Grayson married Cynthia Pierson, had nine children; James Henry married first, Elizabeth Dunlap, had 11 children, second, Lucinda Kessie, third, Keziah Kennon; Sargent Wisdom married Elizabeth Johnson, had three children; Charles Henderson married Martha Hood, had 10 children; Elizabeth married Josiah Wiese, had one child; Shelby U. married Malissa Cunningham, had seven children; and Martha married John N. Cunningham, had eight children. Jefferson, Emma and Mattie died young.

The Gallivan and Hutcheson families joined together with the marriage of two grandchildren born one day apart and just up the road from each other. On Feb. 17, 1916, James Austin Gallivan, born Aug. 6, 1896 and Bessie Lee Hutcheson, born Aug. 7, 1896, were united in marriage in Bolivar. They had three children: James, Victor and Joy Sue. When Joy Sue was small they moved to New Mexico and several years later they moved to California. They have grandchildren living in New Mexico, Indiana and California. *Submitted by Margaret Gallivan Baldock*

James Austin Gallivan and Bessie Lee Hutcheson after their wedding in 1916

GALYAN – Ira Galyan was born Jan. 30, 1887 in Polk County, MO. Ira was the son of Frank Galyan and Mary Phillips Galyan. Ira's father Frank migrated to Polk County, MO from Grainger County, TN. We know that Frank was the son of Pinkney Galyan, but the Grainger County, TN records were destroyed in a fire and we cannot find anymore information on Frank's family. Frank was quite an accomplished fiddle player. Ira told the family, that he played the fiddle at dances for money as he walked to Missouri from Tennessee. He was only 17 years old at the time. Upon arriving in Missouri, Frank made his way to Fair Play and decided to settle there. In those days Fair Play was a bustling little town. The railroad had brought a lot of business to the area and many families settled there. Frank met Mary Phillips, daughter of Mathis and Martha Phillips and they were married.

Frank and Mary had six children: Ira, Ethan, Arleigh, Preshie, Nora and a baby, Phamie, who died at birth. Ethan married Annie Sutherland. Arleigh was a wonderful piano player and made a living all of his life giving piano lessons to many of the people in Fair Play. Arleigh never married. Preshie married William Bunch. Nora married William "Bill" Curl. Ira married Liza Mayse. Liza was the daughter of Charley Mayse and Margaret Suttle Mayse. Liza's parents, Charley and

Margaret, migrated to Missouri from Tennessee and Kentucky. Margaret's parents, the Suttles, were from an old pioneer family in Tennessee. They migrated to Kentucky for a short time, where Margaret met Charley. When the Suttle family decided to move to Missouri, Charley followed them. They lived their entire life in Fair Play. Besides Liza, they also had a son Coy, who married Liza Lynch.

Ira and Liza operated the Fair Play telephone exchange for 30 years. Ira also ran a photo studio in the Fair Play area. They had one daughter, Geneva, who was born in 1917 and died in 1997. Geneva married Raymond Nickels and they lived their entire lives in Fair Play.

Liza died Sept. 12, 1952 at their home in Fair Play. After Liza died, Ira moved in with his daughter Geneva and her husband Raymond. He lived with them until his death Jan. 22, 1976. Raymond and Geneva's son, Gary, and his wife Kay Smith Nickels moved next door into Ira and Liza's house where they live today. Gary and Kay Nickels have one daughter, Gayla Nickels Wells, who lives in Bolivar. Gayla is married to Marty Wells and they have one son Derek.

Ira and Lisa Mayse Galyan

If anyone has any information on the Galyan family that stayed in Tennessee, please contact Ira's great-granddaughter, Gayla Nickels Wells. *Submitted by Kay Nickels*

GAMBLE – The Gamble farm located between Fair Play and Dunnegan has been in the family for over 160 years. Drury Keirsey from Maury County, TN was one of the earliest settlers in Polk County, establishing his residence on what is today the Gamble farm in 1839. Drury's wife was Agnes Thompson. Their daughter Gracy married Obediah Gamble in 1854. Obediah was the son of Ebenezer and Elizabeth (Ashlock) Gamble. Obediah and Gracy raised a large family of which one son was William Drury Gamble, who in 1895 built the house that still stands on the Gamble farm today. William Drury Gamble and his wife Florence Adella Lushbaugh had several children, one of which was Ernest Obediah Gamble who made his living on the farm until his death in 1960. Ernie Gamble was married to Tracy Stauffacher. Ernie and Tracy had four children: Rex, who died at the age of 6; twin girls Violet and Vesta; and a son Glen. Glen for many years was the postmaster and a rural mail carrier for the post office in Fair Play. Glen passed away in 1990. His widow Ann (Gardner) Gamble lives on the Gamble farm today. Their children and grandchildren include: Sheila Ellis of Springfield, married to Max Ellis and their son Todd and daughter Ashley, Brent Gamble of Fair Play, married to Betty Visintainer and their sons Brandon and Brian; Brad Gamble of Bolivar, married to Debbie Fite and their daughters Rachel, Brittany, and Jessie Katelyn. Violet and Vesta Gamble, for several years, were entertainers (Gamble Twins) singing on KWTO radio in Springfield and nationwide on the Korn's-A-Krakin show. Vesta married Gene Blue of Bolivar, who for many years was in the dimestore business on the Bolivar square. Gene passed away in 1993. Vesta lives in Bolivar today. Their children include two sons, Lex of Nevada, MO and Lance of Overland Park, KS, married to Anne Proctor. Violet married William R. (Jim) Morton of Cedar County, who for many years was in the bread business. Jim Morton passed away in 1981. Violet lives today in Houston, TX. Their one son Kim lives today in Kingwood, TX. *Submitted by Kim Morton*

Glen, Violet, Vesta Gamble 1930

GARDNER – According to historical documents, the Gardner family emigrated from England. The family crest, along with some descendants, can still be found in England. The first reported American ancestor was Thomas Sparhawk (1) Gardner who was born 1761 in Cambridge, MA and died on Nov. 4, 1840. He married Hannah on Oct. 15, 1789. She was born Jan. 25, 1771 and died Feb. 23, 1860. From this union were born six children: Hannah, Susanna, Thomas, Mary Sparhawk, Hariat and Thomas Sparhawk (2).

Thomas Sparhawk (2) was born Dec. 12, 1809 and died on Dec. 22, 1866. He married Emeretene Chase on June 16, 1835 in Quincy, IL. They moved to Missouri where were born the following eight children: Hannah Elizabeth, Mary Susan, Rachel Angeline, Hariet Eliza Maria, Lucy Ellen, Thomas Sparhawk (3), William Blagden Rice and Catherine E. Martha.

Ann's grandfather, Thomas Sparhawk Gardner (3) was born on Oct. 28, 1852 in California, MO and died March 8, 1941. He married Nancy Jane Hill on Dec. 25, 1883 in Lawrence, KS. They moved to Evergreen, CO and had 10 children: Harry Ellsworth, Alice Janet, Thomas Sparhawk (4), Henry Gorman, Mary Helen, Claud Melvil, Edith Elmira, Mabel Clair, Clarence and Ann's father, Arthur Kemp, who was born on April 12, 1898. Her father first married Dosha Mae Lynn on May 8, 1917 in Evergreen, CO. Before Dosha's death on Nov. 2, 1925, they had three children: Harriet Elizabeth, born March 7, 1918; Kenneth, born Aug. 23, 1919 and then died on Jan. 18, 1920; and Dimple Bell, born May 6, 1921. Together, with his two young children, Ann's father, Arthur, moved to Bolivar where he met and married Jessie Lois Stewart on March 10, 1929. Together, they had three children: Arthur Stewart, born Feb. 27, 1931; Lois Ann, born Sept. 21, 1932 and Arvel Thomas, born Feb. 14, 1938.

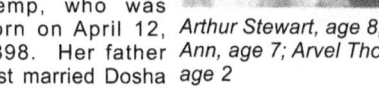
Arthur Stewart, age 8; Lois Ann, age 7; Arvel Thomas, age 2

Ann's father died on Sept. 21, 1967, her brother Arthur Stewart on May 15, 1980 and her mother on Feb. 26, 1981.

Ann was the first to marry and married Glen E. Gamble (Fair Play) on Nov. 23, 1951. They have three children: Sheila Ann, Brent Wade and Brad Kerry. Sheila married Max Ellis (Stockton) and has two children, Ashlie Nichole and Todd Christopher. Brent married Betty J. Visintainer (Springfield) and they have two sons, Brandon Wade and Brian Lee. Brad married Deborah Lynn Fite (Bolivar) and they have three daughters, Rachel Breanna, Brittany Leigh and Jessie Katelyn. Ann's older brother, Arthur Stewart, married Neva Charlene Titus (Bolivar) on Feb. 1, 1953. They have one son, John Kemp. Arvel Thomas, Ann's younger brother, married Patricia Ann Seiner (Bolivar) on Dec. 6, 1963. They have three children, Myrla Lynn, Michael Shane and Mark Cameron. Myrla married Stacy Hall (Bolivar) and they have two children, Broch and Macy. Michael married Jana Russell (Springfield) and their two sons are Shane and Colten. Mark just recently married Ellen Jackowitz (Franklin, TN).

Arvel and Ann continue to live in Polk County. *Submitted by Lois Ann (Gardner) Gamble*

GARNER-ANDERSON - Joel Garner was born 1825 in Tennessee, died 1895 in Dallas County, MO.

Martha Smith Garner, wife of Joel Garner, Grandma of Bertha White

Martha Jane Smith was born in 1828 in Tennessee. Died 1910 in Missouri. Joel and Martha were married in Polk County, MO on Jan. 28, 1846. To this union were born: Permilla Ann, Lavinia Jane, Nancy Angelina, Maragaret Mary Cordelia, Melissa, Lucinda M., James W., Robert Theodore, Francis Marion and Flora Bell.

Joel and Martha are buried in Mount Pleasant Cemetery, Dallas County, MO in the far northeast part. They worked hard to help start and attend the church they loved so much.

Lavinia married John Henry Anderson, March 31, 1872 in Dallas County, MO. Their children: John Willis Perry, Bertha Ruby Mae and Samuel Ezekiel.

Willis married Letha Conley, March 2, 1900, in Polk County, MO and they had five children. He later married Canzada Mary Hensley on Aug. 8, 1921.

Bertha married Thomas Henry White April 24, 1898 in Polk County, MO. They had six children.

Samuel married Edna Belle Scott. They had eight children. Later he married Josephine M. Dowler Cutsinger and had one son.

On July 11, 1899, a young 16-year-old woman, Bertha, gave birth to her first child, a girl, Rosa Bell Frances. While recovering from the birth of her baby, she got word that her mother, Lavinia, had died, somewhere around Deepwater or Clinton, MO. Not knowing the exact place, she never learned where her mother was buried.

Recently through the Internet, it has been discovered there is a Garner Family Reunion every two years at Big Spring, MO. This is a large three-day event. While unable to attend this year, we are certainly looking forward to the year 2004. We'll meet lots of Garners, and with luck find out more about Lavinia and John. *Submitted by Leta Altic Page (great-great-granddaughter of Lavinia)*

GARRETSON - Harold L. Garretson, son of Isaac M. and Clara (Collier) Garretson, married Mary L. Dunn on Jan. 8, 1938 in Osceola, MO. Harold and Mary had four children: Mildred Ethel, born Oct. 29, 1938; Lyle Lee, born Sept. 16, 1940; Fred Earl, born May 1, 1942; and Harold James Garretson, born Sept. 15, 1944. The Garretsons lived in Cliquot, Polk County, MO, where Mary worked as the postmaster for 14 years. Harold worked different jobs for several years but in 1958 Harold and Mary moved to Bolivar where they owned and operated Garretson's Trash Service for 12 years. Their four children all attended school at Cliquot until 1953 when the school district consolidated. Mildred graduated from Bolivar High School in 1956; Lyle graduated from Bolivar High School in 1958; Fred graduated from Humansville High School in 1960; and Harold J. graduated from Bolivar High School in 1962.

Mildred E. Garretson first married Leonard Earnest in 1959. They had three children: Ricky

Mary and Harold L. Garretson

Earnest, Kathy Hommelson and Jeff Earnest. Mildred married Robert McCain in 1980. She owned a title company in O'Fallon, MO until she retired in 1999 and moved to Lake of the Ozarks.

Lyle L. Garretson, known as "Buster," married Sharon Kay Scurlock in 1966. They had three children: Trudi Snow, Greg Garretson and Staci Wendland. Buster and Kay bought Garretson's Trash Service from Harold and Mary in 1970 and continue to own and operate this business in Polk and Hickory Counties.

Fred E. Garretson, known as "Buddy," first married Nancy Smith in 1964. They had two children: David Garretson and Sherri Collier. Buddy then married Shirley Doolin in 1965. They had Michael Garretson and Leslie Williams. Buddy married Kathy Grawbois in 1977. They had Kathleen Boarder. He married Jenna Kemerling in 1982. Bud was a pipe fitter for Ford Motor Co. in Kansas City, MO for several years, and then owned a plumbing company in Lee's Summit, MO until he retired and moved to Hickory County on Lake Pomme De Terre.

Harold J. Garretson, known as "Jim," married Sharon Sue Phillips in 1961. They had James Ray, John and Joe Garretson. Jim was a grain merchandiser, both cash and futures. After his retirement, Jim and Sharon moved to Bolivar where they lived until Jim's death on March 25, 1999. Sharon continues to live here and work at SBU. *Submitted by Trudi Snow*

GARRETSON – Issac M. Garretson was born on March 7, 1884 in Buffalo, NY. He was the son of John Worth Garretson and Clara Sophia Rapalyea. Issac married Clara Louise Collie on June 17, 1908 in Keokuk, IA. She was the daughter of John N. Collier and Louise M. Thaller. They had five children. Mary Louise was born on May 5, 1909 in Chattanooga, OK. Mildred Clara was born on

Issac M. Garretson

Sept. 17, 1910 in Summitville, IA. John Collier was born on Oct. 17, 1912 in Summitville, IA. George Herbert was born on Jan. 23, 1915 in Faxon, OK. He died at Keokuk, IA on Sept. 15, 1923 at the age of 8. Harold L. was born on Nov. 21, 1916 in Faxon, OK.

Issac M. Garretson received his government license as a steam engineer in August of 1906. During WWI, he operated two 500 horsepower steam engines for the government at a power plan in Nashville, TN. During this time Clara and the children were living in Oklahoma, but they moved to Cliquot, MO in Polk County on Jan. 15, 1920. Clara died in Cliquot on Feb. 28, 1920 from a form of the flu, leaving behind five small children.

Issac and the children moved back to Iowa. He then married Alice Irma Seward on Nov. 23, 1923. They lived in Iowa for five years, then moved back to Cliquot, MO in March of 1928. Issac and Alice remained in Polk County until their deaths. They had six children of their own. Their children were Alice Irene, born March 6, 1925 in Keokuk, IA; Arthur Issac, born May 24, 1926 in Keokuk, IA; Elizabeth Lou, born Dec. 22, 1927 in Keokuk, IA; William R., born Aug. 5, 1929 in Cliquot, MO; Nellie Ruth, born Jan. 10, 1931 in Cliquot, MO; and Zella Mae, born Aug. 19, 1934 in Cliquot, MO. Issac and Alice owned and operated a 400-acre farm in the Cliquot area. Issac also would take his threshing machine and thresh wheat for other farmers. He completed 12 years as president on the local school board and six years as chairman of the Township Soil Conservation Board. He was a member of the Polk County Extension Board and a member of the advisory board of Ozark Production Credit Association of Springfield, MO.

Polk County continued to be the home to eight of the 11 Garretson children. They married and lived in the Bolivar, Cliquot and Humansville areas.

Mildred C. Garretson married William Rankin Rowles in Bolivar, MO on Dec. 1, 1932. They had Emma Carolyn Rowles, born on Sept. 17, 1935.

John C. Garretson married Lillis V. Carneal on Dec. 30, 1933 in Humansville, MO. Their children were Issac Alah, born July 25, 1935; Barbara Ann, born Aug. 22, 1937; and Robert Lee Garretson, born Dec. 30, 1950.

Harold L. Garretson married Mary L. Dunn on Jan. 8, 1938 in Osceola, MO. Their children were Mildred Ethel, born Oct. 29, 1938; Lyle Lee, born Sept. 16, 1940; Fred Earl, born May 1, 1942; and Harold James Garretson, born Sept. 15, 1944.

Arthur Issac Garretson married Helen Anderson on May 19, 1948 in Bolivar, MO. Their children were Jerry Wayne, born March 16, 1953 and Steven Eugene Garretson, born Sept. 2, 1950.

Elizabeth Lou Garretson married Thomas Black on April 13, 1947 in Bolivar, MO. Their children were Johnnie Dale, born Feb. 26, 1949; Anna Marie, born Sept. 10, 1953; and William Black, born Feb. 1, 1958.

William R. Garretson married Wanda Floyd on June 19, 1959. Their children were Randy Gay, born Aug. 8, 1961 and Sandra Kay Garretson, born Jan. 30, 1963.

Nellie Ruth Garretson married Earl Ellis on June 11, 1949 in Bolivar, MO. Their children were Teresa May, born June 8, 1952 and Donnie Earl Ellis, born Sept. 3, 1958.

Zella May Garretson married Oren Piper on Jan. 15, 1955. Their children were Irma Ann, born Nove. 25, 1960 and Debbie Lynn Piper, born Nov. 13, 1963. *Submitted by Lyle Garretson*

GAUNT – James H. Gaunt was born Sept. 26, 1806 in Frederick County, VA, the son of John Gaunt and Tabitha Dobyns Mott Gaunt. His parents left Virginia and settled in Hopkins County, KY in 1811 when James was only 5 years of age. He grew up in Hopkins County and there he married Susannah Thomasson on Dec. 12, 1826. She was born April 10, 1806 in Kentucky, the daughter of Samuel D. Thomasson and Hannah Haynes Thomasson.

James H. Gaunt and his wife, Susannah, had at least four children born in Kentucky prior to 1836 — Harden Haines Gaunt (married Emeline West, 1849), Samuel D. Gaunt (married Rebecca Martha Claypool, 1849), John William Gaunt (married Exonia Ann Gearhart, 1856) and Tabitha Gaunt. About 1837/38, James Gaunt left Hopkins County, KY for Missouri. James was accompanied by his wife and children and an extended family that included his half-sister, Sarah Gaunt Wetzel (wife of John Christopher Wetzel) and their children and his nephew, John Mott Gaunt (married first, Mary E. Berry and second, Emily Pyles). The families settled in Polk County about 1838 where they purchased land. James H. Gaunt's land was in Township 32, Range 25—a portion of the county that later became Dade County. In Missouri two more children were born to James and Susannah — Thomas W. Gaunt was born about 1838 and Dixon Gaunt was born in 1841.

James and Susannah Gaunt were pioneers in every sense of the word. Although they remained in Polk (later Dade) County until 1853, they then decided it was time to go west again and embarked on an adventure that would take them overland via the Oregon Trail to Yamhill County, OR where they settled and James became Justice of the Peace. The Gaunt Bridge, located in Lafayette, OR, was apparently a favorite place for weddings, many performed by James H. Gaunt in the 1860s, and thus so named.

James died April 30, 1874 in Yamhill County, OR, three years after the death of his wife, Susannah. They are both buried in the Masonic Cemetery in McMinnville, OR.

Although several of their children and grandchildren moved to Oregon with James and Susannah, one son, John William (Jack) Gaunt remained in Missouri. He married a young woman who lived on a neighboring farm, Exonia Ann Gearhart, daughter of Peter Gearhart and Susannah Alexander Gearhart. Jack and Exonia had eight children. They continued to live near the original family farm (by then in Dade County) until they moved to Dallas County, MO sometime after the Civil War.

Many descendants of James H. Gaunt and Susannah Thomasson Gaunt still live in southwest Missouri, primarily Dallas and Greene Counties, while others have located in many areas throughout the United States. *Submitted by Sarah Gaunt Thompson*

GEORGE – Wiley B. B. George and wife Hannah (Alldridge) George were among the early settlers in Johnson Township. They moved from Knoxville, TN to Polk County in 1838, homesteading northwest of Humansville.

W. B. B. George and James G. Human, founder of Humansville, were first cousins. Wiley's father was Solomon George of Knoxville. The mother of Judge James G. Human was Winnifred (George) Gilliam Human of Knoxville. Solomon and Winnifred were brother and sister. W. B. B. George was a descendant of Nicholas and Margaret (Saward) George who immigrated from Essex County, England to Lancaster County, Virginia by 1625.

W. B. B. George was born April 7, 1812 in Knoxville and died June 23, 1880 in Humansville. He and Hannah Alldridge were married in Knoxville Aug. 9, 1832. Hannah was born on Aug. 31, 1811 and died May 28, 1885. She was the daughter of William and Mary Alldridge of Knoxville. The children of W. B. B. and Hannah George were Mary, 1833-1901, married Thomas Dawson on May 31, 1874 in Polk County;

Solomon, 1835-1864, married Louisa Josephine Earnest in St. Clair County, MO in June 1863 (Solomon A. M. George, a Union army officer, was killed in Arkansas in August 1864 shortly before the birth of his daughter, Josie George);

William, married Josephine Hapsgood Dec. 20, 1868 in Polk County;

Wiley, 1837-1862;

Margaret, married James Hopper;

Melvina, married Joshua Frost on Nov. 5, 1858;

Karen, 1846-1886, married Thomas B. Hopper on April 4, 1865;

Thomas, 1850-1925, married Ella Foster on

Samuel J. George, 1909, Humansville, MO

July 3, 1870.

Samuel Joseph George was born Aug. 24, 1848 in Humansville and died May 19, 1911. He married Rebecca Frances "Fanny" Mashburn on Jan. 9, 1868 in Rondo. Fanny, daughter of Emanual and Polly (Beavers) Mashburn of Elkton, MO, was born Sept. 17, 1852 and died Jan. 13, 1940. Samuel J. George represented Polk County in the Missouri House of Representatives, 1887-1893 and was Humansville's Postmaster, 1896-1906. The children of Samuel and Fanny George were Will, 1869-1961, married Emma and lived in Humansville all of his life; Fred; Mae; Dora; Samuel Jr.

John Blunt George was born Jan. 23, 1872 in Humansville and died Jan. 15, 1963 in Bethany, OK. He married Jennie Harrison Peterman on Dec. 19, 1894 in Humansville. Jennie, daughter of George and Martha (Lindsay) Peterman of Humansville, was born Dec. 11, 1872 in Lathrop, MO. She died October 17, 1941. John and Jennie moved from Polk County to Hinton, OK in October 1909. Their children were Joe, Frankie, Veda, Bert and John.

Joe George was born Dec. 19, 1895 in Humansville and died March 29, 1967 in Oklahoma City. He moved with his parents to Oklahoma at the age of 13. Joe married Blanche Richardson on April 18, 1917 in Fletcher, OK. Blanche was the daughter of Millard and Nettie (Spencer) Richardson and was born Feb. 22, 1898 in Circleville, KS. She died Aug. 21, 1983 in Oklahoma City. Joe served in the 112th Infantry of the US Army during WWI and was wounded in action at Chateau-Thierry, France in August 1918. Joe and Blanche moved from Hinton to Oklahoma City in 1923 where Joe worked for Sharps Auto Supply and, later, Tinker AFB, 1942-1961. Children of Joe and Blanche George are Joe Jr. and Dale. *Submitted by Gregory A. George*

GERSTLE – Marilyn's grandmother, Lexie Gerstle Roderick (1896-1988), loved to tell stories about her own grandma, Granny Gerstle. Granny's maiden name was Nancy Redman (1845-1917). She was born near Memphis, TN. Her family moved to Missouri before the Civil War. They lived on the "Wade Voris place" between Schofield and Halfway.

While the men were away fighting in the war, bushwhackers burned the Redman house. A churn of honey and a feather bed mattress were saved from the fire. A wagon and a team of oxen were hidden away from the house. Nancy's mother was very sick. They put the salvaged mattress in the back of the wagon for her mother to lie on. Nancy drove the oxen team to Marshall, MO where the family had relatives.

During her stay in Marshall, Nancy went to see a fortune teller. Her fortune was, "You will meet a man on the street who will give you a gift. That is the man you will marry." She met a man on the street who gave her an apple. He was a short, strong, German man, who stood barely five feet tall. His name was Frederick Gerstle (1835-1897). She married him.

Frederick was born in Wittenberg, Germany. His mother put him on a ship to America when he was 18 years old. He worked for many years to save enough money to bring her to America. On the day he went to make arrangements for his mother's passage, a letter was waiting for him at the post office. His mother had died.

Nancy and Frederick were married in Marshall and they had a baby girl buried there. They moved south of Halfway in 1869. Two more baby girls were buried in the Gorden Cemetery there. They had two surviving sons, Jim and Luther and one daughter, Emma Viles.

Frederick bought 160 acres from James Gorden for $1200, with a promissory note for $400 at 10% interest. Frederick almost had the note paid off, when one day James Gorden's brother, Sam, came to visit Frederick. Sam told him that James was going to foreclose and take Gerstle's farm. Sam had brought money for Frederick to pay off the debt. Our family still has that farm today.

Nancy and Frederick Gerstle and son Luther

Lexie's father was the oldest Gerstle son, Jim (1873-1959). He was well known for curing fistula in horses. He would ask the horse owner to bring him a single blade ax. Jim would take the horse into the woods, where he would work some magic. We've never known what the secret was, but for many years Marilyn's father found broken axes in the woods near the old home place.

Lexie's mother, Cordie Eagon Gerstle (1873-1955), was good when there was sickness in the community. Lexie hated it when neighbors would come to get her mother in the middle of the night because a baby was to be born.

The Gerstle families are buried at Schofield Cemetery near Halfway. *Submitted by Marilyn Dunseth*

John William Webb and J. Elizabeth Gillihan Webb

GILLIHAN/WEBB – Thomas Gillihan (1783-1840), his wife Lucinda Brown (circa 1785-1840) and their seven children: Frances (circa 1811-1840) who had married Isaac Routh in 1831; Elizabeth (1813-1882) married William Webb; William T. (1815-1849) married Nancy Asbell; Gideon Bedford (1823-1902) married Mary Jane Hensleet, then B.J. Parriott; Martin (1824-1906) married Sarah Howell; Thomas Summers (1827-1901) married Jane Atkin; and Hiram (1830-1853) came to Greene, later Polk County, MO in 1833 from Greene County, IL. They had lived in Greene County, IL possibly five years and before that in Jackson County, TN. In the 1838 Polk County land records, Thomas Gillihan and William Webb secured land in the Township 33. Other related families who came to Polk County with the Gillihans are the Wrights, Smiths, Blairs, Rouths, and Browns. Thomas served on the first Circuit Court, Sept. 7, 1835. He was a widower when he died in 1840. The minor children were placed in guardianship with William Webb, Isaac Routh and Alexander Blair.

William Webb (1813-1882) and Elizabeth Gillihan (1813-1883) were married in Polk County, June 30, 1836. At the time of her marriage, Elizabeth already had a son, Thomas Jefferson Gillihan (1832-1909), married Susan Routh. Of the six boys of William and Elizabeth, only three lived to maturity. Two boys, William and John died in 1861 and shortly there after the Webbs moved to Saline County, and then to Bates County, MO where they spent the rest of their lives. Their children are Eleanor (1838-1871), married John Davidson; Malinda (1838-1879), married Tyre Asbell; Margaret (1840-?), married Charles Brockman; John (1842-1853); Mary (1842-?), married Mr. Pickett; Daniel (1843-1861); William (1845-1861); Richard (1847-1897), married Amanda Fortner; Grace (1849-?), married John Greer; Hiram (1852-?), married Emma Beck; Nancy (1855-?), married Mr. Greer, then Greenbery Grayer; Franklin Pierce (1854-1930), married Idellia Freeze, daughter of John Wilkerson (1820-1881) and Ann Bethia Mills (1819-1873) Freeze of Dade County, MO. Franklin and Idellia had four children: Edward (1878-circa 1900); William Elmer (1880-1957), married Willia Johns (1890-1966) of Webster County, MO, the daughter of Alexander (1864-1947) and Lou Vada Cave (1866-1941) Johns; Bertha (1882-circa 1969), married Earnest Everet Lowery; and Dellie (1884-1885). Idellia died in childbirth in 1884. Both Thomas Gillihan and William Webb were farmers. *Submitted by Glennis Webb Horn*

GILMORE – There have been eight generations of Gilmores in Polk County since 1837. Wilson and Martha (Cates) Gilmore came to Missouri in 1837 from Tennessee. They were among the first settlers around the Brighton area. Wilson was born in 1812 in Tennessee and died in 1890 in Polk County; Martha was born in 1810 in North Carolina and died in 1893 in Polk County. Together they had five children: Amanda M. Brock/Doke; William Barton; Rueben C., a Baptist preacher; James Canon, who died at the age of 15; and Mary Adeline Jones. Wilson and Martha are both buried at Slagle.

William Barton Gilmore was born in 1838. He married Rachel Ellen Bradford. They had only one child, William Asbury. William Barton

Four generations, November 1999. Left to right: Billie Paul, Loyd M., Paul Dwain holding Shelby Paul Gilmore

was killed at Bob Town by bushwhackers (Civil War) in 1864. He is buried at Brighton in a double grave with his brother-in-law Edmond Bradford.

William Asbury Gilmore was born 1862 at the home of his grandfather Wilson Gilmore. He married Emma Carmilia Epperson in 1884. He was also known as "Brother Billy" because he was a Baptist preacher. They had six children: Lola Mae Scroggins, Oma Catherine (never married), William Raif, Paul Pierson, Homer Lee and Opal who died at age 6. William Asbury died in 1941 in Polk County and Emma died in 1954; both buried at Slagle.

Paul Pierson Gilmore was born in 1896. He married Bama Pearl Morgan. They had only one child, Loyd M. Gilmore. They lived in the Halfway/Pleasant Hope area. Paul Pierson died in 1963 and Bama Pearl died in 1973. Paul Pierson served in the army in WWI. They are both buried in Pleasant Hope Cemetery.

Loyd M. Gilmore was born in 1923 at Halfway, MO. He served in the army in WWII, stationed in the Philippines Islands. He married Iva Mae Erwin. They had four children: Billie Paul, Shirley Mae Orrell, Rex Dee and Brinda Lee Johnson. Loyd and Iva are still living near Halfway in the home where he was born.

Billie Paul Gilmore was born in 1947 near Halfway. Billie served in the army in Vietnam. He married Velma Marie Orrell. They have three children: Paul Dwain, Billy Shane and Regina Marie Fergerson.

Paul Dwain Gilmore was born 1972 and married Natalie Dawn Taylor. They have two sons, Shelby Paul and Austin Neil. Billy Shane Gilmore was born in 1976 and married Amy Lynn Maggard. They have two sons, Michael Shane and Shawn Adam. Regina Marie was born in 1979 and married James William Keith Fergerson; they have one child, David Allen Fergerson.

The Gilmores have lived in the Brighton, Slagle, Pleasant Hope and Halfway area since 1837 for 175 years. *By Velma Gilmore*

GILPIN – Thomas Erye Gilpin, the son of Marion and Mollie Gilpin, was born Nov. 25, 1881 in Windsor, IL. Minister of the Gospel D. R. Jones performed the marriage of Thomas Gilpin to Mertie Pearl Paul on Jan. 21, 1900 in Dunnegan, Polk County, MO at the home of her parents Flora Ann (Nickels) and George Paul. Mertie had attended Oakland School in Dunnegan in the 1890s along with her sister Bertha Jane and brother Charles Allen Paul.

Tom and Mertie lived at Dunnegan, MO until they moved to Clearwater, KS in 1904, then to Chase, KS and returned to Collins, MO in 1906. Later, in 1915, they moved again to Laurel, MT. Tom Gilpin was a blacksmith and practiced his trade in these towns until they moved to Snohomish, WA where here he was elected County Supervisor in 1932 and County Commissioner in 1938. In 1948 he was appointed State Superintendent of Highways for Snohomish County, WA.

He became ill in 1955 and bedridden in 1959 from high blood pressure and complications. Mertie cared for him until her death on June 3, 1966 at Snohomish, WA. Tom died Jan. 2, 1967 in Snohomish, WA.

Their five children are, as follows: Zelma Alfred Gilpin, born July 20, 1900 at Dunnegan, MO and died Jan. 12, 1950 at Bradwood, OR; Edna Lula Jewel Gilpin (Vannoy), born March 8, 1905 at Clearwater, KS and died Nov. 4, 1946 at Snohomish, WA; (twins) Winston and Marshall Gilpin born Jan. 2, 1913 at Collins, MO; Paul Robert Gilpin, born Aug. 9, 1917 at Collins, MO. *Submitted by Janet Houtman*

GLADDEN – Charles Leslie Gladden was born Sept. 16, 1860 in Scott County, IN. He died June 28, 1889 in Polk County MO in the northeast part of the county. He is buried in Lindley Creek Cemetery which was near his home. His parents were John Harbor Gladden and Caroline Bell, who are also buried at Lindley Creek Cemetery. John and Caroline were the parents of 10 children: Mary Jane; Alexander Jackson "Elic;" Elijah Barnet "Barney;" John Riley; William H. "Bill;" Sarah Bell; Eugene A. "Jim;" Charles Leslie; Anna N. and Daniel Voorhees "Dan." Barney arrived in the county before other members of the family. The descendants of many of these siblings still reside in the area surrounding Polk County. The Gladden family had resided in Scott County, IN for many years along with their Clendennin, Kimberlin and Whitlatch ancestors. They had arrived there about 1805 according to land records and family letters saved by the earlier generations. They lived near where the Pigeon Roost Massacre took place in 1812.

Charles Leslie Gladden   *Mary Breshears Gladden*

Leslie married Mary Lucinda Breshears on Jan. 16, 1885. She was the daughter of Jesse Carroll Breshears and Rhoda Catherine Jump. Leslie and Mary were the parents of Florence Elnora "Nora" and Phelura Ann "Lura." They lived on the farm until 1888 when they moved to Springfield where he worked for the railroad for a short time and became ill. The family moved back to the farm and Leslie died there.

Mary was married to George W. Holt after the death of Leslie. They had seven children with all but one child dying at a very young age. Their daughter Zella Katherine married Herman Thornton and lived the rest of her life in Idaho. Mary died in 1907 and is buried by Leslie and five of her six children who died young.

Nora married William K. McGee and Lura married Leo Johnson. with both having many descendants in the Polk County area. *Submitted by Jeannie Crawford Cook, a great-great-granddaughter*

GLADDEN – John Harbor Gladden was born Oct. 13, 1821 in Green County, PA, the son of Elijah and Sarah (Whitlatch) Gladden. Sarah was the daughter of Barnet and Elizabeth (Kimberling) Whitlatch.

April 1831, Elijah, Sarah and their five children (their third child was born and died in 1823), along with Sarah's parents, three brothers and two boatmen left Green County, PA and came to Scott County, IN on the boat *Monogahea*, landing at Lee's Landing near Madison, IN. In Scott County, IN, their five youngest children were born.

Elijah died on Sept. 5, 1850 and is buried at Old Kimberling graveyard in Scott County, IN. Sarah died on Sept. 23, 1879 and is buried by Elijah.

On March 17, 1842, John Harbor married Caroline Bell, the daughter of James and Elinor (Crosser) Bell. Elinor died when Caroline was born on Feb. 5, 1824. James remarried, but died shortly after. Caroline was raised by a stepmother.

John Harbor and Caroline's children are Mary Jane, married William Vire; Alexander J., married Emily Wilson; Elijah Barnet first married Anne Clopton, and second marriage was to Nancy Stone; John Riley, married Mahala Manes; William H., married Elizabeth Wells; Sarah Bell, married Josiah Crawford; Eugene A.; Charles Leslie, married Mary Breshears; Ann, married Ellis Sawyer; and Daniel V., married Fanny Ruthford.

Elijah Barnet was born Aug. 19, 1846 in Scott County, IN and married Sarah Anne (Clopton) Chapion on Oct. 6, 1864. On Feb. 8, 1865 he enrolled in the Union Army at Lexington, IN. He was a private in Company H, 144 Regiment of the Indiana Infantry. He was five feet 10 inches tall, fair complexion, blue eyes, light brown hair and was a farmer. He was honorably discharged at Stevenson Station, VA on Aug. 5, 1865.

Elijah Barnet, Sarah Anne and daughter Ida Bell left Scott County, IN for Missouri with his parents, brothers and sisters in 1868. Oldest daughter Sarah Ann was born and died in 1865, Ida Bell was born Jan. 30, 1866.

The men worked on the Frisco Railroad from Rolla to Springfield, which brought them through Pulaski County, MO where Arizonia Ellen was born on Dec. 11, 1869.

John Harbor and Caroline moved to Polk County, MO. John Harbor died on Jan. 31, 1894 and is buried at Lindley Creek Cemetery in Polk County. Caroline died on June 6, 1909 and is buried by John Harbor.

Sarah Anne and Mr. Chapion had no children. In November 1873, Sarah Anne died near Nevada, Vernon County, MO. On Oct. 19, 1874, Elijah Barnet married Nancy Stone,

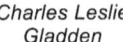

Back row-Arizona (Gladden) Crawford, Edwin Spear and Wanda Bell Spear. Front row-James R. Crawford I, Richard Ward and Robert L. Crawford.

daughter of James R. and Mary (Holt) Stone at Jasper County, MO. Their children: Luna Roxena, married Samuel Griffith; Cora Ann, married Henry Hobbs; Lee Morgan; Harbor Russell, married Dillia Sallie; William Perry, married Alma Wallace; Charlie Edgar, married Josie Baker; Addie Jane, married Jacob S. Sallie; and Ollie Mae, married James Morgan.

Elijah Barnet and Nancy moved to Polk County, Dallas County and Ozark County. Nancy died on March 27, 1922 in Longrun, Ozark County, MO. She is buried at Tree Vine Cemetery near Longrun.

Elijah Barnet moved back to Louisburg, Dallas County, MO between 1924 and 1928 and made his home east of Lindley Creek church. He died on June 4, 1934 and is buried at Lindley Creek Cemetery.

Elijah Barnet and Sarah Anne's daughter Ida Bell married Mark Seaboldt; Arizonia Ellen first married Marion Harris and then married Robert Lanzo Crawford. Robert Lanzo and Arizonia are the great-grandparents of James R. Crawford II. *Submitted by James R. Crawford II*

Florence Elnora "Nora" and Phelura Ann "Lura" Gladden

GLADDEN – Sandy's maternal grandmother, Florence Elnora Gladden, was born in Polk County, MO in the year of 1886. She would be called "Nora." Nora and her sister, Phelura Ann, or "Lura," were the only children born to Charles Leslie and Mary Lucinda Breshears Gladden, who were married in Dallas County, MO in 1885. Leslie was born in 1860 and died in Polk County in 1889. Nora was only 3 years old at the time of her father's death and Lura was not yet 2. Leslie is buried in the Lindley Creek Cemetery.

Mary Lucinda Breshears was born in Polk County, MO in 1866. She would marry again in 1896 to George Washington Holt. They would have seven children, but only one, Zelma, would live past childhood. Mary died in 1907 in Polk County and is buried in Lindley Creek Cemetery.

Mary Lucinda Breshears was the daughter of Jesse Carroll Breshears, who was born in Tennessee in 1830 and died in Polk County in 1902. He would marry Rhoda Catherine Jump in Polk County in 1855. Rhoda Catherine was born in 1836 in St. Louis County, MO and died in Polk County in 1903. Jesse Carroll and Rhoda Catherine would have 11 children. Besides Mary Lucinda, their children were James Knox Polk, John Henry, Naomi Elizabeth, Joseph Carroll, Saphrona Angeline, George Washington, Jesse Simon, Matoke Erickson, Missouri Bell and Lewis Hardin Breshears. Jesse Carroll and Rhoda are buried in Lindley Creek Cemetery.

Jesse Carroll Breshears' parents were John Quincy and Naomi Ann Hogg Breshears. John Quincy was born in South Carolina in 1795 and died in Polk County in 1869. Naomi was born in Kentucky in 1804 and died in Polk County in 1898. They would have 15 children: Mary Albany, Henry Harold, Reuben Dobbin, William Arthur, Sarah P., Jesse Carroll, Susan J., Nancy G., John Wesley, Margaret, Joseph W., Ozais Martin, James K. P., Thomas Henderson Benton and Andrew Jackson. The last five were born in Polk County.

Rhoda Catherine Jump, wife of Jesse Carroll Breshears and mother of Mary Lucinda Breshears, was the daughter of James and Eulila Palmer Jump. James Jump was born in Kentucky in 1804 and died in Polk County in 1880. Eulila Palmer Jump was born in St. Louis County, MO in 1801 and died in Polk County in 1878. They were married in 1830 and would have six children who would live in Polk County: Peter, William Kincaid, Lucinda, Rhoda Catherine, Joseph Henry, and James Knox Polk Jump. Joseph and James were born in Polk County. James and Eulila are buried in Lindley Creek Cemetery.

These are Sandy's ancestors who lived in Polk County. Sandy's grandmother, Nora, was the only one of them that she had the privilege to know personally. Nora did not have an easy life, losing her father at such a young age. As a young person she lived for some time with her Uncle Dan Gladden who lived in Polk County. She also stayed with others and worked for them. She would marry in 1913 in Dallas County to William Kelly McGee and have three children, Minnie Willa, William Kelly and Carl Lawrence McGee. Minnie was Sandy's mother. Nora would lose her husband in 1942 and would live the rest of her life alone, except for the time her children were still at home. She lived most of her married life in Dallas County and after William Kelly's death moved to Springfield.

As a child, Sandy remembers spending time with her grandmother, Nora. She loved having her six grandchildren with her. Sandy remembers her often talking about her grandparents, Bell on her Gladden side of the family and her Breshears and Jumps on her mother's side of the family. Nora Gladden McGee died in 1970. *Submitted by Sandy Maness*

GLOVER - The Thomas and Dorcas Glover family settled in the eastern side of Polk County, MO during the 1830s. They settled along the creeks for good water supply. Land records show they bought land on Hominy Creek, Wilson's Creek, Schulty Creek, Pomme de Terre River and Prater Branch.

The old Glover Cemetery is one-half mile north of Gold (later named Tin Town, after a traveling salesman came through selling tin). The earliest grave there is 1864.

Thomas Glover was born in 1802 in Tennessee. He married Dorcas in 1822. Dorcas was born in 1805 in Virginia. Her father was born in England, coming to America. Her mother was born in Virginia.

Dorcas Glover came to Polk County as a true pioneer woman.

Three of their children were Margaret C. Glover, married Henry Yandell, later a Mr. Page; Newton William Glover; and Susan C. Glover, married Daniel Pain.

William Newton Glover was born in 1842 and is buried in the Glover Cemetery. He married Mary Elizabeth Prater, daughter of Jeremiah and Margaret (Miller) Prater. They had eight children: John, William, Nancy, Wes, Thomas, Mary, Albert and Greenbury. Mary died and Newton married Samantha. They had one son, Charles Glover.

William Newton Glover and children; John Henry, William Newton, Wesley B., Mary Elizabeth (Glover) Bridges and Albert "Ab" Glover.

Newton served in the Union Army during the Civil War. He moved to Halfway. He was a successful farmer, businessman and a Baptist.

William Monroe Glover was born in 1866 at Red Top. He married Mary Treacy/Tressa Mayfield in 1889 at Goodnight. He was a farmer and a blacksmith, later running the store at Tin Town. He died in 1927 and is buried at Rock Prairie.

Mamie Alice Glover was born and reared on the farm at Tin Town. She taught school at the Black Oak School. She married Grover Helton. They had eight children. Dale, Carl, twins Bobby and Barbara live in Michigan. Ruth married Bill Squibb, moving to Texas with the Woolworth Co. as a regional manager. Mary married Ralph Jones. Bill lives in California. Eleanor married Lloyd Hough from Springfield. They had six children. Gary Hough married Barbara Woodall. They have two children. Matthew Todd works with computers in St. Louis, and is married with two children. Rebecca married Tim Hathcock, a fireman. She works in Springfield. *Submitted by Rebecca Hathcock*

GOLDSBERRY - The 1850 Polk County census is the first record of Jonathan S. Goldsberry being in Polk County, MO. Jonathan S. (born Feb. 17, 1816 in North Carolina) was married to Mary Ann "Polly" Johnson (born February 1832) in Polk County on Jan. 30, 1853 by Wm. Hancock, J.P. They homesteaded a place over on Highway H known as the Providence School. Then in 1857 they purchased a place nearby, now owned by Maynard Hobbs. Nine children were born of their union including Jonathan Ignatius May Goldsberry (born May 15, 1869). Jonathan S. had a little singsong rhyme for his family's names: "Mary Amanda Main, Catherine Jane, Emily Adaline, Penny Payne, Ignatius May, Molly and Polly, and old Golie, by golly 'himself!" Two girls, Maude and Delilah, don't seem to have been included in the rhyme and may have passed away in childhood.

Back – Melvin Lewis Goldsberry. Ignatius May and Anna Roberta, Willie Hilman Goldsberry on lap. Opal P. Goldsberry – Skeele on lap. Charles J. Goldsberry – standing

Jonathan Ignatius May was the first Polk County Surveyor, naming several small towns in the county, including Halfway. The story goes that he walked all the way from Bolivar to Buffalo, counting his steps as he went, then turned around and walked back halfway and staked out a township, calling it Halfway. He also named what is now known as Pleasant Hope, "Pinhook" and what is now known as March, he named "Dog Town." Tin Town retains the name that he gave it.

Jonathan I. M. Goldsberry married Anna Roberta Albert on May 26, 1889. The minister who married them, Tifton Peterson, told them there was no need for them to get down off the horses they arrived on, so they were married on horseback. Their union produced 11 children including the firstborn son, Melvin Lewis Goldsberry (born March 23, 1890). Melvin Lewis Goldsberry worked on a dairy farm owned by A. J. Anderson in Kiowa,

201

KS where he fell in love with Anderson's only child, Cyrena Blanche Anderson (born March 31, 1898) and enticed her to run off and elope with him on Sept. 8, 1913, much to A.J.'s displeasure. Not daring to return to the Anderson farm, Melvin and Blanche went to Oklahoma. There Melvin worked for Tom Stutter, a rancher, who had no heirs and who promised Melvin that if he would stay with him until his death, Melvin would inherit all the Stutter estate. However, in 1917 Jonathan I. M. and Anna Roberta visited their son at the Stutter Ranch and persuaded Melvin and Blanche to return to Polk County with them, Blanche and Opal (Melvin's sister) walking behind the covered wagon all the way to Polk County.

Melvin hunted squirrels for breakfast and would soak them in salt water overnight. The meat kept disappearing, so one night Melvin wrapped the squirrel in paper and put it under his pillow, then laid awake all night to see what would happen. In the middle of the night a big bobcat jumped in the window, rolled Melvin's head aside and took the meat. Melvin didn't argue, he just let him go!

Melvin and Blanche had 10 children. The surviving three, Phil and David Goldsberry and Freda Day, currently live in Bolivar. *Submitted by Bonnie Denton*

Edwin McMasters Goodman (1851-1916)

GOODMAN – Edwin McMasters Goodman was born Sept. 12, 1851 in Polk County, MO, the 12th child of Sampson and Sarah (Lingar) Goodman. The family migrated from Tennessee during the 1840s, settling on land Sampson purchased in Jackson Township, Polk County. Edwin was reared and educated in the county and on Sept. 19, 1869, he married America Chumbley, granddaughter of Robert Chumbley.

America was born Jan. 4, 1851 in Claiborne County, TN, the last of eight children born to John Chumbley and Malinda Sharp. Her father died shortly before her birth, and before her 10th birthday, her mother married Joseph Souther. By 1860, Joseph, Malinda, her three youngest children by her first marriage, and two of his sons by a previous marriage, were living in Benton County, AR. It is not known exactly when, how, or with whom America came to Polk County. It is believed that sometime after the Battle of Pea Ridge, the Souther family fled to Missouri, spending time in Orleans in Polk County and Springfield, Greene County between 1863-1865. America's mother died during the Civil War, and her step-father remarried in 1865, for the third time. She, her brother Samuel and sister Margaret may have remained in Polk County, staying with or near other Chumbley relatives.

Edwin and America remained on his father's farm for at least the first year of their marriage. Sometime in the early 1870s they settled on a farm near Verona in Lawrence County. Although he was primarily a farmer, Edwin held a number of jobs during his lifetime, most likely out of necessity. The family moved to Aurora when the mines opened and he became involved in mining. By 1880, they were living in Spring River Township and Edwin was listed as a farmer on the federal census for that year. In 1900 the family was living in Mt. Vernon and he was working as a teamster. On Nov. 8, 1904, Edwin was elected Lawrence County sheriff, an office he held for the next four years. He had previously served as a constable in both Aurora and Mt. Vernon. Prior to his death, Edwin was an ice manufacturer.

He died July 1, 1916 in Mt. Vernon and is buried in the IOOF Cemetery. America survived her husband by another 20 years, living first in Mt. Vernon with her son and daughter-in-law, Homer and Pearl Goodman. During the 1920s she lived in Springfield, sharing a home with her son-in-law and daughter, Joe and Emma Nickel. At the time of her death in 1936, she was living with another married daughter, Arlie Wise and family in Fayetteville, AR. America is buried beside her husband in the IOOF Cemetery in Mt. Vernon.

To this couple were born 11 children, all in the counties of Polk and Lawrence:

Cora Alice Goodman, born Aug. 20, 1871; died Dec. 12, 1927 in California; married Oliver Symphronious Goodman, Dec. 29, 1898 in Keokuk, IA. He was the son of Dr. Thomas Kelly Goodman and grandson of Sampson Goodman.

Emma Goodman, born Jan. 4, 1874; died Feb. 24, 1929, Springfield, MO; married Josephus Nickel Nov. 21, 1897 in Lawrence County.

Addie V. Goodman, born Jan. 17, 1877; died June 2, 1882.

Charles Claudie Goodman, born May 20, 1879; died July 3, 1880.

Albert Goodman, born Sept. 30, 1881; died Oct. 2, 1901.

Edith B. Goodman, born Jan. 11, 1883; died April 19, 1884.

Mabel Elodia Goodman, born Oct. 1, 1885; died April 18, 1961 in Pasadena, CA; married William Earl Scott April 19, 1905 in Lawrence County.

Arlie Clive Goodman, born July 14, 1888; died about 1967 in Springfield, MO; married William Oscar Wise, Sept. 23, 1914.

Othar Harrison Goodman, born Feb. 13, 1891; died circa 1940s.

Homer Albert Goodman, born Jan. 23, 1895 (twin); died Nov. 15, 1972 Mt. Vernon; married Pearl Beard Aug. 1, 1915 in Lawrence County.

Helmuth Earl Goodman, born Jan. 23, 1895 (twin); died Aug. 16, 1966 in Bend, OR; married three times. *Submitted by Sharon Lee Ford*

GOODMAN – John Franklin Goodman was born Sept. 11, 1831 in Tennessee, the fourth of 12 children born to Sampson and Sarah (Lingar) Goodman. The family moved to Polk County, MO during the early 1840s, settling on a farm in Jackson Township while John was still a fairly young boy. He was raised as a farmer and later owned a farm of his own. Although he has been said to have had a sense of humor, John must have had a very serious or sensible side. He was educated and religious and served as part-time Baptist preacher during his lifetime, although it is not known if he was ever ordained.

John Franklin Goodman (1831-1910)

In September 1850, at the age of about 19, John married Orleana (Dobbs) Hurst, a widow eight to 10 years his senior. Orleana was born in Tennessee, but came to Polk County with her parents in the late 1830s where she met and later married Absolom Hurst on Oct. 10, 1839 and bore him five sons. Absolom Hurst died in 1848 while serving during the Mexican War.

John and Orleana were married for 40 years and had the following children:

Harvey Russell Goodman, born Dec. 23, 1851; died April 30, 1889; buried in Turkey Creek Cemetery; married Isadora Josephine Boone, Dec. 7, 1871 in Greene County.

Sarah E. Goodman, born May 11, 1852; died Oct. 28, 1879; buried in Turkey Creek Cemetery; married William Christian, Jan. 13, 1875 in Greene County.

Elizabeth V. Goodman, born March 27, 1855; died Aug. 13, 1922; buried in Turkey Creek Cemetery; married George B. Slatten, Jan. 28, 1872 in Greene County.

Sampson D. Goodman, born 1857; died as a small child.

Barbra Angeline Goodman, born March 17, 1860; died April 21, 1938; buried in Pleasant Ridge Cemetery, Polk County; married James M. Owen, Dec. 1, 1879, in Polk County.

Salena A. Goodman, born Oct. 1, 1861; died July 1, 1865; buried in Turkey Creek Cemetery.

George Washington Goodman, born 1863; married twice, first to Laura Lowry May 15, 1885, Polk County.

Everette (Eva) Rochester Goodman, born Sept. 2, 1872; died March 19, 1965; married Alvin B. Hagerman, 1895.

Sarah Etta Goodman, born Sept. 20, 1874; married Albert Albien Eugene (Al) Chumbley, Jan. 23, 1896.

Mary Catherine Goodman, born Aug. 30, 1876; died April 18, 1955; married Denver Smith Hamilton, Aug. 10, 1908.

John Franklin Goodman, born Jan. 30, 1879; died Dec. 27, 1894.

Nellie May Goodman, born May 26, 1882; died Dec. 28, 1963; married Earl Downing Wilkinson, April 26, 1903.

Charles L. Goodman, born Aug. 23, 1884; married first, May Bristow, second, Frances _____.

Orleana died Aug. 8, 1890 and is buried in Turkey Creek Cemetery in Polk County. John survived her by 20 years, marrying twice more. He married Mary Neff on Feb. 4, 1892 and to them were born twin boys, Arliss and Arvil. Mary died either at the time of their birth or shortly thereafter. Arvil went to live with the widow of his uncle Harvey Russell Goodman, however he did not survive to adulthood. Arliss was raised by his half-sister Barbra Angeline Goodman and her husband, James M. Owen. John Franklin Goodman married a third time to Mary E. Dyer and they had one child, a daughter, Martha Golden Goodman.

John Franklin Goodman died Dec. 12, 1910 in Walnut Grove, Greene County, MO and is buried in Turkey Creek Cemetery in Polk County.

GOODMAN – Sampson Goodman was born Oct. 6, 1806, probably in Tennessee, as indicated on various census records. On Sept. 28, 1827, he married, in Tennessee, Sarah Lingar, daughter of John Lingar. She was born about Oct. 2, 1809 (date of birth calculated from her age on her headstone, 60 years, 9 months, 7 days) in Tennessee. There are various spellings of her surname, but in early records, it is spelled as Lingar. It became Lyngar in Missouri.

Sampson was a man of modest means, a farmer and stock raiser by trade. Though he could not read or write, it has been said that he had more than ordinary intelligence, with a talent for sound judgment. Both he and Sarah were members of the Baptist Church.

Sarah had inherited land from her father in Claiborne County, TN, but in 1842 she and Sampson sold the land to her brother James Harvey Lyngar. It may have been around this time that they decided to move to Polk County, MO

Sampson Goodman (1806-1888)

along with Chumbley and Slatten families from Claiborne County, TN, with whom the Goodmans and Lyngars had intermarried. It is not known if they all traveled together, but by 1850 the families had relocated from Tennessee to Polk County. Sampson acquired land (160 acres total) in Polk County during the late 1840s and l850s, from the General Land Office of the United States. There they lived for more than 40 years. The four youngest children were born in Missouri. Sampson and Sarah appear to have escaped the ravages of the Civil War, experienced by others in their community.

Sarah died July 9, 1870 and is buried in Turkey Creek Cemetery in Polk County. Sampson survived her by 18 years, remarrying on Aug. 20, 1876 to Mrs. Rebecca (Cass) Delk, who was born April 5, 1829 in Missouri. Rebecca died Nov. 20, 1887 in Missouri, and is buried in the Hurst-Linville Cemetery in Walnut Grove, Greene County, MO. Sampson died May 15, 1888 and is buried in Turkey Creek Cemetery, beside Sarah.

To this couple, 12 children were born:

Francis M. Goodman, born about 1827 in Tennessee; married first, Elizabeth _____, married second, Jane R. Conn, Aug. 10, 1870, Polk County, MO.

Elizabeth Goodman, born December 1828 in Tennessee; died Aug. 13, 1922, Polk County, MO; married George H. Slatten June 9, 1858, Polk County, MO.

Nathaniel "Nate" Goodman, born and died between 1830-1840.

John Franklin Goodman, born Sept. 11, 1831, Wilson County, TN; died Dec. 12, 1910, Polk County, MO; buried in Turkey Creek Cemetery; married first, Mrs. Orleana (Dobbs) Hurst, Dec. 23, 1852, Polk County, second, Mary Neff, Feb. 4, 1892 and third, Mary Augusta Dyer March 19, 1895, Lawrence County, MO.

James E. Goodman, born about 1832, Tennessee.

Isaac I. Goodman, born 1837, Tennessee.

William R. Goodman, born 1839, Tennessee.

Newton Jasper "Newt" Goodman, born Dec. 7, 1841, Tennessee; died Feb. 14, 1921, Benton County, OR; married Rhoda Ann Ward June 27, 1861, Polk County, MO. She was born June 16, 1840, Pope County, IL.

Mary Eliza Goodman, born April 12, 1844, Polk County, MO; died Dec. 14, 1911, Republic, Greene County, MO; married Samuel Chandler Chumbley Feb. 1, 1863, Walnut Grove, Greene County, MO. He was born March 25, 1843, Claiborne County, TN.

Harvey C. Goodman, born Feb. 10, 1847, Polk County, MO; died March 23, 1915, Lawrence County, MO; married Madeline Haskey Delk April 3, 1866. She was born Dec. 7, 1845 in Tennessee and died after 1910.

Thomas Kelly Goodman, born March 10, 1849, Polk County, MO; died Dec. 28, 1899 in Arkansas; married Mary Elizabeth Greenhaw May 10, 1871 in Missouri. He was a doctor in both Newton and Izard Counties in Arkansas.

Edwin McMasters Goodman, born Sept. 12, 1851 or 1852, Polk County, MO; died July 1, 1916, Lawrence County, MO; married America Chumbley Sept. 19, 1869, Polk County, MO. She was born Jan. 4, 1851, Claiborne County, TN.

GORDEN - Hugh Gorden was born circa 1735 in Scotland, died Sept. 27, 1834 in Washington County, KY. He was called "Hugh the Patriot" or "Hugh the Immigrant." He settled in Fauquier County, VA and married Sarah Owens, daughter of Nathaniel Owens, in King George County, VA circa 1787. They had 11 children. The Hugh Gorden Bible is in Virginia State Library and Archives.

Elijah Gorden, son of Hugh and Sarah Gorden, was born Aug. 29, 1788 in Fauquier County, VA and died Feb. 20, 1862 and is buried in the Gorden Cemetery.

He married Statia Anne Gootee Oct. 18, 1811, daughter of Joseph Gootee, born May 5, 1795 in Maryland and died Sept. 4, 1865.

He came to Polk County in the fall of 1838/39 from Washington County, KY and settled in Benton Township. His descendants still own property where he settled. He was a farmer.

Children: John T., born May 2, 1813, died Aug. 31, 1863 (bushwhacked); Samuel Owen; Benjamin Franklin, born Jan 3, 1817; James Whalan, born Oct. 12, 1817; Sarah Ann, born Dec. 9, 1821; Elijah Gootee, born June 17, 1824; died Aug. 31, 1863 (bushwhacked); Mary Eleanor (Ellen), born Oct. 17, 1826; Henry Jefferson, born April 27, 1828; William Whitman, born Feb. 22, 1829; Rhoda J., born May 14, 1832; Elizabeth Francis, born March 27, 1835.

Bill Dad, John, Samuel O., Joe, and Dave. Row 2 – Ben, Mollie, Schuyler and Tom

Samuel Owen Gorden, son of Elijah and Statia Anne Gootee Gorden, was born Feb. 11, 1815 in Washington County, KY, died Nov. 12, 1899 after a brief but severe attack of congestion and is buried in the Gorden Cemetery. He resided in the Schofield Community during the remaining 60 years of his life. He was a citizen widely known, and highly respected for his good morals and Christian virtues by all that knew him.

He married Elizabeth Askren, daughter of Josiah and Mary Askren, born March 1, 1817 in Kentucky and died Oct. 17, 1894 in Polk County, MO after having a paralytic stroke. They married Oct. 20, 1836 in Washington County, KY.

Children: John Henry, born Sept. 15, 1837; Joseph Hardin, born Aug. 20, 1839 in Missouri; William A., born Jan. 26, 1842; David Whitman, born Oct. 15, 1847; Dennis Schuyler, born Oct. 21, 1850; Benjamin Franklin; Thomas Jefferson, born Dec. 3, 1855; Mary Ann (Mollie), born Dec. 1, 1844; James, listed in 1850 census and probably died young.

Benjamin Gorden, son of Samuel and Elizabeth Gorden, was born May 9, 1853 in Polk County, MO and died March 13, 1933 and is buried in the Schofield Cemetery. He was a farmer and a deacon at the Schofield Baptist Church. He served one term as sheriff of Polk County in 1890-1892.

He married Martha Willa Morris, daughter of William and Saletha Martha Jenkins Morris, born Aug. 14, 1861 and died March 26, 1941 in Polk County, MO. They married Nov. 13, 1877.

A large crowd of friends and relatives helped them celebrate their Golden Wedding Anniversary in November 1927. They lived most of their life, except for a time in Oklahoma, two years in California, and two years in Bolivar, on their farm in Benton Township.

Martha Willa was known as "Aunt Matt" to her friends. She was an invalid for the last 12 years of her life. The last eight years were in the home of her daughter, Mrs. Sam Jester. Children: Owen, Wilby, Oby and Nora.

Wilby Oren Gorden, son of Benjamin and Martha Willa Gorden, was born April 17, 1882, died Dec. 19, 1964 in Greene County, MO and is buried in Schofield Cemetery. He was a farmer. Wilby had an accident involving a horse as a young man and one of his legs was shorter than the other one. He married Rosa Matilda Lejeune, daughter of Louis and Mary Lejeune, born Sept. 2, 1889 and died June 3, 1970 in Greene County, MO. They married Nov. 6, 1910 in Polk County, MO. Their entire lives were spent in the Schofield Community except a few years spent in New Mexico and California.

Wilby and Rosa Lejeune Gorden

They had two children, Esther Geneice, who married Wade Voris and Louis Benjamin Gorden, who married Faye Jones and Vera Quick Farmer. Both of their children married and lived on a farm within a mile of them. They celebrated their Golden Wedding Anniversary in November 1960 at the home of their son, Louis. They had four grandsons: Larry, Jerry, Dean Voris and Ben Gorden. *Submitted by Jerry Voris*

GORDENS – The Gordens came to Polk County, MO in 1839. They came from Washington County, KY via Virginia and the Cumberland Gap. The Gordens, like many immigrants, fled Scotland after backing the wrong clan. The Gordens settled up and down Hominy Creek, east of Halfway. Hugh Gorden was born in 1735 in Scotland. He died in 1834 in Washington County, KY. He settled in Fauquier County, VA and married Sarah Owens, daughter of Nathaniel Owens, in King George County, VA in 1787. They had 11 children. The Hugh Gorden Bible is in Virginia State Library and Archives. Hugh Gorden's son Elijah J. Gorden settled southeast of Halfway on land presently owned by Louis B. Gorden, Ben R. Gorden and

Seated left to right – Oby, Martha Willa and Benjamin. Standing left to right – Wilby O., Nora Gorden Jester and William Owen Gorden

Brian R. Gorden. Brian R. Gorden represents the seventh generation to live and farm the land patented and homesteaded in 1839.

The first two generations are buried in the family cemetery located on the highest part of the farm. The later generations are buried in the Schofield Cemetery southeast of Halfway.

Elijah J. Gorden and Statia Ann Gootee had 10 children who lived in and around Polk County. One of their children, Samuel O., married Elizabeth Askrens, daughter of Josiah and Mary Askren. They raised stud horses and lived where W. Dean Voris presently lives. This union produced six sons and one daughter. Benjamin F. Gorden, son of Samuel and Elizabeth Gorden, lived on the family farm near Halfway. He was a farmer and a deacon at the Schofield Baptist Church. Benjamin F. Gorden was the sheriff of Polk County from 1890 to 1892. He was the sheriff who chained the train to the tracks following a murder and ended the circus coming to Bolivar for many years. He married Martha Willa Morris, daughter of William and Saletha Jenkins Morris. A large crowd of friends and relatives helped them celebrate their Golden Wedding Anniversary in November 1927. Martha Willa was known as "Aunt Matt" to her friends. She was an invalid for the last 12 years of her life spending the last eight in the home of her daughter Mrs. Sam Jester. Ben and "Matt" had four children: Owen, Wilby, Oby and Nora.

Wilby O. Gorden lived on the family farm from 1882 to 1964. Wilby lived and farmed around Halfway; except for a few years spent in California. He homesteaded a quarter-section in New Mexico in 1900, but sold the homestead and moved back to Polk County. Wilby married Rosa M. LeJeune, daughter of Louis and Mary LeJeune in 1910. To this union were born two children, Esther Geneice (Gorden) Voris and Louis B. Gorden. Esther Geneice married Wade Voris and had three sons: Larry, Jerry and Dean.

Louis married Faye Jones in 1940. They had one son, Bennie Ray. Following 37 months and one day in the United States Army Air Corps, Louis returned to the family farm in 1946. Louis, his wife, Faye and son Ben operated a dairy operation on the farm until 1965. Louis worked several years as a loan officer at Polk County Bank. He retired in 1982. Following Faye's death from cancer, Louis married Vera (Quick) Farmer and currently lives in Bolivar.

Ben, except for time spent at the University of Missouri (Columbia), has lived on the family farm all of his life. Ben taught science for 25 years at Tunas in Dallas County and Halfway R-3 Schools in Polk County. Ben married Karen Pritchard in 1968. Their children, Christa Gorden Owens and Brian Gorden, and grandchildren, Katie and Kassidy Owens, still enjoy walks up and down Hominy Creek, tilling the 100-year-old garden spot, skipping rocks in the spring branch, climbing the big trees and enjoying the rural atmosphere provided by the family farm.

A commercial cow-calf beef operation is presently maintained on the farm by Ben and Brian. The farm established in 1839 by Elijah and maintained by Samuel, Benjamin, Wilby, Louis, Ben and Brian still remains part of the history of Polk County, MO in 2002. *Submitted by Ben Gorden*

GORMAN - Eric and Sonya Gorman moved to Polk County in 1997. Eric was born in Sedalia, MO and lived in various places growing up (Missouri, Kansas, Hawaii and Colorado). Sonya was born in Ft. Huachuca, AZ, then moved to Utah and Nevada briefly and then back to her mom's hometown area of Grand Junction, CO. She lived there from the age of 3. Eric and Sonya met in Colorado in 1990. Eric then moved to Missouri with his family to the Hermitage area in 1991. After graduating college, Sonya moved out to Missouri to be with him in 1993. On July 16, 1994, they were married in Palisade, CO.

They moved to Bolivar in 1997 and have lived in the same home since. The size of the town and its location and the friendly people drew them to this area. They now have dreams of moving to the Aldrich area soon to be out in the country and near the lake so they can enjoy that lifestyle with their children.

In 1996, their son Cody was born at Citizens Memorial Hospital. In 1999, their daughter Kaitlynn was born also at Citizens Memorial Hospital. Cody is now in first grade at Fair Play Elementary. Kaitlynn is a busy, almost preschooler staying at home with mom.

Eric is a deputy for the Polk County Sheriff's Office and has been since February 2001. Before that he worked for a short while at the Bolivar Police Department. Previously, he had worked with a tree service in the Bolivar area.

Sonya has a degree in Early Childhood Education and worked for a couple of years at a childcare center in Buffalo. When they moved to Bolivar, she was a childcare provider for infants and toddlers in her home until Kaitlynn was born in 1999. She currently works at home as a medical transcriptionist.

Eric, Sonya and Cody and Kaitlyn, September 2002

Eric's parents are Charles and Melanie (Rhoades) Gorman. Sonya's parents are James and Nancy (Inskeep) Pollard. Her stepdad is Donald Samson of Colorado. Nancy and Donald are both now deceased (Nancy in 1994 and Donald in 2002). *Submitted by Sonya Gorman*

GOTHARD-HARMON - George Sigel Gothard, the third child of George Washington and Barbara Ellen Hughes Gothard, was born July 28, 1861 in Cedar County, MO near the Needmore community. His family had recently returned from Dallas County, TX.

George W. Gothard served in the Union Army from 1862-1865 near Rolla, MO. His family later settled in the Dallas and Webster County, MO area where George Sigel grew to adulthood.

On July 3, 1892 George S. and Arminta Jane Harmon were married and began their 51 years together.

Arminta "Mint" was born in Dallas County, MO on Oct.

George S. Gothard and Arminta (Harmon) Gothard, July 1942 – 50th Anniversary

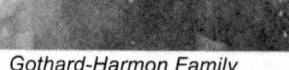

Gothard-Harmon Family

18, 1877, the daughter of David and Jennie E. Dawson Harmon. The Harmons were from Davidson County, NC, where David fought for the southern cause in the Civil War. In the aftermath of the war, David and Jane moved their family to Missouri.

George attended Mt. Olive Baptist Church and Mint went to the Buttermilk Chapel, located west of Mt. Olive and up the hill from her home.

Shortly after their marriage, they settled near Cane Hill in Cedar County, where their first five children were born. In the late 1890s they moved to the Needmore community where they spent the rest of their lives, except for a year in California and two years in Polk County, MO. They bought their farm in 1910 and it stayed in the family until the 1970s. Their house burned in 1925 and they rebuilt.

George made his living as a farmer and worked as a hired hand in the community. He worked hard to provide for his family. In 1934 he suffered a stroke which left him crippled the rest of his life.

Arminta was a small woman with red, curly hair that she wore in a bun. Her youngest daughter, Cuba, recalled many nights when the children would gather around the fireplace and Mint would tell stories of her parents' lives in the Old South. In these stories, her own past would come to life for her children.

They were miles from a doctor so Mint used home remedies to care for her babies. All nine children lived into their 70s and 80s.

She had a large garden and was a hard worker.

Mint had a recurring dream of the cemetery where they would be buried, although she'd never seen it in real life. While driving past Shady Grove Cemetery during WWII, she recognized this as the cemetery in her dreams.

On March 14, 1944, George died after a lingering illness. His funeral was held at Shady Grove.

After living south of Fair Play for two years during WWII, Mint moved back to the "old homeplace" along with her son Frank and his wife Helen.

On March 21, 1951, after a long bout with cancer, Arminta died at her home surrounded by her children. After preparing Arminta for burial, they returned her to the home. As was the custom, neighbors and family sat through the night out of respect for the deceased. As they left her home, her grandsons carried her, followed by her family, through a pathway of flowers that her granddaughters held. Her funeral was held in Needmore Church and she is buried beside her husband in Shady Grove Cemetery in Polk County.

Their children: Ressie Pearl, born April 19, 1894, died April 17, 1973; Lorah Delphia, born Feb. 10, 1896, died Oct. 11, 1968; Gertie Loris, born Dec. 28, 1897, died Feb. 20, 1978; Floy

Georgie, born Oct. 4, 1900, died Nov. 30, 1985; Bessie Gladys, born Jan. 1, 1903, died Sept. 10, 1983; Ruby Marie Ellen, born Feb. 11, 1905, died May 9, 2000; Cuba Dee, born July 12, 1908, died Dec. 7, 1993; Ralph Hiram, born Nov. 13, 1912, lives in Stockton, MO; Frank David, born Dec. 19, 1916, died Sept. 23, 2002. *Submitted by Doug Lane*

GRANT – The Grants and their cousins with deep roots in Polk County compiled a brief summary of their genealogy in the early 1960s. The editor of "Our Family History" noted "the name seems rather ancient."

At the time, their oldest known ancestor was John Grant of Rutherford County, NC born 1794/5. His family moved on to the Chattanooga, TN area. His two sons that moved to Polk County around 1860 were James Morris and Alfred Webster Grant. Other family researchers on the east coast believe John Grant's parents were Alexander and Susannah (Morris) Grant. Alexander appears once in Revolutionary War records. It is believed Alexander's grandparents were William and Mary Grant of Virginia. There is no written record of their origins, but some believe they came from Scotland.

The very first Grant in documented records was a sheriff in Inverness, Scotland at the north end of Loch Ness in 1218. Considerable evidence suggests Grants were flourishing before the late Middle Ages, but recorded history about them is sparse.

In Scotland's old Highland times, the Grants were known as one of the half-dozen more powerful and among the most "clannish" of all clans

The Right Honorable Lord Strathspey, James Grant of Grant, 33rd Hereditary Clan Chief, in Scotland

(extended families). They heavily populated both ends of Loch Ness and a wide valley to the east they still call Strathspey, bordered by the Cairngorm mountains.

The surname Grant was derived from ancient vocabularies meaning a large tall, or in some contexts, an ugly man. There is another theory Grant was close to a word that described a particular moor in ancient Scotland. Whether (or when) the name originated with the Normans (who spoke French), Gaelic people, or Vikings is still a source of debate among 21st century researchers.

Clan Grant was first to adopt a tartan of uniform design "with red and green broad springed sett" for clansmen to wear. Their rallying cry and present motto is: STAND FAST! Sometimes the phrase is accompanied by "Craighellachie," a clan landmark. Craighellachie is a tall, limestone hill where bonfires were lit to signal Grants to assemble to defend their territories or honor, or to socialize. A symbol of the "burning hill proper" dominates the family crest with the words "Stand Fast."

The center of the universe for Grants is the town of Grantown-on-spey, planned and built by the "Good Sir James" Grant in 1775/6. Grantown enjoys a reputation as a popular tourist destination, and is one and one-half miles south of Castle Grant. The castle was the official residence of the Chiefs (head) of Grant until a damaging fire during WWII left it mostly in ruin. The castle has been restored and is under private ownership.

Interest in all things Grant led to the formation of the Clan Grant Society in the US in 1977 and a revival of Clan Grant-UK. The membership of both groups are united in their deep connections to their heritage, their ancestors and their quest to collect and preserve family history, artifacts and property through support and participation.

The advent of the Internet offers a great potential for making new family connections (and has), genealogical discoveries and new friendships on a worldwide basis via websites at www.clangrant.org and www.clangrant-us.org.

Polk County's Grants know they are not even distantly related to President U. S. Grant. But are they Scottish? The true answer, as it does for many in their family lines, remains elusive.

However, Steve Grant (of Springfield, MO) got a clue during his first exploratory visit to Scotland in 1986, when he stopped at a bed and breakfast for the night.

As the front door swung open, the innkeeper blurted out, "Are ye ah Grant?" with that distinctive Highland burr in his booming voice.

"Why, yes" replied the slightly astonished tourist, "from the Missouri Ozarks."

To which to Scotsman announced, "Well laddie, ye luke like "UM!" *Submitted by Ozarks Commissioner of Clan Grant Society US*

GRANT – Members of Grant families (and their cousins) who trace their earliest beginnings to Polk County owe their name and heritage to either James Morris Grant or Alfred Webster Grant.

The two brothers first came to Springfield, MO in 1858 during the emigration of "Scotch-Irish" to the Ozarks Highlands from eastern Tennessee and Kentucky. While James and Alfred went on to settle in the Morrisville area (Looney township) around the start of the Civil War, their other brother, Henry, stayed on in the Springfield area.

Two brothers born a century after those "original" two brothers arrived in Polk County are the only present-day Grants directly related to both family lines.

Stephen (Steve) Edward Grant and Gary Alan Grant have made their respective homes and careers in Springfield. Both were educated in Springfield Public Schools. Steve earned a degree from Evangel University in 1976. Gary has worked for City Utilities (CU) in power production and the gas department since graduating high school. Steve has been on-the-air as a broadcast journalist for KYTV (KY3-TV), and as an announcer for KTXR-FM for an almost identical number of years.

Their maternal great-grandfather William Morris "Uncle Bill" Grant; grandfather Lynn Alexander Grant and mother, Mary Lynn Grant, belong to the second, third and fourth generation descendants of James Morris Grant.

Likewise, their paternal great-grandfather Howard Wayne Grant, grandfather Everett Edward Grant and father, Joe Winn Grant, are among the second, third and fourth generation descendants of Alfred Webster Grant.

Joe Winn Grant and Mary Lynn Grant were both 1948 graduates of Morrisville High School and both were born in 1930. Like his son Gary, Joe also worked for CU and later went on to management positions with Springfield Public Schools and Mid-America Dairymen. Mary Lynn raised their two sons and remained a homemaker.

As with the Scottish clans of old, the Grants were never far from one another and their kin. Along a two-mile stretch of what is now Highway 215 (old Hwy. K), the farms and land on both sides of the roadway was, or still is, owned by Grants. The Grant Manor retirement apartments sit on land donated by Everett Grant. His great joy was to buy a worn-out or overgrown farm and make it productive again. His powerful work ethic led to a spread of 2,000+ acres by the time of his death.

The Grants remain mostly Baptist or Methodist in their upbringing. Well before automobiles, "Lizzie" Boyd Fisher Grant rode side-saddle to church with Lynn and his older brother, Lester, both barely out of diapers. Her husband "Uncle

Castle Grant, ancestral home of the heads of Clan Grant, Grantown-on-Spey

Stephen Edward (Steve) and Gary Alan Grant, at the centennial service of First Baptist Church in Morrisville in 1991. The brothers' great-great grandfathers were also brothers, James Morris Grant (maternal) and Alfred Webster Grant (paternal).

Bill" was known for his fondness for mail-ordering religious books. He spent Sunday afternoons, in spring and summer, stretched out in the grass below their house, reading. Shortly before his death, he told a niece, reading about the life of Christ and watching his sheep "helped him 'know the Saviour better'." *Submitted by Steve Grant*

GRANT – Lester and Lora Morton Grant farmed, raised their family, attended church and schools in Polk County. Lester was born to William "Bill" and Elizabeth "Lizzie" Fisher Grant, Dec. 17, 1895, on their farm between Morrisville and Brighton. He had one brother, Lynn, younger than he. Bill and Lizzie were farmers and believed in education. The boys attended Tuck school and went to Baptist College in Bolivar for their high school education. Lester was drafted in July 1918 to serve his country. He and 70 other young men from Polk County were pictured in the Bolivar paper as they left for Camp Funston, KS. Lester lived at home and farmed with his dad.

Back row – Lester, Lora, Susanne. Front row – Bill Grant, Mark Grant, 1946 or 1947

On Nov. 24, 1926, he married Lora Morton, a school teacher, from Brighton. Lora, born May 24, 1897, was a daughter of Lorenza and Martha Fender Morton. Lester and Lora bought the farm on Highway K (215), two miles east of Morrisville, that joined his dad's farm. Lora continued teaching at Brighton and Flint Hill school until they started a family five years later. Lester and his dad were general farmers producing registered Hereford cattle, dairy cattle, sheep, hogs, chickens and crops of wheat, rye, oats and alfalfa hay. Lester believed in conservation of the soil, therefore he did not grow corn. In later years Lester, with Lora's help, increased their dairy herd and sold quality milk to the dairies in Springfield.

Lester and Lora had three children: Susanne, born December 1931, Bill, born September 1933 and Mark, born October 1936. Even though there was drought at the time and crops were very poor, there was meat, milk, eggs, a little fruit and vegetables to eat or share with hobos and gypsies who came to the door asking for food.

Lester and Lora were active leaders at Brighton Baptist Church, serving as Sunday School Superintendent and Sunday School teacher. Lora was active in the Polk County Baptist Women Missionary Society. She was active in the Parent Teachers Association during the time her kids were in school serving as local and county president. She was involved in getting the hot lunch program started in Morrisville Schools in the mid 40s.

The residents of the Tuck School district paid tuition for their students to attend the Marion C. Early Schools in Morrisville for better educational opportunities. The three children of Lester and Lora Grant all attended 12 years of school and graduated from Marion C. Early Schools. Susanne, Bill and Mark all attended Southwest Missouri State College in Springfield.

Lester died in July 1961 and Lora died in January 1992. Following Lester's death, the farm was sold to Billy and Wanda Beersman who still live there. Lester and Lora are buried in the Slagle Cemetery as well as Lester's parents, William and Elizabeth Grant; his grandparents, James and Nancy Grant; his brother and wife, Lynn and Ossie Grant. *Submitted by Susanne Grant Walden*

GRANT – Bill Grant, son of Lester and Lora (Morton) Grant of Morrisville, MO, met and married Eulala Bray, daughter of Ernest and Georgia (Berry) Bray of Nevada, MO, at Southwest Missouri State University, Springfield, MO where both were students. They married Nov. 13, 1954 at the First Christian Church, Nevada, MO. To this union two children were born: William Kelly Grant, Feb. 1, 1958 and Kimberly Kay Grant, Oct. 23, 1959. Bill and Eulala purchased the "Old President Pike" farm south of Bolivar from his daughter Caroline Pike in 1960. They remodeled the old historic home and buildings and ran a dairy farm for 31 years before turning the farm in to a beef farm in 1986 which it still is today. Kelly and Kim were raised on the farm. Bill and Eulala still enjoy living on the farm and entertaining the third generation (two grandsons). Now Bill operates an extensive hay operation and collects and restores antique tractors. Eulala enjoys hobby of antique collecting.

Kelly married Anne Abney of Springfield, MO in 1988. They have built their home on five acres on the northwest part of the 540 acres. Kelly is a major stockholder and general manager of Bill Grant Ford-Mercury, Inc. which Bill and Eulala purchased in 1976. Kelly and Anne are both graduates of University of Missouri, Columbia, MO. Anne taught school for several years.

Kim married Gregory Horton of Fair Play, MO in 1982. They live in Springfield, MO and are the parents of Bryan Alan Horton, age 11, and David

Bill Grant family – front row – David, Bryan Horton. Second row – Anne Grant, Eulala Grant, Kim Horton. Third row – Kelly Grant, Bill Grant and Greg Horton

Grant Horton, age 7. Greg and Kim own Integrity Home Health Care in Springfield and Joplin, and Integra Home Health Care in Kansas City. Kim owned International Tours in Bolivar for approximately eight years before David was born. Kim is a graduate of Southwest Missouri State University, Springfield, MO and Greg is a graduate of Central Missouri State University, Warrensburg, MO.

Bill and Eulala Grant are members of First Baptist Church, Bolivar, since 1955. They have always been community minded and have held many positions in farm organizations, represented Missouri agriculture on a people to people mission in 1968 to nine countries, including Russia, East and West Berlin and Czechoslovakia. The mission was to promote Missouri products. Bill has served on many dairy and soil conservation boards as well as several terms on the Marion C. Early Board of Education. Presently he is a bank board member. Eulala has taught school and is a member of Federated Womens Groups for years. *Submitted by Eulala Grant*

GRAVELY – The Gravely family moved to Polk County, MO in 1875 after events involving the most famous member of the original settlers, Joseph Jackson Gravely. Joseph Jackson Gravely and Martha Marshall were married in 1850 in Henry County, VA. Both were members of prominent families and Joseph J. was an attorney and Virginia legislator.

Joseph and Martha made the long journey to Missouri in 1854 and settled on Lindley Prairie in Cedar County. They were living there and Mr. Gravely was teaching school, when the Civil War broke out. He joined the army as a lieutenant, was soon a captain, and quickly became colonel of the Eighth Missouri State Militia.

When the war ended, they moved to Stockton, where Mr. Gravely took up the practice of law. He was elected a member of Congress in 1866 and in 1870 was elected Lieutenant Governor of Missouri. The first of April 1872, he adjourned the Senate and came home. He had been gone to Jefferson City all winter. He took sick and, after a few days' illness, died on April 28, 1872.

In November 1875, Mrs. Gravely moved to Bolivar to send her children to school. There were eight Gravely children, five girls and three boys: Nanny M. (Upton), Lewis Gravely, Pattie (Leith), Eleanor (Barkley), Benjamin F. Gravely, Joseph W. Gravely, Minnie (Skinker) and Lutie (Mitchell).

Joseph W. Gravely continued the Gravely name in Polk County. Joe W., as he was known, married Myrtle McDaniel and they had two sons, Francis Gravely (who died as an infant) and Ralph Gravely. After Joe W.'s first wife died, he married Bessie Wolford and they had three children: Ruthe (Utley), Jean (Palen) and Marshall Gravely.

Ralph and Marshall were lifelong Polk County residents. Ralph married Esther Hammontree and they did not have children. Marshall married Ola Creed and their children are Martha (Byrd), Benjamin Gravely and Bill Gravely. Martha married Cecil Byrd and their children are David, Becky and Elizabeth. Bill married Karen Wainscott and their children are Jessica, Page and Scott. The Gravely name continues on in Polk County through Benjamin Lewis Gravely, who married Marquita Payne. They have two sons, James and Andrew Gravely.

The Gravely name was long associated with the *Bolivar Free Press,* a weekly newspaper established in 1868. Joseph W. Gravely purchased the newspaper in 1891 and the Gravely family continued publication until 1966. Joseph W. Gravely died in 1934 and his sons, Ralph and Marshall, continued as publishers of the newspaper. Ralph started working at the newspaper in

1920 and was the editor of the *Free Press*. Marshall started working at the newspaper in 1929 and he managed print shop operations, eventually becoming editor upon Ralph's retirement. Marshall died in an automobile accident in 1965, and the family sold the newspaper in 1966. Ralph died in 1972. The *Bolivar Free Press* was noted as a "Republican Party paper and chronicler of local events," and the Gravely family was devoted to faithfully serving the citizens of Polk County. *Submitted by Ben Gravely*

GRIFFIN – William A. Griffin was born near Cynthiana, KY on June 25, 1810. His parents were Gabriel and Elizabeth Anderson Griffin, whose families were patriots of the Revolutionary War. It is not certain when Gabriel moved his family to Boone County, IN, but deeds show that his Kentucky farm was sold in 1821. Gabriel, Elizabeth and Anthony are buried in Beck Cemetery in Boone County. William Sr.'s siblings were John Collier, Anthony, Washington and Angeline. William Sr. married Catherine V. Shoemaker in Indiana, but they moved to Benton County, IA where William began farming. Twins, Eliza Jane and Mary E., were born in 1839. These girls later married Foster and Wence Cox. Four more girls were added to the family: Julia Ann, Nancy E., Martha M. and Maranda L. This family has always been active in church and community affairs and William was no exception. When Benton County, IA was in its early years, it was home to a band of horse thieves who terrorized the homesteaders and forced a suspension of law enforcement. William was a member of a society called the Iowa Protection Society that formed to bring peace to the area. He was a farmer, but also a skilled musician who played the violin and sang. His daughter said that he often traveled 20 miles to play at "balls." Catherine Griffin died in 1863 and is buried in Benton County, IA. In 1870, William married Amanda Brown and they moved to a farm south of Bolivar, MO. Four children, William Anderson Jr., John Collier, Nathan Lewis and Clara Amanda were born to this marriage. William, Amanda and William's daughter, Amande, are all buried in the cemetery at Mt. Gilead Church near Bolivar. William Anderson Jr., though young in years when his father died, took the responsibility of raising his younger siblings and running the farm. He married Nettie Hayden, daughter of Kenzie and Selena Brown Hayden. They homesteaded in Oklahoma, but made yearly trips to Polk County to visit friends and relatives in Bolivar. They never forgot the place that was their first home. Their children were Pearl, Roy, Winifred, William Kenzie, Bernie, Nettie, Wilma, Zirma, Ruby, Clyde and Claude (twins), and Clifford. William Anderson Jr. and Nettie are buried in Maple Grove Cemetery, Alfalfa County, OK. *Submitted by Doris Griffin*

GRIFFIN – William Griffin, born July 29, 1824—died Oct. 31, 1906, married Elizabeth Harvey, on Sept. 20, 1843 in Decatur, Meigs County, TN. Elizabeth was born 1824—died Aug. 2, 1901. Her father's name is unknown at this time, her mother was Phoebe (maiden?), Harvey, Davis, Gardner. Elizabeth's brother, William H. Harvey, married Sarah Dethrage in Tennessee. It is believed that Sarah died during the move to Missouri and he later married Rebecca C. Griffith. Elizabeth also had a sister, Melvina "Viney" Harvey, who married Calvin Mantooth and lived in Polk County, TN. It's likely that Elizabeth Harvey had other siblings yet to be discovered.

William and Elizabeth's first three children were born near Kingston, Roane County, TN. About 1850 they, along with other relatives who were looking for a better life, decided to leave Tennessee and move further west. They traveled, by wagon and ox team, west through Tennessee, through Arkansas as far as Hot Springs, then north into Missouri. Anderson and Ann (Daniel) Griffin (and her brother Jack), stopped in Texas County and lived a few years before moving on to Polk County.

Buell Wesley and Mary Ellen (Trimble) Griffin. Curtis Buell (5) and Albert Harlow (baby)

The others, Samuel and Filey A. (Robertson) Griffin, William and Elizabeth (Harvey) Griffin, her brother William H. Harvey and his family, eventually made their way to Polk County. William Griffin was a farmer and he settled near the Sac River at Shady Grove. William and Elizabeth's children are Dr. George Washington, married Susan Barbary McIntosh; Elijah, who died during the Civil War; Lavina, married Wm. J. Wright; Arthur married first, Belle Potter, second. Mary Jane Needham, and third to Mary J. Wing; Thomas Asbury, married Frances Armstrong and moved to California; Samuel Andrew, married first, Aurelia V. Chandler, second, Lucy Blair Acuff; John Wesley, married first, Molly Cleveland, second, Alcy Lockman Eddy; William Lester (1860-1861).

William and two sons served in the Civil War, Company D, Sixth Regiment. Elijah died and George W. was discharged due to illness. George married Susan B. McIntosh, daughter of Collon and Mary Jane (Fox) McIntosh, on Nov. 12, 1863 in Polk County. They were the parents of Ophelia Armintis, married James R. Johnson; Elijah Milton, married Cora Ann Eddy; Melcena A. (1869-1882); Horace Elmer (1870-1880); Buell Wesley, married first, Mary Ella Trimble, second, Mrs. Viola Cheek Mitchell; William Collin, married first, Minnie Martin, second, Minnie Parsons; and two infant daughters.

Mary Ella (Trimble) Griffin was born March 12, 1879 and died Oct. 7, 1911 on her son Albert's second birthday. She was the daughter of William Hardin and Nancy Elizabeth (Blackburn) Trimble. Buell and Mary were the parents of four children: Glen (1900-1901); Gladys (1902-1903); Curtis Buell (1903-1941) and Albert Harlow (1909-1970), who married first, Ethel Mary Ammerman, second, Flora Ethel Jones, daughter of Charles Elmer and Nora Alice (Wynes) Jones, of Cedar County.

Albert Harlow Griffin was born Oct. 7, 1909 and died Jan. 25, 1970. Albert H. and Ethel M. (Ammerman) Griffin were the parents of Jean Carroll and twins, Mary Louise and Mary Mae (1934-1934). Baby Mary Mae died at birth and Ethel died soon after. On Nov. 5, 1939, Albert married Flora Ethel Jones, born Aug. 3, 1911 and died Jan. 8, 2000. They were the parents of Charles William (1941-1941), Charlotte Kay and Linda Elaine (1947-1949).

William Griffin's known siblings are Samuel; John, who died in Meigs County, TN; Anderson; Elizabeth, married William Hutcheson; and Sarah, married Daniel R. Box. *Submitted by Kay Griffin Snow*

GRIFFITTS – George Washington Griffitts was born Dec. 11, 1848 in Tennessee. He served in the Tennessee State Militia during the Civil War. He married Martha H. Keen (once also noted as possibly Martha McClure) on Sept. 26, 1869. They had 12 children, the first four in Tennessee and the last eight in Polk County, MO near Brighton. Martha was born Jan. 22, 1852 and died May 1, 1925. There are also letters to indicate the family traveled on two lengthy trips. George and Martha are both buried in the Brighton Methodist Cemetery, Polk County, MO.

Their children were listed on a handwritten Record of Family document as Anna, born Nov. 28, 1870 – died March 7, 1872; Beecher, born Aug. 27, 1872 – died Aug. 10, 1873; ——ne (sp?), born Dec. 14, 1873 – died Sept. 19, 1911; Ri1ey, born 1874 - not known; Perry P., born Aug. 23, 1876 - died Aug. 7, 1948; Francis "Frank" Jerome, born March 12, 1879- died

George and Martha Griffitts family – ca. 1896

1965; Finis, born Nov. 12, 1880 – not known; Marshel, born Jan. 28, 1883 – died not known; Ina Inez, born March 22, 1885 – died Jan. 26, 1972; Ola, born Oct. 2, 1887 – died not known; Quinn S., born Aug. 8, 1889 – died Oct. 31, 1977 and Lottie, born March 20, 1892 – died Sept. 10 or 19, 1900. It appears that three died at young ages.

Riley married Emma Ruby on Oct. 26, 1899 in Morgan, TX.

Perry P. married Jessie M. Fender. Both are buried in Brighton Methodist Cemetery, Polk County, MO.

Francis "Frank" Jerome married Alice Mae Whitman. Both are buried in Brighton Methodist Cemetery, Polk County, MO.

Finis married Ora.

Marshel married Josie.

Ina married Harry Boswell on Oct. 16, 1904 in Bolivar, MO. Both are buried in Slagle Cemetery, Slagle, MO.

Ola married Ed Whittaker.

Quinn married Omah E. on May 28, 1915. Both are buried in Brighton Methodist Cemetery, Polk County, Mo.

Other descendants are also buried at Brighton Methodist Cemetery, Pleasant Hope Cemetery and Slagle Cemetery. Anna died as a young child, probably buried in Tennessee. Beecher also died as a young child and was probably buried in Tennessee. The third name on the record that was not legible, shows no record of marriage or burial. Lottie died at 8 years. Her sister said the family was coming home from Texas in a covered wagon and she died on the way back to Missouri. Lottie is probably buried in Oklahoma.

As an adult, Riley was a lifelong resident of Hico, TX. Perry, Frank and Quinn were lifelong residents of Brighton, MO. Ina was a lifelong resident of Polk County, MO, living mostly in Morrisville and Bolivar. Finis, Marshel and Ola resided in Idaho.

Some of George and Martha's great-grandchildren attended Marion C. Early in Morrisville, MO. *Submitted by Paula Ledford*

HACKER – Barney Jackson Hacker (1892-1973) and Eula Jane Cooper (1892-1969) were born, attended school and were married in Cedar County, MO. Born to this union was a son, Jack Ralston (1925), a daughter, Wanda Zoe (1928) and another son, Bob Max (1933). Barney, better known as B. J., served in the Marline Corps in WWI in France where he fought in the Battle of Belleau Wood and the Argonne Forest. He served his country again during WWII buying horses for the US Calvary. B. J. was a lifelong member of the American Legion and the 40 & 8 Club.

In 1929, the family moved to Humansville, MO and then to nearby Bolivar the following year. There, B. J. first worked at the Ernest Bitzer Chevrolet Agency. B. J. had long been involved in buying and selling horses and mules in the area. He left the car agency in 1936 to return to that occupation. B. J. became well known as a mule trader as he traveled through Missouri, Kansas, Arkansas and Tennessee buying and shipping mules for the Owens Brother's Commission Company of Memphis. The Frisco Railroad was an integral part of his business as he accompanied boxcar loads of mules to Memphis every Saturday. The mules were sold on Monday after which he would return home to Bolivar and repeat the same routine. He retired from that occupation in the 1940s. In the years that followed, B. J. conducted Saturday livestock auctions east of the square in Bolivar as well as a location west of town.

Eula, a graduate of Springfield Normal College (now SMS) was a teacher in one-room schools at Bear Creek, Caplinger Mills and Jerico Springs before her marriage. Once married, she devoted her life to raising her children and becoming very involved in their activities. Eula was an active member of the American Legion Auxiliary, the PTA and several social clubs. She was a member of the Christian Church in Bolivar teaching the "Willing Workers" Sunday school class for over 20 years.

After renting two houses in Bolivar, the Hacker family purchased a home, orchard and pasture on what is now Forest Street. The original white house and barn remain on the property. In 1943, the family moved to a large, brick house on the east side of South Chicago Street where they lived for the remaining years of their lives.

Jack Ralston Hacker married Ann Tostengard of Pipestone, MI and practiced dentistry until 1987. Their oldest son, David, continues that family practice today with the youngest son Jim on the family ranch continuing his father's cattle operation. Daughters: Betsy is a counselor with a private practice and Susan is a respiratory therapist living in nearby towns with their families.

Wanda Zoe Hacker graduated from SMS and taught several years before working in Germany for the US Government. She was married to Ellis Dodge Allen Jr. from Yonkers, NY. He was employed by American Express in Germany, New York and London before returning to Bolivar in 1981. Their son, Ellis Dodge Allen III (Baron), is a restauranteur and a daughter, Lindley Jane, graduated from Drury and UMKC and lives with her family in St. Louis.

Barney and Eula Hacker, 1967

Bob Max married Inezetta Ruth Price of Bolivar. They moved to Valdosta, GA in 1963 where Bob has been involved in raising livestock and producing rodeos. Their daughter, Cheryl, is a nurse practitioner and a pain specialist and son, Barry, is a graduate of Valdosta State University and is employed in magazine distribution. *Submitted by Wanda Allen*

HALE - Thomas and Sarah Hale came to Polk County sometime between 1840 and 1850. Almost all that is known about Thomas and Sarah comes from census records. Sarah's maiden name is unknown. Thomas was born in South Carolina around 1797 and Sarah was born in North Carolina around 1802. Thomas's death was noted in the old *Bolivar Courier* in 1858. The following is the quote from the paper. "Died at his residence 8 miles east of this place on 7th inst. of a lingering chronic disease, Thomas Hale, an old and respected citizen of this county." Children listed for Thomas are William, born in 1828 in Illinois; Mary E., born around 1834 in Arkansas; Thomas, born around 1836 in Illinois; Stephen, born 1838 in Missouri and James, born in 1843 in Missouri.

Stephen Hale didn't live a very long life. He passed on at the age of 23. However, he did leave behind a very long list of descendants. On April 1, 1858 in Polk County, he married Mary Elizabeth Vincent, daughter of Thomas Roy Vincent and Elizabeth Pearman. They had one son, Thomas R. Then tragedy struck. Stephen drowned. His drowning was reported in the old *Bolivar Courier* Aug. 20, 1859. The clipping reads "On Monday last, at or near Owens' Mill on Pomme de Terre in this county, Mr. Steven Hale was accidentally drowned, while engaged in rafting some timbers from said mill to the bridge below. We understand that several unsuccessful attempts were made to rescue the unfortunate man, but to no avail. Coroner Foushee held an inquest over the body on the day following, and a verdict rendered of accidental drowning." According to Polk County marriage records, Mary married a second time to Isaac Wells on March 8, 1866. It is not known what happened to her.

The T. R. and Luzettie (McLin) Hale family: Zettie holding James, T. R. holding Oma, Charlie in back with Bill in front.

Thomas R. Hale and Luzettie McLin were married in Polk County on June 27, 1881. Thomas was born May 10, 1859 and Luzettie was born March 5, 1863 in Nebraska. Luzettie's parents were Perry J. McLin and Julia Moore. They had eight children. They are Charles Linnis, who married Annie Payne; Tommie Russell; Oma, who married a Bagley, James Denis, who married Jennie Reed; George Lee, who married Susie Kaudle; W. W. "Bill;" Gentry; and Gertie, who married Harrison White.

Tommie married Pearl Ashlock March 8, 1916. Pearl's parents were William Francis Ashlock and Sara Eliza Low. Tommie was born April 23, 1895 and Pearl was born May 22, 1897. Tommie and Pearl had four children: Chester, Garland, Jereline, who married Nelson Warren and Marceline, who married Omar Ward.

Chester married Opal Frank May 21, 1938. Chester was born Feb. 19, 1917 and Opal was born April 20, 1920. Her parents were Gus Frank and Jewell Cheney. Chet and Opal's children are Shirley, who married Frank VanCamp; Kay, who married Harold Holt; and Ron. They have three grandchildren, Scott, Steve and Sarah and two great-grandchildren, Spencer and Morgan. *Submitted by Ron Hale*

HALE - David Lynn Hale and Nancy Marie Simpson Hale's ancestors on both sides have been in Polk County since before the Civil War. Jack Glendenning, a local historian, once told Nancy that their families were not on the friendliest of terms. Jack said some of David's relatives had a part in doing away with one of Nancy's great-grandfathers on the place where Ron and Sarah Jump now live.

David and Nancy went to first grade together at Polk school in 1956. Nancy moved to California in 1957 and then returned to Polk in 1966 at the age of 15. The first day of school Nancy was on the bus to go home when David and Kenny Reynolds bounded on board. Kenny sat by Pam Wheeler and David sat by Nancy! Nancy guesses that's where it all "started."

Front: Angela, Steve, Kim, Nancy, Julie, Jason; inset: Codey and David; back: Jay, David, John and Trudy

David and Nancy dated all through high school and graduated in 1968. They were married on Aug. 31, 1968 and moved to Springfield where David was in school and working. They both worked there until their first daughter Kimberly Elaine was born on Feb. 21, 1970. David worked at Springday at the time. On Oct. 29, 1971 their first son Jason David was born. On the day he was born their small family moved back home to Bolivar where they had bought a place on Forest St. David continued working in Springfield until 1975, when he got a job with Missouri Telephone. On June 7, 1976 their second daughter Angela Marie was born. She was their Bicentennial baby. Life in Bolivar was good; their house and family continued to grow and on June 29, 1981, a second son John David was born. Time marched on very quickly, it seems now, and on Aug. 2, 1985 their third daughter Julie Lynn was born. Nancy says, "We've had a good life here in Bolivar. We have had good times and bad times. Our saddest time was when our daughter Angela was killed on Oct. 31, 1996; she was three months pregnant. She and her husband John Jay Follis were married in July of 1993."

Kimberly married Steve Hawk in July of 1996 and they have one son David Leonard, born in August of 1997. Jason was married to Trudy Walker; they have one son Codey Jason, born in January 1993.

Time passed so fast, Their children and grandchildren are growing up and life in Polk County continues to be good. They are now retired and spend a great deal of time woodcarving and spending time with friends and family.

Nancy says, "God has blessed us in many ways. We have five wonderful kids and two very special grandsons and they have four outstanding grandparents: my parents, Marion and Mayme Simpson, and David's parents, L. D. and Eugenia Hale. Our hope is that we can be as good of parents and grandparents to our children and grandchildren as they were." *Submitted by Nancy Hale*

HALE - L. D. Hale was born July 21, 1925 to Charles Linnis and Annie (Payne) Hale, son of Thomas Russell and Luzetta McLinn Hale. L. D. and his siblings Lee, Steve, Roy, Melvin, Raymond, Olen, Verble, Zella, Dollie and AnnaBelle were all raised on a farm near Polk, MO.

L. D. served in the Army during WWII from Oct. 9, 1943 to Jan. 10, 1946. He served in the South Pacific as a truck driver with the 470th AAA Battalion. After returning from the service, he drove a school bus and worked in a garage.

L. D. met Eugenia Purdin Anderson at the O.K. Café on the square in Bolivar. Eugenia and her twin sister Virginia had moved from Humansville to work. Eugenia worked at the USDA while Virginia worked at the County Extension Office.

They were married April 7, 1949 on Eugenia's 21st birthday. L. D. and Eugenia were the proud parents of four sons: David Lynn (born Feb. 15, 1950); Robert Eugene (born March 31, 1952); Donald Ray (born July 27, 1954) and Joe Wayne (born June 7, 1958). God blessed them with a wonderful family and they prayed for God's guidance in raising them. Every Sunday was spent in church and then at Humansville with the Anderson family.

After the death of L. D.'s father, the family moved back to the family farm, and took care of his mother until her death. L. D. worked for the county road-bridge when the boys were teenagers and the boys had part-time jobs. L. D. bought a bulldozer and dump truck in the mid 1970s. Eugenia and the boys helped out with the family business. L. D. enjoyed the work and the people that he worked for.

David married Nancy Simpson on Aug. 31, 1968. They had five children: Kimberly Elaine, Jason David, Angela Marie, John David and Julie Lynn. Robert married Yvonne Sharon "Sheri" Castleberry on Dec. 3, 1971. They had two children, Adam Eugene and Amber Dionne. Donald married Mary Jean Barnett on Dec. 22, 1973. They had two children, Cody Joe and Ashley Nichole. Donald's son Cody died of meningitis at 2 years of age. Joe was working for Hank Deshazo burying telephone cable after graduating from high school. He died in a car accident Sunday, Aug. 6, 1978.

In October 1987 L. D. had a massive heart attack and lost 50 percent of his heart. God blessed his family with nine more years together before he passed away Sept. 14, 1996. L. D. and Eugenia had been married for 47 wonderful years.

That same year Donald's wife, Mary, and David's daughter, Angela, also passed away. Eugenia says, "Our family has experienced many losses but we are thankful for the time we had together. It is with God's help and support we have risen above these deaths and walked on with him."

Eugenia stays busy with family, church, and friends. She volunteers 20 hours a week as a Foster Grandparent in the fifth grade at Bolivar Schools.

The family continues to grow and now includes three great-grandsons: Kim's son, David Leonard Hawk, Jason's son, Codey Jason, and Adam's son, Beau Taylor. *Submitted by Eugenia Hale*

HALE - The boy, Will, was 10 years old when he moved to Polk County. The area was only woods, streams, trails and a few settlements. He attended school in Bolivar.

When Shirley's great-great-grandfather, William M. Hale, arrived circa 1837, Bolivar, MO was a town of log houses and log stores. He carried bricks for 25 cents per day during the construction of the old courthouse. A veteran of three wars, he wore his medals proudly. He made three cattle drives to California, once as a helper, twice as owner of the herd. Apparently, of the colorful adventures of his life, the cattle drives were his most passionate, and often repeated, memories.

On June 20, 1851 he married Sarah Elizabeth Delilah Lindsey. They raised two daughters, Mary Jane and Willie Van. Their home was in Goodson until the twilight of their lives when they moved to Bolivar, nearer to family.

Shirley's great-grandmother, Mary Jane Hale, married Homer Logan Wright in 1868. They made their home in Goodson for more than 20 years before moving to Bolivar. They had nine children. The eldest daughter, Edith, became Shirley's maternal grandmother.

Edith Wright married Rhueben P. Arnold. Two years later, they bought 40 tree-covered acres about one mile southeast of Bolivar. Rhueben cleared the land and built a one-room house. Prior to digging a well, they carried water from a spring in the pasture of adjoining neighbors. After waiting nine years, Grandpa and Grandma Arnold received the best Christmas present ever, for them and us!

On Christmas day 1901 their only child, Shirley's mother, was born. She was so tiny and frail the doctor told the assisting women at the farmhouse that they didn't need to "bother" dressing her because she couldn't possible survive. Evidently he didn't know Shirley's grandma or the spirit within that tiny two and one-half to three pound baby! Shirley's great-grandmother Wright DID dress her. Her Mamma and Papa became the "specialists" that gently nurtured their precious gift. From that pre-

William M. Hale, 1827-1913 and Elizabeth (Lindsey) Hale, 1831-1913

carious beginning they gave Annie Marie Arnold the will to survive, a faith to live by and the lifelong determination to keep on trying, no matter what! Marie attended Forrest Grove School. She told wonderful stories of her early childhood in Bolivar with her cousins, aunts, uncles and friends. In 1911 Rhueben and Edith bought a farm just over the county line in the Prairie Grove community southwest of Buffalo. (Shirley's childhood home.)

Marie Arnold married George Henry Gilpin, Sept. 5, 1920. Mama and Daddy had seven children. Of those, Shirley is the only daughter and she has five very special brothers in Missouri. (One died in infancy.)

Shirley spent a week (twice) with her great-uncle, Arthur Wright, and cousin Dessie on his farm near Bolivar. Dessie made dresses for Shirley. What beautiful childhood memories!

Shirley lives in California now, but will always remember that her family roots are firmly planted in Polk County, MO. *Submitted by Shirley Gilpin Triplett*

Charlie and Annie Hale

HALE - Charles Linnis Hale was born May 4, 1882 in Polk, MO in the family home. He married Annie Justine Payne (born July 5, 1885) on Dec. 27, 1903 in Louisburg, MO. To this union 11 children were born. Lee Merl (born March 29, 1905); Sylvia Verble (born May 2, 1907); Steve Harrison (born Nov. 17, 1911); Henry Roy (born March 19, 1913); Melvin Clarence (born June 5, 1915); Raymond Carl (born Aug. 17, 1917); Olin Merchie (born Nov. 13, 1919); Zella Pearl (born Feb. 18, 1923); Louie Donald (born July 21, 1925); Dollie Marcella (born April 21, 1928), Anna Belle (born July 9, 1931).

Charlie ran the merry-go-round at the Louisburg picnic when horses pulled it.

Charlie worked on the railroad, but he didn't like being away from home. They had a truck farm, a peach orchard and a strawberry patch. They sold the produce to supplement the family income. The summer of 1935 Annie and her daughters canned 45 gallons of peaches. Charlie worked for Retty Shannon farming for $2.50 a day. Her husband was a lawyer in Kansas City. Annie took in laundry. Charlie cracked black walnuts; the children picked out the meats, which they sold to the walnut factory in Polk. When the walnut factory closed they would work after school and on Saturday peeling tomatoes for $.05 a bucket (3-4 gallon). The Baggets had a turkey farm, the children would pick feathers for $.05 a turkey, only at Thanksgiving and Christmas.

The children walked to Polk for school and church. They rode the bus to high school at Goodson.

At 14 Raymond joined the government CC camps. Went to Utah, where he drove a truck and hauled the mail for the army for two years.

When the family moved to the house on top of Shannon Hill, Raymond, Melvin, and Ward Inglis dug the basement with shovels. On March 4, 1938 the original house burnt. The personal family records were destroyed. Charlie bought walnut lumber from Mrs. Shannon to rebuild. Olin, Raymond, Melvin, Tom Sullivan and Charlie built the house that stands today.

Lee and Freda lived in Marionville, MO, no children. Verble and Ray Higginbotham lived north of Springfield, eight children. Steve and Grace lived in Brookline, two sons. Melvin and Inez lived in Yuciapa, CA, two children. Raymond and Wanda still reside in Redlands, CA, no children. Olin lived in Redlands, CA, one daughter. Zella and Everett West live in Bolivar, four children. L. D. lived in Polk; his wife Eugenia still resides in the family home, four sons. Dot Cox "Dollie" lives in Bolivar, two sons and Anna Belle and Bob Stewart live in Coulterville, CA, three children. *Submitted by Robert Hale*

HALE - Donald Ray Hale, third son of Louie Donald "L. D." and Eugenia Lee (Anderson) Hale was born July 27, 1954 in Humansville, MO. Donald was raised on the family farm with his three brothers, David, Robert and Joe. Their mother worked at home and kept a large garden and still enjoys sharing the bountiful plenty of her garden with her boys and their families. Their dad worked on many farms in the area with his grader, dozer and dump truck. He graduated from Bolivar High School with the class of 1972.

On Dec. 21, 1973 in Fair Grove, MO, Donald was united in marriage to Mary Jean Barnett (born Jan. 20, 1956 in Baxter Springs, KS) and they had two children, Cody Joe Hale, born April 30, 1980 and Ashley Nichole Hale, born June 11, 1982. Both Cody and Ashley were born in Shattuck, OK where they were living at the time while Donald worked in the Oklahoma oil fields. Cody passed away on Dec. 12, 1982 at the age of 2 1/2 when he contracted meningitis. In January of 1985, Mary and Donald moved back to Missouri. Mary worked for the Circuit Judge's office for many years prior to her passing away on March 11, 1996. Donald is self-employed and enjoys spending time off at the golf course or the lake. Ashley graduated from Bolivar High School with the class of 2000 and is living in Bolivar and attending Ozark Technical College in Springfield, studying to become a nurse practitioner. She recently became engaged to Jake Roberts and they plan a 2003 wedding. *Submitted by Ashley Hale*

Donald Hale and daughter Ashley

The Robert Hale family

HALE – Robert Eugene Hale (born March 31, 1952) married Yvonne "Sheri" Castleberry (born April 26, 1955) Dec. 3, 1971. They have two children, Adam Eugene (born June 5, 1972) and Amber Dionne Cline (born Jan. 15, 1981).

Robert spent four years in the army; one and a half years in Colorado, and one and a half years in Germany. He was the logistics analyst for the howitzer guns. After returning to Polk County in 1977 he went to work for Hank Deshazo in Halfway burying telephone cable. They bought a home east of Bolivar where they lived until they moved into Bolivar. Robert went into the excavating business with his father and brother David. Eventually he started his own backhoe business in 1986, which he sold in 1999. He is now a truck driver for Indiana Western Express out of Springfield, driving from coast to coast. He always wanted to travel and see the world.

Adam graduated from Bolivar High School in 1990. He married Dawn Marie Carson, Nov. 5, 1996. They have one son, Beau Taylor Hale (born June 16, 1996). They were divorced Feb. 28, 1998. Adam resides with his son in Bolivar. He works with his Uncle Donald as a floor-covering expert.

Amber graduated from Bolivar High School in 1999. She will graduate from Southwest Baptist University with a degree in marketing in the spring of 2003. She played softball for SBU until a car wreck in June of 2001 put an end to that. She married Terry Wayne Cline on May 26, 2001 in Bolivar. They live five miles north on Highway 83.

The family stays close hunting, fishing, and playing softball together. Adam and Amber live close and see each other a lot. Family is an important theme that runs throughout the Hale family. Robert and Sheri were fortunate that they both came from very close families, and they were able to raise their children the same way. Love and faith in God and their families being the most important.

Beau Taylor Hale is the eighth generation of their Hale family to live in Polk County. He and his cousins Codey Hale and David Hawk are the seventh generation to live here all of their lives. That is a long legacy of family and tradition to be proud of. *Submitted by Amber Hale*

HALE - Between 1840 and 1850 Thomas (originally from South Carolina) and Sarah Hale (from North Carolina) came to Polk, MO with three children: William (born in Illinois), Mary E. (Arkansas) and Thomas (Illinois). Stephen was born in 1838 and James M. in 1843 somewhere else in Missouri.

Bill made several cattle drives to California, where they would sell the cattle and horses, sail around the horn to New Orleans, take a steamboat up the Mississippi River to St. Louis. There they bought new horses and returned home. T. R went at least once.

Thomas Russell Hale "T. R." was born May 10, 1859. He was the son of Steve Hale and Mary Elizabeth Vincent (married April 1, 1858). He married Luzettie McLin (born March 4, 1863) on December 27, 1893. They had eight children: Oma, Charles Linnis (born May 27, 1882), William (born Sept. 20, 1884), James (born Jan. 21, 1890), George (born April 28, 1893), Thomas (born April 30, 1895), and Gertie. Their son Gentry (born Feb. 1, 1900; died Jan. 24, 1902) died when he took an overdose of medicine.

T. R. was raised by his grandparents (the Vincents). His father was killed helping build a bridge across Pomme de Terre River. His mother died a year later. They are believed to be buried in a cemetery between Bolivar and Burns, which is no longer there.

Coming home from work (he couldn't swim), he would cross the Panther Creek on his horse. Two panthers attacked him and he shot them. Dorothy Quickbeorner (a granddaughter) remembers seeing the claw marks the panthers made on his saddle when she was a little girl. Panthers are how the creek got its name.

Luzettie (McLin) Hale, Thomas R. Hale, Charlie, Bill, Oma and Jim

Luzettie's parents, Mr. and Mrs. Perry James McLin, lived at Slagle. They didn't want her marrying Tom. The story is, Zetti went to church Sunday, wearing three dresses, one on top of the other, told her mother she had a nose bleed, left the church, eloped with Tom, and went to northern Missouri to live. Years later they returned. They had two small children and a baby. Back then women wore big starched bonnets. Zetti asked her mother for a cup of water for the baby. When Mrs. McLin returned Zetti had removed her bonnet and they realized it was their daughter. All was forgiven. P. J. McLin took his son-in-law into the family blacksmith business and taught him the trade. Later Tom and Zetti opened one of the first blacksmith shops in Polk. T. R. was a farmer and horse trader.

Tom was 57 when he died of pneumonia.

Zetti lived at home with her son Bill until she developed cataracts and was blind. She moved in with Charlie and his wife Annie until she died, Feb. 10, 1953.

Oma and Gertie moved to California. Oma died in a landslide.

Charlie, James, George and Tommy married and raised their families around Polk. Bill owned a threshing machine, traveled during crop time, but returned home in the winter months. He never married. *Submitted by Sheri Hale*

HAMILTON – Edgar Leonard Hamilton Jr. was born Oct. 22, 1920. His father was E. L. Hamilton Sr., born Sept. 2, 1891. E. L. Sr.'s father was George Washington Hamilton, born April 27, 1845. George W.'s father was Wood Hamilton, born Feb. 1, 1816 in Kentucky and he died in June of 1852 at age 36 from pneumonia after plowing in rain.

Wood married Nancy (Robinson) Hamilton in Polk County in 1836. Wood Hamilton had three older brothers who built a water mill on the Little Sac River about 1836. They operated the mill about 1845 when they moved to Arkansas. The millstones were there when E. L. Jr. was young. These stones were round; the sides flat with small ridges from center to circumference. They were about four feet in diameter and 12 to 14 inches thick with a square hole in the center about four by four inches. There were two of the large stones and several of the smaller ones like them. These are all gone now, but E. L. knows where one of the larger stones is.

Wood and Nancy settled near Eudora. They lived there until 1851. Wood built four log pens, which is believed to have been his barn. Each pen was 10 feet by 10 feet and 10 feet between, making a passway 10 feet wide in one direction and a stable on one side and a saddle house on the other by closing the sides in. At the top of the pens, the top log is 30 feet long on all sides, tying the pens together. The pens are approximately 12 feet high. The logs are slotted and tapered at the ends making them lock together, not one has slipped in 150 years. He later built a barn over the pens. The barn and pens are still in use today.

Wood Hamilton also built a house. The house stood until recently when a small tornado did its damage. Large stones, hewn smooth, were used for the foundation and to build a fireplace. He also built a flue for a kitchen stove of handmade bricks.

Thirteen children were born to Wood and Nancy Hamilton, four girls and nine boys. The girls lived to be adults, but only three boys did. Six boys died as infants or very young. George W. Hamilton was the oldest boy to live to adulthood. At 13 years of age he worked making bricks. The brick he made went into a house the family called "The Old Brick." At the age of 16 he enlisted in the army for the Civil War.

On Jan. 15, 1871, he married Susan Ann Lemmon, whose family lived in "The Old Brick." To this union four boys were born: Walter, Charles, James and Benjamin. Susan passed away at the age of 42. This was on July 9, 1889 and hers was the first grave to go in at Oakville Cemetery.

Wood is buried at Coats Cemetery, west of Graydon Springs, as are the young children. When Nancy died at age 50, Coats Branch was flooding, making passage impossible. At this time, there were no funeral homes and family members took care of preparations. So, she was taken

George W. Hamilton and his wife. The small child standing at his father's knee is Edgar L. Hamilton Sr. and the next child is Benjamin and the largest is James.

to Enon Cemetery, northeast of Wishart because it was necessary to bury in the day of death, especially in hot weather.

On May 22, 1890, George W. Hamilton married Martha A. McKnight, who helped him during his wife's illness and with the children after her death. Their children were Leonard, who married Jewell McDonald and had two children; Esther, who married Harry Morton; E. L. Jr., who married Betty Ann Cook; Ruby Hamilton, who married Hoil Wood, they had no children; Llano Hamilton, who married Aggie Belle Schartzer, they had two children; George R., who married Iva June Gilmore; and Hannah Katherine, who married Ralph Sanders. *Submitted by E. L. Hamilton*

HAMILTON – Woods Hamilton was born Feb. 1, 1816 and Nancy Robinson was born May 8, 1820, married in 1836, Polk County, MO. They were one of the earliest settlers of Jackson Township. Woods moved to Missouri when he was very young and Nancy moved in 1836.

Children born to this marriage were born in Polk County and are listed below.

Andrew J. was born Jan. 11, 1837 and died Aug. 22, 1842; James R. was born Sept. 4, 1838 and died in infancy; Joseph was born Dec. 21, 1839 and died young; Isac S. was born 1840 and died in 1842; Frankie A. was born Feb. 24, 1841, died Feb. 20, 1912 and married Alexander C. Lane on Oct. 17, 1859 in Polk County, MO. He was born Aug. 8, 1834 in Van Buren, TN and died Dec. 16, 1902 in Van Zandt County, TX. David P. was born Jan. 28, 1842 and died Aug. 28, 1842; Sarah E. was born Dec. 20, 1842, died 1870 and married Thomas Cossins. He was born 1840 and died 1910. Martha J. was born Feb. 22, 1844, died 1915 and married Jefferson Griffin on Oct. 18, 1868. He was born 1841 and died 1918. George Washington was born April 27, 1845, died Aug. 26, 1928 and married Susan E. Lemon on Jan. 15, 1871. She was born Dec. 10, 1847 and died Aug. 9, 1889. George married Martha A. McKnight on May 22, 1890. She was born June 21, 1858 and died Jan. 10, 1932. Susan E. was born March 9, 1847, died 1882, and married Benjamin Wilson Appleby on Aug. 31, 1873. He was born 1845 and died 1910. John Newton was born May 13, 1846, died Dec. 21, 1927 and married Margaret Jane Towe on Nov. 10, 1870. She was born June 26, 1848 and died Nov. 9, 1927. William Wood was born Feb. 20, 1850, died Sept. 29, 1930 and married Emma Lemmon on Aug. 28, 1873. She was born Sept. 9, 1855 and died Jan. 10, 1929. Thomas B. was born Nov. 18, 1852 and died in infancy.

Excerpts from the book written by James Lemmon Hamilton in 1953: "After Wood Hamilton died, his young widow, Nancy, with her three young girls, Frankie, Sarah and Martha, and some hired help, carried on raising the smaller children and not only finished paying for the land purchased before Woods died but also purchased and paid for additional land."

Frankie Hamilton and Alexander Lane had the following children, all born in Polk County.

Nancy A. was born May 25, 1860 and married William J. Hall on Jan. 24, 1878 in Polk County.

Joseph Woods was born July 14, 1862, died Nov. 22, 1939 in Knox County, TX and married Julie Ann Stephens on Dec. 15, 1886 in Bell County, TX. She was born Sept. 5, 1869 and died 1913.

Mary J. was born June 30, 1866.

Noah S. was born June 14, 1872.

Virgie Emly Bell was born July 28, 1876.

Clerrissa Arminda was born May 14, 1878.

Alexander Lane enlisted in the Civil War as a private, Sept. 16, 1863 in Webster County, MO. He was mustered in Sept. 16, 1863 in Springfield, MO. He served in Company H, Eighth Regiment, Cavalry Missouri State Militia under Captain Moore.

Frankie and Alexander signed the Polk County Loyalty Oath 1862-1864.

Frankie and Alexander left Missouri and were in Crawford County, AR in the 1880 census. Nancy and William Hall had Frankie and Alexander's first grandchild, Thomas J., born about 1879 in Arkansas.

They left Arkansas and were next in Bell County, TX in 1886. They were farmers and traveled between Bell County and Van Zandt County, TX.

On the 1910 census, Frankie was living with her son, Joseph, in Haskell County, TX. Rayma has not been able to find a record of Frankie's death nor has she been able to find her grave.

Rayma believes Frankie was the only child of Woods and Nancy to leave Missouri. She believes there are still descendants of the other children still living there. *Submitted by Rayma Lou Edgar*

HANCOCK - Robert R. Hancock was the son of Ballis and Mary Hancock. Mary Ann Hand was the daughter of Thomas W. and Elizabeth Hand. Robert (1829-1907) and Mary (1838-1897) were married in Pickaway County, OH 1852. They and their children came to Polk County in the early 1880s. The children were: Harvey, 1853-1896; Elizabeth, 1855-?; Robert Thomas, 1857-1946; Ella, 1859-1886; Flora, 1865-?; Oletha, 1867-1880; McPherson, 1871-?; and Eustice, 1875-1875. Robert Thomas aka "Tom" married Matilda Hughey Rector, 1867-1943, in 1884 in Ohio. They followed his parents to Polk County.

Tom and Tillie spent their married life in Polk County except for two short periods in the Kansas City area. Tom was a farmer. They had a

Robert Thomas and Matilda Hughey Rector Hancock

small farm northwest of Bolivar. His father owned acreage next to theirs. The family raised berries, cane, etc. They would take the berries to town and sell them door to door. Tom worked at different odd jobs to supplement his income.

Tom and Tillie had seven children: Calvin McPherson, 1888-1976; Prentice Rector, 1890-1973; Nellie M., 1894-1986; MaryAnn, 1897-1991; Paul Wiggins, 1898-1981; Robert Victor, 1901-1976; and Minnie Lee, 1906-1984.

Around 1924, Tom had problems with one of his eyes. Two doctors came out to the farm, put him to sleep on the kitchen table and took out the eye. He had a glass eye that was a great source of interest to his grandchildren and great-grandchildren.

Calvin married Emil Sutton, 1890-1978, in 1910. They had one child, Richard, 1914-1978. He married Gladys Ware, daughter of Charley and Sarah Ware. They had two children, Carrol and Carl.

Prentice Rector married Nettie Jones, 1888-1971, in 1912. They had six children: Wayne, who died in infancy; Maxine, who married Preston Whitaker, and had two sons Samuel and Michael; Glen, who married Shirley Mustain, and had five children: Donnie, Shirley, Charles, Sarah and Mary; Madge, who married Arzie Walters, and had three children: Laura, Robert and Jimmie; John, who married Mae Sue Sterling, and had three children: Ronald, Steven and Dennis; Prentice Jr., who married Virginia Sterling, and had four children: Cindy, Renee, Tina and Prentice III.

Nellie married Everett Brashears, 1890-1986, in 1911; one daughter Thelma, 1914, who married Herbert Douglas. They had two children, Janice and Dwight.

Mary Ann married Ruby Ables, 1900-1981, in 1919; one daughter Lillie (1920-2002). She married Max Phillips, two daughters, Sharon and Dorothy.

Paul Wiggins married Pansy Summers, 1901-?, in 1920. They had two children: Lois, 1922, who had two children, Patsy and Vicki; and Deryl (1934-1975).

Robert Victor married Eva Russell in 1922, no children.

Minnie Lee married Tom Johnson, 1903-1955, in 1924. They had two daughters, Edith and Dorothy. Edith had two children and Dorothy had three. They spent most of their married lives in California.

Calvin, Prentice, Paul and Robert were all farmers. They lived northwest of Bolivar on farms just a few miles apart. Nell and Everett farmed and then owned grocery stores in Bolivar for many years. Mary and Ruby owned a hatchery and feed store in Bolivar and raised turkeys, hogs, etc. on their farm north of Bolivar.

This family was a close-knit group and good neighbors to others. If one had a problem, the rest were there to help. They also had a lot of fun. Family get-togethers were happy times filled with laughter. What more could anyone ask? Six of the seven couples celebrated 50 years or more of marriage to each other. *Submitted by Carl Hancock*

HANKEY - Jakob Hanggi, son of Johann Jakob and Marianna (Hanggi) Hanggi, was born June 29, 1836, Nunningen, Switzerland. Jacob and a brother, Johann Peter, immigrated to America in 1859. They settled in the mining region of Ontonagon County, MI. In America, the surname, Hanggi, was transliterated to Hankey, and all descendants are using this spelling.

Feb. 24, 1860, Jacob married Maria Antonia Kaiser in Ontonagon County, MI. Maria Antonia "Mary" Kaiser, daughter of Niklaus and Mariann Kaiser, was born May 11, 1840, Grellingen, Switzerland. This couple lived in Michigan and Jacob worked in the copper mines until 1868 when Jacob moved his family to Polk County, MO. Oct. 1, 1868, Jacob Hankey applied for a land patent at Springfield. The family took up residence on the 80 acres of land on Nov. 1, 1868. Final approval of this application was made in 1874, and the patent was delivered June 14, 1875. The location of this land was described as "South half of the southeast quarter of section number 28 in Township 33 of Range number 21." Jacob and Mary lived on this land until their deaths. Jacob Hankey died July 28, 1899, and Maria A. Hankey died Oct. 6, 1899. Both are buried in Schofield Cemetery, near Halfway, MO. They had seven children.

Jacob Hanggi

Caroline, born Nov. 17, 1860, Ontonagon County, MI; died March 28, 1941, Geneva, NE; buried in Schofield Cemetery, Polk County, MO. She married Benjamin Viles Aug. 18, 1880, Polk County, MO. Four children were born to this union.

Josephine "Phenia," born Sept. 10, 1862, Ontonagon County, MI; died March 23, 1933, Polk County, MO; buried Schofield Cemetery, Polk County, MO. She married Wade Gordon Feb. 15, 1882, Polk County, MO. One child was born to this union. She married William Moses Vest Feb. 21, 1891, Polk County, MO. Eight children were born to this couple.

Johann "John," born Aug. 4, 1864, Ontonagon County, MI; died about 1875, Polk County, MO; buried in an unmarked grave in Red Top Cemetery, Dallas County, MO.

Louis Hankey, born March 5, 1868, Missouri; died Jan. 1, 1945, Collin County, TX; buried Princeton Cemetery, Princeton, TX. He married Louise G. Appleton Nov. 24, 1889, Collin County, TX. Three children were born to this union. He married Annie Liz Stephens Nov. 15, 1910, Collin County, TX. Twelve children were born to this couple.

William "Wid," born Nov. 5, 1872, Polk County, MO; died Nov. 26, 1952, Polk County, MO; buried Schofield Cemetery, Polk County, MO. He married Anna Blanche Conley June 12, 1895, Polk County, MO. Ten children were born to this union. This couple lived with his parents. After their deaths, William and Anna continued to live on the homestead.

Mary Ann, born March 25, 1876, Polk County, MO; died Oct. 13, 1949, Polk County, MO; buried Schofield Cemetery, Polk County, MO. She married William Thomas Lambeth Nov. 17, 1895, Dallas County, MO. Eleven children were born to this union. She married Robert O. Percival April 16, 1933, Dallas County, MO.

Rosa Ellen "Rose," born March 24, 1878, Polk County, MO; died Oct. 3, 1962, Springfield, MO; buried Schofield Cemetery, Polk County, MO. She married Mark Isaacks Sept. 5, 1895, Polk County, MO and Benjamin F. Morris Aug. 27, 1899, Polk County, MO. One child was born to each union. *Submitted by Geneva Marie (Hankey) Rudolph*

HARMS - Roy Alvin Harms, born Aug. 2, 1952 in Springfield, MO, was the third of five children born to Daley Linville Harms, born Oct. 14, 1925 in Missouri, and Colleen Moore Arnold Harms Cargill, born May 22, 1926 in Missouri. His siblings are Robert Dale Harms, Paul Laverne Harms, Judith Marie Harms Davis and Lynda Elizabeth Harms Stanley Sterling. His father is a veteran of WWII, serving in the Philippines, and is still actively involved in the VFW, and serves on the burial detail in Sedalia, MO.

The family moved often, with Linville setting up turkey hatcheries with Ralston Purina in Missouri, Arkansas and Ohio. Roy attended several schools growing up and graduated from high school in Vinton County, OH in 1970.

Following graduation, Roy worked for several years on his grandfather's farm in Lincoln, MO and several construction jobs. He saved up enough money to buy a new 1973 Harley-Davidson Sportster for his 21st birthday. His grandfather Gentry Fritz Frank Harms thought this was not a good investment, but felt better when Roy told him that he could sell it at any time and buy six cows with calves.

In 1974, Roy was saved in Bolivar, MO and experienced a life-changing conversion. He attended Central Bible College from 1975 through 1978. He left the spring semester of 1977 to work in the Texas oil fields to pay off his college tuition.

In 1977, Roy and his mother took a trip to Texas trying to locate his brother, Paul. While there he met the pastor at Uvalde Assembly of God, and was introduced to Marsha K. Mooney, who attended the church there. Roy returned to Missouri, and corresponded with Marsha from July 1976 through January 1977. In late January 1977, he loaded his Harley-Davidson and his trunk on a Bolivar Insulation Truck and rode to Bryan, TX. He shipped his trunk to Uvalde by bus, and rode into Uvalde, TX on his bike to court his sweetheart.

Roy and Marsha (Mooney) Harms

Marsha Kaye Mooney Harms, born Oct. 14, 1951, is the eldest daughter of Charles Wesley Mooney, born July 18, 1928 in Texas, and Nellie Ruth Keith Mooney, born June 16, 1930 in Alabama. She was born in Seattle, WA, where her father had been discharged from the US Air Force after serving in the Korean Conflict. Her siblings are Rogerma Suzanne Mooney Boulware and Charles Daniel Mooney. Marsha graduated in 1969 from Tivy High School, Kerrville, TX, and attended Kerrville Business College.

Roy and Marsha were married on June 11, 1977, at the Country Community Church in Kerrville, TX, by Rev. Wes Weston. Roy worked as a derrick hand in the oil fields and Marsha worked for the Texas Department of Health until July 1977, when they moved to Bolivar, MO, so Roy could continue his education at Central Bible College, Springfield, MO.

Two daughters were born to Roy and Marsha Harms, Heidi Kaye Harms (McGinnis), born Sept. 30, 1978 at St. John's Hospital, Springfield, MO, and Heather Suzanne Harms, born March 24, 1981 in Dr. Ruth Rios' Clinic, Bolivar, MO. In October 1978, Roy sold the 1973 Harley-Davidson Sportster to pay the hospital bill for Heidi's birth. Roy assisted in Heather's birth, and since mother had problems, he was handed the tiny baby to clean and wrap while the doctor concentrated on mom.

Heidi and Heather grew up on the family's small farm outside of Cliquot, MO, where the family raised Missouri Fox Trotters and some exotic animals for a time. Both graduated from Bolivar

High School. After the children entered school, Marsha went to work as a legal secretary with the prosecuting attorney's office in Polk County, MO in 1989, and continues to work for the prosecuting attorney in the child support division.

Roy established Harms Tree Service in 1979 and continues to do tree work on a limited basis. He has been actively involved in politics since 1991, serving first as northern commissioner of Polk County and is presently serving as the presiding commissioner of Polk County, following a long line of political service in his family. His great-grandfather John T. Linville and great aunt Amy Linville served many years as the presiding commissioner and county treasurer of Benton County, MO, respectively. Aunt Amy Linville was the first woman elected to serve in public office in Benton County. Roy's aunt, Helen Hyde, served 10 years as county collector of Dallas County, MO.

Roy has been exceedingly blessed and privileged to participate in mission trips in Honduras, El Salvador, Venezuela, and the Los Angeles Dream Center, California. He is an avid hunter and enjoys the great outdoors. *Submitted by Roy Harms*

HARPER – Nelson Harper was born as the first child and only son to Henry Harper and Sally Johnson in 1805, Lincoln County, KY. There are five sisters born later: Malinda, Sally, Susan, Betsy and Matilda. Nelson first appears in the family's obtained records with the registration of a marriage bond with John Garland as the father of Martha Jane Garland, in Warren County, KY in 1834. They were married July 28, 1834 in Warren County, KY. Their children are John Henry, born May 4, 1835; Sarah M., born Aug. 20, 1837; Charles N., born 1840; Mary Elvira, born Feb. 14, 1843; Sidney S., born Feb. 15, 1845; Thomas James, born Jan. 18, 1846; William Bush, born June 20, 1849 and David Joseph, born in 1852.

Sometime after 1852 Nelson takes his family and moves to Missouri. By 1853 Nelson and his family are living in Polk County, MO. On June 12, 1853, Jessie Calvin is the last child to be born. On Aug. 9, 1855 Nelson buys land in Polk County, MO from Levi and Sally Strand. For $400.00 he bought the southwest part of quarter Section 19, Township 32, Range 24, containing 33.88 acres (and other land); these deeds did not list all of the land and the deeds in that part are lacking in particulars.

On Nov. 2, 1861, Martha Jane passed away. As was custom in those times, Nelson decided to bury her on the farm. She is the first person buried in the Harper Cemetery of Polk County, MO. After the death of Martha Jane, Nelson then married Missouri Ann.

As Nelson was a farmer by trade, he did his own black-smithing as most everyone who lived in that time. He raised corn, wheat, barley, cotton and, of course, the family garden. Food was dried in the sun. Both meat and vegetables and roots were kept in a "cave" as they called them. It is called a cellar today. Water was taken out of a hand-dug well with a wooden bucket. Over time the county was split into other counties and part of the farm was then located in both Dade County and Polk County.

Charles Nelson Harper, Potter girl and Mary Elvira Harper

During the Civil War four sons fought. John Henry was in the Sixth Missouri Cavalry, Company D. Charles N. was in the Sixth Missouri Cavalry, Company D. Sidney S. was in the Sixth Missouri Cavalry, Company L. Thomas James was in the 15th Regiment of Missouri Cavalry Volunteers Company C. Of these four boys, two of them died. Sidney died at age 21 years, 4 months and 6 days, from bleeding of the lungs, and Charles N. also died of bleeding of the lungs. There is no date on his stone and both have military headstones in Harper Cemetery, Polk County, MO. Neither one ever married. Nelson Harper passed away May 21, 1879 from pneumonia fever as listed on the Polk County 1880 mortality schedule.

His children with their spouses are John Henry, first married Elizabeth Catherine Neil, second Nancy E. McDaniel; Sarah M. married Huston Chandler; Mary Elvira, first married Leander M. Wheeler, second George Claypool; Thomas James, first married Martha Ann McDaniel, second, Isabell Sanders, third, Nancy Caroline Cheek, fourth, Fannie Prebble; William Bush, first married Mary Jane Malone, second, Jane Donaldson Malone; David Joseph married Nancy Ann Martha Davis; Jessie Calvin never married.

After Nelson's death the children one by one sold their part of the family farm to John Cowan. The family farm had other owners but is now owned by Don McClelland of Aldrich. *Submitted by Verdie T. Harper*

HARRIS – William Jasper Harris was born Aug. 23, 1842 and died Feb. 17, 1913. Henrietta L. Sawyer, his wife, was born Jan. 23, 1851 and died March 15, 1913. William was one of 11 children born in Platte County, MO to Samuel J. and Sophia Harris. Samuel lived 1819-1890; Sophia, 1822-1890.

William and Henrietta has six children: Monroe, born 1867, died 1927 in Duncan, OK. He married Lula Dorothy Henderson. Loren, born 1870, died 1942 and married Nora E. Burton. Dilla, born 1875, died 1957, married Arthur McGee and then James Lucas. Twins, Oliver, born 1881, died 1969, married Carrie Burton; and Olivia, born 1881, died 1939, married Frank McGee. Loren and Oliver married sisters, and Olivia and Dilla married brothers.

William served in the Missouri Infantry Company D, Regiment 35, Aug. 16, 1862 to June 28, 1865. He was discharged in Little Rock, AR. He received a pension of $18.00 per month.

William had bought and sold a lot of land in Arkansas, Oklahoma, New Mexico and Missouri. It is not known how long they lived in Bolivar. They may have moved away and back again. They are buried in Bolivar at the Greenwood Cemetery.

Oliver and Carrie had eight children: Golda Ester (born 1906; died 1935); Everett Raymond (born 1908; died 1984); Eugene Vernon (born 1910; died 1975); Fred David (born 1913; died 1970); Walter Allen (born 1915; died 1997); Della Amberzella (born 1918; died 2001); Flora Mae (born 1920) and Carmel Nadine (born 1926).

Oliver and Carrie moved from Arkansas to Kokomo, IN in 1944.

William was the grandfather of Nadine (Harris) Mittower and Oliver was her father. *Submitted by Nadine Mittower*

HARRIS - In January 1915, Andrew Jackson Harris, a hardware owner and state representative, wife Elizabeth Ann; five sons, Ed, Len, Ben, John, Lowell; four daughters-in-law, Elizabeth "Lizzie," Lola, Maggie, Bertha; a daughter, Nora and nine grandchildren all left Sullivan County in north Missouri by train. Destination: Flemington, in south Missouri. Two daughters, Dora and Sarah, remained in north Missouri.

In a freight train were household goods, farm machinery, wagons, livestock and four sons. A. J. and Ed rode with the women and children in the passenger train. After switching to the Frisco in Kansas City, the passengers soon overtook the freight, which was moved to a siding. Children rushed to the windows shouting "Daddy! Daddy!" Word soon spread that a Mormon family was headed south.

At the Flemington Depot the wagons were unloaded; the farm equipment and most of the furniture and passengers went to the Elkton area. A. J. and three of his sons had bought property there.

One son, Ben and family, and daughter Nora were to live with A. J. After a very short stay, living upstairs, Ben's family moved back to north Missouri (too much togetherness!).

Ed's wife, Lizzie, an independent woman ahead of her time, had decided not to honor A. J.'s dictum that each morning he see the smoke from his son's fires. Ed had arranged for a house in Flemington, too far for A. J. to see their smoke. This pleased Lizzie, but not daughter Norine, who often asked, "Why couldn't you at least have moved to Bolivar?"

After another move to a house where Ruth was born, they bought a house near the school. When Kenton, Ruth's five-year-old brother, was first allowed to see her in bed with her mother, he laid a sweaty crumbled cookie on the pillow with this request, "When he gets through suckin', give him this."

Norine and brother Merrill attended Humansville High School as Flemington schools had only eight grades.

Kenton, youngest son, started to school to Miss Ada McCracken, an extremely popular teacher whom all the kids loved.

Soon, lice appeared in the classroom. Miss Ada, in order not to discriminate, requested that each child's mother comb his head with a fine-tooth comb over a newspaper. When no lice appeared on Kenton's head, he was extremely disappointed. His lament: "But Moma, what will Miss Ada say?"

When Miss Ada decided to leave, the school board was at a loss.

Ed and Lizzie had owned a grocery store in Milan. Ed, also in real estate, had intended to continue in Flemington, but a meeting with the Flemington School Board changed that.

The Board (after checking teachers' exams and records of Ed's and Lizzie's teaching in rural schools in Sullivan County) hired Lizzie to teach the lower four grades and Ed the upper four in the Flemington School.

Lizzie's mother, Electa Van Weye Emberton, came from Green City, MO to keep Ruth. It was a wonderful, warm relationship for the two, but "Grandma" died when Ruth was 4.

Lucy Emberton, Lizzie's sister, from Green City, then came to live with them. This was a really great time for Ruth and Kenton, especially when Aunt Lucy made "East Biscuits."

213

Back left to right: Ed, Ben, Lowell, John and Len; front left to right: Dora, Nora, Elizabeth Ann, Andrew Jackson and Sarah

During this time, when Ruth was 4, she frequently was allowed to go to school on Friday afternoons. To Ruth and a younger boy, Johnny Jones, who also attended, this was a cherished play day.

The students also considered this "time off," although the play was really a learning time. They competed in spelling bees, map games, "ciphering" (at that time rapid solving of math problems at the chalkboard) and other fun learning games. The first one finished was the winner. Ciphering for Johnny and Ruth consisted of rapidly making chalk marks on the board while being timed. The one with the most marks won. Ruth had won several times and Johnny was getting steamed. This last time when Ruth won again, Johnny became enraged, picked up a small pair of scissors and threw them at her. Ruth wasn't hurt but she cried. Johnny ran out the door and down the hill to his home. Ruth was heartbroken as she had a "crush" on him.

The next fall, when Ruth was 5, she started to school to her mother. Kenton was now in his dad's room. The first day of school, Mrs. Harris asked their neighbor, Edison Loy, where he would like to sit. He said, "I'd like to sit with RUKE." They were friends and played together each day at home. That arrangement lasted until Edison marked on Ruth's side of their double desk. She retaliated by squirting lemon juice in his eyes. Immediately, Edison was moved and Ruth was spanked.

Her only other spanking in school (also by her mother) was in second grade. That was a result of her messing up Dee Proper's sandbox architecture. She liked him immediately and he wouldn't pay any attention to her.

A Kansas City reporter, having learned of the Harris family situation (the members, including parents, attending school daily) considered it unusual and published an article in the *Kansas City Star*.

Ruth spent 12 years in the Flemington Schools. For a graduation gift, she was allowed to spend the summer with Merrill in Chicago, IL and Norine in Cleveland, OH, who had come for her graduation.

This was "heavy stuff" for a girl of 17 who had never been farther from home than Jefferson City. She attended the 1934 World's Fair almost daily. She had a "blast" in Cleveland. One highlight was a boat trip on Lake Erie to Cedar Crest Amusement Park. Ruth had ridden one roller coaster in Kansas City. Here there were six or seven...BIG ONES!

Ruth entered STC (later SMSU) in Springfield, MO in the fall of 1934. After graduating she applied for a position at Preston High School in Hickory County, MO and was accepted. Here she met her future husband Selby King, a teacher and sports coach. He later became Preston High School Superintendent. He had taught in rural schools and was attending summer school at STC getting his degree.

Ruth taught at Preston, worked in government offices and became Hickory County Superintendent of Schools. She substituted at Cross Timbers High School (Hickory County) where Selby was teaching. In the fall of 1947, Selby, Ruth, Roscoe and Sada Edde moved to Bolivar, MO where they had bought a Dodge/Plymouth agency.

This was Ruth's first playtime since starting school at age 5. She joined clubs and organizations, and despite gossip that Bolivar natives were clannish and not too fond of newcomers, the Kings found them very friendly and welcoming. They formed friendships that were warm and long-lasting.

While living in Bolivar the Kings were blessed with the arrival of their 1-month-old daughter Elizabeth Ann, who came just in time for Christmas! What a joy!

Elizabeth "Lib" had eight happy years in Bolivar. She had lots of friends, swam, picnicked in Dunnegan Park and enjoyed her adoring grandparents Homer and Grace King of Preston, MO and Ed and Lizzie Harris of Cleveland, OH who visited each summer. Uncles, aunts and cousins were a joy to her. One cousin, Bill Martin of Cleveland, OH, lived with the Kings in Bolivar for his senior year. He and Elizabeth formed a bond that still exists.

Lib attended the first year of school at Wheatland, MO where Selby and Ruth drove each day to teach. Her second and third years were at Mitchell in Bolivar.

Meanwhile, Selby and Mrs. Kellee Murray were commuting to Dadeville High School where both were teaching. In 1960 the Kings moved back to Hickory County. Selby and Ruth had accepted teaching positions in the Hermitage High School, Selby as coach and principal and Ruth as English and French teacher.

Selby spent one term as Hickory County State Representative. The districts were changed, including parts of several counties, and that took care of that. He then went to Weaubleau High School. Ruth joined him there when Lib graduated from Hermitage in 1969.

During Ruth's teaching career she was interested in furthering her education. She took night courses at Drury, an extension course in Adolescent Psychology, N.D.E.A (French) Institute in Coe College at Cedar Rapids, IA, and several summer trips to France, spending as much time as possible at the Sorbourne in Paris.

After 31 years in the county near Preston, they moved back to Bolivar to be near their daughter Lib and her husband Larry Turner, three grandchildren, Mike, Katie and Jenny Lorimore and another granddaughter Ashley Turner (Larry's daughter).

Selby died in 1995. He wasn't privileged to know their beloved great-grandchildren, Jenny's Lyricke Nicole Pierce and Lauryn Grace Lorimore and Katie and Joe Brown's Bailee Ann Brown.

Ruth is now 85 years old and loves living here in Bolivar. She should not like to live any place else. Polk County and Bolivar are great! *Submitted by Elizabeth Ruth Harris King*

John Harvey and Sinthy Grogan Harvey

HARVEY - John Harvey was part Creek Indian. His parents may have died when he was young; he is believed to have lived with a family named Letter. He was a tenant farmer. John was born Oct. 10, 1837 in Tennessee and died April 14, 1910, Morgan Township, Dade County, MO. He married Cynthia "Sinthy" A. Grogan, born April 8, 1836, McMinn County, TN (near Conasauga, GA), died June 1, 1911 in Aldrich, Polk County, MO, daughter of Albert (Allbird) and Mary Grogan of Tennessee, about 1857. The Grogans were Cherokee and possibly Black Dutch.

Their children are listed below.

Hugh L. Harvey was born Aug. 12, 1858 and died July 31, 1860.

William Calvin Harvey was born March 29, 1860, died Sept. 2, 1935 and married Harriet Berlier, born Oct. 6, 1858 and died November 1942.

Emily Emma Harvey was born Oct. 12, 1862, died April 3, 1939 and married Jasper Newton O'Neal on Aug. 16, 1882, born June 28, 1836, died Dec. 12, 1916.

Sarah Frances Harvey was born Oct. 17, 1862, died June 1932 and married Thomas Wilson DePew on Aug. 5, 1881, born April 8, 1863, died May 23, 1935.

Woodford "Wood" Harvey was born Oct. 8, 1863, Polk or Dade County, MO, died May 13, 1950, Seminole, Seminole County, OK, and married Theodosia "Doshey Jane" Smith July 29, 1891 by A. J. Griffin in Polk County, MO, born May 28, 1874, Bolivar, Polk County, MO, died Feb. 23, 1943, Seminole, Seminole County, OK.

Albert Harvey was born Oct. 1, 1864 and married Delia Eden.

Mary Elizabeth Harvey was born April 13, 1869, died June 13, 1961 and married Rufus Asbury Griffin, born April 13, 1868 and died June 16, 1961.

John Leonard Harvey was born Jan. 11, 1871 and married Minnie Depee on Sept. 27, 1901, born Dec. 2, 1879 and died Sept. 6, 1927.

Henry Alonzo Harvey was born Jan. 11, 1871 and died Oct. 20, 1907 and married Almina Painter on Aug. 2, 1895, born 1880 and died Oct. 17, 1910.

Minnie A. Harvey was born 1876 and married John Alexander Ferguson, born May 30, 1877 and died Jan. 17, 1949. *Submitted by Debra Clark*

HARVEY - William H. Harvey arrived in Polk County, MO in the fall of 1853. He was widowed with two children. William was born in 1827 in Wythe County, VA to Allen and Phebe Harvey. Allen was from England and Phebe was born in North Carolina. William had three brothers and three sisters. His sisters were Phebe, Elizabeth and Lavina. He married Sarah Dethrage in Meigs County, TN July 15, 1848. Lavina, born Meigs County, 1849, John, born August 1853 in Arkansas, were his children. William married Rebecca Syrena Griffith Nov. 20, 1854 in Bolivar, MO. Rebecca, born in 1831 in North Carolina, was the daughter of Amanda Cooneater, a Cherokee from Georgia. Children born to this marriage were Artismisa Elizabeth, born Sept. 11, 1855, Phebe Jane and David Alvin, born Aug. 8, 1860. The family farmed 80 acres in Jackson Township, Section 33, Township 33, Range 23.

William H. Harvey was inducted into Company C, Fifth Regiment, Missouri Infantry, Confederate Army, on Jan. 26, 1862. He fought and was taken prisoner in the Battle of Pea Ridge, March 8, 1862. He was exchanged May 17, after contracting the mumps. He was discharged with a disability Aug. 31, 1862. He was shot on the way home at Leadhill, Boone County, AR. He had spent the night in a cabin and had gone to the creek for water when he was killed. Rebecca moved the children to rural Humansville, to be closer to relatives.

Artismisa Elizabeth Harvey Harris

Artismisa Elizabeth, born Sept. 11, 1855, married Joseph Barber Harris Nov. 7, 1871. They met while he was on a cattle drive from Texas to Sedalia, MO. His parents were Dr. Charles William and Mary Barber Harris. Charles was born in New Jersey in 1807 and Mary Barber was born in Maryland.

Charles' mother was from Alsac-Lorraine, Germany. Joseph B. was born April 29, 1841 in Dubuque, IA. The family moved to Texas while he was young. He was inducted into Company C, 11 Texas Calvary. He was captured March 8, 1864 in Lincoln County, TN at the Battle of Shiloh. He was discharged April 22, 1864. Children born to Artismisa Elizabeth and Joseph B. were Mary, Maud, Sarah, Kate and twins who died at birth. The family returned to Polk County in the spring of 1890. Here, Loy W., Charles William and Edith Odessa were born. Loy W. and Charles W. joined the US Army during WWI.

Sarah, born Jan. 21, 1878, was working at a hotel in Joplin, MO when she met and married Johnathan Joseph Norman Jones on June 4, 1904. John Joseph was born Sept. 5, 1887 in Madison County, AR to Lewis Gumm and Cynthia Adeline Dotson Jones. John Joseph was working and studying to be an electrician. Their children were Elva Eleanor and Norma Faye. John moved the family to her parents' farm where Sarah died of consumption Dec. 12, 1912.

Standing: Sarah Harris Jones and Elva Eleanor Jones; Sitting: Johnathan Joseph Norman Jones on lap, Norma Faye Jones

Great-Great-Grandma Rebecca would teach the grandchildren and great-grandchildren the Cherokee language. They would name the food on their plate in Cherokee before eating. She would line the children up on the hearth and have them practice words in Cherokee. She always sat in a rocker by the fireplace. She was ill and the doctor came by every day to see her. Great-Great-Grandma Rebecca is buried in the Longrun Cemetery, Longrun, MO next to her second husband, Cyrus Patterson.

Elva Eleanor Jones, born May 9, 1905, married John Huey Griggs Jr. April 15, 1922 in Kansas City, MO. He was born Aug. 12, 1882 in Chillicothe, MO to John Huey Sr. from Scotland and Mary Jane Minor Scott Griggs from New York.

Children were John Huey III, Charles Richard, Carl Luther, Mary Eleanor, Donald Merle, Elva Cornelia Lorraine, Jerry Allen, Larry Jerome, Dolly La Verne and James Leonard. The family traveled to Kansas, Oklahoma, Colorado, Arkansas and back to Missouri. John worked in the oil fields and farmed. This covers one line of the family from 1800 to 1941. Part of the second and third generation went to school and farmed in Polk County, MO. The family has reached all parts of the mid-west. *Submitted by Elva Cornelia Lorraine Beltz*

David Alvin Harvey

HAWKINS - Keathley "Keith" Hawkins was born about 1807 in South Carolina or Tennessee and died 1862 in Missouri, somewhere in the vicinity of Springfield. He married Rachel Goodnight May 8, 1832 in Montgomery County, IL. Rachel was born Jan. 26, 1811 in Giles County, TN and died on Sept. 29, 1896 in Wishart, Polk County, MO and buried in Enon Cemetery. She was the daughter of John H. and Mary Margaret "Peggy" (Condor) Goodnight.

Keith and Rachel were Modell's second great-grandparents. They moved from Illinois to Barry County, now Christian County, MO in about 1842. They had six children. The first three were born in Illinois and the last three were born in Missouri. They were John Goodnight, Nancy Rachel, Mary Ann, Margaret "Peggy," Amanda C. and Henry Harmon. A lot of Keith and Rachel's descendants are buried in Enon Cemetery in Polk County.

Modell descends through John Goodnight Hawkins and his wife Charlotte M. (Banks) Hawkin, then through their son, Thomas H. Hawkins and his wife, Nettie Ann (Dixon) Hawkins and Thomas and Nettie Ann's oldest son, John Sherman Hawkins and his wife Margaret Elizabeth (Lynn).

John G. was born in Williamson County, IL in 1833 and died Oct. 31, 1887 in Caddo, Blue County, OK. He married Charlotte M. Banks March 4, 1885 in Capris, Newton County, MO. Charlotte was born Sept. 22, 1837 in Missouri and died Feb. 22, 1905 in Dodge, Walker County, TX. She is buried in Shockley Chapel Cemetery outside of Dodge, TX. They had at least eight children. Six lived to be adults.

Charlotte was the daughter of Moses and Charlotte (Grindstaff) Banks who moved from Tennessee in about 1835 to Van Buren, Newton County, MO.

All the other children of Keith and Rachel Hawkins lived in Polk County, MO, except Nancy and her husband, Andrew Jackson Daniel. They lived in Kansas, Arkansas and then back to Missouri.

Henry Harmon Hawkins, Keith and Rachel's youngest child lived most of his life in Polk County and raised a large family there. He died May 23, 1929 in Wishart and is buried in Enon Cemetery, Polk County, MO with his two wives, Lucinda (Sawyers) Hawkins, died 1879, and Sarah Elizabeth (Hook) Hawkins, 1867-1909, and at least six of his children and also grandchildren. He was married to Sarah Elizabeth Hook in 1882 in Polk County, MO. There are many Hawkins descendants still living in and around Polk County, MO. *Submitted by Modell Hawkins Whiteley*

HAYES - Shawn Hayes was born April 29, 1972 in Oklahoma. In 1995 he moved to Polk County. He was attending Central Bible College and serving as Brighton Highway Assemblies youth pastor. Members of the church introduced Shawn to Alysia Whiteley and they immediately fell in love.

Alysia was born June 20, 1978 to Terry and Sherry Whiteley. Her parents settled in Brighton in 1976. Terry started W-Bar-Y Fence Company in 1978. Sherry was a homemaker and mother to Alysia and Josh. Josh was born June 1, 1981. Alysia graduated in 1996 and Josh graduated in 1999 from Marion C. Early.

In 1996 Shawn graduated from Central Bible College. He and Alysia took a children's pastor position at Glad Tidings in Springfield. They were married in December of 1998 and moved to Bolivar. Alysia attended Evangel University for three years in pursuit of a degree in special education. After the arrival of their first child Emory, born Nov. 28, 1999, she chose to put her degree on hold and stay at home with her son. Shawn managed the One-Hour Photo at the Bolivar Wal-Mart for four years. In March of 2002, he became an agent for Farm Bureau Insurance at the Bolivar office.

Church is a big part of their life. They have been serving as youth sponsors at Brighton Highway Assembly since 1999. In 2002 Shawn and Alysia started The Full Life Learning Center, a tutoring program at the church. Alysia volunteers as the center's director and enjoys raising their two children. She stays at home with Emory and their daughter Adelyn, born on Nov. 30, 2001. Their future plans include building

Alysia and Shawn Hayes

their home in Brighton where their children will attend Marion C. Early. *Submitted by Shawn and Alysia Hayes*

HAYTER - William Hayter II, a veteran of the War of 1812, was the father of William, Thomas, Bud, John Jamerson, Job, Mitch, Louisa, Armilda and one other daughter who married a Langford. We think John Jamerson, Job, Mitch and the daughters with their dad came to Polk County in about 1850. They came from East Tennessee in a covered wagon. Two of the three sons that came to Missouri fought for the Union in the Civil War. John Jamerson was too old. The other three sons fought for the South. The Hayters settled on pre-empted land in the southwest corner of Polk near Walnut Grove and near Eudora.

John Jamerson Hayter, who lived near the Walnut Grove area, donated land to the Presbyterian church for the Oak Grove Church in the 1850s and it is one of the oldest Presbyterian churches in the area. Many members of the Hayter family are buried in the cemetery next to the church.

In 1952, there was a Centennial Celebration for the Hayter family. The land near Walnut Grove stayed in the family until the 1980s. It was also noted that the Hayter family celebrated at least a 200-year anniversary since their arrival in the States from the British Isles. John Jamerson Hayter's son Menan and wife Sarah Wheeler Hayter lived on the farm and then their sons Alvin and James Oren Hayter located there. James Oren Hayter lived with his son Albert Oren on the farm until the late 1950s. He then moved to his daughter's home in Lockwood, MO. He lived to be almost 100. The land stayed in the Hayter family until the 1980s. There are still members of the Hayter family living in Polk County. *Submitted by Kay Bird Sewell*

HAZARD - Joel Morris Hazard was born Aug. 17, 1817 in Kentucky. He moved to Polk County before July 12, 1883, where he owned 160 acres east of the Pomme De Terre near Rondo. He rests (Nov. 10, 1896) in the Bolivar City Cemetery. Born in Tennessee in 1834, Adaline (Daniels) rests (March 2, 1916) in the Humansville Cemetery across the highway from the house she lived in with her son Eli. She was a widow (Duncan) when she became Joel's third wife on Aug. 17, 1871. John Jackson Deaver was born Dec. 4, 1853 in Tennessee and moved to Mansfield, MO in 1880 and to Humansville some 10 years later. J. J. Deaver's front-page obituary in the *Star-Leader* carried the headline, "J. J. Deaver, Pioneer Citizen Passes On." He died Nov. 3, 1934, preceded by Emma (Wheat), his wife of nearly 60 years, on Feb. 26, 1934. They rest in the Humansville Cemetery. Alexander Jackson Butler was born in Tennessee on March 5, 1833 and owned 167.75 acres east of Rondo, bisected by the Pomme De Terre, as of April 16, 1870. Unfortunately, there is no record of where A. J. Butler (June 7, 1913, Ottawa, KS) and his wife Nancy (1885, Rondo) are buried, perhaps on the land he once owned.

Jack Hazard (right) great-grandson and Wayne Hazard (left) great-great-grandson to Joel Morris Hazard

Eli Samson Hazard was born Jan. 20, 1875 in Vichey, MO. Etta Viola Butler was born April 2, 1877 near Rondo. They married Aug. 2, 1902, living on the Butler Farm before moving to Humansville where Eli set up a jewelry and watch repair shop in the Hubble Drug Company store. Oral O. "Speck" Deaver was born Jan. 25, 1894 in Humansville. Hazel Courtner was born Feb. 15, 1898 and moved to Humansville prior to her marriage to Speck, in May of 1915. Hazel's parents, Lawrence and Almyra, and sister Bernice Mottesheard, rest in the Humansville Cemetery. Oral was likely known as "Speck" due to his freckles, one attribute of his Irish heritage. He was also known for frequent brawls with his brother, Pete (Clarence). An item in the *Star-Leader* on May 23, 1935 reads, "Night Police, O. O. Deaver landed two drunks in the jail Sunday night. They did not want to go, but there is no use in fooling with Mr. Deaver when he makes up his mind. Humansville is troubled very little with drunks or disorderly conduct." A 1935 expense report indicated he made $30 a month as Night Watch. Oral (Sept. 7, 1956) and Hazel (Sept. 9, 1941) rest in the Humansville Cemetery.

Clifford Scott Hazard was born Dec. 23, 1910 in Humansville and had two older siblings, Arthur and Vivian. Around 1918, the family moved to Texas in an unsuccessful attempt to save his mother from tuberculosis. Lorraine Deaver was born March 28, 1916 in Humansville and, like her younger brother Loren, graduated from Humansville High. She was social editor of the *Star-Leader*, prior to becoming a student nurse at Dimmitt Memorial Hospital. She met Clifford, who was visiting Dr. A. J. Stufflebam while on a trip up from Texas, and began a courtship on one of the hospital porches. Shortly thereafter, she moved to Kansas City with her parents, married Clifford in December of 1938, moving to Texas with him. They migrated to Tucson, AZ for her health, following WWII and Lorraine (July 18, 1979) and Clifford (December 30, 1997) rest there today. They are survived by a son, Clifford Jackson Hazard, of Helena, MT; grandson Clifford Wayne Hazard of Poulsbo, WA; granddaughter Geri LaRoy Borseth and great-granddaughter Jackie Lorraine Borseth, both of Absarokee, MT. *Submitted by: Wayne Hazard*

HEADY - Every family has in its past mysteries that seem to defy solutions. In Paul's family, the most intractable concerns Eli Heady. Born in Sullivan County, IN on Jan. 3, 1828, he married Martha E. Driver there in 1849 and had two sons, William Jefferson and James E. Martha died in 1852 and there is a possibility that Eli married a woman by the name of Rosannah Van Meter in 1853. What is known for sure is that Eli turns up in southern Missouri with only William Jefferson and marries Mary Ann "Polly" Presley, April 11, 1833 to Dec. 8, 1910, in Greene County on Jan. 26, 1857. Polly and her family appear to have been fairly recent residents of the area as they are recorded in the 1850 census for Monroe County, TN. Unlike Eli, who had no known family living in the area, Polly came with, at least, her father and five brothers. The numerous Presleys interred in Hickory Grove and Brighton Cemeteries will attest to this family's presence in the area. What had happened to Miss

Eli Heady 1828-1909 circa 1863

Van Meter and James E. is another mystery.

Eli and Polly raised a family of eight children: Richard, Joshua Bonepart, Thomas S., Martha Ellen, Mary Elizabeth, John Miller, Eli "Dutch" and Charles. Two of the boys married daughters of Charles H. and Mary Jane Parcels Berlew. Richard was married to Martha Ann (1862-1952) on March 4, 1880 and Joshua Bonepart married Almirah Elizabeth (1860-1929) on Oct. 2, 1879. Joshua and Almirah later separated and Joshua went to Arkansas and then Indian Territory where his life as a US Marshal and other activities needs a great novelist's skills to fully recapture. Richard and Martha Ann lived in Polk County, raising their six children: Alba, Birdi, Loarn, Porter, Amy and Charles.

The Berlews were from Ohio and came to Polk County around 1870. Martha Ann's obituary says, "At the age of eight years her father started with his family consisting of three sisters, a brother and mother to bring them to what was at that time considered the West. They followed an old wagon trail and while en route here one sister sickened and died and was buried beside the trail." The family's tragedies weren't over, unfortunately. As recorded in the newspapers of the time, two of the girls of Hiram Berlew, Lida "Libbie" and Mary "Mollie" were drowned in the Dry Sac River on Jan. 1, 1892 while returning from a trip to Springfield. The *Springfield Daily Democrat* for Jan. 5, 1892 gives the tragedy an air of mystery.

Speaking of mysteries, we are back to Eli. He died on Nov. 26, 1909 and he and Polly, along with their grandson, Claudie, are buried in Hickory Grove Cemetery. The Headys of Indiana are an exhaustively researched group but where Eli fits seems to be his own affair and we can only continue to puzzle. *Submitted by Paul Coats*

HEBBERT - The Charles R. Hebbert family became Missourians in 1919 when they arrived by train with their household belongings, furniture, tools, machinery and farm animals. Charles, his wife, Jessie and daughter, Josephine, had left their homestead ranch in Sheridan County, WY. He, with his father and a brother, had been part of the "westward movement and settlement" during late 1800s and early 1900s. The end of WWI had prevented his scheduled military service.

At the end of their train ride to Flemington, they were looking to buy a farm. It was located in gradual hills and hollows about nine miles north, northeast of Bolivar; and about five miles southwest of "Polk Town," their postal address. Starting with 80 acres, "Green Mound Farm" eventually grew to 120 and finally to 220 acres, some of which was timber.

The modest frame house with wood stoves, no electricity or phone, a drilled well with rope pulley and bucket (later a hand pump), a rain barrel for soft water, provided shelter and necessities for several years. Some of the furniture, including a piano, velvet divan, bedroom set, dining table and chairs and a mahogany stand table were given to Jessie by her grandmother with whom she had lived in Ohio. (Charles had met them in McComb while he was attending Otterbein College in Westerville, OH.)

Necessary work on the farm was endless for one man and a team of horses; plowing and planting fields, making hay, planting a vegetable garden, truck patch and fruit trees, cutting trees for firewood and to enlarge fields and pasture, removing tree stumps by digging, dynamiting, burning, pulling with tackle, (and cussing the tough ones), and always oak and persimmon sprouts to cut. One man and a team of horses were ready to rest when opportunity came! Most of the hay and grain were consumed on the farm by horses, cattle, pigs and chickens. For cash income, some cattle, milk, eggs and firewood were sold.

Two sons were born: Frank Mondell in 1920 and Paul Donald in 1923. As the children grew to school age, the Green Mound Elementary Schoolhouse across the road from the farm was convenient. Attending high school necessitated walking a mile to catch a school bus and then riding for an hour; what fun! Christmas programs, pie and box suppers, music parties, etc., provided community entertainment and many local people participated.

Charles Raymond, Jessie Mae, Frank, Paul D. (baby), and Josephine Mondell 1924

When the "Big Depression" came, the farm was paid for and Dad Hebbert had money in the bank (also a good buggy with the back compartment large enough to seat two small boys), then the bank closed, never to re-open. Yet, without a dime from the prevailing relief programs, Green Mound Farm and its residents survived. Through the years, the old farmhouse was remodeled and enlarged, a large barn built, and finally the wagons, buggies, and horses were replaced by autos and a tractor. Charles and Jessie stayed on the farm until they closed the house and moved to their cottage on W. Broadway in Bolivar in 1964.

The children grew, acquired an education, found jobs and occupations, were married, reared families, and now Josephine and Mondell and their children live from coast to coast, and Paul and his family remain in Bolivar and Springfield, MO.

Those who knew Charles and Jessie Hebbert well, remember them as friendly, patriotic, righteous, helpful people who, after about 90 years, occupied their final campground in the Greenwood Cemetery in Bolivar, Polk County, MO. *Submitted by Paul Hebbert*

HEINMAN - Ralph William Heinman was born Dec. 26, 1946, the youngest child of three. He and his sisters, Voila Mae Conner of Independence, deceased 1988 and Frances "Dutch" Oldham of Odessa, were the children of Ralph Frances Heinman, deceased 1984 and Violet Lola Leaton, deceased 1965, in Independence, Jackson County, MO. June 1, 1968 he married Sandra Nadine Nash, born Sept. 21, 1948, the youngest child of Wilbur W. Nash deceased 1991 and Gladys G. (Painter) Nash, deceased 2001, in Kansas City, MO. They lived in Independence, MO and had two children, Shelly Marie Heinman, born March 24, 1969 and Johnny Mack Heinman, born May 1, 1972, both born in Kansas City, MO hospitals while living in Independence, MO. They lived in Independence, MO until about 1985 when they moved to Bates City, MO and lived there about 10 years, then moved to Oak Grove, MO, where they ran an antique and flea market for two years. In about 1997 they moved to Flemington, MO to live on Pomme De Terre Lake. Ralph, best known as "Butch" to his friends and family, worked for Armco Steel which later changed to GST Steel for 34 years until he retired in September 2000. Sandra, also known as "Sandy," worked at several different jobs in her life from real estate, cashing, Citizen's Memorial Hospital to owning her own business.

In January 2002 they opened their second antique and flea market shop in Stockton, MO and now run it with their children and grandchildren. The family spends a lot of time together.

Shelly Marie (Heinman) Woodward now lives in Bolivar, MO and has three girls, Nicole Rachelle Woodward, born April 12, 1988, Kristina Lynn Woodward, born March 21, 1990 and Lindsey Kay Boyd, born May 16, 1992.

Johnny Mack Heinman now lives in Flemington, MO and has three children, Meranda J. Heinman, born July 14, 1993, Cody Mack Heinman, born Feb. 16, 1995 and Dakota Dane Heinman, born July 29, 1998. All the grandchildren were born in the Independence and Lee's Summit, MO area. *Submitted by Sandy Heinman*

HEMBREE - It is February of 1834 when Alexander Brown decides to leave Tennessee and travel westward. He and a group of others make the trek, stopping just outside of St. Louis in Illinois for the winter. When the Mississippi River could be crossed, they again set out. They traveled towards the southwest and ended up in the most beautiful place Alexander Brown had ever seen, Brighton, MO.

Alexander was Melanie's sixth great-grandfather. His descendants started the Fender Chapel Church near Brighton. He died on Oct. 12, 1837, on the west side of the Little Sac River. He always wanted to be buried on the highest spot opposite the river since the day he arrived in Brighton. His wish was fulfilled, and he was the first person to be buried in what is now known as Brock Cemetery. Many other descendants are buried in Hickory Grove and Brighton Cemetery.

Alexander Brown was married to his wife Violet on Feb. 25, 1797 in Tennessee. Ten children were born to them: Thomas, Anne, Elizabeth, Sarah, Dicie, Isham, Zachariah, John, Valetta and Susan.

Alexander and Violet's second oldest son, Isham Alexander Brown, was married to Matilda Tindall of Alabama. To this union 10 children were born: Daniel B., Susan S., Isiah, William Marion, Elizah, John Thomas, Robert, Isom Alexander, Benjamin Franklin and James Henry. Isham and Matilda are Melanie's fifth great-grandparents. Many of Isham Brown's descendants still reside here in Polk County.

Isham and Matilda's second eldest son, William Marion, was united in marriage to Lucinda Floy Swadley on March 11, 1855 in Greene County, MO. They have five direct descendants: David Asbury, Samas James, Mary "Polly" Ann, William Lemman and Margaret Elizabeth. Melanie's third great-grandmother was their

William A. and Clara Johnston

daughter Polly.

Polly was married on March 4, 1877 to Laffayette "Fate" Baldwin. When Grandpa Baldwin died in 1899, Grandma Polly later married Abraham Medsker. Polly and Fate had eight children. Fate died before the birth of his second son, born less than a month later. Lucinda Ann, Melissa Arabell, Amanda Catherine, Etta Mae, Francis Marion, Sarah Marah, Myrtle Emmerline and William Henry were their children.

Melanie's great-great-grandmother was Etta Mae Baldwin. She was married to Fred Hembree in the early 1900s. Together they raised eight children: Clara Mae, Raymond, Grace, Mary, Floyd, the twins Dessie and Ressie, and the youngest son who still survives, Roy Lee.

Melanie's great-grandmother was Clara, and she was married to William Avery Johnston on April 20, 1922. They had 10 children before he passed in 1946: Margaret Marie, Oscar Lee, Calvin Coolidge, Lou Etta, Thomas Junior, Billy Joe, Monroe, Anna Mae, Gilbert Edward and Dortha Faye.

Monroe is Melanie's grandfather. He and Elvena Johnson were married June 3, 1957. They have two daughters, Loretta Marie and Tammy Sue. Melanie is Tammy's daughter. Melanie is the ninth generation to call Polk County, MO home, and her cousin Jennifer's daughter Emily Lynn Drake is now the tenth generation to be here. *Submitted by Melanie A. Strong*

HENDRICKSON – Virgil Clarence Hendrickson, second son of Fred (born April 30, 1893; died May 8, 1971) and Leola (Graham) (born May 6, 1899; died June 12, 1952) Hendrickson, was born on May 11, 1920 in a log home south of Bolivar.

Front: Dorothy, Fred, Leola and Evelyn; Back: Harold, Clark and Virgil, 1945

Paternal grandparents were William (born Aug. 26, 1846; died July 24, 1923) and Lovy (born Feb. 17, 1853; died Aug. 24, 1936) (Roberts) Hendrickson; maternal grandparents were Billy (born Nov. 11, 1876; died Aug. 29, 1951) and Stella (born Dec. 22, 1879; died Jan. 17, 1933) (Kerns) Graham. Virgil had two brothers, Clark (born Aug. 16, 1918; died Aug. 9, 1987) who married Carolyn Roberts in 1943 and had three children: Martha, Don and Ray; and Harold (born Aug. 22, 1924) who married Ann Walker in 1946 and had four children: Elizabeth, Jeannie, Richard and Robert. Virgil also had two sisters, Evelyn (born March 18, 1922) who married Arlie Bacon in 1940 and had three children: Kenneth, Verle and Debbie; and Dorothy (born Jan. 23, 1927) who married Glen Bennett in 1946 and had three children: Dale, Doyle and Fred.

Virgil grew up on the Hendrickson homestead, attended Bolivar schools and graduated from high school in 1940. Following graduation, he worked on the farm until joining the Air Force in 1941, serving his country during WWII until 1945. On Feb. 17, 1946, Virgil married Frances J. Wilson (born Jan. 19, 1928). Her parents were Frank (born Dec. 17, 1889; died January 1959) and Annis (Flint) (born June 23, 1891; died March 11, 1981) Wilson. Her grandparents were Mortimer and Mary (Robertson) Wilson and Samuel and Frances (Hudson) Flint. She had two siblings, Veda (born Dec. 31, 1914; died May 3, 1982) and Raymond (born Feb. 27, 1931; died May 6, 1993). Veda married Lee Griffin in 1937 and they had a daughter, Mary Annalene "Babe." Raymond married MaryLou Kirby and they had three children: Mike, Sherry and Marsha. After divorcing, Raymond later married Joan Seiner in 1967.

Virgil's mother, Leola, passed away in 1952 from a heart attack. Fred later married Florence

Vickery, but that didn't last long. In 1961, Fred married Irma Gallivan. He passed away on May 8, 1971. Virgil owned and operated a farm south of Bolivar most of his life and worked for the Bolivar School System from September 1967 until May 1985. Frances also worked for Bolivar Schools from August 1955 until September 1990. They moved to town in 1976, but still farmed. Their only child, Ronald Kent, was born July 23, 1948. Ron helped his dad on the farm, attended school in Bolivar, graduated from high school in 1966 and married Marilyn Kay Korth of Liberty, MO on May 15, 1971. From that day on Virgil always wanted to know when he was going to be a grandpa. Four years later he got his wish, Kristi Kay was born April 17, 1975, then grandson Derek Kent arrived seven years later on June 26, 1982. He was so proud of his grandchildren, and they loved their "Pop" and "Gram." Derek followed his Pop everywhere and was "taught" to drive on the farm at an early age. Virgil loved children, which was probably one of the reasons he worked at the elementary school. He was always doing or fixing something for someone. Virgil enjoyed life and was a generous giver. He had a stroke in October 1991 and was partially paralyzed. Frances lovingly cared for him at home until it was physically impossible. He was moved to a nursing home in December 1997 and passed away on July 22, 1998. A wonderful person went to his heavenly home. *Submitted by Frances Hendrickson*

HENDRICKSON – Ronald Kent Hendrickson, only son of Virgil C. (born May 11, 1920; died July 22, 1998) and Frances J. (Wilson) (born Jan. 19, 1928) Hendrickson, was born on July 23, 1948 in Humansville, MO. Paternal great-grandparents

Back: Derek, Ron and Marilyn Hendrickson holding Bailey Proctor; Kristi and Jamie Proctor on right

were William and Lovey (Roberts) Hendrickson and Billy and Stella (Kerns) Graham; grandparents were Fred (born April 30, 1893; died May 8, 1971) and Leola (Graham) (born May 6, 1899; died June 12, 1952) Hendrickson. Maternal great-grandparents were Mortimer and Mary (Robertson) Wilson and Samuel and Frances (Hudson) Flint; grandparents were Frank (born Dec. 17, 1889; died January 1959) and Annis (Flint) (born June 23, 1891; died March 11, 1981) Wilson.

Ron grew up on a farm south of Bolivar, attended Bolivar Schools and graduated from high school in 1966. He moved to Kansas City, MO after graduation, took some drafting courses and worked at Simmons Mattress Company. In July 1968 he met future wife, Marilyn Kay Korth of Liberty, MO. Ron was drafted into the Marine Corps in 1969, spent a year in the states and a year of active duty in the Philippines during the Vietnam War. Ron and Marilyn were married on May 15, 1971; lived in Raytown, MO and worked in Kansas City until April 1974, when they moved to Bolivar. Ron operated a backhoe for Dee Aspey and Brooks Kaudle and helped his father on the farm; Marilyn worked for the Bolivar School System. On April 17, 1975, daughter Kristi Kay was born. Ron went to work for Stewart Concrete in Halfway, MO in 1976. Son Derek Kent was born on June 26, 1982.

When Estal and Bonnie Stewart decided to retire, Ron and Marilyn purchased Stewart Concrete Products from them in January 1989. In 1994 more land was purchased in Halfway, the business was expanded and a new office/warehouse was built.

Kristi graduated from Bolivar High School in 1993, from Drury College in 1997 and married Jamie Proctor of Dunnegan in July 1997. They lived in Dunnegan for a while before moving to Halfway. On April 26, 2001, Bailey Michelle Proctor was born. Kristie and Jamie own Bulldog Concrete.

Kristi, Derek, Marilyn, Ron, Virgil and Frances Hendrickson

Derek grew up helping on the farm, graduated from Bolivar High School in 2001, attends Ozark Technical College, works in Springfield, and received the American Farmer Degree. After being diagnosed with terminal cancer in December 2000, Ron was advised to get his affairs in order. Stewart Concrete Products, Inc., with offices in Halfway, Lincoln, Nevada and Spokane, MO sold in June 2001.

Ron left this early world much too early on April 11, 2002, after a courageous and valiant battle with stomach cancer. He was preceded in death by his father, Virgil, on July 22, 1998.

Ron was a wonderful husband, father, son, "Papa," friend and businessman. He was big, tough, kind, gentle, handsome, generous, quick-witted, fun loving, slow to anger, fair, hard-working, funny and always ready and willing to help anyone in need. Ron loved his family and provided well for them. He also loved and believed in God, life, and his country and never met a stranger. He was a generous giver and supporter of various groups, individuals and organizations. Ron was a member of Bolivar United Methodist Church, Halfway Lions Club, previously a Jaycee, stockholder of a Bolivar Bank and on several business and community boards. He also farmed and had land in Hickory and Polk Counties. Ron always thought he was so lucky and so blessed, and he was! *Submitted by Marilyn Hendrickson*

HENRY – Jackson Bazeman Henry was born Aug. 12, 1830 in Harrison County, KY. He lived in Ulyssis, KS where he had a clothing store. He died June 30, 1903 and is buried in Alder Cemetery. His children were William Thomas (born Oct. 7, 1863; died Jan. 28, 1933); George Leonard (born Oct. 26, 1885) and Charlie (born 1873).

William Thomas Henry married Lelia Bell Martin (born July 6, 1888; died Nov. 13, 1976). Their children were John Thomas (born Dec. 6, 1910; died Dec. 17, 1910); Beulah Fern (born May 2, 1912; died Oct. 18, 1987); Glen Art (born Oct. 1, 1914; died March 14, 1985); Nina Irene (born April 17, 1917; died Oct. 1, 1986); Guy Elton (born March 1, 1920); Velma B. (born May 7, 1924) and Charles Edwin (born June 12, 1928; died May 1, 1973).

Darlene's grandfather William Thomas Henry owned a grocery store in Centerville, west of Humansville, MO in the 1930s.

Beulah Fern married Hubert Reed and had a daughter Yvonnia Charlene (born July 29, 1929; died July 21, 2002).

Glen Art married Florene Brown and they had a son Monty Lee Henry (born Sept. 20, 1937; died July 25, 1997). He also married Juanita Pickering and they had four daughters: Linda Lou, Shirley Sue, Glenda Kay and Janice Fay.

Nina Irene married Calvin Purtle. Guy Elton married Joyce and had one daughter Lora Ellen.

Velma B. married Fredrick Martin Latiker on May 9, 1941. Fredrick was born March 22, 1918 and died Dec. 23, 1971. Their children are Fredrick Leon, Brenda Darlene and Jackie Darrell. *Submitted by Velma Hudson*

HENSLEY - According to the 1889 History of Polk County, Benjamin Hensley and family came to Polk County about 1840 and, it is believed, settled in the Shady Grove area. His wife, Ann, born 1807 in Tennessee, died late in 1850. There were several children, including William, born about 1816; Catharine, born about 1818; John B., born Oct. 19, 1819, and James Monroe, born Jan. 27, 1822; all believed to have been born in North or South Carolina. Barnett, born in 1827 and Keyiah and Matilda J. (twins) were born in 1832 and are believed to have been born in Tennessee. Martha J. was born in 1843 and Benjamin Alexander was born Sept. 26, 1848; both were born in Polk County, MO.

The children's marriages were, as follows: William Hensley married Nancy Willis and Catharine is believed to have never married. John B. married Temperance Davis on Aug. 4, 1844 in Polk County, MO and James M. married Francis Jane Brown on April 6, 1843 in Polk County, MO. Barnett married Margaret Potts on March 12, 1848 and Keyiah married John W. Kennon on Dec. 5, 1861. No records were found of Matilda marrying and Martha J. is not mentioned after the 1850 census.

Benjamin moved to Cedar County about 1854 and married Mildred Keeling on May 16, 1858. They had one child, Levi D. in 1860. No further record has been located of this child other than on the 1860 Cedar County census. Benjamin is believed to have died in Cedar County in 1861 or 1862. No record of where he was buried has been found. Mildred died on Aug. 12, 1883 and was buried in Looney Township but the cemetery was not recorded.

Benjamin Alexander Hensley married Mary Jane Wilson on Oct. 19, 1871 in Polk County, MO. To this union were born 12 children; their names were as follows: Elizabeth, who married Thomas Robson; George Monroe, who married Pearl Booth and after her death he married Martha E. Loveless; Mary Octavy, who married Edward

Benjamin A. Hensley and family

Daughtery and after his death she married Thomas Robson; Thomas Mayberry married Iva Keeling; Stacy Alexander married Bessie Smith; Sarah Jettie married Steven Simmons; Ulla A. married Ollie Hammer; Isom Melvin married Inez Ross; Anna Keziah married James Jones; Clara Ethel married William Jones; Bonnie Washington married Mamie Helm; and Roy Austin married Beulah Glenn. All of the children were born in Polk County, MO, many of them being born in the Wishart community.

Benjamin was ordained to the work of the ministry on June 28, 1908 at the Salem Baptist Church at Cliquot, Polk County, MO. He preached in several of the community churches in Polk County as well as Vine Church in St. Clair County. This church no longer stands as it has been torn down. During his later years he lived in the Humansville area and before his death moved to the city of Humansville. He died on Jan. 21, 1920 and is buried in the Humansville City Cemetery. His wife Mary Jane, daughter of Rev. George L. Wilson and Mary Copeland, married Thomas Robertson after Benjamin's death. Her own death came on March 25, 1928 and she was buried beside Benjamin in the Humansville City Cemetery, Humansville, MO. *Submitted by Evelyn Graham*

HENSLEY - James Hensley was born about 1839 in Polk County, MO. He married Matilda Isdell about 1858 in Kansas. She was the daughter of Henry Isdell and Edna Story. At the time of their marriage James was serving in the Sixth Regiment Kansas Cavalry. James and Matilda had four children, two passed away very young. Gideon was born in 1867 and Belle was born in 1869 in Kansas. James died in 1874 in Linn County, KS and Matilda passed away one year later, leaving Gideon and Belle orphans. Eliza Hensley, their grandmother, took them to Texas and Belle died while in her teens.

James Hensley, Company D, Sixth Regiment, Kansas Calvary

Gideon married Bettie Burnett, Aug. 16, 1889 in Hillsboro, TX. There were three daughters born to this union: Noma, Minnie and Effie. They lived most of their lives in and around Cordell and Port, OK.

Effie was born Aug. 3, 1894, in Hot Springs, AR. Effie married Hurbert Anderson in Eldorado, OK on April 30, 1991, who was born in Peoria, IL. Hurbert Anderson was the son of Joseph Anderson and Delila Esleshman, born Sept. 16, 1834, who married in Peru, IN Nov. 11, 1865. Joseph and Delila were married while he was on active duty in the 47th Regiment of the Illinois Infantry. Hurbert was a farmer and taught his children to love nature. He was a good father. Effie was a fun-loving person. She would bring cheer and laughter into a room when she entered. Effie and "Hub" were poor folks most of their lives.

Bettie and Gideon would help them out a lot. Hub went fishing one day and slipped and fell and caught the fishhook in his hand. Mud got into the wound and he got gangrene. He had to go to Oklahoma City to the hospital for a week. They did not have the money to pay the hospital bill. So, the hospital took their farm, which left them penniless. They continued to sink lower financially.

Hub and Effie had a total of seven children, six girls: Ruby Van Hoosen, born March 1912; Widdie Copus, born April 15, 1913; Elsie Parks, born Jan. 23, 1915; Dorothy McConnell, born Nov. 9, 1916; Betty Thomasson, born Aug. 9, 1924; Helen Ackerman, born April 21, 1926; and one son, Joseph G. Anderson, born Nov. 1, 1920. *Submitted by Victoria Thompson*

HENSON - Thomas Henson (born 1801 in Virginia), married Sarah, (born April 25, 1801 in Virginia), likely in Scott County, VA about 1825. Sarah's last name is unknown but some possibilities are Flint or Frieze. They had nine children; five born in Scott County, the next three in Sullivan County, TN and the last in Polk County, MO. Thomas died May 23, 1856 in Polk County; buried in Bolivar City Cemetery. Sarah lived with her oldest son in Humansville and died there April 4, 1876; buried at Humansville Cemetery.

Rebecca Henson, born July 6, 1827, married William S. White on Nov. 15, 1846 in Polk County. Rebecca died Oct. 4, 1847 in Bolivar and was buried in Bolivar City Cemetery.

William Leonard Henson, born Oct. 14, 1828, married Mary Ann Hull on Aug. 15, 1850 in Sullivan County. They moved to Polk County about 1852/1853 and settled near Humansville. They had seven children: Sarah Lucinda (married Richard G. H. Wells, nine children); David Thomas (married Cordia Alice White, nine children); Isabella J; Emeline F.; Mary V. (married John Dorner); Tennessee E. (married Frank Best); Analeatha C. (married William Best). William, a Civil War veteran, died Sept. 21, 1873 in Humansville; buried in Humansville Cemetery.

Hiram F. Henson, born March 12, 1832, married first, Mary Ann Frieze, on Feb. 4, 1852 in Cedar County, MO. They had one son, John Wesley Henson, born in 1854 (married Sarah Parthena Russell, 10 or 12 children). Mary Ann died and Hiram was remarried to Melvina (Kennon) Patterson on June 16, 1857 in Polk County. They had five children: Sarah E. (married Philip Harris, at least two children); Rebecca Jane (married Joseph M. Weese, one child); James Thomas (married Emma Margaret Hocker, 10 children); Laura Levina (married William Thomas, five children); and William P. (lived six days). Hiram, a Civil War veteran, died April 9, 1869 in Polk County; buried in Mt. Olive Cemetery.

Thomas J. Henson, born July 10, 1833, married first, Elizabeth Decker, on March 13, 1853 in Polk County. They had four children: Rebecca Jane (married Morris Kennon); Susan Francis (married James Hayden, one child); Wiley R. (married Prudella Sherwood, at least two children); and Clinton L. (died at age 12). Thomas was remarried to Easter Wright on July 5, 1868 in Polk County. They had four children: Frank (stillborn); Addie Belle (married Eugene McColm, five children); Walter Lee (married Mary Lewis, six children); and an unnamed infant. Thomas, a Civil War veteran, died April 24, 1882 in Polk County; buried in Mt. Olive Cemetery.

Sarah Catherine Henson, born 1835, married Robert S. Wilson on Sept. 26, 1852 in Polk County. They had five children: Benjamin Franklin, James G., Annie, William and Mary.

David Alexander Henson, born April 9, 1837, married Cathrine Pickering on Aug. 12, 1854 in Polk County. They had eight or nine children: Sarah O. (married John E. England, two children); William H. (married first, Sarah S. Flint, one child, second, Frances Matilda Butler, one child); James Leonard (married Adelia Butler, 10 children); John B. (married Anna L. Mead, six children); Rebecca J. (married Leonard Belknap, two children); Mary E. (married James Albert Jones, six children); Hiram Milton (married Louisa Hills, six children); Fred C. (married Georgia Mitchem); and Ora V. (possibly a granddaughter instead of a daughter). David, a Civil War veteran, died Nov. 28, 1887 in Polk County; buried in Salem Cemetery.

James M. Henson, born about 1839, married Julia F. Rawlings on Oct. 18, 1863 in Shelby County, MO. He served in the Civil War.

Susan Jane Henson, born about 1841, married James W. Kennon on Sept. 3, 1863 in Polk County. Susan died between 1870 and 1873, possibly in Polk County.

An unnamed infant daughter, born in 1843, was the first member of the family to be buried in the Bolivar City Cemetery.

HENSON - James Thomas Henson, son of Hiram and Melvina (Kennon) Henson, was born Aug. 2, 1862 in Polk County. He was married on April 27, 1886 in Henry County, MO to Emma Margaret Hocker, daughter of Peter and Emeline (Bogner) Hocker, born April 28, 1868 in Polk

James and Emma Henson family, 1917-1918; front: Ona, James, Emma and Etta; middle: Thurman; back: Hiram, Elsa, Oren, Guy, Nella and Nelson. Thurman's picture was inserted by the original photographer because Thurman had died by the time the photograph was taken.

County. They settled in Polk County and had 10 children, all but one born in Polk County, although in different areas of the county. James died Feb. 9, 1945 in Polk County; Emma died July 11, 1930 in Bolivar and both were buried in Payne Cemetery in northeast Polk County.

Nella Elizabeth Henson, born Dec. 3, 1886, married Bluferd Locke on Dec. 18, 1904 in Polk County. They had three children: Roxie May (married first, William Childers, two children and then married second, William Franklin Graves, one son); Carl (married Vernice Louise Scroggins, one daughter); and Coy (married Mavourneen G. Hook, three daughters). Nella died Sept. 11, 1930 in Brighton, MO and was buried in Payne Cemetery.

Thurman Peter Henson, born May 3, 1888 in Dallas County, MO, died Sept. 18, 1916 in Polk County, buried Payne Cemetery.

Hiram James Henson, born Feb. 21, 1890, married Mary Alma Ables on Nov. 20, 1910 in Polk County. They had six children: Maggie Mae (married Olivar Roy Lee, three children); Neta Wilma (married Harvey Adrain Hook, one daughter); Wauneta Faye (married Cecil Leroy Wollard, two sons); Emma Lorene (married William Leo "Pete" Galyan, three children); Oren Stanley (married Cordie Virginia Hensley, five children); and Thelma Jewell (married Clyde Edward Fish, three children). Hiram died June 21, 1950 in Fillmore, Ventura County, CA and was buried in Santa Paula Cemetery, Santa Paula, Ventura County, CA.

Elsa Leo Henson, born Sept. 17, 1891, married Willis E. McGee on Nov. 18, 1916 in Polk County. They had two children, James Elmer and Opal Louise (married Henry Adolph Robertson, three children). Elsa was remarried to James E. Evans in 1946 and then died June 6, 1962 in Columbia, Boone County, MO. She was buried in Payne Cemetery.

Pearl Emley Henson, born April 12, 1894, died April 15, 1894 and was buried in Payne Cemetery.

Guy Thomas Henson, born Sept. 19, 1896, married Iva May Rowles on May 9, 1920 in Polk County. They had one daughter, Marcella May (married Patrick Joseph Thompson, three children). Guy and Iva moved to California where he died Jan. 6, 1971 in Santa Paula and was buried in the Santa Paula Cemetery.

Oren William Henson, born Dec. 27, 1898, married Mary Elizabeth Lamar on Nov. 2, 1928. They did not have any children. Oren died Aug. 16, 1967 in Buffalo, MO and was buried at Reynolds Cemetery near Buffalo.

Nelson Henson, born March 10, 1901, married Pearl Anna Fellows on Dec. 26, 1920 in Bolivar. They had one son, Thurman Robert (married Wava Lucille Ankrom, two children). Nelson died Sept. 11, 1961 in Humansville and was buried in Payne Cemetery.

Ona Myrtle Henson, born April 12, 1903, married James Clifford Piper on May 28, 1922 in Bolivar. They had four children: Lexie Merle (married Warren F. Smith, no children); James Clifford Jr. (married Elma G. Lawyer, two children); Ona Darlene (married John Vance Keith, three children); and Carolyn June (married Thomas Dale Evans, two children). Ona died March 4, 1986 in Bolivar and was buried in Payne Cemetery.

Mary Etta Henson, born Sept. 25, 1905, married DeWard Wheeler on Aug. 5, 1947 in Bolivar. They did not have any children. Etta died July 26, 1992 in Polk County and was buried in Payne Cemetery. *Submitted by Thelma Fish*

HICKMAN - William Hickman was born 1783 in North Carolina. Wife Patsy was born 1797 in North Carolina. Elizabeth, maiden name unknown, was born 1826 in North Carolina. Husband unknown. Enumerated in 1850 - 1860 Madison Township Cedar County, MO, Census. William (died 1869) and Patsy (died between 1860-1869) in Cedar County. 1870 Eliza Hickman Madison Township;

Family of Lynton "Harold" and Golden Beverly (Shouse) Hickman; Front: Lacy and Logan (children of Lullel and Lisa); middle: Leslie (husband, Charles), Beverly, Harold and Lisa (wife of Lullel); back: Mirian (husband, Lynton) and Lullel; Lullel, Charles and Lynton are the sons of Harold and Beverly taken December 2001 North of Greenfield Sons Creek home of Lester and Vickie (Hickman) Decker

Children: Sophia C., Nancy J., Alex M., Johnson L., Sarah E., Charles M. Elizabeth and her children entered Dadeville after the Civil War in a covered wagon, dying shortly after, townspeople took in her children. Elizabeth died 1872; burial in Rice Cemetery. Johnson Lincoln was born July 12, 1865. He was enumerated in 1880 Morgan Township, Dade County Census at 14, residing at Joseph W. Carmack's. He married Alta Malinda Walker, born Aug. 1, 1868 to Amos James and Martha (Love) Walker. They eloped on March 5, 1886 to State of The Cherokee Nation at Vinita,

Taken summer 2002 in Grove, OK; Harold and Beverly Hickman and their grandchildren, Harold, Beverly holding Blake, Logan, Lacy, Connor and Corban. Logan and Lacy, children of Lullel and Lisa; Corban and Connor, children of Charles and Wendy; Blake, son of Charles and Leslie.

Indian Territory. Enumerated in 1900 Morgan Township and 1910 North Township, Dade County. Children: Euriel, Roy, Martha, Joe, Roscoe, Paul, Margaret, Robert, Delone, Pearl, Lynton, and Gayle. Johnson died May 4, 1926 and Alta died Dec. 17, 1945; burials in Wetzel Cemetery. Lynton "Moose", was born Aug. 1, 1912 at Sons Creek. He attended Draughn Business College in Springfield. He met Roberta Jean Pyle, born April 4, 1916 to Charles and Rada (Campbell) Pyle. They married 1935 in Ozark. Children: Harold, James, Beverly, Vicki, Linda, Sue. Moose said, "My dad died when I was 13, so if I was to have anything it was up to me." Grandma Jean's Christmas traditions: reading the Christmas Story (Luke 2: 1-19) before gifts, on her red tablecloth we wrote our names and the year, then she embroidered it. December 1989 is blank, Moose died the 19th. Burial in Pleasant Grove Cemetery. Harold was born March 20, 1936 at Sons Creek. He graduated from Greenfield, and in 1958 from University of Missouri. He joined the Army National Guard 203 Transportation Battalion Springfield, rank Specialist 5 (1958-1964). He married Golden Beverly (Shouse) on April 24, 1960 at Greenfield. Beverly was born Dec. 15, 1940 in Greenfield to Lullel Oral "Bill" and Edna "Jewell" (Wilson) Shouse. Children: Beverly, Linley, Caroline and Gary. Beverly graduated from Greenfield in 1959. Harold worked at Meeks in Lockwood. Beverly was a telephone switchboard operator at Greenfield. They moved to Polk County in 1961, running Charles C. Meeks dairy farm (295 acres) at Sac River, southwest of Morrisville. Beverly's occupations: teacher's aide, elementary principal's secretary, Post Office, co-owner Cup-N-Saucer Cafe, L & M Grocery (all in Morrisville), doctors' office in Springfield, Bolivar Golf Course "cook," cleaning houses. Children: Lullel, Charles, Lynton, Morrisville graduates of 1980 and 1983. They all attended SMSU in Springfield. Lullel was born July 13, 1962 in Springfield. He began running in college at 19, running long distance and marathons. Lullel's occupation: Construction / stock cattle. He met Melissa Ann Vote, born Feb. 28, 1966 to John and Bonnie (Bays) Vote. (See: Vote Family by Lisa Vote-Hickman). Lisa is a 1984 Morrisville graduate. They married on Aug. 25, 1984 at Morrisville. Children: Logan Ryan and Lacy Diane. Lisa graduated in 1990 from Graff VO- Tech in Springfield. She was a Morrisville PTA Historian, Secretary, and First Vice President 1995-1998, a Home Interior Dealer, paraprofessional at Morrisville March 1, 1999 to May 2002 teaching Morrisville's first Down syndrome student, three year member of Polk County Genealogical Society. Charles and Lynton were born Dec. 10, 1965. Members of Morrisville's 1981-82 IA State Basketball Championship Team. Charles married Wendy Louise (Warner) July 27, 1991 in Springfield. Wendy was born Sept. 12, 1967 to Walter and Joyce (Frazer) Warner. Children: Corban Charles and Connor Matthew. Divorced in 1996, Charles met Leslie (Burnett) McClelland, daughter of Roy and Sharon Burnett, marrying on Nov. 3, 2000 in Arkansas. Child: Blake Zachary. Charles and Leslie work at Tyson's in Arkansas. Lynton married Marian Marcel (McMasters) Langford April 30, 1994 at El Dorado Springs. Marian was born June 17, 1960 in Stockton to James and Evelyn McMasters. Marian first married David Langford; he died young. Their child Jason had twin boys, Calob and Curtis. Lynton's occupation: MFA Manager at Lamar. The Meeks dairy farm sold at auction June 2002. *Submitted by Golden Beverly (Shouse) Hickman*

HICKS – Jonathan Albert Hicks, born Jan. 17, 1845 in Davidson County, TN, third child of Hiram Jehu Hicks and Mary Jones, married Lorinda Vashti Harralson, Sept. 3, 1868 in Polk County, MO, daughter of Vincent Harralson and Martha Dove Hambelton. To this union seven children were born. Strumlow Nelson, born Dec. 16, 1870 in Polk County, MO, married Abbie Caroline

Jonathan Albert Hicks family

Matthews, died July 29, 1911 and is buried in Rose Hill Cemetery, Greene County, MO. Katy Carry Elvina, born Sept. 27, 1873 in Missouri, married Albert J. Matthews, died Aug. 27, 1930, and is buried in Rose Hill Cemetery, Greene County, MO. Dora T. was born May 18, 1879 in Missouri and died before 1906. Noah Travis, born April 28, 1880 in Ash Grove, MO, married Lula Leata Conn, died May 27, 1947, and is buried in Greenwood Cemetery, Bolivar, MO. Vera Wade was born April 1882 in Missouri and died before 1906. Mary Susan was born April 15, 1884 in Greene County, MO and died 1907. Ernest, born Feb. 1, 1890 in Greene County, MO, married Jerlie Stepp, died March 1, 1956, and is buried in Rose Hill Cemetery, Greene County, MO.

Jonathan Albert Hicks and a twin sister, Susan, born near Nashville, TN, had eight siblings. They traveled from Tennessee to Montgomery County, IL (1850 census) then to Marion County, AR (1860 census) and to Polk County, MO (1870 census).

Jonathan was a farmer, five feet 10 inches tall, fair complexion, blue eyes and dark hair.

Jonathan, age 19, living in Brighton, MO, on July 12, 1864 volunteered to serve in the Civil War, mustering into the Union Army, Aug. 11, 1864, at Bolivar, MO, as a private with Company F, 15th Missouri Cavalry. He was involved in a skirmish at Mt. Vernon, MO on Dec. 10, 1864. While on guard duty Jan. 1, 1865 on horseback from Bolivar to Springfield, MO, he tried to dismount but could not; they found his feet were frozen.

Family stories, during Jonathan's enlistment, relate that about once a month he traveled by horseback through the woods 15 miles to the Hicks home place checking on his family, who lived east of Walnut Grove, MO, on Asher Creek.

On July 1, 1865, Jonathan mustered out of the service in Springfield, MO.

On Sept. 3, 1868 in Morrisville, Polk County, MO, marriage vows were read to Jonathan Albert Hicks and Lorinda Vashti Harralson by a relative, Rev. Jacob Hinkle. To this union seven children were born; one of them Ernest, Betty's grandfather.

On Sept. 21, 1887, Jonathan applied for a war pension, his health failing. On Dec. 13, 1888, R. C. Drum, an Adjutant General, stated on his affidavit that hospital records were not on file as to Jonathan's disability.

May 21, 1889, Elijah Hamilton, who served with Jonathan, swore that Jonathan's legs were frozen and he had injuries to the "small" of his back, causing an inability to work.

May 1892, William Rook (brother-in-law) of Cave Springs, Greene County, MO, swore that Jonathan was destitute. Neighbors supplied him with clothing and food, as he had nothing but a cow, calf, and 12 chickens.

In 1895 Jonathan lived in Buckley, MO.

Jan. 20, 1899, while living in Grisham, MO, he again applied for a pension.

June 18, 1900, an affidavit signed by A. E. Tupper and N. W. Long of Sacville, MO as to Jonathan's condition, was described as an eye disease, rheumatism in back, causing him to walk in a stooped position and unable to perform manual labor.

In 1906 Lorinda Vashti enrolled herself and Ernest on the Eastern Cherokee Rolls. Family members submitted numerous affidavits to claim Indian blood through Alexander Brown. Aug. 9, 1907, while living in Morrisville, MO, Lorinda again filed paperwork to be included on the Guion Miller Cherokee rolls. The family was rejected.

Jonathan, living in Pearl, MO, desperate for pension, applied again in 1907.

Lorinda Vashti died Oct. 6, 1912 and was buried in Rose Hill Cemetery, Willard, MO.

Pearl, MO in 1915, Jonathan swore out an affidavit, his health at this time caused him to sign with his mark.

June 14, 1929, Jonathan is living in Bolivar, MO.

July 31, 1925, age 80, another affidavit for his pension was witnessed by W. J. Dodd and Noah Travis Hicks, his son.

From Sept. 21, 1887 to Aug. 3, 1926, a period of 39 years, he applied until finally he is accepted for a pension. Beginning on March 1, 1927 Jonathan would receive $90.00 per month.

Jonathan passed away May 10, 1928 in Polk County, Marion Township, MO, in the home of Milford Hicks (grandson). Extremely ill for one year, he was cared for by Boyd Matthews (grandson), Walter Bush, Milford Hicks (grandson) and Noah Travis Hicks (son).

Jonathan is buried at Rose Hill Cemetery, Willard, MO. His name is listed on the War Memorial along with many friends and relations who served with him in the Civil War.
Submitted by Betty Hall

HOBBS - Silas Hobbs (1814-1887) and his wife, Polly Ann Fanning (1822-1874), came to Missouri from Tennessee. They had eleven children.

Silas and Polly's second son, John Jackson Hobbs (1843-1925), married Mattie Elizabeth Messick (1845-1930) in Mattie's home near Springfield, MO on Feb. 15, 1866. John and Mattie lived their early-married life in Dade County and moved to Polk County near Oak Grove in 1883. In 1912, they moved to Walnut Grove where they lived until their deaths. John and Mattie are buried in Green Lawn Cemetery, Walnut Grove, MO.

John and Mattie's children were Sarah Louise (1866 -), Benjamin Leroy (1871 -), Thomas (1880 -) and John Frank Hobbs (1876-1960). John Frank Hobbs married Nora Minerva Hargrave (1880-1955), daughter of Samual Clayton Hargrave (1846 -1921) and Annis Helen Edge Hargrave. Their children were Ruby Lorene (1900-1973), Coy William Hobbs (1903-1988), Velma Gertrude (1905 -1980), Mattie Helen (1908-1996), Mildred Gwendolyn (1910 -1941), Angeline Luciel (1913 -1996), Georgia Lee (1916 -1996), Lillian Katheryne (1919 - 1963) and Dorotha Loleta (1922 -).

Truman Alfred Hobbs (1913-) wrote about his Granddad, John Jackson Hobbs, "Granddad was 5'11" tall. He had light hair, fair complexion, and carried a straight military bearing all his life. He was a cavalry man, and like others, owned his own horse. He was paid for the feed and use of his horse by the government. Upon release from the army he married and became a farmer a few miles northwest of Walnut Grove in Polk County."

John Jackson and Mattie (Messick) Hobbs are the great-grandparents of the late Bonnie Lee (H o b b s) Underwood, Barbara Dale (Hobbs) Cunningham, Peggy Ann (Hobbs) Blakemore, Nora Etta (Hobbs) Erwin, all of Walnut Grove, MO, and the late Sandra J. (Hobbs) Kelly, of Springfield, MO. Samual Clayton and Annis Helen (Edge) Hargrave are also their great-grandparents.

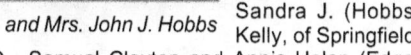
Mr. and Mrs. John J. Hobbs

Information about the Old Soldier's Reunion photograph.

The three-part photograph is a copy of an original photograph of the **(Old Soldier) Civil War Soldier's Reunion** on Commercial St. in Springfield. (The photograph is not dated, however, a copy of a photograph taken of a later *Old Soldier's Reunion* is dated September 1908, so assumption is that the earlier picture was taken before September 1908.) John Jackson Hobbs and Samual Clayton Hargrave, great-grandfathers of Peggy Ann (Hobbs) Blakemore, both fought in the Civil War, and are pictured in the *Old Soldier's Reunion* photograph. Also in the picture are Albert Hayward, Henry Hayward's dad and Carole's Granddad.

(Jay or Alan King can identify some members of the Dadeville Band pictured in the *Old Soldier's Reunion photograph.*)

The document titled *A Brief Sketch of the Organization of the 2nd Battalion, 6th Regt., Missouri Cav. Vols.* was written by John Jackson Hobbs. *Submitted by Peggy Ann Blakemore*

HOCKER - Peter Hocker, born May 29, 1833 in Dauphin County, PA and Emeline Bogner, born

Old Soldiers Reunion

Jan. 5, 1836 in Pennsylvania, were married about 1853 in Pennsylvania. (Their parents were John Peter Hocker and Nancy Welpmer Hocker and Jacob Bogner Jr. and Elizabeth Pogue Bogner.) They had 10 children, three born in Dauphin County, one in Wayne County, OH and six in Polk County, MO. Emeline died March 10, 1892 in Polk County; buried in Payne Cemetery. Peter was remarried to Mrs. Ellen Prater on April 24, 1902 in Polk County. Peter died March 2, 1907 in Bolivar; buried in Payne Cemetery.

Sarah Matilda Hocker, born about 1854/55, married William Henry Shipley on Feb. 5, 1891 in Polk County. They had three children: Roy, Nellie and Clyde (died young). Sarah died Sept. 6, 1907 in Polk County; buried in Greenwood Cemetery.

Martin August Hocker, born May 2, 1856, married Mrs. Emma Haugwood on July 15, 1883 in Polk County. They had two children, Otto and Pauline. Martin died Feb. 11, 1902 in Springfield, Greene County, MO.

Lione Elizabeth Hocker, born Sept. 6, 1859, married William Moses Vest on May 11, 1876 in Polk County. They had six children: William Peter, John Edward, triplets Anna, Lena, Linda and an unnamed infant (buried in Payne Cemetery). Lione died Nov. 10, 1888 in Polk County; buried in Payne Cemetery.

Stephen Edward Hocker, born Dec. 25, 1861, married Laura Belle Jump on Oct. 12, 1891 in Polk County. They had four children: Ernest Edward, Arthur Marion, Pearl and Wilburn. Stephen died Oct. 8, 1942 in Los Angeles County, CA.

Clara Jane Hocker, born Aug. 10, 1867, married Reuben Charles Goff on Sept. 24, 1885 in Nevada, Vernon County, MO. They had 15 children: an unnamed infant, John Landon, Vernie, Clara Jane, Charles Reuben, Alice Elizabeth, Bonnie Bluebell, Roxie Anne, Chauncey Isador, Albert Roy, Mary Lewis, Ruby Anne, Thelma Mae, twins Ada Landon and Anne Landon. Clara died Dec. 8, 1932 in Chelsea, OK.

Painting of Emeline, Lilly and Peter Hocker, circa 1890

Emma Margaret Hocker, born April 18, 1868, married James Thomas Henson on April 27, 1886 in Clinton, Henry County, MO. They had 10 children: Nella Elizabeth, Thurman Peter, Hiram James, Elsa Leo, Pearl Emley (lived three days), Guy Thomas, Oren William, Nelson, Ona Myrtle and Mary Etta. Emma died July 11, 1930 in Polk County; buried in Payne Cemetery.

Martha Nancy Hocker, born June 9, 1871, married Frank Mitchum about 1890/91. They had 11 children: Charles Peter, Earl Jesse, Clifford Harry, Anna Marie, Grace Ruby, Clyde Franklin, twins Loren Alfred and Lila Alice, twins Jim Jackson and John Henry, and Hazel Tillie. Nancy died April 6, 1956 in Batesville, Independence County, AR; buried in Oak Lawn Cemetery in Batesville.

Mary Catherine Hocker, born Jan. 25, 1873, married Samuel H. Wilson on Aug. 19, 1894 in Polk County. They had 12 children: Hubert, Finnie T., John, Peter, Nola Maggie, Homer, Theodore, Lige, Otis, Minnie Belle, Mary J. and an unnamed infant. Mary died Aug. 12, 1917 in Polk County; buried in Mt. Olive Cemetery.

Lewis Peter Hocker, born Feb. 22, 1876, married Chloe Grace Tatum on Sept. 4, 1897 in Polk County. They had eight children: Leonard, Dolis, William Jacob, Sylvia, Rudolph, Irene Grace, James Richard and Venson Peter. Lewis died Jan. 14, 1917 in Polk County; buried in Payne Cemetery.

Lilly Ann Hocker, born Sept. 18, 1878, married Albert Boone on Jan. 1, 1899 in Polk County; one son, James Albert Boone. Lilly died from complications with childbirth on Nov. 17, 1899 in Polk County; buried in Payne Cemetery. *Submitted by Jim Mitchum*

HOFFER - Umphrey Silas "U. S.," born Feb. 13, 1881 in Illinois, the son of Jacob and Carrie (Crumsie) Hoffer and Claudia Grace (Connelly) Hoffer, born March 14, 1883, daughter of Christopher Columbus and Henrietta (Cutler) Connelly were married on Feb. 25, 1903 and reared their nine children in western Kansas near Ellis. In the mid-1930s, they were taking turns caring for Umphrey's stepmother Hannah (Foster) Hoffer in Florida. While traveling through Missouri, they noticed how green and pretty Missouri was compared to the drought and dust storms of western Kansas. They sold everything and moved to Bolivar in September of 1939 with their two youngest children (Wayne and Blanche) as the older ones had married and settled with their families, except for Lester who was teaching and came to Bolivar the following year. They had visited the area previously and purchased the original tract of 79 acres at the top of the hill south of the Roberts Ford Bridge, east of Bolivar, from the bank. Through the years, they bought more acreage and at one time had a total of more than 155 acres. In the fall of 1939 Wayne enrolled at Southwest Baptist College as a freshman and Blanche attended Bolivar High School, from which she graduated.

U. S. and Grace had nine children: Gladys Edith, born June 23, 1904, died Jan. 7, 1990, who married Otto Allen Wahlborg; Beatrice Gertrude, born Dec. 5, 1905, died March 25, 1986, who married Orin Roesch; Nellie Marie, born Nov. 28, 1908, died in 2000, who married three times; Carrietta, born Sept. 2, 1910, died Dec. 5, 2000, who married Roger B. Brown; Lester Connelly, born Dec. 18, 1911, who married Mary Jane Leavitt (daughter of Fred and Georgia May Reed Leavitt) on Nov. 18, 1943 in Bolivar; Ralph Jacob, born Sept. 2, 1913, died Jan. 16, 1968, who married Mary Beth Wildes; Cora Irene, born Aug. 8, 1915, who married Earl Roy Bland; Wayne Nathaniel, born Oct. 21, 1919, who married D. Lucille Sconce; and Daisy Blanche, born April 11, 1923, who married M. Dale Murphy, who was born April 13, 1924 in Bolivar, MO.

All of the children were born in Ellis, Trego County, KS. Over the many years, U. S. and Grace and their nine children were often together. In 1938, before they moved to Missouri, all nine children were together and again in 1959, with the exception of Cora who was living in Texas.

Cora, U. S., Grace and Beatrice, Blanche, Wayne, Carrietta, Lester, Marie, Ralph and Gladys, 1938

U. S. died on Sept. 2, 1959 at the Ozark Osteopathic Hospital in Springfield, Greene County, MO and is buried at Greenwood Cemetery in Bolivar. In his obituary it says, "Because of his jovial, yet gentle disposition, he was loved by all who knew him." Grace died on Feb. 8, 1966 at Burge Hospital in Springfield, Greene County, MO and is buried next to U. S. at Greenwood Cemetery.

Currently Laura Hoffer and her children Bonnie Lucille Hoffer and Silas Taylor Hoffer are living on the farm; the children are the fourth generation of Hoffers on the farm. *Submitted by D. Blance (Hoffer) Murphy*

HOFFER - Wayne Nathaniel Hoffer was born Oct. 21, 1919 to Umphrey Silas and Claudia Grace (Connelly) Hoffer, the eighth of nine children. He attended rural schools in Kansas in grades one, two, four, six, seven, and grades three, five, and eight in St. Cloud, FL. He attended high school at Wakeeney, KS, graduating in 1939.

Front left to right: Autumn McDaniel, Wayne Hoffer, Vonzel, Silas, Lucille Hoffer, Nathan Hoffer, Sasha Camp and Bonnie Hoffer

Sept. 2, 1939 the family moved to Bolivar and Wayne attended Southwest Baptist College for two years. The fall of 1941, he taught at Watson School (north of Bolivar) until January 1942 when he was inducted into the army. He served our country in Australia, New Guinea and the Philippines until Dec. 15, 1945. After discharge, he was employed as a sixth grade teacher at Lebanon, MO. That fall, he enrolled at Missouri University at Columbia graduating in May 1949. Employed by the University as County Extension Agent in 1949, he worked until his resignation in March 1958; most of that time was in Shannon County, and it was there he met his future wife and they were married April 5, 1953 in the First Baptist Church at Eminence. In 1958 they moved to Bolivar. Wayne had bought land from his dad in 1951 and had a broiler house built. While in the chicken business, he also worked in the County Extension Office and ASCS Office.

On April 13, 1961, their son Nathan Wesley Hoffer was born. In 1966, Wayne was employed as sixth grade teacher at Marion C. Early School at Morrisville, where he taught until his retirement in 1986.

Dorothy Lucille Sconce was born Oct. 24, 1931 near Eminence, MO. She was the youngest of the seven children of William Wesley and Lula Pearl (Prince) Sconce. She attended all 12 years of school at Eminence, graduating in 1949. That summer, she attended Missouri Baptist College in Poplar Bluff and Southwest Missouri State Teachers' College in Springfield and taught school in 1949-50. Lucille attended college in the fall of 1950-51 then taught two more years, attending college in the summers.

In the fall of 1952, she met Wayne and they were married April 5, 1953. In November 1957, she was employed as secretary at Eminence High School where she worked until she and Wayne moved to Bolivar. Lucille worked in the County Extension Office in Bolivar from 1959 until 1961 when Nathan was born.

In 1966, when Nathan started school she went back to work and was employed by Bolivar R-I Schools and worked there 27 years until her retirement in October 1993.

Nathan married Laura Lynne Gee in Tucson, AZ on Feb. 14, 1987 and in August 1989, after the birth of their daughter Bonnie Lucille Hoffer (Feb. 27, 1989) they moved on the old Hoffer farm. Oct. 31, 1992 Silas Taylor Hoffer was born in Springfield. Wayne and Lucille feel so fortunate to have their family near. After Nathan's marriage to Vonzel, two step-grandchildren were added to their family.

Wayne and Lucille are members of Mt. Olive Baptist Church where Wayne serves as a deacon and sings in the choir. *Submitted by Wayne N. Hoffer*

HOFFER - Laura Lynne Gee was born Aug. 21, 1963 in Hinsdale, IL, the eldest child of Sydney Taylor and Bonnie Lou (Laird) Gee. Laura has a younger brother, Steven Taylor Gee, who is married to Lisa (Locke) and has two children, Taylor Allison Gee and Ryan Cameron Gee. Her family moved to Dallas, TX in 1967, then to Houston, TX in about 1969 where they stayed until 1976. In 1976 the Gees moved to Tucson, AZ so the parents could operate their business franchises, Kwik-Kopy Printing. Laura graduated from Sabino High School in 1981 and went right to work for The Arizona Bank as a teller that summer. She stayed with the bank and rose to senior teller until 1983 when her mother became terminally ill. Laura left the bank and took over her mother's printing business while her father operated his printing business at the other end of town. Laura's mother Bonnie passed away in September of 1984 in Tucson, AZ. Laura moved back to Houston, TX and took a corporate job with the Kwik-Kopy Printing home office and worked in the legal department. While in Houston, she met Nathan W. Hoffer, son of Wayne and D. Lucille (Sconce) Hoffer. The couple moved to Tucson and was married there on February 14, 1987. Laura was working in banking and a night job in publishing at that time. Their daughter Bonnie Lucille Hoffer, named for both her grandmothers, was born Feb. 27, 1989 at University Medical Center in Tucson. After her birth, they decided to move to Bolivar where they had visited Nathan's parents during previous years. In August of 1989

Silas, Laura and Bonnie Hoffer

they moved to the Hoffer family farm and lived on the place with Nathan's parents. Laura went to work at Teters Floral Products as a secretary for five years and Bonnie was cared for by her grandpa Wayne Hoffer. From the age of 6 months Bonnie and her grandpa Hoffer would check fence and cattle and get in a good long walk, spending the day together. To this day the bond between Bonnie and her grandpa is very special. Laura and Nathan's son Silas Taylor Hoffer was born Oct. 31, 1992 in Springfield. He is named for his great-great-grandfather Umphrey Silas Hoffer and Taylor is his grandpa Sydney Gee's middle name as well as the middle name of his Uncle Steve and numerous other men on the Gee side. Laura left Teters and worked for Janice Barham at The Shoe Box for a while. Laura started at Pitts Funeral Home in the summer of 1995 as a secretary for Sidney Joe and Erlene Pitts. She completed all the required state testing and licensing and became a licensed funeral director on Aug. 13, 1998. She is currently employed at the same location; the name changed to Greenlawn Funeral Home-Pitts Chapel in January of 1997 following the death of Sidney Joe Pitts in 1995. In March of 2000, Nathan and Laura divorced. Laura and the children are living on the family farm. The children make four generations of Hoffers to live there. *Submitted by Laura L. Hoffer*

HOFFER - Nathan Wesley Hoffer was born April 13, 1961 in St. Louis, MO and was adopted by Wayne and Lucille Hoffer. The adoption was done through the Missouri Baptist Children's Home at Bridgeton, MO and he was brought home to the family farm on May 5, 1961. Nathan attended K-12 in the Bolivar R-I school district and graduated in 1979. He worked for Sid and Erlene Pitts at the Pitts Funeral Home in Bolivar, where he discovered that he enjoyed that sort of work. He later attended the Commonwealth College of Mortuary Science in Houston, TX.

He married Laura Lynne Gee in Tucson, AZ on Feb. 14, 1987. Their daughter, Bonnie Lucille Hoffer, was born Feb. 27, 1989. They moved to the Hoffer family farm in August of 1989. In 1991, Nathan ran for public office and was elected the Polk County Coroner. (He still holds that posi-

Vonzel, Bonnie, Sasha, Nathan, Silas and Autumn Rayn

tion.) Their son, Silas Taylor Hoffer, was born Oct. 31 1992 in Springfield, MO. Nathan was divorced on March 21, 2000. Bonnie and Silas reside on the Hoffer family farm with their mother.

Nathan then married Vonzel McDaniel of Fair Grove, MO on Oct. 21, 2000. Vonzel has two children, Sasha Danielle Camp, born on April 7, 1988 and Autumn Rayn McDaniel, born on May 14, 1997. All four children attend Bolivar schools.

Nathan maintains a commercial driver's license and drives locally while also performing his duties as coroner. Vonzel is finishing her degree as an aerospace engineer and has been offered jobs at NASA, Boeing, and other facilities. Nathan and Vonzel maintain their home in Bolivar. Nathan also plays in a local band called Floodwater and has for several years. Vonzel and Nathan also started a home-based business called Soaps of the Seasons, selling homemade soap locally and over the Internet.

HOLMAN – Judy (Stevens) Holman's family has long been residents of Polk County. Enos Organ was born in Virginia about 1803. He had five sons: Andrew Jackson, Cornelius, Jesse, James Perry, and VanBuren.

From this line: James Perry married Mary Jane Blankenship. From their union came six boys and two girls: Cornelius "Neil," Mary Minta, Charles, Jasper, Coy, S. A. "Nettie," Clinton and Cleveland.

Mary Minta Organ married William Frederick Coble, the son of David and Susan (Best) Coble. His siblings were George, Frank, Burton and a half-brother Charles Jessie Barker. From their union came one daughter and one son: Thelma Marie Coble and James Clinton Coble. James Clinton married Josephine Adams and had one son, John Carl, all now deceased.

Thelma Marie, born at Caplinger Mill, married Everett Stevens, born in Chandler, OK and had one son, Billy Eugene Stevens, born on the Polk-Greene County line. Billy married Mabel Moody, born in Chadwick, MO, and had four children: Judy Ann, born in Springfield, MO; Billie Jean, born in Aurora, MO (had two sons and one daughter); Cathey Jane, born in Aurora, MO (had two sons); and Keith Dewayne, born in Aurora, MO, a resident of the Bolivar area with his wife, Beverly (Hopkins) (also a long-time Polk County family) and their daughter, Kalyn.

Judy, a resident of the Eudora area since 1984, had four children (one son was adopted in Germany); Dyle Longpine II, born in Wittlich, Germany; John Everett Longpine, born in Fontana, CA, now a resident of Eudora with his son John Charles; Matthew Glenn Longpine, born in Loma Linda, CA, now a resident of the Strafford area with his wife Natasha (Runouski); and Arlene Michele Longpine (Sinclair), born in Blythe, CA, now a resident of Des Moines, IA with her husband J. R. Sinclair, sons Russell and Bradley and one daughter, Brittany.

Judy is married to Bobbie Ray Holman, born in Walnut Grove and they reside on the long-time family farm once owned by her great-great-grandfather, J. P. Organ, located in the southwest corner of Polk County in Jackson Township. James Perry "J. P." Organ purchased the first parcel of land from Samuel A. J. Malicoat in 1883.

Bob Holman's family background comes also from long-time Polk County residents: Thomas Hensley married Mary Elizabeth Owen and they had three sons and eight daughters. Their son, Everett married Mary Elizabeth Hoel (from Kansas) and had four children: Dwain, Opal, Genevieve and Betty. Opal married Noel "Pete" Holman and had four children; Bob had six children: Debbie, Scotty, Chrystal, Stacy, Shane and Amy; Georgia had six children: Dennis, Cindy, Russell, Steve, Darren and Travis; Larry; and Danny, who died at age 3.

Noel "Pete" Holman was one of 11 children of Ramie Holman and Dollie (Wright). His siblings were Irene, Mary, Frances, Lucille, Marjorie, Ralph, Helen, Lee Allen, Donna Jean and Sue. Ramie Holman's parents were Lafette Holman and Nancy (Neil) who had five children; she died and he remarried Hannah Parrish. Dollie's parents were Doc and Sarah "Sally" Wright. *Submitted by Judy Holman*

HOLMES – Sept. 8, 1792, Moses Holmes and Geney Rogers were married in Orange County, NC. They had seven children: Robert, Rachel, Eleanor, John, William, Ann and Jean. They moved to Maury County, TN in the early 1800s.

Robert Holmes married Rachel Latta (third marriage) and had seven children: Samuel, Margaret, William, Artemissa, Robert, Emeline and Lurena. They moved to Bolivar, MO about 1840, then Bellefonte, AR around 1848. Andrew, son from first marriage (to Jane Mitchell) stayed in Dunnegan.

William Robert Holmes, born Aug. 14, 1844 in Bolivar, MO, raised in Bellefonte, AR, moved back to Dunnegan Springs, MO, in the 1860s. He rode with "Wild Bill" Hickok and served in the Union Army during the Civil War. One day while "on point" near the timber, he heard soldiers but could not tell from which direction they were coming. Suddenly the soldiers popped out of the timber. There was a log down in front of him. As William grabbed the saddle horn on "Baldy," he yelled,

"Get out of here, Baldy!" The horse took off running down the log and carried him into the brush without a shot.

William married Mary Carneal (daughter of Elizabeth and Littleton Carneal of Russellville, KY) and they had seven children: Adelia, Martha Florence, Laura, Mary Elizabeth, Lula, James and Thomas Jefferson.

Thomas bought a farm west of Dunnegan. Dad (Tom) told a story about him and his dad deer hunting one day. As he chased a deer, the deer jumped over a rail fence. As the deer raised his tail, Granddad fired a shot and killed the deer "without breaking the skin!"

Thomas married Jennie Esther Lowry Dec. 31, 1917. Jennie's parents were William Sinclair Lowry and Mary Rebecca Sansom. The Lowrys moved to Dunnegan in 1870 and raised nine children: an infant, Mary Elizabeth "Lizzy," John, George, Charles, Jessie Isabelle "Belle," Jennie, Emily and James.

Thomas Holmes and James Larew (Lula's husband) owned the Larew & Holmes General Store in Dunnegan. Tom and Jennie were talented musicians. Tom played the violin and Jennie played mandolin and organ at the church and "play parties." They were active in the Missouri Farm Club.

Tom and Jennie had three sons: Ivan Thomas, Estel Jefferson and Keith Robert. Jennie died June 14, 1938 from breast cancer.

Ivan graduated from Humansville High School in 1938 and left the farm when drafted into the army June 17, 1941. Ivan married Amy Ruth Williams of Clever, MO, Feb. 14, 1944 and had two daughters: Carole and Carla. Amy died June 1, 1993 with muscular dystrophy.

Estel served in WWII combat. He married Lula Eileen Solomon (Amy's cousin), Clever, June 21, 1947. They had one son, Thomas, who lives in Drexel, MO. Estel Holmes died Jan. 30, 1997 of a heart attack; Eileen died Jan. 11, 1997.

Keith died Nov. 15, 1944 at the age of 14 years.

Ivan Holmes has a Bible given to him by his Granddad William Holmes. The copyright is 1790 and lists Moses Holmes and Geney Rogers' marriage and names and birth dates of Robert Holmes' 14 children. The Bible was on display in Humansville in the 1930s and is the family treasure. *Submitted by Carla Sanders*

HOLT - George W. Holt, son of Johann Henrich Holts and Artemesia "Mecy" Cox, was born Jan. 4, 1846 in Richland County, IL. After his father's death in 1848, he and his mother moved to Lawrence County, IN. On Oct. 15, 1848 Mecy Cox Holt was married a second time to William Edwards. From this union George's half-sister, Lucinda Edwards, was born in 1849. After the death of his mother (1850-1860) George joined Company E, 13th Regiment, Indiana Cavalry of

Front: Mecy, George W., Mary Calvina and Noble; Back: Harvey, Tilden, Anna, Lee and Addie

the Union Army.

After his service George went to Orange County, IN. On July 25, 1867 he married Mary Calvina Abel, daughter of Samuel "Huston" and Mary Ann "Polly" Abel. Mary Calvina Abel was born Nov. 14, 1843 in Orange County, IN. George and Mary Holt were the parents of Mecy, married Marion Sampson; Harvey, married Lucinda Higginbotham; Zendria, died young; Anna, married Drew Williams; Aaron, died young; Samuel "Tilden;" Laura, died young; Barbery, died young; Addie, married Phineas Stewart; Lee, married Etta Boren; and Noble, married Minnie Brooks.

Tilden Holt (1876-1961) recounted that in the early 1880s he and his parents, siblings, and maternal grandparents left Indiana in a covered wagon and headed west. Along the way George and Mary Holt suffered hardships, including the loss of a child. When they reached Polk County, MO they knew they were "home." Indiana relatives with the surnames of Abel, Austin, Pinnick and Lewis also settled there. Many of these family members were laid to rest in Goff Cemetery.

On Dec. 23, 1905 Tilden Holt married Eva "Mae" Trehern. Born Nov. 26, 1881 in Waco, TX, Mae's roots were in Polk County. Her mother, Belva "Dora" Burnes, daughter of Thomas J. Jr. (1837-1872) and Elvira Jane Wright Burnes (1841-1917), was born there on Jan. 28, 1861. Thomas Jr. was born in Murray County, GA, the son of Thomas J. Sr. and Rebecca Childress Burnes. From Polk County Thomas Jr. enlisted in Company 26 of the Enrolled Missouri Militia during the Civil War. The town of Burns was named for Thomas J. Burnes Sr.

Elvira Jane Wright was the daughter of William and Sarah Whiteside Wright. While on a business trip in St. Clair County, IL, William Wright died in 1848. He was brought home to Polk County and buried on his farm. Sarah was interred beside William in 1853 on what is now known as Pleasant Hill Cemetery.

By 1880 Dora Burnes was living with her uncle and aunt, Charles and Elizabeth Wright Brandon in Coryell County, TX. Dora married William H. Trehern (c. 1861-1913) in Texas. William was born in England. Elvira Wright Burnes raised Mae and her brother, William Trehern, in Burns, MO after Dora's death in 1885.

Tilden and Mae Holt moved back and forth between the counties of Polk, MO and Ventura, CA. They were the parents of Fola (1906-1988), married Fern Stewart; Anna "Faye" (1908-1969), married Elvie Lindsey; G. Raymond (1911-1968), married Bobie Johnson; Avia (1913-2002), married Cecil Fellows; Golden (July 30, 1917); Dorothy "Oma" (1920), married Milton "Doc" Booher; and George (1924-1996), married Jackie Henry. Mae Holt died in 1956 and is buried beside Tilden in Santa Paula, CA.

Golden Holt married James "Brooks" Morris (1911-1967) in Polk County. Brooks was the son of Jesse and Mary "Addie" Brooks Morris. Jesse (1888-1973) was the son of James F. and Eliza E. Whitney Morris, grandson of Robert and Lucinda James Morris. Jesse's great-grandparents, John C. and Mary Jenkins Morris, left Alabama and settled in Polk County before 1840. Addie (1890-1982) was the daughter of Theophilus and Sarah Harper Brooks, granddaughter of Thomas C. and Louisa Harper Brooks and great-granddaughter of John and Betsy Courts Brooks. The Brooks and Harper families came to Missouri from Kentucky before 1850.

Golden and Brooks Morris had four children: Brooksie Lee, Joyce May, Ronald Holt and Patrica Gay. They moved to Ventura County, CA (Golden's birthplace) before the birth of Beth and Whitney's mother, Joyce. Joyce May Morris married John Thomas Brodersen, (1935-1976). Beth and Whitney's siblings are Deborah Brodersen Pedersen, John Morris Brodersen (1956-1957) and Heather Brodersen Garnica. Most of their family members still reside in Ventura County, CA.

Thanks to stories of their Polk County heritage told by their dear Grandma Golden, great-aunts Oma Holt Booher and Wilma "Max" Morris Griffin, when they visit there they also have a sense of being "home." Along with their siblings, their cousin Ryan Morris enjoys learning about the family history and memories of life in Polk County, MO. *Submitted by Beth Brodersen Collins and Whitney Brodersen Doud*

HOLT - Zella Katherine Holt was born in northeast Polk County on Jan. 30, 1899 to George Washington Holt and Mary Lucinda Breshears Gladden Holt. She was the third child born of this marriage. Her brothers and sisters were Jesse W., Graydon Arthur, Mary Elizabeth, Ruth Ann, Everett George and Orpha Ellen. Zella was the only child to live to adulthood. Her brother Jesse is buried at Louisburg Cemetery in Dallas County and the other children are buried near their mother at Lindley Creek Cemetery in Polk County. Zella's mother, Mary, was buried there by her first husband Charles Leslie Gladden.

On Jan. 20, 1915 Zella married Herman Thornton of Weaubleau, MO. They first went to California and Montana. Their daughters were born in Montana. Later they went to Idaho and remained the rest of their lives. Their daughters were Virginia Katherine and Emma Josephine. Virginia married Burlin Benham and they had a daughter, Barbara Elaine. Virginia died just a few

Zella Katherine Holt, age 15

months after Barbara's birth so Herman and Zella raised Barbara as their own.

Josephine married Leonard Flint and they had two children. They were Virginia and Butch.

Zella liked to reminisce about Polk County. She always kept in touch with family through her older half-sister Florence Elnora "Nora" Gladden McGee. After Nora's death Zella corresponded with her niece, Minnie McGee Fowler. Herman died on Dec. 27, 1993 and Zella died on Aug. 9, 1994. They lived the last years of their lives on the Snake River in western Idaho in the area of Homedale.

Barbara "Barb" is married to Ron Maxwell and they are the parents of six children. They are Ginger, Daniel, Blaine, Kelli and Mike. In 1998 Ron and Barb made their first trip to Zella's often-talked-about Polk County. Barb got to meet many cousins for the first time and visit the graves of many of her Breshears relatives including her third great-grandparents John and Naomi Hogg Breshears, who are buried in Breshears Cemetery in northeast Polk County. *Submitted by Barb Maxwell*

HOOBLER - John Reynolds and Ann Maria Tibbets Hoobler were the first of the Hoobler family that Nancy knows of to live in the areas of Dallas and Polk Counties. They came from Greenfield, Hancock County, IN with their seven living children about 1870. John was a farmer, served in the Civil War and lived very close to Red Top in Dallas County. He was born April 30, 1826 in Ohio, married Ann Maria Tibbets May 15, 1851 in Campbell County, KY. She died Nov. 9, 1893 in Dallas County; he died March 12, 1902, also in Dallas County. Their children migrated to

Top row: John Robert Hoobler, Malissa Jane Hoobler (wife), Thomas Ransom Agee, Effie Viola Hoobler and Ida Maude Hoobler; Front row: Arthur Cook Hoobler, Myrla Jane Hoobler, John Reynolds Hoobler and wife Ann Maria, Elizabeth Verdot Agee (mother of Malissa Jane Hoobler) and Henry Housten Hoobler, circa 1893

other areas, but some of their children did stay in Polk County. John Robert Hoobler, born March 19, 1852, married Malissa Jane Agee and moved his family from Red Top to Hooker, Texas County, OK in 1908. Martha Ann "Mattie" Hoobler, born Oct. 30, 1854, married John Cook Cowden and moved to Council Grove, Morris County, KS where they lived until their death. William Washington Hoobler, born Feb. 28, 1857, married Catherine "Katie" Clark and moved to Stone County, MO and then on to Morris, OK where they remained until their deaths. Henry Houston Hoobler, born Aug. 12, 1859, married Mary O. "Mollie" Headlee in Dallas County, but made their home in Bolivar, Polk County. Henry and wife were farmers and had one child, Guy Hoobler, born Feb. 10, 1893. Henry died July 18, 1896, Mollie died March 5, 1893 and Guy died July 18, 1896 in Bolivar. They are all buried in Greenwood Cemetery. Emarette Louisa Hoobler, born June 27, 1862, married Peter Munroe Clark Oct. 24, 1882 in Polk County. Peter was a farmer and reverend. He died May 3, 1933 in Bolivar; Emarette died 1903 in Bolivar. They are buried in Mt. Olive Cemetery. Sherman David Hoobler, born May 21, 1865, married Kitty Blan Friend. Sherman and Kitty had three children: Irma Blan Hoobler, Bernie Garrett Hoobler and Grace Dare Hoobler. Sherman remained in Dallas County and married Luna Estelle Fraker. They had two children, Thelma Helen Hoobler and Guy Olen Hoobler. Lawson Brown Hoobler, born Jan. 28, 1868, married Mary Jane "Janie" Brown Aug. 7, 1894 in Dallas County but resided and died in Bolivar. Lawson and Janie's children: Roscoe, Grace, Ray, Ai, Inez. Roscoe, born 1895, married Viva Iora Utterback and remained in Bolivar. They are buried in Shady Grove Cemetery. Ray Hoobler married Maude Winfiel and they resided in Los Angeles until their deaths. Inez "Nina" married Elias L. Manning and they are buried in Shady Grove Cemetery. Grace died shortly after birth. Nancy has very little information on Ai Lawrence Hoobler, only that he resided in California. To the best of Nancy's knowledge this information is correct. Please contact her and let her know of any errors. *Submitted by Nancy Jane Ramsey Norris*

HOOVER - Reva's parents were Claud Hoover and Ressie (Gates) Hoover. They lived most of their lives in or around Pleasant Hope, MO. Claud's parents were William Henry Hoover and Celia Emmaline Milligan (Millican) (Millikan). Her father was Henry Minett Millican. Her mother was Charlette Giles. William was born in Everton, MO. He lived at Pleasant Hope, MO. William and Celia were members of Providence Baptist which is just north of Pleasant Hope, MO. William's father was Henry Samuel Hoover. He was born at Everton, MO. He served in the Civil War. He married Theresa America Reagan, whose father was William Reagan. Henry's father was Samuel Hoover, born in Tennessee (believed to be Hoover Gap). Samuel fought on both sides in the Civil War. He married Frances Stone. They lived in Barry County, MO which later became Dade County, MO. Samuel's father was John William Hoover who was born in Virginia and died in Everton, MO. John married Nancy Sutton on 1799. John's father was "Old" Matthias Huber ("Old" was used to differentiate him from those of his descendants who were named after him). "Old" Matthias Huber married Maria (no last name listed). They first lived in Lancaster County where Matthias took the oath of allegiance to the state of Pennsylvania in November 1778. They moved to Virginia and then on to Tennessee, stopped for a time in Sweetwater Valley, which is where Reva (Choate) Hoover's husband's ancestors came from originally. Matthias purchased 5000 acres in Rutherford County, TN. He had 10,000 acres there which was, and still is, known as Hoover Gap, TN. He was the first member of the family to embrace a religion other than the Mennonite faith, when he became a Methodist. He changed his name to "Hoover." "Old Matthias'" parents were Jacob Huber and Anna. He spelled some of his children's names Hover and some Hoover in his will. He owned two plantations. He willed the 250-acre plantation to Matthias and Jacob. Jacob's father was Hans Huber, who was Reva's earliest US ancestor. He was born in Switzerland. Hans married Margareth Koch, pronounced "cook." They were Swiss Mennonites who fled Switzerland to avoid religious persecution. They went to Germany and then on to America where they settled in Martic Township, PA. This takes Reva's ancestries back to Switzerland.

Reva married Samuel Paul Choate in Harrison, AR. She had lived all her life in the Pleasant Hope and Brighton area. Reva had nine brothers and sisters. They include Raymond Hoover, Gladys Teague, Clyde Hoover, Nora Hoover, Norma Young, Betty Williams, Arbaleta Cossins, Dean Hoover and Kenneth Hoover. Reva and Samuel had three children. They are Paul Wayne Choate, Paula Mae Choate, and Linda Kay Choate. Wayne married Alice Mathis and had two children, Wanita and Wesley. Wanita married Jeffery Watts and had one child, Justin Watts. Wesley married

Claud and Ressie (Gates) Hoover, Reva Choate's parents

Michelle Mears and had Jacob Choate. They divorced and Wesley married Tara Tindall and they had Kamry Choate. Paula married Pat McCoy and divorced. She then married Lanny Meins and divorced. Paula then married Jerry O'Dell and had Nicole O'Dell. Linda Choate married Lendell Morris and they had Thomas Morris. Thomas married Michelle Overby and they had Tyler Morris and Kendall Morris. *Submitted by Reva (Hoover) Choate*

HOPKINS – Edgar "Ed" Hopkins, youngest of eight children of James and Elviria Fox Hopkins, was born Dec. 14, 1875 in Dunnegan, Polk County, MO.

Annettie "Nettie," daughter of William H. and Martha Olinger Rovenstine, was born Aug. 9, 1872 in Atwood, Kosciusk County, IN. Martha died and William, with his four children, moved to Missouri, near Republic in Greene County, MO.

Ed and Nettie married in Republic on Sept. 22, 1897. A son, Clarence "Bud" Edward, was born Sept. 24, 1898 near Dunnegan. They moved to Oklahoma where land was opened for homesteading. A daughter Mabel was born Feb. 5, 1903. After three years they moved back to Missouri, later to a farm west of the Hopkins School. Ed's brother lived on the neighboring farm. After grade school, the children attended Fair Play High School in Missouri. Ed's final move was to a farm one and a half miles from Dunnegan, west of the Dunnegan Springs. It was first homesteaded by William Dunnegan, whose family came to this area and gave Dunnegan its name. Ed and Nettie purchased the farm from his Uncle Solomon and Cordelia Dunnegan Hopkins. Everyone remembers and loved the farm, the threshing, butchering, shearing and swimming in Spring Creek.

Bud married Neva, daughter of Fred and Cora Bush Engleman. She was a teacher. Bud continued farming. He died on Nov. 12, 1938 and is buried in Akard Cemetery, south of Fair Play. Ed was buried beside him on Nov. 2, 1960 and Nettie on Jan. 18, 1959.

On Feb. 5, 1920, Mabel married Ernest Hugh Curl, son of James "Jim" and Mary Jane Ray Curl. After moving to Bolivar, Ernest continued his ministry and Mabel, who loved to sew, became a seamstress. Ernest died March 1, 1981 and Mabel died May 7, 2000 at the age of 97 and is buried at Greenwood Cemetery in Bolivar.

The Curl children were the only grandchildren of Ed and Nettie. They graduated from Hopkins School and Fair Play High School.

Juanita B. was born Oct. 20, 1922, obtained a master's degree and retired in 1983 from the Grandview, MO schools. She married H. Leon Foster, son of Homer and Alta May Copeland Foster on June 13, 1944. Their children are Michael W., born Aug. 2, 1945, Patrick B., born Sept. 5, 1948 and Terrence "Terry" E., born Feb. 25, 1950. Leon worked in Kansas City, MO for a library system and traveled to many states. They moved back to Bolivar in 1986. Leon died and was buried Feb. 23, 1993 at Greenwood Cemetery, Bolivar. Leon served in the army in Salina, KS.

Bueford C. was born Aug. 12, 1924 and enjoyed farming. After his time served in the army in Germany he came back to the farm. He married Neta Ruth, daughter of Ray and Erma Vest, a teacher. Bueford was a mail carrier; he retired and is raising cattle. Their children are Kent C., born April 16, 1952; Daniel "Danny" R., born Feb. 24, 1953 and Freddie W., born June 19, 1955, deceased.

N. Dale was born Aug. 16, 1926 and served in the army in Texas. He married Charlene, daughter of Marvin and Lizzie Ragsdale on Nov. 30, 1947. Dale worked for Boeing in Wichita, KS and their only child Catherine Gayle was born March 20, 1957. He retired from McDonald Douglas and they moved to Bolivar. Charlene died and is buried at Greenwood Cemetery. Dale married Juanita "Cricket" Roach on Nov. 5, 1995.

Dixie G. was born Nov. 5, 1929 and married Clyde L., son of Cleo and Granville Mayse. He also served in the army. They moved to Springfield, IL where Dixie was a bookkeeper for Royal Tire Company and Clyde traveled the area for Hershey, based in Pennsylvania. After retirement, they bought and built on acreage outside of town and raised a garden and fruit trees. Their children are Larry G., born May 12, 1948; Randy L., born March 26, 1952 and David L., born June 10, 1956. *Submitted by Juanita Foster*

HOPKINS - James Hopkins, son of Thomas Hopkins, was born in Wales about 1700. He emigrated to Virginia and died in Orange County, NC in 1758. His son, William, was born in 1737 in Wales and died between 1761-1779 in Orange County, NC. William had a son born in Orange County, NC in 1765, who was named James, after his grandfather.

James, a Revolutionary soldier, enlisted at the age of 16 in June 1781 as a private in Captain Parrish's Company, Colonel Thomas Farmer's North Carolina Regiment, and was at the Battle of Eutow Springs. He was later in South Carolina with General Greene.

James married Elizabeth Billingsley about 1795 in Rowan County, NC and they had eight children. The family moved to Greene County, MO in 1833 and in 1835 settled in Madison Township, Polk County, MO.

Elizabeth died in 1848 and James died in 1849. Both were buried in the family cemetery on their farm one and three-fourths miles west of Fair Play, now called Hopkins Cemetery. On Sept. 6, 1931, a stone furnished by the Quartermaster General, US Army, was dedicated by members of the Rachel Donelson Chapter, DAR.

Solomon Hopkins, the seventh child of James and Elizabeth, was born March 18, 1813 in Wilson County, TN and died Sept. 20, 1853. In 1835 he married Mary Hartley, who was born Oct. 9, 1813 and died Aug. 8, 1896. Both were buried in the Hopkins Cemetery. To this union was born 10 children.

Solomon H. Hopkins, the seventh child of Solomon and Mary, was born March 26, 1846 and died Aug. 8, 1924. He married Cordelia Dunnegan in 1872. She was born Nov. 30, 1845 and died March 12, 1922. To this union was born nine children. They first lived on the farm originally settled by Cordelia's grandfather, William Dunnegan Sr., on Spring Creek, about a mile west of Dunnegan Springs. In 1901, they built a house near the Big Spring, at the edge of the present town of Dunnegan, where they lived until their deaths.

Sitting on porch is S. H. Hopkins, his wife Cordelia and youngest daughter Nellie Hopkins, circa 1910

They were buried at Akard Cemetery at Fair Play. Cordelia was a sister to T. H. B. Dunnegan Sr., the founder of the Polk County Bank of Bolivar.

Solomon C. "Cecil" Hopkins, the seventh child of Solomon and Cordelia, was born on the family farm Aug. 27, 1882 and died Dec. 16, 1968. He left Missouri about 1910 and homesteaded land at Richey, MT. There he married Klova Lee Davis in 1920. Klova was born April 27, 1897 and died Dec. 16, 1978. They had one son, Rex Lee.

After the deaths of Cecil's parents, Cecil and family moved to Missouri and resided in the home near the Big Spring at Dunnegan until their deaths. Cecil and Klova were buried at Dunnegan Cemetery.

Rex, their son, born Jan. 1, 1921 in Richey, MT, married Helene L. LaRew, Feb. 27, 1944. Helene was born April 27, 1925 and died July 5, 1988. She was buried at Greenwood Cemetery.

Rex and Helene had one daughter, Jo Ann, born Oct. 23, 1945. Jo married David Strader April 8, 1978. David was born June 6, 1949. They had two sons, Wesley Christopher, born Oct. 26, 1982 and Daniel Anthony, born Jan. 21, 1985. All currently reside in Bolivar. *Submitted by Rex Hopkins*

HOPKINS - Louise Hopkins was born in Osceola, MO Aug. 13, 1910 but has lived in Polk County for 82 of her 92 years. Her father was Ira W. Woodford, who was manager of the local branch of the Hurley Lumber Company (based in Kansas City) in Osceola from 1906-1913 and then from 1913-1939 in Humansville when he retired. He was born in Lamar, MO and moved to Weaubleau, MO with his family when he was a young man. Her mother was Maude (Burchett) Woodford. She was born near Collins, MO. All the formal education she had was in Vine Hill Country School but Louise always admired her mother's thirst for knowledge for she put forth great effort to educate herself.

Louise graduated from Humansville High School in 1927 and then after two years at SWBC (now SBU) she taught for three years until she was married in 1932. Louise's husband, Basil Hopkins and she were married in Buffalo, MO, by the Rev. J. E. Jackson. Basil was the son of Laura (Holmes) and J. B. Hopkins of Dunnegan. Basil and Louise had one daughter Dixie Lou and farmed for 23 years near Dunnegan until 1955 when they moved to Republic, MO. There they bought and operated the Three Gables Station.

In 1962 they leased the station and moved to Bolivar where they bought a farm west of town where Louise still resides.

Basil and Louise were some of the founders of the Dunnegan Community Bible Church, of which they and their five grandchildren were all members.

Dixie was killed in a tragic tractor accident in 1968 and the children came to live with them until they were all grown and on their own.

The family lost Basil in 1992 but besides the grandchildren, Louise has nine great-grandchildren and four great-great-grandchildren of whom she is very proud.

People told Basil and Louise that they couldn't raise five grandchildren ages 1-12 at 58 years old but they proved them wrong. They are James and Roy Lewis and Kaye Jarrell of Bolivar and Faye Southard and Ray Lewis of Springfield.

Louise's life hasn't always been easy but it has been an experience and a blessing that she would not want to have missed.

James has served in the Air Force Reserves for 20 years, which allowed him to do much traveling which he enjoyed.

Louise has seen many changes in Polk County in her lifetime. Even the weather has changed. During the winter of 1924-1925 she ice-skated on the big pond in the city park for weeks.

Their first family car was a 1916 Model T. The taillight ran on kerosene and she and and her sister took turns blowing it out. Louise has a copy of the tax receipt for 1881 on Basil's Grandpa

Left to right: Dean Rector, George Hurley, Rolla Mirkles, Ira Woodford and Cane Rector.

Holmes 80-acre farm near Dunnegan and the taxes were $3.83.

Basil was a man of great determination. He never started anything expecting it to fail. *Submitted by Louise Hopkins*

HOPKINS – Marsha's Hopkins family ancestry can be traced to the Revolutionary War soldier James Hopkins and his wife Elizabeth Billingsley. They were among the first settlers in Madison Township of Polk County. The land they homesteaded is where the Hopkins Cemetery is located in Fair Play where many of this line of the family are buried. Their son, James A. Hopkins, a Cedar County judge, his wife Sarah Robertson and their children also came to Missouri in 1835 from Tennessee.

One of James A. Hopkins' children, David R. Hopkins, a Civil War veteran, settled in Laclede and Wright Counties after the war. David's wife was Margaret Catherine Jones Wheeler. David died in 1889 and is buried at Macomb in Wright County. David and Margaret's children were Henry Francis, Sarah, John Columbus, George Thomas, Mahala Elizabeth, Martha Eldora and Ralpha Ann.

In 1900, David's son John Columbus Hopkins moved the family to the community of Wishart in Polk County, where John worked for the Frisco Railroad. John's wife was Maud Jane Hensley. John's mother, Margaret, the widow of David R. Hopkins, also moved with the family to Wishart. Margaret died in 1935 and is buried at the Enon Cemetery.

Marsha's grandfather Okley Israel Hopkins was born in Pulaski County, MO on June 20, 1895, the first son born to John Columbus Hopkins and Maud Hensley. He was 5 years old when the family moved to Wishart. His brothers and sisters were William David (married Mary Mayfield, children: Geraldine, Betty, Vida, Virginia, Elizabeth, Ted, John, Norman and Stephen); Georgia (married Robert Pate, children: Captola and Robert); Scharlotte (married Coy Underwood, children: James, Guelda, Ruby Grey and John William); John Paul (married

Front row: Columbus Sullins, Earl, Ollie Etta Perriman Gent holding Raymond; back row: Ruth, Nathan, William, Stephen and Elsie, year 1915

Gladys Holdren, children: Wanda and John); Cuby (married Braz Lawrence, children: John, Bobby, Daniel, Venita, Ruby and Donald); Ruby (married Oscar Wilson, child: Marvella). John and Maud Hopkins are buried at the Enon Cemetery.

On Feb. 20, 1920, Okley married Minerva Ruth Gent, Marsha's grandmother. Ruth was born Jan. 31, 1901 in Polk County, the daughter of Columbus Sullins Gent and Ollie Etta Perriman. Columbus Sullins Gent's parents were Nathan Sullins Gent (son of Josiah Gent and Patty Sullins) and Mary Elizabeth Mitchell. Mary Elizabeth Mitchell was the daughter of Stephen Mitchell and granddaughter of the Mitchell family patriarchs Morris Mitchell and Elizabeth Hoosang. The Gent and Mitchell families moved to Polk County around 1835 from Tennessee and settled near Orleans on the Little Sac River. Most of this family is buried at the Mitchell Campground.

The Hopkins family front row: John Columbus Hopkins (seated), Ruby, Maude Jane Hensley Hopkins (seated) Cuby and John Paul (seated); back row: Georgia, Okley Israel, William Davis and Scharlette, year 1917

Hopkins/Gent family reunion, 2000

Columbus Sullins Gent went by the nickname "Lum." He and Ollie had the following children in addition to Marsha's grandmother Ruth: Nathan Lather; William Ray (married Goldie Mitchell, child, Harold Ray Gent); Stephen Asa; Chester (married Versa Brown, children: Snoda, Donald, Doris, Alice and Carol); Elsie Myrtle (married Ira Landreth, children: Wanda June, Retha and Jack); Earl Perriman; Raymond Simpson Gent (married Anna Kups, children: Raymond Dale and Carl David). Lum and Ollie are buried at the Mitchell Campground.

Okley and Ruth Hopkins farmed in and around Wishart where they raised their family. Their children are Velma; Delsena (married Floyd Stewart, children: Gary, Dean and Kent); Glen E. (married Melba Medlock, children: Carl and Marsha); Harlan (married Dorothy Zumwalt, children: Harlana and Ramona); Maudetta (married first, Kenneth Carns; married second, Augustine Colvin; married third, John Bruhn, children: Vicki, Francine, Jacqueline and Michael); Bonnie (married Richard Kirksey); Stanley (married Barbra Brobisky, children: Tonda and Diane); and Doyle (married Nadine Simpson, children: April, Brent and Amy). Okley died in 1969 and Ruth in 1977. They are buried at the Enon Cemetery. Okely and Ruth's family have remained very close over the years and enjoy getting together for the "Hopkins and Gent Family Reunion" held every two years in Bolivar. *Submitted by Marsha J. Hopkins*

Archibald Hopper, born 1823, Bedford County, TN, died 1900, Polk County, MO

HOPPER - Archibald "Arch" Hopper was born March 24, 1823 in Bedford County, TN. His parents were Charles Hopper Jr. and Susan/Susannah Penn, who were both born in North Carolina. Archibald married Margaret Gibbons in Marshall County on Sept. 22, 1843. Margaret was born November 1823 in Tennessee.

Two children were born to them in Marshall County, TN. A son, Andrew Morrison Hopper, was born in 1845. A daughter, Malissa Elizabeth Hopper, was born July 28, 1846. About this time Arch and Margaret decided to emigrate from Tennessee and head west, crossing the Mississippi River to Polk County, MO. The young couple with two small children began lives as settlers at Johnson Township on March 28, 1847 with 50 acres of Missouri land, to be known later as Humansville, Polk County, MO. Arch and his family planted a peach orchard and ran a distillery making peach brandy for the Government. They also farmed, expanding their holdings to 205 acres.

Arch and Margaret had been on their new settlement but a short time when twins were born to them; Charles H. "Charley" and Sarah C. were born July 20, 1848. Little Andrew Morrison was 3 years old and Malissa Elizabeth was 2 when the twins were born. Other children followed. Nancy Jane was born June 20, 1850. Thomas Hugh was born Jan. 13, 1852. Susan Catherine was born Oct. 7, 1854. James Archibald was born Jan. 12, 1856. Alvin W. was born in 1858. America Evalina "Lina" was born March 27, 1860. Henry Sigel was born Feb. 27, 1862. Margaret Ann was born Dec. 23, 1863. These last 10 children were all born in Humansville.

A few days after Henry Sigel was born, Arch answered the call for volunteers in the Union Army. On March 10, 1862 Arch was mustered into Captain Smith's Company C, Eighth Regiment Missouri State Militia Cavalry and given the rank of corporal at Pittsburg, Hickory County, MO. On the muster roll, dated April 30, 1862, he is listed as a sergeant, and in the remarks section on the roll dated Aug. 31, to Sept. 19, 1862, it reads that he was on "detached service." Arch was discharged from the Union Army Feb. 11, 1863 at Newtonia, Newton County, MO to accept a civil office per order of General Curtis. The civil office was his appointment as constable of Johnson Township where he owned his farm.

Ten months after his arrival home, his wife, Margaret, delivered their last child: Margaret Ann, born Dec. 23, 1863. The next month, on Jan. 25, 1864, Margaret died at age 41 at Humansville. She is buried at Plum Grove Cemetery at Humansville. Arch Hopper, at age 41, was then a widower with 12 children, ages 19 years through 1 month.

On July 12, 1864 Arch married Harriet A. (Ruyle) Mitchell, born Nov. 15, 1831 in Illinois. Harriet was a widow whose husband, John A. Mitchell, had died Oct. 1, 1863 and is buried in Shady Grove Cemetery, south of Humansville. Harriet was left with three children: Mary, age 11 years; Urilla Louise, age 9 years; and Mahlon Adolphus, age 6 years. One year later, on July 26, 1865, a daughter, Harriet Labirdia, was born to Arch and Harriet. Two more daughters were born after Harriet Labirdia. They were Tennessee L., born March 20, 1867 and died April 30, 1867 and Olley, born July 28, 1868 and died Dec. 28, 1871. Both children are buried at Shady Grove Cemetery.

Arch's wife, Harriet, died Nov. 19, 1870. She is buried in Shady Grove Cemetery. On May 4, 1871 Arch married Mary E. Mitchell, no relation to Harriet's first husband. Archibald Hopper died Sept. 4, 1900 in Humansville in his 97th year and was buried in the Plum Grove Cemetery. He was a Master Mason, a Baptist Church member, and a Republican. *Submitted by Joanne L. Franklin*

HOPPER – Archibald Hopper, the writer's great-great-great-grandfather, was born Feb. 24, 1806 to Charles and Martha Hopper in Grainger County, East TN. Later, Archibald and other family members began a westward trek and Archibald found his future wife, Nancy Barcroft, in Madison County. They were married June 15, 1826 and had five children. About 1835 Archibald packed up his family to follow his sister Sarah and husband James G. Human, to Missouri to be numbered among the first settlers of the village of Humansville in Polk County.

Archibald, a farmer, amassed 400 acres of land just southwest of town where he grew crops and nine more children: Margaret Emily, Elisha, Thomas Benton, Sarah I., Rufus G., Erasmus, Nancy Mahubla, Elizabeth and Telitha Orlena. The five Tennessee-born children were Martha Elizabeth, William Carroll, Mary Jane, James Franklin and Charles.

The Civil War took its toll in the first year when Archibald, age 55, joined the Missouri Home Guard at Bolivar July 6, 1861, serving in Capt. Menefee's Company A, 15th Regiment, USRC. He was killed Sept. 19, 1861 at the Battle of Lexington in northern Missouri along the Missouri River where he is buried. He served two months but his official discharge date was Dec. 6, 1861, and the five months service was granted $65.48 that was not paid until July 21, 1864. His death left wife Nancy with five young children to raise ages 3 to 15. Two sons were also drawn into the conflict for the North: Lt. Thomas Benton Hopper and Private Elisha Hopper, both in Company D, 15th Missouri Cavalry.

By 1870, Rufus G., age 23, Archibald's 10th child, was in charge of farming and welfare for his mother, now 68, and three younger sisters. By 1880, Nancy has died and Orlena, with twins Tolbert and Mary (Chaney) Earnest, are living with Rufus. In 1881, Rufus married Nancy Anne Crumb and had five children: Fred Lee, William, Fanny Viola, Letha and Sterling. Nancy Anne did not survive Sterling's birth and Rufus remained on the farm to raise his children alone. Rufus died April 16, 1926, at age 76 and is buried in Shady Grove Cemetery. In 1923, his daughter Viola was killed instantly when a cyclone swept through the area and blew off a chicken house roof that landed on her.

Fred married Myrtle McKee in Humansville Dec. 13, 1909, with S. B. Evans, MG of the Christian Church officiating. Witnesses were Sam W. and Iva (McKee) Goodson, also of Humansville. Fred and Myrtle Hopper had two children born in Polk County, MO before moving to Cass County, MO: Homer and Beulah. In Cass County the family increased with Wilbur J., Orville W. and Elsie May. Strong ties to Humansville kept the family making regular visits riding the train from Raymore, Cass County. Fred's siblings, Fanny Viola, Letha and Sterling made their homes in Humansville and William lived in Cass County.

The writer resides in Cass County near the land of her grandfather Fred and continues the tradition of regular visits to Humansville to visit relatives, albeit many are resting in Shady Grove, Plum Grove and Humansville Cemeteries. *Submitted by Marilyn Hopper Davis*

HOPPER – Archibald Hopper was born in Tennessee in 1823 to Charles Hopper and Susannah Penn. The year after Archibald was born, Charles remarried and we have yet to learn what happened to Susannah. Archibald married Margaret Gibbons in Tennessee in 1843 and came to Missouri in 1847. It is said he raised the first crop where Humansville is now located. Twelve children were born to them: Andrew Morrison, Melissa Elizabeth, Charles H., Sarah Clarkie, Nancy Jane, Thomas Hugh, Susan Catherine, James Archibald, Alvin W., America Evalina, Henry Sigel and Margaret Ann. His wife died in 1864. Archibald married twice more, first to Harrieta

The James Archibald Hopper family, top row: Nora Jane and Luella Catherine; bottom row: James Archibald, Harley James, Charles Arthur and Annie; note: William Archibald was grown and had left home when this picture was taken.

Ruyle in 1864, then to Mary Elizabeth Mitchell in 1871.

Evelyn and her siblings descend from James Archibald Hopper, born in 1856 in Humansville and died in 1926 at his home near Dunnegan. He married Anna "Annie" L. Boyd in 1879 in Bolivar and they had six children: William Archibald, Margaret A. (died at age 9), Nora Jane, Luella Catherine, Charles Arthur and Harley James. Their dad was Charles Arthur Hopper, born July 16, 1895 in Humansville. He was only 9 years old when his mother died Dec. 3, 1905. Their dad's oldest brother, William, may have already left Missouri as records show that he married in Sheridan, WY and his first child was born there in 1907. Nora, being the oldest child, assumed much of the responsibility of caring for her younger sister and brothers. Nora then met and married Charley Carr in 1908. Charley and Nora lived in Clarinda, IA and their only child was born there in 1909. Soon after they moved to Lodge Grass, MT, about 40 miles north of Sheridan, WY where William was living. Soon Charles and his sister Luella joined Nora and William. It is not known why Harley James left Missouri.

Charles "cowboyed" around Wyoming and Montana a few years. He was inducted into the US Army July 19, 1918 at Sheridan, WY and was stationed at the Base Hospital, Camp MacArthur, TX from August 1918 to February 1919. He was honorably discharged at Fort Logan, CO Feb. 10, 1919 and returned to Wyoming. He married Inza Fay Littrell, Aug. 18, 1924 in Sheridan, WY. Their first born, Vivian Lorraine, was born in Sheridan July 3, 1925, but lived for only 12 days. Soon after her death, they moved to Lodge Grass, MT. There three children were born: Boyd Edward, born in 1927, Evelyn Jane, born in 1928 and Phyllis Jean, born in 1930. Charles and Inza divorced in 1936 and Charles remarried. He had another son, Dale D. Hopper, born in 1937.

Evelyn knows there were many Hoppers in Polk County, and she continues to search for anyone who may have a family connection to her. Her great-grandparents, Archibald and Margaret Gibbons Hopper and her grandparents, James Archibald and Annie Boyd Hopper are buried in the Plum Grove Cemetery. Would like to have more information on them and on Archibald's children and their families. *Submitted by Evelyn Hopper Hunter*

HOPPER - Hiram Henderson Hopper, Virginia's grandfather, was one of nine children born to Uriah Henderson, a Civil War veteran, (born Feb. 22, 1825; died Feb. 21, 1897) and Sarah Mackey Ray Hopper (born March 27, 1831; died April 6, 1915); both were from Tennessee.

Hiram (born Aug. 15, 1858; died July 5, 1940) spent his early manhood in Idaho and was a driver of a stagecoach. Evidently he would make visits to Missouri to court Tirzah Elizabeth Litle (born Dec. 10, 1858; died Sept. 20, 1938). Tirzah was caring for her ailing mother. He gave the ultimatum, "Marry me now or never," and so they were wed! Tirzah's parents were James Litle (born March 6, 1833; died April 9, 1905) and Miranda Elizabeth McPherson Litle (born Jan. 15, 1839; died March 5, 1925). They came from Harrison County, WV.

Hiram and Tirzah's son, Burnie Litle, was born Nov. 1, 1899 and died Sept. 16, 1967. He was soon nicknamed "Big Boy" and was known by this name all of his life. Ethel Belle was born March 8, 1903 and died Aug. 23, 2000 and "Babe" became her nickname.

The Hopper family moved to a farm of Benton Dunnegan's near Dunnegan, MO and worked for him the rest of Hiram's life, considering it a good deal.

As soon as quick, energetic and impatient Babe was big enough, she took over many household duties; far sooner than most girls her age, as Tirzah was not well. Hiram, who was considered studious, soon had Babe reading as she would sit on his lap and they would read the comics. He was a staunch Republican and was clerk of the Campbell Township voters.

E. B. and Burnie were in the Oakland school district, but also attended Dunnegan school's sessions. E. B. was eager to learn and this caused problems as the teachers kept moving E. B. up a grade until she was in Burnie's class. He was not happy with this! E. B.'s parents chose to have her repeat the seventh and eighth grade and she didn't seem to mind as she liked school and learning.

Burnie enjoyed hunting and doing things with friends and cousins whom lived nearby. He became a crack-shot and was well known for his squirrel-hunting ability. This provided meat for the table.

Ethel Belle rode the train to Humansville to go to high school and graduated. She did the same to Southwest Baptist College in Bolivar for a summer teaching term. Oh, joy! Her first teaching assignment was at Red Hill in Cedar County. She rode her horse nine plus miles daily and did the janitor work.

Ethel Belle and Lonnie Nottingham (born Dec. 28, 1901; died May 28, 1976) were married Feb. 19, 1927 and began farming, moving twice before buying a farm in the Cedar Grove school district. By now they were the parents of Donald H. (born Oct. 13, 1927; died Feb. 4, 1988), who weighed in at three pounds. He was a tough, little fighter. On July 24, 1933 black-eyed and black-haired Virginia Lee arrived, tipping the scale at seven pounds. Next, Larry Douglas (born Nov. 3, 1942) weighed six pounds and was named for General Douglas MacArthur.

Burnie grew up, never married, entered the army and then worked in Nebraska. Later he lived in Humansville in a boarding home.

Ethel Belle, daughter of Hiram and Tirzah Hopper, age 20

Lon and E. B. were partners in farming and worked long hours, but read the daily paper. Lon was a farm sale buff and E. B. enjoyed it, too. She was active in Polk County Extension clubs (Busy Bee and Rosebud), a 4-H leader, and Republican Committee Woman for Johnson Township. They were known for hospitality, honesty, and loyalty to the Spring Creek Cumberland Presbyterian Church at Dunnegan.

One of the legacies carried on from each generation was the love of reading. Hiram and Tirzah had three grandchildren and each of those homes continues to subscribe to the daily news as begun by the Hoppers. *Submitted by Virginia Nottingham Stauffacher*

HOPPERS - Bill and Charlotte Hoppers moved to Polk County in 1961 when he became superintendent of the Humansville school system. He was born in 1931 at their farm home near Urbana, MO to Bill and Mayme Russell Hopper. He attended school there and eventually got a business degree from SMS, a master's degree from MU and a specialist degree from CMSC. After serving in Germany during the Korean Conflict he worked in the schools of Cross Timbers, Wheatland, Climax Springs and for over 20 years in the Humansville system. He is a member of Hogles Creek Lodge No. 289 AF & AM, OES, and various educational fraternities and associations.

Charlotte and Bill Hoppers, June 22, 1952

Charlotte was born in 1934 in Topeka, KS to Harry and Doris Dieval Burger and attended elementary school in Kansas City, MO. After WWII, ill health forced her father into retirement; the family moved to rural Weaubleau where they operated a grocery store and filling station. She graduated from Weaubleau High School and received a teaching degree from SMS and a master's from Drury University. She started her teaching career in a rural school and then taught in area schools. She retired from the Humansville system in 1991. She is a member of the OES of which she is a Past Matron and she also served as DDGM of the 41st District. She enjoyed dancing with the "Timeless Tappers" and

Bill Hoppers, Doris Burger, Charlotte Hoppers; back row: Steve, Charla and Jarrett Lear, Kris, Marsha and Tara Keller.

china paints in her spare time.

Their elder daughter, Charla Kay, was born in Springfield in 1957. She graduated from Humansville High School and received a bachelor's and a master's from SMSU. She and her childhood sweetheart, Steve Lear, reside on a farm east of Weaubleau and he works for Hermitage Lumber and she teaches business at Weaubleau High School. In 2001 she was recognized as the "Outstanding Business Teacher of Southwest Missouri" and in 2002 she received the "Outstanding Secondary Educator of Southwest Missouri" award presented by MSTA. Their son, Jarrett Steven, graduated from Weaubleau,

Charlotte, Bill, Marsha Dian and Charla Kay Hoppers

attended DeVry College and is employed in Kansas City.

Their younger daughter, Marsha Dian, was born in 1959 in Osceola, MO and was valedictorian of her graduating class in Humansville. She attended Burge School of Nursing and is now an assistant professor of nursing at Cox College of Nursing. In 2001 she received the "Governor's Award for Excellence in Teaching." She and her two children, Tara Lindsay and Kristopher Allan live in their rural home north of Springfield. Kris is a student at SMSU and Tara attends Hillcrest High School.

The Hoppers bought the Tim Jones property in 1962 and Charlotte continues to live there. Bill has been a patient in the Veterans' Home in Mt. Vernon since 1997. *Submitted by Charlotte Hopper*

HUBBERT - Joseph John Hubbert was born Oct. 23, 1886 in Prairie du Chien, WI, the son of Francis Frank and Mary (Hanzlicek) Hubbart. He was one of 12 children in the family, 10 of whom lived to adulthood.

Work brought Joseph to Missouri and he settled in the Polk County area where he met and married Margaret Mary Novak on Aug. 29, 1912. Margaret came to Karlin in 1902 with her parents, Mathais and Anna (Husske) Novak and their children. Margaret was born June 19, 1887 in Fort Dodge, IA.

Joseph and Margaret resided on a farm just outside of Karlin. They had four children, Ludmilla "Lillian," Stephen, Frank and Josephine. Tragedy struck the young family in 1918 when Joseph caught pneumonia during a flu epidemic that affected and killed many young men in the area. Joseph died on Oct. 11, 1918.

After Joseph's death, Margaret left the farm and moved back to Iowa to be closer to her family. It was there that she gave birth to Josephine, a month after Joseph had died. A short time later, Margaret and her four small children moved back to Missouri and the farm. She was told by many that a woman and four small children could never make it alone on a farm, but Margaret was determined and they made it work.

Excitement came to the Hubbert family as well as the whole Karlin Community when, in the late 1920s while a water well was being drilled near the depot, a presence of natural gas was detected. This sparked the interest of many oil promoters who in the mid-1920s leased a part of the Hubbert farm in hopes of finding oil. The derrick became a big attraction for the area, bringing in people from all over. Much to the dismay of all involved they were unable to strike oil.

Through all the hard times, Margaret kept her family together. They were very active in the St. Wenceslaus Church and the community. After the children were grown, Margaret moved to town. She later got remarried to Joseph Mudd and they moved to Texas for a bit before they returned to Bolivar and moved into a house near the Hubbert farm which Margaret's son, Stephen and grandson, Joseph, built for her so she would be close to the family. Joseph Mudd died Nov. 17, 1971.

Stephen married and remained on the family farm where he farmed until his death in 1989. His youngest daughter now lives on the family farm. Frank also married and was a farmer in the Karlin area until his death in 1985. Stephen and Frank were both well known Polk County farmers. Josephine, in turn, also married a farmer and raised her family in Polk County. Josephine died in 2000. Ludmilla "Lillian" joined the convent of the Sisters of Mercy. She became known to many as Sister Mary Natalie. She is now retired and resides in St. Louis.

Margaret died on Nov. 5, 1983 and is buried in the St. Wenceslaus Cemetery along with both of her husbands as well as her children and many other family members. *Submitted by Rita Hubbert Lemmon*

HUCKABY - One warm day on the Sentinel Prairie in Polk County, MO in 1857, a little boy playing near his home noticed a weary old dog trudging up the road. The little boy thought he recognized the dog and ran toward his house. "Ma, Pa," he yelled. "Here comes a dog up the road and it looks just like Joe Huckaby's old dog!" When the family reached the road, coming into view was the heavily laden wagon bearing Joseph and Agnes Huckaby and their children. And so arrived Joseph and Agnes Payne Kinslow Huckaby in Polk County.

Agnes' roots go back to Bedford County, VA where her ancestors settled in the early 1700s. Agnes, born Jan. 20, 1820 in Barren County, KY, was the seventh of 16 children of Jubal Payne (1787-1850) and Rhoda Basham Payne. In 1837, she married Joseph Kinslow, son of Ambrose Kinslow (Kincheloe), in Barren County. Two children were born to the young couple: Page C. on July 31, 1838 and Josephine Ann about 1840. The untimely death of Joseph in the spring of 1840 left Agnes a widow, 20 years old, with two babies.

Agnes Payne Kinslow Huckaby

The son of Thomas Huckaby, who was born in England and emigrated to Bedford County, VA in 1765, Joseph was born Oct. 18, 1789 and moved with his parents to Barren County, KY. He fought in the War of 1812 and on his way home on foot from the Battle of New Orleans he became so hungry that he traded a new, homemade jeans vest to the Indians for two loaves of corn bread. Joseph married Mary "Polly" Bridges and they had nine children, among them: Nancy (married Ben Litteral), Thomas (whose daughter, Martha Jane, married Agnes' son, Page), Joseph, Mary (married J. Payne), William, Nathan and James.

On June 23, 1841, Agnes married Joseph Huckaby, a widower. Agnes and Joseph Huckaby had 15 children of their own: Margaret, John, Juble, Hayden, Allen, Elizabeth, Felix, Wayne, Crit, Martha, Jennie, Mary, Joseph, Joshua and George. Joseph and Agnes were active members of the Hopewell Baptist Church. Agnes served on the "visiting committee" which called upon members who were absent from services or who might have strayed from the straight and narrow path. Joseph Huckaby passed away Jan. 1, 1872, a lifelong "Jackson" Democrat.

Agnes was blind the last 30 years of life but managed quite well. She was one of the last three living widows of veterans of the War of 1812. Described by her great-grandson, Bertie Huckaby, as a small lady, Agnes smoked a corncob pipe as did many ladies of her day. Two of her sons wanted to build a new house for her but Agnes wanted no part of a "closed in" house, which she thought would be unhealthy. Agnes washed her clothes in Lindley Creek near her house. Foundation rocks of the old cabin, clumps of iris and a plum thicket remained in the late 1970s.

Agnes continued to live in the cabin near Lindley Creek, west of Huckaby, MO until her death Aug. 7, 1911 at age 91. Agnes was survived by 11 children, 78 grandchildren, 101 great-grandchildren and four great-great grandchildren. *Submitted by Alice Kinslow Kugler*

HUCKABY - Mary Jane Huckaby was born March 4, 1849. She was born either in Polk County or on the way to Polk County from their home in Barren County, KY. Her parents were Thomas Huckaby and Margaret Bridges. They were married Feb. 7, 1848 in Barren County, KY. Thomas was the son of Joseph Huckaby and Mary "Polly" Bridges and was born in 1822 in Barren County, KY. Polly died about 1838 in Kentucky and Joseph married Agnes Payne. Joseph did not arrive in Polk County until after Thomas and his family. Members of the Bridges and Payne families arrived in Polk County about the same time.

Margaret was the daughter of Benjamin Bridges and Mary Satterfield. She was born May 24, 1829 in Barren County, KY. Thomas and Margaret lived in northeast Polk County as did many of the Huckaby family. Thomas and Margaret were the parents of four children. They were Mary Jane, Catherine, Joseph and Martha. Margaret died in April 1856 when Martha was 1 month old. In 1858 Thomas married Sarah "Sally" Miller. They had a daughter Nancy. Thomas, Margaret, Sally, Joseph and Agnes are all buried at Hopewell Cemetery in northeast Polk County.

Mary Jane Huckaby married James Thomas Southard on Aug. 17, 1873 in Polk County. They made their home in Dallas County near Louisburg where they raised eight children. Their children were Sarah Elizabeth, John Thomas, James Macklin, Rebecca Jane, Emma, Joseph Benjamin, Ida and William. Sarah Elizabeth married George Arnold. John Thomas married Mary Elizabeth Goff. James Macklin married Ida Brown. Rebecca Jane married Charles Lamar. Emma married John Austin. Joseph Benjamin and Ida did not marry. William married Flossie Hite. Mary Jane died on July 15, 1898 and is buried in New Hope Cemetery near Louisburg in Dallas County. Thomas later married Sylvania Russell Norman.

Mary Jane Huckaby Southard

Joseph Huckaby married a woman named Jane. Martha J. married Page Kinslow. Nancy Huckaby married James R. Payne.

A post office and store in the northeast corner of Polk County was named for the Huckaby family as most of them lived in that area. *Submitted by Julie Crawford Graves*

HUDSON - Atha Gregory Hudson was born Nov. 25, 1813 in Halifax County, VA, the son of Daniel and Sally Hudson. According to Atha, his father drowned in a well when he was 3 years old. At the age of 10 he lost his mother as well. He then became an indentured orphan to Joshua Crow in Christian County, KY. Under Joshua Crow's indenture he learned farming and at the age of 14 learned the saddler trade.

At some point under his apprenticeship he met Catherine "Kate" Ann Elizabeth Shipp Lander, the daughter of Henry Lander and Nancy Brasfield. Kate was born July 8, 1820 near Winchester, Clark

Mary Ophelia Kate Brown, Catherine Ann Hudson, Atha Gregory Hudson (left to right) picture taken at their home in Humansville

County, KY. Kate had many suitors, but the most persistent was Atha Hudson. Henry Lander did not approve of the relationship between Kate and Atha, so in 1835 they eloped. Henry Lander was so furious that he immediately disinherited his daughter, some say at the bequest of his wife, the stepmother of Kate.

From the time of their marriage until October 1851 they lived in Trigg County, KY. There they had four sons: Charles William, James W., Daniel B. and John A. From October 1851 until the time of the Civil War, they lived in Cedar County, MO. There two more children were born, Phillip C. and Elizabeth Jane "Betty." During the Civil War, Atha worked in Sedalia, Pettis County, MO. There two more children were born, Ophelia Kate and Mary E. "Mollie." After the Civil War the Hudson family returned to Cedar County, MO and remained until after 1880 when they settled in Humansville, Polk County. Atha and Kate lived there the remainder of their lives. Atha and Kate had a total of nine children, the ninth being Henry Hudson, but the date and place of his birth is unknown, he having died in infancy. Two sons, Daniel B. and Phillip C., did not live until adulthood.

Charles William Hudson was born May 25, 1840 and married Anna D. "Annie" Sutton April 24, 1866 in Sedalia, MO. Charles Hudson served in the Civil War. He was a farmer all his life. They had six children but only two lived until maturity, Alma and Charles B. Charles and Annie are buried in Vernon County, MO.

James W. Hudson married Roseanna A. "Rosa" Lingle, the daughter of John S. Lingle and Elizabeth Cleveland. James W. Hudson was a saloonkeeper. They had five children: Elizabeth, Edward B., Harvey L., Susie and Lilly.

John A. Hudson was born December 1850. He married Kasiah Hudson Aug. 23, 1875 in Cedar County, MO. John Hudson was a butcher by trade. They had two sons, Arthur and Franklin. John A. Hudson died in Polk County, MO, a widower.

Elizabeth Jane "Betty" Hudson married David Abraham Brown, the son of Alfred Young Brown and Lucy Gipson Thompson, July 21, 1871 in Cedar County. Betty and David had two daughters, Mary Ophelia Kate and Minnie B. The couple is buried in Cedar County, MO.

Ophelia Katie Hudson was born March 12, 1862 in Sedalia. She married Cicero Berlin Warner March 19, 1878 in Cedar County, MO. Cicero was the son of Jacob Lingenfelter Warner and Sarah "Sallie" Siler Eller. They had five children, two born in Cedar County, William Berlin and Harry C., and three born in Polk County, Clara Edmund, Emma V. and Alice Purl. Four of them lived until maturity, Harry C. died in childhood. Katie and Cicero are buried in the Humansville City Cemetery.

Mary E. "Mollie" Hudson married Edmund Penn White, Esq. They lived several years in New Orleans, LA where Edmund White was a railroad contractor. Around 1912 they moved to Kansas where E. P. White owned a furniture store. They had four children: Leigh, Atha A., Edmund P. and Hudson G.

Atha and Kate were married for over 77 years. They not only raised their own children, but also raised their granddaughter, Mary Ophelia Kate Brown, the daughter of David and Betty Brown. Aunt "Ophie" as the family called her, stayed with Atha and Kate and cared for them until their deaths. She married William "Willie" McAllister.

Atha Gregory Hudson lived to be 99 years and 2 days. Upon his death, Kate took to her bed never to leave it again. She died a little less than two months later at the age of 93 years and 6 months. They are both buried in the Humansville City Cemetery. *Submitted by Ginette Lynn VandenOever*

HUDSON - Gineth E. Hudson was born Nov. 10, 1922. He served in the United States Army from July 1944 to August 1946 in the 21st Infantry, 24th Division. He received the Purple Heart while serving in the Philippines. Gineth married Jane Meinecke Hudson on Friday, July 13, 1951. To this union four children were born. They are Catherine Sue, born Oct. 8, 1952; Gineth Lee, born March 24, 1954; Dennis Hardin, born June 29, 1956; and Kevin LeRoy, born June 26, 1959. The family moved to Bolivar (Polk County) in January 1957 for Gineth and Jane to attend Southwest Baptist College, which was then a junior college; Gineth graduated in May 1959 and pastored various churches in Missouri. Then in 1966, after Southwest Baptist College became a senior college, they moved back to Bolivar to continue their education. Jane and Gineth both worked for the college and Gineth received his bachelor's degree in education. He taught school at Pleasant Hope and Jane finished her college with a bachelor of science degree in medical technology. Jane began to work for the McCraw, Koon, Kahler Clinic where she worked a total of 17 years for Dr. Kahler (after Dr. McCraw retired and Dr. Koon left Bolivar).

Gineth has pastored Shady Grove Baptist Church on Highway 7 west of Warsaw, Pleasant Hill Baptist Church, near Everton, MO, Jamestown Baptist Church at Jamestown, MO, Immanuel Baptist Church at Bethany, MO, Hopewell Baptist Church near Quincy, MO (22 years) and Lazy Acres Baptist Church near Edwards, MO (has been there 11 to this date). Jane worked at Taylor Health Center at Southwest Missouri State University for seven years, after completing the 17 years working for Dr. Monte Kahler and now after retirement, assists Gineth in the church work at Lazy Acres and they both work as Auxiliary Members at Citizens Memorial Hospital in Bolivar. Gineth served nine years as the hospice chaplain for CMH Hospice.

Back: Ron Molder, Jane, Gineth, Cheryl, Diana Hudson; front: Roxy and Kevin Hudson, Cathy Hudson Molder, Gineth Lee and Dennis Hudson.

Cathy taught business education at Wheatland School for six years after graduating from SBU. Then in 1981 she began working as the Executive Assistant to Donald J. Babb, Chief Executive Officer of Citizens Memorial Hospital and has worked there 21 years. She was the first employee Mr. Babb hired for the hospital. She is married to Ron Molder who teaches seventh grade Life Science at Marshfield, MO. They have one daughter, Sarah Elizabeth Molder, born Oct. 18, 1987. Sarah is a student in the Bolivar Schools. Gineth Lee married Cheryl Losh and they have three daughters: Leah Maxine Hudson (married Joe Love), born Jan. 19, 1980; Rebekah Jean, born April 22, 1984 (Easter Sunday); Erica Jane, born Feb. 7, 1992. Gineth Lee and Cheryl live in High Ridge, MO. Gineth Lee works for Diebold and Cheryl is a court reporter.

Dennis Hardin married Diana Holloway. They have two daughters: Heather Diane, born Jan. 30, 1987 and Rachel Ann, born Jan. 14, 1991. Dennis is Minister of Missions for four churches in Fort Worth, TX. Diana is a schoolteacher.

Kevin LeRoy married Roxy Jo Cravens. They have two daughters, JoBeth Stanford and Katelyn Jo Stanford. At the present time, Kevin works for AMS and Roxy is an accountant at Woods Supermarkets. Kevin worked as Director of Plant Facilities for First Baptist Church in Bolivar for approximately 10 years prior to working at AMS. Kevin served several years as fire chief for the Alert Fire Department and also for the Bolivar Fire Department. *Submitted by Gineth Hudson*

HUMAN - James G. Human was born in Knox County, TN on Oct. 27, 1798. He was the son of Basil Human and Winnifred George. Mr. Human was married to Sarah Jane Hopper (daughter of Charles Hopper and Martha O'Neal) on Jan. 22, 1818 in Knox County, TN.

In 1830, he and his family made their way to Missouri, settling near the Big Spring area. Mr. Human and his wife put up a tent to live in, then built a two-room log house in 1834. Mr. Human, being the first settler, is how Humansville got its name.

Mr. Human homesteaded two sections of land and was granted a patent on Aug. 7, 1837. He later built a log house in 1838. Mr. Human opened up the first business in Humansville. Having formed a connection with a St. Louis house, Mr. Human engaged in a mercantile business. That was the starting of the town of Humansville. He became the first postmaster. Mr. Human was the first judge of Polk County. He also filled the office of representative from Polk County in the legislature in Missouri. He held the office of jus-

James G. Human

tice of peace for years and was holding that position at the time of his death on March 6, 1875.

James G. Human had a total of 19 children. He had 12 children by his first wife, Sarah (who died May 16, 1858 in Humansville): Elizabeth Ann, married Nathaniel Rains; Mahala, who died as a girl; Susan, married Thomas Irick; Eliza Montgomery, married Lawrence Rains; James Madison, who was killed in the Mexican War; William Calvin, who died in 1850; Thomas Jefferson, who was killed in the Mexican War; Minerva Jane, who died as a baby; Levi Boone, married Phoebe Childs; William Carroll, married Maria Caroline King; Sarah, married George King (Maria and George were sister and brother, parents are Thomas W. King and Avy Batten); and Julian Frazier, married Matilda Richter.

On March 23, 1860, Mr. Human married Miss Mary Ann Miller. She lived only a year after their marriage. Their only child James Daniel married Mary Egbert.

On Jan. 7, 1863, Mr. Human married Miss Emily Miller, sister of Mary Ann. Their six children: Ida May, married Fred Lizburn; Mary, married Toll Beers; Felix (one of the triplets), married Lizzie Slagle' the other two triplets, a boy and a girl, died as young babies and Pink Human married Charlotte. (Emily died Dec. 16, 1891 in Sumner, WA. Emily and Mary Ann are daughters of Daniel Miller and Polly Moran.)

William Carroll Human, 10th child of James G. Human, was born in Hillsboro, Montgomery County, IL on May 9, 1836. He married Mariah Caroline King on Feb. 12, 1854 in Humansville. Mariah was born Dec. 2, 1834 in Tennessee. They had four children: Mary Jane married John Wilson; Cinderella Almanza, married Russell Rogers (son of William Rogers and Paulina Jane Skinner); Sarah Josephine, never married; and a son, who died as an infant. On Feb. 14, 1924, William and Mariah were featured in the *Spokane Daily Chronicle*, Spokane, WA, for being married 70 years.

Cinderella was born in Humansville on Jan. 30, 1857 and married Russell Rogers on Nov. 26, 1873 in Humansville. Their eight children are Gladys Josephine, Harry Carroll, Mary Theodosia, Agnes Almanza, Ethel Arena, Arthur Russell, Albert Harrison and Bertha Maud.

Gladys Josephine, first child of Cinderella and Russell Rogers, was born in Humansville on Oct. 6, 1874, married Virgil Herod Kelley on Oct. 14, 1894 in Qunicy, MO. They had 11 children: Frederick Virgil, Eurick Lee, Eugene Russell, James Harry, Arcie Carmel, Nellie Jewel, Albert Clinton, William Floyd, Everett Ester, Paul Edward and Thomas Rogers. This family took advantage of the Homestead Act and traveled to eastern Colorado (Prowers County) by covered wagon in 1915, taking three months to reach their destination and later built improvements on their land. *Submitted by Dorothy (Kelley) Zongker*

HUTCHESON - Charles T. Hutcheson (Hutchison) of Scotch-Irish descent was born Dec. 21, 1796 in Tennessee. He was a farmer. He married Elizabeth Ann Bird in 1816. Elizabeth was born in Tennessee Aug. 15, 1798. According to family legend, Elizabeth was a Cherokee Indian.

Charles and Elizabeth lived in Monroe County, TN before moving to the area where Mississippi, Alabama and Tennessee came together. Charles and family can be found in the 1830 Federal Census for McNairy County, TN and the 1837 and 1840 census for Tishomingo County, MS.

Because of Elizabeth's heritage, the family may have moved about to escape the Trail of Tears relocation in 1838. Sometime in the 1840s the family moved to northwestern Arkansas and is found in the 1850 and 1860 Federal Census for Carroll County.

During the Civil War the family remained loyal to the Union. In August 1862 the First Arkansas Cavalry was formed. Company K was mostly men from Carroll County. Charles and Elizabeth had three sons, two sons-in-law and four grandsons in this unit.

Naturally they and their families were considered traitors by the Confederates and were pressured to leave Arkansas. Undaunted, they packed their belongings and caravaned in 11 wagons to Polk County, MO in 1863 where they settled northeast of Bolivar.

The Descendants of Charles Thomas Hutcheson and Elizabeth Ann Bird by John French and others states Charles and Elizabeth had 11 surviving children.

Margaret Hutcheson (Wyatt) was born Nov. 21, 1817 in Tennessee. Margaret married William Joseph Wyatt Oct. 6, 1838 in Tishomingo County, MS.

William Hutcheson was born July 12, 1819 in Tennessee or Alabama. William married Elizabeth Ann (Jones) Sims. William served during the Civil War as a private in the First Arkansas Cavalry.

Sarah H. Hutcheson (Youngblood) was born Aug. 7, 1820 in Tennessee. Sarah married Theodrick Birgit Youngblood Nov. 17, 1839 in Tishomingo County, MS. Theodrick was captain of Company K, First Arkansas Cavalry.

Nicodemus G. Hutcheson was born 1823 in Monroe County, TN. Nicodemus married Elizabeth M. Gauslin. Nicodemus served in Robb's Battery during the Civil War.

John Grayson Hutcheson was born Sept. 27, 1824 in Monroe County, TN. John married Cynthia Pearson Jan. 7, 1842 in Arkansas. John enrolled in the Missouri State Militia in 1862. He was wounded in the Battle of Springfield. He re-enlisted at Bolivar and served until the end of the war.

James Henry Hutcheson was born Jan. 20, 1827 in Tennessee. James was first married to Elizabeth Ann Dunlap, second to Lucinda E. Ragsdale and third to Kiziah Kennon.

Sargent Wisdom Hutcheson was born 1831 in McNairy County, TN. Sargent married Elizabeth Louise Johnson. He was a sergeant with Company K, First Arkansas Cavalry in the Civil War.

Charles S. Hutchison was born Jan. 8, 1833 in Tennessee. Charles married Martha Ellen Hood March 4, 1855 in Carroll County, AR. He was a farmer and gristmill operator.

Elizabeth Hutcheson was born 1836 in Tishomingo County, MS. Elizabeth married Joseph Weese. Joseph served with the First Arkansas Cavalry and died in the second Battle of Springfield.

Shelby Ulysses Hutcheson was born May 14, 1838 in Tishomingo County, MS. Shelby married Malissa O. Cunningham Feb. 27, 1858 in Fayetteville, AR. He was a private with the First Arkansas Cavalry.

Martha Jane Hutcheson was born Nov. 23, 1840 in Tishomingo County, MS. Martha married John Newton Cunningham June 1, 1862 in Arkansas.

Charles and Elizabeth and family farmed in Polk County and were instrumental in the establishment of the Mt. Olive Church and Cemetery. They are buried in Mt. Olive Cemetery with many of their children. Others are buried at Greenwood and other locations. *Submitted by Robert M. Hutchison*

HUTCHESON - Gene Hutcheson, born Jan. 4, 1921 and Billie Lee Hendrickson, born May 2, 1931, were each born, attended grade school, graduated from Bolivar High School and Southwest Baptist College in Polk County. Their four parents were born and educated in Bolivar.

William Taylor Hendrickson (1846-1923) came to Bolivar with his siblings, Sherman, Evert, Sam, Vie, Eliza and Mester. They were brought by their parents, Davy Crockett Hendrickson (1821-1844) and Lydia Gordon (1819-1875). Lydia had courted Abe Lincoln and it is noted that Abe split rails for her father. Davy's brother, Jesse, settled in Buffalo. The Hendricksons came from Tennessee. At that time you could stake out allotted acreage for each child. They claimed land from Aldrich Road, south to Karlin Lane. Taylor married Lovy Roberts (1853-1944), with an Irish heritage. They had eight children: Charley, Eddie, Bessie, Golden, Myrtle, William Taylor, Della and

William T. Hendrickson   *Oma Pitner Hendrickson*

Fred. William married Myrtle Miller; they had Bess, Troy and Bert. Myrtle passed away; William (1888-1953) married Oma Pitner (1891-1946) they had one daughter Billie Lee. Billie Lee and Gene were married Aug. 2, 1951 at Morton's Wedding Inn in Bolivar. They have two children, Jim (Oct. 19, 1954) and Jill (July 3, 1956). Jim married Jeanette Russell and they have two children, Jimmy (March 10, 1982) who is a sophomore at Pepperdine University and Nicole (May 16, 1984) who is a senior at Glendale High School. Jill married Tom Carter (Oct. 27, 1956) and they have one son Cole (Dec. 16, 1989), a seventh grader at Pershing Middle School. Both families live in Springfield. Gene has been in real estate for 33 years; Billie retired from teaching 30 years in 1991.

Albert and Nellie Hutcheson

Billie's mother's parents came to Polk County from Kentucky. James Albert Pitner (1847-1933) was born in Georgia, came to Bolivar with his parents when 7 years old and settled on a farm southeast of Bolivar. At 16 he enlisted in the 15th Missouri Cavalry and served until the Civil War was ended. He served at

Granby and Wilson's Creek. He had two sons by his first marriage, John and Andy. His wife died and he married Margaret Davidson (1854-1918). They had Etta, Jim, Lee, Eva, Ed and Oma. Jim enjoyed seven of his nine children living in this area.

Gene's great-great-grandfather Charles Hutcheson (1796-1868) and his wife Elizabeth Bird (1798-1874), a full-blooded Cherokee Indian, came to Polk County soon after the Civil War from Kentucky. His grandfather Laban Hutcheson (1858-1934) married Eliza Kazar Watson (1858-1943), who was the youngest of 13 children. Gene remembers the story she told him repeatedly of the bushwhackers during the Civil War coming and stealing their chickens, flour and sugar and once her father was shot at, but he ran and hid in a corn shock fodder and they couldn't find him. Eliza told her stories very dramatically. They had Annis, Ulous, Flora, Maggie, Albert, Zenas, Delbert and Bessie. Albert (1889-1974), Gene's father, married Nellie Gallivan (1893-1984). They had Lois, Eva, Gene and Nell Anne.

Jeanette and Jim Hutcheson, Cole and Jill Carter, Billie and Gene Hutcheson, Tom Carter, Nicole and Jimmy Hutcheson

Gene's grandfather Jim Gallivan (1868-1957) was born in Polk County; his parents were Jeremiah (1812-1908) and Catherine O'Sullivan (1821-1918) from Ireland. Catherine, at the age of 13, leaving her mother crying on the boat dock, left Ireland, working her passage out on the boat. This was during the potato famine in Ireland. In America, she worked in a little café. Jeremiah worked as a paddy of the railroad; one day he went in the café and as the family story goes, he had convinced her to marry him by "sunset." They were probably married by a traveling priest as both were Catholic. Jim Gallivan married Clara Bowen (1878-1947); they had Nellie, Austin, Dennis, Norah and Roscoe. *Submitted by Billie Hutcheson*

HUTCHESON – Robert Lyle Hutcheson and Clara Elizabeth "Betty" Wimberly were married on May 19, 1936. Robert and Betty were born and raised in Polk County and were Bolivar High School sweethearts. Their children are David Lyle, born in 1937; Jean Elizabeth, born in 1938; James Robert, born in 1940; Debra Jo, born in 1955; Daniel Jay, born in 1956; Ronald Carl, born in 1958. Robert and Betty were so happy with the three children they raised in the 1940s and 1950s that they chose to begin again with three more children when the older ones were teenagers. Robert always said they got a second chance as parents to the younger ones to correct any mistakes they had made with the older ones.

The above picture is of Robert and Betty's home, 311 E. Freeman, in Bolivar. This unique house was a home filled with laughter, love, and all the wonderful joys of growing up in the 1940s, 1950s, 1960s and 1970s.

Robert was employed with the United States

Postal Service before he was called to join the army in June 1944. Betty lived at 311 E. Freeman to care for the children while Robert was serving his country in Germany. After Robert returned home and started back with the Bolivar US Post Office, he and Betty settled in to share the "good life" after the war was over.

Robert was an excellent gardener and produced an abundance of vegetables every summer. Betty spent many hours in the hot kitchen canning all of his produce. The children helped with assigned duties (reluctantly) by snapping green beans, shelling peas, shucking corn, digging potatoes, picking tomatoes, etc. Of course, the end results were the most delicious meals anyone could possibly want. One of the dreaded chores was when the children helped Robert wring necks and pluck feathers from the chickens they raised. Robert, Betty and their six children were members of the Bolivar United Methodist Church. This church was a focal point of their lives. Christian values were instilled in their children, as well as honesty and good work ethics.

Robert's paternal ancestors and their wives were Carl Chester and Ena Jewell Greer Hutcheson, William F. and Julia Ann Buckner Hutcheson, William H. and Elizabeth Ann Jones Hutcheson, and Charles Thomas and Elizabeth Ann Bird Hutcheson, all buried in Polk County. These ancestors migrated to Polk County from Arkansas, Kentucky, North Carolina, Tennessee and Virginia. Robert's maternal ancestors and their husbands were Ena Jewell Greer and Carl Chester Hutcheson, Martha Ellis Greever and George Robert Greer, Disey E. Cravens and Charles C. Greever II, Mary Ann Leach and Jeremiah Cravens.

Betty's paternal ancestors and their wives were Otis Tayler and Grace Marie Keeling Wimberly, Charles Tayler and Clara Delphene Scott Wimberly, Isaac and Sara Jane Hall Wimberly, William and Rebecca Wakefield Wimberly. These ancestors migrated to Polk County from Illinois, Ohio, Tennessee, Kentucky and Virginia. Betty's maternal ancestors and their husbands were Grace Marie Keeling and Otis Tayler Wimberly, Caroline Elizabeth Sims and Austin Oliver Keeling, Rebecca Patton Clark and James McGarity Sims, Ophelia Campbell and David Simpson Clark. Betty's female lineage goes back to the Campbell and Polk families who were founders and settlers of Bolivar and Polk County.

Robert died in 1972 at the age of 54. Betty died in 1991 at the age of 72. *Submitted by Jean Raney*

HUTCHISON - Charles Thomas Hutcheson and his wife Elizabeth Bird (a Cherokee Indian) came from Tennessee to Arkansas and then to Bolivar. This was during the Civil War and they were northern sympathizers who did not want to fight in the Confederate Army. Also, Elizabeth was of the Chickamauga Tribe of the Cherokees. This tribe came to Arkansas and Missouri to avoid the "Trail of Tears." Charles T. and some of his sons served in the Civil War on the Union side. Charles T. was born Dec. 21, 1796 in Tennessee. Elizabeth was born April 15, 1798 in Tennessee. They were Baptists and donated the land for the Mt. Olive Baptist Church and were active in starting the church. The church building was moved down the road several years ago and only the Mt. Olive Cemetery remains at the original location. The fact that Elizabeth was an Indian was not revealed for many years because at that time it was illegal for an Indian to live in Missouri. They had a large family, 14 children. Dawanda's great-grandfather Charles Sherman Hutchison, was their eighth child, born Jan. 8, 1833 in Bolivar and died in 1890 of typhoid fever, in Bolivar. He changed the spelling from Hutcheson to Hutchison. That is why Dawanda grew up thinking she was not related to the Hutchesons, but she is. Charles S. married Martha Ellen Hood March 4, 1855 in Arkansas. She was born April 22, 1835 in Illinois and died in 1900 in Bolivar. Her parents were Thomas Hood Jr. (1807-1857) and Sarah Eaton (1811-1857). They are thought to have been killed in a wagon train raid. Charles S. and Martha had 11 children. Dawanda's grandfather, Grant Ulyses Simpson Augustus Hutchison, was one of them. Notice his three middle initials are USA. He was born Jan. 30, 1872 in Bolivar and married Mary Jane Hood Sept. 1, 1893. She was born May 18, 1872 in Bolivar. Her parents were James K. P. Hood (1849-1920) and Margaret Jane Dalton (1848-1930). Margaret was related to the infamous Dalton gang. Dawanda's dad told her that Margaret told him about hiding them on her farm when they were running from the law. They would come riding in on their snorting horses and wearing big black hats. Dawanda's grandfather Grant was caretaker for the Greenwood Cemetery in Bolivar for many years. Dawanda remembers as a child riding with him on the horse-drawn mower as he cut the grass there. He and her grandmother, Mary Jane, raised their family in a house right next to the cemetery (where the new cemetery office now sits). They had 10 children,

Back row: Roy, Ray, Willard, Charles, Mark and Paul; front row: Helen, Grant, Mary, Edward and Pearl

Dawanda's father Ray B. Hutchison was one of them. They others were Charley, Willard, Roy, Mark, Paul, Pearl, Helen, Ed and Edna (died as an infant). Ray was born July 9, 1902 in Bolivar and married Zela Elaine Caldwell Sept. 15, 1923. She was born Jan. 23, 1907 in Bolivar. Her parents were Levi B. Caldwell (1876-1960) and Arzetta J. Heydon (1874-1952). Dawanda's parents moved to Kansas City, MO shortly after marrying; so Dawanda and her brothers, Ray Jr. and Eugene, were born and raised there. They always enjoyed visiting their grandparents (on both sides) in Bolivar. Dawanda graduated from SWBC (now SBU) in 1948 where she met her husband, Howard Karr. *Submitted by Dawanda (Hutchison) Karr*

INGRAM – Dewey and Imogene Ingram came to Polk County in 1950 when Jane, their youngest child, was 2 years old. They were native Arkansans, having been born and raised there: Dewey at Harrison, Imogene at Altus. They were married in 1936 at a small town called Bellefonte. The town is still a popular destination for couples getting married today.

Imogene had two daughters, Sally and Susie, from a previous marriage that ended when her young husband died of cancer in July 1934. They also had a son, born just two months before his father died, who sadly also passed away at the age of 5 months. Father and son are buried in Maplewood Cemetery, Harrison.

Imogene and Dewey had known each other from their schooldays together. After their marriage they worked together for a time at a laundry. Later he worked on the Norfork Dam Project at Beaver Lake and she was able to stay home with the children. Daughters Nancy and Ann had been born, making four children. They moved to Springfield, MO, after Dewey was hired by Frisco Railroad. He traveled and worked as a civil engineer until retirement, sometime in the 1970s.

Family life in Morrisville revolved around school and church activities. At Marion C. Early School, the girls belonged to the marching band and vocal music groups, took part in class plays and enjoyed Junior-Senior Banquets, sports such as volleyball and softball and senior class trips. Imogene attended PTA meetings and games with them; Dewey was usually away on business trips. They loved the weekends when he was at home. He was known by neighbors as a good TV repairman, a hobby that was self-taught. He serviced their car himself, and could often do needed repairs on it, too. He liked to learn new things, and sometimes at leisure, did logarithms just for fun. Imogene was a member of the local Garden Club; many times in warm weather they'd stroll to a neighbor's house where they would compare notes on bulbs and seeds. She also belonged to the Women's Society for Christian Service and helped with many church dinners and bazaars through the years. Imogene and Dewey were also members of the Eastern Star and Masonic Lodges, respectively. Meetings were held upstairs in a building that used to be the Bank of Morrisville. The stairway was narrow and dark and, in Jane's childish mind, it seemed they were climbing almost to Heaven, it was so tall! While the grown-ups were meeting Jane would sit quietly in the outer room, knowing that when they dismissed she'd be allowed in to see the Stations, arranged in a particular pattern and each symbolized by items such as a crown and scepter.

Imogene and Dewey moved back to Springfield in 1967 in order to be closer to shopping facilities, doctors and hospitals. Dewey retired from the railroad after more than 30 years' service. He stayed active with yardwork, recycling, trips to the library. He kept up with local politics and never missed going to the polls to vote. He died June 15, 1992, six weeks after suffering a massive stroke. Imogene, unable to live alone, was joined by a loving caregiver, Bonnie Crawford. Both courageous ladies lost their lives as the result of a house fire: Imogene died Dec. 26, 1995 and Bonnie, on December 28th, the day of Imogene's burial. Imogene and Dewey now rest together in the Morrisville Cemetery. *Submitted by Jane Thompson*

Dewey, Nancy Katherine, Ann Franklin and Imogene Ingram, ca. 1946

INGRAM – Joseph Ingram was born in Kentucky on Feb. 8, 1798. He married Sarah Stotts in Pulaski County, KY on March 12, 1822. They moved from Kentucky to Illinois in 1835 and on to Polk County, MO in 1837. John and Sarah had seven sons and one daughter. Morgan, Isaac, John S., Lemuel Lockett and Charles were born in Kentucky. William, Joseph Frederick and Sarah J. were born in Polk County. Morgan, Isaac and John married sisters, Martha E., Ann D. and Eliza Smallman. Lemuel Lockett married Nancy Jane Collins; Charles married Jane Catherine Mackey; William married Mary Melvina Scroggins; Joseph Frederick married Margaret Jane Keeling; and Sarah J. married George Williams. Isaac, John, William and Joseph Frederick stayed in Polk County while Morgan, Lemuel and Charles moved to Cedar County. Morgan and Lemuel fought in the Civil War as members of the Confederate Army. Joseph fought in the war in the Union Army. It is very likely that Morgan rode with Joseph Shelby's cavalry and that Joseph Frederick was with the Union forces that drove Shelby's cavalry into Arkansas. This was a case of brother against brother. Morgan died in a Confederate army camp at Monticello, AR from an illness. Lemuel surrendered to the Union Army in New Orleans and was released from prison camp in Shreveport, LA. He walked from Shreveport to his home in Cedar County. Isaac, Charles and Joseph Frederick were ministers in the Baptist church. Charles was a member of the first board of trustees of Southwest Baptist College. Isaac also served on the board of trustees. Isaac was a pastor of Slagle and Enon Baptist Churches and Joseph Frederick was a pastor of Pleasant Hill Baptist Church. John and William farmed in Polk County.

Margaret Jane Kelling Ingram and Joseph Frederick Ingram

Joseph Frederick and Margaret Jane had four sons: William, David, John Quincy (Quince) and Charles and one daughter, Mary Jane. William and Charles moved to California and raised families there. Dave, Quince and Mary Jane stayed in Polk County. Dave and Quince were farmers. Mary Jane married William Wright, Dave married Maude Smith and Quince married Arah Hargis. Dave had one son, Archie, who died at the age of 15. Quince had five sons, Joseph, Ralph, Clark, Con and Claude and two daughters, Hazel and Mary. Joseph, Bobby's father, married Dortha Hook and had Marylyn and Bobby. Clark married Maydell Ashcroft from Texas; Con married Dorothy Hendrix from Springfield and Mary married Edward (Bud) Cox from Tennessee. Bobby was born in Polk County but now lives with his wife Sue Latham Ingram in Louisiana. They have two daughters, Teresa and Kimberly, and one son, Mark. *Submitted by Bobby J. Ingram*

JARMAN – William Washington Jarman, son of Josiah Thomas and Luvisa Ann Tindle Jarman, was born April 29, 1869 in Sweet Springs, Saline County, MO. In 1895, Will traveled to Buffalo, MO where he met and married Mary Frances Spears. Mary, the daughter of David and Sarah Frances Warden Spears, was born Nov. 22, 1875 and spent most of her childhood in Pleasant Green, Cooper County, MO. Mary's heritage included Native American ancestors. William and Mary made a handsome couple. He was tall and thin with auburn hair and she was small with brown eyes, dark hair and a beautiful smile.

The Jarman family, 1935, Bolivar, MO. Front – Claude Leona, William (Pa), Mary (Ma), Girtha. Back – Ernest, Flossie, Roy, Troy (Doc), Ora, Alma and Alva

The young couple settled in Bolivar, Polk County, MO in 1900. With hard work they labored on their farm and reared a family of 12 children. Times were difficult but together they overcame the obstacles that confronted them. Ten of their children survived to adulthood and had families of their own:

Claud Estelle, born May 12, 1896, Houstonia, MO, married first, Girtha M. Rush, married second, Gladys Mary Felthoff; Alma, born March 11, 1898, Buffalo, MO, married Lawrence Thomas Polodna; Alva, born March 11, 1898, Buffalo, MO, married first, Elsie Bond, married second, Elva Landreth; Roy Washington, born April 8, 1901, Bolivar, MO, married Clara Myrtle Serls; Flossie Jewel, born Jan. 5, 1903, Bolivar, MO, married Charlie Milford Parsons; Ora, born Jan. 5, 1905, Bolivar, MO, married Dolly Caroline Hurd; Troy Robert, born Feb. 22, 1907, Bolivar, MO, married Ruby Pool; Leona May, born June 20, 1909, Bolivar, MO, married Milford C. Hicks; Ernest W., born April 19, 1913, Bolivar, MO, married Hallie Jane Wind; Girtha Lee, born Sept. 10, 1918, Bolivar, MO, married first, Glenn Howard Cunningham, married second, Robert Gomer, married third, Paul Beary.

The Jarmans endured the loss of two of their children:

Viola, born 1911 and died in 1915, Bolivar, MO; baby boy, born and died in 1915, Bolivar, MO.

These descendants and their children have fond memories of Will and Mary. The Jarmans's home was always a haven for them. The house was built by William and the plumbing and lights were added as they became available in Bolivar. Eventually each room had a light hanging from the ceiling but no wall outlets. Instead, electrical cords ran from adapters in the light socket to operate electrical appliances. The kitchen had an ice box that needed to be filled with ice once or twice a week and a wood cook stove with a hot water reservoir that provided water for bathing. The only indoor plumbing was a lone faucet in the kitchen that seemed to be frozen from November to March. When the snow came there would be a light dusting on the beds and floor upstairs. It was no problem to track yourself downstairs to breakfast in a warm kitchen. The two-holer down by the garden was another place the snow blew in. The game played on those cold mornings was "who could go to the bathroom second."

In the summer the grandchildren would gather to ride stick horses, shoot sling shots, chase a wagon hoop with a tee, and play hide and seek among the corn stocks. When Grandma wasn't looking, the boys would have mud fights in the hog pen. One of the most favorite times was Christmas. The house would be bulging with family anticipating a feast that included roasted hog.

The Jarman family has continued to grow and follow numerous walks in life but their roots will always bring them back to the young couple who made their home in Bolivar. We, their descendants, are pleased to have this opportunity to honor them. *Submitted by Harold Hicks*

JARMAN – Johnny William Jarman Jr. (Sept. 25, 1942 – Jan. 30, 1988) was the second child, but the first son, born to Johnny William (March 11, 1921) and Nora (Stewart) (Sept. 11, 1923-Oct. 6, 1993) Jarman Sr. His family called him Junior at times, but usually Gene, a nickname from childhood that stuck permanently. John Jr. married Rachel Allene Hyde on Sept. 4, 1965. They had two daughters, Rebecca Ann (Nov. 4, 1966) and Ralene Audra (June 27, 1970). Rachel always called him John, as he requested.

Johnny W. Jarman Jr., December 1971

Throughout his life, John was shy and easily embarrassed. He hated when attention focused on him, except within his family. With his family he was playful, a tease and a cut-up. He would chase his children on his hands and knees, growling like a bear, or be their bucking bronco. He teased Rachel and females in the family, drawing squeals and "Yucks!" by sneaking up to land a quick lick of his tongue to a cheek or ear. But the attention of outsiders would mortify him.

Although they lived in the Kansas City area most of their married life, one year John and Rachel lived on the family farm, several miles north of Bolivar. One day during that winter John went to chop firewood. In a short time he returned to the house, slightly opened the front door and called out, "Do you have a weak stomach?" Before Rachel could gather her wits to answer, John pushed the door the rest of the way open. The right side of his upper body—head, shoulder and arm—was soaked with blood, and blood dripped from his fingertips.

As Rachel pressed towels to his head, John explained that on an upswing, his axe had caught in some low-hanging branches. He yanked too hard on the axe handle and didn't quite have control as it came down. There was a gash starting just above his right ear. The axe had cut vertically into the side of his head, through the upper half of his ear. When Rachel said he needed stitches, he flatly refused. She was afraid the bleeding wouldn't stop, so she threatened him by saying his ear would heal in two weird-looking, separate pieces. John agreed to go to a doctor.

Doc Zumbrun stitched the wounds, gave him a tetanus shot and told John to come back to get the stitches out in a week or so. When the week passed, John refused to return to the doctor. He insisted Rachel could remove the stitches. It took a few days to wear her down, but finally she removed the stitches with fingernail clippers and tweezers. There was a scar, but the ear was in one piece.

A couple of months later, they saw Doc Zumbrun in town. They nodded as they passed, but after a few steps the doctor turned and called, "Weren't you supposed to get stitches out several weeks ago?" John stopped and explained the stitches had been removed.

"Let's take a look," Doc said. With people passing by, he grabbed John's head, bent him forward to eye level and carefully examined his head and ear. "Looks fine," he said and walked away, leaving a red-faced, terribly embarrassed John standing on the Bolivar square on a busy Saturday afternoon. *Submitted by Rebecca Ann Jarman, daughter of John and Rachel*

JENKINS – Evart Gray Jenkins was born on Oct. 19, 1924 in Dunnegan, MO, son of Virgil Simon Jenkins, born on June 3, 1890 in Lockwood, MO, died May 28, 1966 in Dunnegan, MO. His mother, Myrtie Cora Gray, was born July 18, 1893 in Egira, CO and died Sept. 30, 1961 in Dunnegan, MO. Virgil and Myrtie were married on April 12, 1914 in Red Oak, MO. They had two other children, Lena Helen Jenkins, born April 10, 1916, died July 11, 1998 and Edna May Jenkins, born April 16, 1919, died Nov. 10, 1983. Evart grew up on the farm in Dunnegan, MO and attended high school in Fair Play, MO graduating in 1942. He then worked on the farm until he entered the United States Army on Oct. 17, 1944. He spent approximately two years in the service during WWII until he was discharged in October 1946. He received the Purple Heart medal from wounds received on Okinawa in June 1945. After returning from the service, he married Juanita Hartley on Dec. 31, 1949. They had two children, Alden Evart Jenkins, born Oct. 19, 1954 and Barry Welton Jenkins, born Sept. 23, 1961. Evart worked for Springfield Grocer Company in Springfield, MO for a short time until being employed by the United States Postal Service. He served as post master in Dunnegan, MO prior to becoming rural mail carrier. He served in this capacity in Dunnegan until he was transferred to Greenfield, MO in 1973. He carried the mail in Greenfield until his retirement in 1979. Shortly after his retirement with the postal service, he went to work at Silver Dollar City in Branson, MO as a production cook. He worked at Silver Dollar City for 20 years until his death on Aug. 10, 2000. *Submitted by Juanita Jenkins*

Evart Jenkins

JENKINS - Joseph and Charlotty, this writer's great-great-grandfather and grandmother, came to Polk County in 1838 as land records show them to have sold their farm in Jackson County, AL in April 1838. They had lived in Crow Creek Valley of that county for 20 years as we find them there in 1819 as squatters in what was then Cherokee Indian territory.

They journeyed to Polk County in a wagon train consisting of brothers, sisters and perhaps cousins. These brothers and sisters were the children of William and Mary Jenkins, who were Virginians by birth, according to family tradition. Family tradition also contends that he was a Revolutionary War soldier. Since he does not appear in the 1840 census or any later census, he either was deceased before the trip or was deceased by 1840. He and Mary were born approximately 1765 to 1775. We do find Mary in her daughter's household in 1850 and 1860 census records.

The brothers and sisters that came in this migration were Richard, Joshua, William, Nancy and Matilda. At the time of their arrival, Richard, Joshua, and Nancy were already married as were Joseph and Charlotty. Richard was married to Mary Sells. Nancy was married to Evan Stewart.

Back – Dortha, Orbie, Mertie, Ollin, Florel, Everett, Agnes, Adrian, Jewell and Emeral. Front – William Henderson and Rhoda Evaline (Craig) Jenkins

William married Polly Ann Rash May 16, 1844 in Polk County. Matilda married Leroy L. Rash March 3, 1846, also in Polk County. Leroy and Polly were children of William Rash, also an early settler of Jackson County, AL.

Joseph and Charlotty were both born in 1801, she in Georgia and he in Kentucky. Their children were Mary, Martha, George, Charlotte, William, Joseph, Richard and John. All of these were born in Crow Creek Valley before their coming to Polk County except Richard and John, who were born in 1838 and 1839 in Polk County.

Mary married John Chesser. Martha married John Morris and then Mr. Dickerson. George W. married Louisa Brooks; Charlotte married Thomas Hale; Joseph married Elizabeth Dickerson. John apparently never married and Richard left home early and no further knowledge is had of him.

William, Russell's great-grandfather, married Elizabeth Slaughter, the widow of John Slaughter. At the time of their marriage, she already had Mary, Martha, Richard, Jemima Jane and Eliza. William and Eliza then had Jane, Lyeida, Mahala and William Henderson Jenkins, Russell's grandfather, born Aug. 3, 1856.

William Henderson Jenkins married Rhoda Evaline Craig, March 24, 1881. They had 12 children of which 10 lived to adulthood, two having died young. The 10 were Dortha, Mertie, Addie Florel, Orbie Edgar, Orlin, Agnes, Alma Jewell, Everett Ora, Adrian Cecil (Bob) and Emeral Clifford (Pat). The writer's father was Everett Ora.

In 1945, William H. and Rhoda Evaline celebrated their 60th wedding anniversary, and all 10 of their children were present to commemorate the happy occasion.

This writer readily admits that there may be inaccuracies in this writing and begs forgiveness if such be the case. In conclusion, the writer visited Crow Creek Valley in September 2002 and walked over ground that William and Mary had once owned. This little valley is a beautiful place and it surely must have been hard for Russell's ancestors to have left behind their little home in the valley. *Submitted by Russell A. Jenkins*

JENKINS – Richard Jenkins was from Kentucky and died sometime between 1850 and 1860. His wife was Mary Sells Jenkins, who was born in Tennessee. Their children were John, William Henry and James Solomon Jenkins. Their son John was born in Alabama and sons, William Henry and James Solomon, were born in Missouri.

James Solomon Jenkins married Margaret P. Birdsong. Her parents were Jessie and Elizabeth Birdsong. They are buried at Payne Cemetery near Polk, MO. Lora's grandfather, Charlie Smith Jenkins, was their only child and was born March 11, 1871, northwest of Huron, MO. He spent his entire life in Polk County, having lived in several different communities but spending the major portion of his years near Huron, MO. He passed away Oct. 12, 1950 and is buried at Payne Cemetery. Charlie Smith Jenkins and Emma H. Manes were married on Nov. 5, 1899 near Sentinel, MO by P. C. Kinslaw. Lora's grandmother, Emma H. Manes, was born March 3, 1880 near Polk, MO and died Sept. 4, 1965. Her parents were Henegar and Levara Ann Wattington Manes. Henegar died February 1943 and Levara died Oct. 18, 1907. Emma Manes Jenkins had one sister, Pearl Manes Mullinex, buried by her father at New Bethel Cemetery, south of Halfway, MO. She also had two brothers, John (Lon) Manes and William (Cap) Manes.

Charlie Smith and Emma H. Manes Jenkins's children were Vivian Jenkins, who never married, born Aug. 29, 1900; Oliver, born Dec. 24, 1902, married Verda Fellers; Iva Jenkins, born Nov. 27, 1904, married Everett Oringdeff; Albert, born Nov. 13, 1902, married Vera Haven; Cecil, born Sept. 21, 1908, married Alta Madison in April 1927 and later married Margaret Bell in September 1935; Oma, born Feb. 16, 1910; William, born March 25, 1912, married Vida McElwee on March 24, 1934; Lola Mae, born May 8, 1914, died 1916; Robert Jenkins, born Feb. 13, 1916, married Jannie Huggins on Sept. 10, 1936; infant girl, born and died Dec. 5, 1918. All of the children were born northwest of Huron, MO.

Lora's mother, Oma Jenkins, married Clyde W. Bass, Sept. 15, 1928 in Bolivar, MO. His parents were William Franklin Bass and Nancy Elizabeth Brown, both buried at Pleasant Hill Cemetery near Bolivar, MO. Clyde was born in Jerico Springs, MO on Sept. 26, 1904. As a young boy, Clyde lived and went to school at Liberal, MO and his family lived at Halfway, MO. Clyde and Oma lived around Halfway and Adonis, MO until 1933. They moved to Humansville, MO in the Rosebud area and then near Flemington, MO. Clyde and Oma had one daughter, Lora Lee, who was born in Humansville, MO. They were farmers and raised stock cattle and Clyde also worked for MFA Feed and MFA Grocery in Humansville. In about 1953, Clyde began work for Hercules Powder Company in the accounting department near Lawrence, KS, where he worked until he retired. Then they sold the farm near Flemington, MO and made their home in Lawrence, KS until they passed away.

Clyde W. Bass and Oma Jenkins, 50th Wedding Anniversary, 1978

Lora Lee Bass married Norman E. Eberhart on Feb. 13, 1955 and they have lived in Lawrence, KS. Norman was raised in Lawrence. They have one daughter, Charlene K. Eberhart. She married David L. Simmons from Cleveland, TN on May 29, 1982 in Lawrence, KS. They have two daughters, Rachel Lora Simmons (born Jan. 11, 1986) and Sarah Katherine Simmons (born Jan. 13, 1990). They live in Leawood, KS near Kansas City, MO.

There are several Jenkinses located in Bolivar, MO that are descendants of Charlie and Emma Manes Jenkins. *Submitted by Lora Lee Bass Eberhart*

JENKINS – Clifford Emeral "Pat" Jenkins was born Jan. 30, 1904 in the small community of Mission, MO northeast of Halfway, MO to William Henderson "Bud" Jenkins (Aug. 3, 1856-Aug. 15, 1946) and Rhoda Evaline Craig Jenkins (Nov. 2, 1863-March 4, 1950). He was the 12th child born into the family. His siblings were Prentiss (died in infancy); twins Dorotha (Mrs. George Cleland) and Daisy (died in infancy); Mertie (Mrs. Charles Farrar); Flarel (Mrs. Gene Cleland); Orby Jenkins; Orlin Jenkins; Agnes (Mrs. Ralph Voris); Jewell (Mrs. Hobart Rodgers); Everett Jenkins; Adrain (Bob).

Since Clifford Emeral had been called "Pat" since a very small child, the story was told about his father waiting, along with the census taker, for the train to arrive at the Cliquot, MO railroad station, to ask his mother, who had been to Bolivar, MO shopping, a very important question. "What did we name that last youngin'?"

Berniece Armstrong and Clifford Emeral "Pat" Jenkins on Easter outing at Bennett Spring State Park, April 1925. Notice Pat's Model T car in background.

Pat moved from the Blue Mound Prairie southeast of Halfway, MO to a farm near Cliquot just before his teenage years. He was saved and joined the Salem Missionary Baptist Church in Cliquot, MO.

He met Berniece Armstrong, who was also a member of the Salem Baptist Church. Pat and Berniece Armstrong Jenkins (Sept. 14, 1907) were married on Nov. 12, 1925 in Bolivar, MO. Both the Jenkins and Armstrong families enjoyed music very much and there were many happy times spent singing together. Pat, singing bass in quartets and Berniece, singing alto, provided music for many funerals throughout their married life.

In 1941, Pat and Berniece became charter members of Calvary Missionary Baptist Church in Bolivar where their membership remained.

Pat learned the electrical trade as a young man while working in Los Angeles, CA. He continued the same work for many years in Polk County while working for The Ozarks Utility, which later became Empire District Electric. He retired to the farm located on the Pomme de Terre River near Burns, MO. Later he moved to a farm near Halfway, MO and finally the last three years of his life lived in Bolivar, MO.

Pat is buried in the Reed Cemetery near Halfway where his parents, grandparents on both sides of the family, and his infant siblings are buried. His wife, age 95 at this writing, still survives him.

Pat and Berniece were the parents of two daughters: Helen Louise, born Aug. 28, 1930 and Mary Evelyn, born Dec. 5, 1941.

Helen Louise Jenkins was married on Sept. 9, 1950 to Paul Harry Roberts, born Dec. 5, 1925. They became the parents of three children: Paula Louise, born Jan. 27, 1953; Krista Helen, born May 14, 1955; Alan Pat, born March 19, 1958.

Paula Louise was married on June 30, 1973 to Terry Richard Moore, born Aug. 2, 1951. They have two children: Mackenzie Jo, born July, 18, 1981, and David Forest, born July 28, 1987.

Krista Helen was married first,on Dec. 28, 1974 to Brad T. Cisco, born July 8, 1954. They have two children: Rachel Krista Cisco, born July 16, 1981 and Jonathan Randall Cisco, born Sept. 5, 1983. They divorced. Krista Helen was married second,to Richard Forrist Nebel, born Feb. 26, 1953. They have two children: Lydia Rachel Nebel, born March 22, 1989 and Richard Forrist Nebel II, born March 9, 1991.

Alan Pat was married Oct. 20, 1979 to Tammy Ann Pitman, born Feb. 5, 1960. They have four children: Paul Alan, born Aug. 3, 1980; Adam Gerald, born May 4, 1987; Lucas Taylor, born May 30, 1993; Annie Elizabeth, born Sept. 30, 1997.

Mary Evelyn Jenkins was married Aug. 20, 1960 to Larry Dean Scroggins, born Nov. 28, 1937. They became the parents of four children: Marla Evelyn, born Aug. 8, 1963; Malinda Diane, born Oct. 31, 1967; Malissa Beth, born Aug. 10, 1970; and Marcia LaDean, born Nov. 25, 1974.

Marla Evelyn was married July 16, 1983 to Kelley Ray Roberts, born Oct. 5, 1960. They have two children: Karaley Evelyn, born Feb. 15, 1988 and Sterling Kelley, born Feb. 5, 1993.

Malinda Diane was married Sept. 5, 1998 to Gregory Wayne Elliott, born Dec. 1, 1964. They have two children: Leah Diane, born April 28, 2000 and Owen Gregory, born Feb. 7, 2002.

Malissa Beth was married July 13, 1991 to Shawn Terry Phillips, born Feb. 18, 1971. They have four children: Shawn Patrick, born July 2, 1984; Samantha Beth, born Aug. 3, 1985; Shane Conner, born June 15, 1998; and Julia Mary, born Aug. 18, 1999.

Marcia LaDean was married on June 10, 1995 to Douglas Winfield Skinner, born Feb. 17, 1972. They have two children: Ryan James Skinner, born March 3, 1998 and Rheagan Hope Skinner, born April 23, 1999. *Submitted by Mary Jenkins Scroggins*

JENKINS-IKERD - John Kelly "JK" Jenkins was born May 18, 1869 in Princeton, Gibson County, IN to William R. Jenkins and Harriet Hatcher. He first came to Missouri with his parents and showed up in the 1880 Laclede County, MO census. His siblings were James, Eveline, Mary Ann (married George W. Laughlin), William E. (married Francis Heatherly), Missouri Drucilla "Zuri" (married Edward Cox), Artalissa "Artie" (married William Franklin Nobles), Charles M. (married Julia Montgomery) and Phillip Frank (married Mary J. Hite and Susie M. Brown).

JK married on April 22, 1888 in Laclede County, MO to Frances Lorine Green, daughter of Charles H. Green. Frances, born July 8, 1865 in Rochester, Monroe County, NY, died Feb. 11, 1955 in Springfield; buried in Pleasant Hill Cemetery, Bolivar, MO. JK died June 14, 1930 at his farm, six miles north of Bolivar, north of the Jefferson Bridge in the Greenwood community. He is buried in the Mt. Olive Cemetery, Bolivar, MO.

They had Charles William Jenkins; an infant; Mary Magnalene "Maggie" Jenkins; Evelyn "Ev" Rebecca Jenkins and Sidney Arthur Niles "Jack" Jenkins.

John Kelly Jenkins first shows up in Benton Township, Polk County, MO in the 1900 Census, then in 1920 Polk County, MO census in Marion Township. He was in Laclede County, MO in 1910.

Charles W. Jenkins was born Oct. 5, 1888 in Missouri; died Dec. 14, 1918 in Bolivar. He married on July 19, 1908 in Polk County, MO to Grace Maude Orrell, daughter of L. H. and Mary A. Orrell, born July 16, 1892, Dade County, MO; died April 13, 1967 in Bolivar. Tragedy struck this family in December 1918, when the flu took three of four children, Johnny W., Mary Lorine, Ray and father, Charley. All buried in the Goff Cemetery. Grace and son Clarence Lu'Allen

John Kelly Jenkins, ca. 1900

235

survived the ordeal.

"Maggie" Jenkins was born June 14, 1893 in Conway, MO. She married on Oct. 9, 1908 in Lebanon, MO to Homer Logan Ikerd, son of Thomas Fleming Ikerd and Martha Jane Rimmer. He was born Aug. 15, 1881 in Conway, MO and died Jan. 4, 1967 in Springfield, MO; buried Mt. Olive Cemetery.

Maggie's death occurred on Sept. 16, 1921 from burns. She had started a fire, but did not think it was burning good enough, so she poured on some coal oil. The flames caught the oil and the can exploded, throwing oil on her clothes. She called her husband telling him the house was on fire, and ran out into the yard with her clothes burning. He tried to tear her clothing off but the flames were too fierce and her clothing was burned off and her body was burned. Homer received bad burns on his hands and face trying to rescue his wife. Their screams could be heard more than a mile away. The fire happened about 5 a.m. and she lived until 12:30 p.m. She was buried at Mt. Olive Cemetery.

She left six children: Alice Rebecca (married Edgar Virgil "Eddie" Derossett); Wm. Henry (married Dean A. Basham); Francis Irene (married Raymond Curtis Carter); Agnes Marie (married Marvin Carl Vest and Cecil Wesley Gilden); Adron Jackson "Jack" (married Jewell Marie Seamster); and Lucy Isabelle (married Otto Johannes Remmenga).

Ev Jenkins was born Aug. 2, 1895 in Stockton, MO; died April 27, 1984 in Stockton; buried Bolivar, MO. Ev married first, Lannie Wilson; second to John Edward Morris on Aug. 12, 1945 in Bolivar, MO. She had two sons, Cloyd Wilson and Eugene Wilson.

"Jack" Jenkins was born June 17, 1900 in Van, Polk County, MO and died after June 1955 in California. He married Norah Martisha Hite, daughter of Hugh Boyd Hite and Martisha Rinck. They had three sons, Jack, Johnny and Dale Gene. *Compiled and submitted by William E. "Bill" Ikerd*

JOHNSON - James Wates Johnson (1811-1888) was born in Virginia, emigrating at a young age to near Nashville, TN. There he met and married Nancy Piper (1814-1883). They came to Polk County, MO in 1834. He was of English descent. Nancy's father William Piper was a native of Ireland, coming to this country in his youth. He was a soldier in the War of 1812 and his body was the second buried in Bolivar City Cemetery. Piper Creek was named for him. James W. owned slaves but fought with the Union Army during the Civil War. He had been promoted to colonel in his regiment of the Missouri Militia before he resigned in 1863. Before the war he had held elective offices in Polk County. He was a staunch Democrat and he and his wife were active members of the Christian Church. James W. and Nancy had eight children, five of whom lived to adulthood: Delilah, Richard M., Samuel R. (Phil), James W. and Abraham L. who became the grandfather of Wilma Beck.

A traveling minister, Rev. McNair from Illinois, visited the settlers from time to time. One day he stopped at the Johnson home at noon and spent a few hours visiting. Some weeks later he returned to ask the colonel if he could marry Delilah. Colonel Johnson was not at home, so Nancy said to the minister, "Young man, if you don't want the worst tongue-lashing you have ever heard, take Delilah and leave before my husband gets home." They left for Illinois. Wilma's grandfather, Abe, as he was called, corresponded regularly with Delilah. She had children.

The four sons of the colonel settled in the Bolivar area and each of them had children. Abraham L. (1861-1924) was married in the early 1880s to Mary V. Hargis (1861-1925). Soon they went to Texas in a wagon, taking along an extra mule. Apparently things there did not meet their expectations — soon they returned to Polk County and settled about six miles southeast of Bolivar. Abe and Mary had three children: Maude, Mattie Chloe and Harry Clark (1889-1967). Harry, Wilma's father, married Lydia Susan Stambaugh (1889-1982) and they had six children: Loren L., Clark W., Wilma L., Freda L., Clifford S. (who died in infancy) and Mary Virginia. They lived near Bolivar and were active in Mt. Gilead Church.

Loren (1910-1993) married Mary Belle Butler (1914-1964). They lived in Cedar County where he was a farmer and she was a teacher. They were active members of Filley Christian Church. Clark (1912-1989) married Hazel Scroggins (1915-1988) and they lived and farmed near Pleasant Hope. Hazel was a teacher. They had four children: Gene Clark, Fred Wates, Barbara Ellen and Betty Kay. They were active in the Pleasant Hope Baptist Church. Wilma was a teacher and counselor in Polk and St. Louis Counties. She was married to David Beck, also a teacher. They retired to Stockton from Rockwood School District, Eureka. They are active in the United Methodist Church. Freda joined the WAC and worked in the Pentagon during WWII. After the war, she worked in California for several years, then went to Eureka and taught for 20 years, retiring to Bolivar where she attends the United Methodist Church. Mary Virginia worked for Polk County Bank before her marriage to Mynatt Scott of Bolivar. He was a teacher and school administrator in Rockwood School District for many years. They had one daughter, Elizabeth Anne. They also retired to Bolivar and are active in the Christian Church.

Colonel James W. Johnson has many descendants living in Bolivar and Polk County. One granddaughter, Helen (Johnson) Phillips, was 104 years old in 2002 and lives in Bolivar. James W., Nancy and other family members are buried in Bolivar City Cemetery. Others are buried in Greenwood Cemetery, Mt. Gilead Cemetery and elsewhere. *Submitted by Wilma Beck*

JOHNSON, NEUHART, FISH AND WAGGONER – Pamela's family patriarch was J. A. Johnson. He was born Nov. 4, 1842 somewhere near Nashville, TN. He was in the Civil War and was a flag bearer for the South. He was in the Civil War three years and was honorably discharged. He married Christina M. (Wyatt) Johnson on June 1, 1862. Christine was born June 6, 1842. She was from around Tishomingo, MS. J. A. Johnson and family moved to Missouri around 1871. They lived in Marion Township in Polk County, MO. J. A. Johnson joined Mt. Olive Baptist Church in 1871. He was an ordained deacon, a licensed preacher and ordained preacher. He was a Sunday School superintendent for 10 years and treasurer for 42 years. The Johnsons had two children. One died in infancy; the other child was Pamela's great-great-great-grandmother Lucinda (Johnson) Neuhart. She was born July 23, 1868. She was married to Henry Neuhart. They had four children. It was told that Lucinda was out picking wild blackberries and stepped on a yellow jackets nest, and that the yellow jackets got up in her hair, as she wore her hair up. She was stung multiple times till she was dead. Lucinda Neuhart died on Oct. 23, 1891. The Johnsons took in Lucinda's four children; one of those children was Pamela's great-great-grandmother, Florence M. (Neuhart) Fish, born March 27, 1884. Florence met and fell in love with Clyde Emmerson Fish. He was born in Gutherie, IA. She married Clyde Emmerson on Jan. 7, 1900. She was a quiet,

Left to right – Blanche McWhorter, Mabel Jennings and Mildred Fish, three sisters

respected woman— a very patient person. Her door was always open to those in need. She was a very good Christian. She took care of her home and raised five children: Blanche McWhorter, Mildred C. Waggoner, Mabel I. Jennings, Clyde Ed Fish and Wayne Fish. The Fishes had two other children that died in infancy. J. A. Johnson died on Dec. 4, 1914; Christina died in 1925. Clyde Emmerson Fish was a respected businessman. He was an insurance man who had his own agency. The Fishes lived in Bolivar for many years. Clyde Emmerson Fish died April 10, 1954. Florence M. (Neuhart) Fish died Nov. 14, 1956. Mildred C. (Fish) Waggoner was Pamela's grandmother. She was the next to the oldest. She was born Jan. 28, 1909. She attended Bolivar schools and graduated high school in 1927. She went to Southwest Bible College and studied nutrition. She started "Grandmother's Headstart." She was married to Oscar Waggoner, born May 8, 1906. They corresponded back and forth from Bolivar, MO to Enid, OK. They would exchange letters and pictures. Mildred was 21 years old when she married Oscar Waggoner, Jan. 7, 1930. Oscar Waggoner was raised in Enid, OK. He had three sisters and three brothers. Oscar Waggoner was the youngest of the six. His parents were Mary (Bewely) Waggoner, from Polk Town, Polk County, MO and John Martin Palmer Waggoner, from Enid, OK. Oscar and Mildred lived in Weatherford, TX for a while, then Ava, MO and finally Bolivar, MO. In 1937 a child was born to them. Her name was Patricia L. (Waggoner) Gaulden-McGhee. She is Pamela's mother. They lived in Bolivar for sometime. Pamela's grandfather Oscar Waggoner worked as superintendent of streets in and around Bolivar, MO. He died Dec. 28, 1975. Mildred continued to live in Bolivar till 1985/86. She moved to Harlem, GA and lived there till her death on Feb. 11, 2002. All these people are buried in Mt. Olive Cemetery. Most of the Neuharts, Fishes and Johnsons are also buried there. This ends Pamela's family line in the state of Missouri. *Submitted by Pamela Moseley.*

JOHNSTON - Polk County, MO has been the home to many generations of Thomas and Mary____ Johnston. Thomas and Mary were buried in a mausoleum in Hickory Grove Cemetery in 1854 and 1843, respectively. Their youngest son, Thomas, was born in the state of Kentucky in 1822. He was married around 1850 to Eliza Eviline Bancom of Tennessee. To this union eight children were born: Thomas, Mary, Elizabeth, John, Rachel, twins Silias A. and Susan and Charles Samuel.

Thomas and Eliza are Tammy's second great-grandparents. They resided outside of Brighton on land that is just south of the Little Sac River. On Sept. 27, 1898 they sold a parcel of land for the sum of one dollar to George Griffin, Christian Fender, Asa Fender, Eliza Blackburn and Jessie Fender for the purpose of building a school and church. Gumbo School and Fender Chapel became the products of this sale. While Gumbo School has long since gone, Fender Chapel is still being used. It is located just off Highway 13, north of the Little Sac River. Thomas and Eliza were laid to rest in Brock Cemetery in 1889 and ____ respectively.

Thomas and Eliza's oldest son Thomas was married around 1872 to Margaret J. Presley. Her parents were Isaac Presley and Martha J. Smith. To this union five children were born: Tipton Monroe, Isaac Joe C., William Avery, Thomas and Liza J. Thomas and Mary were buried in Hickory Grove Cemetery in 1898 and 1903, respectively.

William Avery was born in January 1881 just outside of Brighton and was a resident of the Brighton and Pleasant Hope communities all of his life. He was married to Clara Mae Hembree on April 20, 1922. Clara was born in September 1905 to Fred Hembree and Etta Mae Baldwin Hembree. Clara was the third great-granddaughter to Alexander Brown, the first person to be buried in Brock Cemetery, also located north of the Little Sac River off Highway 13. To this union 10

Margaret J. Presley Johnston and Thomas Johnston

children would be born: Margaret Marie (Wommack), Oscar Lee (1924-2002), Calvin Coolidge, Lou Etta (l928-1929), Thomas Junior (1930-1999), Billy Joe, Monroe, Anna Mae (Thomas), Gilbert Edward (1940-1963) and Dortha Faye (Caffey). William Avery (Bill) and Clara were laid to rest in the Brighton Cemetery in 1946 and 1974, respectively.

Monroe Johnston, their fifth son and Tammy's father, was married to Elvena Marie Johnson on June 3, 1957. Her parents were Elmer M. Johnson and A. Lorrain Swearengin of Christian County, MO. They would have two daughters, Loretta Marie and Tammy Sue.

Eight generations of Thomas Johnston's family have called Polk County, MO home. Counting the fifth great grandparents down to Tammy's great-niece Emily Lynn Drake, there are 10 generations of Alexander Brown's family to have lived or are still living in Polk County. *Submitted by Tammy Sue Johnston*

Back, left to right: Bessie, Elgie, Grace. Front left to right: Charlie, Archie, Nellie.

JONES – Charles Oliver Jones, son of William Smith "Bill" and Martha (Ragsdale) Jones, was born Sept. 30, 1884 in Polk County, MO, west of Louisburg, MO and died Aug. 13, 1935 of cancer in a Springfield, MO hospital. Charlie married Nov. 29, 1905, Nellie Ethel Davison, daughter of Wm. and Ellen (Tarbot) Davison. Nellie was born April 14, 1887 and died March 16, 1965 of liver cancer in Springfield, MO; both are buried in the Lindley Creek Church Cemetery. Charlie and Nellie lived close to her parents, about five or six miles east of Goodson when the children were small, spent a short time in Chanute, KS, finally buying 40 acres of farm land close to his father, from his brother Nate, for a team and wagon ($400 value) in 1908. They farmed this until Charlie's death; Nellie and Elgie carried on until Nellie's death. The land was then to be Elgie's until he died. It was sold in 1981. Charlie and Nellie's children:

Grace Opal was born Feb. 22, 1906 in Kansas, died Jan. 3, 1940 in Buffalo, MO, buried Lindley Creek Church Cemetery. She married Sept. 8, 1925, Glen Carter (1909-1999), son of Erby and Grace (Scott) Carter. Children: Beverly (1933-) married 1950, Ronald Brown (1933-). Children: Sherry, Valerie and Ronald Leon. Beverly has been a bank executive and she and her family have lived in Independence, MO most of their lives. Evelyn Florence (1935-) married 1951, Arcie Fender (1932-). Children: Archie and Jackie Wayne. Evelyn and Arcie have lived near Brighton most of their lives.

Bessie Pearl was born Oct. 10, 1908 in Polk County and died Dec. 7, 1997, buried Harrisonville, MO City Cemetery. Bessie married Oct. 22, 1928, James Buel Walker (1907-1993), son of James and Lula (Walker) Walker of Goodson, MO. (Divorced) Buel studied electricity and did wiring, started an appliance store in Archie and Harrisonville, MO, finally selling real estate. Bessie sold sewing machines after their divorce. Their daughter Wanda Jean Walker (1929-) married Bill Alexander (1928-). (Divorced.) Bill farmed and Wanda taught school. Wanda and Bill's children were: Gayle, Nancy, Sandy and Guy. Bessie's and Buel's son, Vernon Lee Walker (1931-) married Barbara Kay Harvey (1933-). Vernon started the Family Center in Harrisonville, MO, is now retired. Children: Joy, Jil, Jeff and Jay.

Elgie Lloyd was born July 29, 1911, died Nov. 25, 1980, buried Lindley Cemetery, never married.

Gladys Okla was born July 5, 1917 and died Nov. 20, 2000 in Buffalo, MO. She married 1934, Lowell Parscale (l908-1967), son of John and Stella Parscale. Both are buried in the Schofield Church Cemetery, south of Halfway, MO. Lowell was injured in an auto accident and was left with a bad back, but Okla carried on the work on the farm until that was too much to do. Children: Shirley Ann Parscale (1935-) married 1953, Dean Covert (1929-1991). Dean is buried at Schofield Cemetery. Dean farmed and became a minister in the Baptist Church. Their children: Charlotte, Wayne and Eddie. Barbara Lee Parscale (1937-) married 1950, Donald Dunseth (1931-). Donald farmed and milked cows. Their children: Carl and Paul.

Archie Lovel Jones was born Feb. 24, 1923, was married Dec. 7, 1950, Myrtle Ann (Miller) Reed (1926-) the daughter of Jess and Hattie Miller. Archie has done different jobs, but has retired to Louisburg, MO. Myrtle quilts and cans what Archie raises. Children: Dean Wilburn (1959) married Teressa Hine (1958-). Children: Brandon Hine (adopted), Jesse Ryan. Myrtle had two children by her first marriage: Dennis R. Reed and Margaret Rea. *Submitted by Barbara (Parscale) Dunseth*

JONES – Floyd Junior Jones was born Aug. 28, 1930 in Mammoth Spring, AR. He was the third of eight children born to Uriah Clevis Jones and Ollie Harrell. Being the oldest boy, he helped with the farm, hunted and trapped for the family. He attended Bald Nob school through the eighth grade. In the

Back row – Earlene, Gaylen, Keith and Floyd Jones. Front row – Amy Hammoudt, Connie Easterly, Diane Charlton.

fall of 1945, the family moved to West Plains, MO. Floyd went to high school and graduated in 1949. Seeing an advertisement telling about the wonders of electricity he attended the Coyne Electrical School in Chicago, IL. He worked nights at Cook County Hospital. After completing the nine month course, he came back home to West Plains and went to work for Cloud Oak Flooring. One day while working on a conveyer he lost the little finger of his left hand. Hoping to save the finger, they sent him to Springfield and placed him in the care of a young nurse trainee named Earlene. Earlene Ruth Foster was born in Springfield on Sept. 25, 1931. After leaving the hospital he began to call upon Earlene; they courted through the summer of 1951. During this period Floyd decided to join the army; he learned he was to be sent to Japan, and he asked Earlene to marry him. Floyd and Earlene were married on Nov. 22, 1951 and soon after he was shipped to Japan. Then in April of 1953 Earlene went over to stay with him. Their first child Connie Sue Jones was born Jan. 12, 1954 at Johnson Air Force Base, Urumagawa, Japan. In the summer of 1954, the family came home by ship, Floyd was discharged from the army and they settled in Springfield. Floyd joined the Electrical Workers union and went to work at Springfield Electric Service, winding transformers and Earlene went to raising babies. They soon had Diane Marie Jones born on Dec. 6, 1955, followed by Gaylen Lee Jones on Feb. 14, 1957. In 1958 they moved to a farm near Fruitland store. Here they raised pigs, milked, and had a few horses. It was here that Keith Alan Jones was born on June 3, 1967. Then in 1969, the family moved to Dallas County; it was here that Amy Dawn Jones was born on Sept. 19, 1970. The family lived here for almost four years, but the barn was small and land was poor, so in the spring of 1973 the family moved to Polk County. Floyd purchased a 240-acre farm in Halfway, MO that included a hill called Blue Mound and was known as the old Ike Roweton place. It was here that they started seriously milking. Connie, Diane and Gaylen continued to go to school in Buffalo, since they only had a short time left, but Keith and Amy started school at Halfway. Floyd continued to work in the electrical trade, but usually took the summers off to put up hay. In 1979, Floyd purchased another 160 across the road; it is here that Floyd and Earlene now reside in the new house built in 1995. *Submitted by Floyd Jones*

JONES – John Calvin Jones was born in Collin County, TX on July 19, 1882 to Umphrey Mitchell Jones and Ruth Eveline Lawson, who were married there on Sept. 12, 1880. Umphrey was born in July 1853 in Laclede County, MO, one of nine children of Henry T. Jones and Nancy Frances Phipps, who were married June 21, 1831 in Allen County, KY and came to Laclede County, MO before 1850. Henry T. died about 1865 and Nancy Frances about 1877 in Laclede County. Umphrey traveled to Collin County, TX with John W. Lawson and his wife

Calvin and Dessie Jones

Martha Caroline Gibbs, the parents of his bride-to-be.

Umphrey's brothers and sisters were Charles, born 1838; James, born 1839; Margaret, born Sept. 2, 1840, died July 3, 1935 (married David R. Hopkins, lived in Polk County); William, born June 4, 1843; Henry, born June 4, 1843, died Oct. 14, 1927; Matthew, born 1846; Sarah, born 1849; Umphrey M., born July 1853; John T., born August 1855, died Oct. 14, 1927.

Umphrey and Eveline "Ev" came back from Collin County, TX to Polk County, MO with their son John Calvin, known as Calvin, before their second child Minnie M. Jones was born April 23, 1885 (married Charles W. Brown, Jan. 13, 1902 in Polk County, lived in the state of Washington). The remainder of their children born in Polk County were Vina A. Jones, born June 26, 1889, died July 13, 1996, married George Hopkins; Marvin W. Jones, born June 1893, married Grace Haseltine; Lester M. Jones, born August 1894, married Dessie Fox; Jesse R. Jones, born November 1896. Ev died about 1898 and is buried in an unmarked grave in the Slagle Cemetery in Polk County. Umphrey never remarried and lived with his daughter Vina and her husband George Hopkins until his death in 1931. He is buried in the Enon Cemetery.

Calvin grew up in Polk County and there he met Dessie Dell Faulkner, born Sept. 18, 1886, daughter of William A. and Mary Louise (Renfro) Faulkner. Calvin and Dessie were married Feb. 16, 1902 in Polk County. For a few years in the 1920s they lived in California; otherwise, they lived their entire married life in Polk County. They had five children: William Emerson Jones, born June 6, 1903, died Jan. 10, 1999, married Alma Irene Cobb, Nov. 16, 1929; Jewell Eveline Jones, born Nov. 14, 1905, died Sept. 19, 1967, married Leo Wells, Sept. 28, 1921; Loren Leo Jones, born Oct. 27, 1909, died June 21, 1994, married Opal Austin, Aug. 30, 1930; Laura Louise Jones, born July 24, 1912, died Feb. 8, 2002, married Ruby W. Eagon, Aug. 5, 1929; Melby Edwin Jones, born Aug. 18, 1918, died Nov. 28, 1951, married Nellie Bays, Oct. 18, 1940. William, Loren and Laura each celebrated their 60th wedding anniversaries.

Calvin was a carpenter and therefore, they lived at several different places in Polk County. One job that took him away from home for long periods of time was working on the Bagnell Dam. Another was the original bridge on Highway 65 in Dallas County over the Pomme de Terre River. In the late 1930s while living in Slagle, south of Bolivar on Highway 13, he was working on a house when he fell from the roof onto the porch and broke his back. He recovered but somewhat limited his climbing thereafter. Later, in the 1940s, he and Dessie moved to Bolivar but after a series of heart attacks he had to retire and was unable to work. They made Wishart their home late in life. Calvin died July 28, 1964 and Dessie died Sept. 17, 1966. Both are buried in the Slagle Cemetery. *Submitted by Calvin G. Jones*

JONES – Joseph Allan Jones was born Nov. 25, 1867 to Rucamby Pennington Jones and Sarah Ann Brown in Kentucky. Family moved near Ash Grove, MO in 1869. Joe went to school at Kelly - no grades. "We went till you got too big for the teacher to whip." In the spring of 1883 (March 1), he went to Wellington, KS and stayed the summer with an aunt. No school there. Joe went to Sedalia, MO in fall. He lived with his uncle Joe Brown in 1883, where he attended high school. Graduated May 28, 1886. (12 in class, six boys and six girls.)

Joe was married on the day he was 19. Married Emma Frances Sloan, 14 years old, Nov. 25, 1886. Moved to Springfield, MO. He worked at painting and paper hanging trade, which he learned in high school. Lived in Springfield, MO from 1887 to 1893. Had his own business.

In 1893 during one of the worst panics the country ever had, building trades closed down. No work from July 1, 1893 to mid-October. He lost business and home. Moved close to Morrisville, MO to work on a farm, cutting wood at 50 cents per day and dinner. He had a wife and two children when he rented a farm at $1.25 per month. March 1, 1894 he began to paint and hang paper at $1.25 per day and dinner, as well as farming until oldest son got ready for high school, and moved to Morrisville, MO to send children to Morrisville Methodist College.

He took examination for newly created rural mail route in Morrisville in 1905. Seven took the exam. He made 98.5% and got the job. Served mail route until he was 65. Joe was mayor of Morrisville for 20 years.

Joe and Emma had eight children. All were high school graduates; three were college graduates. Children were:

Lee Jones, born Jan. 28, 1889, died July 20, 1977. Teacher and school superintendent at Fair Play, MO. Married Hattie Meek. Had two sons, Bernard and Bobbie. Both died in infancy.

"Miss Bessie" Jones, born Dec. 6, 1891, died Jan. 18, 1969. Single. Taught first grade at MCE for 42 years.

Sarah Jones, born Sept. 1, 1894, died Oct. 22, 1966. Married Harley Bloomer, had six children: Basil, Craig, Marguerite, Mescal and twins, Francis and Joseph.

Faye Jones, born Nov. 21, 1897, died Dec. 19, 1987. Married Cash Willey, had three children: Mary Frances, Billie and Richard Lee.

Bettie Jones, born Feb. 21, 1901, died April 1, 1975. Single. Worked in children's home in Joplin, MO.

Lois Jones, born July 2, 1904, died Jan. 1, 1997. School teacher. Married Rube Dyce, sheep man from Wyoming. No children. (Rube was a Navy Seabee in WWII. Severely wounded in Iwo Jima.)

Dick Jones, born Nov. 20, 1906, died Sept. 17, 1967. School bus driver, mechanic. Married Alyce Schutt, had two children, Joe Lee and Karen. (Dick's name was drawn from the fish bowl by President Roosevelt in 1940, drafted in army. Served four years in Europe. Was in "Battle of the Bulge.")

Vivian Jones, born Oct. 31, 1912, died June 20, 1963. Married Carl Schuler. No children. Divorced. Taught music at home. (Badly crippled with arthritis.)

The Jones family home is the white two-story house on Highway 215 across street from MCE Elementary. Joe was correspondent for *The Bolivar Herald* for 50 years. His motto through life was "Don't worry!" *Submitted by Joseph E. Bloomer*

JONES – Mike and Bunny Jones moved to Bolivar in 1981 to "raise the kids in the country." Mike had grown up in the country in Stone County, MO, the son of Orvil and Iris Maness Jones. Bunny, the daughter of Guy and Leota Ross Sawyer, had lived in the city most of her life. Bunny was born at the home of her parents on her grandparents Marvin and Vesta Ross's farm near Dunnegan, MO. They lived in Polk County until Bunny was about 3 years old. By then her father, Guy Sawyer, had taken a job in Kansas City, thus the move. Bunny and her four younger siblings were raised

Charles Michael, Bunny, Angela Elaine and Mike Jones

in Johnson County, KS and lived there until they all married, had their children, and eventually moved to different areas.

In 1980 when Mike, Bunny and their children Michael and Angela came down to visit Bunny's grandmother at Cliquot, they decided to buy some property in Polk County and set their dreams into motion. That is when they found their "dream place." It had never had a dwelling on the land as it was the east corner of an original 200-acre property. That began the adventure of their lifetimes. Mike and Bunny worked long hours and many years building up their farm. They had chosen to "do it themselves" with their building as the interest rates were 21 percent at that time and they did not want all the debt with the high interest rates on top of it.

What pioneers! They had to have a driveway made, which turned into the deepest worst mud when it rained and even worse when the ground would freeze and thaw in the winter and spring. There were a couple of years that they would have to park cars out by the road and carry the groceries, etc. all the way to the house, while trying to keep the deep mud from sucking the boots off of their feet. When that would happen, they would lose their balance and more than once lost what they were carrying and they would end up on the ground, laughing at what a picture that would make. Eventually they got enough gravel and rock base to keep their driveway built up and could enjoy driving in on solid ground.

Wanting their children to have pets and to experience raising farm animals, they eventually got some dogs, cats, chickens, rabbits, cows, goats, ponies, ducks and yes, stinky pigs! They learned how to butcher chickens and rabbits and raised huge gardens to preserve. The kids enjoyed trips to the nearby Pomme de Terre River to have weiner roasts and swim and play quite often as they grew up.

Since they were the only ones on Bunny's side of the family living in the country, they had company on most weekends and holidays for those first several years, so that the rest of the family could enjoy "getting out of town." Wonderful family visits were accrued and will always be remembered. The "city" families would bring their "toys," such as three-wheelers and the Jones family would ride those while the "city" families would love to get up on the John Deere tractor and drive it around for fun. Such simple pleasures, but add huge, picnic-style meals topped off with lots of

Michael, Bunny, Mike and Angie Jones, January 2002. Mike and Bunny's 30th Wedding Anniversary

watermelon and outdoor games in the summers and you really had wonderful quality family times. While it was a long road to travel, some 23 years have passed. The kids are raised, the animals are a thing of the past and Mike and Bunny, along with their son Michael, still reside on the farm, which is very close to where Bunny was born. Angela lives close to where she was born and to where her mother, aunts and uncles were raised in Kansas. What is the old saying? You always return to your roots. In this case, it appears to be true. Bunny Sawyer Jones is glad that she is living near to what was the beginning of her life. She appreciates the fact that she can walk the lands of her forefathers and that her husband "helped" her choose the country life. After 32 years of marriage and 23 years on the farm, she thinks that she will most likely live her last years where her first years began, being content to be a "country girl" after all. *Submitted by Angela Jones*

JONES – The Jones family has traced its history back to Shadrack Jones, who was born Feb. 22, 1802 and died March 23, 1894. He was born in Sampson County, NC. Shadrack went to Tennessee and married Susan Amanda Garrigus on March 24, 1829 in Maury County. They moved to Laclede County in 1853 and had 15 children, one of which was William Riley Jones. William was born Dec. 15, 1835 and married Susan Whitson on July 16, 1857 in Laclede County. William and several of his brothers fought in the Civil War; he was in the Union Army, Company B of the Missouri Infantry. To this marriage were born 11 children. Of these 11, one was Loranzo Harrison Jones; he was born Nov. 4, 1872 and married Martha Emeline Fincher, born Jan. 30, 1875. They were married Jan. 31, 1892 and to this union were born 12 children. Of these 12, there was a son named Uriah Clevis Jones, born Dec. 2, 1904. He married Ollie Harrell, born Sept. 10, 1906. They were married Nov. 5, 1924 in Mammoth Spring, AR. (For more of these Joneses see the 2000 edition of the *Laclede County History Book*.) They had eight children, of which one was Floyd Junior Jones, born Aug. 28, 1930. He married Earlene Ruth Foster, born Sept. 25, 1931. They were married Nov. 22, 1951 and had five children. Of these was Keith Alan Jones, born June 3, 1967 in Greene County. Keith moved to Polk County with his family in 1973, at the age of 6 years old. He had started school at Buffalo, MO, but finished the year at Halfway. Keith kept very busy on the farm, milking in the evenings and school during the day. The summers were always very full with planting and putting up hay. Keith attended high school at Halfway and was very active with FFA and Choir. When he graduated in 1985, he started college at SMSU, working for an electrical engineering degree. After the death of Cliff Foster, a very close friend, Keith dropped out after one year. In the fall of 1986, Keith started the IBEW apprenticeship program and went to work as an electrician. During this time Keith started piano lessons, from an old family friend, in Springfield. It was this lady who changed his life forever. She first found him a house to buy and in 1987 he moved to Springfield. She then introduced him to a student of hers, a young lady named Jeanine. They got along really well and started to see each other on a regular basis. Jeanine Sue Hancock was born May 7, 1970. She was the daughter of James Hancock and Janice Willis. Keith and Jeanine were married on May 18, 1991 in Springfield, MO. Keith completed his apprenticeship training and became a journeyman wireman and Jeanine started nurse's training. They now have two boys, Zachary Wayne Jones, born June 18, 1995 and Andrew Grey Jones, born Nov. 29, 1997. They continue to live and work in Springfield, but

Keith, Jeanine, Zachary and Andrew Jones

plan to return to Polk County to live in the future. *Submitted by Keith Alan Jones*

JONES – Tom and Ida Jones came to Polk County by train from Ulysses, NE soon after their marriage on June 6, 1921. They settled near Slagle and later, during depression years, moved to near Polk. Tom was born near Galveston, TX on Feb. 12, 1882. Little is known of his young life as he was orphaned at an early age. He was engaged in farm work all of his life; was a progressive farmer, serving on the school board and interested in new farming methods. He died on May 6, 1965 and is buried at Payne Cemetery near Polk.

Tom and Ida Jones

Ida was the youngest child of German immigrants August Herms and Louise Schliesser Herms, who settled near Brainard, NE in 1892. Ida's parents had both died by the time she was 11 years old and she was raised in Oklahoma by an older sister. She was born Dec. 14, 1897 near Brainard and died Sept. 20, 1984. Burial was at Payne Cemetery.

Tom and Ida had five children—Irene Louise, born April 28, 1922; Anna Lee, born June 1, 1923; Calvin Thomas, born Dec. 11, 1924; Arnold Edward, born Feb. 14, 1927; and Judith Eileen, born Sept. 2, 1941.

Irene, a registered nurse, married Gilmer Wallace Dehn, a WWII veteran and Missouri University graduate in 1952. They have four children. Lydia Ann, born May 18, 1953, married David Cushman Welch from Media, PA in 1984. They have two children, Nathaniel Dehn Welch and Travis Cushman Welch. Paul Joseph, born July 24, 1954, married Janet Kay Maples in 1980. They have two children, Andrea Michelle and Jared Paul. Stephen Leonard, born Jan. 4, 1956, has served in the military and is a veteran of the Gulf War. David Lynn, born Dec. 19, 1960, married Joan Reichl from Milwaukee and they have two daughters, Mariel Joy and Julia Marie.

Anna Lee, a social worker and WWII Naval veteran, married Alan Meredith from Marion, OH. They had four children: Edward Alan, born Dec. 12, 1954; Dennis Lee, born Dec. 30, 1956; William Thomas, born June 20, 1958; and Janet Marie, born May 20, 1960. Janet married David Goggin from Dallas and they have two daughters, Amanda Kay and Holly.

Calvin, a farmer and WWII veteran, married Ruth Payne in 1948. They have three children. Rodney Dale, born March 1, 1958, married Julie Brown. They have two children, Nathaniel Brock and Nicole Paige. Robert Gregory, born Feb. 11, 1960 married Elizabeth Marie Boyd. They have two sons, Adam Robert and Calvin Thomas. Mary Elizabeth, born Sept. 4, 1970, married Rick Vance. They have two children, Ryan Alexander and Madison Elizabeth. Calvin died Feb. 17, 1997 and is buried at Payne Cemetery.

Arnold, a farmer and WWII veteran, married Corene Rader on Feb. 13, 1949. They have three children. Carl Wayne, born May 10, 1950, married Patricia Kay Daniels. They have three children, Laura Nicole, Clint Edward and Malissa Kay. Kenneth Edward, born July 15, 1956, married Dawn Michelle Akers. They have three children, Kristi Dawn, Michael Edward and Katie Marie. Sharon Faye, born Dec. 15, 1957, married Raymond Dale Bolin. They have two children, Raymond Chad and Charity.

Judy, a farmwife and genealogist, married Lyndell McKinney on Sept. 2, 1972. They reside on a farm near Halfway. *Submitted by Irene Dehn*

JONES – Wilbur Jones was born July 29, 1917 at Koshkonong, MO, the son of Heman Clarence and Rachel Rebecca (Epple) Jones. Heman was the son of William and Polly (Blackwell) Jones. Wilbur was one of nine children: Westley Loyd (died at 9 months), Gladys Irene, Wilbur Loyd, Zelma Nadine (died at 4 years), Leroy James, Willis Ivan Epple, Alice Nadine, Clarence Arnold and Sadie Mae.

Wilbur started to school in 1923 at Red Ranch, they moved from Koshkonong to Pittsburg, KS in 1924 or 1925, and then in 1926 they moved from Pittsburg to Catron, MO in a covered wagon. It took 21 days; they became farmers, raising cotton and soybeans.

In December 1937, Wilbur went to California, having uncles there as well as Lillie, who had moved there to her sisters from Koshkonong; they were married on May 29, 1938 at San Bruno, CA. Lillie Hilliah Dare Johnston was born at Koshkonong, MO on Nov. 28, 1919 to Vernie Clay and Minnie May (Madden) Johnston; she was one of six children: Lola Lorene, Lillie Hilliah Dare, Nora Jane, Virgil Leon, Ralph Deane and Maryland Virginia (died at 1 year).

Wilbur and Lillie lived in California through the summers picking fruit and cotton, then to Missouri with Wilbur's mother through the winter, then eventually went to work for Colorado Fuel and Iron wire mill, and then the Bethlehem steel ship yards until WWII. Then on Feb. 19, 1943 he went into the army. He

Lillie 24, Wilbur 26, made May 1, 1944

spent 18 months stateside and 18 months in Germany; he was with the 70th tank battalion, keeping the shells supplied to the gunner. He was discharged from the army Dec. 3, 1945. Lillie had been living in Missouri during this time, but they returned to California traveling yearly to "home" Missouri, while working in California; they also had Wayne Noris and Wilma Joyce in California. In 1950 they bought a farm near Walnut Grove, MO where they had Sharlanda Norine and then Valinda Mae. Sold this farm and bought a farm near Aldrich/Eudora, which they rented out and moved to California, buying a home in San Mateo and working at Colorado Fuel and Iron, also having two more children, Keith Allen and Jimmy Lloyd. They moved back "home" to the farm in 1962. Wilbur farmed, milked cows, raised beef, became a beekeeper (great honey), bought a water well driller and drilled many water wells in the Polk County area. Wilbur died Aug. 19, 1987. Lillie sold the farm and moved to Fair Play, MO in 1989 and to Pleasant Hope, Dec. 6, 1995. Of the six children, five live in Polk County. Wayne and Cheri Jones live in St. Louis. Wilma and James Stall live in Brighton; the rest all have Pleasant Hopes addresses: Sharlanda and Mike Schleifer (Mike's family have roots in Polk County 1867), Valinda and John Diacatos, Keith and Sue Jones (Sue teaches at Halfway) and Jim and Wilma Jones. Lillie has 13 grandchildren (10 living in Polk County), four great-grandchildren, with three more to arrive summer 2002. *Submitted by Lillie Jones*

JONES – William Emerson "Bill" Jones was born in Polk County, MO on June 6, 1903. His parents were John Calvin Jones (son of Umphrey M. Jones and Eveline Lawson) and Dessie Dell (Faulkner) Jones, (daughter of William Faulkner and Mary Louise Renfro). He married Alma Irene Cobb, born June 10, 1909 (daughter of George F. Cobb and Lillie Belle Rowland), in Polk County on Nov. 16, 1929 at the home of A. C. Rymer by the Rev. Clarence Salsman. They lived most of their married life in Polk County and purchased a farm in the Schofield community where their six children grew up. Their children were Virginia Maxine Jones, born March 30, 1930, married Herbert G. Lawson (born Jan. 31, 1930) on Dec. 8, 1948; children: Judith Maxine Lawson, born Feb. 19, 1950, married Bobby Gene Carey on Aug. 21, 1972;

W. E. "Bill" and Alma Jones

Brenda Jean Lawson, born March 2, 1951, married Dwight Robert Menefee on Nov. 21, 1970; Mark David Lawson, born Nov. 30, 1958, married Orilla F. Taylor on Jan. 20, 1978. Calvin George Jones, born Oct. 17, 1931, married Emma Lee Fitzgerrell (born May 19, 1935) on May 20, 1956; children: Teresa Gale Jones, born April 21, 1957, married Thomas L. Williams on Feb. 16, 1890; Travis Lee Jones, born Feb. 13, 1959, married Traci J. Hertzberg on Aug. 10, 1985. Harold Lee Jones, born July 26, 1933, married Geraldine Cook (born Feb. 3, 1935) on Sept. 9, 1956; children: Christopher Lee Jones, born June 10, 1963, married Jennifer L. Hardison on June 2, 1990; Eric Steven Jones, born Oct. 5, 1964; Beth Ann Jones, born Aug. 15, 1967, married Donald Edwin Robb on Jan. 20, 1990. Joye Bell Jones, born March 13, 1937, married Donald Sumner on June 26, 1957; children: Twyla Kay Sumner, born July 13, 1958; Kyle Raymond Sumner, born June 21, 1959, died June 21, 1959; Rhonda Lynne Sumner, born Sept. 19, 1962, married first,Mark Chronister on Aug. 22, 1979, married second,Ron Harriman, May 1988. Shelby Laverne Jones, born July 1, 1942, married Frances Kay Blevins (born Dec. 15, 1945) on March 27, 1965; children: Kevin Laverne Jones, born June 28, 1966, married Shelley Hainey on June 10, 1995; Cynthia Kay Jones, born May 6, 1971, married Ray Collins on Feb. 11, 1995; Harlan Gales Jones, born Nov. 27, 1946, married Glenda Darlene Simpson (born April 10, 1950) on Sept. 13, 1969; child: Lesley Erin Jones, born March 25, 1977, married Phillip Preiser on May 27, 2000.

Life during the great depression was difficult for Bill and Alma Jones. There were some evenings that they had only turnips to eat. Slowly life did improve even though Bill continued to farm with horses for several years. Alma's first washing machine was powered by a gasoline engine; before that she did her laundry on the "washboard" for her large family. Electricity came to the Jones farm after WWII. Their first child, Maxine, had polio as an infant which left one leg completely paralyzed. She made several trips to Columbia to the State Crippled Children's Hospital with the Polk County health nurse during childhood. In spite of her handicap she graduated valedictorian of her high school class, graduated from Draughon Business College and worked as a vice president in the trust department in a bank in Kansas City until retirement. Calvin attended the University of Missouri and was an agriculture extension agent in Barton County, MO. Harold attended Southwest Missouri State College and University of Missouri School of Medicine and practiced medicine in Springfield, MO. Joye became a licensed practical nurse and worked in a doctor's office in Springfield. Shelby worked as transportation supervisor for Associated Grocers in Springfield. Harlan attended Southwest Missouri State University and became an accountant in Springfield. Bill and Alma were married for slightly more than 64 years when Alma died Jan. 3, 1994 at the age of 84. Bill lived five more years and died on Jan. 10, 1999 at the age of 95 1/2 years. Both are buried in the Rock Prairie Cemetery in southeastern Polk County. *Submitted by Harold L. Jones, M.D.*

JONES – William Smith "Bill" Jones, son of Thompson and Eliza (Fisher) Jones, was born June 27, 1857 in Missouri. Both Thompson and Eliza were born in Barren County, KY. They left Barren County after 1855 and came to Missouri. They were in Webster County when Thompson enlisted in the army at Springfield, MO Aug. 10, 1863. He was in Company G, Eighth Regular Missouri Cavalry when he was killed by a bushwhacker at Bayou Metre, near Little Rock, AR, Sept. 2, 1863. Eliza then came to Dallas County to be near some of her relatives in Polk County. Eliza married second, Elijah W. Williams, in Polk County and had two more daughters, Eliza Bell and Elvina. Eliza died Nov. 19, 1892 and is buried in Goff Cemetery next to her daughter, Elvina. The children of Elias Thompson and Eliza Jones: Martha Elizabeth was born 1849 in Barren County, KY, married John T. Fisher Jr. and died 1902 in Polk County, MO. Sarah Ellen Jones was born 1851 in Barren County, married Nathan Elliot. Lived in Ardmore, OK 1923. Tabitha Frances was born 1855 in Barren County, married John Henry Williams, lived in Little Rock, AR 1923. William Smith was born 1857, died 1923. James Radford was born 1859 in Missouri, married Meda, died in Oklahoma. David Sigel "Sig" Jones was born in 1862 in Missouri, married Mary Elizabeth Pitts, died Pittsburg, MO.

William S. was married to Martha R. Ragsdale Jan. 10, 1875 in Polk County, MO by George Suiter, Minister of the Gospel. Martha was the daughter of John W. and Mary Ann (Hale) Ragsdale who lived north of Halfway, MO. Bill and Martha did some traveling before they settled down west of Louisburg, near Lindley Church. Martha died April 26, 1900 of the measles, so Bill got a girl in to take care of the children, who he married Dec. 1, 1901. Amanda Frances (Carter) Riley, born Sept. 12, 1882, was the daughter of Harrison. Bill died May 3, 1923 at home and is buried in the Ragsdale Cemetery next to his first wife. Amanda died Oct. 8, 1959 and is buried in Santa Paula, CA, where she moved after Bill died. It was told in the family that when a problem arose, Bill would open a big Bible and the answer would be found on that page. Bill and Martha Jones's children:

Bill and Martha Jones family – back – Nathan, Charles, Marion, Virgil. Front – William R., Florence, John T.

John Thomas was born Nov. 2, 1857 in Dallas County, MO, died July 18, 1931 in Glendale, AZ. John married in 1900 to LuSindae Jane "Sinda" Bonds (1877-1966), daughter of James and Margaret Bonds. Children: Nellie Mae, James Curtis, William Odus, Vonney Lee, Opal Marie and Dortha Hellen.

Florence was born Aug. 10, 1878 in Kansas, died May 22, 1952 in Santa Paula, CA. Florence married first,in 1896 to Robert Meadows (divorced) and had Clarence E. Florence married second,in 1900 to William Foster (1876-1963) and had Charles E., Perry, Gertie, Cecil, Lovell and Leslie.

William Radford "Will" was born March 11, 1881 in Missouri, and died Feb. 2, 1954 at Wheatland, MO. Will married in 1904 to Jemima Elizabeth "Lizzie" Williams (1886-1968), both buried Hopewell Church Cemetery. Their children: Ressie Corlis, Alfred Adrian, Elsie Florence, Jessee Lee, Leo Radford, Velta Elaine, Lawrence Edwin, Henry Wilfred, Clifton Eugene, Martha Goldina and Edna May.

Charles Oliver Jones, born 1884, died 1935 (see separate story).

Nathan "Nate" Jones was born March 9, 1887, died March 19, 1961. Nate married in 1908 to Iva Hogg (1886-1910), both buried Hopewell Church Cemetery. Their children: William Cecil "Willie" and Fern Evelyn.

Marion Thomas Jones was born June 11, 1890, died Dec. 7, 1973. Marion married in 1911 to Zelpha Mae Rush (1891-1980). They are buried Garden of Memories, Buffalo, MO. Their children: Lavern Gale and Laverta Eunice.

Virgil Lester Jones was born Nov. 28, 1894 and died March 23, 1963 in Fillmore, CA, buried Bardsdale Cemetery. Virgil married in 1915 to Fannie Jewel May (1898-). Their children: a son, died as infant, Iris Annalee, Vernice Mae.

William Smith "Bill" Jones and Amanda Riley's children (all children born Polk County, buried in California).

Letha Anne was born Aug. 13, 1902, married Ralph Mashburn, died Santa Paula, CA. Children: Vernon Ralph, Wilda Fern, Norman, Willene Rae.

Arvil Elgie was born Feb. 2, 1904, married Nadena Meaders, child: Willa Dee.

Myrtie Belle was born Sept. 15, 1906, married Mark Condren, children: Dale, Dorothy.

Alma Dorothy was born April 22, 1909 in Purcell, OK, married Wilburn Hobson. Children: James, Wilbur, Shirley, Dorothy.

James Adrian was born Sept. 26, 1913 in Polk

County, married Ethel Mae Keeney, children: Barbara, Beverly.

Vela May Jones was born July 16, 1915 in Polk County, married Christian Christoffersen. Both buried Whittier, CA.

Nora Irene Jones was born Sept. 10, 1918 in Polk County, married Lamond Cooper, child: Gary. *Submitted by Wanda J. Alexander*

JUMP – Donald Robert Jump's grandfather was Robert (Bob) Thomas Terry Boone Jump; he was born in Hickory County, MO in February 1870 and he married Mary Eliza Jump. His parents were John Jr. and Sarah Jane Zumwalt Jump. John Jr. was born in 1832 in St. Louis County, MO. His father John Sr. was born in Kentucky in 1794 and was buried in 1886 in Polk County, MO. John Jump Sr.'s father was Peter Jump who came from England and was married in Lincoln County, KY.

Sarah Jane Zumwalt Jump was the daughter of Jemina (Boone) Zumwalt, who was the daughter of Nathan Boone, son of Daniel Boone.

Mary Eliza Jump was the daughter of Haden and Ellen Barber. She was born in Montgomery County, KS in 1873. Bob and Eliza were married in Polk County on Feb. 25, 1894. They lived most of their married lives north of Goodson on a farm that was close to Panther Creek and Lindley Creek. They moved to an 11-acre farm at the north edge of Bolivar in about 1948. Their house was on the old fairground road and that is now developed with several homes. To this union seven children were born. One son died in infancy and one son, Lonnie, passed away at the age of 2.

Nora Jump was born in September 1885 and married Henry House in 1916. Their children were Willard, Elgie, Melbie and Dorothy Lee. They lived north of Goodson on a farm close to her parents' farm.

Huston Jump was born in 1899 and married Hazel Worthey in 1957. Huston lived with his parents until they passed away and lived in Bolivar until his death at the age of 93.

Bertha Jump was born in 1904 and married Allen Pursley in 1927. They had two children, Iris Hood and Gayford Pursley. They lived on a farm on Highway 83, north of Bolivar.

Donald Robert Jump's father, Arthur, was born in 1909 and married Ada Roberts in 1935. Donald has heard a lot of stories about trying to get started during the depression. Arthur taught school for 37 years in rural schools and later in Bolivar and Halfway. Some of the rural schools were Independence, Eagle Hill, Carter, Roberts, Inglis and Wilmington. They lived on a farm north of Burns.

Adrian Jump was born in 1912 and married Ruth Keith, whose father was Jim Keith. They had two children, Adriana Stapleton and Lonnie Robert Jump. They lived on a farm just east of Huron. The farm is now the 3-Jumps Farm and is owned by Ron Jump.

Back row – Huston, Adrian, Arthur Jump. Front – Nora Jump House, Mary Eliza Jump,, Bob Jump and Bertha Jump Pursley.

The Jump family spent most all of their lives in Polk County. Bob Jump told a story about moving to Polk County when he was a little boy. They moved in wagons and during the move, he lost one of his shoes. Some of the family went back and found his shoe. Bob lived off the land. He hunted and fished as well as farmed. He always tried to pay his property taxes with his earnings from coonskins. Hog butchering day was normally the Friday after Thanksgiving. Most of the family came and spent the day working up the meat and rendering lard. Bob and Eliza probably ate a lot of food that would not be considered healthy by today's standards, but they worked hard and lived to be 88 and 90. They were both members of the Star Ridge Methodist Church. *Submitted by Donald Robert Jump*

JUMP – James A. Jump was born in Bolivar, MO in 1853, the son of either James Jump, 1837, or John Jump, 1839, coming from either Tennessee or Kentucky. His wife Sarah E. was born in 1859. To this union were born daughters: Dell, Donna, Edith and Mary. Mary was born in 1885, Nancy Jane was born in 1890. James had only one son, Alfred L. Jump. He had several brothers, but not sure about sisters. Several relatives served in the Civil War, WWI and WWII. It is believed that all are buried in Greenwood Cemetery. Alfred L. Jump was born Oct. 28, 1886 in Bolivar and died in 1972. His wife Inez Fair Hutchison was born Oct. 20, 1899 in Bolivar and died in 1953. Their children are Lee Olen, 1920-1973, Marion Edward, 1922-2001, Marcella Gale (Vandergrift), 1923-2000, Olivene Joy, 1925-1926, William James, 1927-2001, Richard Guy (Bob), born 1929, Mary Ellen, 1932-1932, Alfred, 1934-1934, Johnny A., 1935-1935, Frances Pearl (Avis), born 1937, Albert L. (Sonny), born 1938, Willa Mae (Brewster), born 1941. Alfred Jump is the grandfather of Ronald Jump and Marion Jump is Ronald's father. Marion served in WWII and was the recipient of several awards, including the Purple Heart and the Bronze Star. He married Betty Sue Thomas, born 1928, on June 16, 1947. To this union were born two sons, Ronald Dean, born 1948, and David Allen, born 1950, father of Don and Linda. Ronald's dad was a farmer all of his life. He had several other jobs. He owned and operated a service station. His last public job was that of Polk County Collector, retiring in 1970, after holding that office for eight years. *Submitted by Sara Jump*

KALLENBACH – Robert Wynes and Bonnie Fay (Small) Kallenbach moved to Bolivar in 1941 when Robert (Bob) accepted a position with University of Missouri Extension as a county agent. He had previously worked for extension in Cole and Jasper Counties and was encouraged by his older brother, Harry, to apply for the Polk County position. Harry had become familiar with the county when he was the driver for Missouri Secretary of State Charles U. Becker (1921-1933), a native of Wishart who made frequent trips back to his home area in the south central part of Polk County.

Both Bob and Bonnie Fay were born and raised near Tuscumbia in Miller County. They were married in 1936 and had three children: Deanne, who was 4 at the time of the move, William Robert (Bill Bob), who was 2 and Rose Fay, who was 6 months old.

They soon bought a house at 807 N. Water where they lived for more than 20 years. Bill Bob often accompanied his father when he went to rural schools in the evenings to conduct balanced farming and 4-H meetings, which gave both father and son an opportunity to become acquainted with people from all over the county. This was shortly after the Rural Electrification Act had

Left to right – Robert Louis, Robert Wynes, Carrie Camille, Bonnie Fay and John William Kallenbach. Row 2 – Karalyn Kay, Charles Hamilton, Deanne and Chuck Murphy, Rose Fay, Bill Bob and Judy Kallenbach, 1974

brought electricity to the rural areas, making it possible for Bob to present slide programs with Bill Bob running the projector.

After her children were teenagers. Bonnie Fay went back to college to complete her degree and taught at Pleasant Hope for several years before Bob accepted a position as balanced farming agent in Gasconade County. She then taught at Owensville until their retirement when they returned to the family farm at Tuscumbia, which became a Centennial Farm—having been in the same family since 1860. After Bob's death in 1975, Bonnie Fay moved back to Bolivar where she lived until her death in 1999.

Deanne married Charles Hamilton Murphy Sr., son of Earl O. and Pauline Hamilton Murphy of Bolivar.

They had two children:

Charles Hamilton Jr. (Chuck), is a reimbursement manager and hospital chaplain in Kansas City. His wife, Dawn, is a human resources director.

Karalyn Kaye, a former elementary school teacher, married Gary Highfill, an otolaryngologist, son of Donald Rex Highfill and Norma Copeland Highfill, formerly of the Pleasant Hope area. They live in Springfield and have three children, Brittany Alexandra, Zachary Daniel and Mallory Kristine. After Charles Sr. retired from the U S Air Force, he and Deanne bought the family farm at Tuscumbia. Charles died in 1988. Deanne continues to live near Tuscumbia on the family farm.

Bill married Judy Lemons, formerly of Buffalo. Bill served in the US Army in 1962 and 1963 and as Polk County clerk from 1971 through 1990. He is a farmer and has bought and sold hundreds of trained coon hounds, mostly Walkers, over the last 45 years to buyers all over the United States. He is an elder of the Bolivar Church of Christ. Since 1978, Judy has worked at the *Bolivar Herald-Free Press* where she is now editor.

Bill and Judy have three children:

Robert Louis Kallenbach is a statewide forage specialist with University Outreach and Extension and an assistant professor at the University of Missouri. His wife, Rachel (Carpenter), is a former music and elementary teacher. They have three children, William Isaiah, born in 1997, Grace Ellen, born in 1998 and Joseph Robert, born in 2002. They live in Columbia.

John William Kallenbach and his wife, Eva Maria (Kincaid, daughter of Fred and Artemisa Kincaid of Bolivar), live in Bolivar. John is a lawyer and business owner. Maria, a former elementary school teacher, is now a cosmetologist.

Carrie Camille Gordon and her husband, John Harrison Gordon, live in Belmont, CA. Carrie is a family nurse practitioner and John is an information technologist.

Rose married Tod Kinerk and has two stepsons:

Wesley T. Kinerk and his wife, Jennifer (Good),

have a daughter, Elizabeth Jane, who was born in 2002. They live in St. Louis where Wesley is in optometry school and Jennifer is an account executive.

Timothy T. Kinerk is a student at St. Louis College of Pharmacy.

Rose was a social worker in Kansas City for 33 years and now works in her husband's real estate business in Salem. *Submitted by Judy Kallenbach*

KATES – Henry P. Kates married Martha A. Choate in Missouri. They had five children: Monroe, Marvin, Emmett, Annie and Pauline.

The Rev. Monroe Harrison Kates married Virgie Pearl Graves in Bolivar, MO on May 24, 1920. He was a lifelong resident of Bolivar. He died in 1961 at the age of 63. Monroe was a Baptist minister. His brothers, relatives and he worked farms for a banker in Bolivar, Grey McDaniels. Saturdays the farmers would go to pick up their pay in Bolivar. Then they would visit, eat and shop. The younger ones would walk the square, roller skate, or see a ten-cent matinee. The teenagers hung out at the "Nifty Café," played the juke box and drank soda.

Marvin married Lois P. Alexander on June 25, 1917 in Bolivar, Polk County, MO. Emmett (called Uncle Nick) married Ruby, Annie married Jim Davis and Pauline married Lucien O'Dell. Pauline wrote "The ABC War Song," and her daughter, Maxine and Dorothy sang it at the County Fair when Dorothy was 12. They won first place; a 24-pound sack of MFA flour and three dollars each!

Virgie Pearl Graves was the daughter of Jim and Florence Graves. She had 16 siblings. One sister, Tommie, married Rev. Wilbur Foster, who was the pastor of a Baptist church. Some of her brothers were musicians. Two played guitar and sang over the radio station KWTO in Springfield.

A relative, Fred Choate, and his wife, Ruby, lived in a huge house on one farm. When harvest time came, the women and children gathered and prepared a mid-day meal (dinner) for all the workers.

Monroe and Virgie Kate had six children: Walter, Kenneth, Curtis, Mildred, Dorothy and Thelma. Dorothy Mae Kates married George Lee Pickel in 1945. He lived in Fair Play, MO. They had a son, Gary Lee, who lost his fight with cystic fibrosis at the age of 3. The family also had three daughters, Patsy, Mona and Lori Pickel. George was killed in an automobile accident in 1965. The family had moved to California. Dorothy remarried and had a son Larry Bates.

Dorothy's childhood memories are of caring people, such as a sweet teacher who invited each girl to stay at her house once a year, church pot lucks, skating on their frozen pond, the big catfish caught in the deep rivers, digging sassafras roots for tea, the call of the whippoorwill and fireflies in the evening.

Dorothy says, "I had wealth in good Christian parents and teachings. This I have passed on to my children." Patsy J. Schell is an in-home care nurse. Mona is a office technician at a veterinarian office; Lori is a teaching assistant and art teacher at an elementary school; Larry is an electrician working on a degree in electron microscopy. All are happy in their lives and have families of their own. They live in the foothills of California. Dorothy says, "I am happy and proud to say my heritage is in good ole Missouri." *Submitted by Lori D. Kelly*

Rev. Monroe Harrison Kates and wife Virgie Pearl Graves

KEITH – Annie Lee McConnell Keith is a descendant of James Hensley, who was born in Polk, MO in about the year of 1839. James married Matilda Isdell about 1858, the daughter of Henry Isdell and Edna Story. James died in 1874 in Linn County, KS. Annie was born in Ventura, CA on June 17, 1939. She married Floyd H. Keith, Sept. 5, 1954 at Santa Paula, CA.

To this union were born five children:

Lloyd Gene Keith, born Dec. 14, 1955 in Ventura, CA, married Margie Pearl Rash, Goodson, MO, on July 4, 1974. They had three children: Faithia Marie, married Glen Gillogly, Hollie Lee, Stephen Lloyd (Tater) and four adopted boys: Derrick, Joshua, Thomas, Ryan.

Mark Leon Keith, born Nov. 28, 1957 in Fresno, CA, married Debbie Baldwin of Goodson, MO on Jan. 11, 1978. They had two children: Jodi, who married Chris Warrick, and they have an 8-month-old son, Christian, and the second daughter is Lori.

Floyd, Annie, Loyd, Danny, Cindy, Charles and Mark

Charles Wayne Keith, born June 22, 1959 in Fresno, CA, married Carla Fowler on March 3, 1979 in Bolivar, MO. They had two children, Jason and Lacey.

Cindy Lee Keith Talburt, born June 22, 1960 in Fresno, CA, married Larry Wayne Talburt on Oct. 27, 1984 in Bolivar, MO. Cindy and her two children, April and Willie, live in Bolivar.

Daniel Allen Keith, born April 19, 1962 in Bakersfield, CA, married Rebecca Hieston of Baxter Springs, KS. They have four children: Joshua, Rachel, Virginia, Elizabeth and make their home in Bolivar.

Annie and her family decided that they would move from California to Bolivar for better surroundings in which the children could grow up. They decided on Bolivar because of their visits with her sister Louise. It turned out to be the right decision because all are active members of the Lord's Church and a benefit to the community. Floyd and Annie started and maintained an upholstery business known as "Keith's Upholstery" for 30 plus years until failing health forced them to turn it over to the oldest son. Floyd preached at Republic for a number of years at the Church of Christ, then started the congregation of the Church of Christ that meets at 1037 West Broadway. Annie is active in the Polk County Genealogical Society, TOPS Weight Management, Daughters of the American Revolution and church activities.

When the family decided to move she had no idea that she had ancestors who had lived in Polk County. Now it has come full circle from James Hensley to his great-great-granddaughter Annie, spanning a little more than 150 years and eight generations. *Submitted by Annie Lee Keith*

KELLY – Floyd Kelley, son of John and Etta (Hunter) Kelly, was born Feb. 25, 1918 near Cabool, MO.

Maggie Belle Paul, daughter of Claude and Martha (Ballard) Paul, was born Nov. 8, 1926 in Polk County.

Floyd, with his family, moved to the Humansville area in 1932. Floyd served in the army in WWII from 1941-1945. After returning from service, Floyd and Maggie were married on Dec. 21, 1945. They moved to a farm south of Humansville in 1952. Here he did general farming and raised cattle and horses. He took great pride in his Appaloosa horses. He also worked for McGregor Wholesale Hardware in Springfield and the Witt Printing Company in Humansville until he retired in 1977 because of his heath.

Maggie graduated from Humansville High School in 1944. She received an AA degree from Southwest Baptist College, a BS degree in education from SMS and a master's degree from Drury College. Maggie worked in elementary education for 36 years before retiring in 1988. Six of the years were in one-room rural schools and 30 years in the Humansville school as an elementary classroom teacher and principal.

Three daughters were born to Floyd and Maggie.

Donna was born on Oct. 31, 1946. She married James Myers in 1966. They live near Bolivar. They have two sons, James (Jim) and Kelley. Jim lives in Springfield. Kelley and his wife, Lee (Burks), live near Aldrich. Both Jim and Kelley have followed their father's profession as carpet layers and Kelley also lays tile. James and Donna also have two grandchildren, Emily Myers of Springfield and Jacob (Jake) Myers of Aldrich. Donna retired from Commerce Bank of Bolivar in 2002 after working there 32 years. She then began working in real estate in Bolivar.

Carolyn was born Sept. 17, 1948. She was married to Bill LeAn in 1971. Carolyn has worked for Teters Floral Products Company in Bolivar for 27 years. She has one daughter, Jo Dee (LeAn) Ryan, who is a teacher in the Humansville High School. Jo Dee and her husband, Shane, have two sons, Hank and Luke. Jo Dee and her husband are planning to build a new home near Dunnegan on the home site where her great-grandfather, Claud Paul, and great-great-grandfather, David Paul, had lived.

Barbara was married to Ronald Hunsaker in 1969. Barbara worked at St. John's Hospital for a few years and has worked in food services at different places as Ronnie was transferred in his work. They are now retired and live in Mesquite, NV. Barbara and Ronnie have one son, Ronald Jr. (Beau), who is now living in Florida and works with computers.

Floyd passed away after a long illness in 1989.

Maggie still lives on the family farm. She attends church at Humansville First Baptist where she teaches a third/fourth grade Sunday School class and also does volunteer work for Hospice. *Submitted by Donna Myers*

KEMP – It was August 1969 when Ronald Nuburn Kemp, his wife Lou Thelen and their three sons moved to Bolivar from Huntsville, TX. Ronald was born July 23, 1936 in Cyril, OK and Lou Thelen was born in Headrick, OK on Sept. 29, 1935. They both graduated from Oklahoma Baptist University in Shawnee, OK. They relocated from Texas, where Ronald was a pastor, to Bolivar where he became the chaplain and an instructor at SBU for seven years. In 1976 he worked for the Missouri Baptist Children's Home establishing counseling centers. In 1980 he chose to go into private practice and established the Family Institute of the Ozarks in 1985.

Ronald Kemp family

Their three sons were born in Fort Worth, TX but their years of public education were completed in Bolivar, MO. Ronald Nuburn Kemp Jr. married Marjorie Ann Cooper on Jan. 21, 1980. Their daughter Serenity Ann was born Oct. 13, 1981 and their son Levi Nuburn was born Nov. 23, 1982 in Stanberry, MO. Luther Harrold (Hal) Kemp married Peggy Ann Campbell on Aug. 7, 1982 and two daughters were born to this union, Laura Alyssa on July 23, 1992 and Erin McKenzie on Jan. 18, 1998 in Overland Park, KS. Wesley Don Kemp married Marla Jo Roweton on Jan. 3, 1986. Their three children include Tyler Don, born in Hinsdale, IL on March 8, 1989, Landon Holt, born in Hinsdale, IL on March 18, 1991 and their daughter Rylee Lou, born in Bolivar, MO on Feb. 12, 1993.

In 1969, as they were unpacking their dishes they almost made the discovery that six plates had come almost full circle. These plates had left Halfway, MO in 1903 with Lou Thelen's grandparents as they relocated into Indian Territory near Olustee, OK. Another circle would be that Ronald's great-grandfather, Andrew Jackson Kemp, was born in Callaway County, MO in 1842.

Andrew Jackson Kemp

According to the history of Callaway County, John Kemp of England married Polly Craighead and settled in Franklin County, VA. They were the parents of six children. Their son Jourdan married Peggy Mattox and his estate was filed on Sept. 20, 1844 in Callaway County, MO. David V. Kemp, one of the sons, married Nancy A. and to this union were born five children. Andrew Jackson Kemp, born in 1842 in Callaway County, was their youngest child. The family records indicate he was married three times and had one step-son and eight biological children. One of the stories repeated about Andrew Jackson is that once a week he would dress in his hunting boots and heavy pants with reinforced knees. Dressed like this, he would use a pole with barbed wire twisted loops on the end to twist rabbits out of prairie dog holes for a rabbit dinner. At other times, he always dressed with a buttoned vest and shined shoes as indicated by the picture. Robert Lesley and John Wesley Kemp were their twin sons. Ronald's ancestor was Robert Lesley, born in Tarrant County, TX and he was the father of Luther Nuburn Kemp, born in Apache, OK, the grandfather of Ronald Nuburn Kemp, the great-grandfather of Ronald, Hal and Wes Kemp and the great-great-grandfather of Serenity Ann, Levi Nuburn, Tyler Don, Landon Holt, Rylee Lou, Laura Alyssa and Erin McKenzie. After many years the Kemps have returned to one of their original roots in the state of Missouri. *Submitted by Ron Kemp Jr.*

KENNON – Reverend James Kennon (son of John Kennon Sr. and Nancy Taylor), born Nov. 22, 1793 in Virginia and Rebecca Bowen (daughter of John Bowen and Sarah Bean), born Dec. 25, 1798 in Grainger County, TN, were married on May 31, 1816 in Grainger County. They had nine children, all born in Grainger County. They moved to Polk County about 1854/55 and seven of their children came, too. James died Jan. 12, 1884; Rebecca died Aug. 10, 1876 and both were buried in Brush Grove (Potts) Cemetery in Polk County.

John W. Kennon, born about 1820, married Rhoda (Lane) Hubbs on Sept. 10, 1838 in Grainger County. Rhoda already had a daughter, Phoebe; John and Rhoda had eight children together. They were William James (married Sarah Potts, four known children); Joseph (or Josiah) Clark (married Mary Elizabeth Fox, 10 children); Luke (married Nancy Caroline Hess, at least one child); Sarah (likely died young); John K. (married first, Catherine LeForse, two children and then Hixey Anna Wells, five children); Leander L. (married Nancy Catherine Hensley, seven children); Tilman Howard (married Sarah C. Worthan, four children); and Haseltine (last found in 1870 census, age 16). Rhoda died in Tennessee and John moved with his family to Polk County by 1860 and married Keziah Hensley on Dec. 5, 1861. John, a Civil War veteran, died between 1884 and 1890.

Sarah Kennon, born between 1817 and 1825, married John Lane on May 8, 1838 in Grainger County. Sarah was living in 1884 in Tennessee, according to her father's probate file.

Nancy Kennon, born in 1822, married Theosophlies Goodwin on Aug. 9, 1845 in Grainger County. They had one child, Samuel S. (married Louisa, three known children). After Theo's death, Nancy and Samuel moved to Polk County, where she died in 1881—buried at Brush Grove.

Elizabeth J. Kennon,, born between 1823 and 1829, married Calvin Maggett on Dec. 23, 1842 in Grainger County. Elizabeth was living in Tennessee in 1884, according to her father's probate file.

Louisa Kennon, born about 1830, married William Crow on Aug. 12, 1848 in Grainger County. They moved from Tennessee to Polk County and then to Washington County, AR. They had eight or nine children.

Lee Kennon, born between 1828 and 1831, married Martha L. Chase on Sept. 2, 1847 in Knox County, TN—one known child, Morris. After Martha's death, Lee married Susan Mitchell on May 17, 1855 in Knox County—one known child, Rachel Rebecca. After Susan's death, Lee married Drucilla Privett circa 1868 in Missouri—one known child, Josephine. Lee was still living in Missouri in 1884 when his father died.

Melvina Kennon, born June 12, 1833, married Benjamin Patterson on Oct. 13, 1853 in Knox County. It is not known what happened to Benjamin. Melvina came to Polk County and married Hiram F. Henson on June 16, 1857. He already had a little son, John Wesley. Hiram and Melvina had five children: Sarah E., Rebecca Jane, James Thomas, Laura Levina and William P. (See HENSON story.) After Hiram's death, Melvina married James Goff on Nov. 29, 1875 in Polk County. James died in 1891. Melvina died Aug. 22, 1906 in Polk County and was buried in Mt. Olive Cemetery near Hiram and three of her children.

Mahala Kennon was born in 1834/35 and came to Missouri with her parents. She likely had two children, Mary and Harman L. Mahala was last found in 1891 in Polk County.

James W. Kennon, born about 1842, married Susan Jane Henson on Sept. 3, 1863 in Polk County. (Susan was the sister of Hiram F. Henson). After Susan's death, James married Rachael Ruth Carter on July 20, 1873 in Polk County. They had two known children, Flora B. and Mary R. After Rachael's death, James married Mary Ellen Crow on Oct. 20, 1881 in Polk County. They had one known child, S. Emma. *Submitted by Darlene Piper Keith*

KIBBY - Milo Edwin Kibby was born Jan. 20, 1870 to Nelson Kibby (1845-1875) and Susan Evaline (Hunt) Kibby (1848-1930). Milo married Merty Simpson (born Nov. 5, 1878), daughter of Johnson and Amanda (Hudspeth) Simpson, on Jan 23, 1895 at Mount Vernon, MO. While living in Lawrence County, two girls were born: Ethel on Aug. 25, 1896 (died April 9, 1905) and Hazel on Dec. 23, 1898 (died Dec. 9, 1944). Within a short time the family moved to Iola, Allen County, KS, where Milo was employed in the steel foundry for approximately 10 years. During this time they celebrated the birth of three sons — Edgar Johnson on Feb. 26, 1904 (died May 17, 1952), Leo Paul on Feb. 20, 1906 (died Oct. 23, 2000) and Olin Everett on April 15, 1909 (died Feb. 24, 1976). While in Kansas, tragedy struck, losing their first born Ethel to a diphtheria epidemic at the age of 9.

In 1910 the family moved back to Missouri, settling on a property that was adjacent to the main road between Springfield and Bolivar. This road was to become Highway 13 in later years. Milo operated a freight wagon service between Springfield and Brighton. While living there, their daughter, Maxine, was born July 3, 1912 (died Nov. 25, 2001). In 1913 they purchased a farm northeast of Brighton in the Pleasant Grove (Frog Pond) School District. Two more daughters were born — Effie Loretta on March 11, 1915 (died Dec. 13, 1974) and Hada Rosalie on March 18, 1920 (died June 23, 1935).

The family enjoyed success at this location and developed many long-lasting friendships within the local community. The children took an active part at the Frog Pond school. The relationships developed there spawn countless stories that continue to be told into the succeeding generations. There Hazel met and married John Frady of Brighton in 1921. In December 1922, Milo, in search of a more prosperous life, sold the farm. He and the oldest son, Edgar, left by train from the Morrisville Station for California to secure employment, and in turn, send for the family. This left Merty and the children to sell the personal property at a public sale and wait for news to join them in California. Soon they, too, got on the train at Morrisville and made the journey.

The stay in California lasted until August 1926, when the call of Missouri brought them back to Polk County, this time to a farm southwest of Halfway just

Milo and Marty Kibby

243

across the road from the New Bethel School. Here the children grew into adults, except Hada, who died at the early age of 15. Maxine married Frank Crockett of Pleasant Hope in 1931. Edgar married Margaret Pinkley in 1932 and Olin married Lorea Snider in 1934; both were from the Buffalo area. Loretta returned to California and married Edwin Brown in 1937. Leo had remained in California where he married Jean McGovney in 1938.

In their older years, Milo and Merty purchased the square rock/stucco house just north of the Walnut Ridge Baptist Church in Van. They both were members of this church. They lived out their remaining years in this home. Milo passed away on Dec. 20, 1950 and Merty on Feb. 11, 1974. Their grandchildren are, as follows: Johnny Lee Frady, Merle (Frady) Warren, LaVaughn (Crockett) Beauchamp, Elvin Kibby, Delcie (Kibby) Choate, Carolyn (Kibby) Glover, Darryl Brown (1941-1969), Byron Kibby, Dwight Kibby, Elaine (Brown) Floyd, Norman Kibby. *Submitted by Dwight Kibby*

KIBBY - Dwight and Majuana Kibby made their home in Greene County for nine years before returning to Polk County to reside in Pleasant Hope. By this time, Dwight had established a career with the St. Louis - San Francisco Railway, eventually evolving into the Burlington Northern Santa Fe Railway. This career spanned 34 years. Dwight and Majuana farmed in both Polk and Webster Counties. They were greatly involved in many community organizations, city government, school organizations, board of education and the fire department. They were also actively involved in the Bolivar Church of Christ. To their happy union were born two children, Sonja Darline on Oct. 20, 1969 and Nelson Wayne on Feb. 20, 1974. Sonja married in 1991 to Eric Jacobson of York County, NE. Nelson married Julie Tucker of Webster County, MO in 1996.

In May 1994, Dwight and Majuana purchased her family (a Missouri Century) farm in Webster County after having lived in Pleasant Hope for 20 years. They are currently semi-retired and enjoying two granddaughters Eryn Rose Jacobson and Alexa Lorea Kibby. They are anticipating the arrival of number three grandchild in the days to come.

Eric, Sonja, Eryn Jacobson, Majuana, Dwight, Julie, Nelson Kibby

Submitted by Sonja Jacobson

KIBBY - Olin Everett Kibby was born April 15, 1909 to Milo Edwin Kibby and Merty (Simpson) Kibby in Iola, KS. The family moved into Polk County, northeast of Brighton, in 1913. Here he attended the Pleasant Grove (Frog Pond) school until he was about 13 years of age when his family moved to California. His family returned to Polk County in 1926, where they purchased a farm southwest of Halfway in the New Bethel community. Here Olin farmed with his family until he met Lorea Vivian Snider (born March 12, 1912, daughter of Everett Snider and Leona (Olinger) Snider), a Dallas County school teacher stuck in a muddy road. His offer to pull her out turned into much more than a "Good Samaritan" act. They were married Jan. 20, 1934 and rented a small farm north of Van. Soon they moved to a larger place, continuing to farm as well as finding outside work when it was available. In 1936, they, like so many

Olin and Lorea Kibby

of Polk County residents, heard of "greener grass" in California.

In California Olin went to work as a roughneck in the oil fields. Because this job required him to work in several locations in southern California, they lived in many different towns. Living in California did not mean their hearts were there. They made many trips to Polk County in their 1936 Ford V8. On one of these trips, they purchased a 70 acre farmstead two miles east of Van.

On Aug. 9, 1940, they were blessed with the birth of their first child Carolyn Charlene. Olin eventually went to work for a welding shop in Oxnard, learning the welding trade. When the war broke out, the draft board reviewed his papers, seeing that he had a "ranch" in Missouri. The lady indicated to him that because of his age (32) and the fact that the US would need food as much as they needed men, he could have an agriculture deferment if he would move back to his "ranch." Polk County was their next stop!

Olin and Lorea set up a farming operation with their small farm as well as rental property. Over the years they were involved in about every kind of farm product, including turkey production. On Oct. 13, 1944, their son Dwight Wayne was born. Olin not only farmed, but established a welding shop and a good reputation as a electrician and plumber. Much of the farm work was done by Lorea, because of Olin's outside employment. In 1956, Olin went to work in Springfield as a welder and followed this occupation until his retirement in 1974. Carolyn and Dwight both met their future spouses at Halfway. Carolyn married Bob Glover in October 1960 and Dwight married Majuana Cass in October 1964.

In 1962 they sold the farm and built a new house in Pleasant Hope. Here Lorea always grew a beautiful garden and graciously shared it with everyone. Olin passed away on Feb. 24, 1976. At this writing Lorea is 90 years of age. Grandchildren of Olin and Lorea are Vivian Glover, Raymond Glover, Sonja (Kibby) Jacobson and Nelson Kibby. *Submitted by Nelson Kibby*

KIFER - Lloyd C. Kifer, born Dec. 11, 1880 in Waverly, KS to J. W. Keifer and Mary Massena Keifer, went to the courthouse and had the "E" taken out of Keifer to be more American, as an adult. J. W. Kifer and Mary Massena Kifer birthed five children: Lloyd C., Albert Keifer, Frank Kifer, Jenny Kifer Stewart and Zoe Kifer Lower. They traveled to Polk County, MO via covered wagon when Lloyd was 14 years old. They lived near Pomme de Terre at Kifer Ford.

Lloyd traveled to Jerome, AZ 1900-1901 to work in copper mines to make money to buy 80 acres northwest of Bolivar. He married Gertrude A. Burks, born Aug 23, 1887, in January 1907. Gertrude was a daughter of W. H. (Bud) Burks and Mary A. Swartz Burks. They had four children: Charles, Gertrude, Elsie, and Emmett.

Lloyd and Gertie were living in the two-room log house on the 80 acres when their son, Charles Everett, was born March 7, 1908. When Charles was 4, the family went west to earn money to plow it into the farm.

Lloyd and Gertie worked hard for the Standard Oil Company in the Taft-Bakersfield area. They managed the cook shack, making meals for the oil crews, cooking for 30 to 50 men. The company furnished plenty of good food and demonstrated how to prepare for many. They had huge cook stoves and walk-in coolers. Meals were served three times a day, family style, and a midnight snack. Charles set the tableware for the men and earned 15 cents a day. Saving enough money to build a house and a barn, the Kifers left California for Missouri where their son, Charles, could go to school. There was no school at the oil compound.

As most family farms were then, they had cattle, sheep, hogs, chickens and a team of horses. There was no electricity and everything was done by hand with the help of horses or mules to plow and put up hay.

Charles was placed in school at Union Grove for four years. It went to five months instead of the normal eight months. His father secured approval and transferred Charles to West Union. After two terms, WU went to five months. Charles was transferred to Woodlawn, with eight months term. He had seventh grade here.

The teacher was Dessa Manuel. Dessa moved to Runyan for the eighth grade level. So did Charles. The last four years of grade school, Charles rode a horse to school most days.

The Kifers decided to raise more chickens and turned the farming over to Charles, who started to Bolivar High School, then at the North Ward School. After graduation, he attended Southwest Baptist College one year.

The Kifers had six laying houses with a laying hen count of 2000. They purchased incubators that held 14,000 eggs to sell baby chicks. Eggs were shipped to New York by railroad, too.

The hatchery grew to 34,000 egg capacity and they were selling 10,000 young chickens a year. The incubators were heated by Delco batteries. This was before rural electrification was available.

Charles met Floris Frieze, daughter of Harmon Frieze and Lillie Dinwiddie Frieze of Aldrich, MO, at Bolivar High School. Floris had a brother, Lowell. Charles and Floris were married Sept. 11, 1930.

Charles and Floris had a son, Robert Earl Kifer, Nov. 22, 1931.

In 1939, the government had worked on a plan where the farmer could modernize and maybe get electricity. Charles Kifer was instrumental in bringing electric energy to the rural areas in this part of the state. Told it wouldn't work, Charles spent many hours working to bring electricity to Polk County. Many people discouraged it, but enough farmers were interested that it was a GO. REA has helped farmers and other businesses maintain and grow.

Charles, Floris and Robert Kifer, ca. 1933

Lloyd was instrumental in helping with the First Christian Church of Bolivar.

Lloyd died in 1948. Gertrude died in 1971. Charles died Oct. 18, 1992.

Robert attended Oak Grove #70 rural school, Bolivar High School, Southwest Baptist College and graduated from Missouri University-Columbia College of Agriculture in 1954.

Mr. and Mrs. Lloyd Kifer and son Charles, 1949

Lt. Kifer had three years' active duty in the United States Air Force, with a tour of duty in Korea and Norton Air Force Base, San Bernardino, CA.

He married Betty J. A. Holt, daughter of Willie and Bess Holt, Sept. 13, 1953.

Robert helped organize the Farmers and Merchants Bank and helped with many other community projects.

Robert and Betty had three children: Thane Holt, Aug. 14, 1957; Thaila Renee, Dec. 11, 1958; and Thora Lynn, April 30, 1961. Thane married Suzanne Marie Brumback, July 26, 1980. Their children are Drew Holt Kifer, July 21, 1986, and Troy Harmon Kifer, April 26, 1993. Thane is with Mid-Missouri Banking. Suzanne is an elementary teacher.

Thaila married Douglas Patrick Pickett of Phoenix, AZ, Nov. 27, 1982. Douglas is a licensed commercial plumber.

Thora married Brian Thomas Anderson of Ephrata, WA, Aug. 23, 1980.

The Andersons and Picketts helped organize Vineyard Christian Fellowship of North Phoenix. The Andersons pastor the Fellowship. *Submitted by Betty Kifer*

KILPATRICK –

Barney and Winona Kilpatrick

Barney McCoy Kilpatrick was born in Lawrenceburg, TN on Jan. 14, 1903. At an early age, his family moved in a covered wagon to Oklahoma, finally settling around Beaver in the Panhandle. His father was a farmer, blacksmith and preacher. He helped establish South Flat Church of Christ. It was there that Barney met Winona Mae Davis. She had been born in Spencer, IN on May 19, 1903. Her family moved to Oklahoma when she was 10 years old. She was a teacher at Logan in a one-room schoolhouse where she taught all eight grades. After marrying on June 24, 1924, they moved to Two Buttes, CO. Barney was a farmer and later drove a truck hauling grain. One trip was to El Dorado Springs, MO. He was so impressed with the beauty of the Ozarks that he moved his family to El Dorado Springs in 1935. Winona was delighted because the trees reminded her of her native Indiana. Their children were Venita Faye, Norma Lou, Carolyn Lea, Shirley Ann and Kenneth Allen. The three older children were born in Colorado and the younger two in Missouri

In 1941, they moved to Bolivar. Mr. Kilpatrick became the International Harvester dealer. For many years his business was on north Springfield Street where the Baptist church building is now located. He later added Hudson cars and IH refrigerators and freezers. Mr. Kilpatrick was involved in many community activities. He was a long time member of the Kiwanis Club. He was the president in 1948 when President Truman and President Gallegos of Venezuela were in Bolivar to dedicate the Simon Bolivar statue. He was the program committee chairman who compiled the official program which featured the history and background of Simon Bolivar and included advertising from national corporations. He also served one term as president of the Chamber of Commerce.

Both of the Kilpatricks were committed Christians who were members of the Church of Christ. He was instrumental in the establishment of the Church of Christ in Bolivar. Much of their time and activities were centered on their church.

Mrs. Kilpatrick enjoyed helping people in the church and her neighbors. They lived a block east of the railroad station and she often fed the homeless men that dropped off in Bolivar. She loved flowers and always had a big garden.

For many years, Kilpatrick Supply Company occupied the site on north Springfield street. He later moved his business to the half-block that Woods Grocery now occupies. When Mr. Kilpatrick's health failed, he sold the business to Paul Degraffenreid and moved to Springfield in 1958. Mr. Kilpatrick died in 1961 and Mrs. Kilpatrick in 1999. They are both buried in Greenwood Cemetery. Still living in Bolivar is their daughter, Carolyn Kilpatrick Roberts. *Submitted by Carolyn Roberts*

KIMES - Marcus Lafayette and Sarah Ashby Kimes and their three sons came to Missouri in 1900 from Howell, TN. They first settled in north Missouri near Monroe City, then moved with their youngest son to a farm one and three-fourths miles west of Humansville. They arrived on Christmas Eve 1904. They were attracted to the area because it reminded them of their Tennessee farm and because of a never-fail spring located close to the home on the property. Marcus died in 1930 and Sarah in 1924. They are both buried in the Humansville Cemetery.

Their son, Travis Jefferson Kimes, attended school in Humansville, engaged in farming and then entered auction college at Trenton, MO. He followed the vocation of auctioneering until he entered the army in 1918 and was sent to France. Upon returning he continued farming, stock raising and auction work. His auctioneer skills were in constant demand and he was greatly respected throughout the county. He was a member of the Humansville Methodist Church, the American Legion and the Masonic Lodge.

In 1917, Travis married Celia Em Taylor at Pikeville, TN. They were married in her family home and then traveled to Humansville on the train. Celia was a beautiful, strong, Southern lady and was famous for her delicious meals. She and Travis raised their four children on the family farm: Travis J. Jr., Norine, Mary Ruth and Robert Taylor Kimes. All attended Elm Grove School and graduated from Humansville High School. Travis Jr. graduated from Colorado Western State College. Norine and Mary Ruth attended college in Springfield, and Robert graduated from Missouri University. Both daughters taught school in Polk County until they moved from the area. Norine married Joe Talley in 1945 and they have two sons, Joe Jr. and Douglas. Joe Sr. died in 1980. They have two granddaughters. Mary Ruth married Joe Greenhaw in 1944. They have one son, Joe Jr. and a daughter, Nancy. They have two granddaughters and two great-granddaughters. Norine and Mary and families now live in the Kansas City area.

Major Travis J. Kimes Jr. served with the Army Air Corps as a pilot from 1940 until his death in a car wreck in 1947. In 1942 he married Katherine Bell in Las Vegas, NV. Their three children are Kay Whalen, Celia Walker and Gary Kimes. They had six grandchildren and the families now live in California.

Robert Taylor Kimes met Jeanette C. Hembree at Missouri University and following his graduation in 1952, they were married in Springfield, MO. Robert entered the U S Air Force the same year and he and Jeanette moved to Mather Air Force Base in California. Upon completion of his tour of duty they moved back to Missouri. They had six children: Robert Jr., Marcus, Jeffrey, Pamela, Julia and Amy. Their son Marc died in May 1997, and he is buried in the Kimes family plot in the Humansville Cemetery with his grandfather, Travis Sr., who died in 1959, his grandmother Celia, who died in 1978 and his uncle T. J.

Robert worked as a teacher, with the USDA, and retired as a land appraiser with the Corps of Engineers. He continued to raise cattle on the family farm and his ties to the home place remained strong. After retiring he and Jeanette built a house on the farm and reside there now. Three of their children and their families and Marc's family live in Missouri. One daughter lives in Tennessee and one son in California with their families. Robert and Jeanette have 12 grandchildren and one great-grandchild.

Robert and Jeanette Kimes Family

The Kimes family continues to gather at the family farm for holidays, hunting season, fishing in the pond, walks in the woods and wonderful togetherness. Marcus and Sarah, Travis and Celia, we all thank you for this great inheritance and we promise to carry on the stewardship you passed to us. Polk County, MO truly is a wonderful place to live and to nurture families. *Submitted by Robert and Jeanette Kimes*

KIMMONS – Elmer Earl and Bertha Hortense Kimmons of Pleasant Hope, MO raised three sons: Billy, David, Gayle. Later in life, Elmer moved to Illinois and Bertha moved to Branson, MO with her son Gayle and family.

Billy raised his family in Pleasant Hope, marrying Joan and having five children: Debra, Gary, Cheryl, Tammy, Cindy. All of them attended Pleasant Hope High School.

Many years later, after moving to Bolivar, Billy worked as a non commissioned officer of the Air Force and later became a real estate broker. In Bolivar, he met his second wife and married Feb. 2, 1972, Stella Bea Clark, daughter of Jasper and Beatrice Clark. They had two children, Kimberly Sue and Billy Earl Kimmons II. Living with them were her three children, Carol, John and Mark Stillwagon from her first marriage.

All attended Bolivar Schools for many years. *Submitted by Kim Conrad*

KINCAID – William (Bill) H. (nmn) Kincaid, Kathryn Lorraine (Parkman) Kincaid and Lorraine's mother, Sarah Kathryn (Coar) Parkman Johnston, moved from Fort Lauderdale, Broward County, FL and Cobb Island, Charles County, MD to Bolivar, Polk County, MO in September 1988. Kathryn came for the purpose of living with Lorraine and Bill. Bill and Lorraine came to Bolivar to live because their son, Chester (Chet) Eugene Kincaid and his family had moved to Bolivar from Maryland about five years earlier. Bill and Lorraine bought a home at 623 E. Division St., Bolivar, Polk County, MO, where Lorraine still resides.

Bill and Lorraine were married Sept. 27, 1941 in the home of Lorraine's grandparents, Mary Emma (Burton) Coar and William Thomas Coar in Burtonsville, Montgomery County, MD. They had two children: Wayne Meredith Kincaid, born Feb. 20, 1949 in Washington, DC, and Chester Eugene Kincaid, born Jan. 29, 1952 in Bethesda, Montgomery County, MD. Wayne died May 19, 1953 of congestive heart failure and is buried in Union Cemetery, Burtonsville, Montgomery County, MD. They have three grandchildren: Jessica Marie Kincaid Ferguson Prentice, Lacey Margaret Kincaid and Shane Taylor Kincaid.

Bill's working career was with the US Postal Service. Lorraine's working career was with US Immigration and Naturalization Service, the US Navy Department, and the U S Treasury Department in Customs. Both retired while living in Fort Lauderdale, Broward County, FL.

Before moving to Bolivar, Polk County, MO, Bill and Lorraine Kincaid lived in Burtonsville and Silver Spring, Montgomery County, MD; in Laurel, Prince George County, MD; and in Fort Lauderdale, Broward County, FL. They had a summer home on Cobb Island, Charles County, MD. They moved to Florida because Lorraine was suffering with arthritis and her doctor in Maryland recommended a move to a sub-tropical climate and it did help her arthritis. While living in Florida, they enjoyed the tropical weather, boating, fishing and the beach, and many visitors. Chet learned to scuba dive and they had many an enjoyable day on the ocean and canals, where alligators and tropical birds and fowl abound.

May 1998 – Bill and Lorraine Kincaid

Lorraine and Bill found Polk County to be a pleasant place to reside, and made many friends here, and enjoy Bolivar. There are lots of friendly people, lots of churches, a university, good law enforcement, good fire protection, good elected officials who take their duties seriously, lots of community activities to attend, and very pretty scenery. The proximity to large farms with cattle, horses, sheep, goats and bales of hay in the fields is conducive to a relaxing atmosphere.

Since moving here in 1988, there have been a lot of changes in Lorraine's life, the most devastating being the loss of Bill on April 11, 1999 and the loss of Kathryn on Dec. 20, 1999. Both are buried in Union Cemetery, Burtonsville, Montgomery County, MD.

Blessings still fill Lorraine's life and Lorraine is lucky to live in this part of the USA. *Submitted by Lorraine Kincaid*

KINCAID – James Frederick "Fred" Kincaid (born Sept. 4, 1916 in Knoxville, MO) married Eva Winans Carman (born May 2, 1919 in Florence, CO) in Excelsior Springs, MO on June 30, 1940. After selling their farm in Stet, MO in 1966, they bought and moved to a farm near Cliquot, MO.

Fred was a carpenter and raised cattle. He constructed over 250 barns and other structures in the Polk County area with the help of Robert Sawyer, Jerry Sukovaty, Cecil Dickson, Lannie Potts and Fred's two sons Frederick Clyde and Charles Ray. He enjoyed quail hunting and fishing with Eva.

Eva was employed by Dryer's shoe store in Bolivar. She was active in the Happy Hustler's Extension Club, enjoyed cooking, sewing, spending time with her grandchildren and fishing with Fred.

Eva and Frederick Kincaid

Fred and Eva were members of the Bolivar Methodist Church. Eva departed this life on May 22, 1996. Fred greatly missed Eva, his wife and companion for over 50 years. On Feb. 26, 2002 he went to be with her forever.

Fred and Eva's oldest son, Frederick Clyde (born Dec. 28, 1942 in Braymer, MO) and his wife, Artemisa Parra Lopez (born March 21, 1945 in Indio, CA) were married Sept. 30, 1967 in Higginsville, MO and moved to Bolivar in 1969 after living in Higginsville and Republic, MO. Fred spent many years in construction, electrical work and real estate. He now works for A-1 Tool Inc. in Wishart, MO. Artemisa "Tammy" worked at the Penguin Restaurant, the Bolivar Nursing Home and Teters Floral Products in Bolivar. She is now a part-time housekeeper. Fred and Artemisa worship with the Bolivar Church of Christ.

Fred and Artemisa's only child Eva Maria (born Jan. 9, 1973 in Springfield, MO) graduated from Bolivar in 1991 and Southwest Baptist University in 1996. After teaching elementary school and working part-time in real estate with her father in Bolivar, she is now a hairstylist at Designers and Co. Maria wed John William Kallenbach (born Dec. 1, 1968 in Springfield, MO) on June 26, 1999. He is the son of William Robert and Judy Kallenbach. John is an attorney with Douglas, Lynch, Haun and Kirksey and owner of A-1 Tool. John and Maria live in Bolivar and worship with the Bolivar Church of Christ.

Second son of Fred and Eva, Charles Ray (born Oct. 7, 1945 in Braymer, MO) married Clara Moss Roberts (born Jan. 10, 1951 in St. Clair County) on Feb. 21, 1969 in Greenfield, MO. Chuck and Clara moved to Polk County in 1976 from Corder, MO with their three children: Julie Raye (born July 9, 1970 in Carroll County), Winfield Scott (born March 29, 1974 in Lafayette County) and James Joseph "J.J." (born March 9, 1976 in Lafayette County). In 1988, their marriage ended after almost 20 years. Chuck moved to Taney County, MO doing survey work until he began work with the Missouri Department of Transportation. Chuck and Clara were reunited in marriage in 1995 and live on a farm in Taney County where Clara dabbles in artwork. Julie, Scott and J.J., all graduates of Humansville, moved to Taney County to be near their parents. Scott and J.J. have worked in Branson, MO with varied employment. Julie, their daughter, has worked in productions of "The Promise" and Two From Galilee" in Branson, MO. She now works in Springfield, MO as a receptionist.

Fred and Eva's only daughter, Carol Rose (born Nov. 8, 1949 in Carroll County) graduated from Bolivar in 1967 and moved to Kansas City, MO in 1972 with her daughter Michelle Lynn (born July 30, 1971 in Springfield, MO). Carol married Ronald Curtis Radford (born Dec. 10, 1948 in Memphis, TN) on Dec. 27, 1976 and had a son Ronald Ray (born Dec. 16, 1980 in Jackson County). In 1985, her marriage ended and in 1990 she returned to Bolivar with her son Ron, who graduated in 1999 from Bolivar, where he currently lives. Carol has been employed with Mercantile Bank and Preferred Title Company in Bolivar. She married Robert W. Baggerly (born Oct. 6, 1959 in Bell County, TX) on Sept. 27, 1997 in Bolivar and now resides in Mathis, TX where he is a route salesman with Schwan's.

Michelle Lynn Kincaid, daughter of Kenneth Wayne Anderson (born Nov. 11, 1947) and Carol R. Kincaid, graduated from Grandview High in 1989 and married Eric Newton Babicky (born Nov. 6, 1966 in Albuquerque, NM) on June 17, 1993. They had two children, Raven Newton (born Oct. 16, 1992 in Jackson County) and Reba Lynn (born Nov. 5, 1995 in Jackson County). Their marriage ended in 1996 and on April 1, 1998, Eric passed away. On Jan. 24, 1998, Michelle married David Lee Carroll (born June 14, 1967 in Springfield, IL), son of David Lee Carroll and Karen Duggins. David and his father work together siding houses. Michelle and David had a son David Andrew "Davy" (born March 11, 1999 in Bolivar, MO). David and Michelle currently live in Bolivar with their children, Raven, Reba and Davy and worship at the Bolivar Church of Nazarene. *Submitted by Maria Kallenbach*

KING - Robert Thomas King was born May 6, 1870 in Warren County, MO. Mary Ella Bean was born Feb. 12, 1871 in Dayton, OH and moved with her parents to Warren County at the age of 5. R. T. and Ella (as they called each other) were married Dec. 25, 1894 in Middletown, MO where their son, Ray, was born Jan. 7, 1896. Another son, Eugene, was born Jan. 15, 1897. They moved to southwestern Missouri, where their daughter, Eulallia Vee, was born March 20, 1900. They were living in Imboden, AR when their fourth child, Ernest, was born Aug. 19, 1905. The family was living in Cedar County, MO in 1911, when Ernest started to school. R. T. and Ella moved their family to a farm southwest of Humansville about 1914, when Vee started to high school. John and Lou (Pratt) King, parents of R. T., also lived with them. Lou died in 1915. John died in 1923. After Ella died in 1940, R. T. sold the farm and moved into town. Later, with failing health, he lived with Vee and Walter Stauffacher and was staying with Ernest King in Pueblo, CO when he died in 1946. Lou, John, Ella and R. T. are interred in the Humansville Cemetery.

King family – Vee, Ernest, Robert, Ella, Eugene and Ray

Small grain crops were grown on the farm. A few cows were milked for the dairy products. Chickens were raised to provide eggs and meat for the table. R. T. also raised sheep and in the spring, black or twin lambs, abandoned by the mother ewe, had to be bottle fed - a delightful task for a visiting grandchild. An orchard produced cherries, peaches and apples. Helping pick apples was a great family gathering in the fall. When the apples were harvested, some would be put through a cider press. Looking forward to that delicious juice made the job of picking apples much easier. Ella's green thumb tended a vegetable garden and filled their front porch with pots of flowers and greenery. Her TLC was freely given to the ailing and she attended at the birth of many neighborhood babies. Her kitchen often had an aroma of bread, baking in the wood burning range. Sitting on her lap, relishing a slice of bread spread with sweet cream butter and liberally sprinkled with sugar, is Margie's favorite memory of her grandmother Ella.

Faithful followers of Christ, they were active members of the Humansville Baptist Church.

Ray King married Wassa Steward of Stockton and with their children, Lorene, Cleo, Harold, Louella, Wayne, John, June, May, Hazel and Donnie, lived on farms near Humansville. Eugene King married Edna Capper of Humansville and lived in northeast Missouri with their children, Deanna Mae and Kenneth. Vee King married Walter Stauffacher and lived on a farm south of Humansville with their children, Paul, Margie, Ralph, Casper and Ruby. Ernest King married Lavita Perry of Collins and with their children, Bob, George, Arlene and Bill, resided in Pueblo, CO.

The only descendants currently living in Polk County are June King and Ralph Stauffacher of Dunnegan. *Submitted by Margie Stauffacher Stoll*

KINSEY - Zacarias Riley Kinsey (Jan. 5, 1844—March 5, 1915) came to Polk County from Bucyrus, OH with his son, Guy Verne (Sept. 14, 1869 – Sept. 22, 1899), probably in the late 1870s or early 1880s. Riley's parents were Jacob and Nancy Maldaman Kinsey (Lancaster County, PA) and Jacob's parents were Daniel and Martha Palmer Kinsey (Pennsylvania). Riley, from Bucyrus, married his second wife, Alla May Walker (May 4, 1855—Sept. 22, 1932) from Nevada, OH, on Nov. 4, 1879 in Upper Sandusky, OH. It is not known whether she arrived in Polk County with Riley and Guy Verne, or whether she came later. Mrs. Riley Kinsey is listed as Ella in Ohio public records, but is shown as Alla May Walker on their marriage certificate. She was called "May," and she had a son Sam White, who is shown on an early census as living with her parents, John and Hannah Walker, in Wyandot County, OH. The Walkers later lived in north central Missouri, as did Sam.

Riley Kinsey had been married to Margaret Lucinda Stevens in Ohio and was either divorced or widowed. He left a family of three daughters in Ohio: Iva Captola (Nov. 14, 1864 – Jan. 17, 1960), Hulda Mae (May 16, 1866) and Ila Kizia (Aug. 11, 1867). According to family members, Riley did not talk about his family in Ohio; he changed his name from Kinsey to Kinzia. He is said to have brought the first Jersey cow to Polk County.

Riley's son, Guy Verne, married Rebecca Hutchison on Nov. 7, 1894. Their children were Effie May (July 5, 1895), who married Walter Lockhart and whose children were Cleo, Thelma Lauren, Jean Marie, Danny, Juanita, Faye Lavern, Wanda Lee and Betty Lou; Maggie, who married a man named Ellsworth and who had a son; Verna Rebecca (Oct. 5, 1900) who married Eugene Clifford Cowden and whose children were Clara Maxine, Helen, Dorothy Jean and Vernon Porter. Rebecca's son, James Guy Leroy Kinsey, was born in 1903.

The Kinseys lived on a farm north of Bolivar

Front – Riley Kinsey with Ina, May Kinsey with baby, Ordy. Rear – LaVinnie Kinsey

and they had the following children who were born and lived in Polk County:

Ada LaVinnie (March 22, 1881 - June 11, 1907) married Thompson Watt and their children were Earnest, Bud, Ersel, Maggie and Gertie;

Ina Elizabeth (Nov. 26, 1887 – Jan. 26, 1943) married Lee Patrick McElwee on Jan. 25, 1906 and their children were Ona Mae, Henry Lee, Vida Jewell, Julia Laverne and Edward Eugene (Henry Lee died just before he was 2 in 1915);

Lola (March 22, 1893 - March 28, 1893);

Ord Alroy (Aug. 26, 1894 – Feb. 27, 1983) married Anna Mae Pilcher on Oct. 23, 1916 and their children were Virginia Mae, James Woodrow, Thomas Shelby, Don Richard and Max Raymond.

As of the year 2002, descendants of each of Riley and Alla May's children who lived to adulthood still live in Polk County. *Submitted by Ona Jenkins*

KINSEY/PILCHER - Ord Alroy Kinsey (Aug. 20, 1894 – Feb. 27, 1983), only son of Riley and Alla May Walker Kinsey, lived most of his life on or near the farm north of Bolivar where he was born, with the exceptions of the short times he spent in a zinc mine in Kansas, a CC Camp, the US Navy, and in a nursing home in Springfield.

"Ordy" was married on Oct. 23, 1916 to Anna "Mae" Pilcher (Aug. 19, 1899 – Feb. 21, 1992) who moved from northern Missouri with her parents, Bart and Amanda Pilcher, and became a neighbor of the Kinseys. Mae and Ordy had five children. Their only daughter, Virginia May (Sept. 2, 1920), was killed in an automobile accident when she was 9 years old. Ordy, Mae and Virginia are buried in Payne Cemetery, Polk, MO.

The O. A. and Mae Kinsey family. Mae and Ordy. Inset upper right – Don and Max in front, Woodrow and Tom in back. Right inset: "Sister"

The Kinsey family spent many hours for many years gathering, hulling, cracking and shelling black walnuts. Ordy scoured the area for these nuts—sometimes buying, other times just "pickin' up walnuts" for local farmers. It was a family affair. Ordy located and the boys picked up the black walnuts. Using their Model-A, with a jacked-up rear wheel and an improvised trough made from a hollow log, the walnuts were hulled and propelled toward the side of the barn where they were left on the ground to dry before they were stored. The walnuts would then be soaked in steel barrels filled with water. Ordy would dip the walnuts from the water, lay them on boards and let them sun-dry. The boys would then pick up the walnuts, sort them and take them to the house.

Beginning at 4:30 a.m. daily, Ordy cracked the walnuts. He used a lard stand with a few inches of water in it and a metal piece placed in the bottom to hold a bucket, punched with holes, filled with walnuts and covered with tow sacks, to hold the heat as the walnuts steamed on the woodstove.

Next he poured the steamed nuts into a hopper and covered them, again with tow sacks, so they would stay hot while he cracked about three bushels a day on a walnut cracker made by a local blacksmith. When the boys returned from school and supper was finished, the family would gather around the kitchen table, each with his/her own pick, listen to their favorite radio programs and pick out the kernels. The walnuts would then be placed behind the woodstove to dry. The next day, Mae sorted the kernels, picking out any small hulls and shells that remained. On Saturday mornings Ordy and Mae went to Bolivar, delivered and sold their walnuts at Barnes Store and spent the day socializing on the square. Occasionally, the boys were allowed to go along.

Picking walnuts was the Kinsey family's vocation; their avocation was fishing. Mae Pilcher Kinsey loved to fish and had quite a fishing reputation. In the summer she often gave up her trip to Bolivar and had Ordy drop her off at Jefferson Bridge where she fished the whole day while he was in town. She was often joined by her sons on her fishing expeditions and she passed the love of fishing, nature and the Pomme de Terre River on to her sons.

Socializing with their neighbors on Sundays and, especially, on Decoration Day at Payne Cemetery was important to this family.

All four Kinsey sons served in the military and all four entered the teaching profession.

Woodrow (Sept. 27, 1922) married Ernestine Stewart, stayed in Bolivar, was employed as teacher and principal by the Bolivar School System for many years and has a son, Timothy Stewart.

Tom (May 11, 1928) married Uarda Lee Wahlborg, taught at Central High School, Greenwood Lab School and Southwest Missouri State University, is an artist and has two daughters, Roxanne Darby and Joy Dawn Fothergill.

Don (May 22, 1931) married Nancy Sue Davis of Elkland, MO, moved to St. Louis, was Department Chairman of Guidance and Counseling at Mehlville High School and has two daughters, Mignon Sue Been and Kristin Lynn Kinsey.

Max (June 2,

1932) married Sue Simmons from Bolivar, taught in schools in Missouri, worked for World Book Encyclopedia in Chicago and had a son, Kent. Both Max and Sue died in the 1980s and are buried in Greenwood Cemetery.

Kinsey grandchildren and their families are located in Illinois, Minnesota, Missouri and Virginia. *Submitted by Don Kinsey*

KINSEY/WAHLBORG - This story is about treasures and connections. In this *Polk County History Book*, being prepared in 2002, Lee Kinsey hopes that some day her children, grandchildren, nieces, nephews, cousins and their descendants yet-to-be-born will find the same joy that she did when she read a little Ogallah, KS booklet titled *In Remembrance: Early Pioneers of Ogallah and Community*. Lee discovered it during the 1980s when her mother, Gladys Wahlborg, sold her home in Springfield, MO after her husband Otto died. In that booklet, written in western Kansas about 70 years after her great-great-grandfather, Henry Cutler, had moved there from Illinois and sent for his family, there was a page that told of the hardship, sadness, strength and pride of that family in those sometimes-trying times. In addition, on pages dedicated to other pioneer families, she found more little jewels of information showing connections between family and friends that she had never understood. Some of that Cutler family, on the maternal side of the U. S. and Grace Hoffer family, became residents of Polk County in the late 1930s. If they search, descendants of Cutler, Hoffer, Kinsey, and Pilcher families may find and enjoy the family histories that unite them.

Front row – Ona McElwee Jenkins with Autumn Brie Raney, Eric Raney. Back row – Dorothy Jenkins Wood Cothrell and Barbara Wood Lake. All except Barbara live in Polk County.

Tom Kinsey, Lee's husband, is a third-generation member of both Polk County Kinseys and Pilchers and she (Uarda Lee Wahlborg) is a Polk County, second-generation Wahlborg and third-generation Hoffer. Although they lived only 20 and nine years, respectively, in Polk County, their roots are deep and these roots tug and pull them back often and have for over 50 years. When they left Polk County, they moved to Virginia for Tom's army service, to Springfield for his educational and teaching career and to Taney County for retirement. Tom's parents were O. A. and Mae Kinsey. He had three brothers, one of whom, Woodrow (Ernestine Stewart)* lives near Bolivar. His other living brother, Don (Nancy Davis), lives in St. Louis and his youngest brother, Max and his wife, Sue (Simmons), lived in Missouri and Illinois, and both died in Chicago in the 1980s. Lee's sisters are Donna Michael (Don (deceased 2002), divorced) Olathe, KS and Lois Price (Steve), Las Vegas, NV. Her brother Berne (Joyce Tye) died in California in 1990. Tom's special cousin, Ed McElwee, Springfield, is like a fourth Kinsey brother; his wife, Virginia Smolnik McElwee, died in January 2002.

The Kinsey daughters, Roxanne Darby (David), Kissee Mills, MO and Joy Fothergill (Kevin), Minneapolis, MN, have the following first cousins. On the Kinsey side are Woodrow's son, Tim (Cindy Bowers), Herndon, VA; Don's daughters, Mignon Been (Mike) and Kris Kinsey, St. Louis; Max's son, Kent (Bobbie), Chicago, IL. On the Wahlborg side are Donna's children: Rex (Vicky Hamm), David (Kelly Jones) and Mindy Chaffee (David), all of Olathe, KS and Powell (Brendy Fry) of Laguna Beach, CA; and Lois's children, Brad Price and Stacy Donald (Quintin). Berne had stepchildren and step-grand-children in California and Kansas. Eddie McElwee's sons are Greg (Teresa), Steve (Jerri) and Jon (all second cousins).

Dustin and Danielle Fothergill and Seth Darby are Tom and Lee's grandchildren. Their step-grandson is Bill Darby (Melissa Brown) and their son Camden is the Kinseys' only great-grandchild. The grandchildren's second cousins are Tim's children, Rachel, Jacob and Rebecca; Mignon's children, Justin and Megan; Kent's children, Tiffany, Heather and Guy; Rex's children, Ryan and Cassandra and Johnny Riley; Powell's children, Theo and Macy; David's children, Jason, Kelsay and Allie; Mindy's children, Lynzie Michael, Erin and Rebecca Rohr, and Elizabeth and Eric Chaffee; and Stacy's children, Ashley and Leslie. Greg's children, Amber, Amy and Adam Davis, and Steve's family, Stephanie, Matthew and April McElwee and Dustin and Wesley Rose are some of Dustin, Seth, and Danielle's third cousins.

In 2002 there are no Wahlborgs in Polk County—the surviving of 40 Kansas first cousins are scattered throughout the United States. There are three generations of Hoffers in Bolivar—Lee's Uncle Wayne Hoffer (Lucille Sconce), their son Nathan (Vonzell McDaniel) and their family, Bonnie and Silas Hoffer, Sasha Camp and Autumn McDaniel. Two families represent the Pilcher tree—Woodrow Kinsey and Fern Triggs Kauffman (Curt), Humansville. There are, however, Kinsey descendants galore. Names are Kinsey, Jenkins, Cockrell, Raney, Netherton, Garzee, Davis (several families), Ballentyne, West, Dodson, Bays, Pursley, Koon, Keith, Ross, Hitchcock, Ray, Moore, Vote, Hickman and Bridges (there may be more).

Two special cousins hold places of honor in the Kinsey family treasure chest. Ona McElwee Jenkins was the first Kinsey grandchild born in Polk County in 1910 and is now the great-great-grandmother of a five-generation family (four of whom live in Polk County). Her sister, Vida Jewell McElwee Jenkins, born in 1919, is the Kinsey walking, talking, family- encyclopedia. *Spouses in parenthesis. *Submitted by Lee Kinsey*

KINSLOW - Page C. Kinslow, his first wife, Mary Virginia (Harrison) and young son, James C., left their home in Barren County, KY during the winter of 1865 and traveled to Polk County, MO to make their home near where Page's mother and stepfather, Agnes and Joseph Huckaby, were living in northeastern Polk County. A family history relates that the young family arrived on Christmas Day 1865 and had Christmas dinner with Agnes and Joseph.

Page C. Kinslow (Kincheloe) was honorably discharged from the 37th Kentucky Volunteer Mounted Infantry, Union Army, Dec. 29, 1864 after serving 18 months of duty and having been wounded in action. He volunteered for the Union Army at age 24 as a married man with one child, served as a private in the same command as his uncle, William Kinslow, and was described as being five feet, eight inches tall, dark complexion, blue-gray eyes and having auburn hair. On Nov. 15, 1863, Page was on patrol duty from Camp Glasgow in Barren County, KY. The patrol left camp about dark to scout the Pikesville road 10 or 12 miles south, then split into pairs. If nothing was found or heard of the enemy, they were to split up and return to camp, each taking his own route back. "After he was returning leisurely alone, by the next day, as ordered, just before daylight, he was shot, in the dark, the ball entering his left cheek and coming out behind the left ear, losing all teeth from eye teeth back in upper left jaw; dressed own wound, never stopped duty, lived on soup for some time; was attacked by broken bone fever June 10, 1864, hauled in wagon to Lexington, KY, moved to Mt. Sterling, KY. In August 1864, paralyzed from attack of blue-erysipelas (from exposure as a teamster in winter of 1863-64), walked on two sticks for a long time after the attack."

Page C. Kinslow

Mary Virginia died in 1874 and in 1877, Page married Martha Jane Huckaby, daughter of Thomas and Sarah (Sally) Huckaby, granddaughter of Joseph Huckaby. Martha Jane was a lovely young woman with brown hair and clear blue eyes. Several children were born to Page and Martha Jane: Aaron, Tom, Joseph, William Haiden, Celia, Sarah and Mary - all survived to adulthood. Three babies died in infancy. Tragically, Martha Jane died in childbirth on June 25, 1898. Page's daughter, Edna, wrote of her recollection of that day as told to her by Page. "They had picked green beans and he helped snap them. She was feeling all right (she had had the measles recently). The beans were on to cook, Page started to shave and Martha Jane started labor. He got on the horse, rode for the doctor and sent one of the children for a nearby neighbor (Eliza Luttrell). At 12 o'clock, the beans were cooked, his face half shaved, his wife and infant baby were dead."

Page was married for a third time to a widow, Eliza Segels Francis Clemens Luttrell, on April 26, 1901. Two children, a son, Otto, who died at 6 months, and a daughter, Edna Kinslow Ballinger Hunt, were born to Page and Eliza.

Page served as a notary of the public. He was a good friend and neighbor. A neighbor told that he would ride his horse to town for supplies and errands for his family and for neighbors. Page, of Irish heritage, was described as being congenial, intelligent and a good conversationalist with a sense of humor. Page and Eliza sold their farm and moved to Bolivar where Eliza died in 1924. Page passed away at the age of 87 on April 6, 1926 at his home in Bolivar following complications from pneumonia. Page and his wives are buried in Hopewell Cemetery in northeastern Polk County. *Submitted by Gene Alvin Kinslow, great grandson of Page*

KIRCHNER — William Matthew Kirchner was born Sept. 21, 1852, at Girbigsdorf, Kreis Sprottau, Schlesien Province, Germany (now Poland), and died Jan. 28, 1931, at his home on a farm in Woodville Twp., Platte Co., Nebr., that was about 2 miles east of Saint Edward, Beaver Precinct, Boone Co., Nebr. He arrived in America on Nov. 1, 1876, and first lived near Saint Joseph, Buchanan Co., Mo. He came by himself to America and had no other relatives here at the time. He is a son of Benjamin Kirchner, but the name of his mother is unknown. His parents and three sisters remained in Germany. The names of his three sisters are also unknown.

He married in the courthouse in Saint Joseph, Mo., Aug. 9, 1885, Sarah Ellen Latier, daughter of Samuel Latier and Lucinda Fuller. Ellen was born Feb. 14, 1870, in Peoria, Peoria Co., Ill., and died Nov. 23, 1950, at her home in Saint Edward, Nebr. She and William were both buried in the Evergreen Cemetery about 1 mile east of Saint Edward.

William Matthew Kirchner, age 60 y. 10 m. 19 d., and his wife, Mrs. Sarah Ellen (Latier) Kirchner, age 43 y. 5 m. 24 d. Taken at Grant City, Worth Co., Mo., on their 28th wedding anniversary, Aug. 9, 1913.

William and Ellen lived for at least 10 years (1885-95) on a farm near Clarksdale, De Kalb Co., Mo. They later lived on farms near Parnell, Nodaway Co., Mo. (1898), Sheridan, Worth Co., Mo. (1902), and Grant City, Worth Co., Mo. (1908). About 1916, they moved to a farm in Platte Co., Nebr. (about 2 mi. east of Saint Edward in Boone Co.), and lived there until his death. Ellen moved to Saint Edward after William died and lived there the rest of her life.

Mr. Kirchner was a farmer during most of his life. While living near Parnell, he worked on the railroad. He had been a member of the German Lutheran Church since early youth and was a member of the Independent Order of Odd Fellows Lodge during the last 40 years of his life (1891-1931). He was in the French and German War that occurred during 1870-71 before he came to America.

Children: (1) Anna Elizabeth, born Sept. 19, 1886, on a farm near Clarksdale, De Kalb Co., Mo.; died Sept. 30, 1886, probably on a farm near Clarksdale; buried at Clarksdale. (2) Charles William, born Oct. 30, 1887, on a farm near Clarksdale, De Kalb Co., Mo.; married Sept. 27, 1911, in Saint Joseph, Buchanan Co., Mo., Louise Christine Krull; died July 16, 1960, in a hospital in Powell, Park Co., Wyo.; buried at Powell. (3) Roy Stanley, born July 17, 1889, on a farm near Clarksdale, De Kalb Co., Mo.

(4) George Franklin, born Nov. 4, 1890, on a farm near Clarksdale, De Kalb Co., Mo.; died unmarried, after 1958, probably in Saint Edward, Boone Co., Nebr.; buried in the Evergreen Cemetery at Saint Edward. (5) John Richard, born Dec. 23, 1895, on a farm near Clarksdale, De Kalb Co., Mo.; married about 1928, probably in Boone Co., Nebr., Esther Brooks; died after 1957, probably in Post Falls, Kootenai Co., Idaho; probably buried at Post Falls. (6) Benjamin Henry, born Mar. 23, 1898, at Parnell, Nodaway Co., Mo.; died unmarried on Dec. 17, 1922, in a hospital in Saint Edward, Boone Co., Nebr., after a car accident; buried in the Evergreen Cemetery at Saint Edward.

(7) Clara May, born May 12, 1902, on a farm near Sheridan, Worth Co., Mo.; married Feb. 21, 1922, in the courthouse in Columbus, Platte Co., Nebr., Clarence Palmer Roberts; were both residing at Genoa, Nance Co., Nebr. 68640, in Mar., 1972. (8) Nellie Murl, born Mar. 8, 1908, on a farm about 3 miles SW of Grant City, Worth Co., Mo.; married Sept. 6, 1927, in the courthouse in Columbus, Platte Co., Nebr., Ivan Glenn Hodge who had died before Mar., 1972. Nellie was residing at 2608 Rees St., Omaha, Douglas Co., Nebr. 68105, in Mar., 1972.

Roy Stanley Kirchner was born July 17, 1889, on a farm near Clarksdale, Washington Twp., De Kalb Co., Mo., and died of a heart attack on Feb. 25, 1972, at his home in Humansville, Johnson Twp., Polk Co., Mo. He attended grade school in De Kalb Co., Nodaway Co., and Worth Co., Mo., and graduated from the 8th grade.

He married (1) in the home of Rev. C. O. Peterson at Grant City, Fletchall Twp., Worth Co., Mo., Dec. 24, 1911, Hattie May Simmons, daughter of George Simmons and Mary Frances "Fannie" Smith. Hattie was born Apr. 5, 1892, probably at Sheridan, Union Twp., Worth Co., Mo. She and Roy lived for about 9 years (1911-20) on farms near Grant City, Mo., and then moved about 1920 to a farm in Jefferson Twp., Cedar Co., Mo., that was about 3 miles NW of Dunnegan in Polk Co. and about 5 1/2 miles SW of Humansville. The farm in Jefferson Twp. was in the NE corner of Section 1, Township 34, Range 25, and was next to the line between Cedar Co. and Polk Co.

Roy Stanley Kirchner, age 44, his wife, Mrs. Lillie Ellen (Newcomb) Kirchner, age 25, and their son, Roy Stanley Kirchner, Jr., age 11 months. Taken in Sept., 1933.

Roy and Hattie were divorced on Feb. 21, 1923, in the courthouse in Grant City, Worth Co., Mo. He then worked as a hired hand (plowing, putting in wheat, and harvesting) in Colo., Nebr., S. Dak., N. Dak., and Kans. for about 9 years (1922-31), when the wages were as little as 50 cents and $1 a day, and later returned to his farm in Cedar Co., Mo.

He married (2) in Humansville, Polk Co., Mo., Aug. 7, 1931, Lillie Ellen Newcomb, daughter of Charles Henry Newcomb and Louisa Catherine Conway; were married in the parsonage of the Baptist Church by Rev. Dan R. Gott who was then the minister. Lillie was born Dec. 7, 1907, on a farm 2 miles NW of Parnell, Independence Twp., Nodaway Co., Mo., and died of cancer on July 14, 1986, in the Citizens Memorial Hospital in Bolivar, Polk Co., Mo. She and Roy were both buried in the Greenwood Cemetery in Bolivar.

Charles Henry Newcomb, son of George Thomas Newcomb and Emily Elizabeth Miller, was born Nov. 15, 1862, in the home of his paternal grandparents (Rev. George Newcomb and Lucy Rand) at Dedham, Norfolk Co., Mass., and died Dec. 3, 1948, at his home on a farm in Jefferson Twp., Polk Co., Mo., that was 5 miles east of Flemington. He and Louisa Catherine Conway, daughter of Fifield Clarkson "Clark" Conway and Susannah "Susan" Adaline Sweeten, were married on May 18, 1891, at Maryville, Nodaway Co., Mo. She was born May 16, 1872, on a farm near Sweethome, Jackson Twp., Nodaway Co., Mo., and died Apr. 12, 1951, on a farm in Cliquot Twp., 7 1/2 miles north of Bolivar, Polk Co., Mo. (the home of Charles Fredric "Fred" Newcomb and Rosalia Grace Newcomb, a son and a daughter). Charles and Louisa (Lillie's parents) were both buried in the Flemington Cemetery about 1/2 mile west of Flemington.

George Thomas Newcomb who was born Dec. 16, 1836, in Quincy, Norfolk Co., Mass., died July 24, 1883, in Orrsburg, Independence Twp., Nodaway Co., Mo., and is a son of Rev. George Newcomb and Lucy Rand. He married Apr. 21, 1859, at Hannibal, Mason Twp., Marion Co., Mo., Emily Elizabeth Miller who was born Sept. 29, 1835, in Ky., died Jan. 11, 1906, in Parnell, Independence Twp., Nodaway Co., Mo., and is a daughter of Hansel Miller and Nancy M. James. George and Emily were both buried in the Parnell Cemetery about 1/2 mile south of Parnell. He was in the Union Army during the Civil War.

Charles Henry Newcomb, age 73 y. 8 m. 17 d., son of George Thomas Newcomb and Emily Elizabeth Miller. His wife, Mrs. Louisa Catherine (Conway) Newcomb, age 64 y. 2 m. 16 d., daughter of Fifield Clarkson "Clark" Conway and Susannah "Susan" Adaline Sweeten. Taken Aug. 1, 1936, in the yard at the SW corner of their home on a farm in Jefferson Twp., Polk Co., Mo., about 5 miles east of Flemington, Star Route.

Lillie moved with her parents in Dec., 1917, from the farm where she was born to a farm in Jefferson Twp., Polk Co., Mo., that was about 6 miles east of Flemington. Her parents moved a few years later to a farm in Jefferson Twp. that was 5 miles east of Flemington where they continued to live until they both died. Her father was

Mrs. Lillie Ellen (Newcomb) Kirchner, age 34. Taken in Dec., 1941.

a farmer and had a large orchard on the second farm. Lillie attended grade school at Elm Grove, a country school near Parnell, and then at Union, District No. 5, a country school about 3 1/2 miles east of Flemington, where she graduated from the 8th grade.

Roy and Lillie lived for 14 1/2 years (1931-46) on the same farm where he had previously lived in Cedar Co., Mo. On Feb. 22, 1946, they moved to a farm about 1 mile east of Humansville where they lived for 14 years (1946-60). They sold this farm on May 17, 1960, and moved shortly thereafter to what was known as the old Earl Quillen farm in the south edge of Humansville where they lived for about 5 years (1960-65). In 1965, they moved to a home in the SW edge of Humansville where they lived until his death.

Mr. Kirchner was a dairy farmer during most of his life while residing in Cedar Co. and Polk Co., Mo. The milking was all done by hand while sitting on a little wooden stool with a kerosene lantern for light. He frequently sang or hummed a church song while he was milking. Cooking was done on a wood stove in the kitchen, while using a kerosene lamp, and heat in the winter was obtained from a wood heating stove in the frontroom. The washing was done in a galvanized tub with homemade lye soap and a washboard, and water was obtained from a pump in the yard. Plowing, harrowing, planting, cultivating, mowing, raking, and putting up hay was done with a team of horses. He drove a team of horses and a wagon to Dunnegan and Humansville and to the High Point Baptist Church which was in the same building as the High Point School in Cedar Co. He later got a Plymouth pickup truck.

Roy Stanley Kirchner, age 69 y. 3 m. 12 d., and his wife, Mrs. Lillie Ellen (Newcomb) Kirchner, age 50 y. 10 m. 22 d. Taken Oct. 29, 1958, in the yard in front of their home on a farm about 1 mile east of Humansville, Polk Co., Mo. (Route 1, Box 73).

Roy had a cream separator, which was turned by hand, and sold the cream at a cheese factory in Humansville. The skimmed milk was fed to hogs. They raised chickens and sold eggs at the Zerkel Hatchery and at the Farmers Exchange in Humansville. Lillie cleaned and graded eggs for the hatchery, and each year she took care of feeding and watering many hens while they were sitting on eggs for hatching baby chickens. They always raised a big garden and sold some produce (potatoes, tomatoes, and onions) which was hauled in a wagon to stores in Humansville. They did a lot of canning, and the fruit jars were stored in a cellar with crocks full of milk, churned butter, and potatoes.

While living in Cedar Co., Roy and Lillie had no electricity, indoor plumbing, running water, or telephone. They had a battery radio. It was not until after they had moved to a farm about 1 mile east of Humansville (in 1946) that they finally had electricity, but there was still no indoor plumbing until after they moved to Humansville in 1960 and no telephone until sometime after 1965. They received a used black and white television set from their son and his wife in 1959.

Roy was forced to quit work and retire after a car accident on Aug. 25, 1955. He was again in a car accident in 1965 which left him nearly unable to walk. He attended the Methodist Church for awhile when he was a young boy, joined the Baptist Church at an early age, and later transferred his membership to the Christian Church in Humansville about 1944 where he and Lillie both remained as members and where he served as a deacon. She was a Sunday School teacher for awhile at the High Point Baptist Church. Roy did a lot of reading and particularly liked to read western stories.

Mrs. Lillie Kirchner sold her home in Humansville on Mar. 7, 1972, and moved 2 days later to 428 West Maupin St., Bolivar, Mo. 65613, to be near her son, daughter-in-law, and three grandchildren who then lived on a place joining hers in Bolivar. She continued to live there until her death.

Children by first wife: (1) Arthur Leslie, known by his middle name, born Oct. 30, 1912, on a farm 2 1/2 miles west of Grant City, Worth Co., Mo.; married about 1943, perhaps in Mo., wife's name unknown. (2) Mable Ruth, known by her middle name, born Dec. 24, 1914, on a farm 4 1/2 miles NW of Grant City, Worth Co., Mo.; probably unmarried in June, 1958. (3) George Floyd, born Mar. 2, 1919, on a farm near Grant City, Worth Co., Mo.; died at Grant City, probably in 1920; buried at Isadora, Worth Co., Mo.

Child by second wife: (4) Roy Stanley, Jr., born Oct. 25, 1932, on a farm in Cedar Co., Mo., about 3 miles NW of Dunnegan.

Roy Stanley Kirchner, Jr., was born Oct. 25, 1932, in the home of his parents on a farm in Jefferson Twp., Cedar Co., Mo., that was about 3 miles NW of Dunnegan, Campbell Twp., Polk Co., Mo., and about 5 1/2 miles SW of Humansville. He attended grade school at High Point, a country school in Cedar Co., about 2 miles west and a little south of the farm where he was born, and at Union, District No. 5, a country school about 3 1/2 miles east of Flemington in Polk Co., Mo., where he graduated from the 8th grade. He then attended the Humansville High School where he graduated in 1949 and was salutatorian of the class that year. During the following year, he again attended the Humansville High School and took post-graduate courses. Much of his time was spent mowing lawns all over the town during summer vacations. He was a member of the Boy Scouts in Humansville with Ray Martin, Jr., as the scoutmaster.

He married in the Church of the Nazarene, 831 East Third St., San Bernardino, San Bernardino Co., Calif., Apr. 7, 1954, Deva Louise Poe, daughter of Jesse "Jess" Fay Poe and Jessie Katherine Thatch. Deva was born June 21, 1932, in the home of her maternal grandmother, Mrs. William "Will" Stewart Thatch (Viola "Ola" June Roth), in the south part of

Roy Stanley Kirchner, Jr., age 21, and his wife, Mrs. Deva Louise (Poe) Kirchner, age 21, who were married Apr. 7, 1954, in San Bernardino, Calif. He was then an Airman First Class in the U. S. Air Force, and they went a few days later to Wiesbaden, Germany.

Wheatland, Wheatland Twp., Hickory Co., Mo. Her parents were then residing on a farm that was about 1 1/4 miles W and 3/4 mile south of Elkton, Tyler Twp., Hickory Co., Mo. Her father was a farmer.

Jesse "Jess" Fay Poe, son of Henry Emmett Poe and Sarah Lou Tillery, was born May 5, 1901, on a farm about 2 3/4 miles SW of Elkton, Tyler Twp., Hickory Co., Mo., and died of a heart attack on Sept. 11, 1951, at his home on a farm about 2.6 miles SW of Elkton. He was buried in the Flemington Cemetery about 1/2 mile west of Flemington, Polk Co., Mo. He and Jessie Katherine Thatch, daughter of William "Will" Stewart Thatch and Viola "Ola" June Roth, were married on Nov. 28, 1925, in the home of Clyde E. Holland, a Justice of the Peace, in Wheatland, Hickory Co., Mo. Jessie was born Jan. 10, 1906, on a farm about 2 1/2 miles SW of Elkton.

Henry Emmett Poe, son of John "Jack" Poe and Elizabeth Minerva Dooly, was born Aug. 30, 1853, on a farm about 2 1/2 miles SW of Elkton, Tyler Twp., Hickory Co., Mo., and died July 10, 1940. He and Sarah Lou Tillery, daughter of Jacob "Jake" Franklin Tillery and Sarah Ellen Carnes, were married on Nov. 21, 1880, at the home of the bride's parents on a farm near Elkton. She was born Apr. 10, 1864, in Mo., probably on a farm NW of Elkton, and died Sept. 30, 1942. Henry and Lou both died at their home on a farm about 2 3/4 miles SW of Elkton and were both buried in the Tillery Cemetery about 3 miles SW of Elkton.

William "Will" Stewart Thatch, son of Thomas Daniel Thatch and Catharine McSpadden, was born Apr. 14, 1871, in Hickory Co., Mo., probably on a farm about 3 miles NE of Elkton in Tyler Twp., and died Nov. 19, 1929, in State Hospital No. 3 in Nevada, Vernon Co., Mo. He and Viola "Ola" June Roth, daughter of John Roth and Sarah [NMN] Diener,

Jesse "Jess" Fay Poe, age about 50, son of Henry Emmett Poe and Sarah Lou Tillery. His wife, Mrs. Jessie Katherine (Thatch) Poe, age about 45, daughter of William "Will" Stewart Thatch and Viola "Ola" June Roth. Their daughter, Lois Jean "Jeanie" Poe, age about 8, born Apr. 10, 1943, on a farm about 2 1/2 miles SW of Elkton, Hickory Co., Mo. Taken about 1951.

Henry Emmett Poe, age about 66, son of John "Jack" Poe and Elizabeth Minerva Dooly. His wife, Mrs. Sarah Lou (Tillery) Poe, age about 55, daughter of Jacob "Jake" Franklin Tillery and Sarah Ellen Carnes. Probably taken in 1919.

William "Will" Stewart Thatch, age 52.5, son of Thomas Daniel Thatch and Catharine McSpadden. He married Viola "Ola" June Roth, daughter of John Roth and Sarah Diener. Taken in Nov., 1923, at Nevada, Vernon Co., Mo.

were married on June 25, 1901, at Elkton. She was born June 25, 1883, in the home of her maternal grandparents (George [NMN] Diener and Mary Ann Mosholder) and died Mar. 15, 1960, in the Big Spring Rest Home in Humansville, Johnson Twp., Polk Co., Mo. William and Viola were both buried in the Lehman Cemetery about 1 mi. NE of Elkton.

Deva attended grade school for 2 years at Shady Grove, a country school about 4 miles west of Elkton, Hickory Co., Mo., and then at Sunny Slope, a country school in Hickory Co. that was about 1 mile north and a little bit east of Flemington, Polk Co., Mo., where she graduated from the 8th grade. She attended the Humansville High School for 3 years and then attended the Weaubleau High School in Weaubleau, Hickory Co., Mo., for 1 year where she graduated in 1952.

Deva moved with her mother to San Bernardino, Calif., in Dec., 1952. Her mother married (2) in the Hall of Justice in Las Vegas, Clark Co., Nev., Dec. 31, 1954, Earl Raymond Daniels, son of Wallace Edgar Daniels and Minnie Virginia Flowers. He was born Dec. 3, 1900, on a farm about 1/2 mile SW of Brushy, Washington Twp., Webster Co., Iowa, and died Feb. 2, 1981. Deva's mother died on Mar. 10, 1989. Her mother and her stepfather both died in the Saint Bernardine Hospital in San Bernardino, Calif., and were both buried in the Montecito Memorial Park Cemetery in Colton, San Bernardino Co., Calif.

Roy enlisted in the U. S. Air Force on July 11, 1951, and retired as a Staff Sergeant on Aug. 1, 1971, after serving for 20 years and 20 days. His occupation during that time was typist and stenographic technician. While in the U. S. Air Force, he was stationed at Lackland AFB near San Antonio, Texas, for basic training; University of Alabama, Tuscaloosa, Ala., for additional technical training (was Honor Student, No. 1 in the class); Camp Lindsey in Wiesbaden, Germany; Wiesbaden Air Base near Wiesbaden, Germany; Parks AFB near Pleasanton, Calif.; Camp Polk, La.; Travis AFB near Sacramento, Calif.; Arlington Hall Station near Arlington, Va.; Fort Myer near Arlington, Va.; overseas again at Wiesbaden Air Base near

Mrs. Deva Louise (Poe) Kirchner, age 26 y. 16 d., wife of Roy Stanley Kirchner, Jr. Mrs. Viola "Ola" June (Roth) Thatch, age 75 y. 12 d., wife of William "Will" Stewart Thatch. Mrs. Jessie Katherine (Thatch) Poe-Daniels, age 52 y. 5 m. 27 d., wife of Earl Raymond Daniels (widow of Jesse "Jess" Fay Poe). Taken July 7, 1958, in front of the W. W. Walker Boarding Home, 605 East Broadway St., Bolivar, Polk Co., Mo.

Wiesbaden, Germany; Office of Special Investigations District 63 in Paris, France (resided in Le Vesinet, France); Directorate, Office of Special Investigations, in Washington, D. C.; Phan Rang Air Base near Phan Rang, Vietnam; Kirtland AFB in Albuquerque, N. Mex.; Johnston Island Air Base on Johnston Island in the Pacific, 720 miles SSW of Hawaii; Hickam AFB near Honolulu, Hawaii; and Travis AFB, Calif., again for retirement processing and discharge.

During three periods of separation while Roy was overseas, Deva lived near her mother and her stepfather in San Bernardino, Calif. This was for about 7 months when there was a ban on dependent travel to Germany, 1 year while in Vietnam, and 1 year while on Johnston Island. During the year when he was in Vietnam (1967-68), they met for 5 days at Fort DeRussy near Honolulu, Hawaii. They continued to live in San Bernardino, Calif., for 1 1/2 months after his discharge and then returned to Humansville on Sept. 20, 1971, and lived there for awhile with his parents. On Jan. 1, 1972, they moved to a home which they bought at 604 South Lillian Ave., Bolivar, Mo. 65613-2330, and where they were still residing in 2002.

Roy Stanley Kirchner, Jr., age 69, and his wife, Mrs. Deva Louise (Poe) Kirchner, age 69. Taken Apr. 22, 2002, in their home at 604 South Lillian Ave., Bolivar, Mo., after being married for 48 years.

Roy attended the Southwest Baptist College in Bolivar and received an Associate of Science degree in General Education on May 19, 1979. His first and only car was a 1955 Ford Customline, bought new in Hayward, Calif., for $2,500 on Aug. 12, 1955, which was still being driven by him in 2002. He is particularly interested in pursuing his favorite hobby of genealogical research which was commenced on Jan. 1, 1957. He was also interested in stamp collecting, coin collecting, old books, old phonograph records, song collecting, tape recording, and computers.

Children: (1) Christena Louise, born Oct. 25, 1959, in the DeWitt Army Hospital at Fort Belvoir, Fairfax Co., Va. (2) Angelena Jean, born May 23, 1963, in the 196th Station U. S. Army Hospital in Neuilly-sur-Seine (a suburb of Paris), Department of Seine, France. (3) Roy Stanley, III, born Apr. 10, 1967, in the U. S. Air Force Hospital at Andrews Air Force Base, Prince Georges Co., Md.

Christena Louise Kirchner graduated at the Bolivar High School in 1977. She married Oct. 29, 1977, in the Center Point Missionary Baptist Church in NE Marion Twp., 3 miles west of Huron, McKinley Twp., Polk Co., Mo., Richard Ervin Barber. He was born Aug. 5, 1947, on a farm 1 1/2 miles south of Polk, McKinley Twp., Polk Co., Mo., and is a son of Claude William Barber and Alma Pearl (Oringderff) Hattersley (adopted name). Richard and Christena were divorced on Feb. 22, 2000, in the courthouse in Bolivar, Polk Co., Mo. They had four children:

(1) Atha Marie, born July 3, 1979, in the Cox Medical Center in Springfield, Greene Co., Mo. She married June 4, 1999, in the Southern Hills Baptist Church in Bolivar, Mo., Benjamen [sic] "Ben" Wayne (Hill) Schatz, born Sept. 16, 1978, in Columbus, Cherokee Co., Kans., son of Daniel Hill and Robin Louise (Kohley) Buttram. (2) Nathan Daniel, born Aug. 8, 1981, in the Cox Medical Center in Springfield, Greene Co., Mo. He joined the U. S. Army on May 31, 2000, for 6 years and was at Fort Bragg, N. C., in 2002. (3) Joshua David, born Nov. 30, 1982, in the Cox Medical Center in Springfield, Greene Co., Mo. He was attending the Drury College in Springfield, Mo., in 2002. (4) Marissa Jean, born Mar. 15, 1987, in the Mount Vernon Clinic in Mount Vernon, Lawrence Co., Mo.

Angelena Jean Kirchner graduated at the Bolivar High School in 1981 and then attended the Southwest Baptist University in Bolivar for 2 years. She married (1) May 23, 1982, in the 1st Assembly of God Church in Bolivar, Mo., Ray Ike Mollet. He was born Oct. 9, 1951, in the Audrain Medical Center in Mexico, Audrain Co., Mo., and is a son of John Adolphus Mollet and Mildred [NMN] Sweitzer. Ray and Angelena were divorced on Sept. 11, 1997, in the courthouse in Mexico, Mo. They had two sons: (1) Glen Roy, born Aug. 30, 1983, in the Audrain Medical Center in Mexico, Audrain Co., Mo. (2) Mike Martin, born Nov. 24, 1986, in the University of Mo. Hospital and Clinics in Columbia, Boone Co., Mo.

Angelena Jean Kirchner married (2) July 25, 1998, in the 1st Assembly of God Church in Centralia, Boone Co., Mo., Johnya "John" Paul Hirsch. He was born Sept. 8, 1954, in the Boone Co. Hospital in Columbia, Boone Co., Mo., and is a son of Joseph Travis Paul Raymond Hirsch and Betty Goldie Davis. They have 1 son: (3) Jesse John Seth, born May 31, 2002, in the Audrain Medical Center in Mexico, Audrain Co., Mo.

Roy Stanley Kirchner, III, attended grade school in Bolivar and attended the Bolivar High School for 2 years. He is unmarried and was living in Clinton, Henry Co., Mo., in 2002.

Compiled and typed by Roy Stanley Kirchner, Jr., 604 South Lillian Ave., Bolivar, Mo. 65613-2330, e-mail royk@ipa.net, phone 417-326-5626, on July 21, 2002.

LADD – Amanda Anna Marie Bauer (Jan. 28, 1888) married Perry Ladd (Aug. 22, 1888) on Dec. 12, 1912. To this union three girls were born: Irene (Aug. 15, 1914-April 20, 2002), Delphia (Feb. 2, 1916-Feb. 19, 1994) and Jewel (Jan. 13, 1918-). They also had a son, Perry Gilbert (Aug. 21, 1920-Nov. 16, 1920).

Perry had tuberculosis, therefore was unable to work; in fact he could barely get a good breath of air. There was no government aid in the '20s, so neighbors and friends helped the family as much as possible. Times were hard, but young men in the neighborhood cut wood and hunted wild game to help the Ladds make their own canned goods and preserved fruit last through the winter. When anyone butchered a hog, the meat and lard were shared with them. Wheat and corn that had been ground at the Goodnight Mill into flour and cornmeal were divided also. Perry Gilbert was born with tuberculosis and lived less than three months. When Tom White heard of the baby's death, he walked up the road to offer condolences and found Perry out at the woodpile, sitting on a stick of wood, wiring the soles of his shoes together so they would be presentable for the baby's funeral the next day.

Marcus and Amanda White and Irene Ladd Salkil

On Jan. 12, 1921, Perry died and Amanda found herself with three small girls to raise. She had a milk cow, also a few chickens and, with neighbors helping, she managed. The girls went to Sunset School, later returning to teach there, and things got better for the family.

As school children trudged down the road, they were greeted with the wonderful aroma of baking bread as they neared Amanda's house. Sometimes, if you were lucky, you were invited in to sample one of the hot rolls and as times got better, there was orange marmalade. The children were always welcome to stop in and warm themselves in the winter, and in hot weather, a cup of cool water from the well was a refreshing treat as they headed home. In the late '30s or early '40s, Amanda married James Marcus White (Oct. 3, 1870) and moved into a little white house. She did beautiful embroidery work and made sure every girl in the community had a pair of snowy white pillowcases (made out of feed sacks), delicately embroidered, to add to her hope chest. Today, 50 or 60 years later, you can still find some of her handiwork in a lot of homes around Sunset and Van.

Marcus died Feb. 21, 1944 and once again Amanda found herself alone, but she gathered her courage around her and plodded on down the road of life. Another generation of children were invited in to eat the delicious bread and get a cool drink from the well. She was always willing to help a neighbor with the birth of a baby, or if someone became ill, she was a compassionate nurse. No matter if it was day or night, she was ready to help.

In the early '50s, she married Charles L. Steinshouer (Sept. 4, 1893). They spent their twilight years in the little white house.

Amanda died on March 31, 1976, leaving Charley alone. He moved to town when he became unable to drive and died Jan. 18, 1983.

The little white house has been empty for two decades now. The barn fell down years ago and weeds grow where pretty hollyhocks once bloomed. Sometimes, as you walk down the road, you can almost smell fresh bread baking, and long for a cool drink of water from the well. *Submitted by Verna Overcash Barbour*

LANDRETH – DAYS IN THE LIFE OF A SMALL TOWN POLICEMAN

Federal agents with guns hid on roofs of the buildings as a special, presidential train rumbled into Bolivar, MO. An armed guard, who was riding on top of one of the train cars, watched the crowd as it descended upon the train. President Harry S. Truman, President Gallegos from Venezuela and other dignitaries gazed out of the coach window.

Today, July 5, 1948, was the third day of Simon Bolivar Days with a colorful parade, square dancing in the street and other festivities. The most significant event of the day was the dedication of the granite statue of Simon Bolivar, which was given to Bolivar because it was the largest US town named after this historic figure.

Standing amid the 9:30 a.m. ceremonies of speeches from the two presidents and other dignitaries was a tall man in a police uniform, who was quietly surveying the thousands of people for any militia action. Ira Landreth, the town's elected official, was also guarding the galvanized water bucket from which the presidents drank. This was just as important a job as the gunmen who surveyed the crowd from the building tops and the secret service men who hid themselves in the crowd.

"This is the highlight of my career," thought Ira as he stood near the president's water. His gun was in his holster and his billy club ready for action. "I'm a part of this most important day in the history of Bolivar," he told himself.

Most days Ira Landreth would be

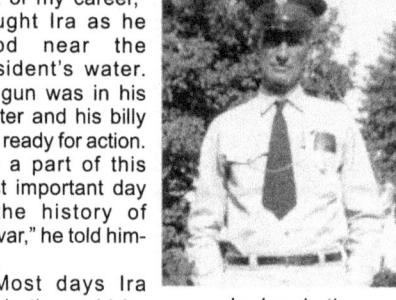

Ira Landreth

seen walking the quiet streets of the Bolivar square, keeping peace among the town inhabitants. His 12-hour shift, from 6 a.m. to 6 p.m., consisted of making the people safe, secure and happy. Perhaps the biggest crime was the loitering of a drunk on the street corner. Ira would simply take the drunk home in his police car to sleep off the alcoholic effect. Crime was so low in this serene town that Ira never carried a gun, only a billy club in his back pocket. Elsie, his wife, would comment about him wearing out so many back pockets.

Ira's son, Jack, remembers his policeman dad making lunch time an exciting time of each day. Ira would cruise home in his '49 black Ford police car, and just as he approached the block near his home, he hit the siren and lights, bringing pleasure to his small son.

Ira Landreth took pride in keeping his small "Mayberry" town safe until he suffered a heart attack which forced him to retire. John Playter, Director of City Services, called Ira a "dependable and dedicated elected official with a sense of humor." Many of the old timers will remember Ira Landreth's smiles and kind words as he made his visits around the town square of Bolivar, MO. *Submitted by Retha Wright, Wanda Murphy and Jack Landreth*

LASTER – Levi Bradley "Lee" Laster and Bertha Jane (Harper) Laster moved to Sunset in Polk County in the early 1930s, following Bertha's sister Gladys and her husband Russell Bryant from Oklahoma. They left Oklahoma because of the "Dust Bowl" of the 1930s. Lee Laster and Bertha Jane Harper were married in Oklahoma in 1924. Lee Laster was born in Oklahoma and was the son of John Neuton Laster and Matilda Harriet Dyer. John Neuton Laster was a descendant of Robert Laster, who was born in Virginia in 1642. This family migrated through Virginia, North Carolina and finally to Johnson County, AR where Lee's grandfather, Stephen F. Laster, was a judge.

Lee served in WWI in France with Company D, Eighth Machine Gun Battalion, US Army. He participated in the Battle of St. Mihiel under the command of General John J. Pershing, where he was wounded and a victim of mustard gas. The damage caused to his lungs by the mustard gas later resulted in his death. Lee and Bertha had three children: Robert Lee, Carl Bradley and Nelda Carol. Lee and Bertha were close neighbors and friends of Fred Fisher. When Lee was near death, leaving by train for a VA Hospital in New Mexico in 1938, he asked Fred to watch over his family after he was gone. This Fred did for several years, then he and Bertha married, having two children of their own: Nancy Marie and Christine.

Bertha Jane Harper was born near Chelsea, OK. She was the daughter of Robert E. Lee Harper of Harper, MO and Nancy Elizabeth Owlsey of Cross Timbers, MO. Robert E. L. Harper was the son of Jacob Talley Harper and Margaret Copenhaver. Jacob Talley Harper was the son of John M. and Nancy (Williams) Harper. "This Harper family was among the very first pioneer settlers in the area of St. Clair County, MO. They felled trees for timber for their homes. Through the spinning wheel and loom came their clothing. When their youngest child George W. Harper was only a baby in arms, his father died, April 15, 1839, leaving his wife and family to rough it alone. Nancy Harper knew no such word as fail and bravely shouldered each added burden. During the horrible reign of the bushwhackers she saw her home pillaged, then stood by to see the house go up in flames. The only thing saved was the old family Bible which one man among the rioters allowed her to carry away." - Excerpts of the Aug. 27, 1935 issue of the *St. Clair County Democrat*.

Nancy Elizabeth (Owsley) Harper was the daughter of William Burton Owsley and May Pauline Walker. William B. Owsley was a direct descendant of Major Thomas Owsley, who arrived September 1677 in the Colony of Virginia.

Bertha Jane Harper was the direct descendant of three Revolutionary War veterans: Major Thomas Copenhaver, Private John Owsley and Private Martin Luther Miller. *Submitted by Nelda C. Darnell*

LATIKER – Sandy Latiker came from the state of Tennessee to Polk County. His wife died in childbirth. They had one son, Henry Franklin, who was born Sept. 26, 1876 and died April 16, 1964. He was raised by Hiram Martin and Sarah E. Martin. Hiram was born Feb. 9, 1836 and died April 3, 1915. Sarah was born Nov. 24, 1838 and died August 10, 1907. They came from Indiana to Humansville, MO.

Henry Franklin married Aurora Bell Manuel; she was born Dec. 10, 1877 and died July 3, 1938. He farmed and raised horses. He was buried in Humansville, MO. The children of Henry Franklin and Aurora Bell are, as follows: Dottie May, Naomi Joe, Mary Elizabeth, Virgil Lee and Fredrick Martin.

Dottie May married James Hammons. Naomi Joe married Edward Earl Messer. Mary Elizabeth married Lake Sloan. Virgil Lee married Marjorie?.

Fredrick Martin was born March 22, 1918 in Humansville, MO. He married Velma B. Henry on

Henry Franklin Latiker

May 9, 1941. They moved to Bolivar in 1943. Their children are Fredrick Leon, Brenda Darlene and Jackie Darrell. He passed away on Dec. 23, 1971. He had worked at Bill Roberts Chevrolet in Bolivar for 30 years.

Fredrick Leon married Roseann Marteniz and they have two children, Anthony Shawn and Lisa Renee.

Brenda Darlene married Billy Berlin Pate and they have two children, Tammy Lynette and Timothy Martin. Tammy Pate married Wade Jerome Bolen and they had twins, Brittani Brooke and Brandon Van. Jackie Darnell's children are Amy Elizabeth, Michael Matthew, Nicholas Darrell and J. D. *Submitted by Darlene Truitt*

LAWSON – John W. Lawson was born in Tennessee in May 1817 and came to Polk County, MO in the early 1800s. He first came to Miller County, MO in the 1840s and is enumerated on the 1850 census there. He next appears on the Taney County, MO census in 1860 and the Pulaski County, MO census in 1870. His parents, Nathan Lawson and Christian High, were married in Charlotte County, VA on Aug. 26, 1802 after which they lived in Kentucky and Tennessee and had a family of nine children. They were David Lawson, born 1809; Andrew Lawson, born Dec. 25, 1812; Nathan Lawson, born March 5, 1813; Martha Lawson, born 1814; William Lawson, born 1815; John W. Lawson, born May 1817; Margaret Lawson, born 1818; George W. Lawson, born 1832; and Calvin Lawson.

The parents of Nathan Lawson have never been proven but there is strong evidence that an older Nathan and wife Mildred, who came from Charlotte County, VA to Washington County, KY, were his parents. This older Nathan was named as a son in the will of a George Lawson of Charlotte County, VA dated Sept. 12, 1786. Christian High was the daughter of David High (born March 2, 1725, died December 1794), Charlotte County, VA) and Susannah Westmoreland (born April 30, 1729, died after 1794 in Virginia).

John W. Lawson and Martha Caroline Gibbs, daughter of Samuel and Jane Gibbs, were married on May 31, 1840 in Blount County, TN and they had nine children that grew to maturity. The first two children were born in Tennessee, the others in Missouri. Their children were Columbus P. Lawson, born March 23, 1841, died March 8, 1901, married Susan Howell on June 11, 1865, Polk County; William Fulton Lawson, born July 4, 1843, died March 16, 1916, married first Rutha in 1860, married second Sarah Elizabeth Wilson on Aug. 6, 1871; Martha Jane Lawson, born July 16, 1844, died Nov. 20, 1926, married Caleb Witt on Jan. 3, 1867, Polk County; Sarah Mary Lawson, born 1848; James R. Lawson, born August 1852, married Mary M. Franks on Dec. 3, 1876, Collin County, TX; Joseph Wright Lawson, born Feb. 18, 1857, died Oct. 11, 1929, married Mary Tabitha Wilson on Nov. 9, 1884; Henry P. Lawson, born Feb. 18, 1857, married Anna Helen Kenning on July 8, 1881, Collin County, TX; Ruth Eveline Lawson, born 1860, died about 1898, married Umphrey Mitchel Jones on Sept. 12, 1880, Collin County, TX; Margaret Melvina Lawson, born Feb. 11, 1862, died July 27, 1949, married John T. Jones on Aug. 5, 1883, Polk County.

Both John W. Lawson and his son Columbus served in the Union Army during the Civil War. It was said that John proudly wore his blue uniform at every opportunity throughout his entire life.

The Lawson family moved from Pulaski County, MO in the late 1870s to Collin County, TX where they are found on the 1880 census. Two brothers, Umphrey and John Jones, moved from Missouri to Texas with the Lawsons and are listed in their household in 1880 as boarders. While in Collin County, TX, Umphrey Jones and Ruth Eveline Lawson were married. They were Harlan's great-grandparents. All returned to Missouri before 1883 when John Jones and Margaret Melvina Lawson were married in Polk County. Even though the Lawsons appeared to have moved often, after their return to Polk County in the 1880s, they lived the remainder of their lives there. So did most of their children. The date of Martha's death is unknown, however John died May 13, 1904 and both are buried in the Enon Cemetery. *Submitted by Harlan G. Jones*

LEE - Asa Lee was born in Newark, Licking County, OH, July 21, 1819 and came to Bolivar in 1844, one of the pioneers of Polk County, MO. He married his first wife, Elizabeth Stephens, April 8, 1841, and she died in 1846. He married Ann Douglass McCracken, April 17, 1853. She died March 30, 1893. Asa, a skilled mechanic and wagonmaker by trade, was a faithful member of the Methodist Episcopal Church. He died April 5, 1903 and was buried in Greenwood Cemetery. He was survived by three children: Leander and Robert B. of Bolivar and Gabriel (Mrs. Gabie Frazier) of Boone County, MO.

Robert Bird Lee was born July 24, 1856 in Bolivar. "Uncle Bob," a member of the Methodist Church and the Modern Woodmen of America, played alto horn in the Bolivar town band. His occupations included farming, working in a livery stable, and helping his son in the Lee Store in Bolivar. Jan. 21, 1883, he married Rhoda Ann Rush, born Feb. 8, 1855, the daughter of Daniel Webster and Rhoda J. Chapman Rush of Louisburg, MO. Rhoda had taught school at Louisburg and was a member of the Baptist Church. They had three children: William Bird in 1883, Letha Ella in 1886 and Rena Faye in 1889, who died of typhoid fever in 1898.

Known to family as Gramp and Mother Lee, R. B. and Rhoda lived in Bolivar until 1934 when they moved to Miami, OK to live with their daughter's family (Mrs. J. A. Robinson). Rhoda died there Sept. 4, 1936, and R. B., Nov. 27, 1943. They were buried in Bolivar in Greenwood Cemetery.

William Bird Lee was born Dec. 8, 1883, north of Bolivar. He was educated at Warrensburg State Teachers College and Missouri State Normal School, receiving an AB degree in 1910. He taught country school and later served as Polk County Superintendent of Schools for two terms. Other pursuits included: salesman for Welch Paper Company of Springfield, MO; clothier in the Lee Store in Bolivar, salesman for Franklin and New York Life Insurance and representative for Silver Burdette Publishing Company.

W. B. was a member of the Methodist Church and served as choir director and Bible class teacher. He was a leader in the community and played trombone in the Bolivar town band.

Jan. 8, 1908, he married Pearl Runyan in Bolivar. Pearl Ann, the fifth child of William Ahab and Eliza Emily (Vannice) Runyan, was born Sept. 5, 1886 near Bear Creek. She attended rural school, meeting her future husband when he was her teacher. Pearl completed a course in Normal Training and taught in rural schools of the Bolivar area. A Baptist in her youth, she became a Methodist after her marriage and was active in the Ladies' Aid Society. She was a 50-year member of the Mizpah Chapter, Order of Eastern Star.

Of their three daughters, Rena Ann, born Dec. 31, 1908, and married to J. Ralph Braithwait, was the only one who continued to live in Bolivar. Letha Faye, born May 29, 1911, married Earl Eugene Josten. Grace Emily, born Dec. 22, 1914, married Morris H. Aliber.

Pearl Ann Lee and William Bird Lee, daughters Faye, Grace and Rena, circa 1926

In 1927 W.B. began his 18 years of representing Silver Burdette textbooks in Iowa and South Dakota, prompting the family move from Bolivar to Des Moines, IA in 1928. "Bird" was affiliated with the Masonic order, maintaining his membership in the three Masonic bodies at Bolivar and in Abou Ben Adhem Temple of the Shrine in Springfield, holding the 32nd degree in the Scottish Rite and Noble of the Mystic Shrine. In addition, he was Chief Executive of the Iowa Schoolmen's Golf Association for 12 years. His second heart attack within two years caused his death on March 24, 1945. Pearl died from pancreatic cancer July 20, 1974, in a hospital in Belmond, IA. Both she and W.B. were buried in Bolivar in Greenwood Cemetery. *Submitted by Ann Riggs*

LEGAN - The Legan family first settled in Dallas County near Long Lane. Jacob Legan moved his family to Halfway where he operated a flour mill in the late 1800s. Jacob and wife Martha Miller had nine children: Stella, Jessie, Ernie, Harrison, Edith, Della, William, Lemuel and Rosa. Many descendants from Jacob Legan are still living in Polk County.

Jacob's son, Harrison, married Mary Lou Campbell and settled in Halfway. They had two sons, Adolphus and Dwight. Adolphus had the nickname of "Bulldog" because as a boy he won a fight with a bigger boy who had been picking on him. Later, many people knew him as "Dog Legan" as the nickname stuck. Adolphus and Dwight graduated from Halfway High School

John and Martha Caroline (Gibbs) Lawson

and then fought in WWII. Adolphus married June Jones during the war. Following the war they settled on a farm northeast of Halfway and raised two sons, Ken and Kyle. Dwight married Pearl Lane of Halfway and moved to Springfield where he raised two children, Lyndol and Vickie.

In 1954 Adolphus was elected to the Missouri House of Representatives and served until 1958, when he became a rural mail carrier for the USPS at Halfway. He was well known around Halfway for his sense of humor. Adolphus was a charter member of the Halfway Lions Club.

Following graduation from Halfway High School, Ken worked five months in Alaska. In January 1965 Ken enrolled at University of Missouri in Columbia where he graduated with a degree in animal science. He married Becky Bodenhamer. Ken served in the US Army where he was a food inspector. In 1971 Ken returned to farm in Polk County. Ken and Becky raised two children, Brock and Stephanie. Ken was elected to the Missouri House of Representatives in 1981 and served through 2002, where he held the office of Minority Whip and was the senior member of the Budget Committee. Becky has taught fourth grade for 26 years at Halfway R-III School. Brock and his wife, Sonja Brinning, make their home in Macon, MO with their daughters, Callie and Shae. Stephanie and husband, Tom Howard, live near Jasper, MO.

Mary Lou Legan with sons Adolphus and Dwight, 1940

Kyle graduated from Halfway High School in 1967. He married Rita Farmer. Kyle is a letter carrier for the USPS in Bolivar. Kyle and Rita live in Bolivar where they raised two children, Mark and Amber. Rita is the librarian at Bolivar High School. Kyle has served on the Bolivar School Board for several years. Mark Legan and wife Angela Payne, are making their home north of Bolivar, where they are raising their sons, Dillon and Drew. Amber and Wayne Sergent live east of Bolivar with their son, Luke.

The Ken Legan family are active members of Halfway Baptist Church, where Ken serves as deacon. The Kyle Legan family are active members of Calvary Missionary Baptist Church, where Kyle serves as deacon.

The Legan family has lived in Polk County for many years. They enjoy living in Polk County and find it a good place to raise their families. *Submitted by Ken Legan*

LEININGER - The Leiningers moved to Bolivar from Illinois in December 1984 as Ray was called to pastor First Baptist Church. Bolivar quickly became home and they began to rediscover and appreciate many of their Missouri roots.

Ray's maternal grandparents, Thomas Henry McNeil and Willie Maud Black, were from Jackson and Bates Counties, MO. He was a lawyer for the KC transit system. His paternal grandfather, William B. Leininger from Berks County, PA, came to Jackson County about 1895. Grandmother Annie (MacKay) Leininger emigrated from Scotland to Jackson County at the age of 9 in 1884. Ray's parents, Louis Lee and Ollie Frances, were born in Liberty and Kansas City. In 1922 Lee was called to preach. Ray is fifth of six children born in St. Louis, August 19, 1940. In 1945 the family moved to East St. Louis, IL where Lee pastored 15th St. Baptist Church, until he died in 1972.

Judy's maternal grandparents, Emmet Arthur and Phaymie (Caldermeyer) Pride from Jasper, IN, moved to E. St. Louis in 1910. Her paternal grandparents, Webb and Ethel (Davis) Tipton, were from Maries County, MO. The Davises started from Pittsfield, IL for Arizona in a covered wagon in the 1890's to get Grandma Davis into a better climate for asthma, but they stopped in Missouri. The Tiptons came from Tennessee, descendants of Col. John Tipton, a Revolutionary-era military man and politician, a leader in the movement to make East Tennessee a separate state. By 1910 the Tipton clan had grown, times were hard and several years of Gasconade River flooding convinced the younger generation to leave the farm. Webb and Ethel moved to E. St. Louis. Webb found work at George S. Mepham Paint Mill, where Missouri iron ore was milled into paint pigment. Eventually, his brothers and father Jacob worked at the paint mill as did Judy's father from 1936-79. By 1940 Webb was called to preach and pastored 15th Street Baptist Church until Ray's dad became pastor in 1945.

Ray graduated from high school in O'Fallon, IL and received a BS in mechanical engineering at the University of Missouri School of Mines and Metallurgy, Rolla 1958-62. Judy graduated from E. St. Louis Senior High School and Washington University, St. Louis with a BA in elementary education in 1962. Ray and Judy married on Oct. 20, 1962 and left for two years in the army. Ray served as the engineer instructor at the Air Defense School, Ft. Bliss, TX.

In 1967 Ray was called to preach. He earned Master of Divinity and Doctor of Ministry degrees from Southwestern Baptist Theological Seminary, Ft. Worth, TX. He pastored Hennepin Baptist Church, Hennepin, OK 1971-73 and College Ave. Baptist Church, Normal, IL 1973-84.

Ray and Judy have three children, Andrew Neil (Sept. 29, 1963) and Elizabeth serve as Southern Baptist missionaries in the Republic of Belarus. They have three daughters, Hannah, Rachel and Rebekah. Elizabeth Ann Moore (June 2, 1965) is a licensed social worker, wife of a pastor, Steve, and mother of four: Katy, Nathan, Emily and Claire. They live in Port St. Lucie, FL. Sarah Ann Jones (May 3, 1967) is a physical therapist at CMH in Bolivar. She and Tom, an optometrist, have four children: Maddy, Abby, Sam and John.

Bolivar became home not only for Ray and Judy, but also for Judy's parents, Ray and Wilma Tipton, who moved to Bolivar in 1988; an immense blessing as Judy is an only child. They died in 1994 and 1999 and are buried in Greenwood Cemetery. Tom and Sarah moved to Bolivar in 1998, making four generations in town.

Ray and Judy say, "Our move to Bolivar has been a blessing from God. We love Bolivar and thank God every day. It is our desire to stay here until the Lord calls us home." *Submitted by Ray Leininger*

LEJEUNE - Louis Joseph Lejeune was the first Lejeune to come to Polk County, MO in 1884. He was born Feb. 19, 1844 in France and died Nov.

30, 1922 in Polk County. He married on Oct. 19, 1874 in Illinois to Mary Margaret Francois, born Feb. 5, 1857 in St. Louis County, MO and died July 24, 1937 in Polk County. Louis was the son of Christopher Lejeune, born 1808 in Alsace-Loraine, France, died in 1890 and Marie Ann Barbier, born 1819 in France, died in 1852. Mary Margaret was the daughter of Joseph Francois and Barbara Thomassin.

When the family landed in New Orleans circa 1847/8, Louis was 4 years old. Christopher is in the 1850 New Orleans, LA census and is listed as a shoemaker. He supposedly had three wives, two of whom were Barbier sisters. He planned to take his young family to St. Louis via the Mississippi River. His wife, Marie Ann, died on the trip. Family tradition says he returned to New Orleans and put the children in an orphanage. Later he returned and took them to Illinois. The children are living in neighboring households in the 1860 St. Clair County, IL census.

Louis became a member of the Catholic Church in Cahokia, IL when quite young. He was in the Civil War and served the greater part of the war as a teamster and endured many hardships of war. He lived in Mooney Township near Pleasant Hope in the 1900 census. In 1910 and 1920 he was in Benton Township where his occupation is listed as farmer.

Louis and Mary Lejeune had 11 children: Louis Joseph, born Sept. 12, 1875, Clinton County, IL, died Aug. 11, 1941, married Vina Barnett, Feb. 28, 1897; Alfred C., born March 8, 1878, died March 11, 1966, married Lucy Dukes, Dec. 29, 1901; Frank V., born Dec. 15, 1880, Quincy, IL, died June 4, 1962, Ventura, CA, married Chloe Faulkner; August L., born April 20, 1883, Belleville, IL, died Nov. 29, 1959, Greene County, married Nora Oglesby, Oct. 22,

Sitting: L to R: Louis Joseph and Mary Margaret Francois LeJeune. Row 2: Rosa Matilda Gorden, Jessie Walter, Volina (Linnie) Van Horn, Clara Mabel Shackleton, William Charles (Willie), Josie May Viles.
Row 3: Frank Victor (Frankie), August Lee (Gus), Alfred Christfor, and Louis Joseph (Lou).

1905; William C., born Sept. 16, 1885 near Slagle, MO, died Jan. 6, 1957, Polk County, married Helen Shackelton, Dec. 27, 1908; infant son, born Oct. 22, 1887, Polk County; Rosa Matilda; Josie Mae, born April 17, 1891, Polk County, died April 12, 1976, Polk County, married Charley Viles, Feb. 5, 1911; Jesse W., born Oct.. 1, 1893, died Oct. 30, 1982, Visalia, CA, married Edith Blankenship in 1914; Clara Mabel, born Oct. 27, 1896, died Nov. 27, 1991, married Floyd Shackelton, Feb. 3, 1917; Linnie Agnes, born Nov. 20, 1900, died July 15, 1971, married Cleo Van Horn, March 14, 1920.

Their daughter Rosa was born Sept. 2, 1888 in Polk County, died June 3, 1970 in Greene County, MO, buried in Schofield Cemetery. She married Wilby Gorden, Nov. 6, 1910. They lived near Halfway in the Schofield community and farmed. They had two children. Geneice Gorden, born Aug. 12, 1916, died Feb. 20, 1996 in Polk County, married Wade Voris and had three sons.

Larry Gene married Hazel Dulin, had three children: Steven Jay Voris married Rebecca Harrison, three children: Timothy Michael Voris, Vincent Josiah Voris, Alethea Marie Voris; Dana Kay Voris married Matthew Bedwell, two children: Joseph Michael Bedwell, Nicholas Matthew Bedwell; Tony Ray Voris married Paula Runge, two children: Wade Alan Voris, Drew McKinley Voris.

Jerry Wade married Linda Wagoner, one child: Louise Renee Voris married Mark Walters, four children: Sarah Elizabeth Walters, Laura Kathryn Walters, Hannah Kaye Walters, Claire Elaine Walters.

Wilby Dean married Mary Ballew, two children: Jeffrey Dean Voris, Stacey Renee Voris married Alex Warden.

Louis Gorden, born Oct. 13, 1918, married Faye Jones. Louis married second, Vera Quick Farmer in 1990. One child, Ben Gorden married Karen Kay Pritchard, two children: Christa Kay Gorden married Darin Owens (div'd), two children, Katelyn Ann Owens, Kassidy Ann Owens; Brian Ray Gorden. *Submitted by Dana Voris Bedwell*

LEMMON - John Smith Lemmon was born in 1811 in Barren County, KY to Jacob Lemmon and Mary Polly Smith Lemmon. He married Permelia Wallace in Henry County, TN in 1828. In 1828 he, his father Jacob, his brother Thomas and his cousin William H. Lemmon came to what is now Springfield, Greene County, MO (*History of Hickory, Polk, Cedar, Dade and Barton Counties* by Goodspeed, page 670).

By 1831, John Smith had relocated to Polk County, MO. In 1835 he built the first saw mill on the Sac River. He and Permelia built a large brick home ("The Old Brick") near the mill, prior to the Civil War. (State of Missouri, *History of Polk County*). It was here that he and Permelia raised 11 of their 14 children to adulthood. This home is located three miles southwest of Morrisville near the Sac River and is still occupied.

According to the biography of his son Dr. Jefferson Lemmon, during the Civil War John Smith "went South with his property and was never heard from again (*History of Hickory, Polk, Cedar, Dade and Barton Counties, Missouri,* 1889 by Goodspeed, pages 670, 671). Although he is never again mentioned in relation to this family, evidence indicates that he left Polk County with Nancy Jane Hambleton Hinkle, who had lived on a neighboring farm and went to Colorado. In Colorado he and Nancy had seven children. It is believed that John Smith died in February 1885 in either Montrose or more likely Crawford, Delta County, CO.

Jacob, Polly, Permelia and several of her children are buried in Old Union Cemetery in Polk County.

A more complete account of the ancestry and history of John Smith Lemmon and his families can be found in the Lemmon file at the Polk County Genealogical Society Library in Bolivar, MO.

LEMMON – Joe Liss Lemmon was born to Mayhew and Lera Mae (Hurd) on Dec. 15, 1929 in the Morrisville area. Joe later moved to Bolivar and married June Charlotte Smith on May 3, 1951. June's parents were Hershel and Ruth (Sage) Smith. Joe and June were blessed with six children: Joe Dale, Patricia Lou, Jerry Glenn, Pamela Lee, Penny Lynn and Jacqueline Kay. Joe worked for various businesses including Standard Mill, Bolivar Grocery Company and Foremost. June dedicated herself to working at home, raising their children. In 1963, Joe joined with Bob Jump in the ownership of Jump's Skelly Station. Later, Joe became the sole owner and changed the name to Lemmon's Service Station.

Joe served two terms as Bolivar ward councilman in the early 1970s. He was elected mayor of Bolivar in 1973 and served in that office until 1991 and then again from 1993 until 1995. When Joe first became mayor, the city had three policemen, but no police cars. They used a city maintenance truck to patrol at night. City funds were very limited; in fact, half of the city street lights had been disconnected to save funds. It looked as though Joe would have to lay off the city's only two maintenance workers. In order to avoid laying off the much needed workers, Joe went to Polk County Bank and took out a $10,000 loan which allowed the city to cover its expenses. A city sales tax had recently failed at the polls, but was placed on the ballot again as quickly as legally possible. Fortunately, it passed.

With the new funds from the sales tax, Joe and the city councilmen were able to accomplish many things, including the paving of many city streets, taking over the responsibilities of the cemetery and Dunnegan Park, building a sports complex and raising the city water towers. Joe also served on a committee to gain funding and approval for a hospital and Citizens Memorial Hospital became a reality in 1982.

In the late 1980s David Delarue, a Polk County native, gave $3,000,000 to the Polk County area. A portion of this gift was designated for the City of Bolivar and significantly increased the city's budget. The city maintained the airport located on west Broadway Street and then in 1992 began work on a new airport at its current location three miles east of town on Highway 32. A new building to house the fire department was also built and completed in 1983.

Since the office of mayor was a part-time position, Joe operated the "mayor's office" from his service station. He was on-call 24 hours a day and residents could call him at the service station or at home. The city was in need of a new building to house its expanding departments and of course, a more official mayor's office. And so, the current City Hall was completed in 1990.

Bolivar's population grew greatly during these years and saw the opening of many new businesses. In 1993 it was recognized as one of the 100 Best Small Towns in America.

Joe also served for many years on the Chamber of Commerce and for 25 years on the Ozarks Community Action Corporation. He was very proud to receive the Bolivar Civic Service Award in 1995.

In 1993, Joe closed his service station and then retired from being mayor in 1995. He and his wife, June, remain in Bolivar and enjoy spending time with their family, which now includes 14 grandchildren and two great-grandchildren.

Jody and his wife, Vicki (Coffey), have two children: Jody Junior (JJ) and Christy. JJ and his wife, Shannon, have two daughters, Chloe and Delaney.

Patty died in an automobile accident in 1969 at the age of 15

Jerry and his wife, Rita (Hubbert), have two children, Keisha and Hank.

Pam and her husband, Roger Grider, have five children: Jason Cooper, Tesa, Tanya, Fable and Landon.

Penny and her husband, Doug Brandt, have two children: Patty and Tony.

Jackie and her husband, Tony Hitchcock, have three children: Mackenzie, Macey and Cooper. *Submitted by Jackie Hitchcock, daughter of Joe and June Lemmon*

LEMONS - Bert and Jewel Lemons moved to Halfway, MO in April of 1943. They had previously rented a home just over the county line. Bert and Jewel were both schoolteachers but after they married on May 12, 1934, they soon started a family and, of course, Jewel quit her job. Wendell Eugene was born on April 11, 1936 and Ransom Jay was born on April 16, 1939. The farmhouse on top of the hill was a very exciting venture for the family. It was the first house they had ever owned. Ardys Lee was born on July 25, 1943 and that completed their family.

Times were hard growing up on the farm. Bert's teaching salary wasn't great and the family raised cattle and chickens, and had a garden and orchard for extra food and money. Ardys and Wendell both took medicine. Bert kept going to school and finally earned his Master's Degree in 1956. He then got a job as a superintendent and could earn a higher salary.

Jewel and Bert Lemons, May 12, 1984, their 50th Wedding Anniversary

Some of the family memories are that in the fall they would sell calves in Springfield and then go shopping and buy clothes. Jewel would buy two dozen donuts at Kresge's for 35 cents a dozen. Ardys loved the ones with chocolate icing, and remembers great times.

The family's sources of entertainment were going to the Lucky 13 drive-in in Bolivar, the skating rink in Halfway and relatives getting together for family dinners. The times they went to the drive-in were great; the whole family would go and Wendell seemed to enjoy it so much. Thursday nights the whole car could get in for one dollar.

Wendell passed away in January of 1956. Bert and Jewel had worried about what would happen to Wendell if they died first. Ardys had told her parents she would see after him and Ransom said he would also care for him, but that was not to be. After Wendell died, Jewel went back to teaching. She went to night school and summer school to finish her degree. The children were always very proud of her for that, knowing how hard it was for Jewel to go to school with young people.

Ransom was very popular in school. He played baseball, basketball and he ran in track. He was very considerate of his younger sister and would, on occasion, even double date. He was involved in a car wreck in 1959 and was injured badly. He was in a coma for two weeks and was never the same. He died in February of 1961. These were sad times for the family and Ardys noticed her parents aging before her eyes.

From 1961 to 1963 Ardys attended Southwest Baptist College. That was a good time in her life and she often brought friends from college out to the farm for one of Jewel's home-cooked meals. Sometimes there would be four or five extra for Sunday dinner. Bert and Jewel both seemed to enjoy her friends talking about their classes and college life.

Bert and Jewel retired from teaching in the early 1970s. They loved retirement and living on the farm. They were very involved in the Christian Church and community work.

Ardys got her degree in 1965 and moved to Kansas City. She soon found a teaching job, teaching English and social studies. After getting her Master's Degree in 1971, she became a high school counselor. Jewel died in 1992 after a long illness and Bert died in 1996. After working for 32 years, Ardys Kenyan is now retired and living in Shawnee, KS and still owns her parents' beloved farm and comes down on weekends as often as she can. *Submitted by Ardys Kenyan*

LEWIS - Franklin Lewis was born in Rondo, MO on Oct. 6, 1900. His parents were Fillmore Lewis and Ella Breeden. He had one brother, Neal, who died at 34 of stomach cancer. He also had two sisters, Gertrude and Lela. Gertrude married Jim Stevenson. Lela died at 19 from typhoid fever.

When Frank was 13, he moved with his family to Mulberry, AR. He rode a horse while his family was in the wagon.

Frank married Beulah and had two children, Everett and Mary Lois. Everett joined the Air Force and made a career of it. Later, Frank and Beulah were divorced.

Staying single for several years, Frank kept himself busy teaching school and playing musical instruments. He was quite a fiddler and while playing at a square dance he met his second wife, Grace Mincher. Frank and Grace were married on June 23, 1935 at Oak Grove Chapel in Cecil, AR.

Frank and Grace Lewis

Grace was born on July 26, 1912 to Ben Mincher and Rachel Evans Mincher. She was an only child. While she was growing up, she lived with her mother, two aunts and an uncle.

Frank and Grace lived in Mulberry, AR and had four children. Jean was born May 13, 1936. During the Depression, Frank moved to California to find work. After he found a job, he sent for his family. They lived in California when the second child was born, Harvey Ray. He was born on June 16, 1937 in Oakland, CA.

They had lived in California for about one year when they moved back to Arkansas. Their third child, Francis Lea, was born on Oct. 12, 1942. Francis passed away when she was 1 month old. She is buried in Cecil at Oak Grove Chapel.

Frank was called up for WWII. He had children at home and was too old to go. He moved his family to Camp Chaffee and became a barber. During that time the fourth child, Bernadean, was born on May 31, 1944.

After the war, they moved back to Arkansas. During his later years, Frank made a living as a commercial fisherman on the Arkansas River.

Frank passed away on Jan. 19, 1954 from stomach cancer. He is buried at Heights Cemetery in Mulberry, AR.

After Frank's death, Grace went to work at the canning factory. She worked there for 10 years. During that time, Jean married Hobert Redd on July 11, 1954. They moved to Halfway, MO. Harvey Ray married Ada Bell Harris. They stayed in Arkansas. Bernadean moved to Missouri with Hobert and Jean and later married Hobert's brother, Ray Dean Redd.

Grace moved to Fort Smith, looking for work and found a job at Saint Edwards Hospital. She worked there for 20 years. During that time, she met and married her second husband, Cleo Fullen. After three years of marriage, he passed away.

Grace spent the rest of her years between Arkansas and Missouri. She broke both hips at separate times. After the last hip, she moved to Halfway. She was taken care of by her daughters until her death on Feb. 20, 2000 from stomach cancer. She is buried at Reed Cemetery south of Halfway. *Submitted by Shae Redd Voris*

John Henry Licklider, 1840-1910, wearing his Confederate War medal

LICKLIDER – John Henry Licklider was the head of the Licklider family of Polk County. He was born Jan. 6, 1840 in Bloomfield, OH, son of Thomas and Jane Melvin Licklider. Both his parents came from old Virginia families that have origins in that state back to colonial times. His family moved to Cooper County, MO where John spent much of his youth. John was a supporter of the Confederate cause in the War Between the States. He was awarded some sort of a medal that he wore on formal occasions through his life.

He married Mary Ann Pike of Polk County, MO on Oct. 1, 1868. They had the following children: Horace Calvin (May 16, 1869 – Nov. 5, 1871); Australia Geneva (Sept. 13, 1870 – July 3, 1882); Allie Babe (March 9, 1872 – April 26, 1946, married Charles Dokes, Oct. 26, 1893); James Monroe (Oct. 25, 1874 – Sept. 28, 1951, married Bertha Loofman, Sept. 8, 1898).

Mary Ann Pike Licklider died in Polk County on July 5, 1878. This left John with a family of young children to raise. John Cook was married to Lorana Caroline Pike, Mary's sister. At about this same time John Cook died, leaving Lorana with her only surviving child of four born to that union, James Thomas Cook (April 25, 1874-Feb. 6, 1947, unmarried). John Henry Licklider and Lorana Caroline Pike Cook were married on Sept. 23, 1879 in Polk County.

John and Lorana lived and supported their families as farmers in Polk County the remainder of their lives. They were strong supporters of the Slagle Missionary Baptist Church. They and many of their descendants are buried in that cemetery.

John and Lorana had the following children: Cora Belle (Sept. 1, 1880 – Oct. 20, 1937, unmarried); Rose Mae (May 7, 1882 – May 18, 1956, married Calvin Slagle, Sept. 27, 1903); Ona Etta (Sept. 25, 1885 – Sept. 11, 1930, married Floyd Mitchell (March 4, 1907); John Flemmer (Feb. 16, 1888 – 1957, unmarried); Laura Ann (June 5, 1889 – Aug. 4, 1943, married Benjamin Freeman Reeves, March 5, 1911); Eddie Lee (June 10, 1891 – March 5, 1945, married Vera Clark, Oct. 20, 1912); Katie (Jan. 24, 1894 – Dec. 13, 1923, married Roane Clark).

John Henry Licklider died in Polk County on Dec. 8, 1910 and his wife, Lorana Caroline Pike Licklider, died on Aug. 8, 1926. *Submitted by Max Reeves*

LIGHTFOOT – Henry Jarrett Lightfoot was born on May 28, 1793 in Virginia. He married Barbara Lambert on June 8, 1819 in Warren County, KY. She was born in 1799 in South Carolina. The family moved to Polk County around 1850. To this union 13 children were born: John, Sarah, David L., Polly, Esau Jackson, Elizabeth, Mahala, Melissa, Melinda, Henry Bannister, Rebecca, Josias, Barbara Dorothy. Henry passed away on July 22, 1861 in Polk County and Barbara in 1865; both are buried in Oak Grove Cemetery near Polk, MO.

Henry Jarrett Lightfoot

Generation 2

John Lightfoot was born on May 13, 1820 in Allen County, KY and married Kezia H. Chapman on June 23, 1842 in Warren County, KY. Kezia was born on Aug. 15, 1822 in Monroe County, KY. To this union 10 children were born: Henry Jackson, Mary Elizabeth, David Nathaniel, John Salatheil, Barbara Malinda, William Alexander, Louisa Frances, infant, Armilda Jane, Zerilda Catherine.

Kezia passed away on June 20, 1891 and John on June 29, 1901; both are buried in Oak Grove Cemetery, Polk County, MO.

Sarah Lightfoot was born 1821 in Simpson County, KY.

David L. Lightfoot was born on Feb. 10, 1823 in Simpson County, KY. He married Sarah Chapman in 1842. To this union seven children were born: David Williams, Carter, Sarah Jane, Jackson B., John Wesley, Henry M. Lightfoot. David's second marriage was to Mahola Taylor on April 5, 1857. She was born in October of 1830. To this union three children were born: Calvin L., Noah W. and Christopher C. Mahola passed away on Nov. 18, 1908 with interment in Payne Cemetery. David married Sally Colston and they had one child, Samuel.

David passed away on Oct. 14, 1892 in Missouri.

Polly Lightfoot was born 1825 in Simpson County, KY.

Esau Jackson Lightfoot was born on May 16, 1828 in Simpson County, KY.

Elizabeth Lightfoot was born 1830 in Simpson County, KY.

Mahalia Lightfoot was born 1832 in Simpson County, KY.

Melissa Lightfoot was born 1833 in Simpson County, KY.

Melinda Lightfoot was born 1834 in Simpson County, KY.

Henry Bannister Lightfoot was born on April 3, 1836 in Simpson County, KY and married Nancy J. Fischer on Dec. 10, 1840. To this union eight children were born: Elizabeth, John Frank, Emma E., James Robert, William H., Josiah,

Chloe E., Clyde A. Henry passed away on June 12, 1910 and Nancy on Nov. 17, 1902; interment is in Oak Grove Cemetery near Polk, MO.

Rebecca Lightfoot was born in 1838 in Simpson County, KY.

Josias Lightfoot was born on Dec. 3, 1840 in Simpson County, KY and passed away on March 21, 1858 with interment in Oak Grove Cemetery in Polk County, MO.

Barbara Dorothy Lightfoot was born in 1842 in Simpson County, KY. *Submitted by Shirley (Seamster) Potts*

Baxter Lightfoot

LIGHTFOOT - Baxter Lightfoot was well-known throughout Polk County. He served one term as Polk County Clerk in the early 1930s. Then he followed in his father's footsteps, becoming Bolivar's longtime City Clerk. He married Juanita Redd of the Van community in December 1931. They were the parents of one son, Harry Beecher Lightfoot, named for both grandfathers.

Baxter, with the help of Juanita, operated an abstract business on the north side of the Bolivar square. He had a partner in this business, Ed Peterson. After Ed's passing, Baxter bought out the Peterson part but kept the name, Peterson-Lightfoot Abstract.

Harry Beecher married Sondra Wilhite and they are parents of Tammye and Mark. Grandchildren are Kendra and Courtney and Adam Baxter Lightfoot.

Baxter died on Feb. 13, 1976. He was a member of Bolivar First Baptist Church and a Republican in political beliefs.

LILLARD – John H. Lillard, the son of Mark and Sarah J. Smith Lillard, was born Aug. 8, 1850 in Cocke County, TN. He is a descendant of John Lillard, who came to America from France in 1685. He married Margaret Elzora Gorman on Feb. 8, 1873 in Polk County, MO. Zora, the daughter of David and Eliza Henry Gorman, was born May 16, 1858 in Tennessee.

John and Zora's children are Marcus Franklin, born Jan. 18, 1875; Ollie V., born Feb. 11, 1877; William T., born Oct. 27, 1881; Esta B., born Feb. 25, 1884; Dessie J., born Oct. 2, 1886; and J. Elmer Lillard, born April 5, 1901.

John died June 3, 1918 and Elzora died Jan. 30, 1930 and are buried in the Brighton Cemetery.

Marcus Franklin Lillard married Mary Ann Buckle on Dec. 25, 1904 in Brighton. Annie, the daughter of Mathias and Maragaret Buckle, was born March 10, 1882 in Harvey County, KS. They lived in Brighton where Mark worked as a farm laborer and Annie was the switchboard operator for the area. Mark died Oct. 30, 1958 and Annie died Oct. 19, 1961 and are buried at White Chapel Cemetery in Springfield, MO.

To this union were born two daughters.

Agnes Viola Lillard was born March 1, 1906 in Brighton. She married Oscar T. Hicklin on June 5, 1926 in Springfield. The son of Jonathan Hicklin and Cynthia Cantrell was born Feb. 8, 1904 in Chesapeake, MO. Their son, Oscar T. Hicklin Jr., was born Dec. 6, 1927 in Brighton. He married Janus L. Holloway on Jan. 31, 1947. She was born June 22, 1931 and is the daughter of George and Gretta Roden Holloway. Oscar T. and Janus live in Springfield. Their children: Terry Lynn, born March 21, 1949, who married Patricia Brummell on May 25, 1972. They live in Joplin. Their children are Bonnie and Jennifer.

Kathleen Kay was born June 11, 1952 and married Thomas N. Ross, son of Clyde and Ruth Ross, July 25, 1890. They live in Springfield. Kathy has one child by a previous marriage, Betsy Clayton, wife of Timothy Leighty. Tom and Kathy have one son, Thomas (T.J.), and a grandson, Clayton Thomas Leighty.

Tammy Sue Hicklin was born April 6, 1958. She married John Groves on July 3, 1988. Tammy has two children, Kimberly and Justin Simmons and a grandson, Brandon Christopher.

Agnes died Jan. 5, 1990 and Oscar died Dec. 30, 1976. They are buried at White Chapel Cemetery.

Julia Mae Lillard was born March 13, 1907 in Brighton and died Dec. 23, 1983. She married Thomas E. Blackburn on Aug. 6, 1924, the son of George and Della Blackburn. Tom was born July 21, 1905 in Polk County and died April 23, 1986 in Springfield, MO. Their daughter Velma Mae was born May 15, 1925 in Brighton. She married Jesse Ward Bowen Jr. Nov. 28, 1946. He was born June 17, 1921. Velma and Jesse live in Nixa, MO. Their children are Deborah K., born March 13, 1950, married John Preble, May 14, 1983 and their children are Matthew and Amanda; Barbara Jean, born March 20, 1953 and has two sons, David and James Carr. *Submitted by Oscar T. Hicklin*

LINDLEY – Elmer Carl Lindley was the son of Abner "Abby" and Adna (Lyle) Lindley and was born June 10, 1893 in Humansville, Polk County, MO. He served in the United States Army from Jan. 8, 1913 through Jan. 7, 1920 with serial number 2280368, Sergeant Quartermaster Corps (cooks and bakers).

He married Chrystle G. (Holford) Spafford in Tacoma, WA on March 24, 1923 and had two sons. Richard L. Lindley, born May 6, 1924, served in the AAF during WWII, traveling to such places as Africa, Island of Pantalarea, CBI Theater and Assam, India. He was also crew chief of P-47 Republic Thunderbolt (jug) Serial Number of 19059640. He and Chrystle had a daughter, Linda Lee Lindley. Richard died Oct. 19, 1999.

The second son was Robert A. Lindley, who was born July 11, 1929. He served in the United States Marine Corps Reserve from January 1948 to April 19, 1953 as a sergeant, serial number 1058706 and had been in Station Ordnance/Rifle Range in El Toro, CA, FMF-PAC (mos4963), rifle marksmanship instructor during the Korean Conflict. He married Ruby E. Jordan; she passed away and he married Barbra J. Hayes. He had two children, Carl Abner Lindley and Gail C. Lindley.

Robert A. Lindley states that his late mother's step-mom was a direct descendant of Samuel Langhorn Clemens...Maude Clemens (Spafford, Brown). *Submitted by Robert A. Lindley*

Steve, Tom, David and Eric. Mary, Kim, John, Martha, Dean. Luke, Carson and Logan.

LISTON - The Dean Carson Liston family moved to Bolivar, MO in August of 1971 from Boulder, CO. The family consisted of Dean, his wife Mary Katherine (Lewis) Liston and five children, Thomas Dean, Stephen Lewis, Martha Sue, David Clay and John Daniel, ranging in age from 4 to 16. They purchased and moved onto a farm approximately two miles from Bolivar. Dean started a certified public accounting practice in Bolivar and maintained it until 1990 when he retired. On the farm the family had a Simmental cow and calf operation until they sold the herd in 1990.

Dean's family consisted of his father, Thomas Beaman Liston, his mother, Mamie Loree (Owen) Liston and his older brother, Leland Lee Liston. Dean was born in Fairfield, IL and he attended school there through his junior year in high school. Dean and his family moved to Boulder, CO in 1944 when his father purchased the Dodge-Plymouth automobile agency. Dean graduated from Boulder High School in 1945 and spent the next eight years attending the University of Colorado and serving two tours of duty in the Marine Corps. He graduated from the University of Colorado in 1953. Tom and Mamie moved to Bolivar, MO in October of 1971 to be near Dean and his family. They lived in Bolivar until their deaths; Mamie in 1977 and Tom in 1979.

Mary's family consisted of her father, Gomer Lewis, mother, Della Ruth (Morris) Lewis and her older sister, Fern Elizabeth (Lewis) Chrisman. May was born in Emporia, KS. The family moved from Emporia to a ranch near Higgins, TX in the spring of 1929. Mary graduated from Higgins High School in 1945 and later graduated from the University of Colorado.

Dean and Mary were married in Boulder, CO in 1952 and lived there until 1971. During this period Dean worked with his father in the finance business, owned an automobile parts store and went to graduate school at the University of Colorado to become a certified public accountant. After graduating from college, Mary taught first grade in Longmont, CO until their first child was born. From that time on Mary was busy being a mother and homemaker. The Lewis and Liston families were always active members of the Methodist Church.

All of the children of Dean and Mary graduated from Bolivar High School. Tom, Steve, Martha and John graduated from Southwest Missouri State University. David graduated from Oklahoma State Technical Institute. Tom went into the marketing business in Denver, CO. Steve is involved in a petro chemical brokerage business in Houston, TX. Martha married Eric Richards and works in the administration office of Poudre School District in Ft. Collins, CO. Martha and Eric have one son, Logan Thomas. Eric is a teacher in the Poudre School District. David served in the Air Force for four years after which he returned to Bolivar, MO and works for Elite Logistics in Springfield, MO. John married Kimberly Kay (Karnes)

Mark and Annie Lillard with daughters Agnes and Julia

and they have two sons, Carson Allen and Luke Daniel. They live in the Kansas City area where Kimberly is a homemaker and John is in the insurance business. *Submitted by Dean Liston*

LOAFMAN - Dr. James E. Loafman of Bolivar, MO, the eldest son of William Perkins and Elender Pulliam Loafman, was born near Bowling Green, KY in 1834. He and his wife Dulcena Vaughn moved to the Polk County area soon after their marriage in April 1860. James' younger brother, William Edward, married his sweetheart, Susan Sawyer, in Missouri in September of 1860. Evidence indicates that their mother, William Perkins' widow, and her second husband, John E. Curtis and family, may have moved west with their two sons. The story is much the same as with James and William's father, W. P. when his parents, Edward and Sally Perkins Loafman moved from Caswell County, NC into the Tennessee area, then forged on and settled near Bowling Green, KY around 1830. It is believed that Edward and Sally may have gone to Kentucky about the same time as Benjamin and Nancy Perkins Loafman left Caswell County, NC and moved to Hickman County, KY. The kinship between Benjamin and Edward is not yet documented, but their lives paralleled greatly.

Dr. James Ervin was tutored by his father until his father's early demise in 1845. James graduated from the University of Kentucky prior to moving to Missouri. When the Civil War broke out, Dr. Loafman moved from Bolivar to Dallas County, MO. There he served as the examining surgeon for the military. He moved back to Polk County after the war.

Married three times, Dr. Loafman was the father of nine children. Records indicate he was the delivering doctor for many Polk County residents. According to one news article, he lived on a 120-acre farm on the east side of Bolivar, in a two-story frame house that burned to the ground. He was active as a Baptist church deacon, a Mason, and a Republican in Polk County along with being a founding member of the Polk County Medical Society.

Late in his lifetime, Dr. Loafman moved to Oklahoma for about four years, probably to be close to his brother William's family around Shawnee, as well as his daughter Ada, near McAlester. He moved back to Bolivar about 1922 and passed away there in February 1923. He was buried in Greenwood Cemetery. He was survived by his wife and five of his children, including James, Fannie Harrison, Delcena Bondridge, Grace Marlowe and Adah.

Dr. Loafman's story is typical of the "move west" by so many children of pioneers moving from the Eastern shores into the Midwest, then the West. Many of his family members have spread from the Virginia area into North Carolina, Tennessee, Kentucky, then up to Missouri, and Illinois, and some down to Texas, with many ending up in Oklahoma and Colorado, as well.

Gail's husband's grandmother told her family: "If the name is spelled LOAFMAN, then they are our kin."

It is the people of such hearty stock as the Loafman family who have made the story of the "Move West" such a success! *Compiled by Gail Thomas Loafman*

LOCKE - James William Locke's great-grandfather James Locke was born in North Carolina and moved to Tennessee, where he married Penelope Bass and later died. His widow and children moved to St. Clair County, MO around 1850. One of their sons, Matthew Milton Locke, finally settled in Cedar County. Two of Matthew's sons, John and William Franklin, moved to Polk County with their grandmother Penelope Locke around 1880. Penelope, John, John's wife Annie, and two of their sons, Bluford and Jeff plus some other family members, are buried at Payne Cemetery near Polk.

William Franklin Locke married Lucinda Hutcheson "Cindy" in Polk County in 1893. Their children were Bessie, James William, Matthew Milton and Anna Ardell. The family moved to Oklahoma around 1907 where William died in 1911. His family moved back to Polk County in 1913 to be near the widow's brother, J. Henry Hutcheson. "Cindy" and children eked out a living on a farm near Roberts' School in the Violet community.

Bessie married Ray Sampson; Matthew married Zula Bailey; and Anna married John Angle. James William married Bernice Shuck, a school teacher at Beef Neck School, in 1924 and moved to California. In 1931, after a seven-year sojourn, James and Bernice moved their family and his mother back to Missouri where he farmed with Uncle Henry Hutcheson. In 1941, James and Bernice bought a farm in the Black Oak school district near Pleasant View Baptist Church.

The Lockes' three sons, James Donald, Russell Lloyd and William Harold "Bill," all graduated from Halfway High School. After college, Donald moved to Phoenix, AZ because of his lifelong struggle with asthma. He married Grace Cassidy and had an outstanding career as an engineer at Goodyear Aircraft Company. He died in 1997 without any children.

James and Bernice Locke and sons Donald, Russell and Bill

Russell married Veda Williams and they had a 36-year career as missionaries in Nigeria. Russell and Veda's five children are Judith Levina, who married Larry Miller; Martin Anderson, who married Pamela McFarling; Stephen Russell, who married Tonya Kell; Charles James, who married Donita Frazier; and Alan Judson, who married Elsbeth Benignus. Russell and Veda and children lived in Bolivar during their furloughs.

Bill, third son of James William and Bernice Locke, was a farmer/truck driver and lived most of his life at Halfway until he died in 1988. He married Alice Joy Berry and their four children are James Freeman, who married Janet Wheeler; John Williams, who married Debra Edge; Janie Jo "Jane," who married Michael McKinney; and Jerald D. "Jerry," who married Terri McCoy. They all still live or work in Polk County with the exception of Jane who lives in Nevada, MO.

At present (2002) there are nine grandchildren, 24 great-grandchildren and eight great-great-grandchildren of James and Bernice Locke. *Submitted by Russell Locke*

LOCKE – Alonzo Crittenden "Crit" Locke, son of Herbert Ivan Locke and Tabitha Lillian (Lily Ann) Owen, was born in Hart County, KY, Jan. 18, 1875. He moved to Humansville, MO with his parents when a small child, coming to Halfway in 1897, where he spent the remainder of his life. He died Nov. 9, 1947 in Halfway. He was buried at Greenwood Cemetery, Bolivar. "Crit" farmed near Halfway. He was a talented fiddle player and possessed a beautiful tenor voice.

He was calm, patient and not very excitable. During the tornado in Polk County in 1929, Crit was having lunch with Clarence Middleton on Clarence's farm when the tornado appeared. Clarence asked Crit to help him carry his wood stove outside to prevent it being blown over and catching the house on fire. Crit's response was "Uncle Clarence, could I have another sup of that soup first?"

He was married to Eva Jane Ashlock in Bolivar, Feb. 26, 1899, by J.B.M. Ramsey (JP). Eva was born in Halfway June 18, 1879, the daughter of William Francis Ashlock and Sarah Eliza Lowe. Eva died Feb. 1, 1970 in Bolivar. She was buried in Greenwood Cemetery, Bolivar. At her death she was one of the last two Charter Members of the Halfway Baptist Church.

This union was blessed with eight children, all born at Halfway:

Olin Alonzo Locke, July 7, 1900-May 12, 1985. Olin married Bessie Pearl Davison (1902-1989) on Aug. 23, 1923 at Bolivar. They were parents of Olin Dayle, Aug. 31, 1925 and Deryll Duane, June 26, 1935. Olin and Bessie are buried at Greenlawn Cemetery, Springfield, MO.

Herbert Ivan Lock, June 24, 1903-July 20, 1990. "Herb" married twice. First to Elva May Alexander (1904-1963) on Jan. 14, 1926 at Bolivar. Herb and Elva had one son, Carl Eugene, Nov. 10, 1930. After Elva's death, Herb married second to Faye Roweton-Standley (1905-1999) on Dec. 25, 1964. Herbert and Elva are both buried at Brighton Cemetery.

William Fred Lock, May 30, 1905-Oct. 1, 1990. Fred married Opal Fern Alexander (1906-1996) on April 8, 1928 at Bolivar. Fred and Opal are buried in Brighton Cemetery. They had no children.

Esther Mattie Locke, Oct. 23, 1909-Oct. 22, 1994. Esther married Harley F. May (1905-2002) on April 20, 1931 in Yuma, AZ. They were parents of Robert Wayne, Feb. 6, 1932-Feb. 4, 1975 and Larry Austin, Jan. 2, 1937. Harley, Esther and Robert are buried in Greenwood Cemetery, Bolivar.

Francis Edwin Lock, Aug. 27, 1913-June 30, 1993. Francis married Zelma Jane Adams (1917-living) on Dec. 31, 1936 in Myrtle Creek, OR. They had Wendell Ray, Dec. 27, 1937 and Barbara Jean, Nov. 14, 1944. Francis was cremated.

Wilbur Clinton "Shorty" Locke, Sept. 2, 1915-June 9, 1978 in Long Beach, CA. Shorty served in combat during WWII. He never married. He is buried in the Inglewood Cemetery, Long Beach, CA.

Mildred Evalee Lock, Nov. 24, 1923 (2002, resides in Kansas City, KS). Mildred married Joseph B. Gottesburen (1920-1984) on Jan. 25, 1944 at Kansas City, KS. They had Robert Lee, June 8, 1945 and Connie Jo, Oct. 4, 1950. Joe is buried in Chapel Hill Memorial Garden, Kansas City, KS.

Wanda June Locke, June 30, 1926-Dec. 21, 2000. June married Roscoe Jerry Mullings (1924-1982) at Bolivar. They had three sons, James Dean, Nov. 5, 1962, Gary Lynn, July 13, 1964 and Ronnie Gene, Sept. 2, 1968. Roscoe and June are buried in the Brighton Cemetery. *Submitted by Kimberley May Mead, great granddaughter of Alonzo C. and Eva Jane Ashlock*

LONGACRE-PERRINE-AYRES – The chosen surname of Longacre is Swedish for "long field." It first emerged in the 1693 census of the Swedes on the Delaware River.

Andreas Peterson Longacre was born in 1653 in Kingsessing, Philadelphia County, PA. Andreas

Peterson Longacre's father was Peter Andersson and his grandfather was Anders Olsson. They came to America in 1643 on the *Kalmer Nyckel*.

Andreas Peterson Longacre died Oct. 10, 1718. In 1681, he married Magdelana Cock, who was born in 1659 in New Sweden, Philadelphia County, PA. She was the daughter of Peter Cock and Margaret Lom.

Children of Andreas Peterson Longacre and Magdelana Cock are Peter Longacre, born Nov. 16, 1682, died May 6, 1739; Andrew Longacre, born 1684, died before 1753; Margaret Longacre, born 1688; Helena Longacre, born 1690; Maria Longacre, born 1692, died before March 28, 1745; Catherine Longacre, born 1696; Gabriel Longacre, born 1697; died June 5, 1723; Brita Longacre, born 1700, died after 1729, married Joseph Tetlow; Magdalena Longacre, born after 1700, died after 1749, married John Townsend; Ellen Longacre, born 1718, died 1722.

Peter Longacre married Barbara Nilsdotter on Nov. 10, 1705, the daughter of Nils Frande and Anna Andersdotter. Barbara Nilsdotter was born 1678 and died after May 24, 1739.

Children of Peter Longacre and Barbara Nilsdotter are David Longacre; Peter Longacre II, born 1711, died Nov. 26, 1770; Sarah Longacre, born February 1713, died May 13, 1758; Andrew Longacre, born 1716, died Feb. 12, 1796; Israel Longacre, born 1725, died Sept. 23, 1784.

Andrew Longacre, born 1716, Pennsylvania, died Feb. 12, 1796 in Frederick County, VA, married Hannah Ireson circa 1738. She was the daughter of Richard Ireson and Sarah Hannah. Hannah Ireson was born July 13, 1715 and died Aug. 4, 1793, Frederick County, VA.

Children of Andrew Longacre and Hannah Ireson are Richard Longacre, born 1740, Virginia; John Longacre, born 1745 in Virginia, died 1814, Jefferson County, TN; Joseph Longacre, born 1745 in Virginia, died November 1806, Frederick County, VA; Benjamin Longacre Sr., born March 31, 1761, Frederick County, VA, died Sept. 22, 1846, Johnson County, MO.

Benjamin Longacre Sr., born March 31, 1761 in Fredrick County, VA and died Sept. 22, 1846 in Johnson County, MO. He married Ruth Carter in Tennessee. She was born circa 1765 in Jefferson County, TN and died before 1830.

Benjamin Longacre was an officer (ensign) in the Jefferson County Infantry on July 8, 1795. He was also the judge of Roane County, TN for many years before moving to Johnson County, MO.

Children of Benjamin Longacre Sr. and Ruth Carter are William Longacre, born circa 1780, Jefferson County, TN; married Patsy Colter on Nov. 28, 1820 in Roane County, TN. He died 1784 in Roane County, TN. Andrew Longacre, born 1785, Frederick County, VA married Ann Longacre on Nov. 26, 1803, Jefferson County, TN and died 1789, Jefferson County, TN. Hannah Longacre, born 1786 in Frederick County, VA and died 1823, Wilson County, TN. Elizabeth Longacre, born 1788, Frederick County, VA. Benjamin Longacre Jr., born July 24, 1789, Fredrick County, VA; died Sept. 17, 1853 in Johnson County, MO. Ruth Longacre, born 1790, Frederick County, VA; married William Hickey, Aug. 7, 1807, Jefferson County, TN. Richard M. Longacre, born October 1791, Frederick County, VA, died Sept. 15, 1871, Cass County, MO. Anna Longacre, born Jan. 22, 1794, Jefferson County, TN; died Dec. 27, 1875, Merced, CA. Rachel Longacre, born Oct. 8, 1798, Jefferson County, TN; died Sept. 1, 1866, Roane County, TN. Phoebe Longacre, born Oct. 28, 1798, Jefferson County, TN; died 1855, Bates County, MO. John Longacre, born July 11, 1802, Jefferson County, TN; died May 13, 1864, Johnson County, MO. Billinda Longacre, born 1804, Jefferson County, TN; died 1839, Roane County, TN. Sarah M. Longacre, born 1806, Jefferson County, TN; married Bryant Breeden, March 30, 1830, Roane County, TN.

Elizabeth Longacre, born 1788 in Frederick County, VA, married Matthew Perrine, Nov. 26, 1803 in Jefferson County, TN, son of Henry Perrine. Matthew Perrine was born circa 1784 in Jefferson County, TN.

The Perrine family were French Huguenots. The first Perrine who came to America was Daniel Perrine (Daniel, the Huguenot). Daniel Perrine was born circa 1640 and died circa 1719. His forebears were affiliated by birth and marriage with the Houses of Barneville, Rosel and Carteret. Daniel Perrine came from the Isle of Jersey in the "Philip" in 1665 and settled at Elizabethtown Plantations, NJ. He married Maria Thorel, born circa 1640 in Rouen, France. Daniel and Maria Thorel Perrine were the grandparents of the above Henry Perrine.

Children of Elizabeth Longacre and Matthew Perrine are Martha Jane Perrine, born circa 1810; Samuel Perrine, born July 22, 1813, Virginia; Andrew Perrine, born circa 1814, Tennessee; Benjamin Perrine, born circa 1818, Orange County, TN; Rhoda Perrine, born May 27, 1821, Tennessee; Lucinda Perrine, born June 24, 1823, died Feb. 23, 1903, married Jackson Vickers on Nov. 4, 1844, Orange County, IN; James H. Perrine, born June 27, 1825, Tennessee; died June 1, 1888.

Martha Jane Perrine, born circa 1810, married John Ayres on July 2, 1829 in Roane County, TN. He was born circa 1806 in Kentucky.

Children of Martha Jane Perrine and John Ayres are Samuel Ayres, born 1831; Susan Elizabeth Ayres, born 1833; Minnie A. Ayres, born 1836; James H. Ayres, born 1837; Sarah Evaline Ayres, born 1839, married Vinson Montgomery Ayers on Feb. 3, 1860; John Leroy Ayres, born 1842; Francis W. Ayres, born 1844; Lucinda Jane Ayres, born 1846, married Vinson Montgomery Ayres on May 27, 1867; Hiram S. Ayres, born 1850; Emily Parentha Ayres, born 1853.

A note on John Ayres. His wife Martha Jane Perrine Ayres died sometime before August 1868. John Ayres married Martha Craig, a widow, on Aug. 6, 1868 in Bates County, MO. She had three children, Sarah, Lowery and William Craig. Together John and Martha Craig Ayres had two children, Thomas, born 1869 and Mary, born 1871. He was divorced from Martha Craig sometime after 1871. In 1880 he was living alone in Robberson Township, Greene County, MO. He was living close to his ex-wife and sister-in-law Lucinda Perrine Vickers.

Lucinda Jane Ayres, born 1846, Indiana, died Jan. 26, 1922, Taney County, MO married Vinson Montgomery Ayres on May 27, 1867 in Osceola, St. Clair County, MO. He was born Feb. 9, 1842 near Albany, Clinton County, KY and died March 30, 1918, Taney County, MO.

Sarah Evaline Ayres and Vinson M. Ayres married Feb. 3, 1860, died on March 22, 1862 in Leavenworth County, KS. There were no children with this marriage. Lucinda and Sarah were first cousins to Vinson M. Ayres. Lucinda and Vinson are buried in the family cemetery at Ditt, Taney County, MO.

Note on Vinson Montgomery Ayres: parents were George W. Ayers Sr., born 1802 in Kentucky and Ruth (unknown), born in 1805. George was the above John's brother.

Children of George W. and Ruth Ayers were David Ayers; George Ayers Jr., born 1829, Kentucky; Williams, born 1832, Tennessee; Henry Ayers, born 1834, Tennessee; Nancy Ayers, born 1838, Tennessee; John Ayers, born 1840, Tennessee; Marion Ayers, born 1841, Tennessee; Vinson Ayers, born 1842, Kentucky; Milly C. Ayers, born 1845, Kentucky; James Ayers, born 1849, Kentucky.

Children of Lucinda Jane Ayres and Vinson Montgomery Ayres are Benjamin Franklin Ayres, born May 7, 1868; Hiram S. Ayres, born Sept. 7, 1869; Sarah A. Ayres, born May 30, 1871; Mary A. Ayres, born Sept. 11, 1874; Amanda C. Ayres, born May 4, 1877; Charles Montgomery Ayres, born Aug. 1, 1879, Taney County, MO.

Charles Montgomery Ayres, born Aug. 1, 1879, Taney County, MO, died March 1, 1963, Maricopa County, AZ. Charles married May 1, 1898 to Ollie Elizabeth Nance, born April 22, 1879 in Taney County, MO, died Dec. 2, 1964. She was the daughter of John (Jack) C. Nance and Malinda Bolen. Jack Nance was the judge for the Eastern District of Taney County.

Charles Montgomery Ayres was the constable of Taney County; he was also a large producer of "moonshine" at the same time. The revenuers finally caught up with him and left Missouri for Arizona.

Children of Charles Montgomery Ayres and Ollie Elizabeth Nance Ayres are Jesse Montgomery Ayres, born March 22, 1899, Protem, Taney County, MO; Vinson Montgomery Ayres, born 1901, Taney County, MO; Benjamin Ayres, born Feb. 18, 1905, Taney County, MO; Amy Faye Ayres, born 1906, Taney County, MO; Meade Ayres, born 1910, Taney County, MO; Elberta Ayres, born 1915, Taney County, MO; Georgia Ayres, born 1917, Taney County, MO; Troy Francis Ayres, born 1919, Taney County, MO; Mamie Ayres, born 1920, Taney County, MO.

Jesse Montgomery Ayres, born March 22, 1899 in Protem, Taney County, MO, married Feb. 22, 1920 to Walsie Ray Tannehill Hampton, born July 9, 1904 in Ozark County, MO. Walsie Ray Tannehill was the daughter of Thomas Benton Tannehill and Maggie P. Gilliam Tannehill. Maggie P. Gilliam Tannehill died during childbirth of Walsie, leaving four other children. Thomas Benton Tannehill adopted Walsie to William and Ellie Hampton of Ozark County, MO. The Tannehill and Hampton families had been friends for many years.

Jesse M. Ayres died in 1986 in Springfield, MO and is buried at Cabool, Texas County, MO. Walsie died in 1995 in Stockton, and is buried in Cabool, Texas County, MO.

Children of Jesse M. and Walsie Tannehill Hampton Ayres are Lloyd Brooks Ayres, born June 28, 1921, Taney County, MO; Florence Loretta Ayres, born July 10, 1923, Christian County, MO; Willard Edward Ayres, born April 20, 1926, Christian County, MO; Hillary Gene Ayres, born March 27, 1933, Ozark County, MO.

Hillary Gene Ayres, born March 27, 1933, Ozark County, MO, died Aug. 16, 2002 at home in Polk County, MO, buried at Rondo Cemetery, married June 3, 1950 to Melda Geraldine DeLoach, born June 3, 1931, Phoenix, Maricopa County, AZ. She is the daughter of Charles Isaac DeLoach, born Feb. 22, 1909, Coyle, Logan County, OK and Veoma Arnold, born June 28, 1909, Robert Lee, Coke County, TX.

Children of Hillary Gene Ayres and Melda Geraldine are Gary Gene Ayres, born May 12, 1951, Glendale, AZ; Alfred Lloyd Ayres, born April 30, 1953, Glendale, AZ; Johnny Earl Ayres, born May 8, 1955, Phoenix, AZ; Roy Edwin Ayres, born Sept. 15, 1957, Phoenix, AZ; Charles Jesse Ayres, born Nov. 21, 1959, Cabool, Texas County, MO; Jgade Keno Ayres, born June 30, 1962, Cabool, Texas County, MO; William Kelly Ayres, born Jan. 7, 1965, Cabool, Texas County, MO.

Gary Gene Ayres, born May 12, 1951, married Jan. 15, 1977 to Ruth Ann Gillaspy, born Oct.

12, 1949, Des Moines, Polk County, IA; daughter of Harry Robert Gillaspy and Juanita Bernice Cowan, both of Iowa.

Children of Gary Gene and Ruth Ann Gillaspy Ayres are Megan Rae Ayres, born Nov. 26, 1977, Phoenix, AZ; Bethany LeAnn Ayres, born Oct. 4, 1980, Springfield, MO.

Megan Rae Ayres graduated from Humansville HS in 1996 and from Northwest Missouri State University in 2001. She married John Kirby Mires, born June 12, 1969 in Nodaway County, MO, on March 18, 2001 in Las Vegas, Clark County, NV. They have one daughter, Jessica Nicole Mires, born March 22, 2002.

Bethany LeAnn Ayres graduated from Humansville H S in 1998. She married Adam Ray Dalton in October 1998. They had one child, Caitlyn LeAnn Dalton, born March 13, 1999. Bethany has one son, Ryan Ashton Ayres, born Nov. 7, 2000. Bethany married John Adams, born Sept. 4, 1970, on Dec. 21, 2002.

These families came to Missouri in the 1820s—mainly in Johnson, Cass, Vernon, Bates, St. Clair and Polk Counties. Many came from Tennessee and Kentucky. During the War Between the States these families were truly divided. Brother against brother and even father against son but that was not unusual, especially in Missouri. Some associated names with these families are Vickers, Barnett, Harley, Ham, Hinds, Oldham, Phipps, Burris, Cockrell, just to name a few. *Submitted by Gary Ayres*

Elizabeth Elmore (Lizzy) Looney Parker, age 100. The picture was taken the day she won Queen for a Day of contestants of various nursing homes in Greene and Polk Counties

LOONEY - Benjamin Looney V. was born about 1795 or 1796. He was on the 1830 census of Tennessee, but he came to Missouri as a widower before 1850. His children were born in Tennessee, most of them in Franklin County. He was the son of Benjamin Looney IV and Mary (Polly) Galbraith Looney. The wife of Benjamin V died in Tennessee and was kin to the Holder family as their minor children had Holder guardians in Missouri. The children were Pleasant, born in 1823, who married Nancy Killian; J. B., born in 1826 and died young; Anthony S., born in 1825; Eliza Jane, born in 1828, married Ruben Alexander in Lebanon, MO, then went to Greene, Polk and Dallas Counties; John, born in 1831; Frances Marion, born in 1833, married Sarah Elizabeth Hogan; Lucy Ann, born in 1835, married Bill Thompson and went to Texas after Bill's death; William Riley, born in 1836, married Betsy Holstein and stayed in the Pleasant Hope area; James Madison, born Aug. 29, 1838, married three times. They were a McGuire, a Holder and Manerva Catherine Gregory. J. M. and Manerva Looney had a daughter named Elizabeth (Lizz) Elnore while they lived at Pleasant Hope. She told of playing with Hullum Alexander's children who were her Aunt Eliza's grandchildren. She also played with the Sallee and Stokes children who grew up around Pleasant Hope. Elizabeth (Lizz) Elnore Looney was born in 1891. She married a Parker. They adopted a boy. She lived to be over 100 years old and is buried at Cuba, MO by her husband. *Submitted by Bruce Dillard*

LOONEY-MITCHELL - Sarah Black Looney was born May 19, 1829 in Ralls County, MO, the daughter of Absalom Looney and Mary Price. Absalom died near Springfield, MO in 1848 and his widow married Samuel Asher on Sept. 14, 1848 in Polk County, MO. After Samuel's death, Mary returned to Missouri. On May 16, 1847 in Polk County, MO, Sarah married Wiley Blunt Mitchell. Wiley was the son of the Rev. John Mitchell and Betsy McVay of Roane County, TN, brother of Rachel Blake and grandson of the Rev. Morris Mitchell. Rachel Blake is the grandmother of Betty Blake, the wife of Will Rogers. Wiley and Sarah had the following children: John Henigar Mitchell, who performed with Buffalo Bill Cody in his Wild West Shows; Mary Ann R. Buckner (Bob's great-grandmother); Rev. William Riley Mitchell; Rhoda Jane Abbott; David M. Mitchell; James L. Mitchell; Martha Didama Meek; Archibald L. Mitchell; and Sarah Ann Miller. Sarah Looney was part Northern Cherokee and wore a headband. Wiley Mitchell died April 8, 1904 is buried in the Bethel Methodist Church Cemetery in Cedar County, MO. After Wiley's death, Sarah lived with her daughter Mary Ann and died on Nov. 23, 1918 in Adonis, MO from arterial sclerosis. She is buried in an unmarked grave in the Adonis Baptist Church Cemetery.

Mary Ann Mitchell married Jesse Franklin Buckner on Feb. 7, 1869 in Cedar County, MO. They had 17 children, including Bob's grandmother, Christina Buckner, who was born Dec. 25, 1886 in Missouri. Mary Ann died April 28, 1923 and Jesse Franklin Buckner died Oct. 28, 1914. They are both buried in the Payne Cemetery. Christina married Finney A. Stewart on July 15, 1906 in Polk County, MO. Finney was born March 4, 1887 in Bolivar, MO, the son of Benjamin M. Stewart and Clora Payne. His grandfather, Joseph R. Stewart, came to Polk County, MO before 1860. Many of the Stewart families moved to the Kansas City area to find work. Christina died Jan. 21, 1919 in Wyandotte County, KS and Finney died March 20, 1974 in Mission, KS. Finney and Christina had five children, including Bob's mother Dorothy Stewart, who was born Aug. 9, 1910 in Kansas City, KS. Dorothy married William Shelby Anderson on Aug. 13, 1927. They had nine children. Dorothy died on July 25, 1979 in Corder, MO and Shelby died Nov. 11, 1981 in Higginsville, MO. They are both buried in Maple Hill Cemetery in Rosedale, KS. *Submitted by Bob L Anderson*

Sarah Looney Mitchell between 1904-1918, Adonis, MO.

LOWE - The Lowe ancestor came to America from Loch Loman, Scotland about 1780, settling in Virginia. Cary Lowe, a son, married Mary Middleton and settled in Louden County, TN. He was editor of the first paper in Louden County. They had one child, Addison Cary Lowe, born Sept. 23, 1823 in Louden County. Addison went to California and spent one and a half years mining gold, to later purchase a section of land in Brighton, MO in 1852. Also that year he married Amma Ti Tuck in Bolivar, MO. Addison and Amma had six children, one son being James Hiram Lowe, born in 1857.

He married Dinah Trantham in 1882. They had four children, one being James Roy Lowe, born in 1904. Roy married Lucy Mildred Ball in 1924.

Roy then purchased the portions of land from his siblings. Roy and Lucy had one child, Virginia Irene Lowe. Irene married in 1943 to Wesley Brice Walker. They had two sons, James Bruce and Rickie Allen Walker. James (Jim) still resides on the land in Brighton. He and his wife, Cyntha Anne Grisham Walker, married in 1965. Three children were born from this union. Sammy Lanee Walker Sawyer, Curt (Mart) Matthew Walker and Shad Daniel Walker. Matt, wife Amanda and son (Colten) now reside in the old homestead built around 1853. Shad and family, wife Jennifer and two sons Caul and McCrae, live on the portion of the land by the spring pond. Through the years the land has been retained and lived on by seven generations. *Submitted by Brice and Irene Walker*

LOWE – Joseph Newton Lowe, son of Jacob Low and Eliza Ramsey "Betsy" Rodgers, was born in Tennessee on June 24, 1818. The family came to Polk County prior to 1840. Joseph died September 1859 near Bolivar. He is buried in the Payne Farm Cemetery, Sentinel, MO. Joseph served in the Mexican War from Polk County as a private, Company H, Second Missouri Volunteers. His occupation was a farmer.

He married Cynthia Ann J. Howe in Bolivar, Feb. 2, 1843.

Cynthia was born in Robinson County, TN March 9, 1826, the daughter of John Wesley Howe and Sarah Williams. Cynthia died May 17, 1903 in Goodson. She was buried in the Ragsdale Cemetery at Halfway.

Joseph Newton Lowe and Cynthia Ann J. Howe had the following children:

Martha Jane Lowe was born in Bolivar, MO circa 1846. Martha died circa 1893. She is buried in Ragsdale Cemetery, although there is no marker for her.

Arminda "Effie Ann" was born in Halfway Jan. 3, 1879. Arminda died Nov. 12, 1957 in Star, Ada County, ID and was buried in Star Cemetery, Star, ID. She married James Elmer Vincent in Halfway April 26, 1899. James was born in Halfway Oct. 25, 1877, the son of Christopher Columbus "Lum" Vincent and Mary Frances Ashlock. James died Jan. 8, 1971 in Caldwell, Canyon County, ID. He was buried Jan. 12, 1971 in Star Cemetery, Star, ID.

Harriet Angeline Lowe was born in Halfway, Polk County, MO circa 1848. Harriet died Nov. 7, 1890. She married Charles Cornelius McKinney in Sentinel, March 31, 1867. Charles was born in Ohio or Pennsylvania October 1846. During the Civil War he served as a private in Company A, Eighth MSM and was wounded.

Sarah Eliza Lowe was born in Sentinel, MO, May 10, 1853. Sarah died Sept. 28, 1936 in Halfway. She was buried in Ragsdale Cemetery. She married William Francis Ashlock in Bolivar, June 25, 1871. William was born in Halfway on Dec. 24, 1848, the son of Francis Porter Ashlock and Mary Frances Barclay. William died Feb. 14, 1940 in Halfway. He was buried in Ragsdale Cemetery. William farmed in Polk County.

Sarah Eliza Lowe and William Francis Ashlock had the following children:

Frances was born in Halfway, circa 1872. Frances died circa 1875 in Kansas on the Oregon Trail. After her death, her parents left the wagon train and returned to Polk County.

Margaret Angeline was born in Halfway, MO March 24, 1874. She died Nov. 5, 1960 in Halfway. She was buried in Ragsdale Cemetery. She married Robert Walter Ragsdale in Halfway, Sept. 10, 1896. Robert was born in Logan County, KY, Nov. 13, 1868, a child of Lewis Ragsdale Jr. and Rachel Black. Robert died April 22, 1942 in Halfway. He was buried in Ragsdale Cemetery.

Dora A. was born in Halfway, Jan. 27, 1877. Dora died of typhoid fever September 1890 in Halfway, at 13 years of age. She was buried in Ragsdale Cemetery.

Eva Jane was born in Halfway June 18, 1879. Eva died Feb. 2, 1970 in Bolivar. She was buried in Greenwood Cemetery. She married Alonzo Crittenden Locke in Bolivar, Feb. 26, 1899. Alonzo "Crit" was born in Hart County, KY Jan. 18, 1875, a son of Herbert Ivan Locke and Tabitha Lillian (Lily Ann) Owen. Alonzo died Nov. 9, 1947 in Halfway. He was buried in Greenwood Cemetery.

William Lewis was born in Halfway Oct. 27, 1882. William died Nov. 13, 1958 in Huron, MO and is buried in Ragsdale Cemetery. Bill was crippled his entire life. He ran a grocery store and made brooms in a shed in the back of his residence. He was never married. He died in a house fire in Huron, Polk County, MO.

Luther Francis was born in Halfway, June 13, 1887. Luther died May 23, 1973 in Humansville. He was buried in Greenwood Cemetery. He married Minnie Belle Voris in Halfway, Nov. 28, 1909. Minnie was born in Halfway June 29, 1891, a daughter of Julius Albert Voris and Martha Malissa Viles. Minnie died Oct. 25, 1969 in Springfield, MO. Her body was interred in Greenwood Cemetery.

Grace Emmaline was born in Halfway, Feb. 8, 1894. Grace died Nov. 5, 1978 in Los Angeles, Los Angeles County, CA. She was buried in Rose Hills Memorial Park, Whittier, CA. She married James Earl Norris in Buffalo, MO, Dec. 24, 1915. James was born in McCloud, Pottawatomie County, OK, May 28, 1894, a son of James Howard Norris and Rosella Florence Jones. James died June 17, 1967 in Norwalk, Los Angeles County, CA. He was buried in Rose Hills Memorial Park, Whittier, CA. In 1920, James was farming in Polk County, MO.

Pearl Elizabeth was born in Halfway, May 22, 1897. Pearl died June 3, 1991 in Memorial Hospital, Bolivar. She was buried in Mt. View Cemetery. She married Tommy Russell Hale Jr. in Halfway, March 8, 1916. Tommy was born in Bolivar, April 23, 1895. Tommy was a son of Thomas R. Hale and Lucetta I. Macklin. Tommy died July 28, 1977 in Springfield, MO. He was buried in Mt. View Cemetery.

Samantha Newton Lowe was born in Sentinel, MO circa 1856. She married twice. She married John H. Manes in Bolivar on June 6, 1880. John was born in Tennessee August 1843. John died before 1900. She married Alvin A. Ayers in Bolivar, Nov. 22, 1903. Alvin was born in Lincoln County, TN, Sept. 4, 1843, a son of Baker W. Ayers and Elizabeth Clark.

Samantha Newton Lowe and John H. Manes had the following children:

William was born in Bolivar, February 1880. William was killed in a tornado when young.

Media was born in Bolivar, June 11, 1892. Media died Jan. 2, 1963 in Atascadero, San Luis Obispo, CA. She was buried in Atascadero, District Cemetery, San Luis Obispo, CA. She married four times. She married Charles Terry Davis circa 1908. She married husband Callahan circa 1911. She married George Victor Valencia in San Luis Obispo County, CA, Oct. 23, 1916. George was born in Santa Ynez, Santa Barbara County, CA, Feb. 3, 1882, a son of Ramon Evaristo Valencia and Emanuela Olivera. George died Dec. 29, 1949 in San Luis Obispo, Gen. Hosp., San Luis Obispo, CA. He was buried in Atascadero, District Cemetery, San Luis Obispo, CA. Media married fourth, Elijah Tudor in California, circa 1952.

Samantha Newton Lowe had the following child:

Louella was born in Bolivar, Polk County, MO before 1903. Louella was born out of wedlock.

Margaret E. Lowe was born near Sentinel, April 9, 1858. Margaret died June 14, 1865 in Polk County at 7 years of age. She was buried in the Payne Farm Cemetery at Sentinel, MO. *Submitted by Larry A. May*

LOWER-HARTLEY – Jesse Andrew Lower, born in Polk County on Feb. 16, 1901 and Elsie Hartley, born in Cedar County on Aug. 19, 1904, were married on Dec. 24, 1921 in Fair Play, Polk County. They first shared a home northeast of Fair Play with Jesse's brother, Henry, and Elsie's sister, Thelma. About 1925, they moved with two daughters, to a farm home east of Fair Play, overlooking Barren Creek and what is now Missouri Highway 32.

Fair Play was a thriving town on the Frisco railroad and Missouri Highway 13 with a stockyard, newspaper, flour mill, livery stable, mercantile store, and multiples of churches and grocery and hardware stores.

Jesse and Elsie lived the hard lives of those days, dairying and raising livestock, growing livestock feed and family food with hand labor and horse power, earning income from sales of milk, lambs, wool, hogs, poultry, eggs, honey, molasses and strawberries.

The children worked hard at farming, gardening and household chores. In the early life of the family Elsie and the older girls helped with haymaking and the grain harvest. They did the family wash with a washboard, cooked family and harvest meals, churned butter by hand, canned fruits and vegetables, helped with butchering and tended a large flock of chickens.

Jesse and the boys, exchanging labor with neighbors, planted and harvested grain and hay, cared for and worked horses, sheared sheep, fed and managed livestock and constructed farm buildings. They supplemented the farm income by hunting and trapping muskrats, possums and skunks for fur.

All family members saved money and improved the family diet by hunting food in the form of rabbits, squirrels and fish and by tending a small orchard and berry patch. Everyone shared in the milking chores and gardening. The milk was cooled in a spring box, family food was refrigerated with ice and water was carried from a spring.

About 1930 Jesse installed a hydraulic ram to provide running water in the house. Around 1938 he erected a wind-charger to provide electric lights to the home and farmstead. Jesse and his brother Henry owned haymaking equipment together and did custom hay baling. Jesse later acquired his own tractor and implements.

The family was active in the community and attended church at Bismont Baptist Church, later at Barren Creek Cumberland Presbyterian Church.

Jesse was the son of Rufus Andrew Lower and Cordelia Belle Osborn, both of the Pickel School district of Polk County. Rufus was the son of John Lower and Martha Ann Walker. Cordelia Belle was the daughter of John Harden Osborn and Hattie (Hettie) Florence Shepard.

Elsie was a daughter of John Edward Hartley and Fannie Mayse of the Bethel/Masters community in Cedar County. John was a son of Richard Hartley and Almira T. Underwood. Fannie was a daughter of Moses Mayse and Melinda "Mellie" Settle.

Jesse and Elsie had 10 children. Elsie and nine of 10 children are living at this writing. Jesse Eugene, the fourth child, died in infancy of pneumonia. In birth order, the children are Beulah Evelyn, Bertha Fern, William Bernard, John Benton, James Richard, Fred Leonard, Betty Lou, Larry Joe and Carol Ann. These nine children graduated from Fair Play High School. Bertha, Bernard, John, Dick, Betty and Ann had children. Bernard, John, Dick, Betty and Ann had grandchildren.

Jesse Lower died at age 84 and was buried in Barren Creek Cemetery on Aug. 25, 1985. Elsie married Luther Leroy Forgey on Aug. 2, 1987. *Submitted by John B. Lower*

LUNCEFORD - William Lunceford, an early settler in Polk County, arrived about 1832 with his wife, Jane and six children. He was a farmer and soon became a landowner, settling in the Marion Township near Bolivar. He soon became active in local affairs by serving as a grand juror on the first Circuit Court in 1835. He also served as a judge of the County Court for two years in 1837 and again in 1852 for a four-year term.

William was born June 4, 1792, probably in the part of Virginia that is now West Virginia. His parents, Reuben Lunsford and Mary Margaret Dennison, lived in or near the town of Greenbrier in Bath County at one time. William's father served with the Virginia Continental Line during the Revolutionary War and received land grants in Ohio. The family moved from Bath County, VA to Gallia County, OH about 1800. William married there about 1815 to Barbara. It is thought that her surname may have been Coffman since they named a son by that name. William and Barbara's children were Martha, Reuben, Coffman and Barbara Ann. His wife, Barbara, died Jan. 15, 1824 in Ohio. William married again to Jane Greenlee on Feb. 13, 1825. His family with Jane were Elbridge G., John D., William F. and Morris W. Family records were kept in a small, red, leather book which William carried around in his shirt pocket. This book was last known to be in the possession of the Loma Lunceford Paulson family of Kansas City, KS.

Children of William mainly lived in Polk County but descendants have spread to Texas, Oklahoma, California, Oregon, Washington, and probably to many other states. His daughter, Martha, married Abraham Slagle in 1833; Coffman married in 1842 to Elizabeth Campbell and Barbara Ann married also in 1842 to Reuben Barnes. His son, Elbridge, married Susan Winn in 1853; John married Caroline Brittain in 1859; William F. married in 1866 to Mary McClure Bagley and Morris married Sarah Higginbotham in 1872.

William died Jan. 14, 1863 in Polk County, leaving his estate to his wife, Jane. His will was dated July 23, 1862. He is buried in the Hensley Cemetery in land that he probably owned at one time. Jane, his wife, is also buried there. Jane was born May 9, 1807 in Virginia and was the daughter of William F. Greenlee and Nancy Casteel. Jane died May 20, 1879. *Written by Audrey Lunceford Ulm*

LYLE – James C. Lyle Sr. was born April 13, 1897, Humansville, Polk County, MO, son of William Lee Lyle (1858-1936) and Nancy Clementine (Garrison) (1859-1901). James married Aug. 18, 1922, Muskogee, OK. Death was April 26, 1952, Parsons, KS. He was a railway express messenger, managed the bag-gage and express cars of passenger trains. His education was to the eighth grade, rural school, Humansville, MO. His spouse, Mary Ann Lipsey, was born Aug. 30, 1899 at Panama, OK (Indian Territory). Her father was John Lipsey (1868-1915) and mother, Mahala Jane (Williams (1879-1942). Mary Ann died Nov. 5, 1953 at Parsons, KS. Both are buried at Oakwood Cemetery, Parsons, KS. She was a telephone operator prior to marriage, a housewife after marriage. Their children: James C. Lyle Jr., born May 17, 1923, Belleville, KS; married Dec. 11, 1942, death was Dec. 12, 2000, burial in Houston, TX. Spouse – Benicia (Nagle), born Jan. 12, 1924 at Parsons, KS. She was very supportive and interested in her husband's education and activities. Daughter of Arthur Nagle (1889-1979) and Bernice McKinney (1898-).

Jim and Bernicia Lyle, February 1998

On Aug. 1, 2000, visitors in the home, cousin Sylvia (Simmons) Thomas and Alva Lyle in Overland Park, KS. On Aug. 2 was Sylvia's brother, Glen Simmons and his grandson, Christopher Buck, born with MD. James and Liz were into family history. Liz is receiving much information and pictures. Children are Ronald Dean Lyle, born May 3, 1947, Parsons, KS, married Aug. 31, 1968, Overland Park, KS, died Feb. 21, 1994, cause ruptured aorta, burial Houston, TX. Spouse, Margaret Ellen Lamb, born Aug. 3, 1950, Overland Park, KS. Their children, Sandra, born Sept. 6, 1977 and Robert, born Sept. 6, 1982.

Marsha Faye Lyle, born May 1950, Parsons, KS, married Geoffrey Heil on April 11, 1970, divorced 1984, married Clet Landry on July 8, 1994. She is manager of wholesale children's clothing business in Houston, TX, no children.

Rodger Kent Lyle, born June 12, 1958 at Lawrence, KS. Married Angela Masera Sept. 12, 1981, divorced 1984. Married Sue Lehman on Oct. 17, 1991, no children. He is sales rep. for Aim Investments, Houston, TX.

Continued children of James C. Lyle Sr. – Nancy Sue Lyle was born Oct. 25, 1926 at Muskogee, OK, married Olen R. Coker on Dec. 19, 1947 in Albuquerque, NM. Details about Nancy Sue's family may be obtained by contacting her. Address 11543 E. 7th ST. Tulsa, OK 74128. James C. Lyle Jr. worked for Panhandle Eastern Pipelines. *Submitted by Liz Ward*

LYMAN - Asa Y. Lyman and Susan Neill were reared between the west Polk County line and Turkey Creek. A. Y. was born in 1856 and Susan in 1858. They were married in the 1870s. In the early 1880s, A. Y. went west with a wagon train from Walnut Grove, MO, to Sublette, KS. Susan arrived later by train. The first three years were good years in Kansas, then drought hit and they almost "starved out." A. Y. and Susan then returned to Missouri and bought the old original Routh Chapel Church and one acre, built in 1880 in Section 18, Township 32, Range 24. With a team of mules and log skids they moved the old church building four miles to the northeast on 40 acres located in Section 5, Township 32, Range 24, one and one-half miles west of Highway 123, on what is now Highway 215. It was converted into their home and rooms were later added. The old church building portion has been recently restored with white permanent siding and a green metal roof. They reared their children at this location: Elsie May, Lloyd, Gertrude, Don and Jay Asa. A. Y. opened the A. Y. Lyman Monument Co. in Aldrich and Humansville in 1900. A. Y. died in 1930 and Susan in 1947. Jay Asa obtained the old home property from A. Y. and Susan in their later years. Jay Asa served in WWI in the 313th Engineers and later worked for A. Y. in the monument business. Jay Asa was married to Jessie Copeland and their children, Jay Jr., Frank X. and Wanda Jean (Taylor), were reared in the same home. Jay Jr. was in the Army Air Force during WWII. When Jay Asa died in 1956, Jay Jr. and Annabel Lyman purchased the old home 40 acres. It is now recognized as a Century Farm.

Jay Jr. and Annabel (Longcrier) Lyman were married in 1948 and he opened a barber shop in Aldrich on Oct 1, 1948. For 20 years, the barber shop was open six days a week, and on Wednesday and Saturday nights. When Stockton Dam and Lake was being constructed, the US Corps of Engineers purchased the barber shop, home, and a small farm at the edge of Aldrich. Their house in Aldrich was moved west of the Little Sac River to 4997 S. 30th Road on an adjoining property just one-quarter mile east of the old Lyman home place. Jay Jr. and Annabel have a son, J. Randall Lyman, and a grandson, Aaron R. Lyman, currently residing in Springfield. The son plans to return to the old Polk County home place upon retirement from employment with the City of Springfield.

For many years, a sign hung in the barber shop at Aldrich that formerly hung in the orderly room at Morris Field in Charlotte, NC during WWII. It read, "So long as you know you are green you grow, but when you think you are ripe, that's when you become rotten." Jay says, Well, after all these years, I know I am still green, I don't smell ripe, but I sure feel rotten sometimes." *Submitted by Jay Jr. and Annabel Lyman*

Jay Lyman Jr – front left; Annabel Lyman – front right; Arron R. Lyman – front middle; James Randall Lyman – back right; Sue Lyman – back left

LYNGAR - James Harvey Lyngar, "Harve," as he was known throughout his adult life, was born Feb. 12, 1821 in Tennessee, the son of John and Mary Lingar. In early records, the surname is spelled various ways, mainly as Lingar, most likely at the whim of those recording it. It is not known if the parents were literate, but James Harvey, who had little formal education, could read and write and he made certain that his children were educated. By the 1840s, the spelling of the surname as Lyngar was accepted as the proper spelling by Harve and his descendants, while his brother and family in Tennessee retained Lingar.

James Harvey and his brother John were orphaned at an early age, Harve at 11 years of age, his brother at about 17. Their father died around 1827-1828 and their mother in 1832. Their sister Sarah was much older and already married to Sampson Goodman, and the mother of four or five children. It has been told that Harve left home at the age of 13 and traveled to New Orleans with a plantation owner. By the time of the 1840 Federal census for Claiborne County, TN, it appears that he was living with his brother and family.

On Jan. 19, 1843 in Claiborne County, TN, James Harvey Lyngar married Eliza Chumbley. She was born in Tennessee about 1824, one of nine known children born to Robert Chumbley and Elizabeth Ford. The Chumbley, Goodman, Lyngar and Slatten families of Claiborne County, TN intermarried and by the early 1840s, members of these families had relocated to Polk County, MO; Harve and his family did not join them until the late 1840s.

Like his father and brother, Harve was a farmer; however, according to one daughter, he left the farm for a while during the 1850s and headed west, hoping to strike it rich in the gold fields. He did not serve in the military during the Civil War, but it is known that he hauled supplies from the nearest railhead at Rolla.

Harve and Eliza had been married a little over 27 1/2 years when she died, Sept. 22, 1870. She is buried in Kings Cemetery in Polk County, MO, the same cemetery as her father, Robert Chumbley.

To this couple were born seven children:

John Franklin Lyngar, born about 1844 in Tennessee; died Jan. 14, 1904 in Greenfield, MO; married first, Missouri A.V. Long, April 24, 1870 in Dade County, MO and second, Anna M. Willard. He was a doctor in Greenfield, MO.

Andrew Chumbley Lyngar, born Oct. 18, 1845 in Claiborne County, TN; died Oct. 23, 1906 in Pittsburg, KS; married Adeline Camilla Spivey, Feb. 17, 1867 in Dade County, MO. He was a doctor in Jasper County, MO and later in Pittsburg, KS.

Wiley Lyngar, born Nov. 18, 1847 in Polk County, MO; died March 10, 1850 in Polk County, MO, buried in King Cemetery.

Emily E. Lyngar, born Aug. 2, 1849 in Polk County, MO; died Dec. 27, 1862 in Polk County, MO; buried in King Cemetery.

Harriet Orleany Lyngar, born Jan. 1, 1853 in Polk County, MO; died March 19, 1922 in Polk County, MO; married Ellis Willingham (Ham) Jones Sept. 20, 1872 in Polk County, MO.

Fannie Josephine Lyngar, born March 25, 1856 in Polk County, MO; died Sept. 25, 1857; buried in King Cemetery.

William V. Lyngar, born Nov. 13, 1860 in Polk County, MO; died Sept. 11, 1870 in Polk County; buried in King Cemetery.

On Sept. 22, 1881 in Greene County, MO, Harve Lyngar married Mary Susan Anderson. To this union was born one daughter, Thedra, in August 1882 in Polk County, MO.

Harve Lyngar died Jan. 28, 1902 in Polk County, 15 days following the death of his wife Mary. They are both buried in Oak Grove Cemetery.

MCALLISTER – Very little is known about two of Polk County's earliest settlers, Thomas McAllister (McCallister) and his son-in-law Wesley Pennington.

Thomas McAllister was born in Kentucky around 1785 and died around 1862 in Bolivar, Polk County, MO. Wesley Pennington was the son of Riggs Pennington and Johanna Osborne. He was born in Kentucky in 1810. Wesley died Dec. 27, 1867 in Brenham, Washington County, TX at 57 years of age.

The first evidence we have of Thomas and Wesley coming to Polk County is from Deed Book A, page 1 where Wesley was appointed Power of Attorney for a William Ross to dispose of bounty land in the state of Illinois on May 11, 1837. Thomas and Wesley also both appear in the 1850 and 1860 Polk County Census. According to these censuses, their primary occupation was farming.

Wesley served in the Black Hawk War as corporal in Captain Edmonston's Company in the extra Battalion of Illinois Rangers from June 1831 to July 1831. He enlisted again in June 1832 as a private through Captain Stennet's Company out of Illinois and was discharged in September 1832.

Shortly after being discharged, Wesley returned to Knox County, IL and married Margaret McAllister, the daughter of Thomas and Sarah McAllister. Wesley brought his wife and in-laws to Polk County sometime before 1837 as indicated by Deed Book A.

On Dec. 21, 1839, Thomas McAllister and his wife, Sarah, purchased three town lots numbered 2, 3 and 6 in block 22 for the sum of $50.00 from Commissioner William Jamison. However, records indicate that the title was warranted and defended on only two of these lots. Thomas and his wife purchased an additional 80 acres for $1718.00 in April 1841. In June of 1854, Thomas sold 4.97 acres for $5.00 to Gibson Hendricks, William Brown and John McReynolds, trustees of the Methodist-Protestant Church, to erect a campground and a place of religious worship, with free access to a spring north of the property. This would become known as Mt. Gilead Church.

Wesley Pennington was able to acquire land in Polk County in 1850 and another 40 acres in 1855 through the Bounty Land Act, having served in the Black Hawk War.

Wesley and Margaret moved about frequently as indicated by the places of birth of their eight children. Four of these were born in Missouri, one in Illinois, one in Texas and two in Arkansas.

Margaret McCallister Pennington died while they were enroute to Texas, probably of pneumonia. They had lots of rain and she had become ill. She died on the south side of the Arkansas River. They waited several days for the river to recede so they could bring her back across the Arkansas River and bury her in or near Van Buren, AR. The exact date of her death is not known, but this happened prior to March 3, 1867 when a granddaughter, Annie Matilda Edison, was born.
Submitted by Cynthia May Beers

Rick and Karen McCaslin

MCCASLIN – Rick and Karen McCaslin moved to Polk County from Camden County in the summer of 1983. They built a home on a lot purchased from Woodrow Kinsey located in the Hutchwood Subdivision in Bolivar.

Rick was born in Oklahoma, moving to Camden County, MO from Kansas in 1965. Karen was born and raised in Camden County. Rick and Karen were married July 12, 1970 in Camden County by Elder Glenn Waldren. They have two children: Rickey L. McCaslin and Kimberly S. McCaslin.

Rick received his draft notice from the Army on Dec. 24, 1970, which was during the last of the Vietnam conflict. The majority of his AIT unit was sent to Vietnam but he was fortunate in being sent to Germany instead. He was part of the Eighth Cavalry unit and he was stationed near Manheim, which is about 30 miles south of Frankfurt, Germany. Rick was stationed there for about 17 months; Karen and their son were there for about 10 months.

After his tour of duty, Rick enrolled in Linn Technical College where he graduated with an associate's degree in mechanics.

Rick was saved July 25, 1974 at the Parrack Grove Missionary Baptist Church in Camden County during a revival. He joined the church and was baptized on August 25, 1974 by Elder Lee Howard of Preston, MO. He was called to preach on Jan. 10, 1975 during the revival services at the Pleasant Grove Church in Camden County and was later ordained a minister by the Goodson Missionary Baptist Church at Goodson, MO. Rick is currently the pastor of the Rock Prairie Missionary Baptist Church at Pleasant Hope, MO.

Karen was saved February 26, 1970 at the Parrack Grove Missionary Baptist Church in Camden County during a revival and baptized Sept. 8, 1974 by Elder Glenn Waldren, Camdenton, MO. Karen enjoys playing the piano and writing gospel songs.

Rickey L. McCaslin was saved June 8, 1986 at the Goodson Missionary Baptist Church during a revival; he joined the church and was baptized on June 22, 1986. He was called to preach May 15, 2002.

Kimberly S. McCaslin was saved August 8, 1990 at home.

Rick works as a carpenter, specializing in finish work, including installation of cabinets and millwork. Rick has built several custom homes from the ground up as well as he is experienced in commercial building.

Karen is a Certified Professional Secretary, she also holds a Life and Health Insurance agent license and she has successfully taken the H&R Block Tax course receiving an A. She has won photography awards from the Ozark Empire Fair. One of Karen's poems titles "From My Heart" can be found on page 84 in the book "A Celebration of Poets" published by The Poetry Guild. The three gospel songs that Karen holds copyrights to are titled "Oh, How I Love Him," "Find Grace in the Lord" and "Welcome Home My Child, Welcome Home."

Karen has worked for certified professional accountants for over seven years, in banking for over nine years, she has worked as a bookkeeper for the Camden County Treasurer, and she also held a temporary position at the Dunnegan Gallery of Art here in Bolivar.

From My Heart – In my quest for the perfect card I found the selection limited and small. But I'm hoping these Birthday regards will be better than…nothing at all! So even though this card definitely is not, what I call classy, elegant or smart, Please notice it's another Forget-me-not sending you wishes… from my heart. *Submitted by Rick and Karen McCaslin, poem by Karen McCaslin*

MCCLELLAND – Phillip Curry McClelland was born Feb. 11, 1851 in Rockbridge County, VA to Robert Wallace McClelland and Dolly Ingert Gregory. He was the third of 11 children. Phillip Curry married Margaret Elizabeth Burkhart, born Feb. 18, 1856 in Sullivan County, TN, the daughter of James Willoughby Burkhart and Mary P.T. Delaney, July 2, 1874 in Sullivan County, TN. To this union nine children were born: James Russell, born April 6, 1876 in Bristol, TN, married Radie M. Harness, Dec. 28, 1898, died April 27, 1918, buried Rice Cemetery, Dadeville, MO; John R., born Aug. 31, 1877 in Bristol, TN, married Margaret "Maggie" Elizabeth Hasket, Oct. 22, 1902, died Aug. 8, 1962, buried Rice Cemetery, Dadeville, MO; George Burkhart, born May 19, 1879 in Bristol, TN, married Mattie Isolene Faulkenberry, Sept. 27, 1900, died Dec. 19, 1941, buried Pleasant Ridge Cemetery, Polk County, MO; Joe Ben, born June 6, 1881 in Cedar County, MO, died Sept. 4, 1881, buried Hackleman Cemetery, Caplinger Mills, MO; Frank Lee, born Dec. 29, 1883 in Cedar County, MO, died Feb. 29, 1884, buried Hackleman Cemetery, Caplinger Mills, MO; Ollie Mae, born March 27, 1885 in Polk County, MO, married Clarence Clinton Wheeler, April 27, 1904, died March 19, 1955, buried Wheeler Cemetery, Dade County, MO; William Theodore, born March 4, 1889 in Polk County, MO, married Maude Esther McConnell, Sept. 17, 1910, died Nov. 7, 1961, buried Masonic Cemetery, Dadeville, MO; Claude Castle, born Aug. 4, 1891 in Polk County, MO, married Bernice Sweet, Dec. 24, 1912, died Dec. 24, 1967, buried in Rice Cemetery, Dadeville, MO; Hugh Park, born Feb. 8, 1896 in Polk County, MO, married Louesa Susong Dunn, Nov. 2, 1915, died Sept. 29, 1955, buried in Routh Chapel Cemetery, Dade County, MO.

First row James, Claude, Hugh, Margaret (wife), 2nd row John, William, Ollie Mae, George

Phillip and Margaret had three boys, James, John and George, born in Tennessee. About 1880 Phillip moved his family by wagon from Tennessee to Cedar County, MO near Caplinger Mills. November 1879, Phillip was in Sullivan County, TN, as he was a witness on John Rhodes Delaney's will (grandfather of his wife). Their first child born in Missouri was in June 1881.

Ben Joe and Frank Lee each died at two months of age and were buried in Cedar County, MO.

Between February 1884 and March 1885 Phillip and Margaret moved from Cedar County to Dade County, MO. Phillip, in 1895, purchased about 80 acres in Polk County, Jackson Township and across the road in Dade County, another 80 acres in Morgan Township. Their house was located in Polk County. On this farm were born Ollie, Claude, William and Hugh. The farm was purchased by their son William in 1915 and farm has since remained in the family.

Phillip and Margaret owned a small log house which they referred as the "Weaner Cabin," where some of the older children lived for a short time after they were first married. Franklin's sister Ernestine McClelland-Neil was born in that cabin.

A neighbor was quoted as saying, "Doc was very honest and a true friend, Margaret 'Maggie' enjoyed her flowers and has a lovely flower garden which she tended with great care. She also enjoyed piecing quilts."

Phillip died Jan. 9, 1908 in St. John's Hospital, Springfield, MO from pneumonia following an appendicitis operation. Funeral services were held up by a severe winter storm, blocking the roads.

Margaret died May 18, 1924 after a severe stroke. Her funeral was interrupted by possibly the worst hailstorm to ever occur in that area. All cars with cloth tops were in shreds, crops and gardens were destroyed, windows were broken, including those in the church. The burial was postponed until the following day. *Submitted by Franklin McClelland*

Great-Grandfather Eugene Frame McColm

MCCOLM – John McColm III was born 1800 in Oldtown, MD. Came to Adams County, OH in 1804. He was the son of John II, born 1772 in Ireland, who married Sarah Smith in 1796 and grandson of John I, born 1730 in Scotland, who married Elizabeth Blair in 1771. Their families came from Scotland to Allegheny County, MD in 1793; the grandparents died here. John III married Hanna Beach, April 24, 1823; their children were William, Nathan and Stephan.

William McColm was born Aug. 21, 1824 in Adams County, OH. Delila Pence, born Nov. 8, 1821, first married Samual Pollard; their children were Mahala, Elizabeth, Morgan and Mary. Samual died in 1847. William McColm and Delila (Pence) Pollard married April 8, 1848. Children were Philip, Lewis, Albert, Melvina (all born in Adams County, OH) and Eugene Frame, born Oct. 22, 1857 in Lewis County, MO.

William and Delila McColm came to Polk County around 1869 or 1870, when Jane's great-grandfather (Eugene) was 12 years of age. At this time they bought the farm where Jane and her two brothers grew up.

Eugene, in March 1884, married Addie Belle Henson, born June 13, 1870. Their children were Minnie, Fannie, Etta, Ada and William "Howard."

Howard, born Feb. 28, 1897 and Millie Jane Bass, born March 18, 1900 were married Dec. 26, 1920. Children were Willa Maxine, Ruth Helene, William Ralph and Elma Jean.

Elma Jean McColm, born Sept. 17, 1931 and Vernon Alonzo Carter, born May 24, 1934, were married on April 21, 1956. Jane's great-grandmother "Addie" died in 1958. At this time, Jane's parents, Vernon A. and Elma Jean Carter, bought the farm. Jane and her two brothers, Michael Kim, born Aug. 18, 1957 and Vernon Mark, born June 7, 1963, grew up on the farm where William and Delila settled in 1870.

The fifth generation is now owner/operator of that farm. Michael K. and Rhonda G. (Stogsdill) Carter moved there in 1995, with their children, JudiAnn (Carter) Sutt, Kimberly A. (Carter) Foster and Michael Lee.

Some things that are still with their family are a stone butter churn, dresser, bed, rocking chair and a Second Grade Public School of Missouri, Teacher's Certificate in their great-great-grandfather's name (William McColm), dated Nov. 12, 1870. The bed, dresser and chair are part of Jane's home today. The rocking chair in the pictures below was used to rock Jane's own children, Larry Curtis Covert, Amy Jo (Covert) Hodges and Emily Rae Francka.

Great-Grandson Michael K. Carter also pictured on right are two more generations, Michael Lee Carter, Zachary and Madison Sutt, to share memories of the same farm.

Jane says, "All of my life has been in rural Polk County. Most people probably considered us to be poor, on the contrary, the memories of our family being together here are such a blessing. Family and the simple things in this life are captured in my thoughts." *Submitted by Addie "Jane" (Carter) Francka*

MCCONNELL – Dorothy Anderson married Willie McConnell, September.1930 in Cordell, OK and they continued to live in Cordell until their fourth child was born. They moved to Saticoy, CA in 1938 and raised their family there.

Their first child, Billy Joe "Junior," born Jan. 30, 1932, Cordell, OK, was married to Dottie Larson, June 16, 1956, in Saticoy, CA. Junior died Sept. 1, 1995 in Medford, OR.

Their second child, Mary Ann, born Nov. 3, 1933 in Dill, OK was married to Everett Clifton on April 5, 1951. Mary Ann died March 26, 1999.

Their third child, Billy Gene, was born May 10, 1935 in Sayre, OK. He married Fayth Gerhold, Jan. 8, 1955, in Saticoy, CA.

Willie and Dorothy McConnell, Effie Anderson about 1969.

Their fourth child, Maxine Rella, was born Aug. 26, 1937 in Dill, OK, died Oct. 18, 1999 in Lodi, CA. She married Walter Dowling, who died Feb. 14, 1981 in Bolivar, MO. Maxine, Walter and their son Billy are buried in the Greenwood Cemetery, Bolivar, MO.

Their fifth child, Annie Lee, was born June 17, 1939 in Ventura, CA and married Floyd H. Keith, Sept. 5, 1954. at Santa Paula, CA.

Their sixth child, Louise, was born Aug. 20, 1943 in Saticoy, CA and married Theo Condren of Goodson, MO, June 19, 1960. They make their home in Bolivar, MO.

Dorothy and Willie were both from financially depressed backgrounds. They were both hardworking and determined workers. In 1938 they moved from western Oklahoma to Saticoy, CA. They both worked for the Saticoy Lemon Packing Company until they retired and moved to Rouge River, OR, where they lived until the death of Willie of lung cancer on May 10, 1978, in Medford, OR hospital. Willie was buried in Greenwood Cemetery, Bolivar.

Willie McConnell was an inventive person. The management at the lemon packing plant ask him to make a machine that would size and pack the lemons. He not only designed and built the machine, to my knowledge; the third or fourth generation is still in use. He was always inventing something.

After the death of her husband, Willie, Dorothy moved to Bolivar where she made her home until she passed away on Aug. 1, 1991. She came here so her daughters, Annie Lee Keith and Louise Condren, would be near and able to care for her in her declining years. Dorothy really enjoyed living in Bolivar. She really enjoyed her vegetable garden which she grew each year until she was no longer able to tend it. When her mother and sisters would come to visit, they would try to come when the different wild berries were in season. They would make pies and tell of days gone by. The highlight of their visit was not pies but poke greens and catfish. Many was the time that all they had to eat was poke greens and catfish.

Dorothy loved her grandchildren and was fortunate to be surrounded by many of them in the twilight of her life. *Submitted by Betty Thomosson*

MCCRACKEN – According to land records, the first McCrackens to purchase land in Polk County, in 1837, were Robert Holmes McCracken and his brothers, Nathaniel, Samuel and James. They had arrived from Williamson County, TN and by 1842 were joined by their parents, Thomas and Elizabeth Holmes McCracken and the rest of the family of 13 children.

The McCrackens settled in what is now northern Polk County and southern Hickory County, roughly in the area of the intersection of Missouri Highway 83 and State Road V.

Thomas McCracken was born in Maryland on Feb. 26, 1778, the son of John and Jean/Jennet Lytle McCracken. John died in Rowan County, NC in 1792. Other children of John and Jean Lytle McCracken were Jennie/Jane, born about 1769; John Lytle, born 1770; Ephriam, born 1772; Joseph, born 1774; Sarah/Sally, born 1775; James, born 1780; Samuel B., born Jan. 11, 1783; Robert M., born Oct. 18, 1785.

Thomas McCracken and his wife Elizabeth Holmes were parents of 13 children. John Lytle, born Aug. 9, 1808, married Elvira McMinn in Tennessee and settled his family near Springfield, MO, in the area that is now near Northtown Mall.

Robert Holmes, born Dec. 26, 1809, married Clarissa Richardson. Their family lived in what is now Hickory County until his death in 1888.

Samuel, born March 30, 1811, married Elizabeth Owings and lived in the same area. He died in 1854, leaving Elizabeth a widow with young children. She eventually followed one of her sons to Quannah, Hardiman County, TX.

Nathaniel, born Oct. 17, 1813, married Arissa Cates. He and Arissa lived on his homestead in Hickory County, where he died at age 84. They are buried in the McCracken Cemetery on that property.

Photo believed to be Thomas McCracken, 1778-1859

James, born Sept. 28, 1815, married first, Intha Ann Kelly, who died only three weeks after their marriage. He married second, a widow, Anne Douglas Ballew. James was a carpenter and was building the first school building in Bolivar when he died during a measles epidemic in 1852. His son, William Thomas Jewett McCracken, first put the McCracken family history in writing in 1930.

Milas/Millice, born Sept. 11, 1815, was physically and/or mentally handicapped and cared for by his brothers until his death in 1865.

Doctor Thomas, born Aug. 7, 1819, was not a doctor. This was his name. He had not yet married when he died three days after his brother

James, with whom he was working on the academy building in Bolivar.

Ephriam, born May 17, 1821, married Susan Reynolds. Ephriam and Susan raised their family in northern Polk County. They are buried in Tillery Cemetery in Hickory County.

Albert Garner, born Jan. 28, 1823, married Mary Ingram. Albert suffered an injury to his leg while in Tennessee. It was amputated after he came to Missouri. He owned and operated Kickapoo Nursery, shipping plants all over the southwest part of the country. He also served as Circuit Clerk in Greene County. Albert and Mary are buried in Springfield, MO.

Margaret Jane, born March 26, 1824, married John Q. "Jack" Appleby. They raised their family near Springfield. Descendants are still in Polk and Green Counties.

Elizabeth Ann, born Nov. 26, 1826, married John B. "Jack" Ingram, a brother to Albert G. McCracken's wife, and lived in Polk County. Jack Ingram also was a nurseryman.

Nancy Malinda, born April 17, 1828, married Rev. Elkanah Spurgeon, a Baptist preacher. She lived only a few years after marriage. Her grave has not been located but Rev. Spurgeon and his second wife's graves have been located in Chariton County, MO.

Joseph Carroll, born Aug. 15, 1830, married Mary Frances Bodine. They were parents of 10 children, nine living to adulthood. Descendants still live in Polk and Greene Counties. "Uncle Joe" and "Aunt Frank," as they were known, are buried in Rondo Cemetery in Polk County. *Submitted by Carol Kramme*

MCCRACKEN – Marcus McCracken was born Oct. 18, 1857 in Polk County MO, the second child of Joseph Carroll and Mary Frances Bodine McCracken. On Dec. 10, 1882 he married Pauline Belle Ammerman, who was born Oct. 19, 1862, the daughter of Sanford and Rebecca Newberry Ammerman.

Marcus and Belle (Ammerman) McCracken with grandson Carroll McCracken circa 1941, black box on Belle's shoulder is hearing aid microphone.

Marcus and Belle lived in the Rondo area of northern Polk County, moving from farm to farm as share-crop farmers. They were parents of six children: Allie Lee, born Jan. 2, 1884, married Floyd Tompkins; Joseph Carl, born Oct 17, 1886, married Annis Lightfoot; Nieta Neola, born May 14, 1889, married first, Rev. Elmer Pitts, who died in 1912, later she married Lester Long; Sanford Ray, born Feb. 11, 1892, married Cuba Beem; infant son, born Jan. 13, 1895, died Feb. 2, 1895; Virgil Stewart, born March 7, 1896, married Mildred Compte; Gladys Marie, born July 4, 1901, married Glen Squibb.

Marcus and Belle died only one week apart in June 1942. They had celebrated 42 years together. During the last four years of their life, their son, Ray, returned from Orange County, CA to Polk County, with his wife Cuba and son Carroll, to care for them.

Marcus had great difficulty supporting his family, so Belle used her talents as the community seamstress. She would move from home to home as the season changed and children grew to sew for a family. When she completed her work at that home she would move to another, rooming and boarding at the home where she worked. Her machine and sewing box, a converted spool cabinet, would be loaded into a wagon or truck and hauled to the next client's home. She continued this long after her children were grown. She was an excellent seamstress, having the ability to design fancy dresses as well as construct everyday utilitarian clothing.

Two sons, Ray and Virgil, served in WWI. Virgil died at age 31 due to illness contracted during the war. Ray lived to the age of 96.

Marcus and Belle are buried in Rondo Cemetery. *Submitted by Jill Holder McCracken*

Ray and Cuba McCracken

MCCRACKEN – Sanford Ray McCracken was born Feb. 11, 1892, the fourth child of Marcus and Belle Ammerman McCracken. At the age of 14, he decided to journey to Colorado and go to work, sending money home to help his mother. He worked in the cook shack on a ranch and later harvested cantaloupes and other fruits and vegetables.

Shortly before he entered the service in WWI, he returned to Missouri. His mother sent him about five miles away to the home of John and Eliza Stokes to get a turkey. While there, his eyes beheld John and Eliza's granddaughter, 14-year-old Cuba Beem. He decided he would wait until she grew up, then he would marry her. Grandpa Stokes wouldn't think of letting Cuba date, but correspondence began between Ray and Cuba. They were married in Orange County, CA on Dec. 11, 1929.

Ray worked on Sunnydale Ranch, as a merchant patrolman in Los Angeles, and for fruit packing houses. Cuba worked in a factory until they discovered she was with child. In the spring of 1939 Ray sent Cuba and their son, Carroll, to Missouri to care for his parents, Marcus and Belle McCracken. This was a difficult decision for the family, but in order for them to have provisions for the winter, Cuba had to get to Missouri in time to raise a garden and preserve its produce. Ray needed to stay in California where he could earn more money. He followed them to Missouri that fall after the fruit packing season in California was over.

They lived the rest of their lives in the same location north of Rondo. Harvest times were community events with the crews moving from one farm to another. For many years Ray pulled his horse-drawn baler from farm to farm. At the age of 90 years, he was feeding big round bales of hay with a big Ford tractor-one bale in front and one behind. He was one proud farmer to be able to accomplish that feat.

Ray and Cuba were actively involved in their community. Cuba was a charter member of the Pleasant Hour Extension Club and remained a member until her death in 1996. Ray helped organize the WWI Veterans Organization in Bolivar. He was a charter member and she was a charter member of the Auxilary. Cuba taught Sunday School at Rondo Baptist Church and helped with Vacation Bible School and other church activities. She served many years as the church clerk, faithfully keeping the minutes of each monthly business meeting.

Like other families, they raised a large garden and various farm animals including chickens, pigs, sheep and cattle. Horses were a necessity for accomplishing every kind of farm work. Ray's big, black and white horses were of stock from his grandmother's horses. During the Civil War, the horse of his grandmother, Rebecca Newberry Ammerman, was stolen. She secured another horse and followed the troops to near Lebanon, MO where she reclaimed her horse. Ray always had a special fondness for those spotted horses and their history. *Submitted by Carroll S. McCracken*

Mary Francis Bodine and Joseph Carroll McCracken

MCCRACKEN – Joseph Carroll McCracken, born Aug. 15, 1830 in Williamson County, TN was the youngest child of Thomas and Elizabeth Holmes McCracken. He traveled with his family by covered wagon to Missouri when he was 12 years old. His generation of McCracken men are said to have been over six feet tall, with blond hair and blue eyes. Photographs of J.C. and Mary Frances show him to be very tall and she, very short, hardly coming to his shoulders.

On Oct. 21, 1855 he was married to Mary Frances Bodine. J.C. and Mary Frances became parents of 10 children. Their daughter, Ivy Olive died as an infant in 1875 and is buried near her parents in Rondo Cemetery. Other children were Henry Clay, born 1856, married Irena Lightfoot; Marcus Alexander, born 1857, married Belle Ammerman; Charles Cornelias, born 1859, married Cora Niblick; Marcellas Bell, born 1860, married Mary Pitts; Theophilus Pope, born 1862, married Alice Butler; W.T. Sherman, born 1865, married Minerva Cooper; Launa Christella, born 1867, married John Kendall; Virginia Florence, born 1869, married Charles Toups; Martha Frances, born 1876, married Charles Niblick.

J.C. inherited the homestead from his father Thomas, with the stipulation that he provide for his brother Millice. He continued to farm it until his death in 1913. He provided for Mary Frances to be supported by the farm until her death in 1922.

J.C. and Mary F. had an orchard of considerable size and transported ripe apples, packed in straw, to Sedalia where they could travel by train to markets in the east. Mary Frances, affectionately known as "Aunt Frank," also dried apples. There are pink dishes in the McCracken Room at the Polk County Museum that were some of the merchandise for which she traded her apples. This trade was made in Osceola, in St. Clair County, where her grandson ran a mercantile store.

J.C. was active in the Mission Chapel Baptist Church, now known as Rondo Baptist Church. *Submitted by Charles McCracken*

MCCRACKEN – Carroll S. McCracken, fifth generation Polk Countian, named for his great-grandfather, Joseph Carroll McCracken, was the only child born to S. Ray and Cuba L. Beem McCracken. At the time of his birth, they were living near Fullerton, CA. At the age of 4, his parents returned with him to the prairie of north central Polk County to live and care for his grandparents, Marcus and Belle Ammerman McCracken.

Carroll attended grade school at Union School #5 which was only a few hundred yards from his home. During some of those years he would arise early, build the fire in the schoolhouse stove and return home for breakfast. This job paid him 25 cents per week.

He was active in 4-H, raising sheep and cattle in his projects. He was also involved in church youth activities at Rondo Baptist Church where he is a member.

Carroll graduated from Bolivar High School in 1952. While there he played football, was active in FFA, serving as chapter president during his senior year and participated in at least one school play.

Jill and Carroll McCracken

After graduation he farmed with his father for several years, then joined a partner, J.C. Meador, in the ownership of M & M Farm Center, the Ford and New Holland farm equipment dealership. He managed this business from 1969 to 1995, gaining the reputation of an honest businessman. In 1995 he "retired" to the farm where he and his wife, Jill, cared for his mother until her death in 1996.

In the 1970s they acquired the 1842 homestead of Thomas and Elizabeth Holmes McCracken, which is across the road from his childhood home, and continues to raise cattle on it.

Carroll served in the Army Reserves in the 1950s and is a member of the Kiwanis Club, American Legion and AmVets Post 114.

In 1974 he was married to Jill Holder Howe, a native of Cooper County, and daughter of Raymond and Neva Walker Holder. She had a daughter, Sarah, and a few years later, another daughter, Raylea, was born. Jill's varied careers include working for the Division of Family Services, being a stay-at-home-mom, teaching home economics, owning a fabric store, custom sewing, and being a Parents as Teachers Educator. She is a member of the Rondo Baptist Church. *Submitted by Raylea McCracken Whiteman*

William H. McCulley

MCCULLEY – William Henry McCulley was born April 26, 1850 in Peoria, IL. His parents were Jackson McCulley and Julie Dixson and his grandparents, Rolla McCulley and Nancy Devers. William H. McCulley married Mary Eugenia "Jennie" Calvin, March 1, 1876.

Jan. 27, 1865, William H. McCulley was mustered into Company M, 11th Regiment, Illinois Volunteer Cavalry as a bugler. Though he was only 14 at the time, he was tall for his age, five feet 10 inches, and was believed when he gave his age as 18. He told his grandchildren, "I fought for the North to make us free." Carrying his bugle, he marched in the Bolivar parades honoring veterans of the Civil War. When the war ended in 1865, he went to Cheyenne, WY, where he opened a leather shop. He went on buffalo hunts with Wild Bill Hickok for the hides. He also was a blacksmith and shoed Wild Bill's horses.

March 5, 1885, William H. McCulley and family moved to Bolivar after hearing about the cheap land and excellent fruit-growing region. He arrived with the first pair of cream-colored horses, 15 1/2 hands high, in Polk County. He took great pride in these horses, taking great care of them. The weekly grooming regimen consisted of coats polished to a high gloss, manes brushed and trimmed, hooves cleaned, and on special occasions, tails elaborately braided. On trips to town, he hitched his high-stepping horses to a fancy, fringed carriage, using the reins to turn the horses' heads at a slight angle in a showmanship style. No one dared pass him on the road. He was a very domineering man.

He was a perfectionist. He kept his property cleared of debris such as corn cobs, feathers, weeds. It was told that he was one of the first homeowners to enclose his property with knee-high hedges, kept immaculately trimmed. Each horse had its own stall and even in the winter months, all mud and snow had to be removed from the horses before entering their stalls. He built separate sheds for his buggies, farm equipment, crops, tack and fodder. He was president of the board of directors of the first telephone company in Bolivar, the Polk County Mutual Telephone Company. He was noted for his exquisite penmanship, put to excellent use in the 1900 censes as the enumerator of Marion Township, Polk County. He subscribed to newspapers from several states where he had previously lived.

When William H. McCulley became ill in 1913 and was unable to care for his farm and livestock, he had a sale. He watched the auction from his window. He hoped that the offspring of his palominos would go to a good home. When the high bidder was the owner of a livery stable that rented out horses and buggies, he broke down and cried.

The children of William H. and Jennie McCulley were Addie May, Josie, Charley William, Judy's grandmother Nellie, and Clyde J. Granddaughter Elva Callaway owned Tots-N-Teens Shop at 110 West Broadway in Bolivar. Another granddaughter, Thelma Price, owned a restaurant, noted for its pies, located off the Bolivar square. Many of their descendants still live in Polk County such as Carrye Ann Leith and Charles Franklin Price. *Submitted by Gae Slavens*

MCELWEE – Lee Patrick McElwee, an Irishman, moved to Polk County sometime in the 1900s, and, although the McElwee name has a Polk County history of less than one hundred years, when Lee died in 1963, he left a slew of descendents, many of whom still live in or near Bolivar.

According to oral history, Lee McElwee's parents, Frank and Mahalie McElwee, lived near Brownington or Vista, MO in the late 1800s and Mahalie died when Lee's brother John was a baby. Frank packed up his three youngest sons and moved to Texas while Lee, who was 12 years old, moved in with friends and stayed in Missouri. The Texas McElwee brothers were Clarence and Les, and they spent the rest of their lives in Texas. John, the only red-headed Irishman, moved to Reno, NE.

In Polk County, Lee married Ina Elizabeth Kinsey on Jan. 25, 1906. Ina was born Nov. 26, 1887, the middle child of Riley and Alla May Walker Kinsey. Lee and Ina had five living children: Ona Mae, Henry Lee, Vida Jewel, Julia LaVerne and Edward Eugene. There were three stillborn-a daughter in 1908, and sons in 1918 and 1928. Their oldest son, Henry Lee, died in 1915 just before he was 2 years old. Ina McElwee died Jan. 26, 1943, when her son Eddie was 12 years old.

Lee worked for a railroad, tried farming and eventually worked as a carpenter.

Ona, the oldest McElwee child, married Alfred Jenkins. Their daughter, Dorothy Cockrell, has three children, four grandchildren and one great-grandchild. Son Richard married Carolyn Stuckey and has three daughters and one grandchild.

Ina and Eddie McElwee, Dorothy Jenkins, Lee McElwee, Bill and Vida Jenkins with Cleo Wayne, Ona and Alfred Jenkins-inset-Judy McElwee

Vida's husband was William Jenkins and their three sons were Cleo Wayne, William Eugene and Gary Lynn. Cleo Wayne, who passed away in 1997, married Grace Owens. They had three daughters and five grandchildren. Second son, William Eugene "Billy Gene," married Lois Woods. They have four children and five grandchildren. Youngest son, Gary Lynn, married Beverly Gaydoo and they have two children.

Judy married Lee Jump, had four children, divorced and later married Carl Vest. She passed away in 1974. Judy's living children are Joyce Stone and Carolyn Ballentyne. Two sons, Larry and Randy, are deceased. There are seven living grandchildren and one grandchild is deceased.

The McElwees' only surviving son, Edward Eugene, married Virginia Smolnik, a Polk County resident from the Bohemian Community of Karlin. She died Jan. 7, 2002 and is buried in the Karlin Cemetery. This McElwee family moved from the Bolivar area in the 1950s and had three sons: Gregory Michael, Steven Eugene and Jon Edward. There are four grandchildren and four step-grandchildren.

The McElwees are a close-knit family and those who are away visit Polk County regularly, often attending the annual McElwee/Kinsey Family Picnic. *Submitted by Ed McElwee*

Back row – Charles, Debbi, Isaac. Front row – Daberath, Whitney, Denver

MCGINNIS – Charles Eugene McGinnis and Debra "Debbi" Louiese Roberts were married June 1, 1979; each lived in Polk County all their lives. They share a common ancestor in Jesse Russell Payne (born Aug. 24, 1839, died May 25, 1922). At the time of printing all four of their living children reside in Polk County and are therefore seventh generation Polk Countians.

The children are Isaac Roberts (born Sept. 1, 1983) Daberath Louiese (born May 27, 1985), Whitney Dayle (born July 4, 1988) and Denver Payne (born March 24, 1994). Ashley Rae (born and died April 4, 1981) is buried in the Payne family cemetery in Polk, MO.

Charles (born March 13, 1956) is the son of Charles "Charlie" Woodrow McGinnis (born Nov. 3, 1913, died Jan. 15, 1979) and Adlene Miller Payne (born Nov. 30, 1918, died Jan. 24, 2002), who were married July 5, 1947. He was their only child. Charlie was a farmer and served in WWII as a PFC in the 262nd Medical battalion. He died of lymphoma. Adlene was a homemaker and also was employed as a cook with the Bolivar R-1 School system. Her death was due to heart failure and she suffered with Alzheimer's. Her last few months were spent in the home of her son and family.

Charles is also a farmer, raising beef cattle and a few AKC dachshunds and Lhaso Apso dogs. Part-time he also works for Pitts Chapel in Bolivar. He graduated from Bolivar High School in 1974 and is active in Bolivar Young Farmers and his children's school activities. Charles enjoys quiet time at home.

Debbi is the daughter of Donald Claude Roberts (born Aug. 20, 1936) and Delores Louiese Gamel (born Aug. 12, 1938) and has three siblings, Donita Pirkle and twins Dwight Roberts and Denise Stutenkemper. All still reside in Polk County.

Debbi (born May 18, 1959) is the Polk County Collector of Revenue after being consecutively elected since 1994. Previous to that, she served one term on the Bolivar Board of Education, having graduated from Bolivar in 1977. She graduated from SMSU in Springfield, MO in 1980 with a degree in agricultural economics. She is involved in several Republican groups as well as Bolivar Young Farm Wives. Each Sunday she, along with her children, attend Calvary Missionary Baptist Church where she is a member and Sunday School teacher. Debbi enjoys travel, reading, watching her kids in activities, and surfing the Internet.

Isaac is currently attending Ozark Technical College in Springfield after graduation from Bolivar in 2002. He is considering pre-veterinary medicine or another career in agriculture.

Daberath also plans to attend OTC after high school graduation in 2003. She is actively involved with FFA, serving currently as President after accepting the gavel from her brother (a first in BHS history).

Whitney is active in cheerleading and the pursuit of all social activities known to teen-kind. She plans to graduate in 2007 and "do something" but she doesn't know what yet.

Denver is in the third grade currently and plans to play Upward Bound basketball again this year. His greatest accomplishment so far is his ability since kindergarten to recite the alphabet backwards and skip every other letter. He is an avid math student as well. *Submitted by Debbi R. McGinnis*

MCINTOSH – On Oct. 21, 1847 the "Carolina Watchman" published at Salisbury, Rowan County, NC an article on the first settlements in the area, noting the 1772 arrival of "about 12 families; McKays, McIntoshes, Mathesons, Campbells and others."

McIntoshes, McKays boarded the ship *Adventure,* bound for the Carolinas, Aug. 19, 1772 from cove at Loch Erriboll, Sutherlandshire, Scotland.

Hector McIntosh, son of Wm. John and Margaret (Monroe) McIntosh, was born about 1755 in Elrig, Scotland; he married Mary McKay, born about 1764 in Scotland. Mary was a daughter of Daniel McKay and Jeannie Campbell. Hector died about 1795 and Mary died about 1818 in Iredell County, NC. Their children are John McKay, William, Alexander and Margaret.

John McKay McIntosh was born about 1783 in Rowan/Iredell County, NC and died about 1840 in Maury County, TN. He married about 1805 in Rowan/Iredell County, NC to Barbary McKenzie; she was born about 1784 in Rowan/Iredell County, and died about 1855 in Lawrence County, AL. Barbary was a daughter of Kenneth and Christian (Gordon) McKenzie. Their children are an infant daughter, Hector, William N., Daniel, Christian, Collon, Elizabeth and John R.

Collon McIntosh was born March 3, 1817 in Iredell County, NC and he died March 23, 1896 near Shady Grove, Polk County, MO. Collon married Mary Jane Fox, daughter of Elijah Milton and Priscilla (Potts) Fox. She was born May 15, 1820 in Burke County, NC and passed away Jan. 7, 1898 near Shady Grove, Polk County, MO. Collon and Jane were married in Williamson County, TN on Oct. 17, 1839. Their children: John Alexander, Elijah Milton, Susan Barbary, Caroline Priscilla, Sarah, Mary Jane, William Collin, Nancy Christine, Daniel Elderidge and James Henry "Tom."

John A. married Mary A. Cotham; Elijah M. died Oct. 7, 1864, Battle at Jefferson City, MO during the Civil War, he is buried in the National Cemetery there; Susan B. married Dr. George W. Griffin; Caroline P. married Charles B. Wingfield; Sarah, no spouse; William C. married first, Frances Zumwalt, second, Rebecca Zumwalt and third, Nora Alice Irick; Nancy C. married Hardin Crane; Daniel E. married Catherine Whitacker; and James H. "Tom" married Ida A. McGee. *Submitted by S.D. Snow*

Stephen Challance and Mary Elizabeth Dowell McKinney

MCKINNEY – Stephen Challance McKinney was born Jan. 5, 1839 in Wayne County, KY and had five brothers and sisters: John D., Alexander, Charles Sr., Rane Chastain and William Franklin.

Mary Elizabeth Dowell was born March 9, 1842 in Polk County, MO and had four brothers and sisters: John, Thomas A., Rueben Warren and George Taylor.

Mary Elizabeth and Stephen Challance McKinney were married Sept. 27, 1858 in Polk County and had 11 children. George William was born Oct. 23, 1859 in Missouri. First wife's name was Pearl, second wife was Iva Foster. He died on May 7, 1933 in Missouri. James Robert, born Sept. 8, 1861, died in 1861. Lee Ann, born Dec. 29, 1862 in Missouri, married Fredrick William Drewer on Dec. 30, 1879 in Beloit, Mitchell County, KS. They had 10 children and Lee Ann died on Oct. 11, 1935 in Warrenton, MO. John Franklin, born Jan. 11, 1865 in Andrew County, MO, married Martha Jane Tharp on Dec. 12, 1885 in Minneapolis, Ottawa County, KS. They had 10 children and John died on Aug. 26, 1948 in Deronda, Alden County, WI. Samantha Alice was born Oct. 26, 1866 in Illinois. First husband was Adam Miles, whom she married on May 22, 1880 in Cloud County, KS; they had six children. Second husband was George M. Kees; third husband was Edward Mills. Samantha died July 27, 1943 in Seattle, King County, WA. Elizabeth Voqua Ellen, born Nov. 28, 1868 in Illinois, married a man with the last name of Stansill and had two children. Samuel S., born Jan. 24, 1871 in Missouri, married a woman whose first name was Bird and had four children. Artiamecia Rachel, born Jan. 14, 1874 in Missouri, married a man with the last name of Davis. Daniel Boone was born June 24, 1873 in Beloit, Mitchell County, KS, married Alice Rebecca Reber and had six children. Robert Benjamin, born Sept. 17, 1881 in Concordia, KS, married Maudie May Frontin. He died on June 1, 1964 in Kingfisher, OK. Lucy (Blossom), born April 12, 1887 in Kansas, married Henry David Reeves and had one child and adopted two. She died on Jan. 22, 1956 in El Dorado Springs, Cedar County, MO.

Stephen died on July 31, 1918 in Manson, Pocahontas County, IA and is buried at Rose Hill Cemetery in Calhoun County, Manson, IA. Mary applied for a pension since Stephen served in the Civil War. He enlisted in the Union Army in the fall of 1861 at Fayetteville, AR as a driver of teams in the Eighth Missouri, General Blunt's division. He was honorably discharged in April of 1863. Mary died on April 9, 1927 in Kansas City, KS and is also buried at Rose Hill Cemetery.

Samantha Alice McKinney, the fifth child of Mary and Stephen McKinney, and her first husband Adam Miles had six children. An infant was born and died in about 1883. Nellie Elizabeth (birth record lists her as Nanny Elizabeth) was born April 4, 1884 in Newport, Barton County, MO, married Edward Clinton Ingram in about 1900 and had eight children. She died on June 8, 1961 in Port Angeles, WA. Elmer Milton was born July 30, 1886 in Newport, Barton County, MO, married Ida Marie Dickey on May 2, 1910 in Coffeyville, KS and had 10 children. He died May 4, 1936 in Kansas City, KS. Ora M. was born April 13, 1889 in Newport, Barton County, MO, married Arthur M. Smales and had two children. She died in 1960 in Seattle, King County, WA. John Albert was born May 21, 1891 in Newport, Barton County, MO and married a woman named Grace and had three children. William Stephan was born March 1, 1893 in Newport, Barton County, MO. First wife was Florence L. and they married in about 1912 in Missouri and had three children. Second wife was Laura Etta French and they married March 2, 1928 in Fruita, Mesa County, CO and had one child. He died Feb. 28, 1956 in Elma Gray Harbor, WA.

Elmer Milton and Ida M. (Dickey) Miles had 10 children. Hazel Iona, born May 19, 1911 in Mission, KS, married William Wesley Cox in about 1926 and had eight children. She died March 25, 1986 in San Bernardino, CA. Leo was born and died in 1913. Ora Leanor, born Oct. 1, 1914 in Cedar Rapids, IA, married Frank Robert McDaniel Sr. on Aug. 17, 1931 in Kansas and had 12 children. She died March 17, 1999 in Olathe, Johnson County, KS. Second husband was Loren Wilson, whom she married on May 12, 1960. Elmer Milton Jr., born July 7, 1916 in Cedar Rapids, IA, married Tessie McBride and had two children. He died Feb. 2, 1971 in Lansing, KS. Alice Marie, born July 18, 1948 in Pittsburg, KS, married Samuel William Cawyer on July 24, 1934 in Sapulpa, OK and they had seven children. She died Sept. 20, 1997 in Port Angeles, Clallam County, WA. Johnnie Veloris, born Aug. 30, 1921 in Pittsburg, KS, married Mary Ellen Wilson on

July 13, 1941 in Kansas City, Wyandotte County, KS and had 11 children. He died Sept. 5, 1984 in Kansas City, Wyandotte County, KS. Donald Wilbert, born May 31, 1924 in Kansas City, Wyandotte County, KS, married Freda Fay Lawson on Sept. 2, 1945 in Kansas City, KS and had three children. He died July 7, 1994 in Kansas City, KS. Paul Wesley, born Sept. 8, 1926 in Kansas City, Wyandotte County, KS, married Violet Lois Sherwood on Dec. 11, 1943 in Kansas City, KS and had six children. He died May 8, 1997 in Osceola, MO. Beulah Margaret was born Jan. 20, 1930 in Oklahoma City, OK. Married first husband Billy Dee Murray in 1947 in Kansas City, KS and had three children. Second husband was William "Bill" Clark, whom she married Oct. 27, 1953 in Kansas City, KS and had four children. Beulah died Jan. 18, 1985 in North Kansas City, MO. Ida Geraldine "Gerry," born Feb. 12, 1933 in Kansas City, KS, married Iva John Long and had six children. *Submitted by Mary Sanders*

MCKINNEY – John Vardaman McKinney was born Aug. 12, 1822 in Wayne County, KY and came to Polk County, MO about 1853 to join an uncle, James Rane McKinney, who had already settled here. John V.'s parents were William Franklin McKinney (born May 15, 1800 in Mercer County, KY) and Mary "Polly" (Boone) McKinney (born Jan. 31, 1802 in Burke County, NC, and a descendant of Daniel Boone, the frontiersman).

John married Rachel L. Payne on Dec. 9, 1841 in Wayne County, KY and they had 10 children, eight of whom lived to adulthood. They were Mary Agnes, born Oct. 19, 1842 in Wayne County, KY; William Franklin, born Jan. 27, 1847; Martha Elizabeth, born Jan. 23, 1849; and Sara Catherine, born Jan. 26, 1851, all in Bates County, MO; James, born about 1853; John Gant, born Oct. 15, 1855; Charles Stephen, born Nov. 5, 1858; and Lucinda Jane, born Oct. 30, 1859, all in Polk County, MO.

When John was age 40, in 1862, he traveled from his home to Arkansas to enlist in the Confederate Army, leaving his wife and nine children, ranging in age from 20 to age 1 in Polk County. There is much information in his Civil War pension file. At Helena, AR, he was captured and taken prisoner by the North, being transferred on the steamer "Silver Moon" to a Union prison camp in Alton, IL. There, in terrible and crowded conditions, he survived smallpox, being kept in the prison from July 1863 to March 1865, at which time he signed an Oath of Allegiance to the North, when the prison was making up companies of Rebels who were now willing to join the Union Army in exchange for pardon. These troops, known as "Galvanized Yankees" because of their thin coating of Yankee over their Rebel leanings, were not used in the war, but were sent north, to Nebraska Territory, to assist settlers, wagon trains and railroad builders by quieting the Indians, who had become very troublesome when troops formerly stationed there were pulled out to help fight in the Civil War.

As reported in the book "The Galvanized Yankees" by Dee Brown, John V. was one of the two oldest soldiers in the company. They were marched across the Nebraska plains in threadbare uniforms and barefoot, in weather reaching 106 degrees. During this march, John contracted sore eyes which resulted in ulceration and partial loss of vision, due to the alkali sand storms they endured on the march. He was discharged due to this on Oct. 20, 1865 at Ft. Conner, Dakota Territory, and returned home. His wife, Rachel, died Dec. 15, 1868, in childbirth at age 45.

John married again on Jan. 27, 1870 to a young widow, Martha Caroline Moore. They had three children, Edwin Elias, born Nov. 25, 1871; Jason Hardin, born June 2, 1873 and Emma Lee, born April 12, 1876.

Martha died of pneumonia on Feb. 12, 1880. She is buried at the Pleasant Hill Cemetery in Polk County, MO.

John married a third time on March 6, 1881 in Polk County, MO to Hannah (Corn) Taylor. He then died about 18 months after his third marriage, on Dec. 24, 1882 and was buried beside his first wife, Rachel, in the McKinney Cemetery in Polk County, MO.

Three sons of John V. McKinney; Charles S., William F. and John G.

Oldest son, William F., married Sarah Elizabeth Dean on Aug. 5, 1873 and they had four children: Alonzo, born June 8, 1874; Lester, born Nov. 4, 1876; Ida Belle, born Nov. 7, 1878; and Augustus, born May 19, 1882.

Alonzo married Clara Ella Noyes on Dec. 29, 1897 and they had three children who lived to adulthood: Floyd Lester, born May 30, 1899; Estella Mayree, born Aug. 16, 1901; and Orra Samuel, born Oct. 27, 1909.

Orra married Hazel Lorese Viles on Jan. 1, 1933 and they had three children: Lyndel Lavern, born Dec. 25, 1938; Myron Wesley, born Sept. 8, 1944; and Sandra Kay, born Oct. 13, 1946.

Lyndel married Nancy Ellen Condren on March 15, 1958 and they had three sons: Gregory Lavern, born Nov. 27, 1958; Wesley Allen, born Aug. 24, 1962; and Jeffrey Lee, born Sept. 27, 1963. Nancy and Lyndel divorced in March 1971, and on Sept. 2, 1972, Lyndel married Judith E. Jones. Lyndel and Judy currently reside on a farm near Halfway, MO. *Submitted by Judy McKinney*

MCKINNEY – Paul Francis McKinney was born Oct. 9, 1912 and passed Dec. 12, 1997. Paul was born in Aldrich, MO, son of George Thomas McKinney (born Aug. 10, 1874, passed Oct. 7, 1958) and Cora Ellen Hamilton (born May 20, 1888, passed Jan. 21, 1947). The marriage of George and Cora immediately created a large family; both were previously married and widowed with three children apiece. Together they had four more children. Children include: Eura, Eunice and Arley Hamilton, Della, Jesse and Olen "Buck" McKinney; together they had Paul Francis, Mary Lou, Dorothy and Elva.

Paul grew up and attended school in Aldrich. He married Edna Faye Adams, Nov. 13, 1937 and within a few years, the couple built a home just outside of Morrisville and lived there nearly 60 years. On Nov. 13, 1997 they celebrated their 60th anniversary shortly before Paul passed.

Paul and Faye were both members of the United Methodist Church of Morrisville; Faye attained her 50-year membership. Paul followed farming and was a board member of the Missouri Farmers Association in Bolivar and Morrisville; he was also on the school board in Morrisville. Paul owned one of the first threshing machines in the area, friends and neighbors would help each other thresh their crops, moving from one farm to another, while the ladies would gather together in the house and cook meals for those working.

Edna Faye Adams was born Oct. 9, 1912 in Walnut Grove, MO and passed Nov. 21, 2000. She was the daughter of Joseph Vincey Adams (born Aug. 29, 1888, passed Aug. 27, 1971) and Ellen Gee Lomas (born Jan. 15, 1893, passed July 5, 1979). She had one sister who survives her, Helen Euliss of Morrisville.

Faye attended elementary school at Sandhill and high school at Morrisville. She went on to college at Bolivar and Southwest Missouri State and worked toward her teaching degree. At first she taught at one-room schools until she attained her degree; eventually she taught at Morrisville, teaching for nearly 25 years. Those that remember her as "teacher" speak very fondly of her; she was a wonderful teacher and her students loved her. She was a gentle spirit who loved children and thought so much of others, a very sweet and gracious lady.

Paul and Faye have three children who survive them: Pat Harralson of Springfield, MO, Carol Edmunson of Brunswick, MO and Paul McKinney Jr. of Morrisville, MO. *Submitted by Tamara McKinney and Pat Harralson*

MCREYNOLDS – Robert McReynolds, son of Robert D. and Mary "Polly" (Walker) came from Knox County, TN to Polk County, MO where he and wife, Sara (Pennington) had six children. Both died in Bolivar and are buried at Mt. Gilead Cemetery. Their fourth son, John, born March 7, 1863 and his wife, Elizabeth (Higginbotham), born Oct. 27, 1866, met at a school function where John's school, CherryVale and "Lizzie's" school, Wilmington, both participated. They were married May 10, 1885 in Polk County and homesteaded on a farm east of Bolivar near Lizzie's parents. They had seven children: Ralph, Maude, Guy, Loah, Gideon, Clifford and Johnie. All the children attended Wilmington school. John's family was of Methodist faith and Lizzie's was Baptist where her father, Gid Higginbotham, was a preacher. Later, John joined the Baptist church and their children were raised Baptist.

John farmed and worked in the timber business-pricing, buying and selling walnut timber. Local walnut timber, being plentiful then, was cut, hauled to a nearby sawmill and used for furniture making and home building. Lizzie was a housewife who tended to the needs of her family and helped with chores. She was a beautiful quilt maker and sewer and taught her daughters and granddaughters this art.

The whole family loved animals but horses were their special thing and all enjoyed working and riding them but Loah loved them most. She rode until quite senior in age and liked to tell the story of her first horse which was a gift from her parents. When she would go to the pasture it would come up and "kiss" her. Then one winter day while moving stock across the river her horse fell and had to be killed.

As the years passed the children grew up, married and moved to their own homes some as far as California and Pennsylvania. John and Lizzie stayed on the farm and enjoyed visits from friends and children and grandchildren. These were special times for them and Lizzie, who was a wonderful cook, would make the best "country meals" with home-cured meat, jellies, garden vegetables and her special chocolate pie. Sundays they attended church – Lizzie going in the buggy pulled by an old, gray horse and John, who loved to walk, would walk across the pasture.

In his later years John took special delight in going to Bolivar where he would be seen visiting with friends. He always walked, leaving home in the morning and walking as far as Highway 32 where someone would always pick him up. After his day, around five o'clock he would go to the post office, sit on the front bench and visit until someone going his way would give him a ride. Usually he didn't have long to wait as everyone knew about this and made sure he had a ride home.

Back then not too many lived to celebrate their 50th wedding anniversary but John and Lizzie did and it was decided to have a yard party with all the trimmings, long tables under the trees and basket food. When the big day in May 1935 arrived, so did family and friends, all bringing baskets. It was a day to remember by all, especially John and Lizzie who never dreamed they had so much family and many friends who wanted to share this important day with them.

John and Lizzie lived on this same farm all of their married lives. Even though the farming did slack off as the children left, family and friends would come by to help. John died on the farm May 5, 1943. Lizzie, with help of family and friends, stayed until 1948 when she moved to her daughter's, Loah (Mrs. Fred Abel) in Halfway where she lived until she died Feb. 25, 1950. Both John and Lizzie are buried at Pleasant Hill Cemetery, east of Bolivar off Highway 32. *Submitted by Loraine Taylor*

MCREYNOLDS – Robert N. McReynolds, son of Robert D. McReynolds and Mary "Polly" Walker was born in Knox County, TN, Dec. 24, 1833. Robert died Aug. 8, 1894 in Bolivar. He married Sarah Ann Pennington in Bolivar, March 30, 1854. He and Sarah are buried in Mt. Gilead Cemetery.

Robert and his brother John W. were in Polk County, prior to the 1850 federal census. Robert was a private in Captain Miller's Missouri State Militia during the Civil War.

Robert N. McReynolds and Sarah Ann Pennington had the following children, all born in or near Bolivar: Mary Margaret "Maggie" McReynolds, March 28, 1855. Mary died July 6, 1930 in Ventura, CA. She married Wesley Fletcher Batten in Bolivar Dec. 21, 1873.

Mary Margaret "Maggie" McReynolds and Wesley Fletcher Batten had the following children, born near Bolivar: Alonzo A. "Lon" was born Oct. 17, 1874. Alonzo died Nov. 10, 1964.

Ida F. was born Jan. 25, 1877 and died Jan. 16, 1878.

James Henry "Jim" was born March 23, 1879 and died May 9, 1959.

Annie E. was born Aug. 2, 1881 and died Sept. 24, 1921.

John W. was born Feb. 9, 1884. John died 1952.

Frank Delmar was born Sept. 19, 1886 and died Jan. 17, 1963 in Ventura, CA.

Charles Edward was born March 2, 1889. He married Alma Enyart in Halfway, April 10, 1910. He married second Lena Ellen Wright in Bolivar, Dec. 31, 1921.

William E. was born June 9, 1891. William died Sept. 15, 1971 in San Antonio, TX. He married Dora Mae Griffith in Weaubleau, MO, Jan. 18, 1914.

Della Mae was born Oct. 6, 1893 and died Jan. 21, 1977 in Madera, CA. She married Llano Claude Gorden in Bolivar, Oct. 8, 1911. She married Jesse D. Pratt in California, circa 1951.

Lena I. was born May 16, 1896 and died July 8, 1896.

Raymond F. was born Oct. 27, 1899. Raymond died July 13, 1950. He married three times.

Alexander R. McReynolds was born Nov. 8, 1856, died Aug. 12, 1901 and was buried in Mt. Gilead Cemetery.

Laura Ellen McReynolds was born Oct. 20, 1860 and died April 11, 1901. She married Martin Taylor Higginbotham in Bolivar, Oct. 26, 1879. Both are buried in Pleasant Hill Cemetery.

John Pennington Wesley McReynolds was born March 7, 1863 and died May 9, 1943. He married Elizabeth Rachel "Lizzie" Higginbotham in Bolivar, May 10, 1885. Both are buried in Pleasant Hill.

John Pennington Wesley McReynolds and Elizabeth Rachel "Lizzie" Higginbotham had the following children, born near Bolivar: Ralph Archie was born June 23, 1886, died July 26, 1973 in Springfield, MO.

Maude Essie was born March 29, 1889, died April 27, 1953 in Santa Cruz, CA. She married Walter Elbert Burchett in Bolivar in Sept. 27, 1914.

Guy Floyd was born Aug. 15, 1892. Guy died Feb. 2, 1976 in Monument, CO. He married Ada Blanche Fuller in Halfway, April 3, 1913.

Loah Claud was born Oct. 12, 1894. Loah died July 17, 1986 in Springfield, MO. She married Fred Olin Abel in Bolivar, Nov. 7, 1915.

Gideon Cheek "Gid" was born Dec. 29, 1896. Gideon died Aug. 17, 1982 in California. He married Martha Alice Honeymon in Bolivar, June 8, 1919.

Clifford Newton was born Sept. 10, 1905. Clifford died March 1, 1990. He married Florence Whitney in Bolivar, Aug. 31, 1926. He married second, Mrs. Wilma E. Brown-Bonner Nov. 21, 1938.

Johnny Gail was born Nov. 22, 1907. Johnny died April 28, 1992 in Charlotte, NC. He married Eleanor Rachel Dotterer, May 22, 1934.

Fannie Elizabeth McReynolds was born Oct. 20, 1865. Fannie died July 22, 1948 in Fillmore, CA. She married Samuel Monroe May in Bolivar, June 29, 1884. Both are buried in Mt. Gilead Cemetery.

Emma Jewell McReynolds was born May 19, 1869 and died Jan. 6, 1930. She married John H. Morris in Bolivar, June 2, 1889. Both buried in Mt. View Cemetery. *Submitted by Larry May*

MCSWAIN – Thomas McSwain was born Feb. 18, 1792 in Cleveland County, NC and died May 21, 1851 near Bolivar, Polk County, MO. His wife Selena Hall was born February 1794 in South Carolina and died October 1874 near Bolivar, Polk County, MO.

The children of Thomas McSwain and Selena Hall were Mary "Polly," who died in a fire at about age 9 in Berea, KY; Elizabeth "Betsy"—Mrs. Travis Cox; Susan—Mrs. William Brown; Hanah J.—Mrs. Resser B. Price; Sarah Ann—Mrs. Wright Bollinger; Margaret "Louiza"—Mrs. Thomas Johnson; Selena W.—Mrs. Baily East; Thomas Jr.—married Malinda East; William—first wife, Florinda East, second wife, Mrs. Martha P. Kemp; Nancy—first wife of Cyrus Patterson; Dianna—Mrs. Tillman Patterson; Serena—Mrs. William H. Moore.

Thomas McSwain, wife, and younger children moved to Polk County, MO in November 1838. Their daughter Susan and her husband, Rev. William Brown, had come first to Cedar County, MO in 1836. Thomas was a stone cutter—stone mason and helped build the first courthouse in Bolivar, MO in the early 1840s. When they arrived in Bolivar there was no church house, no school house, no jail and no permanent courthouse. The town was basically one little store owned by a man named Moore, a tannery owned by a Mr. Wilson, one blacksmith shop, one doctor named DeWitt and one cotton gin.

In the spring of 1851, when he knew he was "sick unto death," Thomas heard the cooing of a mourning dove and had one of his daughters follow it over to "younder Hill" to see where it lit. It lit on a cedar tree which is still there. In accordance with his wishes, that was where he was buried. He thus became the first person buried in what is now the Mt. Gilead Cemetery. His preacher son-in-law, William Brown, suggested that that would be a good place to build a church and in 1853 the Mt. Gilead Methodist Protestant Church was built near his grave. The cemetery continues to grow. The church, now the Mt. Gilead United Methodist Church, which is in a building built in 1932, continues the work started 150 years ago. *Submitted by James Whitman*

MAAS – In 1900 Nicholas Worthington Maas (1874-1946) and Carrie Lenora Jeffries Maas (1871-1941) arrived in Polk County, MO from Polk County, IA. Nicholas had seen several springs (south of the Bolivar square on Business 13) he thought would benefit his butter business. Prior to moving, Carrie had taught the Maytag children (of Maytag Appliance Company) in her school.

The springs did not keep the butter cold and he went broke. They moved to Springfield but returned for him to run the light plant in Bolivar from 7 a.m. to 10 p.m. There was no electricity in the town between 10 p.m. and 7 a.m.

Three sons were born to the family; Richard Harlan (1904-1933), Myron Jefferies (1909-1910) and Joseph Leonard (1905-1992).

In 1911 N. W. started N. W. Maas and Son Creamery and Ice Plant. They also sold coal for heating.

Harlan and Leonard worked in the plant with their father, until Harlan quit to run the Ideal Café on the north side of the square. He married Mary Griffin and they had one daughter, Joan Marie (1926-1969). Joan attended Drury College and worked the major part of her career in Hollywood for such stars as Dinah Shore, Steve Allen and Bob Hope. As Hope's associate producer, she traveled on many of his overseas USO tours. Hope called her "Bolivar Baby" and delivered her eulogy in Bolivar at her death. Mary owned the Style Shop on the east side of the square.

Leonard attended Drury College and the University of Missouri but left school to come home to help run the plant. He married Pauline Hamilton (1911-1997), a student at Southwest Baptist College. Her grandfather, Samuel E. Payne, a trustee and board member of the college, agreed to pay her tuition.

Two children were born to them: Samuel Nicholas (1935) and Carolyn (1936).

Leonard sold the Maas and Son Dairy to Robert and Peg Houk in 1954. He sold the ice cream business to Foremost in 1957.

Leonard and his family were members of the Disciples of Christ Church (First Christian Church) where he was an elder, choir member and Sunday school teacher for many years. He was a charter member of the Rotary Club and served on the school board, city council and as chairman of the Republican Party. He was elected Polk County Collector. He received the Silver

Beaver Award in Boy Scouts and the Community Service Award. Pauline served as treasurer of the Community Concert Association and as president of Chapter EZ of the PEO Sisterhood.

Nick met Jobeth Ellis at Drury College and they married in 1959. He and his father owned and operated the Maas and Son Quarry in Fair Play. Nick opened Maas Automatic Welding in Bolivar until he sold his building and to the city of Bolivar in 2002. He was an avid hunter and black powder enthusiast. He served as an elder and Sunday school teacher for many years. Jobeth taught school for 32 years. She received the Master Teacher and the Southwest District Teacher of the Year Awards. She was the pianist at the First Christian Church for over 30 years.

They had two children, Nicholas Joseph married Kathryn Marie Sears. They lived in Bolivar with their children, Katlyn Faye and Samuel Nicholas Joseph. Betsy (Pauline Elizabeth) married Terry Paul Davidson. They lived in Oklahoma with their children, Hannah Jane, Sarah Jobeth and Samuel Paul.

Carolyn Maas attended MacMurray College and the University of Missouri where she graduated with a nursing degree. She married Dr. Howard Dwight Adams and they lived in Liberty until their divorce in 1985. They had three children. David Hamilton Adams married Diane Sutton. Their children were Aubrey Diane and Caitlyn Mary. Later, another child, Delaney Pauline, was born. Ann Elizabeth married Gregory Allen Fay and their children were Kathleen Elizabeth, Jackson Alexander and Theodore Gregory. Mary Carolyn married Todd Saracini and their children were Ellen Pauline and Joseph Michael.

The "Maas and Son" business sign has alerted Polk Countians to ice cream, butter, milk, ice, coal, agricultural lime and track welding since 1911. Currently it hangs on a building where smaller welding jobs can be done (if he isn't hunting, shooting or flying) on land belonging to Nick Maas. *Submitted by Jobeth Maas*

MACKEY – Joseph M. Mackey, born Sept. 17, 1875, was the son of Newton Perry Mackey and Elizabeth J. Erwin and in the fourth generation of Mackeys born in Polk County. They were all farmers and farmed near Morrisville, MO. Joseph married Maud Duncan, Sept. 18, 1895. Her ancestors came to Missouri in the late 1700s and from six generations back, all lived in Polk County. They all farmed around Morrisville and Hickory Grove, Oakville and Wishart. They were just about kin to every household in the area from one side or the other. They were active in the community of Morrisville and attended the Methodist Church in town. They had eight children: Ona, Earl, Earnest, Otis, Elizabeth, John, Pauline and Kenneth. The children would lose their mother, Maud, to heart problems when Kenneth was only 6 weeks old. Ona was away at college and was taken out of school to help with the younger children. Joseph's brother Hardie and his wife Lucy Scroggins Mackey would take baby Kenneth to raise until the age of 2 and then he was to come back home.

Joseph Marion Mackey

When Otis was a young man, Morrisville had a college. He sold tomatoes one summer so he could attend the college in the fall. He and Earl farmed together for a while and Ona married Payne Bond from Morrisville. Father Joseph would die of cancer in March 1930. The children all stayed together until the youngest graduated from high school. Then John, Earnest and Kenneth went to California and Elizabeth and Pauline went to Springfield to work. Both were married and lived their lives in Springfield. Earl married Martha Wilson and farmed between Morrisville and Eudora. Otis became the postmaster at the Morrisville post office and he and his wife Mary lived their life in Morrisville. *Submitted by Elizabeth Fischer*

MACKEY – Newton P. Mackey and his wife, Elizabeth Erwin, had five children, among them Joseph M. Mackey. Newton and Elizabeth are buried at Morrisville Cemetery. Joseph married Maud Duncan and they had eight children; Otis was their fourth born. A plaque at the entry to the Morrisville High School building lists Joseph as a member of the school board when that building was constructed. Joseph farmed west of Morrisville. Maud died in 1916 and Joseph in 1930; both are buried at Morrisville Cemetery.

Otis was born in 1903 and attended schools in Morrisville. He graduated from the Scarritt-Morrisville Academy (high school level) in 1924. The buildings of the Methodist College were burned soon after, so Otis attended a Methodist college in Fayette, MO. While there he worked in a cold-storage room at a produce company. That job seemed to contribute to a health problem, so he gave up college and traveled to California to work. His older brother, Earl, asked him to return to Morrisville to farm with him. After four years of farming, he was offered the position of manager of the Missouri Farmers Exchange (MFA) in Morrisville, which he held for 13 years.

Cora Mackey Perryman (Otis' cousin) introduced Otis and Mary Kepner. Mary was born in Iowa but was working in Kansas City and attended the church that Rev. Perryman pastored. When he was reassigned to a church in Springfield, they invited Mary to move with them; she would board with them, help with housework and childcare and attend nearby Drury College.

Mary and Otis were married in January 1935. They rented a house in Morrisville for several months and then bought a house on West Elm Street, which would be their home for the rest of their lives together. A copy of the trust deed, dated May 1937, records their purchase of the house.

Mr. and Mrs. Otis C. Mackey, 50th anniversary picture 1985

Otis was appointed postmaster at Morrisville in 1943 and Mary was part-time postal clerk. Otis served as postmaster for 26 years and Mary served as interim postmaster for about two years after his retirement.

Otis always planted a large garden and also kept chickens, a cow, a pig and other animals at times. Mary kept busy with canning and preserving the foods that Otis grew. He always planted a large assortment of flowers also and many of them and the garden produce were given to family, friends and neighbors. In his later years, Otis turned the pasture into an orchard of nut and fruit trees.

Otis and Mary were active members of the Morrisville Methodist Church, he for over 60 years and she for over 50 years. Both supported the church in many capacities.

Otis and Mary had two daughters: Mildred (married Lloyd Jones) and Louise (married Jerry Black). Both graduated from the Burge Hospital School of Nursing and later from Drury College with BS in nursing degree.

Otis and Mary celebrated 50 years of marriage in 1985. Otis died in December 1992 and Mary exactly one year later. Both are buried at Morrisville Cemetery near Otis' parents. *Submitted by Mildred L. Jones*

MACKEY – Thomas Asberry Mackey was born in Polk County in 1844. He was one of 11 children of Samuel A. and Sarah (Wolsey) Mackey. Samuel was originally from Tennessee, coming to Washington County, MO sometime before 1825. He and his family were listed in 1831 in Greene County as one of the eighth members of the first Methodist church organized in Southwest Missouri. His residence was included when Polk County was formed from Greene County in 1835. Samuel is believed to have accompanied his father, John Mackey, from Washington County. Samuel Mackey's sib-

Left to right: Mary Elizabeth Ford and Thomas Asberry Morris Mackey

lings include Elizabeth, who married William Gouty; Cynthia, who married David Welch and settled in Webster County; Andrew, who married Mary G. Walton; Amanda, who married Thomas Griffin; Jane, who married James S. Griffin and settled in Oklahoma; and Stephen.

T. A. Mackey's siblings include Ester (Lill), who married James Wiley Mitchell; James, who married Leah J. Mitchell and settled in Jasper County; William, who married Mary Mathews; Timothy P., who settled in California; Newton Perry, who married Rachel L. Cavin and later Elizabeth J. Erwin and Manerva A. (Cavin) Patterson; Jane C., who married Charles Ingram; Sarah, who married Joseph Lane; Mary A., who married Samuel A. Giles; Samuel A., who married Barsheba C. Gouty and later Sophie Jane Orr and Martha Ford; and Amanda, who died young.

Thomas Asberry Mackey was married to Mary Elizabeth Ford of Webster County. They became the parents of 14 children. These include William Grant, who married Josie Williams; Thomas Edwin, who married Mary Melvina Taylor; Martha, who married Guy Cunningham; Jane (Johnnie), who married Denver S. Hamilton; Noah, who married Cora Cynthia Belle Lee; Mollie, who married a Hudgins; Sarah, who married Henry Freeland and later Henry Herman; May, who married Utah Perryman; Otho, who married Rubie Mitchell; Jerome; Cordie; Timothy; Tennessee; and George Washington, who married Nancy Elizabeth Erwin.

The Mackeys settled around the town of Morrisville and the community of Wishart. Mackey descendants are buried in the Mitchell Campground Cemetery and the Oakville Church Cemetery. *Submitted by Hayward Barnett*

Samuel A. Mackey

MACKEY – Samuel A., born June 1805 and his wife Sarah Wolsey came to Polk County, MO from Tennessee in 1836. They lived first in Washington County, MO as they were listed there at the time of the 1830 census. When they arrived in Polk County they brought with them their five children: Ester, 11; James, 10; William, 7; Timothy, 5; and Newton, 4 and one Negro slave. It is believed they came at the same time as two brothers of Samuel and possibly their father, John Mackey. They were all farmers. Samuel purchased public land near Morrisville. They had five more children: Jane C., Sarah, Mara A., Samuel A. and Thomas A. John, their father, died March 30, 1843 and is buried in Polk County. They were devout lay members of the First Methodist Church South in Springfield, MO and listed as charter members of that church. Samuel died June 28, 1847 of a heart attack. He is buried in the Mitchell Campground Cemetery in Polk County. Seven years after the death of Samuel, Sarah married James Mitchell, Feb. 2, 1854, the widowed preacher of the First Methodist Church South in Springfield. They had three children: Melvill A., Sarah C. and Thomas. There began the first ties to the long time established Mitchell family in Polk County. Sarah's daughter, Ester Mackey, later married James W. Mitchell. Her son, James Mackey, married Sarah J. Mitchell; William Mary Mathews; Timothy went to California; Newton had three wives, Rachel L. Cavin, Elizabeth J. Erwin and Manerva A. Cavin Patterson, the sister of first wife Rachel; Jane E. married Charles Ingram; Sara married Joseph Lane. All of these children stayed in Polk County except for Timothy, it is not known about Samuel and Thomas A. This was the beginning of a long list of Mackey descendants who lived out their lives in Polk County, MO in and around Wishart and Morrisville. *Submitted by Pauline Megerian*

MANUEL – He stood well over six feet tall. Given a tall horse and hat, he could be an imposing figure astride the horse. People in western Polk County knew him because he sought to buy livestock, especially cattle. He would then drive them to Fair Play, where they were herded onto the train and sent to the stockyards in Springfield. Often, James Lafayette "Fate" Manuel would accompany the shipment. On one bitterly cold afternoon, he rode the cattle car to Springfield in a driving sleet and snowstorm. Upon return home, his wife, Mary Louisa Watson Manuel, put him to bed with the chills. He contracted Bright's disease and spent the rest of his life disabled, deceasing in 1913, after what must have been a harsh family experience. Troubles related to his decline in health, coupled with dwindling finances, eventually forced the family to relinquish the farm, which stood on the south side of the road between Bolivar and Fair Play, just a mile directly north of Barren Creek Church.

Fate and Mary Louisa had seven children. Robert became a preacher in Ojai, CA. He was an imposing figure in the pulpit. He stood six feet, five inches tall and weighted nearly 300 pounds. He married a Polk County girl, Nora Wakefield, and they had one son, Charles Manuel, a Marine Corps veteran of WWII and a shop teacher in the Los Angeles school system.

Dessa Jane Manuel, the fourth child of Fate and Mary Louisa, became known across the breadth of Polk County as Miss Dessa. Never married, she became county superintendent of schools, a job at which she worked with all her energy. A teacher at heart, she held the superintendent job from 1928 to 1940, then reverted to teaching, mostly in St. Louis.

Elizabeth "Betty" Manuel married Elmer "Bunt" Brown, also of a Polk County family. They spent a few years in California, but lived the majority of their lives on a farm west and south of Bolivar. Betty worked very hard, while Bunt Brown farmed enough to keep them going. It was said of him that any time he heard a fish or hound bark he was off to the hunt. He was, however, a man of exceptional mechanical talent and could keep just about any farm implement running.

Wellington Sigel "Toby" Manuel fell off a wagon at age 17 when his team bolted. His back injury disabled him and he spent over 20 years in that condition. In essence, his mother spent nearly 25 years nursing the disabled males of her family.

The Manuels youngest daughter, Lafa Ann Manuel (1901-1986), like her siblings, first saw daylight on that Polk County farm. As the Manuel tradition, she attended Barren Creek Cumberland Presbyterian Church and today rests in that cemetery with almost all of her family. Lafa married Avery Edwan Utterback (1900-1966) in 1919. She bore two children, James Ferrell Utterback (1921-) and Helen Louise Utterback Stevens (1933-). The Utterback story is contained in this volume.

The parents of Fate were Payton Manuel and Sarah Malissa Black Manuel, who came from Lawrence County, TN. Mary Louisa's father was William Amsey Watson, son of William Houston Watson, who came from Roane County, TN. All are buried at Barren Creek. These pioneers were known for their work ethic, integrity and tremendous faith in Christ, and are part of the backbone and history of Polk County. *Submitted by Eric A. Stevens*

Charlotte and David Marsch

MARSCH – David Lee Marsch and Charlotte Estelle Highsmith were married Aug. 2, 1997 in Alton, IL and made their first home in Bolivar.

They met in 1994 when they both were freshmen at Southwest Baptist University. They served together on a mission team sent to Winnipeg, Manitoba, Canada. They dated for almost three years before they were married.

David graduated from SBU in December 1997 with a degree in social science education. Charlotte graduated in May 1997 with a degree in communications arts. She started working part-time as an editorial assistant at the *Bolivar Herald-Free Press* during her senior year of college. Six years later, she still works for the BH-FP associate editor. David has worked as a support engineer at Database Systems in Springfield since August 1998. He fixes software problems on Macintosh computers.

The Marsches are members of Southern Hills Baptist Church in Bolivar, where they sing in the choir. Charlotte is finishing her fourth year serving on the Polk County Extension Council and is secretary of the group.

David grew up in Jefferson City. He was born May 5, 1975 in Jefferson City to Ronald Lee and Barbara Joan Marsch. He graduated from Jefferson City High School in 1993. He played violin in the school orchestra and sang in the youth choir at church. He also earned the Boy Scout Eagle Scout Award. He has one sister, Laura Muhlenbruck. She married Russell in 2001 and they live in Columbia.

Charlotte grew up in Shipman, IL. She was born June 9, 1975 in Jerseyville, IL to Earl Dean and Norma Jean Highsmith. She graduated from Southwestern High School in Piasa, IL in 1993. She played the clarinet in band, worked on the yearbook staff in high school, was in 4-H for 11 years and participated in youth group activities at church. She has two brothers; Kent lives in Shipman, and Clark and his wife, Susan, and son, Benjamin, live in Midlothian, TX. *Submitted by Charlotte Marsch*

MARSHALL – James William Marshall was born Sept. 13, 1880 to Rhoda P. (Akard) and Peyton Samuel Marshall on the family homestead near Fair Play, MO. His father Peyton was Cedar County Assessor from 1866-1870. James had eight siblings: Florence (Milas Hensley), Mary

(John Kennon), Martha "Mattie" (H. P. Curl), Ruby (James Harris), Nancy "Nannie" (John Rickman), Rhoda "Elizabeth" (Milton Barkley), Amanda "Fannie" (James Taylor), Joseph (Florence Phillips), James (Icy Wynes), Addie (Alfred Strange) and John L. (lived 4 days). Peyton died on Sept. 7, 1885 and Rhoda died on Feb. 5, 1911. Both Peyton and Rhoda are buried in the Marshall Family Cemetery located on their old homestead in Bear Creek.

James and Icy Marshall, 50th wedding photo, 1950

James married Icy Vernettie Wynes on Aug. 5, 1900 in Cedar County. She was born Feb. 17, 1884 in Bates County to Henry Clay and Malinda (Alsbury) Wynes. After their marriage, they lived in Bolivar and sometime after 1931 moved to Aldrich, MO where James was a farmer. James and Icy had five children: Willard, Wayne, Henry "Clay," Lucile and Claude. James died Nov. 8, 1954 in Bolivar, MO; Icy died Aug. 13, 1947 in Aldrich, MO. Both are buried in Greenwood Cemetery in Bolivar, MO.

Willard Akard Marshall was born April 16, 1902 in Cedar County, MO. He married Ophillia "Opha" Campbell, June 28, 1920. They had two children: Geraldine and Charles Willard. Willard and Opha moved to Ventura, CA. On Nov. 30, 1936, shortly after the move, Willard died from touching a live wire. He is buried in Greenwood Cemetery.

Wayne Garfield Marshall was born Oct. 5, 1904 in Cedar County, MO. He married Opal Louise Hoskins on April 2, 1927. Opal was born on July 8, 1908. They had four children: Robert Wayne, Billie Dean, Wanda and Judith. Wayne died Jan. 8, 1975, Opal died April 19, 1966 and both are buried in Greenwood Cemetery.

Henry "Clay" Marshall was born April 16, 1907 in Cedar County, MO. He married Mary "Ruth" Pike on Oct. 3, 1934. They moved to California. Clay died April 24, 1967, Ruth died on Aug. 12, 1986 and both are buried in Greenwood Cemetery.

Lucille Levena Marshall was born Oct. 23, 1908 in Fair Play, MO. On June 16, 1923, she married Edwin Robert Bean, the son of William and Annie (Drake) Bean, in Bolivar, MO. He was born on June 25, 1906 in Eudora, MO. Edwin was a farmer and owned his own automotive mechanic business located on Front Street in Aldrich, MO. Edwin and Lucille had six children: Edwin "Marshall," Thelma, Dorothy, Betty, James and Terry. Edwin died on Jan. 14, 1975, Lucille died on Jan. 8, 1986 and both are buried in Greenwood Cemetery.

Claud Marshall was born Sept. 25, 1911 in Cedar County, MO. On March 23, 1934, he married Inez Needham in Stockton, MO. Inez was born on May 10, 1913. Claud died on March 23, 1971, Inez died on Nov. 4, 1999 and both are buried in Greenwood Cemetery. *Submitted by Dorothy M. Hudy.*

MASHBURN – Jesse (no middle initial) Mashburn was born March 9, 1917 in Polk County, MO. He was the youngest of six sons born to Jesse Lee Mashburn and Sarah Almeda "Meda" Mashburn, nee Carter. He has lived in Polk County all of his life except for two periods when he lived near Lawrence, KS.

Jesse recalls travelling as a child in a Model "T" to Santa Paula, CA with his father, Jesse Lee, mother, Meda, and brother Ernest "Jack." They were visiting his three older brothers, Clyde, Ralph and Earl, who were roustabouts on oilrigs in California. The going was slow as the roads were unpaved and rutted. To pass the time and break the monotony, Jesse would often run or walk alongside the car. At night, they camped along the road. While in California, Jesse Lee and Jack cut firebacks (clearing land to prevent fires).

When Jesse was 4, he was on a spring wagon with his mother, Meda, who fell out and hurt her wrist. She had pushed Jesse to the floor and he was left alone in the wagon with the horses galloping on. They finally stopped and he bailed out. One of the horses, Stonewall, had a history of being temperamental.

Jesse married Betty Crowell on June 11, 1938. They had four children: Charles Leo, July 26, 1939; Janice June, Jan. 31, 1941; Billy Earl, July 29, 1943; and Gene Allen, Sept. 13, 1946. When she was growing up, Betty would often sing at political rallies with her sister Charlene (Tot). Many people enjoyed listening to her play the piano at the Mount Etna Church north of Bolivar.

On May 18, 1963, Jesse married Berniece Woods, nee Flipps, of Bolivar. Berniece has always been a great step-mom to the four children. She didn't even tattletale on the youngest one, Gene, after he threw a cherry bomb into the Bolivar garment factory where she was a supervisor at the time.

Berniece Mashburn and Jesse Mashburn at Berniece's 80th birthday party

Jesse Mashburn had a tree service in Bolivar for several years. He had a great reputation for doing excellent work and for not overcharging. Long after he quit the tree service business, he would occasionally climbs a tree to trim it. However, after he turned 80, his children strongly suggested he should really stop that kind of activity. Jesse and Berniece lived along Highway 13, north of Bolivar for many years. There, Jesse supplemented their income with an antique and used furniture business, which would have been the envy of Sanford and Son. Jesse would attend auctions across the state and haul enough things home to keep the local auctioneers happy.

Jesse and Berniece Mashburn now make their home in Bolivar.

Also see Jesse Lee Mashburn and John Reynolds Mashburn. *Submitted by Jessica Mashburn*

MASHBURN – Jesse L. Mashburn was born Nov. 27, 1875 in Humboldt, KS. The family moved to Polk County, MO in 1889.

His youngest son tells the story about Jesse L. riding his workhorse all the way to Kansas in the summer of 1896 to plant and harvest a summer crop of flax and broomcorn for his oldest sister Ellen and for her neighbors, a family named Munson. It was said the Munsons, who were Swedish immigrants, claimed that English sounded like shotgun pellets on a tin roof. Jesse L. was able to save $150, enough to marry Sarah Almeda "Meda" Carter in November of 1896 and buy his household goods and furniture from Walter S. White in Bolivar. About 1903, he went by train with the Moore family to homestead in Spokane, WA. It snowed for three days and that was the end of that venture. He decided to head back south to Missouri.

Jesse Lee and Meda raised six sons: Ralph, Feb. 16, 1898; Clyde, Sept. 13, 1899; Earl "Joe," Dec. 23, 1901; Lee, Oct. 30, 1905; Ernest, May 27, 1909; and Jesse March 9, 1917. The four oldest sons made their way to the California oil fields while Ernest "Jack" and Jesse stayed on the family farm. Meda died March 25, 1938. Jesse recalls Meda telling him that her mother brought her on a horse from Tennessee to Polk County, MO, when she was 3 years old. Meda also told him that he was the great-great-grandson of the first elected governor of Missouri.

Jesse Lee Mashburn lived alone in Goodson, MO. He thought nothing of walking the three miles to the family place Ernest farmed. When Jesse was asked if his father never drove, he said that Jesse Lee had trouble getting up a hill on one occasion and subsequently gave up driving as a nuisance. His grandson Gene remembers the small house in which Jesse Lee lived and the eerie shadows his grandfather cast, as he would walk around before bed with his kerosene lantern. Gene also remembers how his grandfather taught him to read the letters on the wood heating stove and how they talked before bedtime.

Jesse Lee lived with his son Jesse and his family for the last several years of his life. He is remembered as being quiet and peaceful. He often sat in his rocking chair, read his Bible and spat in the half-full Folgers can he kept at his side. He died in Springfield, MO, Jan. 20, 1958, when his youngest grandson Gene was 11.

Jesse L. and Meda are buried near the front entrance of the Lindley Creek Cemetery in Goodson, MO.

Also see John Reynolds Mashburn and Jesse (no middle initial) Mashburn. *Submitted by Marika Mashburn*

MASHBURN – John R. Mashburn was born Oct. 9, 1843 in Macon County, NC, the oldest of nine children. His parents were Drury Washington Mashburn, 1818, and Temperance Reid, 1820, both born in Burke County, NC. John is listed in the 1850 Macon County, NC census.

John R. and wife, Charlotte Louisa (Bryson) Mashburn

John fought in the Civil War as a Confederate. One story has it that during the war, John was carrying a soldier wounded in battle and while doing so, the soldier was hit by a cannon ball and killed. The Macon County Historical Society has John's amnesty record of Civil War veterans dated Sept. 8, 1865.

John was a livestock trader. He married Charlotte (Sharlotte) Louise Bryson born in Macon County, NC on Nov. 17, 1848. They married at the Wautawgee Church near Franklin, NC. John and his family moved to Allen County, KS between 1870-1872. Both John's parents died in or near Humboldt, KS. Drury died in 1886. Temperance died prior to that date. In 1889, John moved his family to Polk County, MO. They traveled by wagon and the trip took between a week and 10 days. They were accompanied by "Uncle" Tom Moore (a livestock trader) and his family. The Moore family had been friends and neighbors for years and had moved from Burke County, NC to Macon County, NC to Allen County, KS and then on to Missouri. John's eldest daughter, Ellen Louise, married T. L. Pinkston and remained in Kansas. The Mashburn dog didn't like Missouri and walked back to Kansas where he lived out his years looked after by the neighbors.

John and Charlotte had 10 children: Ellen Louise, Dec. 20, 1868; William Thomas, Nov. 4, 1870; Edward Curtis (Coleman) (Edd), 1873; Jesse Lee, Nov. 27, 1875; Joseph Marcus, April 16, 1877; Samuel W., May 10, 1880; Roxanne "Roxie," Sept. 25, 1882; Grover Cleveland, 1885; John Scott, Aug. 8, 1889; and Metoka Ericson, Nov. 8, 1892. Metoka was the only child who was given an Indian name by Charlotte who was believed to be part Cherokee. Charlotte died from gallbladder problems (she declined surgery which was experimental at the time). John and Charlotte are buried at the Christian Church Cemetery in Louisburg close to the twin cedars.

Many thanks to Beulah Holaday for her many hours of research and sharing her information with the young ones.

Also see Jesse Lee Mashburn and Jesse (no middle initial) Mashburn. *Submitted by Gene A. Mashburn*

Cora, Baylos and Delphia Mayfield, children of Robert and Jane (Dodd) Mayfield

MAYFIELD – Logan Mayfield and Lucinda Tice were married in Polk County in July 1853. They settled in the Rock Prairie area of Polk County. Logan was born in Murfreesboro, TN in August of 1825. Lucinda appears on the 1850 Polk County, MO census in the home of her mother, Nancy Tice. She was born in North Carolina in December of 1826. Nancy's father's name is not known. Logan's parents were William Thomas and Kate Mayfield. William and Kate's 13 children were Ambrose; Tolbert Fountain, who married Nancy Davis first, then Elizabeth Johnston; Baylos Earl, who married Mahala Ann Langston; William O.; Betsy, who married William Baker; Mary "Polly," who married Willis J. Tiller; Elizabeth "Eliza," who married Payton Keel; Nancy; Margaret; Ellen, who married John McCurry; Thomas Logan; Alisha Woodford; and Elisha Elihua.

Logan was married twice. He first married Mary Murray, Aug. 4, 1847, Polk County, MO. Logan's children from his first marriage were William Caleb, who married Margaret Ann Fullerton; Baylos Earls, who married Margaret Charlotte Newport; and Isaac Mayfield. Logan and Lucinda's children were John Wesley, who married Mary E. Steel; Charles Harrison, who married Matilda A. Fullerston; Robert Lee; and Nancy Ellen, who married Jonathan P. Williams.

Robert Lee Mayfield was born July 11, 1863 in St. Louis and died Jan. 6, 1950 at his home in Polk County. He married Nancy Jane Dodd on Oct. 4, 1884 in Polk County, MO. Her parents were Henry Dodd and Martha "Mattie" Lusk. They had 10 children. They were Baylos Henry, George O., Oliver, Paul, Lillie, Delphia, Cora, who married Virgil McAtee, Oma, Franklin and Lewis.

Bay Mayfield married Lessie Earlene McCurry, daughter of Jacob Hamilton McCurry and Samantha Highfill, Aug. 2, 1919 in Cheney, KS. Bay was born June 26, 1888 and died Oct. 8, 1958 in Polk County. Lessie was born Feb. 19, 1895 and died Feb. 21, 1968. They had two children, Ernie Lee Hamilton Mayfield and Clella Mayfield, who married Lloyd Patterson.

Ernie Mayfield married Jewell Evelyn Stoops in 1940. Jewell is the daughter of Irvin Stoops and Lucy Masters. Ernie and Jewell's children are Carolyn, who married Lawrence Shields, Howard, who lived only to the age of 11 and Stan, who married Suzanne Warren. Ernie and Jewell have one granddaughter, Brooke Mayfield. *Submitted by Stan Mayfield*

MAYFIELD – William Mayfield was born in 1782 in Tennessee. He moved from Murfreesboro, TN to Polk County, MO in 1836. He married his cousin, Katie Mayfield. Katie was born in 1785 in North Carolina and died in 1858 in Polk County. William died in 1863 in Polk County. They had eight children, one of whom was Logan.

Logan Henderson Mayfield was born in 1825 in Tennessee and died in 1867 in Polk County, MO. Logan married Mary Murray on Aug. 4, 1847 in Polk County; they had three children. Mary died and on July 6, 1853 in Polk County, Logan married Lucinda Tice, who was born in 1826 in North Carolina. They had four children, one of whom was Nancy Ellen Katheren, who was born in 1865 and died in 1937 and is buried in Polk County. Nancy married Jonathan P. Williams, who was born in 1854 and died in 1900 in Polk County. They had five children, one of whom was Alvin P. Williams.

Alvin P. Williams was born in Polk County in 1894 and died in 1970 and is buried in Polk County.

James Hollis was born in 1871 in Polk County and died in 1903 in Polk County. He married Mae Wilson (Hollis) (Cavin). She was born in 1873 and died in 1964 in Polk County. They had five children, one of whom was Vera Hollis, who was born in 1897.

Alvin P. Williams married Vera Hollis in 1925. She died in 1950 in Polk County. They had nine children: infant daughter (deceased); Hollis A. Williams, born Nov. 9, 1927, now lives in Cheyenne, WY; Wilbur E. Williams, born Aug. 29, 1929 and died Dec. 15, 1994 and is buried in the National Cemetery in Springfield, MO; Gloria K. (Williams) Bilyeu, born Aug. 5, 1931 and now lives in Bolivar; Loria M. (Williams) Staffen, twin of Gloria, also born Aug. 5, 1931 and now lives in Buffalo; Buford G. Williams, born Dec. 27, 1933 and now lives in Springfield; Milda A.

Alvin P. Williams and Vera A. (Hollis) Williams

(Williams) Climer, born June 24, 1936, now lives in Houston, TX; and Robert R. Williams, born Oct. 12, 1938 and now lives in Clear Lake, IA. All of these children were born in Greene County, MO. *Submitted by Robert Williams*

Front: William Cabe and wife Margaret Ann (Fullerton) Mayfield; Standing: Wade Henderson, Mary Treacy, Troy Adam, Rella May and Albert Jackson

MAYFIELD – James Mayfield was born in England circa 1735. He came to America after 1755, settling in Virginia. His three known children were William, Isaac and Betsy.

William Thomas Mayfield was born in 1783 and married a cousin, Catherine Mayfield, in 1802. The family moved west, settling in middle Tennessee. The father, John Mayfield, was killed by Indians in Tennessee in 1790.

William and Catie moved to Polk County, MO in 1836. On the 1840 census he was living in Mooney Township, farming 300 acres. Their children were E. Tolbert, Bailum, Elizabeth, Mary, Ellen, Nancy, Eleanor and Logan Henderson. Will and Catie are buried on the old Mayfield farm cemetery.

Logan Henderson was born in 1835 and married Mary Murray in Polk County in 1847. They had William Caleb, Bailum and Isaac. Mary died in 1853 and William married Lucinda Tice and they had John, Charles, Robert, Nancy and Katie.

William Caleb Mayfield was born Aug. 22, 1848 in Polk County, MO and married Margaret Fullerton. They had 11 children, several who died from an epidemic. Their children: Mary T., Albert, Nora, Wade, Rella (married Lonnie Ethridge and lived on a farm at Pleasant Hope), Millie, Harvey, Troy, Everett, Carl and Jesse. William, known as "Cabe," became a Christian in 1868, joining membership with Rock Prairie Baptist Church. Cabe was known to be honest, hard working, and a well-respected farmer of the community.

Mary T. married Will Glover, a blacksmith and farmer at Tin Town. They had Mamie, Lloyd and Bertha. Mamie taught school at Tin Town and later married Grover Helton and moved to Springfield. They had eight children, one of whom was Eleanor, who married Pate Hough, who worked for the Frisco Railroad. Lloyd married Phoebe and owned several corner grocery stores in Springfield. Bertha married and they moved to Montana where they homesteaded a big cattle ranch.

Pate and Eleanor Hough had six children. Gary married Barbara Woodall. He worked for Paul Mueller Company for 27 years. Then they moved to Indiana where he was corporate safety director for a transportation company. She retired from Kraft Foods in Springfield. He is now back home in Springfield, working in safety. They have two children, Matthew and Rebecca. They still enjoy visiting the old Mayfield homeplace, visiting with kin and researching their family tree. *Submitted by Barbara Hough*

MAYSE - On Nov. 13, 1995 Alta Marie (Sprague) McCrory of Bolivar, Martha (Jeffries) Mayse of Lamar, and Zula (Mayse) Sicard of Fair Play had lunch at a Bolivar restaurant and spent the afternoon reminiscing old times along with sharing their family photographs in Alta Marie's home. This was a special occasion as Martha and Alta Marie had not seen each other for 63 years. They had known each other a short time as children in the lower elementary grades and later as teenagers and as young married couples in Fair Play. In 1934 Martha, her husband, Jesse and infant daughter, "Ann," moved to California, returning to Missouri in 1939 but residing in Barton County. Martha's sister-in-law, Zula Sicard, arranged this enjoyable meeting for Martha, Alta Marie and Zula.

The following are a few news items taken from the *Fair Play Advocate* newspaper. These are examples of the life and times of folks in and near Fair Play from 1915 to 1936. People often visited in homes of relatives and friends. Traveling from one of the small towns in Polk County to Bolivar was considered a big event. Newspaper wedding and birth announcements and obituaries were written much differently than our current time. The newspaper notes of the 1930s can give a person a deeper meaning of hard times during the depression years. Small town newspapers, such as the *Fair Play Advocate*, are studies in sociology and customs of folks living in those places during those years. The dates shown are the publication dates of the Advocate.

July 1, 1915 Shovelers and Rakers in Teams
115 shovelers and rakers in 16 teams worked on the roads Tuesday, June 29. The workers included Tom Leavitt and A. F. Leavitt. Men either worked all day or donated $1.50 in money. This was their poll tax to give them the right to vote.

July 8, 1915 Aldrich News
F. H. Jarnagin put in a concrete walk from his office to the railroad tracks last week.

August 9, 1915 Eudora News
The protracted meeting began at Turkey Creek last Sunday with Rev. James Jeffries and Rev. Wood as preachers.

October 21, 1915 Fair Play News
Dr. W. S. Hopkins, of Springfield, was down (came to Fair Play) Saturday to attend the funeral of his sister, Miss M. E. Hopkins.

January 16, 1916 Dr. W. S. Hopkins Dead
(At the age of 54, Dr. Wellington S. Hopkins died Jan. 12, 1916 of pneumonia at his home in Springfield, Missouri. He had been a medical doctor for about 30 years, 17 years in Fair Play, eight years in Bolivar and five years in Springfield. On March 17, 1887 he married Elsie M. Paynter, daughter of Judge C. W. Paynter. Dr. Hopkins was survived by his wife and two daughters, Mrs. Cleo McKinney and Miss Mary Hopkins.)

February 2, 1916 Aldrich News
Effie Maryellen Jeffries, 6-year-old daughter of Rev. Jeffries, died Wednesday evening of membranous croup. She had been sick only a few days.

February 24, 1916 Mrs. Rebecca Frieze
Rebecca E. Jarnagin was born in Tennessee on December 16, 1832 and came to this section of the country with her parents when only a girl. Was therefore one of the oldest settlers of this section.

In 1850 she married John A. Frieze and to this union 11 children were born, nine of whom are still living; Alfred Frieze and Mrs. John Lowery being two of the children.

In early life she professed religion and united with the Baptist church and at the time of her death was an honored member of that church in Dunnegan.

She had passed even the four score years allotted to man and on February 8, 1916 she went on into the great beyond with her faith strong in the Resurrection.

The funeral service was conducted by Rev. E. C. Waldow and interment was made at the Lindley Prairie Cemetery.

July 12, 1917 Army Registration List
ages between 21 to 31, who registered June 5, 1917.

Madison township were: Porter Leavitt, Edgar Hopkins Leavitt and James Franklin Frieze of Fair Play.

April 4, 1929 Items of Interest
A fine new daughter was born to Mr. and Mrs. Orba Frieze of Fair Play last Sunday morning. Mrs. Frieze was formerly Miss Effie Brown of this city.

June 6, 1929 An All-Day Meeting
There will be an all-day meeting at Oak Grove Church, Sunday, June 9, also meeting Saturday afternoon and evening. Rev. Jim Jeffries and his two boys will be there. Everyone invited to come and with well-filled baskets on Sunday.

September 5, 1929 Fair Play News
Mr. and Mrs. Granville Mayse have taken charge of the Southern Hotel. Mr. and Mrs. Mayse have moved therein. Mrs. Matt Morgan and Mr. and Mrs. Fay Hutchins, who have been running the hotel, have moved into the W. I. Ashlock property on the west side of town.

October 24, 1929   Local News
Mr. and Mrs. Orba Frieze and Mrs. Alfred G. Frieze were shopping in Bolivar Thursday.

February 6, 1930 Revival Closes
The revival, conducted by the pastor, James N. Jeffries at the Fair Play Baptist Church for the past four weeks, closed last Sunday night with large audience present. Notwithstanding the severe weather all four weeks, the meetings were well attended, the church membership was greatly revived, nine young people were converted, and many others interested. There were 13 additions to the church membership.

(in paper during time of revival:) Temperature from 10 above zero. Snow thawed considerable, but still covers the ground about three inches deep on the level with drifts several feet deep in places.

February 27, 1930 A Boy Preacher
Sunday night, February 16, at the Fair Play Baptist Church, Johnny Jeffries, the 11-year-old son of Pastor Jeffries of that church, delivered a sermon that would have been a credit to any ordinary minister. His thoughts were deep, his language good and his delivery excellent. Also, there was the serious, reverent attitude that ought to mark the delivery of a Gospel sermon at any and all times. If Johnny continues to grow in knowledge and power, he will be a great preacher before he reaches middle life.

April 24, 1930 They Broadcasted
Rev. John Wheary and Rev. James Jeffries took a bunch of Fair Play and Wheatland young folks to Jefferson City on Wednesday of last week where they broadcasted in song and speech on station W. O. W. They were given only a half-hour, but the home folks had the pleasure of hearing their boys and girls over the radio. Static was bad that evening and some did not get the program, while others reported that it came in very satisfactory. Besides Rev. Wheary and Rev. Jeffries the following make the crowd who made the trip: Mrs. Wheary, Misses Zula Mayse, Zula Akins, Evelyn Harvel, Erma Miller, Frances Payner, Dorothy Pierce, Ethel Jeffries, Esther Jeffries, Martha Jeffries, Nora Fleeman, Marguerite Engleman, Ruth Sterling, Mary Frances Wheary; Messrs: Ferrell Hammons, Ralph Hammons, Jesse Mayse, King Engleman, Willard Brown, Bernard Potts, Boss Gothard, Johnny Jeffries, Jimmy Jeffries, Fred Manuel, Cortis Hutchins, and Mr. and Mrs. Fay Hutchins. (Eleven year old Johnny Jeffries delivered a short sermon over the radio at that time.)

April 24, 1930 Fair Play School News
Those who attended the free cooking school at Bolivar were Alta Marie Sprague, Wilma Fiddler, Erma Miller, Eunice Miller, Zula Akins, Zula Mayse, Lucille Rowden, Juanita Wright, Neva Engleman, Marguerite Engleman and Thelma Patterson.

May 8, 1930 Local News
A daughter was born Monday to Mr. and Mrs. Orba Frieze of north of town.

June 12, 1930 Fair Play News
You old folks are not the only "tater" raisers in this man's town. Jesse Mayse has a patch of high producers in the south part of town, and they are fine lookers, too. The taste is all right also, as we sample them at the dinner in the Mayse's hotel dining room. (Jesse Mayse was 19 at that time and operated a cleaning and pressing business in Fair Play.)

July 17, 1930 Mayse-Jeffries
Jesse Mayse and Miss Martha Jeffries, both of Fair Play, were united in marriage Friday, July 11. Jesse is the son of Mr. and Mrs. Granville Mayse, who are operating the Southern Hotel; and the bride is the daughter of Rev. and Mrs. J. N. Jeffries. The young married couple have the best wishes of their many friends for a happy and prosperous life together. (This was the first marriage in Fair Play for a long time. Note: Jesse and Martha were married 58 years and one month before his death in 1988.)

October 16, 1930 Fair Play News
C. F. (Foley) Mayse took a truckload of eggs, poultry and cream to St. Louis Monday night for O. L. Thomas. Mr. Mayse tells us that he made the trip frequently.

December 18, 1930 Letters to Santa (below are only two of the letters)
Dear Santa Claus: I am a little boy in the first grade and am seven years old. I want a wagon that I can ride in and an areoplane. I will look for you on Christmas night. Your little friend, Noah Jeffries (During the Second World War, Noah served in Army in Europe) (Note: Noah spelled airplane as shown above.)

Dear Santa Claus: Please bring me a train and a tractor and a little ring. I am six years old and in the first grade. Your little friend, Clyde Mayse (During the Second World War, Clyde served in the Army in the South Pacific.) (Also note: During Second World War if the US had made an

Five generations- taken late 1911 or early 1912. Seated left to right: Frances Jane (Guinn) Hopkins and her husband, James Perry Hopkins and Elsie Lee (Leavitt) Frieze. Elsie holding Jesse Mayse. Standing left to right: Amanda Elizabeth (Hopkins) Leavitt and Cleo Elizabeth (Frieze) Mayse. This James Perry Hopkins was a grandson of Revolutionary War soldier, James B. Hopkins. In this photo the lineage is James P. Hopkins, Amanda Leavitt, Elsie Frieze, Cleo Mayse and Jesse Mayse.

invasion on Japan both Noah Jeffries and Clyde Mayse were among hundreds of military to participate in that invasion.)

December 29, 1930 Dunnegan News

Ed Hopkins and wife and Mr. and Mrs. Earnest Curl and children of Dunnegan were in Fair Play a while last Thursday afternoon.

January 1, 1930 Butler – Jeffries

Mr. Lester Butler and Miss Ethel Jeffries, both of Fair Play, were united in marriage, Saturday, December 20, 1930, at the home of the bride's parents; and the ceremony were performed by the bride's father, Rev. James N. Jeffries. The groom is the son of Mr. and Mrs. W. H. Butler of north of Fair Play. The many friends of these young people will join the Advocate, we feel sure, in wishing for them an abundance of life's blessings and few or none of its handicaps. (Note: Lester and Ethel were married 51 years and 3 months before his death in 1982.)

May 21, 1931 and September 3, 1931 articles concerning James Hopkins, Revolutionary War soldier: "In Honor Of A Soldier" and "Will Unveil Monuments"

In 1931 facts were verified by Mrs. Cleo McKinney of Springfield, MO great-granddaughter to this James Hopkins. Mrs. McKinney was the daughter of Dr. Wellington S. Hopkins and granddaughter of Hiram Hopkins. The following is condensed from those two excellent articles from the *Advocate*.

James Hopkins was born in North Carolina either in 1760 or 1765. He was but a boy when the Revolutionary War broke upon the American colonies. He served with the colors during that war and helped in securing freedom for the colonies and to establish the United States of America.

He came to Missouri in 1835 and with his family settled near Cave Springs, two miles west of Fair Play. He secured government land in this then wilderness and Cave Spring was on the old Hopkins estate. Fourteen years after coming to Missouri, he died in 1849 and was buried in the Hopkins cemetery on the Hopkins farm.

Mrs. Cleo McKinney, a member of the Daughters of the American Revolution, with A. C. Hopkins and others, looked up the army record of their ancestor and verified the fact that he had been a soldier in a North Carolina Regiment during the Revolution. He was honorably discharged for disability received while in service. The National government furnishes monuments for the graves of all soldiers who fought in our wars and one was placed at the grave of James Hopkins on September 6, 1931. Also a marker was place at the grave of his wife, Elizabeth Hopkins. Miss Dorothy Ann and Master Charles Wellington McKinney, great-great-grandchildren of James Hopkins assisted in the unveiling. There were five living grandchildren of James Hopkins present for that special ceremony: Sol Hopkins of Lebanon, age 88, the eldest; Mrs. Mary Jane Easley, age 83, second oldest of Marionville; Mrs. Jennie Camp of Ava; Mrs. Amanda Walker and Alvin Hopkins, both of Fair Play. A sixth grandchild, J. O. Hopkins, was in his home a short distance away, but was unable to attend.

An interesting relic was on exhibition. It was the flintlock rifle owned and used by James Hopkins before and after he came to Missouri. It is a style of weapon not many of the younger generation (of the 1930s) have seen, as it was displaced by more modern guns more than 50 years ago (1880s). This rifle is now (1931) owned by J. O. Hopkins, one of the grandsons.

Mrs. McKinney reported that the Hopkins family emigrated to North Carolina from Wales in an early day. James Hopkins, youngest of three brothers, was born in Orange County, North Carolina in 1764. He married Elizabeth Billingsly, of North Carolina. They had five sons and three daughters, John, Samuel, James, Solomon, Hiram, Mary, Elizabeth and Lucinda. After moving to Fair Play area, local history states he had several skirmishes with the Indians.

Note: The lineage from this Revolutionary War soldier, James Hopkins, to Charles Sicard of Fair Play is as follows: James Hopkins (soldier); his son, James A. Hopkins; his son, James P. Hopkins; his daughter, Amanda Elizabeth (Hopkins) Leavitt {married Henry Wallace Leavitt}; their daughter, Elsie Lee (Leavitt) Frieze {married Alfred Grant Frieze}; they had three children: Cleo Elizabeth, Wayman (died at birth), and Orba; Cleo Elizabeth (Frieze) Mayse {married Granville Boyd Mayse}; they had three children: Jesse O., Zula Audry and Clyde Leon. Jesse and Martha (Jeffries) Mayse have three daughters: Ann, Louise and Dorthy. Zula and Melvin Sicard's son is Leon. Clyde and Dixie (Curl) Mayse have three sons: Larry, Randy and David. Leon and Janet Sicard's five children are: Abby, Patricia, Lea Ann, Charles and Matthew. The first James Hopkins is a seventh great-grandfather to Charles Sicard. Charles and Noreen Sicard now own and live on the Frieze/Mayse land northeast of Fair Play.

(Note: Before her death in 1976, Cleo Mayse told her granddaughter, Ann Denny that Henry W. Leavitt was one-fourth Cherokee Indian. Henry's grandparent that was full-blooded Cherokee Indian endured the hardships of the "Trail of Tears." Ann does not know if that was Henry's grandmother or grandfather.)

March 31, 1932 Fair Play News

Granville Mayse has taken the place long held by Robert Mead as local manager of the Lightfoot Produce House. Granville assumed his new duties last week.

May 18, 1933 Local News

An old-time rail fence was torn down this week on the Albert Forgey farm east of Fair Play and the rails were hauled to town and sold for firewood. One by one these old familiar landmarks disappear.

June 15, 1933 A Garden Story

Here's another garden story, strange but true. Granville Mayse has a barrel full of soil in his garden back of the Southern Hotel and there are 26 holes bored in the sides of the barrel. Out of each hole a cucumber vine is growing and Granville is expecting a real crop of pickles there from. We have heard of that scheme before but Granville has the first exhibition of it we have seen in Fair Play.

August 31, 1933 Fair Play News

William Mayse and family of Woodlake, California, who have been visiting their many relatives here, left last Saturday for their home. They were accompanied by W. E. Hubbard and his two sons and two daughters. Mr. Hubbard had closed his grocery store here and they expect to make California their future home. Miss Lillie Rickman and Miss Zula Mayse also accompanied the Mayse and Hubbard families.

September 14, 1933 Fair Play News

Word has been received by Mr. and Mrs. Granville B. Mayse from their daughter, Zula Mayse, that she arrived in Long Beach, California and had work, and that W. E. Hubbard and family, with whom she went, were there and had made the trip without any trouble.

September 28, 1933 McNeely – Jeffries

Mr. Forrest McNeely, son of Mr. and Mrs. Ben McNeely of near Humansville and Miss Esther Jeffries, daughter of Rev. and Mrs. James N. Jeffries, of Fair Play, were united in marriage last Wednesday, September 20 at the home of the bride's parents, their vows being read by Rev. Jeffries. The groom is a graduate of a business college at Parsons, Kansas, but has decided to be a farmer for the present, so the young couple will make their home on a farm near Humansville. The many friends of the bride here will wish for her and her husband a long life of happiness and prosperity together. (They were married 63 years and seven months before Forrest's death in 1997.)

October 5, 1933 Fair Play News

Mr. and Mrs. L. L. Jeffries and daughter, Juanita; Mr. and Mrs. Granville Mayse, and son, Clyde, left Sunday morning for Woodlake, California where they expect to make their future homes. The trip is to be made in the Jeffries' truck, which has been fixed for sleeping quarters with a place to cook and store some of the furniture that the families are taking with them.

Mr. and Mrs. Cortis Hutchins have taken charge of the Southern Hotel, taking the place of Mr. and Mrs. Granville Mayse who left Sunday for California.

October 26, 1933 Fair Play News

Word from L. L. Jeffries and family and G. B. Mayse and family states that they arrived in California without any trouble and that they all have work. (The 1930s were the depression years. Having some type of employment was very important. Traveling all the way to California in the 1930s without any trouble was a great accomplishment.)

May 3, 1934 Fair Play News

Miss Lydia Jeffries is spending this week with her sister, Mrs. Forrest (Esther) McNeely and husband near Humansville.

August 30, 1934

—An article reported that Soloman Hopkins and Minerva (McSpaden) Hopkins had been married for 70 years. Soloman was 91 and Minerva was 87. They were married August 11, 1864. Their children: Joseph, Henry, Mrs. Nina Jarman, William, Charley and Mrs. Mary Jarman. A daughter, Mador, was dead.

October 11, 1934 Fair Play News

Several women participated in an old-fashioned quilting bee one-day the past week.

December 27, 1934 Fair Play News

Mrs. Amanda Leavitt spent Christmas with Mr. and Mrs. C. Rickman of Bear Creek.

January 23, 1936 "Six in Fair Play Receive Old-Age Pension Blanks"

The state has promised to start paying old-age pension to the most eligible within the next few weeks. Blanks have already been received by six in Fair Play according to a report from H. Cunningham who as a notary has helped applicants fill out the blanks.

As soon as these requisition blanks are returned to the state auditor's office and checked, the pensioners will receive their first checks.

The sum now allotted range from $7 to $12 a month. Those who signed the first applications in September will be paid four months' pension in their first payment. All pensioners as they are certified will receive these requisition papers as the final step before being settled on the roll for good.

The board does not plan to raise the amount of pension this year, but will increase the number of pensioners if more money becomes available.

Those in Fair Play who have received final papers are: Mrs. Amanda Leavitt, Mrs. Mary Galyon, Mrs. Fannie Elrod, Jim Tillery, Franklin Crain and Mrs. Caroline Fisher. Three applicants at Dunnegan will also get the pension: Mrs. Nancy Davidson, Mrs. Mary E. Kennon and Mrs. Nancy Dixon. (Note: that was the beginning of what we now know as Social Security.)

February 6, 1936 "Who Can Beat That?"

Mrs. S. P. Estes of Dunnegan writes, "Here I am again with another dollar to pay for my paper (*Fair Play Advocate*). I can't live without it. I am

Left to right: Alta Marie (Sprague) McCrory, of Bolivar, Martha (Jeffries) Mayse of Lamar, and Zula (Mayse) Sicard of Fair Play. Alta Marie and Martha had not seen each other for 63 years. Photo taken Nov. 13, 1995 at Alta Marie's home, in Bolivar. Zula arranged for the three to be together that day.

nearly 78 years old and still split all my wood. Who can beat that for a woman?"

March 5, 1936 advertisement from Hudson's Grocery Store
- tomatoes 3 cans 25 cents
- hominy 1 can 10 cents
- green beans 1 can 5 cents
- new cabbage 1 pound 3 cents
- green onions 1 bunch 3-1/2 cents
- tender roast beef 1 pound 16 cents
- boiling beef 1 pound 12-1/2 cents
- frankfurters 1 pound 10 cents

May 28, 1936 New Grocery

Clyde Fleeman has opened a new grocery store in the Barker Building on Wall Street. He will also handle flour and feed and buy country produce. He is being assisted by Lester Butler.

November 5, 1936 AMANDA LEAVITT DIES SUDDENLY

Pneumonia fatal to great-great-grandmother The school girl's friend

Amanda Elizabeth Hopkins, second daughter of James and Jane Hopkins, was born near Fair Play, Missouri, March 24, 1858 and died at her home in Fair Play, November 2, 1936, being 78 years, 7 months and 8 days of age.

She was converted when 15 years of age and became a member of the Methodist Church where she was an ardent Christian and devout church worker all the years that she enjoyed good health.

She was married to Henry Wallace Leavitt, July 26, 1874. To this union were born five sons and two daughters, all of whom survive: Mrs. Alfred Frieze, Visalia, California; Mrs. Charles Richman, Bear Creek; Walter S., Humansville; Brooker J. and Porter E. of Springfield; Fred of Nixa; and Edgar H. of Stockton.

The husband died March 8, 1901 when the two younger boys were quite small. This brave, fragile woman with the loyal help of her daughters and sons met this grief with Spartan courage and indomitable will, keeping their home intact and rearing the younger children to useful honorable lives. She was a mother who admonished her children to walk in the ways of the Lord and was always proud that they were obedient and loving to her. Few children shower greater love and devotion on a mother than have these. Her passing was very sudden. She was sick of pneumonia only four days.

After the children established homes of their own, Mother Leavitt took great interest in her grandchildren and any young person with whom she chanced to be associated. She often kept schoolgirls in her home and always found perfection in young people. She kept young in years by living the ideals of these young people. Her home was a place for their comfort and happiness. On cold, wintry nights several of them often stayed in her home rather than brave the cold walk to their homes in the country.

Hers was a sunny, joyous disposition and her peaceful expression in death showed that she had gone to her Heavenly reward.

Her death came as a shock to her many friends. Sorrow over the tragic death of little Nola Lee Leavitt, a great-granddaughter, who was burned to death in her parents' home in Kansas City, October 26, likely was a contributing factor hastening her death.

She is also survived by 18 grandchildren, 5 great-grandchildren, and one great-great-grandchild; three sisters: Mrs. Sarah Bugg, Mrs. W. H. Winton; and Mrs. Monroe Potts, and one brother, Fred Hopkins, all of near Fair Play.

The funeral was held in the Fair Play Methodist Church Tuesday, November 3, conducted by Rev. Henry Hiles, pastor. Interment was in Hopkins Cemetery under direction of Hutchinson-Blue & Wright.

(Note: the newspaper headlines of the death of Amanda Leavitt were in large, all capital letters, all across the top of page one of *Advocate*, with subtitles.)

(The *Advocate* also printed recipes. In the early 1930s people cooked with either wood or coal and recipes that had to be baked would end with the phrase, "cook until done." Around the mid 1930s some folks had cook stoves with temperature gauges and the recipes that had to be baked would end with two phrases: "cook until done" and "cook at (an exact temperature) for (an exact) length of time.") *Submitted by Ann Mayse Denny*

Jesse Mayse and his wife, Martha (Jeffries) Mayse and 4 month old daughter, Doris Annalee "Ann." 1934

MAYSE - Precious memories mean so much to me. I look back to the summer of 1916. I was 4 years old at May 25, 1916. I have tried so hard to think back before that as my oldest sister, Effie Maryellen Jeffries, age 6, had died on Jan. 12, 1916 of membranous croup. My sister, Ethel, age 5, and I were so hoarse we could hardly speak the day of Maryellen's funeral at the Pleasant Ridge Church near Aldrich, MO. Before the funeral, in our home, they had a special song they wanted sung. My dad asked us girls if we had one. My mother said I spoke in a whisper, as I was unable to speak out loud, and said, "Sing, 'We'll Never say Good By in Heaven." My mother, whom I called Mom, said the singer broke down and cried.

I am unable to remember that far back as I was only 3 1/2 years old. But, I do remember the nail on the kitchen door where Maryellen hung her little coat and cap when she came home from school. The fall and winter of 1915 she attended the first grade at Aldrich.

My earliest remembrance was during the months of July and August of 1916. My sister, Ethel and I had typhoid fever. The doctors then starved patients who had fever; Ethel and I were so weak and ill. We became so thin so our mom said she was afraid to pick me up for fear my bones would come through my skin. Our parents changed doctors and called in Dr. Myers who asked mom what Ethel and I wanted to eat. She told him, "Bacon." Dr. Myers told mom to cook bacon as crisp as she could and for us girls to chew it as fine as we could. I remember that bacon tasted so good. Dr. Myers then gave us each a teaspoon of syrup pepsin and we went to sleep. He told mom to increase the amount of bacon each time and follow with the medicine. We began to recover.

While Ethel and I were ill with the typhoid fever, our Uncle Josie Jeffries, his wife, Clara and their sons Hershel and Harley came to visit our family in their covered wagon. Ethel looked out the window and said, "There's a covered wagon!" I rolled out of bed to see and Ethel said, "Mom, Martha is out of bed." I remember Mom coming from the kitchen and picking me up and putting me back into bed.

While our family lived in Aldrich, we moved to another house down below the switchboard where Mrs. Head was the attendant there at the switchboard. She had a little girl my age named Shirley. Shirley loved my black, curly hair and wanted curly hair like me. I had heard my mom say every time it rained my hair would be more curly, so I told Shirley that the next time it rains, for her to stick her head under the drip. She did that. Her mother came running out on the porch and asked, "Shirley, what are you doing? You will get sick!" Shirley told her mother, "Martha said I might get curly hair like her."

In 1918 my parents bought a tombstone for Effie Maryellen. This tombstone has a sweet, little lamb carved on the top of it. Our family all got into a big wagon. My mom and we children sat down in the bed of the wagon. Dad and our neighbor sat high in a wagon seat with two big, brown horses pulling the wagon. At that time, we saw very few Model-T Ford Cars and horses was afraid of those cars. A car came up behind our wagon and the driver honked his car horn. Those horses danced up and down as they were scared. The dirt roads were so narrow and we had to get our wagon over on the side of the road. I was afraid our wagon would turn over. We took Maryellen's tombstone to her grave site at Pleasant Ridge Cemetery in Aldrich.

At that time I had my sister, Ethel, a year older than me, a sister Esther, and a brother, Jimmy. While we lived in Aldrich my sister, Lydia, and brother, Johnny, were born.

I remember the First World War. Our Uncle Marvin Gordon, Mom's youngest brother, had to go to war. After the First World War was over on Nov. 11, 1918, the town of Aldrich had a celebration parade. I remember a big crowd of people. I wanted to get out and march with the parade. I was only 6 years old then. My dad looked down at me and told me the people would run over me; that I was to small to march with them. He asked me why I wanted to march in that parade. I told him, "Because Uncle Marvin is coming home!"

When Lydia was an infant, we moved to a farm near Aldrich. Dad made up a hammock that was attached to two trees. In those days many tramps (hobos) roamed the country out of work. Back then there was no federal or state government assistance for people. Times were hard, a drought, and hardly any work for many people. The trains ran more from town to town then. Those tramps would hop a freight, get off, and beg for food. They always knew where we lived. Dad would never turn any away. Mom always cooked something for them. One even stayed overnight sleeping in the hammock. Dad always talked Bible to them. If they didn't like Bible lessons, they never came back.

My brother, Johnny, was born at Aldrich in 1918, which was a hard year for our family. My parents always tried to raise one or two hogs for us to butcher so on Christmas morning we would have "good old ham and gravy" for breakfast. That year they could only get one small hog. Feed was so scarce and high priced, the pig did not get very fat. My parents butchered the pig anyway. One day, another preacher, with several children, came to visit Dad. These two preachers had many wonderful talks on the Bible. This man told Dad, "Brother Jeffries, this year, we won't have any ham for our Christmas."

After he left, my Dad said to Mom, "Why don't we share one of our hams with him and his family? Our hams will be small, but both families will have ham for Christmas." My Dad quoted the Bible verse from Luke 6:38 "Give, and it shall be given unto you; good measure, pressed down, and shaken together, and running over." Mom agreed.

My dad wrapped one ham up and took it to this family. That preacher cried and said, "No, Brother Jeffries, you have a larger family than I do." Dad said to him, "The Bible says, 'Give, and it shall be given unto you, good measure, pressed down, and shaken together, and running over'." My dad told him now both families will have ham for Christmas. The man cried with joy and thanked Dad.

On Christmas morning as Mom was frying the ham, there was a knock at our door and Dad went to see. A farmer who loved to hear Dad preach had in his arms a very large ham for us. My parents cried and thanked him so much. Dad turned and repeated that Bible verse. Among the Bible verses I had been taught were, "All things work together for good to them that love the Lord" and "Give and it shall be given unto you."

We often moved as our dad was a preacher and different churches would call him to be their pastor. My sister, Susan, was born after we moved to Fair Play. Jimmy was about 4 years old at the time. Our next door neighbors were such nice, elderly people but the man would say bad words. One day, we kids were playing in our yard. A fence was between us and that couple. The man was working in his yard. He was angry about something and let out a big cuss word. Little Jimmy, peeking through the fence said to him, "Oh, Mr., you won't got to Heaven if you say words like that." The man put down his rake and went into his house for a while. Later that evening he was talking to our dad and said, "Mr. Jeffries, if you had told me that, I would have been angry. But a little boy so young, that is something else." Sometime later we were told this man was saved before he died because of the little boy who corrected him.

While we lived in Fair Play, MO, the train brought Uncle Marvin Gordon home from the First World War. After getting off the train, he walked across our field toward our house. My mom saw him and ran to him with her arms outstretched, shouting, "Marvin's home! Marvin's home!" To me, my mom looked like an angel with her long hair blowing in the wind. My dad's brother, Luey Jeffries, had a car. Dad got Luey to take all of us and Uncle Marvin to my grandpa James Gordon's farm six miles south of Stockton. They covered Uncle Marvin up with a quilt to surprise his family living near Stockton. As we drove near the Gordon farm, people were working in the fields. We came along the narrow road. Uncle Luey honked and honked the car horn and people came running from the fields and in wagons following us up the hill to my grandpa Gordon's home. When we arrived at their farm home they asked what was under the cover in the front seat with Uncle Luey. We all laughed and said, "Some laundry." What shouting and hugging went on. What a great day of rejoicing for everyone. I remember I was scared all the car honking and people shouting would scare the horses. While we were there a few days, a big feast was spread with kinfolk and neighbors gathered at Grandpa and Grandma Gordon's home for a great reunion and celebration. Uncle Marvin, who had been a machine gunner in France, came home from the war without a scratch.

During the 1920s I often dreamed. Some dreams were scary, some funny and some crazy to me. My sister, Ethel, had a book on dreams and told what different things in dreams meant. Often she would ask me, "Martha, what did you dream last night?" And we would look it up in that dream book. One time, in 1929 (our family lived in Lamar, MO between 1924 to beginning of 1930, where my dad was the Barton County Baptist Missionary and also supported his large family as a carpenter and as a deputy sheriff) I dreamed of a tall, handsome, blonde, young man with a gold tooth. I told Ethel of this dream. She said, "Oh, that man you will meet someday."

Then, my dad was called back to Fair Play and the first week of January of 1930 he became full-time pastor at the Fair Play Baptist Church. In Fair Play we moved into a two-story house just northwest of the church. Dad went immediately into a big revival there that lasted four weeks. During that revival there was snow and ice on the ground, but the bitter, cold weather did not keep people away from church. There were several conversions during that revival and the church increased in membership.

After church services, we young folks would gather around the piano to sing and my sister, Ethel, would play the piano. The Methodist Church young people would come to the Baptist Church and the Baptist young folks would go to the Methodist Church. Then, one night, after church services, as we were at the piano singing, I looked toward the back of the church. There stood a tall, blonde, young man. He looked up and smiled. He had a gold tooth that shinned so bright. Ethel punched me and said, "Martha, there's your dream man!" I asked her who he was. She didn't know. Later we learned his name was Jesse Mayse, son of Granville and Cleo Mayse. The Mayses operated the Southern Hotel and Jesse had his own cleaning and pressing business at the hotel. I wanted him to ask me for a date. Later Jesse Mayse asked my brother, Jimmy, if I would go out with him and Jimmy told Jesse, "Ask her and see." When Jimmy told me this I said, "Well, Jimmy you sure are a lot of help!" Jesse finally got the courage to walk to where my family lived and ask me if I would go with him to the eighth grade play (My brother, Jimmy, was in that play). Of course I would go with Jesse. That was March 4, 1930. Jesse asked me to marry him on May 18, 1930 and we were married in my parent's home in Fair Play on July 11, 1930. My mom cooked us a wonderful wedding supper. Back in those days married couples did not go on honeymoons. After our wedding and wedding supper, my husband and I moved into the hotel run by my in-laws. (We were married 58 years and one month before he died in 1988).

This was the beginning of the 1930s, the depression was getting worse and worse. Hot and dry climate and people tried and tried but couldn't raise much grain. Little pigs had to be drowned as soon as they were born as there was no feed for them. Times were getting harder and harder. I took over our cleaning and pressing business as my husband, Jesse, began driving a truck for his uncle Folly Mayse. Uncle Folly had two trucks. They hauled cream, eggs, chickens or cattle to Kansas City and to St. Louis. My husband would be gone two to three days at a time on those long hauls for Folly.

Later, my husband and I moved from the hotel to a little, white house just back of the hotel. Jesse's grandpa, Alfred Grant Freize, gave me a little, runt pig. My mother-in-law said it would die; but in my spare time, I cared for that pig like it was a baby. As it grew up, it would follow me everywhere. I talked a lot to this pig and it just grunted back. When I would enter a store to shop, the pig would wait outside until I came out. Then it would follow me home like a little dog. It finally weighed 500 pounds. What a huge pig! Jesse said we had to sell the pig as we needed the money. I cried, but he sold it anyway. It brought $9.00. I cried so hard that Jesse went to where he sold the pig and bought it back. Crazy me. As time went by, we finally had to butcher it. That was just as hard for me. It was a huge, black and white spotted pig.

Our first Christmas of married life Jesse and I were still living in Fair Play. The Baptist Church had a Christmas tree program. Many came and brought gifts to put under the tree of children of the church. Times were hard. Jesse told me, "Let's buy all your brothers and sisters socks. Socks are useful and needed." While other children were getting various toys from under the tree, my little brothers and sisters smiled at all the other children. As they were unwrapping their gifts from Jesse and me, one of my brothers, Jesse Thomas, came to us, smiled and said "Sanks, Mossie and Jess for my socks. All my socks at home are teared." He was very young, always called me Mossie and didn't talk plain at that time. When we got home, I cried, My husband tried to reassure me that my brothers and sisters were proud of their socks. My siblings were always thankful for whatever they received.

The youngest child in our family, Grace Annas, died at Fair Play on March 12, 1933 at the age of 11 months from severe whooping cough and pneumonia. She was buried by her sister, Mary Ellen, at Pleasant Ridge Cemetery in Aldrich. My other brothers and sisters included: Esther, Susan, Ruth, Noah, Paul, Bobby and Philip.

My mother, Effie Caroline (Gordon) Jeffries died in 1967. My dad, Rev. James Nathan Jeffries, died in 1970. They were married almost 60 years before Mother died.

There were 15 of us children born to the same parents. As of this year of 2002, seven of us 15 children are still alive. The others have gone to their Heavenly Home where the soul never dies. I thank my God for Christian teachings and many precious memories. *Submitted by Martha Ann (Jeffries) Mayse*

MEDLEY – William J. "Bill" Medley, Oct. 5, 1873-Dec. 24, 1949, married Cora Hastings, March 28, 1878-Feb. 17, 1961, about 1896. They lived in the community of Tin Town on a farm. They had five children: Claude, Dorothy, Carl, Zelma and Ellis.

Claude Dewey Medley, Sept. 7, 1898-Oct. 8, 1957, married Vercy Lucinda Elizabeth Williams, April 9, 1897-May 27, 1985, on Jan. 21, 1920. He was a farmer and drove a milk truck for Producers Creamery in Springfield, MO. He was on the school board for the Black Oak School near Tin Town. She was a housewife and mother. They had William Dean, Oct. 23, 1920-Nov. 9, 1952 and Vercillia Jean, June 8, 1922-Dec. 1, 1972, who married Cecil Ellison.

Erma Lee McCurry and Dean Medley

W. Dean married Erma Lee McCurry, Feb. 23, 1922-Jan. 20, 2001, on March 10, 1938. She was the daughter of Jacob and Nora Agnes Hill McCurry from Olive in Dallas County, MO. She had four siblings: Ralph, Mary, Howard and Willa Dee McCurry.

Dean and Erma Lee had three children: William Dennis, born June 19,

1941, married Saundra Kay Kenner from Hollister, MO on May 19, 1962; Linda Sue, born July 17, 1945, married Billy Lee Yoast from Bolivar, MO on Jan. 5, 1964; Deanna Lou, born Jan. 13, 1948, married Ronnie Lee Cook on Feb. 16, 1965. Dennis and Saundra had Dennis Allen, Donna Kay and David Kent. Linda and Billy had Shawn Lee, Shane Lee and Shannon Lee. Deanna and Ronnie had Brian Lee.

Dean and Erma Lee farmed on the family farm and after getting electricity, they built a Grade A Dairy barn and milked Jerseys and Guernseys. They had a few hogs, chickens and raised a big garden. There were always flowers to take to Decoration Day at Rock Prairie and Union Grove Missionary Baptist Churches to put on loved ones' graves.

The drought years of the 1950s forced them to move to Tin Town and find work off the farm. Dean went to work in Springfield at Coon Roofing Company as a roofer. Erma Lee found work at a plant in Springfield as an upholsterer. She worked there six years. She would take home scraps of vinyl from the chairs she upholstered and started making purses for family and friends. She decided to apply for a Farmers Home Administration small business loan and received the first loan in Polk County. In 1961 Medley's Upholstery and Purse Shop began. At the height of the business she employed 12 ladies and shipped purses all over the United States and abroad. She became known as "the Purse Lady from Tin Town." Because of health problems she retired and closed the purse shop in June 1991 after 30 years of business. She continued to go to church, sing and play the piano whenever she could.

MERRITT – Samuel Frank Merritt was the first son of Henry C. Merritt and Elizabeth Tindle Renfro Merritt. He also had a brother, John and a sister, Anna. John married Lydia Roberts. Anna married Gene Quinn. He also had a half-brother, Thomas Asbury Renfro and a half-sister, Mary Elizabeth.

Annie and Frank Merritt

Thomas Asbury Renfro married Ellen Eliza Pierce and Mary Elizabeth married first, Walter Lovett and second, Joe Best. Frank was born July 16, 1878 and died Feb. 20, 1954. He married Annie Crawford on May 30, 1902. She was born February 1883 and died Oct. 12, 1950. To this union were born two daughters, Alta and Freda. Alta married Clyde Burchell and they had one son, Richard Gene and a daughter, Betty. Freeda married Ralph Hood and they had no children.

Freda is buried at Slagle Cemetery in Polk County, MO and Alta is buried in Nevada, MO by Clyde Burchell. *Submitted by Deadra Sillavan Ervin*

MEYER – Andrew Meyer I was born approximately 1730 in Auggen, Grand Duchy of Baden, Germany. He was a cabinet maker by trade. He married Anna Gering (Gehring) around 1750 and the couple had four children: Fredrick, Sophronia, Andrew II and John Jacob, all born in Auggen, Baden, Germany.

Andrew Meyer II, born Aug. 14, 1790, married Mary Adolph in 1817. Mary was born in Germany in 1796. Andrew II was a cabinet maker and a farmer. He immigrated to America with his family in 1834, arriving via the ship *Formosa* through the Port of New York, settling in Wayne County, near Mt. Eaton, OH. In 1844 Andrew Meyer II moved his family to Holt County, MO, settling on a farm two miles northwest of Oregon, MO. The couple had 10 children, the first seven were born in Germany and the last three in Mt. Eaton, OH: John Martin, Andrew III, John, Anna Marie, George, Christian, John Jacob, Ludwick Lewis, Gottlieb and William.

John Jacob Meyer was born April 13, 1834. He farmed and lived one and one-half miles northwest of Oregon, MO, near the Andrew Meyer II homestead. He married Minerva Curtis on Oct. 8, 1857. Minerva was born May 13, 1837 in Marion County, IN. They had seven children: James Curtis, Mary Jane, Rebecca Curtis, Hannah Jane, Sumner, Thomas and Laura.

James Curtis Meyer was born July 14, 1858. He married Elizabeth Deborah Lukens of Cadiz, OH on Sept. 4, 1880. Elizabeth was born Jan. 7, 1860. The couple had 12 children, including one set of twins who did not survive: Charles Sumner, Arthur Lee, Edna Lukens, Jennie Minerva, Elizabeth Bessie, James Ralph, Dwight Lewis, Elmer Willie, Russell Walter and William Elmer.

William Elmer Meyer was born May 23, 1904. He married Opal Irene Kuhn on Jan. 9, 1929. Irene was born Nov. 11, 1907. They farmed, lived many years and raised their children on the old James Curtis Meyer homestead, which was designated a Centennial Farm. Their children are Robert James, William LeRoy, Donald Bruce, Richard Max, Ronald Lee, Nancy Ann, Linda Sue, Alvin Dee, Betty Jean and Janet Irene.

Alvin Dee Meyer was born July 5, 1942 north of Oregon, MO on the family homestead. Alvin married Rosalie Harris in Miami, OK on June 30, 1966. Rosie was born June 12, 1947 four and one-half miles north of Forest City, MO on the family homestead.

A job change brought the couple to Polk County in 1987. Alvin became cashier at the Pleasant Hope Bank, Pleasant Hope, MO and began that job on February 2. Rosie started work as a parent educator and secretary for the Exceptional Pupil Cooperative of the Ozarks in Bolivar, MO on June 1. They have two children. Alesia Renee Meyer married Ryan Scroggins. They live in Platte City, MO and are expecting the birth of a son in November 2002. Marsha Gay Meyer married Brad Foster. They live in Nixa, MO and are parents to a daughter, Dani and a son, Eddie, who are Alvin and Rosie's step-grandchildren.

Rosie and Alvin Meyer

Alvin says, "We enjoy seeing row crops grow in the northern part of the county, soybeans and corn, which reminds us of the croplands in Northwest Missouri. We love it down here and we don't know where we could have moved to have liked it any better. There's awesome scenery, lakes, pasture land or wooded areas, hills or flatlands just a short drive away." *Submitted by Alvin D. Meyer*

MIHULKA - Josef and Franciska Kopecki Mihulka and their five children (four sons and one daughter) arrived in America circa 1890 from the "old country," Czechoslovakia. Sue's grandmother, Frances Ursula Mihulka, was 8 or 9 years old when the family boarded ship and set out for a new life in this country. It was a remarkable adventure for a young girl and accounts of the voyage have been repeated throughout the years. They settled in Nebraska and raised corn before relocating to Bolivar.

The family moved to Bolivar in the early 1900s and Frances Ursula worked at the Hotel located north of the square as a desk clerk. There she met Mathew "Big Matt" Duffek, also born in Czechoslovakia, whose family had settled in Sturgeon Bay, WI area. He was traveling by train to the 1903 St. Louis World's Fair. They began corresponding and were married in 1905. They lived in a large two-story house northwest of Bolivar. Three children were born: a son, Milo, who lived only three months and two daughters, Sadie Lucille and Mildred Frances (Sue's mother).

At home the children spoke Bohemian until they started school. Mildred Frances attended the first class held in the North Ward School. She graduated from Bolivar High School and worked in the 5 & 10 Dime Store located on the west side of the square. In the harsh winter of 1928 she caught pneumonia and there was little hope she would survive. A doctor from Springfield was finally called. He performed surgery by removing a rib and inserting a drainage tube. All this was done on the kitchen table. Several months of recovery followed.

In 1933 she married Rodney Francis Sterling. It was during the war and he had found work in an airplane factory in Michigan. As the story is told, they had been seeing each other for some time and one day he came by on his way to Michigan and asked Mildred Frances if she wanted to go with him. She packed a truck and they were married that same day. She always claimed it was the "craziest" thing she ever did. They returned to Bolivar after the war and had two children, Ted and Sue, who still reside in the area.

It has been 112 years since the Mihulka family arrived in America and all have passed on. They are buried in Bolivar Greenwood Cemetery, except great-grandfather Josef. He returned to Czechoslovakia and built a large home near Zumbeck for the elderly. *Submitted by Sue Sterling Schofield*

MILLER - David E. Miller, Barbara's great-grandfather, was born March 9, 1850, in Clarenceville, Quebec, Canada. His parents were Matthew Jameson Miller and Mary Elliott. David married his first wife Lucinda Kincaid, Jan. 20, 1880 in Clarenceville. Their son, Ernest Whittier Miller, Barbara's grandfather, was born Dec. 24, 1880. When Lucinda died on May 20, 1882, David married Hellen Marion Nichols on March 3, 1884 in Clarenceville.

David E. Miller's uncle, also named David Miller, had previously located in Bolivar. Uncle David owned a printing shop and Aunt Nancy Agnes Miller, a millinery store. Their three sons, Almond R. Miller and Charles W. Miller, owned the *Bolivar Free Press* off and on in the late 1870s and through the 1880s. David E. Miller was persuaded to immigrate to Bolivar in December of 1883, and his brother, Elliott Miller, in 1885, by their Uncle David who, in his letters to them, extolled the great resources of and the unlimited opportunities for prosperity in Polk County.

The following item was featured in the July 9, 1885, issue of the *Bolivar Free Press*: "D. E. Miller is making preparations to build a residence during the summer on his farm west of town." The barn has since been torn down, but the house still stands and is located off Lemmon Road, northwest of Bolivar.

Some interesting comments on Bolivar and its people, taken from David E. Miller's letters. Before immigrating to Bolivar, David had worked for a short while in Winnipeg, Manitoba, Canada, with his brother Elliott.

Letter dated Jan. 23, 1884: "It is astonishing how little they know of Manitoba down here. While in conversation with the banker, he learned that I had just arrived from Winnipeg and inquired if it was in this country. Again, when talking with an old doctor here, an intelligent, well-informed man, knowing that I was from Manitoba, he remarked that is up near Chicago, isn't it? Also, the Methodist minister here had to learn of Minnie (David's first cousin) where it was situated. I leave it for Marshal (friend in Manitoba) to decide whether it is the inferiority of this country or the gross ignorance of the people here that calls forth such questions." And "You ought to see the things they make and call sleighs here. They would be fined for driving such things in the north."

April 18, 1884: "A great many have come in from the North during the last year, so the old settlers think their day has come to make money, and they sell out land and everything else for all they can get. They have surveyed a line of railway from Springfield to Bolivar lately, and although the people do not say much, owing to their disappointments in the past, yet they seem quite confident they will get it, and that they will begin work at once."

David E. Miller

November 19, 1884: "Times are rather dull now owing to the election. We have nothing reliable yet as to who shall be president. A good many predict a stagnation in business if the Democrats come into power. I believe they are capable of bringing about more than that if they had rope enough."

December 30, 1884: "Until a few days ago, we could boast of the same amount of snow that you could. It came on the 10th instant and lasted until after Christmas, then it thawed and rained and now everything is slush. If the soil here was as tenacious as Manitoba mud, we would all be mired. I find that in order to keep stock with any degree of comfort and success, shelter is as necessary here as in some colder countries, though there is a class of fogies here who seem to thank they can endure anything."

Barbara's mother, Lorraine Wilkinson, nee Miller, and her sister and four brothers were all born in Karlin, MO. *Submitted by Barbara L. Wilkinson*

MILLER - John Miller was born circa 1809 and died in March 1880 in Polk County, MO. Milla Davis was born circa 1815 and died in March 1870 in Polk County, MO. They were married Jan. 23, 1839 in Grainger County, TN. Their parents are unknown. It is believed that John and Milla Miller are buried in the Trimble Cemetery near Aldrich,

William Anderson Miller, circa 1890

MO in unmarked graves. John and Milla Miller can be found in the 1850 census in Madison Township, Polk County, MO with their two sons, Emanuel and William Anderson. Since about 1850 until the present time, seven generations or more of the family of John and Milla Miller have lived in Polk County, MO.

Emanuel Miller was born May 28, 1844 in Grainger County, TN and died May 22, 1917 in Polk County, MO. He married on Feb. 14, 1864 to Synthia Hays who was born Nov. 10, 1835 and died July 3, 1913. They are buried in the Trimble Cemetery. They had six children: Joseph, married Hannah Coffee; James, married Sarah Mitchell; Sarah Elizabeth (Speed), married John W. Brown; William, died young; Conaway, married Oma Stevens and second, Marie Spidell; a son who died young.

William Anderson Miller was born Dec. 19, 1842 in Grainger County, TN and died Aug. 8, 1919 in Polk County, MO. He married on March 12, 1859 in Polk County, MO to Martha Jane Martin, born Jan. 10, 1844 in Louisville, Boone County, VA and died May 21, 1927 in Polk County, MO. She was the daughter of William Martin Jr. and Wintha Henrietta (Ritter) (Adams) Martin, who settled near Fair Grove, MO about 1850. They died in 1853 of typhoid leaving Martha Jane, her sister Susannah and her brother Bently as orphans.

William Anderson and Martha Miller were the parents of six children. John C. married Louisa Orlena Crain. They had two children, Cora and Nora. James Bently (Tobe) married Irene F. "Rena" Price. They had nine children: Dessa, Maude, Nellie, Lester, Edger "Ed," Ruth, Dorotha "Dorothy," Marie and John Perry. Thomas Marion married Elizabeth Morton. They had six children: Claude D., Grace Louise, Flora Elizabeth, Ralph Morton, Bruce Marion and William Anderson. Ellen "Babe" died young, buried Trimble Cemetery. Hardin D. married Celestia Elizabeth "Lessie" Younger. They had five children: Elgy Faye, died young, Meda Vere, Ira Ingle "Bob," Jesse Barge and Paul Younger. Jonas Jerome "Jone" married Girty Blair. They had three children: Ruby Pearl, Glen Rural, and a son who died as an infant.

William Anderson and Martha Miller accepted Christ as their Savior and lived with a great abiding faith. About seven years before his death, William Anderson was injured by a fall and lived a quiet, peaceful life with his wife, children and many friends until his death. The farm home of William Anderson and Martha Miller was on Route V, west of Highway 123 near Aldrich, MO. It was not far from the Shady Grove Cemetery where William Anderson and Martha Miller are buried. Many of their children and other family members are also buried in the Shady Grove Cemetery. *Submitted by Theron O. Miller, great-grandson of William Anderson and Martha Jane (Martin) Miller*

Martha Jane Martin Miller, circa 1890

MILLER - Henry Fredric Miller was born on Nov. 13, 1878 in Chariton County, MO to John Folkerts Miller (born in Germany on May 14, 1839, died Dec. 26, 1931) and Henrietta Calkins (Nov. 13,1878 -July 16, 1956). On Oct. 13, 1897, he married Barbara Elizabeth "Bessie" Dowell (Jan. 5, 1880 - December 31, 1963). She was the daughter of Simeon Horace Dowell and Rebecca Jane Hayden, from Livingston County, MO.

Henry and Bessie moved to Polk County, MO by about 1910, where son, Horace, attended his first year of school at Rock Prairie. In 1915-1916, Henry and oldest son, Emil, went to Kansas to wheat farm, while Bessie, Horace, Murray and Jean moved back to Marceline, MO until Henry and Emil got settled. When Henry and Emil came back to Chariton County, the family settled south of Marceline, MO, then later bought a place east of Mike, MO. They later sold it and moved to Brookfield so that all the children could attend high school. Horace started ninth grade and graduated from high school in 1925 at Brookfield, MO. In the spring of 1926, the family moved back to Rock Prairie, Polk County, MO and settled next door to the John Partee and Allie Burdett Chapman family.

Henry Fredric Miller and Barbara Elizabeth "Bessie" Dowell, 1955

Henry and Bessie had five children. Henry Emil Miller (Jan. 21, 1899-July 28, 1925) married Hazel Perry on April 10, 1921. Hazel was born Aug. 30, 1902 and died Nov. 15, 1994. Both are buried in Locke Cemetery, Chariton County, MO. Mona Marie Miller (Oct. 17, 1901-Oct. 2, 1902). John Horace Miller (born Aug. 23, 1904) married Georgia Marie Chapman on March 17, 1928. Georgia was born March 3, 1912 and died Jan. 3, 2002. She is buried at Pleasant Hope Cemetery, Pleasant Hope, MO. (See Horace and Georgia Chapman Miller article). Murray D. Miller (March 8, 1908-about 1985) married Nina Eagon on Sept. 3, 1929. Nina was born May 5, 1910. Murray is buried at White Chapel Cemetery, Greene County, MO. Barbara Jean Miller (born Aug. 22, 1919). Jean's first marriage was to William Roscoe Murray on Aug. 8, 1943; they later divorced. Jean's second marriage was to Ernest "Ern" Thaden on April 17, 1948. Ern was born Jan. 21, 1909 and died Aug. 30, 1998. He is buried at Hope, AR.

Henry Fredric Miller died in Polk County, MO on July 16, 1956 at the age of 77. Bessie Dowell Miller died on Dec. 31, 1963 at the age of 83. Both Henry and Bessie are buried at the Pleasant Hope Cemetery, Pleasant Hope, Polk County, MO. *Submitted by J. Horace Miller*

MILLER - One day, in the spring of 1926, on the family farm in Rock Prairie, 21-year-old Horace Miller (son of Henry Fredric Miller and Barbara Elizabeth "Bessie" Dowell) went about his daily chore of rounding up the cattle for milking. The Millers' land and cow pasture came down to John P. Chapman's side yard, and it wasn't long until the Chapman's 14-year-old daughter, Georgia, began to notice him. Soon Horace and Georgia were waving and smiling at each other daily across the pasture. It was on Decoration Day, on the first Sunday of June, when the Chapmans, John, Allie, son Raymond, age 9 and Georgia, age 14, hitched the horses to the hack (a two-seated buggy with no top) and went to Union Grove to decorate graves. The young people always went to these gatherings because there was usually a dinner on the ground.

Horace Miller was there with his horse, Old Ribbon, and the buggy. Horace and Georgia saw each other, smiled and they finally spoke when he asked her if he could take her home. After getting permission, Georgia went with Horace. They dated for the next two years, with Old Ribbon taking them far and wide.

Georgia Chapman and Horace Miller

In March of 1928, Horace proposed to her after Georgia's daddy was consulted. John Chapman was hesitant because Georgia was only 16 years old, but agreed. Plans began to take shape. Georgia's mother made her dress, lavender rayon, long waisted and very plain. Since Georgia was not old enough for Horace to get a license, John Chapman went with Horace to sign the written permission. Driving Old Ribbon and the buggy, the men got caught in a snowstorm on the way back from Bolivar, but arrived safely.

After marrying on March 17, 1928, by C. E. Craig, Horace and Georgia moved to their first home, a two-room house with a back porch. Although they could see cracks between the floorboards, one little King heater kept them warm. They had a bed, a phonograph, a table, two chairs and two-burner kerosene cook stove.

By 1941, they moved to Pleasant Hope, where Horace had started driving the school bus for Pleasant Hope, as he would do for 30 years. For 35 years, he served as mayor, city clerk and treasurer with Georgia supporting him by serving as hostess when the Council met in their home. It was obvious that they were true lovebirds and was a joy for the family to witness. Even when Georgia was in the nursing home, she would say, "He's just so cute!"

Georgia passed away on Jan. 3, 2002, at the age of 89. It was two months shy of their 74th wedding anniversary. Horace still lives in Pleasant Hope, and in August 2002, will celebrate his 98th birthday.

They have three children, Chester L., Velma L. and John H. *Submitted by John H. and Lanita Sconce Miller*

MINCKS - Garley E. Mincks and Sarah Marie (Appleby) Mincks moved to Polk County in the spring of 1940 from Greene County, north of Rogersville, where they lived with Garley's folks, Silas Lafe Mincks and Julia Ellen (Brewer) Mincks.

Garley and Marie bought 20 acres north of Bolivar near Mt. Etna School. Clara Nadine, their daughter, was nearly 3 years old and had the measles so she stayed with her grandparents Ross and Ora Elizabeth (Snead) Appleby, who lived north of Willard, MO.

Garley and Marie worked side by side farming and milking cows, truck farming and cutting wood in the winter. In the early 1950s rural electricity came to the farm, making life a little easier, with running water, ice cubes and ice cream from their new refrigerator and washing clothes in the Maytag wringer washer.

Clara attended eight years at Mt. Etna School and rode the bus to Bolivar High School. In 1954 a new baby boy came to live with the Mincks family, Ross Wayne, who was the apple of his parents' eye.

Clara graduated high school in May of 1955 and married James Clyde Cunningham that fall and eventually moved back to rural Rogersville, MO where they raised their family of four boys and one girl, making lots of visits to Clara's parents' farm.

Both were very active in the Mt. Etna Baptist Church, where Marie taught Sunday school and was the treasurer and Garley was Sunday school director and a deacon.

Garley and Marie lived all the rest of their years on the same farm, adding more land as time went on.

Garley and Marie and Clara Mincks, 1940

Their son Wayne died Aug. 9, 1981 as a result of a truck accident.

Marie died on April 16, 1987, their 52nd wedding anniversary. Garley lived alone on the farm until his death on Jan. 24, 2001.

Garley always said Polk County was the best place in the entire world to live, and he did. *Submitted by Clara Nadine (Mincks) Cunningham*

MINCKS - Lester Mincks was born Oct. 30, 1902, son of Lafe and Julie (Brewer) Mincks. Eula Ann (Smith) Mincks was the daughter of George and Nellie (Baliff) Smith. They grew up and married at Rogersville, MO. From Rogersville in 1927 they moved to Buffalo, MO. From Buffalo they moved to Springfield in 1934, moved to Bolivar (Polk County) in April of 1935 and spent the rest of their lives there.

Lester worked for WPA and River Farm, farming all their lives. Lester's grandmother Liza (Finn) Brewer was a full-blooded Indian. Eula's mother Nellie was born in England and came to the USA at the age of 18 months on a ship with her family.

Lester and Eula were married Jan. 21, 1919. They celebrated their 76th anniversary on Jan. 21, 1995. Lester passed away May 4, 1995 at the age of 92. Eula passed away May 18, 1996 at the age of 93. They are buried in Payne Cemetery in Polk, MO.

They had 14 children, all are still living. Of the 14 children, five of the sons served in the military- Willard, Paul, Boyde and Jay were in Germany and Loyde served in France. They are Bertha Jarvis (Ozark), Leonard Mincks (Bolivar), Chestine Ahart (Bolivar), Willard Mincks (Fair Play), Paul Mincks (Humansville), Cheslie "Big" Mincks (Dunnegan), Leslie "Lid" Mincks (Cleveland, MO), Rose Kirby (Harrisonville), Ruth Neal (Bolivar), Boyde "Butch" Mincks (Bolivar), Loyde "Pee Wee" Mincks (Cleveland, MO), Lester "Jay" Mincks (Flemington), Kenneth Mincks (Bolivar) and Billy Mincks (Bolivar).

Leonard passed away Nov. 9, 2002 and is buried at Payne Cemetery. He leaves behind his wife Fannie.

Their families are: Elmer (deceased) and Bertha Jarvis, children Rick, Joe and Tresea; Leonard (deceased) and Lorene (deceased) Mincks, children Earl, Joyce, Charlotte, Gene, Lennie, Bertha, Garley, Lena, Loyd, Linda, Jeff, and Scott; Bradford (deceased) and Chestine Ahart, children Betty, Georgia, Jerry, William and Helen; Willard and Wanda Mincks, children Larry, Chesley, Marcella, Anna, Willy and Raymond; Paul and Margaret (deceased) Mincks, children Retha, Jean, Paul David, Donnie, Gary, Billy, Cindy and Dale, wife now is Janice; Cheslie and Ileen (deceased) Mincks, children Sharon, Brenna, Suzie and Steve; Leslie and Myrle Mincks (divorced), children Dale, Deanie, Donna, Carol, Rita, Jim, Charles and Pete-Leslie's companion now is Delta Egger; Reuben (deceased) and Rose Kirby, children Emily, Rosie, Richard, Kenny and Robert; Dale and Ruth Neal, children Danny, Roger, Terry, Artie, Jenise and Denise; Boyde and Virginia Mincks, children Michelle, Randy and Debbie; Loyde and Shirley Mincks, children Loyde William, Patty and Penny; Jay and Kay (deceased) Mincks, children Dennis, Cathie, Malinda, Dalinda and Todd-wife now is Marge; Kenny and Sue Mincks, children Butch, Tonya, Shawntell and Derek; Billy and Emma Mincks, child Debra. Billy owned Bill's Feed in Bolivar.

They had 75 grandchildren, eight are deceased. One hundred eighty-five great-grandchildren, six are deceased. One hundred seventy-seven great-great grandchildren, four are deceased.

Their family includes two sets of twin sons, two sets of twin granddaughters, two sets of twin great-granddaughters and grandsons, and one set of twin great-great-granddaughters. They have 451 descendants.

Lester and Eula were longtime members of Mt. Etna Baptist Church, where Lester served as a deacon and longtime Sunday school teacher. *Submitted by Ruth (Mincks) Neal*

MITCHELL - Elizabeth Mitchell was born June 25, 1831 and died Dec. 12, 1884. She was a descendent of the Methodist preacher that held brush arbor meetings in what is now called the Mitchell Campground and Cemetery. She married Alfred Paul Strange who was born Feb. 2,

1825 and died Aug. 5, 1860. They had a good farm in the bend of Highway 32 and Bear Creek River. They had four children, Sarah Ann, Rebecca Ester, Alfred and Morris. Morris was born in 1860, the same year his father died. Soon after her husband died she married a Hudson and they had two children, Tom Hudson, born in 1862 and Martha born in 1866.

Sarah Ann married Andrew Jackson Smith. Sarah Ann was born Sept. 14, 1852 and died July 7, 1929. Andrew was born Oct. 2, 1844 and died Oct. 2, 1914. He was a small man who was part Indian. He fought in the Civil War from 1861 to 1865. He fought for the south and was considered a "rebel." He was in the Battlefield Battle, west of Springfield. In those days you just did not marry an Indian, neither was it good for a Rebel to marry a Yankee! Andrew Smith had been to Dadeville to visit his brother who had settled there. Looking over the country on horseback he stopped at the Strange home. Sarah Ann remembered that he came up about dusk and she was sitting on a log fence. Against her folks' wishes, they were married on Sept. 1, 1870. They bought a farm east of Bethel. There was a one-room log cabin on it. To this union nine children were born: Alfred, Lenny, Bennie, Ira, Cora, Bertha, Mandy, Coy and Creed. After some of the older children were born, Andrew built a two-story house and the cabin was used for a storehouse.

Ira married Ruben Stenson and they had a restaurant in Fair Play. Mandy married Bob Beason and lived in Fair Play. Bertha married Cliff Williams from Fair Play.

Creed, the family says, was a gypsy at heart. He moved around a lot. He was born Nov. 20, 1892 and was the youngest of the nine children. He married Florence Wildey in 1911. To this union two children were born, Naomi and Norman. Florence died on Feb. 5, 1926. Creed then married Violet Smith in 1929 and she had a small son when they married. Seven children were born to this union. Margie was born in Kansas, Ken and Nellie were born in Ava, MO and Jack, Jim and Susan were born in Fair Play. Linda was born in Creston, IA. The family lived in and around Fair Play from 1938 to 1946 and the children went to Bear Creek and Hartley schools. In 1946 they moved to Creston, IA when Nellie was in the seventh grade. She finished high school in Iowa and married and stayed there. Creed and Violet moved back to Lowry City, MO in 1952. Creed died on Jan. 20, 1962 at the age of 69. Violet moved to Clinton, IA after Creed died. She died on Dec. 3, 1983. They are both buried in Kidds Cemetery, west of Lowry City, MO.

Arnold and Nellie Curry

Nellie married Arnold Curry and retired to Polk County in June of 2000. They live between Fair Play and Aldrich on VV Highway. *Submitted by Nellie Curry*

MITCHELL - John Henigar "Jim" Mitchell was born March 22, 1848 in Cedar County, MO. His parents were Wiley Blunt and Sarah Black Looney Mitchell. "Jim" was a blacksmith by trade and came from a long line of Methodist preachers on his father's side and was half-Cherokee Indian from his mother's side. (She, being full blooded.) John married first, Emily Missouri McConely, April 22, 1864 in Lawrence County, MO and second to

Bucking Horse Riders; Back row: Joseph Esquival, Jim Kid, Jim Mitchell, Dirk Johnson, Billy Bullock, Antonia Esquival, unknown; front: Johnny Baker (Cody's foster son) and unknown man; Staten Island, NY 1886

Mary Jane Kirk sometime before 1870 in Missouri. Mary was born Sept. 15, 1848 in Cedar County, MO. "Jim" and Mary were Dottie's great-grandparents. They are enumerated in the 1880 Cedar County, Madison Township census. They moved to Polk County by 1881 and settled in the Shady Grove area where at least two of their 10 children were born. Their children's names were Dorothy, Franklin, Sarah, Mary Alderina, Moses, Jesse, Emma, William Riley, James Albert and Wiley B., with Moses possibly having died in infancy. Dottie descends through their son James Albert Mitchell who was born June 26, 1894, in Aurora, Lawrence County, MO. On Oct. 30, 1920, James married Mary Sierra Roush in Wichita, Sedgwick County, KS, who was born April 10, 1905 in Warren, Huntington County, IN, the daughter of William Wesley and Electa Jane Pearson Roush. John Henigar "Jim" Mitchell was a good friend of W. F. Cody, also known as "Buffalo Bill" and was a scout with him and a performer in his "Wild West" show, along with other notable names such as Annie Oakley, Lillian Smith, Buck Tayler, Nate Salsbury, Sitting Bull, Calamity Jane, Geronimo, Wild Bill Hickok and others. Pictures of him can be seen at various times displayed in the Buffalo Bill museum at Lookout Mountain in Golden, CO where William Frederick Cody is buried. "Jim" was an exceptionally gifted horseman and accounts of his riding skills can be found in various books that have been written about the "Wild West" show. A favorite of Dottie's, in describing the 1886 program, relates that an English spectator described Jim Mitchell's riding of a black mare named "Dynamite" in this manner: "It was necessary for four men to hold her and she had to be blindfolded before he could get on her, and then letting out a scream like a woman in pain, she made a headlong dash and plunged with all her force into a fence, turning completely over head first and apparently falling upon the rider...Poor Jim was dragged out bleeding and maimed, and led away. What was the astonishment of the multitude, when the other refractory animals had had their sport, to see "Dynamite: again lead out, and the cowboy, limping and pale, come forward to make another attempt to ride her...for fifteen minutes the fight went on between man and beast...The cowboy, got upon her back by some superhuman skill, and then he was master." (Quoted from the *London Era* newspaper). While in Munich, Annie Oakley saved Prince Luitpold of Bavaria from being trampled by "Dynamite," the show's most dangerous bronco, shoving him to the ground in just the nick of time. The appreciative prince sent a diamond bracelet to Oakley and a cigarette case to "Dynamite's" handler and rider, "Jim" Mitchell. John Henigar "Jim" Mitchell died Jan. 3, 1917, in Prosperity, Jasper County, MO. His wife Mary Jane and her children moved to Kansas after his death where she married William Hathaway. Mary Jane died Oct. 12, 1936, and is buried in Wichita Park Cemetery, Wichita, Kansas. *Submitted by Dottie J. Keegan*

MITCHELL - The Mitchell family roots in Polk County begin in the 1830s with the arrival of Morris Mitchell, his wife Elizabeth, many children and grandchildren. Stephen, their 10th child and Stephen's oldest son, James Harvey Clark, were among those arriving in approximately 1835 from eastern Tennessee.

James Harvey Clark was born May 19, 1827 in Roane County, TN. At the age of 19 he enlisted in the Second Regiment of Missouri Volunteers and served during the Mexican War from Aug. 3, 1846 to Sept. 17, 1847 in Company H. The Second Regiment served in New Mexico under the command of Colonel Sterling Price.

On March 9, 1848 he married Mary E. Hendricks of Washington County, AR. Mary was born Feb. 13, 1831. They had four children: Sarah Rachel, Martha A., Hugh and Julia E. Mary died on July 15, 1860.

James then married Mary's sister Emily Elizabeth Hendricks on Jan. 3, 1861. Emily was born March 18, 1839. They had five children: Alma P., Ella G., Eula I., Nora M. and Lester Henry Stephen (born Sept. 9, 1874).

James served the Union in Company L, 15th Regiment of Missouri Cavalry Volunteers from Nov. 1, 1863 to his discharge as a sergeant on July 1, 1865. James died May 22, 1888.

Lester Henry Stephen married Nellie Pearl Doty on Jan. 2, 1907. The Dotys' ancestry goes back to Edward Doty of the *Mayflower*, through Ohio and New Jersey. They lived with Lester's

Lester Henry Stephen and Nellie Pearl Mitchell behind 12 of their children in front of their home on Forest in Lee's Summit, MO (late 1927?). The children are, from left to right: Ruth Adeline, Stephen Ray, Harold, Clark, Howard James, Dorothy Ula, Roy Gaylord, Alice Enid, Cliff Zorn, Charlie Paul, Imogene and Glenna Lee.

mother, Emily, on the family farm. Twelve of their 14 children were born on the farm in Polk County (Section 18, Township 33N, Range 24W). When Emily died in 1923, the pension she received from James' service ended. Nellie and Lester sold the farm and moved the family to Lee's Summit, MO, in Jackson County.

Harold Clark was born Aug. 9, 1910, the third child of Nellie and Lester. Harold Clark graduated from Lee's Summit High School. He married C. Virginia Brown on Jan. 6, 1934. Virginia's Brown ancestry goes through Culpeper, VA in the 1730s and ultimately to a town in northern Wales. Harold died Jan. 29, 1996. They had two children, Luann and Gary Clark.

The children and grandchildren of Nellie and Lester have spread from Massachusetts to California and Texas to Idaho and many locations in between. The Mitchells came a long way from Montgomery County, MD, through Washington County, PA and Knox, Roane, and Blount Counties in Tennessee to Polk County, MO, and have gone a long way from Polk County. *Submitted by Gary Clark Mitchell*

1943, Prudie and Jim Mitchem

MITCHEM - James Ellis Mitchem was born March 27, 1870 in Flora, IL. His parents were James Mitchem, a minister, and Susan (Stanley) Mitchem. He came to Dunnegan, MO in 1896. Jim married Prudie Irene Barnes on Oct. 19, 1898. Prudie was born March 3, 1881 in Dunnegan, MO. Her parents were Allen and Alice Barnes.

Jim and Prudie made their home east of Dunnegan until 1943 when they moved to Humansville, MO.

Jim owned a well-digging rig and drilled wells for several years. He also ran a portable saw rig. Jim operated his own feed mill for eight years. He served on the school board and was the caretaker of the Dunnegan Cemetery.

Jim was a very honest man. Around 1923, a gentleman named Mr. Baney gave Jim $5.00 to put red flowers each year on his mother's grave.

Jim did this for several years and then passed this responsibility on to one of his daughters, who recently passed this responsibility on to another family member. Each Memorial Day for over 75 years, red flowers has been placed on the grave.

Prudie was a loving and caring mother who worked very hard raising her family. She was very hard of hearing and relied on her older children to listen for the younger children's cry.

Jim and Prudie had 13 children. Hazel, born in 1899, married George Minor. Esther, born in 1901, married Ray Stovall first and John Bennett, second. James Hallie, born in 1903, married May Little. A boy died at birth in 1905. Bert, born in 1906, married Opal Morris. Edna, born in 1908, married Harold "Dutch" Waider. Maxine, born in 1910, married Ray Huff. Dorothy, born in 1912, married Harold "Shorty" Huff first and Louis Gambrel, second. Dora, born in 1914, married Harrison Mustain. Irene, born in 1916, married Raymond Crites. Marjorie, born in 1918, married Bruce Billingsley. Maude, born in 1920, married Jack Baker. Charlie, born in 1923, married Gladys Thorsland.

Jim died Sept. 13, 1948 in Humansville, MO after having a stroke. Prudie died July 14, 1959. They are both buried in the Dunnegan, MO Cemetery. *Submitted by Maudie Baker*

Lydia Eveline (Mooney) Yokum, circa 1865

MOONEY - John B. Mooney, born circa 1785 in North Carolina or Tennessee, married in Lebanon, Wilson County, TN, Feb. 25, 1807 to Lydia Elizabeth Burns, born 1785 in North Carolina or Tennessee. The Mooneys became the parents of four known children namely: Lydia Eveline, born 1808 in Tennessee; Elizabeth, born 1810 in Tennessee; James E., born circa 1820 in Marion County, AR; and John B. Jr., born 1823.

As John and Lydia's family grew they set out on a migration path to the west around 1820 on the established "Nashville-Memphis Road" through Hardeman County, TN, across the Mississippi River, overland to Marion County, AR, and eventually came to rest in Greene County, Taylor Township, MO in 1827. This area became Polk County, Mooney Township, and a part of the original division of Greene County in 1835. John Mooney appeared to be traveling with a brother, Edward Mooney, his son-in-law Jacob Yoakum, a future son-in-law Cyrus Patterson, and possibly Ezekiel Campbell of Hardeman County, TN.

Mooney Township was named after Rev. John B. Mooney, who settled with his brother, Edward Mooney, on rented Delaware Lands near a small stream called Davis Creek, a tributary of the James River. Rev. Mooney remained at this location permanently as a farmer and may have also served in some capacity for the Cumberland Presbyterian Church of Pleasant Hope, as did the Polk County Burns families, kin of Lydia Burns. It is at this location where the Mooney children were partially raised, became adults and married.

Of the four known children the first, Lydia Eveline, was an exception and married Jacob Yoakum in Hardeman County, TN in 1823, where their first child, John, was born. Jacob was born in Jefferson County, TN, son of Solomon Yoacham and Susannah Adams. Solomon was one of the famous participants of the "Ozark Yocum Silver Dollar Legend."

America Eveline (Yokum) Margam-Ward, circa 1940

Jacob and Lydia Eveline raised 14 children in Taney, Polk, and Dade Counties between the years of 1824-1864 when they left on the California Trail with four daughters and one small son. Two sons and one son-in-law died in the Civil War before 1863 in Missouri. One daughter supposedly stayed on the Yokum farm with her husband, located two miles south of Greenfield on the Turnback River. Eleven of the Yokum children along with their parents lived and died in Butte and Shasta Counties in California. Second child, Elizabeth, married Cyrus Patterson on Aug. 8, 1828 in Gasconade County, MO. They raised eight children in Polk and Dade Counties. Third child, James E., a Mexican War Veteran, married Clarissa "Jane" Murry on Feb. 6, 1840 in Polk County. Five children were raised in Linn County, KS. Fourth child, John B. Jr., married Rebecca G. Russell on Dec. 29, 1842 in Polk County. John B. Jr. died circa 1848, leaving two children. His widow married James R. Harper in 1849, Polk County, raising their children in Dallas County, MO.

The parents of these four children enjoyed a full life when eventually God Almighty called upon them. Rev. John B. Mooney died 1846-1849 and Lydia Elizabeth Burns died after the Polk County 1850 Federal Census. Burials unknown in Polk County. This compiler is the great-great-great granddaughter of Rev. John B. Mooney and Lydia Elizabeth Burns; great-great granddaughter of Jacob Yokum and Lydia Eveline Mooney; and great-granddaughter of America Eveline Yokum, born Oct. 17, 1845, died May 13, 1940, at 94 years old. Her daughter Lucinda Fern Ward lived to be 99 years old. (Compiler's grandmother). May God bless these courageous pioneers. *Submitted by Audrey Lee Becker*

MOORE - Joe Moore was born in a log cabin on his granddad's farm near Center Point Church west of Huron, MO. Joe W. Moore was the son of John Moore and Sarah Ann Bewley. John Moore was the son of Alexander Moore and Ruth Williams Moore; both of whom were born and raised in Hawkins County, TN. Hawkins County is in the extreme eastern part of Tennessee and was settled early. Alexander Moore was born near Red Bridge in Hawkins County and was probably the son of Ewell Moore and Nancy Creed, who came to Polk County, MO before 1840. Ruth Williams's father James was an early settler of Polk County. Most of the Williams family died in the 1850s of some type of epidemic disease. Alexander Moore served in the Mexican War in Captain Robertson's Company H. Alexander received a federal pension later in life.

Sarah Ann Bewley was the daughter of Jesse H. Bewley and Mary J. Davis. Jesse Bewley was born in Barren County, KY near the town of Glasglow. He came to Polk County about 1856 and settled near Huron, MO. Mary's father, John "Jacky" Davis, was an early settler of Polk County. Jesse Bewley was a devout Baptist and even preached in some of the local churches. He served in the federal militia during the Civil War. He received a government pension for his war service. His original farm is now owned by Bill Moore and has always been in the family.

Sallie Hutcheson was born on April 10, 1887

in Polk County near Huron, MO. Sallie's parents were William "Bill" Hutcheson and Julia Ann Buckner Hutcheson. Bill and Julia were born near Carrollton, AR. Their families both came to Polk County after the Civil War. Sallie's grandfather and great-grandfather both came to Missouri after the war. The Hutchesons, Weeses, Johnsons and Cunninghams helped to found the Mt. Olive Baptist Church and Cemetery. Julia Buckner's father, George Buckner, served in the First Arkansas Cavalry during the war. The Southern people of Arkansas called these Union families "Mountain Feds."

Travis, Joe, Kathy, Jessie (Moore) Phillips, Sally and Harold Moore

Joe and Sallie's first child was Jessie Mildred, born in 1908 and died in 2002. Jessie married Burl Phillips of Cedar County, MO. Harold Gardiner was the second child, born in 1909 and married Juanita Berrie of Columbia, MO. The third child was William Travis, who was born in 1913 and married Mary Alice Phillips of Paris, MO. George Donald was the fourth, born in 1917 in Hickory County, MO and lives in Virginia. The fifth child, Ruth Virginia, was born in Polk County in 1931 and now lives in Idaho. Joe and Sallie both lived in the state of California before they were married. Joe was a streetcar conductor in San Francisco. He survived the San Francisco earthquake of 1906, and then came home. Joe and Sallie lived on the Moore family farm and later Joe owned a store at Huron, MO.

They lived in Hickory County near Urbana for eight years and then they moved to a farm three miles northeast of Bolivar. Their children went to Liberty school and went to church at Mt. Olive. Joe farmed and did carpenter work. Sallie raised chickens and turkeys and sold eggs. All of their children went to high school and college. Joe and Sallie sold their farm in 1953 and moved to town. Joe continued to do carpenter work and was a janitor at the Bolivar Christian Church. Joe died in 1972 and Sallie died in 1979. Both are buried at the Mt. Olive Cemetery. *Submitted by Bob Phillips*

MOORE - William Walter Moore was born June 8, 1865 to Thomas Bradford Moore and Phoebe Evaline (Cooper). He was the owner of W. W. Moore and Company, dealers in clothing, furnishings, shoes and hats. The business was located on the west side of the square in Bolivar, MO.

He was united in marriage in 1891 to Luella Agnes Nichols, who was a native of Bolivar. Three children were born from this union, namely, Charles Walter Moore, Helen Moore Underwood and Ruby DeFord Moore, who died at the age of 3.

Mr. Moore died in 1917 at the age of 52. He is buried along with his wife and daughter in Greenwood Cemetery, Bolivar, MO.

MOREAU – James Redd's great-grandfather, Joseph Moreau (May 26, 1820-Jan. 16, 1879), was quite an adventurer in his youth. He was born in France and immigrated to Quebec, Canada. He made three trips to California. One time he went by ship around Cape Horn. Once he went across the Isthmus of Panama, and another time he went overland by wagon train. He almost lost his life on the overland trip, when a man in their group killed an Indian woman along the trail.

Joseph married a Protestant woman from New York State, Mary A. Wright (May 30, 1824-March 15, 1896). Joseph was a Catholic. He wrote to his family about the marriage. He received a letter back, which said he was "dead and buried." He never heard from his family again.

He was living in Michigan when the Civil War broke out. He was recruited by the Union Army in Grand Rapids in 1862. He served with Company D of the Seventh Michigan Cavalry. He fought with Sheridan up and down the East Coast, mainly in Virginia. He survived the Battle of the Wilderness, but he was shot through the right breast at Trevilian Station. His military records note he was missing in action on June 11, 1864.

He had been left for dead on the battlefield, but a family found him and took him home. They pushed a heated ramrod through the hole in his breast to cauterize the wound. They hid him up on the roof of their back porch. When Joseph realized where he was, he told the family to turn him into the Confederate forces or their family might be killed.

The Confederates took him to Richmond and then to prison camp at Andersonville. He survived and was paroled on Nov. 26, 1864. He was taken to a hospital in Annapolis, MD.

He returned to his family in Michigan, but he was in poor health. His wife, Mary, told him how a neighbor had treated her during the war. The neighbor would come and get her horses each morning and work them hard each day. He would return them in the evening for her to feed. Joseph was physically wore out and tired of fighting. He told her that "the state of Michigan was not big enough for both of them." He moved his family to Missouri. They bought a farm on what is now "FF" near "blue mound" at Halfway.

The old wound continued to plague Joseph. He would have "spells" where he would get out of his head. He told his family to hide in the woods or lock themselves in the house. He would often pelt the house with rocks. When the "spell" was over, he would be fine again. But the wound abscessed and finally killed him.

Mary was a friend with Rev. James Schofield, who was also from New York. She was a charter member of the Schofield Church near Halfway. Joseph and Mary are buried at Schofield Cemetery.

James' grandmother was Susan Moreau Peterson (1859-1937). His mother was Minnie Peterson Redd (1882-1971). *Submitted by James D. Redd*

MORGAN - Sarah Elizabeth (Morgan) Safritt was born Jan. 18, 1861 in Hopkins, TX. Sarah's parents were Charles Morgan and Susan McBee. Sarah Morgan married White Safritt and lived in Polk County, MO. White Safritt had two children by a previous marriage, whose names were Lela and Nola Safritt. Sarah is buried in the Fouts-Ankrom Cemetery Halfway, Polk County, MO. White Surfeit is buried in the Pleasant Hope Cemetery, Pleasant Hope, MO, next to his daughter Nola Scroggins.

William Jasper Morgan was an older brother of Sarah Morgan. He was born Feb. 23, 1851 in Hopkins, TX. He married Hannah Ankrom and lived in Polk County, MO. They had 13 children and raised them in Polk County, MO.

They had the following children.

Walter R. Morgan was born on Sept. 8, 1876 in Polk County, MO.

William Richard Morgan was born in Polk County, MO, and married Pearl (Potter) on Jan. 26, 1898 in Polk County, MO. Pearl Potter was born in Missouri. They had two children, Vera L. Morgan, who was born in Polk County, MO and William E. Morgan, who also was born in Polk County, MO.

Jessie Van Morgan was born Feb. 24, 1878 in Mooney Township, Polk County, MO, and was buried in Pleasant Hope Cemetery, Pleasant Hope, MO. He married Etta Self on Nov. 8, 1899 in Polk County, MO. Etta Self was born May 30, 1879 in Polk County, MO. They had two children.

Orlando E. Morgan was born Sept. 29, 1879 in Polk County, MO. He died Aug. 8, 1908 in Polk County, MO. He is buried in the Fouts-Ankrom Cemetery, Halfway, Polk County, MO. He married Lula Yates on Sept. 17, 1879 in Polk County, MO. Lula Yates was born in Polk County, MO.

Elmer W. Morgan was born on Aug. 23, 1881 in Polk County, MO.

Harvey Lon Morgan was born on July 29, 1883 in Mooney Township, Polk County, MO.

Milford M. Morgan was born in 1885, Polk County, MO.

Mary B. Morgan was born Dec. 25, 1887 in Mooney Township, Polk County, MO. She died July 23, 1913.

Lewis Morgan was born on Jan .8, 1890 in Polk County, MO. He died Feb. 18, 1966 in Springfield, Greene County, MO. He was buried in Greenwood Cemetery, Bolivar, Polk County, MO.

Cora E. Morgan was born on Jan. 23, 1892 in Polk County, MO. She is buried in the Schofield Cemetery in Polk County, MO. She married A. W. Arnold.

Olean J. Morgan was born on Sept. 3, 1895 in Polk County, MO. He died in 1957 and is buried in the Pleasant Hope Cemetery, Pleasant Hope, MO.

Marion Morgan was born in Polk County, MO.

Ruby W. Morgan was born in 1898 in Missouri. He married Stella Arnold. They had four children.

Sarah and Jasper had four other siblings. Their names were Lucy Ann (Morgan) Wilson, Loretta (Morgan) Maddy Morrison, Francis Marion Morgan and Charles Morgan and all of them were born in Hopkins, TX. *Submitted by Joan Boswell*

Tommy Morris and Theo Condren at grandparents grave marker, Mt. View Cemetery, Polk, MO July 1998

MORRIS - In Ventura County in the '50s and '60s, it seemed that most obituaries for Santa Paula residents stated, "born in Polk County, MO." Perhaps that is why the city was dubbed "Little Bolivar." One tall tale goes like this: "You can see more Polk County people on the streets here on a Saturday night than back in Bolivar." When did the migration start? An article in the *Ventura Daily Democrat* (May 2, 1905) mentions the Missouri

Society of Ventura County having 101 members from Polk County. In 1962, a Polk County newspaper carried a regular Ventura County feature.

Tommy Morris's grandparents, Jess and Addie Morris, moved back and forth many times, but not nearly as much as did his Aunt Sylvia and Uncle Punch Condren. No one could keep track of which county they lived in from year to year. Other family tree surnames with Polk County/ Ventura County connections include Abel, Brooks, Griffin, Holt, McKinney and McConnell.

By the 1930s, Tommy's father, Bernard Lee Morris (1916-1945) had come to Ventura County with a close high school friend, Ralph Fisher. Twenty years later, Tommy had a similar connection, as he had a high school friend, Gary Moss that was born in Bolivar.

Tommy has continued to discover Polk County connections in Ventura. His optometrist, Dr. Richard Hatcher, has ties to Humansville and two of Dr. Hatcher's employees, Tommy's cousin Violet (Condren) Sweet and Nancy Wyand (Huckaby, Ingles, Shaw, Pitts), also have Polk County roots.

In 1998 while visiting Cousin Theo Condren in Bolivar, Tommy was given a tour of Polk County and its cemeteries. Pausing at a grave marker with the name Eidson on it, Theo said, "You should know Wilber Eidson, he lives in Ventura." Tommy's reply was that he has known a Ed and Bev Eidson for the past 25 years. "That's Wilber!" said Theo. Uncle Punch's sister Tressie L. Condren was Ed's mother. The whole Eidson family moved from Louisburg to Ventura in 1925. An interesting fact is that Ed and Tommy had attended the same church for all those years without realizing this relationship. Also in Ventura at church, another long time friend, Elaine (Terry) Sallee living in Santa Paula, said that she was born in Halfway and had ties to the Rowetons. Was this a similar connection? Viola E. Morris married Roma E. Roweton on Feb. 18, 1930.

Also in 1998, another connection was discovered. Barbara (Morris) Burnell, the granddaughter of Tommy's grandfather's brother, Lee Morris, wrote from Kansas City introducing herself as his second cousin. From this, a small Morris cousins genealogy group was formed. They now needed contact with someone down the line of the third brother, Claude Morris. Claude and Bellzona's (Abel) grave marker was discovered in the Bardsdale Cemetery in Fillmore, Ventura County. Then in March of 2000, the obituary of Claude's son, Gerald Morris, born in Bolivar, appeared in the Ventura newspaper. Gerald's son, Gary, was listed as being from Ventura. This new second cousin lived only three blocks from Tommy's home. Needless to say, they were both amazed and have started a wonderful relationship, which is an ongoing benefit of that Polk County/Ventura County connection. *Submitted by Tommy Morris*

MORRISON - Kenneth Morrison's parents, Paul and May (Peterson) Morrison, had each lived in lots of places before coming to the Humansville area of Polk County in 1926. Paul was born in Daviess County, MO but had moved with his parents, Elmer and Anna (Shipley) Morrison, several times from northwest Missouri to southwest Missouri, to northwest Kansas, to south central Kansas to Texas County, MO, then back to Daviess County, MO. May Peterson was born in North Carolina, moved from there to Tennessee, then Michigan, from Michigan to Kansas, then to Oklahoma, from there to Wright County, MO, where she met Paul and they married in 1920. They lived in Wright County for two years before going back to Daviess County for a couple of years, then living in Bates County a year before moving to Humansville. There must have been something about Polk County that held them here, they made this their home the rest of their days. Paul passed away in January 1980 and May in December 1992. They are buried at Humansville Cemetery. Humansville has been Kenneth's address since birth in February 1930.

Kenneth and Martha (Andrews) Morrison were married in September 1949 and have lived in the Rosebud neighborhood, southwest of Humansville, more than 50 years. Martha's parents were Ray and Pearl Andrews of Flemington, MO. Martha was born August 1931, just over the line in Hickory County, north of Flemington, moving to town at about 8 months of age, then moving back out to the country north of Flemington when about 4 years of age, growing up on the Almon place. Her parents were living on the county line road just north of Flemington at the time of their deaths. They are buried in the Rondo Cemetery.

Left to right: Debbie, Donna, Martha, Kenneth, Kenny, Paul and Dennis Morrison

Kenneth and Martha moved to the farm southwest of Humansville in 1952 and began to milk cows, make hay and raise horses. Horses have always played a big part in the livelihood of the Morrisons, for several generations' back. There always seemed to be at least one in each family that inherited a great love for horses.

Kenneth and Martha have four children, two sons and two daughters, and they all are horse lovers, but it's not hard to see it comes from both sides of the family. Donna, the oldest, and husband Jim Huffman are raising, training and showing Tennessee Walking Horses. Debbie, the third child, is also raising, training and showing Walking Horses. The boys, Kenny, the second child, lives in Shanghai, China; Dennis, the youngest, lives in Clovis, CA. Both loved and showed horses but are unable to keep horses due to their jobs.

Martha and Kenneth lived through some lean years in the early '50s when they were first married and raising their family, but would not chose anywhere else to have lived. They think Polk County has been a great place to live. All of their children were born at the Dimmitt Memorial Hospital here in Humansville, which was a wonderful and well-run health facility with Dr. G. G. Robinson as the family's doctor. *Submitted by Martha and Kenneth Morrison*

MOSIER – June Mosier was born at the home/ farm of Sam and Lora Davis (grandparents on her mother's side) southwest of Aldrich in August 1938. June's parents were Alta Faye Davis and Frank Allen Mosier, son of Cecil King Mosier and Pauline Toalson. Her mother had two sisters, Lois and Francis and a brother, Leonard. Frank Mosier had one brother, George and two sisters, Betty Ellen and Nelda Net. June's grandfather, Cecil, built a home southeast of Aldrich on 40 acres. His mother, Sarah Mosier, owned the adjacent farm. Cecil was a carpenter by trade and worked away from Aldrich frequently. June lived with her grandmother Nelda in Aldrich while he was away and went to the Aldrich High School, which had

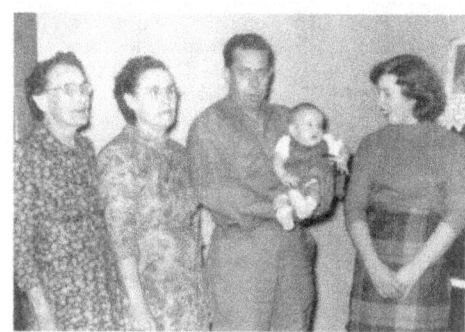

Ella Toalson, Pauline Toalson Mosier, Frank Mosier, Rick Barnhouse, June Mosier Barnhouse Riley

all 12 grades in the same building. That building was destroyed when the Stockton Lake was built. When that school closed June's family moved to Kansas City where she finished high school. Two of her school years were spent at the Orleans one-room schoolhouse; that was so much fun. June could see the school from her bedroom window at the farm where she lived with her grandparents. June rode with her teacher to school each day and then her teacher would bring her home. June's great-grandparents, Schell and Ella Toalson, lived in Aldrich and she spent a few weeks each summer at their home while she was living in Kansas City. She was the one that ran to Rice's Grocery Store on the main street. Grandma Toalson sold milk and eggs to people in Aldrich. There was a well on one side of the house that Grandma kept buckets that were secured by a rope where things were kept cool, long before refrigerators. On the other side of the house there was a cistern where we got water for washing. June's aunt, Ruth Toalson, was a teacher in Jefferson City. She would come home for holidays and would take them Coffman Branch to play in the water and take them to the woods to gather ferns for Memorial Day. June had several cousins that would come to visit, which was so nice since June was an only child. Schell and Ella Toalson were members of the Aldrich Christian Church as well as Pauline Mosier, Alta Davis Mosier and June herself. Dagny Hall, June's daughter, is still a member as is her son Jonathan Hall, making six generations that have belonged to the church. When June was young Aldrich was quite a town. It had an MFA grocery and feed store, a mercantile, owned by the Toalson Brothers, a locker plant, two garages, a barber shop, a tavern, a filling station, café and a switchboard office for the telephone. The operator was June's aunt, Nola Davis. After finishing high school, June married Charles Barnhouse of Bolivar and they had three children while living in Bolivar, Rick and Jeff Barnhouse and Dagny Hall. Rick and Dagny still live in Polk County. Jeff lives in Dade County. *Submitted by June Mosier Barnhouse Riley*

MOSS - Shirley Louise Cooper was born on May 3, 1946 in the early morning. Her parents are Henry R. and Cuba (Gothard) Cooper. They lived on the Barker place, southwest of Fair Play, on the Polk/Cedar County line. Their home had three rooms, with a porch across the front. There was a sister, A. Marie, age 12 and a brother, C. Kenneth, age 8, to welcome her into the world. Their neighbors were the Davises, Browns, Creeches, Wrights and the Owens. On Saturdays, they always went to Fair Play and would do their shopping and visiting with friends. It was really a social event.

In 1952, her parents bought their first farm in Cedar County, behind the Bear Creek School. She started school and would live here for the next four years. In 1956, the family moved to Independence, MO to find jobs. In 1960, her father had a heart attack and died. Life had changed, forever. Her mother supported them by being a cook and put Shirley through high school.

On June 6, 1970, Shirley married Jerry W. Moss in Independence, MO. Jerry had returned from his duty in the army and was employed by Coca-Cola and is still employed there. Shirley worked for a truck line when she married. Then, when their three children were born she became a stay-at-home mom. They purchased their home near her mother to help take care of her. Shirley worked seasonal jobs with the IRS for several years and in 1987, she started driving a school bus for Independence, MO Schools and is still employed there.

Left to right: Tracy, Jerrold and Tammy Moss with parents Jerry and Shirley Cooper Moss

In September of 1980, her brother, Kenny, was killed in a traffic accident. Then on Dec. 7, 1993, her best friend, her mother, departed this life, at the age of 85 years.

In 1958, she became a member of Oak Grove Baptist Church near Masters in Cedar County, where her family were members. This was a very important part of their lives. In 1963, Shirley and her mother became charter members of Charity Missionary Baptist Church in Independence, MO. In 1993, her family and other family members became charter members of Reach Out Missionary Baptist Church in Blue Springs, MO where they are presently members.

In 1973, Jerry and Shirley bought a lot at Price Creek Cove on Stockton Lake. This has become their second home.

She enjoys working in family history and the history of Polk and Cedar Counties. Her family lines are Gothard, Simmons, Davis, Phipps, Hughes, Perkinson and Harmon. Her greatest loves are her God and her family.

Their children: Tamara Renee Moss-Martin, born Oct. 15, 1972 and lives in Independence, MO. Married Michael Q. Martin on Aug. 10, 2001. Tammy is employed as a nurse.

Jerrald Wayne Moss, born Jan. 7, 1975, lives in Independence, MO. Jerrald is employed as a truck driver.

Tracy Michelle Moss, born July 28, 1978, lives in Independence, MO. Tracy is attending college. *Submitted by Tamara Martin*

MOTT - The family of Paul Alan and Carolyn Mustain Mott is, as follows: Paul Alan Mott was born April 11, 1928 near Manes, MO. His parents were Frederick Haydon and Dorothy Cantrell Mott. On June 9, 1950, he married Martha Carolyn Mustain, who was born July 27, 1930 in Bolivar, MO.

To this union were born four children.

Paula Ruth, born Nov. 14, 1951, married Mark Hemingway, March 22, 1975. Their children are Marla Beth, Jessica Lyn, David Mark, Daniel James, John Alan and Laura Marie.

Teresa Elaine, born Feb. 18, 1953, married Raymond Charles Kendall, May 24, 1975. Their children are Paul Mitchell, Jay Irvin and Carody Rae. Mitch is married to Kiley Duda and they have three sons, John Patrick, Benjamin Maxwell and Kyle Christopher.

Dana Rosiland, born Jan. 22, 1955, married Billy Don Warren, Feb. 11, 1984. Their children are William Andres, Christopher Michael and Timothy David.

Anita Carolyn, born Oct. 8, 1957, married Robert Kent Robidou, Aug. 4, 1979. Their children are Robert Bruce, Fredrick Austin and Jeffery Alan.

Paul and Carolyn spent seven and a half years living in Shawnee, OK, where all of their children were born and 37 years in Salina, KS, where Paul was a partner in the accounting firm of Kennedy & Coe, CPAs LLC. They returned to their native state in 1994. *Submitted by Paula Mott Hemingway*

MURRAY - Mary was born in Polk County, MO, Nov. 27, 1850. Her parents were Daniel Davis Murry and Manerva Jane Prater. Daniel's parents were Caleb Murry and Amelia Davis. Caleb operated a mill on the Pomme de Terre River for several years before moving to Iowa. Mary's mother died April 23, 1865 and her father Daniel died Feb. 1, 1866, leaving several young children, including Mary, to seek homes with other relatives. Mary moved to Linn County, KS and lived with William H. Murray until her marriage to James A. Fletcher on March 19, 1871.

To this union six children were born: Grace Elizabeth, Walter William, Etta A., Rosa (died in infancy), Ira Iola and Mary Mae, who also died at an early age.

James and Mary Fletcher lived on a farm northeast of Mound City, KS until about 1889 when they moved to Kiowa, KS and then on to Beaver, Oklahoma Territory. At Beaver, James operated a stage and freight line between the railhead at Meade, KS and Beaver, OT until his death.

James Fletcher died of consumption on Jan. 26, 1892 at Beaver, OT. Grace Elizabeth (Charles Dingus' grandmother) was married to Frank S. Davis at the home of her mother on Jan. 22, 1893. Charles's grandparents met while they were both teaching at an Indian school near Beaver. His grandmother used to speak of some of the hardships of living in a sod house on the prairie, especially in the winter when they would go out and pick up buffalo chips and bring them in to burn in their heating stove to keep warm.

After a short time Mary Fletcher moved back to Linn County, KS to be near some of her brothers and sisters. One of her sisters, Martha Joan Murray Copple, lived next door to Charles's family when he was a youngster in Mound City, KS. His mother referred to her as "Aunt Jo" and Charles never knew why until years later when he started researching the Murray clan. After four years of widowhood Mary again married, this time to John H. Davis. On May 30, 1917 Mary died of stomach cancer. She was buried in the Mount Carmel Cemetery in Linn County, KS.

When Charles and his wife moved to southern Missouri in 1977, they looked at houses all around the Springfield area and finally settled on the house and five acres where they now live.

The irony of it all is that they live less than two miles from where the original Murry family

Grace E., Mary M., Ira I., James A. and Etta A., circa 1890

settled when they came to Polk County and about the same distance from the Prock/Murry Cemetery where some of Charlotte's ancestors are buried. *Submitted by Charles W. Dingus*

MURRAY - William Floyd Murray and Georgia Lee Hawkins met in Bolivar, MO at an early age. He was just out of high school and she was a freshman in high school. They dated seven months, then ran off to Arkansas and got married. This was Dec. 20, 1950. To this union three children were born: Janice Lee on Oct. 31, 1951, Jaquetta Lynn on Dec. 2, 1962 and Jeffrey Mark on April 14, 1964. All three children graduated from Bolivar High School.

Janice is married to Jerry Wells. She had two daughters by her first marriage, Janette Lee and Janell Lynn.

Jaquetta is married to Danny Tidwell and has one son, Jared.

Jeff is married to Margaret Cunningham and has three children, Megan, Josh and Meleah.

Janice's daughter Janette is married to Jeff Jump. Janell is married to Scott Nelson and has two children, Jordan and Jenna.

Floyd's father was Tom Murray. His mother was Zelma (Hensley) Murray. Floyd was born near Wishart, MO on Feb. 21, 1933. Georgia's father was Mark Aaron Hawkins. Her mother was Laura Lee (Dotson) Hawkins. Georgia was born near Aldrich, MO on Sept. 18, 1935. *Submitted by Georgia Murray*

Back row: William Thomas Canole, Elmer Keithly, John Moore, Earl Canole, Molly Bobbitt Canole, Orville Canole, Glessie Canole Moore, Maude Canole Keithly, Ethel McGovney Canole and Alvin Canole; front row: Eugene Keithly, Leon Keithly, Mary Louisa Canole holding Dorothy Canole and Aurice Canole with puppy

MURRAY - Charles Wesley Murray was the son of Caleb Murray and Emillie "Amelia" Davis. Charles was born Dec. 22, 1834 in Lafayette, Tippacanoe County, IN and was the 10th child in the family of 13, seven boys and six girls. He came with his family into the Pleasant Hope Community of Polk County about 1830. The men and boys were engaged in farming. In later years Charles met Joanner Mallard, who was born Oct. 3, 1835, the daughter of George Wright Mallard and Anna Foster.

Charles and Joanner were married in 1856 and continued to live in the Pleasant Hope Community. They had seven children, four who lived to adulthood: Liza, who was married to John Thomas Loftin; Millie, who married John J. Sheridan; Mary Louisia, who married William Thomas Canole; and Anna, who married Robert Burns.

Charles served in the Civil War and, after being injured, returned to his family near Pleasant Hope. He died soon after, on Jan. 3, 1866 and was buried in the Prock-Murray Cemetery where their young children were buried. On Sept. 3, 1868, Joanner married Henry B. Viles, a widower, also with young children. To this union was born one son, Richard Benjamin Viles. Joanner died Oct. 13, 1910 and is buried in the Mallard Cemetery in Dallas County, MO. She was the mother of eight, grandmother of 23 and great-grandmother of 16 children. Three children survived her, Liza Loftin, Mary Canole and Benjamin Viles. Mary Louisa Murray, born April 13, 1861, married William Canole on Nov. 24, 1884. They homesteaded in Polk County and were very much a part of early Polk County history. Ten children were born to this union: Effie, Amy, Grover, Orville, Maud, Glessie, Ona, Alvin, Earl and Opal. William Thomas Canole and Mary Louisa Murray were Imogene's grandparents. *Submitted by Imogene Louise Keithly Hook*

Gayles and Catherine Mustain's 50th anniversary

MUSTAIN - Gayles Mustain was born to Hobart and Rosa Phillips Mustain on a very cold Nov. 7, 1917 near Fair Play, MO. Hobart was a Missionary Baptist preacher and pastored churches for over 60 years.

Gayles married Catherine Brown from Jerico Springs in Cedar County, Oct. 9, 1940.

They lived in the Shady Grove Community. They have three children: Louis, born in August 1941, Elizabeth, born in 1943 and Geraldine, born in 1947.

After the war broke out Gayles was drafted into service and left Nov. 11, 1942. He served his country for three years. He came home with five Battle Stars, a Purple Heart, three Clusters, two Bronze Stars for heroic action beyond the call of duty, and with a rank of staff sergeant.

Outside of four years in Rockford, IL, they have lived in and near Fair Play. They have seen a lot of changes in Fair Play in 62 years. It was a busy town with several stores of all kinds and the town was kept up and clean. They knew everybody and they are still proud of their school and the new buildings that the town has. They go to a little country church, Bismont Baptist, that is way over 100 years old. They now have eight grandchildren and 14 great-grandchildren.

Louis married a Florida girl and still lives there. He is Senior Process Development Engineer for Florida Steel Corporation.

Elizabeth married Fred Maples from Versailles, MO. He worked for Hallmark Cards for 38 years and they live in Independence, MO.

Geraldine married Richard Fink from Fair Play and still has businesses in Bolivar, MO.

Gayles and Catherine say, "We have seen a lot of-country, but are still proud to call Polk County, MO our home." *Submitted by Mrs. Gayles Mustain*

MUSTAIN - The Mustain family is of French descent, driven from France by religious persecution. They first settled in Pittsylvania County, VA. They migrated to western Kentucky and later to Dallas and Hickory Counties, MO.

Lewis Edward Mustain was born April 17, 1871 (died Jan. 22, 1953) in Dallas County, MO. On Nov. 9, 1890, he married Tennessee Jones, born Dec. 5, 1873 (died Nov. 15, 1953). His father was Thomas Edward Mustain Jr. and his mother was Nancy Melissa Jackson. Tennessee's father was Daniel Richard Jones and her mother was Sarah Caroline Mitchell.

Lewis and "Tenny" spent most of their married lives in Polk County, near Fair Play. Their children were Richard Harrison, born Sept. 8, 1891, died May 4, 1977; Melissa Anna, born Nov. 14, 1894, died Nov. 3, 1978; Hobart McKinley, born Dec. 2, 1896, died Dec. 16, 1986; Thomas Lester, born May 3, 1902, died Oct. 13, 1966; Lewis Elmer, born Jan. 18, 1906, died Sept. 2, 1982; Claud Jones, born Nov. 16, 1909, died May 1, 2003; Shirley Immogene, born Sept. 17, 1919, died 1999.

Claud Jones Mustain married Ruth Elizabeth Keeling June 5, 1926. Ruth's parents were Austin Oliver Keeling (born Oct. 16, 1872, died Feb. 25, 1942) and Caroline "Carrie" Elizabeth Sims Keeling (born Jan. 20, 1873, died March 15, 1944).

Claud and Ruth had three children: Kenneth Keeling, born June 17, 1921, died Dec. 9, 1968; Martha Carolyn, born July 27, 1930; Richard Arnold, born Feb. 3, 1932, died April 13, 1932. *Submitted by Carolyn Mustain Mott for Claud J. Mustain*

NEBEL – Richard Forrist "Rick" Nebel moved to Bolivar, Polk County, MO in the fall of 1981 when he was asked to come to Southwest Baptist University to develop a computer system for the university that could keep up with the growth of the school. He moved to Polk County from Jefferson City, Cole County, MO where he had done the same type of work in the Missouri Baptist Building.

Rick was born in Jefferson City, MO on Feb. 26, 1953 to E. Harmon and Dixie Cutler Nebel. He had two older brothers, Larry and Rod Nebel. Rick's paternal side of the family had lived in the High Hill, MO area. The Nebel family originally immigrated to the United States from Bavaria, Germany in the late 1800s. Rick enjoyed traveling back to Germany where the family roots were located. One of his ancestors was the originator of the popular "Werther Original Chewy Caramel Candies" made by the Gustav Nebel family in Werther, Germany.

Rick's ancestor on his maternal side, William Collings, was in the Revolutionary War and is proven by DAR #265867 as was registered by a grandmother, Eulah Mae Riley Cutler. Rick's mother served in the DAR organization for many years.

While growing up in Jefferson City, MO, Rick (a very tall man at six feet, eight inches) played varsity basketball and went on to Louisiana Tech on a basketball scholarship. He decided to pursue a business/marketing degree and returned to Southwest Missouri State in Springfield, MO. Basketball continued to be an enjoyment for him for the rest of his life and he played on various local teams.

Front row – Rachel Cisco, Ricky Nebel and Lydia Nebel; Back row – Jonathan Cisco, Krista (Roberts) Nebel and Richard Forrist Nebel

Rick had furthered his education and received his MBA from Drury University, Springfield, MO in the summer of 1989. He also held several certifications for various computer-related systems and boards. He was the Chief Information Officer of Southwest Baptist University. He was a cabinet member at the university he loved. He also served as the treasurer for the Community Concert Association in Bolivar, MO.

He married Krista Helen Roberts Cisco on Dec. 6. 1986, whom he met at Southwest Baptist University, Bolivar, MO. Krista (born May 14, 1955) is the daughter of Paul H. and Helen Jenkins Roberts, lifetime residents of Polk County, MO.

Rick and Krista are the parents of Lydia Rachel Nebel (born March 22, 1989) and Richard Forrist Nebel II (born March 8, 1991). Rick was also a wonderful step-father to Rachel Krista Cisco (born July 16, 1981) and Jonathan R. Cisco (born Sept. 5, 1983).

Rick's life was taken much too soon by a motorcycle accident while he was riding in the countryside to admire the last of the fall leaf colors. He loved the outdoors. Rick was known as a gentle giant and a man of few words. He had many hobbies and interest and was quietly devoted to his God, his family and his many friends. He was of the Baptist faith. Rick passed away on Nov. 9, 2002. He is buried in the Greenwood Cemetery, Bolivar, MO. *Submitted by Krista H. Nebel*

NEIL – Loyal Edward "Bub" Neil was born April 28, 1918 and has lived in Polk County, MO all of his life. He married Eva Lorene Rotramel on Jan. 28, 1946 and they later had four children together. Loyal had one brother and three sisters. They were Loman, married

Bub Neil

Dorothy Summers and they had four children; Louise Belle, married Paul Taylor and they had two daughters; Leona, married Cleo Asberry Smay and they had one son; and Lovan, married Chester Shough and they had one daughter and later Lovan married James Riggans. They were all born on a farm on Walnut Creek just north of Wishart, MO and most have lived their entire lives in Polk County. Their parents were Ray Thomas Neil and Amanda Rebecca (Stevens) Neil. Ray T. was born in Polk County on March 19, 1888 and was one of nine children. Amanda was born in Illinois on March 31, 1890, one of four children, two whom died very early in life. Amanda moved to Polk County, MO when she was very young. She always told that she came to Missouri in a covered wagon pulled by oxen, not long after she began to walk. They would tie a rope to the little children from the back of the wagon so they

Ray and Amanda Neil

could get some exercise. The rope was so they wouldn't wander off the trail and get lost in the wilderness.

Amanda's parents were William J. and Ina Bell (Hurst) Stevens. William J. Stevens was born in Illinois on May 2, 1863 and moved to Polk County and in the spring of 1938 he had gone to Bolivar and got into a fight and later had to have his hand removed, because of infection. They cut it off at the house and later had to cut off more because it wouldn't heal. He died on Aug. 20, 1938 in Polk County, MO. Ina Bell had their son Charlie bury William's hand in the garden and when William died, they dug it up and buried it with him. Ina Bell was born in Ohio on Jan. 9, 1870 and died July 29, 1956 in Polk County, MO. Ina Bell's father, Phinias Hurst, was in the Civil War and served in the 153rd Ohio Infantry, Company B and is buried at Campbell Grove Cemetery in Polk County, MO. Phinias was born April 22, 1837 in Ohio and died in Polk County on June 30, 1894. Her mother was Elizabeth Jane (Roye) and after Phinias passed away, she went back to Illinois where she died on May 10, 1922. William's parents were Samuel Bateman and Amanda Stevens. Samuel was born March 31, 1843 and died Feb. 23, 1905 in Polk County, MO and Amanda was born Nov. 13, 1843 and died July 29, 1921, also in Polk County, MO.

Ray T. Neil's parents were William Robert and Rebecca Evelyn (Coats) Neil. They were born and died in Polk County, MO. William was born July 19, 1851 and died January 3, 1931 and Rebecca was born Nov. 4, 1857 and died Oct. 1, 1939.

Ray lived his whole life in Polk County and was blind most of his life, but managed to cut out a good living for his wife and children. Amanda worked in the house and on the farm. She would drive a tractor and work just as hard as any man. Ray kept track of the money and always knew exactly what they had, from the money to the cattle and exactly how many bales of hay they had in the barn and could give someone back change, because he kept his money in order and always knew what he had. He did help milk when they had milk cows but later they went to beef cattle.

Loyal and Lorene still live in the house they bought just after they married, some 50 years ago. Loyal had farmed and raised beef cattle and sheep on his Polk County farm all of his life. They bought 70 acres of timber patch across the road from the house where they lived and started clearing it with a crosscut saw and later finished it with a chainsaw, leaving only walnut trees. This made a beautiful, walnut timber for him to sit on the porch and look at and it made some extra income for the family, just in time to buy Christmas presents. Every October day that it was weather fit, they picked up walnuts and took them to Aldrich or Eudora to sell. He has always enjoyed his walnut trees. Now sometimes the grandchildren pick the walnuts, and he still helps. He also enjoys all his chickens, ducks, turkeys, and guineas. *Submitted by Leanna Wilson*

NEIL – At the foot of a long, steep hill in the small town of Aldrich, MO there stands an old barn-like building; it is now surrounded by woods and the foliage of the nearby wildlife sanctuary, but in an earlier time it stood next to the "Neil Produce." The Produce, along with other types of nearby businesses, bustled with activity. Farmers brought poultry, eggs, cream, wool and hides to sell at the Produce, where, in turn, they could buy baby chicks, feed for livestock, ice in hot weather, gasoline and tires. The farm products they brought were sold to merchants in Springfield and Kansas City. Seasonal items such as black walnuts and turkeys also passed through the Produce on their way to market. Those walnuts that arrived at the Produce unhulled were shoveled into a wooden trough placed under the rear wheel of a running Model T Ford. The nuts would fly in one direction – the hulls would scatter nearer the wheel. It was an effective operation, but one had to stand clear of flying objects.

The owner and operator of the Produce was Roy Alva Neil. Roy's great-great-grandfather, Jesse Neil, had come to the area from Tennessee by the year 1838, and had, along with wife Rachel Savage, helped to establish the Turkey Creek Baptist Church, now located between Eudora and Walnut Grove on Highway 123.

Roy was the son of a stockman and was himself so knowledgeable it was said that he could look at an animal and tell you how much it weighed. He kept pasture land throughout his life, raising hogs and cattle. He was married in Bolivar in 1912 to Loutreacy Shuler, the daughter of George H. and Louisa Crone Shuler. At the start of their life together, Roy and Treacy lived in the house near Orleans, where she had been born. It was there that they were blessed with three of their five children—Nobel Mark, born in 1913; Anna Pauline, born in 1915; and Roy Layne, born in 1916. Two other sons were born after the family moved into Aldrich – George in 1920 and Sammy Lee in 1926. Each of the four boys served overseas in the military during WWII and all came safely home.

During the youngsters' growing years, the family lived in a large house less than a block from the Produce and just across from the Methodist Church. From the porch on the west side could be seen Ed Davis's shoe repair shop and the Lyman gravestone establishment. They were close by the 100 feet or so of hitching rack in the back of the "ell" shaped main downtown area. Over the post office and other buildings you could see across the Sac River valley to the Harmon Frieze hill.

Following WWII, business activity in Aldrich began to decline, but the actual demise came with the advent of the Stockton Dam and negotiations by the Corps of Engineers on the purchase of land for wildlife refuge and overflow areas. As they sold their land, some families moved closer to Highway 123; many left the area. Today only memories remain of downtown Aldrich.

Roy Alva and Loutreacy Neil are buried at the Pleasant Ridge Cemetery near Aldrich. Beside them lie two of their sons, Noble Mark and Roy Layne. A third son, Sammy Lee, is buried in a National Cemetery on Long Island, NY. Roy Alva Neil's parents, Prior Lee and Susan Cowan Neil, and his paternal grandparents, Samuel B. and Amanda Tygart Neil, are also buried at Pleasant Ridge, as is granddaughter, Sylvia Elayne Neil, who, in 2001, joined her ancestors in eternal rest. *Submitted by George Neil*

NEILL – James Robert Neill was born Oct. 8, 1826, in Logan County, KY, the son of John Clinton and Sarah Wilson Neill. James was the oldest of four, including John Clinton, Albert and Sylvanus. The family moved to Washington County, AR in the early 1840s, where Sarah died about 1845. John remarried Dec. 25, 1847 to Malinda Johnson. This union produced sons Thornberry and Alexander.

Elizabeth M. Mayfield was born Sept. 13, 1827 in Hickman County, TN, the daughter of Baptist Minister, Rev. James Mayfield, and wife (unknown). Elizabeth was the oldest of the six children, including William, Mary Saphronia, Martha, Elijah and Harriett. The family moved to Washington County, AR in the late 1830s where James' wife died in April 1840. James remarried March 25, 1841 to Matilda Jones. They had eight children together: Mary, Susan, James, Ellender, Lucinda, Armanta, Abigail and Wilburn Green.

James Neill and Elizabeth Mayfield married in Washington County on Jan. 25, 1852, started their family and James took up farming. At the outbreak of the Civil War, they had five living children: William (died in infancy), Mary Jane, Nancy Elizabeth, Susan May, Sarah Ann and John Clinton.

The war was hard for them, as it was for everyone in the region. Bands of ruffians raided farms and towns along the borders. During the war, both James and Elizabeth's fathers were murdered by ruffians; John Neill on May 11, 1862 and James Mayfield in 1865. By the beginning of winter in 1863, James Neill decided they had to leave and move north to someplace safer. He left his family so he could look for a new home. He found a place in western Polk County, MO, near the town of Aldrich. He sent back word for the family to join him. In March 1864, Elizabeth, who was very pregnant, packed up the family in a wagon led by oxen and headed north. By March 23, they were in Miller, in northern Lawrence

County, but Elizabeth could go no further. The next day, she gave birth to her seventh child, Liza. Once Elizabeth and Liza recovered sufficiently, the family joined James in their new home.

In Polk County, James and Elizabeth had three more children: James Sherman, Albert and Allis, though Allis died in childhood, James died at 29 and Albert at 23; neither had married.

The remaining six children grew to adulthood, married and raised families in southwestern Polk County and northeastern Dade County. Mary Jane married John H. Stephenson on Nov. 28, 1875 and had children Wynona and Robert. Nancy Elizabeth married Martin Lafayette Holman on Dec. 21, 1882 and had children Raymond, Claude, Myrtle, Albert and Lola. Susan May married Asa Young Lyman on Jan. 6, 1878, and had children Elsa May, Lloyd, Gertrude, Don Sherman and Jay A. Sarah Ann married Sterling Wells Adamson on May 4, 1884 and had children Frederick, Hugh, Atha May, Merta Ann, Oren, Thomas Edward and Claud Terrell. John Clinton married Permelia Holman, Lafayette's first cousin, Sept. 28, 1884 and had children Mamie Elizabeth, Eltha, Elsie, Belle and Alta Alva. Liza married Robert Frazier McLemore on Nov. 12, 1889 and had children Lester, Floyd, Ralph, Alma, Ethel, Huber, Archie, Virgil and Mabel.

Elizabeth M. Mayfield Neill didn't live to see much of the growth of her family, dying July 21, 1884. James Robert Neill died May 20, 1911. They, as well as many of the Stephenson family, are buried in Rice Cemetery. However, into the 21st Century, descendants of the Holmans and Lymans still lived on parts of their ancestral homes in Polk County. *Submitted by Robert L. Wilson*

NICHOLS – 1849 was the year Phil's family came to Polk County; though he had absolutely no knowledge of that fact when he and his wife Barbara first came here in 1982. It was several years after they settled on their acreage west of Dunnegan when they actually stumbled on this lost piece of the Nichols' family history.

Barbara and Phil had always dreamed of building their own home in the country. They lived in North Kansas City during their first year of marriage and frequently visited Barb's folks' place on the Lake of the Ozarks near Laurie. That's where Phil learned to love the Ozarks' hills and hollers.

They were living in Bellevue, NE in 1981 when they finally made the decision to move to the Ozarks.

Two ancient travel trailers with a small addition served as home for five years as they and their small daughter learned to survive in a strange land; much as their pioneer ancestors had done. They did succeed in building their dream during those years of struggle and strife; one nail, one stone at a time.

Their 34 more or less acres are just across the line in Cedar County. "Though I can step out the back door, walk across the south pasture, climb over the fence and be standing in Polk County before you can finish reading this," says Phil.

It was Phil's great-great-grandfather William Lawrence Boon who actually anchored their history in Polk County.

Phil's father told him several times as a boy that they were related to Daniel Boone on his grandmother's side. Phil attended a reunion near Kahoka, MO in 1960 where he met his then 94-year-old Grandpa Joe. Joseph Franklin Boon, Phil's great-grandfather, died shortly after that reunion and Phil lost the thread of his ancestry for 33 years.

During a trip to Kahoka in 1993 they uncovered Grandpa Joe's obit and discovered that one of Phil's dad's uncles was still living in the area.

They sent a letter to his address which was answered nearly a year later by his daughter-one of the cousins Phil had met at the reunion in 1960. Trading information, Phil discovered that William Lawrence Boon (Grandpa Joe's father) was supposed to have purchased a homestead just east of what is now C&C Farm Supply in Bolivar in 1849. A check of the county records verified this astounding assertion.

William Lawrence and his family farmed in Polk County throughout the Civil War years, moving north to Kahoka in 1866-the year Grandpa Joe was born. A baby girl Amanda Harriet is buried somewhere in the area though they haven't been able to find her in any of the local cemeteries.

Phil says, "Was it happenstance which brought us here over 130 years after my ancestors first set foot in Polk County or something else? Who knows?" *Submitted by Phillip Nichols*

The living children of James R. and Elizabeth J. (Hardy) Nickels, circa 1900-1910. Front row, left to right: Jim, Tom, John and Will. Back row: George, Silas "Bert", Minnie, Eva, Dave and Alice.

NICKELS – James Robert Nickels, born June 2, 1823 in Clark County, IN, married Elizabeth Jane Hardy, born Oct. 31, 1830 in Scott County, IN, on Feb. 20, 1847 in Scott County, IN (daughter of Jonathan Herschel and Jane Minerva Boles Hardy). James and Elizabeth had 13 children, all born in Clark County. In 1879, the family moved to Polk County. James, a Civil War veteran, died Nov. 17, 1907 and was buried in Plum Grove Cemetery next to Elizabeth (died March 29, 1905).

Flora Ann, born Jan. 23, 1848, married George Paul on Oct. 5, 1880 in Humansville—three children: Myrtle Pearl, Bertha Jane, Charles Allen. Flora died April 22, 1901—buried at Plum Grove.

William Perry, born July 26, 1849, married Charity Adeline Carroll on Sept. 24, 1874 in Indiana—12 children: Effie Dean, Daisy Lean, Adah Alice, James Allen, Dallas Jackson "Jake," Corda Pearl, Ora Bell, Carl Ira, Laura Elizabeth Ann, Minerva Mae, Clara Adeline, William Donald. William died Jan. 28, 1940—buried in Dunnegan Cemetery.

John Terrell Nickels, born Sept. 7, 1850, married Theo Docia Belle Fox on Feb. 25, 1883 in Humansville—seven children: Jean Margaret, Frank Eugene, triplets Flora A. (lived two days), Nora May (died at age 5) and Cora Fay, Charles Columbus, Ruby Pearl. John died July 14, 1926 in Santa Cruz, CA.

Thomas Herschel Nickels, born March 7, 1852, married Eudora Jane Matthews on April 3, 1873 in Indiana—nine children: Clara Elma (died at 3 months), Albert Lionel, James Frederick, Harry Jackson, Elmer Clyde, Claude Leslie, Jessie May, Bessie Grace, Kenneth Earl. Thomas died Jan. 26, 1925 in Los Angeles, CA.

Margaret Jane Nickels, born Dec. 2, 1853, married William Franklin Martin on March 8, 1883 in Humansville—one son, James Leroy (died at age 4 months). Margaret died April 24, 1884 in childbirth—buried at Plum Grove (no stone can be found).

Sophia Alice Nickels, born July 28, 1856, married Allen Barnes on Dec. 10, 1875 in Indiana—five children: Frank Orlando, Maude Alene, Prudie Irene, Freddie (died at age 2 days), Clemmie Herschel (died at age 5 months). Alice died March 17, 1937—buried Dunnegan Cemetery.

James Andrew Armour Nickels, born Aug. 10, 1858, married Martha Jane Stark on Feb. 1, 1880 in Lane County, KS—seven children: Georgia (died at age 1 month), Sylvia (died at age 1), William Riley (died at age 1), Della Mae, Nellie Alice, Arthur Thomas, Clara Ethel. James died May 1, 1926—buried at Plum Grove.

David Campbell Nickels, born Jan. 14, 1861, married Mary Elizabeth Law on Oct. 18, 1881 in Indiana—four children: Lily Dell, Elizabeth Leota, Acsah Ann, Frances James. David died March 26, 1947—buried at Plum Grove.

Eva Elizabeth Nickels, born Nov. 8, 1862, married John Martin Ireland on Dec. 14, 1882 in Dunnegan—seven children: Charles Homer, Lula Mae, Marvin D., Goldie Elsie, Mary (died at age 6 weeks), William Chalmer, Jennie Pearl. Eva died Jan. 21, 1928 in Winfield, KS—buried at Highland Cemetery in Winfield.

Minnie Bell Nickels, born May 27, 1886, married Joseph Nottingham on Jan. 11, 1885 in Humansville—10 children: Oma Clyde, Melvin Arthur Earl, Cecil Ernest, two unnamed twin boys (died at birth), Elizabeth Katherine, Nettie Maude, Elsie Pearl, Eva Rena, Fredda Alice. Minnie died March 13, 1961 in Dayton, TX—buried in Rosewood Park Cemetery, Humble, TX.

Charles Robert Nickels, born March 14, 1868, died Dec. 3, 1870 from croup and was buried in Barnes Cemetery, Clark County, IN.

Silas Berton Nickels, born March 27, 1870, married Margaret Elizabeth Fox on March 8, 1891 in Humansville—two children: Marion Joseph, Stella Belle. Bert died April 8, 1949 in Aurora, NE—buried in Hampton, NE.

George Preston Nickels, born May 24, 1873, married Nora Lucetta Gilpin on Nov. 26, 1893 in Dunnegan—nine children: Lucy Pearl, Lawrence George, Otho Lonnie, Roy Lee, Ezra Guy, Virgil Dale, twins Freddie and Eddie (died at age 1 week), George Olin. George died Sept. 29, 1957 in Bradshaw, NE—buried at Plainfield Cemetery in Bradshaw. *Submitted by Julie Wollard Trout*

Jim, Nellie, Ethel and Mattie Nickels; Standing: Arthur and Della Nickels, circa 1898-1900

NICKELS – James Andrew Armour Nickels, born Aug. 10, 1858 in Clark County, IN, married Martha Jane Stark, born May 12, 1852 in Scott County, IN, on Feb. 1, 1880 in Lane County, KS. Mattie was the daughter of Thomas Calvin and Louisa Jane (Johnston) Stark. This family moved to Salina, KS in 1878. James, the son of James Robert and Elizabeth Jane (Hardy) Nickels, moved with his parents and siblings to Polk County in 1879. Jim and a friend, Charles Elmer Cummings, continued on from Missouri to Salina to work for Mr. Stark, Mattie's father.

After Jim and Mattie married, they settled in Salina. They soon moved to Polk County, settling in the area between Humansville and Dunnegan. They had seven children, the first two born in Kansas and the rest in Polk County. Mattie, who had been afflicted with diabetes all of her adult life, died from complications of diabetes on April 25, 1918 at their farm near Dunnegan. She was buried in Plum Grove Cemetery. Jim continued living on the farm with his daughter Ethel and her family. On May 1, 1926, Jim was riding in the back of the family truck and stood up to steady the crate of eggs as the truck rounded a corner. He fell out and hit his head; he died later that night of his injuries. He was buried at Plum Grove next to Mattie.

Georgia Nickels, born in November 1880, died less than one month later of a "summer complaint" near Salina, KS.

Sylvia Nickels, born in 1881, died in 1882 of a "summer complaint" near Salina, KS.

William Riley Nickels, born March 18, 1884 in Johnson Township, Polk County, died 1885 in Polk County and was buried at Plum Grove (no stone can be found).

Della Mae Nickels was born Dec. 26, 1885 and married Henry Weaver Wollard on July 19, 1903 in Dunnegan—a double wedding with her sister Nellie and Weaver's brother Columbus. Weaver and Della had four children: Eunice, Mary, Leland and Cecil. (See Wollard-Nickels story). Della died Feb. 23, 1966 in Bolivar.

Nellie Alice Nickels, born Oct. 25, 1887, married Columbus Elmer Wollard on July 19, 1903 in Dunnegan. They had five children: Aulton, Clara, Charles, Mattie and Cleo James. (See Wollard-Walker story). After Columbus's death, Nellie married Ira Ashlock, a widower, on Oct. 19, 1942 in Polk County. Nellie died Nov. 16, 1962 in Springfield.

Arthur Thomas Nickels, born Sept. 14, 1889, married Oval Wilson on Dec. 17, 1911 in Dunnegan. They had one son, Guy Carl (Sept. 2, 1923-Feb. 17, 2000, buried Rondo Cemetery). Guy married Bonnie Belle Potter and had two sons, Larry Ray and Gary Lee (died at birth, buried Rondo Cemetery). Arthur died Dec. 7, 1970 in Springfield, Greene County, MO and was buried in Rondo Cemetery.

Clara Ethel Nickels, born May 4, 1893, married Claude Marshall Manuel on Nov. 23, 1913 in Dunnegan. They had two children: Juanita, (born and died on Jan. 12, 1921, buried Barren Creek Cemetery in Polk County) and Dorothy Lou Dee (Nov. 23, 1923-Dec. 1, 1999, buried Barren Creek Cemetery). Dorothy married Lawrence Jewell Griffin and had two daughters, Sonya Kay and Sheila Ann. Ethel died Jan. 11, 1980 in Ozark, Christian County, MO and was buried in Barren Creek Cemetery, Polk County. *Submitted by Don Wollard*

NICKELS – William Perry Nickels was born on July 26, 1849 in Clark County, IN, near Lexington, Scott County. He was raised on the farm and attended the Carroll County School nearby. When he was still in his teens, he and his oldest sister, Flora and his brother, John, went to Centralia, IL. They worked there for their uncle, Jake Fisher and his wife, Sallie (Hardy) Fisher, a sister of their mother. After William had worked there for three years at $15.00 per month, he returned to his home near Lexington, IN to marry the girl he had left behind. He was married to Charity Adeline Carroll on Sept. 24, 1874 in Clark County, IN.

William and Adeline rented a farm near New Washington, IN and made this their home for five years. This is where their first three children were born. On Nov. 5, 1879, they moved to Illinois where they rented a farm near Atwood, IL. They lived here for the next six years where two boys and a girl were born. The rent was quite high on this farm so they migrated to Missouri on Feb. 4, 1886. They traveled by train and arrived at the home of his parents near Dunnegan, Polk County, MO on Feb. 6, 1886. William's parents and several of his brothers and sisters had already migrated to Missouri previously from Indiana.

The family lived on his father's farm for a year and then moved to a farm nearby for the next three years. William bought 80 acres of timber and, with the help of his wife and two little boys, built a two-room log house, which was later enlarged to six rooms. They moved into their new two-room home on March 4, 1888, the day of President Harrison's inauguration.

William cleared all of their land, split rails for his fences and cut the logs for his farm buildings. Six more children were born to them on this farm. In the fall of 1890, he became ill with typhoid fever and pneumonia and after his recovery, he was never able to work hard again. Later he carried the mail from the post office at Dunnegan to Mollie, Cedar County, MO, a 10 mile round trip. He made this trip twice a week on horseback and was paid about 30 cents per day. He also worked for 50 cents a day when he was able and made molasses every fall for which he received 10 cents a gallon.

He suffered a paralytic stroke in 1935 that confined him to his bed until his death in January of 1940. After he died, Adeline and their daughter, Adah, lived on the farm, which was located about two miles east of Dunnegan, MO. Adeline died July 29, 1943 in Dunnegan, Polk County, MO. Both are buried in the Dunnegan Cemetery.

William and Adeline had the following children: Effie Dean Nickels Carneal, Daisy Lean Nickels Noblett, Adah Alice Nickels, James Allen Nickels, Dallas Jackson "Jake" Nickels, Corda Pearl Nickels Flint, Ora Bell Nickels Barnes, Carl Ira Nickels, Laura Elizabeth Ann Nickels Worthan, Minerva Mae Nickels Campbell, Clara Adeline Nickels Rhoden and William Donald Nickels.

Gayla is a descendant of William and Adeline's son, James Allen Nickels. *Submitted by Gayla Nickels Wells*

NOFFZINGER – Hobart Webster Noffzinger (Noffy) was born July 24, 1897 in Tinney's Point, Ray County, MO, the youngest of seven children born to Jesse Martin and Iva Jane (Taylor) Noffzinger. He died May 24, 1986 in Bolivar, MO and is buried in the Greenwood Cemetery in Bolivar. His siblings were Ernest, Myrtle, Edmonia, Floy, Lula and Lella. He also had a half-sister born to his father from an earlier marriage. The Noffzingers were of German heritage. Hobart's grandfather David C. was born in Botetourt County, VA and came to Ray County in 1849, possibly by way of Illinois.

On March 6, 1921 Hobart married Geneva Hortene Goll, born June 17, 1901, daughter of William and Mary (Collins) Goll. Two children were born to this union, Mary Jane on Dec. 30, 1921 and Evelyn Frances on Nov. 27, 1923. Mary Jane assisted her mother in a home laundry and currently lives in Butterfield Residential Care Center. Frances is a graduate of Southwest Baptist College, the University of Missouri and the University of Denver. After teaching school for four years, she obtained her master's degree in library science and worked for 37 years at Southwest Regional Library, retiring as Administrative Librarian in 1986. On Sept. 28, 1951, she married Scott Merwin Roberts, oldest son of William Lovell and Irma Ann (Jones) Roberts. Scott was born May 5, 1924 and died of a heart attack on Sept. 16, 1974. He is buried at Greenwood Cemetery. Scott and Frances had two children, Karen Sue, born on Aug. 25, 1953 and Patricia Ann, born on April 16, 1955. On Aug. 24, 1980, Karen married Robert Louis Ebert, born Sept. 25, 1952, son of Lee Moses and Mary W. (Wallbrunn) Ebert. Three children were born to this union: Erin Lynn on Sept. 6, 1984 and Matthew Lee and Megan Lea on Nov. 1, 1986. On July 15, 1978, Patricia married John Michael Roussin, born Nov. 4, 1950, son of Clyde Anthony and Laura Bernice (Hawn) Roussin. Two children were born to this union, Michael Scott on July 2, 1980 and Darin Matthew on May 19, 1984.

Hobart moved to Bolivar, MO in 1929 and soon joined the Joe Brandt Plumbing Company. He eventually formed his own company and remained active in plumbing until his retirement in 1974. During the 1940s he served as Bolivar City Water Superintendent. Prior to his move to Bolivar, he was a farmer and his love of farming remained with him. He became an avid gardener, being noted for his large, beautiful gardens with their bountiful produce, especially tomatoes.

Hobart was noted for his ready smile, his

Row one sitting: Ada "Ade" Nickels, Effie "Eff" Nickels Carneal, Grandma Charity Adeline "Add" Nickels, Grandpa William Perry "Will" Nickels, James Allen "Jim" Nickels, and Dallas Jackson "Jake" Nickels. Back row standing: Donald Wayne "Duck" Nickels, Cordie Pearl Nickels Flint, Ora Bell "Ode" Nickels Barnes, Clara Adeline "Ked" Nickels Rhoden, Laura Elizabeth Ann "Sis" Worthan, Minerva Mae Nickels Campbell, Carl Ida "Pete" Nickels.

friendliness, his devotion to hard work and his ever-present desire to be of help to anyone who needed his services.

The farm home where Hobart grew up had a petrified tree that was widely acclaimed. According to a family legend, when the Noffzingers moved from Illinois to Missouri they were forced to leave their pet dog behind. Some weeks later the dog appeared at their home, presumably having swum the Mississippi River. *Submitted by Frances Roberts*

NORMAN – Thomas James Norman was born March 11, 1811 in Virginia. When he left Virginia his mother gave him a quilt which still exists. He married Lucretia Clay in Sumner County, TN on June 6, 1837. Lucretia was the daughter of Jonathan Clay, who was a cousin to Henry Clay, the orator. Her mother was Martha "Patsy" Taylor, whose father was a cousin of Zachary Taylor, President of the United Sates. Lucretia was born Sept. 7, 1817 in Davidson County, TN.

They moved to Polk County, MO between 1840 and 1843. They had two sons born in Sumner County, George H. Norman, born Aug. 18, 1838 and Jonathan, who died as an infant sometime around 1840. George fought in the Civil War in the Missouri State Guard Company D, Regiment Infantry Eighth. He engaged in the battles at Wilson's Creek, Lexington, Elk Horn, Farmington, Inka, Port Gibson and was killed May 14, 1863 in the Battle of Champion Hill. After they arrived in Polk County the following children were born: Sarah Frances, Martha Ann, William Thomas, Susan Virginia, Caroline Sennie and James Monroe (Norma Jean's grandfather).

Thomas James and his family resided in Humansville and during the Slicker War they were robbed of all of their possessions and their house was destroyed. He and his family resettled in Looney Township, where he lived until July 9, 1863. On that day some men, supposedly wishing to purchase some horses, shot him in the back while he was getting a drink from his well. The story is that the quilt his mother gave him was used to lay him out and the spots of blood were from his wound.

He was buried in the old Brock Cemetery which was not maintained and there was nothing left of his grave site.

After Thomas's death, his wife and their youngest son, James Monroe Norman, resided with Sarah Frances, who married Noah Brock. Lucretia was bedridden for two years before she passed away Sept. 5, 1895 near Brighton in Polk County and she, too, was buried in the Brock Cemetery with her husband.

James Monroe married Susan Melinda Jane Johnson on May 13, 1883. Susan was the daughter of Thomas and Eliza Elizabeth (Baucom) Johnston, who were married March 11, 1849 in Polk County.

All of Thomas and Lucretia's children remained in Missouri, except Caroline Sennie, who married Daniel Tom Irby, and James Monroe and his children. Susan Melinda Jane, his wife, died March 12, 1902 and was also buried in Brock Cemetery. These families moved to Oklahoma. *Submitted by Norma Jean Norman Dunten*

NOTTINGHAM – Thomas Nottingham, Virginia's sixth great-grandfather, came to America from England in 1669. He lived in St. Mary's County, MD, which is located on the mouth of the Potomac River on the Chesapeake Bay. (Died in 1716.)

The journey westward did not begin until the third generation with Virginia's fourth great-grandfather Phillip, who settled in Washington County, KY, (died 1800).

Based on reminiscences told by Virginia's great-grandmother, Mary Nottingham (born May 3, 1823, died Nov. 15, 1889), wife of Benjamin (born Oct. 18, 1823, died March 11, 1901), the family had moved to Noble, IL where many family members contracted a form of malaria. Ben became very weak and it was recommended that they travel to Missouri for his health. Traveling with a team of horses and also, one of oxen, Ben did begin improving with Missouri air.

In 1869 Ben's family homesteaded 120 acres in Polk County. They were charter members of the Dunnegan Baptist Church, built in 1888. He and Bill Routh built the first school house in the Rock School District.

Virginia's grandfather, Charles Elbridge "Eb" (born Nov. 6, 1865, died 1945), was the baby of this family. Married a local beauty, Adelia A. Holmes (born 1867, died 1904), eldest daughter of William and Mary Holmes, also of Dunnegan. They became the parents of six children: Cora A. (born Feb. 2, 1888, died 1941); William B. (born Sept. 26, 1889, died 1938); Orvilla (born Nov. 19, 1893); Arizona (born Nov. 5, 1896); and twin sons, Lonnie (died May 28, 1976) and Connie (born Dec. 28, 1901, died May 1970).

Eb did farming, blacksmithing and carpentering. Adelia "Dele" decided to paint the exterior of the house and, according to stories, died the next day of lead poisoning.

The following years were hard years for this family. Thus, we begin the history of Virginia's beloved father and his wonderful twin. Lonnie and Connie were only 2 years old and no mother!

Virginia's grandfather married Onesta Bell Mitchell. After a few years Virginia's father had a half-sister and five half-brothers. This marriage ended in divorce with Bell and children moving to California and appear to have prospered.

Connie and Lonnie Nottingham at Lon's farm home.

The young children of Eb and Adelia were often given temporary homes with relatives. They all survived this time of hardship, were good citizens and had a strong love of family.

Lon married lovely Ethel Belle Hopper (born March 8, 1903, died Aug. 23, 2000), a teacher, on Feb. 19, 1927. She and her older brother, Burnie, were Hiriam Henderson Hopper and Tirzah Elizabeth Litle Hopper's only children. They were residents of Dunnegan and Lon and Ethel Belle also settled near there, later purchasing a farm near Humansville where the children, Donald H. (born Oct. 13, 1927, died Feb. 4, 1988 as the result of a tractor-hay baler accident), Virginia Lee (born July 24, 1933) and Larry Douglas (born Nov. 3, 1942) graduated from high school, as did Ethel Belle years before.

Connie, so very much like Lonnie, married a California lady, Elsie White. Their yearly vacations to Missouri were Virginia's families' summer highlight.

Don, a Marine veteran and banker, married Dolores Pitts. Dolores Ann was born May 11, 1951. After a divorce, Don wed Helen Brown Pierce. Stepsons were Daniel R. and Scott P. Joe Donald was born Aug. 6, 1968. Grandchildren: Amy Pierce, Emily Pierce and Kyle Don Nottingham.

Virginia, a teacher, married Ralph A. Stauffacher on Oct. 26, 1952. Children: Cathy Lean (born Dec. 16, 1953), Jeanne Beth (born July 1, 1955), Janelle Kay (born March 24, 1957), Shirley Susan (born Oct. 31, 1958) and Alan Nottingham (born Oct. 21, 1963).

A dozen grandchildren: David Adams, Tammy, Jared, Audra, Ashley, Autumn Robinson. Melissa and Adam Stewart. Robert and Stephanie Tummons. Tori Stauffacher and Taylor Adams, great-granddaughter.

Larry, a teacher, married Peggy Costley on May 28, 1977. Children: Rachel Dawn (born Aug. 10, 1980) and Sarah Rose (born May 10, 1984).

Polk County has been home to many Nottinghams, but now there are only a few. *Submitted by Virginia Nottingham Stauffacher*

OBERKIRSCH – When Captain John Govan sailed the ship "Patience and Margaret" from Rotterdam, Holland, aboard were two German-born brothers, Jacob and Michael Oberkirsch. They came from what is now Obernai, France, but was once part of greater Germany. Their family were Bergermeisters, which is sort of like our mayors, and also in charge of the Church's money. They were of Lutheran faith.

Landing Oct. 25, 1748, they settled in Lancaster County, PA. In early 1800 Jacob moved his family to North Carolina, also about then Michael's son Baltzer sold all of his holdings and moved to Chambersburg, Franklin County, PA. How they came to pick that area the descendants don't know, but a cousin who visited the homeland in France said the two towns and terrain were very similar, with a flowing spring running through the middle of town, rolling hills and good farmland. The men were carpenters, farmers, merchants and railroad men. They also fought in the Revolutionary War.

Early 1800s the name was changed to Overcash.

Michael (1721-1782) wed Anna Barbara (1737-1782), children – Baltzer, Jacob, Michael, Margaret.

Baltzer (1761-1846) wed Margaret Fetterhoff (1790-1868), children – George, Phillip, Michael, Jacob, John, Suzanna, Elinor, Rebecca, Elizabeth, Christopher.

Jacob (1785-1871) wed Mary (1790-1868), children – Rebecca, Samuel, Susan, Rosanna, Jacob Jr. (Reva's great-grandfather).

His descendants don't know when or why Jacob left Pennsylvania but were told he left on foot, heading west. They never heard from him again. They were convinced he was killed by Indians.

Back row – Troy and Belle Overcash, Roy and Rosa Overcash, Nelle Overcash. Front row – Wilma, Jacob, Thelma (Troy's girl) and Alice Overcash

At one time he lived in Chicago, IL. Found in some old letters were papers for two grave lots. After contacting the cemetery, descendants were told two babies were buried there but don't have any more knowledge about his wife. He next shows up in Carthage, MO, selling sewing equipment and looms.

His next wife is Sarah Atwood (1840-1870) and they have a son Jacob Pharris (Reva's grandfather).

Jacob dies when Jacob Jr. is about 6 months old, Sarah dies the next year. His Grandfather Atwood raised him.

In 1890 Pharris (1869-1946) married Alice Jelly (1868-1942), children – Roy, Troy, George, Nelle, Wilma. Pharris had a big part in helping establish the Rural Hill Baptist Church at Sunset.

In 1924 he leaves his family and settles in Tahlequah, OK having two more sons, Jacob and Raymond.

Roy (1891-1956) married Rosa White (1899-1985), children – Verna, Leroy, Ruth, Reva, Rena.

Reva (1935) wed Roy Altic (1930-1981), one daughter, Leta.

Leta (1961) wed Gary Page (1949), one son, Kelly.

Kelly (1979) wed Virginia McCaulla (1982) and they have one precious baby girl, Alexis Korrin. The last limb on Reva's family tree.

At the age of 10 Reva learned she had a grandfather, until then they thought he was dead. In the summer of 1944 or 45, their family and Reva's dad's sister and her family went to Oklahoma to visit. They rode in the back of a truck, and they got so sunburned that they had to wear their clothes two or three days before they could bend their arms enough to remove them.

While there the children got to pick strawberries for the neighbors across the highway, and for someone who had never seen tame berries, it was a treat doing so. "I'm sure we ate our share," Reva says.

Reva, her sister Rena and Rena's son Tim visited a cousin Dr. Steven Overcash in Pennsylvania in 2000. Saw the homestead, lots of beautiful crops and old homes that are still standing. It's a pretty country.

Reva's grandfather died in 1946, so the family was very glad they got to see him that one time. *Submitted by Reva Overcash Altic*

ODOR – Elwood Smith Odor was a principle in the history of Polk County, MO. His family had been in the forefront of the struggle for American independence and before that had been prominent in French history, leaving that country to come to a land of religious freedom. The Odors had fought in the Revolutionary War and were from Culpeper County, VA. Their family members belonged to the Culpeper Minute Men. His wife Martha McMorris can trace her roots through marriage to John Marshall, the first Chief Justice for the United States of America; her nephew was Governor of Illinois. Elwood, for a time, was a coal miner in Coshocton County, OH but studied to become a doctor of medicine. He practiced in Wenona, Marshall County, IL before locating to Bolivar in 1867.

Elwood and Martha's children: Celia Ann, who married Dr. Thomas B. Hamilton in Wenona, IL, who died during the Civil War in Nashville, TN. Then she married Capt. James H. Buck in Bolivar and later located to LaPorte, IN.

John Thomas Odor was a pharmacist and farmer. He married Sarah Jane Suiter, daughter of Rev. George and Anne (Hammack) Suiter of Halfway. Their children were George Elwood; Celia Gilly, who married Walter M. Jobes; Martha Xelna, always known as Daisy, she married James Martin Kelsey; and Zula B., who married Walter A. Holstein. John T. and Elwood Smith owned City Drug and started marketing a product called Nature's Remedy that was made in Bolivar. The formula was later sold to A. H. Lewis who moved the manufacturing to St. Louis. Lewis later started marketing another remedy, today called TUMS.

William Samuel followed in his father's footsteps and became a doctor of medicine in Bolivar. He married Caroline Suiter, sister of his brother Joe T.'s wife Sarah Jane. He eventually retired from the practice of medicine and served the county of Polk as treasurer, and many other offices. His son James William married Lottie Day in Springfield, MO. His daughter Jennie Suiter married Charles Ellis York, son of Calvin M. and Mary E. Sutton of Carlinville, Macoupin County, IL. They had one son, Maxfield Samuel York. Max married Nellie Jean Wilson in Los Angeles, CA. They met going to college at UCLA.

Ottoman Cressy was a painter and married Alice E. Lawrence, Buena V. E. Ammerman and Rebecca S. Dunaway, also of Bolivar. He and Rebecca later located to California. His children were Webster Smith, John Smith, Elijah O., Kathryn D., Hobarta Rhuey (Watson), Carolyn C. (Hume), Josephine (Coons) and Rebecca (Randolph). Ottoman and Rebecca are buried in Santa Paula, CA along with his aunt Gilly Suiter Middleton and her husband Isaac Middleton and their daughter Dora Starr.

Otho Gabriel worked in the newspaper business and was the owner and editor of the *Buffalo Register* of Dallas County, MO.

John M. went north and was the owner and editor of the *Minneapolis Herald Tribune*. John passed away in 1897, leaving a wife and three children. *Submitted by Jacquelyn York Sparks*

Roy O. Overcash

OVERCASH – Roy Ozro Overcash (July 26, 1891 – March 2, 1956) was a quiet, unpretentious man who spent most of his life in overalls, except during WWI, when he wore an Army uniform. He wore his best overalls to church and the faded ones for every day. Although "Big Roy" (as called by many because of his six feet, two inches height) was a man of few words, everyone knew that his word was his bond and there were no profane words among those few. The closest he ever came to swearing was when he would say "Dadgum that dadgummed thing!" usually after smashing his thumb with a hammer.

Although Roy was a quiet man, he was not without humor. There is a family story about how Roy was so quiet that once, when cleaning soot from a kerosene lamp, he nearly scared away one daughter's suitor when he "yelled 'BOO'!" at the young man through the lamp globe. The young man, and future son-in-law, was so startled that everyone had a good laugh at his expense.

Roy was a man with many talents who worked hard at a variety of trades and tasks to provide for his family and give to his community. He was a carpenter, farmer, mechanic, hunter and fisherman. He was a Deacon and Sunday School teacher at Sunset Baptist Church. He was regularly called upon to sit up with the sick. At times he was asked to sit all-night watch with a family when someone died, and then to be a pallbearer. And whenever asked to get his pliers, he was "dentist" for his father-in-law, Thomas White.

At one time, Roy owned the only sawmill around for miles. He built a house for his family in the early 1930s. He also helped his neighbors build houses and barns. He helped to build the old Sunset Bridge south of Bolivar. Roy also owned one of the first tractors and threshing machines in the Bolivar area, so he often hired out to work for others at 50 cents an hour. With his mechanic's training (he had gone to a mechanic's school in Kansas City), he kept his equipment and on old truck going with "bubble gum and baling wire."

Because times were hard, Roy sometimes traveled far for the opportunity to work. Probably the farthest he ever went for work was to California. Around 1926, Roy took his wife, Rosa and children and traveled to Ventura. Joining them on that trip were in-laws, Lon and Ethel Sanders and Fred and Flara Sanders. The work was to build piers in the ocean. Roy fell into the ocean at least once during that job.

Although he was a quiet man, Roy may have had a bit of the adventurer in his soul, as hinted at by his willingness to travel. But a stronger indication was when, around 1940, a man named Lucien Yandel offered to take Roy and Rosa for a ride in Lucien's small plane. Rosa was afraid to go, so Roy, who had never been in a plane, took his young daughter, Ruth. She remembers that ride to this day.

Those who knew Roy recall that he was respected, well-liked and considered to be a pillar of his community. Above all, he was a good decent man who always did the best he could for his family, friends and neighbors. *Submitted by Ramona Beth Ammerman*

OVERCASH – Grandma Overcash (Rosa Belle Francis (White) Overcash, July 11, 1899 – Aug. 8, 1985), wife of Roy Ozro Overcash (July 26, 1891 – March 2, 1956), was beloved by her family and their memories of her are cherished. She was a spiritual, loving and generous woman who lived most of her life in Polk County, in the Bolivar area. Grandma was poor in money, but she gave richly to multitudes of people all of her life. Her gifts were of herself, her time and her skills. As a young wife and mother, Grandma provided care to her mother-in-law, Alice (Jelly) Overcash. As a widow in her late 60s, she cared for her mother, Bertha (Anderson) White and a spinster cousin, Maudie Ballinger. Throughout her life she gave thousands of hand-made items to others. She made everything from aprons to quilts, including linens and pot holders, sun bonnets and clothes, crocheted rugs, and doll clothes and dolls.

Grandma was the mother of five, four of which were girls. They were the first recipients of her hand-made rag-dolls. Because they family was poor, new rag-dolls, filled with sawdust, often were the only Christmas present the girls received. The dolls were always completely dressed, underwear included, and usually had sun bonnets as well. Then when granddaughters began to come along, a few of the first girls played with a rag-doll made by Grandma, but home-made was going out of style. The new generations purchased their daughters' dolls.

Years later, one granddaughter, Rachel, recalled the dolls of her childhood that long ago had been loved back to rags and sawdust. Rachel asked Grandma to make her one last rag-doll, to keep forever. When Grandma agreed, little did she imagine what she was getting herself into.

This time Grandma didn't use sawdust; the stuffing was cotton. When Grandma presented Rachel with the results, it was with not one, but two dolls, a little man and woman. The woman had a complete ensemble of bloomers, full slip, dress, sunbonnet and lace-up shoes. She had a gold pendant around her neck and a Holy Bible under her arm. The man was dressed in underwear, shirt, overalls, cap and lace-up boots. He had a tiny pencil in his bib pocket, a wallet in one rear pocket and handkerchief in the other. Grandma was not an artist, but as in the past, the faces and hair were drawn on. Rachel was surprised and deeply touched, because these dolls were truly precious.

Grandma Rosa Overcash

Naturally, once these dolls were seen by the family, all the females (and a few of the males) wanted a rag-doll of their own. Although Grandma was in her late 70s, she still found pleasure in giving and doing for others, especially her family. By the time she stopped making the dolls, she had created and dressed over 100 of them, in all sizes and shapes, each one unique. Today, Grandma's rag-dolls are spread across many states, from Missouri and Kansas to Texas, Arizona and California.

Out of all the dolls Grandma made, those first two were the best...Not the prettiest or the fanciest, but the most precious. They represented Roy and Rosa Overcash. *Submitted by Ralene Audra (Jarman) Hambicki*

OVERCASH – In June of 1935, Roy (July 26, 1891-March 2, 1956) and Rosa (White) (July 11, 1899-Aug. 8, 1985) Overcash were about to become parents for the fourth time. The other Overcash children were Verna (April 2, 1920), Leroy (July 14, 1923-Sept. 30, 1989) and Ruth (Oct. 3, 1932). The small Overcash farm was several miles south of Bolivar, and the family lived in a house that Roy had built. Their home was next to Rosa's parents' farm.

On June 27th, after a normal, full-term pregnancy, Rosa surprised everyone when she delivered identical twin girls. Rosa's mother, Bertha (Anderson) White (March 29, 1883-July 20, 1968), helped with the delivery. The beautiful babies were named Reva Fae and Rena Mae. Because it was almost impossible to tell them apart, a ribbon was tied to the wrist of Reva. It didn't take many days for Rosa to learn that the babies slept much better when placed head to foot in the same basket. From the time of their birth the twins fared better together than apart.

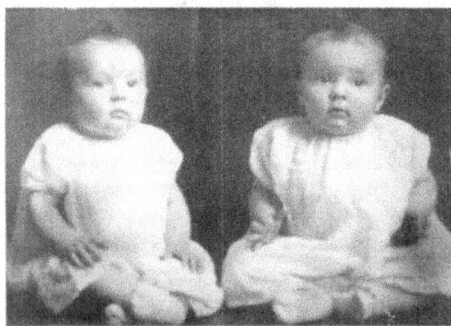

Reva on left; Rena on right 10 1/2 months; all clothes were made by their Mom-excluding socks

Apparently, identical twins were a novelty for Polk County folks, because within a few weeks people began stopping at the Overcash farm. Family, friends and mere acquaintances came to see the look-alike babies, with some folks even making the trek by horseback. Reva and Rena never cared for the spotlight. By the time they were 2 or 3 years old, having a visitor stop by would send them running to hide under the bed.

When the time came, the twins walked with big sister Ruth to a one-room schoolhouse. Through the years the teachers and students had problems telling the twins apart. They attended Pleasant Hope High School, and as young women, they began to forge separate lives. Eventually, Reva went to work in Kansas City while Rena remained on the farm for a while.

One day Rena had stomach pains so disabling she had to go to bed. A few days later Rena learned that Reva had undergone an emergency appendectomy on the same day Rena was in severe pain over 200 miles away. This psychic and physical connection has been so strong that the twins have never been truly comfortable when separated.

In 1953, Rena married Leroy Smith and had two sons, Timothy (Dec. 2, 1954) and Steven (Oct. 25, 1967). In 1960, Reva married Roy Altic and had a daughter, Leta (April 4, 1961). It was a good thing both husbands had out-going personalities and the children got along well, because the families were almost always neighbors.

The twins returned to Polk County in 1962. Roy and Reva bought the Overcash farmstead and lived in the house where the twins were born. Later, they bought the Whites' farm and sold the old homestead to Leroy and Rena. The homes are about a quarter-mile apart.

Today, Reva and Rena are fortunate to have their children, grandchildren and two great-grandchildren nearby. Christopher, Amber and Adam are the children of Tim and Peggy (Fieth) Smith. Kelly is the son of Gary and Leta (Altic) Page. The great-grandbabies are Alexia, daughter of Kelly and Gini (McCaulla) Page, and Lucas, son of Adam and April (McDaniels) Smith.

While identical twins are no longer a novelty in Polk County, at times the twins still create consternation for those folks who mistake one for the other. That is quite understandable, since even Leta, when she was little, called them "Mommy" and "Mommy Nena." *Submitted by Rachel Moritz*

PATTERSON – One Sunday afternoon in the spring of 1947, several members of Elbridge and Julia Patterson's family were gathered at their home near the Polk and Dallas County line northwest of Redtop. It had started just like most Sunday afternoons at their home, family gathering after church for Grandma's delicious chicken and dumplings dinner and visiting. However, after dinner, while the men visited outside, cousins played and the women washed dishes, an ominous storm cloud approached from the southwest. Men and children, after spotting a funnel cloud dipping toward them, scurried into the house for safety since Grandpa's storm cellar was not large enough to hold the whole clan. Once inside, everyone huddled together as a loud, ripping noise was heard overhead. After the tornado had passed, the family went outside to assess the damage— uprooted oak trees, broken windows, house twisted on its foundation, barn and other buildings destroyed and debris everywhere. Someone commented that surely the house would have been picked up and relocated had it not been for the weight of all the people inside.

Since Grandpa was a carpenter, the house was salvaged and continued to be a "haven of safety" for the family for several more years. Elbridge and Julia had reared 13 children in that home—five children born to Elbridge and Mary Klutz Patterson and eight children born to Elbridge and Julia Waggoner Patterson, whom he married after Mary's death.

There are many memories associated with that family home that were recorded by Elbridge and Julia's oldest daughter, Ida Pearl Patterson Smith,

Julia and Elbridge Patterson, 1940, at their home.

a few months prior to her death in March 1998. She recalled memories of childhood days in the old house before Grandpa remodeled it in the 1920s: sleeping on featherbeds, helping grow and preserve food, laundering clothes in the wash house, butchering hogs, rendering lard, making soap, apple butter, cider and molasses, carrying water from a nearby spring to the house, playing childhood games with the neighboring Hayden and Sheridan children, walking to one-room schoolhouses at Rock Prairie, Hasten and Glady Springs, completing the eighth grade twice just to attend the school since there was not a high school within walking distance and attending church services at the Redtop Missionary Baptist Church.

She also recalled memories of the first Stephen Thomas Patterson family reunion, which was to be held at Elbridge and Julia's home but was moved to the Redtop Church due to rain.

Elbridge Thomas Patterson was born Aug. 20, 1867 at Redtop, MO, the son of Stephen Thomas and Sarah Eliza Coble Patterson. Stephen Thomas was born Feb. 6, 1844 in Tennessee, the son of James Turner and Elmira M. Patterson. James Turner, who was born Dec. 28, 1821 in Tennessee, moved to Mooney Township in Polk County about 1850 with his family and parents, John and Catharine Patterson. Many of these ancestors are buried in the Union Grove Cemetery in southeast Polk County where this family first settled. *Submitted by Carolyn Smith Wrinkle*

PAUL – Marjorie Pauline Little Gould was born on a farm north of Dunnegan, MO in Polk County on Aug. 10, 1923 to Hattie Ethel (Paul) Little and James Clyde Little. Her mother's parents were Daniel Henry Paul and Amanda Pearlie (White) Paul, who lived only a half-mile away and made Marjorie's young life very happy.

Marjorie had three brothers and one sister and two aunts and two uncles to cater to her every want and need. She can remember her parent's first automobile. Her father first bought a Model T Ford and the next was a big, old, touring Buick. They had to push it by hand to start it on cold winter days. It took the family to Dunnegan shopping on Saturdays where they sold cream and eggs and bought kerosene, chicken feed and staple groceries like sugar, flower, salt and baking powder and soda. Marjorie remembers that Dunnegan had three grocery stores, a doctor, three churches, a drug store, a railroad depot, a cream station, a post office, a nut factory, a hotel, a grade school and a high school, a hardware and furniture store, a filling station and a feed store.

The family had cows, pigs, gardens and orchards which furnished the other goods they ate. They had a saddle horse, four horses and two mules which Marjorie remembers riding.

Marjorie went to grade school at Rosebud and high school at Humansville and graduated with about 20 classmates. Church played a big part in her life. They attended Spring Creek Cumberland Presbyterian Church at Dunnegan. She was married in that church to William Robert Gould on Aug. 6, 1944.

In the early 1950s, Robert graduated from

Southwest Baptist College; then they moved to Tennessee to attend two more years of college and three years of theological seminary. She has been a preacher's wife for 50 years and has many people who show their love to them. They are now retired and living in Aurora, MO after living in Tennessee, Oklahoma, Kansas and Kentucky.

They adopted two children, aged 3 months and 19 months, who now live in Lawrence County, MO. They enjoyed them even though they were assured that living in a manse was very hard for children because of people's criticism. *Submitted by Marjorie Gould*

Bertha Jane (Paul) and James Volney Culbertson 1909

PAUL – Bertha Jane Paul was born Sept. 14, 1886 at Humansville, MO, the daughter of Flora Ann (Nickels) and George Paul and attended Oakland School near Dunnegan. Bertha's parents are buried in Plum Grove Cemetery, south of Humansville, MO, her mother having died when Bertha was just 14. Bertha married "Bill" James Volney Culbertson, the son of John Fowler Culbertson and Mary Loga Piper, on May 11, 1908 at Sedalia, Pettis County, MO. Bill was born Aug. 18, 1889 near Roscoe, MO. To this union were born nine children.

After their marriage, they started farming about three miles west of Cobb, St. Clair County, MO, then in 1916 homesteaded near Lamar, CO for several years, finally returned to the farm near Cobb, MO and lived there until his death. He was a carpenter on the Osceola Power Dam in 1928 and 1929. He served for some time as a deacon of the Riverview Church and was often called upon to minister to the needs of community members. Bill died June 29, 1935 at the age of 45 years, 10 months and 11 days at his home south of Riverview School in St. Clair County, MO, just one and one-half miles from where he was born. He was buried at Freeman-Holsapple Cemetery near Collins, MO.

Bertha and the four unmarried children lived on the farm until they sold it in the fall of 1936. Bertha lived in Oregon for the next five years until the fall of 1941, then moved to California to join other Missouri homefolk already there. She spent much of her later years going from family to family, visiting grandchildren. Bertha loved to fish and crochet. Bertha died Aug. 15, 1965 in Martinez, CA and was buried beside her husband.

The children: Jewel Phyrne Culbertson (Rector, Welle), born Aug. 18, 1908 at Roscoe, MO, died July 27, 1991 at Martinez, CA, buried Oakman Park, Lafayette, CA; James Lee Culbertson, born Nov. 5, 1910 at Roscoe, MO, died Oct. 25, 1938, buried Ow Yhee Cemetery, Nyssa, OR; Charley Paul Culbertson, born Nov. 19, 1912 at Roscoe, MO, died Feb. 7, 1895 at Nyssa, OR, buried Ow Yhee Cemetery, Nyssa, OR; Lester Silas Culbertson, born Nov. 20, 1915 at Roscoe, MO, died Nov. 8, 1990, buried Odessa Cemetery, Odessa, MO; Loga Lorene Culbertson (Allen, Burkhart), born April 4, 1918 at Beca County, Utleyville, CO, died July 29, 1994 at Bolivar, MO, buried at Freeman-Holsapple Cemetery near Collins, MO; Elmer Dale Culbertson, born Aug. 24, 1920 at Buster, CO, died March 19, 1986, buried Highland Memorial Cemetery, Knoxville, TN; Flora Juanita Culbertson (Powers), born June 16, 1923 at Roscoe, MO, she lives in Pleasant Hill, CA; J V Culbertson, born Aug. 8, 1925 at Roscoe, MO, died Sept. 26, 1988, buried Laurel Cemetery, Cave Junction, OR; Arleta Rose Culbertson, born March 3, 1927 at Roscoe, MO, died June 1, 1939 at Holy Rosary Hospital, Ontario, OR, buried Ow Yhee Cemetery, Nyssa, OR. *Submitted by Jane (Burkhart) Volkart*

PAUL – Charles Allen Paul, the son of Flora Ann (Nickels) and George Paul, was born in Dunnegan, MO on July 5, 1890 and died March 15, 1931 in Seattle, WA. He married Kathleen Edna Eudora Parker on Aug. 19, 1915 in Seattle, WA, the daughter of James Parker and Caroline Flindall. She was born Nov. 28, 1890 in Seattle, WA and died Oct. 10, 1980 in Seattle, WA. She was buried in Lakeview Cemetery, Seattle, WA beside her husband.

They had three sons born in Seattle, King County, WA. The first son was born Sept. 7, 1916 and died Sept. 7, 1916. The second son, Charles Parker Paul, was born Dec. 29, 1917 and the youngest son, James Richard Paul, was born Sept. 5, 1920. *Submitted by Jerri Graham*

PAUL – Dan Paul, the second son of John and Elizabeth (Thomas) Paul, was born on Nov. 17, 1861 on a farm near Nokomis, IL. In the spring of 1867, he, his father, mother, older brother, George and younger brother, David, began their move from Illinois to Missouri. They traveled in two wagons, one being driven by John and the other by George. Their journey led them to the Missouri River, which they crossed by ferry boat on July 4, 1867. The family first settled near Rockville, MO in Bates County. It was here that Dan's sister, Florence, was born on Feb. 18, 1872 and his mother died on Dec. 6, 1872.

Dan's father next married Martha Jane (Cooper) Vannoy on Sept. 17, 1874. They settled in Polk County in 1875. At first, they homesteaded. Then, they bought land located about one and a half miles northeast of Dunnegan, MO that extended almost to Plum Grove Church. It was at Dunnegan that Dan's half-sisters, Corda and Daisy Grace and his half-brother, William, were born. Dan also had a step-brother, Charlie Vannoy, and a step-sister, Maggie Vannoy.

Dan was converted to Christ in early manhood and united with the Spring Creek Cumberland Presbyterian Church at Dunnegan, MO. While just a young man, he was ordained as an elder in the church and held this position throughout the rest of his life. As an elder, he attended Presbytery and sometimes traveled to the location where it was meeting by train from Dunnegan.

Dan was united in marriage to Alcy Parlee White on Aug. 18, 1885. Dan and Parlee made their home on family acreage given to them as a wedding gift by his father. Seven children were born to this union over a span from 1886 to 1905. They were Johnny Elmer, Hattie Ethel, Fred Clarence, James Ira, Ruby Jane, Conaway (Connie) Russell and Dorothy Mae Paul.

Three of Dan's sons, Johnny, Fred and James Ira, served in WWI. James Ira was wounded. Also during the war, the government bought a team of horses from Dan to use in battle.

Throughout their lives, Dan and Parlee were devout in their attendance to Spring Creek Cumberland Presbyterian Church and would sit in the "Amen Corner" of the church. If there wasn't preaching at the C.P. Church, they and the congregation would go to either the Baptist or Christian Church, whichever one had preaching at the time. Visiting preachers came home to eat meals with them.

Dan, a farmer by trade, used horses to work the fields in which wheat, corn, and oats were grown. He also had an apple orchard. He kept chickens, cows, and sheep. In addition, he had honey on the table from the bees that he raised. Dan would send cows and calves to be sold at the stockyards in Springfield, MO, but most everything else was used on the farm.

In 1908, the Dan Paul family moved to a farm south and a little east of Flemington, MO near the railroad track. They continued to live there until 1917. Then, they moved to a farm, which was later owned by Clarence Litle, about three miles north of Dunnegan. It was here that Dan and Parlee would spend the rest of their lives.

Parlee passed away at her home on March 25, 1929. She was 66 years old. She had been converted to Christ early in life and joined the C.P. Church. She was remembered as a strong Christian woman who enjoyed the services and would get really happy and stamp her feet to the music during the hymns.

Dan continued living on the farm with his son, Conaway (Connie) and daughter, Ruby. He passed away on May 27, 1939. He was 77 years old. He was buried beside his wife at Dunnegan Cemetery, which is located one mile east of Dunnegan. *Submitted by Michael Fare*

PAUL – David King Paul was born Sept. 3, 1865 in Nokomis, Montgomery County, IL, the third son of Elizabeth (Thomas) and John Paul. The family moved to Rockville, Bates County, MO in 1867 where his mother died in 1872. His father then married Martha Jane Cooper (Vannoy) Sept. 17, 1874 at Fort Scott, KS before moving the family to Polk County, MO in 1875, settling north of Dunnegan. David Paul was a member of the Cumberland Presbyterian Church and took an active part in the care of the Plum Grove Cemetery. David Paul died Aug. 7, 1934 at the age of 68 and was buried in the Plum Grove Cemetery under the direction of Luckey Funeral Home of Wheatland, MO.

The ordained preacher of the Gospel Elder Allen Bridges united David King Paul in marriage to Belle DeRena Thomas Fox on Dec. 25, 1887 in Dunnegan, MO, at the house of the bride. She was born April 7, 1859, four miles west of Fair Play, MO and moved with her parents, Jane (Thomas) and William Fox at 2 years of age to Little Rock, AR. She lived there until 12 years of age, a member of a family of six children. When her parents died, she returned to Polk County, MO and located in Dunnegan where she lived until she departed this life Jan. 18, 1937 at the age of 80 years, 9 months and 11 days. She was buried beside her husband at Plum Grove Cemetery.

This union was blessed with three children: Nora, Claude and Cora, born in Polk County, MO. Their oldest child, Nora Ellen Paul, was born Nov.

Back – James Ira, Johnney, Fred
Middle – Hattie Ethel, Dan, Parlee, Ruby
Front – Conaway (Connie), Dorothy

David King Paul and family circa 1898

24, 1888 and died Nov. 4, 1906 of typhoid fever at the age of 17 years and was buried at Plum Grove Cemetery.

Claude William Paul was born Oct. 25, 1892. His military headstone reads "PVT HO CO 354 Infantry WWI". He received a Purple Heart for his military deeds. Claude was a farmer in Polk County his entire life. He died April 19, 1962 at Dunnegan, MO at the age of 69 years and was buried at the Plum Grove Cemetery. He married Martha Jane Ballard, Feb. 3, 1924, in Polk County, MO. Martha was the daughter of George Thomas Ballard and Margaret Frances Holbert Ballard, who had moved to Dunnegan in 1903. Martha Jane (Ballard) Paul was born Nov. 16, 1895, a member of a family of seven and died Feb. 21, 1983 at the age of 87 and was buried beside her husband. Their children, Maggie Belle (Paul) Kelley and Wilberta Jane (Paul) Hulett, still reside in Polk County.

Cora Nellie Paul was born Oct. 18, 1895 and died July 28, 1947 in Lindsay, CA. She married Lee Watson Williams, Nov. 15, 1914, in Humansville, Polk County, MO. Their children are Neta Belle Williams (Summers), Walter Williams and Marie Williams (Brown). *Submitted by Maggie Belle (Paul) Kelley*

PAUL – George Paul was born Jan. 18, 1854 in Bernards Township, Somerset County, NJ, the son of Elizabeth Thomas and John Paul. The family moved to Nokomis, Montgomery County, IL in 1857 where his two brothers, Daniel Henry Paul (born Nov. 17, 1861, died May 27, 1939) and David King Paul (born Sept. 3, 1865, died Aug. 7, 1934), were born. In the late spring of 1867 the family left Illinois for Missouri. Father and son each drove a team with covered wagon and crossed the Missouri River by ferryboats on July 4, 1867.

George's mother died on Dec. 16, 1872 near Rockville, Bates County, MO after the birth of his sister, Florence Paul, Feb. 18, 1872. His father then married Martha Jane Cooper Vannoy in Fort Scott KS, Sept. 17, 1874, giving George his stepsiblings Charley (born Dec. 1, 1865, died May 12, 1927) and Maggie Vannoy (born about 1869). His father purchased land in Township 34, Range 24 of Polk County on April 14, 1875 and moved the family to Dunnegan, MO. George married Alice Shaw but is listed as divorced on the 1880 Polk County census with the family including his three youngest siblings, Cordie Paul (born Feb. 27, 1876, died March 8, 1899), William Alexander Paul (born Aug. 5, 1877, died Oct. 28, 1955) and Daisy Grace Paul (born Dec. 10, 1879, died Dec. 20, 1972), all born in Dunnegan, MO.

George Paul married Flora Ann Nickels, Dec. 5, 1880 in Dunnegan, Polk County, MO in the presence of Wm. P. Nickels and Allen Bridges, by Elder Benj. L. Smith, at the home of her parents, James Robert and Elizabeth Jane (Hardy) Nickels. Flora was born Jan. 23, 1882 in Lexington, Clark County, IN and came with her family to Polk County in the fall of 1879. To this union four children were born in Dunnegan, MO: Raymond Paul (born and died Oct. 21, 1882), Mirty Pearl Paul (Gilpin) (born Feb. 25, 1884, died June 1, 1966), Bertha Jane Paul (Culbertson) (born Sept. 14, 1886, died Aug. 15, 1965) and Charles Allen Paul (born July 5, 1890, died March 15, 1931). Flora Paul died April 22, 1901 of pneumonia in Dunnegan at the age of 51 years and was buried at Plum Grove Cemetery.

George Paul married Luella Garrison, Dec. 4, 1901, in Humansville by Elder Allen Bridges. She was born July 4, 1880 in Humansville, the daughter of John H. Garrison. Three of their children survived to adulthood, Mildred Irene Paul, Nina G. Paul and Beulah F. Paul. George Paul was engaged in the saw mill business for several years, ran a blacksmith shop and at one time operated the Humansville Roller Mill. In 1906 he owned a small store at Cobb, MO. He moved Luella and the three youngest girls to Vera Cruz, MO about 1911, then on to Brinkley, AR the fall of 1912 and died at home Thursday, Aug. 7, 1913. The body was brought back to Dunnegan and buried at Plum Grove Cemetery by the Knights of Pythias Lodge of which he was a faithful member for years.

Luella married John Taylor at Yellville, AR and moved to Hollywood, CA, 1925. She died on Oct. 31, 1951 in Northwood, CA of cancer and was buried in the Valhalla Memorial Park Cemetery. John Taylor died Oct. 23, 1962 at North Hollywood and was buried beside Luella. *Submitted by David Paul Williams*

PAUL – John Paul, the son of George Paul and Harriet Testor (both of Engand), was born near Morristown, NJ, Dec. 12, 1829 (date from obit.), where he resided until about 25 years of age. Then John moved to Illinois, living in Montgomery and Macoupin Counties and in 1867 moved to Rockville, Bates County, MO. He followed farming all his life and by his thrift and industry accumulated a competency. On April 17, 1875, he purchased land situated in Township 34 of Range 24 of Polk County, for the sum of five thousand dollars. John Paul was a highly respected citizen of Dunnegan serving as justice of the peace and was otherwise honored. On April 22, 1878, John Paul, as a member of the Directors of School District No. 4, Township 34 of Range 24, gave one acre of land for the Plum Grove schoolhouse site. He died Feb. 17, 1898 in Dunnegan, MO of pneumonia and was buried in Plum Grove Cemetery north of Dunnegan.

John Paul

While living in New Jersey, John Paul married Elizabeth Thomas, Feb. 22, 1853, by which four children, George, Daniel, David and Florence, were born. George Paul was born Jan. 18, 1854 in Bernard's Township, Somerset County, NJ, died Aug. 7, 1913 in Brinkley, AR of Bright's disease and malaria, buried in Plum Grove Cemetery. Daniel Henry Paul was born Nov. 17, 1861 in Nokomis, Montgomery County, IL, died May 27, 1939, Polk County, buried in Dunnegan Cemetery. David King Paul was born Sept. 3, 1865 in Nokomis, Montgomery County, IL, died Aug. 7, 1934 in Polk County, buried in Plum Grove Cemetery. Florence Paul was born Feb. 18, 1872 in Rockville, Bates County, MO, died July 23, 1948, Webb City, MO. She married William Elsworth Reid, Oct. 19, 1893, in Polk County, MO.

After the death of his first wife, John Paul married the widow of Caleb Vannoy, Martha Jane Cooper Vannoy, Sept. 17, 1874 in Fort Scott, KS. She was born Aug. 14, 1844 in Bloomington, IN, died March 25, 1922 in Polk County, MO at the age of 77 years, 7 months and 10 days and was buried beside John Paul. They had three children, Cordie, William Alexander and Daisy Grace. Cordie Paul was born Feb. 27, 1876 in Dunnegan, Polk County, MO, died March 8, 1899 of consumption, buried Plum Grove Cemetery. William Alexander Paul was born Aug. 5, 1877, Dunnegan, Polk County, MO, died Oct. 28, 1955, Polk County, buried Plum Grove Cemetery. Daisy Grace Paul was born Dec. 10, 1879, Dunnegan, Polk County, MO, died Dec. 20, 1972, Polk County, buried in Lindley Prairie Cemetery in Cedar County. Daisy married Charles Michael Baker, Jan. 2, 1900 in Polk County. John Paul had two stepchildren. Charley Vannoy was born Dec. 1, 1865, Booneville, IN, died May 12, 1937, Stratford, CA, buried in Plum Grove Cemetery. Maggie Vannoy married Thomas D. White, Oct. 28, 1890 in Polk County, MO and lived at the time of her mother's death in Nashua, MT. *Submitted by Joyce Burkhart*

PAUL – William Alexander Paul was born Aug. 5, 1877 in Polk County, near Dunnegan, MO, the son of John Paul and Martha Jane (Cooper-Vannoy) Paul. This life-long resident of Polk County was a farmer by trade.

William's father was born near Morristown, NJ, Nov. 12, 1829 (date on headstone) where he resided until about age 25 years, then moved first to Montgomery and Macoupin County, IL, then moved to Bates County, MO in 1867. John Paul's first wife, Elizabeth (Thomas), died leaving John Paul with four children, three boys and a girl. William's mother, Martha Jane Cooper, was born Aug. 15, 1844 near Bloomington, IN, moved with her parents to Illinois, grew to womanhood, then married Caleb Vannoy and moved back to Indiana. When Caleb Vannoy died she and her two children, a boy and a girl, then moved to Rockville, Bates County, MO where she met John Paul.

William's parents married Sept. 17, 1874 in Ft. Scott, KS. The family then moved to Polk County, MO near Dunnegan in 1875. Here William, his older sister, Cordie and younger sister, Grace, were born.

"Bill" William Alexander Paul married Parthena Ashlock, Aug. 7, 1898 in Polk County, MO, the only daughter of Henry Ashlock and Jane (Phillips) Ashlock. Parthena (Ashlock) Paul was born May 19, 1876 in Polk County and died April 26, 1942 in Polk County and was buried in the Plum Grove Cemetery. This union was blessed with two children, both born in Polk County near Dunnegan, MO: Jewel Jane Paul, born Sept. 29, 1910 and Zola Mae Paul, born May 15, 1914.

William and Parthena Paul and first child Jewell Paul circa 1912

Jewel Jane Paul married Teddy Arthur Hammons, June 23, 1928 in Bolivar, MO. He was born Nov. 16, 1907 in Cedar County, near Dunnegan, MO. They are both buried at Humansville Cemetery, Humansville, MO. Their only child, Wendell Dale Hammons, was born Jan. 29, 1929 in Dunnegan, MO.

Zola Mae Paul married Floyd Herbert Stiles, Nov. 26, 1933 in Bolivar, MO. Floyd was the son of Hugh Stiles and Ethel (Peery) Stiles. He was born May 12, 1909 in Collins, St. Clair County, MO. They took up residence on his grandfather's place near Collins, MO – soon to be a centennial farm. Floyd died June 8, 1990 in Cox Medical Center South, Springfield, MO. Their two children are Tamalene Jane Stiles and Herbert Joe Stiles, both born in St. Clair County, MO.

On Aug. 30, 1947, the widowed "Bill" William Alexander Paul married the widow of Manuel LaRose, "Mollie" Mary Idelle George (LaRose), the fourth of five children born to William Aldridge and Josephine Alwilda (Hapgood) George. They lived in Dunnegan for two years, then moved to Wheatland. William Alexander Paul died Oct. 28, 1955 and was buried in Plum Grove Cemetery beside his first wife. After the death of William Alexander Paul at Wetzel Hospital, Clinton, MO, Mollie continued to live in Wheatland until her death on Jan. 26, 1965. She was buried in the Hermitage Cemetery, Hermitage, MO. *Submitted by Zola Mae (Paul) Stiles*

PAYNE – Elijah F. Payne was born in 1806 in Kentucky. In 1830 his home was near Hopkinsville, KY. Five years later, on Sept. 21, 1835, across the Ohio River in Gallatin County, IL, he married Kisiah Phipps, the daughter of Daniel and granddaughter of John Phipps.

It's easy to speculate that Elijah and Kissiah traveled in the company of other family members using the most logical mode of travel, going by boat down the Ohio River to the Mississippi River and north to St. Charles, MO, then west on the Missouri River. The 1840 census records Elijah living in Carroll County, MO as a 34-year-old farmer with a wife, daughter and son, both children being born in Missouri.

Elijah moved his growing family to Johnson County, AR: Mary Ann, James, Martha, Daniel, Oliver, Lucy, Missouri, Rachel, George Jackson and Jasper McWilliams ("J.M.") who "said he was nine years old when the family returned to Missouri" about 1863, locating on 80 acres just south of the Polk County line.

J.M. married Nancy Elizabeth Barcley in September 1876 in Pleasant Hope, MO. Two years later he was ordained as a Baptist minister by Rock Prairie Church. He served churches in Polk and Dade Counties, Indian Territory and Springfield, MO.

To Mr. and Mrs. Payne was born a large family. Their children were Pearl, married R.M. Clark; Elijah David, married Isabelle Howe; Otto; Tabitha, married Marion Thompson of Polk County; Daniel married Maud (unknown); Edward F., lived in Kansas; Cora, married M.A. Snodgrass; and Corina.

Elijah and Kisiah were living with J.M.'s family in Polk County when Elijah died in 1879. He is buried in Union Grove Cemetery; Kisiah was still living with the family in 1880. No other records are located for her.

George Jackson Payne was born in March 1848, the first of Elijah and Kisiah's children to be born in Clarksville, AR. He joined the Confederate Army, Company E, Arkansas Cavalry, serving from August 1863 to August 1865.

George married Octavia Tennessee Prater on Sept. 13, 1867 at the home of her parents, Jeremiah and Emiline (Taylor) Prater of Mooney Township, Polk County, MO. George, like his father, was a farmer and raised a large family: Robert, married Ella Rush; Columbus, married Anna Rebecca Cox; George Clinton, married Ollie Walker; Henry Walter, married Laura Argo; Charles Mack, a life-long barber, married Jane F. Rose, the daughter of Granberry and Elizabeth (Utt) Rose of Greene County. She was the granddaughter of Kindred Rose, an early pioneer who was credited with the naming of Springfield. Octavia died July 15, 1885 at 38 years of age; she and her young children John Wesley, Laura and twin sons are buried in Prock Cemetery.

George was remarried Oct. 10, 1886 to Cordelia M. Harmon, the daughter of David Harmon of Dade County, MO. Children born were Addie Maud, married L. Dorsey; David Ray, married Georgia F. (unknown) – both are buried in Rock Prairie Cemetery; Alfred "Hugh," a life-long barber, married Julia Mankins; and Orin, born 1899.

George and Cordelia donated the land for the building of Pleasant Hope Baptist Church. George died Oct. 12, 1904 at age 66. Cordelia died July 8, 1922. Both are buried in Rock Prairie Cemetery.

Front row – Anna (Payne) House, Elizabeth (Bewley) Payne, Jesse R. Payne Sr., Martha (Payne) Roberts, Nancy (Payne) Emory
2nd row – Jesse R. Payne Jr., John H. Payne, William E. Payne, Dwight L. Payne, Isaac C. Payne, James L. Payne, Andrew J. Payne

PAYNE – Jesse Russell Payne Sr.'s, paternal ancestors came from England in the 1660s due to deprivation of religious freedom by an act of British Parliament. The Payne group settled in Pennsylvania. The early Jesse Payne served in the Revolutionary War. Later his family migrated to Hawkins County, TN. It was there that Joseph C. Payne, the father of Jesse Russell Payne Sr., was born April 9, 1798. In 1819 Joseph C. married Anna Johnson, who was an identical twin and a cousin of President Andrew Johnson. To this union 11 children were born from 1820 – 1844. They were Polly Ann, Elizabeth, James, Sarah, Elbert, Alsey, John H., Ellender, Jesse Russell, William and Lucinda. Jesse Russell Payne Sr. was born Aug. 24, 1839. The first person buried in the Payne Cemetery near Polk was their son, Elbert, who died in 1852 at the age of 23.

While still a small boy, Jesse's parents, Joseph and Anna, and family migrated from Tennessee and settled on Sentinel Prairie near Polk, MO. Joseph became a successful farmer and owned some of the best land in this section. He was a Democrat and his early religious faith was that of a Quaker, later becoming a Baptist. He died in 1858 at the age of 60 and his wife Anna Johnson died in 1873 at age 75.

Jesse Russell Payne Sr., a son of Joseph and Anna, bought a farm adjoining his father's and made this his lifetime home. He married Sarah Elizabeth (Lizzie) Bewley, daughter of William and Martha (Davis) Bewley of Rondo, MO, on June 14, 1874. Elizabeth's birth date was June 30, 1855. They became the parents of 10 children: William Elbert (1875); Anna Elizabeth (1877); Nancy Catherine (1879); John Houston (1882); Martha Pearl (1885); James Luther (1888); Jesse Russell Jr. (1891); Andrew Joseph (1893); Isaac Columbus (1896); and Dwight L. (1900).

The house where Jesse R. and Lizzie lived and raised their family is still standing and is the home of a Payne family member. Two fireplaces were used to heat the home. In early years, a community and family gathering was held at the home to celebrate birthdays. The first ones were in honor of Jesse Sr. and later continued to honor Elizabeth's birthday. This custom, now called the Payne Reunion, is still being observed by relatives and friends. In 1999 there were 270+ in attendance at the July celebration.

Jesse Russell Payne Sr. died March 25, 1922 at the age of 82. Sarah Elizabeth died Dec. 15, 1945 at age 90. She died at her home near Polk on the same farm where she had spent the last 71 years of her life. She was survived by all 10 children, 67 grandchildren, 72 great-grandchildren and two great great grandchildren. *Submitted by Eva Voris*

PAYNE – Jesse Russell Payne Jr. was born Jan. 31, 1891, the seventh child of Jesse Russell Payne Sr. and Elizabeth (Bewley) Payne, one of 10 children. They lived on a farm near Polk, an area called the Payne Prairie. There were crops to be planted and harvested and many animals that needed care. Jesse Jr. became interested in treating the sick animals and growing better crops. He decided to get more schooling to learn improved methods for farming. He worked his way through high school and college.

Jesse R. Jr. attended Inglis Grade School, Bolivar Academy, Springfield Normal (now SMSU), William Jewell in Liberty and then the University of Missouri at Columbia, where he graduated in 1916 with a BS degree in agriculture. He majored in botany and veterinary science. He was on a rifle team, debate team and a football team.

As a young man he taught at Inglis School. The enrollment at the beginning of school was 70 pupils; several students being nearly as old as he. Some students attended after harvest season and would be out during spring planting.

Jesse R. Jr. and Grace Elva Estes met at Springfield State Normal College in 1914 where both were students. They were married June 28, 1917. Her parents, Jacob A. Estes and Margaret (Nigh) Estes, were both teachers and lived at Newtonia, MO. Grace taught school in Newton County for several years before marriage. She had one sister, Maye Estes, who married Elbert House in 1922.

Jesse R. Payne Jr. was inducted into the US Army during WWI and was sent to Waco, TX. He was in the cavalry division where he served as a veterinarian and caretaker for the horses. After the war ended, he returned to his farm.

Front row – Jesse Russell Payne Jr., Grace Estes Payne, Roa Elizabeth (Mrs. Ferrol Wainscott)
Back row – Ava Estes (Mrs. Cecil Pitts), Iva May (Mrs. Gene Rust), Eva Margaret (Mrs. Paul Voris)

Jesse and Grace lived on their farm in the Star Ridge District near Rimby where they raised their family. Their four daughters were Roa Elizabeth, born Aug. 25, 1918; Ava Estes, born Jan. 1, 1921; Eva Margaret, born July 3, 1922; and Iva May, born Jan. 19, 1925. A son, Marvin Wilson, was born and died on Oct. 5, 1919.

The farm home was near Rimby Store, Star Ridge Church and School. The four girls went to elementary school at Star Ridge.

Telephone poles and lines were installed in the community about 1920. Several neighbors were on a "party" line. They could call each other by ringing what was called "shorts and longs."

It was not considered rude to "listen in" on other people's conversations. It was a means to learn about sickness, deaths, births, celebrations, etc. The switchboard at Rimby could be used if you needed to call someone "outside" the immediate area.

Star Ridge Church was a common gathering place for all. Denominations did not seem to matter. To go to church during the '20s most people either walked or drove horses hitched to wagons or buggies. Grace Payne organized a Sunday School and many families in the community were faithful to attend. Both Jesse and Grace were highly respected for their integrity and knowledge and their willingness to help others in need. Both were faithful Baptists.

Grace died Aug. 2, 1947 at age 52 and was buried in Payne Cemetery.

In 1950 Jesse R. married Mildred Borgstadt Payne, former wife of Andrew, Jesse's deceased brother. They lived their last years in Bolivar. Jesse died Dec. 22, 1981, being nearly 91 years old. Mildred died Aug. 11, 1995. Both were also buried in Payne Cemetery. *Submitted by Ava E. Grannemann*

PEMBERTON – William H. Pemberton was born about 1826 in Tennessee or Virginia and died Jan. 30, 1888 in Phoenix, AZ. He was married to Martha Bower, who was born about 1825 in Tennessee, and she died May 13, 1880 in Prescott, AZ. His mother's name was Mary.

William and Martha had about 11 children: they are James or Jarues G., who was born about 1842 in Missouri; Rachel, born about 1844 in Missouri; Mary Jane, born July 17, 1844 in Missouri, died Sept. 20, 1933 in Prescott, AZ, buried in Citizens Cemetery, Prescott; Ahab born between 1845 – 1861; Henry, born about 1848 in Missouri; Louisa, born about March 1850; Eliza, born about 1852 in Missouri; William A., born in 1855 in Missouri; Nancy Adeline (Addie), born Jan. 15, 1857 in Missouri, died March 14, 1915 in Prescott, AZ, buried in Mountain View Cemetery, Prescott; John A., born in 1860 in Missouri, died about April 1883 in Clear Creek, AZ from smallpox; and Samuel Bender (Cathy's line), born May 13, 1864 in Bolivar, Polk County, MO, died May 21, 1936 in Prescott, AZ, buried Mountain View Cemetery, Prescott, died from old age.

Marriages – Mary married Henry J. Joyce, born about 1822 in North Carolina. He died before 1897, they married Nov. 25, 1868 in Benton County, AR; she then married William Pleasant Allred (uncle of Leatha Arizona Roy) July 26, 1897 in Prescott, AZ. Mary never had children. Eliza married Samuel Cox, born about 1848 in Arkansas; they married Nov. 25, 1866 in Polk County, MO. They had three children: Lizzie Belle, born October 1867 in Arkansas, died about 1903 in Del Rio, Yayapai County, AZ; James Cox, born November 1869 in Arkansas; and Walter S. Cox, born December 1871 in Arkansas and died Nov. 17, 1942 in Mint Valley, Prescott area, AZ. Nancy married Robert Stringfield, born about 1853 in Arkansas and died Nov. 1, 1891 in Prescott, AZ from a wagon accident. They were married July 4, 1869 in Benton County, AR. They had six children: Olive May, born 1861, Albert Walter, born Nov. 28, 1872, Vada M., born June 1878, Bertha Elizabeth, born March 1882, Elizabeth, born about 1888 and Alice Louise, born May 9, 1890. Samuel Bender married Mary A. Weston, born about 1861 in California, died Dec. 6, 1888 in Prescott, AZ; they married Feb. 5, 1885 in Yayapai County, AZ. He then married Letha Arizona Roy, who was born Dec. 25, 1878 in Del Rio, AZ and died Dec. 22, 1932 in Prescott, AZ. There was one child to this union, Samuel Henry (Cathy's grandfather). They divorced. He then married Alice E. Postle, born Feb. 17, 1870 in Prescott, AZ, died March 30, 1945 in Prescott, AZ.

It is unknown when William came to Polk County; he moved to Benton County, AR between 1860 and 1870, he then moved again to Prescott, AZ about 1875. *Submitted by Cathy (Pemberton) Filliaux*

PERKINSON – Amy Elizabeth Harwell was born in 1760, when Virginia was still a colony. She married Archibald "Archer" Perkinson on Sept. 6, 1790 in St. Andrew's Parish in Brunswick County, VA. Amy and Archer moved to Henry County, VA. There are records of them selling land in Martinsville, VA in 1835. We have no further records of Archer.

In the 1830s, imaginations were sparked when tales were told of good land at $1.25 an acre west of the Mississippi. The oxen-drawn wagons started rolling out of Virginia and Amy would join her sons and their families as they pulled out for Missouri. The trip would be over 1,000 miles long with mountains and mighty rivers to cross. We have been told that Amy Elizabeth walked most of the distance because she had a toothache and could not stand the jolting of the wagon. She would have been well up in years when she made the trip.

Some wondered why she ever left Virginia. Amy Elizabeth was born before the Revolution. She married and raised six children. She had been a pioneer all of her life. Maybe, she decided to help her children carve out homes in the new frontier.

The Perkinsons acquired land in Polk County along the northeast banks of Little Sac River about four miles above the junction with Big Sac. In 1841 Dade County was formed and included this land until 1845, when it became Cedar after Cedar County was created. This is near Needmore and Price Branch area of the Stockton Lake, today.

In the 1840 Polk County Census, Hezekiah and William Purgison (Perkinson) are listed with nine people in each household. William's includes a 70 to 80 years old female (Amy Elizabeth).

In 1844 Amy resided with her son William's family. Here is a family story that has been passed down through the years.

It was a cold, snowy day when 6-year-old Cassandra, daughter of Hezekiah and Susannah Perkinson, saw Grandma's red shawl lying on the snow, and questioned why it was there. Grandma had walked a few yards from the house and fallen. After checking, the family found that she had died. Grandma always went out to a thicket of trees everyday to pray. She prayed that the Lord would let one moment of time close the scene of her life. Her prayers were finally answered.

Amy Elizabeth Perkinson was buried on the property of Garrett Philpott, a brother of Susannah Perkinson, about three miles northeast of the Perkinson home. She was not the first one to be buried at that location, but she was the oldest, being born in the 18th century. The property grew into the Lindley Prairie Cemetery, which now contains seven generations of her descendants. Her flat tombstone reads: Elizabeth Purkeson, 1760 – 1844. *Submitted by Shirley Cooper Moss*

PERRY – Alfred and Jane Loftin, natives of North Carolina, migrated to Missouri shortly after their marriage. Alfred, born Dec. 7, 1814 in Guilford County to Thomas and Mary (Thomas) Loftin, married Zuretha Jane Perry on April 20, 1837 in Davidson County. She was born Oct. 12, 1818 to Jordan Perry and Elizabeth Barr. By September 1838 the couple, accompanied by Jane's younger sister, Julia, were in Pulaski County, MO where Julia met and married A. J. Dodd. About 1842 Alfred and Jane moved to Polk County, bought a tract of land north of present-day Pleasant Hope and established their home. It was there that their six children were born and grew to adulthood.

By 1850, Alfred's brother, Thomas Loftin and half-brother, Merrell D. Lambeth, had settled with their families near Alfred and Jane. At the onset of Civil War, Thomas Loftin and Alfred's son, John, enlisted in the Confederate Army. Another son, Frank, later joined and was killed in 1864. Alfred, crippled and unable to actively serve in the military, supported the Confederacy as evidenced by inclusion of his name on Polk County's List of Rebels. Because his life was threatened numerous times, Alfred, at Jane's urging, left his family and went alone to a relative's home in Arkansas.

In 1863 Alfred and Thomas Loftin, then based in Arkansas, traveled with four friends to southern Missouri for a family visit. While meeting at a predetermined place near Alpena, AR for the return trip, the party was ambushed. Having only one weapon among them, Alfred, Thomas and three of their friends were killed. They were buried in a crude, shallow grave by local women and children near the site of the ambush.

In Polk County Jane and her children did not escape the ravages of the Civil War. During a terror-filled night, they were forced from their home at gunpoint and watched as the house was ransacked and burned to the ground by bushwhackers. Afterward, Jane and the children went to a home for widows and orphans near Pleasant Hope where they remained until the close of the war.

When her son, John, returned from the war, Jane and family moved back to the farm and lived in the original, old log cabin that Alfred had built when they first came to Polk County. About 1874 she married Albert G. Byrd of Webster County and moved to his place near Marshfield where she remained until her death on Feb. 26, 1899. She is buried in Pleasant Hill Cemetery near the Byrd family home.

Zuretha Jane (Perry) Loftin circa 1890

Six children of record were born to Alfred and Jane Loftin:

John Thomas (1844–1905) married Minerva E. Viles (1857-1942), a daughter of Charles W. Murray and Joanner Mallard and stepdaughter of Henry B. Viles. They are buried in Viles Cemetery near Pleasant Hope.

Benjamin Franklin (1846-1864) died unmarried.

Mary Elizabeth (1849-1907) married first, Alfred Davidson and second, Joseph C. Julien and lived in Marshfield, MO.

Samantha (1852-1920) married Timothy C. Freeman (1843-1921), a son of William Freeman and Nancy Walling. They settled in Berryville, Carroll County, AR.

Atha (1855-1912) married George Allen Stewart (1842-1902), a son of Richard Stewart and Arlinda McCabe. They lived briefly in Chariton

County, MO before settling near Blair, Washington County, NE.

William Bradley (1859-1932) married Dora Isabel McDaniel (1864-1947), a daughter of John Pemberton McDaniel and Susan Catherine Russell. They lived near Marshfield, Webster County, MO several years, then settled near Thornfield, Ozark County, MO. *Submitted by Carol Loftin Peek*

PERRYMAN – Jacob and Margaret Knight Perryman came to Missouri in what was then Polk County with seven of their eight children from Tennessee. He was born in North Carolina to Isaac and Margaret Perryman in 1780 and was married in 1798. His children, Benjamin Franklin, Sarah, James Henry, Elizabeth F., Jacob Green, Thomas Knight and Willis. Absolom and Sarah Perryman remained in Tennessee with their families.

Jacob (Perriman) Perryman was one of the settlers of Cass Township, in Greene County, MO. He died in Polk County, near Brighton, MO in 1848 and his wife Margaret moved in with her daughter, Elizabeth and Williamson Johnson and their 12 children in Looney Township, Polk County. She was born in North Carolina in 1778 to Thomas Knight and Elizabeth Simpson and died about 1851. She may be buried in Greene County. Benjamin F. and Sarah Wood Perryman lived in Boone Township with their 11 children: John G., Margaret Jane, Louisiana Rosana, Martha E., Thomas Jefferson, Jacob Green, Owen Wood, Owen Franklin, Sarah Malissa, James M., William, Benjamin Franklin. Benjamin F. was born in 1799 in Tennessee and died in 1847 in Greene County, MO. He married Sarah Wood in 1820, the daughter of Owen Wood. She was born in Virginia and died Feb. 28, 1856 in Greene County, MO. Their son John G., born Dec. 13, 1821 in Rutherford County, TN, married Mary Lemmon on Aug. 10, 1848. She was born Dec. 7, 1830 in Missouri to Jacob and Mary Lemmon and died Nov. 6, 1860, buried in Cave Springs Cemetery in Cass Township, Greene County, MO. Their children were William C., Jacob Lemmon, Owen Wood, Sarah Susan, Amanda Jane and James G. His second wife was Cassandra Nancy Grishman, daughter of Joseph Van Grishman, born in Tennessee on May 2, 1835 and died March 22, 1919 in Springfield, MO. Cassie and John G. are buried in Ash Grove Cemetery. Their children were John B., Mary Louise, Burton T., Nancy E., Emma Josephine, Lura L., George W. and Walter L. Emma Josephine, born Nov. 22, 1870 and Aaron Miller Ritter married on Dec. 4, 1902 in Springfield, Greene County, MO. Their children: Miller Perryman and William Howard. Aaron was born May 25, 1834 in Indiana to Jacob Ritter and Elizabeth Miller and died Aug. 2, 1923. Emma died Sept. 7, 1921, buried in Clear Creek Cemetery in Greene County, MO. Miller Perryman Ritter, born Sept. 3, 1903, died Aug. 6, 1969, was born in Greene County, MO and married Anna Mae Crane on Feb. 27, 1933 in Liberal, KS, daughter of Raymond Leslie Crane and Estella Viola Fox. She was born March 7, 1915 in Sitka, Clark County, KS. Their children were Dolores Jean, William Aaron, Wanda Marie, John Raymond and Warren Miller. Miller was a mechanic and his family lived in Ashland, Clark County, KS. He died in Ft. Dodge, Ford County, KS and is buried in Ashland Highland Cemetery, Clark County, KS. Dolores Jean was born Sept. 22, 1933 in Sitka, Clark County, KS. She married Robert Eugene Appleby on March 5, 1951 in Greensburg, KS, son of Roy Sneed Appleby and Iona Mae Jarvis. He was born Oct 18, 1930 in Ashland, Clark County, KS and died Sept. 14, 1973, Springfield, MO. Robert was a carpenter and a member of the Christian Church. He is buried in Crestview Memorial Gardens, Bolivar, Polk County, MO. Their children: Teresa Susan, Robert Roy and Dana Jean. Her second husband is Frank Thomas Dickerson. Teresa Susan, born July 22, 1952, married Danny Barker, son of William Dwight Barker and Mary Ethel Pridgen. Danny was born Oct. 16, 1951, married July 2, 1971. Their children: Travis Aaron, March 1, 1972, Missouri, Daniel Curtis, Nov. 9, 1979, Missouri, William Robert, Jan. 13, 1981, Missouri. Daniel (Curtis) married Heather Jo Shadwick on Oct. 17, 1998, one child: Peyton Daniel, April 19, 1999, Missouri. Robert Roy Appleby, born June 24, 1955 in Meade, Meade County, KS, married Lavonne Deane Marllette, daughter of Arnold Marllette and Christelle English. She was born July 12, 1956 in Arizona, children: Rachael Lea, Dec. 10, 1983, Missouri; Joshua Thomas, April 14, 1986, Arizona; Rebekah Anne, June 7, 1989, Georgia. Dana Jean Appleby, born Sept. 25, 1963 in Missouri, married David Lawayne Peak on June 8, 1988 in Arkansas, son of Roy Peak and Glenda Bodenhamer. He was born June 14, 1966 in Arizona. Children: Megan Mae, March 8, 1986, Missouri and Nicholas David, May 30, 1989, Missouri. *Submitted by Dana Peak*

PETERSON - John Peterson was born March 23, 1788 in Egg Harbor, NJ. His parents were George Peterson and Judith Horn. John married Sophia Goforth, who was born May 13, 1794 in Burlington, NJ. She was the daughter of Samuel Goforth and Mary Brown. Mary Brown was the daughter of Revolutionary War soldier Henry Brown. The family moved to Williamsburg Town, Clermont County, OH. The History of Clermont County notes that "after 1830 the bears became scarce, only a few remaining in their old haunts. The last one was killed by John Peterson, a hunter of skill and daring. He was returning to his home on a moonlight evening when he saw a large, black object sitting in the road not far from his house. He called his dogs and they came at once and had a lively tussle with the bear, which escaped across the East Fork. Nothing more was seen or heard of the animal until the fall of the following year when Mr. Peterson was hunting wild turkeys in the Elklick Hills when his dogs started up a bear which made a sudden attack on the hunter. He aimed at him, but his rifle misfired and to escape the onslaught of the dogs, the bear ran up a tree. Again Peterson fired, wounding the animal, which slid down the tree and attacked him. The dogs fought him off and Bruin once more escaped. About a year later the tracks of a bear were seen, and a party of men was organized to hunt him down. An exciting chase followed for five or six miles when the bear was killed by Mr. Peterson who saw from the marks it bore that it was the same animal that he had tried to kill on two previous occasions."

The children of John and Sophia were Jesse, Samuel G., George A., Sarah, Mary and Elizabeth. Jesse Richard was born Feb. 18, 1825 in Ohio and departed this life on March 27, 1900. He is buried at Schofield, MO. He was married to Elizabeth Jane Kain on June 19, 1851. She was born in Ohio Feb. 6, 1834 and died Aug. 27, 1913. She is buried beside her husband in Schofield, MO. Jesse and Elizabeth were Lou's great-grandparents. They moved from Ohio or Illinois to Halfway, MO by 1880 as they were enumerated on the census for the county. They were parents of nine children: William Randolph, Tiffin, Clara Belle, John, Sophia Jane, Mary Hester, Elizabeth, Thomas and Richard. Lou descends through Thomas Peterson. He was born Sept. 30, 1869 in Clark County, IL. He married Matilda Jane Snodgrass on Oct. 27, 1892 at her family's home in Schofield, MO. She was born Sept. 13, 1870 in Dallas County. They were the parents of Marvin Levitt, Ethel Gertrude, Nellie Jane, William Ralph, Clifford Thomas and Harrold Richard. Thomas and Matilda moved to Indian Territory in 1903 near Olustee, OK. The original sale bill lists the following property to-wit: two mares in fold, three cows, two three-year-old heifers, three calves, two brood sows, two fat hogs, six shoats, some hay, some corn, about 25 bushels of wheat and oats, farming implements, wagon and hack, one Deering reaper, and household and kitchen furniture. Terms—a credit of 12 months will be given on sums over five dollars, without interest if paid when due, otherwise to draw eight percent interest from date. Sums of $5.00 and under cash. Purchaser required to give bankable note before removing property. Six percent discount for cash over $5.00.

Thomas Peterson Family

Lou's grandmother Matilda Jane sewed $200.00, resulting from the sale, into the staves of her corset because she was fearful of being robbed on the train that took them into Oklahoma. Harrold Richard Peterson, born Nov. 12, 1910 in Oluste, OK was Lou's father. On Jan. 6, 1932 he married Lucille Castle, who was born Sept. 22, 1910 at Pecan Gap, TX. She was the daughter of George Thomas and Hattie Lee Mann Castle. To this union were born a daughter, Lou Thelen and a son, Dwight Harrold Peterson. Lou Thelen married Ronald Nuburn Kemp on Aug. 3, 1957. They had three sons, Ronald, Hal and Wesley. Dwight was born Dec. 7, 1937 in his Aunt Ethel's home in Altus, OK. On Nov. 27, 1958 he married Janis Marie Stoup, who was born Jan. 12, 1942. To this union were born a daughter, Debora Dawn on Jan. 22, 1960 and a son, Donald Wayne Peterson on Oct. 25, 1963. *Submitted by Lou Kemp*

Jessie (Moore) Phillips, Burl E. Phillips

PHILLIPS - Jessie Phillips was born on the Moore family farm west of Huron, MO on Feb. 12, 1908. Jessie was born on her grandmother Julia Hutcheson's birthday and she had a grandson, Sam Phillips, born on her birthday, thus covering a period from 1857 to 1979. Jessie was the oldest child of Joe and Sallie Hutcheson Moore; both from pioneer families of Polk County, MO. Jessie lived in Hickory County, MO in the Pleasant View Community. Her family moved to Polk County and Jessie went to high school at Bolivar. Jessie's class of 1926 was the last class to graduate from the North Ward School building. She drove a horse and buggy to town every day to high school. After high school, she taught school. She then attended Southwest Baptist College and graduated in 1929. Jessie then worked at the Polk County Courthouse from 1929 to 1939 in the circuit clerk's office as deputy Circuit Clerk. She then worked in Springfield at the MFA Milling Company office.

On April 7, 1942 Jessie married Burl Phillips of Bear Creek of Cedar County. Burl was born in Bear Creek or Paynterville on July 22, 1910. Burl's father was Noah P. Phillips and his mother was Leila R. Ahart Phillips. Both of Burl's granddads were Union veterans of the Civil War. Burl's family on both sides had come to Missouri from East Tennessee.

Two weeks after their marriage, Burl entered the US Army at St. Louis, MO. He trained at Camp Chaffee in Arkansas and then left the county in November of 1942 and after 19 days landed at Casablanca, Morocco in North Africa. Burl then went to Italy and he was sent back to the US and was in England and later crossed Europe into Germany, meeting the Russian Army at the Elbe River.

Jessie and Burl's first son, Joe Burl, was born on March 17, 1943 in Springfield, MO. Joe went to school at Bear Creek and Stockton and received a BS degree from Southwest Missouri State College and a law degree from the University of Missouri at Kansas City. He married Carol Sims of Stockton and they have three children: Bron, Tondra and Bren. Joe is a lawyer and at present, Associate Circuit Judge of Cedar County, MO.

After the war, Burl and Jessie lived in Springfield for five years. On Dec. 22, 1948, their second son, Robert Harold Phillips, was born at the old St. John's Hospital. They moved to Bear Creek in 1951 to the family farm. Bob went to Bear Creek grade school and Stockton High School and went to the University of Missouri at Columbia. He graduated in 1971 with a BS in agriculture. Bob has farmed since 1972. Bob married Julia Hammond of Fayette, MO on Nov. 14, 1976. They have lived at Bear Creek since that time. Julia is a registered nurse and has worked at Cedar County Memorial Hospital since 1977.

Bob and Julia have three children, Samuel Robert, James Edwin and Carrie Phillips. Sam works at T&M Stone near Aldrich, MO. Jim is a junior at SMSU. Carrie is a freshman at SMSU. All the children were active in 4-H and FFA in school. Jessie passed away on Feb. 4, 2002, eight days short of her 93rd birthday. Burl is still at home near Bear Creek, just a few hundred feet from the old, one-room school he attended as a kid. *Submitted by Carrie Phillips*

PHILLIPS - Mathis Phillips was the fourth child of Jacob Phillips and Jane Miller Phillips. He was born in Roane County, TN on Feb. 12, 1831. He came to Missouri with his parents and siblings in the fall of 1846. Mathis' parents settled in Bear Creek, Cedar County, MO.

In approximately 1849, Mathis headed for the California gold fields. Family history tells us he joined up with a member of a wagon train, apparently in the Westport, MO area, who agreed to haul his back pack if Mathis would assist the wagon master, but he would have to walk as it was necessary to keep weight to a minimum and walk he did.

Mathis kept a notebook with almost daily entries on his journey over the Oregon-California trail, but the record of the trip west and most of the time spent in California has been lost. Copies of his notes from May 1853 until his arrival home are in the possession of some of the family members. He often made daily entries of his gold dust and nuggets. It appears he may have had his findings assayed and stored every night. His daily entries varied from 0 to as high as $98.00. The average amount of dollars he recorded was much lower than the top figure. Something must have discouraged his prospecting as he apparently went to work for the mine operation at $5.00 to $6.00 per day before he decided to return to Missouri.

Mathis left the gold camp at Rough and Ready, CA on Sept. 29, 1853. On Oct. 1, he was in Sacramento where he bought "a ticket" for $100.00. This must have been for a passage to Panama as he took a riverboat to San Francisco, then a ship down the coast. We see that he docked in Acapulco, Mexico on Oct. 11 and went ashore. On Oct. 16, he landed in Panama. An entry was made on October 19, stating, "Set sail for New Orleans." No mention was made as to how he crossed the Isthmus of Panama, but it is presumed he walked, as that would only be a short hike for a man who had walked from Missouri to California. On October 28, he logged his arrival at New Orleans where he transferred to a riverboat and arrived in St. Louis, MO on November 6. He was back home by Nov. 20, 1853.

Mathis Phillips

On Sept. 11, 1855, Mathis Phillips married Martha Simmons. Martha was the daughter of John and Elizabeth Smith Simmons. He obtained land south of Bear Creek and established a prosperous, well-improved farming operation. Mathis and Martha had six children. They were Mary Phillips Galyan, Uriah Phillips, Margaret Elizabeth Phillips Ray, Connaway Phillips, Laurinda Phillips Morgan and Martha M. Phillips Baker.

Tragedy struck the family on Nov. 29, 1866 when Martha died. Martha's sister Victoria Carolina Simmons began helping Mathis care for the children. About one year later, on Dec. 3, 1867, Mathis married Martha's sister, Vickie. However, Mathis' children always knew her as Aunt Caroline. Mathis and Caroline did have one daughter, Sarah Florence, born in 1868, but she passed away on 1870.

From all the family stories of Mathis, he must have been a very outspoken individual who was not afraid to speak his mind and give his opinion. He has the honor of being the only person in Cedar County's Madison Township who voted for Abraham Lincoln in 1860. His was one of the four votes in the county. It should be said that Lincoln received every vote cast in the county four years later.

Mathis and Martha have several descendants today still living in Cedar and Polk Counties. *Submitted by Gary Nickels*

PICKERING – Jonathan Pickering, born Nov. 5, 1809 in Greene County, TN, and Rebecca Thompson, born April 10, 1812 in Tennessee, were married on Sept. 2, 1830 in Tennessee. Their parents were Enos and Elizabeth (Harrold) Pickering and James and Catherine Thompson. They had eight children, three born in Tennessee and the rest in Polk County, MO. They moved in 1839 to Polk County, along with several other families. Rebecca died June 27, 1862 and was buried at Salem Cemetery. Jonathan was remarried to Mrs. Margaret Ann (Ladd) Phillips on April 7, 1863 in Polk County. They had three children together. Jonathan died Nov. 10, 1874 in Polk County and was buried at Salem Cemetery near both of his wives.

Enos Pickering, born Feb. 24, 1833, married Mary Elizabeth Devin on Feb. 23, 1854 in Polk County. They had four children: Martha Ann, Margaret Isabelle, Mary Frances and James Alexander. Enos, a Civil War veteran, died April 8, 1928 in Polk County; buried at Salem Cemetery.

Elisabeth (Bettie) Pickering, born Aug. 10, 1835, married James B. Hicks on April 20, 1854 in Polk County. They had nine children: Sarah J., Rebecca, Nancy Ann, Mary C. (died at age 1), Amanda M., John F., Hiram T. (died at age 7 months), Margaret E. and Laura O. Elisabeth died May 13, 1884 in Polk County; buried in Salem Cemetery.

Cathrine Pickering, born Feb. 14, 1836, married David Alexander Henson on Aug. 12, 1854 in Polk County. They had eight or nine children: Sarah O., William H., James Leonard, John B., Rebecca J., Mary E, Hiram Milton, Fred C., and Ora V. (Ora may have been a granddaughter instead of a daughter to Cathrine and David.) Cathrine died Dec. 3, 1908 in Polk County; buried at Salem Cemetery.

Mariah Pickering, born May 12, 1840, married first, Francis Marion Morrow on Jan. 21, 1858 in Polk County. They had two children, Lucy Ruth and Rebecca Ann. Francis died during the Civil War and Mariah married Joseph Byers Morrow on July 24, 1862 in Polk County. (Joseph is not known to be related to Francis Morrow.) Joseph and Mariah had one son, Thomas Sherman. Mariah was living in Webster County, MO in 1874 when her father died.

John Pickering was born between 1845 and 1848. He was living in Arkansas in 1874 when his father died.

Hiram Pickering was born about 1849. He was living in Webster County in 1874 when his father died.

Rebecca Jane Pickering, born April 11, 1852, married George W. Jones on Nov. 26, 1871 in Polk County. They had nine children: Ida Francis, Della May, Isaac Nelson, Lewis Oscar, Will, Rebecca Christina B., James A., Agnes and George Everett. Rebecca died Jan. 17, 1912 in Polk County; buried at Salem Cemetery.

Johnathan T. Pickering, born 1857, married Margaret Tennessee Holmes on Nov. 7, 1878 in Polk County. They had six children: Sarah Elizabeth, John Henry, Minnie, Harley B., James M. and Hiram W. Johnathan died in 1945 in Polk County; buried at Dunnegan Cemetery.

William Francis Pickering, born May 24, 1864, married Mary Ashlock on April 6, 1884 in Polk County. They had five children: Obediah, Martha, Ellen, Jim and Carl.

Mary Caroline Pickering, born Dec. 26, 1886, married Thomas M.S. Mead on Feb. 27, 1881 in Polk County. They had two children.

Margaret Isabel Pickering, born Jan. 6, 1868, married John Thomas Forgey on Aug. 5, 1883 in Polk County. They had five children: Alonzo M., Grace, George Nelson, Homer Conway (a WWI soldier, died overseas in 1919) and Jessie May (died at age 4). Margaret died Nov. 20, 1961 in Polk County; buried at Salem Cemetery.

PICKERING – Enos Pickering, born Feb. 24, 1833 near Rheatown, Greene County, TN, and Mary Elizabeth Devin, born April 23, 1832 in Pike County, MO, were married Feb. 23, 1854 in Polk County. They settled near Cliquot and had four children, all born in Polk County. Enos served in the Civil War (Union Army). Mary died Sept. 18, 1909 in Polk County; buried at Salem Cemetery. Enos died April 8, 1928 in Polk County (age 95) and was also buried at Salem.

Enos and Mary Pickering, circa 1905-1909

Martha Ann Pickering, born Nov. 1, 1858, married Samuel Harden Meade on April 22, 1877 in Polk County. They had two children. Margaret Eliza Meade (March 23, 1878 – June 12, 1966, buried Salem Cemetery) married first, Sylvester Wisdom in 1916 and then second, Alonzo Miles Burnum on Sept. 21, 1939. Margaret did not have any children. Nelson Ebenezer Meade (Oct. 29, 1879 – July 5, 1976, Bakersfield, CA) married Edith Nora Weese in 1911 or 1912. They had one son, Carl Samuel Meade. Martha died Aug. 10, 1947 in Bolivar; buried at Salem Cemetery.

Margaret Isabelle "Belle" Pickering, born March 23, 1861, married first, Nathan P. White on May 1, 1879 in Polk County. They had one son, James Robert White (Feb. 25, 1880 – Dec. 10, 1918, buried Belle Plaine Cemetery, Sumner County, KS) who married Iva Leah Markle on May 27, 1901 in Polk County. They had four children: Junior Bert, James Shelby, Isabelle Lucille and Kenneth Olin White. Margaret married second, John Lewis Ables on Dec. 14, 1890 in Polk County. They had four children. Mary Alma Ables (Dec. 5, 1891 – July 3, 1973, buried Greenwood Cemetery) married first, Hiram James Henson on Nov. 20, 1910 in Polk County and had six children: Maggie Mae, Neta Wilma, Wauneta Faye, Emma Lorene, Oren Stanley and Thelma Jewell. Alma married second, Grant DeWitt on May 19, 1945 in Polk County. Bertha Annis Ables (Dec. 25, 1896 – Nov. 10, 1976, buried Salem Cemetery) married Charles Alvin Lawson on Feb. 10, 1915 in Polk County and had five children: Harold Raymond, Bernice Isabel, Opal Marie, Hazel Annis and Lois Jean (died at age 5). Otto Francis Ables (Sept. 6, 1901 – July 1, 1966, buried Sunny Slopes Cemetery, Corona, CA) married Lena Davison on Aug. 31, 1926 in Polk County and had three children: Wilma Jean, Shirley Marie and John Hamilton. Martha Pearlee Ables (July 2, 1904 – May 4, 1955, buried Glendale Cemetery, Louisville, NE) married Charley Devin Hammons on Jan. 24, 1923 in Polk County and had five children: Margaret Mabel, Maurice Bernard, Mary Louise, Charles Robert and John Myron. Belle Ables died Jan. 16, 1941 in Cliquot and is buried at Salem Cemetery.

Mary Frances Pickering, born Jan. 6, 1863, married first, John W. Knightly in 1886 in Missouri. They had three children: Mary F. Knightly (1887-1890), Bertha Knightly (1890-1892) and William John Knightly (Jan. 17, 1893 – Jan. 25, 1951, buried Calvary Cemetery, Wichita, KS). William John married Mary C. Roach and had three children: William John Jr., Mary Demontfort and a daughter (first name unknown), wife of Jack Farrell. Mary Frances married second, Ellsworth Hatfield in 1906 (no children). Mary died July 1, 1920, likely in Wichita, KS.

James Alexander Pickering, born Feb. 18, 1870, married Sarah Agnes Lyons on March 26, 1889 in Polk County. They had four children. William Thomas Pickering (April 20, 1890 – April 21, 1890, buried Salem Cemetery) was the oldest. George Washington Pickering (July 21, 1891 – Dec. 31, 1960, Kansas City, MO) married first, Marie Blanchard in 1915 and then second, Freida Poe in 1941. Martha Elizabeth Pickering (Jan. 14, 1896 – Aug. 27, 1972, buried Salem Cemetery) married John Payton Jr. on Sept. 1, 1917 in Polk County. They had one son, Willard Gordon Payton. James Albert Pickering (April 12, 1902 – June 5, 1988, Merced County, CA) married Thelma Daughtery on Feb. 21, 1929. They had one son, Robert George Pickering. James Alexander died Nov. 25, 1943 in Cliquot and was buried in Salem Cemetery.

PILCHER – Bartlett Burk (Aug. 30, 1867-Feb. 15, 1957) and Amanda Virginia Butler Pilcher (Oct. 12, 1879-Jan. 13, 1962) moved to Polk County from Gallatin, MO in the early 1900s. They reared five children—Anna "Mae," Thomas "Shelby," Gracie Ellen "Grace," Orville Estes "Mike" and Mary Elizabeth "Lizzie" and helped rear two grandchildren—Mike's children, Jimmy and Rosetta Pilcher.

There is a photograph available of Bart Pilcher's parents, but their names are unknown to the family. Amanda's father was James Monroe Butler, possibly a Native American, and her mother was Mary Hammond Butler. There were several Butler brothers and sisters. Both of these families lived in north Missouri near Gallatin.

Mae (Aug. 19, 1899-Feb. 21, 1992) married Ord Alroy Kinsey. Their children were Virginia Mae, James Woodrow, Thomas Shelby, Don Richard and Max Raymond.

Shelby Pilcher (Dec. 15, 1901- April 26, 1986) never married. He spent his life in Polk County, most of the time living in the family home.

Grace was born Jan. 27, 1904 and died in Arkansas in the 1990s. She married William Henry Moore and lived in Missouri and Oklahoma. Their daughter was Viola Mae "Vicki."

Mike (Jan. 23, 1906-April 7, 1975) married Viola Johnson and they had two children, Jimmy and Rosetta. Several years after Viola died, Mike married Stella Thornton and they had a daughter, Liebe Michael.

Front - Shelby, Mike, Grace and Mae
Back – Bart and Amanda Pilcher with baby Mary "Lizzie"

Lizzie, or Mary, as she preferred to be called (May 7, 1908-March 21, 1992), married George Triggs. Their children were Fern Amanda and Floyd William. Lizzie and George were divorced and later she married Andrew Clift. Children from this marriage were Leora Joetta and Velda Joan.

Most of the third-generation Pilcher family moved from Polk County.

Virginia Mae Kinsey (deceased).

Woodrow Kinsey married Ernestine Stewart and remains in Bolivar.

Tom Kinsey married Uarda Lee Wahlborg, lived in Greene County and is retired in Taney County, MO.

Don Kinsey married Nancy Davis and lives in St. Louis, MO.

Max (deceased) married Sue Simmons (deceased) and lived in Missouri and Chicago, IL.

Vicki Moore married Robert Smith and has lived in California and Oregon.

Jimmy Pilcher (deceased) married Janet Cooper (deceased) and lived in Kansas City, KS.

Rosetta Pilcher (deceased) was married to and divorced from Gale Goodman and lived in Springfield, MO.

Leibe Pilcher, married to Jimmy Carter, lives in Oklahoma.

Fern Triggs married Curt Kauffman and lives in Humansville, MO.

Floyd Triggs (deceased) married Lorraine Barrett and lived in Texas.

Joetta Clift, married to Reuben Leatherman, lives in Arkansas.

Joan Clift married Maurice Herie (deceased) and lives in California.

There are 34 great-grandchildren and numerous great-great-grandchildren.

Bart and Amanda Pilcher, Shelby Pilcher, Viola Johnson Pilcher, Jimmy Pilcher, Mae and Ordy Kinsey, Virginia Mae Kinsey, Kim Kinsey and an infant son of Max and Sue Kinsey are buried in Payne Cemetery, Polk, MO.

Grace Pilcher Moore, Bill Moore, Rosetta Pilcher Goodman, Max Kinsey and Sue Simmons Kinsey are buried in Greenwood Cemetery, Bolivar, MO.

Mike Pilcher and Stella Thornton Pilcher are buried near Halltown, MO; Mary Elizabeth and Andrew Clift are buried near Harwood, MO. *Submitted by Tom Kinsey*

PIPER – John Lewis Piper was born April 21, 1842 in Scott County, IL. His parents were James Piper and Harriett (Little). John Piper married Biddy Ann (Peak) in Hancock County, IL in 1866.

John and Biddy Ann were Stephanie's second great-grandparents. They homesteaded 160 acres in Polk County, MO in 1877. John and Biddy Ann had eight children. These children were Alfred, George, Charles, James Edward, Isaac Walter, Lee Etta, Luther and Sydney. John and Biddy Ann are buried in Payne Cemetery in Polk County.

Stephanie's great-grandfather, Isaac Walter Piper, married Ruby Dell (McBride) in 1900. They had nine children: Marie, Mildred, Willard, Russell, Vera, Harold, Bernard, Marjorie and Roger. All of these children except Marie were born in Polk County.

Marie Swanee Piper never married and was a school teacher all of her adult life.

Mildred Piper married Homer Platt. They were both school teachers by profession. They went to Canada where they homesteaded a farm, eventually coming back to Polk County. They didn't have any children.

Willard Piper married Eva (Fisher) and they had the first grandchild of Isaac and Ruby Dell Piper. His name is Quinton Piper.

Russell Piper married Ida (Bowen) and they had one son, Leland. Both Leland and his mother are currently residing in Polk County.

Vera Piper married John Livezey and they moved their family to Oregon. Their children were Johnnie, Rex and Lauradell.

Harold Piper married Laura Annalee (Allison) and they raised their family in the Polk County area. Their children were Harold Duane, Shirley, Carroll, Donnie and Gaylord. Gaylord and his wife, Lorna, and their children live in the house that first belonged to Marie Piper.

Bernard Piper married Cecil Fern (Miller) and they raised their two sons near Flemington. Cecil is still living and resides in Polk County. Stephanie's father, Kenneth Piper, married Bonnie (Gordon) and has a farm in Hickory and Polk Counties. Stephanie, her husband, Greg Burke

Back row: Harold Piper, Homer Platt, Isaac Walter Piper, Vera Livezey, Willard Piper, Harold Piper, Cecil Piper, Roger Piper
Middle row: Laura Piper holding Donnie Piper, Wanda Piper holding Karen Piper, Russell Piper holding Leland, John Livezey holding Clayton Piper, Ida Piper, Marjorie Potter, Bernard Piper, Quinton Piper.
Sitting: Carroll Piper, Shirley Piper, Max Potter, Rex Livezey, Harold Duane Piper, Kenneth Piper, Johnny Livezey.

and her son, Garrett, live in Kansas. Her sister, Kim and her daughter, McKenna live in Iowa. Kenneth's son, Kevin, and his wife, Nancy (Whitney) live in the house that Bernard and Cecil had built north of Flemington. Stephanie's uncle, Clayton Lee Piper, preceded his father, Bernard, in death.

Marjorie Piper married Harold Potter and they had one son, David Max Potter. Marjorie is the only living child of Isaac and Ruby Dell (McBride).

Roger Efton Piper married LaWanda (Bullington) and they raised their children on the land that was homesteaded by part of the Piper family. Their children are Karen, Sharon and Efton. Wanda still owns the farm in Polk County.

Isaac and Ruby Dell (McBride) Piper and their children, except Vera (Piper) Livezey, are buried in Flemington Cemetery in Polk County.

Beginning with Stephanie's second great-grandparents and descending to her child the family has had six generations living all or part of their lives in Polk County, MO. *Submitted by Stephanie Piper Burke*

PITTS – Cecil Otto Pitts was born on May 23, 1919 in Benton County, MO. He was the second child of Clarence "Jack" and Pearl Pitts and one of eight boys and one girl. The family moved to an area near Rimby in 1924, where the children attended Star Ridge School. After a few years, they moved to Kansas.

In the 1930s Cecil moved back to a Polk County farm near Rimby to live with and help an older uncle. It was during this time he became interested in a neighbor girl, whom he later married.

Times were hard and jobs were scarce in the '30s. Cecil joined the US Navy in January 1940. By the time of the bombing of Pearl Harbor, Cecil had been assigned to a ship as a boatswain mate. His ship had been in Pearl Harbor, but he was being transferred to a ship on the East Coast and was at sea in December 1941. Almost all of his six years of enlistment was spent aboard ship in the Pacific.

In November 1943, Cecil had a short leave and he and Ava Payne were married. Ava was teaching at Cole Camp, MO and she returned to her job and Cecil went back to his ship a few days after their wedding. Letters were often delayed and lines in them censored for national security. Those were anxious days as loved ones waited for news of their men in the service.

In March 1946, after six years and three months, Cecil was honorably discharged from the US Navy. He had attained the rank of Chief Warrant Officer. Cecil and Ava bought a farm in the same area where Ava's family had lived. Three daughters were born: Mary Linda in 1947, Grace Anna in 1949 and Sara Ruth in 1952.

Cecil was very community minded. He served on many boards. He spent 26 years on the Bolivar School Board. He was a faithful deacon of Louisburg Baptist Church. He was the presiding judge of Polk County for two terms, and at the time of his death, he was serving as chief appraiser for the Polk County Equalization office.

Cecil died in April 1985 and is buried in the Payne Cemetery near Polk, MO. *Submitted by Sara Ruth (Pitts) Shadwick*

Cecil Otto Pitts

This poem was written by Patty Fly Peavy in 1998 about her days at Pleasant Hope School.
Oh how I'd like to walk those halls
    I walked so long ago,
from class to class where I would learn
    to face the world as so.
We'd start each day with pledge and prayer,
    And learn of loyalty
And respect of others also there,
    The best in each to see.
While whispering in class one day
A hand gently rested upon my head.
    It belong to Mr. Tillery,
    Not a word was said.
He called me "Pollyanna"
    And had to tell me why.
This would be remembered
in many days gone by.
Miss Miller spoke of "horse sense"
We should not forget to use
With what we learned from books at school,
    Along the path we'd choose.
We had no fear of guns and harm,
    As scholars do today.
What happened to that golden rule
    Learned the old-fashioned way?
Pleasant Hope…My School!
There's a message in the name.
May others passing through it's doors,
    Attest to it's acclaim.
Submitted by Patty Fly, 1998

POLODNA – Frank John Polodna was born Dec. 5, 1876 in Prairie du Chien, WI. Frank's parents, Joseph and Anna Kozelka Poledna, immigrated from Kucer, Bohemia in 1865. Maria (Mary) Sophia Lanka was born to Joseph and Rosalia Cejka Lanka in Prairie du Chien on May 1, 1878. Frank and Mary married on Jan. 10, 1898. After the birth of their fifth child, Frank, Mary, the children and widower Joseph Poledna moved to Polk County, MO in the summer of 1909. In Karlin they purchased a 40-acre farm and settled into a small, one-room log cabin. Stray cat in the area became a nuisance so Frank eliminated the problem. One evening Mary placed her shoes under the bed and retired. To her dismay in the morning, she found her shoes had been destroyed by mice. Within a year Frank built a sturdy, two-story home which no doubt helped reduce the mouse problem. Their home is still standing.

While living in Karlin the Polodnas had six more children. The primary language spoken in the family was Bohemian. The Polodnas were members of the St. Wenceslaus Catholic Church. With hard work the farm grew to 160 acres and they built a home and added a dairy. Ten of their 11 children grew to adulthood.

Lawrence Thomas, born Dec. 30, 1898, married Alma Jarman;

Andrew Joseph, born Oct. 30, 1900, married Caroline Petronilla Novak;

Emma Christine, born Oct. 23, 1902, married Forrest Sterling Davis;

Leo Frank, born, Oct. 18, 1904;

Bessie Catherine, born, Nov. 25, 1906;

Frank John Jr., born June 3, 1909, married first, Catherine Lehar, married second, Jessie Ables Johnson;

Caroline Mary, born Nov. 8, 1910, married Lewey Raymond Elbert;

Louis Matt, born April 21, 1913, married Christine Lehar;

Lucy Julia, born May 21, 1916, married Edward Hejna;

John Alfred, born Aug. 17, 1919, married Evelyn Marie Elkins;

Dorothy Alice, born Jan. 8, 1924, died Oct. 17, 1938.

Wedding Day; Jan. 10, 1898, Frank John Polodna and Maria (Mary) Sophia Lanka

On Jan. 1, 1919, Lawrence Thomas Polodna, the eldest son of Frank and Mary, married Alma Jarman, daughter of William Washington and Mary Frances Spears Jarman. From this union seven children were born:

Hollis Lawrence, born March 17, 1920, married first, Anna Belle Ward, second, Sue Tecklin Brown;

Forrest Franklin, born Aug. 7, 1921, married Betty Ann Kennemer;

Helen Frances, born Sept. 19, 1923, married Forrest Allen Flynn;

Eugene Robert, born March 27, 1926, married first, Barbara A. Forrest, married second, Dolores Ann Gifford, third, Linda Marie Blocking;

Leo Thomas, born and died May 16, 1928;

Eva Joan, born May 27, 1931, married Richard Krtek;

Anna Marie, born Oct. 9, 1938, married Donald George Jackett.

Lawrence worked as a carpenter, nurseryman, and as a employee of Maas Ice Cream. He was a hard worker and built the family home in Bolivar with oak lumber since it was the most affordable at the time. Due to the wood being so hard, Lawrence had to hand drill a hole for each nail. Alma enjoyed music. When she heard a song she could in turn play the piece on the piano even though she had never had piano lessons and could not read music.

We, the descendants of Joseph and Anna Polodna and Joseph and Rosalia Lanka, are thankful for our ancestors' strength of character. Leaving behind their lives in Bohemia and setting sail for a new country took great courage. We are thankful to them for the blessing of freedom. *Submitted by Betty A. Polodna*

Grandpa with Garland and Bill; John, Charles, Clara and Florence

POOL – Clara Bell Straw Booth was 27 years old when she married Charles Parker Pool, a 71-year-old Civil War veteran in Fayetteville, AR in 1915. She was the last widow in Missouri to draw a Civil War pension. Clara Bell Straw was born in Polk County on July 24, 1888 to William Jack and Elizabeth (Kettner) Straw and moved to Arkansas early in life. She first married Clyde J. Booth and they had four children: Golda, Glen, Viola and James. Then she married Charles Pool and they then had five more children: Charles Thomas, who died young; Ernest John, born Nov. 10, 1918, who married Allie Peterson; Florence, born Oct. 4, 1922, who married Harry Wilson; William, born Jan. 13, 1925, who married Shirley Courtney; and Garland, born Nov. 4, 1927, who married Robbie Self. After Charles P. Pool died Jan 18, 1933 in Arkansas, Clara and the children all eventually ended up in Polk County, MO.

According to a 1979 BH-FP story, Mrs. Pool did not begin until 1948 drawing the Civil War widow's pension to which she was entitled, though she did receive money for the children. Her widow's pension was held up in enforcement to a law designed to penalize those who married the veterans simply to draw the pension, and once she started to draw it, it was less than $150 per month.

Bill, Florence, Clara, John and Garland Pool

Charles Pool was injured in battle and his left leg was amputated above the knee. He spent the rest of his life on crutches, but Charles was a vigorous, active man well into his 80s. He and the other children tell tales of the elder Mr. Pool striding into the Arkansas Mountains to hunt squirrels and other small animals to feed the family and carrying back the game in the crock of his crutches. There was no Civil War stories or memorabilia in the house. Mr. Pool never spoke of the Civil War. It was a bad memory for him. He wanted it in the past. He had served with Company D, Sixth Regiment in the Virginia Volunteer infantry as a private. At 17 years old he passed for 18 and mustered in and he served for three years. Records of this information were obtained from the Military Service Administration, National Archives, in Washington, DC.

Up until he was 85 he had a beautiful garden. There wasn't a weed in his garden. He kept his pocket full of seed and would stick one in the earth when he saw an empty spot. He would sit down in the garden and scoot backwards, hoeing in front of him.

John, William and Garland Pool (his three sons) all served in WWII.

The home place where Charles and Clara lived and raised their children in Arkansas is now in the Devil's Den State Park. The rock foundation is all that is left. But there is a plank there that says, "This is the Pool home place."

Clara Bell joined Enon church after moving back to Polk County, MO and spent the remaining years of her life living with her children after she was unable to live by herself. After she was about 95, she was taken to Stockton Nursing Home, Stockton, MO and lived the remainder of her life there.

Clara Bell (Straw, Booth) Pool was born in Polk County on July 24, 1888 and died May 8, 1990 at the age of 101 years, 9 months, and 14 days and is buried at Enon Cemetery in Polk County. In 1990 at the time of her death she was survived by 6 surviving children, 37 grandchildren, 100 great-grandchildren, 47 great-great-grandchildren and 6 great-great-great-grandchildren. *Submitted by Charlotte DeBauche*

PORTER – Martin Taylor Porter Jr. and Linda Jo Porter were married in June of 1965. In July of 1976, Martin and Linda Porter moved to Bolivar with their three sons Tony (Brian Anthony), John (John Christopher) and Randy (Martin Randall). The Porters purchased Meador Seed Company from JC and Joan Meador. They later changed the company name to Porter Seed House. It still operates under that name.

The Porters attend First Christian Church in Bolivar. The boys were 2, 7, and 9 when they moved to Bolivar, and were involved in JYF at church, summer sports baseball, mighty mite football, and Tony in scouting. As the boys grew up, they were active in Jr. High and High School athletics. They were all members of the FFA, where Tony served as president his senior year of high school. All three boys were active in teenage Republicans with Tony and John both serving as president. John was a member of the National Honor Society in high school. Tony traveled to Austria and Germany with the concert choir his sophomore year. They all worked at the seed house during their high school and college years.

Martin, in addition to running Porter Seed House, raises cattle on his farm west of Bolivar. He also developed Porter Place Subdivision on the south edge of Bolivar. He was active in the Bolivar Booster Club when the boys were in high school. Martin served terms on the boards of the Sheltered Workshop and the Senate Bill 40. He was an avid quail and pheasant hunter for many years and still enjoys fishing. Martin took the family snow skiing in Colorado each winter while the boys were in school and enjoyed late-summer trips to the lake for water skiing, boating and jet-skiing.

Linda is a lifetime member of the CMH Auxiliary and has been active, over the years, in PTA and PTO. In the early 1980s, she served as president of the Polk County chapter of the American Heart Association where she helped with blood mobiles and other community activities. Linda belongs to the Nu Chi chapter of Beta Sigma Phi, Bolivar 20 Club and is active in Republican politics. She has been on the Republican Central Committee since 1980 and is currently serving as chairwoman. She has been a member of the Republican Women's Club since the late 1970s, served as advisor to the teenage republicans organization and is a Charter member of the Polk County Pachyderm Club.

Tony graduated from Bolivar High School in 1984 and attended SMSU where he graduated in 1988 with a degree in agricultural economics. Tony is a member of the Gamma Beta chapter of Kappa Alpha order. He married Gena Chaney in 1986. They had two children, Austin Taylor Porter, who was born in 1987, and Andrea Marie Porter, who was born in 1989. Tony owned and operated Preferred Commodities, Inc., a commodity futures and options brokerage service, before returning to manage Porter Seed House. He and his family are active at the First Christian Church where Tony serves as an elder and trustee. Tony married Lisha Renee Cloyd in 2002. Lisha has two sons, Dustin and Jared. She is a cosmetologist at Visible Changes in Bolivar. Tony was active in Bolivar Young Farmers, Farm Bureau and Bolivar Rotary Club. Tony is on the Agricultural Advisory Committee for Congressman Roy Blunt.

John graduated from BHS in 1987 and attended SMSU, before transferring to SBU, where he graduated in 1992. He was married to Gina Rose Helton in 1992 and moved to Oklahoma where he attended Oklahoma City University Law School. John graduated law school in 1995. Gina transferred from SBU to Central Oklahoma State University, where she graduated in 1995. They returned to Bolivar, where John was employed by the John Parks Law Firm in Humansville, MO. John then went to work for the Douglas, Lynch, Haun and Kirksey law firm in Bolivar, where he also served as prosecuting attorney for the city of Bolivar. In 1998, John was elected prosecuting attorney for Polk County. In 2002, John was re-elected to that position. Gina teaches English and Spanish at the Buffalo Middle School. John and Gina have two daughters, Abbi (Abbigail Elizabeth), born in 1995, and Alex (Erin Alexis), born in 1998. John and his family are active at the United Methodist Church of Bolivar. John is a member of the Polk County Pachyderm Club. Gina is active in the Genesis Club and the Republican Women's Club.

Randy graduated from BHS in 1992 and attended SBU in Bolivar. He transferred to OTC in Springfield and completed his education at Drury University, where he graduated from the School of Architecture in 1999. He married Tanya Brand in 1996. Tanya graduated from SBU in 1995 and received her MBA from Drury University in 1999. They reside in Bolivar, where Randy is employed by Ed Kurtz of Design Group Architects. Tanya opened TM Clothing Company on the square in Bolivar in 1999. Randy studied in China the summer of 1998. Tanya was able to join him for two weeks. Randy and Tanya worked with the committee that helped get the YMCA in Bolivar. They attend the First Christian Church in Bolivar. Tanya is a member of the Genesis Club, Republican Women's Club, and is on the Board of the Polk County Health Department.

Austin Porter has played baseball through the Legion Program and in the summer sports program. He played mighty mite, middle school and freshman football. He wrestled in the USA youth program. He also wrestled in middle school and is currently involved in the high school program. Austin is an active member of the Bolivar FFA.

Andrea has been active in basketball since her second grade year. Her team went to the AAU 10 and under tournament in Orlando, FL in 2000. She now plays middle school volleyball and basketball. She also played summer sports softball and soccer.

Abbi Porter plays summer sports softball, soccer, and basketball. She plays in the bell choir at the United Methodist Church and has been a member of the girl scouts.

Alex Porter takes ballet lessons and attends the Polk County Christian pre-school. *Submitted by Linda Porter*

POTTS – Bonnie Potts and her mother Florence Herndon have been doing their part from 1995 to about 1999 to save all the stuffed animals they could find in Polk County. They may not be saving endangered species, but they travel from garage sale to garage sale, saving the animals, by buying up all the teddy bears, bunny rabbits, elephants and whatever else they can find available. Eventually, the animals find homes with children in Old Mexico, delivered by Don Tuter, a missionary to that country. He comes to Bolivar twice a year to collect clothing, food, tools and toys. "He just takes everything." Potts said, "One year he suggested we collect stuffed animals." So they started hitting the garage sales. They started out buying them for 25 cents apiece and they thought that was good. Then they started asking "How about if we give you 10 cents apiece" now they go on the second day and say, "What will you let us take them off your hands for?" The animals go from garage sale to Florence's house. She washes them and repairs them, putting on new eyes, restuffing, sewing up rips in seams and adding new ribbons. Once Florence has finished her part, Bonnie inspects them to see what else they might need.

The two worked on this special project for four or five years starting about 1995. The garage sale season starts in April and the two hit the road the whole summer and then spend the necessary time it takes to repair and to stuff all the animals. In 1996 they collected 824 stuffed animals. When Tuter picked them up he was very happy that the fuzzy animal search went well. *Submitted by Dairen Potts*

PRICE – The youngest child of Gladys and Otto Wahlborg, Lois, attended North Ward School and Bolivar High School, and although she physically left Bolivar when she was 19 years old, it still has a special place in her heart.

Lois' memories include standing in line for the Saturday matinee at the Drake movie theater as a youngster and having vanilla cokes at Rexall Drugstore. When she was a young teenager, Jester's Drugstore became the place to have a coke and meet friends. During these years, the Penguin Drive-in and Ripples' Café were popular places to go. Other memories are of the closing of the city street for the children with their sleds on a cold, winter night, summer days at the sandy-bottom swimming pool, sunrise services on Easter morning at Dunnegan Park, community concerts at the old Pike Auditorium at SBU, the carnival that came to town each year, the Halloween parade that made its way around the city square, band concerts on the courthouse lawn each morning Saturday night, Dunnegan Park for lots of picnics and long walks with friends, the city siren, noon, and evening, the ring of the Methodist church bell each Sunday morning, the small-town atmosphere when rooting for the home team, the thrill of being at the game in 1960 when the Bolivar High School basketball team won the state championship and the opportunity to go to Washington, DC as a high school senior. These are some of the memories of Bolivar, MO that she holds dear.

Brad Price and Stacy Price Donald, Lois' grown children, have their own Bolivar memories. Her parents lived close to Dunnegan Park and all of their grandchildren loved to go there. This was the place where they became better-acquainted with their cousins. They would return home hot, out of breath, bursting with excitement and telling tales of their expedition to the park.

Steven and Lois Price celebrated their 35th wedding anniversary in July 2002. In addition to Brad and Stacy, the Prices have two darling granddaughters, Ashley and Leslie Donald.

Steve and Lois and their children, when they were young, used to take trips to Bolivar from California to visit her parents. On these trips her family developed a special fondness for Bolivar, and in their eyes Bolivar, MO, was the perfect small town. Steve, born in North Dakota and raised in California, has gone so far as to claim that Bolivar is his hometown. *Submitted by Lois Price*

PRITCHARD – Elvis Pritchard came to Polk County in 1912 to marry his long-time sweetheart, Olive Lindsay. The Lindsay family, Fred and Mary, had arrived here from Dekalb County, MO about 1909 or 1910, except for Olive, who was teaching school there. In those days, a teacher's certificate was issued after completing a two-year course in "normal school." So she began teaching at a young age. After joining her parents here, she taught at Black Oak school, north of Burns.

It has always been interesting to the family to know how Elvis made the trip here from Dekalb County with his possessions. He drove his cows along the road to the railroad station, about 10 miles to Maysville, MO, with his team and wagon and an extra horse. The wagon contained farm implements and various supplies such as feed and his personal property. His younger brother came along to help with the animals. He had rented a railroad car that stopped overnight in Kansas City. There, they milked the cows, giving it to the children who came to watch the trains come in. Arriving at Bolivar, they unloaded and drove the animals about 10 miles northeast to a little farm near where the Lindsay family had settled.

Elvis and Olive were married on Dec. 22, 1912. Two children were born to them, Herbert in 1914 and Leota in 1915. Most of their lives were spent living near where they first settled.

Herbert grew up and married Leila Moffitt, whose parents were Asbury and Nan Moffitt. One daughter was born to Herbert and Leila, Karen. She married Ben Gorden, son of Louis and Faye Gordon. Two children, Christa and Brian, were born to them. Christa is now Christa Owens and has two daughters, Katie and Kassidy. Brian is still single.

Leota married Clark Barham (the Barhams are elsewhere in this book). They became the parents of Randell in 1936 and Doris in 1946. Randell married Janice Vincent, daughter of Roy and Pearl Vincent. Randell owns and farms the land of both sets of his grandparents along with other land owned by the family. They had two children, Cindy

Elvis and Olive Pritchard December 1912

and David. Cindy is married to Bernard Francka Jr. They have three children, B. L., Mallory and Samuel. David is married to Lisa Sanders and they are the parents of Jenny, Brad and Ben. Doris is married to Dean Haguewood. Her daughter is Tammy, married to Jody King, son of Charles and Marge King of Billings. Tammy and Jody have one son, Sterling. Of the five generations mentioned, most have lived in Polk County and nearby counties thus far.

Elvis and Olive Pritchard are buried at Greenwood Cemetery in Bolivar, as also are Herbert and Leila Pritchard and Clark Barham. The older Lindsay family, except for Olive, are buried at Goff Cemetery north of Burns. The older Prichards came from Wales in the 1630s.

Pritchard relatives remain in Dekalb County and also at Waynesville, MO. Other Pritchard families in Polk County are not known relatives of ours. *Submitted by Cindy Francka*

Herman Pufahl and Florence Mattie (Whaley) Pufahl

PUFAHL - This is a story of how two cousins who were immigrants from Provence Posen, Kingdom of Prussia, or Germany (depending on which relative was telling the story), became part of Polk County's rich history. The cousins' names were Theodore Rechow (pronounced wreck'-o) and Herman Pufahl. Gottlieb and Wilhelmina Pufahl arrived at the Port of New York on June 28, 1871 with four children (one other had become sick and was buried at sea). Herman was, at that time, 3 years old. The family went to Wisconsin where others from their homeland had settled. Sometime during the Civil War, Theodore, who was at the time a member of the Kansas Cavalry, rode through Bolivar. He was so impressed with the area that he moved to Bolivar after the war and set up a law firm. Later, Herman came to Bolivar from Iowa, where his family had settled. During those days, a young man who aspired to become an attorney could apprentice himself to a practicing lawyer, study for a number of years and then attempt to pass the bar. That is what Herman did on Oct. 31, 1893. He then became a member of Mr. Rechow's firm (at sometime Mr. Rechow became known as "Judge" Rechow). Herman later married Florence Whaley, daughter of Andrew and Elizabeth Jane Whaley, who for some years ran the Whaley House, located on the northwest corner of Main and Broadway. Four children were born to that union: Helene Whaley, 1896; Elizabeth Mary, 1900; Herman Andrew, 1909; and

*Front – Quintin, Leslie and Ashley Donald
Back – Stacy Donald, Steve, Lois and Brad Price*

Robert G., 1911. Herman became well-known in the area as an attorney. Herman spent a short time as Polk County Prosecutor, but didn't care much for being the prosecutor and soon returned to the full time practice of law. The law office was located upstairs over what is now the Shoe Box on the south side of the square. The Pufahls lived for some time in a farmhouse they had remodeled, then moved next door when Mrs. Whaley broke up housekeeping. The first house was located at the present west end of Mitchell school and the second just west of the first. Both houses were torn down to make room for the expansion of the school, a reason Mr. Pufahl would have applauded as education was very important to him. Helene married A.F. (Pete) Leavitt, Elisabeth married Lowral D. (Sandy) Elrod, Herman Andrew remained a bachelor and Robert married Anita Scott. The Pufahls became grandparents to four: Lorraine Leavitt (Mrs. Carl Bridges), Eugenia Elrod (Mrs. Bill Miller) (Mrs. Bill Davis), Jean Pufahl (Mrs. Larry Parsons) (Mrs. David Vincent) and John Pufahl. Their great-grandchildren are Rodney and Karen Miller; Lori (Mrs. AJ Ellis), Lisa (Mrs. Major D. Hammett II) and Robert Parsons; and Jeannie and Robert Pufahl. Great-great-grandchildren are Caitlin and Abby Ellis and Mason, Liam and Mali Hammett. Descendants of both Theodore and Herman still reside in Polk County, continuing to weave threads in the tapestry of family history that was begun so many years ago. *Submitted by Jean L. Pufahl Vincent*

PURSLEY – When Ada LaVinnie Kinsey Watt, from the second-generation, Polk County branch of the Kinsey Family tree and her husband, Thompson Watt, named one of their daughters, they reached back to the preceding generation and gave part of her mother Alla May's name, and also part of her sister Ina Elizabeth's name, to Maggie May Elizabeth Watt (who would marry John Davidson, divorce, then marry Fred Sanders). This began a family tradition of preserving family names that is still evident in a little twig on this family tree who is named McKinsey Kay Hitchcock.

Maggie continued the tradition when naming her Davidson daughters by passing on one of her own names to Elizabeth Marie and one of her mother's names to Vinnie Lorene. Marie married Phillip Eugene "Phil Gene" Pursley (who passed away May 18, 2001). He is from another long-time, Polk County family. Vinnie married Bud Bridges.

Phil and Marie, their three daughters, their grandchildren and their great-grandchildren is one of the few families (if not the only one) from the Kinsey three that all stayed and reared their families in Polk County, and this family carried on the name-preserving tradition "big time."

The Pursleys' first daughter, Phyllis Marie, named for both Mom and Dad, married David Davis. They have a daughter, Sharon Marie, who married Gary Koon and the Koons have a daughter named Julie Beth. Vickie Aline is the second Davis daughter and she married Danny Ray Ross; they have two children Lacey D. and Colby.

Another of the Pursley daughters, Dixie Carol, married Danny Hitchcock. Their children are Lorna Marie, who married Jimmy Ray

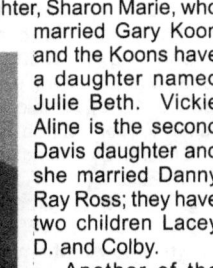
Phillip Eugene and Marie Elizabeth Pursley 1989

and whose children are Tyler, Tanner, Trevor and Lisa Marie, and son Tony Edward, who married Jackie Lemmon. The Hitchcock children are Cooper, Macey and McKinsey Kay.

Daughter Freddie May (named for her stepgrandfather and her grandmother) married Larry Eugene Moore. One of their daughters is Glenda Marie, whose husband is Roger Vote, and whose children are Mark, Rebecca and Joseph. Son Terry Eugene, who was named for both his father and his grandfather, is divorced and has a daughter, Brook Elizabeth. Freddie May and Larry's other daughter, Carol Sue Hickman, once cried because she wasn't named Marie, but is proud to be named for her Aunt Dixie Carol. Carol Sue is divorced and has two sons, Clint and Cory.

Although Ada LaVinnie's other granddaughter, Vinnie Lorene, spent most of her life in California, she and husband Bud have returned to Polk County. They have two sons. Timmy Lee and his wife, Debbie, have two children, James and Christina. Mark Allen is divorced and has a son, Timmy. *Submitted by Marie Pursley*

Mrs. Wilma (Johnson) Beck. Mary, James, Caleb and Karri Pursselley.

PURSSELLEY – John Robert Pursselley started Frogpond School in the fall of 1932 at the age of 5 and graduated from the school in the spring of 1941 at the age of 13. John lived about one and a half miles from the school and walked if the weather was nice. When the weather was bad, his parents took him to school in their Model A Ford. John walked to school with Floyd Ray and Edith May Pierce, who lived up the road and sometimes met others at the corner.

John attended school with kids who were also his neighbors and the families sometimes got together. Brown and Mae McArtor and their children Bud, Bob, Jane were neighbors to the southwest. The Lathams, Bill, Rebecca, Norma Jean, and Alma, were neighbors on the south. Horace and Nora Cribbs were neighbors to the west. John played with the Cribbs kids and was sometimes watched by the older girls. Steve and Gary Cribbs are still neighbors to the west. The Ruzicka boys, Tony, John, and Jim, were neighbors to the north. Marion and Lela Doke with their children, Dewey and Herman, were neighbors to the southeast.

John and the other kids enjoyed playing together during recess. The games that they played include ball, ante over, dare base and blackman along with races and jumping games. When the weather was bad, they played marbles inside on a sand table. John admits that he wasn't very fast or coordinated but had fun anyway.

One memory John has is of the Thanksgiving program in 1934 or 1935. The kids were let out early so that they would be able to get their chores done and get back for the program. When they arrived that evening, it was just beginning to snow. When the program was over, there was over a foot of snow on the ground. John and his parents tried to get home but their car got stuck in the deep snow. They had to go back to the school building where some of the men had to break the lock to be able to get in out of the storm. Several families had to spend the night. John remembers being scared they were going to get arrested for breaking into the school.

John also remembers his first crush. Her name was Gladys Hoover. She was in the eighth grade, John was in first.

John's son Scott and his wife home school their children. When they started home schooling, John asked if he could name their school. He named it Frogpond to keep memories alive. His grandchildren who now go to Frogpond live on the same farm John grew up on. On John's 50th wedding anniversary his last teacher from Frogpond came to the anniversary party. There the new Frogponders got to meet the lady who taught their grandfather. Her name was Miss Wilma Johnson. She now lives in Stockton. *Submitted by Ruth Pursselley*

PURSSELLEY – A few months after he came home from service in the Spanish-American War, John Washington Pursselley married Minnie Cochran from Pleasant Hope in 1900. Minnie's brother, Albert, owned the Cochran Hotel which sat on the corner of Tillery and Adams streets in Pleasant Hope. John W. Pursselley's great-grandson, John Scott Pursselley and Peter Bradford now own an auto repair shop on the same property.

A miller by trade, John W. owned and operated the Brighton Mill from 1907-1919. In 1919 John and Minnie moved with their five children, Norma, Nella, Alfred, Nina and Neta, to Morrisville, then Mt. Vernon and finally to Springfield. In Springfield, John W. owned a corner grocery.

While in Mt. Vernon, Alfred met and married Veda Moore. They had one child, John Robert Pursselley. In 1949 John Robert met an Ozark county girl named Ruth Billingsly. They were married in 1950 and have three children: Robbi, Krista and John Scott.

John W. Pursselley's brother, W.T.W. Pursselley,

John W. Pursselley's flourmill at Brighton, MO circa 1907

was the Polk County sheriff from 1920-1924. He owned several farms in the area and willed one of them to John Robert. John W. and then Alfred Pursselley had life estate on the farm because John Robert was only a baby. The farm was a hog farm and a sheep farm with a few milk cows and is now a beef cattle farm.

John Robert and Ruth lived on the farm until John Scott married. John Robert and Ruth were then missionaries to England until their retirement. John Scott now lives on the place and raises beef cattle.

Robbi married David Almanzar and now lives in Colorado where David is the pastor of a church. They have four children: Jonathan, Courtnii, Jordan and Cody. They also have three grandchildren: Jacob, Hannah and Gracie.

Krista married Ken Dowell and they are missionaries to England where they teach in a Bible college. They have two children, Rachel and Eli and one grandchild, Isaac.

John Scott married a city girl named Cheryl Conn, whose only knowledge of cows was that they gave milk. They have four children, Mary, James, Caleb and Karri. John Scott works for the City Utilities in Springfield and also co-owns an auto repair shop in Pleasant Hope.

The kids raise and milk dairy goats along with helping on the farm. Cheryl has learned a lot about cows in the years she has lived on the farm and now would never want to live in town again.

John Robert and Ruth also live on the farm now and are happy having grandkids and great-grandkids all over the place. As far as they are concerned, the more the merrier! *Submitted by John Scott Pursselley*

QUICK – James Fred Quick was born March 30, 1895 in Polk County.

His parents were James W. Quick and Anna Clark Quick; she was born May 16, 1866, daughter of James and Martha (Ragsdale) Clark.

Anna and James W. Quick was married Oct. 28, 1892. They also had two daughters, Minnie Davison, born Aug. 27, 1893 and Oma Knight, born Oct. 9, 1896.

Anna and her husband moved to Oolaga, OK shortly after their youngest daughter was born. After family difference, Anna moved back with the three children and was later divorced.

Anna stayed in the family home on the homestead and cared for her mother, Martha. After her mother's death, Anna inherited the family home and the 40 acres on which it stood.

Fred was only 8 years old when they returned to Missouri and since he was the only boy in that family, he was expected to do the farm work. With the help of a nearby uncle, Dan Davison and two older cousins, he did learn. He found it to be hard work and not much time for play but also an enjoyable time in his life.

Fred enlisted in the Army during WWI at the age of 22. Although he had never driven before, they had him to drive a supply truck and deliver ammunition to the front line at Luxembourg, France (know as the Hindenburg Line). He drove for the 89th Artillery Division until the close of WWI. He came home on a troop train to Bolivar and then walked the 13 or so miles to the home of his mother near Halfway. His name appears on the statue that stands on the northwest corner of the courthouse lawn.

He purchased 40 acres that joined his mother's land and also did the farming for her. He met his wife-to-be shortly after his return home. Winifred Lane was a teacher at the Clark school and boarded with his aunt Hannah Davison.

Fred and Winifred were married Dec. 2, 1923. Winifred was born to Harry L. and Flora Means Lane.

After Anna's death on Jan. 22, 1929, Fred purchased the family farm from his two sisters and kept this land in the family along with the 40 acres he already owned. In the early 1940s, he was able to purchase another 80 acres that lay next to the home.

It was upon this farm that he and his wife, Winifred (Lane) Quick, spent 50 wonderful years and raised six children: Fred G. Quick, Floradelle Barham, Annabelle Looney, Vera (Farmer) Gorden, Irene Mayfield and Lonnie (Gene) Quick. Fred often remarked that his children were the best crop he ever raised. It is on this farm that the family has so many good memories, fishing, hunting, wading, and swimming, not only enjoyed by his children but the grandchildren and his great-grandchildren.

Fred was faithful to take his family to church and was made a deacon at Halfway Baptist Church. He served on the Clark school board and was a charter member of the MFA Farmers Exchange in Halfway.

After Winifred died on June 9, 1974, Fred remarried Opal Lane Quick, a younger sister of Winifred.

They sold the farm and moved into Bolivar, where he lived until his death, June 29, 1995. Fred lived to be 100 years old and would often tell us the first 50 were the best.

Roy and Lucy Ortner owned the farm for about 20 years. When they chose to sell, Gary and Judy Barham became the owners. Gary Barham is a grandson of Fred Quick. Gary and his wife Judy (Ragsdale) Barham, are also the owners of the homeplace of Joel Ragsdale. Gary is the fourth generation of James Clark and fifth generation of Joel Ragsdale. *Submitted by Reanna Mayfield Smith*

RAGSDALE – Joel Ragsdale and Jane (Alread) Ragsdale were married on Christmas Eve in 1824. They came to Missouri from Kentucky and settled north of Halfway.

Joel's name appears on the Polk County census for the year of 1840. Joel and Jane had eight children and the youngest was an infant when Jane died.

Jane was only 44 years old when she died and according to the custom of those days, she was buried in the edge of the garden near their home. About a year after Jane's death, Joel remarried and brought his wife, Verlinda Winsdom, to his house beside the garden.

Joel and Verlinda had seven children.

Joel was a farmer and businessman and owned a large amount of land. When he and Jane's two oldest children married, they each received 1,000 acres of land. He operated two freight lines into the south from nearby Bolivar and also owned a saddle and harness shop in Bolivar.

According to Ragsdale family history, like most of his neighbors, Joel owned slaves when the Civil War began. He worked to help secure a northern victory, much to dismay of many of his neighbors. In fact, Joel was excluded from the church he belonged to because of his efforts.

To protect his family, Joel often slept in the woods near his home on bedding that was dyed black to elude would-be attackers. His activities were varied and he reportedly monitored the movements of General Sterling Price as he made his way across Missouri to the historic battle at Wilson's Creek.

Despite his efforts to protect his family, Joel and Jane's 19-year-old son, Absalom, was killed in an ambush intended for Joel. Absalom was buried in Ragsdale Cemetery, only a short distance from his mother.

Even though the end of the war brought the northern victory Joel had worked so hard for, no doubt it was a bitter victory. Not only had he lost a son, but also several members of the Ragsdale family were estranged because of differing Civil War loyalties. Several years after the end of the war, family members established contact and reunited a family torn apart by the confusion of war.

Although Jane's was the first burial in the garden, two more would follow by 1853. Others would be added through the years, and in 1881, Joel deeded one acre of land to be legally established as Ragsdale Cemetery. Today, there are more than 150 graves in the cemetery and the most recent burials were in 1990.

Joel died on July 4, 1883, at the age of 77. He is buried between Jane and Verlinda. Many of Joel's descendants lived in the area, and several are instrumental in helping preserve Joel's garden cemetery.

Ragsdale graveyard, stone of Jane, Joel and Velinda Ragsdale

Without a doubt, when Joel buried Jane in the edge of the garden that October day in 1850, he had no idea of the legacy the garden-turned-cemetery would create, or about the people that would one day know the story of Joel Ragsdale because of it.

Children by Jane were Sally Ann (born May 31, 1829), John W. (born May 18, 1831), Lewis A. (born Aug. 11, 1833), Martha J. (born May 13, 1835), Margaret (birth unknown), Hannah R. (born Jan. 15, 1840), Absalom (born July 4, 1842) and Susan V. (born March 26, 1844).

Children by Verlinda were Lydia (born Jan. 25, 1851), Elisa I. (born Aug. 5, 1852), Lucinda (born Aug. 7, 1854), Joel (born Oct. 20, 1856), Velinda C. (born Feb. 9, 1859), James Grant (birth unknown) and Abraham Lincoln (birth unknown). *Submitted by Vera Gorden*

RAGSDALE – Our Ragsdale history began in 1644 when Godfrey Ragsdale II was born on a land grant near Jamestown in Henrico County, VA. Godfrey II was the son of Godfrey I who came to America from Wales or England sometime between the settlement of Jamestown and 1642. Godfrey I and his family were massacred on April 29, 1644, with only the baby Godfrey II surviving, and he died in 1703 leaving a will. Our line is from Godfrey II's son Benjamin, who was born in 1698. This story will skip several generations to get to John W.

John W. Ragsdale was born May 18, 1831 in Morgan County, IL, the son of Joel and Jane Alred Ragsdale. Joel was born in 1806 in Tennessee and died in 1883 in Polk County. Jane died in 1850 in Polk County with a baby 3 months old, and Joel married again in 1850 to Verlinda Wisdom and had another child before the year's ending. Joel and Lewis Jr. (also of Polk County) were the sons of Lewis Ragsdale Sr. Joel lived two and one-half miles north of Halfway and started a cemetery behind his house there, now known as Ragsdale Cemetery. John W. was the second child of eight of Jane and Joel's family. Joel and Verlinda had eight more children.

John W. married on June 22, 1853 to Mary Ann Hale, born Dec. 14, 1833, the daughter of Thomas and Sarah Hale. John received his education in the district schools, converted in 1843, joined the Methodists, but in 1876 joined the Baptists and was ordained in 1880. Mary Ann died Sept. 3, 1866 and John married second in 1876 to Margaret Jane Jackson. Against most of his children's wishes, he went to live with his daughter Susan in Guyman, OK after his wife died. He died Jan. 9, 1912 and is buried in rural Guyman, Camp Cemetery, beside Susan and her husband. The following were children of John W. and Mary Ann.

Sarah Jane Ragsdale (1854-1930) married Issac F. Suiter (1853-1885); both buried in Ragsdale Cemetery. Their children were Wesley (1885-1906) and Ethel, who married Russell Smith.

Martha Rebecca (1856-1900) married William S. Jones (1857-1923), son of Thompson and Eliza J. Jones. They lived west of Louisburg. Both are buried at Ragsdale Cemetery. Martha and William's children are as follows: John Thomas (1875-1931, Glendale, AZ) married Lusinda Jane Bonds; their children were Nellie Mae, James Curtis, William Odus, Vonney Lee, Opal Marie and Dortha Hellen. Florence (1878-1952, Santa Paula, CA) married first Robert Meadows, divorced; their child was Clarence. She married second William Foster (1876-1963, California) and their children were Charles E., Perry, Gertie, Cecil, Lovell, Leslie. William Radford "Will" (1881-1954) married Jemima "Lizzie" Williams (1886-1968) and their children were Ressie Corlis, Alfred Adrian, Elsie Florence, Jessee Lee, Leo Radford, Velta Elaine, Lawrence Edwin, Henry Wilfred, Clifton Eugene, Martha Goldina and Edna May. Charles Oliver (1884-1935) married Nellie Ethel Davison (1887-1965) and their children were Grace, Bessie, Elgie, Okla and Archie. Nathan "Nate" (1887-1961) married Iva Hogg (1886-1910) and their children were Wim Cecil "Willie" and Fern Evelyn. Marion Thomas (1890-1973) married Zelpha Mae Rush (1891-1980) and their children were Lavern Glen and Laverta Eunice. Virgil Lester (1894-1963) married Fannie Jewel May (1898-) and their children were a son that died young, Iris Annalee and Vernice Mae.

Lavina (circa 1859-died after 1870) who died young.

Mary Ann (1861-1946) married in 1882 to Westley Wellington Rice (1860-1927). Both are buried in Crudington Cemetery. Their children are listed as follows. Charley Evert (1883-1940) married Addie Arnold and their children were Floyd, Bertrum and Wilby. Walter Emmett (1885-) married Gertrude Sanford and their children were Ray Harold, Laurene Thurston and Letha Grace. Luvania Alice (1888-1938) married Archie Day and their children were Ruby and Elsie. Virginia Margaret (1890-1935) married Percy Thornsbury and their children were Paul, Charles and Madaline. Elsie Eunice (1895-) married Floyd Jay Highfill and their children were Denzil, Gwinevere and Helen. Ernest Albert (1902-1924).

Susan Virginia (circa 1863-1933) married in 1884 to Rev. William Sam Hodges (1858-). Susan died and is buried at Guyman, OK beside father, husband and a son, James R. (1899-1922). Their children were Arthur S. (47 in 1933), Roscoe H. (45), Vest T. (41), Bessie S. Odneal (39) and John R. (34). *Submitted by Archie Jones*

Vivian and Elsie Rathbun 1938, "A dream come true"

Vivian and Elsie Rathbun 1938, "soon baby makes three"

RATHBURN - James Arthur Rathbun, born Jan. 22, 1884 in Hickory County, MO and Eva Williams, born Feb. 5, 1875, were married April 18, 1909 in Humansville, MO. James' parents were Jacob Washington and Lucinda Catherine Kee Rathbun. Eva was the daughter of George W. and Julia A. Williams.

Jim and Eva's first son, Vivian Williams Rathbun, was born Aug. 24, 1911 in Humansville, MO. A second son, James Lee, was born Aug. 17, 1916 in Humansville but died March 17, 1922 and was buried in the Humansville Cemetery.

Hence, Vivian was raised as an only child. He attended Humansville Schools where he enjoyed music and played the trumpet in his high school band, as well as a private band in the Bolivar, MO area.

The Rathbun family lived on a small farm north of the Humansville city limits on Highway 13. Jim was a rural mail carrier, part-time carpenter and farmer. Eva was a full-time homemaker who sold eggs for extra money. Vivian helped his father with carpentry work and farming and he also exhibited architectural skills.

In 1933, Vivian began selling Raleigh Products in Hickory and Cedar Counties, door to door, farm to farm. The summer of 1934, Lee Hyatt introduced her daughter, Elsie Marie Hyatt, to Vivian, her friendly Raleigh Salesman. He was captivated immediately. The couple became engaged and Elsie began a one-year teaching assignment at the High Point Grade School in the fall of 1934. Vivian and his dad, Jim, began building a bungalow on an acre of land just below the family farm. Jim and Eva had given the couple the land as a wedding gift.

Vivian and Elsie were married June 2, 1935 and worked together on their new home. They picked up Blossom Rock, native only to this area, to build and decorate their front porch. All those rock came directly off their one acre of land. A baby girl, Barbara Joan, arrived at their home, before breakfast, June 28, 1938.

In the spring of 1941, Vivian began to experience stomach problems. Elsie presumed her husband had an ulcer. Oct. 8-18, 1941, Vivian was bed-ridden at home and then he was hospitalized October 18-28 at the new Humansville Hospital. He had never previously complained about not feeling well and doctors were perplexed. Oct. 28, 1941, the doctor finally told Elsie that Vivian had stomach cancer; he passed away that same day. He was buried in the Humansville Cemetery.

Elsie and Barbara, now 3 years old, moved to El Dorado Springs, MO to live with Elsie's parents, Henry Clay and Lee Hyatt. Their dream bungalow was sold. Elsie left for Kansas City in the spring of 1942. She lived with her brother and family. Barbara remained with her maternal grandparents until January 1945 when the three of them moved to Kansas City where Elsie had bought a large house for her daughter, parents and sisters.

Jim Rathbun continued to farm on a small scale. Eva began selling Raleigh Products after Vivian's death. She died Feb. 2, 1948 at the age of 73. Jim remarried and after Bessie's death, sold the farm and in 1956 moved to town. He died April 19, 1958 at 74 years. Both Jim and Eva are buried in the Humansville Cemetery. *Submitted by Barbara Joan Rathbun Tucker*

RECTOR – Clarence Charles Rector was born Oct. 7, 1906 near Humansville, MO, the fifth child of Ulysses Grant Rector and Sarah Elizabeth Ball Rector. He lived most of his youth in the same general area.

On Dec. 25, 1926, he married Jewell Phyrne Culbertson at the Osceola County Courthouse. Their son Linval Dean was born July 23, 1929, daughter Naomi Fay was born July 19, 1931 and daughter Norma Gay was born June 24, 1933.

Clarence supported his family by farming. In late 1935 they moved to Iowa, near Red Oak, where Nova was born April 18, 1936. In late 1936, the family, along with Bertha Jane Culbertson (his widowed mother-in-law) and four of her children, moved to Nyssa, OR near her two sons Lee and Charley Culbertson. Early 1937 saw the Rector family moving to Martinez, CA where Clarence was employed as a carpenter (a trade he had learned from working on the Osceola Dam) for General Chemical Corp.

Clarence and Phyrne were divorced in 1954 and he married Blanche Reeves in 1955. He retired from General Chemical Corp in 1968.

Clarence was an avid fisherman and raised red bone coonhounds that he hunted with for many years until an auto accident left him unable to do so. Another hobby was raising fighting cocks which he sold, never fought.

Clarence died of cancer on New Year's Day 1977 and is buried in the Freeman-Holsapple Cemetery. He was survived by four children and 10 grandchildren. *Submitted by Naomi Fay Rector Hytholt*

REDD - After the Civil War, 10 families came to the area from Allamakee County, IA. They traveled on a barge down the Mississippi River. One of the families was the Redd family.

Andrew Jackson was born Aug. 19, 1829 in Guernsey County, OH. He was the son of Peter Redd and Hannah Dolman. Peter Redd was born in 1803 and Hannah Dolman was born in 1807. They were both from Guernsey County, OH.

Andrew Jackson Redd and Lovina Barham were married on June 21, 1855 in Allamakee County, IA. Lovina was born Feb. 18, 1833 in Cole County, IL. She was the daughter of Nathan Barham and Jackness Webb. Nathan Barham was born in North Carolina around 1806 and Jackness Webb was born in Kentucky around 1810.

According to a special census in 1890 of Civil War veterans and their widows, Andrew served in the Thirteenth Iowa Infantry, Company B, Oct. 20, 1864 through July 21, 1865, which was the end of the war. This infantry was included in the campaign against Savannah, GA, also known as Sherman's March to the Sea.

Andrew and Lovina had 12 children. Seven of the children were born in Waukon, IA in Allamakee County. The oldest child was 13 while the youngest was a baby when they floated down the river to Missouri between 1868 and 1870. The last five were born in Halfway, MO in Polk County. Andrew purchased 160 acres from John Bayless on Highway H south of Halfway.

Cansaida was the oldest born April 27, 1856. She died on July 4, 1916. Rufus Richter was born on July 10, 1857. He died on March 3, 1935. Alameda was born Jan. 31, 1859 and died Dec. 3, 1946. Andrew Walter was born March 19, 1860 and died June 10, 1935. Welcome B. was born July 21, 1862 and died Feb. 1, 1939. Nathan was born May 9, 1864. He died Sept. 6, 1884 after being stabbed during a fight. He is buried at Reed Cemetery in Halfway, MO. Hannah Jennie was born March 3, 1868 and died Oct. 6, 1964.

The children that were born in Halfway were Eliza Ann, Elizabeth, Daisy, James Schofield, and Samuel Farr. Eliza Ann was born on Oct. 18, 1870 and died Nov. 23, 1916. She is buried in Caldwell, ID in Canyon County. Elizabeth was born on May 16, 1872 and died Aug. 25, 1955. Daisy was born on Jan. 1, 1873 and died on Sept. 8, 1873 when she was just 8 months old. James Schofield was born Sept. 11, 1874 and died on

Andrew Jackson Redd

Jan. 24, 1962. Samuel Farr was the last born on Aug. 31, 1876 and died on Sept. 1, 1967.

Lovina died Nov. 16, 1907 when she was 74 years old. Andrew lived for 13 years as a widower. He passed away Feb. 24, 1920. They are buried at Reed Cemetery in Halfway, MO. *Submitted by Hobert Redd*

REDD – Rufus Richter Redd was born July 10, 1857 in Waukon, IA in Allamakee County. He was the son of Andrew Jackson Redd and Lovina Barham. He was next to the oldest in a family of 12 children, six girls and six boys. He lived in Iowa until he was 12. His family was one of 10 families that floated down the Mississippi River, on a barge, to Missouri. They settled on a farm south of Halfway.

Rufus Richter Redd

On Aug. 12, 1886, when Rufus was 29, he married Zella Belle Lewis. She was a daughter of Abraham Lewis and Margaret Voris Lewis. Belle was born in May of 1862 in Indiana. She had several brothers and sisters.

Rufus and Belle had six children. James Edwin was the first. He married Minnie Petersen. They had four children, one of whom died young. The children's names were Wilbur, James Denzil and Verian.

Alice was the second child. She had one child, Kenneth Redd, out of wedlock and then married Tom Andrews and had a girl named Wanda.

Joseph was the third child. He married Leona Blair. They had two girls, Geraldine and Leota Fay. Geraldine survived polio when she was a little girl.

Andrew Jackson was the fourth child. He was born on July 28, 1895. He married Lottie Barham and they had four boys: Hobert, Herbert, Ray Dean and Tom R.

Jennie was the fifth child. She married James Dennis Hale and they had 13 children: Ruth, Clifford, Adrian, Dorothy, Erma, Edna, Elgi, Orlan, Willa, Avajean, Jimmy and Carl.

Vinna was the last child born on March 29, 1903. She married Arl Lockhart. They had four boys: Leroy, Earl, Wayne and Curtis.

One of Belle's granddaughters, Verian Shadwick, remembers her as having long, brown hair that never turned gray. She also said that she was a very generous and kind person who never spoke ill to or about anyone. She loved to read the *Kansas City Star* newspaper, especially the continuous story. In one of the publications, she read that tea was soothing to burns. She had burned her foot with a coal from the stove and decided to give it a try. She brewed the tea, put it in a wash pan, sat down in her rocker to soak her foot in the tea and promptly fell asleep. She woke up the next morning with a very black, but no longer hurting, foot.

Verian also remembered her grandfather Rufus. He was shucking corn one fall when the weather quickly turned cold and rainy. He went home cold and wet, suffering from rheumatism. He never fully recovered. He walked with a cane and later was partially bedfast for the rest of his life.

He was also known to have a sack of soda sitting next to his bed that he could wet his thumb, dip into the soda and lick it off to help with his indigestion.

Rufus passed away on March 3, 1935. He is buried in Reed Cemetery at Halfway, MO. Belle wanted to live to see her grandsons come home from WWII. She passed away in 1949. She is buried next to her husband at Reed Cemetery. *Submitted by Alan F. Redd*

REDD – Andrew Jackson Redd was born July 28, 1895 north of Halfway. He was the son of Rufus Richter Redd and Zella Belle Lewis Redd. He had two brothers, James Edwin and Joseph. He also had three sisters, Alice, Vinna and Jennie.

Andrew was drafted to the United States Army during WWI. He was a Private First Class in Field Artillery. He was stationed at Fort Raleigh, KS. He was in the services about six months.

Andrew was united in marriage to Lottie Barham on Oct. 7, 1923. Her parents were Thomas Barham and Rebecca Hannah Felthoff Barham. Lottie was born on June 30, 1894 south of Burns in Polk County, MO. She had one sister, Myrtle and four brothers, Roy Levi, Charles Emmett, Joel Benjamin and Claud Jessie.

To this union came four boys: Hobert Andrew, Herbert Barm, Ray Dean and Tom R. They were living north of Burns when the first and second children were born. Hobert Andrew was born on Nov. 11, 1924 and Herbert Barm was born on Sept. 20, 1926.

Later they moved to a place of 117 acres north of Halfway, during which the third son, Ray Dean, was born on Aug. 20, 1932. They then moved in with Lottie's parents and Tom R. was born on Sept. 12, 1936.

Andrew and Lottie lived at another place northeast of Halfway with 160 acres and in Halfway north of the MFA. He was also known as "Papoo" or "Jonah." Lottie was known as "Mom." He had two hats, a Sunday Stetson and an everyday Stetson.

Andrew Jackson Redd

One night, Papoo woke Mom because he heard something in the chicken house. All of the chickens were making noise and Papoo thought someone was stealing his chickens. He ran and got his gun, had it pointed out the window ready to shoot. Mom was very calm about the situation. She told Papoo that the man stealing the chickens probably had a family and that he did not need to shoot him. Just then the milk cow came walking out of the chicken house.

At the age of 71, Papoo passed away on Aug. 9, 1966, from heart failure. He is buried at Reed Cemetery in Halfway, MO. Mom lived for 18 years as a widow. She lived in Halfway for sometime. Finally, she moved to a small house next to her youngest son until her death on Dec. 6, 1984. She was 90 years old. She is also buried at Reed Cemetery. *Submitted by Mike Redd*

REDD – Hobert Andrew Redd was born Nov. 11, 1924 north of Burns in Polk County, MO. He was the oldest son of Andrew Jackson Redd and Lottie Barham Redd. He had three brothers, Herbert, Ray Dean and Tom R. He attended school at Union Ridge and Halfway High School.

In early spring of 1944, Hobert was drafted to WWII. He was inducted at Fort Leavenworth, KS. He was assigned to the 222nd Ordinance Company, United States Army and went through basic training at Camp Chaffee, AR. After basic training, he went to Aberdeen, MD and attended Small Arms Mechanical Maintenance School. After graduation, he went to Camp Gruber, OK. He guarded North African POWs from the famous General Rommel's company. Seattle, WA was the next place and finally to Pearl Harbor in Oahu, HI. After the war ended, he left Hawaii and went to Fort Ord, CA, the to Fort Leavenworth, KS, and finally home to Halfway, MO. He was discharged as a staff sergeant.

Hobert Andrew Redd

He bought 77 acres from Roy Barham, north of Halfway. During a trip to Arkansas to take his father to visit a cousin, he met his future wife. Hobert was united in marriage to Jeanne Lewis on July 11, 1954 at his parents' home. Jeanne was born on May 13, 1936 to Frank Lewis and Grace Mincher Lewis. While in a hurry to pack, Jeanne forgot her wedding dress, so she wore Lottie's dress.

Hobert and Jeanne had two children, Alan Frank and Dale Andrew. Alan was born May 31, 1955. He married Debbie Floyd and they had two children, Kimberly Ann and Courtney Alan. Dale Andrew was born Sept. 9, 1956. He married Debbie Brown and they had two children, Jamie Lynn and Justin Andrew.

In 1959, they bought 80 acres, the Pond Place, from Hobert's dad. They lived there for about one year and then bought another 40 acres, across the road, from Ott Wright. They have had two house fires. The first one burned only part of the house. The second fire destroyed the whole house.

Hobert worked for 15 years in road construction. He has milked cows, run a sawmill, farmed and operated a dozer. When he was young, he worked at the Missouri State Prison in Jefferson City.

He is an avid hunter and fisherman. He had gone to North Missouri, Colorado, Wyoming, Canada, and Newfoundland hunting deer, elk, antelope, caribou and moose. He has also hunted rattlesnakes, alligators and wild hogs. He has been to the Gulf of Mexico to deep-sea fish many times.

Hobert and Jeanne both love to travel. They have taken many trips with family members. They have been to almost every state in the union including Hawaii. *Submitted by Dale Redd*

Ray Dean Redd

REDD – Ray Dean Redd was born on Aug. 20, 1932 in Halfway, MO in Polk County. His parents were Andrew Jackson Redd and Lottie Barham Redd. He had three brothers, Hobert, Herbert and Tom R.

He went into the United States Army in 1952 during the Korean Conflict. Due to a previous leg injury, he was unable to go overseas. He had surgery while at Camp Polk, LA. He was given a medical discharge in 1953.

In 1954, he bought 80 acres in Halfway from Edgar Breshears and started milking cows. He married Bernadean Lewis on Aug. 7, 1960. His brother had married her sister. She was born May 31, 1944 to Frank Lewis and Grace Mincher Lewis.

To this union came five children: Darren Ray, Kevin Lee, Michael Alan, Tara Shae and Shawna Dale.

Darren Ray was born Jan. 9, 1961. He was married twice and had four children: Shannon, Chilua, Darek and Jared.

Kevin Lee was born Aug. 9, 1962. He married LaDona Powell and they had three children: Brandon Lee, Andrew Jackson and Kayla Dawn.

Michael Alan was born Aug. 19, 1966. He was supposed to be named after his grandfather, but he was born just 10 days after Andrew Jackson Redd passed away. Dean and Bernadean decided not to name his Andrew Jackson because of Lottie. Mike had married twice and has one child, Taylor Dawn.

Tara Shae was born Nov. 26, 1968. She married Randy Voris and they had three girls: Kelli Shae, Katelyn Rae and Kamryn Lynn.

Shawna Dale was born July 16, 1972. She married Mike Grisham and they had three children: Dalton Michael, Samantha Dale and Abby Dean.

Dean and Bernadean milked cows and farmed. They enjoyed going to horse shows with Darren and Kevin. Later they went to sporting events with Mike, Shae and Shawna.

Dean was also a very avid hunter. He went to Colorado to hunt for deer and elk. His first trip was in 1954. He missed the year he was married and the last four years of his life. He hunted with his cousins and brothers.

He and his brother bought one of the first self-propelled combines in the area. They did custom fescue combining. Dean was very good at keeping the combine running smoothly. Folks who also had combines were always calling to ask him what was wrong with their machines.

He later sold the farm to his son, Kevin. They moved to Columbia where he passed away from cancer on March 1, 1997. He is buried at Reed Cemetery in Halfway, MO.

Bernadean moved back to Halfway to help take care of her mother and to be with her children and grandchildren. *Submitted by Kevin Lee Redd*

REDMAN – John Perryman Redman was born in the state of Tennessee in 1820, the son of John Polk and Nancy Hamilton Redman. When he was 8 years old he was left to the care of his mother when his father died. His siblings were William H., Nelson C. and Elizabeth Redman.

After a few years, Nancy Hamilton Redman married James Cobb. They had a daughter, Almira Cobb. While Almira was still young, her mother and possibly her father died. She was raised by her brother John and moved to Polk County with him where she married Dudley Smith on Sept. 8, 1853. She appears to have died within a few years.

John grew to adulthood and married Artemecia Bird Stockton, the daughter of Robert and Nancy Ragland Stockton. After the death of his wife, Robert also moved to Polk County to be near his family and died there in the late 1800s. John became involved in community life in Meigs County, TN where at one point he was a justice of the peace. Then in 1849 or 1850 he, along with his brother, William H. Redman, moved to the Polk County area.

In Polk County John was a farmer and, in the tradition of his Hamilton ancestors, a cattle trader. He is reported to have taken several cattle drives from the Polk County area to the west where they were sold for profit. With these profits he bought several parcels of land and also loaned money to many of his neighbors.

In 1862 John became involved in the cause of the South. He, along with many of his neighbors,

Tennessee Redman Reeves 1850-1911

joined the forces organized under General Sterling Price. He was elected a sergeant at the formation of the company. They soon found themselves in the midst of the conflict. John was wounded and taken prisoner at the battle of Pea Ridge, AR. He, along with the others taken in this battle, was brought under guard through Springfield, within 13 miles of his home, then on through Rolla to the military prison in Alton, IL. In Alton John succumbed to pneumonia and his wounds on March 25, 1866. He was buried in an unmarked grave and is listed among the dead on a large monument erected years after the end of the war.

John was survived by his wife, Artemesia, and the following children: William C. (born 1847; died Aug. 12, 1869; married Anna Rooks); Robert S. (born about 1849); Tennessee (born Dec. 14, 1850; died June 15, 1911; married James Coleman Reeves on June 13, 1869); Elizabeth (born 1855; married William Wiley Oct. 17, 1872); Artimesia (born March 27, 1856; died April 22, 1894; married John W. Elles); John Wilson (born November 1858; married Laura B. Shriner Dec. 5, 1888); Thomas Freeman (born about 1861; married Florence Mae Gott on June 10, 1888).

Artemesia Stockton Redman later married John Roach, a widower of the area, and they had one child. Joseph H. Roach was born in April 1869. Artemesia appears to have died between 1880 (Census) and 1885 (John Roach's next marriage). Family tradition says she was buried in the Enon Cemetery, though no stone has been found. *Submitted by Randall A. Reeves*

Picture taken in Nebraska 1909, the Charles Robert Reeves family

REEVES – Charles Robert Reeves was born Nov. 15, 1870, Polk County, MO. He is the son of Robert Jasper Willis Reeves and Mary Elizabeth "Liza" Anderson. Grandson of Elijah Reeves, Elizabeth Ashbrook and Jordan A. Anderson, Mary Elizabeth Watkins. On Oct. 9, 1895 he married Francis Catherine Crow, born Aug. 12, 1870, daughter of Andrew Jackson "Jack" Crow and Mary. They were married by A. E. Crawford in Polk County, MO. Charles Robert farmed around Fair Play, MO and later in Nebraska City, NE. Children are William Oscar, Mary Ann, Robert L., Charles Edward, Roy L., Rosie and Dorthey. Charles died Oct. 31, 1930 in Union, NE. Francis died March 29, 1941. Burial at Cowles Cemetery, also known as Wyoming Cemetery, Nebraska City, NE.

William Oscar Reeves was born Sept. 20, 1899. In 1920 he married Victoria Leatha Bell Mead, born May 10, 1902, Bolivar. Children are

Lester, Wilma, Mary, William and Marjorie. William died 1944, Lincoln, NE and Leatha died Oct. 29, 1973, Minnesota. Burials are at Oak Hill Cemetery, Plattsmouth, NE.

Mary Ann Reeves was born Aug. 5, 1900. She married Victor Coy, Edward Ranard, 1915 and Olaf Jordet, 1941. Children of Mary and Edward are Raymond, Richard, Robert and Eunice. Mary died Nov. 25, 1979. Burials at Cowels Hill Cemetery, Nebraska City, NE.

Robert L. Reeves, born May 10, 1902, died 1916 at age 14.

Charles "Charlie" Edward Reeves was born March 17, 1904, Union, NE. On Aug. 1, 1925 he married Katharina "Katherine/Susie" Schneider, born April 27, 1907, daughter of Christian Schneider and Maria Mosblach, Nebraska City, NE. Children are Grace, Betty, Charlotte, Hazel, Francis and Donna. Charlie died June 9, 1977, Nebraska City, NE and Katherine died Aug. 5, 1991, Maryville, MO. Burials at Cowels Hill Cemetery, Nebraska City, NE.

Grace Marie Reeves, born Aug. 6, 1926, died Dec. 2, 1994. Married Alfred Hummel, April 16, 1950. Their children were Cheryll, Catherine and Charles.

Betty Jean Reeves was born Jan. 3, 1930. Married Robert Moeller Aug. 28, 1949. Their children were Robert Jr. and Bobbie Marie.

Charlotte Katherine Reeves was born Oct. 1, 1935. Married Leonard McComas June 5, 1953. They had Pamela.

Hazel Joan Reeves was born June 16, 1940. Married Duayne Holland, Aug. 16, 1957. Their children were Raymond, Deborah, Therese, Kenneth, Steven, Tamara, Lawrence and Douglas.

Francis Louis Reeves was born and died Jan. 26, 1953.

Donna Christine Reeves was born Oct. 25, 1954.

Roy L. Reeves was born April 18, 1908 and died 1908.

Rosie Reeves was born Nov. 20, 1909. Married 1924, Bud Study. Their children were Viola, Janelle, Doris, Donald, Ester, Lewis, Marilyn and unknown. Married 1962 to Frank Drewel. Rosie died Aug. 24, 1973, Nebraska City, NE.

Dorthey Catherine Reeves was born Sept. 29, 1915. On Sept. 5, 1931 married Ocie Mullennax. Their children were Belva, Robert, Clifford, Melvin, Edward, Christopher and Docie. Dorthey died Aug. 11, 1968, Nebraska City, NE. Burial at Camp Creek Cemetery. *Submitted by Donna Reeves*

REEVES – Robert Jasper Willis Reeves was born May 1, 1851 in De Soto County, MS. Parents were Elijah Reeves and Elizabeth Ashbrook. On March 4, 1870, Robert married Mary Elizabeth "Liza" Anderson, born June 28, 1856, daughter of Jordan A. Anderson and Mary Elizabeth Watkins. Robert's father died shortly before his birth. At about age 2 Robert came to Missouri with his family. Siblings are John W., Roy L., Charles Robert, Elizabeth Jane, Ann, James and Anna Eliza. His mother later married Samuel Forgey. Robert and Liza farmed in Polk County, MO. They had 13 children: Charles, Reley, Elizabeth, James, Johnie, Mary, Mina, Stella, Deldie, Ada, George, Ida and Elnora. Robert died Feb. 4, 1919. Liza died Sept. 9, 1918. Burials at Barren Creek Cemetery.

Charles Robert Reeves was born Nov. 15, 1870. On Oct. 9, 1895 he married Francis Catherine Crow, daughter of Andrew Jackson "Jack" Crow and Mary. Children are Oscar, Mary, Robert, Charles, Roy, Rosie and Dorthey. They moved to Union, NE. Both are buried at Cowles Cemetery, Nebraska City, NE.

Reley C. Reeves was born May 20, 1872 and died Nov. 12, 1889.

Elizabeth Coque Reeves was born Feb. 1, 1876. On Nov. 30, 1892 she married Marshall Wakefield, son of Charles Wakefield and Mary. Children are James Willis, Charlie Benjamin, Grace Mae, Marshie Nannie and Mary. Elizabeth died March 26, 1967 in Oklahoma.

James Bender Reeves was born March 6, 1878. On Dec. 24, 1902 he married Lillie B. Mead, born 1884, daughter of James Mead and Dyalthia McGee. They had one child, Margaret. James died Dec. 28, 1921.

Johnie Reeves was born May 1879, died 1888 at the age of 9 years.

Mary Jane Reeves was born June 27, 1881. On March 25, 1900 she married James Mead. Children are Fred Glen, Obe Willis, Amanda Caroline, James Henry, Magnus Everette, Lewis R., Floyd Leroy, Earnest Veron and Allen. Mary married Joseph Barkley. Mary died Sept. 1, 1968, burial at the Barren Creek Cemetery.

Mina May Reeves was born July 12, 1883. On July 28, 1899 married William Edwards Jr. son of William Edwards and June. Other marriages: Bill Campbell, Hugh Smith and Walter Moore. Mina died May 18, 1969.

Stella Ann Reeves was born Jan. 31, 1889. On Oct. 30, 1906 she married David Elmer Blacketer. Children are Ruby, Lee Otis, Hollis Cecil, Hester Mae, Mildred Maxine and Hershel Kenneth. She married C. P. Barnhouse. Stella died Nov. 27, 1969.

Deldie C. Reeves was born and died March 1891.

Ada Ethel Reeves was born Feb. 23, 1894. On June 25, 1910 she married Andrew Jackson Stroud, son of William Stroud and Martha Ann Gillispie. Children are Bessie Ann, Flora Elizabeth, Alta May, Clyde, Lula and Willia Mae. Ada died Nov. 25, 1937.

George Landen Reeves was born Aug. 1, 1895. He married Lucille Waggener. On Feb. 22, 1923, George married Cynthis Rich. Children are George Lee, Albert, Juanita Dora, Carrie Margaret, Robert Charles and James Richard.

Ida Francis Reeves was born Feb. 3, 1898. On Oct. 31, 1913 Ida married Bert Stroud. Children are Ida Mae, unknown, Cleta Irene, Cleo Bell, Cletis Marie, Viola Betty, Paul Clifford, Violet Jean, Vera Louise and Edna Rose. Ida married Howard Rhay, June 25, 1946. Children are Fred, Lloyd, Allen, Robert and Maxine. Ida died July 25, 1964.

Elnora Bell Reeves was born Oct. 18, 1900. On Nov. 5, 1916 Elnora married Joseph Yeager. Children are Joanna, Ruby Bell, Raymond Franklin, Betty Mae, Jack Oren and Willie David. Elnora died Sept. 17, 1970. *Submitted by Hazel (Reeves) Holland*

Mary Elizabeth Anderson Reeves and husband Robert Jasper Willis Reeves

REEVES – The earliest member of this branch of the Reeves family to come to Polk County was George Washington Lent Marr Reeves. George was born in Tennessee on March 30, 1821. His parentage, as of this time, is still unknown. The earliest official record of George is his purchase of land

James Coleman Reeves and friend Jim Pitner

and his marriage to Francis Elizabeth Smith in Obion County, TN on Dec. 22, 1842.

The family resided in Obion, TN where George was granted a franchise to operate a ferry on Reelfoot Lake. Here the family grew and most of their children were born. Their children were Mary Jane (born Oct. 16, 1845; died April 29, 1912; married Charles Newton Chapell, Aug. 9, 1864); Elizabeth George (born July 6, 1847; died Nov. 28, 1928; unmarried); James Coleman (born May 17, 1848; died July 23, 1935; married Tennessee Redman, June 13, 1869); John Thomas (born Feb. 15, 1853; died between 1893 and 1900 in Joplin; married Mary Edwards, June 27, 1878; this family later moved to Springfield where the sons worked for the railroad); William Henry (born Aug. 15, 1855, appears to have died before the family moved to Polk County); twins Jenetta and Loretta (born in 1857, Jenetta died young; Loretta had at least one daughter, Bertie, raised by her grandparents); and Nancy Belle (born September 1860; died 1940; married Benjamin Franklin Crum in Joplin).

George moved his family to Polk County in 1858 and became a farmer here. He was involved in the Civil War, choosing the Union Cause. He farmed here until the mid 1870s when he moved to Joplin, in Jasper County. He died in Jasper County on Feb. 9, 1888 and is buried in the National Cemetery in Springfield.

Francis, after the death of her husband, moved to Springfield where she lived with her two oldest daughters. She died in February 1904 and is believed to be buried by most of her children in the Enon Cemetery in Polk County.

James Coleman Reeves is the member of this family that has the strongest connection to Polk County. He also was a supporter of the Union Cause and was in the same unit as his father. He was one of the last two survivors of his company. He lived most of his life in Polk County. He died at the home of his son in Harrisonville, MO on July 23, 1935 and was buried in Enon Cemetery. His children were James L. (born April 2, 1870; died Nov. 2, 1871); John Thomas (born Feb. 1, 1872; died March 14, 1872); George E. (born Jan. 21, 1873; died May 17, 1959 in Creston, IA; married Dec. 23, 1894 to Cora Wilson); Charles N. (born Dec. 31, 1874; died April 17, 1959 in Kansas; married Emma Moore June 7, 1914); Flora Mae (born Feb. 4, 1877; died November 1907 in Nebraska; married J. William Mead Sept. 22, 1898); John Perryman (born March 21, 1879; died Sept. 26, 1952; married first Minnie Wagoner March 10, 1901 and second Helen Billsley); William A. (born and died in 1881 while the family was in Texas); Mary Ellen (born April 2, 1882; died April 1, 1964; married Albert Robertson); Walter Eugene (born Sept. 30, 1884; died Nov. 14, 1956; married Minnie Ince Oct. 10, 1904); Benjamin Freeman (born Feb. 17, 1887; died Jan. 14, 1954; married Laura Licklider March 5, 1911); Francis Elizabeth (born Jan. 12, 1890; died April 10, 1956;

married Fred Robertson March 2, 1909); Ernest William (born June 16, 1892; married first Belle Edwards, second Pearl Mae Choate); twins born Oct. 9, 1895 Robert Stockton (died June 8, 1959, married Leathas Livingston Sept. 18, 1912; and Ruby A. (died Nov. 28, 1970, married Frank Atkins).

The Smith family had its origins in Obion and Weakley Counties in Tennessee. Half of the known family settled in Polk County. The family as we know it consisted of the mother listed in census records only as M. Smith; her children Francis Elizabeth, wife of George W. L. M. Reeves and William H., who both settled in Polk County; a sister Idotha, who is the wife of Jerome Cooley, and an apparent half-brother W. H. House.

William H. Smith was born about 1829 in Tennessee, married to Sarah Ann Ray June 6, 1849. He buys land about this time next door to George Reeves from what appears to be George's brother. They live side by side for a time, then both move to Polk County in 1858.

The family of William and Sarah consisted of Martha J. (born August 1850, married Dec. 3, 1871 to William Jackson Oringdorff); Robert Roy (born 1851); Mary Susan (born 1853, married Dec. 30, 1870 to John Oringdorff); William H. (born 1854, married Jan. 31, 1875 to M. C. Derossette); Idotha Francis (born 1855, married Aug. 4, 1872 to Hiram Welch); Madison Monroe (born 1857, married Mrs. Alta McNeece April 21, 1878); John W. (born April 1859, married July 13, 1872 to Sidnie Price); Rebecca Delilah (born 1861, married May 16, 1880 to Archibald Firth McNeece); Thomas B. (born January 1865, married June 7, 1887 to Alice Price); Anne Belle (born 1867, married Sept. 22, 1884 to Even Jones); and Lavina Florence (born 1869, married June 26, 1886 to Noah Wadley). *Submitted by Ben Reeves*

Florence and William Elsworth Reid and family

REID – Florence Paul was born Feb. 18, 1872 in Rockville, Bates County, MO, the youngest daughter of John Paul and Elizabeth B. (Thomas) Paul, both born in New Jersey. Her mother died Dec. 16, 1872 in Rockville, Bates City, MO, leaving her father to take care of three boys, George, Daniel Henry, David King and infant Florence.

Her father married Martha Jane (Cooper) Vannoy, the widow of Caleb Vannoy, Sept. 17, 1874 in Fort Scott, KS. John moved his family, which now included Martha's children Charles and Maggie Vannoy, to Polk County, MO in 1875, settling in Johnson Township, near Dunnegan. At the age of 9 years, Florence Paul is listed on the 1880 Polk County Census, Johnson Township, with her family which now included an additional three children, Corda, William Alexander and Daisy Grace Paul. She was remembered by her siblings to be a tomboy.

Florence Paul of Dunnegan Springs, MO was united in marriage to William Elsworth Reid of Bolivar, MO, Oct. 19, 1893 at the residence of John Paul in Polk County, MO by Reverend G. T. Jeffers. John Paul's will written March 22, 1888, said the girls were to receive 200 dollars apiece as they married. On March 28, 1902 W. E. and Florence Reid of Benton County signed papers as one of their heirs of John Paul selling Maggie Vannoy White's land in Polk County. William Elsworth Reid was a minister in Webb City, MO for many years.

Their children were Raymond Reid, born Nov. 25, 1894, married Ester; Beulah Carrie Reid, born April 15, 1896, died May 1972, married Walter Hensley who died April 1963 and resided in Tulsa, OK; and Lucy May Reid, died at age 3 or 4 and is buried east of Elkton, MO.

Florence (Paul) Reid was remembered by the younger generation as a kind lady that attended numerous family reunions. She died July 23, 1948 in Webb City, MO. *Submitted by Paula Boulanger*

Cora and Will

RENFRO – Cora Renfro was the daughter of Thomas Asbury Renfro and Elnora McKnight Renfro. She also was a twin to Nora Renfro. Cora's mother died when she was 16 years old. She was washing clothes outside and the water tub tipped over on her causing severe burns. This is recorded in the old Death and Birth record book in the Polk County Courthouse. Elnora died March 22, 1885. Nora died July 1884, leaving Tom to raise Cora. She was always close to Mary Renfro Steele, her half-sister.

Cora was married to William Rogers. He was the son of George and Fannie Rogers. She was born May 10, 1884 and died Dec. 9, 1935. He was born July 17, 1883 and died July 1, 1936. Both are buried in Slagle Cemetery, Polk County, MO.

Cora was very ill and wanted Mary Renfro and Joe Steele to be married before she died. Joe and Will had worked in the Marble Head Quarry. After they were married on Dec. 5, 1935, they went to Cora and Will's home in Springfield, MO and stayed with them until she passed away. Cora and Will had no children. *Submitted by Debra Tennison*

RENFRO – Thomas Jessie Renfro was the first son born to Thomas Asbury Renfro and Ellen Eliza Pierce Renfro. He was born Oct. 10, 1906 and died July 28, 1971. He married Thelma Lorraine Polling on Aug. 10, 1935. She was born Feb. 21, 1914 and died Nov. 26, 1984. To this union were born one son, Thomas Gale Renfro and two daughters. Alice Orlean Renfro married James Whitman and they had one son, John Paul. Lau-

Thomas, Jess, Thelma holding Laurel, Alice and Thomas Gale Renfro

rel Virginia Renfro married Ronald Moore and they had two daughters and two sons. Their children are Laura Elaine, Ronald Dean, Angela Dawn and Nathanial Thomas.

Jessie was a farmer all his life. He worked hard and always lived in the Morrisville area. Thelma always loved to play the steel guitar and sing gospel songs. She was a good cook. Fried chicken, mashed potatoes and strawberry shortcake was her specialty.

Jessie and Thelma are buried in Slagle Cemetery beside her mother, Eva Tyo and stepfather, T. A. Tyo. *Submitted by Melinda Manes*

RENFRO – Woodrow Wilson Renfro was the sixth child of Thomas Asbury Renfro and Ellen Pierce Renfro. He was born Oct. 1, 1915 in Morrisville, MO. He died April 25, 1980 and is buried in Sugar Creek Cemetery, Russelville, MO. He married Ellen Elizabeth Hughes on Jan. 1, 1938. Two daughters and two sons were born to this union. They are William Woodrow, James Hughes, Linda Lee and Terry Diane.

Woodrow Renfro, WWII

Woodrow served in WWII. He worked for 30 years as a nursing assistant with the Veterans Administration Hospital in Leavenworth's Hospital in Leavenworth, KS. He loved his wife and kids and always took care of them. He loved to come and visit his brother and family, Jess Renfro, in Morrisville, MO and then go to Springfield, MO to visit his sister Mary Steele and her family.

He and Jess loved to play pranks on their sisters Mary and Bessie. One time they shut the cellar door on the girls and wouldn't let them out. They continued to yell down at them telling them that the snakes would get them. Boy, did they get it from their mom and dad! They continued to play fun pranks even when they were older. *Submitted by Becky Wilson*

RENTFROW – James Rentfrow married Sarah "Sally" Yoast on Dec. 22, 1823 in Knox County, TN. Sarah, the daughter of Francis and Barbara Yoast, was born June 28, 1799 in Virginia. She had many siblings, most of who migrated to Polk or Hickory Counties in Missouri. There were Jacob, Polly, Elizabeth, John, Andrew, Peter, Francis and her twin Catherine. Catherine married Sampson Tillery and is buried in Tillery Cemetery, Hickory County. The ancestry of James Rentfrow is unknown. He was born March 11, 1800 in Virginia.

The happy couple lived in Knox County until 1832 when they relocated to Madison County. They farmed there until 1837. Humansville was to be their permanent home. They settled there in 1838 and homesteaded some 640 acres one and one-half miles southeast of the town. The family home was reportedly a lovely building with an ornate staircase. Unfortunately it was destroyed in a fire.

James was very active in the United Methodist Church of Humansville. The first service of the church was in the living room of his home. He was a licensed minister and a blacksmith. Many of his letters to his children exist and give an insight into his life. Sarah acted as midwife to area women. They had 12 children. Son Andrew F. served in the Missouri state legislature and in different capacities in Polk County. Son Peter was elected Public Administrator for Polk County.

The 12 children are listed below.

Mary was the second wife of John C. Rogers and had six children. She died near Azle, Parker County, TX.

John died at the age of 17 and is buried in Shady Grove Cemetery.

Peter married first, Nancy Jane Luttrell and had 10 children; married second, Sallie A. Weese; buried at Adonis-Oak Grove Cemetery beside his wife Nancy.

Catherine married first, William Oakes and had three children; secondly she was the third wife of Asa Hail Kennedy and had three children; died in Hugo, Choctaw, OK.

Barbara Elizabeth married John Wallace Richards as his second wife; had three children; buried at Shady Grove Cemetery near Humansville.

Sarah Jane was the third wife of Lemuel Robinson Oakes. It is believed there were no children.

Andrew F. never married and died at the age of 71 and is buried at Shady Grove Cemetery near Humansville.

James Joseph married Ruey Ann Bennett and had five children; buried at the Humansville Cemetery.

Susan Minerva (a twin) married LeRoy Bennett and had four children; buried at Santa Ana, CA.

Her twin, Harriet Amanda, married Samuel Bennett and had three children; buried at Santa Ana, CA.

William Marion died at the age of 2 1/2 months and is buried at Shady Grove Cemetery near Humansville.

Hester Ann married Joshua Johnson Jones and had three children and is buried at Rice Cemetery, Dade County.

James Rentfrow died Jan. 2, 1881 and is buried beside his beloved wife Sarah at Shady Grove Cemetery. Sarah died June 22, 1871. *Submitted by Mary Jefferson*

REYNOLDS – Thomas M. Reynolds was born in 1794 in Delaware. He served in the War of 1812. He died in White County, IN on May 13, 1865. He married Polly Beaucamp on March 26, 1823 in Pickaway County, OH. She died Feb. 7, 1841. Both are buried at Pretty Prairie Cemetery near Battleground, IN.

Thomas and Mary "Polly" had seven children: Mary, Emilia, Jeremiah, Mines and Risdon were born in Pickaway County, OH; John and Moses were born in Indiana. The family lived on a farm in the southeast part of White County, IN.

Mines was born Oct. 31, 1831, died Nov. 22, 1898 in Polk County, and is buried, along with his wife, in Barren Creek Cemetery west of Bolivar. Mines married Elizabeth Dysart on March 25, 1860 in White County, IN. Elizabeth was born on April 29, 1838 and died Aug. 22, 1895. They had nine children: Fulton, Thomas Miles, George, Lyda, Emily, Alfred, Cora, Carlton and Cary. Mines walked with his hands behind his back, and so did Tom and Tom's son Sim.

Thomas Miles was born on July 25, 1862 in White County, IN. He died April 13, 1948 at his home west of Bolivar. He married Orah Ann Runyan on June 9, 1886. She was the daughter of Abraham and Mary Ann Runyan. Tom came to Missouri to help drive and to get the family settled, then he was to return to Indiana to study to be a doctor. But, he and Orah Ann fell in love, married and he remained in Missouri. They had a short but happy marriage. She died a few days after their last child, Ora, was born. They also had three sons, Abe, Sim and Frank.

Frank married Golden Beason on June 15, 1913 in Fair Play. They had two children, Luella, who was born March 15, 1914 and died March 5,

Thomas M. Reynolds

2001 and Anna, who was born April 15, 1918. Luella married Fred Engel in California and they divorced. She later married Marvin Anderson. Anna was married to Carl Carson on Jan. 20, 1956 at Fair Play by Lewis Mead. Carl was born July 26, 1921 and died Jan. 13, 2001 and he had retired from the Navy.

Neither Luella nor Anna had children.

Frank was born March 3, 1892, four miles west of Bolivar where he lived all his life. He died Feb. 21, 1955 at his home. Golden was born March 18, 1895 northwest of Aldrich, the daughter of John and Caroline Beason. She died March 31, 1969 at St. John's Hospital in Springfield. Both are buried at Barren Creek Cemetery. Both had belonged to Barren Creek Church.

Frank was a farmer, dairyman and stockman and sold oak lumber in later years. He loved to trade hound dogs, knives, guns and horses. Golden loved to quilt and work with flowers. Many people in the area have beautiful quilts that she quilted. The family milked cows by hand for many years; those were Jerseys, for the butterfat content of the milk was important then.

Oldest child of Tom was Abe and he was born Oct. 6, 1887 and died Dec. 8, 1956 and is buried at Barren Creek Cemetery. On Oct. 4, 1910 he married Elsie Pope and they had one child, Verda, who was born Dec. 11, 1911. They divorced. Abe was badly injured in WWI. He sold many apples and grapes. Verda married and lived in California and had two children. *Submitted by Anna Carson*

REYNOLDS – Sim was born Feb. 14, 1890 and died Aug. 6, 1961. He was a farmer and veterinarian. He took a correspondence course and was self-taught. On Dec. 4, 1913 he married Blanche Hopkins, who was born April 25, 1894 and died June 30, 1983. Their children are listed below.

Oliver was born Oct. 17, 1914. He married Eseline Strange on April 17, 1944 and they had two children, Timothy and Karen. They divorced and he later married Irene Davison.

Emojean was born Aug. 26, 1916 in a log cabin west of Bolivar. She married Bill Jenkins on Oct. 28, 1939 and had one child, Ronald, who was born Oct. 8, 1942. Bill died on Aug. 13, 1972. Emojean remarried on June 1, 1975 to Lawrence Hembree, who died on Nov. 2, 2001. She was a teacher and school librarian at Bolivar Schools until retirement. She lives in Bolivar.

Charles was born Sept. 9, 1918 west of Bolivar. He married Jean Hunter on Dec. 26, 1945 in California. They had four children: Vicki, Valene, Charles Jr. and Vanessa. Charles died in April of 1989.

Elizabeth was born Feb. 11, 1921. She married Dolen Hammons on March 17, 1939. Dolen had a son from a former marriage named Jim. Elizabeth cared for him as if he were her own. Elizabeth and Dolen had a daughter, Jacqueline. Elizabeth and Dolen spent several years in California, returning to Missouri in 1946 where she was a secretary at Fair Play Schools. She retired as a caseworker with Missouri Division of Family Services. Dolen died on Jan. 28, 1998. Elizabeth lives in Bolivar.

Jerry was born July 7, 1926. He married Opal Hemphill. He died on Feb. 1, 1997. Opal died on Jan. 16, 2000. Jerry served 13 years with the US Foreign Embassy Service and had assignments in Singapore, Nigeria, Israel, Italy, Somalia and Sweden.

Ann was born Sept. 2, 1929. She married Don Brown on Dec. 24, 1949 in Bolivar. Don was born July 9, 1924. Don was a US Army Warrant Officer and retired in July of 1974. They bought and operated an insurance business. Don died May 31, 1997. Their two children are Nancy and Steven.

Nancy married Kevin Simmons on May 15, 1976 and they had two children. Kelly was born Oct. 8, 1980 and they adopted Tyler on March 1, 1987. They divorced. Nancy died Jan. 27, 2001. Kelly married Justin Mauck on June 2, 2001 and they have one son Andrew.

Steven was born March 25, 1956. He first married Debbie Pierce and had one child, Matthew and they divorced. In 1985 he married Paula Bray and they have three children, Derek, Jessica and Zachary.

Ora, youngest child of Tom and Orah Ann, was born June 29, 1895 and died April 4, 1979. She was married to William Curl on April 8, 1923. Bill died July 17, 1927. She worked as a music teacher, schoolteacher and as a caseworker in Polk County Welfare Office. They had two children, Edwin and Mary Anna.

Edwin "Pete" was born Nov. 4, 1924. He married Dil Palmer on Oct. 10, 1947 in Springfield. Pete served in WWII in the Air Corps, then as a basketball coach. They had two children, Gregory and Bob.

Mary Anna was born Nov. 1, 1926. She married Jerry Tindle on Dec. 12, 1948. They had seven children: Martha Ann, Jerry, Bill, Kenneth, Carl, Mary and Rebecca. *Submitted by Ann Brown*

REYNOLDS – Alfred was born March 14, 1869 in White County, IN and died Nov. 18, 1925, southwest of Bolivar and is buried in Mt. Gilead Cemetery. He married Josie Burleson on Sept. 18, 1895. Josie was born Feb. 20, 1871 and died March 8, 1956. Their children are listed below.

Naomi was born June 8, 1896. She married Roy Payton on March 25, 1917 and had three children, Verdin, Vergil and Wilma.

Troy was born Feb. 25, 1899. He died May 20, 1963 and is buried in Greenwood Cemetery. He married Iva Ammerman who contracted typhoid fever and gave birth to twin boys and all three died within one week. He married again and she left a son, Clyde, born to their marriage. Troy married again to Myrtie Campbell who had a son by a former marriage, Ben Campbell and he married Anna Lee Cunningham. Troy and Myrtie had two children, Alfred and Barbara.

Delphia was born Oct. 14, 1907 and married Ray Manes and had two children, Thurman and Harold Dean. They later divorced. She later married Perry Lockhart.

Alfred was born Nov. 30, 1932 and married Ethel Mae Redford and later divorced. They had two children. Alfred is now married to Jean Swartz. Alfred is a barber in Bolivar and has done that for 46 years and Alfred's son Randy has barbered for 22 years.

Barbara was born July 1, 1934 and married Bud Campbell on Sept. 26, 1951. They had two children, Roger and Russell. She is now retired after working in a law office.

Another descendant of Mines Reynolds and Elizabeth was Cora, born Jan. 23, 1871 and died Oct. 23, 1932. She married Billie Haden on Feb. 2, 1893. He was born Nov. 17, 1862 and died Jan. 4, 1963. Both are buried at Red Top Cemetery. Their 11 children were Charley, Iola May, Lola, Lillie, William, Dan, Lena, Carl, Carrie, Alice and Oba.

Carl was born April 7, 1904 and married Lela Seiner; they had no children but became active in the Assembly of God Church in Bolivar. Lila helped organize it.

Two other descendents of Mines and Elizabeth were Carlton "Cat" and Cory. *Submitted by Alfred Reynolds*

RICHARDSON – Jesse Richardson Sr. was born in the early part of the 1760s in Lincoln County, VA. According to pension records, he was in Virginia when he volunteered his services in the Revolutionary War in 1778. Tax records indicate he owned land in Pulaski County, KY in 1835. Jesse Sr. moved to Polk County, MO, where he purchased land on what is now part of the Triple C Ranch. The Richardson Family Cemetery is on this property. Jesse Sr. had three sons that we are aware of. Jesse Jr., born in 1819, married Elizabeth Ann Stewart of Polk County on March 15, 1842. Elizabeth Ann is the daughter of Evan Stewart and Nancy B. Jenkins. Evan and Nancy were from Tennessee and settled about eight miles north of Bolivar in 1836.

During the Civil War, Jesse Jr. was arrested on the Arkansas and Missouri border. He was not a soldier but was put in the Union prison camp in Springfield, MO, where he died May 20, 1863. He and Elizabeth had eight children. Nancy, born in 1845, married Peter Davis. Virginia T., born in 1848, married Joshua Hayden and died in 1875 of measles. George W. was born in 1850. Newton Jasper was born in 1853 and died in 1920. John Evan was born in 1855 and died in 1862. Francis Marion was born in 1856 and died around 1939. He was a successful farmer in the Cuyama Valley in California. Caroline, born in 1860, married Joseph Cox. Jesse E. (daughter) was born in 1863. After the death of Jesse Jr., Elizabeth auctioned the Richardson property off on the courthouse steps for $425 to William Pill as documented in Jesse's probate.

Newton Jasper married Margarete Clarinda "Clarina" Warren (born 1856; died 1940) from Warsaw, MO in 1875. They lived on property south of the original Richardson property in Polk County. They sold this property and moved to Bakersfield in 1917, where he worked as a gardener for the city. Margarete "Nanny" is remembered for wearing a sunbonnet, smoking a corncob pipe and always having a spittoon in her house. She had both legs amputated and ended her life confined to a wheelchair. She is fondly remembered for the beautiful quilts she made.

Newton and Margarete had 14 children. Four died at a young age; Claudie (born 1883; died 1884), Birttie Mae (born 1892; died 1894), Bessie Elizabeth (born 1899; died 1900) and Minnie Zoe (born 1902; died 1902). Jesse was born in 1876 and died in Santa Maria, CA in 1953. Francis Marion was born in 1878 and died in 1940 in Bakersfield, CA. John W. "Willy" was born in 1881 and died in 1962 in Bakersfield. Walter Loranza was born in 1884. James "Frank" was born in 1887 and died in Bakersfield in 1977. Matty Myrtle was born in 1889 and died in 1927. Maggie Bell was born in 1894 and died in 1966. Newton Henry "Newty" was born in 1897 and died in 1959. Orpha and Olpha were born in 1904. Orpha died in 1984 and Olpha died in 1950.

Newton Jasper's sons moved to Kern County, CA around 1910. John W. and his brother, Francis Marion, came to Bakersfield first. Walter came to Taft, where he married Clara Lois Kofahl in 1913. She was working in a boarding house for oil workers in Shale. Walter was 29 and Clara was 16. Clara was born in Licking, MO. Walter worked as an oil worker. They had four children. Marguerite Lenora Romley was born in 1916 in Bolivar. Roy Leonard was born in 1921. Betty Lois Hannagan was born in 1923. Roy and Betty were born in Taft. In 1925 they moved from Taft to Bakersfield into the house Walter built on property purchased from his mother. In 1929 Walter worked as an oil worker in India for a year. During the Depression, Walter found work wherever he could. Clara picked chickens for 25 cents a piece. She was an excellent cook and never turned a hobo away when they came to the door. Patricia was born in Bakersfield in 1932. During WWII (1943) Walter, Clara and Patricia moved to Grass Valley, CA, where Walter worked as a steamfitter at Camp Beale. Walter died in 1973 in Bakersfield at the age of 89. Clara died in 1993 in Walnut Creek, CA at the age of 96. They are both buried in Bakersfield. At this writing, their four children and grandchildren are living in California. *Submitted by Betty Richardson Hannagan and Suzanne Hannagan Foster*

Frederick A. and Kate (Van Bargen) Richner circa 1920; the first Richner family in Polk County

RICHNER – Frederick Richner was born in Bern, Switzerland in 1840. He came to America from Switzerland when he was 16 years old. The census of 1860 showed that he was living in Diana, Lewis County, NY, near Watertown. Later Frederick moved to Cincinnati, OH and met and married Katherine Van Bargen in 1877. Katherine had come to America from Switzerland, also, with her parents in 1859 when she was 7 years old. She was born in 1852.

They had two children while living in Cincinnati, OH. The children were named Charley and Adolph "Ollie." Frederick had been working as a cheese maker. Then, Katherine decided that they should go further west. In 1881 they took a train west and stopped in Springfield, MO. At the station they met Philip and Fredericka Schleifer who sold them 80 acres of land for $250. This took place around Dec. 5, 1881. This land was near Van, MO. Frederick spent the rest of his life farming. They were the first Richners in Polk County, MO.

Frederick and Katherine then had four daughters named Nellie, Carrie, Lulu and Esther. Charley, 3, and Adolph "Ollie" Frederick, 2, at the time of the move, grew up near Van. Charley married Maude Scroggins and moved to California to live. Adolph "Ollie" stayed in Polk County and lived here all of his life as a farmer except for a couple of years when he worked in Garden City, KS.

Adolph's "Ollie" date of birth was Nov. 11, 1879. On Nov. 20, 1915 he married Ethel Hook. Her family lived near Wishart and later sold their farm and moved eight miles southeast of Bolivar.

After a year of marriage, Adolph "Ollie" and Ethel bought a farm about three miles southeast of Slagle, MO. They raised their three children there. Their sons, Weldon and Ralph, and their daughter, Pauline, went to grade school in Wilson District and went to high school at Pleasant Hope.

Weldon, the oldest child of Adolph "Ollie" and Ethel, married Volda Payne. They lived most of their married life in the Rock Prairie Community. He worked for Springfield City Utilities and was a farmer. They had two sons and a daughter. Volda's father, Ray Payne, gave the land for the Rock Prairie Cemetery on the north side of the road. The Richners in this area attend the Rock Prairie Missionary Baptist Church.

Gary, their oldest child, had also stayed in Polk County. He married Betty Meyer on Dec. 27, 1960. Their two sons, Mike and John, have also made their home in the Rock Prairie Community.

Sue Carol, Weldon and Volda's daughter, married Larry Vest and they have two sons. Fred, their youngest child, married Claudia Fetters and they have two daughters.

Ralph Richner, Adolph "Ollie" and Ethel's middle child, also has spent most of his life in Polk County. He married G. Karleen Davison on Dec. 25, 1941. He served in the Army Air Force during WWII for two and a half years. He spent most of this time working for Frank Horton and Company, a consulting engineering company. After working out of Bolivar they decided to move closer to his work in Fulton, Licking, Poplar Bluff and DeSoto, MO. In 1958 they decided to move back

Newton Jasper Richardson family. Back row: Francis Marion, Orpha, James "Frank," Olpha and Newton Henry; between back row and front on end: John W. "Willy;" Front: Matty Myrtle, Newton Jasper, Margarette Clarinda, Maggie Bell; between back row and front on right end, Walter Loranza.

to Bolivar to be closer to family. He also worked for Allgeier, Martin, and Associates, another consulting engineering company. He retired in 1983.

Karleen Richner's family also lived in Polk County for several generations. Her paternal great-grandfather lived in Halfway at the time of his death on June 25, 1858. His name was Milton M. Davison. His second child was Karleen's grandfather, George Thomas Davison. George Thomas Davison's 13th child was her father, Melvin M. Davison. He was the manager of the Farmer's Exchange (MFA) in Bolivar and Halfway, owned a grocery store, and built a few houses in Bolivar. Karleen's great-grandfather on her maternal side, Thomas Standley, came from England and after marriage to Sarah Jane Amos, also from England, moved to Polk County, MO near Violet (northeast of Bolivar). Thomas and Sarah Standley's son, W. S. Standley, married Phoebe Ann Erwin and they lived most of their married life in the Violet community northeast of Bolivar and owned a store and ran the post office in the community. Their daughter, Eunice M. Standley, married Melvin M. Davison and they lived in Halfway and Bolivar most of their married life.

Ralph and Karleen Richner had three children: Robert, Janice and Patricia. They attended Bolivar High School. None of them stayed in the Bolivar area. Robert married Ann Thompson. They have five children. Janice married John McGaughey and they have one daughter. Patricia married Dennis Miller (deceased). They had one son. She then married Steve Larson. He also has one daughter.

Adolph "Ollie" and Ethel Richner's other child, Pauline, taught school in the Wilson School District for one year. She married Leroy Fay Redfearn and had one son, Kenneth. Kenneth has two sons. Pauline and Fay have lived most of their married life in Houston, TX.

A book on the Richner name published by the Halberts Family Heritage shows the estimated number of the households in different countries with the Richner name; Switzerland 878, United States 389, Germany 48, France 21 and Italy 8. There are currently only five households in Polk County with the Richner name. *Submitted by Ralph Richner*

RIPPLE – During the long winter evening, after chores were done and supper was over, the children looked forward to sitting around the stove while their mother read to them from Harold Bell Wright's *Shepherd of the Hills*. They soon made their first vacation trip to Missouri to explore the "Ozarks" and see an authentic "hillbilly."

Then in early 1953 Evan and Neva Ripple moved their family of four, Neva's mother, Anna Montgomery and the family dog, Toby, to their new home north of Bolivar. Coming from northern Iowa they were looking forward to the milder winters and farming their own 80 acres. They had purchased the Molly Cheek farm located across from Spring Valley Church and, Buddy, Willy, Judie and Duane all attended South Ward School in Bolivar.

In addition to his own farm, Evan worked at the cheese plant and picked up odd jobs whenever possible. Neva also worked at Teters Nursery and later managed the roller rink on North Main for several years.

In 1955 they embarked on a new opportunity, purchasing the Hiway Café which was located under an auto parts store on Springfield Street. Having had no prior restaurant background it was a family run business with "Pop" Ripple running the front and "Mom" Ripple in the kitchen baking pies, frying chicken, hamburgers and her famous tenderloin sandwiches. It soon became popular with the morning and afternoon coffee drinkers as well as the regulars at lunchtime where a daily special plate lunch cost less than $1.

Being a popular hangout for high school and college students, it offered several pinball machines as well as a jukebox with all the latest records, six plays for a quarter. Sunday nights and Wednesday nights were jammed with college students and their dates sharing fries and a Coke before curfew. Other nights during the week Pop would run a delivery service to the girls' dorms with orders of sandwiches, fries, chips and cases of pop.

Having sons that played sports, Pop contacted all the out-of-town teams and was soon staying late and feeding the players and coaches some good home cooking before they made the bus trip home.

With the graduation and senior trip of their oldest son, Buddy, they started a tradition of opening early the morning the seniors left for Washington, D. C., with complimentary sweet rolls, donuts and drinks for all seniors and their parents. They continued this from 1957 to 1966 when their youngest son graduated and went on the senior trip.

After Evan's death in February of 1969, Neva sold the business and returned to Iowa until 1988 at which time she returned to Ozark, MO where she resided until her death in November of 2001.

Their daughter, Judie, and her husband, Kenneth Deane, reside in Bolivar. Buddy and his family live in Ozark, MO; Willard and family in Fort Lauderdale, FL; and Duane and wife in Keosauqua, IA.

Love and laughter with people young and old help make enduring memories of Mom and Pop Ripple and the Hiway Café. *Submitted by Judie Deane*

RITTER – John Jacob Ritter was born April 3, 1777 in North Carolina. He was married to Barbara Garber in 1805. John migrated with his widowed mother to near Nashville, TN when he was 15, then returned to North Carolina for two years, then he went to Kentucky. John moved near Dayton, OH and married Barbara, daughter of John Garber and Barbara Zook. Barbara was born Sept. 1, 1785 in Rockingham County, VA. Their children: Jacob, Michael, John, Sarah, David, Susan, Benjamin Franklin, Samuel and Martin Enoch.

Jacob was born Jan. 1, 1806 in Dayton, OH; he is the descending line to Teresa. Jacob married Elizabeth Miller Oct. 26, 1826 in Wayne, IN, daughter of David Miler and Sarah Hardman. Elizabeth was born June 5, 1809 in Montgomery, OH. Children of Jacob and Elizabeth are Lucinda, Barbara, Sarah Anne, Aaron Miller, Amanda Ellen, Martha Emeline, William Henry Harrison, David Miller, John Newton, Benjamin Franklin, Theodore, Clarinda Jane, Lorinda and Elizabeth Miller. Jacob and Elizabeth were pioneers of St. Joseph County, IN, being one of the first families that settled there.

Aaron Miller Ritter was born May 25, 1834 in St. Joseph County, IN. He was married three times. His last wife Emma Josephine Perryman was born Nov. 22, 1869 in Greene County, MO. Married Dec. 4, 1902. Aaron came to Springfield, Greene County, MO in 1860. Where the airport is today in Springfield was part of Aaron and his brother David's farm and the road in front is named Ritter after them. North of Springfield on Highway 13 is a little school that is named Ritter School; the land was given by the Ritter brothers. The railroad ran through their land and they had a store and railroad stop called Ritter Station. They both farmed and had cattle, horses, and 120-acre apple orchard, which was one of the largest in the Ozarks. Their barn burned during WWI, it had 3000 bushels of wheat in it. The wheat had been sold to the army and it was thought that

German sympathizers set the fire. It had to be used as feed. Aaron and Emma had two children, Miller Perryman Ritter and William Howard Ritter.

Miller Perryman Ritter was born Sept. 3, 1903 in Springfield, MO. He was married Feb. 27, 1933 in Liberal, Ford County, KS to Anna Mae Crane, born March 7, 1915 in Sitka, Clark County, KS. Their children are Dolores Jean, William Aaron, Wanda Marie, John Raymond and Warren Miller.

Aaron Miller Ritter, Miller Perryman Ritter, and Emma Perryman Ritter, circa 1905

Dolores Jean Ritter was born Sept. 22, 1933 in Sitka, KS. She married Robert Eugene Appleby March 5, 1951. Robert was born Oct. 18, 1930 in Ashland, KS. Children are Teresa Susan, Robert Roy and Dana Jean. Robert went to Bolivar School and graduated there. Robert "Bob" and Dolores lived the first four years of their marriage in Kansas and moved to Bolivar in 1955. Robert Eugene was a carpenter, helping build Bolivar High School gym, Southwest Electric, SBU dorms, Morrisville gym, and many others.

Teresa Susan Appleby was born July 22, 1952 in Ashland, KS and married Danny Gene Barker July 2, 1971 in Bolivar, MO. Danny was born Oct. 16, 1951 in Humansville, MO. Children are Travis Aaron Barker, March 1, 1973; Daniel Curtis Barker, Nov. 9, 1979; and William Robert Appleby, Jan. 13, 1981. Teresa attended Bolivar School and Danny went to Fair Play. They dairy farmed for 23 years. They have owned Teters Florist in Bolivar for the last seven years.

Daniel Curtis Barker was born Nov. 9, 1979 in Bolivar, MO. He married Heather Shadwick Oct. 17, 1998. Their child is Peyton Daniel Barker, born April 19, 1999. *Submitted by Teresa Barker*

ROBERTS – Amos Hall Roberts was born on Jan. 23, 1884 to William Henegar Roberts (born March 20, 1856, died March 20, 1926) and Ann Elizabeth Hall (born March 7, 1863; died Aug. 21, 1884) and died March 28, 1976. On Feb. 21, 1905 he married Martha Pearl Payne (born Sept. 8, 1885; died April 21, 1963). For the first two years of their married life they lived in Adonis, the area where his father lived. They then purchased a farm at the corner of Highway D and 64 in Polk. That farm remains in the family today. The original house, which was located due east in the Lindley Creek bottom, was moved to its present location in 1914. Amos and Martha also built a small house on the original home site that the family still refers to as the "weaning house." Four of their sons along with their wives used the "weaning house" as their first home.

Amos and Martha had 13 children, losing two in infancy. They are listed below along with their spouses.

Annie Elizabeth (born Jan. 5, 1906) married Russell Hightower Walker (born Aug. 25, 1903; died Jan. 15, 1993) on Nov. 20, 1924.

Fred Payne (born Dec. 4, 1907; died July 16, 1991) married Mabel Elva Walker (born Oct. 10, 1905) on Dec. 23, 1928.

Amos Roberts family 1942
Front row: Annie, Amos, Martha, Ada, Atha;
Middle row: Ester, Clifford, Fred, Albert;
Back row: Leslie, Claude, Jesse, Cleo

Atha Pearl (born Oct. 2, 1909; died Feb. 9, 2001) married Ruby Leonard Ragsdale (Nov. 2, 1904; died Feb. 5, 1988) on Feb. 17, 1929.

Ada (born March 24, 1911) married Arthur Jump (born Aug. 12, 1909; died Sept. 28, 1988) on Oct. 19, 1935.

Claude William (born May 14, 1913; died Dec. 21, 1987) married Ruby Golden Inglis (born Dec. 12, 1917; died Sept. 27, 1991) on Nov. 25, 1934.

Clifford Leo (born March 10, 1915; died Nov. 6, 1999) married Laura Elnora Combs (born July 24, 1917; died March 5, 1997) on April 14, 1940.

James Albert (born Oct. 2, 1917) married Jewell Delphia Walker (born Aug. 9, 1919) on Oct. 21, 1939.

Amos Cleo (born Jan. 8, 1920; died Jan. 15, 2000) married Willa Mae Kelley (born June 18, 1927; died March 19, 1990) on Nov. 16, 1946.

Cletus (born Jan. 8, 1920; died Jan. 8, 1920).

Jesse Andrew (born Jan. 28, 1922; died Aug. 19, 1974) married Bertha Fern Lower (born April 10, 1924) on Dec. 23, 1945.

Willard Elbert (born Sept. 24, 1924; died Nov. 7, 1924).

Leslie Erwin (born Dec. 31, 1925) married Elta Alene Noblitt (born April 24, 1928) on Nov. 4, 1946.

Ester Avington (born March 12, 1928) married Nadine Elizabeth Rader (born July 4, 1927) on April 15, 1949.

Amos and Martha were devout Missionary Baptist and attended Sentinel Missionary Baptist Church while their health allowed. Many happy memories were created during family gatherings in the Roberts' home especially at Thanksgiving and Christmas. The rooms were filled with laughter, conversation and many children.

Amos and Martha left a legacy of love of God and respect of family to their children and grandchildren. Many of their descendants still live in Polk County. Those living now number 102. With the exceptions of Amos' parents and his son Jesse, the entire lineage listed above, upon their passing, have been buried at Payne Cemetery in Polk, MO. *Submitted by Donita Pirkle*

ROBERTS – Donald Claude Roberts married Delores Louiese Gamel at the home of her parents (Willard and Fern Jones Gamel) near Halfway. Don is a great-grandson of Jesse Russell Payne, the grandson of Amos Hall Roberts and Martha Pearl Payne and the son of Claude William Roberts and Ruby Golden Inglis. He was born Aug. 20, 1936, in Polk in the "weaning house," the common name for the small house that sat in the back of the farm owned by Amos and Martha. Several of their children used it as their first home as newlyweds.

Dolores was born Aug. 12, 1938 in Halfway and moved several times with her family, attending 19 different schools before she graduated in 1956 from Pleasant Hope High School. She met Don at a pie supper in Halfway and they married on Sept. 22, 1957. To this union were born four children: Debra "Debbi" Louiese (McGinnis), May 18, 1959; Donita Lynn (Pirkle), May 29, 1960; and twins Dwight Craig and Denise Leah (Stutenkemper), Feb. 13, 1963.

In 1940 Don and his parents moved to the Jim Payne farm in Polk where Garland Dale (born March 22, 1940; died Sept. 22, 1999) was born. The family then moved in 1946 to the farm on Highway 32 east of Bolivar. On this farm they were very active in raising turkeys and at times had as many as 1,000 hens. In addition to that enterprise they operated a dairy, raised sheep and had huge gardens. Claude was always pleased to share from his two-acre watermelon patch. In June 1959, Don and Garland opened the Roberts Sale Barn on a portion of the family farm. Don attended The Reisch Auctioneer School and held many farm, household and estate sales over the years.

Dolores was also active in the business, assisting in roles as clerk, bookkeeper, etc. As their children became old enough, they, too, assumed jobs within the family business. Dwight and Donita as well as several grandchildren are still active in the livestock auction.

Through the years many family gatherings were held in Claude and Golden's house including daily lunch for the men and the hired hands. The grandchildren begrudgingly rose early to help dig potatoes behind the horse and plow, picked high from the cherry trees, picked low for walnuts and groaned when it was butchering or apple butter making day. And yet as maturity approaches and generations pass away, those memories become precious. Many pleasant hours were passed eating melon straight out of the patch complete with salt that Claude kept in a Tupperware shaker in his overalls, shucking corn in the shade and being rewarded with Golden's homemade ice cream, and putting up with Claude's antics as he tried to scare his grandchildren by dressing up in various costumes and chasing them around the yard. To date they are convinced that the "Boogie Man" is still in the crawl space to the attic in the north bedroom.

Don, Delores, Donita, Dwight, Denise and Debbi

Besides the auction business, Don and Dolores also raised beef cattle and rented bulls to many farmers throughout the area. Today they remain active in the family business and enjoying their grandchildren, Isaac Roberts McGinnis (born Sept. 1, 1983), Daberath Louiese McGinnis (born May 27, 1985), Whitney Dayle McGinnis (born July 4, 1988), Denver Payne McGinnis (born March 24, 1994), Sarah Donn Pirkle (born Oct. 2, 1986), William Colfax "Cole" Pirkle (born May 17, 1990), Jacob Glenn Roberts (born Feb. 11, 1980), Dustin Craig "Dusty" Roberts (born May 9, 1986), Adam James Roberts (born June 18, 1988), Devon William Statenkemper (born Nov. 21, 1983), Donald "Cody" Stutenkemper (born April 20, 1986) and Dakotah Diane Stutenkemper (born Jan. 14, 1992). *Submitted by Dolores Roberts*

William and Agnes Roberts

ROBERTS – Agnes Lee Hammons was born in Dunnegan, MO on Oct. 7, 1903. William Henry Roberts II was born in Bolivar on Aug. 15, 1900. They met when Agnes Hammons was teaching at Humansville and Bill Roberts was a partner with his brothers, Harold and Luther, in the Chevrolet dealership at Humansville. At the time she was in a graduate education program at Missouri University. Her major professor didn't think female teachers should be married. Because she feared that she wouldn't receive her master's degree, they were married very quietly on June 3, 1931. As the minister at her church, Cumberland-Presbyterian, was in the midst of a remodeling project on his home, they were married in Bill's 1931 Chevrolet.

Agnes continued teaching until Mr. Roberts became the Chevrolet dealer in Bolivar. She then joined him working as the office and finance manager. She worked full time until her late 80s. After that she visited the dealership every day that her health permitted. Bill III joined the dealership in 1955 and later became the owner and president.

The Robertses had two sons, William H. Roberts III and Lee Melvin Roberts.

Mr. Roberts also farmed and showed Tennessee walking horses. His most famous horse was Missouri Chance. In his younger days, he also enjoyed the Missouri version of fox hunting. Mrs. Roberts joined him one night, but she couldn't see much enjoyment in sitting in the dark listening to the dog's bark while chasing an animal, perhaps a fox. When one of the men declared that "Old Red" was leading the pack and then seconds later "Old Red" came trotting into camp alone, she decided that fox hunting was not for her.

Mrs. Roberts loved spending time with her boys and working in her flowerbeds, but she felt most comfortable sitting in the front office at the dealership writing up car deals and greeting customers. Both Mr. and Mrs. Roberts were longtime members of First Baptist Church.

Both sons graduated from Bolivar High School as salutatorians of their class. Bill graduated from Missouri University with a degree in business. He was a member of Beta Theta Pi social fraternity. Lee graduated from Drury University with a degree in biology. Both sons worked at the car dealership. Lee later moved to Republic, MO where he owned Lee Roberts Chevrolet for many years. Bill married Carolyn Lea Kilpatrick on Nov. 30, 1958. They had six children: William IV, Anne, Nancy, Mary, Matt and Mark. Lee married Georgia Brockman. They had four children: Margaret, Melvin, Alice and Ellen. *Submitted by Bill Roberts Jr.*

ROBERTS – William Henry Roberts III was born in Dunnegan, MO April 18, 1933. His parents were Agnes and William Henry Roberts II. They moved to Bolivar in 1937 when Bill Sr. bought the Chevrolet dealership. Bill Jr. began school at North Ward with Veda Bruner as his teacher. His second grade teacher was Ada McCracken. During the second grade year a new student, Carolyn Kilpatrick, joined the class, moving from El Dorado Springs. Both Carolyn and Bill continued through the Bolivar School system graduating in 1951 as valedictorian and salutatorian of the class. Bill was senior class president and participated in varsity basketball, band, glee club, boys quartet, clarinet quartet, B club and the junior and senior plays. Carolyn was the senior class secretary, cheerleader, FHA president, band, mixed chorus, the drum and bugle corps and the junior and senior plays.

Bill Jr. and Carolyn Roberts

After graduation Bill attended Missouri University, graduating in 1955 with a BS in business. He was a member of Beta Theta Pi social fraternity. Among the honors he received was the Wall Street Journal Award for outstanding student in security analysis. During college, he began his sales career by selling Chevrolets to his fraternity brothers. After graduation, he began working as a salesman at Bill Roberts Chevrolet.

Carolyn attended Harding College in Arkansas and Abilene Christian College in Texas but graduated from Missouri University in 1955 with a degree in elementary education. She taught third grade at Robberson School in Springfield for three years.

Carolyn and Bill were married Nov. 30, 1958 at Stone Chapel in Springfield but made their home in Bolivar where they have lived for 44 years. Bill became a partner in Bill Roberts Chevrolet in 1956 and later became the owner and president. His children tease him about his three waves, a raised hand to strangers, a full-hand wave to friends but a big raised arm wave to his customers! Carolyn worked part time at the car dealership until the arrival of their child, William Henry Roberts IV, on March 4, 1961. She became a full-time mother as other children were born: Anne Elizabeth on Sept. 17, 1962; Nancy Agnes on July 25, 1965; Mary Caroline on Dec. 8, 1969; Matthew Christopher on Dec. 9, 1971 and Mark Kilpatrick on Oct. 31, 1974.

All of the children attended the Bolivar Public Schools where they were involved in various activities. Anne and Nancy were valedictorians of their classes.

Bill IV graduated from Southwest Baptist University and married Anissa Fisher in 1992. They have one son, William Logan. Bill has won many golf tournaments and was voted one of the Ten Best Golfers in the Ozarks. He has won the National Deaf Golf Tournament several times and has been a member of the US Deaf Golf team when they participated in international tournaments in England, Pennsylvania and South Africa.

Anne graduated from Johns Hopkins University where she was a member of Phi Beta Kappa honor society. She received her MD from Yale University and completed a residency in internal medicine from Mayo Clinic. She married Dr. Fernando Cavero in 1992. They have four children: Raleigh, Sydney, Devin and Emilia.

Nancy graduated from Southwest Baptist University with degrees in math and business. She received her master's degree in business systems from Arizona State University. After graduation, she worked for Ernst and Young. She is married to Dr. Mark Houston, who is an assistant professor in marketing at Missouri University. They have three children: Jon, Elise and Wil.

Mary attended SBU and SMS, majoring in elementary education. She is a preschool teacher at Polk County Christian School. She is married to Craig Preston who is general manager of Bill Roberts Chevrolet. They have two children, Nicholas and Alexander.

Matt graduated from William Jewell College with a degree in economics. He married Martha Morrison who also graduated from William Jewell. After graduation they lived in Vienna, Austria for three years. When they returned to Raleigh, NC, Matt enrolled in North Carolina State University where he received a doctorate in agricultural economics. He is an extension specialist at Ohio State University. During the time that they were in North Carolina, Mardi received a master's of divinity degree from Southeastern Seminary. They have two children, Sam and Ben.

Mark graduated from Southwest Baptist University with a degree in mathematics. He graduated summa cum laude and received the Life Beautiful Award. He received a master's degree in bio-statistics from St. Louis University. He and Amy Whatley were married June 1999. They live in Bolivar where he is employed as office manager of Bill Roberts Chevrolet and Amy is a first grade teacher at the primary school.

Both parents and all six children made professions of faith at First Baptist Church. They are all active members of their churches. *Submitted by Mary Preston*

Henegar and Martha (Rule) Roberts

ROBERTS – Henegar Roberts was born in Anderson County, TN on April 11, 1831 to Moses and Maria Roberts, who were Virginians. He had one brother, Joseph and one sister, Cynthia. Henegar's parents moved to Illinois where they died between the years of 1831 and 1837 in Carrolltown, Greene County, IL. They died a day apart. Henegar was taken by an uncle, Stephen Portwood, back to Tennessee.

Henegar married Martha Rule, the daughter of Rev. Henry and Nancy (Tarwater) Rule on May 5, 1835 in Knoxville, TN. Martha Rule was born Nov. 17, 1838 in Knox County, TN.

Rev. Henry Rule, a Methodist preacher (born May 12, 1813; died July 4, 1911) and Nancy Tarwater Rule (born Jan. 23, 1813; died June 1911) were married July 31, 1834 in Knox County, TN. Both are buried in the Flemington Cemetery, Flemington, MO.

The Rules were also the parents of William, James, Harriet Ann Cox, Parthena Adeline Trotter, Matthew Andrew, Amanda Elizabeth and Nancy Jane Collins White. Both the Rules and the Tarwaters were of German descent.

Henegar and Martha Rule Roberts moved from Knox County, TN to Polk County, MO in the year 1856. Most of their married life was spent in the Adonis area where Henegar was a farmer and a stockman. The Rule family settled in the Flemington, MO area.

Henegar served in the 26th Regiment Enrolled Missouri Militia during the Civil War. He was a member of the Agriculture Wheel and a Republican in politics. Henegar and Martha were faithful members of the Oak Grove Missionary Baptist Church at Adonis, MO.

Henegar and Martha were the parents of eight children: William H., Andrew Leroy, Nancy Jane Rush, Sarah Ann Williamson Jones, Adaline Vest, Joseph M., Orlie Orestas and Arthur J.

Henegar and Martha Rule Roberts are buried in the Oak Grove Cemetery at Adonis, MO.

Henegar's sister, Cynthia Lovelace Roberts, married Cajah Manes in Tennessee and moved to Polk County, MO near her brother. Nothing is known about Henegar's brother, Joseph. *Submitted by F. David Roberts*

Children of William H. Roberts Front: William Henry Roberts II, Iva Lee Roberts Johnson, Loretta Catherine Roberts Tillery and Rena Roberts; back row: Harold Leroy, Amos Hall, Francis Henegar and James Luther Roberts.

ROBERTS – William Henry Roberts was born in Knoxville, TN on March 20, 1856, died March 20, 1926 and is buried in Oak Grove Cemetery in Adonis, MO. He came to Polk County with his parents in 1856. He was the eldest son of Henegar and Martha Rule Roberts. He grew up on the Adonis Community and made his home there most of his life except for a time when he lived in Bolivar, MO where he served a term as county clerk at the turn of the century. He was a Republican, member of the Oak Grove Missionary Baptist Church, and a successful stockman and landowner. He died on his birthday from complications of diabetes.

William Henry married first Anne Elizabeth Hall (March 7, 1863; died Aug. 21, 1884) on July 25, 1878. Two children were born to this union: Fred (May 6, 1881; died Jan. 15, 1883) buried at Oak Grove Cemetery in Adonis, MO and Amos Hall (born Jan. 23, 1884; died March 28, 1976). Amos Hall married Martha Pearl Payne (born March 8, 1885; died April 21, 1963) on Feb. 21, 1905 in Polk County, MO. They were the parents of 13 children: Annie Elizabeth (Mrs. Russell Walker); Fred Payne; Atha Pearl (Mrs. Ruby Ragsdale); Ada (Mrs. Arthur Jump); Claud William; Clifford Leo; James Albert; Amos Cleo; Cletus (died in infancy); Jesse Andrew; Willard Elbert (died in infancy); Leslie Erwin and Ester Avington. Amos and Martha lived on a farm in the Polk Community in Polk, MO. They are both buried in the Payne Cemetery, Polk, MO.

Anne, Mary, Nancy, Matt, Bill IV, Bill III, Mark and Carolyn

William Henry Roberts married second Elizabeth Ellen Pitts (born July 9, 1866; died June 5, 1951) on Feb. 17, 1886 in Polk County, MO. Eight children were born to this union: Loretta Catherine (Mrs. Orla C. Tillery) (born May 3, 1887; died Sept. 17, 1987), buried in Greenwood Cemetery Bolivar, MO; Iva Lee (Mrs. Herman C. Johnson) (born Aug. 28, 1889; died June 16, 1981) buried in Oak Grove Cemetery, Adonis, MO; Francis Henegar Roberts (born June 14, 1891; died April 16, 1964) buried in Greenwood Cemetery, Bolivar, MO; Carolyn "Carrie" (born Jan. 12, 1894; died Nov. 12, 1899) buried in Oak Grove Cemetery, Adonis, MO; Rena (born April 1896; died Feb. 9, 1980) buried in Greenwood Cemetery, Bolivar, MO; William Henry II (born Aug. 15, 1900; died June 4, 1984) buried in Greenwood Cemetery, Bolivar, MO; Harold Leroy (born Sept. 12, 1902; died June 22, 1992) buried in Greenwood Cemetery, Bolivar, MO; James Luther (born Nov. 13, 1904; died Nov. 29, 1988) buried in Greenwood Cemetery, Bolivar, MO. *Submitted by Paul H. Roberts*

Francis Roberts Family
Front row: Ruth Ellen Roberts Clark, Francis Henegar Roberts, Dorothy Grace Adams Roberts and Carolyn Roberts Hendrickson; back row: Thomas Sylvester, Paul Harry and Francis David Roberts

ROBERTS – Francis Henegar Roberts was born in Adonis, MO to William Henry and Elizabeth Ellen Pitts Roberts on June 14, 1891. He died April 15, 1964. His father, William H. Roberts, traveled to Missouri with his parents, Henegar and Martha Rule Roberts in 1856 from Knoxville, TN. The family lived in the Adonis, MO community where they were farmers and stockmen.

Francis Roberts' mother was Elizabeth Ellen Pitts Roberts, the daughter of Francis M. and Mahala Zumwalt Pitts. Francis M. Pitts was the son of Barney Pitts of Hickory County, MO and Mahala Zumwalt Pitts was the daughter of Adam Zumwalt of Polk, MO. Both families were of the very earliest settlers in their communities.

Francis H. married Dorothy Grace Adams on Feb. 22, 1914. Dorothy was born May 2, 1894 and died Jan. 9, 1972. She was born in Dunkirk, NY. Dorothy was a schoolteacher who lived near Flemington, MO. Dorothy was also an accomplished pianist and played for the silent movies being shown in the Humansville, MO theater. She had moved to the Flemington, MO area as a young girl with her parents, Sylvester and Carrie J. Rhodes Adams from Dunkirk, NY.

Carrie J. Roberts had immigrated to the United States from England in 1874. Carrie J. Rhodes Adams (born July 24, 1866; died June 7, 1918) and Sylvester Adams (born Oct. 29, 1860; died March 8, 1926) came to Missouri from the state of New York. Sylvester was a railroad man and was originally from the state of Michigan. Both are buried in the Flemington, MO Cemetery.

Francis and Dorothy Roberts were farmers in the Humansville, MO and Flemington, MO area except for the term that Francis served as the county clerk of Polk County in Bolivar, MO as his father had done at the turn of the century. Francis was a Republican in politics.

Francis and Dorothy were privileged to celebrate 50 years of marriage. They were longtime members of the Humansville Baptist Church and became members of the First Baptist Church in Bolivar, MO after their retirement to Bolivar. They are both buried in Greenwood Cemetery, Bolivar, MO.

Francis and Dorothy Roberts were the parents of five children: Thomas Sylvester (born Sept. 12, 1917; died Sept. 10, 1983). Tom married Alma Sinden of Jefferson City, MO on June 30, 1945. They had one son, Samuel Thomas. Carolyn Elizabeth Roberts was born Oct. 5, 1919. Carolyn married Clark Delbert Hendrickson, Bolivar, MO on June 6, 1941. They had three children: Martha Frances, Donald Charles and Howard Ray. Ruth Ellen was born Oct. 21, 1922. Ruth Ellen married John E. Clark of Stockton, MO on March 13, 1942. They had four children: John Robert, Stephen Edward, Scott Elton and Joy Dee. Paul Henry was born Dec. 5, 1925. Paul H. married Helen Louise Jenkins of Bolivar, MO on Sept. 9, 1950. They had three children: Paula Louise, Krista Helen and Alan Pat. Francis David was born Sept. 1, 1936. David married Patricia Louise Harris of Butler, MO on Aug. 31, 1962. They had two children: Brent David and Tricia Beth. *Submitted by Alan P. Roberts*

ROBERTSON – During WWII, the ban on married women teachers was lifted, and Lero Robertson Tinsley took the teachers' exam in 1944 and started teaching in Flint School the next September. Starting in 1945, she was a student at Southwest Baptist College during the summer terms. Sometimes her daughters, Joyce and June, visited her college classes. Often, though, she dropped them off, and they walked up the lane to their Grandpa Ike's house.

Grandpa Ike's farm was just up the hill from Salem Church. Next to the lane was a little path the cows had made waling from their pasture up to the house. One day Joyce made the mistake of walking in the cow's path. By the time they reached the house, she was literally crawling with tiny seed ticks! The big, gray "dog-ticks" sometimes burst and spilled out millions of little seed ticks. In those days Missourians had never heard of Lyme disease. Deer were seldom if ever seen either, which was probably related to the overabundance of wolves. Farmers were paid a bounty for shooting wolves.

Although he lived well into the automobile age, Grandpa Ike never owned a car. When he needed to travel a distance, he would arrange with a neighbor, usually Clyde Ryan, to take him. If he had business in Bolivar, he would make the trip by train. Most of the time, Cliquot had all he needed to supplement what he raised on his farm. On occasion Grandpa Ike would send Joyce and June with a short list to the store at Cliquot. He would give them the money, plus a nickel apiece for candy.

Once Grandpa Ike took June and Joyce to Bolivar on the train, and when they got there, he bought them ice cream cones. Joyce was very upset when her dip fell onto the pavement. Knowing the way to a little girl's heart, Grandpa Ike went back to the store and got her another one. Then before going home, Joyce's stiff new shoes began to rub blisters on her feet, which were used to being bare all summer. Grandpa Ike saw no problem with taking her shoes off, though Joyce's mother was mortified later to think of her daughter running around Bolivar like a country bumpkin.

Sometimes Grandpa Ike would go out to the woods and shoot a squirrel for dinner. It was cooked in the little pressure cooker on the black cast iron wood stove in the kitchen. All these years later, June and Joyce still remember the delicious smell of squirrel and dumplings cooking, and the sound of the little valve jiggling on the cooker.

The salt, vinegar, toothpicks and square spoon holder had their place, permanently sitting in the middle of the kitchen table. Beside the table, there was a large flour chest with a breadboard that opened out as a breadboard. Nearby, Grandpa Ike kept a large calendar on his wall, which also served as a diary where he jotted down the weather and any other noteworthy happening of the day.

A door from the kitchen led out to a rather large porch that was high off the ground. The girls used to sit there and dangle their feet while Grandpa Ike told stories about his childhood with four brothers and five sisters.

Before they knew it, evening had come, and there was their mother, back from school to pick them up. Those carefree days with Grandpa Ike grew into a storehouse of pleasant childhood memories. *Submitted by Joyce Robertson Tinsley*

I.B. Robertson with grandchildren Wayne, June and Joyce Tinsley

ROBERTSON – In 1799 Samuel Robertson was born in Kentucky to Nathan Robertson and Anne Leach. This marriage had nine children. They moved between Kentucky, Illinois, Indiana and Iowa. Samuel also as an adult lived in these states. On July 12, 1843, Zachariah Robertson was born of Samuel's second wife, Amanda Elizabeth White, his first wife being Mary Parks. Samuel was the father of 11 children. Samuel died in 1876 and is buried in Powshiek, IA.

Zachariah raised his family in southern and southeastern Iowa, having married Hannah Jane Leek Sept. 5, 1867 in Marengo, Iowa County, IA. Hanna's parents were James and Elizabeth Leek. Hanna was born Aug. 5, 1850 in Zanesville, OH. Zachariah and Hanna had 10 children: Emma Lucretia (born 1868) married John Remley Wysong in 1904; Polly Ann (born 1870) married James Madison; Amanda Elizabeth (born 1876) married Sam Show; Joseph Thomas (born Jan. 31, 1878) married Antonia Dvorak; Albert Arthur (born Dec. 9, 1878) on Sept. 5, 1907 in Polk County married Mary Eliza Reeves (born 1882 to James Colman Reeves and Tennessee Redman Reeves); Charles Alonzo (born 1880); Jeremiah Zachariah (born 1882) married Amanda Zora Stevens; Jesse Anderson (born 1885) married

Zelpha Nora Waggoner in 1911 and secondly, Ella Victoria Waggoner in Polk County; Fred Cleveland (born 1890) on March 2, 1909 also married a daughter of James Colman Reeves, Fannie Elizabeth Reeves (born Jan. 12, 1890) in Polk County, MO.

In the 1900 census Zachariah is in Jefferson Township, Poweshiek, IA but in 1901 his father decides to move to Missouri bringing his five youngest boys with him. They came in a railroad boxcar and settled in Polk County. We have different things of these early days such as Fred's 1904 grade card from the Bolivar school. In 1906 Charles Alonzo dies but the other four boys and their father stay around, from Cliquot to Morrisville and Bolivar. Zachariah died Sept. 8, 1920 and is buried in Greenwood Cemetery, Hanna Jane died in 1923 and was buried beside her husband.

Children of the four boys are

Albert Arthur; Dora Angus married Orval Neal; Dewey married Billie Erwin; Myrtle Lodean married Charles Hejna; Paul Lee married first, Darcus Scurlock and second, Jean McCracken Holms.

Jeremiah Zachariah: Glen, Charles, Alfred, Howard, Samuel, Virgil, Loulinda and Jerry Lee.

Jesse Anderson: Nora Agnes, Erma Geneva, Wilma Ann, Majorie, Golden Leona.

Fred Cleveland: Mattie Elsie married Clarence Jenkins; Amanda Elizabeth married William Lee Orrell; James Cleveland; Delbert married Lillian Amos; John Marion married June Hargis; Raymond Marshall married Dorles Etheline Wood; Henry Adolph married Opal McGee; Ernest Cleveland married first, Betty Frincais Ricchetti and second, Lula Ma Nuccum; Willard Carl married Betty Jo Gordon; Luther Ray married Dora Lee LaRue; Luther's twin Lucy who died young; Dixie who also died young; Albert Eugene married Mary Lou Barber; Robert Dale married Wanda Hart.

Jerry and Jesse moved into the Springfield area in the mid 1900s but Albert and Fred stayed here with their families helping Polk County to become this great place to live that it is. *Submitted by Edward Ray Robertson and family of Fred Cleveland Robertson*

Halfway Baseball Team, Delbert Barham is first on left, Arthur Roderick is third from left and Floyd Shackelton is second from right, others unknown.

RODERICK – Sara's great-grandfather, Arthur Marion Roderick (born 1894; died 1974), often said his great-grandparents, John and Elizabeth Ratcliff (born 1815; died 1863), were among the early settlers at Halfway. Their daughter, Mary (born 1835; died 1913), married John M. Eagon (born 1830; died 1893). The Eagons' daughter, Malissa (born 1866; died 1953), married Porter Roderick (born 1861; died 1919). John Ratcliff died in Texas. The others are buried at Reed Cemetery.

Arthur said the family had a secret that he didn't know about until his grandma, Mary Eagon, was on her deathbed. He was staying with her one night when she began to sob. She was ashamed to tell Arthur that she was part Indian. John Ratcliff's Indian name was Running Horse. Arthur was proud of his heritage. After all, he figured that Indians were here first.

Arthur was close to his grandma. She was a widow, and he had stayed with her when he was younger. He had seen her work very hard, yet she lost her farm. He was determined to buy it back. Several years later, Arthur and his wife Lexie bought it. They were living there when they died.

Arthur loved the game of baseball. He had an opportunity to go to St. Louis to play in the major leagues, but he decided not to go. He said he had a wife, a baby and a farm with a mortgage. He just couldn't take a chance like that. He continued to play for area teams until he was an "old man."

He batted against Satchel Paige when he came through the country with a touring black team. He got a hit off of Paige. Arthur said it was late in the game and the black team was so far ahead that Paige really wasn't throwing his best. Arthur also faced a very young Dizzy Dean. Arthur connected with the ball, but he didn't reach base. Another player on Arthur's team said, "At least you hit the ball. I never even saw it."

Arthur managed the Halfway Farmers Exchange from 1924 until 1937. Halfway was a bustling little town then, but there were difficult times during the Depression. One man asking for credit to buy flour and meal said, "If you can't sell it to me today, I'll have to come back tonight and steal it. I have four babies at home starving to death."

Arthur was also on the school board for a number of years. He worked hard to get the rock high school built in 1937. He said he wore out a car driving people to Jefferson City to lobby for a new high school at Halfway.

Sara's mom said that Grandpa Arthur was a very generous man, but he was also hot tempered and probably got into more fights and arguments than he should have. She said it was probably the "Indian coming out in him." She said he was one of the most interesting people that she ever knew, and she wished that Sara could sit just one evening and listen to him weave one of his stories. *Submitted by Sara B. Dunseth*

ROSS – There have been a long line of Ross families in Polk County since the early 1930s. David Francis Ross married Sarah Sally Lemmon and their children were, as follows: John Jacob, William, Francis, Bolivar, Mary Letta, Jane, Cordelia, Orlena, Paulina and Labrytha.

David and Sarah's son John Jacob married Susan Katherine "Kate" Cargile and they had one child, Thomas Francis Ross.

Thomas Francis Ross married Eulalia Monroe Woodard and they had the following children: Monroe (he married Nora Creed); Ruby (she married George Booher); Roma Jane, never married; Mary Ruth, died at age 6 months; John (married Verna Myrtle Kinney); Elta (married Webster Hughes); George Woodard (married Myrtle Hicks); Rachel (married Charles Moore); Marvin (married Vesta Fuhr); and Lee (married Grace Hembree).

Marvin T. Ross, "The Checker Man"

Thomas and Eulalia's son Marvin and wife Vesta had the following children: Leota (married Charles Guy Sawyer); Robert (married Dorothy Starner); Lucille (married Charles Onas Hill); and Marvena (married Joseph Hall).

Marvin and Vesta's daughter Leota and husband Charles Guy Sawyer had the following children: Bunny (married Mike Jones); Debbie (married Bob Franz); Sherri (married Carl Olson); Charles Guy Jr. (married Kathy Flinn); and Danny (married Mindi Hendrickson).

Guy and Leota's daughter Bunny and her husband Mike had Charles Michael and Angela Elaine. Daughter Debbie and husband Bob had Megan Elizabeth and Jeremy John. Daughter Sherri and husband Carl had Bruce Andrew and Kenneth Clark. Son Charles Jr. and wife Kathy had Nicole Renee and Charles Ross. Son Danny and wife Mindi had daughter Danah. *Submitted by Charles Michael Jones*

Thomas and Eulalia Ross and children

ROSS – Polk County, MO had many fond memories for Leota (Ross) Sawyer Recknor.

Leota's great-grandfather was John Jacob Ross who owned the 209-acre Ross farm on the Sac River, located a few miles south of Morrisville, MO.

John J. Ross was one of 10 children born to David Francis Ross and Sarah Lemmon Ross. He was born in 1840 and served in the Civil War. In 1866 he traveled from Tennessee to Arkansas where he met Susan Catherine Cargile. They were married and moved to Morrisville, MO and their first and only home was the Ross farm.

It was here in 1867 that their only child Thomas Francis Ross was born on Oct. 15, 1867. He died May 29, 1947. When Thomas "Tommie" was a young boy, he was with his father in Bolivar one day and they met the famous Frank James. He had been pardoned from prison and was in

Marvin (left), niece Velma (center) and Marvin's brother Lee

Bolivar selling books that he had written about his brother Jesse James and himself, also books on Cole Younger and brothers. John J. Ross purchased some of the books.

Thomas grew up to marry his childhood sweetheart Eulalia Monroe Woodard. Her parents were Hiram Monroe Woodard and Martha Ann (Bland) Woodard. Hiram served in the Civil War and was captured along with his group of men and sent to Rock Island Prison until the war ended, and then he was released. Due to the conditions there, he had bad health and died young in 1869. Later, Martha Bland Woodard married James Benge.

Thomas Francis and Eulalia had 10 children, five boys and five girls. One daughter Ruth died at the age of 6 months. At this time there were two homesites on the Ross farm, one for Mr. and Mrs. John J. Ross and the other for Tommie and Eulalia and their children. Their four girls (Ruby, Roma, Elta and Rachel) grew up and became schoolteachers and homemakers and most of the boys (Monroe, John, George, Marvin and Lee) were farmers. At early ages they helped their father Tommie tend the farm, cropping the river bottom in corn with grain crops and hay on the upper land, using horses and white nosed mules. Times were primitive by today's standards. Tommie Ross never owned an automobile. Saddle horse and buggy were their transportation. Times seemed to be simpler, no electric bill, no water or fuel bills, no insurance of any kind, no upkeep or payments on cars. The farm and home were theirs and mostly all food was produced and grown on the farm. They raised cattle and hogs, chickens and geese, horses and mules. They had their own milk, eggs, meat, lard, butter, fruits and canned goods from gardens and truck farms. Enough milk was separated to cream and extra eggs were sold in Morrisville to buy the necessities for raising a family and schooling them. The necessities were usually kerosene, matches, tobacco, coffee, sugar, flour and thread. No fast food then, everything was made from scratch by the good cooks.

Taxes had to be paid on the farm and usually a load of hogs and cattle that went to market once or twice a year would provide the cash needed.

John and Marvin Ross

The children of Tommie and Eulalia were schooled in Morrisville, MO. Marvin, being next to youngest, graduated from 12th grade in 1928 from Marion C. Early High School, before that known as Scaritt Morrisville College. After graduation Marvin went to Kansas City, MO and drove home a new 1928 Model A, right off the assembly line. Then he worked on a ranch in Oklahoma and later one in Kansas, making money to pay for his car.

In July 1932, Marvin met and married a lovely red-haired girl, Vesta. She was of German descent and a hard worker. Vesta Fuhr was born in 1912 and the oldest of 10 children born near Billings, MO to Robert and Ota (Brashears) Fuhr. The Fuhr family had two girls and eight boys. Six of the boys served in WWII and all returned home safe by the grace of God.

When the Ross sons and daughters began to marry, they needed a home. Thus a smaller house on the Ross farm was built for them to use until they bought farms and homes of their own. This house was called the weaning house and more than one of the children lived there for a while.

When Marvin and Vesta were married, the weaning house was being called home by Ruby Ross Booher and her family. They lived there several years, so Marvin built a one-room cabin on the Ross farm and there he and Vesta began their married life.

Marvin Thomas Ross, graduation from Marion C. Early High School

The Ross farm had been in the family many years before 1933 when Leota, the first of four children born to Marvin and Vesta, arrived with the help of Dr. Harold from Morrisville. Today his office building still stands at the end of Main Street. Also, another house remains closer to the Methodist Church, where Eulalia Ross (Leota's grandmother) gave birth to her first son, Monroe. The house belonged to Eulalia's mother (Martha Woodard Benge) and was used as a boarding house. It is getting quite old now.

Leota's memories are living near and having Virginia and JoAnne Booher as her first playmates, until she was past 4 years old. In November of 1934, Leota's brother Robert "Bob" was born, but not before Marvin added another room to the cabin and then a third child, a daughter Lucille, was born.

All the while, the country was coming out of a deep depression. In the late 1920s times were very bleak for America. The banks went broke and closed their doors, and people with money lost it and some lost their homes; people were starving. In 1933 Franklin D. Roosevelt was elected as President and began programs to help the people. Soup lines formed and work programs such as WPA and CCC Camps started up. Leota's father, Marvin, had a good team of work mares and was hired by the WPA to help built roads; long, hot tiring hours, but the pay was so appreciated.

The CCC Camp provided boys and young men with work, building fish hatcheries, parks, agricultural improvements, forestry, etc. Part of the wages paid were required to be sent home to help out families. Roads, bridges, schools, dams, buildings, etc. helped the economy and people began to hope again.

The whole country was under terrible drought conditions. The crops and pastures dried up and there wasn't much livestock market. Marvin had a few head of cattle and horses and when he came home after a hard days' work, he'd hitch the horses to the wagon and take barrels to the Sac River and he would fill them with water and take to the livestock.

Years before, down near the Sac River, Pitt Woodard and slave labor had built a mill called the Woodard Grist Mill. Leota's great-grandfather (Hiram Woodard) had worked in the mill as a young man, helping grind the corn, wheat, etc. into flour and meals. In 1866, the Sac River flooded and the entire mill except for the foundation and large, flat grinding stones was washed away.

When Marvin built his house, he hauled a large millstone up to use for his front door step. Later, Leota's daughter (Bunny) got that same stone to use as her front porch step.

In 1937, Marvin and Vesta Ross moved from Polk County to Lawrence County, MO. Their fourth child, another daughter (Marvena), was born there. Leota, Bob and Lucille all began school at Mt. Comfort. Leota was sad to leave her Grandpa and Grandma Ross and playmates Virginia and JoAnne Booher, but there were return visits and some of these included fishing trips down the Sac River. Leota would be fixed up with fishing gear consisting of a tree limb with hook and bobber and the bait was usually fat bacon. Off she and her cousins, Virginia and JoAnne, would go, down the dusty trail with Leota chattering all the way. As they neared the river, JoAnne would say, "Leota, be quiet or you'll scare all the fish away." What fun to see the bobber go under and pull out a wiggily perch three inches long. Then they would get tired of fishing and gather mussels from the gravel bar and on the way back to the house, would pick up paw-paws on the bluff. Some people like them, Leota didn't!

While living in Lawrence County, Leota learned to milk cows and do chores. Her family lived on stock farms with lots of work to do.

In 1943, Marvin went to Polk County and bought two stock farms located between Fair Play and Bolivar. Here he had 20 to 25 head of dairy cattle and some beef stock and saddle horses. The cows had to be milked by hand twice daily. There was lots of hard work on the farm, rocks to pick, wood to saw and barn chores. Leota's mother grew big gardens and canned lots of vegetables. When farmers didn't brush hog the pastures, there were lots of blackberries to pick and can and make jams and jelly. But Oh! Those pesky chiggers!

The family were not strangers to hard work. After moving back to Polk County, Leota, Bob, Lucille and Marvena went to a country school called Pickel. The teachers were all dedicated, the course of study was good and Mrs. Marvin Hopkins, the county school superintendent, did her job well.

Leota and Bob graduated from eighth grade in 1947. The graduation commencement was held at the Pike Auditorium with several of the

Bob, Leota, Marvin, Marvena, Vesta and Lucille Ross

rural school attending. Leota and her brother Bob graduated from Fair Play High School in 1951; at that time Fair Play was a very busy little town. Leota loved school; it was so much easier than working those hours on the farm and more fun with all her school friends. After high school Bob attended Bolivar College (SWBC) which was only a two year college then.

Leota married Guy Sawyer in January of 1951 and they lived in Johnson County, KS from 1955 to 1988. They raised their family of five children there. Their children are Bonita Sawyer Jones, born 1952; Debra Sawyer Franz, born 1954; Sherri Sawyer Olson, born 1956; Charles Guy Sawyer Jr., born 1958 and Daniel Bruce Sawyer, born 1961. All are happily married and have families of their own. Leota has 11 grandchildren and five great-grandchildren. The children all attended Shawnee Mission, KS schools and were saved and baptized members of Greenwood Baptist Church of Shawnee, KS.

In 1954 another drought hit Missouri. Marvin and Vesta had lots of cattle and not nearly enough crops and pasture. The temperatures were record breaking with 112 degrees and 114 degrees recorded one day and animals died from the heat. Marvin had a big livestock dispersal sale and he and Vesta went to Kansas City where they were employed until they retired. They sold the 320-acre farm to Truman Griffin. Marvin and Vesta lived in Polk County until their deaths. Vesta died on July 21, 1991 and Marvin died on June 11, 1995. They are buried in Morrisville Cemetery along with others of the Ross family.

Thomas F. Ross died in May of 1947. Eulalia lived with children until her death in August of 1955. They are buried in Morrisville Cemetery. The 209-acre Ross farm was sold in 1987 or 1988.

Leota Ross Sawyer Recknor moved from Johnson County, KS to Lawrence County, MO in 1988 with her husband Bert. She lives one mile from where she lived from 1937 to 1943 as a young girl. She is happy to have so many memories of her life spent in Polk County. *Submitted by Leota Ross Sawyer Recknor*

ROSS – Clyde Elliott Ross "Hoover" was born May 21, 1926 near Morrisville, MO in Polk County. He was a veteran of WWII. Clyde was an army infantryman and also military police. He was awarded the Bronze Star.

Clyde married Ruth Evelyn Staas on May 21, 1948. They shared a loving union for 52 years. Ruth, the daughter of James and Frances Cunningham Staas, was born Sept. 28, 1929 in Polk County, MO. Clyde and Ruth have three children: Phyllis Jean, Thomas Nelson and Cheryl Renee. All three children graduated from Marion C. Early High School in Morrisville, MO.

Phyllis Jean Ross was born on Dec. 24, 1949. She married Jerry Hall on May 20, 2001 and resides in Springfield, MO. Phyllis has two children: Brian Keith Taylor (nicknamed "Cottontop" by his grandfather, Clyde Ross) and Natalie Dawn. Brian was born Oct. 4, 1969. He married Sonya Kay Presley, June 2, 1990 in Eudora Baptist Church in Eudora, MO. Brian and Sonya have four children: Tiffany Kay, Keith Elliott, Michael Gene and Bryant Levi Taylor. Brian, Sonya and their children reside in the Aldrich area in Polk County in the home of Brian's deceased grandmother, Tillie Taylor. Sonya is the daughter of Mike Presley and Julia Kay Curtis Presley. Sonya was born January 15. Natalie Dawn Taylor was born Jan. 3, 1977, the first baby born in Polk County in that year. She married Paul Gilmore Oct. 17, 1998. Paul was born November 30. Paul was raised in the Pleasant Hope area. Children of Natalie and Paul Gilmore are Shelby Paul Gilmore and Aus-

Phyllis, Clyde, Ruth, Cheryl and Tom

tin Neil Gilmore. Brian and Natalie area also the children of Gene Taylor, son of Keith and Ruth Taylor, also of Polk County.

Thomas Nelson Ross was born Feb. 28, 1953 in Springfield, Greene County, MO. He married Kathleen "Kathy" Kay Hicklin July 25, 1980 in Springfield, Greene County, MO. Kathy is the daughter of Oscar T. and Janus Holloway Hicklin. Kathy was born June 11, 1952 in Springfield, Greene County, MO. They have two children: Betsy Leanne Clayton, born Nov. 11, 1971, she married Timothy Leighty on Oct. 7, 2000. They have a son, Clayton Thomas Leighty. They live in Lee's Summit, MO area. Tom and Kathy's son, Thomas "TJ" Nelson Ross Jr., was born March 18, 1982 in Springfield, MO. TJ loved to fish in Slagle Creek with his grandpa, Clyde Ross.

Cheryl Renee Ross was born Sept. 29, 1963, in Springfield, Greene County, MO. Cheryl married Louis Gomes and they reside in Honolulu, HI. Cheryl and Louis own and operate Ground Transport, a transportation company.

Clyde retired from Kraft Foods in Springfield, MO after 32 years of service. Upon retirement he spent time taking care of the farm and enjoying his grandchildren and great-grandchildren. Clyde passed away on June 27, 2000 from a heart attack and is greatly missed by all that knew and loved him. He is buried at the Morrisville Cemetery. Ruth still lives in their home in Polk County. *Submitted by Tom and Kathy Hicklin Ross*

Elta Ross Hughes and her students 1923

ROSS – This photo above was Elta Virginia Ross Hughes and her students taken around 1923. Can anyone identify any one of these children?

Elta was born Nov. 14, 1900, the sixth child of 10 to Thomas and Eulalia Ross of Morrisville, MO. Her siblings were: Monroe, Ruby, Roma, Rachel, George, John, Marvin and Lee. Ruth died in infancy.

As a young girl she taught school at Fair Play and Brookline, MO. She gave up teaching to marry Webster Wayne Hughes of Republic, MO. They had four children: Blanche Eulalia, Wayne Woodard, Frances Zana and Chester Monroe who died in infancy.

Frances fondly remembers her childhood days at Grandpa and Grandma Ross's in Morrisville, MO. They would have huge family reunions. There would be lots and lots of little cousins to play with. After a big dinner of fried chicken, ham, biscuits, red-eye gravy, home-grown vegetables, homemade cobblers, pie and cakes, the kids would dash off to Sac River, which ran through the back of the Ross's farm to swim and fish. There were always horses to ride, chickens and pigs to feed, wild berries to pick and eat. Living in a small town like Republic didn't have all of these fun things to do.

Mr. Hughes, Frances's dad, had an old Studebaker car. They would go through Springfield, MO and pick up the rest of the clan, sometimes there would be seven or eight people in the car. She remembers one special time back in the 1940s when they were returning from Morrisville, the old car broke down in Brighton. The town was closed up. There was a little white church along the side of Highway 13. The pastor of that church invited them to sleep in the church that night until morning when they could get the car fixed. He brought sheets, blankets and pillows and the kids got to sleep on the ground under the stars. What a treat!

Frances is proud she was born in Polk County. Glad her mother chose to go home to be with her own mother in Morrisville, where she gave birth to Frances. *Submitted by Frances Zana Hughes Etheridge*

George and Myrtle Ross family

ROSS – George Woodard Ross was born Sept. 13, 1902 in Polk County, MO. His parents were Thomas Francis and Eulalia Monroe Woodard Ross and the great-grandson of Polk County pioneer, David F. Ross. George married Myrtle Leona Hicks on Oct. 2, 1920. Myrtle, daughter of Nelson S. and Ellen Hicks, was born Feb. 9, 1903 in Sacville, MO. George lived most of his life in Morrisville area working the farm. George also worked in the shipyards in California. George died July 15, 1979, Myrtle died Nov. 18, 2001, and both are buried in the Morrisville Cemetery, in Polk County, MO.

To this union was born four sons and two daughters: George Wilbur, Leone Faye, Clyde Elliott, Joseph Lawrence, Dorothy Mae and Daniel Lee Ross. George Wilbur Ross was born June 26, 1922 in Polk County. George was killed in an auto accident in January 1970 in Springfield, MO. He left two daughters, Linda Lorene Ross and Michele Ross, and his wife JoAnne.

Leone Faye Ross was born Aug. 15, 1924, Polk County, MO. She married Earl Janes on Sept. 20, 1946. Earl was born Dec. 18, 1919. They have one daughter, Carol Denise Janes, born Sept. 20, 1951. Faye and Earl reside in Byron, CA.

Clyde Elliott Ross was born May 21, 1926 near Morrisville, Polk County, MO. He married Ruth Evelyn Staas on May 21, 1948, a loving union they shared for 52 years. Ruth, the daughter of James and Frances Cunningham Staas, was born Sept. 8, 1929 in Polk County, MO.

Joseph Lawrence Ross was born Sept. 3, 1930 in Polk County, MO. He married Blanche A. Hall on Aug. 20, 1950. She was born March 3, 1927 in Christian County, MO. Joe and Blanche have five sons: Roy Douglas, David Lawrence, Dwight Richard, Mark Allen and Sean Ross.

Dorothy Mae Ross was born July 9, 1935 in Polk County, MO. She married George Allan MacDougall on Jan. 25, 1955. He was born May 19, 1933 in Oakland, CA. Dorothy and George have four children: Debra Lynn, George Allan Jr., Gordon and Gregory Bruce MacDougall. Dorothy and her family live in Fairfield, CA.

Daniel Lee Ross was born Nov. 18, 1942 in Polk County, MO. He married Aneta Williams on Oct. 31, 1964. They have one son, Daniel Lee Ross Jr. *Submitted by Phyllis Jean Ross Hall*

Taken in 1979, seated: Joe, Sean and Blanche; back row: Mark, David, Roy and Dwight Ross

ROSS – George Woodard Ross was born Sept. 13, 1902, and died July 16, 1979. Myrtle Leona Hicks Ross was born Feb. 19, 1903 and died Nov. 18, 2001. Both are buried at the Morrisville, MO Cemetery.

George Woodard Ross was the seventh child of Thomas Francis and Eulalia Monroe Woodard Ross. They lived on a farm south of Morrisville, MO. George was born and raised on the farm. As a young man, he broke mules and also horses. He met and married Myrtle Leona Hicks on Oct. 2, 1920 at the Bolivar County Courthouse in Bolivar, Polk County, MO.

Her parents were Nelson and Ellen Cavener Hicks.

George and Myrtle had six children and all four of their sons were in the military service. Five of their six children attended Marion C. Early School at Morrisville, MO.

George Wilbur "Tommy" Ross was born June 26, 1922 and died Dec. 31, 1969. He was a Navy veteran. He was killed in a car wreck in Springfield and is buried in the National Cemetery in Springfield, MO. He married Mary Lou Craig and they had one daughter, Linda Lorene Ross. Later he married Joan St. John and they had one daughter, Michelle Ross.

Leona Faye Ross was born Aug. 15, 1924. She married Earl Janes and they live in California. They had one daughter, Denise Janes.

Clyde Elliott Ross was born May 21, 1926 and died June 26, 2000. He served in the Army. He lived in Polk County all his life, and is buried in the Morrisville, MO Cemetery.

"Joe" Joseph Lawrence Ross was born Sept. 3, 1930. He served in the Army.

Dorothy Mae Ross was born July 9, 1935. She married George MacDougall and lives in California. They had four children: Debra Lynn, George Jr., Gregory and Gordon.

Daniel Lee Ross was born Nov. 18, 1942. He served in the Air Force and retired in 2001 from the Chrysler Corporation. He married Anita Williams and they had one son, Danny Jr.

Danny Jr. is a minister and officiated at his grandmother Myrtle Ross's funeral in November 2001.

During WWII, George and Myrtle Ross moved to the state of California with their three younger children in 1943 and worked in the defense plants for five years. In 1948 they moved back to Lockwood, MO and lived the rest of their lives in Missouri. Their last residence was at Springfield, MO. In Myrtle's retirement years she loved to piece quilts and pieced many lovely quilts for her children and grandchildren.

"Joe" Joseph Lawrence Ross married Blanche Adalyn Hall in Springfield, MO on Aug. 26, 1950. Her parents were Roy Franklyn and Willie Myrtle Hall. Joe and Blanche Ross had five boys.

Roy Douglas Ross was born Oct. 30, 1952.

Twins David Lawrence and Dwight Richard Ross were born Aug. 18, 1955.

Mark Allan Ross was born March 5, 1963.

Sean Drew Ross was born in Aug. 28, 1967.

Joe Ross retired from the city of Springfield in 2000. Previously Joe and Blanche owned and operated a Tastee Freeze in Springfield, and Joe worked in the grocery business for 45 years and was manager for A & P and Safeway for several years. They celebrated their 50th wedding anniversary in August 2000 and now enjoy their motor home. They have just returned from a trip to Mt. Rushmore. Joe and Blanche Ross also enjoy visiting their 13 grandchildren and one great-grandchild. *Submitted by Joe Lawrence Ross*

ROSS – John Jacob Ross was the fifth child of Thomas and Eulalia (Woodard) Ross.

He was born on their farm at Morrisville, MO in Polk County. The farm was south of Morrisville. He was born on Feb. 24, 1898. He married Verna Myrtle Kinney on Nov. 30, 1926. Her parents were William and Lottie Kinney.

John and Verna Ross had three children, Ruby Naomi, Ralph J. and Mary Lee Ross.

John J., daughter Ruby Naomi, with Verna Myrtle Ross

Ruby Naomi was named after two aunts, one being her aunt Ruby Ross Booher. Ruby Naomi was born in Laverne, OK on Sept. 7, 1927. She married Lee Weder and had one son, Rodney Lee Weder. Later she was divorced and married Leo Raymond Koppes and they had one daughter, Anna Marie Koppes. Rodney Lee, John's grandson, was a paratrooper and while in Vietnam he lost his leg. Both of Ruby's husbands have passed away.

Ralph J. Ross was born at Laverne, OK on Jan. 11, 1929. He married Martha Ring. They had a daughter, Cynthia Jean. Ralph J. worked the railroad and retired disabled. They lived in Kansas City, KS. He died Jan. 23, 1993 and was buried at Kansas City, MO Cemetery. His wife Martha Ross died in 1994 and also is buried there.

Mary Lee Ross, named after Uncle Lee Ross, was born at Morrisville, MO. She was the only child of John's born in Polk County. She married Austin Dunnihoo from Shattuck, OK. They have two sons, Ross Nelson Dunnihoo and Vernon Dunnihoo.

All three children of John Ross graduated from the same high school at Laverne, OK. Ruby married in her junior year at Goodland, KS but got her GED later.

Ruby's parents were divorced when Ruby Naomi was 6 years old. She never saw her father again until she was 13 and then after she married she saw him more often, but not too many times. They lived in Oklahoma and he lived in Missouri. She never got to know her dad very well. She does remember that he liked raisin pie and all kinds of homemade bread. Since they lived in the country, they never got to the store often. Ruby says, "Mom made biscuits, homemade bread and cornbread, so Dad got spoiled. Mom always made pies for him and she made the best pies and pie crust I've ever eaten even though I worked in a bakery for two years, nothing was ever as good as Mom's."

Dad liked to walk and did a lot of it. He used to live later in the country at Marionville, MO right on the old Route 66. He married Ruth; they got married on a Valentine's Day, Ruby doesn't remember the year. They lived on a milk route and got their milk picked up each morning. *Submitted by Ruby Naomi (Ross) Koppes*

ROSS – Robert T. Ross is the second of four children born to Marvin T. and Vesta Ross. He has three sisters, all living.

Robert was born on Nov. 25, 1934 in a two-room house two miles southeast of Morrisville, MO. Some earlier generation townsfolk often referred to Morrisville as "Shavetail," but that is another story. This two-room house had no plumbing, electricity or ceiling and was covered with tarpaper-type siding. It was located on what was known as the Ross farm, which had been in the Ross family for several generations.

In the late 1930s his family moved to a farm in Lawrence County three miles southwest of Halltown. Robert started his first grade of school at a one-room schoolhouse named Mt. Comfort.

During WWII, in either 1943 or 1944, they moved to Polk County. Robert's father bought two farms, which were located between Fair Play and Cliquot. One of these farms was located on a "farm to market" road. Roads that were well graveled and maintained were referred to as "farm to market" roads.

Here, Robert walked about one and one-half miles to attend Pickel School, a one-room schoolhouse with no electricity and two outhouses. He graduated from the eighth grade and went to high school at Fair Play. He graduated from Fair Play in 1951, one of 26 graduates. He then went to Southwest Baptist College, a two-year junior college, graduating in 1953.

While attending both grade school and high school Robert did his studying by a kerosene lamp. He walked about one mile to catch the bus to high school. They attended Bismont Baptist Church and drove there in a Model A car.

They primarily made their living by raising dairy cattle, bucket feeding calves, and selling grade "C" milk. They generally milked between 20 and 25 cows by hand. They raised their hay and put it up loose, either in stacks or the barn loft or both. Teams of horses performed their farm work.

Robert clearly recalls the 18-inch snowstorm that occurred on Oct. 31, 1951 and the record heat wave in July 1954 when temperatures soared between 110 and 114 degrees.

Upon graduating from college Robert went to Kansas City, MO to seek employment. There he met and married Bobbie Starner, who had moved

Robert T. and Bobbie Ross with children; left to right: Karen, Robert E., Diana (seated) and Shelly.

to Kansas City from Rich Hill, MO. While in Kansas City they had two children, Robert E. and Karen.

In 1958 they moved to the Springfield, MO area and two more children were born, Diana and Shelly.

Robert worked at the Dayco Rubber plant from 1962 until 1997, retiring with 35 years of service. During this time he was president of Local Union 662 for 28 years, representing the workers.

Robert currently has a burial plot in the Morrisville Cemetery and will be a fourth generation Ross to be buried there. When Robert and his wife Bobbie are laid to rest in this cemetery, Robert will have come full circle and they will thereby become permanent residents of Polk County. *Submitted by Robert T. Ross*

ROSS – Lula's grandfather, Thomas Francis Ross, born Oct. 15, 1867 in Morrisville, MO, died May 29, 1947. He was married to Eulalia Woodard Ross. She was born Nov. 25, 1866 in Morrisville, MO and died Aug. 13, 1955. They were the parents of 10 children. Lula's mother, Rachel June Ross, eighth child, was born June 1, 1905 in Morrisville, MO and

Back: Rachel June Ross Moore and Charles E. Moore; Front: Lula Jane and Lois June Moore

died June 1, 1985, at her daughter Lula's home in Las Vegas, NV. Rachel June married Charles E. Moore from Dade County, MO. They met when she taught in Dade County. Charles Moore was born Jan. 29, 1881. He died from injuries sustained in a truck accident near Republic, MO in July 1937. They had been married only seven years. Charles and Rachel were married April 20, 1930 at her sister Elta Hughs' home in Republic, MO. Charles and Rachel Moore had two daughters, Lula Jane Moore and Lois June Moore. Lula married Walter Cooper from Oklahoma City, OK. Lois married John Roller in Springfield, MO. Lula had three sons: Jack, Charles and James Cooper. Lois had no children by John Roller. Lula married Leland W. James in Las Vegas, NV. He had two children from previous marriage, Vicki Lynne and Jesse. Leland and Lula had one child, Rebecca Lynne. Lois married Jack E. Delay in Las Vegas, NV. They had five children: Sherry, Mark, Charlotte and Cynthia. Their fifth child, Deborah, died at birth. Jack died July 18, 1992. Lois June Moore Delay remarried John Roller. They now live in Fort Smith, AR. Leland James died Sept. 2, 1997. Lula now lives with her daughter, Rebecca, son-in-law, Samuel Vignone and their two sons, David and Daniel, in Springdale, AR. *Submitted by Lula James*

ROSS – Henry Ross, son of Samuel Ross and Judith Acock, was born Feb. 21, 1816 in Logan County, KY. He came to Polk County, MO in 1832 when he was 16 years old. On March 19, 1840 he married Mary Elizabeth Tarbutton. Mary was born March 16, 1822 in Kentucky. She was the daughter of James Henry Tarbutton and Sarah Hall. Henry was a blacksmith and farmer.

In the 1850 census he and Mary were living in Polk County, MO. In the 1860 census, Henry's household was enumerated in Wright County, MO and in the 1870 census; Henry was again living in Polk County and remained there until his death Oct. 29, 1896.

Henry and Mary had nine children. They were Andrew (born April 27, 1841); Sarah Jane (born March 25, 1843); Nancy Ann (born Jan. 19, 1845); William Henry (born Sept. 21, 1846); Rachel Frances (born Aug. 31, 1848); Martha Margaret (born Jan. 23, 1850); Mary Ellen (born May 9, 1853); John Robert (born Sept. 24, 1856); and Temperance Angeline (born May 1, 1859). Mary Elizabeth Tarbutton Ross died April 4, 1860 and is buried at Nancy Newton Cemetery in Wright County, MO.

Henry married Matilda Henderson (Mrs.) before 1863. She was born Dec. 17, 1825 in Kentucky and died Nov. 5, 1904 in Polk County, MO and is buried at the Schofield Baptist Church Cemetery. Henry and Matilda had four children: Elijah Warren (born 1863), James Josiah (born 1865), Samuel T. (born 1869) and Lulu (born 1874).

Henry was a participant in the establishment of the Schofield Baptist Church in Polk County and the Antioch Baptist Church in Wright County. He was received into the Antioch Church by letter Nov. 5, 1866. His name appears in the original members of Providence Baptist Church organized Sept. 4, 1839 in Polk County, MO. Henry began his military service in the Civil War March 24, 1862 at Sims Creek, MO. He was a private in Company H of the Eighth Regiment of the Missouri Cavalry commanded by H. D. Moore. He was helping to recruit for a new company to be sworn into the US Army when his organization was attacked. He said that he was shot in the head by a few enemy men. A physician was called to treat Henry who was suffering from paralysis on his left side. He had difficulty in swallowing and his head was drawn to the right side. He also suffered from hyperemia or overflow of blood to the head. This condition was the result of camp fever suffered by Henry. He was honorably discharged, Special Orders #69 April 15, 1863 at Lebanon, MO. The physical description given of Henry at age 74 years was that he was five feet, ten inches tall with fair complexion, dark hair and blue eyes.

Henry died Oct. 29, 1896 in Polk County, MO and is buried at Schofield Baptist Church Cemetery. *Submitted by Wayne Smith*

ROSS – Judith Ross was born about 1783 in North Carolina. Her parents were Robert Eaton Acock (born circa 1753) and Mary Blanchett (born circa 1760). Judith married Samuel Ross (born circa 1776 in North Carolina) on Dec. 7, 1803 in Logan County, KY (which parts of Logan County later became Todd County). Samuel died on Feb. 18, 1826 in Todd County.

Judith and Samuel had nine children: Nancy (born Feb. 3, 1806); James (born March 1808); Sarah Jane (born May 22, 1810); Martha (born March 15, 1812); Robert (born Jan. 3, 1814); Henry (born Feb. 21, 1816); Polly (born Jan. 4, 1818); Judith Ann (born July 22, 1820); and Rachel L. (born Dec. 6, 1824). James Ross married Elizabeth or Betsy Hall on Sept. 28, 1831 in Todd County, KY. James and Betsy also settled in Polk County. Robert married Lurana (unknown) and both are buried at the Slagle Baptist Church in Slagle. Henry Ross lived in Polk County and his life is detailed later in another history. Rachel married Asa R. Williams on July 31, 1845 in Polk County. Rachel and Asa along with Rachel's sister, Martha, were in the 1850 Polk County census but are not in the 1860 Polk County census. No other information has been gathered on Nancy, Sarah Jane, Polly and Judith Ann.

Judith lived in Kentucky until after the 1830 census. Judith and five of her children lived in Polk County by the 1840 census. Judith and her son, Henry, were charter members of the Providence Baptist Church. Providence Baptist church was organized on Sept. 4, 1839 about two and a half miles northwest of Pleasant Hope. Judith does not appear in the 1850 Polk County census.

Judith's father Robert Eaton Acock died in Todd County, KY on March 22, 1848. Robert Acock Sr. was a Revolutionary War soldier. He enlisted April 10, 1778 in the North Carolina Third Infantry. He was discharged on Oct. 19, 1778 on Connecticut after he fought in the battles of Brandywine and Germantown.

Judith's siblings were Sally (born circa 1785); William B. (born Feb. 21, 1788, died Oct. 20, 1833); Henry (born circa 1790 and whose family settled in Dade County, MO); Allen (born circa 1792); Winifred (born circa 1795); John (born circa 1796, died 1832); Robert Eaton (born circa 1799, died March 15, 1861 and also lived in Polk County); Thomas (born circa 1803); and Mary M. (born Nov. 22, 1811).

Married in Christian County, KY were Sally to Stephen Faulkenton on April 25, 1807; William B. to Rachel Marshall on July 14, 1809; Winifred to John Porter on Aug. 3, 1819. Married in Logan County, KY were Henry to Madlene Sears on April 9, 1812; Allen to Sarah Hansbrough on Oct. 22, 1814; John to Betsy Simmons on Feb. 11, 1812; Mary M. to Amos Coffman on May 26, 1831. Robert Eaton married first, Margaret Walker Ewing and later Lucy Champe McCulloch on June 9, 1858 in St. Clair County, MO. *Submitted by Dayna Pearson*

ROSS – Robert Ross was born Jan. 3, 1814 in Logan County, KY, son of Samuel Ross and Judith Acock, who were married Dec. 7, 1803 in Logan County, KY. Judith Acock was the daughter of Robert Acock and Mary Blanchett who were married July 25, 1780 in Warren County, NC. Robert Acock was a soldier in the Revolutionary War, who received a pension in Todd County, KY.

Samuel's parents were James and Mary Ross. James Ross researchers say that it was James who married Mary Mitchell, daughter of Robert and Margaret Mitchell of Guilford County, NC. Robert Mitchell secured his grant near the Guilford Battleground, and his family moved to Tennessee after the war. His brother, Adam Mitchell, secured his grant on North Buffalo.

James Ross was born in Ireland about 1741, and was said to be in Virginia by 1750. Henry, James and John Ross, who were believed to be brothers, all lived on Horsepen Creek in Guilford County, NC about 1773. James' family was in Davidson County, TN by 1788. Before 1800 they were in Logan County, KY. At the March 1798 term of court in Logan County, KY, an order read: "Ordered that the place Logan Courthouse now stands a town be established by the name of Russellville," and James Ross was named a trustee. He left Kentucky and went with his daughter Margaret and her husband John Dickey, to Giles County, TN in 1808, where he was one of the commissioners appointed by the Legislature to locate and lay off the town of Pulaski. James' sons, Adam and Robert Ross, left Giles County, TN in the 1830s and located in Pope County, AR.

Samuel Ross, a blacksmith, died in Todd County, KY in 1826. Judith and her sons, James and Robert Ross, were still on the tax list in 1835. Before 1840 Judith with her children and members of her Acock family were in Polk County, MO. The oldest church noticed in Polk County was Providence, organized Sept. 4, 1839 near Pleasant Hope. The constituent members were Judea "Judith" Ross, Nancy Ross, Sarah Ross, Henry Ross, James Driskill and Martha (Acock) Driskill, James W. and Sarah Tiller.

Robert Ross was a blacksmith and preacher. He received his license to preach filed in Lawrence County, AR, where he was one of the early preachers of the New Hope Baptist Church.

"To All to whom these present may come: Greeting. This is to certify that our beloved brother Robert Ross after being duly set apart for ordination by the United Baptist Church at Providence, was duly ordained a minister by the undersigned ministers as a Presbyterian in case done in presence of the church on the 3rd day of November A.D. 1850. William Tatum, James Bradley, and William B. Senter, Presbytery. Filed and recorded this 21st day of September, A.D. 1865. H.W. Harlow, Clerk J.W. Townsend D.C."

In the *History of Polk County Baptist Association of Missouri*, "Eld. Ross was a man of few words, mild and peaceable in his habits, but when aroused he could carry his audience with him, as he would tell the story of the cross. His first wife died in the triumph of faith; his second wife survives him. Eld. Ross died in faith Nov. 29, 1889." He was instrumental in the organization of Slagle Baptist Church. His wife Lurana was born in Kentucky June 1, 1816 and died June 28, 1884. After her death he married Mary Slagle. Robert and Lurana Ross are buried at Slagle Cemetery. Their children were Samuel, born 1835 in Kentucky, Margaret, born 1836, John, born 1839, William H., born 1842, James Thomas, born 1844, Robert A., born 1848, Mathias, born 1850 and Eda Ann, born 1853.

James Thomas Ross with his Bible circa 1890

James Thomas Ross was ordained elder by the Free Will Baptist Church at Friendship No. 2 at Scott County, AR on Sept. 29, 1890. *The Arkansas Magnet* reported "Eld. J. T. Ross, Freewill Baptist evangelist for Logan, Yell and Scott Counties, recently returned from a trip over his territory, and reports the religious and educational interest on the up-grade many points." He married Mary Ann Hudson Dec. 28, 1865 in Lawrence County, AR. She was the daughter of Evan and Mary Hudson of North Carolina. Their children were Cindy Lurany "Lou," Martha Ann "Mat," married William H. Chappell, twins Margie Alzira and Nancy, Mary E., David Washington, married Mattie Wallace, Robert Evan, married Emma Wilson and then Minnie Ellen Casteel. In the 1910 census of Richland Township, Yell County, AR there were listed eight children, but only three living. They were Lou, David and Robert. Lou Ross married William Thomas Howard of Chattanooga, Hamilton County, TN on Sept. 25, 1887, in Logan County, AR. Their youngest child was Virgil Aubrey Howard married to Elsie Skinner. He had a wonderful memory of many stories about his family, which led to this research.

James Thomas Ross died in 1917 and Mary Ann in 1911. They are buried near Waveland, Yell County, AR at Moore's Chapel Cemetery. *Submitted by Ina Lou Howard Willingham*

Dec. 7, 1979, Toombs pigs

ROTRAMEL – Butchering days at the Rotramel farm. Home butchering is a dying art, but this Polk County family has not let the old way slip away yet. Each winter for the past 52 years, the Bill Rotramel family of Bolivar gathers with family and friends to butcher hogs. Almost all the hog is used somehow. Besides the bacon, ham, tenderloin, ribs, liver and fat, which is rendered into pure lard, the feet and ears are used somehow, too. As the old saying goes, "they used everything but the squeal." Our forefathers weren't wasteful people.

Dad gets the fire going under the scalding vat, real early and by 9 a.m. the business of killing and butchering hogs was ready. Dad kills the hogs with his .22 rifle. Aims for the head, and hogs are then pierced in the throat, to let them bleed. The hog is then lowered into a scalding vat, lowered by hand with the use of chains. The water has to be just right so the hairs can be scraped with hand scrapers. After this is done the hogs are hoisted, feet first, on a bar for weighing and gutting. The throat is slit all the way around to let the hogs bleed out. The carcass is allowed to hang for a while in the cool air to let the meat cool down before the butchering starts.

While the meat is cooling down, mom cooks up the meal for the crew, which is fresh-fried liver. That is the family tradition. After the meal, dad, his father-in-law, Con Potts, Glen, Fred, Larry, Deryle and Putter went to work cutting up the five hogs that had been slaughtered that morning, while the women went to work processing the meat. The hogs were lowered one by one from the hoist onto a large cutting table. Dad and Grandpa did the cutting and slicing off the hams, ribs, shoulders, tenderloin and bacons.

Inside the smokehouse mom, Bill's wife, daughters Joyce and Wilma and Bonnie cut the meat for sausage and prepare the lard for rendering. The sausage is cubed and mixed with seasoning. Then Larry, Bill's youngest son, put the sausage through an electric grinder.

Mom (Darlene) makes her own sugar cure for the hams, puts it on and lets the meat set for several days before hanging.

When time and effort are considered, one would have to ask the question, "Why take the trouble to butcher at home?" Because dad says we've done it for a long time. The family all gets together and enjoys taking part in all steps. Dad knows that we wouldn't miss this for anything. We would even skip school to help on butchering day, even the grandkids, too.

I like the opportunity to watch every step of the process all the way through to the table. "You know the meat is good." We probably don't save money when the work is done, but we like to do it because it's family tradition and a dying art.

Mom's rib eye gravy and cured ham can't be beat; it's the best meal. *Submitted by Joyce, Deryl, Wilma and Larry*

ROTROCK – Daniel "DR" Rotrock was born in Clay County, IN to Benjamin and Elizabeth (Ingersoll) Roderick. This German surname has many spelling variations within the family; Rotrock, Rodruck, Rodrick, Rothrock and Roderick are a few.

Daniel married Rebecca Jane Prater (Prather) on Aug. 16, 1855 in Vermillion County, IL. Rebecca was born on Feb. 2, 1839 in Danville, IL. Between 1866 and 1868 they moved to Polk County, MO. Daniel served with Company E, Ninth Iowa Cavalry during the Civil War using the post office address of Buffalo, Dallas County, MO. Rebecca was a midwife in the Shady Grove area.

Daniel and Rebecca had 12 children: Mary Ann, Emily Louise, Stephen A., William H., Tereace A., Cyrus, Loura, Armilda "Milda ," Nelson, Sopha, Margaret and Albert Y. Daniel died in 1895 in Polk County. Rebecca died in Dade County, MO on Feb. 14, 1923. Both are buried in Trimble Cemetery.

Crain family, Back: Palmer, Walter and Warner; Front: Oscar, Emily, Ada, Addie, Elijah Downey and Ida (Crain) Downing

Emily Rotrock was born April 27, 1863 in Illinois. She married Nelson Crain in Bolivar, MO on Aug. 30, 1883. He was born on May 5, 1836 in Grainger County, TN to Pleasant and Ruthy Crain. They had nine children: Ernest "Palmer," Arminta "Mintie," Clarence, Oscar, Ida, Charles "Walter," Warner "Curley," Addie Agnes and Ada Louise. Emily died Nov. 27, 1952 and is buried in Pleasant Ridge Cemetery. Nelson served with Company E, MSM Cavalry during the Civil War. Nelson died March 31, 1904 and is buried in Trimble Cemetery next to his first wife, Rutha Abbott.

"Palmer" Crain was born Aug. 24, 1890 in Aldrich, Polk County, MO. He married Elva Belle Ashlock on Dec. 19, 1920, in Aldrich, MO. She was born Dec. 24, 1896 in Cliquot, MO to Obediah and LaVerne Jane (Allen) Ashlcok. Palmer served with the US Army 20th Combat Engineers in France during WWI. For a time, Palmer and Elva operated a restaurant in Aldrich. They had two children: Richard Lee and Edith "Florene." After Elva died on Jan. 12, 1929, Emily helped raised the two small children. Palmer worked for the K.C.C.&S. 'Leaky Roof' Railroad. Palmer died Jan. 2, 1968. Palmer and Elva are buried in Pleasant Ridge Cemetery.

Richard Crain was born in Aldrich, MO and married Dorothy Bean, the daughter of Edwin and Lucille (Marshall) Bean. They had one daughter, Carmen. Richard operated a pool hall in Aldrich before they moved to St. Louis, MO where he was a bus driver for Public Service Company Bi-State Transit Systems. Richard also had a son, Richard Jr. by his second wife, Ethel Maxine Street. Richard was a veteran of WWII serving with the

32nd Division, the first division sent to Australia for service with General MacArthur's Army of the Pacific.

Florene Crain was born in Aldrich, MO and married Curtis "Mac" McDaniel, the son of Grover and Katie (Peters) McDaniel. They moved to the Kansas City area and had one daughter, Karen. Mac was a veteran of WWII. *Submitted by Carmen R. Willis*

ROWAN – Eli Rowan was born Oct. 8, 1823 in DeKalb County, AL. His parents were William Rowan and Mary. They were married in Virginia about 1813. Eli married Delpha R. Lee about 1850. She was born Nov. 5, 1835 in Tennessee.

Eli and Delpha were Anna's second great-grandparents. Eli moved from DeKalb, AL to Hawkins County, TN, then Lawrence County, AR and finally to Polk County, MO about 1840. He died of typhoid pneumonia in 1887 after living in Missouri for 47 years. He is listed in the Polk County, Union Township, 1850 census living with his mother, Mary and wife, Delpha. Mary is listed in the 1844 tax assessment list with one horse valued at $15 and one cattle valued at $6.

Eli and Delpha were the parents of 13 children. They were America C., Nancy C., John, Samuel, William Joseph, Sarah, Catharine, Minerva, Delpha, Laura Belle, Hattie, Henry and Kiley L. Eli and Delpha were farmers, and bought 40 acres of land near Aldrich in 1852 for $1.25 per acre. They are buried in Routh Chapel Cemetery between Aldrich and Bona in Dade County, along with two of their children, Delpha and Kiley.

Anna descends through William Joseph Rowan, born April 5, 1860 in Lawrence County, AR, where the family spent time in 1860 and 1861, but were listed in both Polk County, MO and Lawrence County, AR 1860 census. He married Alice Emmaline Berlier, born March 29, 1867 in Coal County, IL. Her parents were Michel Berlier, who emigrated from France in 1848, and Mary Ann Brown. He traveled from New Orleans, LA up the Mississippi River to Cincinnati, OH, where he became a naturalized citizen, married and moved to Illinois before finally settling in Polk County, where he homesteaded in 1862 near Aldrich. That land has been owned and occupied by his descendants to this day. William and Alice were the parents to eight children who were Austin Eli, Anna's grandfather; Ora, who died in infancy; Elmer; Norman; Flay; Cliffton; Leo and Flossie.

Austin Eli, Anna's grandfather, married Mamie Elizabeth Neill Oct. 19, 1905 in Polk County, MO at the home of her parents, John Clinton Neill and Permelia Holman. The Neill family has owned land in Polk County since 1819. Born to Austin and Mamie were three sons: Howard Clinton, Richard William and Lowell Norman.

Howard and Inez Rowan 1928 wedding

Elmer married Carrie Boyd and had three children: Leslie, Theadore and Ruth; Flay married Maudie and had two children, Eldon and Grace Anna; Cliffton married Lucille Armstrong and had one child, Cliffton Lee; Leo married Elva Stephens and Flossie married Virgil VanHoosier and had one daughter, Dixie.

Howard Clinton Rowan, Anna's father, married Wanda Inez Dixon July 4, 1928 at the home of a minister in Polk County, MO. Her parents were Floyd Joseph Dixon and Nancy Anna Hamilton. Children born to Howard and Inez were Howard Clinton Jr., Anna Jane and Nancy Sue. Howard and Inez farmed near Aldrich for several years until his health required him to leave the farm, when he became manager of the MFA store in Aldrich. Howard Clinton Jr. still lives on a farm in Polk County, and his son lives on the homestead of his second great-grandfather, Michel Berlier.

"Church was an important part of our lives at Pleasant Ridge Baptist Church, where we could be found at every service. We enjoyed Sunday dinner with friends after church, at our home or someone else's on most Sundays," Anna says.

William and Alice Rowan along with most of their children are buried at Pleasant Ridge Cemetery, as well as Michel and Mary Ann Berlier, Austin and Mamie Rowan and their children, John C. and Permelia Neill and their children. Anna has fond memories of growing up in Polk County, where she always felt safe and doors were never locked. The neighbors always pitched in and helped each other harvest crops, build barns and butcher their meat. Money was not plentiful, but love and friendship was. *Submitted by Anna J. Shaw*

Walter, Max and Osra Roweton, 1944

ROWETON – Andrew Jackson Roweton was born Feb. 20, 1832 in Ross County, OH. He came to Missouri during the Civil War. He was a Union soldier. He was the son of Levin Roweton (1780?-1844) and Nancy Hibbs (Noble) Roweton (1801-1870) and the oldest of five children. Andrew came to Webb City, MO at some unknown date and on Dec. 19, 1869, he married Frances Elizabeth Webb, the third of eight children of Thomas C. Webb and Mary A. (Carr) Webb. Frances' father, Thomas C. Webb and her brother, Auston C. Webb, were both killed by the bushwackers on July 17, 1863. Andrew and Frances moved to El Dorado Springs, MO after they were married and remained there until around 1896 when they moved to Halfway, MO. Andrew made a will in December 1896 and died in January 1897. Frances E. (Webb) Roweton lived for 53 more years after Andrew died. She died at the age of 101 March 9, 1950 and is buried in Goff Cemetery, Halfway, MO.

To this union six children were born: Mary Syrene Roweton Cornelius, 1870-1952; Thomas Jefferson Roweton, 1872-1958; Charles Erasmus Roweton, 1874-1932; King David Roweton, 1878-1961; Etta Frances Roweton Fulbright, 1883-1967; and Johnny Roweton, died as small boy, no dates known. Max Roweton descends through Thomas Jefferson Roweton. He was born March 29, 1872 in El Dorado Springs, MO. He married Ida Mae Bailey (birth date unknown). She was the daughter of Samuel J. Bailey and Mary Jane (Jackson) Bailey. Thomas and Ida Mae had nine children.

Max's father, Walter A. "Buck" Roweton, was their fifth child and their first boy. He was born March 19, 1904. He grew up in and around Halfway, MO, attending Halfway schools through his eighth grade year. He went to the San Jacquin Valley in California at age 14, where he worked on a grape ranch for about three years. He then worked for Eisman Hardware and Grocery in Visalia, CA. He and his brother, Roma, returned to Polk County in 1927 and he farmed near Halfway and was a county ASCS Chairman until 1944. In 1929 he married Osra Ann Legan, a teacher from Halfway. Osra was the daughter of Ernie Josiah Legan and Emma (Mapes) Legan and was born July 5, 1905. Max is their only child. His full name is Doran Max Roweton and he was born Sept. 13, 1935 in Halfway, MO. In 1948 his parents bought the Western Auto Store in Bolivar, MO, which they owned and operated until 1975. Max still owns and operates the store at this writing, and he is also a farmer. On Aug. 16, 1959, Max married Ellen Rose Douglas in Bolivar, MO. She was born April 2, 1937, the daughter of Elvin S. Douglas Sr. and Florence (DeLisle) Douglas. Both were born in 1909 and died 1979.

Max and Rose are the parents of five children: Vicki Kay Roweton Morgan, born 1960 and her husband is Bruce Morgan; Kendal Allen Roweton, born 1961; Denni Gay Roweton McColm, born 1962 and her husband is Steve McColm; Marla Jo Roweton Kemp, born 1964 and her husband is Wesley Kemp; and Kelly Doran Roweton, born 1965 and his wife is Susan Casanova Roweton. They have 17 grandchildren. *Submitted by D. Max Roweton*

ROWLES – John Rowles was born in Oxford, England on Feb. 26, 1835. As a young man, John was a bodyguard for Queen Victoria, later coming to America with a young male friend on a sailing vessel. John worked his way across country and met a young woman in Polk County named Debora Christena Milliken (daughter of Hiram Milliken) as she was horseback riding. Remnants of a rock fence that John helped built remain along Highway 83 north of Bolivar. John and Debora were married and homesteaded land about five miles north of Bolivar along what is now South 115th Road. John and Debora had four children: Marion, Jane, Susan and William.

Front: Jack and Deborah Rowles; Back: Marion, Will and Susie Rowles

Following Marion's line, Marion married Elizabeth Weaver, daughter of Elias and Anna Hadden Weaver who had moved to Polk County from Illinois with Elizabeth and their two other daughters, Mary and Lillie. Marion and Lizzie lived most of their married life on the homesteaded Rowles property and in a log house raised their family of five children: Edward, Susan, Christena, Mae and Edna. Marion had a team of mules that he used to work the land and often offered fruit and vegetables for sale in Bolivar that were grown on the family farm. Lizzie often helped with the birth of neighborhood babies.

Continuing through Christena's line, Christena graduated from Bolivar High School in 1927 and taught Cooper School the following year, having her younger sister, Edna, in first grade. Christena had a pie supper that fall and about six months later married the young man who auctioned the pies and box suppers for her, Earl "Pick" Blackwell. Earl was one of children (Cora, Albert, Oliver, Lorene, James, Elsie, Earl, Lola, Arnold and Chester) of William Preston "Billy" and Nancy Elizabeth Eskew Blackwell of Hickory and Polk Counties.

Earl and Christena lived in Flemington a number of years, losing two children, Betty Jean and Gerald Wayne, to diphtheria in 1933. With their daughter, Patricia, the couple moved to Rondo during WWII, where Earl and Christena operated Blackwell Feed Grocery and Gas, a country store, for almost 40 years. Earl also ran a trucking business for 58 years, hauling cattle and feed for area farmers.

Edward Shoemake and Patricia Blackwell Shoemake have two daughters, Christy Shoemake Johnson and Deborah Shoemake Hoffren. Edward served with the US Navy in the Korean and Vietnam Conflicts and later worked for the state of Missouri after Navy retirement. Edward and his parents, Glen and Audrey Findley Shoemake, and a sister and brother, Glenda and Danny Joe, lived in Dunnegan and his grandparents, Joe and Myrtle Mallory Shoemake, lived in Fair Play during Edward's younger years. Joe Shoemake was a veteran of the Spanish American War. Edward is spending his retirement years traveling.

Christy and Tom Johnson with their three daughters, Janet, Denise and Kimberly, live in southeast Missouri where Christy is a teacher and Tom is a Baptist Minister. Deborah Hoffren and her husband, Todd, are computer analysts in South Texas. Christy's in-laws, Charles and Loretta Johnson, bought and live on part of the Rowles Homestead. Christy and Tom still own a portion of the Rowles homestead as do others in the Rowles family.

Patricia Blackwell Shoemake traveled with her family as a military dependent and taught school in California, Midway Island, Guam, Kansas and Missouri. Patricia is pursuing local Community Theater in her retirement years and is proud to be a fourth generation Polk Countian. *Submitted by Patricia Blackwell Shoemake*

RUNYAN – Abraham M. Runyan, born April 5, 1831 in Hamilton County, TN, was the youngest of nine children of John Wesley (born 1778, Shenandoah Valley, VA) and Nancy Mullendore Runyan (born 1786, Sevier County, TN). As a young adult, he taught school and farmed. Abraham met Mary Ann Jarnagin (born Aug. 6, 1833 in McMinn County, TN, the fifth of eight children of William Caswell and Elizabeth Bowen Jarnagin) in 1851 while going to Missouri with a wagon train. According to family stories, Abraham stopped to help fix Mary Ann's broken wagon at a river crossing. They were married in Polk County Feb. 10, 1852. At one time they had a grocery store in Fair Play. After the Civil War, the family moved four miles west of Bolivar where they farmed and raised stock. Their 11 children were Isaac A. (born Nov. 28, 1853), William Ahab (born Jan. 4, 1855), Binam W. (born Aug. 21, 1857), Nancy Elizabeth (born June 30, 1859), Sarah Mullendore (born June 28, 1861), Mary Angeline (born Oct. 29, 1863), Susan Malinda (born Feb. 27, 1866), Laura Belle (born April 15, 1868), Orah Ann (born March 7, 1871), Timmey Abraham (born Dec. 30, 1874) and Sherley Simeon (born July 6, 1877). In the late 1800s Abraham, known for being industrious and frugal, gave a plot of land located about three and a half miles west of Bolivar, on which Runyan School was built. The family was members of Barren Creek Presbyterian Church and moved to Aldrich sometime before Abraham's death Sept. 12, 1895. Mary Ann died Nov. 18, 1911. They were buried in Barren Creek Cemetery.

There were several members of Abraham and Mary Ann's family who lived in Polk County, leaving descendants. There is a picture of Polk County officers from 1908, of which Binam and his daughter (the only woman with 17 men) were members.

Orah married Thomas Reynolds and that line has descendants still living in Polk County.

William Ahab Runyan, with his wife, Eliza Emily born May 22, 1858 in Crawfordsville, IN to Peter and his second wife, (Emily Trout Vannice), farmed and raised horses near Bear Creek at Walnut Lane Farm outside Bolivar after their marriage Oct. 15, 1874. They reared a family of 10 children: Ohmer Holister (born June 12, 1876), Golden Idell (born Feb. 6, 1879), Merlie Abraham (born July 24, 1881), William Winfield (born Feb. 15, 1884), Pearl Ann (born Sept. 5, 1886), Ada Grace (born June 15, 1889), Mary Cordelia (born Sept. 2, 1891), Tavner Isaac (born May 16, 1894), Clayborn Teller (born July 8, 1897) and Roscoe Vannice (born May 11, 1901). In 1907 "Uncle Bill" and Emily moved their five sons and two of their daughters to Homestead Act Land in McAlister, NM. There they were members of the Methodist church. Mrs. Runyan died Dec. 13, 1930 and her husband, on Feb. 7, 1936 and they were buried in the Browning Cemetery near Jordan, NM.

50th Anniversary, Eliza and William 1924; front: Eliza and William Runyan; middle: Ada Hill, Mary Montgomery, Golden Poe and Pearl Runyan; back: Tavner, William, Roscoe, Ohmer and Clayborn Runyan

Pearl Runyan and her sister Golden (Mrs. Thomas A. Poe) stayed in Missouri when the family moved west. Pearl, a schoolteacher married William Bird Lee (born Dec. 8, 1883 to Robert B. and Rhoda Rush Lee) on Jan. 8, 1908 in Bolivar. Their three daughters were Rena Ann (born Dec. 31, 1908, died May 18, 1947), Letha Faye (born May 29, 1911, died Sept. 19, 1998) and Grace Emily (born Dec. 22, 1914). W. B. was an active Mason, Shriner and member of Eastern Star. He owned the Lee store and sold insurance. Also, Bird directed the Methodist church choir and taught the adult Bible class, and Pearl was active in the Ladies' Aid Society and Eastern Star. The girls attended South Side School and took piano lessons from Miss Caroline Pike and Mrs. Bucholtz at Southwest Baptist College. Faye was a charter member of the Bolivar High School Royal Rooters, and Rena was active in debate and drama, while both were in the chorus. Rena was graduated from Bolivar High School, but Faye and Grave moved with their parents to Des Moines, IA in 1927. A heart attack caused W. B.'s death March 24, 1945. Pearl's death July 20, 1974 in Belmond, IA was caused by pancreatic cancer. They were buried in Greenwood Cemetery. *Submitted by Barbara Reed*

RUNYAN – Abraham M. Runyan was born April

Runyan School House

5, 1831 in James County, TN, the youngest child of John and Nancy (Mullindore) Runyan.

The story told from one generation to the next is that Abraham rode a horse on the trip to Missouri and led a group of wagons. He had been a schoolteacher in Tennessee and intended to return as he has a fiancée back there waiting for him.

The Jarnagin wagon broke down when they were on the Mississippi River Bridge. Abraham helped fix it. This is where he first saw Mary Jarnagin and in the story, he gave her a big red apple. She and her mother had their own wagon and were coming to Missouri to visit her brothers, Fred and Houston. Abraham first went to Barry County, MO, as that was where Mary and her mother were going.

Abraham and Mary Ann Jarnagin were married in Bolivar on Feb. 10, 1852. They bought property about four miles west of Bolivar. They were the great-grandparents of Anna Carson.

Runyan School, west of Bolivar, was named for Abraham. In probate records one piece of property is listed as "less 1 1/2 acres for school."

They had 11 children but at present there are several of his descendants living in the Bolivar area but none with the name Runyan.

Abraham died Sept. 12, 1895. Mary died Nov. 18, 1911. They are buried at Barren Creek Cemetery, west of Bolivar. *Submitted by Anna C. Carson*

RUSSELL – Thomas Simeon Russell came to Polk County, MO about 1855. He was born Dec. 18, 1834 in Jefferson County, TN, the son of William Russell II and Elizabeth Shadon.

Feb. 25, 1857 he married Martha Jane Worthan, the daughter of Richard and Mary Elizabeth (Abbott) Worthan. Richard was born Dec. 19, 1820 in Virginia, and Mary was born in North Carolina on Jan. 17, 1821. Richard and Mary are buried on the family homestead near the junction of Highway 13 and BB Highway.

To this union of Thomas and Martha there were 12 children born and raised about four or five miles northwest of Bolivar, near the original location of Harmony Primitive Baptist Church. Thomas was a farmer and Primitive Baptist Preacher. The 12 children were Mary Elizabeth, Sarah Parthena, Nancy Melvina, Martha Ellen, Louise Jane, Ida Belle, William Isaac, Virginia Tennessee, James Hensley, Rebecca, Thomas Simeon and George Henry.

All of Thomas and Martha's children lived to adult-

Louetta (Ware) and George Henry Russell, baby Lena (Russell) Hancock

hood, married and produced their own families.

Mary Elizabeth married John E. McElhaney April 1, 1877, and after his death July 6, 1893, she married George Suttee March 14, 1894.

Sarah Parthena married John W. Henson Sept. 17, 1876.

Nancy Melvina married William Perry March 15, 1888.

Martha Ellen married Isaac M. Wilson Nov. 3, 1878. Later she married John Bell Feb. 28, 1892.

Eliza Jane married Porter B. Woods April 26, 1883.

Ida Belle married Thomas I. Hamlet July 15, 1888 and then John Henry Brewer Nov. 9, 1893.

William Isaac married Martha Angelia Scotten Sept. 8, 1891.

Virginia Tennessee married John Morgan Hollis Feb. 22, 1891.

James Hensley married Julia A. Scotten Sept. 8, 1895.

Rebecca married Hiram R. Scurlock Nov. 3, 1895; then John S. Brown May 23, 1931.

Thomas Simeon Jr. married Sarah Belle Gerkin Sept. 16, 1903.

George Henry married Louetta Ware Aug. 21, 1904.

Thomas Simeon Hill Russell served in the Union Army during the Civil War. He served first in the Missouri Home Guard; then he enlisted in Company E, Eighth Cavalry, March 13, 1862, where he served until he was medically discharged, March 7, 1864.

Thomas Simeon and Martha Jane Russell are in Barren Creek Cemetery, Polk County, MO, where they rest along side a large number of their descendents. *Submitted by Eva Hancock*

RUYLE – Aaron Ruyle was James Bradford Hoodenpyle's great-grandfather. He was born June 17, 1781 in North Carolina. His parents were Henry and Catherine. He married Elizabeth and arrived by wagon train in 1830 in what is now Polk County. Aaron became an extensive landowner and had numerous slaves in the early days before the Civil War. Born to Aaron were 11 children: Elizabeth, Lavina, Ann Jasper, John, Leander, Franky, Gideon, Phebeann, Alvis and Aaron Jr. Aaron's' will left to Elizabeth, his wife, the cabin, half the land in cultivation, $100, a faithful servant (Silvey), two horses, one wagon and a yolk of oxen. To each of his children he left a slave, $100 and some land. To William, Elizabeth Jane, and Melseny, children of Aaron Jr. (deceased) he left $400 each for the purpose of buying the land from his widow.

William served in the Civil War and was taken prisoner in the fall of Vicksburg, MS July 8, 1863. Elizabeth Jane married Benjamin Uttley. Melseny married John Apperson in 1873, and they had six children: Anna, Golla, Georgia and three who died as infants. Anna married Adrian Bradford (great-grandson of Dr. Hamilton Bradford, an early settler of Polk County) and had three children: Reva, Ford and Athleyne, all born in the log cabin. Golla and Georgia never married. They were born, raised and died in the cabin built by Aaron Ruyle in 1830.

Reva Apperson Bradford married Earl Hoodenpyle in 1918. They had four children. Reva died in 1928. Her children "James" Bradford, 9; Bill, 7; Bob, 5; and Betty "Christina," 1 1/2 were left in the care of John Apperson and his two daughters, Golla and Georgia, on the Ruyle farm.

Bradford spent 30 years (1941-1971) in the USAF as a pilot. He married Aileen in 1947. They have two children, James Jr. and Sandra, four grandchildren and three great-grandchildren. Bill served in WWII in the Army and was a homebuilder until his death. He married Vickie. They had two children, Mike and Debbie; and two grandchildren. Bob served in the Navy in WWII in the South Pacific. He has wood products manufacturing plant in Kansas. He married Betty and has two children, Lorie and Leslie, and one grandchild. Christina married Harlan Graham. He served in the Army in WWII. The have spent most of their married life on the Ruyle farm. They have three children: Sherry, Reva and Cindy; four grandchildren; and three great-grandchildren.

These four children, Bradford, Bill, Bob and Christina, still own the Ruyle farm near Brighton in Polk County.

Rev. E. Slavens held the first church service in Polk County in the original log cabin built by

The Ruyle farmhouse near Brighton in Polk County, log cabin is on the west with the chimney built in 1830; the second story on the right was added in 1900s.

Aaron Ruyle. The first white child born in Polk County was born in this cabin. The old log cabin is still there. It has been wrapped completely inside and out. The cabin was added on to in 1900, modernized in 1950 and restored in 1976. It is now occupied by Nathaniel McKnight (a descendant of Aaron Ruyle) and his wife, Bobbie. *Submitted by James Bradford Hoodenpyle*

SALLEE – Oliver Perry Sallee, son of John Kalvin and Permelia Hudson Sallee, born March 10, 1863, married Nancy Ellen Etheridge and had nine children. Almost all of them have been buried at Rock Prairie Cemetery northeast of Pleasant Hope, MO. They are Bertha, died as a baby; Fred married Ethel Curlin and had five children; Ethel married Samuel Self and had two children; Jacen (Jase) married Addie Case and had one child; John married Alta and had two children; Ava, died at age 21 (it is said she was engaged to be married to Ott Murray and when she knew she wouldn't live, she asked Ott to marry her sister, which he did); Oliver Richo married Zella Choate and had three children; Glenn married Clara Tuckness and had two children and after Clara died, he married Nellie; Gola Mae married William Ott Murray and had 12 children. Ulissus Grant was Perry's baby brother who died two weeks after Perry's mother died.

Perry and Nancy lived all their lives in and around Pleasant Hope, as did their children and grandchildren. Gola and Ott Murray raised their family east of Pleasant Hope on a farm. Roscoe married two times but had no children of his own: however, he raised Louise Comstock Stokes Murray's two boys as his own. He was dad to them. Ruth married Glen William Mayfield and to this union four children were born. Jack married Marjorie. James (Jim) married Mildred Mayfield (Glen's sister) and reared four children. Maxine married Claude Bolin and had three children. Peggy Lou married Kyle Jones and reared four children. Johnny Lee married Patsy Finley. Gene Tuney married Georgianna Patterson and had three children. Freddy Orville married Gladys

John Kalvin Sallee

North and raised her daughter as his own. Betty Sue married Ralph Trentalange and had Susan. Billy Ray married Bridget and had Tammy. He married Sue Ellis. Mineriva Jane married Billy Wayne Duff and had Charles Wayne (Chuck). Later she had Teresa Ann, Caroline Kay and Jimmy Lee. Then she married Roy Gott and had Donna Sue, Timmy and Lisa. Jane died Feb. 10, 1993, with cancer.

Perry's brother Sebern (Dick) also lived at Pleasant Hope with his family. He married Mary Violet Crockett who bore him six children and died when the twins were almost a month old. Their children were Anne, Mahlon Calvin (Cal), Zoe, Lois and the twins Mary Alice and Sebern Albert. Cal, Zoe, Lois and Alice lived to adulthood. Sebern purchased and operated the Roller Mills in 1881 and afterward for several years. After his first wife died, Sebern married Zorah B. Grove who bore him a son, Finis. She died within a month and the son lived less than four months. All are buried in the cemetery at Pleasant Hope. *Submitted by Kay Dillard*

SALLEE – Relod Cecil Sallee, daughter of George and Addie Blackburn Sallee, was born on

Bottom row, left to right: Addie, Doy, Pauline, George; top row, Relod, Beach and Opal circa 1916 – 1918

Aug. 23, 1903 on a farm south of Brighton. She had an older brother, Beach Blackburn Sallee and an older sister, Opal. She has three younger siblings who were Audra, Pauline and Doy Sallee. Relod and Audra had diphtheria in 1909. Audra succumbed to it, but Relod survived. She attended the Fender Chapel Church that her grandfather helped to build in 1875. She attended Johnston School that stood by the church. It was also called Gumbo. After she graduated, she went back the next year to learn more as she was not allowed to attend the Pleasant Hope High School because of the distance and because her parents didn't send her older siblings. They probably didn't want her riding a horse that distance and probably couldn't afford to pay for her to board at the hotel in Pleasant Hope. A 14-year-old who wanted more education probably didn't realize that. Mr. Emory Parrish was one of her teachers.

Relod's home was on a bluff where there were many copperhead snakes, so walking was dangerous. It was nothing to see three or four copperheads on the path to the mailbox at the foot of the hill, but no one in her family ever was bitten.

As Relod got older, her brother's friend noticed her and began riding his horse down the same road that her friends and she walked to church on.

Later he bought a new buggy and she rode in it. He was Orville Stokes, son of Henry and Leona Alexander Stokes, and her only sweetheart. They married on July 27, 1920 and moved to Springfield. They returned to her father's farm in October when her mother passed away so she could help care for her two younger siblings. Water had to be carried from the spring and clothes were washed by using a washboard. There was no indoor plumbing. The garden supplied the family with food during the summer and much canning was done so there would be food through the winter. Corn was taken to the Goodnight Mill to be ground into cornmeal as was wheat for flour. The kerosene lamp and lantern were the lights at night as there was no electricity then. Relod accepted Christ as her saviour in her early teens.

Orville and Relod reared four children: George Henry, Grant, Wanda and Arvilla. They lived the rest of their lives at Brighton. She was an excellent seamstress, making her girls' dresses from feed sacks without patterns. She continued milking cows after Orville died until she fell in the barn loft while feeding hay at the age of 78. She was instrumental in erecting a fence around the Brock Cemetery near Sac River in southern Polk County where her great-grandfather Christian Fender is buried as well as two of Orville's baby brothers. Their grandchildren are W.G. (Billy George) Fieth of Bolivar; David Fieth, Bruce Dillard and Dwight Stokes of Brighton; Michael (Mike) Stokes, Randy Stokes and Phillip Dillard of Pleasant Hope; Peggy Fieth Smith of Willard; and Richard Stokes of Harrisonville, MO. Kenneth Dillard and Janet Stokes preceded them in death due to automobile accidents. Relod and Orville celebrated 59 years of marriage. All four of their children have lived to celebrate their 50th wedding anniversaries and live in the Brighton, Pleasant Hope and Willard areas. Relod died Jan. 20, 1998. She was a remarkable lady. *Submitted by Arvilla Feith*

SAWYER – James Ervin Sawyer married Mira Katherine Able on Dec. 10, 1865 in Morrisville,

Front row – Charlene Sawyer Neil, Mattie Ethel (Harris) Sawyer, Charles Ervin Sawyer, Alma (Sawyer) Wilson. Back row – Elvin Leon Sawyer, Neva (Sawyer) Gannaway, Charles Guy Sawyer, Velma (Sawyer) Fisher, Ernest Robert Sawyer. Taken November 1961 – Charley and Mattie Sawyer's 50th wedding anniversary.

Polk County, MO. They were the parents of the following children: John William, born Aug. 30, 1866; Stephen Wiley, born April 6, 1868; Robert Bertie, born May 17, 1870; Sarah Jane, born Nov. 18, 1872; Mary Lucinda, born Feb. 2, 1875; Ervin Sebern, born Oct. 20, 1877; and Lillie Virdell, born Sept. 22, 1880.

Their son John William married Louisa Clementine Jones in Polk County, MO on June 14, 1888. Their children were as follows: Stella Mae, born Oct. 21, 1889; Charles Ervin, born Sept. 24, 1891; Ethel Cora, born July 12, 1893; Willie Elizabeth, born July 14, 1895; Frank Robert, born Sept. 18, 1897; Dollie Myrtle, born Dec. 19, 1899; Ratha Alice, born Jan. 24, 1903; and a baby born Aug. 11, 1906.

John William and Clementine's son Charles Ervin married Mattie Ethel Harris on Nov. 23, 1911. Their children were as follows: Ernest Robert, born March 30, 1913; Lillie Velma, born Nov. 26, 1914; Ralph, born in 1916; Alma Mae, born July 25, 1918; Leo, born in 1920; Elvin Leon, born May 31, 1923; Neva Francis, born Jan. 31, 1927; Charles Guy, born June 26, 1930; and Helen Charlene, born Feb. 14, 1933.

Charles (Charley) and Mattie's son Charles Guy married Leota Ross of Polk County, MO on Jan. 20, 1951. Their children were, as follows: Bunny, Debbie, Sherri, Charlie and Danny. Guy and Leota's daughter Bunny married Mike Jones and they have two children, Michael and Angela.

Bunny was born in Polk County at her parents' home near Dunnegan. When she was preschool age, the family moved to Kansas City where she and her siblings were raised in Johnson County. After Bunny and Mike were married and had their children, they decided to move back to Polk County to raise the children. They have lived here since 1982 on the farm they bought. There have been many Sawyer families living in and around the Polk County for many generations. Bunny Sawyer Jones hopes that Polk County will always be a place to be proud to call home. *Submitted by Bunny Sawyer Jones*

SAWYERS – Willis Sawyers was born in Robertson County, TN on March 18, 1847 to James Henry Sawyers and Phoebe Ellen Warren. When he was about 4 years old, the family moved to Polk County, MO. Willis joined the Union Army, Missouri Cavalry as a private on Aug. 19, 1863. He was discharged Jan. 11, 1866 near Joffa, MO. Upon his return, he married Nancy A. Hall Bridges. Nancy was born Oct. 16, 1846 in Barren County, KY to William G. Bridges and Nancy Greer. Willis and Nancy were married Aug. 1, 1867 in Polk County by J.W. Rutherford, J.P. Their first son, James William, was born Nov. 26, 1869, followed by Oliva on Feb. 29, 1870, I.V. (an infant) Jan. 18, 1872, Richard on Feb. 1, 1874 and Phoebe Ellen on March 18, 1877. Willis, Nancy, James William and Oliva show up on the 1870 Polk County census. Willis moved the family by covered wagon in 1880 to Oregon for about nine months, then on to Idaho for eight months. Why they made the trip, we don't know. They then returned to Polk County. Willis passed away on May 8, 1910. His funeral was performed by the Rev. Henry Bridges, Nancy's brother. Nancy passed away on Dec. 16, 1911. She is buried in Mountain View Cemetery.

Benjamin Coonis' family began their trek from Madison County, KY with Benjamin's father, Tarleton Cunnius. Tarleton left Kentucky and moved to Alabama, where he married Katharine Nicholas in 1822 in Jefferson County. They then moved to Arkansas. Benjamin was born in Conway County on Jan. 30, 1846. The family finally settled first in Collin County, TX where Tarleton remarried, and then on to Wise County, TX. Tarleton was an original member of Peter's Colony. Benjamin returned to Arkansas to enlist

Sawyers family 1918 Bolivar, MO

in the Union Army for the Civil War. He enlisted on May 5, 1864 as a private in the First Arkansas Cavalry. He was discharged in August of 1865 at Fayetteville, AR. Benjamin and Sarah settled in Greene County but would visit the family in Polk County. James William married Lilly May Coonis on March 8, 1896. Lilly was born Feb. 15, 1880 in Missouri. Lilly's parents, Benjamin Franklin Coonis/Cunnius and Sarah Ann Penter Coonis, were married Oct. 29, 1866 in Franklin County, MO by the Rev. Spain. Sarah was born May 5, 1848 in Illinois.

James William and Lilly May lived for a while in Joplin, then moved on to Goodson. The stay in Goodson was brief, after which they settled in Bolivar. They had 12 children all together. The first, an infant, died shortly after birth. He was followed by Frank, Houston, Edna, Beulah, Avis, Oren, Lester, Emmett, Helen, Hazel and James William Jr. The family moved to California in 1922. Somewhere around this time, the "s" was dropped off of the name.

Their first stop, once in California, was a town named Santa Paula. Santa Paula had become known as "Little Bolivar." So many people who had lived in Bolivar had moved to Santa Paula during this time. Willis Sawyer's baby brother, Monroe Sawyers, lived in Santa Paula. The entire family stayed in California. *Submitted by Susan Sawyer Roland*

SCHLEIFER – Philip Schleifer was born in Alsace Loraine, France, Jan. 26, 1832. He came to the United States at the age of 17 in 1849. His trade was that of a stonemason. In 1856 he married Johanna Fredericka Reister, born April 15, 1840 in Baden, Germany. Her mother brought her, a sister and brother to the United States in 1850. To this union were born 11 children: Fredericka, Elizabeth, Julia, Charlie (died as an infant), Lewis, Amelia, George, Charlie, Phillip Jr., Rose and Fred. In 1862, while living in Cooper County near St. Louis, MO, he enlisted in the 52nd Regiment

Approximately 1885 – Johanna Fredericka Schleifer, her daughter Elizabeth and son-in-law and their three children.

325

Missouri Militia (Union). They moved to Polk County in 1867 and continued his stonemason work, building several river bridge piers, dams, as well as building piers for the railroad. He helped to lay some of the rock foundations of the stores around the square of Bolivar and built the stone jail house at Hermitage, MO, in 1870-1871, which is now a historic site and visitor center. Phillip died March 25, 1888 of malaria fever contracted while working on the Current River railroad, near Van Buren, MO. The Schleifers were some of the original settlers of the Van community, building the rock house still standing 134 years later. Some of his descendants still own and farm the original homestead. *Submitted by Mike Schleifer*

SCROGGINS – Rollo L. Scroggins, a lifelong resident of Polk County, MO, was born July 11, 1904 near Pleasant Hope, MO. He was one of five children born to Edward Paris Scroggins, who was born April 27, 1882 and died March 1, 1966, and Nell Catherine Apperson Scroggins, who was born Feb. 9, 1886 and died Oct. 20, 1978. Both of his parents are buried in the Pleasant Hope Cemetery, Pleasant Hope, MO. Other children born to Edward Paris Scroggins and Nell Catherine Apperson Scroggins were Walter Charles, Edward Del, Vanda Elizabeth and Julia Helen.

Rollo and Erma Scroggins wedding day.

Erma and Rollo Scroggins – 50th wedding anniversary.

Rollo's paternal grandparents were Edward George Washington "Bud" Scroggins (born 1858 and died 1930) and Julia Elizabeth Mitchell Scroggins (born 1858 and died 1945). His grandmother Julia Elizabeth Mitchell Scroggins came from the early pioneer family of Mitchells who lived in the Morrisville, MO area. Both paternal grandparents are buried in the Slagle Cemetery, Slagle, MO.

Rollo, as a 20-year-old, was married to 17-year-old Erma Jean Flanagan on Nov. 6, 1924, whom he had met when her family moved from the Springfield, MO area to Pleasant Hope, MO. Erma was born to Alfred Turner Flanagan and Ada Rebecca Adkins Flanagan. Erma was one of nine children. Other siblings were Arnie, Harry, Zelma, Ava, Evelyn, Wilma, Lora and Laura. Both of Erma's parents are buried at Clark Creek Cemetery near Willard, MO.

Rollo and Erma made their home in the Pleasant Hope and where three of their four children were born. Helen Louise Scroggins, born Dec. 3, 1926; Loy Edward Scroggins, born Aug. 7, 1930 and Lee Roy Scroggins, born Sept. 21, 1932.

In the year 1935, Rollo and Erma left the Pleasant Hope area. They purchased and moved to a farm on the Pomme de Terre River, which was located north of Bolivar, MO, near the old wrought-iron bridge known as the Francka Bridge. On this farm, their fourth child, Larry Dean Scroggins, was born on Nov. 28, 1937. Larry and his wife, Mary Evelyn Scroggins, have continued to live in the same house that Larry was born in and have raised their four daughters there.

Rollo was well-known for his farming abilities. He was successful in raising crops on the river bottom farm, raising turkeys for many years, as well as being a stockman. Rollo served on the local MFA board, held various offices locally and served in the same capacities on the state level. He was instrumental in helping start the Farmers and Merchants Bank, which later became the Commerce Bank. Rollo and Erma were members of Center Point Missionary Baptist Church for many years. When they moved to Bolivar, MO, in retirement, they became members of the Calvary Missionary Baptist Church. He served as a deacon in both churches.

Rollo and Erma were very proud of their family of four children. Louise Scroggins was married to Warren George Jones on June 6, 1954. They had two children: Terry Dean (born Nov. 2, 1955 and died July 20, 1986) and Kristy Ann (born March 26, 1958). Kristy was married to Michael Jones on Sept. 15, 1979. They had three children: Caleb Michael (born May 6, 1985), Kylie LaRae (born Jan. 12, 1989) and Kinleigh Teri (born Feb. 1994).

Loy Scroggins married Leta Jeffries on Nov. 11, 1952. They had two children: Steven Kent (born Nov. 6, 1958) and Michael Wayne (born June 2, 1961). Steven married Cheryl Yarbrough on Sept. 17, 1999 and they had one child, Mackenzie Joy (born April 14, 2002).

Lee Scroggins married Mary Lou Davis on Oct. 18, 1969. They had three children: Douglas Lee (born Dec. 9, 1970), Craig Daniel (born March 17, 1972) and Bradley Todd (born Aug. 22, 1973). Douglas married Melissa Bacon on April 25, 1992 and they had two children: Autumn Nicole (born Oct. 13, 1992) and Kirkland Douglas (born Nov. 9, 1995).

Larry Scroggins married Mary Evelyn Jenkins on Aug. 20, 1960. They had four children. Marla Evelyn Scroggins (born Aug. 8, 1963) married Kelley Ray Roberts on July 16, 1983. Their children are Karaley Evelyn Roberts (born Feb. 15, 1988) and Sterling Kelley Roberts (born Feb. 5, 1993).

Malinda Diane Scroggins (born Oct. 31, 1966) married Gregory Wayne Elliott on Sept. 5, 1998. Their children are Leah Diane (born April 28, 2000) and Owen Gregory (born Feb. 7, 2002).

Malissa Beth Scroggins (born Aug. 10, 1969) married Shawn Terry Phillips on July 13, 1991. Their children are Shawn Patrick (born July 2, 1991), Samantha Beth (born Aug. 3, 1995), Shane Conner (born June 15, 1998) and Julia Mary (born Aug. 18, 1999).

Marcia LaDean Scroggins (born Nov. 25, 1974) married Douglas Winfied Skinner on June 10, 1995. Their children are Ryan James (born March 3, 1998) and Rheagan Hope (born April 23, 1999).

Rollo and Erma Scroggins are buried in the Pleasant Hope Cemetery, Pleasant Hope, MO. *Submitted by Larry Scroggins*

SCURLOCK – Simeon M. Scurlock was born Jan. 16, 1845 in Jackson County, OH to David Scurlock and Mary Buck. On March 11, 1869, he married Lucinda Ware in Jackson County, OH. She was the daughter of William Ware and Mary Vernon. They moved to Dallas County, MO by 1870 with other members of the Ware family. Simeon and Lucinda had several children born in Dallas County, MO: Mary Jane, born 1870; Hiram Russell, born 1871; Eli Martin, born 1873; Elexander, born 1875; Francis Marion, born 1876; Henry Dimmon, born 1879; Minnie Ellen, born 1881; and Lillie Ethony, born 1883. Simeon died in Dallas County in August of 1883, before his last child, Lillie, was born in December. On Aug. 1, 1886, Lucinda (Ware) Scurlock married Simeon Scurlock's brother, Andrew J. Scurlock. They had three more children: Ira Eden, born 1887; Stella, born 1889; and Owen, born 1893.

Francis Marion and Ginetta Frances (Wine) Scurlock; children – Bert, Amy, Clifford and Lonnie Scurlock

Sometime between 1883 and 1898, Lucinda and Andrew moved their extended family to Polk County, MO. Andrew died in November of 1898. Lucinda died in July of 1938 and they are buried at Barren Creek Cemetery in Polk County, MO.

Francis Marion Scurlock, the fifth child of Simeon and Lucinda Scurlock, grew up in Polk County and remained in the community his entire life. He married Ginetta Frances Wine on Dec. 22, 1901. She was the daughter of Loring Corneluis Wine and Amanda Jane Wilson. To this union four children were born: Amy Frances, born March 8, 1904; Burtis Eugene, born Dec. 23, 1905; Clifford Martin, born March 23, 1911; and Lonnie Wesley, born Dec. 16, 1913.

Francis Marion Scurlock served his community as a barber for many years before his death on Sept. 1, 1945. Ginetta Frances (Wine) Scurlock had passed away six years before him on Nov. 7, 1939. They are both buried at Barren Creek Cemetery in Polk County, MO.

Amy Scurlock married Edgar V. Derossett. They had four children: Charles Frances, Virgil, Mary Belle and Harold Dean. Amy died in 1937 due to complications from surgery. She and Edgar are buried in Greenwood Cemetery in Bolivar, MO.

Burtis died at the young age of 21 in 1926 of typhoid fever. He never married.

Clifford Scurlock married Leona Jones and they had two children: Gary Martin and David Allen. Clifford died in May of 1971 and is buried at Greenwood Cemetery in Bolivar, MO.

Lonnie Scurlock married Wanda Lucille Covert on April 17, 1936. Lonnie and Lucille lived in Bolivar, MO. Lonnie and Lucille had two daughters: Shirley Jean and Sharron Kay, who are still living in Polk County, MO. Lucille died Sept. 9, 1995 and Lonnie Aug 21, 1998. Both are buried in Greenwood Cemetery in Bolivar, MO. *Submitted by Shirley (Scurlock) Laird*

SCURLOCK – Lonnie Wesley Scurlock was born Dec. 16, 1913 to Francis Marion "Frank" Scurlock and Ginetta Francis Wine. He was the youngest of four children. Lonnie married Wanda Lucille Covert on April 17, 1936 in Cedar County, MO. She was the daughter of Ernest Edward Gibson Covert and Jesse Vinson (Brown) Covert. Lonnie and Lucille lived in Bolivar, MO during most of their adult lives. To this union, two daughters were born. Shirley Jean was born Dec. 31, 1936 in Polk County, MO. Sharron Kay was born May 30, 1945 in Polk County, MO.

Shirley Scurlock married Loren William Laird on Jan. 27, 1956 in Polk County, MO. They had

Lonnie W. and Lucille (Covert) Scurlock

two daughters: Catherine Diane, born Nov. 5, 1958 and Karen Jean, born May 15, 1961.

Catherine Diane Laird married Edward Preston Akers on April 2, 1977. They had two daughters: Hillary Diane, born Oct. 16, 1977 and Kendra Gail, born on Aug. 26, 1981. Hillary Akers married Robert Talburt on Aug. 21, 1998. They have three children: Bayley Rhys, born Feb. 29, 2000, Keegan Parker, born Feb. 20, 2001 and Sophie Grace, born April 10, 2002. Kendra Akers has one daughter, Alexis Gayle O'Hara, born Feb. 13, 2001.

Karen Jean Laird married Elvin Foster on May 15, 1993.

Sharron Kay Scurlock married Lyle Lee Garretson on Sept. 3, 1966 in Polk County, MO. They had three children: Trudi Kay, born June 6, 1967, Gregory Scott, born Feb. 6, 1970 and Staci Anne, born June 7, 1971.

Trudi Kay Garretson married Steven Bruce Snow on Aug. 19, 1989. They have one son, Zachary Steven Snow, born May 4, 1993.

Gregory Scott Garretson married Julie Ann Turner on Jan. 15, 1992. They have two children: Britnie Jae, born Jan. 13, 1994 and Hunter Isaac, born April 13, 1998.

Staci Anne Garretson married Charles Flint Wendland on Dec. 22, 1995. They have two sons: Tanner Reed, born March 19, 1997 and Dayne Anthony, born Feb. 16, 1999.

Lonnie worked for the Coca-Cola Bottling Company for several years before beginning a long career at Teters Manufacturing Company. After retiring from Teters, he worked part-time for The Flower Patch as a delivery driver. Lonnie enjoyed spending time with his family and friends, walking and riding his bicycle. Lucille worked as a seamstress for Braithwait's clothing store before she started to work for Teters Manufacturing Company. She also retired from Teters. After her retirement, Lucille enjoyed visiting with family, baking, crocheting and quilting. Lucille died Sept. 9, 1995 and Lonnie died Aug. 21, 1998. Both are buried in Greenwood Cemetery in Bolivar, MO. *Submitted by Staci (Garretson) Wendland*

SEAMSTER – Stephen Salee Seamster, son of Williamson Shaw and Susan (Rigsby) Seamster, was born Jan. 17, 1836 in Barry County, MO and moved to Polk County, MO in the 1860s. He first married Minerva Jane Peake on March 18, 1863 in Hancock County, IL. She was born on June 12, 1845 in Illinois. To this union, eight children were born: Rebecca, Mary Alice, Marinda Ellen, William Jonah, Susan Elizabeth, Poett Ann, Tomas and Oscar Lee. Minerva passed away on Aug. 14, 1887 with interment in Payne Cemetery near Polk, MO.

Stephen remarried on Dec. 30, 1888 in Polk County to Etta Mariah Pate. Etta was born on May 20, 1869. To this union six children were born: Finnie Lutis, Arvie Otis, Avis Bethuel, Martha Cordelia, Artie Elgie and Ezra Selvanis. Stephen passed away on Oct. 17, 1920 in Polk County and Etta passed away on March 17, 1965 in Sentinel, MO, both are buried in Payne Cemetery.

Rebecca Seamster was born on Aug. 26, 1866 in Hancock County, IL and passed away on July 30, 1951 in Loveland, CO. She married John Dean Swift on Jan. 1, 1880 in Polk County, MO. To this union nine children were born: Lavonna Ellen, Izella Grace, Antha Jane, Cynthia Orilla, Jon, Orpha Alice, Ora Rebecca, Viola Virginia, Herthel Alma. Rebecca passed away in Loveland, CO on July 30, 1951 and John on Dec. 26, 1904 in Lamar, CO.

Mary Alice Seamster was born on Jan. 1, 1869 in Polk County, MO. She married Jessie More and had two children: Walter and John.

Marinda Ellen Seamster was born on Jan. 1, 1868 in Polk County, MO.

William Jonah Seamster was born on March 14, 1872 in Polk County, MO. He married Florence Hutchenson on March 23, 1894. Florence was born on Jan. 29, 1876. To this union four children were born: Nellie, Frederick C., Jennie B. and Bertha B. William passed away on March 3, 1960 and Florence on April 9, 1946.

Susan Elizabeth Seamster was born on Nov. 26, 1875 in Polk County, MO.

Poett Ann Seamster was born on March 24, 1879 in Polk County, MO and passed away on Sept. 24, 1880 with burial in Payne Cemetery, Polk County.

Tomas Seamster was born on Aug. 10, 1880.

Oscar Lee Seamster was born on Dec. 29, 1886 in Polk County, MO. He married Grace E. Barnes. To this union five children were born: Everette Nolan, Elgie Vinson, Elsie Jewell, Evan Hubart, Velma Cloe. Oscar passed away on Aug. 1, 1919 with interment in Payne Cemetery near Polk, MO.

Finnie Lutis Seamster was born on June 1, 1890 in Polk County, MO and married Mary Agnes

In the picture are Stephen and Etta with their children. Believe the children to be Oscar, Finnie, Arvie, Avis, Martha, Artie and Ezra as baby. (Went by the oldest being the tallest but not sure.)

Shaw on July 20, 1913 in Polk County, MO. Mary was born on March 22, 1893 in Polk County. To this union one child was born, Obie Neal. Finnie passed away on Jan. 27, 1976 in Polk County and Mary on June 19, 1981 in Clay County. Interment is in the Hopewell Cemetery, Polk County, MO.

Avis Bethuell Seamster was born on Oct. 19, 1893 in Polk County and married Myrtie Richards on Nov. 20, 1920 in Hermitage, MO. Myrtie was born on March 27, 1901. To this union two children were born, Alpha Cleo and Jewell Marie. Avis passed away on Jan. 10, 1974 and Myrtie on Dec. 6, 1989; both are buried in Payne Cemetery, Polk County, MO.

Martha Cordelia Seamster was born on Jan. 21, 1897 in Polk County, MO; she married Ray Duncan. To this union one child was born Alpha Willis Duncan. Martha passed away on April 4, 1977 in Kansas City, KS and Ray on Sept. 18, 1970 in Kansas City, KS.

Artie Elgie Seamster was born on Jan. 21, 1897 in Polk County, MO and he married Bessie Baby Lightfoot on July 20, 1920 in Sentinel Baptist Church. Bessie was born on Sept. 11, 1901 near Pittsburgh, MO. To this union 11 children were born: Nola Mae, James Willard, Junior Lee, Donnie B., Johnnie Dean, Alvie Kenneth, Edsel Ray, Juanita Francis, Betty Jean, Charles Elgie and Shirley Faye. Bessie passed away on Feb. 23, 1952 near Sentinel, MO. Artie remarried to Gertrude McNatt on Aug. 9, 1953. She was born on Aug. 4, 1914. Artie passed away on July 14, 1979. Artie and Bessie are buried in Payne Cemetery. Gertrude passed away on April 18, 2000 with interment in Nemo Cemetery.

Elza Selvanis Seamster was born on March 1, 1901 and married Vinnie Skinner. To this union one child was born, Linville Dee. Ezra passed away on April 16, 1976 with interment in Payne Cemetery, Polk County, MO. *Submitted by Ted L. Young Jr.*

SECHLER – The name Sechler was recorded in Cologne, Germany in the year 1135. The name

Nancy Kezia "Kizzie" (Grove) Sechler and Paul Samuel Truth "True" Sechler

referred to craftsmen who worked with leather pouches for coins. The name was introduced in North America in the Revolutionary War in 1775. Michael Sechler of Montgomery County, PA is listed in the pension files of that state. The Sechler ancestry goes back to Rudolph Sechler who lived in Lancaster County, PA. His son, Henry, was the father of Christian Sechler.

The Christian Sechler family left China Grove, Rowan County, NC in the mid-1800s. They settled first in Prairie Grove, Dallas County, MO. Christian Sechler's family headed to California during the Gold Rush era, but their wagon broke down in Bradleyville, Taney County, MO. During the Civil War, Christian was a cook for the Confederate Army. The family lived in Taney County until Christian's death in 1885. He was buried in the original part of the Bradleyville Cemetery.

Paul Samuel "Truth" Sechler (1853-1893), Christian's fourth child, came to Polk County as a very young man to teach school. He later married "Kizzie" Grove, one of his students. Her parents owned land in Mooney Township, Polk County. Paul Samuel, better known as "True," acquired a farm of 294 acres from his in-laws. He built a home with a large fireplace near a large spring. "True" cleared about three acres annually. He would cut the stumps below the ground so he could plow and plant wheat in the fall.

The school where "True" Sechler taught was called Pleasant Grove, "Frog Pond," probably named after the Grove family.

"True" Sechler and his wife, "Kizzie," raised 10 children on this farm: Mattie Whittaker, Zella Faucett, Mollie, Brad Armstrong, Tina, Alma Wells, Alvin, Raymond, and twins Loren and Lois Slagle. Descendants of Alvin and Raymond still farm the original farm and additional land between Brighton and Pleasant Hope, MO. Six generations of the

Alvin Truth Sechler and Raymond Grove Sechler WWI – 1918

Sechler family have farmed this same land. Raymond G. Jr. continues to live and farm the land attained by his grandfather, "True" Sechler. Chester and his family still live and farm acreage adjoining the original farm.

In spite of the great success of this family, "True" Sechler was injured in a logging accident and eventually committed suicide, due to the severity of pain from the injury. Members of the Sechler family are buried at Brighton, Pleasant Hope, and Reed Cemeteries near Halfway, MO. *Submitted by Raymond G. Sechler Jr.*

SELL – Brent DeRosset's great-grandfather was Rolen Clement Sell. He, in turn, was the third great-grandson of Henry Sell.

According to the history of the Sell family by James Sell in 1931, Henry Sell, along with 13 other Sells, came to America from Germany in 1729. We only have record of one son for Henry, that being Jacob Sell, born Dec. 10, 1742 and died Oct. 23, 1825. Jacob's wife was Christina (last name unknown) born 1753 and died 1820. The Sells located in Adams County, PA, near Littlestown, Hanover and Gettysburg.

We have record of nine children for Jacob and Christina. Jacob, Daniel, Abraham, Maria, Margaret, John, David, Peter and Henry. The last four were reported to have gone to live in Starke County, OH.

Brent's third great-grandfather was Rolen, and he is believed to be a descendant of one of the four that went to Ohio, possibly John. In an interview with Rolen by M. W. Sell a few months before Rolen died, he asked Rolen what his grandfather's name was and he thought that the name was Anthony. Rolen's father was Harrison Sell and his mother was Elizabeth Champer.

Harrison Sell was born and lived in or near Stubensville, OH. Later the family moved to Springfield, MO. He is buried in a small cemetery about 10 miles south and west of Stockton, MO. His wife is buried in Mt. Comfort Cemetery about 10 miles north of Springfield near Highway 65.

Rolen was born Dec. 12, 1847 and died Nov. 21, 1941. On Dec. 8, 1869, he married Ezenith Ann Murray, born May 30, 1852 in Wyandotte County, OH, who was the daughter of D. C. Murray. Ezenith came with her father to Missouri in the fall of 1867 and located near Springfield, MO.

Rolen and Ezenith were the parents of 12 children, which included two sets of twins. The children were Arthur, Edwin Hamilton, William Walter, Clara Eldora (who married George Donald McKnight, and these would be Brent's second great-grandparents), Ora May, Olive Celestia, Ira V. and Iva Lee (twins), Jerema Ann, Ida Leaora and Ina Leonna (twins) and Andrew J. In addition to these, Rolen and Ezenith took three grandchildren into their home and raised them, making a total of 15 children. In the spring of 1882, Rolen and Ezenith moved from Fair Grove, MO to a farm three miles west of Moorisville, MO and this is where they raised their family.

They joined the Concord Baptist Church, now called Oakville Baptist Church. He donated land for the cemetery where he and his wife, who died Sept. 15, 1922, along with several children and friends now rest. In a writing by Iva, a daughter of Rolen, Susan Ann Hamilton was the first to be buried in the cemetery. *Submitted by Brent DeRossett*

SELL – Verna C. Slagle Sell was born on March 4, 1913, in Polk County, the daughter of Wade H. and Ida May Scroggins Slagle. She had four brothers: Dennis, Willis, J. Frank and Keith. Verna was a descendant of the pioneer Slagle families who came from Tennessee and settled in Polk County in the 1830s. She was a great-great-granddaughter of John S. Slagle Sr. and Anna Metheny Slagle (children: William, Jacob, John, Elizabeth, Abraham, Harmon, David, James, Coon and Charity).

She was a great-granddaughter of Jacob and Francis Dunlap Slagle (children: John A., Elizabeth, Maria E., William, James, Hanna, Mary Ann and Cordelia Katherine) and a granddaughter of James P. and Barbara Barham Slagle (children: William, Alice, Benjamin, Frances, Charles, Wade, Ella and Emma).

Arthur Gilbert Sell was born Oct. 11, 1910. He was the son of Arthur G. and Alta Gist Sell of Morrisville, MO. He had a brother, Rolen and five sisters, Eula, Rema, Lorena, Edith and Ezenith. Arthur, Rolen and Rema were raised in the Oakville community by their grandparents, Rolen C. and Ezenith Ann Murray Sell, after the death of their father in 1912. The other four sisters returned to Illinois with their mother, Alta.

He was a great-great-grandson of Anthony Sell and Catherine Cale/Kail Sell of Stubenville, OH, originally from Pennsylvania (children: Gabriel, John, Mary, Sarah, Anthony III, Benjamin, Sophia, Harrison, Peter, Catherine, Ann and Margaret). He was a great-grandson of Harrison and Elizabeth Champer Sell (children: Wilson, Katherine, Benton, Portius, Rolen C., George M., Reubin W., Lander and Urban), who migrated from Wyandotte County, OH by wagon train in 1869 with the David C. Murray family. David Murray and his family settled in Greene County, MO. Arthur's grandparents, Rolen C. and Ezenith Ann Murray Sell, were married after the families settled in Missouri (children: Arthur G., Edwin, Walter, Clara, Ora, Olive, Ira, Iva, Jerema, Ina, Ida and Andrew).

Arthur and Verna were married at Enon Baptist Church, Wishart, MO on Dec. 13, 1931. They joined Verna's brother, Dennis, in Bakersfield, CA in 1940 seeking work. Arthur, Verna and their two other children (Leon and Esther) returned to Missouri in 1942 after Verna's father's health worsened. Her mother needed help on the farm and with the care of Wade, who was blind for 18 years before his death in 1944.

Arthur G. Sell, Verna Cordelia Slagle Sell, children: Leon Sell and Esther Sell circa 1942

Arthur and Verna moved to Kansas City about 1945 and lived in the Kansas City area for 27 years while raising five children: Leon Sell, Esther Sell (Schultz) 1938-2001, Shirley Sell (Burgert), Evelyn Sell (O'Dell) and Gilbert Sell. Arthur worked in the construction trade for J.D. Spears while in Kansas City. They returned to southern Missouri upon retirement in 1972, locating on a small farm on Stockton Lake near Aldrich, MO. Verna died in 1986 and Arthur in 1996. Both are buried in Slagle Cemetery, Slagle, MO. *Submitted by Evelyn M. Sell O'Dell and Shirley L. Sell Burgert*

SELL – In 2002 a monument was erected at Oakville commemorating the beginning of the

Rolen and Ezenith (Murray) Sell

cemetery, church and school. Rolen Clement and his wife, Ezenith Ann (Murray) Sell, donated the land for this in 1889.

Rolen Sell was born Dec. 12, 1849. Ezenith was born Sept. 15, 1852. They were married in 1869. Rolen died on Nov. 11, 1941 and Ezenith died Sept. 22, 1922 and both are buried at Oakville Cemetery along with some of their 12 children. Rolen and Ezenith were farmers. Others are buried at Pleasant Ridge Cemetery, Walnut Grove, Springfield and Stockton. Rolen's father, Harrison Sell, is buried south of Stockton.

Even after raising a family of 12 children and helping others, Rolen's estate was divided among the ones he left behind.

Rolen and Ezenith's son, William and his wife, Eliza Belle (Burney), lived on a farm between Morrisville and Oakville. It was there that they raised their family of seven children: Zelma, Ruby, Glen, Woodrow, Raymond, Lawrence and Samuel Sell. *Submitted by Elsie Sell*

SELVEY – The Ron and Donna Selvey family arrived in Polk County in July of 1973. Their oldest

Rolen Clement Sell Family

Ron and Donna Selvey Family

daughter, Rhonda, was a sophomore at Missouri Southern College in Joplin. Their son Roger was a junior in high school. Their daughter Peggy was in the seventh grade and Cammie started kindergarten that year.

Ron was transferred here as a sergeant with the Missouri State Highway Patrol after having served 20 years in the Newton and McDonald County areas. He continued to work in Polk, Hickory and Dallas Counties until his retirement in 1989.

Since retirement, Ron volunteers many hours in Polk County serving as an AARP 55 Alive driving instructor, spending many hours with his tractor and in his spare time you might find him on the golf course. He is also very active in Zion Lutheran Church.

Donna has spent the last 18 years as a part-time sales associate at Davolt's Hallmark Shop. She has taught many beginner bridge groups and enjoys church work and the grandchildren. Also she can be found at either Bolivar golf course on a sunny day.

Their daughter Rhonda is married to Dale Penn, a major with the Missouri State Highway Patrol. They live in Jefferson City where Rhonda teaches second grade. They have three girls. Dayla lives in Bolivar and is employed at Citizens Memorial Hospital day care. Sarah is a junior at West Point Military Academy and Chelsea is in the seventh grade.

Their son, Roger and his wife, Bobbie, live in Plano, TX. Roger is a regional vice president with GlaxoSmithKline Pharmaceutical Company. Their son, Brad, lives and works in Denton, TX and daughter Beth is a sophomore at the University of Arkansas in Fayetteville.

Their daughter Peggy is married to Will Beatty and they make their home in Bolivar. Will works at Associated Grocers in Springfield and Peggy is also a sales associate at Davolt's Hallmark Shop. They have three children. Hannah is a freshman at Ozarks Technical Community College in Springfield, Bryan is in the eighth grade and Luke is in kindergarten.

Their daughter Cammie is married to Bill Wine and they, too, make their home in Bolivar. Bill works at Kraft in Springfield and Cammie is a registered nurse at the Birth Place at Citizens Memorial Hospital. They have three children: Lyndsay is a freshman, Abby is in the first grade and Payton is 2.

Ron and Donna think Polk County is a great place to live and plan to stay here. *Submitted by Donna Selvey*

SERLS – Clara Myrtle Serls Jarman was born Sept. 21, 1905 in Polk County where she lived her life in the town of Bolivar and later on a farm outside of town. She and Roy Washington Jarman raised four children, two girls and two boys. Clara was one of five children born to Iva Mae Jump and John J. Serls Jr. The other children were Rose Lee, Eva Lena, Ralph J. and an unnamed baby who died in infancy.

Clara's mother, Iva Mae Jump Serls, and grandmother, Sarah Jane Zumwalt Jump, also lived their lives in Polk County. Iva Mae was born December 1885 and her mother, Sarah Jane, was born December 1841.

The Jump family moved to Polk County during the 1840s from St. Louis, while the Zumwalt family came from the St. Charles area in the late 1830s. At this same time Nathan Boone, the youngest son of Daniel Boone, the famous frontiersman, moved his family to settle in Ash Grove area in Greene County. These families moved together because Sarah Jane Zumwalt's mother was Jemima Boone Zumwalt, daughter of Nathan Boone, granddaughter of Daniel Boone. Sarah's father was Henry Zumwalt, son of John D. Zumwalt.

They lived on farms as did most families during that time and both the Zumwalt and Jump families consisted of 12 children each. During the Civil War, some family members left Polk County for Indian Territory and Texas while others remained to live out their lives there. Of the families remaining in Polk County, some stayed on farms while others moved into the town of Bolivar to live. *Submitted by Diana Kahler Jones*

Clara Myrtle Serl 1921

SHAW – Winneford was the daughter of William Shaw Sr. of Civil District No. 10, Springfield, Robertson County, TN. He was born 1792 in Tennessee before it became a state in 1796. Her father fought in the War of 1812 with Andrew Jackson in the Battle of New Orleans. He served under Colonel John Cocke, Second Regiment of West Tennessee Militia (November 1814-May 1815) with Richard Crunk group. By the Congressional Act of 1850, William Shaw received land by warrant in Jefferson County, IL. He also received land from John Cook. These papers say that he was living in Walnut Hill, Marion County, IL in 1851. He later sold this land to his son, James Warren Shaw. His second wife, Jane, of Virginia married in Kentucky about 1836, and she died between 1855-1860 around Walnut Hill, Marion County, IL by the Illinois State Census. The widowed William Shaw Sr. lived with his younger son, William Shaw Jr. and his wife, Sarah Shook, and four girls on the farm owned by his oldest son, James Warren Shaw. Then William Shaw, Jr. moved to Wayne County, IL about 1865 and died on Feb. 5, 1878. His will says that the treasurer of Polk County, MO had $100 to be passed on to his two sons: William Charles Shaw and John Duncan Shaw. (They were minors and never received it. So there may be more family connections in Polk County, MO.)

Also, note on the 1850 census for William Shaw Sr. in Robertson County, TN, there are three Mays boys: Daniel (15 years), William (14 years) and James (13 years). These may have been one of the unknown sisters of Winneford who married a Mays gentleman.

Now for Winneford Shaw. She was born April 23, 1819 in Springfield, Robertson County, TN. She married Jackson Warren, son of Seibert and Mary Bushrod (Swift) Warren of Robertson County, TN. Mary, along with some of the Warrens, were buried in a group around the gate of Shook Cemetery in Walnut Hill, Marion County, IL. Winnie and Jackson Warren were supposed to have been married around 1837 in Robertson County, TN. They are first recorded on the tax assessment for Polk County, MO in 1854. When they left Tennessee the 1850 census listed them as having four children: Margaret (12 years), France, female, (10 years), Riley (7 years) and Lewis A. (4 years.) In 1870 census list them at Bolivar Post Office, Benton Township, Polk County, MO. Also, there is a 15 year-old child named Mary F. Warren and Alexander Warren who is 13 years old. Their oldest daughter has married Perry Viles and becomes his second wife and lives next door.

On the 1880 census, Winnie says, "She was born in Tennessee, her father born in Tennessee, and her mother was born in Virginia."

Also her granddaughter Margaret C. Price is in the home. Winnie and Jackson are buried at Mt. Gilead Cemetery. Their tombstones look like the king and queen on a chessboard. Other Warrens buried around them are Bertie G. Warren, Jackson Warren, John N. Warren, Lewis Warren, Mack Warren, Nancy Warren, Norah Warren, Riley W. Warren, R.W. Warren, Winnie Warren, Infant Warren. As you look at the Mt. Gilead Cemetery plat map, you will see the family members all gathered around them. Winnie Warren died May 21, 1903.

Winnie's siblings were an unknown sister (born. 1818 in Tennessee); herself; unknown sister (born 1820 in Robertson County, TN); James Warren Shaw, born Sept. 4, 1822, Springfield, Robertson County, TN and died Sept. 7, 1899, Walnut Hill, Marion County, IL. James W. Shaw had three wives and 16 children. Many are still in that location.

John Westley Shaw was born 1825 Roberston County, TN and died August 1854 in Walnut Hill, Marion County, IL, child: William Thomas Shaw, Phebe Shaw, married Martin Grove in Marion County, IL; Susan Shaw, not sure if she stayed in Tennessee or if she moved with the family. William Shaw Jr. born 1832-1836 in Robertson, TN and died Feb. 8, 1878 in Wayne County, IL, married Sarah Shook on Jan. 26, 1854 in Marion County, IL *Submitted by Marlene Olson*

SHAW – James and Permintney Shaw were both born in Tennessee. They married in about 1842. They came to Missouri before their son James D. Shaw was born in 1842. He always seems to be close to Duncan and Mary (Thrower) Shaw, also from Tennessee. Four sets of their children have the same names. By the 1850 census, James and Permintney Shaw had a total of four children: James D. (1842), Margaret J. (1844), Sarah E. (1846) and Martha A. (1849). They lived next to Duncan Shaw by the enumerator listing. Susan Shaw was born in 1851 in Polk County, MO.

Permintney Shaw, first wife of James Shaw, died on June 20, 1852 and is buried at Ragsdale Cemetery in North Benton Township, about two and one-half miles northeast of Halfway. By October 1853, James Shaw married in Polk County to Bersheba (Keeth) Shaw who becomes his second wife, according to Book A, page 14. They have four children, according to 1860 and 1870 census: Rhonda (Rheda) E. Shaw (1855), Mary Jo Shaw (1857), William Bennett (1859) and Margaret Shaw (1865), which is confusing because first wife already named a child Margaret Shaw in 1844 and Duncan Shaw had a Margaret Shaw in 1848.

The 1900 census lists child # 1 of James Shaw, son James and Mary E. (?) Shaw as being married 33 years (1867), living in Missouri. Mary has had 10 children with eight of them living at present. The two found in their household are Walter D. Shaw (born July 30, 1877 and died Oct. 17, 1902, spouse Iva (?) Shaw – Walter is buried at Ragsdale Cemetery) and Earthy M. Shaw (born August 1880). On May 6, 1887 James D. Shaw is listed as living in Dallas County, MO.

The next child of James and Permintney C. Shaw was Margaret J. Shaw, born in 1843 in Polk County, MO. The birth record of her fourth child was a male on Nov. 20, 1883. The father was Benjamin F. Rafferty, born in 1839 in Kentucky. Possibly Margaret J. Shaw was the second wife of Benjamin F. Rafferty because the 1880 census lists two children as being born in Ohio. These were Rolla A. Rafferty (born 1867) and Silas G. Rafferty (born 1871). Then there are two other children listed as Joseph (born 1876) and Walter J. Rafferty (born 1879) born in Missouri. So who was the other child of Margaret and Benjamin Rafferty?

Sarah E. Shaw was born in 1846 in Missouri. She married W.J. Self. The May 1887 application of James D. Shaw, Administrator of James Shaw's probate will, she is said to be living in Dallas County, MO.

Martha A. Shaw (born 1849 in Missouri) married Montgomery Mosier in Polk County in 1885. M. Mosier is on the bill of sale.

Susan Emily Shaw "Ellen" (born 1851 in Missouri) married Joel K. Duncan (born 1849 in Bradley County, TN). In July 1883 their third child, Pyrmintay Jane Duncan was born. Their fifth child, John A. Duncan, was born Sept. 16, 1886 in Polk County, MO. Benjamin H. Duncan was born in December 1888 in Benton Township, Polk County, MO. Susan was the daughter of James and his first wife Permintary Shaw.

Rhoda Shaw was born December 1855 in Polk County, MO. She was married Feb. 26, 1884 in Polk County, MO to L.C. Vanbuskirk, born in Iowa. She was widowed by the time of the 1900 census with three children: Riley Vanbuskirk, born in December 1884; Luther Vanbuskirk, born in January 1887 in Missouri and Harrison Vanbuskirk, born April 1889 in Missouri. Rhoda was the daughter of James and Bathsheba (Keeth) who were married on Oct. 27, 1853.

Mary J. Shaw was born 1857 in Polk County, MO. Mary J. Wilshire signed the receipt in the probate will for her share.

William Bennett Shaw, born in 1859 in Benton Township, Polk County, MO, married Rebecca E. (Sampson) Shaw on Sept. 17, 1887 in Polk County, MO.

SHELENHAMER-SHIRLEY – Rollin Milton Shirley, born Nov. 26, 1895 in Carroll County, MO, was the son of George Frank and Viola Mildred (Wilmore) Shirley. Etta Jewell Austin, born Aug. 2, 1900 in Carroll County, was the daughter of Ira Oatha and Mary Adaline (Keltner) Austin. Rollin and Jewell married on Feb. 8, 1917 in Carroll County and had four children, all born in Carroll County. Cleo "Gen" Genevee (Nov. 16, 1917-June 2, 1993) married Robert Eugene Harper and had one daughter, Mary Jane. Gen was buried in Ottumwa, IA. Rollin Milton Jr. (Jan. 1, 1920-Jan. 26, 1971) married first, Martha Walker and had one son, Ronald Milton (stillborn). He married second, Stella Irene Phillips and had two children, Jack Milton and Patricia Eva Lynne. Junior was buried in the Humansville Cemetery. Emma Maxine, born March 2, 1923, married James Bysor Shelenhamer and had four children: James Rollin, Emma Frances, Judy Ellen and Jerry Bysor. Alma Dean, born March 23, 1927, married Herbert Ozro Thomas "O.T." Lamb and had four children: Ronald Thomas, Richard "Rick" Dean, Reginald Shirley and Ranea Alice. Rollin, Jewell and their three youngest children moved to Humansville, Polk County, MO in the fall of 1937 where Rollin opened a grain and feed store and then later a Maytag Appliance store. Rollin died Feb. 6, 1963; Jewell died July 7, 1970. Both were buried in the Humansville Cemetery.

George Washington Shellenhamer, born Feb. 16, 1844 in Dauphin County, PA, was married to Rebecca Ann Lingle, born Nov. 4, 1844 in Dauphin County, on Sept. 20, 1866 in Linglestown, PA. George served as a soldier in the Union Army from Pennsylvania from 1862 to 1864. They had 10 children: William "Bill" Franklin, Katie J. (died at age 12), Robert Scott (died at age 5 months), John Jacob, Charles, Joseph, Laura Mae, Nancy Jane, Sylvester "Wess" and James Blaine. After moving to Missouri and then to Oklahoma, George and his family returned to Missouri, settling in Henry County. George, Rebecca, Bill and Laura moved to Humansville in 1920. Somewhere along the way, George changed the spelling of his name from Shellenhamer to Shalenhamer. Others in the family changed it to Shelenhamer. George died May 24, 1929 in Humansville; Rebecca died Jan. 18, 1926 in Humansville and both were buried in the Humansville Cemetery. Siblings Bill and Laura never married and remained in Humansville where Bill died in 1955 and Laura in 1968. They were buried next to their parents in Humansville Cemetery.

James B. "Jim" Shelenhamer, born Oct. 26, 1885 in Warren County, MO, married Nellie Ellen Bysor, daughter of Peter Bazil and Lucy Ellen (Boyd) Bysor, on Jan. 15, 1911 in Henry County. Nellie was born July 3, 1884 in Henry County. They had five children, all born in either Henry or St. Clair County, MO. Reva Ellen (Oct. 6, 1911-Jan. 23, 1990) married Forrest Dale Selvidge—no children. Reva and Dale were buried in Freeman Holsapple Cemetery in St. Clair County, MO. Leta "Sunny" May, born March 16, 1914, married Carl Lee Mumford and had one son, Joe Lee. Ruby Frances (Dec. 1, 1916-Aug. 11, 2002) married Alfred Breeze Grimes and had two children, Jimmie Charles and Linda Lou. Ruby and Alfred were buried in the Humansville Cemetery. Veta Nell (Aug. 5, 1919-June 23, 1920) was buried in Adkins Cemetery, Henry County. James Bysor, born Aug. 30, 1922, married Maxine Shirley, as mentioned above. In 1925, Jim, Nellie and their family moved to Humansville, where he was employed by the Farmer's Exchange until he retired. Jim died Oct. 5, 1977 in Humansville and was buried in the Humansville Cemetery next to Nellie, who had died Feb. 28, 1956 in Humansville. *Submitted by Emma Franklin*

SHELENHAMER – Bysor and Maxine (Shirley) Shelenhamer were married Sept. 1, 1940 in Ozark, MO. They settled in Humansville where they owned and operated the school buses for the Humansville School District. In 1959 they sold the school buses and moved to Bolivar, MO, where Bysor purchased the Ford dealership. In 1967 Bysor and Maxine returned to Humansville, where Bysor was a farmer and the owner of a used-car lot located on the farm. Bysor and Maxine are long time members of the Humansville Baptist Church. They had four children, all born in Humansville.

James Rollin "Jim" Shelenhamer married Donna Lorraine Shuler and had four children: James "Jimmy" Charles, Lori Ellen, Jeffrey Rollin and Jody Bysor. Jim lives on a farm northeast of Bolivar with his wife, Carolyn (McFee). Jimmy, born Dec. 22, 1964, was studying to be a veterinarian at the University of Missouri when he was killed in an automobile accident on May 19, 1984. Lori and her husband, Kevin Sean Fullbright, live in Tulsa, OK, where she is a newscaster for KOTV. Jeff, a pastor, and his wife, Martina Renee (Mitchell), live in Bolivar with their children, Brittaney Renee and Garret Rollin. Jody, owner of Shelenhamer Construction, and his wife, Robin Jacqueline (Vines), also live in Bolivar with their children Kayla Jacqueline, Jacob Bysor and Mariah Catherine.

Emma Frances Shelenhamer married Hardy Delano Sheldon and had two children, Shirley

Front – Jerry and Judy; middle – Maxine, Bysor and Emma; Back – James

Denise and Steven Delano. Emma, a retired teacher, lives in Bolivar with her husband, Carl Benjamin "Ben" Franklin. Shirley, a psychologist, and her husband, Matthew Gerard Trudzinski, live in Fenton, MO with their children, Michael Francis and Amara Catherine. Steve, a builder, and his wife, Angela Rae (Stewart), live near Bolivar with her son, Christopher James.

Judy Ellen Shelenhamer married Larry Lee Wollard and had two children, Julie Lynelle and Justin Lee. Larry and Judy, both retired, live northwest of Bolivar. Larry spent many years working in law enforcement and Judy retired from the education department at Southwest Baptist University. Julie, a genealogist, and her husband, Brian Rand Trout, live northwest of Bolivar with their children, Christian Dean and Jonathan Rand. Justin lives in Bolivar and works in Springfield as the art director for Big Sports magazine.

Jerry Bysor Shelenhamer married Deborah Vaughn Shults and had two children, Jennifer Vaughn and Jerry "Jay" Bysor II. Jerry, a school principal, lives in Cypress, TX with his wife, Elizabeth Lynn (Baker). Jennifer and her husband, Tremain Ray Washington, live in Houston, TX with their children: Brandon Michael and Brianna Michelle Reece and Jarvis Alexander Washington. Jay, owner of Bolivar Concrete Construction, and his wife, Jennifer Nicole (Tinkle), live in Bolivar with their children, Taylor Nicole and Abby Beth. *Submitted by Maxine Shelenhamer*

SHOEMAKE – Shortly after her birth on Dec. 13, 1941 at the home in Bear Creek, Cedar County, the family of Maye Shoemake moved to a farm in Polk County just south of Humansville. Currently, many Amish products are sold from that place near the Plum Grove School area. Just a few memories remain of living there along with two other families—the Glen and Audrey Shoemake family and the Gerald and Jean Akins family from Kansas City. Her memories are most vivid of living on the 159-acre farm her family purchased, known as the Red John Campbell Farm, when she was 4.

One of the best things about the farm was Rock School, a one-room school, which became part of their farm when it was decided not to reopen it. After the children cleaned it out, it made a great roller-staking rink until their dad, Dwight Shoemake, filled it with hay. Their great-grandfather, Thomas Mallory, taught at Rock School many years before Maye's family lived there.

There was no television, but they did have a radio and dynamic imaginations. Favorite radio programs were the Grand Ole Opry, Red Skelton, Father Knows Best, Ozzie and Harriet, and the Carter family's early morning music program that followed the news with Joe Slattery.

Farm life was not all work without its rewards. Her best friends were her pets, which included a young, white nanny goat, lambs named Fibber McGee and Molly, and her Jersey/Hereford cow also named Molly. She helped raise many bucket calves that easily became pets as well as "pony" rides and later steaks and hamburgers.

The Shoemake children, Don, Maye, Wanda and Geraldine, walked three quarters of a mile to catch the Fair Play school bus, meeting the Worthan children, Donna Jean, Iris Ann and R.C., at their corner. Don participated in FFA and the three girls were in baton twirling. All were active in 4-H Club. A favorite event at Fair Play School was the countywide all-day track meet.

Her dad, Dwight, farmed with a team of horses, Dick and Jim, and she enjoyed watching him groom them each morning. She would often drive them to the field while he drove the truck loaded with seeds and fertilizer. She always dreamed of having her own pony but loved working with the horses and even riding them bareback sometimes.

Her grandparents, Joe and Myrtle Shoemake, lived in Dunnegan and often took the grandchil-

Log cabin and smoke house of Rowles farm about 1920

Shoemake children Don, Maye and Wanda with pet lambs – Fibber, McGee and Molly

dren down the street to Dunnegan Springs where they enjoyed playing in the icy cold creek and taking a refreshing drink from the sparkling spring. Grandpa Joe always brought his stainless steel cup for this special treat.

During the drought of the mid 1950s, Maye and her 14-year old brother, Don, would take the truck to Dunnegan Springs to wait their turn on the low-water bridge for the men with the gas water pump to fill their barrels. Their dad, Dwight, took a job in Kansas City with the Santa Fe Railroad, Which left the farming for their mom, Edna, and five children. After their public auction sale in August 1955, the family moved to Kansas City, KS.

Their roots remain in Polk County since their mom, Edna Rowles Shoemake, has given each of the four remaining children their own 10-acre tract of the original John Rowles farm. It is located five miles north of Bolivar and was settled by their great-grandfather who came from England in 1835. *Submitted by Maye Shoemake Gulley*

SHOEMAKE – North of Bolivar on the right side of Highway 83, about a half-mile before the first curve, sits an old, two-story frame house that once was surrounded by farmland. Now it's surrounded by houses. Straight down the road that splits off from Highway 83 at the curve and continues north a couple of miles is the old Rowles farm. It's to the left and extends for a half-mile to the point where the road forms a "T."

On this farm in a log cabin on Nov. 27, 1939, Don Shoemake was born. His mother, Edna (Rowles) Shoemake, had also been born there. Edna's parents, Marion and Elizabeth Rowles, then lived on and owned the farm. Both are now deceased. Sue Rowles, the oldest sister of Edna, also lived there. Siblings Ed, Christena and Mae had married and moved away. Edna had moved to a farm in Cedar County when she married Dwight Shoemake.

Ed Rowles farmed with horses for many years along the Pomme de Terre River. About 1946 he semi-retired to the above mentioned frame house and farmed the 80 acres with a tractor. He sold most of his horse-drawn farm equipment and a kerosene refrigerator to Dwight Shoemake. Ed and his wife, Anna, had no children and later moved to a house in Bolivar. They are both deceased.

Sue Rowles never married but had a special friend, Clifford Woods, from the early '30s until her death in 1986. Mr. Woods is now deceased.

The life of Christena (Rowles) Blackwell is presented elsewhere in this book.

Mae (Rowles) Peace and husband, Bill, are both deceased. They are survived by their only child, Billy Lloyd.

SHOEMAKE – Four more children, Maye, Wanda, Louise (Lou) and Douglas, were born to Dwight and Edna Shoemake between the years of 1941 and 1953.

In 1949, Dwight bought a model "M" John Deere tractor. That made Don about the happiest boy in Polk County. In 1950 the REA brought electricity to the Shoemake farm. Dwight promptly went to Bolivar and bought a new Frigidaire electric refrigerator and a new Frigidaire electric stove from Boss Gothard. That made Edna about the happiest woman in Polk County.

Not everybody in that area southeast of Dunnegan got electricity in 1950. The REA went right by one person who saw no need for electricity. Besides, he thought the minimum monthly charge of about $3 was outrageous. The aforementioned kerosene refrigerator was bought from the Shoemakes by a neighbor who was not reached by the REA. The men loading the refrigerator decided to save time by not draining the water reservoir on top of the refrigerator. When they loaded it onto a Dodge pickup, the springs bottomed out.

The Shoemakes moved to Kansas City, KS in 1955. Douglas was killed in a car wreck in 1976. Dwight and Edna Shoemake live their separate lives in Kansas City, KS. Dwight is a car dealer. Edna is retired from a career in nursing and does ceramics. Maye, Wanda and Lou live in or around Kansas City, KS. Don lives near Houston in Crosby, TX.

Don, Maye, Wanda and Lou all own part of the original Rowles farm. *Submitted by Don Shoemake*

SHORT – Elbert Lavern Short was born Jan. 27, 1917 near Halfway (Polk County), MO and passed away April 20, 2002, Bolivar (Polk), MO. He was called "Elbert" by the military and "Lavern" by his family. He prided himself on being a US veteran and a "Campbellite." His paternal great-grandfather, Francis M. Coy, was a "traveling preacher" who helped to found several Christian churches, including Halfway, Polk, and Prairie Grove (1869).

Elbert Lavern Short – 1942

Lavern was proud of his service in WWII with the Sixth Infantry (Red Star) Division, First Infantry Regiment, Company H, June 5, 1941-Oct. 25, 1945. He was among the first troops trained at Fort Leonard Wood (had training under Generals Eisenhower, Lear and Patton). In September 1943, the division was shipped from Camp San Luis Obispo, CA to Hawaii for tropical training. In January 1945, the division arrived in Milne Bay, New Guinea, ready for combat. For 12 months,

Gene, Dorothy, Marie, Dean, Lavern, Mildred, Glenn, Lizzie, and J.E. Short – 1947

the service men fought not only Japanese troops but also heat, rain, insects and almost impenetrable jungles.

After winning victory over Japanese troops in New Guinea, "The Red Start Division" landed Jan. 9, 1945 on the beaches of Lingayen Gulf, Luzon, Philippine Islands. Casualties were heavy as the men fought their way to Manila and Bataan. Lavern received a crippling leg wound, had teeth knocked out and suffered lifetime hearing loss. He was awarded a Bronze Star "for heroic achievement" on March 9, 1945, while serving as a forward observer for an 81 mm mortar platoon.

Lavern's parents were John Elbert and Susan Elizabeth ("Lizzie") Huckaby Short. His siblings were Garland, Glenn, Mildred (Lavern was the fourth child), Dean, Marie, Dorothy and Gene. Garland was killed in 1934 in a car accident. The four surviving brothers rendered military service for their country (Glenn and Dean in the Air Force, Lavern in the Infantry and Gene in the Artillery). The husbands of Marie and Dorothy served in the Marine Corps and Mildred's husband was a vital part of the war effort. As of April 20, 2002, Marie and Dorothy are the sole surviving family members.

On June 26, 1943, in the home of Rev. Frank Lytle of rural Halfway (Polk), MO, Lavern married Maxine Virginia Wise, born near Everton (Dade), MO, Dec. 10, 1921. She was the daughter of Albert Gallatin and Goldie Hall Wise. She graduated from Greenfield High School in 1939, received a bachelor of science in education degree from Southwest Missouri State University in 1942 and master of science in education degree from Drury University in 1968 with further graduate study at Oklahoma State University, Stillwater. She taught in high schools at Cole Camp, Walnut Grove and Dadeville with 13 years at Southwest Missouri State University.

Lavern completed a bachelor of science in education degree from SMSU in 1946, then taught history and coached at Dadeville High School. In June 1948, he began duties as the rural mail carrier at Dadeville, later being transferred to the Halfway office. His patrons were like family.

A son, John Allen, was born June 15, 1948, in Lockwood (Dade), MO. He graduated from Dadeville High School in 1966, earned a bachelor of science degree from Southwest Baptist University in 1970, rendered Marine Corps service, earned a master of science degree from SMSU in 1972, taught for two years for Meramec Valley Schools and began work in 1975 as a personnel officer for Nevada Rehabilitation Center, Nevada, MO. He retired June 30, 2001 as the center's assistant superintendent.

John's son, Linden John, was born July 7, 1981, at Nevada (Vernon), MO. He graduated from Nevada High School in 2000 and received a bachelor of science accounting from SMSU in December 2002.

On July 8, 1989, in Nevada, John Allen married Maureen Strumph Fairfield, mother of Ian,

John, Maxine, Lavern and Susan Short

Ben and Megan. Megan began dietetics study at SMSU in the fall of 2002. Maureen is administrator of the Barone's Alzheimer Unit, Nevada City Hospital, Nevada, MO.

A daughter, Susan Elaine, was born Oct. 16, 1958, Lockwood (Dade), MO. She graduated from Bolivar High School in 1977, earned a bachelor of science degree from SMSU in 1981, taught for the Lakeland Schools as a disabilities resource teacher, worked as a learning disabilities teacher/supervisor for Higginsville Rehabilitation Center and served as a case manger for the Missouri Department of Mental Health.

On June 17, 1983, Susan married Norman Lloyd Akin in Springfield (Greene), MO. Norman was born June 21, 1958, son of Rebecca and Phillip Akin. He served for six years as an Army Missile Control Crewman, earned a bachelor of science degree from Central Missouri State University in 1984 and began work as a missiles inspector. In 1989, he became a maintenance supervisor at Western Missouri Mental Health Center, Kansas City, MO.

An annual Company H reunion developed from a visit of former military comrades to the Short home in 1954. Lavern thought it was a privilege to lead 48 reunions; death caused him to miss the 49th. God, family and friends always were important to Lavern. *Submitted by Maxine Short*

SHULER – George H. Shuler was born in 1855 in Morgan County, IN. His parents were Charlton Shuler and Phoebe Warthen. On Dec. 9, 1877, he married Louisa Crone, daughter of William Crone Jr. and Susan Ballinger, also of Morgan County. William's father, William Crone Sr., was born in Monoghan County, Ireland in 1772. With his family – at least two sons and wife – he had sailed to America in the early 1830s. Sadly, his wife died at sea.

George H. visited the Orleans region of Missouri sometime between 1883 and 1884. Impressed by the area, he returned home, packed up the family and moved. His younger sister Mary Ellen and her husband, Oliver Perry Stiles, joined the migration, along with the Charles Mosier family. The three families loaded their horses, wagons and all household goods onto the train on which they traveled to Sedalia, MO. From there, they set off in wagons to settle near Orleans.

Upon his arrival to Polk County, MO, George purchased several parcels of land: March 8, 1884, 45 acres; May 24, 1884, 100 acres; and Aug. 4, 1884, 80 acres. Several of George and Louisa's children were born in their new house, built not far from the Sac River between Orleans and Aldrich. It remained in the family for many years, eventually passing into the hands of George and Louisa's youngest child, George Lindsey.

George and Louisa were the parents of seven children: Albert, Minnie Mae, Cora Ellen, William Charlton, Walter Wiley, Loutreacy and George Lindsey. On Feb. 8, 1899, George H. died of pneumonia at the age of 43 and was buried in the Pleasant Ridge Cemetery, Polk County, MO. In 1902, Louisa married John T. Pitner, who died in 1925. Louisa died Nov. 17, 1933 and was buried beside her first husband, George, in the Pleasant Ridge Cemetery.

George Lindsey Shuler was born March 29, 1889 in Aldrich, Polk County, MO, the seventh and last child born to George H. and Louisa Crone Shuler. His father died in 1899 when George was less than a year old and his mother remarried when he was 4 years old. George attended school in Orleans and was president of his graduating class from Bolivar High School in 1918. In September of that year, George enlisted in the Army, training on the campus of Drury College, Springfield, Greene County, MO. The war ended before his training was complete, but several pieces of correspondence he had with his mother have survived. It is interesting to note that their letters reflect more concern about local deaths due to the Influenza of 1918 than of WWI.

On April 8, 1923, in Bolivar, MO, George married Lucile Geneuve Davis. Lucile was born March 7, 1906, in Polk County, the daughter of John Marshall Clay Davis and Joanna Kirby. George and Lucile began their married life on the family farm where George had been born. They were the parents of five children, all born in the same house as their father: Elizabeth Marian married Junior Bond; Victor Crone "Bill" married Dixie McBride; Kelton Roger (April 7, 1929-Sept. 18, 1952) married Shirley Ann Mead; George Marshall "Marsh" married Peggy Layman; and Linda Marie married Dean Gann.

George L. was an innovative farmer. As a long time member of the Registered Jersey Association, his dairy cows were frequently studied for production and butterfat content. He pioneered the practice of terracing and the use of alfalfa in the region. He was a leader in the effort to bring REA to the Aldrich area and served on the Aldrich School Board and Producers Creamery Board of Directors. In 1966, he was featured in *Who's Who in the Midwest*. A man of strong faith, he served as a leader in the Aldrich Christian Church.

In 1980, Lucile died of a heart attack and George passed away in 1987. Both are buried in the Pleasant Ridge Cemetery. *Submitted by Bill Shuler*

SHULER – There is recorded a Johnst Schulcer living in Germany in the early 1800s. Johnst Schulcer was Emogene Corum's great-great-great-grandfather. When a religious war broke out, he immigrated first to Holland. At that time he changed the spelling of his last name to Shuler. Johnst came from Holland to Virginia where he married Sarah Cornett on Dec. 1, 1825. John and Sarah had eight children: James Johnst, Charlton B., Martha Ann, Delilah Ann, Julia Ann, Ephraim, George, John Kendrick Jr. and a girl who lived with them, Mary Ann.

Charlton B. was Emogene's great-great-grandfather. Charlton B. Shuler was born Sept. 15, 1828 in Grayson County, VA. When Charlton was a child, his family homesteaded in Indiana. There he married Phoebe Pucket Wartham in 1849. Charlton and Phoebe had four children: Sarah Jane, William Adkins, George H. and Mary Ellen. Charlton B. died Feb. 21, 1908.

George H. was Emogene's great-grandfather. George H. Shuler and Louisa Crone Shuler were married Dec. 9, 1877 and moved to Polk County from Indiana in 1884. Their children were Albert "Hoggy," Minnie Mae Shuler Boone, Cora Ellen Shuler McKinney, William Charlton (W.C.), Walter Wyley, Loutreacy Shuler Neil and George Lindsey.

George H. and Louisa lived near the small town of Orleans. George H. had a mill at Orleans in the late 1800s. In 1899 George H. was building a house between Walnut Grove and Eudora when he died of pneumonia at the age of 44. Louisa died in 1933. George H. and Louisa are buried at the Pleasant Ridge Cemetery near Aldrich.

William Charlton was Emogene's grandfather and he lived from April 17, 1887 to Sept. 1, 1968. W.C. married Emma Burros on Feb. 8,

Mittie B. Hawkins Shuler and Roy B. Shuler 1981

1905. Emma lived from April 11, 1889 to April 4, 1968. Charlton and Emma had seven children: Earl, Roy Buford, Kenneth Ira, Ruth Mae, June Anna, Lois and Charles Dean.

W.C. and Emma also lived near Orleans when they were first married. W.C. homesteaded in New Mexico for five years and then returned to Polk County, where he bought a farm about two miles west of Bolivar. W.C. and Emma lived on the farm until 1959 and then moved into Bolivar. W.C. and Emma are both buried at Pleasant Ridge Cemetery.

Roy Buford was Emogene's father. When Roy was very small and his family lived on the river at Orleans, he wanted to run off to the river all the time. His mother had someone to hide there and give him a good scare. He did not go back anymore.

Roy married Mittie Hawkins on Dec. 29, 1926. Mittie's father was William Littleberry Hawkins and her mother was Mary Alma Griffin Hawkins. William and Mary Alma's children were Ross, Arnold, Cletis, Mittie, Bessie, Mable, Kimble, Mark, Elsie and Hobart.

Tom Hawkins was the father of William L. Tom died in 1900 and is buried at Pleasant Ridge. Tom had two sons: William L. and Armstead.

William L. inherited a small acreage west of Aldrich from his father. He built a log house there and a blacksmith shop. He lived and made his living there until they moved into Aldrich late in life. William L. lived from 1875 to 1945 and Alma lived from 1877 to 1952. They are both buried at Pleasant Ridge.

Roy and Mittie had three children: Roy Wayne, Feb. 18, 1928; Mary Emogene, Feb. 27, 1930; Marlyn Ray, July 9, 1935 to December 9, 2000.

Roy and Mittie owned a farm between Fair Play and Bolivar. Roy was a farmer and a carpenter. Roy and Mittie moved into Bolivar in 1962. Roy built many houses around the Bolivar area. Mittie was a wonderful artist and cloth was her canvas. She made many quilts in her lifetime and each one was a work of art. Roy lived from May 27, 1907 to April 7, 1999. Mittie lived from Dec. 22, 1905 to Dec. 13, 1994. They are both buried at Pleasant Ridge.

Mary Emogene married James T. Corum on Aug. 8, 1948. James lived from Feb. 6, 1928 to Oct. 11, 1993. James is buried at Greenfield, MO. James was the son of Arthur and Lorine Coursey Corum. James was a preacher for the Church of Christ for over 30 years. The James Corum family still worships with the Noble Hill Church of Christ. James and Emogene have five children: Lawrence Wayne (Larry), May 5, 1949; James Ray (Jim), April 8, 1951; Sheryl Anne, Jan. 17, 1955; Lori Jean, Jan. 20, 1962; and Patty Lynn, July 19, 1963.

Larry married Sharon Rose Cass. Sharon is the daughter of Norman and Betty Cass. Sharon was born Sept. 11, 1951. Larry is currently a student at SMSU and a farmer. Sharon is a teacher at Pleasant Hope Schools. Larry and Sharon live in Polk County. Their children are Curtis Roy, Cassi LaRae' and Coby Ernest. Curtis married Mary Catherine Lynch. Their children are Natasha Tegan Lynch and Tanner Lawrence. Cassi married Larry Harper. Their children are Wyatt Corey, Chloe Elizabeth and Clancy Jo. Coby married Shelia Pyle. Their children are Kylie Louise and Kasey Lynn.

Jim married Mary Robin Hamner. Mary is the daughter of Temple and Eunice Hamner. Mary was born July 27, 1952. Jim was employed by Burlington Northern Railroad for several years. Mary is employed by Funding Friends. Their children are Jacob Littleberry, Mary Rose and Anni Nadine. Mary Rose has two children: Mallory Robin and Levi Ray.

Sheryl married Jimmy Earl (Jim) Loftis. Jim is the son of Clinton and Louella Loftis. Jim was born July 16, 1948. Sheryl is self-employed and Jim is employed by Burlington Northern Railroad. Jim and Sheryl also live in Polk County. Their children are Joshua James and Katie Abigail (Abbie). Abbie married Eli Mabary.

Lori married Jeffrey Bruce Burns. Jeff is the son of Dan and Joann Burns. Jeff was born May 6, 1958. Lori and Jeff own their own business, Hotrod Express, in Blue Springs, MO. Their children are Jessica Elizabeth and Jeffrey Justin.

Patty married Ronnie Ray Wilson. Ronnie is the son of Harry and Florence Wilson. Ronnie was born April 9, 1958. Patty is employed by Southwest Electric and Ronnie is employed by Wilson Heating and Cooling. Ronnie and Patty also live in Polk County. Their children are Caleb Ray and Bailey Renee. *Submitted by Emogene Corum*

SHULER – George H. Shuler was born in 1855 in Morgan County, IN, the area to which his grandparents, John Kendrick and Sarah Cornett Shuler had migrated sometime in the early 1830s, having left southwestern Virginia to try their hand at homesteading. The son of Charlton and Phoebe Warthen Shuler, George on Dec. 9, 1877, married Miss Louisa Crone, the daughter of William and Susan Ballinger Crone, also of Morgan County. During the first years of their marriage, there in Indiana, three children were born to them – Albert, Minnie Mae and Cora Ellen.

George Shuler 1855-1899

In 1883-1884 George H. and his brother-in-law Oliver Perry Stiles made a trip to Polk County, MO. Upon their return to Indiana, both gathered their families, packed their belongings and loaded the family, horses, wagons and household goods onto a train. Another family, the Mosiers, also accompanied them.

On reaching Sedalia, MO, the families unloaded all their gear and set off in their wagons to continue the journey to Orleans, a thriving trading post of some 150 residents, schools, churches (two), blacksmiths (three), bootmakers (two), a gristmill, grocery store (two), a general store, a tanning factory, a tavern, physicians (three), a tailor, a tinsmith, a Post Office, a distillery and water-powered mills (three), and the latter located along Little Sac River.

George built his family a house and it was here that the last four children were born: William Charlton, Walter Wiley, Loutreacy and George Lindsey. That three-room home stayed in the family for many years. Daughter Loutreacy and Roy Alva Neil lived there after their marriage and their first three children were born there. The house later passed to Treacy's younger brother, George Lindsey and his wife, Lucile Davis, and is where all five of their children were born.

George H. Shuler died of pneumonia on Feb. 8, 1899. His obituary reads "The funeral services were held at the home by friends, after which the remains were taken charge of by Aldrich Lodge No. 181 and conveyed to Pleasant Ridge Cemetery where they were laid to rest with all the honors of Odd Fellowship."

Over the intervening years, George and Louisa had acquire some additional parcels of land so that, in the distribution of his estate, each of the children received somewhere between 350 to 385 acres of land in their inheritance. About four years after George's death, Louisa married John T. Pitner and moved to Bolivar with her family. She died on Nov. 17, 1933, and is buried beside George H. Shuler in Pleasant Ridge. They had seven children; all except Minnie Mae are buried at Pleasant Ridge Cemetery:

Albert, born Nov. 6, 1878, died July 1, 1956, married Ella Beal. Issue: Carl, Lennie Madge, Hubert Mark, Thelma Louise and Leon.

Minnie Mae, born May 3, 1881, died Jan. 16, 1941, married Robert Scott Boone. Issue: Cleo, Robert Theodore, Floy, Herman, John Dell and Mary.

Cora, born May 20, 1883, died Jan. 21, 1947, married first George T. Hamilton. Issue: Eure, Eunice and Arley. Cora married second Thomas McKinney. Issue: Paul, Mary, Dorothy and Elva.

William Charlton, born April 17, 1887, died Sept. 1, 1968, married Emma Burros. Issue: Earl, Roy Buford, Kenneth Ira, Ruth, June Anna, Lois and Charles Dean.

Walter Wiley, born Feb. 3, 1890, died Feb. 10, 1963, married Golden Owens. Issue: Louise, Leta, Betty, an infant who died, Henry and William J.

Loutreacy, born Aug. 24, 1893, died Feb. 7, 1980, married Roy Alva Neil. Issue: Noble Mark, Anna Pauline, Roy Layne, George and Sammy Lee.

George Lindsey, born March 29, 1898, died Nov. 12, 1987, married Lucile Davis. Issue: Elizabeth Marion, Victor Crone, Kelton Roger, George Marshall and Linda Marie. *Submitted by George R. Neil*

SIBLEY – The story begins with Uncle L.I. "Speed" and Aunt Grace Sibley Schreiner and son, Larry, living just west of flat bridge (Pomme

Row 1 – Mike and Erylene; Row 2 – Amy, Jamie Sharp and Jeremy, Sarah Sibley

de Terre River) on 470th Road during the 1950s. Larry and wife Sharon Erven Schreiner now live in Springfield. Uncle Edward "Ed" Hale and Aunt Ruby V. Shelton Sibley, married Dec. 11, 1937, of Wichita, KS, came to visit the Schreiners and fell in love with the area. Uncle Ed bought a 60-acre farm on 190th Road in Van about one mile east of flat bridge in 1960. The Sibleys raised hogs and farmed, and Uncle Ed had a milk route, then worked for MFA when he retired. They now live in Bolivar, retiring from the farm in 1998. Michael "Mike" Eugene, born Aug. 11, 1949 (son of Joseph "Joe" Richard Sibley – Grace, Ed and Joe are siblings) and Ines Erylene Fergason Sibley, born May 10, 1951, married Aug. 21, 1971 and children Jeremy Michael, born Oct. 15, 1974 and Amy Leah, born April 20, 1979, of Wichita, KS, came to visit the Ed Sibleys in the 1970s and 1980s. Mike transferred with Southwest Bell Telephone to Springfield, MO in 1979 and the family lived in the country west of Willard, MO. When opportunity arose, Mike Sibley moved his family to a 40-acre farm on 475th Road adjoining Ed Sibley in 1985. Mike is a "weekend farmer" with cattle and haying. Erylene volunteered at Halfway Schools with the PTA working at the local, council and state levels. Since 1995 Erylene has worked as elementary secretary/lunch clerk at Halfway Schools. Jeremy graduated from Halfway in 1993. He was on the basketball team that placed third in the 1992 State Basketball Championships. He went on to Crowder College, Neosho, graduating in 1995 with an associate's degree in agriculture mechanics. On Aug. 26, 2000, he married Sarah Ann Tindle of Fair Play. Jeremy milks for a neighbor and Sarah works at Citizens Memorial Hospital. They live in Van. Amy graduated from Halfway as salutatorian in 1997. She went on to SMSU in Springfield with graduation pending May 2003. On June 12, 1999, she married Jamie Dean Sharp of Halfway (Sharps are from Buffalo, Dallas County). They have a daughter, Jaeden Leah Sharp, born July 22, 2000. Jamie graduated from Drury's Police Academy in the spring of 2002. The Sharps live in Bolivar. Mike currently serves as a board member and Jeremy currently serves as assistant chief and both are volunteer firefighters and first responders for the Halfway Fire and Rescue. Erylene is currently serving as treasurer. Mike and Jeremy are also part of the Polk County Fire and Rescue Training Association, and Mike is currently president of Local Emergency Planning Committee. Erylene and Sarah are novice genealogists. Sibleys are members of First Baptist Church of Bolivar. The above Joe Sibley moved his family from Wichita, KS in 1978 to El Dorado Springs, MO, then to Bolivar in 1986. He married Helen Romance Shelton on Feb. 2, 1948 in Wichita, KS. (Helen and Ruby are sisters). Other children include Brenda Kay Sibley Spevak Wannow, Conyers, GA: Mary Jane Sibley Logue, Wichita, KS; Gary Edward Sibley; Janet Lee Sibley Palenik, Springfield, MO; and Susan Renea Sibley Long, Halfway. Other grandchildren include Sarah Ann Spevak and Katlin Elisabeth Wannow; Rachelle Dawn Sibley, Danielle Renea Sibley, Halfway and Heather Ann, Tasha Lynn and Sean Michael Sibley and Kelsey Sibley; Tyler James Palenik. Joe and Helen Sibley are buried at New Bethel Cemetery, Halfway. *Submitted by Erylene Sibley*

SIMMONS – James Simmons was born about 1810 in Tennessee. He was the son of James and Purry (Warbleton) Simmons. On Sept. 28, 1831, he married Clarissa Davis in Grainger County, TN. Clarissa was born about 1814. In the late 1830s, they would join both of their families on the wagon train out of Tennessee to Missouri.

They are listed in Madison Township on page 190, line 23 of the 1840 Polk County census. James bought land in Township 33, Range 24, Section 7. This area is north of Shady Grove Cemetery.

James' will was dated Oct. 7, 1846, and evidently he died shortly after, as his will was filed in probate on Oct. 19, 1846. The will is in Polk County Will Book A on page 30. On Dec. 11, 1846, Clarissa gave birth to a son and named him after his father.

Clarissa remained in the Shady Grove area, near James' family and her siblings. At dwelling 547, the 1850 Polk County census lists Clarissa Simmons, age 37, born in South Carolina, with her six children: Merrit, 17; Rachel, 15; Nelly (Ellen), 13; Perren, 11; Anderson, 6; and James, 3. By the 1860 census, Clarissa is at household 1587, age 45, born in Tennessee and children are Rachel, Ellen, Anderson, James and Clarissa C. as 10 years old. We believe Clarissa C. Davis (last name listed when she married) is a relative to Clarissa Simmons.

In the 1880 Mortality Schedule of Polk County, Madison Township, recorded by Dr. Wooldridge, Clarissa Simmons is 65 years, born in Tennessee, died September 1879 of typhoid fever. She had been in Polk County, MO for 45 years.

Children:

Merritt, born 1832, Tennessee. Marriages: Esther Phipps, Oct. 27, 1859; Annie E. Rumley, Dec. 31, 1879; Parmelia Worley, June 3, 1902, all Polk County, MO. Children are John A., Alfred S., Francis Cordelia (Cooper), Richard S. and Sam C. Simmons. We have no information on Merritt after 1902 and would appreciate any help.

Rachel, born 1835, Tennessee. Children are Clinton Vernon and Etta (Cooper). Rachel died 1913, buried at Gum Springs Cemetery, Cedar County, MO.

Ellen, born 1837, Tennessee. Married Peter Minnox, June 18, 1869, Polk County. Listed in 1880 Taney County, MO census. Children: William, 9; Birdie, 7; and Christopher, 6.

Perren, born 1839, Missouri. No record after 1850.

Anderson, born August 1843, Missouri. Married Caroline Fields, Polk County, MO. Children: Carol, Oba, Maggie, Benjamin, Thomas, Orie, Ella, Susie and Omer. Anderson died 1923; buried Gum Springs Cemetery in Cedar County, MO.

James, born Dec. 11, 1846, Missouri. Married Harriet Crain, Polk County, MO. Children: Lonnie, Della, Emma and Andrew. James died Aug. 24, 1894, buried in Trimble Cemetery in Polk County, MO.

Listed in 1860 census with Clarissa Simmons: Clarissa Catharine Davis, born August 1850, Missouri; married Samuel C. Phipps, Sept. 3, 1866, Polk County, MO, 10 of their 11 children: Riley, Merrit, Stanford, Edwin, Gracy, George, Louise, Samuel, Sarah and John. Clarissa Phipps died 1917, buried in Liberty Cemetery, Cedar County, MO. *Submitted by Dean Gothard*

SIMMONS – Two young men, James and Jehu Simmons, were born in North Carolina in the 1770s in a country in the process of being formed. The young men grew to manhood and chose mates for life. James married Purry Warbleton in Orange County, NC on March 14, 1797. James Warbleton and David Passmore were the bondsmen. Jehu married Martha Moore in Orange County, NC on Feb. 4, 1800. The bondsman was Robert Moore.

In the 1800 census of Orange County, NC on page 537, three Simmons families are listed. James and Purry, 26 to 45 years old with one male under 10 and two females under 10. Jehu and Martha, 16 to 26 years old with one male under 10. A Ruth Simmons was the third Simmons listed on page 537. She could be a parent to one or both of these young men. She was listed as 45 or over, with two males 26 to 45 years and one female 10 to 16 years living with her. We have never found a record of Ruth's husband.

Ruth Simmons and Abigail Passmore were the daughters of William Craig of Orange County, NC. They were both listed in his will in Orange County. Abigail's husband, David, was the bondsman for James Simmons. From the book *Pioneers of Dickson County, TN* on April 8, 1817, Ruth Simmons' estate is entered. David Passmore was the administrator of Ruth's estate.

In the early 1800s, James' and Jehu's families moved to Grainger County, TN. Jehu died in 1835. On July 15, 1836, the estate was settled and the heirs were John Simmons, Elizabeth Crain, Martha Simmons, James Simmons, Robert Simmons, administrator and Green

Simmons, administrator.

Around 1838, James, Purry and Martha (Jehu's widow) and their children moved to Missouri. The families settled along the Bear Creek and Little Sac River. In the 1840 Polk County census, there are eight Simmons families and two of their daughter's families listed.

By 1848, James had died. In Polk County land transactions (Book C on page 243), Joseph and Katherine Simmons of Cedar County paid $30 per family as they signed for the selling of the land, belonging to James Simmons, deceased (Section 8, Township 33, Range 24). It seems that Joseph moved back to Polk County to care for his mother and the land listed above was James' and Purry's land. Their children are Joseph and the eight families. The families are listed as John and Elizabeth Simmons, Clarissa Simmons, the wife of James (deceased), Jehu and Katherine Simmons, of Polk County, Thomas and Eliza Hopper, William and Lucinda Alexander, Jehu and Eleanor Jackson, William and Susan Simmons and Alice Ezell of Cedar County.

In the 1850 census records of Polk and Cedar County, the Simmons shown listed are Purry, age 75, Jehu, John, Joseph, Clarissa, Robert, John, Green, William, Jehu and Eleanor Jackson; Grundy and Martha Huff and John and Elizabeth Crain; Ally Iseral (Ezell); William and Lucinda Alexander; and Thomas and Eliza Hopper families. They totaled 98 people. Neither James Sr., James Jr. or Martha are listed in the 1850 census.

In the book, "The Wilderness Prophet," by Claud J. Mustain, Daniel R. Murphy, a Baptist preacher and neighbor from Tennessee, made notes of going 14 miles to Mt. Zion for the funeral of Parify Simmons and her five grandsons on March 18, 1855. Purry's life had ended. *Submitted by Greg Lane*

SIMMONS – Merritt Simmons was born in 1831-1832 in Grainger County, TN to James and Clarissa Davis Simmons.

Cordie and Charles Cooper; Merritt Simmons; Coy, Merit and Mandy Cooper

Merritt's parents came to Polk County between 1837-1839 and settled in the Shady Grove area near James' parents, James Sr. and Purry Simmons and numerous other relatives. At the age of 11, Merritt homesteaded 40 acres in Township 33, Range 24 in Polk County, next to his father's land.

Merritt's father, James, died in the late 1840s, leaving Clarissa alone in a new land with small children.

In Polk County, on Oct. 28, 1859, Merritt married Easter Phipps, born 1841-43 in Clay County, KY, the daughter of John and Priscilla Phipps.

In the 1870 Polk County, MO census, Merritt and Easter are listed with their children, John A., Alfred S. and Cordelia. Their fourth child, Richard, was born in 1874.

Between the birth of Rich in 1874 and 1879, Easter died. We have been told that she is buried in Gum Springs Cemetery in an unmarked grave.

On Aug. 31, 1878, Merritt sold a parcel of land near Liberty Cemetery in Cedar County (Section 17, Township 33, Range 26) for $200. This land was located near Easter's relatives, the Phippses.

On Dec. 31, 1879, Merritt married for the second time to Anna Rumley, daughter of Samuel and Elizabeth Rumley, in Polk County. Anna had three children when she married Merritt. Merritt and Anna had one son, Sam C., born in 1881.

Sometime after their marriage they moved to the Bear Creek area in Cedar County. Five of their children were married between 1888 and 1893 in Cedar County. A newspaper clipping stated that Anna was present when her daughter Magnus "Bug" married Andy Belcher on Dec. 9, 1893 at the Simmons residence in Cedar County. Anna died between the time of the wedding and the 1900 Cedar County census. Merritt is listed as living with his daughter Corda and her family.

Anna's daughter, Sultana Agnew, died in 1897 and is buried in Lindley Prairie Cemetery, one row from Merritt's daughter, Corda Cooper. Corda died in childbirth in 1905 and is buried with her newborn baby, beside the other babies that she lost. At her death, she left three sons ranging from 18 months to 15 years.

Merritt married a third time in Polk County. The record lists Merritt Simmons of Hartley, MO, County of Cedar and Parmelia Worley of Aldrich being married by R.R. Fleeman, MG, on June 3, 1902.

The 1902 marriage is the last record that we can find on Merritt Simmons.

Merritt and Easter's children:

John A., born 1860 in Polk County, married Nancy Katherine Routh, March 30, 1880; died 1901, buried Trimble Cemetery, Polk County.

Alfred S., born 1868 in Polk County, married Magnus "Bug" Rumley, Aug. 10, 1888, in Cedar County; died Sept. 23, 1928, buried Greenfield Cemetery, Dade County.

Cordelia Frances, born Jan. 22, 1870 in Polk County, married Charley Cooper, March 16, 1888 in Cedar County; died Aug. 24, 1905, Cedar County, buried Lindley Prairie Cemetery, Cedar County.

Richard S., born Sept. 21, 1875, married Cynthia Elizabeth Cooper, Feb. 17, 1898, Dade County; died July 19, 1928, Dade County, buried Gum Springs Cemetery, Cedar County.

Merritt and Anna's children:

Sam C., born 1881, married Iva Chism, Feb. 22, 1904, Cedar County; died 1936, buried Lindley Prairie Cemetery, Cedar County.

Anna's children:

Magmus, born July 1872, married Alfred S. Simmons, Aug. 10, 1888, Cedar County; died May 26, 1932, buried at Greenfield Cemetery, Dade County.

Sultana B., born 1875, married W. H. Agnew, Sept. 30, 1891, Cedar County; died 1897, buried Lindley Prairie Cemetery, Cedar County.

Louvina A., born September 1877, married Andrew R. Belcher, Dec. 9, 1893, in Cedar County; died Jan. 24, 1939, buried in Dade County. *Submitted by Jerrald Moss*

SIMMONS – Jehu Simmons was born around 1794 in Orange County, NC. He was the son of James Simmons and moved with his family to Grainger County, TN at a young age. On Dec. 21, 1817, he married Catherine Woods in Grainger County. They would raise their family and would join the wagon train from Grainger County to Polk County, MO, around 1839. In 1840, Jehu was listed on page 153 with seven children.

Jehu and Catherine would live more than 25 years in Polk County. Jehu's last will and testament was in box 67 of Polk County and it is dated in 1860.

"State of Missouri, County of Polk. The last will and testament of Jeheu Simmons considering the uncertainty of this Mortal life and being of sound mind and memory do make and publish this my last will and testament in manner and forms following (that is to say) first I give and bequeath unto my son William W. Simmons deceased his daughter living Martha Coffee, late Martha Simmons ten dollars, and to Rebecca Delby late Rebecca Simmons deceased her son Joseph T. Delby ten dollars and to Marthy Huff, late Marthy Simmons ten dollars, and to my son Jehu Simmons ten dollars, and to my son Mathew, ten dollars, and to my daughter Catharine E. Chaney, late Catherine E. Simmons, ten dollars, and to son Henry C. Simmons ten dollars, and lastly as to all the rest resident and remainder of my real estate of the following described lands to wit the north east quarter of south west quarter of section thirty three in township thirty three of range twenty four, also S.E. of S.W. quarter of section 33 in township 33 of range 24 also north west of south east quarter of section thirty three township thirty three of range 24 and goods and chattels and whatsoever kind and nature soever I give and bequeath the same to my said beloved wife Catharine Simmons during her natural of life or widowhood whom I hereby appoint sole Excutrion of this my last will and testament here by revoking all former wills by me made in witness where of I have here unto set my hand and seal this the twenty first day January in the year of our lord one thousand eight hundred and sixty."

Jehu and Catharine Simmons' children:

William W. Simmons, born 1820s Grainger County, TN; married Mary Davis Hopper, Nov. 3, 1842. Died by 1845. Will in Polk County, MO Box 63. Daughter Martha Simmons, 1844/45; married Gilbert Coffee June 26, 1858.

Martha Simmons, born 1828 in Grainger County, TN; married Grundy Huff, Feb. 12, 1847.

Rebecca Simmons, born 1830 in Grainger County, TN; married William Delby Aug. 24, 1848. Died before 1860. Son Joseph T. Delby, born 1849.

Jehu Simmons, born 1832 in Grainger County, TN; married Milly Chaney.

Mathew Simmons, born 1836 in Grainger County, TN.

Catharine E. Simmons, born 1838 in Grainger County, TN; married James H. Chaney July 5, 1856.

Henry C. Simmons, born 1840 in Polk County, MO. *Submitted by Tracy Moss*

SIMMONS – John Simmons was born in Grainger County, TN in about 1805. He was the son of Jehu Simmons and Martha Moore Simmons. John married Elizabeth Smith, June 2, 1832, in Grainger County, TN.

John had three brothers, Robert, Green and James. There was also one sister, Elizabeth, who married John Crain. John and his siblings migrated to Missouri in the late 1830s. This was after the death of their father Jehu. Their mother Martha Moore Simmons, widow of Jehu, also migrated to Missouri with her family. The Simmons families settled along the Bear Creek River. In the 1840 Polk County, MO census there were eight Simmons families and two of the daughter's families listed there. There was Jehu, James, James, John, Joseph, Martha, Robert, William, Elizabeth and John Crain and Jesse and Ally Iseal Ezell. These 10 families totaled 74 people.

When Cedar County was formed in 1845, the

county line would put part of the families in Polk and part in Cedar County. John Simmons lived near Alder School and Church.

John and Elizabeth Simmons' children were Victoria Carolina Simmons Phillips, Marion Simmons, Martha Simmons Phillips, Mary Simmons Phillips, Parthenia Simons, Elizabeth Simmons Campbell, James T. Simmons, Louisa Simmons Baker, John R. Simmons and Amanda Simmons.

John Simmons

Several of the Simmons children married into the Phillips family of Cedar County and some made their homes in Polk County. John and Elizabeth's daughter Martha married Mathis Phillips and they had six children. Tragedy struck the family and Martha died in 1866. Martha's sister Victoria Carolina later married Mathis and helped him raise the children. Mary Simmons married William "Billy" Phillips. Billy was Mathis Phillips' brother. There are also several other Phillips' family members who married into the Simmons family. Two of the Simmons children married Campbells.

The Simmons family was an old pioneer family of Tennessee, North Carolina and Virginia. Since their migration to Cedar and Polk Counties in Missouri, there are many descendants still living in this area today.

John Simmons died in 1886 in Cedar County, MO. Elizabeth, his wife, died in 1875. Both are buried in Alder Cemetery, Cedar County, MO. *Submitted by Derek Wells*

SIMMONS - Addison Lyle was born in the early 1800s and married Ester Alexander, who was born in 1808. Their son Ezra Alexander was born Dec. 30, 1833 and died Jan. 6, 1906 in Cedar County, MO. Ezra married Clementine A. Richardson on July 26, 1855 in Kingston, TN. Clementine was born Aug. 12, 1834 and died March 9, 1912 in Cedar County, MO. To this marriage were born William Lee, Samuel Logan, John Henry, James Thomas, Adna Jane, Alice Martha and Mary Susie.

William Lee Lyle was born Aug. 20, 1858 and died June 6, 1936 in Muskogee, OK, where he was buried. He married Nancy Clementine Garrison on March 30, 1879. She was born April 28, 1859 and died June 27, 1901, as a result of childbirth. She is buried with her infant son in Humansville, MO cemetery. Other children of this marriage were Lewis Alexander, Mary Clementine, Ara Maple, Ida Belle, Ora Lee, Zula, Pearl E., Margaret Larinda, Floy Jane, James Carl Sr. and William Lester for a total of 12 children. James C. Lyle Jr. was born May 17, 1923 and died Dec. 12, 2000. He married Benicia Nagle, born Jan. 12, 1924, on Dec. 11, 1942. He was the son of James C. Lyle Sr. and Mary Lipsey.

Lewis Alexander Lyle was born on April 4, 1882 in Cedar County and died Sept. 6, 1953 in Humansville, MO. He married Addie Daisy Hamlett on May 22, 1910 in Cedar County, MO. Addie is the daughter of William B. Hamlett, who was born Jan. 27, 1833 and died Nov. 8, 1916 in Cedar County, MO, and Mary (Reed) Blodgett, born Oct. 3, 1846 and died Feb. 1, 1935. William B. and his first wife Amanda (Phillips) had eight children. William B.'s second marriage was to Mary Ann Reed Blodgett. He had a total of 16 children. Addie, daughter of William and Mary, was born Nov. 21, 1885 in Cedar County, and died Feb. 10, 1921. To this union were born two children: Genevieve Marie and Charles Vernon.

Genevieve Marie, born July 7, 1919 in Exeter, CA, died July 2, 1997 in Hickory County, MO and she married Benjamin Stephen Simmons on Oct. 3, 1934. Benjamin was born on March 12, 1910 in Stockton, MO and died Aug. 27, 1980 in Springfield, MO. Bennie was a longtime resident of Bolivar, a retired mechanic in the US Navy, member of Bolivar American Legion Post 138 and a member of Calvary Baptist Church. He was the son of Stephen T. Simmons (born Feb. 17, 1875 and died Jan. 1, 1929) and Sarah Jetty Pauline Hensley (born June 2, 1883 and died Sept. 2, 1916). Steve and Sarah married on Oct. 16, 1904. Both are buried in Shady Grove Cemetery near Humansville, MO.

Bennie and Genevieve are the parents of twin girls, Sue Carol and Sylvia Lee and also Lewis Austin, Doris Irene, Glen Raymond and Mary Marie. Sue Carol was born Feb. 5, 1936 in Bolivar, MO, married Rex Raymond Kinsey on Nov. 7, 1952 and died on March 27, 1987. Max was born June 2, 1932 and died Sept. 1, 1984 in Chicago, IL. Both Sue and Max grew up and went to school in Polk County.

Sylvia, twin to Sue, was born Feb. 5, 1936. Sylvia married Jerroll Theo Breshears (also a twin, born Oct. 18, 1934) on Oct. 30, 1954 in Cliquot, MO. One son, Bruce Earl Breshears, was born to this union. Sylvia's second marriage was to Robert Hall Cruse on Aug. 29, 1964. Sylvia then married Calvin Don Thomas on Oct. 13, 1977; Cal was born Nov. 13, 1939 in Moorhead, MN.

Sylvia and Calvin Thomas 22nd wedding anniversary

Lewis Austin Simmons was born Jan. 5, 1937 in Bolivar, MO. He died on Aug. 26, 1981, having never married. His death was due to a beating when someone stole his car in New Orleans. Glen Raymond Simmons was born May 9, 1939 in Bolivar and married Dec. 23, 1960 to Elizabeth Helen Burec, born Oct. 2, 1941. Glen was known as Aquaman because of his love of fishing. Mary Marie Simmons was born March 7, 1941 in Bolivar, MO and married Robert John Box (born Feb. 13, 1936) on March 31, 1959. *Submitted by Sylvia Thomas*

SLAGLE – The name Slagle originated in Germany; it started out as VonSlagel. John Slagle Sr. was born in Virginia or Pennsylvania in 1770. His wife's name is unknown, but she was born in 1780. They had a total of four girls and nine boys. John Sr. and seven of his sons came to Polk County prior to 1841. They founded the community of Slagle Village, also know as Slagle. Several landmarks held the Slagle name: Slagle School, Slagle Store, Slagle Post Office, Slagle Creek and the Slagle Church with its cemetery. All that stands today to mark the town is a sign along the road, "Slagle." The church is still in use today and the cemetery holds a lot of the Slagle ancestors. Slagle Creek still runs close by the church.

One of John Sr.'s sons, Jacob, nicknamed "Jake," was born on Nov. 17, 1796. He married Francis Dunlap in 1818 and was an Indian fighter in Missouri. They had nine children. Two of their sons William E., nicknamed "Big Bill" and James P., nicknamed "Big Jim," served in the Civil War. They were very large men; due to their size, they had to supply their own horses to ride.

Jacob and Francis had a daughter Elizabeth Jane born Feb. 3, 1822. She married E. James Ballinger, who was born June 18, 1823. They were married on March 16, 1845. The Ballingers purchased land from the US Government, settling beside land connected to some of the Slagle homesteads. They had seven children. Their son Silas was born April 18, 1858. He married twice. His second wife was Mary M. Swadley, nicknamed "Mollie." She was born March 1878. She was half-Cherokee Indian. Her mother was full-blood Cherokee and was believed to have come with the Indians on the Trail of Tears.

The Slagle Family taken 1991; Jamie, Jeremy, seated are parents Donald and Janett holding Janel.

Silas and Mollie's daughter Mary Elizabeth was born Jan. 5, 1899. She married Walter F. Durham, who was born Sept. 6, 1900. Mary and Walter had six children. Mary died young and Walter remarried. Gertrude Durham, the daughter of Walter and Mary, was born Nov. 21, 1924. She married Otis Cowden, who was born March 13, 1912. The Cowdens had the following children: Lela, Ronnie, Jane, Beverly, Margie, Janett, Connie and Ronda.

One of John Sr.'s other sons, Abram, born in 1806, had a son William Lunceford Slagle. William also served in the Civil War. After the death of E. James and Elizabeth Jane Ballinger, William purchased their land from their children. William's land was left to his children. His son Calvin married Rose Licklider and they left their share of land to their children. Their son Glen married Faye Campbell and they had the following children: Glenda, Ronald, Linda, Donald and Anita.

By family agreement the land was passed down to Donald and his wife Janett (Cowden) Slagle. Janett is a great-great-great-granddaughter of Jacob Slagle. The land the Slagles own today also contains the piece of land the Ballingers homesteaded on. So far they seem to be the only Slagles left in the area still carrying the last name Slagle and owning original Slagle-Ballinger property. Donald and Janett have three children: Jamie, a sergeant in the US Army, Jeremy and Janel. *Submitted by Janett (Cowden) Slagle*

SLAGLE – South of the Bolivar Speedway, where Bruce Wheeler spent many Saturday nights, is an 80-acre tract of rural heaven that is the childhood home of Ginger Boswell Wheeler. This 130 year-old farmhouse and surrounding 80 acres is the childhood home of Rena Mae Slagle Boswell, too. Rena and her husband, Floyd, a Polk County farmer, well-driller, carpenter and school clerk, raised Ginger and her older brother Charles on the same land and in the same house that was built by Rena's father, William Lunceford (W.L.) Slagle, when he returned from the Civil War.

W.L. built a six-room house, a mortise and tenon barn and a granary. Rena and Floyd added a covered porch to the house in the 1930s and an indoor bathroom in 1966. The 1940s gaslights were replaced by electricity in the early 1950s. Water piped from the well to the house replaced the cistern. Outdoors, they added a cellar, wellhouse, hog barn and chicken sheds. In the early

1940s the daily cattle workings were added to the barn. Bruce and Ginger make a great effort to maintain this living history. Because of them, this farmhouse, out-buildings and 80 acres are now a Missouri Century Farm.

Each generation has made improvements to preserve this home of heritage, but very little has changed since W.L. lived inside. W.L. was one of many children born to Abraham and Martha Slagle. Abraham and his father John Sr., a transplant from Virginia, gave this community its namesake in 1831.

A green sign with white block letters alongside Highway 13 shows drivers that they are passing by the town of Slagle, a community that belongs to the past. Most of what the Slagle community founders accomplished cannot be seen today.

Located where Pitts Mobile Home Sales now sits was at one time the Slagle Store. Directly north of the store was the post office. These two establishments made up what was known as the Slagle Trading Center circa 1831-1880. The store later became Slagle's Meat Market, where Rena worked in the 1960s. The post office was closed in the early 1900s, its letters then handled by the Morrisville station.

Southwest of the Trading Center runs the baptismal waters of Slagle Creek, a stones-throw away from the Slagle Creek Missionary Baptist Church. Ginger tells stories of fire and brimstone summer revivals and bone-chilling February baptisms where the congregation would trek to the creek and the preacher would break ice to perform a baptism. The family wonders if Abraham Slagle and four of his six brothers – Jacob, John Jr. (Jack), James and Conrad (Coon) were submerged in the clear, cold water of the creek that bears their name following a sermon in the church that they helped build.

Behind the Slagle church is Slagle Cemetery. This aged graveyard received David Slagle, Abraham's younger brother, as the first pioneer to lay to rest in the red clay. To follow was Abraham himself, W.L. and his first wife, Emma

Double veranda stretches length of original house built by W.L. Slagle (center) maintained by Almedia (right) and Rena Mae (left) until inherited by Ginger (not in photo).

Jane, along with their children Austin, Calvin, Ruby and Bill. Still later was W.L.'s second wife, Almedia and their daughters Annie and Rena, along with many other Slagle and Boswell descendants.

Between the church and the creek stands what remains of the "new" Slagle School. The original school, according to narrative, was only a log cabin with a dirt floor. Rena and Charles attended the Slagle School. They closed the school one year before Ginger would have started first grade in 1950. She attended Marion C. Early School in Morrisville because the day of the one-room schoolhouse was long-gone.

Gone – but not forgotten. The story of how the Slagle family settled here, fought the Civil War, built a community and a legacy still lives. Bruce and Ginger's daughters, Paula, Dawn and Sandra tell these stories to their children. They speak of their grandmothers and great-grandfathers as if they just stepped out to do chores and will be back at any moment. They won't be back, they know that. But they can still watch them. They hope they are proud of the efforts made to preserve their heritage. The family wonders if they even knew they were creating a legacy?

SLAGLE – Ella C. and Emma V. Slagle were twin sisters born on March 25, 1872 near the community of Slagle which was named for their family. They were the daughters of James P. and Barbara L. Barham Slagle. James was born in Henry County, TN on Nov. 22,

Ella C. and Emma V. Slagle

1828. Barbara was a native of Kentucky as she was born there on June 3, 1833. James and Barbara were married in 1855. He was judge of the eastern district court of Polk County. Ella and Emma both attended Southwest Baptist College in Bolivar.

Ella married Dr. Dan Hammontree. Their home still stands just off the square in Bolivar. They had two children who were Ben and Esther.

Emma married Austin Marion Erwin on March 27, 1892. Their children were Paul and Ruth. Emma died at the birth of her second child on February 10, 1896. She is buried at Slagle Cemetery. *Submitted by Dennis Erwin*

SMITH – Hershel James Smith (April 2, 1911 – Oct. 28, 1988) and his wife, Ruth Marie (Sage) Smith (Sept. 19, 1914 – Dec. 2, 1998) and their two children, June Charlotte (July 5, 1933) and Jerry Gail (Jan. 5, 1938 – Oct. 10, 1994), moved to Polk County in November of 1950. Hershel was hired to manage River Farms, owned by J.B. McCarty and later Vernon West of the state of Maine. Hershel's wife, Ruth, was the secretary and bookkeeper for River Farms.

Hershel and Ruth bought their own farm while still managing River Farms. He later retired from being manager of River Farms, and on Sept. 27, 1973, they moved inside Bolivar. He worked several years for Lemmon's Service Station and Vestal Equipment. Ruth worked for Dorothy Baker and Marilyn and Frank Follis of Greenview Nursing Home as a nurse's aide. They had lived in Springfield, MO and the state of California, but they loved living in Polk County the most. They retired after

Mortise and tenon barn built by W.L. Slagle. Low side of barn is the dairy workings added by Floyd and Rena Boswell.

many years and their biggest joy was being with their grandchildren and great-grandchildren.

Their daughter, June, married Joe L. Lemmon (Dec. 15, 1929) on May 4, 1951. Joe served as mayor of Bolivar from 1973 until 1991 and 1993 until 1995. They also owned Lemmon's Service Station for many years. June was a homemaker until the last two children were in high school. She then worked part time at the *Bolivar Herald Free Press*, then at Citizens Memorial Hospital. She worked in the Polk County collector's office for 10 years. They were blessed with six children:

Joe Dale and his wife, Vicki (Coffey), have two children: Jody Junior (JJ) and Christy. JJ and his wife, Shannon, have two daughters: Chloe and Delaney.

Patricia Lou died in an automobile accident in 1969 at the age of 15

Jerry Glenn and his wife, Rita (Hubbert), have two children: Keisha and Hank.

Pamela Lee and her husband, Roger Grider, have five children: Jason Cooper, Tesa, Tanya, Fable and Landon.

Penny Lynn and her husband, Doug Brandt, have two children: Patty and Tony.

Jacqueline Kay and her husband, Tony Hitchcock, have three children: Mackenzie, Macey and Cooper.

Hershel and Ruth's son, Gail, graduated from Bolivar High School and enlisted in the Air Force for four years. While in the Air Force, he had his fiancée, Lavonne (Bonnie) Lois Thomas (Oct. 7, 1937) come to Las Vegas where they were married on Aug. 19, 1957. After leaving the Air Force, they made their home in Bolivar.

Gail was employed by Southwest Electric Cooperative. He was a great friend to the youth of Bolivar. Gail coached baseball and football for more than a decade in the '70s and '80s. He drew up the plans for the Bolivar Sports Complex and was instrumental in its being built. The muscular Smith could be seen digging in the dirt, building fences, building dugout benches, hauling off rock and mowing grass at the complex almost any evening or weekend. He squeezed in time for family and to coach – sometimes two teams at once – or to fill in for absent umpires. He climbed light poles to replace burned out bulbs or did whatever was needed. Gail served as president of the youth program at times and always served on the board.*

Gail and Lavonne (Bonnie) were blessed with four children.

Sherill Lynn Cowden has one daughter: Megan. Megan and her husband, Brian Breesawitz, have one daughter: Taylor.

Dennis Gail and his wife, Kim (Jones), have two sons: Matthew and Jared.

Sheila Annette, and her husband, Scott Crockett, have two children: Meleah and Tanner.

Darren Paul and his wife, Wendy, have one daughter: Morgan.

These are the descendants of Hershel and Ruth Smith. June Smith Lemmon says, "they taught us to be clean, honest, truthful, to do an honest day's work for our pay, and to always trust in God. For this their family is thankful and so proud to be their children. We now strive to pass these values to our children and grandchildren."

*Taken from an article by Bill Breshears, published in the *Bolivar Herald Free Press* in October 1994. *Submitted by June Lemmon*

SMITH – James H.M. Smith was born January of 1806 in Mercer County, KY, eldest son of James H. and Prudence (McGee) Smith. The Smith and McGee families moved to Kentucky from Virginia shortly after Kentucky had been "discovered" by Daniel Boone, Col. Logan, and others.

About the years of 1821/1822 the Smith family migrated to Howard County, MO. In 1829 James H.M. was married to Mary Ann Looney, daughter of John and Mary (Garrison) Looney, in Ralls County, MO. In 1830 James H.M., Mary Ann and daughter Ellender were farming in Ralls County, MO. Also living with this family were three brothers of James H.M. Smith: George W., John and Hugh. James H.M. Smith had been appointed guardian of two of his brothers when they were orphaned after the death of their father, James H., in 1827.

In 1834 this family was living in that part of Greene County, which in 1835 became Polk County, near the village of Brighton. Mary Ann Looney Smith must have died sometime during this period because in January of 1835 James H.M. married Martha Williams, daughter of John T. and Mary (Russell) Williams.

In the year of 1838 James H.M. Smith filed an early land claim in Polk County and his father-in-law sold his land entry claim to him. Both land entries were located in Township 32, Range 22.

J.J. Hetherington, great-great-great-great-grandson of James H.M. Smith

James H.M. and Martha became prominent landowners in the Looney Township area. They farmed and raised cattle, horses and mules. James H.M. filled the office of justice of the peace for several years. Their farm became a part of the famous Butterfield Trail lines.

Looney Township produced the first woven cloth in the county, which came from the loom of Martha Williams Smith. Martha Williams was born in Monroe County, KY and moved to the Polk County area about 1830. Her father, John T. Williams, paid rent to the Indians the second year he was in this county. The rent was two sides of bacon and five bushels of shelled corn.

James H.M and Martha raised daughter Ellender Ella; they had eight known children of their own: Lenna H., John M., Ephraim G., Annis Jane, James F., Hugh L., William T. (he was also known as "Big Bill" Smith and at one time weighed over 400 pounds) and Margaret E.

James H.M. Smith died Sept.16, 1867.

Thanks to Carl Locke and Jack Glendenning for this information: "This is a single grave on land that was probably owned by the Smiths at that time. The location is between the north and south-bound lanes of Highway 13 that is a short distance north of Missouri Highway 215. It is on privately owned land just on the east side of a small branch." This grave is now unmarked.

Martha, also known as Aunt Patsey, stayed on the farm until her death in September of 1897. She is buried at the Old Ruyle Cemetery, Polk County, MO. *Submitted by Judith Smith*

SMITH Randall Smith's great-grandfather John T. (Turner?) Smith, born circa 1827, lived in Polk County in 1840, 1850 and 1859 with his mother Elizabeth Smith. According to John's census report, he, his mother and father all had been born in South Carolina. His father's name remains unknown.

Next door lived James M. Lewis. John T. Smith married his daughter Sarah Ann Lewis born April 27, 1838, on July 31, 1859.

James M. Lewis, born Nov. 17, 1804, married Elizabeth Anderson, born Feb. 18, 1814, on Dec. 5, 1833. Their other children were Richard, born Jan. 5, 1832, Mary Jane, born June 7, 1839 (she married Andrew T. Hutson); and Easter Emmaline, born June 4, 1860. Prior to the Civil War, John, Sarah, James Lewis and his daughter, Emaline, all moved to Johnson County, Spadra Township, AR.

Next door to James Lewis lived Elizabeth's father, John Anderson, born circa 1786. His wife's name in unknown. Their children were James, born Feb. 6, 1809; William, born April 19, 1811; Matthew, born Jan. 24, 1816; Matilda, born Nov. 26, 1819 (she married Buford Maxwell); July, born Dec. 20, 1820; Andrew, born Sept. 11, 1822; Alexander, born Dec. 19, 1823; and Christopher, born Oct. 20, 1825.

John Anderson married second, Elizabeth (unknown) Smith, Oct. 28, 1840, in Polk County, MO (marriage record), born 1790. She was the widowed mother of John T. Smith. In the cen-

John Turner Smith and Sarah Elizabeth Preskitt with their family

sus of 1830 and 1840 in Polk County, MO, she is head of household. John Anderson lived nearby.

Children of John T. Smith and Sarah Ann Lewis were Easter Emaline, John Turner, Julia Elizabeth, Isaac Davis, Nancy Jane, Lewis W. and Ressie, all lived in Spadra Township, Johnson County, AR. The family moved to Wise County, TX about 1880.

John Turner Smith married Sarah Elizabeth Preskitt Sept. 11, 1884 in Talmadge, Wilbarger County, TX and then moved to Duncan, Stephens County, OK. Their children were Harvey Lee, Charlie Everett, Walter Frazier, Gean Percy, Millage Carey, Ora Elsy and Roy Elmer.

Millage Carey Smith and family lived in Rolla, Phelps County, MO. His son Randall Millage Smith prepared a detailed family genealogy. A copy was placed in the Bolivar, Polk County, MO Library along with a detailed genealogy of the John Anderson family. *Submitted by Randall M. Smith*

SMITH – Among the ante-bellum migrants from Tennessee to Missouri was William T. "Billy" Smith. He was born in Grainger County, TN, Oct. 19, 1839, to Samuel Smith and wife, Elizabeth Dyer. His grandfathers were Thomas Smith and Joseph Dyer, whose farms were on the Holston River below Tampico.

Billy Smith came to Polk County in 1856, possibly in conjunction with his sister, Lavinia and her husband Alfred Wilhite. The Wilhites bought 160 acres near Bolivar, July 10, 1857.

Although the 1860 census does not list Billy in Polk County, he was certainly there March 14, 1861, when he married Rebecca Chandler. Three Chandler sisters married men in the Smith family tradition: Louisa J. and Conaway Wilhite, April 26, 1857; Elizabeth and Robert C. Brim, July 26, 1859; Rebecca and Billy Smith. They were daughters of John Chandler and Catherine Nicely, also from Grainger County. The parents had married in Grainger on Dec. 31, 1832 and moved to Polk County in 1856.

Although his brothers in Tennessee and Alfred Wilhite went with the Confederacy, Bill differed. Perhaps reacting to guerilla threats, he enlisted in Company L. Sixth Regiment, Cavalry, Volunteers, July 22, 1862. He was discharged Dec. 28, 1864.

Despite being bed-ridden much of her life, Rebecca had six children: Willie Lee, July 3, 1863 – Dec. 2, 1904 (married Mary Denton?); Joseph Nelson (or Noble), Aug. 18, 1865 – April 28, 1929 (married Emma Bradshaw); Catherine Elizabeth, Oct. 13, 1867 – April 1, 1905 (married Isaac Newton Evans); Hallie, 1871 - ? (married Monteville F. Roberts); Addie Florence, March 24, 1875 – May 12, 1936 (married Shelton Mitchell); John "Bob", 1882 - ? (married Nell McGrory).

Billy and Rebecca's final location in Polk County was a farm south of Eudora, purchased Sept. 22, 1879. There Billy died Sept. 22, 1884. He was buried across the county line in the Turkey Creek Cemetery near Walnut Grove. Rebecca joined him Aug. 20, 1920.

One of their sons, Joe, was the grandfather of the contributor of this sketch. Joe seems to have left the Polk County farm for Ash Grove while in his teens. He may have worked for Dr. Thomas Doolin whose daughter, Ophelia, inspired the name Ophia for his only child. Subsequently, he worked with Howard Hampstead in the produce business. In nearby Walnut Grove, on Feb. 16, 1890, he married Emma Bradshaw, daughter of James Winborn Bradshaw and Lavinda Malderine Edmonson. James was born in North Carolina on May 6, 1848 to William Nelson Bradshaw and Sarah Leanna Foust. He died in Walnut Grove on Sept. 3, 1888. Lavinda Edmonson was born in Missouri on May 27, 1852 to Allen Edmonson and Polly Julian. The Edmonsons were from Virginia by way of Tennessee. Polly was one of the Cave Spring Julians whose ancestors came early to Maryland and subsequently from North Carolina via Tennessee.

Emma Bradshaw Smith died March 30, 1892, not long after the birth of her daughter, Ophia. Joe married Dolly Blankenship on May 10, 1894. Ophia married William E. Smith (no relation) on July 22, 1916, then principal of the Walnut Grove school. Both became eminent historians. They are memorialized in the W.E. and O.D. Smith Library of Regional History in Oxford, OH. *Submitted by J.W. Smith*

338

SNODGRASS – In July 1969, the Arlin Kent Snodgrass family came to Bolivar from Springfield to make their home. Kent, who was born Jan. 15, 1942, grew up on the Webster-Dallas county line at the homesteaded family farm near

David Snodgrass, Doran Snodgrass, Steve and Laney Norton, Jan Snodgrass Norton, Kay and Kent Snodgrass

Elkland; his wife, Kay, was raised in Christian County. Her family includes the Andersons and Mongers of the Oldfield and Lindenlure areas and the Days and Johnsons of the Rogersville area. Their 3-year-old daughter, Jan Elizabeth and their son, David Kent, who was born Jan. 26, 1970, completed the family. Both Kent's and Kay's families were pioneer settlers in Webster and Christian Counties, his family coming from Arkansas and Kay's from Virginia through Tennessee. Their family histories are recorded in county history books of those respective counties. Polk County ties include the David and Rebecca Platt family and the Walter and Isabelle Lafferty families. Rebecca Snodgrass Platt of the Dunnegan area and (Isa) Belle Snodgrass Lafferty were Kent's great-aunts, sisters of his grandfather, David Richard Snodgrass. The Platts lived north of Bolivar, off Highway D, in a square rock house that could be seen to the east of Highway D near the Sac River Bridge. The Laffertys lived in a white house near the MFA feed mill. Kent's cousins include Barbara Platt McColm and Eula Lafferty Gallivan. The Platts are buried in Greenwood Cemetery, as is Kent, who passed away Aug. 31, 2002. Kent's parents are Joseph Arlin and Marjorie Edwards Snodgrass of Elkland; Kay's parents are Joe Hiram and Dorothy Day Monger of Ozark.

Kent came to Polk County in 1969 to work as branch manager of Production Credit Association, with an office on North Main next to the Newland Cleaners. The office eventually relocated to South Main, next to Blue's 5 & 10 Store. Before David was born, Kent participated, along with Don Fullerton, in a beard-growing contest, said to improve the chances of an expected baby being a boy! Don, the father of three girls, became father of twins, a boy and girl. Kay gave birth to one son to complete their family.

Kent continued working at PCA for some time, then worked for Carroll McCracken and J.C. Meador at M&M Farm Center so that Kay could finish her college degree at SBU. She eventually received a master's degree from SMSU. After teaching sixth grade at Stockton for four years, Kay moved to Bolivar R-1 in 1982 and has been the middle school library media specialist since 1985, setting up two new school libraries during her career.

Kent and Kay rented a farm near Mt. Olive Church from Jim Raney for a short time and then bought the farm where they raised their children from Henry and Sylvia Dedmon. The farm they own is the old Teegarden farm north of the Stone Age Station. It has quite a history, also, with many tales shared by Leroy Seiner, who lived there as a boy and by Ardis Allen, who delivered gas there to two bachelors.

Eventually Kent and Kay established their own business, Hy-Tech Marketing and Dairy Sales, now located in the old Stone Age Station building on west Highway 32. This building has a history of its own – with stories being shared of fish fries held in the yard, using the old, concrete picnic table and bench and grill that still exist. It was also the bus stop at one time and was operated by Wayne Engledow as a gas station. Bill Hines, father of Kay Long and Dixie Jenkins, helped to construct the building and etched the star and moon into the front of the building, which is owned by Gene Engledow.

Kent, Kay, Jan and David became members of the First Christian Church of Bolivar. A full-circle story is that Kent's father, Arlin, was baptized at this church as a boy in the late 1920s when he came to Bolivar to visit the Platts and Laffertys and attended a revival meeting at the church. Kent and Kay joined FCC during the time Lloyd Morgan was pastor and Kent's funeral was held there. Kent was very involved in the Christian Church building project, devoting much time and knowledge to the design and construction of the activity building addition to the church.

Jan and David each graduated from Bolivar High School. Jan graduated from Phillips Junior College and now lives with her family in Nixa. David graduated from SMSU and continues to live in Bolivar where he operates the family dairy equipment business. Jan and David were active in showing dairy cattle at county fairs and at the Ozark Empire and Missouri State Fairs. *Submitted by Kay Snodgrass*

SPARKS – Mark and Susan Sparks moved to the Ozarks in 1986. First settling in Springfield, then moving to Brighton a year later, they finally ended up on a 40-acre farm just north of Cliquot in 1988.

Zaq, Susan and Mark Sparks

Mark was born April 3, 1963 to Larry J. and Janet H. Sparks of Springfield, MO who both have long family histories in the Ozarks. Larry and Janet divorced in 1965 with Janet receiving sole custody of Mark. Janet and Mark moved in with Janet's parents, J.D. and Mary Lee Heflin of Springfield, MO. Mark has always said that nothing much happened to him until the age of 7 when he received a magic set for Christmas. This led to Mark performing at children's birthday parties and various other local events through high school. He moved to Kansas City in 1983 to pursue his lifelong dream of making a living as an entertainer. When a near-fatal fire eating accident that summer led to several weeks of inactivity and being under doctor's orders to stay indoors, Mark took a job as manager of the magic shop at US Toy. This proved to be too confining, leading him to accept a job offer to perform at the 1984 World's Fair in New Orleans.

Born Feb. 18, 1959, Susan was one of three children born to Maynard and Shirley Denolf of Fort Atkinson, WI on a small farm on the banks of the Rock River. Her younger brothers are Joel and Michael. Maynard passed away on April 2, 1968 of heart problems caused by a childhood case of rheumatic fever. Shirley, a widow at the age of 29 with three children under the age of 9, kept the family together and never remarried. Susan left Fort Atkinson shortly after graduating from high school to pursue a career in entertainment. This took her all over the lower 48 states and in 1984 she landed a performing job at the World's Fair in New Orleans.

Mark and Susan hit it off immediately. They both had a sense of adventure and the desire to be successful in their chosen field. For the next two years they traveled around the country, performing at various venues. Then they decided to start a family and moved to Mark's hometown of Springfield.

Married in 1987, they moved to the farm in Polk County where they currently live. The farm purchased by Susan's mother Shirley in 1988 who was gracious enough to open up the land to allow her mother, Evelyn Miller (widow of Glenn Miller of Fort Atkinson, WI) and Mark and Susan to build houses on the property.

The Sparks' son Zaqary Joseph was born on Sept. 17, 1989. Zaq has been home schooled his entire life which has allowed him the freedom to pursue his interests in the culinary arts, farming and performing across the United States with his parents.

As of this writing, Susan is president of the Polk County Genealogical Society for whom she oversaw the purchase of the former Polk County Library building to be used as the group's headquarters and research center. In her "spare time" she produces the entertainment at several events around the country. Mark is vice president of Louisville, KY-based Triangle Talent, Inc., where he manages the Specialty Acts Division. When he's not working out of his home-based office or doing the occasional performance, Mark can be found in his sailboat on Stockton Lake. *Submitted by Mark and Susan Sparks*

STAAS – William Henry Staas was born Jan. 28, 1859 in Missouri and died March 3, 1940. He married Nancy Jane Wilson. Nancy was born Sept. 28, 1871 and died Nov. 22, 1939. They lived in the Wishart, Polk County area. Their daughter, Betty Staas, was born in 1898 and died in 1974.

Charles S. Staas served in WWI as private of the 356 Infantry 89th Division. He was killed in action in France on Nov. 5, 1918 and buried there. Later his parents brought his body home.

Mary Staas was born in 1901. She married George Franklin Stevens in May of 1919, the son of Bateman and Amanda Stevens. He was born Aug. 25, 1884. His family came to this area when he was 11 years old and spent the remainder of his life here. He died Jan. 27, 1948. Mary died in 1979 and both are buried at Enon Cemetery, Polk County, MO.

Everett Staas was born in 1903 in Polk County, MO. He died in 1928 from pneumonia.

James Gordon Staas was born June 18, 1907 in Wishart, Polk County, MO. He married Frances M. Cunningham, daughter of Joseph and Fannie

James and Frances Staas

Fite Cunningham, on Oct. 15, 1925. Frances was born March 24, 1909 in Wishart, Polk County, MO.

Children of James and Francis Staas are Mary Frances Staas who was born July 2, 1927; Ruth Evelyn Staas, born Sept. 28, 1929; "Jean" Annabel Eugenia Staas, born Aug. 28, 1931; Virginia Louise Staas, born June 23, 1933 and died Dec. 7, 1996 from cancer; William Joseph Staas, born April 3, 1934; Betty June Staas, born March 10, 1935; James Leroy Staas, born Aug. 11, 1939; Dorothy Sue Staas, born March 28, 1942; Judy Kay Staas, born April 14, 1944; Linda Joyce Staas, born Sept. 6, 1946; and Deborah Jane Staas, born Sept. 29, 1953.

James worked for MFA Grocery Stores and Frances was employed with Lester E. Cox Hospitals in Springfield, MO. They lived and raised all of their children in the Wishart community. Upon their retirement they moved to Springfield, MO. James died Jan. 19, 1988 and Frances died June 20, 1993. They are buried at Enon Cemetery in Polk County, MO. *Submitted by Ruth Evelyn Staas Ross*

STAMBAUGH – Amos Stambaugh lived in Van community of Polk County. His ancestors came from Alsace-Lorraine on the Rhine River near Germany. Several brothers came to American before the Revolutionary War and settled near Spring Grove, York County, PA.

Amos left Pennsylvania after his friend, Lester Wolf, wrote that land in Polk County was cheap. He moved to Polk County and worked until he made enough money to buy land. Earliest records give his first land purchase as January of 1870 when he bought 200 acres of Pomme de Terre River bottomlands for the sum of $1,011.50. Family history maintains that he borrowed money at 20 percent interest to buy this land.

Amos married Samantha Virginia Hanes in her parents' home in Schofield, Polk County, on March 26, 1871. Her parents, Peter and Susan Hanes, were from Iowa, where she was born on Oct. 8, 1852. They built their first home after they were married, down near Deer Creek bottom since they were unable to dig a well. In 1890, they moved the house, which was a one-and-one half story with a very steep roof, to it permanent location closer to the road. Amos and Samantha started housekeeping using orange crates for furniture. Each time he took a wagonload of wheat to sell in Springfield, he would bring back either good furniture or good dishes.

Amos and Samantha raised 10 children – five boys and five girls, which included one set of twins. They were born adhering to the pattern of girl-boy-girl-boy from oldest to youngest, including the twins. Amos spoke with a heavy German accent, which is apparent from a statement he made circa 1921 when he said, "Shentlemen, Ma, what do you want with more berries? You have more sham and shelly now than you can ever use."

Amos' hard work paid off, for between 1870 and 1909 he bought 1,000 acres of Pomme de Terre River bottomlands. He intended to build an empire by giving each of his five sons, at the time of their marriage, a complete farm that would adjoin his. The only stipulation attached to this gift was that they live on this farm and work the land, otherwise they did not receive the land. Only three sons (Orin, Charles and Jesse) accepted his offer. The rest of their children's names were Melvin, Lewis, Jennie, Alma, Celestia, Dessie and Lydia.

While Amos worked on his farm, Samantha worked hard at her household duties. She sold eggs for three cents per dozen and butter for 10 cents per pound. They raised sheep, then carded the wool and spun it into yarn. She knitted all the socks and mittens worn by her family and wove cloth, then handmade all their woolen clothes. She also wove carpets for the floors. When their neighbors became ill, they could depend on Samantha for nursing. Her daughter, Jennie and she took care of many cases of smallpox without contracting it themselves. In order to avoid it, each day they took a small amount of cream of tarter, which was believed to purify the blood.

The Stambaughs were listed in the Polk County newspaper as being one of the prominent families of Van, MO. They were instrumental in founding the New Bethel Church. Family social activities included ice cream, socials, Sunday school entertainments and Fourth of July picnics at Bolivar or Halfway. They went to these picnics in a wagon and would spend the night. Van also held a three-day picnic.

Amos built their second home on 160 acres of prairie land in 1909 after all their children had left home. This was a move of 6 miles but made them closer to Bolivar and to their youngest daughter, Lydia, who had married Harry Johnson and moved in with his parents. The Stambaughs farmed here until 1918, when they moved to Bolivar. He bought a two-story house and built a barn and a buggy shed, dug a cistern and planted fruit trees. He grew tobacco and rolled cigars, which he sold and used the rest for his pipe. Amos died on June 25, 1926, following a kidney infection. He thought he had recovered, but upon arising, he fell through the bedroom window and the resulting blood loss killed him. He was buried at the Mt. Gilead Cemetery, Bolivar, MO. Samantha lived with her oldest daughter, Jennie, in Halfway until her death on July 11, 1934, following two strokes. *Submitted by Mary Virginia Johnson Scott, granddaughter of Amos and Samantha Stambaugh and daughter of Harry and Lydia Stambaugh Johnson*

STAUFFACHER – Casper K. Stauffacher's paternal grandparents, Caspar and Marge (Kuelper) Stauffacher, came to Polk County in 1907 with their children: Clara, 14; Tracy, 12; and Walter, 11. They moved to their newly-purchased farm, 240 acres of fertile soil and wooded areas, located three miles south of Humansville. This farm straddled old Highway 13 a half mile south of Cedar Grove school.

Caspar, born in Cincinnati, OH in 1869, was the second of six children of Kaspar Stauffacher, who immigrated from Switzerland in 1859 and Sidonia Deckert, who immigrated from Germany in 1866. Kaspar served three years as a drummer boy with the 17th US Infantry in the Civil War before marrying Sidonia and settling on a farm west of Marysville, KS.

Marge, the oldest of seven children, immigrated from Germany in 1882 with her family. Caspar had a fourth grade education but was very adept at raising hogs and managing the modest fortune that he profited from this vocation. He raised various field crops, including a special maize called kaffircorn, which was especially good as chicken feed.

A fourth child, Alfred, was born in 1910. All the children went to Cedar Grove school. In 1917, Clara married a neighbor boy, Merton Stone and moved to their farm east of the Stauffachers. They had two children, Perla and Wally. In the mid

The original Stauffacher family in Polk County about 1928, Tracy, Alfred, Caspar, Marge, Walter, Clara

1920s they moved to Springfield. Merton died in 1969 and Clara in 1983. In 1918, Tracy married Ernest Gamble and moved to their farm, half way between Dunnegan and Fair Play, on old Highway 13, which is still know today as the Gamble farm. They had four children: Rex, Violet, Vesta and Glen. After Ernest died in 1960, Tracy moved to Fair Play where she lived until her death in 1976.

In 1921, Walter married Vee King, who taught at the Cedar Grove school in 1920/21. They settled in with Caspar, Marge and Alfred. In 1922, Caspar, Marge and Alfred moved to another farm that he owned, a mile west of Dunnegan, after arranging for Walter and Vee to buy the Humansville farm.

In 1941, Caspar died at the Dunnegan farm from pneumonia. Alfred took over the farm and married a neighbor lady, Pearl Platt. Marge bought a house in Dunnegan and moved from the farm, where she lived until her death in 1946.

Alfred and Pearl had two daughters, Anita and Eva. Alfred had a respiratory ailment and the family moved to California in 1955, where Pearl taught school for many years.

Meanwhile, Walter and Vee raised five children: Paul, Margie, Ralph, Casper and Ruby. A daughter, Ruth, died as an infant in 1926. All five children attended Cedar Grove rural and Humansville High schools, then left the farm to make their own lives. For a number of years, Ruby lived with her husband, Bill Underwood and their three children, Barbara, John and Glenda, on a farm between Dunnegan and Fair Play until Bill's death in 1980.

Walter was diagnosed with cancer in 1971. In 1974, no longer able to keep up the farm, Walter and Vee sold the farm and moved into a mobile home between Dunnegan and Fair Play. Walter succumbed to cancer in 1977. Vee moved into the Big Springs Rest Home in Humansville where she died from heart failure on July 4, 1983.

The Dunnegan farm was leased by Ralph Stauffacher and his wife, Virginia (Nottingham) Stauffacher. They raised five children: Cathy, Jeanne, Janelle, Shirley and Alan, who all grew up and moved away with their own families.

Today, 95 years later, Ralph and Virginia are the last of the Stauffachers living in Polk County. Ralph is semi-retired from farming and Virginia has just retired after teaching for 25 years in the Bolivar school system.

Annually, on the third Sunday in July, as many as possible return and gather for family reunion at Dunnegan. *Submitted by Casper King Stauffacher*

STEELE – Mary Elizabeth Renfro Steele is the fourth generation of Alfred and Mariah Witt Pierce's descendants to be born in and live in Polk County.

She was born Jan. 13, 1913 and was a twin.

Mary and Joe Steele on their 40th wedding anniversary – Dec. 5, 1975

Her twin, Asbury Jackson, lived only three days. He is buried at Slagle Cemetery next to his grandfather Alfred Jackson Pierce.

She moved to Springfield, MO when she married Joe W. Steele, her husband of 46 years. Two daughters, Jeanette Mae (Nov. 4, 1936) and Reta Lea (June 29, 1942) were born to this union.

Mary was a homemaker first, but she responded to the call of Pleasant Valley School when a cook was needed. She was the first cook to serve hot lunches to the children. She worked from 1948 through 1951. She also was a cook and or manager in several Springfield public schools for about 15 years.

Mary's husband, Joe, was known as "Jack Hammer Pete." He worked at the Marble Head Quarry using a jack hammer, and that is how he earned his name.

In later years he worked for Masters and Jackson and became a "dynamite monkey." He was skilled in his craft, never having blown off any part of his body. He was an expert with dynamite and was in demand for special jobs.

In 1967 Bob and Jeanette Springer took Joe and Mary to Wyoming to visit Reta and Jim Dyson. Everyone went on a sight-seeing trip through a deep canyon. Joe observed the enormity of the mountains and calmly stated, "If I had a big stick of dynamite, I would level this country so it would be good for something!"

After Joe died in 1981, Mary moved back to Polk County. She lived in her own home for two years. Then she lived in the Bolivar Nursing Home until her death on Dec. 1, 1987. She was extremely proud of her Polk County heritage.

Her legacy lives on in her descendants: One daughter, Jeanette Mae Steele Springer and three granddaughters: Rebecca Jeanette Springer Wilson, Debra Jean Springer Tennison and Melinda Jo Springer Manes. Seven great-granddaughters: Deadra Jeanette Sillavan Ervin, Amanda Julian Wilson, Meleah Joann Manes, DeAnna Jolene Tennison, Dianna Jonette Tennison, Martisha Jobeth Manes and Abigail Jacquelyn Wilson. Two great-grandsons, Anthony Daniel Wilson and Robie Dale Manes and one great-granddaughter, Drea Jeanette Sillavan, who live in Bolivar.

She also has one daughter, Reta Lea Steele Dyson, living in Osceola, MO, one granddaughter, Janell Cynthia Dyson Dennis and two great-granddaughters, Megan Lea Dennis and Mandi Lea Dennis, who live in Clinton, MO. *Submitted by Reta Lea Steele Dyson*

STEPHENS – Gerald Stephens was born in Cedar County on a farm near Stockton, MO on Sept. 6, 1919. His parents were John C. Stephens and Lula Peach Stephens. To this family five children were born: Vivian, Melva, Claudina, John D. and Gerald. Gerald attended Independence Grade School and graduated from Stockton High School in 1937. He attended Springfield Teachers College, now recognized at Southwest Missouri State University. Gerald returned to his home area, teaching for two years at his former grade school in the Independence community.

Gerald later moved to Kansas City where he was employed at the National School of Aeronautics. In 1941-1942 this school began to train women to work in defense plants. In this setting, he met Helen Marie Talley. She was the youngest daughter of George Benedict Talley and Effie May Bonjour Talley. George and Effie were married April 7, 1908 in Neuchatel, KS. Helen's older siblings were Walter Oliver and Alberta Leora. Gerald and Helen road the train to Springfield, MO and were married July 25, 1943 in Ozark, MO.

Gerald was inducted in the US Navy Air Corps in 1943 and attended ground school at William Jewell College in Liberty, MO. After ground school, he was transferred to flight training in Yankton, SD, then to Iowa City, Ottumwa, IA and finally to Pensacola, FL where he was commissioned Navy Ensign in 1945, then assigned to a squadron of the Amphibious PBY Flying Boats.

The PBY squadron was no longer needed in the war zone because of the surrender of Japan, so Gerald flew light bombers SNB at the Air Gunnery School in Opalaca, FL, near Miami. Helen

Our family on our 50th wedding anniversary

joined Gerald in Pensacola.

After attending the training school in Kansas City, Helen worked for North American Aviation helping to build B-25 bombers. Her specialty was to wire bomb racks.

After the war, Gerald went to photography school in Aurora, MO and later worked in a studio in Mountain Grove, MO.

Helen had met Betty Brathwait of Bolivar, MO, when they both worked at North American Aviation in Kansas City. After the war, Betty encouraged Gerald and Helen to come to Bolivar and establish a photography business. Gerald and Helen moved to Bolivar in 1946, establishing a home and business and have continued to be contributing members to this community. They are the parents of three children, Michael Joe, born Sept. 28, 1946, Mark Davis, born Oct. 27, 1954, and Meleah Lynn, born May 8, 1964. They have four grandchildren: Mary Helen, Carmen Marie, Nancy Michelle and John David. *Submitted by Gerald Stephens*

STERLING – The Sterling family came from Livingston County, MO to Polk County in 1908. Prior to the 1840s, when the Sterlings and Shumates migrated to Missouri, the families were from Virginia and Maryland.

James Benjamin Dixon Sterling, his wife, Susie Shumate Sterling and their eight children moved onto a 40-acre farm located south and west of the West Union School. Sterling a

James and Susie Sterling Family 1945
Front – Henry, Phyllis, Chloe, Mima, Lura
Center – Ida, James, Susie, Carl
Back – Ward, Grace, Rodney, Kenneth, Wayne and Maude

farmer and carpenter, revised the plans of his small house he had built near Spring Hill and built his new home three 1/2 miles north of Bolivar and about one-half mile west of the Frisco Highline tracks.

His brother, Francis, and his family moved to Polk County about the same time and they settled in the Fair Play area.

Jim Sterling was appointed to serve on the West Union School board of education, which meant he helped hire a teacher each year and made sure the building stayed in good repair. This school would represent the formal education of his 13 children as all graduated from the eighth grade at that location. Because of the distance and the cost for rural students to attend, none of the 13 children went on to high school in Bolivar.

Sterling and his family farmed the area and he worked on building projects to supplement the family income. He built a house on north Main in Bolivar to sell and later he moved in closer to Bolivar, with a small farm just north of town on the extension of what was then Burns Street (and has been renamed Chicago Street in recent years). He, his wife and daughter Chloe lived in that home until his death in 1952. The original home near West Union School remained in the family through the years with his son Wayne living there many years and Wayne's grandson and his family living there today (2002).

James B.D. Sterling's father, William Clark Sterling, served in the Confederate Army under the command of General Sterling Price.

The Sterling children scattered across the country from coast to coast. Maude, the oldest, married a neighbor boy, Charles Loyd. They moved to Inglewood, CA where they had a son, Morris. Susan Grace married Bill Swope and they lived in Missouri, Michigan and then Bolivar. Their children were Bill Jr. and Mary Francis.

James Henry was the oldest boy and he married Lucille Vaughn. They lived in Independence, MO for many years with their daughters, Helen and Velma. Mima Sterling married Cullen Fellows. They lived in Michigan and Bolivar with their children Jimmy Charles, Donna and Jack. Ida Blanche Sterling married Nelson Ashlock. They lived north of Bolivar in the Cliquot area with children Betty Sue, Wayne and Dixie.

Rodney Francis Sterling married Mildred Duffek of Bolivar and lived there throughout his life with his children, Ted and Sue. Lura had one son, Bob Johnson and was married for many years to Orval Galyan of Dunnegan. They lived in and around Bolivar and she was a long-time city clerk. Chloe lived at home with her parents and never married.

Walter Wayne Sterling married Emma Ammerman of Bolivar. They had three children, Mae Sue, Kenneth and Virginia. They lived in the Bolivar area throughout their lives and he was known for selling apples and apple cider on the square in Bolivar during the harvest season. Phylis, or Sis, as she was called, married Ted Bates and they lived in and around Bolivar.

Carl Sterling married Freda Engledow and they had two daughters, Linda and Christa. Carl lived in Wayne, MI and then for many years in Bolivar, where he and Rodney had a construction company that built many business buildings in Bolivar.

Kenneth Clark Sterling married Mary Denison and lived in Dearborn, MI, Boston and Chicago before returning to Bolivar. He ran a print shop and was president of the Bolivar Chamber of Commerce and the Kiwanis Club. His two children were Jim and Diane Sterling. Jim Sterling managed or owned the Bolivar Herald-Free Press from 1967 to 1999.

Ward Sterling was the youngest and he married Dorothy Moffatt, who was originally from Burns. They had two daughters, Vicki and Cathy. Ward lived in Wayne, MI for many years before returning to Bolivar.

Two children, Velma and Eugene, lived only short lives, dying as infants.

James (1866-1952) and Susie (1871-1960) Sterling are buried in Greenwood Cemetery in Bolivar. *Submitted by Ted Sterling*

STERLING – Kenneth C. Sterling was born near Bolivar on April 18, 1912. He was married to Mary Elizabeth Denison Sterling in 1941 at Greenfield Village in Dearborn, MI. He lived to be 80 years old, dying in Bolivar in 1992.

Kenneth was the son of Jim and Susie Sterling. He graduated from the eighth grade at West Union School north of Bolivar. He left for Michigan at 13 to join his brothers and sisters. His first job was carrying water for the Wayne County Road Department. Later he would work for the Ford Motor Company on the company farms and in construction of the Henry Ford Museum and Greenfield Village.

Along the way he took night classes at Wayne State University and worked in the Ford labs in the development of uses of soybeans. He was involved in the early development of plastic products and during WWII he worked on government projects at the Willow Run Bomber Plant. He had tried twice to enlist but had been turned down because of bad feet, which had been injured playing baseball.

After the war, Sterling headed vegetable packing companies in Boston and Chicago and conducted early experiments on precut French fries and salads. The latter, which are common today, did not come into general use for 25 years after his presentation in cellophane bags in super market produce coolers.

Bad health struck him during his early 1940s, and after 100 days hospitalized in the Mayo Clinic, he moved his family to Missouri, believing he had only a year to live. In Missouri, he felt he had enough family to help his wife and children survive. Needing something to do, he found a print shop would be a good

Kenneth and Mary Sterling children: Jim and Diane 1951

business. He learned the business in about six weeks in Chicago, bought a used offset press and copy camera and moved to Bolivar. He opened Ozark Offset Printing Company in a small shop on east Locust Street that had been built by his brothers Carl and Rodney.

Six years later he had defied the odds, was president of the local Kiwanis Club and president of the Chamber of Commerce, and active in getting the first modern factory – Pantsmaker – to locate in Bolivar.

Kenneth Sterling would live 40 years in Bolivar, dying suddenly while doing yard work prior to a fishing outing. He had spent many days fishing on area rivers and lakes and had owned KFTO Boat & Tackle Company along with Sterling Office Supply. For many years his businesses were in the old South Ward School Building.

His wife, Mary, preceded him in death, dying in 1974. He was married to the former Velma Hammons for about 10 years prior to his death.

He had two children, Jim and Diane, and four grandchildren. Jim, who operated or owned the Bolivar Herald-Free Press from 1967 to 1999, has two daughters, Elizabeth and Stephanie.

Diane has two children, Christine and Travis. Travis Biebel was named by his coaches as the outstanding offensive lineman for the first winning Missouri Tiger football team in 13 years. *Submitted by Jim Sterling*

STEVENS – Born in Santa Paula, CA, Helen arrived to Avery and Lafa Utterback on July 8, 1933. She soon learned of her Polk County ties since the family made an annual fall trip back to Fair Play to visit while the orange trees rested. Helen's brother Jim recalls that his maternal grandmother, Mary Louisa Watson Manuel (see Manuel), saved newspaper cartoons for him to read. She would also roast him a pan of peanuts and he would go upstairs and spend hours reading the cartoons during those visits. It was a special treat for a growing young man.

The little family, minus Jim, moved back to Polk County in 1947 and Helen attended Fair Play High School. She became a cheerleader for the Hornets in her senior year. Helen recalls walking to and from the bus on cold mornings in the late 1940s. "My fingers were always very cold," she says with emphasis.

Upon graduation in 1951, she entered Southwest Missouri State in Springfield, MO that summer, where she graduated first in 1954. She returned in 1972 to complete a second degree and teaching certification for elementary education. In 1952, she met Charles T. (Tom) Stevens of Nevada, Vernon County, MO and they married Dec. 27, 1953. They were one of the lead couples of the highly successful SMS Promenaders, a square dance team. Upon Tom's graduation in 1955, they began an Army career, which spanned 16 years, ending when Tom retired due to blindness in 1971.

Their oldest, Mark Thomas Stevens, was born Nov. 6, 1956 at Ft. Jackson, SC. Diana Lynn Stevens Pixler was born Jan. 16, 1959, their youngest, Eric Allen Stevens on Oct. 16, 1961. Both Diana and Eric were born in Augusburg, Germany. During Tom's military career, they lived in Germany for five years, Tom served two years in South Vietnam and had several other military assignments.

After a short stay in Springfield (1971-74), the family moved to Columbia, MO, where Tom continued his education at the University of Missouri-Columbia. Upon graduation from Glendale High School, Mark attended Ozark Bible College, where he met and married Marsha Louise Mountcastle. He also attended Emanuel School of Religion and Kansas State University. They have three children: Rachel Marie, Aaron Thomas and Hannah Louise. The family currently resides in Manhattan, KS, where Mark, a lieutenant colonel, serves as an inspector general in the National Guard. Marsha owns her own private business.

Diana Lynn also attended Ozark, marrying Scott Pixler of Montrose, CO. They have three children: Nathan Andrew, Sarah Elizabeth and Myra Christine. They reside in Phoenix, AZ, where Scott ministers at the First Christian Church.

Eric Allen Stevens attended Central Christian College of the Bible and Cincinnati Christian Seminary. While studying at the former, her married Rebecca Ashworth and they have three children: Michael Allen, Christopher Joel and Duncan Alexander. Eric currently ministers at Kentucky Road Christian Church in Mexico, MO.

Polk County is an integral part of family history for the Stevens children, Mark, Diana and Eric. There are especially fond memories of visiting Grandma Utterback on the farm near Fair Play and visiting Aunt Betty and Uncle Elmer, Aunt Dessa and other relatives in Bolivar. *Submitted by Mark T. Stevens*

STEWARD – Robert Allen Steward was born in Springview, NE on Oct. 31, 1939. On March 3, 1966, he married Lillian Alice Townsend in Springfield, MO.

Lillian was born on April 13, 1943 in Scottsbluff, NE.

It was 1987 when Robert Steward moved his family to Polk County from Cedar County, though the children had all gone to school at Humansville School in Polk County. In fact, Robert had gone to Humansville school his eighth grade year.

Robert and Lillian (Townsend) Steward had four children.

Allen Mark, born Sept. 13, 1967 in West Plains, MO, graduated from Humansville High School in 1985.

Amy Lin, born Sept. 18, 1969 in Springfield, MO, graduated from Humansville High School in 1987.

Duane Robert, born Sept. 21, 1971 in Springfield, MO, finished the 10th grade at Humansville High School and graduated in 1989 from Halfway High School.

Alicia Robin, born Oct. 20, 1973, finished the seventh grade at Humansville High School, before the family moved to Halfway in the summer of 1987. She graduated from Halfway High School in 1992.

Amy went to Southwest Baptist University in Bolivar for two years before marrying LaRon Beemer and moving to Columbia to finish her college. They and their three children are currently (2002) in Ann Arbor, MI where LaRon is getting his master's degree at Michigan University.

Robert worked out of Bolivar as a contract trucker, hauling cattle feed for the Moorman Manufacturing warehouse.

Allen also hauled feed for Moorman for a little while. He also worked for Polk County Concrete before going to St. Louis to college. He married an Illinois girl (Sharon Hamilton) and they now reside in O'Fallon, IL with their two children.

Duane has his own concrete construction business, working out of Willard where he and Tammy now live with their children.

Alicia married Gary Coursey and they currently live in Polk County, just out of Halfway. Gary has his own business installing tiles and hardwood flooring. They have three little girls.

Robert is now semi-retired but helps Duane (hauling gravel) and Gary in the tile installation some.

Lillian has an upholstery and drapery business and does sewing machine repair working out of the home at Halfway. *Submitted by Lillian Steward*

STEWART – Since 1836, Stewarts have been in Polk County, coming from Tennessee. They were of Scottish descent. Born in 1796, Evans Stewart and his wife Nancy Jenkins were both born in

Augustus Shelby Stewart, Annie Susan (Patterson) Stewart 60th wedding anniversary November 1948

Tennessee. They were lured to this county by the offer of free land once the Army gave the clear sign. Settling on the Sentinel Prairie north of Bolivar, they acquired much land and with slaves and their older children, built their homes and lived peacefully. Evans's father was Hamilton Stewart of Virginia and Nancy's father was a Revolutionary soldier. Evans and Nancy were the parents of 11 children, nine boys and two girls. Evans fought in the War of 1812.

The Civil War brought catastrophe. Evans was too old to soldier but had pro-South views. He went north until the end of the war. Returning to his homestead he found that his wife had died, his home burned by Union soldiers and his slaves were gone. Sometime later he married Melvina Todd Bridges.

Evans's son, Francis Marion, returned to Polk County after the war, having fought in seven battles and skirmishes, including those at Cane Hill and Long Lane and at one point rode with Shelby's raiders. He escaped without a scratch. His home had also been burned by Union soldiers and his wife and younger children were nowhere to be found. Eventually, he went north to the Missouri River and at Jamestown in Moniteau County saw a mare tied to a hitch. Stepping away, he asked for the mare to be untied and he called the mare's name. She came right to him. Waiting, his wife, Rebecca, came out with newly purchased supplies. What a surprise!

While Marion Stewart and his family remained around Jamestown for three years following the war, a son Augustus Shelby was born Aug. 27, 1866. He was called Gus, but his middle name comes from the beloved general Marion had had fought with. Francis's wife was Rebecca Zumwalt, the daughter of Jesse Zumwalt.

In 1888, Gus took as his wife, Annie Patterson, the daughter of Tillman and Dianna (McSwain) Patterson. They acquired and farmed land near his family near Pomme de Terre River, Mt. Etna area. They were the parents of one son, Sidney Harold (Harley) and three daughters, Grace, Rebecca and Lelia. They also raised a niece, Exie, whose mother had died.

They took their family to Fillmore, CA for a time and ran a delivery business and boarding house. They returned to Bolivar before WWI, where they remained until 1951. Gus followed farming and carpentry.

They made their home with their son, Harley, his wife, Elva and two granddaughters, Ernestine and Harlene. The granddaughters believe their grandparents were a big influence on their lives.

Upon Harley's death in 1951, they moved to California to live with their daughters. Annie died in 1953 and Gus, nearly blind, lived past 107 years. He is probably the oldest person from Polk County to live as long. His three daughters each lived past their 101st birthdays.

Their two granddaughters and a great-granddaughter and her three children make seven generations of Stewarts to have lived in Polk County. *Submitted by Harlene Esther*

STEWART – Orlin Stewart married Loreta Morgan on Dec. 30, 1937. Orlin was a coach and teacher at Golden City, MO high school and Loreta was an elementary teacher. They moved to Bolivar in the summer of 1938 so that Orlin Stewart could teach at Southwest Baptist College. He coached basketball as well as many other sports. He retired from SWBC in 1973. Loreta finished her college after all of her children had started to school and retired in 1981 after teaching 26 years in Bolivar.

Orlin B. Stewart, the middle child of five children, was born on the Stewart Farm northeast of Bolivar on Feb. 1, 1909 to Otis and Jennie Kifer Stewart. He graduated from Bolivar High School

Bob, Orlin, Bill and Reta Stewart; Bonnie holding Lori, Loreta and Ann Stewart

in 1929 where he was an outstanding athlete. He attended the University of Missouri one semester and was injured playing football. He came back and attended SWBC where he played basketball and then attended Southwest Missouri State Teachers College where he played both football and basketball, graduating in 1933. He received his master's degree from the University of Missouri in 1957.

Loreta Morgan Stewart, the youngest of two children, was born May 1, 1917 to Bern D. and Maude Stansberry Morgan on the Morgan farm four miles east of Golden City, MO. She graduated from Golden City High School in 1935 where she was a top student. She graduated from SWBC in 1954, the University of Missouri in 1959 and received her master's degree from the University of Missouri in 1968.

Bob R. was born on Jan. 26, 1940. Reta Sue was born at Hoffman Hall on March 19, 1942, the boys dormitory where her parents were house parents. The Stewarts moved to the farm that Orlin had purchased from the estate of Jesse Stewart, Orlin's grandfather. William Joseph (Bill) was born in the Stewart home on the farm on Oct. 22, 1944. Orlin and Loreta lived in the original home built by Jesse Stewart until each of their deaths. They remodeled the house several times. Orlin died on May 19, 1984 and Loreta died on April 12, 1999.

Bob married Bonnie Fowler, born on July 18, 1942, on Aug. 10, 1963. They had two children, Lori, born May 2, 1967 and Lane, born June 24, 1970. Lori married Tracy Norcross, born March 14, 1967, on Aug. 19, 1989. They had three daughters: Abigail, born on June 29, 1994; Madeline, born on March 25, 1997; and Olivia, born on Jan. 4, 1999. Lane married Ellen Dowley, born on March 29, 1971, on June 3, 2000.

Reta married Glenn Johnson, born on Jan. 13, 1939, on Sept. 5, 1970. They had one son, Kevin Johnson, born on July 28, 1973. After this marriage ended in divorce, Reta married Edwin L. Smith on July 30, 1982. Their home, built in 1994, adjoins the Stewart property.

Bill married Ann Whitney, born on Sept. 29, 1946, on Aug. 21, 1966. They had two children, Morgan, born on Nov. 27, 1970 and Kasey, born March 21, 1973. Morgan died of Neuroblastma on April 23, 1976. Since 1978, Bill and Ann have lived in the home where Bill's grandparents moved when they married on Jan. 13, 1904. They have restored much of the home to its natural state. Kasey married Jason Roark on June 6, 1992. Jaden Roark was born on April 30, 1996. After this marriage ended in divorce, Kasey married Mike Sallee on Nov. 9, 1999. Kylin Sallee was born on Jan. 21, 2001.

Bob, Reta and Bill, like their parents, are graduates of SWBC and the University of Missouri. The Stewart Farms northeast of Bolivar have continuously been in the Stewart family since 1904. *Submitted by William J. (Bill) Stewart*

STEWART – Evan Stewart, born in Hawkins, TN in 1795 and Nancy Jenkins, born in Kentucky in 1801, were married in 1817. They moved to Polk County, MO, north of Bolivar about 1830. Nancy died in May 1865. Evan died Sept. 12, 1889. Evan's son, Francis Marion Stewart, born Aug. 12, 1838, the next youngest of 11 children, married Rebecca Zumwalt on Aug. 4, 1858. Rebecca was born in Franklin County, MO on Aug. 30, 1837 and died on Nov. 15, 1902. Marion died on Jan. 1, 1920.

Jesse Thomas Stewart, son of Marion and Rebecca Stewart, born Dec. 19, 1861, near Bolivar, the second from the oldest of eight children, married Poet Ann Hutcheson, Feb. 7, 1882. They had three children, Otis, Arvel and Elsie. Poet Ann was born May 1, 1860 and died in June of 1890. On Dec. 6, 1893, Jesse Stewart married Mary Ann Weese and had two children, Orion and Jessie. He died on his farm northeast of Bolivar on March 27, 1930.

Otis Jesse Stewart, great-grandson of Evan Stewart and oldest son of Poet Ann and Jesse Stewart, was born Jan. 17, 1883. He married Jennie Kifer on Jan. 13, 1904 and they moved to a farm northeast of Bolivar. Otis died on Sept. 29, 1940.

Jennie Kifer, daughter of Joseph William and Mary Ann Kifer, was born on Jan. 10, 1887 and died on Aug. 5, 1967. Joseph Kifer, son of Andy and Ann Barger Kifer, was born near Latrobe, PA, March 22, 1856. As a young man, he left Pennsylvania and came to Paola, KS, where he became a blacksmith. About a year later he wrote home for Mary Ann Massena to join him. They were married on May 7, 1876. Two years later they moved to Waverly, KS where they lived for 16 years. In 1894, the family moved to a farm near Bolivar, where they lived until Joseph's death on Dec. 30, 1936. Joseph and Mary Ann had four children who lived to be adults: Lloyd, Jennie,

Back – Leslie, Maxine, Orlin, Loreta, Dorothy, Lloyd
Front – Lorene, Reta, Jennie, Bob, Edith December 1942

Albert and Zoe. Mary Ann was born March 2, 1859 and died Sept. 28, 1939.

Otis and Jennie Stewart had five children: Lloyd, born Jan. 16, 1905 and died Nov. 15, 1978; Edith, born Feb. 2, 1907 and died March 24, 1996; Orlin, born Feb. 1, 1909 and died May 19, 1984; Leslie, born Nov. 27, 1911 and died Feb. 3, 1977, and Lorene, born March 11, 1917 and died Sept. 28, 1998. Lloyd married Dorothy Dale on May 26, 1934. They adopted a son, Dale, born Nov. 4, 1947. Orlin married Loreta Morgan on Dec. 30, 1937. They had three children, Bob, born Jan. 26, 1940; Reta, born March 19, 1942; and Bill, born Oct. 22, 1944. Leslie married Maxine Cherrington in the early 1940s. Lorene married Alvin Schaeperkoetter on March 12, 1950. They had two children, Carl, born Jan. 25, 1953 and Irene, born Feb. 16, 1954. None of the grandchildren got to know Grandpa Stewart, but they were extremely close to Grandma Stewart. They all enjoyed her cooking and her storytelling. *Submitted by Reta Stewart Smith*

STEWART – Sidney Harold (Harley) Stewart, born Sept. 15, 1892, was the second child of four and only son born to Augustus Shelby and Annie Susan (Patterson) Stewart. They lived on a farm in the Mt. Etna area of northern Polk County.

Harley came to Bolivar and completed his high school and began teaching in the county rural schools at the age of 16. After five years of teaching, he joined his family in Fillmore, CA, a few years later returning to Bolivar at the time of WWI.

On June 3, 1922, Harley married Elva R. Roberts, the daughter of Orlie O. and Mary (Glover) Roberts from the Adonis community. Elva was born Jan. 21, 1898. She was also a county rural school teacher.

The first manager of the newly organized MFA in Bolivar, Harley had to give up due to illness, which kept him out of the work force for a time. Then he went to appraising for the Federal Land Bank. In 1934 he became Bolivar's postmaster. It was in 1940 that he went into the car salvage and tire business, as a Firestone Tire dealer. Then came WWII and he suffered with the country in all kinds of shortages. For his business it was tire shortage. During this time Harley served on the Polk County Draft Board.

Sidney Harold (Harley) Stewart 1946

Following the war his business got going again and later he had the Goodyear Tire dealership. Along with the tire business Harley was appointed the county director of Revenue, Motor Vehicle licensing.

Harley served three terms on the Bolivar School Board and as president for one of those terms. He was a leader in the Polk County School consolidation in 1951.

He grew up attending Mt. Olive Baptist Church, later joining the Bolivar First Baptist where he served in different areas. His wife Elva was also active in the church having come from Oak Grove Baptist, Adonis.

Always active in Democratic politics, he served as county chairman and was the old sixth District chairman in the 1930s. Mrs. Stewart was active in Democratic politics and helped organize the county WPA work during the Depression.

A charter member of the Bolivar Kiwanians, Mr. and Mrs. Stewart were members of the Order of the Odd Fellows and Rebeccas.

Following her husband's death, Mrs. Stewart continued as the Director of Revenue, Motor Vehicle Registration. She passed away on July 25, 1969. Mr. Stewart died Sept. 17, 1951.

They had two daughters. Ernestine Kinsey and her husband Woodrow live in Bolivar and have been local school teachers. Mr. Kinsey at one time was the Bolivar High School principal. They have one son, Timothy Stewart Kinsey, a financial analyst for the Department of Energy in Washington, DC. He has three children, Rachael, Jacob and Rebecca. Harlene Esther and her husband Dean also live in Bolivar. Dean has been a Goodyear Tire dealer as well as a cattleman and breeder of Missouri fox trotting horses. Harlene and her former husband, Robert W. Johnson, opened the first Coin-O-Matic laundries in Bolivar and Fair Play. One daughter, Roberta (Johnson) Doke, lives in Brighton, MO. She and her husband, Jim, are the parents of three children, Jamie, Jennifer and Jay Robert. The Dokes operate a propane gas business in Bolivar. *Submitted by Ernestine Kinsey*

STOKES – Orville Richard Stokes was born between Brighton and Pleasant Hope on a farm on Sept. 27, 1898 to Henry and Leona Stokes. He attended grade school at Persimmon Grove and New Hope. Sam Mullings never forgave him for helping him throw rocks at the boys' outhouse because Sam got the whipping while Orville escaped punishment! Orville went through the fifth grade. At the age of 12 he started working for farmers to help make a living for his parents and siblings. However, he could do most any math in his head. Among those he worked for were John Tice, Finis Laney and Noah Brock. Later he cut and hauled wood to Springfield with a team of horses and wagon to sell on the city lot. Highway 13 was a gravel road then. He was hired to help pave it when he was older.

From the time he was a young man he had a good horse to ride, then a buggy, next a car. He married Relod Sallee in 1920. They raised four children. Only one of these ever got switched, the youngest. One day after a rain storm Orville started after the cows that were across the swollen creek. He told his daughter who liked to go with him to stay at the house. As he was on a tree that lay across the creek he looked back and saw her on the bank. As quick as he could he got to her. She got some buckbrush tea that day!

Orville worked at the Frisco Shops for a short time, but he was a farmer at heart so he returned to the farm. His wife was a great helpmeet on their 240-acre farm where they raised corn, wheat and oats. Corn and wheat were taken to the mill to be ground for food for the family. The rest was feed for the horses, milk cows, chickens, geese and hogs. Some was sold for cash. When the wheat and oats were threshed, new straw ticks were filled for mattresses to sleep on. His sons and he also rented farmland to raise corn for a cashcrop to help pay off the debt on the farm. They were never afraid of hard work. There was a large bullhorn to blow to summon Orville to the house from the field if he was needed but usually to tell him dinner was ready.

For a month or two at a time an old gentleman, Bob Tindle, another called Tobe, a cousin, Allen Rice or one of their fathers or brothers would be at their house. Nieces and nephews were often there for a week at a time. They all liked Relod's cooking and Orville's hospitality. A neighbor, Nicholas Cox, lost his farm. Orville built him a one room building in their yard for him to live in. When he later got sick he was moved in their home and cared for until he died.

Orville and Relod Stokes 1977

Orville accepted Christ as his Saviour in his early 50s and joined the Noble Hill Baptist Church by baptism where he remained a member for the rest of his life. He had a son, Grant Stokes, who became a Baptist minister.

Orville was a jolly person. If he could get someone to laugh he was happy. In his later years he enjoyed having quarters in his pocket to give to a grandchild that came and other children also. He had tractors after 1941, but his farm was never without his good horse to ride and enjoy. His last horse died at an old age in the fall before he died in January 1980. He seemed relieved to know she was gone for he knew he could not care for her that winter. *Submitted by Grant Stokes*

STOKES – Richard Allen Stokes was born in February 1831 in Bedford County, TN to Thomas and Mary Robberson Stokes. He married Molinda

Front left to right – Richard, Emaline, Mary Jane and Polly Ann; Standing – Jimmy, Charlie, Johnny, Henry and Silas circa 1895

Emaline Montgomery on July 15, 1851 in Polk County, MO. She was the daughter of James and Mary A. (Polly) Thompson Montgomery. She was born on Jan. 9, 1834 in Blount County, TN. After she and her parents moved to Polk County, they ran a relay station for the stagecoaches where the Good Samaritan Boys' Ranch is located south of Brighton. Richard met Emaline there and fell in love with this tall, reddish-haired young lady. They bought a farm just south of there and reared their family. Their oldest son, Silas, married a Humansville girl, Martha Ann Norman. Their next three children were girls: Mary Jane, who married John Rice; Polly Ann, who married William Daniel Fender; and Elizabeth. Then came five more sons: James Thomas and John Richard, who were both noted fiddlers; George, who died at age 1; Henry Edwin, who married Mary Leona Alexander; and Charley Allen, who married Blanche Walters. James (Jimmy) married America Best and Johnny married Martha Virginia (Virgie) Benge. Richard was devoted to Emaline. It is said that on cold mornings he would warm a rug for her to stand on while she dressed. On cold evenings they sat before the fire roasting apples and potatoes. In summer they sat on the porch facing the west and watched the sun set, side by side. Richard was slim and straight. He had mild, hazel-gray eyes, black hair, a long, black beard and Roman nose. He was always ready to smile, was a good conversationalist and told many amusing stories. Emaline possessed an unswerving faith and trust in God. They were a happy devoted couple and are buried in Brighton Cemetery.

Richard's brother, Russell, married Emaline's sister, Rebecca, and had three girls and two boys. Russell was 10 years old when he came from Tennessee with the Robberson Caravan. He served four years in the Civil War. He was a farmer in Polk County. He and his wife are buried in Greenlawn Cemetery in Springfield. Russell was born Sept. 21, 1821 and died April 2, 1908. Rebecca was buried April 10, 1923. Their children were Mary Elizabeth, born Aug. 6, 1868, married William Henry Hughes; Sarah Malissa, Nov. 24, 1860-Dec. 2, 1917; James Wilbur, Oct. 12, 1871-Feb. 2, 1934; Rufus Sylvester, Dec. 10, 1873-April 5, 1925; Luella Belle, Sept. 20, 1878-April 5, 1925, married Harry Chisler.

Henry and Leona Alexander Stokes had eight children. Ethel married Floyd Nelson and died Dec. 30, 1924 during childbirth. Floyd and Ethel had four boys: Jack lives in Pleasant Hope; J.R. Arvel, whose name was later Orville Richard, married Relod Sallee; Claude Edwin married Rachel Witt and their son John lives in Pleasant Hope; Ruby married Purn Taylor and is 95 years old and lives in Tulare, CA. Geneva married Ralph Tucker and has two boys and three girls, with their son Pete living at Pleasant Hope. Beulah married Hubert Mason and they had two girls, Leona Bell Horton and Beauetta Hogan. Sons Charles and Chester both died as babies. *Submitted by Beauetta Hogan*

STOKES – Christian and Dorothy "Dollie" (Proctor) Fender settled here between 1836 and 1841. Their daughter, Mariah Elizabeth married Elizah "Lige" Blackburn. Their eight children were Jennette "Nettie," married Robert P. Hammontree; Dorothy Carolyn "Carrie," married Isaac Presley; Martha "Mattie," married Pony Presley; George, married Della Vineyard; Christian, died young; Mahlon and Mable, twins (he married Cora and she married Clarence Scroggins, Clarence died early, then she married Burley Presley); and Addah Ursula "Addie," married George Washington Sallee. Christian Fender and his son-in-law Lige Blackburn hauled lumber from Arkansas to build the Fender Chapel Church in 1875. Addie and George W. Sallee reared their family in Polk County. Their children were Opal, Audra, Beach, Doy, Pauline and Relod, mother of Mrs. Wanda Dillard.

Wanda Dillard

Relod married Orville Richard Stokes in 1920 and moved to Springfield from July to October when her mother Addie passed away. They moved back to Polk County so Relod could help care for her siblings. They later bought a farm in the Brighton vicinity and lived there for the rest of their lives. Orville Richard Stokes' parents were Henry and Leona (Alexander) Stokes who lived between Brighton and Pleasant Hope. Their children were Ethel, Claude, Geneva, Charles, Chester, Beulah, Ruby and Orville. Charles and Chester died young and are buried in the Brock Cemetery, as is Christian Fender; this cemetery is near the Sac River south of Brighton. When Orville was born, his name was spelled Arvel, but it got changed when he registered for the Army in WWI.

Thomas Stokes, son of John Stokes from Tennessee, married Elizabeth Pettigrew Robberson's daughter Mary. In 1831, they came to Missouri to homestead land in Greene County where Ebenezer and Robberson Prairie is now. Some of their boys were grown then, but Mrs. Dillard's great-grandfather was just a baby and Elizabeth carried baby Richard as she rode from Tennessee to Missouri.

When Richard was a young man, he drove a freight wagon for the Union and Confederate armies from Rolla to Springfield. Along the Butterfield Route John Thompson had a store or a restaurant or both, located where the Good Samaritan Boys' Ranch is now. Richard met his wife-to-be there, because she worked there with her parents. Her name was Molinda Emaline Thompson. Later Richard's brother Russell married Molinda's sister Rebecca. Richard later bought a farm just south of the Polk County line in Greene County. George Henry Stokes owns the farm today. Richard and Molinda's children were Silas, John, George (died young), James, Polly Ann, Mary Jane, Elizabeth, Charlie and Henry, Mrs. Dillard's grandfather.

Wanda (Stokes) Dillard graduated from Pleasant Hope High School in 1945 and has always had a Brighton address. She taught school at both Pleasant Hope and Brighton. The Brighton school in the rock building was where she taught and it is behind the Hiway Assembly of God Church on Highway 13.

Her husband of 52 years is Edmond Wayne Dillard. They have three sons, Bruce, Kenneth (deceased), Phillip and wife Caroline Kay as well as three grandsons, Gregory, Daniel and Eric (Kenneth's son). She has two brothers, Grant and George Henry Stokes, and a sister, Arvilla Stokes Fieth. She and her husband, children and great-grandchildren all belong to the Fundamental Baptist Church in Pleasant Hope where she is the church pianist. *Submitted by Wanda Stokes Dillard*

STORMENT – William Riley Storment was born in 1860 in Jefferson County, IL. He and a brother toured Missouri as young men and Riley decided to make Missouri his home. He moved to Polk, MO and settled on a high hill southwest of Polk, MO in what he described as the heartland of Missouri.

He met Laura Payne, who was born in 1864 in Polk County, MO. Her family were long-time settlers of the Polk area. Laura's father was James Franklin Payne and her mother was Elizabeth (Hunt) Payne. Riley and Laura were married in 1883 in Polk County, MO. To this union four children were born: Earl, Mary, Omer and Golden. Riley and Laura lived in a little cabin at the foot of the big hill.

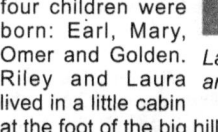
Laura and Riley Storment and old family home, 1916

Riley was a blacksmith. He made tools and also did work for other people in his shop. They made split shingles from red oak trees and the shingles were sold for homes that were being built in the area.

Laura raised a lot of ducks and geese. Some were sold for food; however, Laura also picked their feathers which were sold for pillows and feather beds. She saved $900.00 from the sale of feathers and with that money they built their dream home on the big hill.

The hill where they built their home was covered with limestone rock. Riley started mining the limestone rock. The mined limestone was then burnt and became what was called burnt lime or birdlime. The burnt lime was used for mortar or cement as well as a neutralizer for soil. This process took a lot of hard work.

Riley hired a lot of men to cut wood and work at the "kiln," a furnace for burning the limestone. At one time Jesse James and the Younger boys worked for Riley and Laura; however, they did not know who they were.

Riley sold the burnt lime in Buffalo, MO. He drove a beautiful team of oxen and took wagon loads of burnt lime to Buffalo and it took a week to make the trip. Farmers who lived along the road would let him and the oxen spend the night. Riley would get a meal and the oxen were also fed by the farmers. Laura stayed at home and kept the crew working in order to have another load of burnt lime ready to go for the next week. It must have been a hard way to make a living for their family. Riley and Laura are both buried in Payne Cemetery at Polk, MO.

On Dec. 1, 1914, Golden Storment married Oscar Warren. They had nine children: Jewell, Nelson, Choloada, Eldon, Vanbuna, Arnol, Arbie, Norris and Delma.

Riley and Laura were Eldon's grandparents. He is proud to have a heritage of people who were so willing to work for what they believed in and cared for. He lived a part of his life on the big hill. His son, Rex, and his wife, Diane, have built a big, beautiful, new home on the same place. Eldon's grandparents would be proud to know that their great-great-great-grandchildren are still enjoying the beautiful farm. It has been in the family for over 100 years.

On Sept. 11, 1949, Eldon Warren married Virginia Anderson from Humansville, MO. Their children are Rex, Vanetta and Cynthia.

Rex married Diane Hibbs from Carthage, MO. They have two children, Justin and Emily. Vanetta married Frank Robertson of Bolivar, MO and they have three sons, Sheldon, Albert and Travis. Cynthia married Bill Wood of Weaubleau, MO and they have two children, Joshua and Amanda. Eldon and Virginia have grandchildren who all enjoy their Polk county heritage very much!

Eldon served in the Air Force so that his family could hold and enjoy and look to the future in hope, peace and love. *Submitted by Rex Eldon Warren*

STOUTZENBERGER – In the fall of 1977 when the Maurice Stoutzenberger family became a part of Polk County, it was the return of Stoutzenbergers to the Ozarks. The first Polk County Stoutzenberger was Ezra, the son of a large family of Stoutzenbergers from the East. He became a part of Polk County in the 1890s when he homesteaded a 160-acre farm in northern Polk County, in the area of Adonis. Ezra was married to a local girl, Mary Belknap, and owned the Sentinel store with his father-in-law, William Belknap. Erza and Mary had three children, one of whom was born in Polk County, William. William, his younger sister, Vivan and brother, Eugene, grew up in the Kansas City area. William Ezra Belknap Stoutzenberger married a Lee's Summit area girl, Dorothy Leone Nicely. They had three children, Olive Jean, Maxine and Maurice.

Maurice, his wife, Shirley and their youngest, Earl, once again lived on the Stoutzenberger farm. Maurice worked nights at Porter's seed house, while trying his hand at hog farming, then moved onto work with the Longs in their hardware store. At the opening of Citizens Memorial Hospital, Maurice was there working in the housekeeping department. After leaving the farm, while at CMH, Maurice started a "retirement" business, Me-Shy

Maurice, Shirley, Earl and Catherine

Locksmith. Shirley was employed much of this time at Bolivar Mill, working for Keith Parminter.

Both Maurice and Shirley, living in Bolivar, have not regretted the move to Polk County from what had been their home state of Iowa. The move to Missouri meant leaving family in Iowa. Their oldest son, Belknap, Council Bluffs, IA, who is now married to Evelyn with three children, James, Sarah and Aaron. Their oldest daughter, Eula, Carson, IA, is married to Kevan Green, with their three children, Adam, who was a resident of Polk County and announced races at Bolivar race track one year; Kelli; and Cassandra. Their youngest daughter, Mary, died in 1981, leaving a daughter, Tina Boruff, who then came to Missouri, was raised by Maurice and Shirley and graduated Bolivar Schools in 1993.

Polk County also became home to Shirley's parents, Arthur John Cave and his wife, Pauline. Shirley cared for their needs from 1989 until their deaths in '95 and '96.

Eugene Stoutzenberger also resided in Polk County for a few years, with his wife Hazel. Gene and Hazel were drawn to Bolivar by Hazel's family ties, Hazel being an aunt to Bob Barr of Bolivar.

Earl also is happy to be a part of Polk County. Earl worked for Bill Roberts Chevrolet, for CMH, then in 1993 bought Me-Shy Locksmith from his father. Catherine worked 10 years for Jack Day at Bolivar Glass and Window Company. She then went to work with Earl at Me-Shy in 1996. They raised Catherine's children at Bolivar, Jesse Boyd of Bolivar, graduated in 1992; David Galloway of Bolivar, graduated 1994, married to Tia, children: Daniel, Devin, Andrea, David and Darien; Hollie Galloway/Stapleton graduated 1996, married to Keith with a son, Ethan, living in Aurora, MO. *Submitted by Earl and Catherine Stoutzenberger*

STOVALL – David William Stovall was born in Hardin County, KY on Feb. 22, 1831. His parents were James Stovall and Nancy (Standiford) Stovall. David is the sixth generation of Bartholomew Stovall who immigrated to America from England in 1684 at the age of 21.

David married Mary Margaret Carpenter in 1853. She was the daughter of Lovell Carpenter and Sarah (Hutcherson) Carpenter. Her ancestors came to America in the early 1700s and were of German descent.

David spent much of his childhood in Knox County, MO. At the age of 15, he and a cousin decided to run away from home to seek their fortune. David had 80 cents in his pocket and his cousin had none. After two days the only job offer was for three dollars a month, which was far below what they had anticipated, so they returned home. David later decided to become a doctor. He received his MD degree from Keokuk Medical Center College in Iowa.

Being a doctor, he was active in the Civil War. He was sympathetic to both sides. His son Sterling said the first time he saw his father, he was walking down a path returning home from the war. David told him he had put on civilian clothes and hid his uniform and gun on a ledge above a cave entrance. Whether he actually joined either side has not been proven, but after the war he named a son Robert E. Lee Stovall.

David Stovall moved to Polk County a few years after the Civil War. He continued his medical practice and was noted for driving a team with white mules. The mules knew the way home and this allowed the doctor to doze when returning from late night calls. He often took sick children home with him to provide medical care for them. Some would stay for several weeks. Sometimes money would be scarce, but there was always plenty of food on the table as many people could only pay him with food items.

He was one of the founders and a charter member of the Dunnegan First Baptist Church, which was established in June 1888. He served as one of their deacons.

David and Mary had seven children. They lost their two daughters, Carrie and Amanda, and a son, Smith, before they were grown. Their son, Robert, died in 1891 at the age of 21 and is buried in the Dunnegan Cemetery. Their three sons, Tom, Charles and Sterling married and had families.

In 1892, David and Mary and their sons, Tom and Charlie, moved to Howell County. Although he continued his medical practice, he and his sons also owned and operated a sawmill in Howell County. Tom married Ella Cleveland Kentch. Charles married Gertrude Hiler.

David's son, Sterling Stovall, remained in

Right to left – Serenia and Sterling, Tom, Charlie, D.W. and wife Mary Margaret, rest unknown, probably Mary's relatives, Carpenters or possibly Nances.

Dunnegan. He married Serenia Wollard and they had three children: Carl, Ray and Faye. Carl died as an infant. Faye married Carl Wright and had two sons, Dale and Rex. Ray married Esther Mitchem and they had nine children: Chester, Violet, Ray, Daisy, Eddie, Darlene, Irene, Ronnie and Janice. Ray Stovall was very proud to have served in WWI although his health was affected by the exposure to mustard gas, which resulted in his death when he was only 55 years old. Ray Stovall lived in Polk County, MO all his life and is buried in the Dunnegan Cemetery. Ray's son, Chester, served in WWII in Burma and was one of Merrill's Marauders.

David William Stovall died April 2, 1906 in Howell County and is buried in the Epps Cemetery. *Submitted by Ray Stovall*

STOVALL – Ray Wann Stovall and Esther Fern Mitchem were married in Dunnegan, MO on Feb. 7, 1923. They were born and lived in Polk County all of their lives, as their mothers before them.

They had nine children: Chester, Violet, Ray, Daisy, Edgar, Darlene, Irene, Ronnie and Janice in that order. Edgar died before age 3 and Janice before 9 months. They are buried in Dunnegan Cemetery.

Ray was born April 17, 1892, the second son of Serenia (Wollard) and Sterling Price Stovall. His siblings were Carl Bartlett, who died at age 2 in 1891 and one sister, Faye, born Nov. 1, 1897.

Ray was a soldier in WWI for two years and stationed in France. He returned from service with a heart condition, probably the results of mustard gas used in his training. He died in his sleep on Nov. 15, 1948, at the age of 56. He was buried in Dunnegan Cemetery, with military honors.

Ray Wann Stovall

Esther was born Sept. 26, 1901, the second daughter of Prudie (Barnes) and James "Jim" Mitchem, who had 13 children with one dying in infancy. Her siblings were Hazel, Hallie, Bert, Edna, Maxine, Dorothy, Marjorie, Dora, Irene, Maudie and Charlie. Esther grew up on the south hill bordering Dunnegan Cemetery. She remembered many times her dad coming in to tell her mom that someone was digging a grave and had been invited to eat with them. (Her grandparents, Alice and Allen Barnes, also owned land and lived to the southwest, bordering the cemetery.)

Esther had barely learned to walk when she was stricken with infantile paralysis (polio). She recovered but was left with a crippled foot. She was never able to walk very far, so did not get to attend school very often. She had a strong love for learning and read her siblings' school books and later her own children's books. Her reading comprehension was above average. She read all of her life and kept a dictionary and atlas near her chair to look up new words or places.

She had very busy hands through the years with many skills. She loved to develop pictures, crochet, tat, braid rugs, piece quilts, stencil paint, appliqué, and made hundreds of doilies, quilts and afghans to share with family and friends.

Esther also developed the skills needed to raise a large family in that day, such as milking, gardening, canning, drying fruit, baking bread, making cheese, hominy, kraut and pickles to name a few, along with the usual cooking, sewing, washing on a washboard, also rendering lard and making lye soap. Her children were healthy and never went hungry.

Esther and her family operated the Dunnegan Telephone switchboard during the late 1940s until an ice storm put the switchboard out of business. She also helped her brother Hallie at the Fair Play switchboard.

In 1957, Esther met and married John Bennett (see Bennett) from Flemington. They operated the Fair Play switchboard until 1961. They bought a home near Bear Creek and lived there for a few years before moving to Humansville, MO. They enjoyed a trip to his birthplace in North Carolina and also drove to visit relatives in California and Nevada.

They moved to Bolivar in their later years. John died on Nov. 24, 1977. Esther moved into a senior citizen's apartment and enjoyed many years living next door to Dora Mustain, one of her younger sisters. Esther died April 1, 1991. She and John are both buried at Dunnegan Cemetery. *Submitted by Daisy Fowler*

SUNSET BRIDGE - You know how in your life there's always "the one that got away?" Well, this story is about the bridge that got away.

Can you fall in love with a bridge? Marilyn did. Her name was Sunset, and she spanned the Pomme de Terre River in southeast Polk County. During Marilyn's halcyon days growing up in Pleasant Hope, she was our great escape-our Polk County version of the French Riviera. When

you're young, it doesn't take a lot to amuse you, and the warm, slightly muddy water beneath Sunset Bridge lushly filled the summertime bill.

Once sampled, one could never forget the distinctive "thumpa, thumpa, thumpa" sound a car made as it gently rolled over its wooden floor boards.

The bridge remained a part of the past Marilyn refuses to let go of, even after she left the area. In the late 1980's, she was stunned to hear it was "FOR SALE." A new bridge was planned, and a requirement for federal funding was preserving the rustic beauty in a historical setting. She couldn't comprehend why maintaining it as a pedestrian bridge with another built adjacent wasn't considered. At least it should have remained in Polk County.

Sadly, Anne Arundel County in Maryland was chosen to receive "our bridge" for use in a hike and bike trail spanning a 140-foot canyon. In 1987, it paid $1,800 to have the antique masterpiece shipped disassembled, with the pieces marked for reconstruction. Eighteen hundred dollars for a piece of Polk County history! *Our history*! It belonged to this Marilyn-not that Maryland!

When Sunset Bridge was nearly reconstructed, the girders gave way as it was being lifted by a crane. High drama ensued. A worker on the bridge grabbed a cable and swung away, narrowly escaping injury. The bridge twisted, folded up, and rolled into a ditch. The old bridge was a total loss, with its crossbeams gnarled as much as 180 degrees on themselves. The sun had set on Sunset Bridge.

While heartbroken at its tragic demise, Marilyn found solace in its sense of "Missouri justice." It was a *Missouri* bridge that belonged only in *Missouri*, and like all good Missourians, it wanted to "show them."

The bridge had held its own since being built in 1885, first spanning the Pomme de Terre River at Burns between Bolivar and Halfway, then being moved in 1928 to the site Marilyn loved near Van Town, where she mistakenly thought it would remain forever.

Historically speaking, if the bridge had talked, what amazing stories it might have told. Veterans from the Civil War to Vietnam crossed its span, plus folks hurrying to pie suppers and creek baptisms, and people like Marilyn who wanted to dip their toes in cool water on a hot summer day and enjoy laughter with friends. To those of this generation, Sunset Bridge wasn't just a place; it was a state of mind, a symbol of our golden youth.

Recently, Marilyn passed the old bridge route and the trees she remembered surrounding it had vanished. The beautiful, old metal bridge was replaced by a graffiti-strewn, modern-day, concrete monstrosity. Absent was the "thumpa, thumpa, thumpa" because there was no oak floor. The new bridge was safer, but the magic was gone. She realized, regrettably, "You can't go home again."

Things like Sunset Bridge should be preserved, not so much for themselves, but for what they represent. Perhaps what she grieves for most isn't the bridge but the memories it evokes of those youthfully idyllic lazy, hazy, crazy days of summer.

When Sunset Bridge went down, a little of Marilyn went with it. Yet it remains forever erect in her memory. For over a century, it truly was a "bridge across time." *Submitted by Marilyn Hood Hayes*

SUMMERS – Robert Wilson Summers, born July 27, 1830 and Hannah Rafferty, born Feb. 17, 1831, married in Madison County, OH, Dec. 9, 1852. To this union eight children were born: Immanuel Clinton, born 1855; William Elmore, born 1857; David Matthis, born 1859; Emma Jane, born 1863; Mary Ellen, born 1865; Joseph Rafferty, born 1867; Hannah Mariah, born 1869; Robert Benjamin Franklin, born 1871.

Robert W. and Hannah came to Missouri around 1866 and settled on a farm southeast of Halfway. Hannah passed away June 9, 1889 and is buried in Prairie Grove Cemetery in Dallas County southwest of Buffalo, MO.

Susan Abigail (Agee) Summers; Grace Fern (Summers) West

Robert then married Susan Abigail Agee, Aug. 28, 1892. To this union four children were born in Polk County. They were Omer Alvin, 1894-1973; Owen Wilson, 1896-1981; Grace Fearn (Fern), 1898-1989; Walter Loyd, 1902-1980.

Omer, Owen and Grace all left Missouri and settled in California. Walter married Minnie Estelle Trimble, August 1920. To this union one son was born, Bertram Loyd, on Nov. 11, 1921. Minnie passed away in September 1927 and is buried in Englewood, CA.

Bertram (Bert) was married to Gladys Irene Austin, May 14, 1949. To this union six children were born. They were Charles Loyd-May 8, 1950; Alva Gene-Dec.16, 1951; James Ivan-Nov. 29, 1952; Berta Irene-June 11, 1955; Victor Olin-May 22, 1958; Kelly Brent-May 27, 1967 (stillborn). Bertram passed away in August of 1984.

Robert, Susan, Walter, Bertram and Kelly are all buried in the Prairie Grove Cemetery in southwest Dallas County.

Part of the farm may have been swamp land as Walter told his grandchildren something about that. Another part of the farm had an original prairie. Wildlife ran freely and abundantly. Walter farmed some of the place, raising corn, soy beans and wheat. He raised registered Herefords for beef cattle. Walter did some custom bailing of hay for farmers in Dallas and Polk Counties.

Bert worked at a sawmill at Burns for a while, then later he worked for George Willard feed mill, an MFA milling company in Springfield.

Walter sold the farm due to ill health. The farm had been in the Summers family for over 100 years. He moved to Springfield and died at Cox Hospital in December of 1980. *Submitted by Charles Loyd Summers*

SUNSET SCHOOL – Imagine walking nearly two miles to school on a pair of stilts (two long poles about four feet long with a step nailed about 12 to 18 inches above the ground to place your foot). That's what the kids at Sunset School did several times a year. The boys were so good on them that they even jumped ditches, still keeping the stilts on. The girls weren't quite so proficient.

Sunset was a one-room schoolhouse about four miles east of Highway 13 on Y Highway, though at the time it was just a dirt road. The upper classmates helped the first, second and third graders with their lessons every day. They studied and played together whether it was "Bear Around the Corner," "Ante Over," "Jack, May I Cross Your Bridge?" or jump rope, everyone participated, even Teacher. Sometimes the children climbed over the fence into the woods and held a sapling tree down while another one climbed out onto the limbs, then let loose and whanged you back and forth while the rider rocked to keep it in motion as long as possible. Man, the fun you could have if you had an imagination!

The last Friday afternoon of the month was reserved for competition such as spelling bees, geography, arithmetic and songs. The older students who had already graduated eighth grade would come and participate as well as any parent who could get away to come have fun and visit. Some of the schoolmates were Altic, Ballinger, Brown, Combs, Laster, Fisher, Kibby, Overcash, Russell, Steinshouer and Worthy.

In the fall there was a pie supper when the girls brought a pie done up in the fanciest wrapping, hoping a boy she liked would bid on her pie, then they could sit together and eat it, providing he was the highest bidder. It was not uncommon for a pie to bring $20. The money went toward improvements for the school.

About a week before Christmas, four or five older kids were allowed to go out into the woods to choose a tree for trimming. What an honor! All the children made fancy decorations (such as you could make with paper, crayons and paste). These were proudly hung onto the tree.

There was always a pageant about the Christmas Story with singing and special pieces by each child, then at the end of the program every child

Front left – right: Coneta Fisher – Ruth Overcash – Anges White – Mozel Watson – Ethel Mae White – Dora Ella Worthey – June Fisher – Carl Fisher. 2nd row left – right: Teacher Mary Ellen Whitman – Betty Atwood – Hazel Atwood – Kenneth Fisher – Robert Ladd – Lois Ballinger – Mavis Ballinger – Bonnie Whorthey. Back left – right: George Watson – Floyd White – Willie White – Lee Ballinger – Ernest Worthey – Keith Fisher.

was given a sack of candy, apple and orange. Simple things, yes, but times were simple back then.

During WWII every child was urged to gather as much scrap metal, iron, tin or rubber as they could find to be used in the war effort. If you had a family member in service, you probably hung a sing in the window, "Brother in Service" or "Son in Service" or "Remember Pearl Harbor." Pearl wasn't spelled out, it was just half of a small pearl glued to the sign. So much patriotism back then, but our boys were fighting for our freedom, and everyone was so proud of them.

The one-room schools were disbanded about 1951, so the kids loaded up on the bus and went to Pleasant Hope where they made more friends. The years spent in the one-room schoolhouse were some of the happiest of all. Today many still correspond with their classmates though they live thousands of miles apart. So strong was that bond of friendship, because you had spent eight years together in one small room. *Submitted by Ruth Ella Overcash Lane*

SWIHART – By 1970 after 20 years of hectic life in southern California, Sam Swihart and his wife, Beverly, decided to make the move to a quieter, slower-paced area where they could devote more time to their 10 children. Sam was in the contracting business; most of his jobs were out of state. This allowed him to make his base of operations anywhere in the country. In 1971, after more than a year search, realtor Gene Hutcheson took the couple out to a small farm in Polk Town only a few miles north of Bolivar; as far as Beverly was concerned, it was love at first sight.

The farm was the site of an old grain mill, which had been converted to a tomato canning factory in the 1940s during WWII. Charles and Emma Mathews, along with Charles's parents, had built the house originally and raised their family there. Now, only 80-year-old Emma remained and she was pleased that the house would again hear the shouts and laughter of small children. The Polk School was across the road, but the seven Swihart children still in school were saddened to find out that it would close before they would have a chance to attend. The children still at home would finish school in the Bolivar schools.

The old farm house had no indoor plumbing, very little electricity, no insulation, no air conditioning, and only a small oil stove for heat. Needless to say, there were a few adjustments to make. Nonetheless, the kids loved the farm. Sam and Bev descended upon the Extension office with every problem or question about farming or animal raising that came up. They soon were calling the Swiharts by their first names and were a great help.

In the 18 years the family lived there, they and their children developed friends and memories they would cherish the rest of their lives. Sam recalls they even provided some entertainment for the neighbors as well while they were in the learning process. In one instance when he plowed a two-acre garden across the furrows for lack of a disk or harrow, and looking up from the tractor he noticed six or more pick-up trucks stopped on D Highway watching him bounce up and down off the tractor seat. The newly erected outhouse with the large brightly painted flowers on the side got some attention, too.

All of the Swihart children are grown now and most have moved out of Polk County; all are married and have provided Sam and Bev with 32 grandchildren and nine great-grandchildren at last count.

Sam and Beverly still reside in Polk County; however, they have built a much smaller home on a couple acres on Highway B, five miles north

of Bolivar.

Beverly still works as an aerobics instructor at Citizens Memorial Hospital. When Sam retired, a friend asked, "Where are you going to go to retire?" "Why would I go anywhere," Sam replied, "I already live in the greatest area in the country!"

Once in a while, the whole family still gets together, and it is never very long till the conversation turns to the old farm house at Polk Town and all the happy years spent there......and a unanimous thanks to God for leading them to Polk County, MO. *Submitted by Sam Swihart*

TAFT – Lillie and George Taft were loving par-

Lillie Loretta Eagon and George Kirk Taft were married on Dec. 28, 1904 in Halfway, MO

ents to William Kirk Taft, Marjory Juliette Taft Jones and Amy Belle Taft Fish. Lillie taught school in Polk County for two years and Marjory taught at the Brush Creek School.

In later years they lived on a 40-acre farm three miles south of Halfway. Lillie was an excellent cook and baked wonderful homemade bread in her wood cookstove. The grandchildren still remember the protective beekeeper suit George used to gather honey during a time he had beehives.

William ("Willie" as a child, later "Bill") told about the time that he saw a car for the first time. He was living about a mile west of Halfway and was walking to Sunday school at the Halfway Christian Church. Sherman Goings came by in a Model T won in a Caper's Weekly contest. It frightened William so much that he crawled under the fence and started to cross the field. Sherman called to him, asking him to ride along to church.

William remembered seeing cattle herded from Halfway to Bolivar and seeing horsedrawn hearses going to Halfway for funerals. He remembered his relatives hiring a music teacher for weekly group music lessons. George played the fiddle. His Aunt Amy Eagon played the piano and organ at church. William learned to play the violin and harmonica.

George's parents were James Madison Taft and Mary Jane Bell Taft, who came to Halfway by way of Wisconsin and North Dakota. They had a mill and lived in a house standing on the north side of the road in Halfway. George's brothers were Wills, who moved to California and Willie who died at 18.

Lillie's parents were John T. and Mary Ann Eagon. Other siblings were May Glover, Jesse Eagon, Julia Larimore, Joseph Eagon, Nellie Larimore and Lenora, who died in infancy. John T. was a Polk County sheriff who died in 1913.

John T. Eagon's parents were Jesse W. Eagon and Elizabeth A. John T.'s siblings were Mary C. (Lane), Sarah M., James W. (Withrow), Cinthia (Gregg), Francis and Rebecca (Campbell).

Jesse W. Eagon's (born 1835) father was Jesse Eagon (born 1801). Jesse W.'s siblings were Hannah (William H. Messer), Rebecca, Barnard, Mary, John M. and James L.

Mary Ann Eagon was the daughter of Samuel Hadlock, also a sheriff (born 1838, died 1899) and Juliette Savage (born 1839, died 1938). Other children were Belle A., wife of J. W. Messer and Ella L., wife of J. L. Eagon. Samuel and Juliette Hadlock are buried in the Reed Cemetery near George and Lillie Taft. John T. Eagon is nearby.

Lillie's great-grandfather was Samuel Hardin Hadlock (born Feb. 19, 1801 in New York) who came with his wife, Mary Ann Eliza Owen (born March 10, 1807 in Connecticut) and father David Hadlock (born 1767 in New York). Their children were George, Green, Benjamin, Mary Ann, Samuel, Uodusky, Zachary and John Hardin. These Hadlocks are mostly buried in the old Hadlock Cemetery on the old Hadlock home place south of Bolivar. *Submitted by Rosemary Lillian Taft McLaren*

THIESSEN – Gerald Robert Thiessen was the son of William Lewis Thiessen and Martha Margaret Shepherd. He came with his family to the Morrisville area in Polk County in the spring of 1952 from Omaha, NE. His parents were married Sept. 23, 1939 in Gleenwood, IA. They were the parents of four children: Ernest Lewis, Verna Elaine, Gerald Robert and DeElda Fay.

William Thiessen was the son of Lewis August Thiessen, born March 4, 1880 in Millard, NE and Phoebe Williams, born Jan. 8, 1880. William told stories of his grandparents John Detlaf Thiessen and Christiana (Tidke) Thiessen arriving from Germany in 1865. They lived and farmed in Nebraska for 34 years and then moved to Calgary, Alberta, Canada. They moved their household goods, farm machinery and horses by train. William's father, Lewis, stayed with the horses in the boxcar, taking one week to make the trip. After several years in Canada, they moved back to Omaha, NE, leaving one son, Will, behind in Canada.

A Military Ball, Captain and Mrs. Gerald R. Thiessen

Martha Margaret Shepherd was born in Sarpy County, NE. She was the daughter of Ernest Vaughn Shepherd and Cora Alta Petty. She is a direct descendant of William Shepherd, who died around 1810, and Rebecca Moxley. Rebecca Moxley Shepherd was a descendant of William Moxley, who was born in England around 1610 and died in Westmoreland County, VA in 1668.

Gerald worked for Marjorie and Elmer "Smitty" Smith from the time he was 11 years old. He graduated from Marion C. Early High School in 1964. His academic background includes a bachelor's degree in chemical engineering and a master's degree in engineering management from the University of Missouri at Rolla. He also studied law at George Washington University in Washington, DC. He graduated from the Armed Forces Staff College and has completed the Advanced Operational Studies Fellowship, a War College program, at the School of Advanced Military Studies, Fort Leavenworth, KS. He is a registered professional engineer in the state of Virginia.

Col. Thiessen completed a career of more than 27 years in the US Army. His last assignment was as the Garrison Commander at Ft. Leonard Wood, where he was responsible for management of the installation. His military assignments also include two tours with the Third Engineer Battalion of the 24th Infantry Division, Fort Stewart, GA, where he served as commander, executive officer and assistant division engineer. Col. Thiessen was the deputy district commander of the St. Louis District of the US Army Corps of Engineers. He also served in staff assignments as chief of the Forces and Arms Control Division; plans and policy directorate of the US European Command in Stuttgart, Germany; installation engineer with the Defense construction Supply Center, Columbus, OH; and as the plans and programs officer with the Military Assistance Advisory Group-Iran in Teheran, Iran. He has served as an instructor at the US Army Engineer School, when it was located at Fort Belvior, VA and on the faculty of the School of Advanced Military Studies, Ft. Leavenworth, KS. He served in numerous unit officer troop assignments in Vietnam; Fort Leonard Wood, MO; and Fort Meade, MD.

Among his military awards are the Bronze Star Medal, The Legion of Merit, The Defense Superior Service Medal, the Defense Meritorious Service Medal, the Meritorious Service Medal (six awards) and the Army Commendation Medal (two awards).

He is married to the former Christine Fisher of Sunset. Christine attended Armstrong State University and is a retired registered nurse. Their principal hobby is landscape gardening on the family farm, where they returned after completion of his military career. They have three children: Eric, who attended Georgia Institute of Technology and lives in Atlanta; Nancy, who attended the University of Missouri and is an accountant in Overland Park, KS; and Heather, who attended the University of Missouri and is currently working on a master's degree in anesthesiology at St. John's Hospital and Southwest Missouri State University. *Submitted by Heather Anne Thiessen*

TINSLEY – In the 1600s, land is Virginia was considered the property of England. The king sent governors to distribute land to newcomers and to oversee the settlers. One of those newcomers was our ancestor, Thomas Tinsley (circa 1618-circa 1702), who arrived in Jamestown, VA in 1638. The crown of England made a land grant for each person the planters transported from England. Twelve years after his arrival, Thomas was able to finish transportation for six new immigrants and was granted his first 300 acres.

Thomas Tinsley built his home, Totopotomoi, 12 miles north of the present Richmond, VA. Thomas took part in Bacon's Rebellion in 1676, which was the beginning of the long struggle for American independence.

As was the custom, the eldest son, Thomas II (circa 1640- February 1716) received most of his father's holdings. Thomas II married Sarah Jackson (1665-March 9, 1744). Philip, one of their seven children, was arrested in 1768 for "permitting unauthorized divine services in his home." Of course, in those days there was no "Bill of Rights" that gave people freedom to worship as they chose, and everyone was expected to attend the parish church, which was Anglican.

With his wife, Margaret Vawter (1696-1764), Thomas III (1684-July 16, 1764) had seven children, but his three daughters are not named in his will. His fourth son, Joshua (1730-June 1815) was named executor of his will, along with his mother.

Joshua's son, William (Nov. 16, 1763-Feb. 28, 1835) served in the Revolutionary War. Fifty-four years later, William applied for a pension, made possible for veterans of the Revolutionary War by an act of Congress in 1832. William had moved to Kentucky in 1796. William and wife Sarah Samuel (1772-1863) had 10 children. In his 1835 will, after bequeathing everything to Sarah for her remaining days, he first mentions his youngest daughter and then equally divides his estate among his 10 children. After Sarah paid the bills, she received $389.55 and signed for it with an "X" as her mark.

Andrew J., Charles C., Louis A. and Wayne Tinsley, four generations, 1938

William's son, Archibald (born Nov. 16, 1799) was the first Tinsley of our line to be born outside of Virginia. He was born in Shelby County, KY and on April 3, 1822, he married Polly Yeats (born 1805). They were the parents of Jeptha Dudley Tinsley (May 1, 1831-July 23, 1912). Jeptha left Kentucky for Illinois at the age of 19, and on Dec. 24, 1858, he married Catherine Elizabeth Hoagland (Feb. 4, 1842- Jan. 26, 1910). They moved to Hickory County, MO in 1870 and then to Flemington, MO in 1903. Uncle Jep's obituary begins: "One more of our good old pioneers has passed away. The gate of heaven have swung wide to receive another saint if the doctrine they teach us be true."

Jeptha and Catherine's first child of 10 was An-

Back row: June, Wayne and Joyce; Front row: Lero and Louis; 1955

drew Jefferson Tinsley (Nov. 21, 1859-Oct. 30, 1947). Andrew married Mary Catherine Sapp (Sept. 28, 1862-Feb. 3, 1919) on Feb. 12, 1882, and their oldest surviving child was Charles Cleveland Tinsley (Jan. 28, 1855-Nov. 22, 1955). Charles married Florence Wilson (Oct. 19, 1886-Nov. 13, 1920), and their oldest child was Louis Andrew Tinsley (May 11, 1910-Nov. 21, 1957).

Louis married Lero Robertson (born Jan. 12, 1915) on Dec. 23, 1933 and they had three children: Wayne (born June 26, 1935); June (born June 30, 1937); and Joyce (born April 14, 1941) who are the 11th generation of Tinsleys in America. Wayne's son, Jeff (born July 5, 1962) has two young sons, Jeremy (born Oct. 22, 1990) and Jesse (born Feb. 20, 1993), who carry the name into the 13th generation of our Tinsley line. *Submitted by Wayne Tinsley*

TITUS – Titus Syrach DeVries, born 1630 in Vires Drenthe, Holland, died Jan. 26, 1668, in Flatbush, Kings, NY, married Jannetje Teunis Nyssen on March 7, 1659; Teunis Titus, born 1665 in Flatbush, died Mansfield Square, Burlington, NY, married Mary Barre, Dec. 20, 1699, in New York. Their son Francis, born about 1712, died May 14, 1784 in Middleton, Buck, PA, married Mary Clark June 19, 1734 in New Jersey. She died before June 30, 1783 in Buck County, PA. They owned 175 acres in Falls Township, Buck, PA. Sons Francis Jr., John, Samuel and Timothy owned 856 acres. Samuel born 1745, died December 1819 in Loudoun County, VA, married Deborah Feathers, Nov. 1, 1770, in Reformed Dutch Church Centerville, Buck, PA. Their son Tunis, born about 1781 in Plumstead Township, Buck, PA, died 1848, Goresville, Loudoun, VA, married Sarah Purdam, Aug. 15, 1803 in Loudoun County, VA. Their son, Jeremiah, born Sept. 10, 1810, died 1896 Coles County, IL, married Susanah Goodhart Oct. 1, 1838 in Loudoun, VA, born Jan. 14, 1817, died Jan. 15, 1886. Their four children: James Washington, born Feb. 22, 1839 at Leesburg, Loudoun, VA, died June 2, 1933 in Lowry City, St. Clair, MO; siblings Jonas, Jack and Matilda Roberts. James left Virginia about 1854 for Ohio, lived in Oakland, IL, married Caroline Roberts, born April 27, 1842, died March 15, 1904, daughter of Jacob and Sara Hanks Roberts. After her death he married her sister Sara Jane. He served with the Illinois Volunteers Company H, Regiment 79 during the Civil War and was discharged on Dec. 15, 1864 due to multiple wounds he received in the Battle of Murfreesboro, TN. He was imprisoned twice, once in Libby Prison in Richmond, VA, where he almost starved to death before becoming an exchange prisoner. He gave the Southern guard the Masonic sign and then was nursed back to health. James and Caroline had 10 children: William Devaul, born Nov. 26, 1860, died Jan. 3, 1861 in Ohio; Louesta Eveline, born Jan. 15, 1862, died Nov. 20, 1936; Martha Allice, born Jan. 18, 1866, died April 24, 1954; Lidia Adaline, born March 20, 1868, died Aug. 30, 1963; Thomas Jeremiah, born July 10, 1870, died July 14, 1887; Sara Jane, born July 18, 1873, died Feb. 17, 1874; James Francis, born Feb. 28, 1875, died July 8, 1887; John Henry, born Nov. 19, 1877, died June 15, 1966; Ira Newton, born April 11, 1881, died April 11, 1893; and Myrtle Ellen, born July 14, 1884, died July 1, 1886.

Neva's grandfather, John Henry, married Orah Rosamond Huebner on Dec. 25, 1898 in Lowry City, St. Clair, MO, daughter of Charles and Jennie Crissman, born Jan. 24, 1874, died March 1, 1919. Their children: John Charles, born July 12, 1900, died Feb. 14, 1982; Mary Bertha, born May 26, 1902, died Jan. 27, 1987; Ruth Celestia, born Feb. 24, 1904, died Sept. 24, 1944; Jewell Huebner, born Dec. 12, 1908, died Oct. 13, 1972; Myrtle Ottilla, born May 3, 1912, died Sept. 17, 1981; James Harold, born Nov. 2, 1914, died Nov. 23, 1995; and Rosa Louise, born March 1, 1919, died April 11, 1995.

Neva's father, John Charles, married Neva Mae Blackburn on Aug. 12, 1930, born March 12, 1911, in Mabel, Daviess County, MO. He served in the Navy aboard the *USS Wood* ship. He came to Polk County in the late 1920s and was employed by the Ozark Utilities Company as an electrician. He later started his own business and remained quite active in the operation of it until about 1976. They had one daughter, Neva Charlene, born Aug. 14, 1934 in Bolivar, Polk County, MO, who married Arthur Stewart Gardner on Feb. 1, 1953, born Feb. 27, 1931, died May 15, 1980 in Bolivar, Polk County, MO. They had one son, John Kemp, born Aug. 13, 1968. *Submitted by Neva C. Gardner*

TOOMBS – Isaac Marion Toombs was born Aug. 2, 1889 in Long Lane, MO. His father was James

Back: Loretta, Clyde, Connie, Delbert, Isaac holding Robert; Front: Leroy and Ralph (seated), 1932 Fayetteville, AR

Isaac Toombs of Bedford County, TN (June 28, 1853-Feb. 15, 1913). His mother was Nancy Elisabeth Rose Toombs of Grove County, KY (March 12, 1851-May 29, 1943). Isaac had seven brothers and one sister, all born in Long Lane, MO: William Thomas Toombs (Jan. 5, 1875-June 29, 1877), Mary Elisabeth Toombs (Nov. 16, 1876-Jan. 3, 1877), George Canada Toombs (Dec. 18, 1879-April 4, 1883), Joseph Delbert Toombs (May 22, 1882-Jan. 24, 1883), Henry Elbert Toombs (May 22, 1832-May 18, 1966), Charles Elmer Toombs (July 3, 1884-June 14, 1979), Jacob Alvin Toombs (July 17, 1887-March 22, 1965) and John S. Toombs (April 4, 1892-1978). Isaac married Constance May Hardy (Sept. 12, 1892 in Ada, KS- Nov. 23, 1977) on June 25, 1913 in Long Lane, MO. Connie was the daughter of William Henry Hardy (July 7, 1847, Canada-Jan. 6, 1923, Los Angeles County, CA) and Elisabeth Owen Hardy (Aug. 14, 1853-Nov. 22, 1935, Los Angeles County, CA). She had four brothers and three sisters: Pearlie Hardy (Nov. 1, 1874, Milford, NE- Oct. 26, 1953), Willard Stanley Hardy (Dec. 26, 1876, Milford, NE-April 2, 1964), Leslie Owen Hardy (Nov. 25, 1878, Milford, NE-July 11, 1895), Florence Edna Hardy (April 28, 1881, Milford, NE- Oct. 20, 1963), John Myron Hardy (April 15, 1885, Ada, KS-Jan. 13, 1972), Roy Elmer Hardy (Sept. 20, 1895, Clayton, MO-Jan. 7, 1981).

Around 1913, Isaac and Connie headed to New Mexico to homestead 360 acres of land. Clyde Buford Toombs was born July 29, 1914, in Nobe, NM (February 1999, Pasadena, TX); Loretta Pearl Toombs, April 11, 1917, Nobe, NM; Leroy Alvin Toombs, July 3, 1919, Nobe, NM. Isaac, Connie and the three children moved to Springdale, AR in 1919 for a short time. Then they moved to Watts, CA in 1920 where Delbert William Toombs (Dec. 27, 1921) and Ralph G. Toombs (Oct. 24, 1925) were born. After leaving California in 1928, the family moved to a farm in Greeland, AR where Robert Lee Toombs (Nov. 10, 1931) and a baby girl, who died at birth in 1934, were born. In 1936, the family moved to Polk County on a farm near Aldrich, MO. Through all the moves, Isaac's occupation was farming, working in orchards and raising cattle and other livestock on the land.

Of the six children, only one remains in Polk County today. Ralph Toombs and his wife, Jo, purchased the Aldrich farm, 120 acres, from Isaac and Connie in 1964. Isaac and Connie retired in Holden, MO in 1964. Connie died Nov. 23, 1977 in Warrensburg, MO and Isaac died Sept. 3, 1987 in Bolivar, MO. Both Isaac and Connie were buried at the Pleasant Ridge Cemetery in Polk County.

One of the most noted events that the Toombs family wants to share with others is the tradition of the "Easter picnic," also known as the "Toombs Spring." The neighbors in the Pleasant Ridge area used to get together for wiener roast some time in the spring each year. For a few years in the beginning it was held at different neighboring farms. After that it was moved permanently to the large spring north of the Toombs' home, thus the name "Toombs Spring." Isaac and Connie Toombs started this tradition after the depression years and carried it on for a good 20 years. In 1964 when Ralph and Jo Toombs purchased the farm, they also took over the duty of continuing the tradition. It became known as the "Easter picnic" and was held on Saturday night before Easter. The event consisted of a bonfire, a wiener roast and all the fixings. The neighbors shared in a lot of good times, good food and good memories. As the families grew and spread out, the crowds became larger and depending on the weather, there would be as many as 50-75 people attending. Due to health reasons, the tradition had to be discontinued around 1980. *Submitted by Gene Toombs*

TOOMBS – Ralph G. Toombs, born Oct. 24, 1925 in Watts, CA, is the son of Isaac and Connie Toombs. (See family history of Isaac Toombs). Ralph attended Pleasant Ridge School and Aldrich High School. After graduation, he was drafted in the Army, and he fought in WWII (Nov. 25, 1944-Aug. 3, 1946). He is married to Mary Joan "Jo" Scheel.

Jo was born Dec. 30, 1929 in Humbolt, IA. She is the daughter of Vernon Alva Scheel (Aug. 22, 1898, Iowa- died Aug. 24, 1967, Branson, MO) and Erma Marie Bryan Scheel (Sept. 23, 1902, Iowa- March 9, 1998, Springfield, MO). Jo had two sisters: Dorothy Maxine Scheel Day (Feb. 24, 1926, Humbolt, IA- July 9, 1996, Springfield, MO) and Verna Lee Scheel Leever (Sept. 26, 1928, Humbolt, IA) of Elwood, IN. Jo and her family moved from Humbolt, IA to Springfield, MO in 1935. They lived there for about two years, then moved to Polk County south of Bolivar for three years. In January 1940, Vernon and Erma Scheel purchased the farm known as the Dr. Andy Baker Place, located between Aldrich and Eudora on Highway 123. The Scheel family and Erma's parents, Walter Emmet Bryan (1878, Iowa-1945, Aldrich, MO) and Gertrude Lee Parkhurst Bryan (1880, Iowa- 1956, Springfield, MO), resided on the farm outside Aldrich until 1963. Jo and her sisters attended Pleasant Ridge School and high school at Morrisville, MO.

The Scheel and Toombs families were neighbors; consequently Ralph Toombs and Jo Scheel came to know each other. Upon Ralph's return from the service in 1946, they became engaged and married May 14, 1948 in Aldrich. After their wedding, Ralph and Jo lived in Corpus Christi, TX for 12 years. During this time Ralph was employed by Bell Telephone and Sinclair Refinery. Raymond Glen Toombs was born Sept. 22, 1954 in Corpus Christi, TX. In June 1960, the Toombs family returned to Polk County. Gene Allen Toombs was born Jan. 16, 1963 in Springfield, MO. In 1964, Ralph and Jo purchased the farm belonging to Ralph's parents (Isaac and Connie Toombs) who had lived there since 1936. The farm consisted of 120 acres southeast of the Pleasant Ridge Cemetery. Ralph worked as maintenance supervisor for Hoffman-Taff Chemical Company, which later became Syntex Agri-Business, for 30 years and then retired to work on the farm and raise cattle.

Glen, Gene, Ralph and Jo Toombs, August 1970

Glen Toombs married Wilma Rotramel on July 4, 1975 in Bolivar, MO. They reside in Fair Play, MO and have two sons, Travis Glen Toombs, March 6, 1977 and Chad Anthony Toombs, May 11, 1979.

Gene Toombs married Dr. Franka Figari on Aug. 31, 1997 in Poteau, OK. They reside outside Fair Play, MO and have two sons, Jesse Allen Toombs, April 30, 1999 and Jacob Dwayne Toombs, Oct. 4, 2001. *Submitted by Ralph Toombs*

TRIMBLE – Walter Trimble was born in Scotland about 1700 and came to America in 1730. In 1746, he was living in Augusta County, VA. His will was signed and witnessed on May 26, 1791 in Green County, TN. His wife was Rosanna Atten; her date of birth is not known. She died Feb. 28, 1801 in Washington County, TN.

Major William Trimble was born about 1736 in Virginia and he died Nov. 4, 1831. He married Susannah Clarke about 1763. Their children are James (1744-1847) married Harriett Triplett; William Clark; Robert (1788-1852), married Susan Triplett; and Walter, born 1791 in Fleming County, KY, died in 1848 in Hempstead, AR.

William Clark Trimble was born in 1781 in Washington County, NC. He died in 1866 in Dallas County, TX. He married Phoebe Smith in 1813, Fleming County, KY. Children: Green Clark; Walter Ulyssiss (1816-1873); Thomas Dudley (1817-1899); Allen Smith (1819-1852); Mary Ann; William A.; Andrew Jackson (1828-1892); Nelson Scott (1830-). William married Bethaney Hayworth in Edgar County, IL.

Green Clark Trimble was born Sept. 15, 1813 in Fleming County, KY. He died Sept. 7, 1896 at Shady Grove. He married Sarah A. Roger, daughter of Josiah and Sarah Rogers, on May 1, 1833 in Edgar County, IL. Sarah was born Nov. 30, 1816 in New York. She died May 24, 1896 at Shady Grove. Both are buried at the Trimble Cemetery. Children: Jefferson; Aceneth; Nancy Ellen; Josiah; Angeline; Polly Anne, born in Edgar County, IL; William Hardin; Winfield Scott; Johnathan James and George Washington, born in Lawrence County, MO. Green Clark's father, William C. Trimble, and several of his children left Edgar County, IL and settled near Dallas, TX. It is likely that Green Clark, his brother, Thomas Dudley and their families decided to stop near Round Grove, Lawrence County, MO to make their home. Green Clark ran an inn near Red Oak in Lawrence County at one time. Later Green, Sarah, Johnathan and William Hardin and family moved to Polk County.

William Hardin Trimble was born April 6, 1850 in Lawrence County, MO and died on Aug. 14, 1923 near the community of Shady Grove. He married Nancy Elizabeth "Lizzie" Blackburn in Lawrence County on June 23, 1871. Lizzie was a daughter of William and Sabra (Watson) Blackburn who had moved to Lawrence County about 1861 from Washington County, AR, where William had been in the tanning and lumber business. (Descendants still have the record book kept by William Blackburn where he made the first entry on Dec. 28, 1861.) Lizzie was born Aug. 9, 1848 and died Feb. 11, 1920 at Shady Grove. Both are buried at the Trimble Cemetery. Children born to this union are Ida Cordela, married Andy Hays; Charles Alva (1874-1874); Gilbert Elbert, married Lillie Mae Sawyer; Mary Ella, married Buell Wesley Griffin (see Griffin family); Albert, married first, Belle Adams and second, Eula Z. Fox; Clara Alta, married Andrew J. Griffin, and Eugene (1886-1892).

Ida C. Trimble was born Dec. 6, 1871 in Lawrence County, MO. She died May 16, 1958 near Fair Play. She married Andrew A. Hays on March 9, 1898. Children: Sabra, Clara, Ira Eugene, Leona Irene and Howard Hadley.

Gilbert E. Trimble was born March 14, 1876 and died Oct. 23, 1946. He married Lillie Sawyer on Oct. 14, 1909. Children: Irene Juanita, Yuma Lee and Nancy Elizabeth.

Trimble Cemetery is located southwest of Fair Play on land once owned by the Trimble family. *Submitted by Shelly McKay Bobbitt*

TROST – Johann Melchoir Trost was born May 25, 1824 in Frickenhausen Noerdlinger, Kingdom of Weiertlemberg in Germany. He was granted citizenship June 20, 1862 in Cincinnati, OH, under the name John Trost.

He was married to Rosina Catharina Gehring Sept. 9, 1852 in Philadelphia, PA by Lutheran Minister G. A. Reichert. She was born June 24, 1826 in Lvensback, Gerabornn, Germany. She came to America March 18, 1851 to visit relatives.

Their children were Fredrick, John Gotleib, Edward, August and a daughter. They died when the children were young, and the baby daughter was adopted. John and a brother (possibly Edward) were apprenticed to learn a trade. They ran away, coming to Missouri. Edward and John were going to Kansas to homestead land. Edward accidentally killed himself stepping down from a wagon with a loaded shotgun. John buried him and returned to Missouri.

John Gottleib married Elizabeth Ann Dotson (Dodson) on Nov. 28, 1886. She was known as Betsy until moving to California and she became Betty. Their children are Fred Alexander, Sarah May, Rose Etta, John Edward, William Thomas, Lucy Delilah, Elbert James and George W. They all lived in Polk County part of the time.

Most of the Trosts moved to California. Three of the young men strung power lines. The three brothers worked three levels of the power pole- top, middle and bottom. Fred began a house moving business, moving houses, apartment buildings and churches. Brothers and his children helped in this business. Lucy married first in Polk County. She left with her brothers and mother to move to California. Etta married Bruce Newland and lived in Polk County the rest of her life on a farm adjoining her parents' farm. Kathy's Grandma May married Sherman Bloomer and lived in Polk and Dade Counties the rest of her life.

Many of the Trosts were veterans. Their names are listed on the monument in the courthouse lawn of Polk County.

Kathy knows little about the elder Trosts. Grandma May did not talk about her dad much. He was killed by lightning Aug. 14, 1920 near Eudora and is buried at Pleasant Ridge near the flagpole.

The Trosts lived on a farm not many miles from the Bloomer farm. Prior to May's marriage, they moved for a short time back to Kansas. May was born in Kingham, KS.

May was unable to attend many years of school. She had to go to work at age 13. She did housework until her marriage to Sherman Bloomer. *Submitted by Kathy Bloomer*

TUCK – An indentation in the back step of Nancy's house is the result of six generations of Tucks stepping out their back door. The rock step was moved from the house Nancy's great-great-great-grandfather built on his farm near Brighton, to the house Nancy's grandparents built, where Nancy now lives, on the same 600 acres that the Tucks originally inhabited.

Nancy's family has resided in Polk County since 1838, when her great-great-great-grandfa-

Gus Tuck, Morris Tuck and Herbert Tuck

ther, Joseph, and his wife, Elizabeth Bond Tuck, traveled by wagon from Blount County, TN to near Brighton. Joseph and his son, Joseph Benjamin, raised and sold mules to the US Army. The family still has tools they used to render lard, bake in the fireplace, brand cattle, shoe mules and horses, and repair the family shoes that stepped out the back door onto the rock step.

Joseph Benjamin was the only child who remained on the farm in Polk County. Joseph married a neighbor, Emma Eugenia Mitchell, daughter of Cynthia Harris and Colonel Bill Mitchell. Joseph and Emma had three sons, Herbert Cloud, Morris Benson and Augustus Cary.

Morris left Polk County to attend the St. Louis School of Pharmacy where he graduated in 1916. After serving in France during WWI, he ran Tuck Drugs in Ada, OK. Gus remained on the family farm, where he raised Tennessee Walking horses and registered Hereford cattle until his death.

Nancy's grandfather, Herbert, traveled to Toronto, Canada to attend veterinary college. He went on to work for the Missouri Department of Health, working to prevent the spread of tick fever from Texas cattle crossing into southern Missouri. Herbert "Doc" Tuck married Francis Marie Graves and had three children, Joseph Benjamin, Elizabeth and Eugenia. "Doc" Tuck continued to work for the state of Missouri as deputy state veterinarian in Jefferson City. Eventually, Herbert, Marie and their three children returned to the family farm in Brighton where he continued to work as a veterinarian. He finished his career working with Tuck, Gray and Sprague at the Union Stockyards in Springfield.

Nancy's father, Joseph Benjamin Tuck, received his education from Southwest Baptist College, Southwest Missouri State College, Kansas State University and the University of Iowa. He taught at Union University and Marion C. Early and Bolivar High School and operated a dairy farm. He married Rosemary Stratton, and they have two daughters, Elizabeth Ann and Nancy Eileen. Joe and Rosemary still live on the family farm.

Nancy has the privilege of living on the farm in the house that "Doc" and Marie built. Nancy mar-

Mules on the Tuck farm in Brighton

ried Dan Ellis and has two children, Nathaniel Benjamin and Alexandra Marie. Nancy was the last of this line of the family to bear the name Tuck and although the name does not continue, the love of the land does. Her family has had a long connection to Polk County. She hopes it will continue as descendants of Joseph Tuck reside on the farm and step into the world from the rock step sitting at the backdoor. *Submitted by Nancy Ellis*

TUTER – Caption for the Wednesday, March 30, 1994 *Bolivar Herald-Free Press* Newspaper, page 3-B: "The family of Raymond Tuter of Bolivar, who died recently, gathered at the log cabin located next to the North Ward Museum on March 22. Raymond had lived in this cabin as a boy, and two of his siblings, who are in the picture, Fern (Tuter) Freeman and Kenneth Tuter, were born there in 1919 and 1922, respectively. Solomon and Edna Tuter, their parents, moved their family into the cabin in about 1915. Solomon drove a buggy around the county selling McConnell products. He was an 'old-time medicine man,' Kenneth said. The cabin was located on a farm four miles west of Missouri, 13 and one miles south of Route T before it was donated to the Polk County Historical Society and moved to its present location in the late 1970s. Raymond's wife, Hildred, still lives in Bolivar." *Submitted by Fern Hood Freeman*

TYGART – The story of the Tygart-Griffin family

Tuter family

legacy in Polk County, MO begins with James Coy Tygart of Georgia, son of John Tygart and Eve Huett Tygart who were from South Carolina. James Coy and his parents resided in McLemore's Cove in Walker County, all having been previously living in Tennessee at one time or the other as this area lies close to the borders of three adjoining states in and around the high terrain country of Walden's Ridge and Lookout Mountain rising above the Tennessee River and Chickamauga River Valleys. James Coy married Sarah Elizabeth Griffin circa 1838 in Georgia, soon moving to Marion County, TN. Later, James Coy and his family would move back to Walker County before moving on to Arkansas, arriving there by late 1849 or early 1850, first settling in Johnson County. From here, they moved to Benton County as land records indicate James Coy began to purchase several parcels of land in 1854 in and around Apple Orchard, later to become the city of Gentry.

By trade, James Coy was farmer and a justice of the peace. Sarah Elizabeth was from Tennessee and was known as "Betsy" when she was young, going also by "Sally" in later years. She was the daughter of Daniel Griffin Sr. and Mary (Aon-ta-ta-quas-ta, her Cherokee name). Daniel Sr.'s mother, Sarah Ocoore, was a full-blooded Cherokee of the Wolf Clan. She married John Griffin, a white trader in the Old Cherokee Nation, who was originally from North Carolina. As of this writing, little is known about James Coy's ethnic make-up other than he was of Irish stock. Betsy's parents were both half-blooded Cherokees. Daniel Sr.'s family of 12 is listed on the 1835 Henderson Roll, but he and his wife never emigrated from Tennessee, as did some family members.

Known children of James Coy and Sarah Elizabeth "Betsy" Griffin Tygart and their marriages are, as follows: Martin "Mart" F., married Mary Jane Lefors; Martha A., married first, David Hall, second, James Madison Perkins; Amanda "Mandy" Jane, married Samuel B. Neil "Neal;" Susan and Jane disappear from the record and may have died on the trail to Missouri; John, became a Civil War casualty; Nathan Nabors, married Mary Jane Cheek; Sarah Ann, married John Wilke Perkins; Joseph J., married Mary Ellen Phipps; Thomas Henry, married Tharby Ann Neil (Thomas was the last child of Sarah Elizabeth Griffin Tygart who, on or after Thomas' birth of Feb. 10, 1858 in Bentonville, AR, died of childbirth complications. No information has been located to date concerning either her burial or gravesite).

Samuel B. and Amanda Jane Tygart Neil circa 1920

Following Sarah "Betsy's" death, the family moved to eastern Dade, western Polk County, just east of Bona during late 1860 or early 1861. Here lived relatives and other allied family members such as the Perkins, Cheeks, Neils, Griffins, et al., who could provide comfort and support during this tumultuous Civil War period. Mandy had become the matriarch of the family, responsible for the remaining children since she was the eldest female still at home. James Coy, Methodist by religion, was a Northern sympathizer caught up in the many conflicts of his day along the troubled Arkansas-Indian Territory borders where he lived. He steadfastly remained behind to look after his property interests after first ensuring his family's safe location to Missouri. However, Betsy's relatives, the Griffins, were mostly Southern sympathizers. Thus, it would appear that these families were very much at odds in their beliefs. Herein is yet another example of how this tragic war tore families apart in these most trying of times as conflicting ideologies would most certainly have severely strained, if not altogether destroyed, such precious family relationships. *Submitted by Dr. Dennis M. Neil*

UNDERWOOD – Abraham Alexander Underwood was a native of Pennsylvania. He married Martha Ellen (Nettinger), who was a native of Ohio. They grew up there, were educated and married in the east and resided there until 1870 when they moved to Bolivar, MO. A. A. Underwood was one of five children. When the Civil War came, he enlisted for service in the 101st Ohio Volunteer Infantry from Bucyrus County, OH. He saw considerable hard service, including the greatest battle of modern times, Gettysburg and he was also in a number of other important engagements. After a gallant service of two and a half years, he was mustered out and honorably discharged.

He studied law and, after coming to Bolivar, built up one of the largest practices in southwest Missouri. He was one of the leaders of the Democratic Party in this section of the state. He was a candidate for Congress in 1876 and, in later years, a judge of the county court.

His family consisted of eight children, namely: Jennie, Gertrude, Mary, Sherwood, Alex, John, Jay and Thomas.

Mr. Underwood died Oct. 23, 1911 and is buried in Greenlawn Cemetery, Springfield, MO.

UNDERWOOD – Enoch Underwood was born on May 19, 1802 in Spartanburg County, SC. His parents were John Underwood and Mary Jane "Jenny" Utley. Enoch married Sarah "Sally" Owings on Dec. 9, 1830. Sally was born on Feb. 22, 1802 in Roane County, TN, the daughter of Edward Owings and Elizabeth Sumpter.

In 1842, Enoch Underwood, his wife Sally Owings and several other relatives left Roane County, TN for Missouri. Enoch, Sally, their five living children and Sally's niece settled in Polk County, while other family members continued to Dade and Cedar Counties. Their first year in Polk County was spent in Bolivar and in 1843 they moved to land at Connel's Prairie, located on the Bolivar Prairie. Enoch and Sally's children were Almirah, Franklin, Laurinda, Polly Ann and William. One additional child died in infancy. As William and Franklin reached their maturity, they settled on land near their parents at the extreme western edge of Polk County, just south of what is now Highway 32 near Fair Play.

William Underwood served in the Union Army in the Eighth Missouri S. M. Cavalry, Company D from 1862 until 1865 under Captain Gravely. He provided his own horse but later made a claim of $125 because his horse ran away due to lack of feed. He also spent part of the war serving in the local facilities that were treating wounded troops.

Franklin Underwood married Nancy J. Wakefield in Polk County on Feb. 11, 1855. They had seven children, but the first three died before reaching school age. The remaining children were C. Fremont, Jerome G., Nancy E. and Lorinda E. Jerome participated in the Oklahoma Run of '89 but returned to Missouri when his wife died in 1890 of typhoid. Jerome's son Claud died in 1918 in Europe during WWI.

William Underwood married Martha P. Fox on March 5, 1866. They were the parents of 14 children, 12 of whom lived to adulthood. The children were Sarah J., Margaret A., Enoch S. (died in infancy), John F., James C., William M., Thomas W., Lizzie M., E. Pearl, G. Nimrod, Dolly A., Robert M. (died in infancy), Grace C. and Benjamin H. For about 40 years, William was connected with the Farmers' Bank at Fair Play, serving much of that time as vice president. He provided most of the money to build the old Christian Church in Fair Play. At one point, William also owned more than 1,000 acres, making him the largest landowner in Polk County at the time. According to family history, his wife Martha was the first in the county to own a sewing machine.

Glenda descends through Ben Underwood, William's youngest. He married Bessie Bell on March 12, 1911, in the middle of a bridge separating Polk and Cedar Counties. They had seven children, who were W. Frank, Fred B., Farrell, J. Gordon, Maxine, Billy P. and Bernard Enoch. Billy and Enoch both served their country during WWII, with Enoch continuing in the Navy through most of the Vietnam War.

Billy, Glenda's father, was a prominent dairyman in the county and he served many years on the Fair Play and Polk County school boards.

All Underwoods buried in Akard Cemetery descend from Enoch Underwood, and most Underwood relatives in Polk County can trace their roots to the original brothers who settled in Polk, Dade and Cedar Counties. No family member lives on the original land bought by Enoch, but the eighth Underwood generation is currently living in Polk County. *Submitted by Glenda Underwood Kooney*

UNDERWOOD – John Jay Underwood, president of Springfield Stone and Fuel Co., was born near Bolivar, Polk County, MO on Aug. 25, 1872. He was the son of Abraham Alexander Underwood and Martha Ellen (Nettinger). The father was a native of Pennsylvania and the mother of Ohio. They moved to Bolivar in 1870. He was one of eight children: Jennie, Gertrude, Mary, Sherwood, Alex, Charles and Thomas.

He was reared in his native community and received his education in the schools of Bolivar. His sisters were graduates of Southwest Baptist College.

In 1911, he was one of the incorporators of Springfield Stone and Fuel Co., a general stone contracting business.

Mr. Underwood was married Sept. 9, 1895 to Carrie Farrer, a daughter of Bucher and Elizabeth (Rafferty). Three children were born to this union, namely, Edna, Earl and Mary.

He was divorced from Carrie and remarried to Alta T. Underwood and resided in Los Angeles, CA until his death on Oct. 13, 1953. He is buried in the Forest Lawn Cemetery, Glendale, CA.

Politically, Mr. Underwood was a Democrat. He was a member of the Christian Church and fraternally belonged to the Benevolent and Protective Order of the Elks, the Knights of Pythias and the Modern Woodmen of America.

UPTON – George Mark Upton is J. C. Mahaffey's maternal great-grandfather. Since the family had

Front row: John F., William, Martha, P. E. "Pearl;" Back row: Benjamin F., Grace, Lizzie M., G. Nimrod, Dolly A., Margaret, Thomas W. and William M. circa 1899

been residents of Bolivar and Polk County for generations, they did not discuss family history very much. What J. C. knows, he remembers hearing during family discussions while growing up. His great-grandfather had five brothers. His father, Joseph, was a Bolivar attorney and district judge.

He was the first to occupy the law offices that are now home to the Douglas, Lynch, Haun, Kirksey and Heidemann law firm.

J. C.'s great-grandfather Mark was born in 1879 and grew up on a large Victorian house on the corner of East Broadway and Albany, right across the street from what is now Butler Funeral Home. The house is still there. J. C.'s great-grandfather continued living in the house with his family. At an early age, he began working in what was later the Rexall City Drug Store on the west side of Bolivar square. The store began business in 1871 and, until it closed more than 100 years later, was the oldest drug store in the state in continues operation. J. C.'s great-grandfather completed pharmacy school in St. Louis and became part owner and operator of the pharmacy, somewhere around 1900. His partner was Louis Howe, who created and first compounded the product now known as TUMS and other well-known drug products of the day such as Nature's Remedy. As the products grew in demand, he sold his share of the pharmacy to J. C.'s great-grandfather and moved to St. Louis to begin production on a much larger scale.

Around 1900, Mark married Corda Martin, a local girl. They raised two daughters, Elisabeth (J. C.'s grandmother) and Wilma. He was very active in the community and at one time served as mayor. J. C.'s mother Betty vividly remembers both the store and the big house that creaked and made strange noises when she slept there in a second-floor bedroom, especially when it was windy. The store was so full of so many items to explore and examine.

When J. C.'s great-grandfather died in 1937 at 57, his grandfather and grandmother moved from El Dorado Springs to Bolivar to take over operation of the pharmacy. J. C.'s mother grew up in that store. Her favorite memory is the fountain-made Cokes. They are a thing of the past, and the movie magazines, also gone. The soda fountain was a social gathering place for all generations. They are also gone. When J. C.'s grandfather (Robert L. Woodfill) died in 1976, his uncle, John Mark Woodfill, took over the store. It was sold in the 1980s. *Submitted by J. C. Mahaffey*

UTLEY – James Utley was born Nov. 18, 1808 in Kentucky. His parents are unknown, but the 1880 census recorded they were both born in Virginia.

James married Mary Elizabeth Acock on Jan. 30, 1832 in Logan County, KY. Elizabeth was born Sept. 20, 1814 in Kentucky. Her parents were John and Elizabeth Simons Acock.

Between 1834 and 1840 James and Elizabeth migrated to Polk County. Many of Elizabeth's family members were in Polk County, including her grandfather Robert Eaton Acock. It is unknown if they arrived together or separately. These families primarily settled around Slagle. James and Mary Elizabeth had the following 10 children: John W., Nov. 31, 1832-Aug. 11, 1901; Elizabeth Jane (Slagle), Nov. 28, 1834-April 27, 1910; Martha A., Sept. 27, 1836-1840; James T., May 9, 1840-Dec. 21, 1856; Benjamin F., July 9, 1842-Nov. 16, 1921; George H., Feb. 20, 1845-unknown; Sarah A., Aug. 23, 1846-Oct. 14, 1880; Mary Margaret (Bradford), about 1849-unknown; David Columbus, April 7, 1853-March 12, 1933; and Theodosia V. (Mitchell), about 1858-unknown.

In 1862 Polk County, in accordance with General Order No. 3, listed the names of men and women reported to be rebels or rebel sympathizers. James Utley's name appeared on this list. In the Polk County Record Book titled *Names of Men arrested and gave Bond for good behavior AD 1861 and 2* (sic), James was again listed. A fellow Polk County resident was arrested on June 14, 1862 for being in the Rebel Army and was fined $3,000. James helped provide security for his bond.

His wife, Mary Elizabeth, died on Sept. 7, 1871 and was buried in the Slagle Cemetery beside two of their children who preceded her in death. Most of the Utley children are buried in this cemetery.

An interesting item was found in the *Register of Dogs for Looney Township in Polk County, Missouri for 1878*. It recorded that James Utley lived in School District 4, Township 32, Range 22 and owned one dog. It is said, "a dog is man's best friend," and James may have agreed. But after remaining a widower for 12 years he married a second time. Possibly he desired a companion of the two-legged variety. On Nov. 1, 1883, he married Edith "Eady" Tindle, the widow of John W. Tindle.

On Jan. 19, 1895, James died at the age of 86 years, 2 months and 1 day. He is buried in the Slagle Cemetery next to Mary Elizabeth. Edith Utley died April 15, 1924 and also is buried in the Slagle Cemetery.

James' probate records are lengthy and indicate he had household goods, farming implements and equipment, livestock and crops as well as land at the time of his death. A few items included in the inventory of his estate were four beehives valued at $1 each, a kettle at 75 cents, and a saddle at 50 cents.

Virginia Stokes, daughter of James Almon and Martha Benge, referred to James as "Jimmy." She also recorded that he was the uncle of her father's first wife, Mary Jane Utley Benge. Virginia remembered the Utley children raised large families in Polk and Greene County, MO. She said, "They have always been fine upright citizens." *Submitted by Cecilia Tarry Sneed*

VAN BUREN – Jean's great-grandparents, Alfred Van Buren and Sally Ann Atkinson Shadwick came

Standing left to right: Charles, William, Frederick, Lewis; seated left to right: Callie, Al Van Buren and Sally Mack Shadwick

to Halfway, MO in 1892 from Moniteau County, MO.

Four children were born in Cole County, MO: Fredrick B. (born 1883), William D. (born 1885), Charles L. (born 1888) and Jean's grandfather, Lewis J. (born 1890). One child was buried at Splice Creek Cemetery and two were born in Polk County, Callie A. (born 1895) and McKinley "Mack" (born 1897).

Fredrick B. married Nina Brock in 1919. Two children were born: Byron (born and died 1921) and Samual A. who married Alice Ross 1946; their children were Fredrick S., Bryan I. and Sherry.

William D. lived in Calgary, Alberta, Canada from the age of 17 and is buried in Canada. He came back to Missouri only once, when Jean's father Warren was very young.

Charles "Harry" married Irene Bartum in 1912. Four children were born: George L. who married Inez P. Morris in 1950, one son, Mark; Ben who married Lillian, two daughters, two sons; Marie G. who married Glenn Ratcliff in 1946, their children were Carol and Reva; Martha I. who married Joseph H. Foust in 1953, their children were Sherry, Brian and Valerie.

Lewis J. married Lora F. Roweton in 1916. Five children were born: Marlyn A. who married Agnes D' Ella in 1946, their children: Susan, Steven "Bud;" Warren E. who married Verian S. Redd in 1940, their children: June, Jean, Francis "Frankie;" Jerry, Ann; Wanda W. who married Oscar Hamilton in 1942, their children: Linda, Joseph "Joe," Oscar L.; Earlyn D. who lived in Kansas City, MO after graduating from high school; Dorothy L. who married Walter Bortka in 1950, their children: Paula, Lynn, Gregory, Gail.

Callie married Curry Marriman in 1924. Mack lived and worked in Montana and Wyoming; he was a conductor on the Northern Pacific out of Livingston, MT.

Alfred Van Buren built their home on Missouri Highway 32 east of Route J and Route FF, but when they grew older they lived in Halfway. Alfred Van Buren's grandfather, Hardy, was born in North Carolina; later the family moved to Tennessee, and Hardy married Catharine Miller in Tennessee. Alfred Van Buren's father, Nelson, was born in Tennessee. Hardy and a brother, John, with their families came to Missouri, settled around California, MO and Nelson married first, Rebecca Cruse and second, Ruth McGinnis. *Submitted by Jean Shadwick Oldham*

VANDERFORD – John A. Vanderford was born near Philadelphia, OH Oct. 7, 1833 and died in the home of his son, L. A. Vanderford, near Brunswick, Carroll County, MO at the age of 91 years, 1 month and 19 days, suffering from cancer. He was the son of John Vanderford (born Dec. 25, 1807, died June 12, 1869, and is buried in Reed Cemetery, Halfway, MO) and Jane Hobson, buried in Ohio. John Vanderford and Jane Hobson were married March 3, 1831. John Vanderford then married his second wife, Erlinda Cox, on Aug. 23, 1838. The family traveled to Missouri from Ohio when John A. Vanderford was about 6 years old. The family traveled in covered wagons with the grandparents, Eli and Susannah Ratcliff Vanderford. Eli was born in Maryland and Susannah was a native of North Carolina. Eli and Susannah Vanderford settled in Dallas County, MO along with another son, A. R. Vanderford. Eli and Susannah Vanderford are both buried in the old cemetery in Buffalo, MO.

John Vanderford and Erlinda Vanderford settled in the area which became Halfway, MO. He purchased land (Township 33, Range 21) at the land sale of Jan. 11, 1839 and had a log cabin near the small stream running through Halfway. Other children besides John A. Vanderford were Susannah (Darby); Armenta (Eagon); Ruth (Messer); Lucinda (Vaughn); Axa A. (Coy); Jesse R.; Margaret (Ellis); Martha M.; Dennis W.; and William Vanderford (settled in Nebraska). Both John and Erlinda Vanderford are buried in Reed Cemetery, Polk County, Halfway, MO.

John A. Vanderford was a farmer. He married first, Nancy J. Ratcliff (1837-Dec. 3, 1867). She is buried in Reed Cemetery, Halfway, MO. One child was born to this union: Mary Ellen Vanderford, born July 2, 1863 and died Nov. 5, 1886, buried in Reed Cemetery, Halfway, MO. Mary Ellen Vanderford was married on Sept. 6,

John A. Vanderford and Mary Cornelia Woodle Vanderford

1877 to William Beverly Vanderford. They were the parents of two sons: Oren (March 18, 1868-April 28, 1890) and Pheno (Feb. 24, 1884-April 28, 1968).

John A. Vanderford married second on May 27, 1869 to Mary Cornelia Woodle (June 12, 1844-May 5, 1918). Mary Cornelia Woodle was the daughter of William Woodle. She was born in Iowa, but came to Missouri with her parents from the state of Wisconsin. Her parents are buried in the Pleasant Grove Cemetery in Dallas County, MO.

John A. and Mary C. Woodle Vanderford were the parents of seven children: Nora A.; Argus V.; Oren L.; Landon A.; Genevieve (Mrs. Dan Bates); Teresa "Ressie" (Mrs. S. W. Armstrong); and Albert M. Vanderford.

John A. and Mary C. Vanderford traded their farm at Halfway, MO for a farm near Brunswick, MO. They moved to that farm in about 1894. They are buried in Lower Cemetery in Brunswick, MO. They were members of the Brunswick Christian Church.

One daughter, Teresa "Ressie" Alice Vanderford, remained in the Polk County area. She was married on April 27, 1892 to Sterling Webster Armstrong. They moved to the Pleasant Hope, MO community on a farm. Later they moved and farmed in the Bolivar, MO area. They were the parents of 13 children: G. A. Armstrong; James Paul; Mary Lucille (Clifton Rowan); Raymond McClain; Leland Earl; Helen Marie (Homer Hamilton, Owen Merriman); William Roy; Vera Bernice (C. E. "Pat" Jenkins); Anna Mae (W. S. Miller); Ralph Glenwood; Lula Cornelia (Alvin Kinslow); Ada Clementine; and Eva Mildred. Ressie Vanderford Armstrong (Feb. 8, 1874-Aug. 4, 1938) and Sterling Webster Armstrong (June 28, 1866-June 23, 1956) are both buried in the Greenwood Cemetery, Bolivar, MO. *Submitted by Helen Jenkins Roberts*

VAN VOORHES-VORIS – Steven Koert/Coerten was born about 1600 in Hess, Drenthe, Netherlands; died Feb. 16, 1683/84 in the Flatlands, Kings County, NY. He married Aaltejen Wessels, born circa 1605; she died before 1664. The second wife was Willempie Roelofse Seubering, born circa 1619 in Holland; died circa 1690. On April 15, 1660, the family sailed for the "New World," on the de Bonte Koe (The Spotted Cow). He arrived in New Amsterdam (New York) with a wife, six children and a son-in-law. Steven Coerten never used the name Van Voorhees, although his children did. It seems that the name "Van Voorhees" was first used by relatives in the homeland (Netherlands) when addressing letters to those in America.

A child of the second marriage was Lucas Stevense Van Voorhees, born circa 1650 in Holland; died after 1724 in Flatlands, Kings County, NY, married second, Jannetje Minne. They had a son Albert Lucasse Van Voorhees, born May 10, 1698; died Oct. 28, 1734 in New Brunswick, NJ.

Albert Van Voorhees and second wife, Catyrntie Cornell, born Sept. 4, 1703, had a son, Cornelius Voorhees, born Sept. 6, 1725 in Somerset County, NJ. Cornelius' first wife was Magdalena Van Nuys, born circa 1731 and died before Aug. 27, 1806. Cornelius dropped the "Van" from his name. He spent the years 1752-1765 in Harlingen, NJ and then moved to the Conewago Colony (circa 1769) in Pennsylvania where his last child was born and then married his second wife, Johanna Longstreet, circa 1770. We do not have a death date for Cornelius and we do not know if he moved to Kentucky. His children gave a power of attorney to Garret Terhune, Mercer County, KY to collect a legacy left to them as heirs of Magdalena Van Voorhees by her brother, James Van Nuys of Millstone, NJ, in 1806.

Albert Voris, born March 25, 1753, Somerset County, NJ, died Feb. 18, 1830 in Pleasureville, Henry County, KY, was a son of Cornelius and Magdalena Van Voorhees. Albert was in the Revolutionary War. He served as a private in the Pennsylvania Rifle Regiment. He was the first to change his name to the "Voris" spelling. He married Anna Banta, daughter of Hendrick Banta and Maria Stryker, on April 2, 1783 in Conewago, York County, PA. Anna was born July 29, 1767 in York County, PA; died Feb. 16, 1836 in Johnson County, IN. Albert and Ann had 14 children, all born in Kentucky. His will has the spelling "Voris." His tombstone had "Vories." His father was "Voorhees."

Albert and Ann's oldest son was Cornelius A. Voris, born March 25, 1784 in Kentucky, died June 8, 1863 in Pleasureville, KY. He married first Catherine Woodfill/Woodfield on June 3, 1804 in Shelby County, KY, second, Mary Mitchell Banta on Jan. 20, 1834 in Switzerland County, IN. Catherine, daughter of Gabriel Woodfield, a Methodist Minister and Susanna Gudschall, born April 7, 1786 in Kentucky, died July 27, 1833 of cholera in Pleasureville, KY.

In 1823 the first building was erected in the Dutch Settlement, at the place now known as Pleasant, IN. It was of hewed logs, one-and-a-half stories with gallery. It had neither a fireplace nor a stove. Major Cornelius A. Voris was one of the most prominent of this organization. He would come to these meetings in mid-winter carrying a kettle of coals and this was all the heat they had.

Albert Voris, Cornelius and Catherine's oldest son, born March 5, 1805 in Shelby County, KY, died Nov. 11, 1873 in Polk County, MO. In 1850 census he is listed as a miller. In 1860 and 1870 he is listed as a farmer. He married Keziah Banta on Feb. 26, 1825 in Switzerland County, IN. Keziah was born May 18, 1808 in Kentucky; died May 25, 1863 in Polk County, MO and both are buried at Reed Cemetery. *Submitted by Rev. Dr. Steven Jay Voris*

VICKERS – Madison Vickers was born in Kentucky on Nov. 8, 1815. His parents were Edward and Elizabeth Vickers of Virginia. The family moved to Orange County, IN, where Madison married Rhoda Perrine on July 28, 1842. Rhoda's parents were Matthew Perrine and Elizabeth "Betsy" Longacre Perrine. They were married in Jefferson County, TN on Nov. 26, 1803.

The family moved from Orange County, IN to Johnson County, MO in the 1840s, then moved to Greene County, MO in the early 1850s, living there during the Civil War. However, Madison never fought in the Civil War.

The Vickers family moved to Humansville in Polk County in 1865. Humansville was only a trading post run by Mr. Human. Madison farmed the land where Humansville is today. The family is listed in the Polk County 1870 census.

On Oct. 27, 1870, Madison and Rhoda bought 80 acres of land in the eastern part of Cedar County near the Polk County line and lived there until their deaths. Madison died Oct. 30, 1902 and Rhoda died July 26, 1902. They are buried in the Alder Cemetery east of Stockton, MO.

Their children are listed below.

William Riley, born in Orange County, IN, September 1843, died May 13, 1915. Married Perlina Molder on July 24, 1878. Seven children were born: James E., Osha B., John, Berthena, Rosa Jane, William Franklin and Joe.

Elizabeth Caroline, born in Orange County, IN, June 23, 1847, died Feb. 9, 1915. Married Joseph Routh on May 18, 1888. They had no children.

Benjamin, born in Johnson County, MO, June 5, 1850, died April 8, 1927. Married Rachel Goodson (date unknown). She died and he married Mary E. Simrell on Dec. 5, 1890. Seven children by Rachel: William, Sarah, Charles, John Thomas, Dora Caroline, Henry Franklin and Fred Lee.

Edward, born in Greene County, MO, Nov. 5, 1852, died April 6, 1937. Married Dora Perrine

Madison and Rhoda Vickers, 1890s

on June 18, 1876. Five children: Annie, Cyrus, Jim, Sammie and Jessie.

Samuel, born in Greene County, MO, June 15, 1856, died March 19, 1952. Married Minerva Newcomb on Aug. 15, 1876. Four children: Jim, Madison Andrew, Mary "Mollie" and John.

Sarah Emmaline, born in Greene County, MO, June 15, 1861, died Dec. 1, 1947. Married George Chaney on Feb. 13, 1895. Two children: Delphia Caroline (died at age 1) and Rhoda Esther. Rhoda married Isaac Phipps and they had two children, Luella and Murle.

John Wesley "Doc," born in Greene County, MO, Aug. 19, 1863, died Dec. 18, 1946. Married Callie Youngblood on Feb. 24, 1894. Six children: Steward, Walt, Charles, Sarah, Alma and Coy.

Many of their descendants have resided in Polk County. *Submitted by Luella Phipps*

VILES – William "Billy" Viles was born Oct. 26, 1797 in Caburrus County, NC. He married Martha "Patsy" Banta in Switzerland County, IN on March 13, 1820. Billy and Patsy had eight children who lived to adulthood. They were Nancy A., born Sept. 21, 1822; G. Perry, born April 20, 1824; Henry B., born Feb. 1, 1828; Benjamin F., born Feb. 1, 1828 (twin to Henry); John W., born March 20, 1832; Moses R., born Dec. 20, 1834; Washington A., born 1839; and Martha J., born May 15, 1841, all in Switzerland County, IN. The family moved to Polk County, MO in 1842, where they homesteaded some land. Billy was a Baptist preacher. He died Dec. 18, 1870 and is buried in Viles Cemetery on his old homestead in Polk County, MO.

The family was badly divided in the Civil War. Billy, his sons Benjamin, John W. and Washington A., as well as his two sons-in-law, Elijah W. Roberts and James E. Mayfield, were all on the rebel list of Polk County, while his sons Henry and Perry, and two of Perry's sons, fought for the North.

Henry B. married Sarah Loftin on July 27, 1850 in Polk County, MO. The couple had five children: Martha L., born July 28, 1951; Ann C., born Aug. 26, 1855; Mary F., born Nov. 11, 1857; Virginia A., born Sept. 3, 1861; and Joseph S., born July 14, 1862.

Benjamin F. married Mary Owens on Feb. 26, 1852. They had five children who lived to adulthood: John C., born Nov. 1, 1855; Frances, born 1862; William "Wink," born March 1, 1863; Martha B., born Sept. 16, 1867; and Eliza J., born Aug. 16, 1873.

Henry B. Viles, born 1828

Henry served on the Union side in the Civil War. His twin brother, Benjamin, was a Southern sympathizer. There is an interesting story passed down about how Ben was hanged from a tree in his front yard by a gang sympathizing with the North. This was witnessed by his wife and 7-year-old son. His wife managed to cut him down and revive him, but the strain and stress caused her to have her expected baby prematurely. Ben's wife's family had slaves, and they sent over a 16-year-old slave girl to care for the baby, who was so small he could be put in a four cup measure and a saucer could be set over the top. She kept him in a little box full of cotton, and kept him greased, because his skin was underdeveloped. Incredibly, the baby, "Wink" Viles, lived and grew to be a large man and lived a long, full life. When the war was over, the young slave was given her freedom, but she stayed on and raised Wink, and they developed a close bond which lasted all their lives.

Henry's son Joseph S. married Martha E. Gerstle on July 21, 1889. They had six children: Charles W., born May 31, 1890; Denis A. "Gus," born Jan. 28, 1892; Wilby L. "Jack," born Aug. 30, 1894; Rufus B. "Doc," born June 5, 1896; Verda E., born Nov. 11, 1899; and Joseph C., born May 30, 1907.

Charles W. married Josie LeJeune on Feb. 5, 1911 in Polk County. They had five children: Hazel, born March 22, 1912; Freeman A., born Sept. 9, 1914; Raymond C., born Jan. 22, 1917; Maxine M., born July 26, 1927; and Doris Maydean, born April 23, 1929.

Hazel married Orra S. McKinney (born Oct. 27, 1909) on Jan. 1, 1933. The couple had three children: Lyndel L., born Dec. 25, 1938; Myron W., born Sept. 8, 1944; and Sandra K., born Oct. 13, 1946.

Lyndel married Nancy E. Condren on March 15, 1958. They have three sons: Gregory L., born Nov. 27, 1958; Wesley A., born Aug. 24, 1962; and Jeffrey L., born Sept. 27, 1963. Lyndel and Nancy divorced in March of 1971 and he married Judy Jones on Sept. 2, 1972. Lyndel and Judy are now retired from dairy farming.

Myron married Janet Manard on Aug. 15, 1964 and they have two daughters: Shannon L., born July 7, 1969 and Rebecca J., born June 9, 1971. Myron is a retired president and CEO of Empire District Electric Co.

Sandra married Gary Cooper on April 16, 1965. They have two children: Brian R., born Feb. 9, 1967 and Shonda R., born April 2, 1970. Sandra and Gary divorced in 1982 and Gary died Aug. 11, 1985 of diabetes complications. Sandra cooks for Citizens Memorial Hospital in Bolivar. *Submitted by Myron McKinney*

VINCENT – The 2002 phone directory for Bolivar and surrounding towns lists six Vincent families. Fifty to 100 years ago the name was much more numerous. Although the Vincents listed in the directory may trace back to a common ancestor, they do not all share the same original ancestor in Polk County. This writing is about Thomas Roy Vincent. There are three different accounts of Thomas Roy Vincent and his descendants. They don't agree on his birthplace; one says England, another says St. Louis. They also disagree on whether James Thomas Vincent was the oldest child of Thomas Roy or the fifth oldest child. They do agree on the rest of the information unless otherwise noted.

Thomas Roy Vincent was born Oct. 14, 1811 and died April 22, 1900 near Halfway, MO. He is buried at Lindley Creek Cemetery along with his wife and several of his descendants. He married Elizabeth Pearman, born Nov. 22, 1820 in St. Louis and died April 25, 1892. She was the daughter of Eulila (Palmer) Pearman. Eulila's first husband was James Pearman and her second husband was James Jump.

Thomas Roy and Elizabeth were among the early settlers in Polk County, arriving in the late 1830s. Their nine children were James Thomas Vincent, born Feb. 14, 1838 in Lindley Creek, Polk County, married Lucinda Catherine Ashworth Feb. 9, 1858 in Polk County; Mary Elizabeth Vincent, born 1841-1843, married Stephen Hale, April 1, 1858; Christopher Columbus Vincent, born March 17, 1844 in Polk County, MO, died Dec. 21, 1926 in Polk County, married Mary Frances Ashlock, Aug. 31, 1865; William L. Vincent, born 1846; America Isabelle Vincent, born Nov. 14, 1847 in Missouri, married James W. Howe, July 6, 1864; John Lonson (or Lanson) Vincent, born Nov. 3, 1849, died July 5, 1889, married Minerva Jane Potter, Nov. 2, 1871, buried in Lindley Creek Cemetery; Lucinda Kathryn Vincent, born 1852, married Joseph R. Howe, July 26, 1868; Joseph H. Vincent, born 1856, married Sarah C. Inks, Feb. 11, 1875; and Arena Susan Vincent, born 1862, married John Wesley Howe, Jan. 23, 1879.

Christopher Columbus and James Thomas served in the Union Army during the Civil War. Although Civil War records are not totally clear, it is believed they served together in the same unit. They fought with the Polk County Home Guard at Wilson's Creek. Following the unit's disbandment, they enlisted in the Eighth Missouri State Militia Cavalry. The enlistment location is listed as Robberson Mill in Polk County. History tells us the Eighth Missouri State Militia Cavalry had a distinguished service record. They were involved in numerous skirmishes and battles in Missouri and Arkansas. They were also involved in repulsing General Sterling Price's 1864 raid. One of the family stories that has been passed down tells us the Christopher Columbus Vincent had his horse shot out from under him in an 1862 battle.

Space and available information does not allow for a detailed listing of descendants. One can be assured that it is a large number just in Polk County. Some of the families that have married Vincents and their descendants include: Andrews, Ashlock, Ashworth, Barham, Barker, Box, Breashers, Bridges, Carson, Derosset, Hale, Hinkle, Howe, Huckaby, Ingram, Leith, Potter, Price, Reed, Spear, Spurgeon, Standley, Ward, Warren, Westfall, Willis, Wommack and Wrinkle. *Submitted by Morris Westfall*

VINEYARD – Rebecca Susan Scott was born Feb. 15, 1865 and died April 29, 1896. She and her family were living at Brighton, MO and she is buried at Brighton Cemetery along with her baby. The child was stillborn April 29, 1896. She was married to William Lathem Vineyard. He was born Feb. 10, 1854 and died Nov. 14, 1918. He is buried at Fairview, MO. There were six children born to this union.

Sarah Jane Vineyard was born Oct. 28, 1877 and died Dec. 25, 1973. She married Arthur Swadley on Sept. 7, 1900 at Brighton, Polk County, MO. They resided most of their lives in Bois D'arc, MO. Six children were born to this union. Arthur and Janie are buried at Clear Creek Cemetery near Willard, MO. Their two sons, Bonny and Nuel, are also buried there.

James Monroe was born Dec. 14, 1880 and died Dec. 13, 1969. He is buried in Ponca City, OK. He was married to Ida McColla.

John was born March 27, 1886. His death date is unknown. James and John traveled to Oklahoma to work the oil fields and spent their lives making their homes in that area.

Nancy Mahalia was born June 30, 1888 and died April 7, 1973. She married France Marion Julian on Aug. 7, 1907. They celebrated their 60th anniversary on Aug. 9, 1967. France attended Southwest Baptist College in 1905 and courted Nancy in a horse and buggy. They had two daughters. Noreva Marion Julian was born Dec. 24, 1908. She married Eugene J. Gifford on June 30, 1935. They had no children but claimed their nieces and nephews as their own. Vivian

France and Nancy Julian, 50th wedding anniversary, 1957

Martisha Julian was born March 15, 1919 and married Wallace Marvin Springer on May 18, 1934. They celebrated their 60th anniversary on May 22, 1994. They had one son, Bobby E. Springer, who married Jeanette Steele and had three daughters, Rebecca, Debra and Melinda; and one daughter, Barbara L. Springer, who married Howard E. Bolin and had one son, Thomas, and one daughter, Tambra. Bobby and Jeanette celebrated their 40th anniversary in 1996 and Howard and Barbara celebrated their 40th anniversary in 1997. France and Nancy Julian and Eugene Gifford are buried in Clear Creek Cemetery near Willard.

Ida Vineyard was born around 1891 and traveled to California and died there.

The last child born was an infant born in 1896 while living in Brighton. *Submitted by Vivian Julian Springer*

VODICKA – Joseph Frank Vodicka Jr. came to America in 1904 from Austria-Hungary with his parents, Joseph and Marie (Beron) Vodicka and eight siblings. After getting off the ship in Ellis Island, NY, the family headed to Karlin, MO to settle. Joseph's older brother, Frank, had already made a trip to Polk County and had returned to Austria-Hungary to bring his parents and the rest of the family to live there. Joseph was born March 28, 1888 in Austria-Hungary.

In 1918 Joseph obtained his US naturalization and became a US citizen. Joseph served in the US Army from 1917-1919. Upon returning home from the Army, Joseph met and married a local girl, Genoefa "Effie" Helen Dvorak. Effie was born Jan. 1, 1898 in Howells, NE, the oldest child of Karel and Katherine (Glodowski) Dvorak. As a young girl Effie came to Missouri to visit her uncle and aunt, Joseph and Frances (Korn) Dvorak. They took such a liking to Effie that they asked Karel and Katherine if she could come live with them all the time as they had no children of their own. Effie then moved to Missouri and was raised by Joseph and Frances, who later adopted her.

Joseph and Effie lived their lives and raised their family in the Karlin Community. The Vodickas had eight children: Mary, Frances, Angela "Angie," Adela "Dell," Joseph, Charles "Chuck," Celestine "Sally" and Edward. Farming was the family's main livelihood. Farm life was hard work and everyone had his or her part to do. In addition to farming, Joseph and Effie also ran a general merchandise store and feed mill in Karlin for many years. Joseph also served as the postmaster of Karlin for 20 years after Joseph Dvorak retired. The family was also very active in the St. Wenceslaus Catholic Church located in Karlin.

After the trains stopped coming to Karlin, the community faded and businesses were closed. Joseph remained postmaster until that, too, was stopped. He then turned back to farming full time with his family.

In 1947 Joseph died, leaving Effie and the children to continue farming. Like their father had done, Joe and Chuck served in the military. Joe served in WWII while Chuck served in the Korean War. Sadness came to the family in 1952 when Chuck was killed in Korea during the Korean War. Edward, being the last son to get married, took over the family farm and Effie bought a house in Bolivar where she lived until 1982 when she suffered a stroke. She then moved to Willard to live with her daughter until her death in 1987.

Joseph, Effie and Charles are all buried in the St. Wenceslaus Cemetery in Karlin, The church has been gone for years, but the cemetery remains in use and many of the family members are buried there. *Submitted by Jami Hubbert*

VORIS – William "Earl" Voris was born in 1896 in Polk County, MO. His was the 10th generation after the first forefather came to America in 1660. Following is a brief history of his family.

The common ancestor of the Voris family migrated from the Netherlands and first settled in New York. This family and later generations gradually moved westward.

In 1852 Albert Voris of the seventh generation brought his wife Keziah (Banta) and their eight children from Switzerland, IN to Missouri in covered wagons. One of the eight children was Henry Banta Voris, born in 1827, who had married Mary McGregor in Indiana. They and their two young children came with this dad Albert to Missouri and settled in the eastern part of Polk County.

During the Civil War Henry B. joined Company F, 15th Regiment, Missouri on Aug. 11, 1864 and fought for the Union. He received an honorable discharge July 1, 1865 at Springfield, MO as a corporal. When Henry died in 1882 his widow, Mary received a pension of $8 a month from the US government.

The oldest son of Henry and Mary Voris was William Albert, born in 1849. In 1870 he married Lucy Groves. They had six children, four reaching adulthood. They were Edward, Serena, Henry and Calvin. The wife and mother, Lucy, died in 1882 at the age of 31. William A. then married Delila Rosanah "Rosa" Jones in 1884. Rosa was born in 1865 in Callaway County, KY, the second of 10 children of Calvin and Sarah Rogers Jones. In 1880 she came by wagon train from Kentucky to Halfway, MO. Rosa met and fell in love with William A. Voris, though he was older and had four children. The Jones family decided to move back to Kentucky, hoping to take Rosa back with them. However, she married William and stayed in Missouri. William and Rosa became the parents of nine children. They were Arthur, Maggie, Ben, Ralph, Charley, Grace (Voris) Evans, William Earl, Merle (Voris) Peterson and Glen. They lived on a farm near Halfway, MO.

William "Earl," the seventh child of William A. and Rosa (Jones) Voris, was born Aug. 23, 1896. He attended Knapp Elementary, a rural school near the home. He worked on the farm with his dad until 1918 when he was drafted into the army. He was in training camp nine months, but before he had to go overseas the armistice was signed.

In 1919 he married Lillie Roweton. They lived on a farm near Halfway where their five children were born. They were Paul Thomas, Audrey Ruth, Roselen Mae, Claud Earl "Buster" and Lendell Glen.

William Earl was a hard-working, diversified farmer, keeping work done when needed; his place neat at all times, including fencerows. He was a good community supporter and served on the Halfway School Board for several years.

In 1958 William Earl and Lillie Voris moved to Bolivar when he was elected Polk County treasurer. He served in this post for four years. For a short time he worked as a custodian of the Methodist Church of Bolivar. In May 1963 he suffered a heart attack and died a few weeks later. His wife Lillie continued to live in Bolivar until her death on Jan. 1, 1984. Both are buried in Reed Cemetery near Halfway. *Submitted by Carol (Voris) Morris and Judy (Voris) McElwain*

VORIS – The first Vorises in Polk County were Henry and Mary, their children and his parents, Albert and Keziah.

Children of Albert and Keziah.

Henry Banta Voris, born Dec. 20, 1827 in Switzerland County, IN, died Feb. 21, 1882 in Polk County, MO and is buried at Schofield Cemetery. He married Mary Skeen McGregor on July 7, 1848 in Switzerland County, IN. She was daughter of Alexander McGregor and Martha Rogers. She was born Jan. 19, 1830 in Indiana, died May 16, 1902 in Polk County. Henry and Mary settled three miles east of Halfway in 1855. There is indication that they came, bought land, and went back to Indiana, then returned the next year.

Catherine, born 1829, married John Manford on Feb. 27, 1851 in Switzerland County, IN.

Pelina (Paulina), born Oct. 21, 1837 and died Nov. 1, 1868.

Mary, born 1839, died 1895 in Dallas County, MO, and married John Polly on March 22, 1855 in Switzerland County, IN.

Margaret, born June 8, 1840, died Oct. 1, 1900 in Mulberry, Franklin County, AR and married Abraham Lewis on July 27, 1854 in Switzerland County.

Martha, born Nov. 8, 1843, died Nov. 11, 1918 in Greene County, MO and married John J. Grove on March 31, 1859 in Polk County.

Jane was born in 1845.

Susan Ann, born 1848, married William Barclay on April 12, 1866 in Polk County.

Julius Albert, born December 1849, married Martha Melissa Viles on May 25, 1869 in Polk County.

Children of Henry and Mary:

William Albert "W. A." Voris, born May 12, 1849 in Switzerland County, IN, died May 23, 1925 in Polk County and is buried at Reed Cemetery. He married first, Lucy Ellen Grove, on Feb. 7, 1870, daughter of Daniel Grove and Ann Kemper. Lucy was born Jan. 14, 1851 in Indiana, died Jan. 25, 1882 in Polk County; married second Rosa Jones on Oct. 25, 1883 in Polk County. Rosa was born Dec. 16, 1865 in Kentucky, died Feb. 21, 1937 in Polk County.

John Mose, born March 26, 1851, died Nov. 30, 1936 and married Eliza Bell Cowden on Jan. 1, 1879.

Lewis A. Voris, born May 7, 1853, died Sept. 20, 1879.

Martha, born circa 1855, married William Albert Cowden on Nov. 17, 1872 in Dallas County.

Sarah A. "Sallie," born Sept. 28, 1857, died Oct. 5, 1879 in Polk County of typhoid fever.

Amanda Jane, born 1859, married Daniel B. Morrison on March 25, 1883 in Dallas County.

Charles, born March 9, 1862, died Dec. 15, 1893, married Annie C. Clayton on April 21, 1889 in Polk County.

Indiana "Aunt Den," born July 25, 1864, died March 13, 1945, married Edwin Van Gilder on Dec. 14, 1893 in Dallas County.

Miannie "Miami," born April 29, 1869, died Feb. 25, 1880.

W. A. and Lucy Voris had six children.

Edward Lewis Voris, born Jan. 20, 1871 in Polk County, died July 8, 1938 of ptomaine poisoning. He married Jessie O. Parrish on Dec. 27, 1896 in Polk County.

Serena Ann, born March 27, 1873, died Jan. 14, 1955 in Covine, CA.

Mary Eliza, born May 28, 1875, died Nov. 6, 1879, Polk County.

Indiana, born Aug. 16, 1877, died May 28, 1878, Polk County.

Henry J., born June 13, 1879, died Feb. 8, 1950, Monrovia, CA.

Calvin Clark, born Oct. 30, 1881, died Sept. 7, 1959, Polk County, married Orva Lewis on Sept. 8, 1909 in California. He lived in Monrovia, CA but died on a trip back to Halfway.

Children of W. A. and Rosa Jones Voris:

Arthur Leroy, born July 2, 1885, died June 28, 1937 in Rogersville, Greene County, MO, and married Lucinda Jane Manroe on March 24, 1916.

Maggie, born Feb. 11, 1887, died May 24, 1924 in Polk County.

Ben Harison, born Nov. 3, 1888, died April 27, 1967 in Polk County.

Ralph Nelson, born Sept. 22, 1891, died May 28, 1950 in Greene County, married Agnes Jenkins on March 22, 1919 in Dallas County.

Charley Robert, born Nov. 18, 1894, died April 9, 1954 in Polk County, married Clara Lea Angles on Nov. 26, 1924.

Grace Leona, born Sept. 12, 1895, married Thomas W. Evans on April 29, 1931.

William Earl Voris, born Aug. 23, 1896, died May 22, 1963, married Lillie Mae Roweton on Dec. 20, 1920.

Eula Merle, born April 2, 1903, died July 12, 1996 in Polk County, married Benjamin Cecil Peterson on April 19, 1925.

Glen, born Dec. 27, 1908, died Feb. 28, 1990, married Juanita Buck on Sept. 10, 1933.

Children of Ed and Jessie Voris:

Front row: William Earl, Lendell Glen and Mrs. William Earl (Lillie Roweton); Second row: Mrs. David Dunseth (Rosie Voris), Paul Thomas Voris, Claud Earl "Buster" Voris, Mrs. David Gallivan (Ruth Voris), taken 1946

Wade and Geneice Gorden Voris

Guy, born Jan. 17, 1898, died Jan. 22, 1898.

Hazel, born Nov. 4, 1899, died Oct. 16, 1986, married Ezra Towner "Dick" Walker on Dec. 30, 1930 in Sidney, NE. They lived in Scottsbluff, NE.

Morrison "Moris" was born March 25, 1903, died May 17, 1945 in Port Renfrow, B. C., Canada. He died in a logging accident. He married Dorothy Helen Walker on Aug. 26, 1929 in Anaheim, CA.

Catherine, born Oct. 8, 1906, died Nov. 11, 1906.

John Mose, born Aug. 31, 1910, died Oct. 20, 1991, married Lillian McKinney on July 16, 1932. Mose was a teacher.

Wade Wallace, born July 30, 1914, died Oct. 25, 1996 in a tractor accident, married Geneice Gorden on July 3, 1938 in Scottsbluff, NE. *Submitted by Tony Ray Voris*

VOTE – John Vote was born 1808 in Pennsylva-

Sina Elzina Johnson and husband Guy Warren Vote, great-grandparents of Lisa Ann Vote Hickman

nia. Family story tells the spelling changed from "Vought" or "Voight" to "Vote" at immigration to "Americanize" or by John to ease spelling. He married Anna Mary (Kern), born 1810 in Wurttemburg, Germany. Enumerated in Thompson Township, Seneca County, OH 1850. Occupation: Shoemaker. 1870 Census Genoa Township, DeKalb County, IL. Children: Elizabeth, Mary A., John M., Anna W., Susan, William H., Jacob G., Margaretta, Charles F. and Franklin P. John died June 30, 1893. Anna died July 23, 1877. Both buried in Illinois. John Martin was born Dec. 20, 1839 in Flat Rock, OH. In 1856 at 17, he enlisted in the army, as a private in Company K, 52nd Regiment, Illinois Volunteers. He fought in the Civil War Sept. 6, 1861. Wounded at Battle of Shiloh, discharged as corporal Dec. 17, 1864; for promotion as 1st Lieutenant. He wrote letters for a pal, for "His Girl," Eleanor Almeda Hackett, friend unknown. Married Dec. 6, 1865 at White Water, WI. Eleanor was born Sept. 30, 1848 to Abraham Hackett and Mary (Randall). They arrived in Callendar, IA in spring 1871 in a covered wagon, losing their first three children on the way. Children: Johnnie, Mary, Eddie, Jacob, Burdette, Cora, Guy, Lillian, William, Harry, Sylvia and Clarence. John Martin was justice of the peace for 20 years, then constable at Fort Dodge, IA. John died Dec. 12, 1903. Eleanor died Sept. 2, 1911. Both buried in Iowa. Guy Warren was born April 27, 1873, Kalo, IA. He married Sina Elzina (Johnson) on July 3, 1895 in Fort Dodge, IA. Sina was born Sept. 24, 1880 at Gowrie, IA to David and Rhoda Johnson. Children: Daisy, Dewey, Florence, Clarence, Sina E., Bernetta, Laura, Edwin, Ava, Hazel and John W. Guy died July 29, 1959. Sina died Aug. 22, 1954. Both buried at Aldrich, MO. Lisa Vote Hickman's great-grandparents were the first generation of five to live in Polk County, arriving during the early 1900s. John William Sr. was born May 15, 1923 in Fonda, IA. Schooled at Eudora. He married Mildred (Long), born April 12, 1921 in Ash Grove, MO to William Riley "Bud" Long and Magdalina "Maggie" Mae (Metcalf) Beesley. Married Nov. 13, 1939 in Eudora. Children: John William Jr., Ronald, Roger, James, Richard, Mary, Earl and David. Drafted in the army at 21, a farmer. He served Aug. 22, 1944 to Sept. 22, 1944, a veteran of WWII. Grandpa was sick, so Grandma and the oldest boys worked for neighbors, raised acres of cucumbers to sell to feed the family and pay bills. Grandma kept the family together. The boys married or

John William Vote Sr. and Mildred (Long) Vote on first date, 1939

were in the service. Grandpa was losing the farm. March 30, 1971, he left us at age 47. Lisa was 5 years old. He is buried at Aldrich. Grandma moved to Bolivar, working at Bolivar Nursing Home, met resident Ray Bigler. Married Aug. 28, 1976 at Wheatland. Ray died March 21, 1980. Grandma died Monday March 1, 1999 in her home at Bolivar. Her children were with her and Uncle David was singing, "You Are My Sunshine" the way Grandpa sang it to her. Grandma and Grandpa Vote had eight children, 34 grandchildren, and 41 great-grandchildren as of March 1999. John William Jr. was born July 2, 1940 west of Morrisville. Schooled at Eudora and public schools. Recruited and served in the Marines 1958 to 1962. He was a boxer, stationed in California and the Far East. Married Bonnie Jeanette (Bays) on Jan. 25, 1963 at Eudora. Born Jan. 26, 1946 at Huron to Charlie Joseph Bays and Myrtle Lorene (Seiner). Children: Ronda Yvonne, Regina Jeanette, Melissa Ann and John Joseph. Resided at Eudora (tree farm), Grisham's, Crain's by Sac River, "Old Slagle School House," Bolivar and Gentry, AR. Their children graduated 1982, 83, 84 and 86 from Marion C. Early, Morrisville. Dad's jobs: butchered for Hormel, six years, Bolivar and Siloam Springs, AR, Bill Grant's milk-

Grandma "Vote" and her children

ing, farming for 16 years. Their children and families: Ronda and David Butler. Children: Heather and Brian. Ronda remarried October 2000 to Ray Wood, Peculiar. Regina and David Phillips. Children: Derrick and Rachel. Aldrich. Melissa "Lisa" and Lullel Hickman. Children: Logan and Lacy, Walnut Grove. John and Kim (Bruebeck). Children: none. Divorced 1989. John has a child, McKenna Mae Vote. *Submitted by Lisa Ann (Vote) Hickman*

Family of John W. Vote Jr. and Bonnie Jeanette (Bays) Vote; front: Regina Jeanette and Melissa Ann; middle: John Jr., Ronda Yvonne and Bonnie Jeanette; back: John Joseph

Heather Dawn Butler, Logan Ryan Hickman, Brian Allen Butler, Lacy Diane Hickman, Derrick Scott Phillips, Rachel Diane Phillips, McKenna Mae Vote.

WAGGONER – Phillip Waggoner married

John and Celia (Baird) Waggoner, note, this is a picture of original that is in possession of their grandson, Cameron Seiner

Catherine (Fellers) on Nov. 11, 1790 in Tennessee, daughter of Adam G. and Mary Magdaline (Huber) Fellers. Children in Phillip's will of Dec. 12, 1812: Barbara, Catherine, Nancy, John G., Abraham G., Jacob G., Henry G., Eve, Samuel D. and Rachel. Abraham (born 1796 in Tennessee) married Ellender (Perry) on May 27, 1825. She was born 1802 in Tennessee. Children: Nancy, Eliza, Mary, Tennessee (F), Mahala, John and Abraham Lincoln. Ellender died 1830-1838 and on April 8, 1838, Abraham married Arrilla D. (Spain), born Dec. 20, 1815 in Tennessee. They had 12 children. Surviving children: Samuel, Margerette, Martha, Mary, Ellen, James, Rachel and Ethline. Enumerated in Civil District, No. 5, Davidson County, TN 1850 census. Abraham fought in the War of 1812 as a Tennessee Volunteer. Abraham enlisted 1862 as a private of Com-

Family of George "Lee" and Eliza June (Waggoner) Seiner; front: George Lee and Eliza June; middle: Marie, Cameron, Annie, Hurbert, Sadie; back: Earnest, Bess, Oscar, Jim, Nora, Cecil and Lela

pany B, Fifth Regiment, Tennessee Cavalry Volunteers. Abraham died Feb. 27, 1863 in Rosedale, TN. Abraham told everyone he freed his slaves, believing it morally wrong to own slaves. Three bushwhackers came to his house at night, called his name, and shot him dead. The children were hidden in the courthouse, while the women buried him in the dark, under an apple tree. They gathered to mourn him when the tree bloomed. Arrilla died Oct. 31, 1907 in Nashville, TN. John Waggoner, born Dec. 22, 1834 in Tennessee, married Celia Ann (Baird) on July 3, 1858 in Tennessee. Celia was born Nov. 24, 1835. Child: Eliza Jane, born April 23, 1874 in Tennessee. The first record of these Waggoners living in Polk County would be John and Celia residing in an area called "Four Mile Loop" near Aldrich. John was employed by the Campbells occupying a log cabin in the woods as their homestead. Enumerated 1900-1920 Marion Township, Polk County, MO census. John died April 28, 1927 and Celia died April 11, 1920. Burials at Mitchell Campground, Aldrich. Eliza married George Lee Seiner, born Oct. 3, 1869 in Tennessee. Oct. 26, 2000 quote from their son Cam Seiner, "They almost lost Ernie and Annie to sickness traveling to Missouri from Tennessee. There was a storm, traveling in a covered wagon they put ropes on the wheels and staked them down. The horses broke loose, it took a day and a half to find them." Enumerated 1900-1920 census of Marion Township, Polk County. Children: Earnest, Anna, Oscar, Nora, Bessie, Jim, Cecil, Lela, Sadie, Marie, Cameron and Erwin. George Lee died July 29, 1951; Eliza died June 23, 1915. Burials in Greenwood Cemetery. Earnest was born July 13, 1892 in Texas. Married Edna Mae (Graham), born Nov. 25, 1893 in Colorado, daughter of Walter S. and Ida Mae (Putnam) Graham. Earnest and Edna married July 13, 1913 in Bolivar. Enumerated in 1920 Marion Township, Polk County. Children: Opal, Willard (March 25, 1916-May 3, 1916), Ruth, Lorene, Earnestine, Dorothy, Charles, Helen, Robert and Joann. Earnest died Jan. 13, 1965 and Edna died Aug. 13, 1974; burials in Greenwood Cemetery. Lorene, born Dec. 6, 1919 in Bolivar, married Charlie Joseph Bays on April 19, 1941 in Bolivar. (See Bays/Darman family by Regina Phillips)

Waggoner and Seiner families have had seven generations to live in Polk County. *Submitted by Ronda Vote-Wood*

WAHLBORG – When Otto Allen and Gladys Edith Hoffer Wahlborg and their children moved from rural Trego County, KS to rural Polk County, MO in 1943, they were following a precedent for migration and independence inherited from both families. Otto was the eighth of nine children of Swedish immigrants and Gladys was the first of nine children of Umphrey and Grace Connelly Hoffer.

In Wahlborg history, Johan Bengtsson and his brother Gustav came to the United States from Sweden around 1886 looking for a better life. After moving to America, Johan began having trouble receiving his mail, as there were so many Johan Bengtssons. John and Gustav decided to change their last name to Wahlborg. "Wahl" for Vason, their home in Sweden, and "borg" for village. After settling in Wisconsin, John Bengt Wahlborg sent for his future wife, Johanna Bengtsson-Bertilsson, who arrived with Johan's sister at Ellis Island in May 1887. At that time in Sweden, each son's last name was determined by his father's first name with "son" added, and each daughter's last name was her father's first name with "dotter" added. In all the writings available, however, it appears that Johanna was referred to as Bengtsson-Bertilsson, instead of Bengtsdotter, with no explanation provided. When Johanna arrived in the United States, she, speaking no English, was put on the wrong train in New York, traveled toward a wrong destination and, finally, joined Johan in Wisconsin. They married in September 1887. In Sweden, Johan was a shoemaker, in Wisconsin, a lumberjack, and in Kansas, a farmer. After a few years, John, Johanna, and their first five children moved to western Kansas where their last four children were born.

U. S. and Grace Hoffer had both moved to western Kansas from Illinois as children; he with his father who had come from Switzerland to Illinois (where Umphrey was born) to Kansas; and she in a prairie schooner. Her parents had moved to Kansas, married, moved back to Illinois, had three children, her father died, and her mother returned to Kansas. U. S. and Grace Hoffer moved to Polk County from Kansas in 1939.

Otto and Gladys, both born in western Kansas, were married in 1928, and soon after their marriage faced the Depression, dust storms and poor wheat harvests. Once, as Gladys and her older children related many times, a can of cream was spilled while they were on their way into town to sell it and buy their weekly food supply. That catastrophe resulted in their returning home empty-handed. They endured the many hard times of that era in western Kansas, and on a trip to visit Polk County relatives, they purchased a farm four miles east of Bolivar, a few miles from the Hoffers; home. They moved from Kansas with three children, Uarda Lee, 11, Berne, 9, and Donna Deanne, 3. Late that September, Lois was born.

Their arrival in Missouri would bring satisfaction to Gladys, as she loved Missouri, its trees, and her family, but Otto, affectionately called "Swede" by some, yearned for western Kansas and his relatives who still lived there. A wheat farmer in Kansas, he first tried farming in Missouri, but found it to quite different and soon began other work in Bolivar. In 1949 the family moved from the farm into town where Otto worked at various jobs, served as a city judge and retired from the Bolivar Water Department; Gladys worked as a clerk at different stores in Bolivar and retired from Teters Nursery.

When Otto suffered kidney failure in 1975, he

Front: Uarda Lee, Lois, Donna and Gladys Wahlborg; back: Berne and Otto Wahlborg

and Gladys moved to Springfield where he underwent kidney dialysis until he died in 1977 at age 75. Gladys remained in Springfield until her death in 1990 at the age of 85. They are buried, along with their son, Berne, who also died in 1990, in Greenwood Cemetery.

Although Otto and Gladys' children left Bolivar as young adults, they continue to remember it fondly as "home." *Submitted by Donna Wahlborg Michael*

WAINSCOTT – Sterling Evans Wainscott was born in Bates County, MO Sept. 15, 1884. His parents were Charles Burton Wainscott, born Nov. 29, 1884 in Benton County, AR and Pernecy J. Evans Wainscott who were married Feb. 22, 1872. Charles Burton Wainscott enlisted in the Confederate Army under General Shelby in Polk County, MO and served until the close of the war. The Charles Burton Wainscott family resided in Polk County and other Missouri counties for several years. It was while they were living in Bates County, MO that Sterling was born.

While Sterling was still a child, the family moved to Hazelton, KS where he later met and married Christa Jewel Landreth on Nov. 8, 1913. Shortly after their marriage, they moved to the Aldrich, MO community to a farm located on Bear Creek in Polk County. While living in Aldrich, Ferrol Evans Wainscott was born April 21, 1915 and Chester Lee Wainscott was born April 13, 1917.

Sterling farmed some and was a partner with Coy Stewart in operating a hardware supply store in Aldrich. Christa taught school in nearby rural schools. Chester and Ferrol attended Kinder School. They later moved to Springfield, MO so Christa could take college credits at the Teacher's College (now Southwest Missouri State University). In 1927 their home and all its contents burned while they were away for the weekend. So they moved back to Hazelton, KS, lived with relatives and worked in the wheat fields.

In 1928 the Wainscotts returned to Cliquot, MO

Earnest and Edna Mae (Putnam) Seiner; front: Robert, Edna, Earnest, Joann; middle: Lorene, Ruth, Earnestine, Opal; back: Dorothy, Charles and Helen

where Sterling farmed and Christa taught school in several nearby rural schools. They remained in Polk County for the rest of their lives. They moved to several different communities in Polk County where Sterling continued to farm and did some carpentry. Christa taught school and eventually gave private piano lessons. They moved to Bolivar in the 1950s and remained there until their deaths. Christa died June 21, 1959 of cancer, and Sterling died Feb. 20, 1961 of a blood clot.

Their sons, Ferrol and Chester, graduated from Bolivar High School. Ferrol married Roa Elizabeth Payne on May 21, 1939. They spent their entire married life in Polk County. He was a successful farmer for 50 years in the Polk Community. Roa taught school for one year at Mt. Etna in Polk County before getting married. After her marriage, she devoted her time to raising five children, managing the house and working on the farm. She was also a skilled seamstress and enjoyed teaching others in the Polk 4-H as well as in the surrounding communities. Their children are Jo Ann, Sept. 12, 1940; Elva Rosalie, July 27, 1944; Christa Mae, March 13, 1947; Victor Evans, Aug. 16, 1948; and Karen Sue, Nov. 23, 1949. All of their children graduated from Bolivar High School and attended college. Ferrol and Roa lived near Polk until 1989 when they moved to Bolivar. Ferrol died Sept. 9, 1997 of congestive heart failure.

After graduating from Bolivar High School, Chester taught school at Concord School in Polk County. He served in the Air Force during WWII. After his stint in the service, he returned to Polk County and married Wanda Jo LaRew on Nov. 1, 1941. He graduated from Missouri University. He and Wanda always lived in the Bolivar community where Chester was a successful banker for over 50 years at the Polk County Bank, where he eventually became president. Chester and Wanda remained in the Bolivar community their entire married life. Chester died June 10, 1997. *Submitted by Rosalie Wainscott Grogan*

WALKER – When Esther Payne Davis' grandfather, James Wiley Walker, was in his 91st year, in July 1934, he left the following testimonial:

"I am in my 91st year, a veteran of the unhappy struggle of a country divided against itself, the Civil War, when our country was less than 100 years old.

"I served in the armies of the Civil War three years. I say armies because I fought on both sides of the war when hunger forced me to join the other side. We were so starved; we ate grains of corn picked from horse manure. Sometimes it was brother against brother, as my brother and I fought on different sides at different times.

"I grew up to manhood on Belle Creek, GA, making my home in that vicinity until the 4th of March, 1885, when I left with my family and came to Missouri. I settled in Polk County four miles east of a small county town called Pleasant Hope.

"This same place has been my home for 49 years, the 10th of last March. I have been a farmer all my life except three years I served in the armies of the Civil War.

"I am now in my 91st year, having been born in McDowell County, NC, March 15, 1844.

"I am happy to have been able to survive these 90 years to tell where and how I spent my youth, those days mixed with troublesome yet enjoyable times." J. W. Walker, March 15, 1844 – September 1934.

Contributed by his granddaughter, Esther Payne Davis, native of Polk County.

Esther's mother was Ollie Walker Payne, one of eight children. She, with the others, left Georgia for Missouri when she was 7 years old and told of riding on the train, so crowded some had to sit on laps. *Submitted by Esther Payne Davis*

WALKER – Noah Spencer Walker, born Jan. 3, 1804 in North Carolina, married Lois Ann Walker, born May 23, 1816 in North Carolina, on Aug. 28, 1834, possibly in Maury County, TN. It is not known at this time whether the two Walker families were related. Lois was the daughter of Thomas and Bethanna (Woolard) Walker. Noah and Lois had five children, the first two born in Maury County and the rest in Polk County. A large number of families migrated from Maury and Williamson Counties in Tennessee to Missouri between 1835 and 1840, settling in what is now Polk and Cedar Counties. The Potts, Wakefield, Fox, Church, Wollard and Walker families were part of this migration. Lois's parents and younger siblings Mary Ann, Harriet, Anna Eliza and Thomas Alfred came along.

Bethanna died in 1845 in Polk County and was buried at Spencer-Hufford Cemetery. Thomas and his son went back to Tennessee (all of the girls had married already except Anna Eliza, who stayed in Missouri). Thomas died in 1875 in Maury County. Noah died March 17, 1846 in Polk County and was buried at Spencer-Hufford. Lois was remarried on Nov. 28, 1847 in Polk County to Asa Simpson, a widower with three daughters. Lois and Asa had three children: Benjamin Franklin, 1848-May 21, 1870, buried in Polk County; Narcissa Harriet, born 1850; and Rhoda Ellen, born 1854. Lois and Asa separated before 1860. Lois died Feb. 21, 1865 in Polk County and was buried in Walker Cemetery, Cedar County, MO.

Edward Gray Walker, born Aug. 6, 1835, married Mary E. Fox on July 9, 1857 in Polk County. They had seven children: Thomas Smith (married Juda Ellen, three children, buried Plum Grove Cemetery); Henrietta E.; Maria Louise (died at age 2, buried Walker Cemetery, Cedar County); Joseph; Noah S.; Delilah; and Edward W. (married Elizabeth A. Robards). Edward, a Civil War veteran, was shot and killed Jan. 6, 1872 in Polk County while working in his fields. He was buried in Plum Grove Cemetery.

Wiley Jordan Walker, born Jan. 10, 1837, died Dec. 27, 1838, likely in Maury County.

Calvin B. Walker, born July 5, 1840, married Mary Jane Harper on Sept. 1, 1861 in Cedar County. They had nine children: Walter (stillborn); Parthena Elizabeth (possibly married William M. C. Fox); James Columbus (married Mary Belle Litle, 11 children); Letha Anne (married William A. Rodgers, at least one child); William Edward (married Louella Taylor, three children); Charles Benjamin; Narcissa Kathleen (married Albert Sidney Shirer, two children); Mary Ella or Eleanor (married Asa L. Potts); and Arthur (lived two days). Calvin, a Civil War veteran, died Jan. 3, 1899 in Polk County and was buried at Plum Grove.

Mary Jane Walker, born Jan. 10, 1843, married Henry McBride Wollard, her third cousin, on Jan. 27, 1867 in Polk County. They had four children: Serenia Murtilla (married Sterling Price Stovall, three children); Theodore Allen (married Martha Viola Ellsworth, no children); Columbus Elmer (married Nellie Alice Nickels, five children); and Henry Weaver (married Della Mae Nickels, four children). Mary died July 23, 1889 in Polk County and was buried at Plum Grove.

Martha Ann Walker, born Dec. 3, 1844, married John Lower in December 1868, likely in Cedar County. They had six children: Rufus A. (married Cordelia Belle Osburn, one child); Thomas Edward; Mary Emmeline (married Charles T. Summers, four children); John F. (married Lucy E. Blair, three children); Ida Elvira (married Martin E. Henry, three children); and Frederick Robert (married Myrtle E. Beebe, one child). Martha died Dec. 10, 1893 in Polk County and was buried at Barren Creek Cemetery. *Submitted by Don Vincent*

WALLEN – Prior to 1623 the Wallen/Wallin name

Elisha Wallen "Roundabout" Plantation in Virginia, now is owned by DuPont Company

had possibilities of connection to Wallenstiens of Central Europe, Bohemia. Some Wallens drifted north to Holland then came to America by ship. Tracey Proctor's family left Europe, due to the religious war Protestant Revolt.

Ralph Wallen's birth date is unknown. He died in 1633. With wife Joyce, he docked at Plymouth, MA Feb. 10, 1623, from sailing over on the ship *Ann*. They were members of Francis Eaton Co. of the New Plymouth Colony. They later moved to Providence, RI and had two children, Ann and Thomas. Thomas Wallen I was born in 1627 in Providence, RI. He married Mary Abbott in 1651 and had four children. Mary died in 1669. Tom married Margaret Colewell on June 9, 1669 and had two more children. Thomas Wallen II was born in 1662 in Providence, RI. He married Sarah Elwell May 10, 1695 and they had 11 children. Elisha Wallen I was born July 26, 1708 in Salem County, NJ. He married Mary Blevins. They had nine children. Elisha was a big landowner and owned the "Roundabout Plantation" in Virginia. Elisha Wallen II was born in 1732 in Prince George County, MD. He married Catherine Blevins. They moved to Washington County, MO prior to 1811. He was in the Continental Army. Elisha Wallen III was born Nov. 30, 1795 in Tennessee. He married Mary Hughes Oct. 10, 1815. He was a private in the War of 1812. They had 19 children. George Washington Wallen I was born Dec. 2, 1839 in Washington County, MO. He married Arminta Grider Jan. 7, 1858. They had five children.

He was in the Civil War for the Union. He was captured by Confederates and died in their prison. George Washington Wallen II was born in 1860 in the same county. He married Elizabeth Howard and they had four children. They moved to Phoenix, AZ in 1898. Hiland Wallen was born in Oakland, CA April 4, the year unknown and married Fern Church. They had four children. He worked for the railroad. Charles Hiland Wallen was born in Clarksdale, AZ Nov. 11, 1919 and married Katherine Rosalie Walker May 25, 1946. He was in the US Navy during WWII. They had two children. Kelly Doyle Wallen was born June 28, 1948 in Burbank, CA. He served in the US Navy. He is married to Adrienne and they live in Newhall, CA. They have no children. Tracey Wallen Proctor was born March 13, 1951 and married William Jennings Proctor Dec. 17, 1999. They live in Humansville, MO and have one son Clint Thomas Trevarthen. *Submitted by Tracy Proctor*

WALTERS – James Volney Walters (Volna J. Walters) was born on Nov. 27, 1827 in Bowling Green, Warren County, KY, the oldest child of William W. Walters and Penelope Field (Fealds/Healds), who were said to have originated in Virginia. His siblings were Nancy Jean, Mary, Voltaire Q., Stanford E., Sarah Louisa and William Lewis Walters.

It is unclear exactly when James' family left

Kentucky and began their journey to Missouri, but the Walters family is listed in the 1850 St. Clair County census, and William and Penelope are believed to be buried in Horn Cemetery.

On Aug. 15, 1846 at age 18, James V. Walters joined the US Army at Bolivar, MO. He was a private under Captain Smithson in Company E, Third Regiment of Missouri (Mexican War) Volunteers. However, he served less than two months before being discharged on Sept. 29, 1846 at Fort Leavenworth, KS.

According to family legend, as a young man James married a preacher's daughter "on a dare" and became the father of a child. The 1859 St. Clair County, MO court records related to his father's estate, name Mary Ann Walters, wife of James V. Walters as one of the heirs. It is unknown who this woman was, where they were married and whatever became of her and the child.

Sometime after the death of his mother in 1852 or 1853, James left Missouri, never to return. He first tramped to Oregon with a group of Missouri men where he lived from 1853 to 1856, and then on to California. After living in California from 1856 to 1861, James joined the Army once again. On Sept. 12, 1861, he was inducted into Company A of the Fifth California Infantry at Yreka, Siskiyou County, CA under Captain Joseph Smith. This tour of duty was considerably longer than his first, and took him primarily to the territories of Arizona and New Mexico.

James was mustered out of the Army on Nov. 30, 1864 at La Mesilla, New Mexico Territory. The US government made no funds available for the men to return to their home states, so many of them, including James Walter, remained in New Mexico.

After his army discharge, James worked as a logger, teamster, farmer and as a scout or guide for newcomers to New Mexico. He received a homestead and married a young Hispanic woman, Frances Baca, on Feb. 12, 1869. They had 12 children and were true pioneers, according to the book *Pisacah, A Place of Plenty*, by Lillian H. Bidal.

After a full and interesting live, James Volney Walters departed this life at age 76, on June 26, 1904 at Lower Penasco, NM. He is buried in Elk Cemetery where his military tombstone marks his final resting-place.

James Volney Walters

The 12 children of James Volney Walters and Frances Baca Walters were Felicita "Lizzie," Mary Ann, William, Nancy, Lucy, Edwin, Anomia, Bess, Vivian, Metta, Bertha and James Volney Walters Jr. *Submitted by Kathy Anderson Goins*

WARE – William (1815-1875) and Mary Vernon Ware (1807-188?) moved to Dallas County in 1869 from Jackson County, OH. They came with other families: Scurlocks, Pummills, Thomas, etc. All 10 children of William and Mary, most of them married with children of their own, came with them. That must have been quite a wagon train.

The children were Anderson (1827-1913), Richard (1829-1904), Tinsley (1831-1920), Marion (1834-1856, died in Ohio); Alesey (1837-1905), Smiley (1842-still living in 1920 in Montana), Clarinda (1845-1901), Riley (1848-1928), Lucinda (1851-1938) and Harrison (1855-1934).

In the late 1880s Riley, his wife Eliza Pummill, and his sister Lucinda Scurlock moved to Polk County. Riley and Elizabeth had nine children: Charlie (1870-1950), Della Mae (1872-1874),

Ware family, Back: Henry Elbert, Artie, Louetta, Louella and Charlie; seated: Leander, Riley, Eliza

Louella (1875-1946), Cora R. (1878-1937), Louie (1882-1915), Louetta (1886-1970), Artie (1888-1973), Henry (1892-1972) and Leander (1896-1973).

Charlie married Sarah Carter, Louella married Elmer McGee, Louetta married Henry Russell and Artie married Elda France. These are the families that stayed in Polk County. All of them had large families. They lived near each other in northwest Polk County near Fair Play.

Charlie Ware was a very self-sufficient farmer. He made his own tools, grew all of their fruit, vegetables, and meat animals. In the summer he grew watermelons, cantaloupes, apples, etc., and sold them in town. He would hook up the team of horses and take them to Bolivar on the wagon. Charlie and Sarah grew their own cane and had a sorghum mill where they made molasses. He knew how to find and harvest bee trees. The children all worked hard on the farm and worked for neighbors to earn extra money. The children were Hiram, Otis, Ethel, Oma, Lena, Archie, Henry, Orpha, Orie, Frances and Minnie.

Louella and Henry Russell had a threshing machine that he took farm to farm in the summer to harvest crops for neighbors. That was the hottest work you can imagine. It was hot and sweaty and the straw would stick to the skin and itch like crazy. Henry and Louella had seven children: Eva, Verda, James, Floyd, Mildred, Virgil and Betty. *Submitted by Lois Smith*

WARREN – Ira P. Warren was born Aug. 12, 1821 in East Aurora, NY and Ardelia Ward Warren was born in 1833 in New York. They married in Independence, IA and they moved to Bolivar about 1880. They were the great-grandparents of Ruth Warren Munn.

Ira was mayor of Bolivar from 1883-1885. Ardelia was a milliner. They owned a building on the west side of the public square. They had two children, Joseph R. and Almeda Warren. After their daughter's death in 1893, they moved to Wirth, AR and he was postmaster there. After his death in 1907, Ardelia moved back to Bolivar. She passed away in June 1911.

Ira had a sister, Sarepta Whitney. She is buried at Pleasant Hill Cemetery at Halfway. *Submitted by Ruth Warren Munn*

WARREN – William Franklin Warren was born Jan. 17, 1853 in Clark County, KY (died Feb. 18, 1913) and married Elizabeth "Gunn" Warren who was born Feb. 27, 1855 in Irdell, NC (died Aug. 13, 1918). William was a doctor who started his practice in Pettis County, MO and Elizabeth was a teacher and they had six children: Lee, Earnest, Earl, Edith, Guy and Mable. Both William and Elizabeth are buried in Mt. View Cemetery, Polk, MO.

In the late 1880s William and Elizabeth moved to Bolivar where he opened his doctor's office. About 1890 he moved to Huron, MO and built a beautiful home and his office was inside of his home. He also opened a drug store in Huron and that helped get the town started. Shortly thereafter he opened another office in Polk, MO which helped get that community started.

Doc Warren made all of his house calls in a horse and buggy. He really loved people and took a lot of garden products, canned food, chicken and many things as payment. During the winter they always kept rocks on the stove and put them in the floor of the buggy to help keep them warm on house calls.

Lee Warren was born April 9, 1874 in Pettis County, MO (died Nov. 20, 1952 in Bolivar, MO) and moved to Polk County with his parents. He married Bernice Ellen Willis who was born Dec. 21, 1876 in Kentucky (died Aug. 2, 1952 in Bolivar, MO). Both of them are buried in Payne Cemetery in Polk County, MO. They had nine children: Oscar, Ruth, Carl, Ruby, Olive, Curtise, Marjorie, Joe and Winford. Lee and Bernice lived in Polk County all of their lives and enjoyed cattle and horses.

Oscar Warren (born March 22, 1894 in Pettis County, MO and died Sept. 5, 1969 in Polk, MO) married Golden Storment (born Dec. 1, 1914, Polk, MO and died Oct. 1, 1973, Polk, MO). Both Oscar and Golden are buried in Payne Cemetery in Polk, MO. They had nine children: Jewell,

Doc Warren and wife Nettie

Nelson, Choloada (Schaub), Eldon and Arnol Warren, Polk, MO

Nelson, Choloada, Eldon, Vanbuna, Arnol, Arbie, Norris and Delma. Oscar and Golden had cattle, lots of sheep, and also raised chickens and sold eggs to the hatchery for many years. They also cut saw logs with cross cut saws, which were sold to the sawmill. The sawmill was run by a steam engine and those same engines were also used to thrash grain.

Four of the Warren children served during WWII, three sons: Nelson, Eldon and Arnol and one daughter, Choloada. Although all four came home from the war, this was a huge sacrifice on the part of the Warren family.

On Sept. 11, 1949, Eldon married Virginia Anderson (Humansville, MO) and they had three children, Rex, Vanetta and Cynthia.

Rex married Diane Hibbs (Carthage, MO) and they had two children, Justin and Emily. Vanetta married Frank Robertson (Bolivar, MO) and they had three sons, Sheldon, Albert and Travis. Cynthis married Bill Wood (Weaubleau, MO) and they had two children, Joshua and Amanda. Eldon and Virginia have five great-grandchildren.

Eldon is proud to have had the opportunity to buy both of his grandfather's farms south of Polk, and he had been able to put other land together with the family farms. He is honored to be the "steward" of the land. Eldon says, "We all love and hope to pass the land on to my family in better condition than when I got it."

Eldon is the only great-grandson of Doc War-

Justin, Eldon, Rex, Logan held by Eldon

ren who still carries the Warren name and lives in Polk County. He has a son, Rex, a grandson, Justin and a great-grandson, Logan. The Warren heritage will be in Polk County for a long time as Logan makes seven generations of Warrens to reside here.

During WWII, Eldon had the rank of sergeant and served in the Air Force in the European Theater. He served three and a half years. His job was a teletype operator, cryptographic technician 805, radio operator and he received and sent coded messages all over the world. Today he is a rancher and enjoys raising prime Charolais cattle and quality alfalfa hay. *Submitted by Eldon Warren*

WARREN – (Letter written by Rex Warren after July 4, 2001.)

"After last Wednesday's Fourth of July celebration, I felt compelled to write and express my appreciation to some heroes in my life. I have had the good fortune of living in a family and community that fosters love of nation and of each other. Growing up inside this bubble of devotion I learned at an early age what kind of men it takes to set standards, professionally, personally and spiritually.

"First let me start with my father, Eldon Warren. He was drafted into the US Army/Air Corps in WWII and spent most of his wartime years in France manning an emergency air base. It was front line and was to be used for planes that had received damage on bombing missions and could not get home. His base changed hands several times during his stay and was a constant target for whoever was not in possession at the time. He was bombed by the German Air Force on numerous occasions and was injured when the truck he was on became the recipient of one of those bombs. The control tower he used had no glass left in it and the base was filled with bullet and shrapnel holes. He came home, got married, had a family, and works on the farm still today. He has said very little of his experiences, but over the years has shared at least this much.

"Uncle Nelson Warren was drafted into the Army/Air Corps in WWII and spent the most of his time in the Pacific Theater. He towed airplanes and worked in the motor pool. Uncle Arnol Warren was drafted into the Army and served in Germany and Austria as part of the occupational forces after the war as a member of the military police. Aunt Choloada Warren (Schaub) enlisted in the WACS and worked in the Pacific Theater in Australia, New Guinea, and New Zealand as a dental technician and helped build false teeth for wounded soldiers. (According to her brothers she probably saw more of the horrors of the war than the rest.)

Uncle Rolla Anderson served in occupied Italy.

Uncle L. D. Hale served in the motor pool in the US Army in the Pacific.

Uncle Joe Tinsley served in the US Army in the Pacific.

Uncle Paul Stephens served in the US Army in the Pacific.

All are Polk County veterans.

Ed Hibbs (father-in-law) served in the Marine Corps as a fighter plane mechanic on the *US Essex* and was a witness to several kamikaze attacks. He also witnessed the sinking of the Yorktown.

"All of these men came home and raised families and continued to served their country by working and paying taxes and tending to their day-to-day business of life. Some are gone; some are still here and hopefully still willing to tell a little bit of themselves. They shared a time in our world that is unparalleled. They went from the horse and buggy to the moon and I do not recall them ever complaining about the changes happening in their world.

"Eldon went from rural Polk County to a world at war. He saw the advent of radar and was one of the first to use it. (An instrument that I use every time I start a trip in my airplane.) He saw the change from coal oil lamps to hold back the darkness to atomic energy, from tobacco poultices for home remedies, to the use of antibiotics and laser surgery.

"Much is always made about heroes, as is should be. But I contend that we don't have far to look to find them, but we must look. I am ashamed to admit that for a long time I didn't realize that I sat across the breakfast table from a real hero and that I have spent most of my life in the presence of men and women of great valor. Thank you all very much." *Submitted by Vanetta Robertson*

WARREN – Doc and Nettie Warren came to Polk County in the late 1880s. They settled in Huron where he set up his medical practice. William Franklin Warren grew up in southern Pettis County. He was born Jan. 17, 1853 in Winchester, Clark County, KY. His parents were William Warren and Malinda Tribble. William had several professions, including that of schoolteacher. Eliza Genette Gunn, better known as "Nettie" was the daughter of John Gunn and Delia Allison. John was also a physician. Nettie was born Feb. 27, 1855. Doc and Nettie had eight children. The children were Robert Lee; Ernest; C. Earl; Edith, who married Edwin Pitts; Oscar F.; Homer Guy; Roy G. and Mabel C., who married a Johnson.

William Lee, known around Huron as Lee,

Dr. William Franklin and Nettie (Gunn) Warren

married Bernice Elaine Willis in 1892. Lee was born in Sedalia, Pettis County, MO on April 9, 1874. Bernice, known as "Bunny," was born Dec. 21, 1876 in Anderson County, KY. Her parents were James E. Willis and Mary Ellen Gordon. Lee and Bunny had nine children. They were Oscar Hoy; Carl Lyle; Curtis Paul; Joe; Ruth, who married a Greathouse; Ruby A., who married J. H. "Jim" Cansler; Margie, who married a Delozier; Winifred, who married a Childress; and Mary Olivia.

Oscar Hoy Warren married Golden Storment, daughter of Riley Storment and Laura Payne. They were married Dec. 1, 1915. Oscar was born March 22, 1894 and Golden was born Oct. 14, 1897. Oscar and Golden had nine children. They were Jewell, who married Don Ottens; Nelson; Choloada, who married Ray Schaub; Eldon, who married Virginia Dee Anderson; Vanbuena; Arnol, who married Lucille Black; Arbie, who married Deloris Carson Norris and Delma, who married Clarence Hembree.

Nelson married Jereline Warren, daughter of Tommie Hale and Pearl Ashlock. Nelson was born Sept. 15, 1917 and Jereline was born July 17, 1922. They had two children, Gary and Jeanie, who married Charles Barnes.

Gary Warren married Patty Breshears on Aug. 28, 1966. Patty's parents are Glen Breshears and Pat Love. Gary and Patty have two children, Suzanne, who married Stan Mayfield and Todd. They have one granddaughter, Brooke. *Submitted by Todd Warren*

WATKINS – Alva Watkins was born Feb. 25, 1905 in DeSoto, MO to Richard and Mary Magdalene Watkins. Richard was a Civil War Union Army man. "Maggie" was the daughter of Confederate parents. Her father, Samuel Bridges, had several slaves and owned several acres of land in northeast Polk County. After Maggie and Richard met and fell in love, they knew they could not stay around here so they went to the state of Virginia to get married. They lived in the mountains of Virginia for a few years. While there, they had two children, Elsie Watkins Grant and Albert Watkins. The family later moved to DeSoto, MO, where Alva Watkins was born.

There isn't much history about Richard Watkins' side of the family. He did have a second family but nothing has been recorded. Richard was much older then Maggie.

Maggie was one of eight children born to Samuel and Rachel Bridges, one sister, Maude and six brothers, Fred, Cleave, Tom, Jerry, Clarence and Bert.

Albert Watkins died when he was 22 years old in 1925. Bertha and Elsie Watkins have passed away in later years. Richard died in 1913. Maggie died when she was 89 years old in 1966.

The Watkins family moved from DeSoto, MO to Goodson, MO during the year of 1909. Another daughter Bertha was born. Richard was postmaster at Goodson until his death in 1913. After Richard died Maggie and the four children moved to Hickory County near Huckaby, MO and lived there for two years. They later moved to Buffalo, MO in 1915. During their stay in Buffalo, Maggie met and married V. G. "Gate" McKinney in 1917. They moved to the Burns community in Polk County where Alva presently lives on the same farm. During the first year, another daughter was born, Van Buena McKinney. She resides in Cerritos, CA as of this writing.

Alva's growing up years saw some pretty tough times. He and Albert had farm chores to do: milking, putting up hay and may other chores. The boys hunted rabbits, which furnished them extra spending money as well as a delicious family meal. Albert and Alva would dress rabbits for people and make an extra nickel for cleaning them. In the summer the boys fished a lot, mostly on Lindley Creek. Their Grandfather Bridges taught the boys how to fish. The family enjoyed the catch for the day on many occasions.

Alva received his formal education at McKinney Grade School, a one-room country schoolhouse near Burns. As soon as he graduated from school he went to work for a road construction firm helping to build Highway 32, Highway 65, Interstate 44 and Highway 13. In his later years of working, he worked in building construction of churches and helped to build some of the Southwest Baptist College buildings. During Alva's teen years and early twenties, Alva hunted and sold fur for extra money to help with expenses.

Alva met and married Wilma Cornelius, daughter of William "Bill" and Rena Roweton Cornelius, in 1926. Wilma had five sisters, Dolly, Frances, Rosa, Myrtle and Lola and three brothers, Ode, Jack and Ed. The Corneliuses lived in the Burns community also.

Alva and Wilma had three daughters, Ruth Watkins Legan, Ethel Watkins Lunceford and Dale Watkins Ritsema. Their family had grown to nine grandchildren, 15 great-grandchildren and 11 great-great grandchildren as of this writing.

Wilma and Alva worked hard on the farm. Alva was gone from home working in construction a lot of the time. That left Wilma alone to do the farm chores while he was gone. She was a hardworking woman and loved her many beautiful flowers. Wilma passed away Jan. 1, 1994. Wilma loved her family dearly and was a devoted mother and grandmother. Her prayers and deep faith in God has been a blessing to all her family and friends. Their lives centered on their faith in God, families and church family.

Times were hard in the early 1900s. People were just happy to survive. Alva has seen many changes in the community and the nation. The Burns community where Alva lived most of his 98 years has changed a lot. When he was a young boy, there were two stores, post office, blacksmith shop, gristmill and a lumber mill. The families in the community could sell their eggs, chickens, milk and cream to the general store. Another change was the Pomme De Terre River. It was much larger back in those days than it is now. Lots more water ran in it and fishing was good. As years have passed all of the businesses do not exist in Burns. People now travel to Bolivar to buy their family supplies and groceries.

Polk County has been a good community to live in. It's home and always will be. The people in Polk County are really friendly, helpful people. *Submitted by Dale Ritsema*

WATKINS – Phillip M. Watkins was born March 1, 1796. He is the son of Robert Watkins. Phillip was born in Kentucky and immigrated at an early age to Tennessee. On Oct. 13, 1823 he married Mary Elizabeth Lay, who was born Jan. 15, 1807, in Sumner County, TN by William Montgomery, J. P. Mary was born in Kentucky. Phillip was a farmer and moved to Polk County, MO about 1849. He was a veteran of the War of 1812. He served in the Battle of New Orleans. Phillip and Mary had 13 children born to them. They are Susannah, 1828; Sarah Jane, 1829; George W., 1832; Mary Elizabeth, 1834; John T., 1836; Margaret, 1840; Phillip "Dick," 1842; Nancy; James, 1845 and other names unknown. Phillip died April 4, 1879 in Polk County, MO.

Mary Elizabeth died Aug. 11, 1886 in Polk County, MO. Both are buried at Brush Grove Cemetery.

Daughter Mary Elizabeth Watkins was born June 28, 1834 in Polk County, MO. On Aug. 3, 1855, she married Jordan A. Anderson, born 1832, Tennessee, at Bolivar, Polk County, MO by William B. Senter, M. G. Jordan is the son of William Anderson and Mary Coggins/Scoggins. Jordan and Mary had 15 children. They are Mary Elizabeth, 1856; Robert A., 1857; John Thomas, 1858; Frances, 1860; Susan C., 1862; William H., 1863; James H., 1864; Phillip M., 1870; George W., 1872; Charles W., 1873; Drewery, 1874; Solly, 1878; Nancy, 1866 and two unknown. Jordan served in the Civil War. Jordan also went to work in the gold mine in 1849 in California along with his brothers. He returned to Missouri and farmed. *Submitted by Deborah (Holland) Mellegaard*

WELLS – Richard George H., son of Lawrence Boone and Jane H. (Whillock) Wells, was born March 25, 1847 in Jefferson County, TN. Sarah Lucinda, daughter of William Leonard and Mary Ann (Hull) Henson, was born June 12, 1851 in Sullivan County, TN. They came to Missouri with their parents, grew up in the Polk County area and were married Aug. 2, 1868 by the Rev. J. Bowman in Humansville.

Sarah Lucinda's grandparents, Thomas William and Sarah Henson moved from Scott County, VA to Sullivan County, TN before 1840. They had eight children: Rebecca, William L., Hiram F., Thomas J., Sarah Catherine, David A., James M. and Susan Jane, when the family moved to Polk County, MO in the early 1840s. An infant daughter died shortly thereafter. Thomas, a blacksmith, died May 23, 1856 and is buried in Bolivar City Cemetery between his daughters, the infant who died in 1843 and Rebecca White, who died in 1847. His wife Sarah, who died April 4, 1876, is buried near their son, William, in Humansville Cemetery.

It isn't known if William Henson, born Oct. 14, 1828 in Scott County, VA moved to Missouri with his parents in the early 1840s as he appears on the 1850 Sullivan County census in the home of Jonathan Hess. William and Mary Ann, daughter of David and Isabelle (Matthew) Hull, were married in the Hess home on Aug. 15, 1850. They moved to Polk County, MO after Sarah's birth and had six more children: David A., Isabella J., Emeline F., Mary V., Tennessee E. and Analitha C.

William Henson enlisted in the Union Army at Bolivar in 1862 initially serving in Company I, 27th Regiment, Missouri Volunteers and later with Company I, 30/32nd Com. Battalion Infantry Missouri Volunteers. He was seriously wounded at Missionary Ridge near Chattanooga and given a Certificate of Discharge for Disability in July 1865. However, his pension application and subsequent inquiries were lost or ignored by the government. Consequently, Mary Ann didn't receive a widow's pension after his death in 1873. Guardianship records in Carroll County, MO indicate the minor children, orphaned when Mary Ann died in 1876, finally received a settlement for their father's pension claim in 1889. Place of Mary Ann's burial is unknown; perhaps she's in a unmarked grave near William who is buried next to his mother, Sarah Henson and granddaughter, Mary Jane Wells, in the Humansville Cemetery.

Richard's father, Lawrence Boone Wells, was from a family of nine children (Mary Ann, Humphrey, Henry E., Felix W., Lawrence B., Elizabeth, Rebecca, Sarah B. and Jacob P.). He was born in Greene County, TN to George and Mary (Earnest) Wells. Both the Wells and Earnest families strongly supported Bishop Asbury's efforts to establish Methodist churches in the Kentucky and Tennessee wilderness. The Rev. George Wells, born 1765 near Annapolis, MD, was still active in the ministry and performing weddings two years before his death in 1859 and is buried with Mary in the cemetery of Bethesda Methodist Church near Greenville. On Dec. 23, 1834, their son, Lawrence Boone Wells, married Jane H., daughter of James and Deborah (Rector) Whillock. They moved to Dallas County, MO in 1856 with their 10 children: Minerva Jane, Mary Ann, Samuel P., Maria D., Elizabeth Caroline, Sarah R., Richard George H., William, Jeremiah F. and Joseph S. Jane, who died Oct. 18, 1861, and Lawrence, who died June 5, 1884, are buried in Bowers Chapel Cemetery near Urbana, MO.

Their son, Richard George, was nearly 18 when he enlisted in the Union Army in 1865. Pvt. Wells served in Company H, 14th Missouri Volunteer Cavalry, and was discharged Oct. 26, 1866. After his marriage to Sarah, in 1868, the couple lived a few miles west of Humansville in Cedar County. They had nine children: William Lawrence married Dora Rains; Sarah Nellie married Hiram Hoyt; Joseph J. married Bessie Pool; Lucy Weltha married James Butcher; Thomas J. married Minnie; James Leonard married Lucy Hiatt. Three other children died young. The Wells family moved to Oklahoma Territory about 1896. Richard died Jan. 9, 1900 in Logan County, OK. Four years later, Sarah married Peter Cooper. Following his death in 1915, Sarah lived with her children who were then scattered from the Midwest to the Pacific Ocean. She traveled around the country with a large trunk spending a few weeks or months at each home. Her grandchildren looked forward to her lengthy visits and the little treasures hidden away in her trunk. We have a collection of seashells from Grandma Cooper and a book published in 1865 *The Life and Times of Abraham Lincoln* that belonged to her father, William Henson. The book contains inscriptions by W. M. Catron, one of which reads, "M. C. Stotts, May 21, 1810." William Henson and Fred Catron married sisters, Mary Ann and Emaline Hull, but the identity of W. M. Catron and M. C. Stotts remains a mystery. Sarah died Aug. 2, 1930 and is buried next to Richard in Oakland Cemetery, Crescent, OK. *Submitted by Fran Miller and Marilyn Davis*

WELSH – Barnett Welsh (April 16, 1810-April 4, 1887) was probably born in Virginia and named after his father, who was also Barnett. It is said that his father had a strong "Dutchie" accent, and it is believed that he emigrated from Wales Province before 1800. The younger Barnett is first found in Licking County, OH, having been born in 1810. He married Mariah Overturf "Mary" (May 16, 1813-Jan. 25, 1852).

Mary's lineage is from German immigrants. Valentine Overturf is the immigrant who arrived in Philadelphia in 1753. He raised his family in Pennsylvania; his son Simon married Mary Debolt and they raised 10 children, including Mary. They emigrated from Pennsylvania to Licking County, OH in 1809. Valentine's father was Baltasar Oberdorff of Wertheim of Wertemberg, Germany.

The number of children of Barnett Welsh is somewhat in question. Mary bore at least nine, listed below.

Lucinda Belle (1831-1912), Jeremiah (1833-1858), William (1836-1856), Jesse (1838-1907), George W. (1841-1867), Richard Hiram (1843-1881), Mary K. (1845-1864), Sarah Jane (1847-1888) and John (1850-1870).

Barnett and Mary Welsh arrived in Missouri from Licking County, OH about 1847; their two youngest children were born in Polk County, MO. Mary's tragic death in January of 1852 shocked the whole community.

Barnett married Minerva "Nervy" Ruth Garrison (April 30, 1827-Feb. 22, 1898) of Laclede County, MO in 1857. Barnett and Nervy had a family of six more children. They were David Morgan (1857-1889), Francis Seigle (1861-1926), Robert L. (1864-1924) married Covington, Lenora Ann "Laura" (1866-?) married Fausett, Lanetta Florence "Nettie" (1867-1944) married Thomas R. Hutchinson and an infant born dead.

Barnett was a prominent farmer in Polk County for many years. He was deeply interested in the spiritual life of his family and was especially vocal on his deathbed in urging them to join him in eternity.

As many others, some of the younger Welsh clan got the itch for their own place, probably also attracted by the Oklahoma land rush of the 1890s. But Jesse Welsh (Barnett and Mary's fifth child) did not do that. However, he was married three times and twice widowed. His children and spouses are, as follows:

First marriage to Martha Jane McCrory of Tennessee (born Aug. 31, 1839 and died Jan. 25, 1882). Issue: William Franklin (1861-1941), Mary Jane (1863-1915), Rhoda Adeline (1865-1953), Lucinda Belle (1867-1950), Laura Eleanor (1870-1954), infant son (1872-1872), Samuel Morgan (1873-1875), James Benton (1875-1965), Louisa May "Ida" (1878-1952) and Jessie Easter (1881-1964).

Second marriage to Nancy A. Dysart-Potts (Nov. 29, 1851-March 31, 1897) on Feb. 28, 1883. Issue: Charles Erastus (Feb. 5, 1884-Aug. 1, 1884), Elmer Austin (1887-1952). Nancy had four children by a former marriage.

Third marriage to Sadie Jarnagan (1867-1923) on April 24, 1898. No issue.

Rhoda's son, Jesse Houston Watson, prepared a unique genealogy of this Welsh family. Part of his work is summarized above. Jesse's mother, Rhoda, married William Houston Watson. (See Watson elsewhere) One of Jesse's strongest recollections was that his mother was buried after a tremendous snowfall. Several men and the pallbearers carried her casket from the road to graveside where services were conducted in sub-freezing weather. *Submitted by Tom Stevens*

WESTFALL – In 1899 or 1900, Warren Lee and Olive Bernice (Seavey) Westfall moved to Polk County from Winigan, MO in Sullivan County. They were accompanied by their five children and settled on a farm northwest of Halfway in

Westfall family circa 1900-1910; back: Lawrence, Linley and Roy; front: Mabel, Warren, Olive and Mina

the Dewey Community. Warren was the son of William and Mary (Simons) Westfall. Warren was a Civil War veteran, serving in the Union Army and a first cousin to William Harrison Westfall, the train conductor killed by Frank and Jesse James in Gallatin County. His grandfather, Reuben, was a captain in the Cavalry during the War of 1812. His great-grandfather, Jacob Jr., served as lieutenant in the Revolutionary War and was later promoted to captain. They were descendants of Jurian Westphal (Dutch spelling) or George Westfall (English spelling). Jurian was born in 1629, probably in Prussia. He came to America (New Amsterdam) by way of Holland in 1642, apparently as part of the Huguenot migration.

Olive was the daughter of George W. Seavey, a Union officer during the Civil War. Her mother was Mary Allen Pierce. Her great-grandmother was a Blake. Both the Blakes' and Seaveys' original immigration ancestors date their entry to New England in the 1630s.

The descendants of Warren and Olive are, as follows:

Lawrence Lee, born Jan. 1, 1880, married Nora Davison, June 29, 1902. They lived in Polk County for a short time and had five children but have no descendants living in Polk County at this writing.

Mina Bernice, born July 23, 1882, married Walter Lewis Hale, Jan. 7, 1904. They lived in Polk County and had three sons. One son died as a child, the other two moved to California and raised their families on the West Coast.

Linley Blanchard, born July 23, 1883, married Mertie Vincent, Feb. 13, 1910. Mertie was the daughter of Christopher Columbus and Frances (Ashlock) Vincent. (For additional information see Vincent genealogy.)

Linley and Mertie had two sons. Raymond Earl "Johnny," born Feb. 28, 1911, married Faye Neill, Buffalo, MO, Nov. 21, 1937. Faye was the daughter of Daniel Clinton and LuElla (Barrett) Neill. Johnny and Faye operated a retail grocery store in Halfway in the late 1930s-1940s and later established the Bolivar Candy Company, a wholesale confectionery and institutional supply business, which they operated for 25 years. Johnny was a state representative in the Missouri Legislature from January 1969 until his death following open-heart surgery in August 1971. He and Faye had one child, Morris G. Westfall, born April 5, 1939. Morris married Sharon Douglas, Willard, MO Dec. 19, 1964. She is the daughter of Efton and Juanita (Hall) Douglas. Sharon is related to the Hall and Stokes families that reside in the Morrisville and Walnut Grove area. It is interesting to note that Sharon's Great-Great-Grandfather Stokes fought at Wilson's Creek under the Confederate Flag, while Morris' Great-Grandfather Vincent served in the Union Army at Wilson's Creek. Morris and Sharon reside on a livestock farm south of Halfway. Sharon taught music in the Stockton and Halfway School for 27 years. Morris served in the Missouri House of Representatives from October 1971 to May 1981 and as state senator from January 1995 to December 2002. They have two children, Craig and Christi Westfall and one grandchild, Cody Ray Westfall. Cody Ray is believed to be the only sixth generation descendant of Warren and Olive Westfall carrying the Westfall name.

Linley and Mertie's second son, Glen Lovel, born Oct. 18, 1921, married Veroka Parrott, Bolivar, MO. Veroka was the daughter of Kinsey Kern and Ruby Gladys (Franklin) Parrott. Glen and Veroka lived on a farm near Halfway for many years before their deaths. They had two daughters, Kaylen Kern, born March 2, 1946 and Glenda Michelle, born April 25, 1951. Kaylen had one son, Wyatt Jeffries and they live in North Carolina. Michelle lives near Halfway and has two children. Her son, Kris Wilson, lives in Bolivar and her daughter, Kortney, lives in Springfield.

Warren and Olive Westfall's fourth child was Roy Lesley, born Jan. 3, 1887. He married Jessie Wilson and resides in the Halfway community. They had two sons. Elmo was born Jan. 9, 1912 and married Roxie Cummins. Elmo and Roxie had two children, neither of whom lived in Missouri. Roy and Jessie's second son, Roma Wayne, was born March 13, 1915 and married Virginia Nell Polly, daughter of Luther and Nellie (Bowser) Polly. Roma and Virginia raised their two children in the Halfway community before moving to Springfield. Their son, Larry, born Jan. 24, 1943, resides in the Halfway community. Their daughter, Carol Sue, born Sept. 7, 1944, lives in Greene County, and has three sons, Jimmy, Jeff and Mathew Ingram.

The fifth child of Warren and Olive Westfall was Mabel Edith. Born Aug. 4, 1890, she married Feb. 27, 1910 to Joseph Henry Newland. They had five children but only Arthur Joseph raised his family in Polk County. Arthur was born March 31, 1915 and married Thelma Lois Ashlock. They had one daughter, Shirley Ann, born June 16, 1940. Shirley married Charles Ealy, who is serving his sixth year as mayor of Bolivar. Charley and Shirley have three children, Danny of Blue Springs, Judy Myers of Springfield and Barbra Haynes who lives in Morrisville and has three children. The youngest child of Joseph and Mabel Newland was Mabel Olive, born Nov. 19, 1918. She married Archie Crawford, Feb. 14, 1942 and lived in Polk County for a short time. *Submitted by Craig L. Westfall*

Bertha Ruby Mae Anderson White

WHITE – Bertha Ruby Mae Anderson (March 3, 1883-July 20,1968) married Thomas Henry White (Sept. 5, 1877-Oct. 7, 1955) on April 24, 1898. They had six children. Bertha was not a woman of great distinction or renown, but she is remembered and honored as a loving and devout person who had the hardiness, strengths and abilities of her pioneer ancestors. She was the very capable helpmate needed by her strong, farmer husband.

Bertha had the skills and talents expected of young women in those days; sewing, needlework, and quilting, cooking, canning and baking, housekeeping and gardening. Everyday chores were hard work and unending. Her range was a woodburning stove. The yard was her laundry room. To do laundry for her family, wearing a sunbonnet, long sleeves and long skirts, Bertha would use lye soap she made herself, build a fire in the yard, haul water from the spring to pour into a large cauldron for washing and tubs for rinsing. Stains were scrubbed on a washboard and clean clothes hung on lines to dry. Heavy flatirons were heated for ironing. She went about her daily work while whistling hymns and old ballads. When the wind was right, the sound of her whistling would carry over the fields to approaching visitors.

Bertha was never one of those women who squealed at the sight of a mouse. With her husband in the fields or building fences from daybreak to dusk, she had to be self-sufficient. She milked the cow and set traps for rats that ate the grain in the barn. She tended the vegetable garden, plucking bugs and fat horned worms from the plants and pinching heads off so they wouldn't return. She killed many a snake with a stick or garden hoe, not a few in the path to the outhouse. When a chicken was needed for the stew pot, she wrung its neck and flung it away to run headless until its blood was drained. Feathers were plucked, washed and dried to be used later when making pillows and mattresses. Bertha did what had to be done.

Although the living was pretty primitive, Bertha was a stickler for cleanliness. No one came to her table without first stopping at the wash basin to use the lye soap. Dishes were washed in water as hot as the hands could stand, rinsed with scalding water and dried with pristine towels.

Bertha was also a midwife, assisting with births whenever called. She delivered several of her own grandchildren, including the totally unanticipated Overcash twin girls. She doctored her family, herself and the farm animals with old-time recipes, plants and potions.

Each morning Bertha wound her long hair into a big bun on the back of her head and anchored it with long hairpins. At night, she would let her hair down and brush it 100 strokes. Many of the grandchildren loved to brush her hair, as it touched the ground when she sat in a chair. Long after her husband died, and her hair had turned white as snow, Bertha had it cut and permed so it would be easier to manage. Not long afterwards, a picture was taken of Bertha with her short, curled hair, her smile showing the teeth she never put in at home. No one looking at that picture would ever imagine the history of that pretty woman. But, luckily, some of her granddaughters inherited a bit of her strength. *Submitted by Rene' Belinda Ammerman*

WHITE – Thomas Henry White was born Sept. 5, 1877 to James and Mary Frances Ballinger White. He was the youngest child, having been born a few months after his father was killed in an accident involving horseback riding. No date can be found of his father's death.

Tom had two sisters and four brothers: David Ella, Meartillas, Archable Stephenson, James Marcus, John and Dudley Walter.

On April 24, 1898, he married Bertha Ruby Mae Anderson, and to this union four girls and two boys were born. Rosa Belle Francis married Roy Ozro Overcash. They had four girls and one boy. Martha Elizabeth married John Henry Worthey and had five girls and one boy. Later she married Charles Delbert Graves and had one boy. Ethel Golda Mae married Alonzo Everett Sanders. They had one girl and three boys. Flora Lara married Hershel Fredric Sanders (brother to Alonzo) and had one girl. She later married Orman Dean Blurton and had another girl. Jesse Harvey married Lula Mae Greenwood and had four boys and three girls. Leo Henry married Lucille Brown, later marrying Novella Nadine Nowland. There were no children for either marriage.

An interesting fact about Tom's marriage to Bertha was throughout their 57 years together, they never spent one night or day alone. Tom's mother made her home with them until her death. His brothers, brothers-in-law, children, grandchildren, nieces or whoever needed a place to live, were made welcome. At one time there were 11 people living in a two-room log cabin. One son recalled he had to sleep on an ironing board.

Tom's nickname was "Poppy" and he was called that by family and neighbors. His unique way of talking sounds funny today, but at the time it was just "Poppy's talk." If he wanted to hold someone on his lap he would ask if he could "nuss" them. Getting a stick of wood or bucket of water was "fetching."

Thomas White

Schooling was only through the third grade, as he had to quit to help make a living for the family, as lots of boys had to do in those days.

He could write his name and add a little but not much else. He bought 40 acres and farmed it with a team of horses, keeping the land cleared with an axe and mattox, while helping neighbors clear their land also.

On Oct. 7, 1955, his brother-in-law brought some paw-paws to him and as they were going to the yard to eat them, he had a massive heart attack and died instantly.

Poppy lived rather a dull life by today's standards. That's not the real story here. The real reason for this story is that he had a gift. His gift was being able to heal babies who had thrush, which is a disease of the mouth, caused by a fungus. People brought babies to be healed and he never accepted compensation of any kind, as he considered it a God-given gift to be used for helping others. All he did was puff a small breath of air into the baby's mouth. Within a couple of days the baby was well.

Call it Ozark superstition, black magic or whatever you want. Old wives' tales say it was the fact that he had never seen his father was why the gift was given. Laugh if you will, it worked on all the babies brought to him. No one was turned away. *Submitted by Rena Overcash Smith*

WHITLOCK – During weekends, a young Air Force sergeant from Polk County, MO was employed at a convenience store in Fink, TX, near Lake Texoma. One Saturday, as he sat on the Coke cooler-case, a girl walked in the door and made her way to the counter. As he later revealed to friends, he nearly fell off the Coke-case trying to see if there was a ring on her finger. It turned out that the girl was the owner's daughter and the sergeant later admitted to a case of "love at first sight." In 1971, Donald Clay Whitlock and Laurie Marie Albright were married and, after his "hitch" in the Air Force, made their home in Polk County. They spent their married life in the Pleasant Hope community.

Donald was born in Springfield, MO to Scotty Clay and Mildred (Freeman) Whitlock on Jan. 2, 1948. He was raised in the Pleasant Hope community where his family operated a farm. Growing up, he and his brothers, David, Darrell and Dale, were responsible for daily chores and spent their days outdoors having many adventures. He raised and showed cattle and was active in 4-H and FFA. After high school, Don enlisted in the Air Force (1967-1971), serving in Korea and Thailand during the Vietnam War. While stationed in Texas, he met, fell in love with and married Laurie. Don farmed for many years. He owned and operated a school bus for 12 years for Pleasant Hope Schools. In 1978 he became a rural mail carrier for Pleasant Hope, retiring in 2001. He served as church trustee for the Pleasant Hope Methodist Church. He served his community as a member of the board of education, city council, and the fire and rescue board of directors. He held a private pilot's license and loved flying, building and remodeling planes. He also enjoyed hunting, fishing and golf. Donald died of melanoma on May 8, 2001. If a man's wealth is counted by his friends, Donald was a wealthy man.

Laurie was born on Oct. 7, 1946 in San Diego, CA to Willard Ellis Albright (March 3, 1922-March 23, 1998) and Eileen McKinley (born Jan. 21, 1926). Both parents were born and raised in Guernsey County, OH. Her father served in the Navy during WWII having survived the attack on Pearl Harbor. She and stepsisters Patti and Lana were raised in the Pottsboro, TX area by her father and stepmother, Patsy Ruth (Moser) (Sept. 24, 1927-May 16, 1996). She graduated from Denison (Texas) High School. She earned her BS degree from East Texas University and later her MS degree from Southwest Missouri State University. Laurie taught secondary science for three years in Texas, one year in Morrisville (1976-1977) and for 24 years (1977-2001) in Pleasant Hope, retiring from teaching in June 2001. She has been involved in many student-oriented activities and programs, professional projects, programs and committees, and church and community activities. Laurie enjoys her family, traveling and seeing new sights.

Laurie and Don

Donald and Laurie have two sons, Justin Clay (born Oct. 14, 1971) and Jim Ellis (born Aug. 6, 1973). Both sons graduated from Pleasant Hope High School, and Jim earned BS degree from Southwest Missouri State University. They were active in FFA and enjoyed riding horses and working with livestock. The family enjoyed camping, vacations and family celebrations. Justin, his wife D'Nette (Perkins) and son Coltin Clay (born Dec. 22, 2000) live in Amarillo, TX. Jim lives in Pleasant Hope and has a son, Austin Ellis (born Aug. 13, 1998). *Submitted by Laurie Whitlock*

WHITLOCK – One afternoon while listening to "Walking in a Winter Wonderland" on the radio, a mother-in-law revealed to her son's bride the love story of a young soldier returning from the war and courting a young lady. As the man wooed and won the hand of this lady, she remembered, he would hum and sing the song that inspired the story. She always thought back to those early days when she heard that song. Scotty Clay Whitlock and Mildred Elene Freeman were married Jan. 19, 1947. In 1951 they moved onto their farm north of Rock Prairie in southeastern Polk County. In 1957, they moved to a farm nearer to Pleasant Hope and lived in that area the rest of their lives.

Scotty was born in Springfield, MO on Nov. 11, 1923 to Oren "Bernie" and Rocena (Scott) Whitlock. He and a younger sister, Theda, were raised in the Ebenezer community, and he graduated from Pleasant Hope High School. He served two years in the Army during WWII (January 1945-December 1946). For most of his life, he farmed in the Pleasant Hope area. He enjoyed working on the farm and being outdoors. His wife, Mildred, was the love of his life. He died May 19, 1996.

Mildred and Scotty

Mildred was born in Springfield, MO on April 29, 1926 to Enoch and Florence Freeman. She, her brother, Adrien and sister, Wanda, were raised in the Sparta area where they attended grade school. Later the family moved to Springfield and she graduated from Central High School. After graduating, she worked for Levy-Wolf Department Store and for Southwestern Bell Telephone. When she married Scotty, she began her career as a farmer's wife, mother and homemaker. She loved and enjoyed her family, her children and grandchildren. She died June 23, 1993.

Scotty and Mildred raised four sons and have four grandsons. Donald Clay (deceased, May 2001) and his wife Laurie who lives in Pleasant Hope have two sons: Justin Clay and his wife, D'Nette, and son Coltin Clay live in Amarillo, TX; Jim Ellis lives in Pleasant Hope and has a son, Austin Ellis. David Eugene and wife Janet, of Halfway, have two sons, Dustin Travis and William Cody. Darrell Laverne lives on the family farm in Pleasant Hope. Dale Allen and his wife, Sheila, live in Amarillo, TX.

Scotty, Mildred and the boys worked side by side on the farm. In the early 1960s, the Whitlocks were named Farm Family of the Year. When the sons were younger, they were involved in the daily chores of farming, rode horses and roped cattle, and were involved in 4-H and FFA. They all attended Pleasant Hope schools. Scotty liked to gig-fish and he and his sons loved hunting. Mildred loved singing and listening to music, especially her son, Darrell, playing guitar. They all enjoyed family get-togethers, big dinners and music parties. *Submitted by Jim Whitlock*

Elizabeth Hagewood at Memorial Stone

WILLIAMS – Elizabeth (Williams) Hagewood (of Raytown, MO) spent part of her youth in the Fair Play area, graduating from Fair Play High School in 1939. Her ties to the area are through her paternal great-grandparents, Elijah and Matilda (Oliver) Williams, and her maternal great-grandparents, Richard and Lucy A. (LaCompton-Dwyer) Hays. Elijah and Matilda Williams (married 1820) had 11 children. They are Frederick Oliver, Elizabeth Jane and William (married brother and sister Hiram and Elizabeth Susan Hopkins), Nancy Rebecca (married Clayton Smith Devin), Enoch F. and Elijah Matilda (married sister and brother Sarah and Joseph McCarroll Carter), Mary Ann "Polly" and Sarah "Sally" (both married Rev. Erasmus P. S. Roberts), Thomas Edwin (married Betty Jane Milliken), Malinda Josephine (married Luke Pickel, George Welsh and Enoch Benton Keeling) and Alvin Elijah (Elizabeth's paternal grandfather, married Mary Elizabeth "Polly" Lower in 1868).

Elizabeth's paternal grandparents, Alvin Elijah and "Polly" had five sons: Henry Ulysses (married Ellen (Anderson) Wilcox, Alvin Luther (married Etta, last name unknown), Ambrose (married Frida (Vogal) Bennet), Toby (infant), and Sidney (Elizabeth's father, married Dorcas Ella Hays, 1908).

Elizabeth's great-grandparents Richard and Lucy (Dwyer) Hays (who came to Bolivar in 1869, married 1851) had five children: John T. (married Golden Nickels), Mary Elizabeth "Molly" (Dorcas' mother, married Frances Benson Hays, 1881), Florance Anne (married James P. Roberts), R. Belle (married Mack Holland) and E. Ella (married John Hess),

Lora, Alvin and Elizabeth with parents Sidney and Dorcas Williams

Elizabeth's maternal grandparents, Frances Benson and "Molly" (Dwyer) Hays, had seven children: Truman Dwyer (married Cordia Wakefield), Hattie Belle (married Sam McCurdy), Lucy Virginia (married William Genung), Golden Relief, Francis James (married Mary Quinn and Ella, last name unknown), Richard Benson (married Lydia Phillips, Lilly (Hutchins) Frieze) and Dorcas Ella (Elizabeth's mother, married Sidney Williams). Sidney and Dorcas Ella (Hays) Williams had five children: infant son, Grace Elizabeth (infant daughter), Alvin (married Barbara Miller and Faye Hendricks), Lora Mae (married Larry Akers) and Elizabeth Belle Williams (married Floyd E. Hagewood in 1941). Elizabeth grew up knowing many cousins. On the Williams side was the daughter of Ambrose and Frida Williams: Anna Marie (married Everett Chaney and Roy Austin of Humansville, MO). Among those on the Hays side were the three daughters of Truman and Cordia (Wakefield) Hays: Ida (married Rev. Lewis Mead), Willma (married Paul Degraffenreid) and Dorothy (married C. Pitner and Raymond Dryer). Many of their children and grandchildren are still around the area. Growing up, Elizabeth's grandmothers were both named Mary Elizabeth and known as "Polly" and "Molly." Many of her relatives are buried in Polk County and surrounding counties. Some are in Greenwood Cemetery in Bolivar and in Barren Creek Cemetery, east of Fair Play. Elijah and Matilda Williams are buried in a cemetery in a cow pasture northwest of Bolivar.

Floyd E. and Elizabeth (Williams) Hagewood have three children: Clarence Eugene, Donna Kay (Keith-Lujan) and Ellen Louise. Elizabeth has four grandsons and three great-grandchildren. All of her married life has been in the Kansas City and Raytown, MO area. Her church work has been her blessing all these years. *Submitted by Elizabeth Hagewood*

WILLIAMS – Through Donna's mother, Elizabeth (Williams) Hagewood (Raytown, MO), she became interested in the Williams family. Donna's great-great-grandfather was the Rev. Elijah Williams, born Jefferson County, TN in 1801. They only know of three sisters, Jane (married John Talley), Nancy (married John M. Harper) and Elizabeth (married Absalom Woods).

In the 1830s Elijah helped to start many Baptist Churches in Missouri and owned land east of Fair Play to Bolivar. He married Matilda Oliver in 1820, the daughter of Frederick and Rosanna Oliver. Matilda had two known brothers, the Rev. Frederick J. and A. T. Oliver. Elijah and Matilda Williams are buried in the Heydon/Williams/Devin Cemetery, a small 145-year-old, neglected cemetery in the middle of a cow pasture just northwest of Bolivar. The past decade Donna's mother, her cousin and Donna herself are the only ones doing its upkeep. They know of 15 buried there, many of them related by marriage. To honor them, Donna's mother purchased a monument listing their names and had it placed in the cemetery. They would like to find out who Elijah's parents are and possibly see some pictures of them.

Elijah and Matilda Williams had 11 children. They are Frederick Oliver, Elizabeth Jane and William (married brother and sister Hiram and Elizabeth Susan Hopkins), Nancy Rebecca (married Clayton Smith Devin), Enoch and Elijah Matilda (married sister and brother Sarah and Joseph McCarroll Carter), Mary Ann "Polly" and Sarah "Sally" (both married the Rev. Erasmus P. S. Roberts), Thomas Edwin (married Betty Jane Milliken), Malinda Josephine (married Luke Pickel, George Welsh and Enoch Benton Keeling) and Alvin Elijah (Donna's great-grandfather, married Mary Elizabeth "Polly" Lower, 1868).

Polly was one of eight children of George and Elvery Lower. Elvery (married 1836) is believed to be the sister of Moses Carter. Two of Moses and Cynthia's children married Elijah's children, another daughter (Elvira) married William Lower (Polly's brother). It is said that the Carters were known as the "Singing Carters of Springfield." Also, someone remembers seeing "Little June" on stage peeking around "Mama's" skirt. Could it be June (Carter) Cash?

Now back to the cemetery! Among those buried with Elijah and Matilda Williams are Clayton and Margaret (West) Devin (in-laws of Elijah's daughter Nancy Rebecca), William and Martha Mitchell (Devin) Heydon (Martha was Clayton and Margaret's daughter, a sister-in-law to Nancy Rebecca and two of their sons married Polly's sisters), George Heydon (infant son of William and Martha) and William and James Heydon (grandsons of William and Martha Heydon and great-grandma Polly's nephew).

Liz Hagewood at Barren Creek Cemetery

Alvin Elijah and Polly Williams had five sons: Henry Ulysses (married Ellen Anderson), Alvin Luther (married Etta, last name unknown), Ambrose (married Frida Vogal Bennet), Toby, and Sidney (Donna's grandfather who married Dorcas

Mary Elizabeth "Molly" (Dwyer) Hays and family Ella Hays, 1905).

Sidney and Dorcas Williams had five children: infant son, Grace Elizabeth (infant), Alvin (married Barbara Miller and Fay Hendricks), Lora (married Larry Akers) and Donna's mother, Elizabeth Belle (Williams). Elizabeth married Floyd Eugene Hagewood and had three children: Clarence Eugene, Donna (Hagewood) Keith-Lujan and Ellen. They have four grandsons and three great-grandchildren. More information and pictures welcomed! *Submitted by Donna Lujan*

Clayborn M. Wilson and wife Mollie Robertson, Willie, Rufus and Emma

WILSON – Clayborn Monroe, son of Williams M. Wilson and Martha Ann Coats, was born Oct. 27, 1858. His father, William, from North Carolina and his mother, Martha, from Tennessee, homesteaded land in Missouri. Clayborn "Clab" was the only surviving child of William and Martha Ann. Around age 17 he was given acreage on the backside of his parents' property to remove him from the contagious family. They had tuberculosis.

On Dec. 6, 1886, he married his first wife, Mollie Robertson. They had four children: William A. "Willie" on March 14, 1888; Lillie Ethel on June 11, 1890; Rufus Earl on July 28, 1892; and Emma Marie on Aug. 24, 1894. Lillie died in 1891. His wife, Mollie, died July 14, 1896 of tuberculosis. (Emma was less than 2 years old). Five months later Rufus died at age 4.

Clab married Clara Jane Millican on Sept. 4, 1898. Mrs. Millican's children were Marvin, 10 years, Mack, 7 years, and Zelma, 4 years. Zelma and Emma were the same age when they became sisters. From this marriage came three daughters. Nellie M. arrived Oct. 12, 1899, Martha A. followed on Aug. 24, 1902 and Ethel A. on Oct. 23, 1906. Clab spent his life as a farmer between Eudora and Morrisville, MO. and his family stayed active and involved in the Oakville Baptist Church and were well known in the Eudora community. He had a smokehouse, hen house, cellar and barn built on the farm through the years. Clab sent his son, Willie, to college in Sedalia where he contracted tuberculosis. Willie died at home Feb. 10, 1907 at the age of 19.

Now, just like Clab, Emma was the only surviving child from his first marriage. At age 15 she went to Coachella, CA with her mother's brother, Ragon Robertson and wife June. June was a doctor for the Indians and Mexicans. Emma had many interesting stories to tell about her life in Coachella. Clab made a trip to California to visit her and sent $50 twice so she could come home. They made their trips to and from California on the train. After three years, she married Les Jackson and remained in Coachella, CA. Clab's father, William, moved in with them at the time of his wife Martha Ann's death. He died five months later. Life surely was a struggle with so many deaths in a short period of time.

Nellie married Jim Hayter and lived in Eudora. They had three children, a son E. L., daughters, Maxine and Velma Lee. Martha became a schoolteacher and married Earl Mackey, a farmer near Morrisville. Ethel married Jake McKenzie and moved to Lancaster, CA. They had no children. Ethel returned to Missouri after Jake's death around 1977. About 1935 Earl and Martha moved to the home place to take care of Clab ad Clara. They had three children, Martha Earlene, Kenneth Leon and Joe Wilson. Clab died in 1940 and Clara followed in 1941. *Submitted by Maxine Killingsworth*

WILSON – William M. Wilson was born July 3, 1818 in North Carolina and came to Missouri maybe with other members of his family. He homesteaded land between Morrisville and Eudora. Martha Ann Coats, born July 24, 1830, came to Missouri possibly with her family from Tennessee. There is an Elizabeth Coats buried in the Coats Cemetery who is 30 years older then Martha Ann. The Coats Cemetery is said to be on the Coats farm.

They were married June 1, 1848 in Polk County. He served in the military during the Civil War and drew a small pension from the government. Together they had five children: Robert P., Benjamin F., Mary E., Michael and Clayborn Monroe. They stood by while four of their children died of tuberculosis., plus Mandy, the wife of Robert and maybe three small children of Robert and Mandy. Clayborn was given some land on the backside of William's farm and he separated himself from the family to escape the tuberculosis.

William M. Wilson

When Clayborn was just a small child, it is said that the bushwhackers came to the farm looking for William, and Clayborn promptly told them where he was working. Soon as Martha Ann discovered what had happened she blew the warning on the old conch-shell; it could be heard for miles. William hid in a two-room cave on the farm and was never found.

William loved the company of his grandchildren. Emma recalls that when she and Zelma were around 5 years old, he taught them to say the alphabet backwards. That was before they could say the alphabet correctly.

When the railroad came through it traveled by the side of William's property and could be seen from his kitchen window. He never failed to go to the window to watch "Old John" go winding by. Later when Martha Ann was ailing, he took her to the doctor in Springfield 26 miles away on "Old John." Martha Ann died at the age of 77 with rheumatism and William moved in with his son, Clabe and Clara and family. He told Clara "all he wanted for his supper was sweet clabber milk and a biskit." He never went to bed on a full stomach. He died just five months after Martha Ann when his runaway horse flipped the buggy over at the age of 90. *Submitted by Earlene King*

WILSON – Isaac Wilson was born Aug. 15, 1810 in Greene County, TN. Nancy Bolten was born April 10, 1810 in Kentucky. They were married on June 23, 1831 in Campbell County, TN. Their daughter, Elizabeth, was born in 1840 in Tennessee. Between the years 1840 and 1843 they came to Missouri by wagon. William F. was born in Missouri in 1843, Isaac Newton "Newt" Wilson was born in 1847 in Buffalo, MO. Isaac enlisted in the Mexican War in August 1847. He served in Company B, Gilpin Battalion. He was discharged at the end of the war in 1848. His discharge papers describe him as five feet, nine inches, hazel eyes, dark hair and a ruddy or dark complexion.

He and Nancy traveled to Arkansas in 1849 and their son, Hiram H. Wilson, was born there. It was thought that they had relatives in Arkansas and maybe he was looking for work.

They returned to Polk County, MO in 1850 and his occupation was listed as a farmer. Sometime before 1860 they moved to Dallas County. They farmed there on a land grant he was given by President Lincoln in 1861.

Isaac enlisted in Company A, Dallas County Regiment of Missouri Home Guard in May 1861. He was discharged in August 1861 at the age of 51. Isaac and son, William F. Wilson, enlisted Aug. 19, 1861 in Company I of the 24th Regiment of Missouri Volunteers. They were mustered in the Civil War at Camp Weston in Rolla, MO. They marched with their company to Laclede County, MO. While they were there they were captured by the secessionists on Jan. 25, 1862 and were taken prisoner. They were then marched through Springfield on to a Confederate prison camp at Van Buren, AR. This was in the dead of winter and because his feet got wet and cold, Isaac's feet were injured.

Some war records say that he and William escaped the Confederates in their retreat at Pea Ridge, AR. Others say Isaac was traded by the Confederates. Isaac's feet were in such poor condition, and he was not able to march, so he was medically discharged on Sept. 12, 1862 at Helena, AR. Isaac then returned to Nancy and kids in Dallas County, MO. William was rejoined with Company I of the 24th Regiment. He was wounded and listed as missing in action at the Battle of Pleasant Hill, LA on April 9, 1864.

Isaac enlisted again with Company I, 16th Missouri Cavalry in July 1864 and was discharged in July 1865. He had been at the Bush Creek Station in Springfield to escort stages and then to Linn Creek, MO.

Isaac and Nancy resided in Dallas County until 1884 and they moved to Polk County near Brighton. Isaac died there March 8, 1885. Nancy resided in Brighton until her death in 1888. Both are buried in the Brighton Cemetery. Their son, Hiram H. Wilson, and his family continued to live in Polk County, many of them in the Pleasant Hope area. *Submitted by Dennella Wilson Burchfield*

WILSON – About 1862-1864, Humansville expanded in population with the arrival of Ishmael (1815) and Sarah Annie Wilson (June 1, 1821-April 23, 1876) and their eight children. They left Texas after the death of Sarah's father for whom Ishmael had served as administrator of his properties. The move from Texas may have been prompted by connections to Wilsons in the Humansville area. They purchased their farm just northwest of the town where it adjoined the Cedar County line.

In 1865, Amanda, their ninth child, was born. The other children, all Texas-born but who grew up and schooled in Humansville, were John M., Elizabeth, William David, Daniel Webster, Abraham S., Cassandra Miranda, Mary C. and Sarah Annie.

John M. (1841) was in merchandising with a store on the square and was married Sept. 29, 1870 to Mary Jane "Mollie" Human (Dec. 23, 1854-after 1938). She was the daughter of Mariah and William Carroll Human, and granddaughter of James G. Human, the founder of Humansville. Mollie's sister, Almanza (Human) Rogers, stated there were four daughters: Dorothy, Kathryn, with Rosie and Stella dying young. An 1880 census names Maria, Blanche, Grace and son Carroll. This family lived in Contra Costa County, CA and that is where Mary Jane is buried in Lafayette Cemetery near Walnut Creek.

Elizabeth (1845). Her history is unknown.

William David (May 1848-1930) married in Humansville Aug. 19, 1877 to (believed to be) Mary Jane Pike. They had two daughters, but Will lost all three to typhoid in Fort Worth, TX. Will later married Amanda Kelley. He was a stock trader at the Fort Worth Stockyards.

Daniel Webster (Oct. 11, 1850-Feb. 22, 1919) had close ties to the area as he married July 17, 1874 to Sarah Jane Hopper (Nov. 12, 1855-Dec. 3, 1944) who lived just over the Cedar County line. They were married at the home of her parents, William Carroll Hopper (1829-1880) and Rhoda Ray (1831-1907). Daniel and "Sallie" moved to Fort Worth, TX where only four of their nine children reached maturity: Sarah Annie E., Carrie Jane, Mary Amanda and Daniel II.

Abraham S. "Abe" (November 1851-after 1920) became a mining engineer and explorer of sorts. He left Missouri to work the Colorado mines; next, he owned an electrical engineering firm in Dallas, TX. Adventure beckoned in Old Mexico where he owned a large opal mine operation. With Lou Folley he had children: John, Minnie, Gilbert and Andrew. At the outbreak of the 1910 Mexican Revolution, the family barely escaped with their lives and a pocketful of opals that financed their return to Texas.

Abraham S. Wilson

Cassandra Miranda (October 1854-1916) married cowhand William Marshall in 1871 in Missouri; he was killed on a cattle drive. There was a son, William. Cassie then married Charles Hunt Christian and had five children: Francis Charles, James Frederick, Tisha Maud, Claud Kitty and A. Odell. The two daughters set down roots in California after their marriages. Cassie is buried in Ashland, OK.

Mary C. "Mollie" (February 1855-1930s) married Missouri-native Thomas R. Morris (born 1856) and had four children: Gaba Ella, Evalena, James S. and Sadie M. In 1900, the family was in Ardmore, OK, but by 1920 they were living in Erick. Mollie died alone in Coalgate, OK.

Sarah Annie (May 18, 1860-Jan. 14, 1912) was age 15 when her mother died, and she went to live in Texas with maternal Aunt Amanda (Chandler) and Weldon Bobo, the founder of Bedford. Sarah married Tennessee-born William J. Thomas, a worker on the Bobo farm. Five of

Sarah Annie Wilson

their eight children were born in Bedford: Thornton Jane, Elbe, Ishmael C., Effie Irene and Willie Mae. Land selling for 25 cents an acre took the family to Oklahoma where Annie Amanda, Leslie Webster and Lura Stella were born. Sarah died of typhoid in Roff, OK.

Amanda (1865), the only true Missourian, was born in Humansville, but after her mother's death Ishmael sold his lands and the whereabouts of Amanda and her father became unknown.

The mother, Sarah Annie Wilson, was the daughter of early Texas Ranger Captain Eli Chandler and Mary Butler. She is buried in Shady Grove Cemetery near the graves of Martha and Fleming Wilson. (Unknown if these Wilsons are related.)

The writer, a great-granddaughter of Ishmael and Sarah, continues to search for more of their history. Comments and/or additional information welcome. *Submitted by Paula Currey*

Rufus K. and Clarissa C. Wilson

WILSON – The household of Rufus K. and Clarissa Davis Wilson, near Wishart, MO, must have been a lively and productive one.

Rufus had a rich heritage, rich in values but not monetarily. His father, George Lewis Wilson, was born in Kentucky in 1824, married Mary Copeland in Arkansas at the age of 19 and moved to Missouri with his new bride a year later.

They settled in Polk County. George became a minister. In *The History of Polk County Baptist Association*, published in 1897 by the *Bolivar Herald*, the writer states of Rev. Wilson: "He wishes it distinctly understood that he never exacted a definite salary from any church…He served the church at Enon three years and received…for the three years work $8.50."

George and Mary Wilson had 11 children. The eighth child and sixth son was Rufus K. Wilson, born Feb. 20, 1859, died Nov. 14, 1920. He was Betty's grandfather.

Rufus K. Wilson married Clarissa Catherine Davis (born May 28, 1862, died April 15, 1921) and they, too, settled near Enon Church. They had eight children.

Arthur K. (King) born Oct. 10, 1880, died Dec. 17, 1952; Lewis, born May 10, 1885, died 1956; Albert Rufus, born Jan. 18, 1888, died July 11, 1974; Elza, born Sept. 25, 1890, died Sept. 12, 1956; Lennie Leonard, born March 13, 1895, died Sept. 30, 1979; Minnie Ada, born Feb. 12, 1898, died Aug. 24, 1960; Herman Austin, born Sept. 25, 1900, died Nov. 20, 1975; and Zona Lee, born Aug. 28, 1905, died Nov. 30, 1992.

No doubt the Wilson children learned many things growing up on their farm. They knew how to live off the land they inhabited; they knew how to survive in bad weather and hard times; and they were taught respect for all those around them.

Undoubtedly they learned spiritual truths as their parents and grandparents understood them and practiced them in their lives. They understood death and saw not only their elders die, but also two of their brothers, both at 18 months and a sister at 16.

When Rufus's older sons were teenagers, they helped build their family home from the trees on their land. Using a team of horses and a wagon, they hauled the logs they had sawed. The home was situated on top of a hill in a picturesque setting overlooking a large meadow of white daisies.

The strong family values Rufus and Clarissa had brought to their marriage were passed on to their children, five of whom remained in Polk County. Minnie Ada married Clay Standley Crain on March 5, 1916, who was also from the Wishart area. Betty is one of their offspring, along with her sister, Geneieve Gladys "Jennie" and her brother Wilson Standley "Buddy." Clay and Ada operated Farmers Exchange stores in Wishart, Eudora and Walnut Grove.

Ada died at age 52 of a cerebral hemorrhage in their home near Bolivar, and Clay, at age 62 (died 1960) after spending three years unconscious, the result of head injuries from an accident on icy roads.

When Rufus and Clarissa died, the two youngest children, Herman and Zona were still at home. They cared for their dying parents and kept the farm going.

Zona wanted to attend Southwest Baptist College in Bolivar, but no funds were available. She prevailed upon the Dunnegans at Polk County Bank in Bolivar, who loaned her $500 on a signature note. She graduated SWBC and went on to nurses' training at Missouri Baptist Hospital in St. Louis. While there, she was instrumental in a Kellogg Foundation research project to determine why so many newborns died of diarrhea. Eventually, she became the director of a school of nursing in Michigan.

Before Betty was school age, her mother, Ada, became very ill with a form of crippling arthritis. Her sister, Zona, took off a year from her nursing job and came to live with them in a rural area of Polk County, expressing confidently that she believed she could restore Betty's mother to good health.

Betty watched as Zona fed her mother spinach three times a day, made her go outside to get every ray of sunshine available on her body and gently exercise her painful, immobile limbs. Betty witnessed first-hand the love and sacrifice she had for her sister, and for them. All during this dismal situation Zona filled their home with humor and laughter, and gave them hope. She often asked Betty's mother, "Guess what you're having for lunch today." Relatives relate that Zona believed spinach would heal almost anything, including boils and colds.

Zona's methods worked. Betty had her mother back in good health in the year Zona predicted it would require.

The Wilsons, from Betty's viewpoint, were best known for their family reunions. Since Zona lived away, when she came to Polk County to visit, there

367

was always a reunion, sometimes in a park as the Wilsons grew in numbers, but usually at someone's home. There were long tables of delicious food and long afternoons under shade trees visiting and sharing of their lives. The kids played but often stopped to listen to what their elders were telling.

Betty says, "Families are a wonderful part of our lives. The Wilsons have given me a rich heritage of which I am proud to be a part." *Submitted by Betty Sue Crain McDonald*

WILSON – Wayne and Rowena (Young) Wilson moved to Bolivar in October of 1973 to take over the MFA Insurance (now Shelter Insurance) office of the late Bud Kruse. Wayne grew up in Springfield, MO and Rowena grew up in Marshfield, MO. They both attended school in their respective towns before graduating from

Wayne, Rowena, Leah, Lisa, Lindsey and Craig

Southwest Missouri State where they met.

It didn't take long for Wayne and Rowena to become active in the community. Wayne became a member of Rotary, Bolivar Booster Club, Chamber of Commerce and Polk County Fair Board, just to name a few. Rowena was active in PTA, was a homeroom mother, Girl Scout Leader and a member of Now Group and Beta Sigma Phi Sorority.

Wayne and Rowena started the first Horsemanship 4-H Club in Polk County. The name of the club was Pocomo Wranglers and had a record number of members. Wayne, Rowena and Lisa were very active in the Missouri Quarter Horse Association.

In 1978 a hospital district was formed. Wayne was elected as vice-chairman of the board. He and the other board members spent countless hours looking at hospitals, plans, interviewing candidates for administration as well as doctors. Wayne is still vice-chairman of the board for Citizens Memorial Hospital.

Rowena was a charter member of the Ladies Auxiliary for CMH and served as treasurer for a number of years. Rowena is on the board of Citizens Memorial Auxiliary. Wayne and Rowena have always given generously to Bolivar with their time and talents.

Wayne and Rowena kept the location of their office the same but remodeled the original office (that once was a house at 332 S. Springfield) in 1987 to house their operation and added three other offices.

Their daughter, Lisa, attended Bolivar schools from second grade through high school and graduated in 1984. She went on to the University of Missouri where she met her husband, Craig Lehman (of Billings, MO). They both graduated from UMC and pursued their teaching degrees away from Bolivar. In June of 1995 Craig, Lisa and their two daughters, Lindsey and Leah, moved to Bolivar. Craig worked for Wayne and Rowena in their Shelter Insurance office for three years. Wayne and Rowena retired June 30, 1998 and Craig is now the Shelter Insurance Agent in the same location where Wayne and Rowena first settled. Lisa is a teacher in the Bolivar School District.

Craig is a member of the Bolivar Rotary Club, serves on the Polk County Fair Board and has served on the board for the Bolivar Chamber of Commerce. Lisa is a member of the GFWC Bolivar Genesis Club, a Girl Scout leader and has been involved with the Miss Bolivar Pageant.

The girls are involved in various activities in the community, such as soccer, basketball, softball, Girl Scouts, church choir, piano lessons, horseback riding lessons, tennis and golf.

Both families attend the Bolivar United Methodist Church. *Submitted by Lisa Lehman*

WINFIEL – Carl Dean Winfiel was born Jan. 7, 1939 northwest of Bolivar on a Dunnegan mail route in Cliquot Township in the old Union Grove School District 41. He attended this one-room school eight years; it has since consolidated into the Fair Play System. Dean's parents, Howard Winfiel and Helen Squier, were Polk County natives.

Dean attended Fair Play High School and graduated from Wheatland High School in 1956. He later graduated from Missouri Southern State College, Joplin, MO, obtaining an accounting degree.

On June 5, 1960, Dean married Verna Sue Crawford at the Nemo Baptist Church in Hickory County. Verna was born Jan. 20, 1942; her parents were Henry Clay Crawford and Fannie D. Samples, native to Hickory County.

Dean and Verna have two children; daughter Ramona Sue, married Danny Ray Dryer of Fair Play; they have two daughters, Amy and Erin Dryer. Son Jerry Dean married Cynthia Renee Underwood of Fair Play; they have two sons, Kyle and Kelly. Both children-in-law, their parents and grandparents are native of Polk County.

Dean has followed the accounting profession since 1958. His early accounting work in Kansas City, MO required a top-secret clearance. Since late 1964 he has been involved in public accounting with emphasis in income tax preparation. In conjunction with the accounting and consulting work, Dean has been a registered securities representative since 1987.

Dean Winfiel and his family belong to Mount Zion Baptist Church; he has pastored small country churches in Polk, St. Clair and Hickory Counties since 1963.

Dean's maternal great-great-great-grandfather, E. M. Campbell, was an organizing member of Mount Zion Baptist Church. Dean and Verna's granddaughters, Amy and Erin Dryer, are members of Mount Zion, thus spanning eight generations.

Dean Winfiel's Polk County ancestors include his parents and paternal grandparents: Noah Albert Winfiel, Sarah Jane "Sally" Sawyer, Cyrus Miles Winfiel and Barbara Dickerson, John Dickerson and Melinda Skaggs, James Ervin Sawyer and Myra Catherine Abel, Stephen Sawyer and Sarah Johnson, Hartwell Johnson and Liddy (?), John Abel and Mary Prichett.

Dean Winfiel's Polk County ancestors also include his maternal grandparents: Charles Ashton Squier and Ophelia Sims, James McGarity "Mac" Sims and Rebecca Patton Clark, David S. Clark and Ophelia Campbell, William Clark and Margaret Moore Clark, who is said to be the first white baby born west of the Allegheny Mountains and Ezekiel Madison Campbell and Rebecca Patton Adkins. E. M. Campbell was Polk County's first surveyor.

According to the *History of Hickory, Polk, Cedar, Dade and Barton Counties*, 1889, pages 281-284 have three sets of Dean Winfiel's great-great-great grandparents living in Township 32, Range 23 during the period of 1838 to 1842, the E. M. Campbells, Hartwell Johnsons and Stephen Sawyers, while a fourth set of great-great-great-grandparents, the William Clarks, lived in Township 33, Range 23.

Dean and Verna Winfiel remain in Polk County residing two miles north of Aldrich where Granddad Noah and Grandma Sally Winfiel lived. They also own a home and office and live part-time in Joplin, MO where they still own and manage a very vibrant tax practice. They work part of each week with their son in his Bolivar tax practice. *Submitted by Dean Winfiel*

WISDOM – Arley H. Wisdom and Oma Jean Wisdom purchased 170 acres in Polk County from Orval and Velma Meadors and heirs, January 1957. Original entry dated June 26, 1865 and Sept. 13, 1858: The United States of America to Dennis North and John Fisher. There was once a Fisher school.

Arley was born Sept. 18, 1922 in Talequah, OK. Oma was born Oct. 14, 1933 in Tioga, TX. Arley and Oma's parents moved to California to better their lives during the Great Depression. Arley and Oma met in 1948 in Sacramento, CA and married on Nov. 4, 1951 in Reno, NV. Arley's two sons, Arley Edward Wisdom, born May 8, 1942 and Thomas Harvey Wisdom, born Feb. 25, 1944, came to Urbana, MO with their family in 1957. Children of Arley and Oma are Arleta Jean (Wisdom) Uzzell, born March 26, 1953; Margo Janice (Wisdom) Evans, born June 17, 1954; Gary Stephen Wisdom, born Sept. 8, 1956; and Guy Richard Wisdom, born July 2, 1957. All six children were born in Sacramento, CA.

Sons of Gary and Guy live on the farm in Polk County. It has been their home for 45 years. Guy's son Joshua also lives on the farm, which makes the third generation.

The first time they were in Missouri they liked the four seasons, rolling hills, meadows, creeks and bottom fields and never wanted to live anywhere else. This farm fulfils the life they worked for. There is a lot of history there: Indian mounds, map tree and the covered well. Carl Crain showed Arley where he drank water from many years ago. The place where it was had dirt and leaves filling it in. Arley hand dug it all out.

"Missouri Bound." There is excitement for the Wisdom family. Arley and Oma loaded the one and a half ton 1941 Dodge cab-over truck with 14-foot bed, with everything they owned. Son, Arley Edward was 15 and rode with his dad to help if needed. Son Tommy, 13, rode with his mom, only 24 years old, to help with Arleta, 4 years old, Margo, 3 years old, Gary, 15 months old and Guy, 3 months old. They looked like the grapes of wrath going down Highway 99 from Sacramento in the 1950 Plymouth station wagon with Gary's stroller tied on the back. The old truck could only go 35 miles per hour when they took to the mountains on Route 66 at Barstow. Six days later, they arrived on the county gravel road, which looked like a tunnel where tops of trees met above the road.

"Home At Last." Neighbors Evelyn Moore brought two hot apple pies when she saw the truck, station wagon and a brave mom and dad with six children turn into the drive.

Soon they were so glad to meet their surrounding neighbors. Dudley and Christine (Bridges) Huckaby have two daughters and a son, who were the ages of the Wisdom children, as did Glen and Arlene Winslow, Jack and Ruby Payne and Carrie and Bill Greer.

Forty-five years later, 14 grandchildren, eight great-grandchildren, they are living happily ever after. *Submitted by Oma Wisdom*

WITT – Elisha Witt and Phoebe Dodd never saw Polk County but many of their descendants settled in this beautiful country. Elisha was a descendant of John and Lucy Littlebury.

John was born in 1710 in Virginia and Lucy in 1713 in Virginia. John and Lucy had nine children. John was the son of William who was a Huguenot and was one of 20 Witts who came from London, England to America in 1699.

Elisha served in the Revolutionary War at the age of 17 and 18. He was a guard of prisoners. He served at different times throughout the war. He was on the war field when Cornwallis surrendered. In June of 1794 he bought a farm from his father, John, and lived there for 10 years in Amhurst County, VA. Elisha and his family joined a migration, moving west. After crossing the mountains he continued going west, while most of the other Witts moved south. They settled in Estill County, KY while Nathen was then a baby. He purchased 3,500 acres and lived there until his death. He is buried there on the farm. A DAR marker has been placed there on his grave.

Nathen and Nancy Witt were pioneers of Polk County, MO. They came here about 1830. They had a 40-acre farm here located about two miles north of Bolivar. The location would be just about where the soccer field and north end of the college is now located.

Nathen was born Oct. 20, 1794 in Virginia and died in September 1843 in Polk County, MO. Nancy was born in 1803 and died in January 1864. He first married Francis Kimball and they had one son, Milton. Francis died in Kentucky. Nathen and Nancy were then married and came to Missouri.

Their first child was born in St. Clair County, MO in 1825. They had seven more children in Polk County.

Milton married Drusilla, John married Susannah, James Allen married Louisa Jane, William married Clarinda Chapman (he was named after his great-grandfather), Angelina married Alfred Pierce. They had one daughter. Margaret Jane married John Pierce, Alfred's brother, Louisa married Henry Pointer and Caleb married Martha Jane Lawson; he died in the Civil War. Maria Witt married Alfred Pierce. Maria was his third wife.

Maria and Alfred had four daughters and one son. Their children: Julia Ann married George Woody, Rebecca married William Bridges, Alex married Ida F. Lindsey, Alice Belle married Henry Small Brown and Ellen Eliza Pierce married first, John Drake and second, Thomas Renfro. She had four sons by John, and Tom had twin daughters by Elnora McKnight. Nora died soon after birth and Elnora McKnight Renfro died when Cora was just a baby. Tom and Ellen had three daughters and three sons. Their first-born was Bessie Coren who married Lloyd A. Anderson, Thomas Jessie married Thelma Poling, Hazel Orlean died when she was 15, Ashbury Jackson, born Jan. 13, 1913, lived only a few days, a twin to Mary Elizabeth, Mary Elizabeth married Joseph Steele and Woodrow Wilson married Ellen Hughes. *Submitted by Jennie Springer*

Tom and Ellen Pierce Renfro

WOLLARD – Washington Murry Wollard was born March 10, 1817 in Maury County, TN to Churchill and Mary (Fox) Wollard. Churchill was a War of 1812 veteran; Churchill's father, uncles and grandfathers served in some way during the Revolutionary War. Murry's great-great-great-great grandfather Captain William Woolard came to America in 1670.

Sarah Roseanna "Sally" Walker, daughter of Noah Walker and Mary (Sparkman), was born March 25, 1816 in Tennessee. She married Murry on Feb. 11, 1836 in Williamson County, TN. They settled in Maury County. Murry's obituary says they left March 22, 1840 and arrived in Fair Play, Polk County, MO April 24, 1840; Sally's mother came with them. After making one crop near Fair Play, he moved onto the homestead near Dunnegan in Polk County. Other family would settle nearby: Sally's sister, Delila and husband Thomas Fox; Murry's uncle William Ross Wollard; Murry's grandmother Rebecca (Fatheree) Wollard was living with her son William in 1860; Murry's cousin Rev. Nathaniel Wollard came to the area that is now Dallas County in 1837; and many of Murry's Fox relatives would also settle in the area.

Murry and Sally had nine children, the oldest born in Tennessee and the rest in Polk County; they are listed below. He owned a large amount of land in Polk County and when his children married, he gave the newlyweds a parcel of land from his holdings. His obituary says that he introduced the first thoroughbred shorthorn cattle into this area. Much of the information listed herein was taken from the family history written or dictated by Murry himself in his later years. All of the children's marriages are listed in Polk County records except one.

Nancy Kissrah/Kissiah Wollard, born April 16, 1838, married William Henry Miller on Aug. 19, 1859, had eight children and died in Meeker, OK.

William James Wollard, born June 17, 1840, married first, Lydia Jane Darby, Aug. 9, 1859 in Cedar County, four children; married second, Martha Melinda (Fox) Austin, Sept. 20, 1871. He died March 19, 1883 in Polk County and was buried in Salem Cemetery near Cliquot.

Henry McBride Wollard, born Oct. 5, 1842, married Mary Jane Walker on Jan. 27, 1867, had four children, died Jan. 18, 1927 in Polk County and was buried in Dunnegan Cemetery.

Thomas Harlin Wollard, born Jan. 4, 1844, died Sept. 4, 1869 at his parents' home, buried Plum Grove Cemetery near Dunnegan.

Allen Barrett Wollard, born July 28, 1847, married Narcissus Adeline Holmes on Nov. 4, 1875, had 11 children, died Aug. 17, 1918 in Polk County and was buried in Plum Grove Cemetery.

Delana Ann Wollard, born Oct. 17, 1849, married Rev. Isaac W. Bridges on May 3, 1874, had at least seven children and moved out of Polk County with her family.

Joseph Wilks Wollard, born March 28, 1852, married Mary E. Williams on Jan. 28, 1875, had five children and moved out of Polk County, probably to Kansas.

Elizabeth Demaris Wollard, born Nov. 11, 1854, married Harvey Elijah Mitchell on Oct. 22, 1876 and had one child before moving out of Polk County.

Barton Marshall Wollard, born Jan. 11, 1857, married Elizabeth Jane Holmes on Sept. 25, 1879, had five children, died 1937 in Dunnegan and is buried in the Dunnegan Cemetery.

Murry died Aug. 23, 1903 at home. He was buried in Plum Grove Cemetery next to Sally, who had died Feb. 5, 1897 at their home. A barn that Murry and his sons built is still standing; the outside walls are newer but the inside still shows the wooden pegs that were hand-made and used to put the structure together. Barton inherited the home place and later passed it on to his son, Nelson. Nelson had no children and after he and his sister died, the land that had been owned by the Wollards for 155 years was sold. *Submitted by Justin Wollard*

Serenia Wollard Stovall, Theodore Wollard, Columbus Wollard and Weaver Wollard, circa 1935-1940

WOLLARD – Henry McBride Wollard, son of Washington Murry and Sarah Roseanna (Walker) Wollard, was born Oct. 5, 1842 near Dunnegan, Polk County, MO. He enlisted in the Second Kansas Cavalry (Union) as a blacksmith in 1863 and was mustered out in 1865.

Mary Jane Walker, daughter of Noah S. and Lois Ann (Walker) Walker, was born Jan. 10, 1843 near Dunnegan. Her maternal grandmother was Bethanna (Woolard) Walker, a first cousin of Churchill Woolard, making Mary J. and Henry M. Wollard third cousins. Henry and Mary were married on Jan. 27, 1867 by his uncle, Thomas Fox, JP and they settled near Dunnegan on land given to them by Henry's father. They had four children, all born at home near Dunnegan where Henry and Mary lived out their lives. Their children, listed below, also lived and were married in Polk County. Mary died July 23, 1889 at home and was buried in Plum Grove Cemetery. Henry died Jan. 18, 1927 at home and was buried in Dunnegan Cemetery.

Serenia Murtilla Wollard, born Sept. 30, 1868, married Sterling Price Stovall on July 3, 1888. He was born Sept. 3, 1863 in Appleton City, Bates County, MO and died Aug. 2, 1951 in Humansville, MO. Serenia died Aug. 11, 1950 in Dunnegan. Both were buried in Dunnegan Cemetery. They had three children. Carl B. (Aug. 1, 1889-July 10, 1891) was buried at Plum Grove Cemetery. Ray Wann (April 17, 1892-Nov. 12, 1948) married Esther Fern Mitchem; both buried at Dunnegan Cemetery. They had nine children: Chester Carl, Violet Ruth, Oral Ray, Daisy Mae, Lorris Edgar (died at age 2), Shirley Darlene, Mary Irene, Ronnie Lee and Janice Charlene (died at age 8 months). Fay Xenie (Nov. 1, 1897-Jan. 29, 1990) married Carl Wright; both buried at Dunnegan Cemetery. They had two children, Ralph Dale and Rex Wayne.

Theodore Allen "Bud" Wollard, born Jan. 11, 1871, married Martha Viola Ellsworth on May 22, 1895. She was born April 17, 1878 in Indiana and died Nov. 16, 1944 in Cliquot, MO. Bud died Oct. 8, 1941 in Bolivar, MO. Both were buried in Dunnegan Cemetery. They had no children.

Columbus Elmer Wollard, born Nov. 19, 1873, married Nellie Alice Nickels on July 19, 1903. She was born Oct. 25, 1887 in Dunnegan and died Nov. 16, 1962 in Springfield, MO. He died June 4, 1940 in Springfield. Both were buried in Plum Grove Cemetery. They had five children. Aulton Parker (Oct. 14, 1904-Jan. 20, 1981) married Zelda Belle Watkins; both buried at Salem Cemetery, no children. Clara Mae (Jan. 18, 1907-Oct. 8, 1966) married Orval Ray Wells; both buried at Greenwood Cemetery in Bolivar, no children. Charles Elmer Wollard (May 5, 1914-Feb. 6, 2001) married Lucy Carlene Hawkins; both buried at White Chapel Cemetery, Springfield, three sons: Charles Kent, Richard Lee and Robert Brent (lived only 1 day). Mattie Juanita Wollard (Jan. 22, 1920-Nov. 26, 1981) married first, Joe Francka and had one daughter, Janna Sue (died at age 2); married second, Leonard Robert Bell and had three children: Larry Dean, Ronald Leon and Sherril Ann. Mattie and Leonard are both buried in Maple Hill Cemetery, Kansas City, KS. Cleo James Wollard, a girl (June 12, 1925-stillborn) is buried at Plum Grove Cemetery.

Henry Weaver Wollard, born Aug. 9, 1880, married Della Mae Nickels on July 19, 1903. She was born Dec. 26, 1885 in Dunnegan and died Feb. 28, 1966 in Bolivar. Weaver died Oct. 24, 1950 in Bolivar and both were buried in Plum Grove Cemetery. They had four children: Eunice Edith, Mary Viola, Leland Rechow and Cecil Leroy (See Wollard-Nickels story). *Submitted by Judy Johnson*

WOLLARD – Henry Weaver Wollard, born Aug. 9, 1880, married Della Mae Nickels on July 19, 1903 at Della's home near Dunnegan, MO. This was a double wedding with her sister Nellie marrying Weaver's brother Columbus. Della was born Dec. 26, 1885 in Dunnegan and died Feb. 28, 1966 in Bolivar. Weaver died Oct. 24, 1950 at his home near Bolivar and both were buried in Plum Grove Cemetery. They lived in several places in Polk County before settling northwest of Bolivar in 1937 with their son Cecil. They soon moved into a house of their own next door. They had four children, all born near Dunnegan.

Eunice Edith, born Sept. 17, 1905, died March 24, 1974 in Bolivar, married James Lloyd Bell on Jan. 22, 1925 in Polk County. He was born Sept. 12, 1902 in Humansville and died Jan. 17, 1994 in Bolivar; both buried at Greenwood Cemetery in Bolivar. They had six children: Marjorie Juanita, Georgia Opal, Gladys Marie, James Leonard, Dorothy Lea and Kathryn Louise. Marjorie married first, Lonnie Phillip Willis and had one son, Lonnie Phillip Willis Jr.; married second, Willis Allen Minor and had one daughter, Lori Ann. Marjorie, born Aug. 14, 1925 in Polk County, died Jan. 16, 1995 in Springfield and was buried at Mt. Vernon IOOF Cemetery in Mt. Vernon, Lawrence County, MO. Georgia married Ray Musgrove and has four children: Connie Rebecca, Paula Marleen, Dennis Dewayne and Nancy Ann. Gladys married Richard Moore and has two children, Shirley Marie and Donna Mae. Leonard married Lillian Rosicka and has two children, James Henry and Janice Lee. Dorothy Lea married Marvin Eugene Brown and has two children, Deborah Lynn and Randall Todd. Kathryn married Gary Max Greer and has three daughters, Tambra Lynne, Terri Ranae and Toni Machelle.

Mary Viola, born Aug. 25, 1907, died March 21, 1978 in Bolivar, married Lee Everett Fowler on Jan. 14, 1926 in Polk County. Mary was buried in Plum Grove. They had three children: Henry Troy, Ruby Evelyn and Willa Mae.

Seated: Weaver, Cecil and Della Wollard; standing: Mary, Leland and Eunice circa 1935

Leland Rechow, born Dec. 18, 1910, died Oct. 11, 1989 at his home near Bolivar, married Jewell Ellen Stewart on March 16, 1935 in Buffalo, MO. Leland is buried in Salem Cemetery near Cliquot, MO; Jewell lives in Bolivar. They had four children: Lela Louise, Deryal Lee, Donald Dale and Judith Kay. Lela, born Feb. 10, 1936, died March 11, 1936 and was buried in Salem Cemetery. Deryal married Trillma Irene Jump and has three daughters: Brenda Kay, Sharon Lea and Connie Sue. Don married Linda Faye Shelton and has two children, Amy Lynette and Jared Dale. Judy married Norman Frederick Johnson and has two children, Angela Kay and Randall Wayne.

Cecil Leroy, born July 27, 1917, died April 4, 2000 in Bolivar, married Wauneta Faye Henson on Oct. 19, 1938 in Bolivar. Faye was born Nov. 30, 1916 in Cliquot and died Sept. 23, 1999 at her son's home near Bolivar (which was just down the road from her own). Cecil and Faye were buried in Greenwood Cemetery. They lived on a farm northwest of Bolivar next door to Cecil's parents, who lived in a house Cecil, Leland and Lloyd helped to build for them. Later, Eunice and Lloyd Bell lived in that same house. Cecil and Faye had two children, Marvin Leroy and Larry Lee. Marvin married first, Sandra Kay Harding and had one son, Scott Leroy. He married second, Betty Jean (Crow) Coy. Marvin was born July 22, 1940 at his parents' home near Bolivar, died July 14, 1998 in Springfield and was buried in Maple Park Cemetery, Springfield. Larry married Judy Ellen Shelenhamer and has two children, Julie Lynelle and Justin Lee. *Submitted by Larry Wollard*

WOOD – Ferda Ray Wood was born Jan. 23, 1892 at Hartville, Wright County, MO. His father was William Robert Wood, born Aug. 21, 1866 and died June 15, 1940. His mother was Ollie Wagoner, born Jan. 22, 1872 and died Sept. 17, 1897. Ray grew up on a farm and attended Little Creek Rural School in Wright County. Then, on to Hartville High School by riding his bicycle four and one-half miles. He completed his high school in the academy department at Southwest State Teacher's College. He received his teaching certificate at the age of 17 in 1909 and promptly went to teaching the remaining school term at Mt. Olive in north Wright County. He taught in rural Wright County schools for four years.

Ray Wood

Ray married Nora Caroline Lemons on Nov. 13, 1911 and continued to teach for five years in the elementary school in Hartville, MO. He also served as principal of the grades. Ray and Nora had four children: Juanita born July 6, 1912 and died April 4, 1996; Frank born Jan. 11, 1914 and died Feb. 11, 1985; Geneva, born Dec. 30, 1916 and died April 16, 1997; and Dorless, born Dec. 14, 1920.

In the spring of 1919, he was elected county superintendent of Wright County Schools where he served for eight years. Nora's health declined and she was admitted to the Tuberculosis Sanitarium in Mt. Vernon, MO in 1926. Ray accepted the position of superintendent of schools in Stockton, MO in 1927 and moved his family so they could be closer to their mother. Nora died Sept. 16, 1930, while he was at Stockton and was buried at Little Creek Cemetery in Hartville, MO. In 1931 he accepted superintendent of schools in Bolivar, MO where in 1956 he retired after serving 28 years.

He married Dora A. Denney in 1931 and she taught in the Bolivar High School for a period of time. Dora was born in Mountain Grove, Wright County, MO and got her first teacher's certificate when Ray was county superintendent of Wright County. She was teaching at Walker, MO when she married Ray.

Ray and Dora Wood

Ray received his BS in 1926 at SMS and AM from Missouri University, Columbia, MO. All his college work, both graduate and under-graduate, was done during summer sessions except for one spring term. He was a member of Missouri State Association of Schools, Missouri State Association of School Administrators, a life member of National Education Association, American Association of School Administrators, served 15 years on Legislative Committee for Missouri State Teachers Association, and member of Missouri State White House Conference on Education. During his membership on the sub-committee of finance for the Missouri Citizen Commission, his work was recognized as the most extensive study of education ever made in Missouri. He served as member of the Advisory Committee to State Superintendent of Schools for 10 years. He took an active part in forming a retirement program for Missouri teachers and starting the hot lunch program for school children.

Ray and Dora continued to live in Bolivar after his retirement in 1956. They were active members of the First Baptist Church where Ray taught a Sunday school class. Ray was a member of the Chamber of Commerce, Rotary Club and was on the City Council when they formed the Bolivar Industrial Development Committee. They procured Pantsmaker Garment to Bolivar, furnishing several hundred people employment.

Ray took great interest in improving school and was always available to assist in any way he could. He was very proud of the citizens of Polk County in passing school bonds so new schools could be built and new education courses could be offered to make Bolivar a AAA school system.

Dora died in May 1973 and Ray died in August 1973. They are both buried in Greenwood Cemetery in Bolivar, MO. *Submitted by Dorless Robertson*

WOOD – In 1854-1855 Isaac Wood (1816-1873) and his wife, Susannah, homesteaded in southwestern Polk County 167 acres on Turkey Creek

Left to right in auto: Charley McDonald-driver, Beatrice Wood (Prater), Floyd McDonald Wood, Deedie Wood (lying down), Walter Wood (5 years old), Coy Wood and Hoil Wood; left upper insert: Lum Wood

between Eudora and Walnut Grove. The 167 acres was passed on to one of Isaac's sons, C. L. A. "Lum" Wood. (As a fifth generation Wood descendant granddaughter, Lewalta still lives today on 25 acres of the land.) Lum (1855-1941) and his wife, Alta Kinder Wood (1859-1900), raised their five children, D. M. "Deed," Coy, Ethel (Jones), Hoil and Edith (Box) on the homestead.

The emphasis of this story is on Lum Wood's son, Deed "Deedie," Lewalta's grandfather, as told to her by her Grandmother Floy, Deed's wife. Deed married a Polk County girl, Floy McDonald (1887-1984) in 1906. She was the daughter of John and Clementine Blair McDonald of the Eudora-Aldrich community. Deedie and Floy with their son, Walter, born in 1909, rented the "Bowman Place" about three-fourths of a mile west of the Wood homestead where their daughter, Beatrice (Prater), was born in 1913.

One day as Floy was working in the house and caring for the baby during the summer of 1913, 4-year-old Walter was watching from the front porch as Deed was raking hay with a team of horses in a field southeast of the house. Suddenly, something spooked the horses, causing a stampede runaway. The team left the field running northwest, between the front of the house and the road, over ditches and among trees. Deedie was knocked off the Sulky rake seat and dragged under the rake until it was stopped by hitting a tree. Seeing all of this from the front porch, 4-year-old Walter ran into the house crying, "Mama, Mama, Daddy horses!" Floy ran to reach Deedie and to get help.

Deed was taken by wagon to the Walnut Grove Frisco Depot where he was transported by train to Burge Hospital in Springfield, MO. There was nothing they could do to help him. His back was broken and spinal cord severed at the thoracic spine. At the age of 29 he would be permanently paralyzed from the chest down, losing all feeling and function of his lower limbs including bowel and bladder control. Thankfully, he could still move and use both arms and shoulders. His 26-year-old wife, Floy, the mother of his two small children, would now become the family's breadwinner and principal caregiver, including doing urinary catherization every eight hours.

Shortly after the accident, Lum Wood bought for his son Deed and his young family a 37-acre home two miles south of the homestead on what is now Highway 123, one mile north of the Greene-Polk County line. (A great-great-grandson, Brad Hayter, owns and lives there today.)

In a cooperative effort of family and friends, a wagon/cart was made as can be seen in the above photo, fastened to the side of the automobile in the picture. The cart, 66 inches long and 26 inches wide, became Deedie's "legs" to freedom from being helplessly bedridden. He would lay on the cart on his stomach and using both arms while holding specially cut sticks that reached to the floor or ground he could wheel his cart by himself allowing him a new degree of mobility! While Floy did the farm milking chores outdoors, Deedie could watch the children, including lifting baby Beatrice when she was crying or needed her diaper changed. Also, Hoil Wood was good to come to help his brother and family when needed.

Deed developed strength in his arms and shoulders enough that, by using his wagon and two sticks and the land terrain being level enough he could go from the house to the barn or chicken house to help. Walter started the first grade at Rice School. Deed reviewed the 1915-1916 grade card, signing it the first three-quarters. He died May 1916, three years after his accident. The cause of death most likely was kidney failure or pulmonary embolism. Antibiotics and anticoagulants were not a part of medicine in 1916.

As for Floy, Lewalta took her (her grandmother) to Bolivar when she was 90 to renew her driver's license and to Wommack's. As she said, "I never did like the idea of seeing my name on a tombstone but it's got to be done." After the two chores were finished she said, "Now let's go and have some fun." They went to KFC and Wal-Mart! Lewalta asked her that day, "What was my Grandpa Deedie like?" A smile came over her face and a twinkle in her eye as she answered, "He was a tease." Lewalta never heard her complain nor say that life had been unfair. She lived to be 96 and is buried in Turkey Creek Cemetery beside her husband Deedie in the Wood family plot. *Submitted by Lewalta Wood Myer*

WOODARD – Daniel Woodard and his wife lived in the Carolinas. They had two children, both sons. Pitt Woodard (Aug. 15, 1768-April 14, 1849) is the son that Ruby E. Ross descended from. He went to Tennessee and met and married Elizabeth Smith (May 11, 1778-Nov. 22, 1844). They moved near Brighton, MO in the late 1820s or early 1830s. They brought a few slaves with them. They and four of their slaves were the first members of the Woodard clan to be buried at the Hickory Grove Cemetery in Polk County, MO. They and their six children and slaves were charter members of the Methodist Church there.

Pitt Woodard and his Negro slaves built the Woodard Mill located on Sac River in Polk County; also a two-story log house. A flood washed the mill away in about 1866 and it was never rebuilt. The old log house was torn down in about 1896.

Pitt and Elizabeth Woodard had six children: four girls and two boys. Two of the girls married McKnights (George and Monroe McKnight). One of the girls, Rebecca, married a Faulkner. Leta Huon is a descendant of Rebecca Woodard Faulkner. One of the girls married a Vann. The two Woodard boys were Edward Pitt Woodard and Thomas Smith Woodard.

Thomas Smith Woodard (March 20, 1803-Nov. 9, 1865) was married Oct. 26, 1825 to Susan White Fambrough (also spelled Fambro) (Sept. 2, 1803-Sept. 18, 1871) and they had 14 children. Three died in early childhood. The other 11 lived to be adults: six boys and five girls. Three of the sons were preachers and three were in the Civil War.

William "Billy" Smith Woodard was an itinerant Methodist preacher for more than 50 years.

Frank Woodard-never married, was accidentally shot and killed near Bolivar, MO.

Hiram Monroe Woodard-father of Eulalia Monroe Woodard.

John Woodard-a preacher.

Wesley Woodard-a preacher.

James Woodard-married Alzana Lemmon. Alzana was a granddaughter of Jacob and Mary Lemmon. Alzana's parents were Smith and Permelia (Wallace) Lemmon. James Woodard was killed in the Battle of Vicksburg, MS in 1863.

Elizabeth "Lizzy"-married Hancock.
Jane Woodard-married Hopkins.
Mary Woodard-married McGee.
Lucinda Woodard-never married.
Matilda-married McMasters.

Frank, Hiram Monroe and James Woodard joined the Confederate Army in the 1860s.

Hiram Monroe Woodard (Sept. 27, 1834-March 27, 1869) was a farmer, teacher and soldier in the Civil War. On Nov. 3, 1857, he was married to Martha Ann Bland (Nov. 23, 1839-Jan. 25, 1918) at Humansville, MO by the Rev. John Yoast. Hiram taught at Tuck School, which was between Morrisville and Brighton in Polk County, MO. He also taught at Slagle School and Humansville. As a boy, he worked in his father's mill, the one built by his grandfather, Pitt Woodard. When he was not busy, he studied his books. He went to school a mile south of Morrisville, about where the Old Union Cemetery is located.

Martha Ann Bland's parents were Elliott (Oct. 3, 1813-July 4, 1896) and Virginia Adeline (Clay) Bland (Sept. 27, 1818-Jan. 27, 1862). They moved from Tennessee to Humansville, MO in a covered wagon, arriving Nov. 23, 1839. Martha Ann Bland was born that night in Humansville and lived there until she married. She was the second oldest of 10 children. Nine were born in Humansville, MO. Her older brother, Johnathan Clay Bland, was born in 1837 in Tennessee. He died of pneumonia in his teens in Humansville. The other siblings were Susan Virginia Bland, born 1842, married Henderson Moore; Mary Adeline, born 1845, married Logan Vann; Sarah Loucretia, born 1848, married Julius Fay; George, born 1849, died in infancy; Florence Eulalia (1853-1860); William (1855-1861); Robert (1857-1860); and Finis Bland (1860-1861). Elliott Bland was born in Virginia, went to Tennessee and married. He enlisted in the Seminole War. With a government land grant he settled at Humansville, MO. His wife's parents were Johnathan and Martha Anne (Tayler) Clay.

Hiram Monroe and Martha Ann Bland Woodard had three children:

Susan Adeline "Addie" Woodard (Jan. 20, 1859-April 1919). She and her parents are buried at Hickory Grove Cemetery.

A boy, not named, was born July 4, 1861.

Eulalia Monroe Woodard (Nov. 25, 1866-Aug. 15, 1955), she loved to sing church songs.

During the Civil War, Martha Ann Bland Woodard was shot in the head as she was riding with her husband, a soldier (each on their own horse) as he returned to camp, near Stockton. The bullet dented the top of her skull but did not kill her. She used to let her grandchildren feel the dent, and Ruby Eulalia Ross remembered feeling the dent.

Hiram Monroe Woodard died of pneumonia in 1869. Martha Ann (Bland) Woodard then married James Almon Benge (1829-April 18, 1882) on Sept. 22, 1872. They were married by the Rev. Rueben Gillmore. They had one child, Martha Virginia "Vergie" Benge, born Aug. 18, 1873. Vergie married John Richard Stokes and they had six children: Faye, Fern, Marie, Bryer, Lynn Almon and Raymond "Manz" Stokes. Vergie died Nov. 4, 1960 and is buried at Brighton Cemetery.

Thomas Francis Ross was the only child of Susan Catherine "Kate" Cargile (Feb. 25, 1843-May 10, 1929) and John Jacob Ross (July 22, 1840-April 13, 1920). They were married Dec. 20, 1866 and rode horseback from Quitman, AR to Morrisville, MO. They lived on a farm south of Morrisville. There were four houses on the farm. Both are buried in the Morrisville Cemetery.

November 26, 1950 at Republic, MO, home of W. W. Hughes Ross relatives

Elliot Bland, born October 3, 1813, died July 4, 1896 father of Martha Ann Bland

Thomas Francis and Eulalia Monroe Woodard Ross on their 60th wedding anniversary, February 16, 1947

Ruby E., Virginia June, George Robert and JoAnne Booher

John Jacob Ross, born July 22, 1840, died April 13, 1920 and Susan Catherine "Kate" (Cargile) Ross, born February 25, 1843 died May 10, 1929. They are buried at Morrisville Cemetery.

October 31, 1987-three generations- Kenneth, JoAnne, Bryce Daniel, Danny and Karrolyn Booher

Joseph and Annie Ophelia Miller Booher, JoAnne Booher is their namesake

Thomas Smith Woodard, born March 20, 1803, died November 9, 1865 husband of Susan White Fambrough Woodard. Buried at Hickory Grove Cemetery.

Susan White (Fambrough) Woodard, born September 2, 1803 died September 18, 1871, wife of Thomas Smith Woodard.

Hiram Monroe Woodard, born September 27, 1834, died March 27, 1869 and Martha Ann (Bland) Woodard, born November 23, 1840, died January 25, 1918. Buried at Hickory Grove Cemetery.

Family picnic at Martha Ann (Bland) Woodard Benge's house about 1911, Morrisville, MO

Thomas Francis Ross (Oct. 15, 1867-May 29, 1947) married Eulalia Monroe Woodard (Nov. 25, 1866-Aug. 13, 1955) on Feb. 16, 1887. They lived on a farm south of Morrisville, near his parents, and had 10 children; all nine who lived to adulthood were raised on their farm.

Francis Monroe Ross (Sept. 4, 1891-Sept. 26, 1956) married Nora May Creed on March 1, 1913 at the Bolivar Courthouse.

Ruby Eulalia Ross (Feb. 21, 1893-Nov. 10, 1991) married George Robert Booher (Jan. 11, 1878-July 17, 1958) on Dec. 25, 1927 at her parents' home in Morrisville, MO. They had two daughters: Virginia June and Jo Anne Booher. The family lived at Morrisville for 20 years before moving to Springfield when Virginia June finished high school at Marion C. Early, where she was valedictorian of her class. Ruby was teaching at Collins School in 1922, north of Morrisville, when she met her future husband, George. Ruby earned a Bachelor of Science in education degree from SMS College and taught 31 years in Missouri and Indiana. She taught at these Missouri Schools: Heelstring in 1912, Luck, Pearl, Elm Grove, Fair Play in 1921, Collins, Lindsey Chapel, Halltown, Wiley in 1927, Swadley in 1948, Salem, Chesapeake, Charity in 1955 and Windyville. Ruby and her husband, George Robert Booher, are both buried at the Morrisville, MO Cemetery.

Roma Jane Ross (Oct. 7, 1894-Nov. 2, 1971) taught at Swadley and Fair Play.

Mary Ruth Ross (Jan. 18, 1896-June 9, 1896). She and Roma Jane are both buried at Morrisville Cemetery.

John Jacob Ross Jr. (Feb. 24, 1898-March 8, 1978)-he married Verna M. Kinney on Nov. 30, 1926 and they had three children: Ruby Naomi, Ralph and Mary Lee Ross.

Elta Virginia (Nov. 14, 1900-July 19, 1983)-she married Webster Wayne Hughes on Feb. 13, 1923.

George Woodard Ross (Sept. 13, 1902-July 16, 1979)-he married Myrtle Leona Hicks on Oct. 2, 1920 at Bolivar, MO.

Rachel June (June 1, 1905-June 1, 1985)-she married Charles Moore on April 20, 1930 at Elta Hughes in Republic, MO.

Marvin Thomas (Aug. 19, 1907-June 11, 1995)-he married Vesta Roberta Fuhr on Oct. 19, 1932 at Springfield, MO.

Lee William Ross (Dec. 3, 1908-March 21, 1973)-he married Grace Ann Hembree on July 17, 1929 at Springfield, MO. They are both buried at Salem Cemetery near Mt. Vernon, MO.

Joseph Booher (May 9, 1845-Aug. 1, 1925) married Annie Ophelia Miller (Jan. 21, 1850-Oct. 19, 1935) on May 14, 1868 at Mill Point, TN. They were both born and raised in Bristol, VA. They had a house built in Bristol, VA with a spring running under the kitchen. They had eight children (four boys and four girls) and all were born and raised in Bristol, VA. After their children were grown, they left Virginia and went to Oklahoma where Joseph homesteaded. Annie was not happy in Oklahoma, so they moved to Morrisville, MO and bought a 97-acre farm in 1911. Annie was musical and played the violin. Joseph farmed until his death. Both died in Morrisville and are buried in a family cemetery there. Their eight children are listed below.

Samuel Jesse Booher (April 22, 1869-June 11, 1951)-he got his master's degree at Kings College in Virginia. He homesteaded and taught at Riverside, WA. He is buried on his farm at Riverside.

Carrie Helen (Jan. 30, 1871-April 6, 1947)-she was a great fiddler. She married Bill Massey and had one child, Nellie Massey. Buried in the family cemetery at Morrisville.

John Ensor (April 4, 1873-Aug. 28, 1946)-homesteaded in Oklahoma. He married and had one son who died young. John is buried in the family cemetery at Morrisville.

Joseph William "Bill" (Oct. 10, 1875-Dec. 11, 1961 at Rivertside, WA) married Lillian Prickett and had four children: Harry Freeman, Delphia, Shirley Dean and William DeWayne Booher. They had a store and lived at Collins a while. Both are buried in Riverside, WA.

George Robert Booher (Jan. 7, 1878-July 17, 1958)-he left Bristol, VA and moved to Kansas and Washington where he taught school for 20 years. He also homesteaded in Riverside, WA. He was musical and played the violin, piano and French harp by ear. In 1927 he moved to Morrisville, MO and on Dec. 25, 1927, married a schoolteacher, Ruby E. Ross. He farmed and was postmaster at Morrisville in 1940.

Roxie Belle (March 22, 1880-June 14, 1880) buried at Bristol, VA.

Mary Josephine Booher (Aug. 6, 1881-Oct. 26, 1961 at Springfield, MO) lived with her parents on their farm one and one-half miles north of Morrisville. She and Susan are both buried at the Morrisville Cemetery.

Susan "Susie" Glynn Booher (March 10, 1885-April 5, 1959 at Springfield, MO). She did lovely needlework.

Virginia June Booher (Dec. 11, 1929-Sept. 14, 1987 at Indianapolis, IN) married on Aug. 8, 1954 to George Edward Jackson (Nov. 4, 1928-April 12, 1994). They both got their master's degrees in Bloomington, IN and taught business education. Virginia taught in Missouri, Kansas and Indiana for 33 years. She was a Phi Beta Kappa and was the Outstanding Business Education Teacher of the Year in Indiana in 1981. She had a music minor and enjoyed playing the piano. She and her husband were both stamp collectors. Both are buried at Greenlawn North Cemetery in Springfield, MO.

Jo Anne Booher (April 23, 1931 at Morrisville, MO) attended Marion C. Early School for 10 years and finished high school at Springfield Senior High, getting a two year PTA Teacher Training scholarship to SMS. She got her master's degree from the University of Missouri at Columbia, where she had a Gregory Scholarship. She taught/supervised vocational home economics for 18 years. Eight of those years were with the State Department of Education as a state supervisor. The last three years she was an assistant professor at Southwest Missouri State University. She also taught at Marionville and Houston, MO. She plays the violin and piano, and is a stamp collector. On June 3, 1973 she married Kenneth James Booher (Dec. 13, 1916 at Kansas City, KS-Feb. 18, 1997 at Springfield, MO) in St. Luke Methodist Church at Springfield, MO. The Rev. Paul Reed officiated. She helped raise a stepson, Paul Daniel Booher (June 29, 1958 at Oakland, CA) who married Karrolyn Beth Dorman, and they now live in Coral Springs, FL. Jo Anne also has an older stepson, Kenneth John Booher (Dec. 7, 1946 at Oakland, CA) who now lives in Spokane, WA. Her husband was a 20-year Navy veteran and a 32nd degree Mason. He was assistant manager at Battlefield Mall when they married. He is buried at the Morrisville Cemetery. Jo Anne has three grandchildren: Bryce Daniel, Bradley Alan and Kimberly Jo Booher (her namesake). *Submitted by Jo Anne Booher*

WOODARD – Pitt Woodard, son of Daniel Woodard and Sarah Pitt, was born Aug. 15, 1768 in North Carolina. As a young man, he headed west to White's Creek in Davidson County, TN with his parents and brother Edward. Daniel Woodard purchased 320 acres on White's Creek at a cost of 240 pounds on Feb. 7, 1795. Pitt married Elizabeth Smith (born May 1, 1778 in Virginia), daughter of Thomas and Elizabeth Smith on Nov. 19, 1795, and they raised their family on the Woodard farm on White's Creek. Pitt and Elizabeth were both devout, praying, shouting Methodists. They founded the first Methodist church in that area and Pitt served the church in the capacity of class leader, steward and trustee. The church also held camp meetings for many years at Woodard's Campground on the Woodard farm.

Pitt and Elizabeth Woodard's 11 children were James W., Sarah Margaret Vann, Mary, Rebecca Faulkner, Thomas Smith, Elizabeth McKnight, Martha B. McKnight Mitchell, Cynthia Luter, Jesse, William W. and Daniel A. Woodard. When Pitt again headed west, more than half of his children and their families went with him. They moved to Cooper County, MO; then in 1836 they traveled south and made their home in Polk County, MO, along the Little Sac River.

Pitt, now 68 years old, built a two-story house, the living room of which was 24x20 with a huge stone fireplace. He also constructed a dam across the river and built a flourmill, which served Polk County for more than 30 years. William Winton brought his family from Tennessee the following year and settled on land adjoining Pitt's. There, they established the Hickory Grove Methodist Church where the two families and Pitt's slaves worshipped together. During the winter months, services were held in their homes, because the church building had no source of heat.

In a sermon preached at Hickory Grove Methodist Church on its 50th anniversary, Pitt's grandson, William S. Woodard, said of Pitt, "In politics he was a Whig-decidedly so-by trade a tailor, and practically a farmer. He was five feet, eight inches high, compactly built, walked erect, had blue eyes, fair complexion and a good countenance.

"He was in good circumstances, was energetic, moved about briskly and made things go. He was systematic and correct in his business transactions. He was well informed, took and read the *Methodist Magazine* and the *Nashville Christian Advocate*. During the last years of his life he read the Bible almost constantly, reading it through several times in a year. He lived a consistent Christian life, and died peacefully."

Pitt Woodard died April 14, 1849 in Polk County, MO. His wife Elizabeth died Nov. 22, 1844. They were buried in the Hickory Grove Church Cemetery. They left behind a strong Christian legacy. By 1893, Pitt and Elizabeth Woodard had more then 20 descendants who were Methodist preachers. A number of their descendants were also gifted writers and musicians. *Submitted by Clara Olson*

WOODARD – Polk County had far fewer slaves and slave owners than some of the counties in Missouri. However, one early slave owner was Pitt Woodard. Pitt's father, Daniel Woodard of Davidson County, TN, divided his slaves between his two sons at the time of his death. According to Daniel's will, dated June 16, 1820, Pitt inherited "Jacob, Aggey, Jinney, Sall, Cloey, Henry, Alexander, Minerva, Ennos and Jacob." Pitt's father had purchased Aggey, her daughter Jenny, and another girl named Sarah in 1798 for $450. Pitt's brother, Edward, inherited "Pegg, Isaac, Sarah, Silvey, John, Anderson, Charlotte, Sindey, Eliza and Anzeda, them and their increase."

Edward remained in Davidson County, TN whereas Pitt moved west and eventually settled in Polk County, MO. Little is known about Edward's slaves. In his will dated Sept. 15, 1848, Edward left his entire estate to Pitt's grandson, Robert Pitt Faulkner. Robert's inheritance included 31 slaves.

The slaves Jacob Woodard, his wife Agnes "Aggey," their daughter Jenny, and Jenny's daughter Cloe were charter members of the Hickory Grove Methodist Church where they worshipped with Pitt's family. Jacob Lanius wrote in his journal of a place called Woodard's Mill, "Here there is a good society…Bro. (Pitt) Woodard…is a man of wealth, and has a drove of servants. My soul was warmed last night when I saw the Negroes come in to prayer. This is as it ought to be."

In 1887, Pitt's grandson William S. Woodard recalled "Woodard's Jacob and Agnes—'Grandsir and Granny' we called them—were pure blooded Africans. They were very old, I suppose almost 100 years. Grandsir was the miller, and Granny kept their cabin as clean and neat as a pin. She could beat the world cooking 'possum and making hominy. Some of the richest treats of my boyhood were realized in eating 'possum and hominy, and finishing with ginger cake, in their cabin. They were truly pious and served the Master simply and sincerely. Their bodies were buried not far from their last earthly home.

"Aunt Jenny was their daughter-a good woman-and died near Springfield after the war. Cloe was their granddaughter. Her services were always in demand on wedding and court occasions, as she was reputed the best cook in the country. The last I ever heard of her she was keeping a boarding house in Fort Leavenworth, KS. Most likely she has served her last guest, and gone to be a guest in the guest chamber above."

The "Negro property" in Pitt Woodard's estate settlement included Aggy, Jane, Cloe (valued at $400), Alexander ($700), Alfred ($650), Mary Ann ($300), Caroline ($400), Eveline ($500), Moses ($350), Jacob ($300), Minerva, and three boys named Emons ($200), Billy ($200), and Henry ($125). Pitt told James Faulkner, Thomas S. Woodard, and William McKinght to "see to and take care of Aggy and Jane so long as they live." Elisha Luter received Mary Ann. Thomas S. Woodard received Jacob. James Faulkner purchased Emon, Billy and Henry. Martha B. McKnight received the use of Minerva. *Submitted by Kena L. Jacobs*

WOODFILL – "Frank" Woodfill is Betty's paternal grandfather. As with her maternal side (Upton), her Woodfill predecessors had lived in Polk County and surrounding areas for generations. Family history did not seem necessary to discuss. Betty could never convince her father, Robert Leeper Woodfill, to tell her about his relatives. He was an only child but with many aunts, uncles and cousins. When she would deplore the fact that she had no first cousins, his reply was, "You don't know how lucky you are!" He obviously did not enjoy the many family gatherings he felt forced to attend as a boy.

Betty does know that her grandfather was the Bolivar stationmaster for the Frisco Railroad that had several trains stopping in Bolivar every day. He handled everything: selling passenger tickets, sending Morse Code messages to other stations, switching tracks to sideline some of the railroad cars and changing the semaphore signals that were controlled by huge levers inside the station. As young kids, Betty and her brother fruitlessly used to try to move those huge levers just a little. Her grandfather was not only in charge of all freight that arrived daily but probably did most of the lifting and carrying himself. Most all goods and supplies arrived by freight train until around 1945. That train station was a fascinating and mysterious place to her.

Betty's grandfather was a big, tall, quiet man, walking each day from his home to the station, which was at the west end of town. He married Oma Leeper around 1900 and they had one child, Betty's father, Robert Leeper Woodfill, born in 1903. They lived about one-half block from North Ward School, now the Polk County Historical Museum. Oma was one of the few women of the era and area to have attended college (in Kansas). She baked the world's best bread and the aroma would reach North Ward school ground.

At recess, Betty and her friends would sneak off to her house for a warm slice with apple butter while listening for the bell signaling the end of recess and they would race back. Oma was also known for her beautiful roses. Betty's grandfather died at 56 in 1936. Oma continued to live in the house until her death at 88. It is still there (in 2002).

Betty's father married Elizabeth Upton in 1924, uniting two longtime families of Polk County. Betty's brother, John Mark Woodfill, lived in Bolivar all his life, never married, and died at age 70 in 2000. Her father took over the Rexall City Drug Store in 1937 upon George Mark Upton's death. All the Woodfills and Uptons are buried in the two Bolivar Cemeteries. In 2002 Betty Cord Woodfill Mahaffey, her two sons and two grandchildren are the present survivors of the Woodfill and Upton clans. *Submitted by Betty Mahaffey*

FFA fishing trip, White River at Kimberling City, MO 1949; Bob Wooten, Joe Sprague and Bob McArtor

WOOTEN – Robert Wooten would like to introduce the Clarence and Ethel (Snodgrass) Wooten family of rural Polk County. (Origin-Burt and Maude Snodgrass [six children] plus Luisa and Albert Wooten [five children].)

Clarence and Ethel's family had a Halfway, MO address. Born-Burley Albert, Robert Lee and Virginia Evelyn.

Extended families include Burley and Betty (Lee), two children-Terry and Denny; four grandchildren, four great-grandchildren. Robert and X-Peggy (Thomas/Brown), four children-Ricky Ray, Debbra, Tammera and Anita; nine grandchildren, one great-grandchild. Evelyn and Dean Painter (deceased), three children-Melisa, Mike and Lori; five grandchildren, three step-grandchildren.

Burley, Robert, Evelyn, Ethel and Clarence Wooten, 1952

Precious memories- Rural Halfway.

Robert's family could only have eggs to eat on Sunday, especially Easter. Their eggs and cream were sold at Halfway for extra grocery money. They had homemade light rolls during the week; store-bought on Sunday if they had company.

Momma walked Bobby Lee (Robert) to school his first day, holding onto his hand. He just didn't want to go (bashful). That's two miles as the crow flies from the house to Providence School.

Fishing and hunting was their fun. Later roller-skating and basketball.

Momma was pleased when Dad took her fishing for her birthday. Times sure have changed.

They finally got electricity in their house in 1946. There was one bulb in each room with extension cords for the radio and refrigerator.

Robert joined the Navy after high school at Pleasant Hope. He saw some of the world but still landed in Polk County along with brother Burley's and sister Evelyn's families.

"Space is limited to include all our memories. Thanks for this opportunity," says Robert. *Submitted by Robert Wooten*

WRIGHT – Arthur Booker Wright, the eighth of 17 children, was born Dec. 18, 1875 to William J. and Lavina (Griffin) Wright. He married Margaret Izora Medsker. They had four children: John Otis, Eula Frances, Arthur Cecil and Lola Juanita.

A.B. and Izora Wright had no grandchildren until they were in their 70s, then had three within 11 days. Their three grandsons, David Strange, son of Juanita and James Clay Strange Jr., and twins Ronald and Donald Wright, sons of Cecil and Pauline (Heagerty) Wright, were born in July 1945. The Wrights later had two granddaughters, Charlotte Wright and Ellen Kay Strange, both born in 1947.

A.B. Wright had been a grocery merchant and farmer until 1928 when he traded the family homestead farm of 160 acres in Cedar County for a hardware store in Fair Play. He was later elected probate judge of Polk County and served from 1935 to 1947. Eula Wright managed the hardware store after her father was elected judge.

John Otis was a repairman for Standard Oil Company of Bolivar. Cecil was a shoe repairman and harness maker and helped with the store until he moved to Mt. Vernon, where he was employed at the Missouri State Sanatorium. Juanita worked in the probate office with her father, then in the Selective Service office and the Polk County Health Division. From 1956 to 1985, she worked in the office of Bolivar Manufacturing Company.

Juanita Strange is the only surviving member of the family except the grandchildren.

William J. Wright was born July 15, 1841, the 11th child born to John and Jane Wright. He was married to Lavina Griffin. He died March 31, 1908 and is buried in Shady Grove Cemetery in Polk County. Lavina Griffin was born Sept. 29, 1849 in Roane County, TN, the daughter of Elizabeth Harvey and William M. Griffin. She died Aug. 13, 1913 and is buried in Shady Grove Cemetery.

William J. Wright fathered 17 children. The oldest, Alice, died when she was about 2 years old. She is buried in Shady Grove Cemetery. Arthur Booker Wright was the eighth child of William J. and Lavina Griffin Wright. He was born Dec. 18, 1875 and died Aug. 13, 1976. He is buried in Shady Grove Cemetery. He married Margaret Izora Medsker. She was born Aug. 15, 1897, the daughter of the Rev. I. L. Medsker, a Methodist minister. She was called Zorie. She is buried in Shady Grove Cemetery. *Submitted by Juanita Strange*

WRIGHT – It was the early 1940s and life was difficult for Polk County farmers. Marvin and Lucille (Courtney) Wright, along with their children, Nora Lee and Robert Lewis, owned a hill farm about one mile north of Aldrich, MO. The Wrights had been in the area since the first Wrights, John and Jane Wright, came to Polk County in 1834, buying 240 acres of river bottom land in 1838. Wrights had been farming the hills and bottoms since that time.

Marvin and Lucille raised cattle, hogs, sheep, and milked cows. Lucille, like many farm wives, raised chickens and sold extra eggs in town. Feed for the chickens were sold in 100-pound sacks. Women used these sacks for many needed items.

The plain muslin sacks were made into bedding, tea towels and underclothing. Printed sacks were used to make dresses, shirts, aprons, sleepwear and sunbonnets. They sometimes even used the string from the sacks for crochet thread.

Roy Neil's Feed and Produce store in Aldrich was a popular place for the women to buy their chicken feed. It was common practice for the ladies to go in on Saturday and pick out the sacks of feed they wanted in a bag made of a fabric they liked. It usually took about three sacks to make a dress, but many times the ladies could only afford to buy one or two sacks of feed at a time. Roy was kind enough to put a nametag on the selected sack and save it for the ladies until next time they needed feed and came into town to make their weekly purchases.

Nora Lee, Lucille and Robert Wright, circa 1942

Lucile was a plump little woman who usually needed three sacks to make a dress but had come across a pretty pattern with which she could make one with just two feed sacks. She was proud of this fact and made it known around town. One Saturday she was in Aldrich buying her chicken feed in Roy's store. Curly Crain, who spent many Saturdays "loafing" around the store, was also there. Curly saw Lucille with her flowered chicken feed sack and knew she was planning to make a new dress. He jokingly remarked, "I don't understand how you can get a 200-pound woman into a 100-pound feed sack!" Being a good-natured easy-going lady, Lucille just smiled and went on about her business. She never forgot this exchange with Curly and told the story many times over the years, laughing heartily each time.

This favorite old-time story is retold by Magda L. Neill, the wife of Lucille's grandson Joe L. Neill. Joe is the son of Thomas J. Neill and Nora Lee (Wright) Neill. *Submitted by Magda Neill*

WRIGHT — The John Wright family was part of the group who were among the first settlers in the area that later became southwestern Polk County, MO. They came in 1832, three years before Polk County was organized.

John and Jane Wright settled on the rich bottomland of the Little Sac River area that became Shady Grove. Some of the others in the group were Thomas and Lucinda Gillihan, their daughter, Frances and husband, Isaac Routh, a M. E. minister; Reuben and Lavina Smith; and Jane Wright's brother, Hezekiah Brown, who married Eveline Barnes in 1833.

They left Jackson County, TN late 1829 and appear on the 1830 Greene County, IL census record near several Brown families. The men are listed on the 1833 Greene County, MO tax list.

More families from Jackson County, TN joined the group in the 1830s, including the families of Alexander and Rebecca (Brown) Blair; Blueford Maxwell and wife; Gideon and Margaret Brown; John and Matilda Anderson; Benjamin Hensley and his wife; and probably others.

John Wright and Jane Brown were married about 1819, probably in Tennessee. John was born in the 1790s and died March 8, 1846. He is buried in Brown Cemetery, Union Township, near Stockton Lake. Jane was born about 1802 and lived nearly another 20 years after John died, dying April 15, 1865 and is buried in Brown Cemetery.

They belonged to the Methodist Church. Four sons and five sons-in-law served in the Union Army in the Civil War.

They had 14 children: two died young, names unknown.

Anna married Josiah Brown, probably son of Hiram Brown. Descendants state he came to Missouri, age 16, on the same wagon train with the Wrights. Children: Mary, John Hiram, Naomi, Eak, Sebert, Rebecca M. (Barclay), Josiah, William Jasper and Susan Margaret (Rice).

Hiram married Mary Whitehead. It appears Hiram died before his father and John's heir, listed as Morris Wright of Dade County, is Hiram's son.

Elizabeth married Isaac Whittenberg, son of Peter Whittenberg. Children: Mary J. (Rogers), Francis A., John Earnest, Milton Walton, Martha L. (Williams), Warren P., Robert Young, Sarah S. (Phillips), Laura C. and Artelia (Holder).

Lucinda married first, Alberry Brown, brother of Josiah Brown, children: John H. and Mary Sarah J. Lucinda married second, James Owen, son of Elbert Owen. Owen children: Susan E., Nancy L. (Maxwell), Lucinda (Maxwell), Rebecca F. (Berlier), Harriet A. (Blair), James A., Ida F. (Harness) and Nelson D.

Josiah married Elizabeth J. Gothard, daughter of John Gothard. Children: Mary, John W., Eliza J. (Davis), Elizabeth (Blair), R. Caroline (Beason), W. Hiram, Josiah, Fannie A. (Davis), Thomas J., Wilson and Loyd M.

Louisa Jane married Armstead Owen, brother of James. Children: Debby Lucinda (Hawkins), Samuel T., Mary E. (Davis), James W., Sarah C. (Summers Stowers), Amanda P. (Beason), Emma Jean (Barrett Griffin), Joseph Henry.

Thomas J. married Harriet Lucy Gothard, sister of Elizabeth. Children: John T., Josiah A., William R. "Dick," George, Marion, Fraim W. and Florence (West).

John married Mary M. H. Wood, daughter of Isaac Wood. Their child: Marion D. Mary married second, Thomas D. Dotson.

Rebecca married James Tyler Gothard, brother of Elizabeth. Children: Josephine (Fleeman), Samuel M. and Mary E.

Mary J. born 1839-1840, probably died in the 1850s.

William J. married Lavina Griffin, daughter of William Griffin. Children: Alice, W. Elijah, Arvilla (Coffman), Charles C., Austin, Minnie "Nin" (Simmons), Walter, Arthur Booker, Jacob B., Thomas B., Carry L. (Hays), Coy, Mollie (Eddy), Clarence, Erma J., Erie and Ethel (Renault).

Frances Margaret "Fanny" married John F. Tindle, son of William Tindle. Children: Lucinda J. (Abbott), Laura (Shriner Akins), James and Thomas M.

Many descendants still live in Polk County. *Submitted by Betty Ammerman*

WYNKOOP — John Thornton Wynkoop was born March 26, 1855 in Loudoun County, VA, died Jan.

Front left to right: Eugene Nelson Chandler, Ida Jane, Inga, Jimmie Muriel, John Maurice, John Thornton, Martha Belle and Anna Rowena Wynkoop; back row: Amos Attlee Wynkoop, Daisy (Wynkoop) Chandler, James Oscar Chandler, Laura Lee, William Jedidiah (Billy), Letha Mauda, Susie Mae and Adelbert Marion (Dell) Wynkoop

20, 1941. He was the son of Cornelius Benton and Martha J. (Hardin) Wynkoop. John Thornton's fourth great-grandfather, Cornelius Evertsz Wynkoop, came to the Dutch colony of Rensselaerwyck (now New York) in 1651 from the Netherlands. He was 24 years old. Over time his descendants migrated through Pennsylvania and into Virginia. At the end of the Civil War, Cornelius Benton and Martha J. Wynkoop, their five children, with at least two of Martha's brothers, John and Albert Hardin and their families, moved to Saline County, MO.

Amos and Tina (McGill) Wynkoop

On Sept. 2, 1879 in Saline County, MO, John Thornton Wynkoop, known as "Thornton," married Ida Jane Bond, born Jan. 1, 1858 in Lee County, IA, died Sept. 17, 1950. She was the daughter of William Jedidiah and Rachel (Guyer) Bond. Both Jedidiah and Rachel were born in Indiana. They were parents of six children, four boys and two girls: William Edward, Ida Jane, Benjamin Frank, Amos Martin, Effie and Joseph Alford. Ida Jane Bond descended from English Quakers. Her family came to America about 1755.

Jedidiah Bond and Thornton Wynkoop brought their families to Polk County in 1882-1883. Jedidiah and Rachel bought land just west of the Flint Hill-Oak Grove Cemetery near the Greene County line. Thornton and Ida and their two small children settled on 40 acres of land one mile west of Gulf, now Eudora. Gulf was so named for the Gulf Railroad. The land where the family settled had a log cabin with two big, black cherry trees on each side of the cabin door. Thornton and Ida were parents to 13 children, four boys and nine girls. Eleven of the children were born at Eudora, MO.

Daisy Alice, born Oct. 14, 1880 in Saline County, MO, married James Oscar Chandler at Bolivar, MO. They moved to Colorado in a covered wagon. Later they moved on to Idaho and Washington. William Jedidiah "Billy," born Jan.

Rev. Dell, Anna Pearl, Opal and Verda Wynkoop

30, 1882 in Saline County, MO, married Lula Ann Beason, Sept. 22, 1908. They lived at Eudora, MO. He died Feb. 4, 1924. Laura Lee, born July 13, 1884, married Jeffrey Calvin Hagerman, Dec. 27, 1905 and lived in Orange, CA. The Rev. Adelbert Marion "Dell," born July 21, 1886, married Verda May Brown, Dec. 26, 1909. Verda died Aug. 26, 1955. He married second, Mary Belle (Carter) Levi, on April 29, 1958. He lived all his life in the Eudora community. He was a pastor for more than 60 years. He served many of the churches of Polk and surrounding counties, including the Sharon Baptist church, renamed Edora Baptist Church. Susie Mae was born Jan. 7, 1888 and married Homer Leondous Haynie, Aug. 24, 1911. They lived near Wellston, OK. Dr. Letha Mauda, born April 15, 1890, married John Israel Haines, Sept. 22, 1908 and married second, Dr. Emmett Riley Cole. Mauda lived in Polk County before settling in Norman, OK. Amos Attlee was born June 18, 1892 and married Tina Jane McGill, Nov. 21, 1917. Except for the time Amos spent in the Army during WWI he lived all his life near the place he was born. His farm was just across the road from his parents' home. His daughter, Barbara Stine, still lives on her father's farm. It is one of five small farms her grandfather, Thornton Wynkoop, acquired in his lifetime. Amos was the last child born in the log cabin. He was about 1 year old when the family moved into the new house. The new house must have seemed large compared to the one-room cabin. The new house had four rooms, two rooms down and two upstairs and a pantry under the stairs.

Inga Clark, Muriel Kennedy, Maurice Wynkoop, Anna Box, Belle Acuff, Amos Wynkoop and Dell Wynkoop, 1953

Martha Belle, born Feb. 23, 1894, married Ernest William Acuff, April 5, 1916. He died July 11, 1957; she married second, Theodore Franklin Evans, on Aug. 27, 1959. Both of her husbands were ministers. Anna Rowena was born Jan. 17, 1896 and married William McKinley "Willie" Box on Dec. 19, 1915. Ida Beatrice, born March 9, 1897, died Feb. 10, 1898.

The twins, Jimmie Muriel "Muriel" and John Maurice "Maurice" Wynkoop, were born May 16, 1900. Muriel married John Henry "Jack" Kennedy and lived in Arkansas and Missouri. Maurice married first, Mary Eliza Coffman, Dec. 20, 1919. They were parents to two children, LaVonne and a boy who died as an infant. He married second, Berniece Rosalie Pyle, Oct. 10, 1931. They were parents of two boys, Byron Thornton, who died in infancy and Nathan Dale. He married third, Myrtle May Lyman, Jan. 22, 1939. Two daughters were born of this union, Carol J. and Daisy A. Myrtle (Lyman) Wynkoop died March 12, 1950. Maurice married fourth, Mable (Barnes) Metcalf. Maurice was a farmer/carpenter. He lived most of his life in or near the Eudora community. LaVonne married George Hanch; Nathan Dale married Linda L. Guy. Linda died March 18, 1992. He married second, Sue Pledger. Carol J. married Ray E. Fite. Daisy married Ronald D. Lindsey, who died April 29, 1997. Daisy A. married second, Dwane Winkel. Thornton and Ida's youngest child, Inga, born Nov. 19, 1903, married Thurman F. Clark, Sept. 21, 1924 at Aldrich, MO. They lived in Wichita, KS.

Thornton and Ida Wynkoop were grandparents to 37 grandchildren. In 2000 their granddaughter, Carol J. (Wynkoop) Fite, compiled and published *Tracing Their Steps, Some of the Descendants of Cornelius Evertsz Wynkoop*. The book followed the family from the year 1651 to 2000. Three hundred and forty of the family members recorded were direct-line descendants of Thornton and Ida Wynkoop. *Submitted by Carol Wynkoop Fite*

YEAGER – Edwin Dale Yeager was born on Sept. 18, 1931 in a farmhouse near the Hickory-Polk County line on Highway 83. The Homer Yeagers, Edwin's grandparents, moved to Polk County in 1951 from a farm in Hickory County. Homer Elbert Yeager was born June 2, 1878 and died May 21, 1957. Homer married Mollie Viola Walker on Nov. 28, 1901. Mollie was born Nov. 9, 1879 and died Nov. 30, 1975. They had one son, Dale Yeager, born Dec. 2, 1902 and he died Sept. 14, 1946. Dale was a trucker and stockman. He married Edith Elizabeth Emmett on Sept. 6, 1924. Edith was born May 6, 1907 and died Oct. 1, 1984. They had three children. Lena Maybell was born May 19, 1925 and died June 13, 2002. Bobbie Jean was born Jan. 10, 1929. Edwin Dale was born Sept. 18, 1931.

Ed Yeager

The Yeager family is buried in Flemington Cemetery. Edwin attended first, second and third grades at Prairie Valley School, located on Highway 83, north of the Hickory-Polk County line.

In 1940, Edwin's family moved to a farm north of Flemington; in 1942 they moved to Flemington.

Edwin finished grade school in Flemington and attended Humansville High School, where he graduated in 1949.

After graduating he did farm work. In 1951 he joined then Army Reserve and took basic training at Ft. Riley, KS. In August 1951, Edwin was stationed at Camp McCoy in Wisconsin. He contracted polio and was flown to Fitzsimmons Army Hospital in Denver, CO. He was treated in Fitzsimmons Army Hospital for nine months and released in May 1952.

Edwin moved to the greater Kansas City area and was employed by Westinghouse Electric until the company moved out of Missouri in 1960.

Edwin had purchased a new 1960 Corvette from a Kansas City Chevrolet dealership and they asked him to sell automobiles for them. He was in the automobile business until he purchased his own business in 1968.

Edwin married Patsy Ann Carpenter from Wheatland on June 11, 1955. Patsy was born Nov. 25, 1936. They did not have children. They had a home in Raytown, MO until the spring of 1968 when they moved to Wamego, KS.

They purchased the Western Auto Dealer Store and Hardware, Wamego, KS. Edwin and Patsy managed the business from 1968 until July 1990. In 2000, they sold their building and property in the city of Wamego. In 2002 they sold the farm where Edwin had raised Black Angus cattle, just two miles north of Wamego on 80 acres.

They moved back to Polk County and travel the United States in their motor home. *Submitted by Ed Yeager*

YEARGAIN – William Richard "Bill" Yeargain and Opal Marie Ragsdale were married on Nov. 26, 1943 in Springfield, MO. William returned to military service in California and Opal finished teaching that year before joining him.

Twenty-two years earlier on Nov. 26, 1921 in Quincy, IL Bill was born one of five children to Homer Hayden Yeargain and Fern Marie Seeger Yeargain. Hayden Yeargain was descended from pioneering families who were instrumental in the settling of Quincy. Fern's family was from Atchison, KS and Buchannan County, MO. The Yeargains moved to the Bolivar area when Bill was a young boy and he graduated from Bolivar High School in 1941. He entered the United States Coast Guard on June 26, 1942 and served as fireman in San Francisco, CA. Opal was born Oct. 8, 1924, one of three daughters, to Marvin Walter Ragsdale and Lizzie Ellen Moore Ragsdale. Marvin was descended from the Ragsdales who settled in the Halfway, MO area in the mid-1800s. Lizzie's family had moved to Halfway from Hale, MO in the early 1900s. Both of Lizzie's grandfathers served in the Union Army; the Ragsdales were also supporters of the North and there is much history recorded about their efforts to advance the Union cause.

After WWII, Bill and Opal returned to Bolivar, purchasing the Yeargain Salvage business from Bill's father, who, along with Bill's grandfather, August Seeger, had started the business in 1936. But this was not Bill and Opal's main reason for returning to the Midwest. They were bringing home a son, Marvin William, born Aug. 2, 1945 and they planned to raise him in a community with solid morals and values. It wasn't long until the family grew to seven with the addition of Marcia Ann on Dec. 31, 1946, Linda Sue on Sept. 10, 1948, Charles Richard on July 22, 1951 and Phyllis Marie on Oct. 24, 1952.

W. R., Bill, Marcia and Opal Yeargain

Carrying on the family tradition of service to their country, their son Marvin William (also called Bill) served in the US Air Force during the Vietnam era; Linda's husband, Robert Leslie Thieman, Lockwood, MO, served in the US Army at that same time. Bill and Opal's grandson, Capt. Nathan Lys Thieman, is currently serving in the US Army.

Possibly one of Bill and Opal's greatest joys has been their involvement in the church they helped found in the early 1950s. Berean Fundamental Baptist church was blessed to have Opal as pianist for many years and Bill as a deacon.

Recently, while reminiscing with their dad, Bill and Linda were kidding him about how, as teens in the 1960s, they thought their parents were crazy for moving back to Bolivar and passing up that opportunity to stay in California. Bill Sr. quickly replied that they should be grateful-after all, who knows how they might have turned out if they had been raised in California! *Submitted by Linda S. Thieman*

Jim and June York

YORK – In 1961 the James York family moved to Bolivar. With him was his wife, June, his oldest daughter, Sandra, his youngest daughter, Linda and his son, James Allen II. The move was precipitated by a change in employment.

James York had been hired as the Polk County Baptist association missionary after pastoring a small Baptist church in Amsterdam, MO prior to the move. He earned his seminary degree from Midwest Baptist Theological Seminary in Kansas City after graduating from William Jewell College. Brother Jim, as he was called, served as the Polk County Baptist missionary until 1968 when he accepted a position at Southwest Baptist College in the office of development. While employed at SWBU, Jim also helped establish Resource Development Corporation in Springfield, MO, specializing in estate planning to fund charitable organizations such as SWBU.

June York came to Bolivar as a full-time pastor's wife and mother. After her youngest son entered school, June enrolled on a part-time basis in Southwest Baptist College, receiving her degree in elementary education in 1969. After graduation, she was employed as a fourth and later a fifth grade teacher in the Bolivar School System, retiring in 1990. Many area residents remember the science experiments and hands-on learning style of "Mizyork." Jim and June York continued to reside in Bolivar, MO and celebrated their 60th wedding anniversary in 2002.

Sandra, the oldest daughter, enrolled in Southwest Baptist College and attended until her marriage in 1963. After living in various locations, Sandra and her family moved back to Polk County in 1976 and enrolled her daughter, Donna Woods, in Bolivar Schools until her graduation in 1981. Her son, Richard Woods, attended Bolivar Schools until his graduation in 1997 and then graduated from Southwest Baptist University in 2001. Richard currently lives and works in Bolivar. Sandra currently lives in Bolivar and is employed as a school administrator in the Dallas County R-I school system in Buffalo.

Linda York enrolled in Bolivar High School, graduated in 1965 and attended Southwest Baptist University receiving her degree in music education in 1985. She won the title of Miss Bolivar and competed in the Miss Missouri Contest in 1965. Linda currently lives in Webster County with her family and is employed by the Missouri Highway Patrol as a driver examiner supervisor.

Allen York attended Bolivar schools, starting his school career at Leonard Elementary School. He graduated high school in 1975 and attended Southwest Baptist University, graduating with a degree in music education in 1980. Currently, Allen and his family live in Edmond, OK and Allen is employed as a minister of music. He and his family enjoy making apple butter each fall in Bolivar using an old-fashioned copper kettle.

Even though the York family can't be called "real" natives, the family has had roots here for over 40 years. Their roots have grown strong in the nurturing soil of family and friends in Polk County. *Submitted by June York*

YOUNG – Thomas Young, son of Thomas K. Young, was born in 1841 in Roane County, TN and died in 1922 in Polk County, MO.

The family had moved to Maury County, TN before coming to Polk County in 1853 where Thomas, his brothers and sisters grew up.

The Youngs were farmers and pursued life much as they had in rural Tennessee. Then came the Civil War and their lives were totally disrupted. The father, Thomas K., was killed early in the conflict, and the mother took the younger children and fled to Texas with other people who had lost homes as the war went on in Polk County.

Thomas has married Matilda Sutherland in 1861 and within two years he joined the Union guard Company A, Seventh Provisional Regimental Missouri Militia. Many skirmishes occurred in Polk, Cedar and Dade Counties. Stockton, county seat of Cedar County, had the courthouse barricaded and soldiers guarded it. Thomas was one of the guards. In the fall of 1863, Col. J. O. Shelby led Confederate Troops in a raid through Missouri. They burned towns and took prisoners. When they struck Stockton, 25 guardsmen were killed, several captured, others wounded. Col. Shelby moved on toward Boonville, MO and left Stockton burning. Thomas Young was one of the wounded. He and other injured men hid in a cave situated under the town. A doctor finally found them and treated their wounds. Due to his injuries, Thomas was discharged from the militia the following January and he returned home to Polk County.

Thomas Young

He and Matilda had six children: Frances, John W., James Owen, Thomas Grant, Mary Elizabeth and Lonnie.

Frances married Jacob A. Meek and lived near Aldrich, MO. They had five children. John W. married Sadie Owen and had three children. James Owen married Mary Needham and had seven children. Mary Elizabeth married William L. Mitchell, a descendant of some of the earliest settlers of the county. Elizabeth and William had seven children: Carol, Madge, Lulu, Glen, Ray, Opal, Jack and Thomas Keith. Thomas Keith married Ruth E. Crussell, daughter of David Nicholson and Florra (Hargrave) Crussell. Their children: William David and Kate Ruth. William David married Jean Ann Trantham. Their children: Thomas David and Deborah Ann. Kate married Robert Alan King. They had no children.

In 1875 Thomas Young's wife, Matilda, died. He married Lavica Catherine Griffin. They had three children who died in infancy. Lavica died in 1890. Thomas married Rhoda Adeline (Box) Neil, the daughter of Daniel R. and Parthena (McGee) Box, early settlers of Polk County. Rhoda was the widow of Prior Neil by whom she had seven children. Thomas and Rhoda had one child, Homer Walter Young. He was born in a log cabin southwest of Fair Play, MO. As time went by, the United States became involved in WWI. Homer served in the US Cavalry.

He married Zulah Mitchell. Their children: Mitchell H. Young and Ethel Young.

Cemeteries of Polk County are final resting-places for many of Thomas Young's descendants. *Submitted by Ethel Young*

ZAHNER – It was the spring of 1996 when Bruce and Janet Zahner retired to Pleasant Hope in Polk County. Janet was born in Springfield, MO but he is a native of California. Bruce retired after working 26 years as an air conditioning mechanic with an aircraft company in Newport Beach, CA.

Jim and Rosa Phillips, 1956

Never in Janet's wildest dreams did she think they would ever retire in Missouri, even though Janet has family and many memories here. Bruce and Janet lived in southern California for 34 years near his family. Now, Bruce says, it is time to be near and enjoy Janet's family. Since moving here, they have made many friends and have been able to catch up on family history. They live only five miles from the Brighton Cemetery and Janet looks forward to Decoration Day to adorn the graves of family members. Her mother and father, Bill E. and Hilda L. (Phillips) Blackburn, plus one brother, Billy Joe Blackburn, are buried there. Janet's mother's parents, Jim and Rosa (Scroggins) Phillips, are buried there as well as his parents, Jim A. and Sarah (Hall) Phillips. Janet's great-grandfather, Jim A. Phillips, who lived near Brighton, was the first probate judge to serve in the new Bolivar courthouse in 1913.

Janet laughs now when she thinks back at some of her memories. For instance, she used to think her grandparents' house was so large. She can remember running from one end of the screened-in porch to the other end dodging the mud wasps, only to discover later, that the porch (before the house was torn down) was really quite small. She can remember playing in her grandfather's red barn, which still stands today on Highway 13 and North Dry Sac River. Johnston School was located right next to Ggrandpa's house. Janet's sister, Kay Skidmore, attended school there. Janet's most fond memory is how Gandma and Gandpa used to end each day. He would read his Bible and she would sit listening while doing mending by hand.

Bruce and Janet have never regretted moving to Pleasant Hope. However, they do miss Bruce's family. They have two daughters in California: Brenda Gaylene, married to Peter PoChing with two children, Karina Eileen and Kaylene Brianne. Their youngest daughter, Deborah Jean Zahner, had a lung disease called cystic fibrosis and died in 1988.

They are able to visit California at least once a year, but are always happy to return to the slower lifestyle of Polk County. There have been many changes since they started coming here to vacation in 1963. Janet remembers when her aunts would wear hats and gloves to shop the stores on the square in Springfield. She remembers Doling Park and the simple pleasure of roller-skating. She remembers the family reunions at Gandpa's home in Brighton and him going to the garden to pick a fresh watermelon to serve.

But they live in the present, accept progress and they are pleased to be residents of the Midwest. *Submitted by Janet Zahner*

Taken on Zulauf farm south of Halfway, three miles

ZULAUF – Jacob Zulauf and Katherine Magdaline Sept were married in 1905 in Larvevarde, Romania. A daughter Katie was born there. At that time, Romania was part of Germany. In 1907, Russia was taking control of Romania. Because of Jacob and Katherine's fear of communism, Jacob Zulauf, his wife (posing as his sister), infant daughter, his brothers and two friends fled. After committing mutiny and stealing a ship, they arrived in the United States of America in 1907. They arrived in Philadelphia and their two friends entered the United States as Zulauf's. They all entered on one passport and $250.00, which was stolen, by passing it back to the next person. They settled in Isabelle, SD. They were unable to speak or understand English at the time of their arrival. Jacob was a carpenter by trade. He worked in a flourmill in Eureka, SD and farmed in Isabelle.

Seven more children were born, two babies died, and the living children were Fredrick, Pauline, Edwin (born on June 14, 1918), Lillian and Benjamine. In November of 1924, typhoid fever struck their family. Jacob and his daughter Katie died on what was to be Katie's wedding day. Fred, Edwin and Pauline were critically ill.

Edwin left home in his early teen years to make his own way in life. He served in the army during WWII. He was a parachute folder. He received a medical discharge. In 1943 he met Willa McColm on a bus, she worked in an airplane plant in Kansas City. Ed switched seats with a lady who was sitting by Willa. They became acquainted and, in 1943, Edwin Robert Zulauf and Willa Maxine McColm were married. Willa was born Jan. 4, 1922 and was raised on a farm near Halfway. She was the daughter of William Howard McColm and Millie Jane Bass McColm. This farm has remained in the McColm family since 1896. Owners William and Delila McColm were Willa's great-grandparents. Willa's sister Elma Jean Carter's son, Michael Carter, owns and operates that farm today.

Edwin and Willa spent most of their married years in the Halfway area. Edwin was employed as a bus driver and then as custodian at Halfway schools. He died of a heart attack at the age of 51.

On Sept. 25, 1944, Mardel Carol was born. On March 12, 1951, Retha Jeanine blessed their home. Both girls were raised in the Halfway community and attended Halfway School for all 12 years.

Mardel married Johnny William Dohle on June 27, 1962. They were dairy farmers until Johnny had kidney failure in 1980. He passed away on July 6, 1987. They lived in the Providence community. Johnny was the son of H. L. "Bill" and Wanda Dohle. On Feb. 1, 1964, Deborah Jean blessed this home. Debbie was raised on the farm and attended Pleasant Hope schools. Deborah's great-grandpa, John Jacob Dohle, was also from Germany.

On Aug. 1, 1980, Debbie married Martin Todd Graves, the son of Joe and Betty Graves of Morrisville. Debbie and Todd have one son, Chad Wayne Graves, who was born Oct. 6, 1981. Chad attended Morrisville School and is an avid Dobro player with Ripplin Waters Bluegrass Band.

Retha Jeanine was married on Dec. 21, 1969 to Karl Dean Ryan. They operated a dry cleaning business in Bolivar and Buffalo. Jeanine has worked in the nursing profession most of her life, living in several states, the most recent being South Dakota. Karl and Jeanine have two daughters, Sandra Jean Barnhouse and Kristi La Donna Marshall. They have one grandson, Ryan Christopher Martin.

At the present time, most of these families are in or near Polk County. Mardel has lived all 58 years in Polk County and thanks God every day for the USA. From Romania to Polk County-the Zulauf/McColm roots run deep. *Submitted by Mardel Skinner and Jeanine Ryan*

ZUMWALT – Laura Elizabeth Zumwalt was born Sept. 21, 1911 at Mohawk, MO. Her parents were Eldred Candred "Bud" (Dec. 21, 1887 to Sept. 22, 1974) and Lunnie Mae (Richards) Zumwalt (Sept. 22, 1889 to April 7, 1978, married Nov. 10, 1907). She would be the third of seven daughters. The young family moved three or four times before settling for several years at a farm northwest of the Fairview Methodist Church at Huron.

The girls often walked barefoot to within a short distance of the church before stopping to wipe their feet and put on their socks and shoes. Sometimes Papa would hook the team of mules to a wagon and they would ride to church. After church, their home was a popular place for visitors. Laura remembers Mama killing another chicken, scalding it, plucking it and cutting it up to make enough for everyone!

At a young age each sister learned to quilt to help make money for the family. A company in Kansas City would send the tops and supplies. The family would quilt and finish the edges, mail it back and receive a check. They might also make a little money by staying for a few days with a new mother in the neighborhood.

Laura attended Pickel School near Cliquot for

The Fred Cloyed family, Joan, Jerry, Laura and Fred

a few weeks before moving to Huron and attending Greenleaf through the ninth grade. She and next younger sister, Ada, then attended the Academy at Southwest Baptist College for two years and finally finished at Bolivar High School. Laura did not receive a diploma because the superintendent would not accept her ninth grade work from Greenleaf. During this time, she and Ada lived with their maternal grandmother, Laura Lunetta (Dobbs) Richards (June 5, 1865 to June 18, 1953) and her second husband, John Kinder, in a house on the northeast corner of Walnut Street and Springfield Avenue.

Laura took the teachers' test at the county superintendent's office, passed and was hired to teach at Greenleaf starting in 1933 at $40 per month. She started classes that summer at Southwest Baptist College. She would continue teaching and taking summer classes until receiving her associate degree in education in July 1938. During this time Ma and Mr. Kinder moved to a house on East Locust Street where Laura would stay while taking classes. She spent some nights a few blocks away with Aunt Sally Hunter (sister of Grandma Elizabeth Zumwalt), who was in poor health. Besides Greenleaf, Laura also taught at Concord, Moore, Union and Inglis.

After church one night in July 1931, Laura was introduced to Frederick Earl Cloyed (March 28, 1913 to Aug. 8, 1980). He walked her home and that first date never ended! They were together for church, at friends' homes or outings with friends to Pomme de Terre River. They might drive to Bolivar for a movie or just visit with friends on the square. In 1938 Fred got a job with St. Louis Public Service Company. They were so lonely during this separation that Laura finally declined a teaching contract. The two married on June 25, 1941.

Fred was the older son of Earl Avery Cloyed (Jan. 30, 1886 to Jan. 7, 1971) and Coessie Antha (Thomas) (Dec. 16, 1889 to March 27, 1983, married Dec. 10, 1905). Fred was born on a farm west of Polk but spent several years in California until the family returned to the farm when he was about 16. Fred loved playing every sport, especially golf, which he learned as a caddie in California. His hunting and fishing put lots of food on the table. He played his share of practical jokes and had a hearty laugh. He could repair anything, so working on St. Louis City buses fitted his skills.

Jerry Lee was born Aug. 14, 1942 in St. Louis. There were many friends plus three Cloyed cousins to play with, but his parents were anxious to return to Polk County. In late February 1946 they started living and working with Earl and Coessie on the farm. Joan Kay was born Sept. 23, 1947 in the hospital at Humansville.

About 1950, Fred and Laura bought a farm adjoining to the north of his parents and built a house. Jerry attended school in Inglis until consolidation. He attended sixth grade at the new, red brick school at Polk while Joan started in first grade that year. Laura started working on her bachelor's degree at Southwest Missouri State College and teaching at Goodson, Halfway and finishing her almost 30-year career at Bolivar. She had received her BS at SMSC in 1961 and retired in 1975.

On Nov. 13, 1985 Laura married Frank R. Payne (Dec. 11, 1909 to July 20, 2000). This added a wonderful, extended family to Laura's life.

Jerry and Joan both graduated Bolivar High School and SMSC. Jerry lives at Lamar and works for the Soil Conservation Service. He married Suzanne Stultz (Dec. 10, 1947) at Shelbina on Aug. 7, 1966. She is a pre-school teacher. Valerie Ann (May 21, 1968) married Bernard Waggoner on Aug. 6, 1988. Their children are Jacob Taylor (Oct. 19, 1993) and Jenna Suzanne (June 24, 1997). Laura Jean (Jan. 6, 1970) married Jon White on May 30, 1992. Their son is Drew Michael (March 15, 1996). Karen Diane was born Nov. 13, 1979.

Joan taught elementary grades for a few years and married Dale Dean Cox (Sept. 5, 1947) on June 3, 1972. Teresa Antha (Nov. 4, 1975) married Jonathan Chastian Bishop on May 25, 2002. Dale is a 4-H youth specialist and Joan is an elementary counselor. They returned to Polk County six years ago to live on the farm where Joan was raised. *Submitted by Joan K. (Cloyed) Cox*

Jettie Orval Sallee, Berniece Zumwalt Sallee and Jettie Leroy Sallee (29 months old)

ZUMWALT — Berniece Zumwalt was born Jan. 24, 1910 at Mohawk, MO. She lived her entire life in the Polk County area and passed away Jan. 24, 2002 in Bolivar, MO. Her parents were Eldred Candred "Bud," born Dec. 21, 1887, died Sept. 22, 1974 and Lunnie Mae (Richards) Zumwalt, born Sept. 22, 1889, died April 7, 1978, married Nov. 10, 1907. She was the second of seven daughters in the family, which moved three or four times before settling for several years on a farm northwest of the Huron Methodist Church. She attended Greenleaf School and graduated in 1924.

On Oct. 19, 1934, she was appointed acting postmaster for Polk, MO and commissioned postmaster on March 16, 1935. The Postal Service would only provide supplies such as stamps and scales for weighing letters and packages. She had to provide a building and furnishings for the post office, a safe for storage of stamps and cash and bins for sorting mail. With help of her family and friends, a building and counter with sorting bins was built. A small safe was purchased through Mr. Hutcheson in Bolivar, MO for $10. A wood burning stove, small table and chairs made up the rest of the furnishings. While postmaster, she paid for electricity, wood for heating and maintenance on building. She even bought gravel for a parking area. This had to be moved around several times by kids growing up in the area, Jerry Ward, Gary Warren and Jettie Leroy Sallee. They had plenty of help from Donna (Bybee) Reynolds and Deanna Bybee. When they got it all moved around, a new load of gravel would arrive and we would start all over again. Looking back, it is amazing what could be done with a couple of play toy John Deere tractors and wagons. Berniece retired from the post office Dec. 31, 1974 and continued to live in the house built by her grandfather, James M. Zumwalt, next to the post office.

James M. Zumwalt, born Oct. 17, 1841 in Polk County, MO, died March 26, 1917, had been the first postmaster for Polk, MO opening an office in his store on April 23, 1880. James M. was married on Dec. 6, 1868 to Elizabeth Long, born Aug. 20, 1852 and died May 1, 1940. James was the son of Adam, born July 1, 1807, died July 5, 1870 and Loretta M. (Byrnside) Zumwalt, born December 1820, died Feb. 6, 1884, married Aug. 25, 1837. Elizabeth was the daughter of Noah, born Nov. 20, 1809, died July 3, 1863 and Nancy (Serel) Long, born Oct. 17, 1820, died April 15, 1872.

On Jan. 1, 1936 Berniece married Jettie Orval Sallee, born Aug. 4, 1907, died Jan. 18, 1951. Jettie O. was the son of Merritt Orval, born Aug. 1, 1884, died Oct. 26, 1923, and Mary Edith (Newsum) Sallee, born Aug. 13, 1887, died Dec. 24, 1965, married Oct. 28, 1906. Merritt was the son of Joseph Thomas, born Nov. 22, 1847, died Aug. 8, 1924 and Sarah Jane (Crawford) Sallee, born April 6, 1853, died Jan. 30, 1914, married Jan. 11, 1872. Mary Edith was the daughter of Albert and Rose (Wilson) Newsum.

Jettie Leroy Sallee was born on Dec. 9, 1947 in a house southwest of the town of Polk, MO and west of the schoolhouse and Mt. View Baptist Church and Cemetery. This was known as the Allen place. Berniece added a crib to the furnishings of the post office so she could keep working and take care of her son. Leroy attended school at the new Bolivar R-1 school, built in 1952 at Polk, MO and Bolivar High school in Bolivar, MO. Following graduation he attended Central Technical Institute in Kansas City, MO for one year prior to enlisting in the US Air Force. During an almost 23-year career in the Air Force, he worked as an instrumentation technician and engineer testing parachutes, air refueling systems and aerial delivery systems. He completed 567 parachute training and test jumps and approximately 1,000 flight hours in numerous flight test aircraft. After retiring from the Air Force, he worked 10 years at Edwards Air Force Base, California as lead instrumentation operations engineer for the C-17 Flight Test Program. *Submitted by Jettie Leroy Sallee*

ZUMWALT — Johnnie Zumwalt was born on June 1, 1918 at Cliquot, MO, the daughter of Eldred Candred "Bud," born Dec. 21, 1887, Polk County, MO, died Sept. 22, 1974 and Lunnie Mae (Richards) Zumwalt, born Sept. 22, 1889, Polk County, MO, died April 7, 1978, married Nov. 10, 1907. Both are buried in Mt. View Cemetery, Polk, MO. Johnnie was the sixth of seven daughters. She was 6 months old when the family moved to the Huron, MO community. She attended Greenleaf School at Huron, MO, one year at Bolivar High School and graduated from Emma D. High School, Goodson, MO. She also attended Draughon's Business University, Springfield, MO.

Johnnie and John Shipley 1941, Oct. 12, 1940, 1st Anniversary

Johnnie met John Franklin Shipley Jr., born Oct. 2, 1918, Bolivar, MO and died Nov. 18, 1999, buried in Greenwood Cemetery, Bolivar, MO, son of John Franklin Sr., born Jan. 14, 1874, Bolivar, MO and died Jan. 21, 1948 and Lula Mae (Richardson) Ship-ley, born Jan. 19, 1884 and died July 16, 1954, married Oct. 12, 1904. Both are buried in Greenwood Cemetery, Bolivar, MO. He was ninth of 11 children. He attended all 12 years in the Bolivar School District.

Johnnie and John were married on Oct. 12, 1940. They had two children, Marlin Dee, born March 20, 1947, Burge Hospital, Springfield, MO and Elderine, born Jan. 13, 1949, George Dimmitt Memorial Hospital, Humansville, MO.

In 1937 Johnnie was employed as stenographer by Missouri State Social Security, later known as the Department of Health and Welfare. Following the birth of Marlin Dee, she became a "stay-at-home mom" and successful homemaker. John served in the US Army during WWII from March 1943 to January 1946 with the 78th Infantry (Lightning) Division, Company C, 303rd Combat Engineer Battalion. He was employed by Bolivar Hardware for many years. They were charter members of Second Baptist Church, Bolivar, MO.

Elderine and Marlin Dee Shipley July of 1949

In 1955 the family moved to Baxter Springs, KS where John worked for Yellow Freight System; in 1965 he transferred to Liberal, KS as branch manager; in 1966 he transferred to the home office in Kansas City, MO, but lived in Overland Park, KS. Johnnie was a member of the Leawood China Painters. John retired in 1980 and they returned to Bolivar in 1987. They both came "back home" and he to familiar territory for fishing, hunting and gardening. Johnnie joined the Woodlawn Willing Workers Quilting Club.

Marlin presently resides in Belton, MO. He was married Aug. 19, 1972 to Norma Hogan, born Nov. 30, 1947, died Aug. 6, 1989, buried in Cleveland, MO. They had two children: Terri Lynn Shipley, born Jan. 12, 1976, Kansas City, MO, married June 12, 1999 to Bryan Leonard; Tara Lynn Shipley, born March 27, 1977, Kansas City, MO, married May 4, 2000 to Will Ruble, divorced 2002. They had one son, Blake Ruble, born Dec. 20, 2000.

Marlin graduated from Baxter Springs High School. He served in the Air Force as a radar repairman from 1967 to 1971 and served a tour of duty in Vietnam. He graduated form Emporia State University in December 1973 with a degree in accounting. He worked for Sprint from 1974 until retiring in 2002. Norma graduated from Emporia State University in 1973 with a degree in elementary education. Terri graduated from Northwest Missouri State University in Maryville, MO in 1999 with degrees in elementary education and learning disability education. She also received her master's degree in elementary education from St. Mary's University. Tara is a cosmetologist in Belton, MO.

Elderine presently resides in Columbia, MO. She was married Nov. 20, 1971 to James Morris Milligan, born Nov. 1, 1947.

Elderine graduated form Shawnee Mission West High School in Overland Park. She received accounting certificates from Draughon's Business College in Kansas City, MO and Tulsa, OK. Over the years she worked in health insurance, banking and as an accountant for a CPA firm. Jim served in the US Army during the Vietnam Conflict in an infantry unit and received a Purple Heart. He graduated from University of Missouri, Kansas City with degrees in biology and chemistry and earned a master's degree in fisheries biology at Kansas State University. He is employed by the US Fish and Wildlife Service. *Submitted by Johnnie Z. Shipley*

Childers 131, 170, 219
Childress 63, 224, 361
Childs 231
Chisler 345
Chism 163, 335
Chitten 68
Chittenden 35, 55
Chittenden School 56
Chittenden School House 45
Chittim 29
Chitty 175
Chitwood 187
Chlorsey 166
Choate 21, 53, 60, 118, 137, 158, 159, 225, 242, 244, 309, 324
Chrisman 257
Christ Church 40
Christensen 167
Christian 202, 367
Christian Church (Disciples of Christ) 82
Christoffersen 241
Chronister 240
Chumbley 202, 203, 262
Church 119, 359
Church Growth Today 40
Church of Christ 40
Church of God 40
Church of God Bible School 56
Church of Jesus Christ of Latter Day Saints 40
Church of The First Born 40
Church of The First Born Cemetery 50
Church of The Nazarene 40
Cisco 235, 286
Citizens Advantage (HMO) 111
Citizens Memorial Healthcare 108, 109, 111
Citizens Memorial Hospital (CMH) 108, 109, 110, 111
Clark 10, 11, 36, 49, 56, 73, 139, 153, 157, 159, 160, 165, 171, 174, 181, 195, 215, 224, 225, 232, 245, 256, 261, 268, 281, 289, 295, 297, 304, 315, 349, 368, 376
Clark Cemetery 50
Clark/Finley Spring 8
Clarke 350
Clave 34, 158
Claxton 166
Clay 16, 135, 290, 371
Claypool 138, 198, 213
Claypool Cemetery 50
Clayton 69, 150, 257, 318, 356, 365
Cleavengter 171
Cleland 235
Clemens 248, 257
Clendennin 200
Cleveland 207, 230
Clifford 25, 55
Clift 299
Clifton 264
Climer 273
Cline 186, 210
Clingman 73
Clinton 22, 86, 152
Cliquot 11, 18, 25, 35, 43, 56, 58, 62, 63, 71, 73, 93
Cliquot Township 11, 18
Clopton 200, 201
Cloyd 160, 161, 301
Cloyde 160
Cloyed 149, 160, 161, 378
Clyde 25
CMH 96
CMH Administrative Center 111

CMH Ankle & Foot Clinic 111
CMH Cardiovascular Center 109, 111
CMH Diabetes Education Center 111
CMH Endocrinology Center 111
CMH Eye Specialty Center 111
CMH Senior Health Center 111
CMH Sports Medicine Center 111
Coar 245, 246
Coats 35, 56, 143, 216, 287, 366
Cobb 238, 240, 307
Coberly 116, 117, 188
Coble 63, 68, 155, 223, 292
Cochran 55, 303
Cochran Hotel 74
Cock 259
Cocke 329
Cockrell 248, 260, 266
Cody 122, 260, 281
Coerten 354
Cofer 84
Coffee 279, 335
Coffey 255, 337
Coffman 21, 22, 73, 117, 130, 261, 320, 375, 376
Coffman-Howe Cemetery 50
Cofland 149
Coggins 120, 362
Coggins Clinic's 106
Cogswell 186
Coker 155, 262
Coldsmith 178
Cole 69, 131, 376
Cole Lumber Company 94
Coleman 25, 96, 147, 180
Coleman Store 25
Colewell 359
College Hill 55, 56, 73
College Hill Methodist Church 39, 40
College of the Ozarks 25
Collie 198
Collier 178, 197, 198
Collins 56, 73, 224, 233, 240, 257, 289, 314
Collins School 56
Colonel Coffee's Rebels 14
Colonial Springs Healthcare Center 110, 111
Colorado 27
Colston 173, 256
Colter 259
Columbia 106
Colvin 162, 227
Combs 59, 96, 146, 164, 313, 347
Comer 184
Community of Christ 40
Community Publishers of Missouri, Inc. 89
Community Springs Healthcare Facility 111
Company A 12
Company B 12
Company D 12, 13
Company E 12
Compte 265
Comstock 324
Conavle 129
Concord 56, 73
Concord Church 32
Concord Missionary Baptist 40, 44
Concrete 25
Condor 215
Condren 240, 264, 268, 283, 284, 355
Conethard 32
Congress Spring 27
Conley 125, 159, 197, 212

Conn 44, 203, 220, 304
Connelly 222, 358
Conner 124, 217
Conrad 169, 181, 245
Conway 249
Conyngham 169
Cook 63, 97, 133, 142, 158, 159, 184, 200, 211, 240, 256, 278, 329
Cooley 309
Cooneater 215
Coones 189
Coonis 142, 160, 325
Coons 291
Cooper 56, 73, 99, 125, 161, 162, 163, 177, 182, 208, 241, 243, 255, 256, 265, 283, 284, 285, 293, 294, 296, 299, 309, 320, 334, 335, 355, 362
Cooper School 50, 56
Cooper School House 41
Copeland 69, 149, 150, 163, 219, 225, 241, 262, 367
Copenhaver 252
Copple 285
Copus 219
Corben Cemetery 50
Coren 369
Corn 268
Cornelius 21, 193, 194, 322, 362
Cornell 354
Cornett 333
Cornwallis 127, 186, 369
Corum 156, 333
Cosgrove 12
Cossin 63
Cossins 80, 119, 174, 211, 225
Costley 290
Cotham 267
Cothrell 248
Country Hearth 99
Country Hearth Gift Shop 99
Countryside Veterinary Clinic 106
Countryside Veterinary Clinic-Large Animal Service 106
Countryside Veterinary Small Animal Clinic 106
Coursey 333, 342
Courtner 216
Courtney 53, 301, 374
Courts 145, 224
Covert 163, 164, 173, 237, 264, 326, 327
Covington 363
Cowan 16, 28, 57, 164, 213, 260, 287
Cowden 10, 33, 54, 61, 69, 123, 144, 145, 164, 180, 192, 224, 247, 336, 337, 356
Cowden Knob 28
Cowdin 164
Cowdon 164
Cowen 25, 164, 165
Cowin 164
Cox 73, 116, 133, 146, 178, 184, 195, 196, 207, 210, 224, 233, 235, 267, 269, 295, 296, 311, 314, 344, 353, 378
Coy 56, 73, 130, 308, 331, 353, 370
Coy District 62
Coy School 56
Craig 73, 234, 235, 259, 319, 334
Craighead 18, 243
Crain 11, 18, 29, 44, 53, 93, 119, 145, 153, 161, 165, 166, 169, 275,

279, 321, 322, 334, 335, 367, 368, 375
Crain No. 1 Cemetery 50
Crain No. 2 Cemetery 50
Crane 57, 122, 267, 297, 312
Crank 30
Cravens 157, 166, 230, 232
Crawford 4, 29, 68, 117, 134, 142, 145, 150, 166, 182, 189, 192, 200, 201, 229, 233, 255, 278, 307, 363, 368, 379
Crawford County 8, 10
Crawley 44
Creative Years Day Care Center 78
Creech 284
Creed 132, 138, 167, 193, 206, 281, 282, 316, 373
Crees 140
Crestview Memorial Gardens Cemetery 50
Cribbs 137, 303
Crippin 167
Crisis Pregnancy Resource Center 79
Crissman 349
Crites 282
Crockett 167, 244, 324, 338
Crone 23, 170, 287, 332, 333
Cronje 25
Crook 167, 168
Cross 60, 176
Crosser 200
Crosslin 19
Crosswhite 137, 184
Crouch 117
Crow 157, 168, 230, 243, 307, 308, 370
Crowe 157
Crowell 272
Crum 308
Crumb 227
Crumsie 222
Crunk 329
Cruse 118, 336, 353
Cruso 119
Crussell 21, 377
Cruz 53
Culbertson 53, 119, 148, 180, 293, 294, 305
Culp 177
Cumberland Campground 45
Cumberland Presbyterian Church 33
Cummings 66, 131, 288
Cummins 363
Cunningham 25, 92, 126, 127, 157, 168, 169, 176, 181, 196, 221, 231, 233, 271, 275, 280, 283, 285, 310, 318, 339, 340
Cunninghham 181
Cunnius 325
Cunnyingham 11, 32
Cunnyngham 31, 141, 169
Curl 53, 196, 225, 272, 275, 310
Curlin 73, 324
Curr 129
Curran 87
Currey 367
Curry 263, 281
Curtis 227, 258, 278, 318
Cusanbury 139
Cusick 162
Cutler 222, 248, 286
Cutsinger 197

D

D' Ella 353
Dade County 9, 10, 11, 32,

57, 62, 68, 102, 111
Dade County Family Medical Center 111
Dadeville 32
Dailey 139
Dake 154, 155, 183
Dale 344
Dallas County 9, 10, 11, 16, 21, 25, 28, 34, 35, 36, 43, 55, 56, 62, 103, 111
Dallas Institute-Gupton-Jones College of Mortuary 105
Dallas, TX 105
Dalrymple 55
Dalton 79, 136, 232, 260
Damascus Road United Pentecostal Church 40
Damker 163
Dan and Stan's Pharmacy 112
Daniel 171, 174, 207, 215
Daniels 216, 239, 251
Darby 247, 248, 353, 369
Darman 358
Darmon 129, 130
Darnell 252, 253
Darrow 149, 150
Daughtery 219
Davey 165, 166
Davidson 118, 147, 172, 173, 199, 232, 270, 275, 296, 303
Davis 10, 11, 16, 23, 25, 27, 36, 53, 56, 73, 94, 97, 117, 128, 133, 134, 136, 138, 143, 151, 153, 165, 169, 170, 171, 172, 180, 190, 192, 207, 212, 213, 218, 226, 227, 242, 245, 247, 248, 251, 254, 261, 267, 273, 279, 282, 284, 285, 287, 295, 299, 300, 303, 311, 326, 332, 333, 334, 335, 359, 362, 367, 375
Davis Mill 8, 25, 36
Davis No. 1 Cemetery 50
Davis No. 2 Cemetery 50
Davison 19, 27, 29, 56, 61, 73, 84, 117, 118, 125, 139, 146, 147, 150, 159, 160, 169, 171, 172, 173, 174, 186, 193, 194, 195, 237, 258, 299, 304, 305, 310, 311, 312, 363
Davolt 100
Dawson 199, 204
Day 139, 150, 181, 202, 291, 305, 339, 346, 350
de Graffenreid 174
de Rosset 175
Deal 158
Dean 119, 167, 189, 194, 268
Deane 312
Deaver 216
DeBauche 301
Debolt 363
Decker 219, 220
Deckert 340
Dedmon 339
Deer 80
DeGraffenreid 140, 174
Degraffenreid 133, 161, 174, 245, 365
Dehn 239
Delameter 169
Delaney 120, 255, 263
Delaplain 24, 79, 89
Delarue 255
Delarue Trust 5
Delay 320
Delby 335
DeLisle 177, 322
Delk 203
DeLoach 259

Delozier 361
Demaree 148
Demontfort 299
Denby 40
Denison 342
Dennen 174
Denney 370
Dennis 133, 341
Dennison 261
Denny 276
Denolf 339
Denton 202, 338
Depee 215
DePew 214
Deragowski 87
DeRosset 328
Derosset 355
DeRossett 175, 328
Derossett 63, 65, 174, 175, 183, 236, 326
Derossette 309
Derrossett 174, 175
Deshazo 68
Dethrage 207, 215
Devers 266
Devin 54, 65, 92, 93, 154, 175, 298, 365
DeVries 349
Dewey 26, 44
DeWitt 116, 269, 299
Diacatos 240
Diamond 144, 145
Diamond, MO 113
Diass 164
Dickenson 55
Dickerson 41, 93, 175, 176, 178, 234, 297, 368
Dickey 28, 36, 81, 267, 320
Dickinson 59, 60
Dickson 246
Diener 250, 251
Dieval 228
Dike 123, 124
Dill 118, 173
Dillard 118, 260, 324, 325, 345
Dillon 189
Dingus 285
Dinwiddie 244
Diocese of Springfield-Cape Girardeau 87
District of Louisiana 8
Ditmars 74, 93
Divin 86, 191
Divine 12
Dixon 68, 69, 176, 183, 215, 275, 322
Dixson 266
Do It Best Corp. 97
Doak 74
Dobbs 202, 203, 378
Dodd 21, 68, 164, 176, 177, 221, 273, 296, 369
Dodson 165, 168, 248, 351
Dohle 163, 176, 177, 378
Doke 21, 147, 199, 303, 344
Dokes 256, 344
Dolman 306
Dominguez 80
Donald 302
Donaldson 151, 152, 153, 213
Donnegan 179
Donnell 123, 177
Dooley 165
Doolin 198, 338
Dooly 250, 251
Dorman 73, 125, 181, 182, 373
Dorner 219
Dorsey 129, 183, 295
Dotson 174, 215, 285, 351, 375
Dotson-Dodson Cemetery 50
Dotterer 269
Doty 281
Doud 224
Dougherty 192

382

Douglas 82, 97, 102, 108, 130, 163, 177, 212, 322, 363
Douglas & Douglas 102
Douglas, Douglas & Lynch, P.C. 102
Douglas, Haun, Kirksey & Heidemann, P.C. 102
Douglas, Lynch, Haun & Kirksey, P.C. 102
Douglas, Lynch, Munton & Haun, P.C. 102
Douglass 177
Dowell 267, 279, 304
Dowler 197
Dowley 343
Dowling 264
Downing 321
Downs 149, 182
Dozer 120
Drake 26, 39, 54, 94, 119, 187, 188, 217, 237, 272, 369
Drewel 308
Drewer 267
Driskill 321
Driver 216
Drum 221
Dryer 31, 57, 63, 92, 93, 365, 368
Duda 285
Dudley 170
Due 139
Duff 324
Duffek 278, 341
Duffy 136
Dugan 119
Duggins 246
Duke 34
Dukes 254
Dulin 122, 139, 255
Dunagan 178, 179
Dunagin 179
Dunaway 56, 131, 177, 178, 186, 291
Duncan 145, 216, 270, 327, 330
Dungan 72
Dunigan 179
Dunivant 182
Dunlap 124, 125, 127, 196, 231, 336
Dunn 178, 197, 198, 263
Dunnagan 178, 179
Dunnage 178
Dunnaway Cemetery 50
Dunnegan 11, 16, 18, 22, 24, 26, 30, 36, 48, 54, 55, 56, 57, 62, 63, 65, 74, 89, 91, 92, 93, 94, 108, 118, 119, 173, 178, 179, 180, 225, 226
Dunnegan Baptist Church 39
Dunnegan Bible Baptist 40
Dunnegan Cemetery 50
Dunnegan Christian Church 40
Dunnegan Estate 23
Dunnegan First Baptist 40
Dunnegan High School 56, 57
Dunnegan Mercantile Company 26
Dunnegan Springs 26
Dunnegan Store 26
Dunnigan 179
Dunnihoo 319
Dunningham 178
Dunseth 21, 199, 237, 316, 356
Dunten 290
Durham 30, 125, 164, 180, 184, 336
Dvorak 31, 191, 315, 355, 356
Dwyer 365, 366
Dyce 238
Dye 180
Dyer 186, 202, 203, 252, 338
Dysart 24, 189, 310, 363
Dyson 133, 341

E

Eagan 129, 181
Eagle Hill 57, 72
Eagon 30, 33, 61, 151, 152, 169, 180, 181, 199, 238, 279, 316, 348, 353
Ealy 24, 103, 181, 363
Earhart 184
Earley 69
Early 62, 74
Earnest 197, 198, 199, 227, 362
Earp 181, 182
Easley 27, 118, 275
East 269
Eastburn 54
Easterly 237
Eastern Star 112
Eaton 232
Eaves 65, 74
Ebenezer Campground 68
Ebenezer Hall 68
Eberhart 235
Ebert 289
Eckerle 69
Eckols 152
Eddings 63
Eddy 207, 375
Eden 215
Edgar 211
Edge 84, 143, 221, 258
Edgewood 57, 73
Edison 117, 263
Edmondson 21, 130, 131
Edmonson 53, 338
Edmonston 263
Edmunson 268
Edwards 64, 69, 132, 173, 224, 308, 309, 339
Edwards Mill 25
Edwin 145
Egbert 231
Egger 280
Eidson 57, 63, 73, 138, 166, 284
Eighth Missouri Cavalry 12
Eighth Missouri State Militia 14, 16
Eighth Missouri State Militia Cavalry 12
Eighth Regiment State Militia Cavalry 11
Eisenhower 331
El Dorado Springs 87
Elbert 300
ElDorado Springs 111
Eldridge 173
Elkins 300
Elkland 35
Elkton 27
Elkton Baptist Church 45
Eller 230
Elles 307
Elliot 135, 240
Elliott 30, 106, 188, 196, 235, 278, 326, 371
Ellis 197, 198, 270, 303, 324, 351, 353
Ellison 277
Elliston 24, 147
Ellsworth 73, 155, 247, 359, 369
Elm Grove 57, 73
Elrod 275, 303
Elwell 359
Ely 74
Emanuel Chapter No. 24 30
Emberton 213
Emett 182
Emma D. High School 29, 57, 60
Emmert 182
Emmett 149, 154, 181, 182, 188, 376
Emmons 116

Emmons Cemetery 50
Emory 161, 295
Emprey 93
Endicott 158
Engel 310
Engelbret 184
England 219
Engle 142, 169, 181
Engledow 120, 168, 339, 342
Engleman 178, 225, 274
English 8, 92, 297
Enon Cemetery 19, 50
Enon Missionary Baptist Church 40, 49
Entlicher 93
Enyart 184, 269
Epperson 200
Epple 239
Erickson 132
Erie 27
Erna 27
Ernst 128, 152
Erven 84, 155, 182, 334
Ervin 19, 57, 63, 258, 278, 341
Erwin 16, 56, 63, 182, 183, 187, 196, 200, 221, 270, 271, 312, 316, 337
Erwin-Blue Funeral Home 105
Esicks 158
Eskew 323
Esleshman 219
Esquire Theater 79
Esquival 281
Essex 104
Estes 120, 275, 295
Etheridge 318, 324
Ethridge 273
Eudora 18, 25, 27, 29, 33, 35, 49, 56, 57, 62, 65, 68, 74
Eudora Baptist 40, 46
Eudora Cemetery 50
Eudora Church of God 40
Eudora Springs 10, 27, 36
Euliss 69, 183, 268
Evangel Assembly of God 40
Evans 12, 16, 65, 157, 172, 173, 183, 184, 189, 219, 220, 227, 256, 338, 356, 368, 376
Eveloff 184
Everett 123
Everly 184
Eversoll 184
Eversoll's Station 104
Ewart and Train Charcoal Company 27
Ewing 43, 184, 185, 320
Exodus Ministry 40
Ezell 68, 147, 335
Ezzell 121

F

Fair Grove 14, 29, 73
Fair Grove School District 71
Fair Play 8, 11, 13, 18, 22, 23, 27, 32, 35, 39, 40, 41, 44, 48, 53, 55, 56, 57, 58, 60, 64, 72, 74, 80, 93, 112
Fair Play A. F. and A. M., No. 44 27
Fair Play Assembly of God 40
Fair Play Baptist Church 40, 80
Fair Play Christian 40
Fair Play Church of God 40
Fair Play Free Methodist 40
Fair Play Lodge 112
Fair Play Lodge No. 55 27
Fair Play Presbyterian 40
Fair Play School 58
Fair Play School District 57

Fair Play Store 37
Fair Play United Methodist 40
Fair View 57, 72
Fair View United Methodist 41
Faircloth 131
Fairfield 332
Fairlamb 173
Fambro 371
Fambrough 371, 372
Family Affair 96
Family Eye Care 94, 98
Family Institute of the Ozarks 94
Fanning 221
Fare 293
Fargo 130
Farmer 59, 92, 142, 143, 146, 155, 156, 158, 203, 204, 225, 254, 255, 304
Farmers Exchange 34
Farmers Mutual Fire and Lightening Insurance Company 27
Farrar 235
Farrell 299
Farrer 352
Farris 169, 184
Fatheree 369
Faucett 327
Faulkenberry 263
Faulkner 185, 238, 240, 254, 371, 373, 374
Faulkner Lumber Company 94
Fausett 363
Fay 371
Fayette, MO 10
Fealds 359
Feathers 349
Feith 325
Felix 147, 162, 163
Fellers 235, 357
Fellows 149, 161, 189, 220, 224, 341
Felthoff 125, 126, 127, 233, 306
Fender 41, 60, 81, 146, 147, 150, 206, 208, 236, 237, 325, 344, 345
Fender Chapel Baptist Church 41, 81
Fender Chapel Church 62
Fenner 157
Fergason 334
Fergerson 200
Ferguson 11, 215, 246
Fetterhoff 290
Fetters 311
FFA 74
Fiddler 274
Field 180, 359
Fielder 150
Fielding 152
Fields 10, 19, 134, 334
Fieth 292, 325, 345
Fifteenth Missouri Calvary 12
Fifteenth Regiment 11
Fifteenth Reserve Corps 12
Fifth Regiment, C. S. A. 12
Figari 106, 350
Figueroa 149
Filliaux 296
Fincher 239
Findley 140, 323
Finger 150
Fink 286
Finley 324
Finly Creamery 61
Finn 280
Finney 138
First Assembly of God 41
First Baptist Church 75, 79, 80, 85
First Christian Church (Dis-

ciples of Christ) 82
First National Bank 112
First Presbyterian Church 78
Fischer 69, 256, 270
Fish 84, 219, 220, 236, 348
Fisher 30, 41, 59, 60, 93, 148, 161, 166, 168, 170, 171, 173, 185, 186, 205, 206, 240, 252, 275, 284, 289, 299, 314, 325, 347, 349, 368
Fisher Creek 58
Fite 197, 340, 376
Fittro 129
Fittroff 155
Fitzgerald 36
Fitzgerrell 240
Fitzwater 185
Flack 131
Flanagan 326
Fleeman 59, 103, 186, 187, 274, 276, 335, 375
Fleenor 187
Fleming 27
Flemington 18, 27, 28, 35, 58, 71, 72, 73, 93
Flemington Cemetery 50
Flemington Christian 41
Flemington Methodist 41
Flemington Missionary Baptist 41
Flemington Seventh Day Adventist 41
Flemington Township 11, 18
Fletcher 131, 140, 269, 285
Flindall 293
Flinn 316
Flint 13, 58, 73, 93, 146, 149, 187, 188, 217, 218, 219, 224, 289
Flipps 272
Florence 240
Flowers 251
Flower's Mill 22, 28, 31, 35
Floyd 198, 244, 307
Fly 188, 189, 300
Flynn 300
Folley 367
Follis 209, 337
Force 178
Ford 172, 173, 183, 195, 202, 262, 271
Ford Motor Company 103
Ford Motor Credit 103
Forest Grove 60, 73
Forest Grove School 60, 88
Forgey 93, 149, 157, 189, 190, 261, 275, 298, 308
Forkner 102
Forrest 300
Forsee 73
Forster 173
Fort Scott 9
Fort Sumter 11
Fortner 146, 199
Foster 84, 141, 183, 186, 188, 190, 199, 222, 225, 237, 239, 240, 242, 264, 267, 278, 285, 305, 311, 327
Fothergill 247, 248
Fourshee 92
Foushee 208
Foust 338, 353
Fouts-Ankrom Cemetery 50
Fowler 69, 132, 142, 190, 193, 224, 242, 343, 346, 370
Fox 8, 11, 35, 60, 73, 92, 93, 118, 121, 122, 143, 154, 162, 190, 191, 207, 225, 238, 243, 267, 288, 293, 297, 350, 352, 359, 369
Fox School 59

Frady 243, 244
Fraker 225
France 360
Francios 117
Francka 86, 87, 183, 191, 192, 264, 302, 370
Francois 254
Frank 68, 160, 208
Franklin 31, 34, 120, 121, 133, 134, 145, 187, 192, 193, 227, 330, 363
Franklin County 8
Franks 253
Franz 193, 316, 318
Fraser 73, 140, 193
Frazer 220
Frazier 12, 14, 137, 160, 253, 258
Free Press 91
Freedom 41
Freedom Fellowship 41
Freedom Missionary Baptist Church 41, 49
Freeland 271
Freeman 56, 150, 160, 256, 258, 293, 296, 351, 364, 365
Freeze 199
Freize 277
Fremont 14, 31, 135
Fremont, MO 36
French 30, 121, 134, 143, 144, 231, 267
Fricke 148
Friehedge 59
Friend 225
Friends of the Polk County Library 5
Friendship Missionary Baptist 41
Frieze 21, 84, 154, 175, 193, 194, 219, 244, 274, 275, 276, 365
Frisco 28, 29
Frisco High Line 27, 32
Frisco Lines 36
Frisco Railroad 23, 25, 29
Frog Pond 64
Frogs N Friends 78
Frontin 267
Frost 16, 194, 199
Fry 248
Fugate 173, 174
Fugateville 28
Fugitt 78
Fuhr 316, 317, 373
Fulbright 26, 69, 132, 154, 171, 194, 322
Full Gospel Assembly of God 41
Fullbright 330
Fullen 256
Fuller 145, 171, 195, 249, 269
Fullerston 273
Fullerton 10, 53, 56, 64, 151, 152, 153, 195, 265, 273, 339

G

Gabbert 131
Gabel 83
Gad's Hill 16
Gage 187
Galbraith 147, 260
Gale 131
Gallaher 155
Gallatin 195, 196
Gallegos 24, 91, 245, 252
Gallivan 196, 218, 232, 339, 356
Galloway 346
Galyan 196, 197, 219, 298, 375
Galyon 275
Gamble 12, 21, 197, 340
Gambrel 282
Gamel 267, 313
Gammon 149
Gann 332

383

Kinsey 247, 248, 263, 266, 299, 303, 336, 344
Kinslaw 235
Kinslow 177, 229, 248, 354
Kinzia 247
Kirby 93, 94, 124, 147, 170, 217, 260, 280, 332
Kirchner 249, 250, 251
Kirk 281
Kirkendall 169
Kirkland 103
Kirksey 102, 227
Kite 122
Klaus 68
Kleeman 68
Klondike 28, 31
Kluttz 121
Klutz 292
Knapp 62, 73
Knapp District 62
Knapp School 43
Knight 69, 129, 160, 297, 304
Knightly 299
Knox 122
Koch 225
Koert 354
Kofahl 311
Kohley 251
Koon 230, 248, 303
Kooney 352
Kopecki 278
Kopfer 194
Koppes 319
Korn 86, 191, 192, 356
Korth 218
Kozelka 300
Kramme 265
Kroutil 191
Krtek 300
Kruger 168
Krull 249
Kruse 368
Kuechel 182
Kuelper 340
Kugler 229
Kuhn 278
Kups 227
Kurtz 301
Kuykendall 167
KYOO 103
KYTV 89

L

Laclede County 16
LaCompton 365
Ladd 251, 252, 298, 347
Ladd's Chapel 42
Lafferty 339
Lain 178
Laird 164, 222, 326, 327
Lake 248
Lake Stockton 44
Lamar 113, 184, 220, 229
Lamartinville 31
Lamb 262, 330
Lambert 256
Lambeth 212, 296
Lamke 103
Landacer 65
Lander 230
Landers 21
Landreth 57, 227, 233, 252, 358
Landry 262
Lane 32, 56, 121, 143, 146, 161, 162, 163, 174, 205, 211, 243, 254, 271, 304, 335, 348
Laney 17, 18, 63, 73, 344
Langenburg 32
Langford 165, 216, 220
Langley 34
Langston 117, 273
Lanka 300
Lanning 138
Lappin 79
Larcom 147
Laremore 54
LaRew 226, 359

Larew 26, 223
Larimore 31, 348
LaRose 295
LaRoy 216
Larson 264, 312
LaRue 316
Lash 122
Laster 186, 252, 347
Laswell 148, 149
Latham 10, 233, 303
Lathem 74, 75
Latier 249
Latiker 96, 218, 252, 253
Latimer 167
Latta 154, 223
Laughlin 235
Lavrenz 83
Law 288
Lawrence 68, 118, 171, 173, 226, 262, 267, 271, 272, 273, 281, 287, 288, 289, 291, 300, 333
Lawrence County, MO 86
Lawson 74, 116, 117, 237, 240, 253, 268, 299, 369
Lawyer 220
Lay 362
Layman 332
LCMS 83
Leach 232, 315
Leaky Roof 26
LeAn 242
Lear 228, 331
Leatherman 299
Leaton 217
Leavitt 24, 222, 274, 275, 276, 303
Leazer 182
Lebanon 9, 69, 79
Lebanon, MO 90
LeBow 134, 166
Ledford 21, 208
Lee 62, 68, 69, 73, 74, 118, 136, 140, 155, 219, 253, 271, 322, 323, 374
Leek 315
Leetch 153
Leever 350
Leffleman 191, 192
Lefors 352
LeForse 243
Legan 30, 54, 61, 84, 104, 253, 254, 322, 362
Lehar 300
Lehman 262, 368
Leighty 257, 318
Leininger 254
Leith 62, 73, 125, 206, 266, 355
Leith School 62
LeJeune 67, 185, 203, 204, 254, 355
Lemmon 8, 12, 24, 29, 31, 32, 36, 63, 64, 68, 92, 136, 137, 211, 229, 255, 297, 303, 316, 337, 338, 371
Lemmon Mill 36
Lemmon Store 29
Lemmons 56
Lemmon's Mill 31
Lemon 211
Lemon-Lemmon Cemetery 50
Lemons 152, 241, 255, 370
Lenox 173, 179
Lentz 136
Leonard 25, 379
Letter 214
Letterman 193, 194
Level III Trauma Center 108
Levi 376
Lewis 53, 126, 169, 179, 219, 224, 226, 256, 257, 291, 306, 307, 338, 356
Lexington, KY 82
Liberty 42, 62, 73, 141
Lick Skillet 31, 33

Licklider 256, 308, 336
Lightfoot 24, 25, 93, 193, 256, 257, 265, 327
Lightfoot Mill 31
Lighthouse Assembly of God 42
Lighthouse Missionary Baptist 42
Ligon 137
Lillard 148, 257
Lincoln 11, 231, 366
Lindley 187, 257, 355
Lindley Creek 17
Lindley Creek Cemetery 50
Lindley Creek Church 27, 42
Lindley Creek Missionary Baptist 42
Lindley Prairie 35
Lindsay 169, 199, 302
Lindsey 209, 224, 369, 376
Lingar 202, 203, 262
Lingle 230, 330
Lininger 21, 138
Linn Creek, MO 12
Linville 213
Lion's Club 75
Lipe 100
Lipsey 262, 336
Liston 257, 258
Litle 228, 290, 292, 293, 359
Litteral 229
Little 35, 121, 282, 299
Little Niangua River 8
Little Pomada Tarr 8
Little Pomada Tarr River 8
Little Sac River 8, 22, 25, 31, 32, 34, 36
Littlebury 369
Littrell 228
Lively 31
Livezey 299, 300
Livingston 309
Lizburn 231
Llewellen 131
Lloyd 119
Loafman 258
Lock 258
Locke 29, 145, 219, 222, 258, 261, 338
Lockhart 56, 247, 306, 310
Lockman 207
Lockwood 116
Loftin 34, 286, 296, 297, 355
Loftis 333
Logan 30, 125, 338
Lom 259
Lomas 268
Long 56, 118, 119, 140, 181, 185, 186, 221, 253, 258, 262, 265, 268, 334, 339, 357, 379
Longacre 258, 259, 354
Longcrier 262
Longpine 223
Longstreet 354
Loofman 256
Looney 10, 32, 54, 118, 138, 139, 155, 260, 281, 304, 338
Looney Township 10, 18, 85
Lopez 246
Lorimore 214
Loring 191
Losh 230
Louell 31
Louett 31
Louett's Garage 31
Louisburg 72
Louisiana 27
Louisiana Purchase 8
Love 143, 146, 220, 230, 361
Lovelace 314
Loveless 218
Lovett 133, 178, 278
Low 130, 208
Lowe 148, 258, 260, 261
Lower 93, 150, 154, 155, 244, 261, 313, 359, 365
Lowery 199, 259, 274

Lowry 202, 223
Loy 192, 214
Loyal 133, 172
Loyd 341
Lucas 213
Lucas Knob 28
Lujan 187, 365, 366
Lukens 278
Lunceford 82, 92, 129, 182, 261, 362
Luncefore 74
Lunderman 73
Luney 19
Lunsford 261
Lunsford-Lindsey 140
Luny 19
Lushbaugh 197
Lusk 140, 176, 177, 273
Luter 373, 374
Luttrell 10, 28, 92, 131, 154, 155, 248, 310
Luttrell Mill 31, 36
Lyle 257, 261, 262, 336
Lyman 21, 39, 130, 262, 287, 288, 376
Lynch 102, 120, 197, 333
Lynd 173
Lyngar 202, 203, 262
Lynn 73, 197, 215
Lyon 11
Lyons 299
Lysle 118
Lytle 264, 332
Lyttle 36

M

Mead 116
Maas 24, 82, 169, 269, 270
Mabary 333
MacArthur 228, 322
MacDougall 319
Mack 353
MacKay 254
Mackey 43, 68, 69, 183, 233, 270, 271, 366
Macklin 261
Madden 239
Maddox 173, 184
Maddy 254, 283
Madison 8, 235, 315
Madison Township 10, 11, 18
Maeland 131
Maggard 200
Maggett 243
Mahaffey 352, 353, 374
Mahan 116
Mainess 63
Maki 180
Maldaman 247
Malicoat 223
Mallard 285, 296
Mallernee 152
Mallory 323, 331
Malloy 25
Malone 213
Maloney 128
Manard 355
Manes 164, 185, 200, 235, 261, 309, 310, 314, 341
Maness 201, 238
Mankin 73
Mankins 295
Manley 149
Mann 89, 297
Manning 59, 225
Manroe 356
Mantooth 207
Manuel 65, 143, 244, 252, 271, 274, 289, 342
Mapes 322
Maples 239, 286
Maranatha Baptist 43
Marek 179
Margam 282
Marian Township 19
Marion C. Early 62
Marion C. Early Consolidated School 62
Marion C. Early District 57
Marion C. Early School 55

Marion Township 8, 10, 18, 92
Markey 93
Markham 106
Markle 299
Marks 39
Marlin 9
Marllette 297
Marlowe 258
Maroney 68
Marriman 353
Marris 166
Marsch 271
Marsh 173, 182, 193
Marshall 68, 69, 119, 123, 133, 206, 271, 272, 291, 320, 321, 367, 378
Martenziz 253
Martin 24, 63, 69, 72, 73, 92, 93, 106, 145, 189, 190, 207, 214, 218, 250, 251, 252, 279, 285, 288, 326, 353, 375
Martin Cemetery 50
Martin Randleman Spring 11
Martiz, Inc. 103
Mary 193
Masera 262
Mashburn 30, 155, 164, 165, 199, 240, 272, 273
Mason 33, 165, 345
Masonic Lodge 62, 112
Masonic Temple 112
Massena 343
Massey 165, 373
Massey and Patterson 33
Masters 261, 273
Matheny 53
Matheson 267
Mathews 271, 348
Mathias 140
Mathis 159, 225
Matlock 121
Matthew 362
Matthews 129, 147, 220, 221, 288
Mattison 144, 145
Mattox 243
Mauck 96, 310
Maupin 90, 178
Maxwell 57, 68, 177, 224, 338, 375
May 113, 130, 155, 240, 258, 261, 263, 269, 305
Mayes 174
Mayfield 53, 143, 146, 160, 201, 226, 273, 287, 288, 304, 324, 355, 361
Mayfield Cemetery 50
Mays 329
Mayse 196, 197, 225, 261, 274, 275, 276, 277
MBF Farm Properties 21
McAllister 88, 230, 262, 263
McArtor 64, 93, 195, 303, 374
McAtee 273
McAtt 104
McBee 283
McBride 34, 267, 299, 300, 332
McBroom 10
McCabe 296
McCain 197, 198
McCallister 262, 263
McCammack 119
McCarroll 154, 155
McCarty 71, 337
McCaslin 263
McCaulla 291, 292
McClain 93, 177
McClelland 57, 213, 220, 263, 264
McCloskey 179
McCluer 92
McClure 10, 94, 136, 207, 261
McClure and Company 33
McClurg 12, 14

McColla 355
McColm 97, 155, 177, 219, 264, 322, 339, 378
McComas 308
McConnell 17, 189, 219, 242, 263, 264, 284
McCord 177
McCowden 164
McCoy 225, 258
McCracken 16, 71, 72, 99, 119, 122, 149, 188, 194, 213, 253, 264, 265, 266, 313, 316, 339
McCrackens' Haberdashery 99
McCraw 24, 230
McCrory 18, 64, 65, 74, 274, 276, 363
McCroskey 74
McCullen 89
McCulley 266
McCulloch 320
McCurdy 63, 122, 365
McCurry 93, 273, 277
McCutcheon 134
McDaniel 25, 119, 155, 206, 213, 222, 223, 248, 267, 297, 322
McDaniels 242, 292
McDearmon 171, 172
McDonald 92, 165, 211, 368, 371
McDowell 66
McElhaney 324
McElwain 356
McElwee 235, 247, 248, 266
McFarland 39, 139
McFarling 258
McFee 330
McGaughey 312
McGee 62, 138, 142, 184, 200, 201, 213, 219, 224, 267, 308, 316, 338, 360, 371, 377
McGhee 146, 236
McGill 375, 376
McGinnis 212, 266, 267, 313, 353
McGovney 244, 285
McGregor 356
McGrory 338
McGuire 21, 54, 148, 184, 260
McHaffey 173
McHenry 170
McIntosh 184, 207, 267
McKay 267, 351
McKee 227
McKeehan 122
McKenna 87
McKenna Hall 87
McKenzie 33, 267, 366
McKie 130
McKinght 374
McKinley 364
McKinley Township 11, 18, 50
McKinney 62, 73, 122, 127, 137, 147, 239, 258, 260, 262, 267, 268, 274, 275, 284, 333, 334, 355, 357, 362
McKinney Cemetery 50
McKnight 63, 137, 211, 309, 324, 328, 369, 371, 373, 374
McLaren 348
McLaughlin 78
McLellan 180
McLemore 288
McLin 208, 210, 211
McLinn 209
McMahan 171
McMasters 220, 371
McMasters Cemetery 50
McMillen 143
McMillin 82
McMinn 11, 12, 23, 264
McMorris 291
McMurray 121

386

McNair 155, 185, 236
McNatt 327
McNeece 309
McNeely 275
McNeil 254
McNutt 147
McPheeters 21, 133, 144, 145
McPherson 228
McRay 179
McReynolds 68, 69, 84, 129, 154, 263, 268, 269
McShane 18
McSpadden 250, 251
McSpaden 275
McSwain 168, 177, 269, 343
McTosh 66
McVanzandt 92
McVay 260
McWhorter 236
Meacham 168
Mead 22, 39, 65, 116, 118, 170, 190, 219, 258, 275, 298, 307, 308, 310, 332, 365
Meade 58, 116, 299
Meaders 240
Meador 127, 186, 266, 301, 339
Meadors 368
Meadows 57, 144, 240, 305
Means 304
Mears 225
Medicine Water 27, 36
Medley 53, 277
Medlock 227
Medsker 217, 374
Meek 238, 260, 377
Meeks 220
Megerian 271
Meinecke 230
Meins 225
Mellegaard 362
Mellentine 167
Melton 12, 24
Melvin 256
Menefee 227, 240
Mercer 178
Meredith 239
Merle Norman Cosmetics 99
Merrifield 173
Merriman 354
Merritt 278
Messer 181, 348, 353
Messick 221
Metcalf 357, 376
Metheny 328
Methodist Episcopal Church 85
Methodist Episcopal Church South 39, 43, 85
Mexico 84, 95
Meyer 73, 278, 311
Meyer Cemetery 50
Meyers 93
Michael 358
Michem 168
Mickel 173
Mid-Missouri Bank 91
Middleton 183, 258, 260, 291
Mihulka 278
Milburn 193
Miler 312
Miles 267, 299
Miles for Smiles 111
Miller 19, 32, 40, 59, 72, 73, 74, 84, 117, 126, 129, 131, 137, 140, 148, 149, 153, 157, 158, 169, 170, 173, 174, 182, 185, 201, 229, 231, 237, 249, 252, 253, 258, 260, 267, 274, 278, 279, 280, 297, 298, 299, 300, 303, 312, 339, 353, 354, 362, 365, 366, 369, 372, 373
Miller, MO 74
Miller-Curtis 143

Millican 63, 225, 366
Millican Spring 49
Milligan 69, 225
Millikan 225
Milliken 116, 365
Mills 199, 263, 267
Millsap 138
Mincher 256, 307
Mincks 280
Minglin 177
Minne 354
Minner 188
Minnesota 36, 113
Minnox 334
Minor 282, 370
Minton 43
Mires 260
Mirkles 226
Misenheimer 121
Mission 28, 31, 43, 62
Mission Baptist 43
Mission Cemetery 50
Mission Chapel Baptist 41, 43
Mission Chapel No. 1 43, 45
Mission Church 62
Mission Post Office 62
Missionary Baptist 43
Mississippi 10
Mississippi River 10
Missouri 79
Missouri Baptist Convention 90
Missouri Cavalry 12
Missouri Hospital Association 109
Missouri Sleep Institute 111
Missouri State Fair 104
Missouri State Guard 12
Missouri State Militia 12
Missouri University Law School 102
Missouri Volunteer Regiment 27
Mitchell 11, 18, 19, 21, 22, 30, 32, 33, 39, 43, 63, 68, 70, 73, 92, 121, 122, 133, 136, 147, 159, 164, 171, 174, 185, 190, 206, 207, 223, 226, 227, 228, 243, 256, 260, 267, 271, 279, 280, 281, 282, 286, 290, 320, 326, 330, 338, 351, 353, 354, 365, 369, 373, 377
Mitchell Campground 43
Mitchell Campground Cemetery 19, 50
Mitchelll 68
Mitchem 128, 132, 219, 282, 346, 369
Mitchum 59, 222
Mittower 213
Mix 28
Mizpah Chapter No. 230, Order of the Eastern Star 112
Mobley 156
Modern Lodge 112
Modern Lodge No. 144 30
Modern Lodge No. 184 30
Modern Woodmen of America 32
Moeller 308
Moffatt 342
Moffitt 302
Mohawk 31, 62
Mohawk Junction 31
Molder 230, 354
Molder Cemetery 50
Mollet 251
Molley 25
Monegaw Springs 16
Monett 95, 113
Monger 339
Monroe 347
Montgomery 8, 9, 10, 19, 62, 68, 72, 235, 312, 323, 344, 362
Moody 174, 223

Mooney 8, 10, 11, 212, 213, 254, 273, 282
Mooney Township 8, 10, 11, 19, 49
Moore 21, 43, 53, 62, 73, 80, 83, 96, 116, 119, 124, 126, 138, 139, 143, 148, 169, 170, 172, 183, 184, 186, 188, 192, 208, 211, 235, 248, 254, 268, 269, 272, 273, 282, 283, 285, 297, 299, 303, 308, 309, 316, 320, 334, 335, 368, 369, 370, 371, 373, 376
Moore Cemetery 50
Moran 231
More 327
Moreau 283
Morgan 10, 92, 125, 177, 195, 196, 200, 263, 264, 274, 283, 298, 322, 333, 339, 343, 344
Morgan Cemetery 50
Morgans 82
Morganville 32
Moritz 292
Morris 57, 59, 142, 145, 158, 159, 181, 194, 203, 204, 205, 212, 224, 225, 234, 236, 253, 257, 260, 269, 282, 283, 284, 353, 356, 367
Morrison 18, 121, 283, 284, 314, 356
Morrisville 10, 18, 29, 31, 32, 33, 35, 36, 41, 43, 44, 51, 53, 62, 63, 68, 72, 73, 74, 93, 112
Morrisville Assembly of God 44
Morrisville Cemetery 36, 50
Morrisville College 68
Morrisville Faith Baptist 43
Morrisville First Baptist 43
Morrisville Journal 32
Morrisville Lodge No. 261 32
Morrisville Station 29, 32, 56
Morrisville United Methodist 43
Morrow 11, 58, 116, 117, 298
Morton 197, 206, 211, 279
Mosblach 308
Moseley 68, 236
Moser 364
Mosholder 251
Mosier 53, 129, 155, 284, 330, 332, 333
Moss 163, 171, 186, 284, 285, 296, 335
Mott 153, 198, 285, 286
Mottesheard 28, 216
Mounce 119
Mound View-Mt. Zoab Cemetery 50
Mount Pleasant 32
Mountain Grove, MO 101
Mountain View, MO 90
Mountcastle 342
Moxley 348
Mozier 106
Mt. Bethel 62, 73
Mt. Bethel Presbyterian 43
Mt. Etna 62
Mt. Etna Baptist 43
Mt. Etna School 63
Mt. Gilead Cemetery 50, 88
Mt. Gilead Church 88
Mt. Gilead United Methodist Church 43, 88
Mt. Herman 62, 73
Mt. Moab 43
Mt. Olive Baptist 43
Mt. Olive Cemetery 50
Mt. Olive Church 43
Mt. Pisgah 43
Mt. Tabor Campbellite–Christian 43
Mt. View 43

Mt. View Baptist Church 35
Mt. View Missionary Baptist 43
Mt. Zion Cemetery 50
Mt. Zion Methodist 44
Mt. Zion Missionary Baptist 44
Mt. Zoar Cemetery 50
Mt. Zoar Missionary Baptist 44
Mudd 229
Mueller 120
Muhlenbruck 271
Mulanax 74
Mullendore 323
Mullennax 308
Mullindore 323
Mullings 63, 123, 258, 344
Mulloy 25
Mulloy's Station 32
Mulvey 188
Mumford 330
Munn 10, 360
Munson 272
Munton 102
Murdock 68
Murphy 19, 44, 79, 138, 139, 144, 222, 241, 252, 335
Murray 10, 32, 35, 73, 92, 168, 183, 214, 268, 273, 279, 285, 286, 296, 324, 328
Murray Mill 32
Murry 282, 285
Musser 144
Mustain 153, 212, 282, 285, 286, 335, 346
Myer 371
Myers 83, 156, 166, 242, 276, 363
Myres 166

N

Nagle 262, 336
Nagles 163
Nahon 123
Nance 259, 346
Narcross 116
Nasalroad 126, 155
Nash 217
Nashville 19
National Park Service 5
National Register of Historic Places 5
Nations 166
Neal 73, 152, 153, 280, 316
Nebel 235, 286
Nebraska 86
Needham 65, 93, 143, 146, 164, 170, 207, 272, 377
Neff 69, 73, 174, 182, 202, 203
Neher 176
Neil 53, 68, 169, 173, 213, 223, 263, 286, 287, 333, 334, 352, 377
Neill 10, 262, 287, 288, 322, 363, 375
Nelson 83, 131, 189, 285, 345
Neosho 68
Neosho, MO 19
Netherton 69, 248
Nettinger 352
Neuhart 154, 236
Neuhart Park 24
Nevada, MO 12
New 131
New Bethel 63, 73
New Bethel Cemetery 50
New Bethel Church 51
New Bethel Methodist 44
New Home 63, 73
New Hope 63, 73
New Life Assembly 44
New Life Cemetery 50
New Life Community 44
New Market 9, 32, 63

New Orleans 19
New Town 27
New York 113
Newberry 119, 265
Newcomb 249, 250, 354
Newland 92, 181, 351, 363
Newman 131
Newport 267, 273
Newsom 131
Newson 131
Newsum 96, 379
Niangua 25
Niangua County 11, 22
Niangua River 22
Niangua Trace 8
Niblick 265
Nicely 338, 345
Nicholas 325
Nichols 163, 278, 283, 288
Nickel 202
Nickels 128, 149, 154, 188, 197, 200, 288, 289, 293, 294, 298, 359, 365, 370
Nickerson 68
Nicodemus 84
Nielson 187, 188
Nigh 295
Night Owl Theater 36
Nilsdotter 259
Noble 44, 69
Nobles 235
Noblett 153, 190, 313
Nodurfth 54
Noel 41, 171
Noffzinger 289
Noland 30, 171
Norcross 343
Norman 173, 229, 290, 344
Norris 164, 224, 225, 261, 361
North 324, 368
North Benton Township 51
North Carolina 113
North Green Township 9
North Ward School 39, 54, 91
Northeast Marion Township 10
Northern 133, 149
Northern Organization of the Presbyterian Church 39
Northwest Baptist Church 81
Northwest Marion Township 10, 50
Norton 339
Norway 113
Nottingham 146, 154, 187, 228, 288, 290, 340
Novak 120, 229, 300
Nowland 364
Nox 32, 62
Noyes 268
Nuburn 94
Nuccum 316
Nunn 53
Nutt 132
Nyssen 349

O

Oak Grove 63, 73, 74
Oak Grove Cemetery 50
Oak Grove Missionary Baptist Church 22, 44
Oak Grove School 22, 40
Oakes 310
Oakland 27, 32
Oakley 118, 281
Oakville 32, 40, 44, 63
Oakville Cemetery 44, 50
Oakville School 44, 63
Oakwood 32
Oberdorff 363
Oberkirsch 290
O'Brien 87
O'Connell 87
O'Connor 116
Ocoore 351
Odell 10, 152, 159

O'Dell 169, 225, 242, 328
Oder 65
Odom 133
Odor 119, 291
O'Dwyer 87
Ogden 147
Oglesby 176, 254
O'Hara 87, 327
O'Kelley 138
Oklahoma 10, 95, 113
Old City Cemetery 23
Old Franklin House 23
Old Freedom Meeting House 44
Old Freedom Meeting Place 45
Old Rock Prairie Church 44
Old Shady Grove 42
Old Timer 24
Old Town 27, 39, 85
Old Union 43
Old Union Cemetery 44, 50
Old Union Hardshell Baptist 44
Old Walnut Ridge Church 49
Olde Building 99
Oldham 55, 123, 124, 143, 184, 217, 260, 353
Olinger 225, 244
Olive 177
Oliver 365
Olivera 261
Olson 316, 318, 329, 373
O'Neal 130, 170, 171, 214, 230
O'Neil 189
Open Bible Church of God 44
Organ 223
Oringdeff 235
Oringderff 65, 251
Oringdorff 309
Orleans 27, 32, 33, 43, 56, 63, 64, 73
Orleans Mill 10, 32, 34, 36
Orr 271
Orrell 160, 200, 235, 316
Ortner 304
Osage 19
Osage River 8
Osage Township 8
Osborn 261
Osborne 262
Osburn 359
Osceola 16, 25, 74, 86, 87, 113
Osceola, MO 87
O'Sullivan 196, 232
O'Toole 8
Otradovec 72, 191, 192
Ottens 361
Overby 225
Overcash 72, 124, 186, 252, 290, 291, 292, 347, 348, 364
Overmeyer 35
Overshiner 160
Overturf 363
Owen 27, 57, 93, 130, 171, 202, 223, 257, 258, 261, 348, 350, 375, 377
Owens 10, 41, 53, 60, 92, 123, 203, 204, 255, 266, 284, 302, 334, 355
Owens Cemetery 50
Owings 264, 352
Owlsey 252
Owsley 252
Ozark 64, 73
Ozarks 16

P

Pace 14, 146
Pack 151
Padgett 147
Page 197, 201, 291, 292
Paige 316
Pain 201
Pain Management Clinic 111
Painter 215, 217, 374

387

Pake 72
Palen 206
Palenik 334
Palmer 63, 141, 149, 164, 188, 201, 247, 310, 355
Palsten 32
Pane 19
Pangborn 93
Parcels 216
Parke 124
Parker 12, 68, 138, 188, 260, 293
Parkhurst 350
Parkman 245
Parks 219, 315
Parkview Bone and Joint 111
Parkview Geriatric Wellness Center 111
Parkview Healthcare Facility 111
Parkview Physical Medicine and Rehabilitation 111
Parkview Senior Living Community 111
Parkview Wellness Center 108
Parminter 346
Parriott 199
Parrish 21, 33, 36, 73, 122, 126, 167, 185, 223, 225, 324, 356
Parrot 10, 82
Parrott 178, 363
Parscale 173, 237
Parscall 164
Parsons 32, 165, 207, 233, 303
Passmore 334
Pate 226, 253, 327
Patison 142
Patrick 136
Patten 56
Patterson 8, 10, 19, 33, 45, 63, 93, 122, 187, 193, 194, 215, 219, 243, 269, 271, 273, 274, 282, 292, 324, 343, 344
Patton 153, 331, 368
Paul 125, 130, 200, 242, 288, 292, 293, 294, 295, 309, 318
Paulson 261
Paxton Springs 30
Payne 8, 24, 31, 33, 84, 119, 141, 143, 146, 147, 173, 193, 206, 208, 209, 210, 229, 239, 254, 260, 266, 267, 268, 269, 295, 296, 300, 311, 312, 313, 314, 327, 345, 359, 361, 363, 369, 378
Payne Cemetery 50
Payner 274
Payne's Prairie 33
Paynes Prairie Post Office 34
Paynter 162, 274
Payton 299, 310
Peace 331
Peak 297, 299
Peake 327
Pearman 208, 355
Pearson 96, 231, 281, 320
Peavey 189
Peavy 300
Peculiar 29
Peculiar, MO 29
Pedersen 224
Peek 297
Peery 295
Peine 121
Pellham and Phillips 83
Pelz 148, 149
Pemberton 296
Pence 264
Penn 186, 227, 329
Penninger 184
Pennington 262, 263, 268, 269
Pennsylvania 28, 31, 113
Pentecostal Church of God 44
Pentecostals of Bolivar 44
Penter 325
Percival 212
Periman 187
Period of Silence 10
Perkins 258, 352, 364
Perkinson 285, 296
Perriman 226, 227, 297
Perrine 258, 259, 354
Perry 135, 143, 183, 247, 279, 296, 324, 357
Perryman 68, 270, 271, 297, 312
Pershing 252
Persimmon Grove 53, 64, 73
Persimmon Grove School 63
Petelin 186
Peterman 199
Peters 119, 322
Petersen 306
Peterson 61, 73, 166, 201, 249, 257, 283, 284, 297, 301, 356
Petiford 68
Petticoat Junction 30
Pettigrew 345
Pettit 136
Petty 348
Pfitzner 191
Phelps 68, 189
Phillips 4, 25, 41, 43, 60, 84, 130, 133, 159, 171, 175, 187, 189, 196, 198, 212, 235, 236, 272, 283, 286, 294, 297, 298, 326, 330, 336, 357, 358, 365, 375, 377
Philpott 296
Phipps 158, 163, 165, 169, 187, 237, 260, 285, 295, 334, 335, 352, 354
Pickel 64, 73, 175, 242, 365
Pickel-Meade Cemetery 50
Pickering 93, 116, 117, 175, 189, 218, 219, 298, 299
Pickett 199, 245
Pickle School 64
Pierce 60, 70, 119, 143, 146, 164, 165, 187, 188, 214, 274, 278, 290, 303, 309, 310, 340, 341, 363, 369
Pierson 196
Pike 119, 167, 206, 256, 272, 298, 323, 367
Pilcher 247, 248, 299
Pill 311
Pin Hook 33, 74
Pine 162
Pinkard 65
Pinkley 244
Pinkston 273
Pinnick 224
Piper 153, 198, 220, 236, 243, 293, 299, 300
Piper Creek 31
Piper Creek Mill 33
Pipkin 177
Pippen 58
Pirkle 267, 313
Pischer 157
Pitman 235
Pitner 93, 231, 308, 332, 333, 365
Pitt 373
Pitts 31, 93, 119, 144, 145, 149, 160, 165, 193, 223, 240, 265, 284, 290, 295, 300, 315, 361
Pitts Prairie 35
Pixler 342
Platt 73, 299, 300, 339, 340
Playter 252
Pleasant Hope Cemetery 75
Pleasant Grove 64
Pleasant Grove Freewill Baptist 44
Pleasant Grove School 65
Pleasant Grove School House 44, 45
Pleasant Hill Cemetery 50
Pleasant Hill Missionary Baptist 45
Pleasant Hill Sabbath School 41, 81
Pleasant Hope 8, 14, 18, 23, 25, 28, 31, 32, 33, 34, 35, 36, 41, 42, 44, 45, 51, 55, 64, 65, 72, 73, 74, 75, 93, 95, 106, 110, 111
Pleasant Hope Assembly of God 45
Pleasant Hope Cemetery 50
Pleasant Hope Cumberland Presbyterian Church 44, 45
Pleasant Hope First Baptist Church 45, 71, 72
Pleasant Hope Fundamental Baptist 45
Pleasant Hope High School 45, 65
Pleasant Hope Institute 64
Pleasant Hope Lodge No. 467 33
Pleasant Hope Lodge No. 8 33
Pleasant Hope Mill 32
Pleasant Hope, MO 74
Pleasant Hope Normal Academy 64
Pleasant Hope Roller Mill 37
Pleasant Hope School 64, 71, 75
Pleasant Hope School District 64
Pleasant Hope United Methodist Church 44, 45
Pleasant Lodge 112
Pleasant Lodge No. 160 32
Pleasant Prairie 32, 33, 43, 68
Pleasant Prairie Institute 68
Pleasant Retreat Academy 64
Pleasant Ridge 65, 73
Pleasant Ridge Cemetery 50
Pleasant Ridge Missionary Baptist 45
Pleasant Vale 65, 73
Pleasant Valley 65
Pleasant View Missionary Baptist 45
Pledger 376
Plum Grove 65, 73
Plum Grove Cemetery 50
Plumer 92
Plummer 92
Plugugly 16
Poage 39
PoChing 377
Poe 250, 251, 299, 323
Pogue 221
Pointer 369
Poledna 300
Polick 72
Poling 369
Polk 8, 10, 74, 94, 98, 153, 171, 232
Polk Christian Church 45
Polk Community Hospital 108
Polk County Bank 91, 108
Polk County Baptist Association 43
Polk County Christian 65
Polk County Classics 89
Polk County Commission 92
Polk County Community Center 84
Polk County Courthouse 9, 85, 105
Polk County Genealogical Society 2, 4, 5, 21
Polk County Genealogical Society Library 5
Polk County Home Guard Infantry 12
Polk County Humane Society 106
Polk County Library 21
Polk County Missionary Baptist Association 84
Polk County Post Office 34
Polk County Public Library 5
Polk County Regiment Home Guard Infantry 11
Polk County Southern Baptist Association 78
Polk County Times 89
Polk Post Office 34
Polk Town 34
Polk Mt. View Cemetery 50
Pollard 173, 174, 204, 264
Polling 309
Pollock 185
Polly 54, 356, 363
Polodna 31, 62, 191, 233, 300
Polodna Home 31
Polson 140
Pomada Tarr 8
Pomada Tarr River 8
Pomme de Terre 51, 64
Pomme de Terre Bridge 14
Pomme De Terre Cemetery 50
Pomme de Terre Cumberland Presbyterian 45
Pomme de Terre Lake 83
Pomme de Terre River 8, 10, 11, 22, 23, 25, 28, 32, 36, 44, 45, 92
Pool 233, 301, 362
Pope 117, 193, 310
Poppe 147
Porter 82, 122, 128, 178, 301, 320
Portwood 314
Postle 296
Pottebaum 144
Pottenger 141
Potter 65, 89, 207, 213, 283, 289, 300, 355
Potter Knob 28
Potts 65, 73, 92, 120, 143, 164, 218, 243, 246, 257, 267, 274, 276, 302, 321, 359, 363
Powell 43, 307
Powers 29, 293
Prater 63, 126, 167, 169, 201, 221, 285, 295, 321, 371
Pratt 137, 187, 246, 269
Prather 321
Pratt 137, 187, 246, 269
Prebble 213
Preble 257
Preiser 240
Prentice 246
Preskitt 338
Presley 41, 60, 81, 144, 216, 237, 318, 345
Preston 96, 314
Price 12, 22, 35, 164, 188, 208, 248, 260, 266, 269, 279, 281, 302, 304, 307, 309, 329, 341, 355
Prichard 302
Prichett 368
Prickett 373
Pride 254
Pridgen 128, 297
Prince 222
Principia 34
Pritchard 73, 126, 204, 255, 302
Pritchett 10, 174
Privett 243
Prock-Murray Cemetery 50
Proctor 146, 147, 148, 197, 218, 345, 359
Proffitt 195, 196
Proper 214
Propp 113
Prottsman 68
Providence 64, 65
Providence Church 56, 65
Providence Missionary Baptist Church 23, 44, 45
Providence School 45
Provolt 155
Pruitt 83
Pucket 333
Pufahl 152, 153, 302, 303
Pulliam 258
Pulse 180
Pummill 360
Purdam 349
Purdin 120
Purgison 296
Purity Rebekah No. 305 27
Purkeson 296
Purrington 83
Pursley 71, 241, 248, 303
Pursselley 3, 303, 304
Purtle 218
Puthuff 24
Putnam 358
Pyland 57, 130
Pyle 220, 333, 376
Pyles 198

Q

Quantrill 16
Quennoz 143, 146
Quick 127, 148, 159, 160, 173, 203, 204, 304
Quickbeorner 210
Quillen 250
Quinn 65, 278, 365
Quintin 248

R

Radcliff 84
Rader 83, 239, 313
Radford 246
Rafferty 330, 347, 352
Ragains 66
Ragland 307
Ragsdale 74, 139, 147, 159, 160, 172, 173, 176, 225, 231, 237, 240, 261, 304, 305, 313, 314, 376
Ragsdale Cemetery 50
Railey 188
Raines 320
Rains 11, 35, 67, 82, 158, 231, 362
Rains Building 112
Ralph 182
Ramey 29, 148
Ramsey 61, 92, 119, 189, 224, 225, 258, 260
Ranard 308
Rand 68, 249
Randall 357
Randleman 10, 139
Randolph 291
Raney 97, 174, 232, 248, 339
Range Cemetery 50
Rapalyea 198
Raper 167
Rash 234, 242
Ratcliff 61, 65, 66, 92, 181, 316, 353
Ratcliff District 62
Rathbun 305
Ratliff 73
Rawlings 219
Ray 125, 150, 225, 228, 248, 298, 303, 309, 367
Rayfield 182
Rayn 223
Raynolds 69
Rea 128, 237
Reagan 121, 225
Reaves 178, 190
Rebels of Polk County 14
Reber 267
Rechlau 177
Rechow 55, 302
Recklyle 177
Recknor 4, 316, 318
Rector 211, 212, 226, 293, 305, 306, 362
Red Top 25, 28, 65
Redd 21, 29, 36, 56, 126, 127, 256, 257, 283, 306, 307, 353
Redfearn 312
Redford 84, 310
Redgrave 144
Redman 199, 307, 308, 315
Reece 302
Reed 19, 27, 28, 93, 173, 188, 208, 218, 222, 237, 323, 336, 355, 373
Reed Cemetery 41, 49, 50, 71
Reedy 56
Rees 93
Reeves 120, 168, 183, 190, 256, 267, 306, 307, 308, 309, 315, 316
Reichert 351
Reichl 239
Reid 272, 294, 309
Reister 325
Remington 73, 193
Remington Arms Co. 27
Remmenga 236
Renault 375
Renfro 31, 119, 133, 185, 238, 240, 278, 309, 340, 369
Renfrow 8
Renken 143
Rentfro 66
Rentfrow 26, 30, 309, 310
Republic, MO 96
Reser 183
Rex 34
Reynolds 119, 130, 150, 154, 171, 173, 208, 265, 310, 311, 323, 379
Reynolds County 16
Rhay 308
Rhoades 96, 204
Rhoden 289
Rhodes 139, 189, 315
Rhuska 72
Ricchetti 24, 316
Rice 24, 32, 34, 65, 68, 132, 143, 150, 190, 305, 344, 375
Rice's Mill 34, 35
Rich 188, 308
Richards 59, 72, 121, 142, 145, 257, 310, 327, 378, 379
Richardson 30, 94, 98, 199, 264, 311, 336, 379
Richardson No. 1 Cemetery 50
Richardson-Gallivan-Elliot Cemetery 50
Richman 276
Richner 311, 312
Richter 21, 231
Rickman 272, 275
Rife 119
Riggans 286
Riggs 253
Rigsby 327
Riley 240, 284, 286
Rimby 18, 34, 36, 48, 57, 69, 160
Rimby Assembly of God 45
Rimmer 236
Rinck 236
Rinder 156
Ring 188, 319
Rinks 168
Rios 212
Ripple 312
Rising 118
Ritsema 362
Ritter 122, 128, 279, 297, 312
Ritz 129

River of Life Community 45
Riviere 179
Roach 184, 225, 299, 307
Roark 174, 343
Robards 359
Robb 240
Robberson 344, 345
Robbins 73
Roberson 12, 171, 185
Roberts 18, 22, 24, 57, 65, 73, 78, 84, 93, 96, 116, 133, 136, 210, 217, 218, 231, 235, 241, 245, 246, 249, 253, 266, 267, 278, 286, 289, 290, 295, 312, 313, 314, 315, 326, 338, 344, 349, 354, 355, 365
Roberts Chevy 96
Roberts School 45, 66
Roberts-McGinnis 84
Robertson 93, 133, 137, 160, 174, 207, 217, 218, 219, 226, 308, 309, 315, 316, 345, 349, 361, 366, 370
Robidou 285
Robinson 176, 211, 253, 284, 290, 310
Robison 128
Robson 218, 219
Rock 65
Rock Prairie 25, 34, 65, 73
Rock Prairie Cemetery 50
Rock Prairie Missionary Baptist 45
Rock Prairie School 66
Rodebush 53
Roden 257
Roderick 29, 169, 199, 316, 321
Rodgers 59, 92, 166, 181, 235, 260, 359
Rodrick 321
Rodruck 321
Roesch 222
Rogers 19, 118, 148, 166, 223, 224, 231, 260, 309, 310, 350, 356, 367, 375
Rohrs 75
Roland 325
Rolla 11, 34
Roller 320
Romania 84
Romley 311
Rondo 18, 34, 57, 62, 67, 72
Rondo Baptist 43, 45
Rondo Institute 67
Rondo No. 1 Cemetery 50
Rondo No. 2 Cemetery 50
Rook 68, 221
Rooks 307
Roosevelt 238, 317
Root 130
Rosamond 349
Roscoe 16
Rose 73, 248, 295, 350
Rose Bud 72
Rose Hill 67, 72
Rose Hill Schoolhouse 46
Rosebud 67
Rosebud Community 67
Rosebud Good Neighbor Club 67
Rosebud School 67
Rosicka 370
Ross 4, 24, 25, 30, 34, 61, 68, 69, 73, 84, 101, 121, 122, 150, 157, 167, 193, 194, 219, 238, 248, 257, 262, 303, 316, 317, 318, 319, 320, 321, 325, 340, 353, 371, 372, 373
Roth 250, 251
Rothrock 321
Rotramel 286, 321, 350
Rotrammel 124

Rotrock 119, 169, 321
Rouark 194
Roundtree 59
Rountree 92, 130
Roush 281
Roussin 289
Routh 40, 146, 199, 262, 263, 290, 335, 354, 375
Rovenstine 225
Rowan 57, 322, 354
Rowden 274
Rowels 134
Roweton 18, 97, 98, 177, 187, 243, 258, 284, 322, 353, 356, 362
Roweton's Home Center 97
Roweton's Western Auto 97
Rowland 240
Rowles 56, 198, 220, 322, 323, 331
Roy 296
Roye 287
Rozets 175
Ruark 171
Ruble 379
Ruckman 73
Rudolph 212
Rueb 144
Rule 19, 92, 93, 314, 315
Rumley 173, 334, 335
Rummel 68
Runge 255
Runouski 223
Runyan 67, 73, 253, 310, 323
Rush 25, 186, 193, 233, 240, 253, 295, 305, 314, 323
Russell 8, 84, 145, 184, 188, 197, 212, 219, 228, 229, 231, 282, 297, 323, 324, 338, 347, 360
Russell-Hamlet 143
Russia 84
Rust 295
Ruth 92
Rutherford 183, 325
Ruthford 200
Rutledge 171, 188
Ruyle 8, 10, 43, 84, 85, 96, 140, 169, 227, 228, 324
Ruyle Cemetery 50
Ruzicka 191, 192, 303
Ryan 132, 184, 242, 378
Ryason 195
Ryder 170
Rymer 23, 65, 121, 240
Rynish 87

S

S & S Towing Service 95
Sac River 10, 22, 23, 81, 92
Sac River Band 10
Sack River 8
Sacred Heart 86
Sacred Heart Church 87
Sacred Heart Parish 86, 87
Sacred Heart Roman Catholic 45
Safferty 39
Safrit 121
Safritt 283
Sage 255, 337
Sager 150
Saint Joseph 14
Salama 120
Salem 46
Salem Baptist Church 39
Salem Cemetery 50
Salem Missionary Baptist Church 46, 49
Salem, MO 90
Salkil 252
Sallee 33, 34, 41, 60, 158, 260, 284, 324, 343, 344, 345, 379
Sallie 200
Salsbury 281
Salsman 36, 84, 240

Salzman 126
Samples 57, 368
Sampson 196, 224, 258, 330
Samsoe 131
Samson 204
Samuel 349
Sanborn 14
Sand Hill 67, 73
Sanders 23, 66, 139, 164, 185, 211, 213, 224, 268, 291, 302, 303, 364
Sanderson 36
Sanford 305
Sansom 223
Santamaria 153
Sapp 349
Saracini 270
Sargent 69
Sarkey 159
Satterfield 144, 229
Savage 287, 348
Saward 198
Sawyer 2, 4, 59, 128, 161, 164, 187, 193, 200, 213, 238, 239, 246, 258, 260, 316, 318, 325, 350, 351, 368
Sawyers 128, 145, 215, 325
Sawyers Cemetery 50
Saxbury 173
Saxby 62
Say 19
Saye 8, 10, 11, 18, 19, 92
Sayres 158
Scarritt Institute 68
Scarritt Morrisville College 68
Schaeperkoetter 344
Schafer 156
Schartzer 211
Schatz 251
Schaub 361
Scheel 350
Scheer 192
Schell 35, 146, 242
Schiltz 167
Schleifer 174, 240, 311, 325, 326
Schliesser 239
Schmick 72
Schneider 308
Schnell 35
Schnell Spur 35
Schnelle 83
Schoaley 131
Schoff 186
Schofield 35, 68, 73, 255, 278, 283
Schofield Cemetery 35, 50
Schofield Chapel Missionary Baptist Church 45, 46, 68
Schofield School 67
Schooley 68, 172
Schreiner 334
Schulcer 333
Schuler 177, 238
Schultz 328
Schutt 238
Schwarting 145
Scoggins 362
Sconce 222, 223, 248, 280
Scorggins 93
Scott 82, 137, 161, 171, 188, 202, 215, 232, 236, 237, 303, 340, 355, 365
Scotten 324
Scribner 158
Scroggins 36, 41, 60, 70, 72, 74, 84, 174, 183, 200, 219, 233, 235, 236, 270, 278, 283, 311, 326, 328, 345, 377
Scrouge Out 68
Scrounge Out 74
Scudder 25
Scurlock 84, 145, 164, 198, 316, 324, 326, 327, 360
Seaboldt 200, 201

Seamster 236, 257, 327
Sears 124, 270, 320
Sears Catalogue Store 112
Seat 160
Seavey 363
Sechler 64, 327, 328
Second Baptist Church 78
Secrest 167
Sedalia 9, 104
Seeger 376
Seiner 96, 103, 130, 164, 197, 217, 311, 339, 357, 358
Self 11, 19, 139, 148, 176, 283, 301, 324, 330
Sell 44, 63, 137, 328
Sells 234
Selvey 83, 328, 329
Selvidge 330
Senter 79, 321, 362
Senter Missionary Baptist 42, 46
Sentinel 35, 51, 52, 67, 72
Sentinel Church Cemetery 50
Sentinel Missionary Baptist 46
Sentinel Prairie 35, 36
Sentinel-Pitts Farm Cemetery 50
Sentinel-Town Cemetery 50
Serel 379
Sergent 54, 84, 254
Serl 329
Serls 233, 329
Settle 261
Seubering 354
Seward 198
Sewell 74, 216
Seyer 87
Shackelton 196, 255, 316
Shackleton 254
Shade 63, 73, 84
Shadon 323
Shadwick 54, 128, 297, 300, 306, 312, 353
Shady Grove 27, 35, 46, 68, 73
Shady Grove Baptist 46
Shady Grove Cemetery 46
Shady Grove Methodist Church 42, 46
Shady Grove Mill 34
Shady Grove No. 1 Cemetery 50
Shady Grove No. 2 Cemetery 50
Shady Grove School 46
Shadygrove 35
Shalenhamer 330
Shanghai 35
Shannon 10, 23, 210
Shannon County 16
Sharar 117
Sharon 27, 35, 40
Sharon Missionary Baptist 46
Sharp 119, 173, 202, 334
Shave Tail 35
Shaw 25, 284, 294, 322, 327, 329, 330
Shay 139, 165
Shearer 83
Sheet 166
Sheetz 28
Shelby 12, 130, 233, 343, 358, 377
Sheldon 330
Shelenhamer 330, 370
Shellenberger 148
Shellenhamer 330
Shelton 32, 147, 334, 370
Shepard 261
Shepherd 131, 348
Shepperds Grove 35
Sheridan 283, 286, 292
Sheridan Cemetery 50
Sherman 127
Sherwood 219, 268
Shields 273

Shiloh Cumberland Presbyterian Church 45
Shimkus 194
Shimkuss 171
Shiner 130
Shipley 55, 139, 221, 284, 379
Shireman 150
Shirer 359
Shirley 330
Shockley 122
Shoemake 134, 135, 323, 330, 331
Shoemaker 194, 207
Shoffner 24, 62, 129
Shofner 183
Shoman 134
Shook 329
Shooley 69
Shore 269
Short 54, 56, 143, 146, 331, 332
Shough 286
Shouse 220
Shrader 189
Shriner 307, 375
Shryer 166
Shuck 60, 258
Shuler 21, 53, 84, 167, 170, 287, 330, 332, 333
Shults 330
Shumate 341
Sibley 334
Sicard 274, 275, 276
Sidebottom 69
Sigler 11
Sikdmore 126
Sikes 130, 152
Sillavan 278, 341
Silvery 126
Silvey 126
Simmons 162, 163, 165, 219, 235, 248, 249, 257, 262, 285, 298, 299, 310, 320, 334, 335, 336, 375
Simons 124, 336, 353, 363
Simpson 24, 35, 96, 138, 208, 209, 227, 240, 243, 244, 256, 257, 297, 359
Simpson's Mill 28, 35
Simrell 354
Sims 68, 119, 153, 231, 232, 286, 298, 368
Sinclair 159, 223
Sinden 315
Siscoe 161
Sisk 157
Sisters in One a-Chord 84
Sixth Provisional Regiment 14
Skaggs 29, 149, 154, 190, 368
Skalicky 191
Skeele 201
Skelly Service Station 104
Skelton 167, 331
Skillet 35
Skidmore 126, 129, 377
Skinker 206
Skinner 84, 117, 231, 235, 321, 326, 327, 378
Skopec 191
Slack 140, 141
Slagle 8, 25, 30, 35, 36, 41, 54, 64, 68, 70, 92, 124, 125, 127, 128, 138, 148, 168, 169, 183, 231, 255, 256, 261, 309, 321, 327, 328, 336, 337, 353
Slagle Cemetery 35, 50
Slagle Creek 35, 48
Slagle Creek Church and Cemetery 68
Slagle Creek Missionary Baptist Church 35, 46
Slagle Meat Market 35

Slagle Post Office 35
Slagle School 70
Slate 160
Slater 28, 165
Slatten 202, 203, 262
Slattery 331
Slaughter 234
Slavens 10, 85, 266, 324
Sloan 8, 10, 29, 49, 69, 92, 238
Smales 267
Small 177, 241
Smallman 10, 233
Smay 286
Smith 4, 8, 10, 12, 19, 25, 29, 30, 33, 35, 59, 64, 65, 71, 72, 78, 84, 95, 96, 103, 105, 119, 124, 125, 130, 131, 138, 139, 153, 157, 163, 167, 168, 173, 176, 183, 184, 197, 198, 199, 214, 219, 220, 227, 233, 237, 249, 255, 257, 264, 280, 281, 291, 292, 294, 298, 299, 304, 305, 307, 308, 309, 320, 325, 335, 337, 338, 343, 344, 348, 350, 359, 360, 364, 371, 372, 373, 375
Smith Mill 35
Smithson 8, 10, 19, 25, 360
Smolnik 248, 266
Snapp 33, 119
Snead 280
Sneed 122, 353
Snelling 123
Snider 244
Snipes 166
Snodgrass 82, 88, 89, 295, 297, 339, 374
Snow 72, 198, 207, 267, 327
Snowdale 180
Snyder 11, 106, 174
Social Order of the Beauceant 112
Socialist Hall 35
Solomon 224
Sommerhauser 128, 129
Soultiere 157
South 83
South Africa 113
South Benton Township 51
South Carolina 30, 113
South Dakota 113
South Green Township 9, 51
South Prairie 36
South Ward School 91
Southard 226, 229
Southeast Marion Township 10
Souther 202
Southern Baptist Convention 81, 84
Southern Hills Baptist Church 48, 78
Southside Missionary Baptist 48
Southwest Baptist College 54, 69, 79, 90
Southwest Baptist University 69, 78, 90, 102
Southwest Electric Cooperative 102
Southwest Marion Township 10, 11, 50
Southwest Missouri Conference 68
Southwest Regional Library 19, 20
Sovereign Grace Reformed 48
Spafford 257
Spain 325, 357
Sparkman 369
Sparks 4, 291, 339
Spear 84, 200, 355
Spears 233, 300, 328

389

Speed 279
Spence 33, 106
Spencer 84, 199
Spencer-Hufford Cemetery 50
Sperry 24
Spevak 334
Spidell 279
Spillman 41, 132, 133, 140
Spillman Cemetery 50
Spinks 53
Spivey 262
Sprague 274, 276, 351, 374
Spring Creek 36
Spring Creek Cumberland Presbyterian Church 47, 48
Spring Hill 74
Spring Valley Cemetery 50
Spring Valley Church 47
Spring Valley Missionary Baptist 48
Springer 341, 355, 369
Springer Cemetery 50
Springfield 9, 11, 14, 22, 29, 82, 83, 94, 95, 98, 104, 105, 109, 110, 113
Springfield Leader 89
Springfield, MO 14, 90, 91
Sprout 26
Spurgeon 125, 265, 355
Square Deal Mercantile 28
Squibb 119, 201, 265
Squier 368
St. Alban's In The Ozarks Episcopal 45
St. Andrew Lutheran Church 83
St. Catherine Church 87
St. Catherine Mission 87
St. Catherine of Siena 45, 86, 87
St. Catherine of Siena Parish 87
St. Clair County 9, 11, 16, 65
St. Elmo Commandary No. 43 Knights Templar 112
St. Genevieve District 8
St. John 319
St. John's Hospital 109
St. John's Regional Medical Center 90
St. John's School of Nursing 90
St. Jude Mission 87
St. Louis 23, 25, 36, 103
St. Louis County 8
St. Louis District 8
St. Louis, MO 99
St. Wenceslaus 86, 87
St. Wenceslaus Catholic 46, 86
Staas 318, 339, 340
Stack 143, 146
Stacy 147, 171
Staffen 273
Stafford 133, 191
Stalcup 117
Stall 240
Stambaugh 236, 340
Standgard 136
Standiferd 121
Standiford 346
Standley 21, 24, 29, 66, 160, 178, 258, 312, 355
Standly 178
Stanek 191, 192
Stanfill 105
Stanford 166, 230
Stanley 57, 164, 184, 212, 282
Stansberry 343
Stansill 267
Staples 120
Stapleton 241, 346
Star Ridge 36, 69
Star Ridge Cemetery 50
Star Ridge Methodist Episcopal 48
Stark 288

Starkey 19, 30, 155
Starner 316, 319
Starridge 36
Statenkemper 313
Stauffacher 197, 228, 246, 247, 290, 340
Steel 17, 193, 273, 286
Steele 119, 122, 133, 309, 340, 341, 355, 369
Steffens 120
Steinshouer 132, 252, 347
Stenbeck 83
Stennet 263
Stenson 281
Stephen 282
Stephens 82, 84, 101, 211, 212, 253, 322, 341, 361
Stephens Photography 101
Stephenson 185, 186, 288
Stepp 220
Stepp-Hicks 146
Sterling 89, 108, 119, 120, 132, 212, 274, 278, 341, 342, 346
Sterrett 187
Stevens 130, 167, 176, 178, 223, 247, 271, 279, 286, 287, 315, 339, 342, 363
Stevenson 140, 256
Steward 247, 342
Stewart 28, 65, 72, 73, 106, 107, 122, 124, 129, 139, 146, 160, 174, 183, 184, 197, 210, 218, 224, 227, 234, 244, 247, 248, 260, 290, 296, 299, 311, 330, 342, 343, 344, 358, 370
Stewart Concrete Products 61
Stidham 176
Stiles 157, 295, 332, 333
Stillwagon 245
Stillwell 123, 124
Stine 376
Stinecipher 46
Stinson 11
Stites 125
Stock 166
Stock Yards 75
Stockton 8, 9, 12, 14, 83, 85, 92, 103, 111, 117, 191, 307
Stockton Cemetery 50
Stockton Dam and Reservoir 22
Stockton Lake 22
Stockton, MO 83
Stoddard 50
Stogsdill 264
Stokes 23, 54, 55, 60, 118, 131, 132, 136, 147, 181, 187, 260, 265, 324, 325, 344, 345, 353, 363, 371
Stoll 247
Stone 68, 73, 82, 154, 155, 200, 225, 266, 340
Stoner 143, 146
Stoops 193, 194, 273
Storment 345, 360, 361
Story 219
Stotts 233, 362
Stoup 297
Stout 43, 179
Stoutzenberger 345, 346
Stovall 124, 132, 282, 346, 359, 369
Stowers 375
Strack 134, 153, 154
Strader 84, 155, 226
Strafford 29
Strain 22, 27, 29, 32, 36, 39, 143
Strain's Mill 8, 25, 36
Strand 213
Strange 272, 280, 281, 310, 374
Stratton 351
Straw 301

Street 119, 321
Streeter 106
Strepey Cemetery 50
Stretch 118
Stringfield 296
Strobel 192
Strong 134, 217
Stroud 308
Strumph 332
Stryker 354
Stuart 129, 171
Stuckey 155, 266
Study 308
Stufflebam 89, 216
Stultz 378
Stunkel 80
Sturges 94
Stutenkemper 267, 313
Stutter 202
Stutzman 180
Suddarth 178
Sudduth 118
Sugar Lip 36, 69, 72
Suiter 240, 291, 305
Sukovaty 246
Sullins 183, 226
Sullivan 181, 210
Summerhauser 128
Summerlott 145
Summers 21, 119, 123, 124, 212, 286, 294, 347, 359, 375
Sumner 240
Sumpter 352
Sunderland 154
Sunset 36, 69, 73
Sunset Church 69
Surfeit 283
Surgical Services 111
Sutherland 30, 165, 196, 377
Sutherland Cemetery 50
Sutherlin 165
Sutt 264
Suttee 324
Suttle 196, 197
Sutton 151, 152, 212, 225, 230, 270, 291
Sutzman 180
Svoboda 143, 144
Swadley 125, 217, 336, 355
Swartwood 162
Swartz 244, 310
Swearengin 237
Swearington 141
Sweden 113
Sweet 263, 284
Sweeten 249
Sweitzer 251
Swift 327, 329
Swihart 348
Swingle 93
Swinney 154
Swope 341
Syphert 178

T

T M Clothing 78
Tabor 129
Taco Bell 107
Taft 180, 348
Talburt 242, 327
Talley 245, 341, 365
Tannehill 259
Tapestry Press, Ltd. 85
Tarbert 173
Tarbet 173
Tarbot 237
Tarbutton 320
Tarry 132, 353
Tarter 130
Tarwater 314
Tatum 222, 321
Tayler 281, 371
Taylor 18, 56, 57, 96, 128, 131, 138, 147, 165, 173, 200, 240, 243, 245, 256, 262, 268, 269, 271, 272, 286, 289, 290, 294, 295, 318, 345, 359
Taylor-Milliken Cemetery 50

Tea Garden 99
Tea Garden Cafe 99
Teague 168, 225
Tecklin 300
Teegarden 99
Teeter 127, 128, 150
Temple 23, 92
Tennessee 8, 10, 84
Tennis 189
Tennison 309, 341
Tenth Missouri (Rebel) Calvary 14
Terhune 354
Terrell Cemetery 50
Terrill 80, 177
Territory of Louisiana 8
Territory of Missouri 8
Territory of Orleans 8
Testor 294
Teters 61, 100
Teters Floral Products 100
Teters Florist 100
Teters Florist Inc. 100
Tetlow 259
Texas 95, 113
Thaden 279
Thaller 198
Tharp 167, 187, 267
Thatch 182, 250, 251
The Buttermilk Academy 62
The Eclipse 33
The Fair Play Advocate 27
Thelen 242, 243
Thieman 376, 377
Thiessen 186, 348, 349
Thomas 119, 122, 141, 160, 161, 166, 167, 219, 237, 241, 258, 274, 293, 294, 296, 309, 336, 337, 360, 367, 374, 378
Thomassin 254
Thomasson 93, 198, 219
Thomosson 264
Thompson 44, 63, 67, 130, 139, 163, 170, 175, 176, 197, 198, 219, 220, 230, 233, 260, 295, 298, 312, 344, 345
Thomson 69
Thorel 259
Thornsbury 305
Thornton 200, 224, 299
Thorsland 282
Three Mound Prairie 10, 30, 31, 36
Thrower 329
Thruston 189
Thurston 189
Tibbets 224
Tice 273, 344
Tidke 348
Tidwell 178, 285
Tiller 33, 41, 60, 273, 321
Tiller Cemetery 50
Tillery 21, 69, 96, 250, 251, 265, 275, 300, 309, 314, 315
Tillery District 69, 71
Tillery School District 69
Tilton 23
Tilton and Sanders Hotel 23
Tin Town 34, 36, 48, 49, 53
Tin Town Missionary Baptist 48
Tindall 146, 217, 225
Tindle 19, 130, 133, 174, 233, 278, 310, 334, 344, 353, 375
Tinker 30
Tinker Cemetery 50
Tinkle 330
Tinsley 120, 137, 160, 315, 349, 361
Tipton 139, 254
Tipton, MO 10
Tirey 192
Titus 134, 153, 154, 197, 349
Toalson 129, 284
Todd 16, 124

Tolbert 55
Tolfree 91, 94
Tolliver 78
Tompkins 119, 265
Tonka 100
Toombs 349, 350
Torrance 132
Tostengard 208
Totten 14
Toups 265
Tow 117, 173
Towe 211
Townsend 105, 259, 342
Tracy 16
Trantham 260, 377
Trehern 224
Tremont 31, 36, 86
Trentalange 324
Trevarthen 359
Tri-County Association 84
Tribble 361
Triggs 248, 299
Trimble 117, 207, 347, 350, 351
Trimble Cemetery 50
Trinidad 84
Trinity Lutheran Church 83
Triplett 209, 210, 350
Trost 136, 351
Trotter 314
Trout 4, 288, 323, 330
Troyer 188
Trudzinski 330
Truitt 253
Truman 24, 91, 113, 245, 252, 318, 365
Tuck 60, 71, 73, 136, 184, 260, 351
Tucker 121, 122, 131, 178, 244, 305, 345
Tuckness 142, 324
Tucknuss 176
Tudor 261
Tulsa 113
Tummons 60, 136, 147, 290
Tupper 221
Turkey Creek Cemetery 48, 50
Turkey Creek Church and Cemetery 65
Turkey Creek Methodist 48
Turkey Creek Missionary Baptist 49
Turkey Creek Missionary Baptist Church and Cemetery 48
Turnbo 35
Turner 84, 120, 142, 146, 147, 214, 327
Tuter 302, 351
Tuttle 119
Twenty-Sixth Regiment Enrolled Missouri Militia 12
Tye 248
Tygart 53, 171, 287, 351, 352
Tyler 138
Tyo 309

U

Ulm 261
UMC School of Law 102
Umdenstock 121
Underwood 16, 93, 131, 221, 226, 261, 283, 340, 352, 368
Union 71, 72, 73
Union Grove 36, 49, 71, 73
Union Grove Church 49
Union Grove Missionary Baptist 49
Union Grove No. 1 Cemetery 50
Union Grove No. 2 Cemetery 50
Union Ridge 71, 73
Union School 27
Union Township 10, 11, 18, 51
United Baptist Church of

Jesus Christ 79
United Kingdom 75
United Methodist Church 46
United States Reserve Corps 11
University of Missouri 96, 106
Upshaw Prairie 41
Upshur Prairie 41
Upton 24, 206, 352, 374
Urbana 72, 111
Urich 78
Ussery 99
Utley 24, 97, 131, 132, 140, 206, 352, 353
Utopian Community 34
Utt 295
Utterback 73, 225, 271, 342
Uttley 324
Uzzell 368

V

Valencia 261
Van 36, 49, 72, 73
Van Bargen 311
Van Buren 353
Van Buren Township 10
Van Church 49
Van Gilder 356
Van Hoosen 219
Van Horn 254, 255
Van Meter 216
Van Nuys 354
Van Post Office 36
Van Town Church 49
Van Voohrees 354
Van Voorhees 354
Van Weye 213
Van-Choate 158
Vanbuskirk 330
VanCamp 208
Vance 239
VandenOever 230
Vanderford 30, 36, 123, 160, 181, 187, 353, 354
Vandergrift 241
VanGilder 73
VanHoosier 322
VanKannon 35
Vann 371, 373
Vannice 253, 323
Vannice Cemetery 50
Vannoy 74, 125, 200, 293, 294, 309
Vanzant 72
Vaughn 35, 119, 258, 341, 353
Vaughn's Stand 35, 36
Vawter 349
Venezuela 24, 91
Vermillion 53, 73
Vermont 113
Vernon 326
Vest 18, 21, 59, 73, 118, 136, 180, 182, 212, 221, 225, 236, 266, 311, 314
Vickers 158, 259, 260, 354
Vickery 218
Victor 36, 69, 72
Vignone 320
Viles 73, 93, 94, 147, 176, 199, 212, 254, 255, 261, 268, 286, 296, 329, 354, 355, 356
Viles Cemetery 50
Vincent 35, 84, 152, 153, 171, 208, 210, 255, 260, 302, 303, 355, 359, 363
Vines 330
Vineyard 345, 355
Violet 36, 48, 50, 51, 53, 65
Vire 200
Virginia 10, 113
Visintainer 197
Vodicka 31, 191, 355, 356
Voelker 188
Vogal 365

Vogt 167
Voight 357
Volkart 148, 293
Volprecht 194
VonSlagel 336
Voorhees 354
Vories 354
Voris 21, 117, 118, 122, 139, 176, 196, 199, 203, 204, 235, 255, 256, 261, 295, 306, 307, 354, 356, 357
Vote 130, 220, 248, 303, 357, 358
Vote-Hickman 130
Vought 357

W

Waddelow 152, 153
Waddill 93
Wade 122
Wadley 309
Waggener 308
Waggoner 84, 119, 130, 133, 164, 236, 292, 316, 357, 358, 378
Wagoner 122, 255, 308, 370
Wahlborg 222, 247, 248, 299, 302, 358
Waider 282
Wainscott 74, 129, 206, 295, 358, 359
Wakefeld 120
Wakefield 12, 27, 126, 232, 271, 308, 352, 359, 365
Walden 181, 206
Waldorf-Astoria 94
Waldow 274
Waldren 263
Wales 75
Walker 32, 33, 36, 68, 122, 128, 154, 157, 158, 170, 171, 173, 182, 188, 190, 194, 209, 217, 220, 237, 245, 247, 252, 260, 261, 266, 268, 269, 275, 289, 295, 312, 313, 314, 320, 330, 357, 359, 369, 376
Wall 175
Wallace 131, 200, 255, 321, 371
Wallace/Wallis 136
Wallbrunn 289
Wallen 136, 138, 146, 187, 359
Wallenstien 359
Waller 130, 139
Wallin 359
Walling 296
Wallis 63, 123, 138
Wallula 36
Walnut Grove 73, 74
Walnut Grove, MO 42, 48
Walnut Grove Post Office 32
Walnut Grove School District 68
Walnut Hill Farm 16
Walnut Ridge Missionary Baptist 49
Walter S. White Undertaking Co. 105
Walters 159, 212, 255, 344, 359, 360
Walton 190, 191, 271
Walula 27
Wanita Watts 159
Wann 30
Wannow 334
Warbleton 334
Ward 77, 123, 157, 165, 200, 203, 208, 257, 262, 282, 300, 302, 355, 360, 374, 379
Warden 233, 255
Ware 120, 154, 155, 212, 323, 324, 326, 360
Warford 32
Warner 117, 128, 185, 220, 230
Warren 24, 25, 31, 69, 116, 120, 128, 142, 143, 146, 208, 244, 256, 267, 273, 285, 311, 325, 329, 345, 355, 359, 360, 361, 363, 379
Warrick 242
Warsaw 12
Wartham 333
Warthen 332, 333
Washington 186, 330
Washington Township 8, 10, 92
Waterman 121, 122
Watkins 30, 73, 119, 120, 145, 160, 189, 307, 308, 361, 362, 370
Watson 18, 29, 63, 64, 68, 69, 72, 73, 89, 141, 232, 271, 291, 342, 347, 350, 363
Watson School 71
Watt 247, 303
Wattington 335
Watts 159, 225
Wayne County 8
Weatherby 92
Weatherly 188
Weatherwax 119
Weaver 10, 34, 51
Webb 78, 165, 166, 199, 306, 322
Webster County 9, 10, 11
Weder 319
Wedgeworth 168
Weeden 127
Weese 73, 169, 219, 231, 283, 299, 310, 343
Weinberg 169
Weiser 74
Welch 82, 84, 148, 149, 239, 253, 271, 309
Welle 293
Wellington 169
Wells 72, 73, 116, 117, 123, 132, 136, 182, 184, 197, 200, 208, 219, 238, 243, 285, 289, 327, 336, 362, 370
Wells Cemetery 50
Wells School 71
Wellspring Baptist Fellowship 49
Welpmer 221
Welsh 84, 93, 362, 363, 365
Welsh Slave Cemetery 50
Wendland 198, 327
Wenman 122
Wentzel 134
Wenzel 134
Wessels 354
West 8, 49, 72, 131, 136, 164, 175, 198, 210, 248, 337, 374, 365, 375
West Africa 84
West Bend 9, 31, 32, 36
West Indies 84
West Looney Township 11, 51
West Union 72, 73
Western Auto 97
Western Auto Associate Store 97
Western Auto Store 97
Western Auto Supply Company 97
Westfall 30, 355, 363
Westherwax 119
Westmoreland 253
Weston 212, 296, 366
Westphal 363
Wetzel 198
Whalen 143, 144, 245
Whaley 302, 303
Whatley 314
Wheary 274
Wheat 216
Wheeler 18, 21, 32, 59, 121, 127, 138, 186, 208, 213, 216, 220, 226, 258, 263, 336
Whelchel 19
Whelchel Mill 28
Whillock 362
Whitacker 267
Whitaker 30, 212
White 36, 68, 83, 116, 117, 131, 155, 173, 177, 189, 197, 208, 219, 230, 247, 252, 257, 272, 279, 283, 286, 293, 298, 302, 303, 304, 306, 309, 310, 311, 322, 323, 327, 330, 347, 363, 364, 370, 372, 376, 377, 378, 379
White Cemetery 50
White House 24
White Palace 94
White Palace Livery Stable 94
Whitehead 375
Whiteley 215, 216
Whiteman 266
Whiteside 224
Whitlatch 200
Whitlock 132, 190, 364, 365
Whitman 41, 60, 72, 74, 208, 269, 309, 347
Whitney 56, 224, 267, 269, 300, 343, 360
Whitson 239
Whittaker 208, 327
Whitted 150
Whitten 149
Whittenberg 375
Whittenberg Cemetery 50
Whorthey 347
Wicker 31
Wickliff 121
Wiese 196
Wikle 155
Wilcox 72, 129, 184, 365
Wilcox-Wilson Cemetery 50
Wildes 222
Wildey 281
Wiley 68, 307
Wilhite 96, 176, 257, 338
Wilhite-Long 176
Wilkerson 19, 123, 124, 199
Wilkins 72
Wilkinson 33, 125, 176, 202, 279
Will Dickey Wild West Circle D Show 28
Willard 95, 262, 347
Willard B. Erwin Funeral Home 105
Willey 53, 137, 191, 238
William 150
Williams 8, 10, 19, 25, 68, 77, 89, 123, 132, 137, 138, 144, 148, 153, 155, 161, 165, 169, 175, 176, 184, 192, 193, 194, 198, 224, 225, 233, 240, 252, 258, 260, 262, 271, 273, 277, 281, 282, 294, 305, 319, 320, 338, 348, 365, 366, 369, 375
Williams Cemetery 50
Williamson 36, 96, 116, 148, 149, 314
Williamson Mill 36
Willingham 321
Willis 24, 131, 218, 239, 322, 355, 360, 361, 370
Wills 123, 177, 182
Willson 169
Wilmes 185, 186
Wilmington 72, 73
Wilmore 330
Wilshire 330
Wilson 10, 44, 56, 69, 72, 73, 92, 117, 120, 130, 136, 139, 151, 152, 164, 165, 166, 171, 175, 183, 188, 200, 217, 218, 219, 220, 222, 226, 231, 236, 253, 267, 269, 270, 283, 287, 288, 289, 291, 301, 308, 309, 321, 324, 325, 326, 333, 339, 341, 349, 363, 366, 367, 368, 375, 379
Wilson Creek 35
Wilson School 72
Wilson School House 16
Wilson-Coats Cemetery 50
Wilton 121
Wimberly 153, 232
Wimmer 155
Winchell 143
Wind 233
Winders 102
Wine 65, 116, 118, 326, 329
Winfiel 225, 368
Winfrey 136
Wing 207
Wingfield 267
Wininger 181, 182
Winkel 376
Winkelmann 87
Winkler 119
Winn 261
Winsdom 304
Winslow 369
Winton 32, 36, 41, 133, 146, 148, 276, 373
Wisconsin 86, 113
Wisdom 141, 299, 305, 368, 369
Wise 202, 332
Wishart 18, 36, 49, 62, 72, 73, 157
Wishart Christian 49
Wishart Southern Methodist 49
Wishart Township 11, 18
Witt 57, 131, 173, 253, 340, 345, 369
Wolf 340
Wolfe 122
Wolford 206
Wollard 18, 26, 118, 171, 176, 219, 288, 289, 330, 346, 359, 369, 370
Wollard Cemetery 50
Wolsey 270, 271
Women's Clinic of Bolivar 111
Wommack 24, 113, 237, 355
Wommack Monument Co. 113
Wood 31, 130, 140, 157, 181, 211, 248, 274, 297, 316, 345, 349, 357, 358, 361, 370, 371, 375
Woodall 201, 273
Woodard 10, 25, 36, 41, 63, 131, 132, 135, 136, 167, 316, 317, 318, 319, 320, 371, 372, 373, 374
Woodard Mill 36
Woodfield 354
Woodfill 353, 354, 374
Woodford 226
Woodham 143, 146
Woodin 172
Woodlawn 72, 73
Woodlawn School 73
Woodle 123, 354
Woodmansee 36, 84
Woodruff 141
Woods 100, 120, 123, 124, 266, 272, 324, 331, 335, 365, 377
Woodson 116
Woodward 32, 69, 217
Woody 150, 369
Woolard 359, 369
Wooldridge 334
Wooten 74, 374
Word of God Christian Academy 72
Word of God Fellowship 49
Worden 32
Workman 149, 188
Worley 125, 334, 335
Wortham 188, 189
Worthan 25, 143, 149, 193, 243, 289, 323, 331
Worthan Cemetery 50
Worthey 241, 347, 364
Worthy 347
Wright 8, 10, 49, 57, 66, 122, 127, 130, 147, 165, 170, 199, 207, 209, 219, 223, 224, 233, 252, 269, 274, 283, 284, 307, 312, 320, 346, 369, 374, 375
Wrinkle 119, 292, 355
Wyand 284
Wyatt 12, 196, 231, 236
Wykle 155
Wyman 166
Wynes 162, 207, 272
Wynkoop 130, 375, 376
Wynn 158
Wyrick 185
Wysong 315

X

Xerxes 36

Y

Yandel 291
Yandell 201
Yarbrough 326
Yates 74, 116, 117, 283
Yeager 49, 182, 188, 308, 376
Yeargain 376
Yeats 349
Yoacham 282
Yoakum 282
Yoast 27, 69, 278, 309, 371
Yoast Station 27
Yokum 282
York 291, 377
Young 10, 39, 53, 116, 168, 169, 170, 191, 225, 314, 368, 377
Young Hickory 36
Youngblood 196, 231, 354
Younger 16, 279, 317, 345

Z

Zagony 14
Zahner 377, 378
Zatina 87
Zidlicky 119
Ziegel 64
Zimmerman 89, 108, 149, 188
Zion Lutheran 49
Zion Lutheran Church 83
Zongker 231
Zook 312
Zulauf 378
Zumbrun 234
Zumwalt 11, 34, 51, 52, 92, 160, 161, 227, 241, 267, 315, 329, 343, 378, 379

Dolpha and Lillie Busby Scroggins, 1914

Morrisville, MO, about 1925–Troy Overcash, Benny Barham, Walter Calloway

Thomas, Rebecca holding Joel, Myrtle, Lottie, Emmett, Roy is standing by his dog with the white handkerchief tied around his neck, August 14, 1904.

Mother Rosa Overcash and 1 month-old twins Rena and Reva Overcash, 1935

www.ingramcontent.com/pod-product-compliance
Lightning Source LLC
Chambersburg PA
CBHW081157230426
43666CB00016B/2841